LIFE

OF

CHRIST

LIFE
OF
CHRIST

By
HALL CAINE

DOUBLEDAY, DORAN & COMPANY, INC.
New York   1938

PRINTED AT THE *Country Life Press*, GARDEN CITY, N. Y., U. S. A.

107066
232.95
C/23

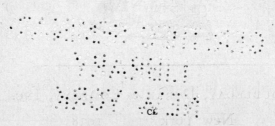

COPYRIGHT, 1938
BY DOUBLEDAY, DORAN & COMPANY, INC.
ALL RIGHTS RESERVED

FIRST EDITION

Introductory Note

MORE THAN FORTY-FIVE YEARS ago our father, the late Sir Hall Caine, conceived the idea of writing in narrative form a Life of Christ. About 1893 he began the work, which intermittently occupied him for the rest of his life. As it developed, and his exhaustive research into the subject continued, he felt more and more that a simple elucidation of Biblical problems would aid growing generations whose falling away from the Church was due in part to their inability to reconcile in their own minds some of the conflicting ideas set forth in the Bible.

Before he had gone very far he realised that he had set himself a work requiring not only an unconceivable amount of study and investigation, but one upon which a man's whole life could well be spent. For nearly forty years he continued his study, making many visits to Palestine, exploring all the available published material relating to Christ's life and having translated for the benefit of his work many relevant documents available only in museums and literary collections.

When he died he left behind more than three million words of text and notes, including early and later versions of several chapters; versions altered as his opinion and thought were extended. All of these words were in his own minute and characteristic handwriting, one which only secretaries long associated with him were competent to decipher. This Life of Christ he would never allow to be published during his lifetime, because he felt, to the end, that his research must go on and on. Brought together now, however, in the form in which he originally intended it, is the complete book, on which eight years of study and collation have been spent.

We have followed his words without alteration, even though occasionally some passages restate an idea, and although there may be lines which, had he lived, he might have altered. But in general we have preferred to be faithful to his text and to present this great work of scholarship and inspiration without undue editing.

G. R. Hall Caine

Derwent Hall Caine.

Foreword

THE PRINCIPAL OBJECT *of this book is to tell, as simply as I can, and in the order I think best, the true story, as far as my knowledge goes, of the life of a Jewish working man, who lived in Palestine, under the rule of the Roman Empire, chiefly in the reign of Tiberius Cæsar, nearly 2,000 years ago, and probably hundreds of thousands of years after the creation of the world and man.*

He was born poor, lived poor, and died penniless. Like all great men he loved humanity with a deep love. Especially, he loved the poor, the weak, the oppressed and the sinful, and he passed the few years of his life among them with a tenderness of sympathy for their sufferings which it is often difficult to think of without tears. He became a man of great wisdom, perhaps of great learning, certainly of great genius. As far as we can see he was a prophet taught by God, yet he preached no doctrine that was new to the world; he promulgated no new creed; he founded no new faith; he established no new Church; he made no religious organization; he authorized no sacraments or sacred writings; he recognized no mysteries; and he ordered no rites or ceremonies. On the contrary, he protested, from first to last, against most or all of these.

The religion that is now called by his name began very humbly. It was born in the valleys and hills of Galilee and brought up in the streets of Jerusalem. It had no altar, except the flowers of the field, and no temple except the open air, whose only dome was the sky. It had no priests or bishops or paid clergy. It had no money or other possessions. It knew no distinctions among its converts of race or sex or colour or class or degree or nationality. It asked nothing of its members but that they should love God and each other. That was the first and last of its commandments.

By a small group of persons in Palestine, the prophet of the Galilean hills was, in his last days, or soon after them, believed to be the Son of God in the special sense that he was the Christ who had been promised by the wisest of His people, and had to die to save the world from its sins. Because he believed the same, himself, and openly proclaimed his belief, he was put to death on a different accusation, at the instigation of an obscure high priest of his own people, who has no other claim to remembrance than comes of association with his name, by an equally obscure Roman governor who has no other right to a place in history. There are now 650,000,000 persons in the world—one-third of the inhabitants of the globe—who believe he was right and his executioners were wrong.

He died the death of a criminal of the lowest class, but he was the highest spiritual power that ever existed on the earth. He is still the purest and most sublime expression of the soul of God as it has moved with many falterings in the hearts of men throughout all ages, and of God's wish and will for the eternal welfare of His children.

But the object of this book is not only to trace, through many tragic happenings, the divine life which was lived in Palestine during thirty odd years, nearly twenty centuries ago—a life which, in the records that have come down to us, is sometimes clear and beautiful, sometimes obscure and contradictory, and not rarely enshrouded in almost impenetrable darkness. To do that alone, inspiring task as it is, would be to do it imperfectly or not at all.

The spiritual life of Jesus of Nazareth did not, in my judgment, begin in Galilee during the reign of the Emperor Augustus or of Tiberius Cæsar, nor in Jerusalem during the last days of David when God told His people that there should never be wanting a man to sit on his throne, nor with Moses on the top of Pisgah, after he had promised his follower through the wilderness a prophet greater than himself; nor with Abraham on the way to the gates of Ur, when he made his covenant with God, who was to lead his little company of the chosen race to a land they knew not of, where they would establish a divine kingdom that would be a blessing to all the world; but with those hopes and fears and visions of primitive man, which were older than any pagan fable of which they had any knowledge, and as old as man himself.

Hence it is also the object of this book to show, as far as my humble powers will permit, that the greatest fact in the story of the human family has not been concerned with its material welfare, with the battles it has fought and won, or the empires it has seen rise and fall, or with the revelations it has made in the realm of mind, or the marvellous discoveries it has achieved in the world of nature, but with the development of the human soul from age to age as a seeker after God and, above all, with the silent and perhaps unconscious growth of the Christ hope in the heart of man— the divine Messianic dream of a deliverer, a Redeemer, a Saviour, which, through all the travail of his wanderings, his sufferings, his sins and his repentance, has gone before him like a pillar of fire by night and a pillar of cloud by day.

Hall Caine./

Contents

BOOK I: BEFORE CHRIST

CHAPTER I THE BIBLE

CHAPTER II PRIMITIVE MAN

CHAPTER III THE FLOOD

CHAPTER IV THE PATRIARCHAL PERIOD

CONTENTS

CONTENTS xvii

CONTENTS

CHAPTER XXVII THE LAST SUPPER

CHAPTER XXVIII GETHSEMANE

CHAPTER XXIX THE TRIAL

CHAPTER XXX THE TRIAL (*Continued*)

CHAPTER XXXI BEFORE PILATE

CHAPTER XXXII THE CROWN OF THORNS

CHAPTER XXXIII THE WAY OF THE CROSS

CONTENTS

CHAPTER XXXIV THE THREE DAYS

CHAPTER XXXV THE RESURRECTION

CHAPTER XXXVI THE RESURRECTION (*Continued*)

CHAPTER XXXVII AFTER THE RESURRECTION

CHAPTER XXXVIII AFTER THE RESURRECTION (*Continued*)

CHAPTER XXXIX THE ASCENSION

BOOK III: AFTER CHRIST

CONTENTS

CONTENTS

BOOK I
Before Christ

CHAPTER I

The Bible

I. The Sacred Book of the Hebrews

BEFORE THE DAWN of history there must have been, as we now see, a deep gulf of time—hundreds of thousands, perhaps hundreds of millions of years. It is more than probable that during incalculable ages man (if he existed at that period) peered into the dark void in vain. What had happened at the beginning? When had man and the world been created? For what purpose had they been called into existence? What was to be their ultimate destiny?

It must have been a great mystery. Time, itself, must have been a mystery. It is still a vast island in the ocean of eternity whereof man, living inland, has never seen the shore. When he tries to calculate in Time he has to set up an artificial starting-point determined by himself. To such of us as are Christians, it is a moving fact that, for the better part of 2,000 years, a vast majority of the human family has, for all practical purposes of life, counted the world's events from the traditional date of the birth of Jesus of Nazareth.

It was not long before that traditional date that man began to have his first glimpse into the dark period before the dawn of history. It came to him, as far as we can see, first in crude imitations of scenes in nature, drawn on stone, which were usually found in caves, then in writings of a kind on cylinders of clay and, finally, in books—what he called sacred books.

There were many of these books, belonging to different races. When they were written man did not always know. Some of them, like the Vedas of the Brahmins, were believed to have existed from all eternity. Others, like the teachings of Zoroaster, were of unquestionable antiquity. Some were comparatively recent. Late in the history of man, as we now count it, there came from a little country on the east of the Mediterranean the sacred Book

3

of the Hebrews. It is with this book, mainly, that we have here to deal.

As a recognizable and complete writing in the twenty-four books of the Jewish Canon, it can hardly be earlier than the third or fourth century before the death of Christ. Sections of it are as old as the eighth and ninth centuries. Fragments of it (such as David's immortal Lament over Saul and Jonathan) are clearly older, and are probably contemporary with the events they record. Thus the Bible as a whole covers little more than a span in the unmeasurable stretch of time, yet it claims to go back to the beginning of all things, which, according to its own chronology, took place about 6,000 years ago.

II. God as Author of the Sacred Book

It is of the essence of nearly all sacred books that they are believed to be, directly or indirectly, written by God; because God, and God only, being the Creator or first cause of the world, could know what happened before man came into existence. This is especially so in the case of the sacred Book of the Hebrews. It contains a small portion which, according to His own account, was written by the actual hand of God Himself; a longer part which was written at His dictation, and a still longer part which was revealed to man by His Holy Spirit.

The substance of this message, so far as we can see, is that of many gods, the God of the Hebrews (often nameless, but sometimes called Yahweh, sometimes, by a corruption, called Jehovah, generally called the Lord) is the old true God; that He had chosen their race out of all the races of man to be His peculiar people; that He had bound them to Him by a covenant, whereby they were to inherit the earth, to establish a Kingdom of Heaven on earth, and, under the rule of a representative of the Supreme Being, the first cause of all things, to become a blessing to all nations; that He had created the world in six days, counting from morning till evening; that He had made man in one of these days; that the world was, as far as we can judge, His only creation, and man His sole or principal concern.

Besides this, there was much in the sacred Book of the Hebrews which enabled man to find the mirror of his soul; to penetrate the darkness of the mysteries which had, he thought, estranged

him from God; to see through the histories of what he believed
to be God's relentless punishment of his transgressions. His infinite
mercy and righteousness; to feel the same joyous thankfulness in
the stress of daily life as the prophets and psalmists of later days
felt and expressed in glowing and magnetic words in the heavy
hours of suffering and captivity. The Hebrews lived and fought
and died for their sacred Book. They felt that what was so inspiring must have been divinely inspired. It was the Book of God.

III. The Book of the Christians

About 200 to 400 years after the last parts of the Hebrew
books came the Book of the Christians. It was written from
beginning to end in its first form in the second half of the first
century of what we call the Christian era. It consists almost exclusively of an account of the life, teaching, miraculous works and
the Resurrection from the dead of the Great Being whose name
it bears, and of the lives, teaching and miraculous works and
inspiring deaths of the first generation of his followers. In its
completed form (after it had been translated into Greek from
the native tongue of the people for whom it was written, and
after many writings of doubtful origin had been cast out) it was
called by a name which must have been startling to the people of
its time—the *New Testament of Our Lord and Saviour, Jesus
Christ.*

Who was this Lord and Saviour, Jesus Christ, and who were
these followers, assuming Greek and Latin names, for whose
writings equality was claimed with the teaching of God Himself?

The early Christians had their ready answer. They did not
doubt that what they called the Scriptures (by which they could
only have meant the sacred Book of the Hebrews) had been written by the inspiration of God. And when, after the death of their
Founder, they wrote the final verses of their own Gospels and
letters about him, they believed, and sometimes said, that he was
God, or the Son of God, and that they, too, who wrote about
him, were divinely inspired. Thus, when Christianity became an
organized religion, they coupled the two books together and called
them by a Greek name, meaning, Their Book, Their Bible.

For many centuries thereafter every word of the Bible as a
whole was believed by the Christians to be as absolutely the Word

of God as if God had written it Himself. No Christian was permitted by his Church to question this under pain of excommunication or imprisonment, or even death on the gallows or at the stake. Thousands of Christians, who accepted the divine origin of the Bible, died voluntarily the most terrible deaths as witness to their faith in it. To thousands of others, the belief in its divine inspiration was a lifelong consolation. In the unsearchable wisdom of their Founder, which defied the mutations of time, the wise and the learned found strength. In his spiritual insight into the uttermost sanctuaries of their souls, the humble and heavy-laden discovered forms of praise which could never otherwise have known utterance in speech. Millions passed out of life with the sweet words on their lips of the great soul who was their Lord and Master, and had, as they believed, purchased with his blood their everlasting redemption. Millions are still doing so.

IV. Creation Stories

Centuries passed like this. For fifteen centuries the foundation of religion knew no fundamental change. Only in the eighteenth century of our own era was the divine inspiration of the Gospels seriously questioned. Then came a staggering challenge, both to the theory of the Hebrew part of the Bible and the accepted ideas of its origin. The biblical theory of the world as the sole creation of God seemed to be shattered by the discoveries of astronomy, which showed that the earth was only a tiny speck spinning like a midge among the heavenly bodies in an illimitable universe which must have existed through incalculable ages. The so-called Mosaic story of the creation of the world in six days appeared to be destroyed by the revelations of geology, which proved that the making of it must have been going on for hundreds of thousands or perhaps millions of years. The story that man, as a human being, had been made from the dust in a single day, seemed to be annihilated by facts which showed that he had ascended through endless ages from humbler forms of life. Could it be believed any longer that God had been the author and inspirer of a book which gave the lie to laws of nature, which He had Himself created? It was one of two things—either God had not written the Hebrew part of the scriptures or He had not created man (what we call man) at all.

Later came the study of other natural laws which appeared to discredit the Christian as well as the Hebrew part of the Book. The Christian part contained a record of events which, so far as man knew, were outside the human experience. Miracles were still said to have happened—miracles, in the accepted sense of the word, had never happened. The sun was still believed to have stood still. The stars were declared to have changed in their courses—the stars could never have changed in their courses. Man was said to have risen from the dead—man could never have risen from the dead. It would not do. Once dead, man was dead for ever. If any of these unnatural events had ever occurred, the world must long ago have fallen into chaos.

Still later came the objections of secular education. The Bible, as a whole, contained statements which conflicted with what had been believed (by the pagans) to be established historical facts; such as that Abraham and Moses and even Jesus of Nazareth had never existed. Above all, it presented in prominent places a picture of the Deity Himself which was so brutal and barbaric as to outrage the human spirit. Again, it seemed to be one of two things—either the Bible was not a God-made book, or else God was not a God of mercy and righteousness, but often an entity of malignant ferocity.

V. Interpretation of the Bible

It was not, at first, that man could face what he called this "blasphemous proposition." He could neither deny the sure laws of nature nor sacrifice a book which had been so precious to his soul. He told himself there must be some explanation. The Bible had said its last word, whereas science and history and general education were constantly changing. Who was fallible and presumptuous man to wipe out the possibility of the supernatural? If God had created the heavens and the earth (and who could say he had not?) nothing was impossible to Him. What was called miracle to-day must be according to law tomorrow. To harmonize the Holy Book with the sure laws of nature it was only necessary to find some new interpretations.

Man found many new interpretations. One of them was that the Bible was not to be understood literally, but spiritually. Sometimes it had a hidden meaning which the Almighty had deliberately left man to find out for himself. Oftentimes it was an allegory. God was not necessarily the actual writer of any part of the Bible. He was not in reality a being who had walked the earth in the image of a man. The six days in which He had created the world were not meant to be six periods of twenty-four hours each. The peoples of the Bible were not always to be taken as flesh and blood creatures, and the accounts of their doings were not be read as we read secular history.

Soon, very soon, man tired of this allegorical interpretation, although it had devout and learned sponsors. It was little better than dead sea fruit to hungry souls who wanted something to live and die by. It robbed the sacred Book of its reality. It reduced it to the condition of a fable. Humanity was gone from it, and, if God Himself remained, it was only as an abstraction.

Still other interpretations followed. One of these, still current both within and without the Churches, is that the Bible is to be read as a means of inculcating doctrine, not in abstract discourse, but in a form like that of a romance which appeals more directly to the emotions and the imagination. Much of it was first written in poetic form, either epic or lyric, and was probably intended to be sung. Thus, it is a poem, a parable, a prolonged song, a divine drama, and the last thing we ought to ask of it is whether its incidents or characters are real or imaginary.

It was labour lost. Man soon wearied of this arrogant and arid interpretation also. And now let us ask ourselves if there is not a simpler and more natural explanation of the conflict between certain of the records of the Bible and the laws of nature, the facts of history, and the purest and best aspirations of the soul. Let us leave the writers who are saying that the Bible by its own unaided glories alone is the sublimest record of man's spiritual adventures to such comforts as they can extract from their astonishing belief, and ask ourselves what is the Bible, if we judge of it, as we judge of other books, by its internal evidences alone?

VI.   The Writers of the Bible

The Bible is, for the most part, the history of a little people who lived for 1500 years, or thereabouts, in a small country called Palestine, which lies between the Syrian desert and the Mediterranean. During the greater part of that time this country was separated, except for caravan routes, from the larger centres of pagan culture, which lay east and south of it.

The writers of the Bible, its compilers, editors, scribes and translators were, as we clearly see, a large number of persons of various nationalities, chiefly Hebrew. Some of them were scholars, prophets and kings, physicians, professors of the best rabbinical schools, and graduates of the most famous pagan universities, of the highest education possible to their times, the noblest intelligence, the most exalted ideals and, in a few cases, of the most transcendent genius. Others were priests, soldiers, brigands, tax-gatherers, farmers, shepherds, herdsmen and fishermen, often of humble intellect, imperfect spiritual development and even of low and gross personal morality.

Their Book, as it comes down to us in irregular form and confused chronology, consists mainly of a vast number of more or less circumstantial stories of God or gods, of kings and queens, of masters and servants, of the poor and of the rich, of base and unworthy women, and of pure and noble ones. These stories are often told with a vividness and power which are without parallel in literature, but not rarely with amazing crudity and almost astounding insincerity. Clearly, the original writers gathered their material partly from the events of their own time, partly from such fragmentary documents on clay as had descended through them from earlier ages, partly from the general stock of tradition, the tales of old men, and partly from the idle talk of the traders by caravan who passed constantly through their country from Persia to Egypt, from Baghdad to Damascus.

The majority of the original Hebrew writers wrote in obvious good faith and without collusion or premeditated design or knowledge of each other's writing, except in the case of the New Testament, where collusion and premeditation are of the essence of the divine intention. Clearly, they did not write with the desire of glorifying their own race, for there is no other book in the world in which the Hebrew is so furiously condemned or held up to such scorn for his frequent lapses into shameless idolatry. Neither did they always write for the glory of their God; for, notwithstanding marvellous and miraculous passages to the contrary, in no other writings by the pen of man is the God of Israel so degraded from the place as the tender Father of His children which the human soul assigns to Him. If such, then, is the Bible, when judged by its internal evidence alone, are we to say that it is the Book of God in the sense that from first to last it is His inspired message to man and the world, and the foundation of religion?

It is impossible. Worse, it would be blasphemous. It would make God responsible not only for all the errors man has made in the slow progress of his intelligence, but also for the sins he has committed and for what he has always declared, not always honestly, to be God's command.

God does not write in books, but in hearts; not in language, but in lives; not in the letters of the alphabet, but in character and conduct, and, above all, in the beliefs of His children. For what men may have written and thought and said about God or for what He is believed to have done, God Himself is in no way responsible. Whatever that may have been, it has been merely according to the measure of man's knowledge of Him. The Bible is not an account of what God has said of Himself, but of what man, in the various stages of his spiritual development, has said about Him. It is the history of man's progress as a seeker after God—that and no other. The discoveries of astronomy, of geology, and, later, of evolution do not touch Him, or if they do it is only to make clear His infinite majesty and power. They only touch the writers of the Bible, whose eyes were sometimes blind, and whose beliefs, as we now see them, sometimes bordered on paganism.

What, then, is the Bible? Not an allegory, a poem, a parable, a drama or a discourse, but a picture of God as it has evolved itself through the eyes and out of the hearts and minds of millions, from the day, perhaps, of primitive man who trembled at the thunder, thinking it the voice of an angry and vengeful Deity, to the time of the loving and beloved human Being between whom and God Himself one-third of the inhabitants of the globe can now no longer distinguish.

This is not to say that the Bible is not God's Book. Far from it. In a higher and purer sense than that of its plenary inspiration, it is God's message to man, illustrated by pictures drawn from every phase of human life, with its ignorance and knowledge, its sins and sorrows, its progress and backslidings, its scenes of spiritual exaltation, and even its exhibitions of savage barbarity.

Then let us not think we have discredited the Bible, that we have found it out, because we have discovered some of its errors and contradictions. Rather, let us try, as one of the most learned of the fathers of the Church, Origen, said, to build up the history of religion, the belief in God and the hope of the Messiah, not from doctrine, but from human history. To do so, we must go back in the spirit of children to the little we know or can surmise of the condition of primitive man, and then forward to that country, "east of the flood," where, as far as we can see, man, as we now know him, emerged from the dust, or, it may be, from the jungle, and so on through the principal incidents of the Bible story, until we see the maelstrom of man's passions and sins and efforts at atonement culminate, for a vast majority of the human family, in Christ.

Only so shall we see in the story of Jesus of Nazareth, his place and his mission, the ever-present controlling force which the Greeks called Fate, and we call God—man's purpose and God's overruling, man's will out on the world's mad waters, but God's will out there too, for the world is God's and its waters.

CHAPTER II

Primitive Man

I. The Age of the World

IF WE ASK THE MAN of science of to-day when the universe began he will say not 6,000 years ago, as *Genesis* tells us, but hardly less than 200,000,000,000,000,000 years since; that the sun could never have been created, as the Bible says, as the sole light to light the world, inasmuch as it is the source of all light and heat, and only one of an innumerable multitude of stars of still greater light and heat. If we ask him when the earth began he will say 2,000,000,000 years ago*; that it was born out of the sun in gaseous masses, which continued to swirl in space until they found their places in the firmament; where they formed themselves into a globe of fiery matter wherein no life could exist; that they gradually cooled down, becoming first liquid and then plastic, and finally made themselves into mountains and valleys and oceans and streams, and then gave birth to life of all kinds, vegetable, animal and human.

If we ask the man of science of to-day when man began he will say 300,000 to 400,000 years ago; that he did not come into existence in a day, or as a thought in the mind of a Creator, but through prolonged periods from the humblest forms of life in the grass or the jungle, until late, very late, so late in the history of the world as to be almost within a hand-clasp of our own time, he assumed the form in which we now see him.

Such figures are bewildering and staggering. To help us to comprehend them, to realize them, to grasp them, a modern scientist has offered a homely illustration. If we climb to the top of Cleopatra's Needle on the Thames Embankment and paste a postage

*Sir J. H. Jeans gives the following table:

	Years
Age of earth	about 2,000,000,000
Age of life on earth	300,000,000
Age of man on earth	300,000
Age of astronomical science	3,000
Age of telescopic astronomy	300

12

stamp on the top of it, and then go on day by day pasting postage stamp on postage stamp, we shall have to make a pillar of postage stamps that will reach as high as the peak of Mont Blanc, and then count each postage stamp as a year, before we shall have attained to the number of years since man first appeared on the earth.

But the facts which appear to destroy the natural part of the biblical story of man are of immeasurably less consequence to humanity than those which disturb his spiritual activity. The astounding facts of the archæologists omit the greatest event in human experience. They omit God. Of God the man of science, as such, knows nothing. Unable to prove the existence of God by his gigantic telescope he leaves Him out of his reckoning. Yet he is well aware that the history of humanity without God would be no more than the rattling of dry bones in a golden sarcophagus. If he is a man with a heart, as he usually is, he sees that although God is beyond the reach of the most searching of his instruments He is the Ultimate Reckoning, the Moving Spirit of the Cosmos (let him call it what he will), and without God all discussions of natural facts are reduced to futility.

The most learned scientist who would say that when he uttered the word science he covered the whole ground of human knowledge would be more ignorant of the primal forces which govern the world and guide its destiny than the veriest dustman who knows what God has been to him in his time of trouble and in the hour of death.

On the other hand the Bible account of the creation, notwithstanding its errors of chronology and its violation of the laws of nature, is full of God. It begins and ends with God, and has thereby become the corner-stone of a religion which has brought strength and comfort to one-third of the inhabitants of the globe.

How did this amazing paradox come to pass? It is difficult to say. But recognizing its reality may we not now, without irreverence, put aside for the moment the first chapters of *Genesis,* written or compiled by men of the far past who knew little of natural law, and, accepting the astounding revelations of science which have come to us 3,000 years later, admit that before the Bible was written and before the facts they describe took place there must have been an unrecorded gap of time in which primitive man not only lived but learned and suffered?

What, then, was primitive man in those unfathomable ages? What were his occupations, his hopes and fears and visions?

It will be said that outside the Bible we have no authority for any such answers. That is not so. We have one authority more searching into the mysteries of the spiritual world than any the scientist has yet employed in solving the problems of the physical universe. We have the authority of the human soul. The stupendous figures of science are beyond the comprehension of the brain of man. They dazzle us, they bewilder us. We cannot see man as he was when he emerged as a worm from the sand of the desert, or perhaps as an anthropoid ape from the jungle. We can only see him when he has become a man like ourselves, living in a world such as we live in. But that is enough. Only the eye of the spirit can see the things of the spirit. And who will say that the things of the spirit were not as clear to the brain of primitive man as they are now to the brain of the man we call civilized?

What, then, was primitive man, after groping through the darkness of unknown and unknowable ages, after deceiving himself and deceiving others with his fables and futilities, after moulding his God with his own hands as the clay is moulded in the hands of the potter? Making his God a changeable and even a barbarous God, he comes at length to see that from the beginning, whatever else He may have been, He has been the Holy One of Eternity, the almighty, invisible omnipotent Being of whom it was said that as the heavens were higher than the earth so were His ways higher than our ways and His thoughts than our thoughts.

II. The Birthplace of the Human Family

With the eye of the spirit, then, we see primitive man for the first time as he enters the valley of the Euphrates, which is believed to be the birthplace of the human family. Even then he was not a brutal savage. According to the ethnologists he is more probably an innocent, helpless and even a timid creature. Nevertheless, he is an animal, and the first call he hears is the call of his physical nature. That is the call of hunger, and he becomes a hunter. But the occupation of a hunter in a country infested by wild beasts is a perilous one, and soon afterwards he becomes a shepherd. As a shepherd he leads his flocks in the cool of night from pasturage to pasturage, and shelters himself and his family from the heat of day in tents made of the skins of the sheep he slays for his food.

Time passes—hundreds, perhaps thousands, of years. The world in which he finds himself is no Garden of Eden, filled with fragrant and fruitful trees, in which he has no need to work because nature provides everything. On the contrary, it is a hard and barren land, sown with thorns and thistles, for it is an island of Caleb, with sights and sounds he cannot understand. From east to west, from the glowing south to the frozen north, it is full of wonders. He hears the roar of the distant sea as well as the song of the neighbouring birds. He sees the pine trees which clothe the strong hills with (as Goethe beautifully said) the living garment of God. He looks on death as well as life. Perhaps the sweetest and most joyous sight he sees is the frollicking of his young lambs in the spring on the fresh grass of the valley, and the sternest and saddest the outstretched body of his dead camel in the winter by the frozen foot of the glacier on the north.

There are moments when he is happy and content. "How wonderful! How beautiful!" He says something like this to himself, with the glistening eyes which are perhaps his only speech.

But the world rolls on, he sees the giant forces of nature about him—the majesty of day and night, the coming of winter and summer, the thunder and lightning, the storms and the calm. The volcanic land he lives in is also full of terrors. An earthquake breaks out under his feet, and he and his children are swallowed up in a hole in the ground. An eruption of lava pours down from the mountain, and his flocks and herds are burnt to bones and ashes. A tidal wave rolls up from the gulf on the south, and when its tumultuous waters ebb they carry his possessions back into the sea. An epidemic comes floating up through the thick and silent air from a poisonous swamp, and it lays him low with disease and he dies in pain.

"Why am I here? Why am I suffering?"

Perhaps in some mysterious way the memory comes back to him of an earlier existence in which a good God and a bad God contended for the mastery of his soul, and he, as a rebel against the good God, was cast out of Heaven for his sin.

How did primitive man come by his sense of sin? With his limited brain, what inner common sense told him? Where was the earthly Torch which communicated from the heavenly Torch the certainty that he had offended against God? Not for thousands of years after man came into existence could he have received from his great conqueror, Moses, the mighty message from his Creator which told him the difference between right and wrong. Is it possible that in the meantime God had been so unjust, so merciless, so cruel as to leave His children on earth in the dark about the sins for which He punished them?

It is difficult to think that primitive man believed this. He believed something more evil and terrible—that no Jehovah but Satan was the Supreme God of All. Nearly all the early religions bear trace of a belief in which Satan was the supreme deity, and the god to be obeyed if not worshipped. Plato himself, in his confession of earthly impurity, hints at a belief in evil as a curse contracted by man before he was born into the world. When St. Paul says that as often as he would do well, evil is present with him, he appears to be speaking of sin as the heritage of a previous condition, and when Origen writes of the Fall he seems to be thinking of it as the sequel, not merely to the transgressions in the Garden of Eden, but of a premundane state in which man was pure spirit, not body. Hence, to account for the origin of sin, we cannot omit mysterious consciousness of an earlier existence. The God of Moses is a just God, but He is also a jealous and vengeful God. Man, in some former state, has offended against Him. How shall he make his peace with God? Only by prayer and repentance. This is religion, and nothing else is.

And here we are on the verge of the most beautiful and at the same time the most dangerous part of faith. Before the Bible story of the creation of man and the world, as written, it was believed that the gods were not one but innumerable. There were the gods of the heavens, the gods of the earth, and the gods of the sun and the moon and the stars. They lived together in some heavenly position. Some were good gods and some were bad. Dissension broke out among them. Certain of them rebelled against the Supreme God of All, and to punish them for their rebellion God cast them out from the paradise of His presence, and, little by little, from these filterings and imaginings there emerged the clear idea of one sole God, all-creative and omnipotent.

III. What Was God?

God has been presented as a being who differed in spirit and even in body at various periods of the history of man.

According to the earliest biblical records He was in bodily form like a man. We are told that man was created by God in His own image. But this tells us nothing about man's body or appearance. We know without being told that man is a creature who walks erect on the earth, has arms and legs and is of a certain size, and that he is a limited creature who can only be in one place at one time.

The statement that God created man in His own image is really intended to tell primitive man something about God Himself; and what it tells us is that He, too, is a being who walks erect on the earth and has arms and legs, is of a certain size and can only be in one place at one time.

Such is primitive man's infantile idea of God. He is a being like man to look upon, with man's limitations in relation to time and space.

All this is seen by us now to be an utterly childlike and foolish conception of the Creator and Controller of the mighty universe which covers millions of miles from the earth to the sun and must have existed through millions on millions of years. But it was the only conception of God which spoke to the undeveloped mind of primitive man. It helped him to realize God to his eye and mind— to know Him. Later in the development of the mind of man, God lost His limitations. He was no longer a being in the likeness of man. He became an invisible presence, a mighty unknown and unknowable being, whose face had never been seen by any man. *He became a voice.* By this last human faculty He spoke to His creatures. So Moses heard the voice of God coming from the burning bush. And 2,000 years later Paul heard the voice of the Son of God speaking from the sky.

The prophets perhaps believed they heard the voice of God, but this is not certain. More probably the invisible spirit of God was thought to speak to them in dreams, in conditions of trance and ecstasy.

This marks an immense development in man's conception of God. God is now a spirit. A mighty invisible spirit who lives in the heavens, and can be anywhere and everywhere at the same time.

Farther than this conception of God man appears never to have attempted to go. It was enough even for Jesus of Nazareth, who, more than any one before his time, liberated the idea of God from any thought of form or bodily shape or space or time. Hence his rejection of the Temple as the only home of God.

God lived neither in the Temple nor in the mountains, but in the spirit of man, and therefore He could be worshipped only in spirit and in truth.

IV. The Real Birth of Religion

To return to primitive man : what, then, does the idea of God mean to him, who is helpless and innocent and ignorant of material love? At first he does not know. He realizes at the beginning that he is in the midst of powers, strong, cruel and insatiable, which are immeasurably greater than himself and capable of sweeping him into the darkness of death.

But at length he becomes conscious of something evil waking within himself. The impulse of the material man, in a world so full of warring elements, is to protect himself against his fellow-man, to subdue him, to rule over him and, if need be, to destroy him. Out of this fierce struggle for existence, this quickening of the will to live, comes his earliest consciousness of his moral relation to the giant powers about him. He has usurped their right over life and death, and therefore he is in danger of being driven from the face of the earth. As a result he becomes afraid, and perhaps his fear is the beginning of his religion.

Quick on the heels of his consciousness of sin comes the desire for forgiveness. This is an animal as well as a spiritual impulse. Little as we have yet learned of savage man, we know that in the presence of his conquering enemy his impulse is not to fight but to supplicate, creeping like a dog the closer to the feet of his master because the whip is over him.

In what way, then, can the mere belief in the existence of magnified man dwelling in the skies be called a religion?

It may be conjectured that religion begins in primitive man at the moment when he presents the spectacle of religious brotherhoods holding communion with their gods. But how can communion be established between feeble and transient man who lives on the earth and the omnipotent powers which exist only in the distant and unsearchable heavens?

Are we not compelled to conclude that religion can only begin when the brain of man has become so civilized that he can think of a Creator who is the first cause of his existence as a being as closely related to him as master to slave, and that as often as he offends against him he must sue for his forgiveness and obtain it, or he will be swept to the door of death?

But even when we see that sin and the fact of punishment is the beginning of religion there remains a still more perplexing question.

It must have been so in the case of primitive man. With the eye of the spirit we see him at the first consciousness of his sin, prostrating himself on the earth and crying out to the gods of fire and flood and tempest whom he thinks he has offended.

This was without doubt the beginning of prayer with man in a state of nature. Perhaps it is all that prayer is now until it takes the form of praise and thanksgiving. But as time went on, and man's brain began to enlarge, and his soul to increase, he saw that as a means towards forgiveness prayer was not enough. It was only a kind of begging, such as a vanquished man might address to his conquering enemy. He must do more if he is to appease the anger of his enemy. So we see primitive man in the next stage of his spiritual development, building pyramids of stones, perhaps on the mountain tops where he thinks his gods live, and then taking the best of his flock, carrying it up the mountain side, killing it, laying it on his altar, setting fire to it and leaving it to burn to ashes.

V. Sacrifice

This was the beginning of sacrifice. But primitive man, under the burden of his guilt, soon realized that even that was not enough. So deep was his sin, or so terrifying his fear of punishment, that he must give blood for blood. Blood, always blood, must be shed if he is to be saved from the wrath of his avenging god.

That is a fearful ordeal. Seeing that when, as a shepherd, he slaughters a sheep for his daily food its life remains until its blood has ceased to flow, he concludes that the blood must be the life. Therefore, he takes the best-beloved of his lambs to his altar on the mountain top, binds it alive to his piled-up stones, kills it, and then stands aside until its pathetic eyes have ceased to look into his eyes, and the last drop of its blood has been shed.

This is, perhaps, the beginning of the blood sacrifice. But as time goes on and his brain becomes still larger, primitive man thinks he sees that even that is not enough. After some fearful calamity, perhaps some frightful slaughter, primitive man begins to believe that the wrath of his god will not be appeased until he has given human life for human life, the life he had loved for the life he hated and had taken away. So we see him in the intoxication of his pre-religious delirium, taking his first-born son, perhaps his only son, the being on whom his hope in life reposes, the sole medium of his continued race, and going up to his altar in "the high places," binding his sin-offering to the stones, raising his knife and killing him; and then eating his flesh and drinking his blood in the belief that as an atonement for his sin he is eating and drinking in communion with his god.

This is called human sacrifice, and it is known to have prevailed as a means of pacification in nearly all the mystical religions. Josephus, the Jewish historian, speaks of it as a "mad course" which had survived down to his own day. We know that it existed in the time of Abraham. Is it blasphemous to say that in its terrifying resemblance to the most exalted rite in the purest of modern religions it still exists, and that devout people of our own day are deriving from it to this hour the sweetest comfort of their souls?

"What have I done? Why do I suffer?"

This is the cry which seems to go up from primitive man through endless and unfathomable ages if it is true, as the scientists (and even many of the theologians) now tell us, that between the origin of man and the beginning of history there was a great gulf of time in which man lived and died either as a soulless animal or else spiritually unredeemed.

There seems to be only one way out of this tragic dilemma, and that is belief in the doctrine of original sin. Nearly all the early religions bear trace of it. Even the Hebrew religion leaves us without doubt that before man came into the world he knew God and was a fallen angel.

VI.   The Beginning According to the Bible

The sacred Book of the Hebrews does not tell us where or how God began, but it contains in its opening passage a more sublime expression of the Godhead than can be found elsewhere in the whole range of books.

In the beginning God created the Heaven and the earth. And the earth was without form, and void; and darkness was upon the face of the deep. And the Spirit of God moved upon the face of the waters. And God said, "Let there be light," and there was light.

Here is a conception of the Godhead which was apparently written not less than 3500 years ago, yet it is still in harmony with the latest developments of religion, and not out of harmony with modern science. God is a being without limitations of time or space or power. He is not the sun or the moon or the stars, because He created them. He is not anything on the earth below or in the heavens above, because He made them. He is a mighty, universal, omnipotent and invisible spirit which pervades the universe and lives apart, having no partners, no father or mother, no wife or child (as certain other sacred books say), and can be anywhere or everywhere at the same time.

This is the first passage in the Bible, and never had book a more magnificent opening.

Later there is another passage of only less sublimity. It describes the origin of man.

And the Lord God formed man of the dust of the ground, and breathed into his nostrils the breath of life; and man became a living soul.

Here, again, is a conception of the origin of man which is also in harmony with religion and not out of harmony with science. Down to this day man has no scientific knowledge which in any way disturbs it. Man is not a beast of the field. He is not one with God. He is not God. But God has endowed him with the highest attribute of His own divinity. He has made him godlike, His servant, His son.

Such is the first conception of God and of the origin of man in the Hebrew religion.*

---

*Days of the Creation of the World according to Josephus:

1. In the beginning God created the Heaven and the earth, and so on. And He named the beginning of light morning and the time of rest evening. [Thus it was one day of twenty-four hours.]

2. Placed the Heaven over the whole world. He also placed a moist and rainy firmament round it, for affording the advantage of dews.

3. Appointed the dry land to appear. On the same day he made the plants and seeds to spring out of the earth.

4. He adorned the Heaven with the sun, the moon and the other stars, and appointed their several courses that the seasons might be signified.

5. He produced living creatures, both those that swim in the water and those that fly in the air.

He also assorted them as to society for procreators, that their kind might increase and multiply. (*Continued on next page.*)

But, unhappily, *Genesis* is the work of many writers, and in the writings of some of them the conception of God is brought down from its first sublime height to certain of man's humblest limitations. One of them concerns the creation of woman, and that is an amazing story. After God had created man, He remembered that He had omitted to make a helpmeet for man, as for all other creatures of the earth. Therefore, causing a deep sleep to fall upon Adam (now the name of the first man) He took out one of his ribs and made it a woman, and then gave the woman to the man, who said:

> This is now bone of my bones, and flesh of my flesh; she shall be called Woman, because she was taken out of Man. Therefore shall a man leave his father and his mother, and shall cleave unto his wife; and they shall be one flesh.

Here is a conception of God and the exercise of His power which has nothing to do with reality as we know it.

VII. The Garden of Eden

But there is yet one other conception of God in *Genesis,* and that is clearly intended to show the origin and penalty of sin. God is now no longer a supreme deity of the universe. He is not the only God, but one of many gods, walking the world as a man, with angels to attend on Him, and demons to torment Him. He has planted a garden in the fairest part of the earth, and put His earthly children into it, to dress and to keep it. The garden is called Eden and it is a place of peace and delight, wherein man might have lived for ever a life that would be innocent and happy.

In this earthly paradise man was doubly blessed—in body and in soul. He had no work to do, because nature did everything. If he were hungry he had only to stretch out his hands to the trees; if thirsty, he had only to stoop to the streams. It was always spring in Eden, for there the softest of zephyrs caressed the sweetest of flowers.

6. He created the four-footed beasts and made them male and female. On the same day he created man.

Josephus omits that God created man male and female. Also that He had created man in His own image.

Accordingly, Moses said that in six days the world and all therein was made. The seventh day was a day of rest, a release from labour; whence it was that man celebrated the seventh day and called it Sabbath, which denotes rest in the Hebrew tongue.

Where Eden stood (if it ever stood anywhere) it has not been given to us to know.*

Notwithstanding the mention of rivers that flowed through and about it, we have never yet discovered its geographical situation. Nor is it necessary that we should do so. Eden is everywhere. Like Ovid's place of peace in the Golden Age, it is the beautiful picture of every poet and the beautiful poem of every painter.

In this paradise, man had all knowledge and power. He was sinless and he was immortal. Only one limitation did God put upon his dominion. In the midst of the Garden, which was full of fragrant and fruitful trees, there was one tree called the Tree of the Knowledge of Good and Evil. Of all other trees man might eat and be welcome, but of that tree he should not eat because (as heathen mythology told mankind many years later) it was the food of God. Therefore, on the day he ate of it he would surely die. With this sole injunction, and the command that he should increase and multiply and replenish the earth, God left His children—the Man and the Woman He had given to be with him—in the Garden He had made for them.

But hardly had He gone when another spirit appeared to them. This was a beast of the field, but standing upright like a man, and endowed with the gift of speech. He was called the serpent (a name common to evil spirits in early mythology), and was understood to be a demon at war with God, one of the fallen angels, akin to the Satan of Milton, who, in an earlier existence, had rebelled against God and been cast out of Heaven on to the earth, where he spent his strength in destroying the faith and trust of His children.

Tempting the woman first, as the weaker vessel, the serpent told her that what God had said of the consequences of eating of the Tree was untrue. If she and her husband ate of it they would not die. On the contrary, they would live and acquire the knowledge and power of God Himself. The woman yielded to the temptation,

---

*Josephus states that the Garden of Eden was watered by one river which ran round about the whole earth, and was divided into four parts. These four parts are understood to have been:
1. Phison, which runs into India, and is by the Greeks called the Ganges.
2. Euphrates, as well as
3. Tigris, which go down to the Persian Gulf.
4. Geon, which runs through Egypt and arises from the east and is called by the Greeks the Nile.
Note. These are not the names given in *Genesis*.

and, having eaten of the tree, she persuaded her husband to eat of it also.

Having done so, they became conscious of sin, and in their shame they covered their bodies, which were naked, with leaves. Then God returned to the Garden to see how His children were faring. They heard Him coming, in the cool of the evening (for He had now the audible footsteps of man), and they concealed themselves in the trees. God called to Adam, but Adam made no answer. At length God found him and his companion, and charged them with what He saw to be their disobedience.

Admitting his offence, Adam blamed the woman whom God had given him, saying she had tempted him. The woman blamed the serpent, saying he had belied her. The serpent alone was silent. God punished all three: the serpent, to return to his former condition as a beast of the field; the woman to become a slave to her husband and to bear his children in sorrow and pain; and the man (and, consequently, his offspring to the last generation) to earn his bread by the sweat of his face, to till the ground, which would be cursed with thorns and thistles for his sake, and, above all, to die. And then, taking counsel of the angels, who appeared to have been with him, God cast Adam out of the garden and put a cherub at the eastern gate of it with a flaming sword that turned every side to keep the way of the Tree of Life for ever.

VIII. Atonement

Such is the Bible story of the Garden of Eden. For 6,000 years at least, according to the chronology of the Bible, it was accepted as an account of the origin of sin. For nearly 2,000 years it has been called the Fall of Man. It asserts the inborn depravity of man, in Adam's disobedience to God. It implies that man is predestined to damnation. Unless by an act of sacrifice and redemption, he cannot save himself. Thus the story of the Fall as a pagan theory, which recognizes only one effective will in the universe—the will of God. From this alienation from God man has to be redeemed. An atonement has to be made. Man has sinned.

For hundreds of years after the story was written it attracted, so far as we can see, little attention among the Hebrews. They simply did not believe it, or, believing it, they did not regard it as an actual happening. What, then, was it? When the Christian

Scriptures came to be written the greatest of the Christian apostles called it a similitude, and said, in words of equal majesty and sublimity, which have since been repeated as often as a Christian has died and been committed to the grave, "For as in Adam all die, even so in Christ shall all be made alive."

"Does this mean," asked a modern scientist, "that without the Fall there can be no atonement—without Adam there can be no Christ?"

But the hope of the Messiah originated at the same moment as the consciousness of sin—the certainty that somewhere and at some time a divine being would come from Heaven to the world to atone for man's transgression, and make his peace with God.

Human history, from its inception in the work of Origen, obviously begins with the events recorded in the opening of the Book of *Genesis*. The world had no existence for him until it became such a place as now—with mountains and villages, rivers and streams, forests and fields. And so man had no reality as man, until he was such a being as we now know—a creature walking erect and holding dominion over all the beasts of the field.

After a period of violent resistance to the will of God, a period of violence and warfare, having its origin in sensual aspirations after the divinity, creating gods of his own, man, who, according to the Bible, had emerged with human life in the valley of the Euphrates, apparently fled from the penalty of his transgressions to the higher lands in the mountains of southern Persia. There he existed for unknown ages. He had separated himself from the tribes called respectively the Semites and the Babylonians. The one tribe, the Semites, had led the lives of shepherds and hunters, but retained the purity of their faith. The other tribe, the Babylonians, had become first agriculturists and afterwards craftsmen, the first and greatest authors of commerce and masters of the arts. In this character they had finally come to regard themselves as the masters of the world.

IX. *The First Sacrifice*

When the gates closed on the Garden of Eden primitive man must have carried out with him from the vast universal chaos in which the earth was sown with thorns and thistles two memories that were to abide with humanity for ever.

The first of these memories must have been the memory of the

Almighty, the second the memory of his sin against God, with its deathless penalty. Between these two, man, in the first hours of his degradation, must have gone through a bitter struggle. What was God in relation to man that He should impose upon him and upon his children to the end of all generations this everlasting punishment? Was He a malignant or a benevolent power—the enemy of man or his friend and father?

If we are to accept the spirit rather than the letter of the Bible, we can hardly resist the conclusion that to primitive man, fresh from the Garden of Eden, God was his bitterest enemy. He had put him in a place of temptation. He had left him the victim of an evil spirit of His own creation, who could do nothing but destroy him.

What was the result? The first we hear of man after the gates of Eden have closed upon him is that in his ignorance and anger he sets up gods of his own making, gods peculiar to himself and his family—images made with his own hands, sometimes in the fashion of beasts, sometimes of creatures that are half beast and half man.

In one case it is a god of the earth who can yield him, or not yield him, the food whereby he lives; in another it is the god of the sun who can fructify, or not fructify, the earth on whose grass his flocks are fed; in another it is the god of the moon whose light may lead him over trackless and barren wastes from pasturage to pasturage, or it is the god of the stars who can help him to foresee the future and give him dominion over his enemies. To each of these gods in turn primitive man, as we have seen, set up his altars and offered his prayers and sacrifices, until at length he comes to make the human sacrifice, the sacrifice of his first-born son, with the eating of his flesh and the drinking of his blood.

X.   Memories of Eden

This is, perhaps, the moment when there came back to primitive man the other memory which he brought out of the Garden of Eden. After all, God, at the beginning, had been a just God. He had loved His children. If He had cast them out of His presence and made them to work and to suffer, it was because they had wantonly disobeyed Him. But again and again since then He had taken pity on them in their lost condition, and offered to receive them back to His favour. And at length, according to a legend of mysterious origin, He had listened to the prayer of the purest and most innocent of His angels in Heaven, asking that he should be permitted to come down to earth and win such of God's children as repented of their sins and were worthy of His forgiveness back to Himself and His state of blessedness.

God had granted that prayer, but in doing so He had demanded a terrible sacrifice—that God's own beloved Son, the being who had been with Him from the beginning, should share the death that had been the punishment of His sinful creatures.

In God's good time he should come down to the earth.

The Son of God had accepted that condition, and some day and somewhere he would come to the earth in the form of a man, and die that his fellow-men might live.

Adam and Eve had two sons. The elder, Cain. The younger, Abel. They had also daughters. The two sons took different courses. Abel became a shepherd. Cain became a husbandman. They had resolved to sacrifice. How they came to think of this, Josephus does not explain. Cain brought the fruits of his husbandry. Abel brought the first fruits of his flock. God was better pleased with Abel's sacrifice. How they know this we do not know. Perhaps Abel prospered more than Cain. Cain became jealous of Abel and he killed him, and hid his body. God came to Cain and asked what had become of Abel. Cain gave at first an evasive reply. God knew and charged Cain with being the murderer of his brother.

God did not inflict death upon Cain, but He made him accursed. He cast him out of the land in which he lived and made him a wanderer on the face of the earth. Cain fled away.

Here, in Josephus's account of the history of Man (as in the Bible's), comes a long and unbridgeable gap.

CHAPTER III

The Flood

I. The Germ of Idol Worship

FEW ATTENTIVE READERS of the sixth chapter of *Genesis* can fail to have been shocked by the passage which appears to denote in primitive man, just emerged from the Garden of Eden, a condition of astounding barbarity. It reads:

And it came to pass, when men began to multiply on the face of the earth, and daughters were born unto them, that the sons of God saw the daughters of men that they were fair; and they took them wives of all which they chose. And the Lord said, My spirit shall not always strive with man, for that he also is flesh; yet his days shall be an hundred and twenty years. There were giants in the earth in those days; and also after that, when the sons of God came in unto the daughters of men, and they bare children to them, the same became mighty men which were of old men of renown.

What does this mean? Is it merely the record of appalling sensuality such as, on the word of St. Paul, God "winked at" for the peopling of this world? Or has the perplexing passage another and higher meaning? In the opinion of the present writer it means both, and at the same time it is the first link between sinful man and his hope of a Messiah.

It takes us back to the last and most barbaric of the sacrifices of primitive man—the human sacrifice of his first-born son for his sins and the sins of the world. As for us, we see that rite as it was first practised in the valley of the Euphrates. We see the stricken father going up to the altar on the mountain top to take the life of his son, and we see him coming down with a broken heart after fulfilling the barbaric act at the "temptation" of his God. And we see his fellow-men, his enemies until now, perhaps, looking on with pity at the suffering inflicted upon him.

But what can his fellow-man do for him? He can do nothing. He cannot even speak to him. Unless we are prepared to believe

28

that when man was created he was endowed with the gift of speech, we have no choice but to believe that he may have been thousands of years on this planet before he had learned to speak.

The dark mystery of the origin of language presents a problem which, in the present state of knowledge, may never be solved. But archæology tells us that, as far as we can judge from the fossil remains which have been unearthed in various parts of the globe, it was the practice of primitive man to wander over the world not in large communities, but in small and scattered bands. Therefore, few and rare were his needs of speech with his fellow-men. His physical necessities he found for himself, as a hunter and shepherd, and he provided for the calls of his spiritual nature by creating his own gods.

At first these gods were few because his physical and spiritual needs were few. But as his numbers became greater his gods increased until at length every power in nature became a god to him. These powers were mighty to heal or to help. By prayer and sacrifice he could appease them. As a consequence, there were long periods of time in which primitive man in his spiritlessness was little better than a closed-up soul. The result was hatred and strife between primitive man and primitive man. As often as they met they clashed, sometimes about their natural possessions (such as their wells and streams), but more frequently about their altars and places of sacrifice and prayer. Perhaps this was the beginning of what was afterwards called holy warfare, which of all kinds of warfare has been the most bloody and blasphemous.

II. First Human Speech

But at length, no one knows when or how, perhaps slowly and gradually, perhaps swiftly and unexpectedly, perhaps at some rapturous moment of common joy, more probably at some terrible time of common calamity, there came to primitive humanity, like an angel's whisper, the great gift of human speech, and it was the golden bridge which for the first time united man to man.

But it was more than that. With the unity of speech came the unity of faith. Primitive man began to see that their many gods had all the time been the same God; that they had only been minor gods at the best—the gods of the rivers and the streams, of the storm and the sunshine, of the sun and the moon and the stars—

while over them was the Supreme God of All, the God of the universe, the God of peace and order, and that He had called on them to live and worship in communion together.

Even this was not all. The time of the coming of human speech may have been the time of the beginning of human sacrifice. And, for all we know to the contrary, it may also have been the time when back from man's earliest days on earth came the dream of the God-man who was to come to earth to save him from the penalties of his sin, and to take his load of suffering from his back as one man may take a load of wood from the back of another.

What joy, what rapture, must have come to primitive man from the birth of language until the beginning of religion! Perhaps, as some writers say, man was then on the plains of Shinar, having wandered so far from his first home in search of pasturage for his flock. But tired of his life as a tent-dwelling nomad, in the midst of perpetual dangers, he was longing to return home to the fruitful lands under Ararat, partly because they were his first home since he came perhaps from the jungle into his inheritance as a man, and partly because he had led himself to believe that it would be there that his Redeemer, his Saviour, his God-man would first appear.

It is a glorious picture that comes to the eye of the mind at the thought of this moment in the depths of unrecorded time. Perhaps it was the spring of the year, when the earth was beginning to awake from the sleep of winter. We see a great company of the united people turning their faces westward, and with the image of their new-born Redeemer going before them, marching through the flowers of the desert that would be the same to them as the footsteps of God, and singing some crude version of the song which, thousands of years later, was to come, in the splendour of speech, to the lips of the greatest of their psalmists.

> The Lord is my Shepherd; I shall not want. He maketh me to lie down in green pastures; He leadeth me beside the still waters; He restoreth my soul . . . Yea, though I walk through the valley of the shadow of death, I will fear no evil; for Thou art with me; Thy rod and Thy staff they comfort me.

How moving, how inspiring! Are we forbidden to believe that the great doctrine of evolution, which is too often concerned with the wriggling of worms in the sand and the cries of monkeys in the trees, may not extend to spiritual as well as physical developments?

And is it blasphemy to say that the first visible symbol of the Messiah may have revealed itself in the idols of primitive man?

III. Idols and Idolatry

It is a common belief that idolatry is the truest form of religious worship. The Jewish law expressly forbids it, and the Bible is full of contemptuous references to the absurdity of man making an idol with his own hands and then kneeling down to it and worshipping it. In the dialogue between the king and Daniel about the image of Bel and his power of consuming the food left out for him by night, the king asks the prophet, "Dost thou say this is not a living God?" And Daniel is made to laugh and reply, "O king, be not deceived, for this is but clay within and brass withal and cannot eat or drink anything." Even St. Paul at Athens, in the spirit of that marvellous intellect that almost utterly failed, is made to say that while God "winked" in the past at the ignorance which caused man to think that the Godhead was like gold or silver or stone graven out of man's device, He now commanded them everywhere to repent of such unrighteousness.

How pitifully foolish! Is it blasphemy to say that this is as utterly untrue as it would be to say that such is the meaning of the adoration of the figure of the Virgin in the churches and streets of Rome? Except in the lowest forms of idolatry the idol has never been worshipped for itself—for the God that has been supposed to dwell in it. Not until the crude physical image has been confused with the spirit it has symbolized has the idol been more than a doll to the child that plays with it. In the highest of pagan civilizations (such as the civilization of Athens) the idol has been nothing more than the representation (often the inspiring representation) of the spirit it has stood for.

It must have been so with primitive man. Through the dim twilight of the unrecorded ages we see man waiting and watching for the leader, the Redeemer, the God-man who was to save him in his helplessness and loneliness from the great forces which had beset him from the beginning. He was long in coming. Years, perhaps incalculable years, had passed and He had not come. On the contrary, He had seemed to recede before man in his journeying, just as the mirage of the desert which had looked so fair to his eyes as he rode towards it on his camel, under the golden mirror of the evening sky, receded at the fall of night. What wonder, then, if in the strain of his hope deferred he began at length to yield to the call of his animal nature, and give cause for the astounding picture of sensuality·which finds expression in the passage from GENESIS which stands at the head of this chapter?

If this was so with primitive man can it have been otherwise with primitive woman? We read that by means of what is called "sacred prostitution" there were mighty men in those days, men of renown. Can we wonder, then, that in her long pilgrimage from the barren plains of Shinar to the fruitful meadows under Ararat primitive woman, yearning for the day that was to witness the advent of the Deliverer, and knowing that she was the only medium of the continuance of her race, may have told herself that the Great Being who was to come might come the quicker if He came as the fruit of her womb?

This is no dream, no fable. In the early years of human history there was no shame in supernatural conception. On the contrary, there was honour and glory. Did not the mother of Plato, after his death, openly boast that he had been supernaturally born, having had a god for a father? And is it a matter for surprise that primitive woman, on her way from the wilderness of Mesopotamia back to her birthplace, may have made herself believe that when the God-man came it would not be as a winged angel, descending from the skies, in the form of a charioteer, but as a child, an innocent and helpless child, who was to become a king and then die for the salvation of his nation?

This was a pitiful delusion, but it lived in the world for endless ages afterwards. Who will say that in the festival of Christmas it is not living in the world now?

However this may be, we can see its beginnings. Primitive woman, on the plains of Shinar, helped out perhaps by the craft of corrupt priests, began to leave the entrance to her tent unlatched when she lay down at night in the hope that "mighty man" in the form of the image which her people carried before them by day might creep in to her unseen, and not leave her until the gleams of morning began to sweep through the desert sky.

Nor is this a fable. History is full of such stories. One of the latest and worst of them may be found in Josephus, cheek by jowl with his fond and foolish words about Jesus of Nazareth, and it is a story of how a pure woman was persuaded by a sensual priest to give herself in the darkness of a Roman temple by night to a licentious scoundrel, in the belief that she was giving herself to a god and thereby would give birth to god-like children.

IV. The Children of Adam

As a consequence of these sinful practices (for we hear of no others that had excited the wrath of God) there was war, bitter and bloody war, between two at least of the tribes, with which the folly of man appears to have been chiefly divided. One of these tribes may have encouraged the practice as a love of the beautiful, and perhaps as a means of peopling the earth with mighty men, while the other seems to have been as strongly opposed to it, believing it to be a breach of the covenant made with God when He created man, male and female, and pledged one man to one woman.

Clearly, God sided with the latter, looking upon "sacred prostitution" as a challenge to His divinity, and saying that the wickedness of men was great on the earth, which was filled with wickedness, that the thoughts of men's hearts were evil continually, that He repented that He had not exterminated him off the face of the world with water, thereby admitting that when He had first created man He had utterly failed.

The sequel was natural, and it needs no supernatural aids such as are described in *Genesis* to make us believe in them. When primitive man, weary of his wanderings in the wilderness of Mesopotamia, so full of danger, returned to the valley of the Euphrates, he must have found himself in the midst of still greater perils.

To the north of him was the Black Sea, which at intervals overflowed its broad banks and poured terrible torrents into the valley below, while to the south was the open mouth of the Persian Gulf that swept tidal waves like champing horses to the foot of Ararat, leaving the flat bed of the two rivers, the Euphrates and the Tigris, between under deep and prolonged floods such as destroyed all life that lay beneath them.

That floods of this character took place at some early period of the world's existence is now beyond question, so widely diffused in the sacred books of the past is the belief in such phenomena, but whether any of them was the flood described in the Bible is open to serious question.

When the Flood of Noah took place (if it ever took place) we do not know. Without wanting in admiration of the researches of the historian, or of the marvellous discoveries of the archæologists, it is impossible not to see that the dates of one are constantly receding, while the remains of the other are going deeper and deeper under the surface of the earth, and thereby giving evidence of earlier and still earlier deluges.

In the light of this fact it is impossible not to sympathise with Luther when he said, in discussing the date of the greatest event in human history, that it did not so much matter when it occurred as whether it occurred at all. Applying Luther's thought, then, to the biblical story of the Flood, we are on easier ground when we ask: Why did the Flood take place? And what purpose did it serve in the scheme of creation?

Cain became a fugitive and a vagabond, and dwelt in the land of Nod, on the east of Eden. He married a wife. Whose daughter she was, if not his father Adam's, is a circumstance which is not recorded. He had children who were both good and bad. One, Enoch, his eldest son, was translated to Heaven without death. The posterity of Cain became exceedingly weakened. They were intolerable in war, and violent in robberies.

Meantime, Adam, and Eve, after the death of Abel, had other children. One of their sons was called Seth. The later sons of Adam and Eve proved to be of good dispositions, and lived in a happy condition till they died. They were the inventors of that kind of wisdom which is concerned with the heavenly bodies and their order.

Adam predicted that the world was to be destroyed at one time by force, at another time by the violence of water.

Seth's posterity worshipped God for seven generations. Then they forsook God. Many angels of God companied with women, and begat sons that proved unjust. They were despisers of all that was good.

At length came Noah, a man greatly favoured of God for his righteousness. He was of the tenth generation from Adam.

God saw that the wickedness of man was great in the earth. He revealed to Noah His intention of destroying the whole race of mankind, for He repented that He had made them. But Noah found grace in the eyes of the Lord, and he and his family would be preserved and the new race should be pure, although the span of their lives would be cut short. It had formerly been about 1,000 years each, but this would be cut short to 120 years only. So God brought on the world the Deluge.

V. The Flood

Noah was told to build an ark of gopher wood, large enough to carry not only himself and his family, but also every living thing of all flesh, two of every sort, male and female, with food in plenty. The dimensions of the ark are given in *Genesis*. It was to be 300 cubits in length, fifty cubits broad and thirty cubits in height. A cubit was equal to twenty inches of our modern measurement, or, say a foot and a half. The ark, therefore, would be 450 feet long, seventy-five feet in beam and forty-five in height. There were three stories, only one window and one door. Presumably the upper story was under cover. There is no reference to oars or sails.

A vessel of these dimensions would be ludicrously small and unsuitable for its intended purpose of accommodating its incongruous freight. Even if Noah had been capable of rounding up the required specimens of every living animal and bird, it is difficult to imagine that they could all be assembled and exist in concord during the Deluge, crowded between decks with neither light nor ventilation. Such a miscellaneous menagerie would require a vast fleet of ships, each of greater size than the ark.

After God had given the signal, it rained for forty days on end, until the flood was fifteen cubits higher than the earth. While the flood prevailed on the earth anything that had lived on the dry land had died, but God remembered Noah, and made a wind to pass over the earth, whereupon the waters were assuaged, and when in the tenth month they had so far subsided that the top of the mountains were seen (Ararat itself being the highest) Noah began to prepare for his return to earth.

First, he opened the window of the ark and sent forth the raven to see if the waters had dried up on the ground, but, after flying to and fro, the bird returned to his hand. Seven days later he sent out a dove, but she, too, came back to the ark, having found no rest for the sole of her foot. After seven other days he sent out the dove again, and she returned in the evening with a leaf plucked from an olive tree in her mouth, and by that Noah knew that the waters were dying down on the slopes of the mountains. Yet another seven days later Noah sent out the dove a third time, and then she came back no more, and from that Noah knew that the face of the ground was dry.

At length the ark settled on the earth, and God commanded Noah to come out of the ark, and he came, bringing his sons and daughters with him, together with the animals which, for the better part of a year, must have made it a pest-house. Then Noah built an altar and made a burnt-offering to God for their deliverance, while God blessed him and his family as He had blessed man at the beginning, telling him to increase and multiply and replenish the earth, and promising that never again would he destroy the world with water, but, as long as it remained, seedtime and harvest, summer and winter, night and day should not cease.

VI.   Did the Flood Actually Take Place?

How far it is possible to accept this story in *Genesis* as a record of actual happenings is, to say the least, very doubtful. There is at least poetic fitness in the hypothesis of the Flood around the mountains of Ararat, inasmuch as they are about an equal distance from the Black Sea and the Caspian and from the Mediterranean and the Persian Gulf. But Ararat consists of two mountains, the great Ararat and the little Ararat, and both are entirely above all possible vegetation, the first being about 17,000 feet above the sea and covered with perpetual snow, and the second being about 13,000 feet above the sea and also covered with perpetual snow. Only the slopes of the great Ararat are covered with fields and verdure. This occurs about 5,000 feet, all above that height being sterile.

Whether, therefore, the biblical story of the Deluge and of Ararat being the resting-place of Noah's ark is of any historical value may at least be questioned. On the other hand, it is necessary to admit that the tradition of the Deluge covering that part of the earth is of very ancient date, and is by no means peculiar to the Jewish scriptures. A flood is believed to have destroyed Ur of the Chaldees. It is said (by Loisy) that this suggested the biblical story. But this is doubtful.

VII. The Tower of Babel

The sons of Noah proved to be a group of graceless ingrates, and, distrusting the promise of God, they devised an impious means of protecting themselves from His further vengeance by setting about the building of a tower which should reach to the sky and have a temple at the top of it that would be an entrance to Heaven.

It was not to be. Seeing that they were too few for so great an enterprise, and perhaps reflecting that they would all be dead and buried before they could finish it, the sons of Noah postponed their scheme until after the birth of a big line of generations of Noah, and then began again with a different motive.

Finding a suitable place on a plain in Shinar, which is believed to have been another name for Babylon, they made bricks of the alluvial soil they lived on and set about building the tower which was to protect them from such another calamity as that with which God had so nearly overwhelmed them.

But God heard of their impious attempt to defeat His will, and with His angels He came down to the builders, who were now of one language and speech, and confused their tongues, with the result that they stopped in their work and fled away in fear to every known part of the earth.

It is admitted that no more appalling picture of human terror can be found in the world of books than that which rises to the eye of the mind from the few words which tell of how, in the confusion of speech, every man looked upon every other man as his foe, and fled from him in terror.

It is the second of the three sentinels on the lonely road between man and God, and it has probably stood there for thousands of years with its naked arms outstretched against the wintry sky.

And now, if these two stories—the Flood and the Tower of Babel—are not to be regarded as pure mythology to which humanity has never yet found the key, what are we to say of them?

In all humility we are compelled to say, first, that they are obviously out of chronology, inasmuch as they pre-suppose a world which must have been thickly peopled at a time when, according to their own calculations, it was sparsely inhabited; next, that they assume a second creation of man and a second Creator; next, that their principal incident, the Flood, would carry greater conviction as an actual happening than it can possibly do as an event produced by supernatural agency; next, that they are entirely without sequence or design and could be dropped out of the Bible without the continuity of the Book being in any way disturbed; and, finally, that they are reprehensible and disjointed and could hardly be more imperfect as examples of the narrative art if they had been written not by instructed priests of the sixth century in their Temple at Jerusalem, but by illiterate bedouin shepherds, riding their camels over the rugged road between Baghdad and Damascus.

VIII.　Babel and Babylonia

Happily or unhappily (we can hardly say which) there is still another sentinel on the lonely way between God and man. It is the story of the dispersion of mankind after the Flood and the downfall of the Tower of Babel. We are told that on reaching a place of safety, certain of the tribes of primitive man divided and scattered themselves on the earth. Two of these tribes were shepherds called the Semites and the Babylonians. The Semites, who are believed to have derived their name from Shem, the eldest son of Noah, may be rightly described as the forerunners of the Hebrews, and they were probably the first cause of the violence which broke out in the valley of the Euphrates against the practice of "angel marriages". The Babylonians are thought to have been the tribe that violently opposed the Semites in this sensual practice, and brought about the adoration of images for their own sakes.

On parting from their half-brothers, the Babylonians, the Semites travelled far into the lonely lands on the north-east. There they lived for centuries as tent-dwelling bedouins, forbidding as a deadly sin the making of images of any kind, particularly the images of gods (such as might tempt lustful men to acts of sin), leaving no nation or empire behind them in the land of their adoption, and worshipping only, as their fathers had done before them, the mighty and invisible Being, whom eye had never seen and ear had never heard, under the silent circuit of the sky.

Meantime, their half-brothers, the Babylonians, had gone their different way and become a great people. They travelled south-west and made their central home in Arabia. There they had first become agriculturists and afterwards traders, establishing the caravan route which crossed the eastern hills and commencing the commerce of the world. Afterwards they joined themselves to the Sumerians, a small tribe of their own blood which had come up before them and become the craftsmen of the East.

One third of the vast country they lived in was stark and naked desert, chiefly of sand. But there was gold and stone in it also, and with these they built cities and temples and fortresses, for they did not forget to become soldiers who had to protect the possessions they had.

It does not appear that on coming into Arabia and joining themselves to the Sumerians they repented of the corruption of the religion for which they had slaughtered their fellow tribesmen in the valley of the Euphrates. On the contrary, they seem to have multiplied their excesses by making images of the most beautiful of their kind and worshipping them. Few and rare are now the references to the God-man who is to be born of a woman and bring in a golden age of peace. They think the golden age is with them, although it is an age of luxury and corruption and war.

Unquestionably, the Babylonians were a great people. They have left a mark on the world which time will not efface. But on coming into Arabia they became a grossly sensual and barbaric race, believing themselves to be the crown of creation and the masters of the earth.

IX.   The Fall of Babylon

No race has ever reached this apex of arrogance without sooner or later crashing down to a fall. How the Babylonians fell in those early days before 4,000 B.C., which is believed to be the beginning of recorded history, we cannot say. What we do know is that with other tribes of primitive men, of whom the Sumerians were the first, and they themselves were the second, they returned to the valley of the Euphrates. Why they returned we do not know. When we try to penetrate the mystery of their return, we are like children awakening from sleep in the first gleams of the dawn and harkening with bated breath to inarticulate voices that come to them from afar. But the voices are very insistent, and they seem to tell of some terrible disaster which fell on the Babylonians at the time of their pride.

What was it? Perhaps it was an eruption from one of the volcanic mountains farther east which wiped out as by one sweep from the mighty hand of nature the little triumphs of puny man. We have no tablets of stone or cylinders of clay to tell us of that calamity in the prehistoric age, and if we are to see it at all it can only be by the eye of the spirit, added to the presence of the broad wastes of desert sand which it has apparently left behind it.

First, then, we see it as a flame of fire leaping up in the high places of the eastern sky; then as a cloud of lava dust, yellow and grey and black, rising through the air and blotting out the sun. Then we see the sun itself going out through the gloom like a dying eye, and the darkness descending on the earth and covering it as with a pall. We hear the domes of the temples of the priests falling under their load of volcanic ash, and the windows of the houses of the people wrenching open before the flight of terrified birds.

We see the people struggling through the dust, waist deep in the streets, and leading their moaning women and weeping children, their sheep and goats and gazelles to what they believe to be places of temporary safety. Later, we see "the mighty men of great renown" snatching up their neglected images from their discarded altars, and singing their prayers and petitions to their dishonoured gods:

> Marduk, O Marduk,
> Away with the demons who would destroy us,
> Marduk, O Marduk, away, away.

Finally, we see the affrighted people, abandoning all hope, going back from their buried homes in Arabia to the cradle of their race at home. The night is dark, the way is long, and the lava dust is deep. Often their camels drop to their knees and are unable to rise again. But the men push on with their children in their arms and their women dragging at their backs. Sometimes, in the silence of the desert storm, they hear the sepulchral groans of the dying creatures they have been compelled to leave behind them.

Thus the heavy night wears on, and when morning breaks on the wayfarers, and the first light of the sun filters down on them, they look back for a moment on the wilderness they have crossed. It is nothing now but a wide waste of blackened sand, as quiet as a sleeping child and as smooth as a shallow sea after a storm. But under the sand lie the ruins of a buried empire and the bones of dead men.

Such is the last of the sentinels in the lonely road of primitive man as we see him with the eye of the spirit, by tradition and by imagination, through the dim twilight of the unrecorded ages. Without books or monuments or inscriptions to guide us, we know he was there as surely as we know that the day is near when, out in the desert places, we look up at the last star of night and see it touched by the first rays of the arisen sun.

And now, what of the future? In what way will primitive man be different when he emerges into the full light of history and begins his faltering march through Time? What new beliefs will be here, what hopes, what dreams? Will he have left behind him the myths and legends of the religion of fear for the light and power of the religion of a God who is a God of love, not of revenge, of peace, not of war?

If, as certain of the chronologists tell us, it is now 10,000 years since the Flood took place (if it ever took place) and the whole human family as God had created it was wiped off the earth and the world began again, with the result (as an illustrious scientist has said) that the poorest pauper of to-day is better fed and better clothed than were the richest men of the days of Noah; that the most neglected and ignorant of humanity has a better conception of God and of his own place in the scheme of the universe than the kings of Egypt had 5,000 years ago—can it be denied for so much as a moment that the movement of man has ever been Godward, and that the central course of his progress has been the ever-increasing belief in the God-man, the Son of God, who is to bring in a more blessed condition some day, somehow and by some means?

> Unfathomable Power is o'er him—
> The might of Unknowable Mind,
> And fathomless Time is before him,
> And fathomless Time is behind.

CHAPTER IV

The Patriarchal Period

I. A Re-editing of the Scriptures

WHEN the Flood took place we do not know. One of the approved chronologists of Scripture gives its date as 2500 years before Christ, or else 2066, he does not know which. He may well not know, since the effort to make the dates of the Bible agree with those of archæology is an activity hardly more worthy of an instructed intellect than the solution of a cross-word puzzle. All we know is that if the great cities which stood on the banks of the Euphrates had been built before the Flood they must have been exposed to the destruction which we are told overwhelmed everything. Yet we know by inscriptions on monuments in our museums that some of these cities were founded 5,000 years before Christ and were still standing 3500 years later.

In like manner it has not been given to us to know when the building of the Tower of Babel took place. An Egyptian priest of the third century says it was about 100 years later than the Flood, but, as we do not know the date of the Flood itself, this statement means nothing.

We engage in a more fruitful inquiry when we ask ourselves which of the two events has left the more enduring mark on the welfare of the world and on the history of mankind. It is difficult to see that the story of the Flood has left any mark whatever. We might drop it out of the Bible and the story of man and the world would remain undisturbed. The story of the Tower of Babel is immeasurably more closely linked with the history of the world, for it offers an explanation, however inadequate, of the distribution of mankind over the world, the formation of great races and the differences of groups of language which are the forerunners of modern civilization. Therefore, the story of the Tower of Babel may not be, as in the Bible, the sequel to the story of the Flood, but the story of the Flood may be the sequel to the story of the Tower of Babel.

There is much to say for this re-editing of the Scriptures. If we think of primitive man as he must have been when he settled in the plain of Shinar, we see how easy it is to follow the development of the human family without supernatural aids of any kind. After his long pilgrimage in the wilderness as a tent-dwelling nomad, man wishes to settle down in a pleasant and fruitful valley as a tiller of the soil, to see the fruits of the earth spring up under the fructifying sun by day and to sleep cool in his tent by night, instead of tramping before his flocks under the light of the moon. But he speedily realizes that he is in the midst of yet greater perils than before. To the north of him there is a vast sea (the Black Sea) which at intervals overflows its banks and pours a terrifying torrent of water on to the plains below, while to the south of him is the gigantic mouth of an ocean (the Persian Gulf) which sweeps tidal waves up to the foot of the mountains of Ararat. Floods are frequent in the land he has come to live in, but they are of short duration, and, reluctant to leave his new home, the first abiding-place he has yet known, he builds towers of refuge to which he can fly for safety until the waters have subsided.

Many such floods we know something about, and the ruins of one such tower is still to be seen, standing broad-based on the alluvial soil. It is obviously the foundation of a gigantic structure only twenty-seven feet high, but nearly 200 feet long and 140 feet broad. There is nothing to say when it was erected or when destroyed, but tradition plays over it like a miasma that is foul or fair according to the spirit in which we look at it. Tradition says it was built by Nimrod, a son of Noah, in the first generation, a century after the Deluge. But it is more than probable that it was built at least a century earlier and was intended to save the people of the valley of the Euphrates from the fearful calamity that was constantly threatening them.

It is possible that some such calamity came at length, and that seeing it coming, like rolling lava from the mountains and champing horses from the gulf to the south, they fled from the place of refuge to the higher lands on the east. It is an appalling picture of human terror which rises to the eye of the mind at the thought of this natural explanation of the disappearance of the people of the known earth—no less terrible than the scene of the flight under fear of supernatural vengeance.

II.　The Semites and the Babylonians

We are now at the gateway of history, and therefore we go back to the Bible, which is, after all, our earliest authority. We read that after the Flood the families of men divided themselves into nations. Many of these nations are to some extent known to us. But apart from the Sumerians, a very ancient people, believed to have come from Central Asia and to have been the inventors of cuneiform script (a kind of picture writing on the clay of the country), there were only two nations of whom we know much. They are the Semites and the Babylonians, closely akin to each other and yet broadly divided.

The Semites, who are understood to have derived their name from the eldest son of Noah, may be roughly described as the forerunners of the Hebrews. A portion of them were worshippers of idols, but the greater part were strongly opposed to all forms of idolatry. It is probable that they were the first authors of the violence which, in the plain of Shinar, followed the introduction of angel-marriages, and therefore religious differences must have been the first cause of their separation from their fellow-pilgrims.

Although some writers believe that the Semites had their origin in Arabia, it is certain that when they parted from the Babylonians they made their way to Mesopotamia. There they must have quarrelled among themselves—the less orthodox, under the name of Semitic-Babylonian, remaining in the south-east, while the stricter sect, under the name of Beni-Israel, travelled far into the lonely lands in the north, where they worshipped, under the open sky, with its sun and moon and stars, the vast invisible Being who had no temples, no name, no habitation, and no gods.

Assuredly this forbade, as a deadly sin, the making of images—particularly such images as tempted the animal passions of either women or men by representations of the Great Unknown whom eye had not seen and ear had not heard, and perhaps this was the first cause of the injunction against image-making which has remained among the Hebrews to this day. They were only shepherds, keepers of sheep, but they were also a great people. Although they left no trace behind them of their sojourn in the land of their adoption, establishing no nation or empire, they fought then, and have fought since, on every battlefield of the human soul.

Meantime, the Babylonians had gone their own way, and were leaving a mark on the annals of time that can never be effaced. After parting from their twin brothers, the Semites, they appear to have travelled south and made their central home in Arabia. There they became the first craftsmen and builders of the world. One third of the vast country is still stark and naked desert, but there was gold and stone in it, and with these they built temples and made images of their gods after the likeness of the most beautiful among his kind, for when man made his idols he had no model except himself. They built villages and cities and citadels and fortresses, for they broke into many nations and followed different occupations, not that of the shepherd only, but also of the agriculturist and trader, and soldier and sailor, thus beginning among the caravans that crossed the roadways of the desert the commerce of the world. As a result they became rich, and, being rich, they became corrupt. They did not repent of the corruptions of their religion, for which they had slaughtered each other in the valley of the Euphrates.

III. Ur of the Chaldees

About 7,000 years ago the vast area that lies between the Mediterranean Sea and the Caspian Sea entered into history. It was then an arid and forbidding wilderness. Much of it is still so.

A hundred miles north of the Persian Gulf and midway between the river Euphrates and a range of grey sandstone hills that form the border of the Syrian Desert there was, until recent years, a great round mound of earth, bricks and rubbish. We have long thought that under this mound lay the remains of a crude home of primitive man, but now we know, by the marvellous discoveries of archæology, that it was a city of great magnitude and importance. It contained palaces, temples and towers which in their barbaric splendour have perhaps never been surpassed. It took tribute from the cities about it, and was for a time the capital of an empire that was mistress of all the known world.

It enjoyed a high degree of material civilization. It had gold and lapis lazuli, and it fought its battles with spears and daggers. We used to think that its inhabitants were little removed from the condition of naked savages unable to read or write or count above ten, but now we know that they kept ledgers and accounts, and that their commercial activities had a startling resemblance to our own.

As late as 2300 years before Christ its government was a tyrannous monarchy based on the theory of theocracy. It was ruled by a king called the Ur-Gur, who claimed divine honours and was believed to be the Son of God. Human sacrifices were made to him, prayers were offered to him, and he presented them to his heavenly father and particularly to his heavenly mother, with whom he was believed to be in constant intercourse.

As far as we know, he was understood to have been born of a virgin, or at least of a woman who had associated with angels.

Nevertheless, as a natural man he had wives and concubines, and took delight in all human pleasures. He lived in his palaces a life of luxury and grandeur. His soldiers and statesmen, his merchants and traders lived in their lofty houses lives of comfort and wealth. How the tens of thousands of his slaves lived has not yet been revealed to us, nor are the archæologists ever likely to tell us, for the hovels of the poor of all ages are buried in ruins before they have fallen into the rubbish heaps of decay.

The religion of the inhabitants of the buried city was clearly idolatrous. Their supreme god was the moon-god, Nannar, or Sin. But they had other gods and some of them were of the foulest, including demons and the gods of fecundity. That way lay the lowest abuses of paganism, with wicked vices which it is impossible to describe. Thus the city at the mouth of the Euphrates was, at the beginning of the third millennium before Christ, a sink of bestial sensuality.

Its name was Ur of the Chaldees.

How had it come to pass that, in the incalculable period between the flight of mankind from the Tower of Babel and their return to the valley of the Euphrates, they had risen so high and fallen so low? The answer to that question must be conjectural, and yet it need not be unreasonable. The student of biblical history and of the recent discoveries of archæology cannot fail to see that the year 5,000 B.C. marks a climacteric period in the human story. About this time a vast immigration of the inhabitants of the world had returned from their places of refuge to the valley that had been the cradle of the human family. Had this been due to a great but unknown spiritual urge, or to some such natural calamity as the writer has just described? He thinks it had been due to the latter.

Clearly, the Babylonians had been the first to arrive. The three great nations into which they were already divided established themselves on the banks of the Euphrates and the Tigris. Having long ceased to be sheep-keeping nomads, and continuing to be chiefly craftsmen, they had built (perhaps at various periods) three great cities at about equal distances apart—Ur, Babylon and Nineveh. Being warlike people they had fought among themselves until one of them had asserted its supremacy. Then they had settled down to the calmer activities of commerce.

IV. Babylonian Laws

Time passed, apparently a long time, and then it was discovered that peace had its conflicts no less than war. If they were to live and work in community, they must have law. A great king named Hammurabi promulgated a code which was, on the whole, founded on wisdom and righteousness. This was about 2,250 years before Christ.

The Babylonian code consisted of three different parts. The first part concerned commerce, and it was written on thousands of tablets. The second part concerned morality, the relation of nation to nation, of man to woman, and of woman to man. Some of its enactments were copied by another great lawgiver of another great race coming later, and one of them, which proclaimed the rights of women, brought the greatest and most mighty of Hebrew kings, notwithstanding the splendour of his intellect and the nobility of his heart, to the bar of eternal justice. The third part concerned the rites of religion and the duties of man to his god.

When the Babylonians came back to the valley of the Euphrates they did not leave their religion behind them. Perhaps they did worse—they altered and degraded it. The Babylonian cosmology ceased to be the monotheism of primitive man in the desert, with its minor gods who were the representatives of a single and supreme one. It became a polytheism, and had a trinity of gods of equal and sometimes of rival authority, the god of Heaven, the god of earth and the god of the watery elements. Each of the three gods had a human as well as a spiritual existence. They were made male and female and held sexual relations. Therefore, they had offspring, and thus the religion they stood for became grossly sensual. It was the theory of angel marriages over again, but now highly organized and of undisputed acceptance.

The Babylonian religion had other aspects more analogous to our own. Confronted by the mysteries of life, it found their explanation in the fixed laws of the seasons. The mystery of death it found in the mystery of sleep, wherein man lay down at night tired and weak and weary and awoke in the morning strong and full of new life. The Babylonian religion could not allow itself to believe that anything that had lived could die, therefore it found its mystery of resurrection in the law of nature whereby the seed sank in the ground and apparently died, and then sprang up in flowers and fruit.

But there was one mystery of life for which the religion of the Babylonians could find no explanation, and that was the mystery of evil. This led to a belief in the existence of demons. The demons were the enemies of the gods and were always opposing them. They lurked everywhere. They could make themselves invisible. They lived in graves and came out in various shapes, often those of serpents.

This led to a highly complicated system of priesthood. The priests were a class set apart by the gods for the prohibition of man from the temptations of the devils. But afterwards they became the agents of the devils, and to propitiate the devils they sculptured them in golden cubes and serpents that flamed like fire, and called on men to bow down to them. Thus the Babylonian religion became a system of mixed devil worship and sensuality.

Further time passed, and then, at the height of the material prosperity of the Babylonians and the depth of their spiritual degradation (probably about 2,000 B.C.), another race came back to the valley of the Euphrates. These were the Semitic Babylonians and perhaps the object of their immigration was little better than a desire to share in what they heard from the caravans of the success of their forerunners. Certain of them, having become craftsmen during their time in Arabia, appear to have been received by the Babylonians, and to have become citizens of the cities on the banks of the rivers, where, accepting the altered religion, they perished in their shame.

The rejected, who had remained nomads, probably established themselves in the little mud-built towns on the outer fringe of the valley, among the circles of scrub grass which surrounded pools and wells of water. Probably they travelled north and founded the city of Damascus, and the towns of Tyre and Sidon. Certainly they went down into the peninsula of Palestine, and there broke up into the numberless tribes which we read of in the Bible, and came to be known by the general name of the Canaanites.

V. The Beni-Israel

Still further time passed, and then (about 1800 B.C.) another tribe of the Semites came down to the Euphrates. These were the Beni-Israel, the sons of Israel, who afterwards became the Hebrews. Where they had come from we cannot say, except that it was from the far north-east. After parting from their half-brothers on the heights above the plains of Shinar, they had gone on and on until they had reached lands in which the foot of man had never yet trod. But it was not for nothing that they had lived alone with nature—with the sun and the moon and the stars as the only symbols of their God. That God had still been the invisible and universal Being for whom they knew no name; yet they had knelt before Him at the close of day when His light went down in the golden gleam of the western sky to rise again in the gleams of the morning.

Why they had turned back none of us can tell, but, judging by the account in the Bible of the days of their first generation, we see that it had certainly not been from a desire to share in the prosperity of those who had returned before them. Looked at in the only other way, the coming of the last of the Semites from the east to the west was one of the greatest events in human history, for it was inspired by the spirit of a crusade. The mysterious means by which rumour passes over the wilderness, like the breeze that breathes over the earth at the coming of the dawn, had perhaps brought accounts of the idolatry of their people in the land of Canaan, where they had planted groves for the idols and were worshipping the Babylonian Baal. Therefore, the caravan must go with a message they had received from the sky.

Their journey was a long one, and children were born and old men died and were buried by the way, so that when, with their flocks and herds, they came near to the south-west of the Syrian desert, their numbers had so far dwindled that they consisted of one family of 138 souls only. Their shepherd-king, by virtue of age, was a man named Terah, but clearly their leader was his eldest son.

This eldest son was one of the world-men whom God sends once in a thousand years to point the right path to the multitudes who are going astray. So few are they in the history of mankind that we can count them on the fingers of our hands. They are not usually kings or conquerors, but simple men, shepherds or tillers of the soil, who have lived alone with nature and have some great thought in their hearts.

This man is one of them. On his way to Canaan he stops before the barred and bolted gate in the high walls of Ur. We see him there in the early morning with his sheep bleating about his feet, and the debauched and dissolute city within lying silent in its drunken sleep.

He is God's messenger to men, and the world will never be the same place again.

All this about Ur of the Chaldees, with whatever else may yet reach us through the dark door of tradition, by authentic history and the discoveries of archæology, would be of little account to the spiritual part of the story of humanity, and would perhaps be allowed to lie buried for ever under its mound of earth and bricks and rubbish, but for its association with his world-name which leaves the mystery-making name of Adam himself in the dust of the forgotten ages. That world-name is Abraham.

VI. *Abraham*

It has been said that Abraham was an astronomer or astrologer who lived in Ur of the Chaldees about 2,000 B.C. There is no reliable authority for that statement. Nothing is known of Abraham outside the Bible. We have no evidence of his existence earlier than 900 B.C. Therefore, we have no clear way to the story of his life and message for mankind except through Scripture. If we cannot convince ourselves of his deathless reality on that authority alone, we must leave the father of the Hebrew nation and religion and the ancestor of the founder of Christianity to the not-too-tender mercies of those who, satisfied of the reality of forgotten kings and princes whose pots and pans they grub out of graves, describe him as a legendary figure and his mission as a myth.

What, then, does the Bible say about him?

When Abraham was born we do not know. According to the Bible he was tenth in the line from Noah. It is impossible to learn from this the period of his life. It may be sufficient to say that even in the Scriptures there is a long and unbridgeable gulf between the first appearance of man on the earth and the beginning of Abraham's story.

Where Abraham was born is equally uncertain. The Bible, our best and earliest authority on this subject, tells us that after the Deluge, the sons of Noah journeyed from the east to the plain on which they built their city and tower. This led the Jewish historian, Josephus, to say that Abraham's father came from "beyond the flood," which meant the eastern side of the Euphrates. It has long been the common belief of mankind that it was from there, if from anywhere in particular, man emerged in some unknown condition from the hand of his Creator, into the first recognizable form of human life.

However this may be, we know that some 4,000 to 5,000 years ago many races of men were living in that quarter of the globe, and that among them was that small but vigorous group called by the collective name Semites. One little family of this group was at some period called the Beni-Israel, the sons of Israel, the Hebrews. Apparently, they were mainly shepherds, and merely to find better pasturage for their flocks and herds they travelled westward. Some of them appear to have taken a north-westerly course in the direction of what we now call Syria. Others seem to have taken a south-westerly course towards Egypt. In this simple and natural happening the greatest story in the world began.

In the opinion of the present writer, the father of Abraham took the south-westerly course, and so came to the wilderness which we now call the Syrian desert, perhaps to the wilderness of Sin, which was afterwards associated with the first tragic experiences of his people. To the writers of the Bible, from the prophets to the authors of the Gospels, a wilderness or desert was not always an arid waste. It was sometimes a free field on the bosom of nature, which sang like the bird and blossomed like the rose, and sometimes a tractless plain full of locust trees and wild honey. The wilderness that was the first home of Abraham, and probably his birthplace, seems to have been a place like this.

Abraham himself is frequently called the Hebrew, a name which came, it is thought, from Eber, a descendant of Shem. He, too, like his father and brothers, was clearly a shepherd. When they came from the country of their origin they were not only looking for fertile fields for their flocks, but also for cities in which to sell them, and at that age of the world there would be few larger or nearer than Ur of the Chaldees. Even the king of the Chaldeans could not live on his magnificence alone. Like the humblest of his subjects, he needed food for his sustenance. Hence it is easy to think of Abraham leading his sheep and goats across the Syrian desert to the profitable market of Ur, and to the productive soil that is said to have lain immediately in front of it.

It is there we first find him in the Bible. Clearly, he lived long in the neighborhood of Ur, perhaps married there, and saw some of his kindred born there. But it is unlikely that he ever lived in the city itself. He probably encamped with his family and servants in his goatskin tents on the desert plains about it. We read that he had 318 servants, so he probably became rich and acquired the character of a desert king. He was almost certainly the head of his tribe. With him were his wife, a beautiful young woman, named Sarah, his brother Nahor, with his wife Milcah, and their father, now an elderly man.

Although it is unlikely that Abraham ever lived in Ur, it is inconceivable that he never entered it, or that, judging by his subsequent conduct, he looked on the polluted life of the Chaldean city with anything but repugnance. He saw there, not only the cow which was the symbol of one of the chief of the Chaldean gods, but also, and probably for the first time, the hideous idols of the devils which had to be propitiated in order to avoid evil, or perhaps to indulge in it. Above all, he saw the strife, the sensuality and the superstition which the worship of many gods, especially the gods of human fecundity, produced. And at evening, his day's business being done, he must have carried the memory of all this with him when he went—a big man with slow step, perhaps—through the city gate to his goatskin tents on the desert roads.

VII. *Abraham's Conception of God*

What happened to him then it is not hard to imagine. Out there, with nothing but the open sky above him, nature awakened in him a spirit and a soul. He told himself that if there were so many gods, the gods of the sun and the moon and the stars, there would be strife among them, a ferocious campaign of deity against deity, even as there was strife among the worshippers. But there was no strife. On the contrary there was peace and perpetual harmony. The sun and the moon rose and set, morning and evening, day by day, year by year, according to their seasons, and the stars moved steadily in their courses.

What did this mean to the son of the desert? It meant that if these were gods, however grossly worshipped, there was a mightier God who, by some divine law, guided and controlled them. That God was invisible, universal and everlasting, the creator of man and the sole power and will of the universe. More than that, he was One, without incarnate gods in the persons of earthly kings, without sons in human form who married the daughters of men, and without heavenly partners.

Above all this, and as a part of it, there came to Abraham, lying out in his tent under the sky, the further thought that this great and only God was not a god of vengeance, who, in His anger against the creatures of His own creation, had swept them off the earth by a deluge; or had need to indulge in foolish fears of what humanity could do to thwart His designs. He was a god of law and order, of righteousness and mercy, a universal and eternal father of His children, who was quick to forgive and was not the cause of the evil they suffered from, except so far as it was the punishment of their sin.

If such was the thought that came to Abraham, the Hebrew, whether as roving enthusiast, as seer, or as diviner, the day on which he arose from his couch in the sunrise, with the free air of the desert about him, and the fever-ridden city in its restless sleep in front, was one of the greatest days in human history.

VIII. God's Promise to Abraham

From that day forward, Abraham was more to his followers than a desert king. He was the representative of God, a kind of pre-Messiah. In the rapid development of his sublime thought he came to believe that God spoke to him in dreams, telling him to separate his people from other peoples that he might keep himself free from their idolatrous corruptions, to leave the Babylonian plains that were the hotbed of voluptuous religions and go to a country he would show him, and he would make him a great nation, that would be a light to the world, and through him and his seed all the families of the earth would be blessed.

This was the promise to Abraham—not merely the promise of a land but of a service—a service to all mankind. By faith in this promise Abraham obeyed the call of his God to go out into a place which he should afterwards receive as an inheritance; and he went, not knowing whither he was going. For reasons unknown to us he had to leave some of his people behind him, and among them was his brother, Nahor. But he took his wife, Sarah, and his father, Terah, and Lot, the son of his other brother, who had been born during their stay in the land of the Chaldees and had died there.

It is a thrilling thing to think about—this little family of strangers and pilgrims on the earth, with nothing in their hearts except the message which they believed they had received from the sky, leaving behind them the rich but licentious cities of the Babylonian plain and crossing the waste to look for a city that had foundations, whose builder and maker was God.

We see Abraham in front, the big man, with solemn face and slow eyes, in his black bedouin cloak and hood, seated on his camel, facing the broad Syrian desert to the north-west, and followed, not only by his father and wife and kindred and his flocks of sheep and goats, but by the innumerable spirits of the unborn generations of mankind to whom God was to be One and a just and righteous God.

In that pilgrimage, inspired by faith alone (for we hear of no more material reason for the migration), the Messianic hope of the Hebrew people appears to have begun.

IX. *Canaan*

After Abraham and his family had crossed the Syrian desert he found himself on the eastern borderland of the narrow strip of grey-green country which is now called Palestine.

It was then a larger country than it is now, but not much bigger than Wales. Notwithstanding rapturous descriptions of its loveliness which have come down to us through the centuries, it is impossible for any travelled man, who can detach himself from the emotions evoked by its sacred associations, to think it can ever have been beautiful. There are thousands of more beautiful countries in the world, and some of it is ugly.

By reason of a "fault" in the crust of the earth, an important part of it is below the level of the sea, and lies, for considerable periods, under a temperature of almost unbearable heat. It has one mountain of noble form and height (Hermon, 9,150 feet); one gorge (going up from Jericho to Jerusalem) of awesome grandeur; one river (the Jordan), of which there will be more to say later; and one lake (Galilee), which has been called "the eye of the land," but is usually dark, stern, forbidding and liable to sudden and dangerous storms.

It is in large part rocky and barren, but it has tablelands of rich pasturage and a few well-wooded forests. It has a backbone which runs down its middle from north to south, and it is bounded on the east by a long range of hills that are often steep, stark, black and precipitous, and on the west by the Mediterranean, where its flat coast is, for the greater part of its length, an open roadstead, with a few small seaports.

It is probable that Abraham entered Palestine over the range of low hills on the south-west of Damascus, a Syrian city of great age, which was the market for the whole of the eastern deserts and had long been associated with Mesopotamia. The scene from there towards the west is highly impressive. The ancient city lies midway between the last of the Syrian hills and the snow-clad heights of Hermon, with a long stretch of the dark cedars of Lebanon beyond and a glimpse of the blue waters of "the utmost sea" (the Mediterranean) in the distance. It is not difficult to believe that to the tired pilgrims from the arid desert Palestine might seem at first sight to be a land of plenty and of infinite beauty and charm.

It was called Canaan.

X. *The Canaanites and the Land of Promise*

Its inhabitants, when Abraham and his followers entered it (probably about the eighteenth or nineteenth century before Christ), were a number of kindred groups of the Semite people who, before his time, had taken the north-west course from the country beyond the Euphrates. They were called by the collective name of Canaanites, meaning traders, which appears to indicate their principal occupation—not that of agriculturists or shepherds, but of petty merchants, perhaps hawkers, trading with the caravans crossing their country from north to south and from east to west, from Assyria to the seaport of Tyre, and from Damascus to the cities of Egypt.

It is believed that they had been in Canaan some 200 to 400 years before Abraham arrived, and that they considered the country their own. Being of the same stock as himself, they still spoke a dialect of the same language, but they had remained pagan. Although none of the Canaanite gods have yet been unearthed (unless the woman and serpent dug up in 1928 should prove to be one), it is believed that they worshipped the Egyptian gods and kings, and their religion called for human sacrifices.

They were a little race, short of stature and slight of build. At the time of Abraham's coming, they were not yet a settled people with a united government. They had few towns of any size, but many villages which, grouped together, were governed by native rulers. Subdivided into many principalities, from the highlands of Asia Minor on the north, to the delta of Egypt on the south, and dependent on other Semitic tribes for protection from the powerful states surrounding them, they suffered not only from internal dissensions, but from the pressure of external enemies.

Nevertheless, they were a peaceful, a sluggish, but not an uncivilised people. Certainly, they received Abraham and his large family in a friendly spirit, and he, on his part, made no attempt to take possession of any portion of their country. It is significant that when he came into Canaan he did not know that he had entered the land promised to him by God. For a long time he did not settle anywhere. He and his people lived in tents as in a strange country; and by no impulse that we can see, except that of following the divine guidance which had led them away from Ur of the Chaldees, they travelled southward.

In doing so, they must have passed by the many-coloured springs of the Jordan, which glisten over the western slopes of Hermon on their way through what was afterwards called Cæsarea-Philippi and is now called Banias, to the valley of the Jordan. Their course would be towards the site of what we still call

Capernaum and along the shores of Galilee, where (there or a little south of it) nearly 2,000 years later the greatest of Abraham's descendants was to say the mysterious words which are perhaps the foundation of the Christian faith: *"Before Abraham was I am!"*

Abraham's first resting-place seems to have been Shechem, now called Nablus, a city which stands about midway between Damascus and the borders of Sinai. It was at Shechem he learned that Canaan was the Land of Promise. It was a goodly land, with a well of sweet water between two noble but rocky mountains, covered in summer-time, in its interstices of soil, by the red and white carpet of the lilies of the field. There, as Abraham believed, God in person renewed the promise He had first given him in dreams on the desert roads outside the walls of Ur; that He gave this land to His children as an inheritance; that they should become a great nation, more numerous than the sands on the seashore or the stars in the heavens; and that through them all the families of the earth would be blessed.

It is significant (and may later prove to be a fact of the utmost importance) that this appearance of God to Abraham, perhaps in a dream, is the only evidence that connects Palestine with the Land of Promise. It is also significant that not even then did it come to Abraham to think that he had a divine right to make war on the Canaanites, and to take possession of their country. Another and far higher interpretation of the promise of God lived in the soul of the shepherd king. After building an altar at Shechem, he travelled peacefully to Bethel, twenty miles to the south, and built a second altar there. How much farther south he went we do not know, but if he followed the usual caravan course he must have passed through places which still ring down the ages with the echo of the footsteps of the greatest of his children until he came, perhaps, to a dirty mud-built Canaanite city with flat-roofed houses of one story, built on a round breast of barren rock, with a maze of crooked lanes for streets, in which half-starved dogs prowled and howled and children, with faces disfigured by scabs and sores and half blind from the poisonous flies that clung to their eyelids, played and sang among the heaps of rubbish and dung. This city was then called "the City of Shalim," after one of the Canaanite gods.

It is now called Jerusalem.

XI. *Folk Tales of Abraham*

Immediately after the patriarch's arrival in Bethel, a famine broke out in the land (a frequent occurrence), and Abraham went down into Egypt and sojourned there, probably with his family and flocks, on the rich feeding grounds which, even in the driest years, never failed along the long banks of "the river of Egypt" which the Greeks afterwards called the Nile.

On the way to Egypt, a corrupt and cowardly thought is said to have occurred to him. As Sarah was a beautiful woman, the Egyptians would say, "This is his wife!" and they would kill him in order to possess her. So to protect his life, and perhaps obtain money and other gifts in exchange for her honour, he told Sarah to say, when they came into Egypt, that she was his sister.

Sarah, perhaps a little woman with timid eyes, in the submission that was natural to a half-pagan woman, agreed to this shameful enterprise; and in due time things turned out as Abraham had expected. The princes of the Egyptians saw that Sarah was fair, gave presents of sheep and oxen and asses and camels and man-servants and maidservants to her husband, and took her to the house of their pharaoh. But hardly had they done so when plagues fell upon the king and his country, and in a way that is not explained to us, Pharaoh saw that through the Hebrew woman he had sinned, or been on the point of sinning, against his god or gods. So he called for Abraham, reproved him bitterly for the lie he had told and caused the woman to tell, which had laid him open to the punishment of his gods, gave him back his wife and sent him away with all that he had.

According to the writers of *Genesis*, Abraham was so far from being ashamed of his shameless conduct that he repeated it not long afterwards. On his return from Egypt to Canaan he went down to a part of the south country which, partly by reason of its association with a similar incident coming a little later, is believed, perhaps wrongly, to have been even then the land of the Philistines, the so-called "people of the sea," a race which, in spite of conjecture to the contrary, were sensual and barbaric.

On reaching Gerar (presumably the capital of the Philistine kingdom) Abraham, according to his chronicler, adopted the same device to save his life and to gain a bribe at the price of his

wife's honour. "She is my sister," he said, and he told Sarah to
say, "He is my brother." At this, the king (Abimelech) sent for
Sarah and took her; but, before he had come near her, he and his
women were smitten with sickness, the one being made impotent
and the others barren. Recognizing in this, after the true heathen
psychology, the hand of his deity, he thought his god appeared to
him in a dream, telling him that, although he had acted innocently, he had acted wrongly, and must at once return the Hebrew
woman to her husband and send them away.

Abimelech called for Abraham and reproved him, asking why
he had brought a great sin upon him and his kingdom. And then
Abraham, with astonishing self-righteousness, replied that he had
thought that the fear of God was not in that place, and that he
had been afraid that the people of Gerar would slay him for his
wife's sake. Furthermore, by way of justification, he added the
explanation (never before heard of) that Sarah was in fact his
sister as well as his wife, being the daughter of his father but
not of his mother. After that the king gave him back his wife,
and a thousand pieces of silver beside, and then Abraham, who
was hailed as a prophet, prayed to God for Abimelech and his
queen and his maidservants, and they were healed and bore
children.

Other heathen stories of Abraham's life in Canaan are told in
the early chapters of *Genesis,* and one of the most puerile is an
effort on the part of the narrator (who was still a pagan in his
conception of the deity) to show that a great prophet must also be
a great warrior, and win glory for God by war.

XII. Sodom and Gomorrah

On returning from Egypt, Abraham had settled for a time near
Bethel. That region was then, as it is now, a bleak and barren
country, and soon the herdsmen of Abraham and of his brother's
son, Lot, were quarrelling about pasturage. Upon this, Abraham
said to Lot, "Let there be no strife, I pray thee, between me and
thee, and between my herdmen; for we be brethren and thy
herdmen. Is not the whole land before thee? Separate thyself, I
pray thee, from me; if thou wilt take the left hand, then I will
go to the right; or if thou depart to the right hand, then I will
go to the left."

Then Lot lifted up his eyes and saw the plain of Jordan (from that point he certainly could not), that it was well watered everywhere as far south as the cities which stood in the vale of Siddim —the bed of what was afterwards called the Salt Sea. So he separated himself from Abraham, and pitched his tent towards Sodom and Gomorrah.

A little later four kings of Lower Babylon made war on the kings of Sodom and Gomorrah, defeated them, carried off their goods and victuals, and took Lot and his women and possessions away with them. Upon hearing of this, Abraham, who was then living in the south, armed his servants to the number of 318, pursued the four Babylonian kings and their armies as far north as Damascus, routed them by night with the strategy of a trained soldier commanding a powerful army, rescued Lot and his family and brought them back.

After this victory, Melchisedeck, the king of Salem, proclaimed Abraham, in true pagan metaphor, the priest of the Most High God, the possessor of Heaven and earth; while the king of Sodom offered him a reward, which Abraham, lifting up his hand to Heaven, refused (with a disinterestedness which sat strangely upon a man who had so lately accepted gifts as the price of his wife's honour), with a solemn oath that he would not take so much as a thread or a shoe-latchet from the Sodomite sovereign lest he should say: "I have made Abraham rich."

The Hebrew scribes of a later age were not even yet done with the father of their people. Looking back through the mists of time, and trying, perhaps, to account for the fearful convulsion of nature which (probably about the period of Abraham) rent the country in twain and sank a great part of it 1200 feet below the level of the sea, they conceived a story of man's sin to explain the reason for the earthquake. In doing so, they made the desert king, who, at Ur of the Chaldees, conceived the sublime thought that God was an invisible and universal spirit, return to the idea that he was just such a visible and limited being as, according to the writers of a thousand years later, had walked in the Garden of Eden, and knew no more than he saw or was told to him.

The men of Sodom were sinners before the Lord, so God came down in the form of a man to Abraham, and after sitting with two of His angels under a tree at the door of Abraham's tent, and eating bread which Sarah had baked for them, announced

His intention of destroying the city. At this, Abraham, more merciful than His Maker, began to plead for his fellow-men, and to ask God not to destroy the righteous with the wicked.

"Shall not the Judge of all the earth do right?" he said. If fifty righteous men were to be found in the place would God destroy it? No, if fifty righteous men were to be found in Sodom, God would spare it for their sakes. If forty-five, if forty, if thirty, if twenty, nay, if ten righteous men were to be found in Sodom would God spare it? At last, relenting in His spirit of vengeance, God promised that He would spare the city for the sake of ten. And then, according to the writers of *Genesis,* God went His way to Sodom to see for Himself what had been done there.

Meantime, in the evening of the day, the two angels who had gone before Him arrived at the gate of Lot's house in Sodom. What happened there, and thereafter, to the angels, to Lot, to his daughters and sons-in-law, is, in its moral enormity, beyond the pen of a modern writer to describe. Next morning, the angels arose and said to Lot, "Arise, take thy wife, and thy two daughters which are here; lest thou be consumed in the iniquity of the city."

Lot and his family fled from Sodom; and then the Lord rained brimstone and fire both on it and on Gomorrah, and on two other cities of the plain, and on all their inhabitants, and they were seen no more, being consumed as in the smoke of a furnace and swallowed up, perhaps, in the eruption of what we now call the Dead Sea—a broad stretch of grey water which still lies in its unearthly silence at the bottom of a deep declivity like a dead eye on the face of the earth, staring up at a dumb sky in which no bird sings, in the midst of gaunt sandhills and slime-pits that might, in their unequalled desolation, belong to the mountains of the moon.

Happily, it is no longer necessary to faith to believe any of these paganized stories. They have neither father, nor mother, nor kindred in the authentic history of Abraham. That they are still to be found in the sacred Book that is the earliest charter of our religion (together with much of the two first chapters of the Bible which, like certain Babylonian legends which closely resemble them, would make havoc of the sublime and sovereign law of nature as we know it) is only interesting as showing how hard has been the fight of the religious consciousness of man with his human development to rise to the height of Abraham's conception of God as an invisible and omnipotent spirit. Nine centuries after Abraham the shadow of Ur of the Chaldees was over this memory still.

It is a relief to pass from these feeble efforts of darkened intellects struggling towards the light to the sweet and human, if sometimes tragic, domesticities of the real life of the simple shepherd king with his wife and children.

XIII. Abraham, Sarah and Hagar

Ten years after Abraham entered Canaan he was still living in tents in the neighbourhood of Hebron. This was even then an ancient city. Its present inhabitants tell you that it is the oldest city in the world, and that it was the first of the sanctuaries of the Canaanite gods. It stands like a grey-clad sentinel on high lands (3,000 feet above the sea) about twenty miles south of Jerusalem. With its crooked streets and open spaces, it looks like a little market-town that might have been used in ancient days by the shepherds in the green wilderness about it for the sale and purchase of their sheep and cattle, and perhaps by the caravans of Egyptian traders going up to Syria as a resting-place on their long journeys to the north.

Abraham's flocks and herds grazed on the rolling plains under this ancient city. His family of bondmen and bondwomen may have consisted by this time of hundreds of souls, but his immediate household appears to have comprised four persons only: himself, his wife Sarah, her handmaiden Hagar (perhaps a true daughter of the East, with large black eyes) and his steward Eliezer, a Syrian of Damascus, a kind of master-slave, who had married and had become the father of a child, who would, according to the law of the country, become his owner's heir in the absence of legitimate issue.

Abraham was now a prince among his people, but the hope of his life was unfulfilled. Although he had lived so long in the Promised Land, he was still as far as ever from possessing it. By the light of the promise which had been made to him in the Chaldean desert, he had read the secret which seems to be hidden to this day from the kings and rulers of the earth—that no nation has ever from the creation of the world been conquered by the sword. Only by patient obedience to the command which tradition told him had been given to man and woman from the beginning (to be fruitful and multiply and replenish the earth), only by the peaceful penetration of the ever-increasing multitude of his people, could Canaan become the kingdom of Heaven. And that was in God's hands alone.

But the time was long and Abraham's heart was heavy. When he had thought God appeared to him in a vision and said, "Fear not, Abraham, I am thy shield and thy exceeding great reward," he had asked God what He could give him, seeing that he was going childless towards the grave and the heir of his house was a home-born slave. To this God had replied that the child of his steward should not be his heir—that a son of his own body should be the inheritor of the promise and the saviour of his people.

Yet his wife continued to be barren, and it seemed to him that he would go to his death without offspring. At length Sarah herself saw things as they were. She knew that, according to the belief of her race, for a woman to die without leaving a child behind her was to have her name rooted out of the earth, so she said to her husband, "Behold now, the Lord hath restrained me from bearing; I pray thee go in unto my maid; it may be that I may obtain children by her."

This was an ancient Hebrew custom, of which there are other examples. A wife's maid was neither her husband's slave nor his concubine, she was the wife's individual possession. A woman's children by her maid were not the sons of sin and shame, but the legitimate heirs of her husband. Yet a touch from the hand of nature (especially woman nature) has again and again made havoc of man-made laws, and it was so in this case.

No sooner had the Egyptian woman become aware that she had conceived than she gave herself airs in the eyes of her mistress, as if to show how much more she was to the husband than his wife had been. Upon this, Sarah, seeing herself despised by her maid, said to Abraham, "The Lord judge between me and thee!" Abraham answered his wife that the maid was in her own hand, and that she could do with her as she pleased. And then Sarah dealt so hardly with Hagar that she fled away.

Out in the wilderness an angel appeared to the girl (angels, according to the chroniclers, were always appearing to Abraham and his people) and told her that the Lord had heard the cry of her suffering; that she was to return and submit herself to her mistress; that a son would be born to her; that he would be a wild man with his hand against every man and every man's hand against him; but that he would be the father of a great multitude and dwell among his brethren. On this, Hagar returned to Sarah, proud and confident, perhaps in the thought that God was on her side. And soon a son was born to her and she called his name Ishmael.

XIV. Isaac

Not long afterwards, in fulfilment of another promise made by another angel appearing to Abraham, Sarah herself gave birth to a child and called his name Isaac. And now a further spasm of the woman heart took hold of both mistress and maid. Seeing herself mocked by Hagar, as by one who was saying that her own son, being the first-born, was the true heir to his father's inheritance, Sarah said to her husband, "Cast out this bondwoman and her son, for the son of this bondwoman shall not be heir with my son, even with Isaac."

Abraham had no choice but to agree, for he had been told from Heaven that through the son of Sarah his seed should be called and the promise of God be fulfilled. So he rose early in the morning, gave bread and water to Hagar, put her child into her arms, and sent her away once more.

Then out in the broad wilderness again, not far from Hebron and the caravan road to Egypt, the outcast mother with her son suffered sorely. The bread and water which Abraham had given her were soon spent, and, in her agony at the child's pitiful torture from thirst, she put him under a shrub lest she should see him die, and sat herself down a good way off and wept. But God, we are told, heard the voice of the child, and the angel of God called to the young mother and said, "What aileth thee, Hagar? Fear not. Arise, lift up the lad and hold him in thine hand, for I will make him a great nation."

Hagar did as she was told to do, and her eyes being opened, she saw a well of water and gave the child drink. After that, the lad grew and dwelt in the wilderness, and became an archer, and in due time his mother took him a wife out of Egypt (perhaps from one of the caravans that passed through Hebron, a fact of importance in subsequent history), and Abraham swore an oath to God that he would deal fairly by his son, Ishmael.

XV. Abraham and the Sacrifice of Isaac

About this time (a little earlier or a little later, for the chronology of *Genesis* is uncertain) Abraham established among his people the rite of circumcision.

It had not always been a rite, and it did not begin among the Hebrews. It had been known in Egypt from the earliest antiquity, and even the Canaanites had practised it before the Hebrews entered Canaan. Some of the surrounding tribes, particularly the Philistines (if they had yet taken their place in history), did not know circumcision; and to others who did, it was probably no better than a ceremony which admitted a youth into the prerogatives and duties of adults. In early times the descendants of Abraham used it mainly as a mutilation inflicted on prisoners of war; and, in later ages, a roving Israelite chieftain of great power and celebrity sent its grosser results as physical proof to his king of the number of the enemy he had killed in battle.

Abraham was the first to give it a religious significance. To him it had no racial distinction. It was a dedication to God of the children of the promise, whether they were Hebrew or not; a rite of tremendous spiritual exaltation separating the heirs of everlasting life from the heathen. So he circumcised his son Isaac when he was eight days old, and his son Ishmael by the Egyptian woman (although here there is a manifest error in chronology) when he was thirteen years of age.

But out of the exaltation of the rite of circumcision there came the deepest pang in the life of the Hebrew patriarch. He was living at Beersheba, south-west of Hebron, when he thought the command came to him from God to sacrifice his son, Isaac.

To make a human sacrifice to the deity was not in itself an unheard of demand. Pagan peoples, as far back as history goes, are said to have given up their eldest sons as burnt-offerings to their gods. The mystical religions are full of such human sacrifices. In later times, as we read in *Psalms,* the Hebrews gave the blood of their sons and daughters to the Lord God of Israel.

The Jewish historian Josephus, who calls it "a mad course," reminds us that Ahaz the King of Judah burnt his children in the fire according to the practice of the Canaanites. The kings of other nations, at times of national calamity (believed to be the consequence of national sin), sacrificed their sons (before the practice of redeeming them had begun) to appease the wrath of their idols.

It may have been a mad course; it may even have been a barbaric one; but who will say that the motive behind it may not have been an early and crude form of what we now call the Messianic hope?

However this may be, the temptation to Abraham, in its human character, was terrible. He had been told that through Isaac his seed were to inherit the earth and become a blessing to all the nations. By faith in that promise he had lived and toiled and suffered; and now he was old and his wife was old and they might have no more children—was he to kill the son who was flesh of his flesh and heart of his heart, and thereby put the promise aside and cut off his line for ever?

A more agonizing situation it is impossible to imagine. It is more tragic than anything in Æschylus, more pitiful than anything in Homer. Did Abraham believe (as the writer of *Hebrews* believed) that when God commanded him to sacrifice the son whom he loved he intended to raise him from the dead that the promise might after all be fulfilled?

None the less, the story of it is terrible. What happened with the mother who had yearned for her son before he was born, and had now to lose him at the command of the God who gave him, we are not told. What happened with the father, and with Isaac himself, is recounted to us only in a few words of almost naked simplicity, and in the deep wells of quivering silence which the modern writer feels it to be scarcely less than sacrilege to explore.

XVI.   The Burnt Offering

Early in the morning Abraham arises in his tent on the plains of Beersheba, cleaves the wood for the burnt-offering, calls two of his young men to carry it, saddles his ass, and, with Isaac his son, sets off for the place in the mountains (afterwards, contrary to all probability, identified with Jerusalem) of which God has told him. On the third day he sees the place afar off, and on the fourth he comes to it.

He tells the young men to stay there with the ass while he and the lad "go up yonder" and worship, and come to them again. Then he takes the wood of the burnt-offering and lays it on Isaac, and, carrying the fire for the kindling in his own hands, together with the knife for the killing of the sacrifice, he and his son begin to climb the mountain together.

Perhaps it is early in the morning, and a heart-breaking sun is shining. Isaac is prattling in the joyous innocence of youth as he strides up the hill, while Abraham is silent. Presently, the boy stops for a moment and says, "Father, here is the fire and the wood, but where is the lamb for the burnt-offering?"

And the father replies, perhaps in a choking voice, "My son, God Himself will provide a lamb for the burnt-offering."

And so they go on again, the lad with a cheerful heart, the father with a sad one.

At length they reach the place for the sacrifice. Abraham builds the altar while Isaac runs about with boyish alacrity to lay the wood on it. And then at last comes the dread moment when the father, almost stifled with sobs, perhaps, lays hold of his son and binds him to the altar, and then lifts the knife to slay him. But before he has done so, an angel of God calls to Abraham and says, "Abraham, Abraham, lay not thy hand on the lad, for now I know that thou fearest God, seeing thou hast not withheld thine only son from Him."

What happens thereafter is of little consequence to the wonderful story. That the scribes of the tenth century believed the invisible God of the universe had to tempt His servant to a barbaric act in order to prove his faith is of no value now in the history of religion. That Abraham was willing to sacrifice his beloved son as an atonement for his sins is first and fundamental.

XVII. The Death of Sarah

The next event in the life of Abraham, as recorded in the Bible, was the death of Sarah. Apparently, he was not with her when she died. The conditions of his calling had always required that he should travel from place to place in Canaan, according as the rain fell and the sun shone here or there and provided pastures for his sheep and cattle. On these journeyings Sarah had accompanied him as long as her strength permitted, but when age and infirmity overtook her she had to remain in the rest and security of Hebron. It was there she had died while Abraham was away with his flocks in the wilderness of Beersheba.

What follows is deeply moving. Abraham returned to the Canaanite city to mourn for Sarah, and to arrange with the inhabitants for the place of her burial. The account of their long-winded bargaining will be recognized by all who know the East, both in its pitiful pathos and its palpable insincerity, as typical of the Orient.

Although God had promised Canaan to Abraham as an inheritance, and he had lived so long in the land, he began by speaking of himself as a stranger and a sojourner among them; and then, standing up before his dead, the big, slow-eyed man begged for a place in which to bury it. The Canaanites replied that he was a prince among them, and might bury his dead in their own sepulchres. Neither Abraham's religion nor his worldly wisdom would admit of this subterfuge, so he asked for a cave in a field near the gate of the city belonging to a Hittite named Ephron, and he offered to pay for it. The Hittite replied that the field was worth 400 shekels of silver; and what was that between him and Abraham?

The price was a preposterously high one (more than ten times as much as was paid 2,000 years later for a similar burial-place for strangers in the neighbourhood of Jerusalem), but Abraham sealed the bargain immediately, weighed out the silver in the value of the money of the time, and the field with the cave became his, according to Canaanite law (it was still called "the field of Abraham" ten centuries afterwards), as a burial-place for his wife and family.

Then alone, quite alone, as far as we can see, and perhaps with his own hands, Abraham buried Sarah in the land which, long years before, God had given him for an everlasting possession. The scene of the burial, as we see it by the eye of the mind, is one of the deepest tenderness—the old husband and the old wife at their last parting. She had been his from the days of her beautiful girlhood, when she left father and mother and came to him from the country east of the Euphrates, and they became no more twain but one flesh until death should part them; his comrade when they had crossed the wide Syrian Desert, not knowing whither they were going; his companion in the scorching heat and freezing cold of their homeless wanderings in the Canaanite country.

True woman and true wife! Unsmirched by the slanders (now seen to be unhistorical) with which the paganized writers of more than 1,000 years later befouled her memory, she comes down to us through the ages as one of the purest examples of faithful and beautiful womanhood. She was the mother of one son only, yet also the mother of millions of the sons of Israel still unborn. Neither Jew nor Christian is permitted to-day to stand by her tomb in the cave by the former gate of Hebron; but may God rest her stainless soul for ever!

XVIII. Isaac and Rebekah

The death of Sarah appears to have strengthened Abraham's desire that the promise should be fulfilled that through Isaac his seed should inherit the earth. He had heard that although his brother, Nahor, and his sister-in-law, Milcah, were dead, they had left a son named Bethuel, who had both sons and daughters, so, not being willing that Isaac should marry one of the daughters of the Canaanites, he sent his eldest servant to his own country to find a wife for Isaac among his own kindred.

This servant, who was probably Eliezer of Damascus, took camels and servants and went off on his long journey to Mesopotamia. It appears to have been in the middle of summer, for, when at length they came near the city of Nahor, the camels knelt down by the moist grass about the well outside the city, as if waiting for somebody to slake their thirst.

It was the evening of the day, when the young women of the city came out to draw water; and among them, with the golden light of the eastern sunset on her face, came a young girl of perhaps fifteen or sixteen years of age, very beautiful with her black eyes and hair, and with her bare feet striding lightly over the grey sand, clad from neck to knees in the long blue gown of her country, and carrying her brown pitcher on her shoulder.

Abraham's servant asked her to allow him to drink a little water from her pitcher, and with alacrity she permitted him to do so. Then, with a cheerful word, she drew water for his camels also. Meantime, the man stood watching the girl in silence, and wondering if the Lord of his master had already made his journey prosperous or not. At length he asked her whose daughter she was, and being told she was the daughter of Bethuel, the son of Nahor, he knew that God had led him to the house of his master's brethren.

A little later he was in the house itself. Nahor and Milcah had indeed gone, but there were Bethuel and his son, Laban, and his daughter, Rebekah, the sweet girl of the well. He was made welcome in the house in the desert and meat was put before him, but he would not eat until he had told his errand. He was the servant of Abraham, the Hebrew, who had grown rich in silver and gold and flocks and herds since he left his native country, and who, by Sarah his wife, lately dead, had had a son named Isaac. And not being willing to take a wife for his son from the daughters of the Canaanites about him, Abraham had sent his servant to find a wife from among the people of his own kindred; and behold, while he stood by the well outside the city, Rebekah had come forth with her pitcher on her shoulder, and the Lord God of Abraham had told him that she was the maid he had chosen for his master's son. Would they not let her go back with him?

There was some parleying, after the manner of the East, and then Bethuel and Laban turned to the girl, herself, and said, "Wilt thou go with this man?"

And the girl, knowing no more than she had just heard, but with the faith of her great ancestor in her big eyes, answered bravely, "I will go."

Next day, or soon after, Rebekah, with the blessing of her father and her brother, who, at their last praying, called after her, "May you be the mother of thousands of millions!" left the home of her childhood and went away with Abraham's servant to the land of which she, in her turn, knew nothing.

As they drew near it, Isaac, walking in the field, saw that the camels were approaching. Rebekah saw him also, and, being told who he was, she lighted off her camel and covered her head, according to the custom of her people, which required that a man should not choose his wife for the beauty of her face but have her chosen for him by God, who alone joined man and woman together in that union which could never be put asunder.

And then Isaac took Rebekah into his dead mother's tent, and she became his wife and he loved her—no priest intervening, no rite or ceremony being observed, and God taking no part except the supreme one of giving the right woman to the right man.

XIX. *The Death of Abraham*

Where Abraham was at the time of this first and most beautiful of the marriages recorded in the Bible, we do not know. It has been said that he must have died before his servant returned to Canaan. We could almost wish it was so. But the Bible tells us that in fact he married another woman, Keturah, and that at an unnatural time of life, he had six other sons, whom we never hear of again.

Then, at a great old age, full of years and honour, Abraham died and was buried at Hebron (in the field he had bought from the Hittite for the companion of his earthly pilgrimage) by both his sons, Isaac and Ishmael, and thus, in that last hour of separation, the promise was fulfilled which was made to Hagar in the wilderness that her son and the son of Sarah, though separated in life, should stand by the sepulchre of their father, and so dwell together as brethren.

Such is the story of Abraham, the Hebrew. It is a great story, however disfigured by interpolations and soaked in the supernatural. Abraham did not live to see the fulfillment of the promise which he believed he had received from God that his seed should inherit the earth, and when he died he possessed no more of the land of his hopes than was sufficient to make his grave. But his heart never failed him, and when his time came to go he laid him down with a will. We do not read that he had any hope of a personal immortality or any expectation of an individual resurrection. But his God was the everlasting God who ruled over all, and he descended into death without fear.

He was not the Messiah, or yet the pre-Messiah. He was only a simple shepherd; but unless we believe the crude and contradictory Babylonian, Chaldean or Canaanite stories of his corruption and cupidity (long since discredited by students of history), he was from the beginning to the end of his life a mighty man, and to his people his voice was as the voice of God. Others might transcend him in knowledge and wisdom and power, but by few or none, for 2,000 years at least, was he to be surpassed in that highest quality of the religious mind which is faith.

By faith he rescued the soul of man from the gods of an earlier age, created in man's own image to pander to the lowest of his lusts, and gave him instead a universal, invisible and omnipotent God who ruled the universe in righteousness, and further than that the knowledge of mankind has never yet gone, and is never likely to go. By faith he took a little shepherd family out of a polluted world and made it an eternal and indestructible nation, who have fought and won on every battlefield of human thought. While the idols and heroes he left behind are still lying in the dust and clay of the Chaldean desert, his name is alive on the lips of the innumerable army of his children all over the earth. Great warrior of peace! Without striking a blow he conquered the world for God.

CHAPTER V

The Children of Abraham

I. Jacob and Esau

THE FIRST FACT in the married life of Isaac and Rebekah (the irregular chronology of *Genesis* is obviously wrong in this particular) is an almost literal repetition of the degrading incident attributed to the life of Abraham.

Famine had fallen on Canaan again, and Isaac is said to have been told by God not to go into Egypt (the natural resort of the inhabitants of Canaan in such circumstances) but to remove from the fields of Beersheba to the more fruitful plains on the west, which are now definitely called the plains of the Philistines. There, according to the story as it has come down to us, he behaved exactly as his father is said to have done a few years before him, in the same place and under the rule of the same king, or of a king with the same name.

Knowing that Rebekah was a beautiful woman, and fearing that the Philistines might kill him in order to take possession of his wife, he gave it out that she was his sister and he was her brother.

Although the rectitude of the woman was in this case endangered rather than assailed, the normal consequences were equally degrading. Looking out of his windows, King Abimelech saw Isaac "sporting" with his wife, and, forming an opinion of their true relations from these signs of their connubiality, he sent for him and rebuked him for a deception which might have brought guiltiness upon his people—thus leaving us again with the humiliating conclusion that (according to the unknown chronicler) it was not the Hebrew patriarch but the pagan king who had any true conception of the sanctity of marriage, or else with the certainty that the incident, being thrice repeated in the lives of father and son, can never have occurred at all.

The next fact in the lives of Isaac and Rebekah is the birth of their children. They were twins. The first to come is described as a "redskin," being covered with hair as with a garment. He was called Esau, and he grew to be a mighty hunter and to be loved by his father, because Isaac liked to eat of his venison. The second, who was called Jacob, was smooth-skinned, and he became a shepherd and was beloved by his mother for reasons that are not explained to us. We see Esau as a large-limbed, red-headed fellow, with a swinging step and a ready smile; and Jacob as a smaller person with watchful eye.

The clash about inheritance, which had come between Isaac and Ishmael while they were children, came now between Esau and Jacob when they were men. According to the Canaanite law a man's property would be in land and cattle. The land was the gift of God to His people, and the purchase of land was on a fifty years' lease at the longest. Therefore the lease of his land would be the substance of what Isaac had to leave to his sons. The eldest son of a Hebrew, even if he were a twin, took a double share of the property of his father at his death, as well as having the sole right to worship God with sacrifices. Hence Jacob may have felt a galling sense of his accidental and unnatural disability, and, if so, this is the sole excuse for his own conduct, as well as for the conduct of his mother.

We read that Jacob was cooking a dish of lentil stew when Esau came home from the fields tired and faint, and as he thought dying.

"Give me a mess of your pottage," he said, and Jacob, seeing his opportunity, replied, "First sell me your inheritance."

Upon this, Esau, asking himself what good his inheritance would be to him if he died, sold it and sealed the sale with an oath (apparently good in Canaanite law), which Jacob required of him. Then, in contempt of his lost inheritance, he went out and married two daughters of Hittites—an act of disloyalty to his own race which is said to have been a grief of mind to his father and mother.

After the inheritance came the blessing, and this was clearly a ceremonial of Hebrew origin only, being the act by which a father in the hour of death conveyed to his eldest son the spiritual essence of the promise of Abraham. We are told that Isaac became blind, and thinking his death was approaching, he sent for his beloved son, Esau, and told him to go out into the field and find venison, so that (contrary to our experience of dying men) he might eat of the savoury meat he loved, and bless him before he died.

Setting more store by his father's spiritual (and perhaps political) blessing, than he had done by his material inheritance, Esau went out with alacrity on this errand. But Rebekah had overheard what Isaac had said to Esau and, thinking to outwit her blind husband, she revealed it to Jacob, telling him to go to the flock and fetch her two kids of the goats that she might dress them and he might take them in to his father before his brother returned, and thus obtain the blessing intended for Esau. To this Jacob objected that, blind as his father was, he would detect the deception, seeing that Esau was a hairy man and he was a smooth one, but Rebekah (perhaps a woman of quick temper and tongue) protested that the curse might fall on her if she failed in her enterprise. So Jacob hastened to fulfil his mother's command; the kids were cooked, their skins were put on Jacob's hands and neck, and he went into his father's tent to steal his brother's blessing.

Things fell out at first as Jacob had expected.

"Who art thou, my son?" said Isaac, and the smooth liar replied, "I am Esau, thy first-born. Arise, eat of my venison that thy soul may bless me."

"How is it that thou hast found it so quickly?" asked Isaac, and Jacob answered, without a qualm, "Because the Lord thy God brought it to me."

Beginning to suspect, Isaac said, "Come nearer, my son, that I may feel thee and know whether thou art my son Esau or not."

Jacob was compelled to do as his father desired and then Isaac said,

"The voice is the voice of Jacob, but the hands are the hands of Esau. Tell me, art thou my very son, Esau or not?" Jacob answered, "I am."

"Kiss me, my son," said Isaac, and Jacob kissed him. Then the blind man ate of the food and blessed his second instead of his elder son, saying he should be lord over his brethren, and that the nations of the future would bow before him.

But hardly had the imposter left his father's presence when Esau came back in hot haste from his hunting, and then over the scene of shameless treachery came a moment of heartbreaking pathos such as can hardly be equalled in the whole range of books.

"Let my father arise," said Esau, "that he may eat of his son's venison and his soul may bless me."

"Who art thou?" said the blind man.

"I am thy first-born," replied Esau.

Upon this, Isaac trembled and said, "Then who was he that was here before thou camest, and brought me his venison, and I did eat of it and blessed him?"

There was no need for an answer to that question. Esau broke into bitter tears, and then recovering himself, he said, "But bless me, even me also, my father."

At that, the blind man blessed his beloved son as well, although with a lesser blessing, not taking back the blessing he had bestowed on his brother, for that was impossible, but saying it should come to pass that Esau would live by the sword, and that when the dominion came to him he would break the yoke of his brother from off his neck.

After that Esau made it known that he would not disturb the days of mourning for his father's death which he believed to be at hand, but after they were over he would kill his brother.

Hearing of this, Rebekah was in terror for the lives of both her sons, Jacob's at the hand of Esau and Esau's at the hand of the Canaanite law. Therefore, making pretext of Esau's marriage with the daughters of the Hittites, she persuaded Isaac that it was necessary to remove Jacob from the temptation of marrying a woman of the Canaanite people by sending him to her own country to take a wife of one of her brother's daughters. So under the cover of another falsehood, Jacob fled to the Syrian desert from fear of Esau's vengeance.

Isaac did not die, as he expected, at that time, or for at least twenty years afterwards, but lived to a great old age, and was then buried at Hebron with Abraham, his father. Except that he carried on the line of his race, he did nothing that is of consequence in the history of his people. We see him as a stodgy and rather stupid person with heavy eyes, without inspiration or even ordinary intelligence. Pious writers in all ages have tried to see the hand of God in his folly, in the deceit of his wife and the poltroonery of his younger son. The modern mind sees nothing in the stories of any of these but indelible stains on the deathless record of the forefathers of the Hebrew race.

II. Jacob's Flight from Esau

In his headlong flight from Esau's vengeance, Jacob slept first at Bethel. This was the stony place in the middle of Canaan at which Abraham had built the second of his altars to the invisible God. But, Jacob, so far as we can see, knew nothing about that. What he did know was a very ancient heathen story. Before it was thought that the cherubim and the seraphim flew on wings through the illimitable sky, it was understood that Heaven and earth were not far apart; that the deities dropped down a celestial ladder after dark and raised it again in the morning; and that by means of this ladder their angels descended and ascended on their way from Heaven to earth, and from earth to Heaven.

This was the substance of Jacob's dream as he lay out in the open at Bethel, with a stone for his pillow. When he awoke in the morning, he perceived, it is said, that the place of his sleep was the house of God and the gate of Heaven; and remembering (what only a pagan might know) that stones were sometimes inhabited by deities, he raised the stone on which his head had rested and anointed it with oil—just as he might have done if he had been a heathen in Ur of the Chaldees.

Apparently, Jacob left Canaan by the road on which Abraham entered it. After he had crossed the Syrian desert and come to the country of his mother, he had an experience which repeated in every essential particular, that of Abraham's servant, Eliezer, when he went to Nahor in search of a wife for his father, Isaac.

Outside the city of Haran (said to have been south of Ur) he came upon a well which was surrounded by a flock of bleating sheep and a company of shepherds who were waiting, according to the custom of their country, for the hour of sunset to water them. He asked the shepherds whence they came, and they answered from Haran. He asked if they knew Laban, the son of Bethuel, and they answered that they knew him.

"Is he well?" asked Jacob, and the shepherds replied, "He is well"; and then, pointing to a radiant young girl who was leading another flock to the well, they said, "Behold, here comes Rachel, his daughter."

Jacob kissed his cousin Rachel, and told her he was her father's brother—brother being a name frequently employed in the Old

Testament, and sometimes in the New, to indicate almost any kind of close relationship. Rachel ran back to tell her father, and soon afterwards Jacob was in Laban's house.

It was an entirely pagan household, consisting of three persons only; Laban himself, a shrewd and unscrupulous schemer, an elder daughter Leah, who is called the tender-eyed—a name which sufficiently describes the home she had been born and brought up in, probably a huddled heap of wooden booths in the middle of animal dung-hills, swarming with poisonous flies which, (as still in the East) produced ophthalmia—and the bright eyed and beautiful Rachel.

Laban welcomed Jacob as "flesh of his bone," and set him to work in his sheepcote. After a month he was so satisfied with his temporary servant that he asked him what wages he should pay him to remain. But Jacob, in the meantime, had fallen so deeply in love with Rachel that, instead of taking wages, he offered to serve Laban seven years in return for her. Laban accepted this offer with a large show of disinterestedness, concealing the fact that, according to Chaldean law, Jacob as first cousin to the girl had the first right to her.

III. Jacob Works Seven Years for Rachel

The seven years' service for Rachel passed for Jacob like a walk in the sunshine, so great was his love for the girl. But when they were over he claimed his wife and probably indicated to Laban his desire to return home. Laban had no intention of allowing him to go, so he laid schemes to prevent it. What form of marriage was made, what priest officiated and what pagan cult consecrated (if any such were necessary) we do not know, but we read that, according to Chaldean custom, Laban gathered together all the men of the place and gave a feast which lasted seven days and was an orgy of drunkenness and gluttony.

On the evening of the first day Laban carried out his design. After darkness had fallen, and (according to the Jewish historian) they were "all drunk and in the dark" he took Leah, the tender-eyed, instead of Rachel, the beloved, and led her to Jacob's room and Jacob went in unto her.

In the morning Jacob saw what had been done to him, and he fell on Laban with bitter reproaches. The smooth-tongued deceiver had his excuses ready. It was contrary to the custom of the country that a father should marry his younger daughter before his elder one; but let Jacob, making no fuss, fulfil the six remaining days of Leah's marriage celebration and he should have Rachel also, on condition that he served a second period of seven years for her. To these hard terms, Jacob, out of his love for the younger sister, consented; and after a week Rachel also became his wife, but with what truncated festivities we do not know.

The second half of the fourteen years passed in penniless drudgery for Jacob, who, in his dependence upon his father-in-law, was paying the penalty of his own earlier duplicity. He had now two wives but no money, so he accepted a further service of six years on terms of a co-partnership whereby he shared with Laban in the earnings of the sheepcote. This gave Jacob an opportunity for his natural unscrupulousness, so he set himself to defeat the laws of nature on which Laban relied. By the exercise of arts unknown to modern biology he became richer than his master in flocks and herds and manservants and maidservants, and then the god whose stone he had anointed at Bethel appeared to him again and told him to return to the land of his fathers. Jacob was nothing loth to do this, so, taking advantage of Laban's absence at the sheep-shearing, he escaped with all his possessions, including his wives, who had their own grievances against their father on the ground (difficult to understand) that he had sold them and "destroyed their money."

IV. Laban's Meeting with Jacob

Three days later, Laban returned from his sheep-shearing, and finding that Jacob had gone he went in pursuit of him. On the seventh day he overtook him, and then came a scene of blatant hypocrisy on both sides.

Laban began with suave oriental insincerities. Why had Jacob crept away secretly, carrying off his daughters as if they had been captives taken by the sword, instead of waiting until he could kiss them and part from them with mirth and song?

But coming down quickly to the real object of his pursuit he demanded to be told why Jacob had stolen the images of his gods which had been the guardians of his house and family.

To this Jacob replied that he had crept away secretly because he knew that at any time Laban might turn him off penniless; but as for the images of his gods let Laban search his tents for them and, if he found them there, the person who had stolen them should die.

Unknown to Jacob, the thief was his beloved wife, Rachel, who, like her father, was obviously still a pagan. While her father and husband were parleying, she hid the images of the gods in the howdah of the camel on which she had travelled, and lay on them, and when Laban came last to her tent she told him that the custom of women was upon her and begged him not to ask her to rise.

· Thus Laban's search became fruitless, and, after Jacob had fallen on him with merciless reproaches, they made a covenant of peace together which meant little to either. After that, the unscrupulous old heathen returned home and so passed, to our infinite relief, out of the pages of history.

A little later, Jacob discovered the images which Rachel had stolen, and (as we are told by Josephus) he hid them in the cleft of an oak and purified his tent of idolatry. How far he purified his heart of it also will be seen by his subsequent conduct.

V. Jacob Wrestles with an Angel

On his way back to Canaan, over the caravan route through the Syrian Desert, and near to the western border of it, he had passed over the ford Jabbok, when an event of illuminating significance is said to have occurred to him. Having disposed for the night of his two wives and his two women-servants and his eleven sons, and being alone, an unknown man appeared to him and wrestled with him. This was no spiritual wrestling in prayer with God, but actual physical wrestling as between man and man. The wrestling lasted all night, and in the course of it Jacob's thigh was put out of joint. Towards morning the man tried to escape and Jacob began to suspect that his adversary was a supernatural being, an angel, who had descended to earth by the celestial ladder which, according to heathen belief, the deities let down from Heaven at nightfall, and by which (like the modern ghost) they had to ascend to Heaven at daybreak.

"Let me go, for the day breaketh," said the man.

But Jacob replied, "I will not let thee go unless thou bless me."

The man thereupon blessed him and said, "Thy name shall be

no more Jacob but Israel, for as a prince thou hast power with God and has prevailed."

Next day, as the sun rose upon Jacob he halted on his thigh, and he told himself he had seen God face to face.

This amazing narrative was not intended to be read as an allegory, but as a circumstantial story of an actual physical happening, for the priestly writers of the ninth century tell us that down to their day the children of Israel did not eat of the steak which is in the hollow of the thigh because God touched it, and in the more backward parts of eastern Europe down to our own time, the Jew who drags a leg behind him is said to have Jacob's limp. What, then, are we to make of it? That it has every relation, except the remotest, to the sublime and universal religion of Abraham is not to be maintained for a moment. But that it has a clear affinity to a primitive belief in local deities (the river-gods as they are usually called) who protected their borders by resisting the attempts of foreign peoples to cross them is plainly apparent.

Thus Jacob, as the only possible authority for the story if the incident ever occurred at all, is seen to have descended during his twenty years' residence with Laban, not only to the excusable paganism of Rachel, who had hidden the harmless images of the gods in the howdah of her camel, but to one of the oldest and crudest of religious beliefs. In short, making all allowance for the confusion of his faith, between the faith of his grandfather and the faith of his uncle, Jacob was returning to Canaan as an almost primitive heathen.

VI. Jacob and Esau in the Syrian Desert

But here, in the history of Jacob, come two incidents of such tenderness, such beauty, such humanity, and in one case such magnificent magnanimity in his domestic relations as tempt us to forget his religious degeneration.

The first of these concerns Esau. On his way back to Canaan through the Syrian Desert (the Bible says by Mount Gilead), Jacob heard that this brother was coming on in his direction. That part of their father's abbreviated blessing which predicted that Esau would become a man of the sword, and that when the dominion came to him he would break the yoke of his brother from off his neck, had apparently been fulfilled, for Esau was now a powerful chieftain with 400 armed men at his back.

This threw Jacob into a panic of terror. Remembering the treachery he had practised on his brother twenty years before, and stricken with fear of the vengeance that would now fall on him, Jacob divided his people into two companies, with vast droves of cattle and camels and colts to each, and sent them on separately, so that if one company should be destroyed by Esau's soldiers the other might escape. Finally, he sent his two wives also before him, telling them that if, when they came face to face with his brother, he should say, "Who art thou, and whose are these?" they should answer, "We are thy servant Jacob's and these are his present to my lord Esau; and behold he cometh behind us!" Last of all, and alone, walked Jacob himself, quaking with dread and bowing his face to the ground.

But no sooner had Esau heard that Jacob was coming his way than, with magnificent magnanimity, he ran to meet him and embraced him and fell on his neck and kissed him. Then, looking around at the droves of cattle and camels and colts that had been sent as a present, he said, "I have enough of my own, my brother; keep what thou hast for thyself."

And then Esau, too, to our immeasurable regret passes out of history (except for a brief moment at the burial of his father)— the man of the field, the man of the sword, the robbed, the dishonoured and the disinherited, but the one gentleman yet born of the children of Abraham.

The second of the domestic incidents in the life of Jacob concerns his beloved wife, Rachel. In spite of the ungeographical reference to Mount Gilead, it is probable that Jacob and his company returned to Canaan on the road by which Abraham entered it, and that on his way to his father's house beyond Hebron he took the usual southern course under Hermon, by the springs of the Jordan, along the shores of Galilee and across the plain of Esdrælon.

His first resting-place was Shechem, and there he bought a part of a field belonging to Hamor, the prince of the country. Another and more sinister incident is associated with Jacob's visit to Shechem, but the modern writer, who does not wish to befoul his page with the unhistoric obscenities of the scribes of one of the most polluted periods in Hebrew history, is glad to emerge from this to one of the most pitiful sequences of incidents in literature.

Jacob's second resting-place was Bethel, where, on his flight from the vengeance of Esau, he had built an altar and anointed a stone. He did so again on his return, and there at Bethel, or a little to the south of it, the deepest tragedy of his life fell on him —his beloved wife, Rachel, died.

VII.   The Wives of Jacob

The story of the married lives of the two wives of Jacob is deeply moving. It is difficult to say which of the two women is more deservedly the object of pity. That Rachel loved Jacob from the moment he kissed her at the well is clear enough from the fact that she makes his seven years' service for her pass over him like a summer day. But it is less clear, although almost equally certain, that Leah loved him also from the beginning.

Even making allowances for the subjection of a woman to her father in an eastern country, it is obvious that in the hard throes of Leah's unrequited affection for Jacob she permitted herself to become a party to the deception that was practised upon him. Perhaps she compelled herself to believe, that once married to her, Jacob would transfer his love to her. If so, she paid a bitter and lifelong price for her mistake. We are told, in one place, that Jacob loved Rachel more than he loved Leah, and in another that Jacob hated Leah. In those early ages there was only one way in which a wife could win the love of a husband who hated her, and that was to bear him children. With all the yearning of her soul and body Leah tried to do this, and she succeeded. After the birth of the first of her sons she said, "Surely God hath looked upon my affliction, and now my husband will love me."

And after the birth of the last of them she said, "Now will my husband dwell with me because I have given him six sons."

The story of Leah's struggle to win Jacob's love is pitiful enough, but the story of Rachel's struggle to retain it is still more tragic. During the first seven years of her married life Rachel was barren, and not all her certainty of Jacob's affection could conquer her fear that her sister, by bearing him children, would sooner or later capture her husband's love from her. The accounts we have of the eastern arts, which, in her envy of her sister, she tried to employ, are (to those who understand them) more pathetic than repellent. It was not so much that, as in the case of Sarah, she prayed for children lest, dying without offspring, her name should be rooted out of the earth, as that she wished for them as the means of retaining the great love that was slipping away from her. So deep was her distress at her childless condition that at one moment she said to Jacob, "Give me children or else I die."

At length God remembered the unhappy woman, and she bore a son and called his name Joseph, saying, "God hath taken away my reproach."

This was in Haran, during the last of Jacob's fourteen years' service in the desert, and when, six to seven years later, she followed him into Canaan and they were somewhere south of Bethel, God remembered her again and gave her another son, and he was called Benjamin. And then she died, almost certainly in childbirth, perhaps the most heartbreaking event that can enter into a woman's life.

If Rachel loved Jacob with all her heart and soul, Jacob loved Rachel, and, all things considered, that is the purest and the best that can be said of him. Apart from Rachel's love for her husband we know little about her. She was quiet and silent, perhaps with large, liquid, patient and melancholy eyes, one of the earliest and most beloved of the sweet sisterhood of beautiful women of the Bible who were faithful wives and tender mothers.

It seems reasonable to think that Jacob, in the grief that lasted as long as he lived, intended to bury her by the side of his mother and grandmother in the field of Abraham at the gate of Hebron. We see him with his company carrying her on his camels, or perhaps shoulder high, along the rugged "robbers' " road to the south, and over the broad round breast of barren rock where stood the rude Canaanite city which, after many transformations, was to be called Jerusalem.

Apparently it was in summer, and we have no reason to think that embalmment was known to the Hebrews at that time. So we are told that Rachel was buried on the way between Bethel and Bethlehem. This is not altogether certain, but we are still shown her tomb a few miles to the south of Jerusalem. It is a crude structure, which appears to show both in material and design that it could not have been built earlier than the sixth century after Christ or perhaps until the Middle Ages. But that is a matter of little consequence now. What ever we may think of the traditional site of Rachel's rest, no one with the heart of a man can pass it on the road without wishing to go down on his knees to it.

VIII. The Sons of Jacob

Ten years after the death of Rachel (Isaac also being dead) Jacob was settled in the neighbourhood of his father's former home in the vale of Hebron—a silent and severe upland with thin grass and few trees, but not without beauty. What had become of the inheritance he had bought from Esau we do not hear, but we gather that he had grown rich in flocks and herds, and that he was carrying on the combined occupations of shepherd and husbandman, with rights of pasturage and cultivation (but not of ownership, unless it was at Shechem) in more favourable parts of the Canaanite country for many miles around.

In this industry he had the help of ten of his sons who were the sons of Leah and her handmaidens, and ranged in age from thirty years downwards. The two sons of Rachel do not appear to have taken part in the work of the farm and the sheepcote—Benjamin being a boy of about ten, and Joseph, who was about seventeen, being the indulged son of his dead but still beloved mother.

It was a time when ancient ideas concerning the potency of dreams had been widely revived among the Hebrews, who believed God revealed the future to His chosen people in figurative visions of the night, and then, having hidden His intentions, endowed specially gifted persons with the power of interpreting them. Joseph considered himself one of the inspired. He was not only a dreamer of dreams but also his own diviner. His dreams were chiefly concerned with forecasts of his future supremacy over his brethren. In one of them he was binding sheaves in the field, when his own sheaf arose and the sheaves of his brothers made obeisance to it. This was interpreted to indicate his forthcoming greatness and the subservience of the other sons of his father. Both his dream and his interpretation excited the envy and hatred of his elder brothers.

We read that on one occasion Jacob reproved Joseph for his pompous priggishness; but we also read that Jacob "observed his sayings," which probably means that he recognized the voice of God in them. He loved Joseph more than his other sons and made him a coat of many colours, with long sleeves such as were worn by priests in pagan countries, and which, reaching to his feet, made it difficult for him to do manual labour.

Jacob was by this time growing old, and the next step in his favouritism of Joseph was little less than foolishness. In the time of harvest, while his ten other sons were at work as far from home as Shechem (about fifty miles north of the Vale of Hebron), he sent Joseph to see how they and their work were faring—in a word, to oversee them.

What happened cannot be a matter for much surprise. Seeing Joseph coming, the brothers said among themselves, "Behold the dreamer cometh!" and straightaway they conspired to kill him. From this fell design they were dissuaded by Reuben, the eldest of the ten. But, according to the earliest versions of the story, they stripped Joseph of his pretentious coat, tied him about with a rope and, despite his cries of anguish, lowered him into an empty pit and left him to die there. The later version has an added incident, namely, that while they were engaged on this work of revenge they saw a company of Ishmaelites coming from Syria, with camels laden with spices for Egypt, and that Leah's fourth son, Judah, said, "What will it profit us to kill the lad; let us sell him to the Ishmaelites."

These Ishmaelites (wild men who wore big golden earrings) were their cousins in the third degree, being the children of Abraham's son, Ishmael. But taking no thought of this kinship, the brothers hauled the lad out of the pit and sold him for twenty pieces of silver to his kinsmen, who carried him off with them to Egypt.

Then setting themselves to consider how best to escape the suspicions of their father, they killed a goat, dipped Joseph's coat in its blood, and took it back to Jacob, saying, "We have found this and do not know whether it is thy son's coat or not."

The country of Canaan was at that time, and for ages afterwards, infested by wild beasts, therefore Jacob came to the conclusion which the brothers expected. The old man was overwhelmed with grief. The coat was indeed his son's coat, and an evil beast had devoured him. The ten brothers made show of comforting their father, but he refused to be comforted, saying, "I will go down to the grave mourning for my son."

IX. *Joseph and His Brethren*

The Ishmaelites who took Joseph into Egypt sold him as a slave to an officer of the king's guard. He became a valuable possession, and gave so many proofs of loyalty and capacity, that at some time during the next few years his Egyptian master made him a free-man, with control over his household.

In this character he had one grievous misadventure. He grew to be a young man of great personal attractions, and as a conse-quence his master's wife made unworthy advances to him. How he preserved his chastity in spite of her temptations has for centuries been a cause of laughter loud and long according to the character of those who have read and believed his story. The end came when the master's wife, taking advantage of her husband's absence, laid hold of Joseph to compel him, and he, to escape from her embraces, left his coat in her hands and fled.

The story bears points of resemblance to a well-known Egyptian story, of much earlier origin, called "The Two Brothers," but the conduct of the scorned and rejected woman after Joseph had fled from her seems to establish its truth. With no reason to publish her shame, she cried aloud to all her household, thereby showing that she knew the Egyptian law of the time which (copied later by the law of Babylon and still later by the Hebrew law) enabled a guilty woman to protect her own reputation and to punish her unresponsive lover by denouncing him publicly and at once. When the men of the house came running to her assistance she said, "See what the Hebrew has done. When I lifted up my voice against him, he fled and left his garment in my hands."

She repeated this accusation to her husband when he returned home, and as a result Joseph was cast into prison.

The writers of *Genesis* tell us that the Lord showed mercy to Joseph, and therefore he was confined in the house of the guard of the king of Egypt. Having regard to the character of the criminal, and the nature of the crime for which he was condemned, this act of clemency seems doubtful. The prison in which Joseph was confined was more probably such a place as may still be seen in Eastern countries—an underground vault with no light and little air, immediately under the palace of the king, where his kingship indulges the unaccountable pleasure of being lulled to sleep at night by the cries of his victims, chained to the pillars which support his chamber.

In a noisome place like this, Joseph lived for some time, and was then joined by two other prisoners who had fallen from Pharaoh's favour. These were his chief baker and chief butler, who, being troubled by dreams, appealed to Joseph for their interpretation. For the chief baker Joseph predicted an evil end by hanging, and this speedily came to pass. For the chief butler he predicted an early restoration to his sovereign's favour, and, when the butler was about to regain his butlership, Joseph begged to be remembered by him. Apparently, the man made this promise, but, in the manner of his kind, he forgot until the time came when Pharaoh also, after a feast, became troubled with dreams which none of his magicians could interpret; and then Joseph was sent for.

X. *A Man Discreet and Wise*

What follows reads like one of the diversions of modern pantomime. Apparently it was written in the seventh century, and was intended to account for succeeding incidents in the history of the Hebrew people. The pharaoh of Joseph's time (believed to have sprung from Arabian blood) is said to have been the first king of his family, and to have claimed divine knowledge and wisdom; but the chief of the dreams that troubled him was the simplest sooth conceivable.

It concerned seven fat kine which were eaten up by seven lean kine. This presented no difficulties to Joseph. He was far from being a prophet inspired by God; but he was a clear-minded man, who saw deeper into events than most people. His means of divining dreams which men dreamt by night was that of studying the incidents which disturbed them by day. Applying this method to the case of Pharaoh, he saw that the king of Egypt was concerned about the material welfare of his nation, which depended then, as it does now, on the periodical rise and fall of the Nile. In the years of its rise the river brought plentiful harvests to the long stretches of land which bordered its banks, while in the years of its fall it left arid wastes incapable of cultivation. So Joseph, taking small chances, interpreted the king's dream to mean that there would be seven years of abundance in Egypt followed by seven years of famine.

Pharaoh took this reading of his dream as a divine revelation (whether from Joseph's Hebrew God or Pharaoh's Egyptian deity does not appear), and Joseph, seeing his advantage, proceeded to say, "Let Pharaoh look out for a man discreet and wise and set him over the land, and let this man gather all the food of the good years and lay it up under Pharaoh's control for the seven years of famine, that the people of Egypt may not perish."

The king "fell" to this obvious suggestion and replied, "Forasmuch as God hath shown thee all this, there can be none so wise and discreet as thou."

The result was that Joseph, then thirty years of age, the son of a shepherd, a Chaldean by birth and a Hebrew by parentage, was taken from the prison to which he had been committed on a charge of attempted criminal assault on the wife of his master, and made ruler over a people whom history and archæology now tell us were at that time the most cultured in the world.

Joseph's government was both hard and inhuman. He taxed the Egyptian farmers in Pharaoh's name twenty per cent on their corn, and restrained them from selling it to foreign countries. Thus, long before the years of plenty came to an end, Egypt was the granary of the world, and Pharaoh was enormously rich, while Joseph, who had been married in the meantime to the daughter of a pagan Egyptian priest, lived in affluence and prosperity, drove in the chariot next after that of the king, and wore clothes of the royal purple.

Then the famine came as Joseph had predicted, and soon the Egyptian farmers, who were famishing, approached him for succour. The conditions on which he gave it were that they should sell their cattle and farms to Pharaoh at Pharaoh's price, and then work for him on a twenty per cent royalty or rental. Thus the whole of the land in Egypt became the property of the king, and its former owners the tenants of the king.

Within two years the famine spread "over all lands." Naturally, it was being sorely felt in Canaan, an arid country, watered by one river only, but Joseph does not appear to have thought of that. Although he must have known that to escape from a similar famine his grandfather Isaac had fled from Beersheba to the country called the plains of the Philistines, and his great grandfather

Abraham from Bethel to Egypt, he made no effort to help his own people. Worse than this, he had been living fifteen years in Egypt without so much as letting his father know that he was still alive.

XI. The Egyptian Governor

Two years after the beginning of the famine in Egypt, Canaan was perishing of hunger, and Jacob, then growing old, and hearing that there was corn in Egypt, and perhaps receiving rumour of the great Egyptian governor who had saved it for Pharaoh, sent ten of his sons to buy corn there, but kept back Benjamin, his youngest son, who was all that remained to him of his beloved wife, Rachel.

"Go down to Egypt," he said, "that we may live and not die."

Fifteen years had passed since the brothers had sold Joseph to the Ishmaelites on the plains of Shechem, and after the silence of that period they had concluded that he was dead. The last thought that could have entered their minds was that he had become the governor of Egypt and held the welfare of the world in the palm of his hand. Therefore, on coming into his presence, they bowed their faces to the ground before him, thus fulfilling the prophecy of their obeisance which had angered them in his interpretation of his dream.

But Joseph probably by this time a tall, slight, sleuth-like person in oriental garments, recognised his brothers immediately and proceeded to punish them in a way which it is difficult to understand. Speaking to them by an interpreter he said, "Ye are spies who have come to spy out the nakedness of the land."

If this accusation meant anything in that hour of Egypt's greatest wealth and security, it was probably intended to mean that a group of rude shepherds in sheepskins had crossed the jealously guarded frontiers of Egypt to find out the weak places in its fortifications for the benefit of surrounding nations that wished to take possession by force of the corn for which, thus far, they had been required to pay dearly.

The brothers replied that they were not spies but good men, and, though their number was large, they were the ten sons of one man who had had twelve sons in all; that the youngest was at home with his father, who was lonely and old, and another was dead.

At this reference to Benjamin we catch the first light on Joseph's intentions. "By the life of Pharaoh," he said, "ye are spies. But hereby shall I know whether you be true men or not. Let one of ye be bound in prison here while the others go back and carry corn for the famine of your families, and then come again, bringing your younger brother with thee—or else see my face no more."

How, in any event, this amazing device was to satisfy Joseph that his ten brothers were true men and not spies, or to do anything except excite suspicion of his own identity, it is difficult to understand. The men had no choice but to consent, so one of their number (Simeon, the second son of Leah) was left bound in Egypt while the other nine returned home.

On reaching Canaan and telling Jacob what conditions the governor of Egypt had made, and perhaps urging him to accept them, they found the old man obstinate and in grief. Apparently he had changed his mind about the cause of Joseph's death, for he said, "Me have ye bereaved of my children. Joseph is not, Simeon is not, and now ye would take Benjamin also. My son shall not go down with ye to Egypt, for his brother is dead and he alone is left; and, if anything should befall him on the way, then shall ye bring my grey hairs with sorrow to the grave."

But the famine continued in Canaan, and when Jacob's company had eaten up the corn they had brought out of Egypt Judah said to his father, "Send the lad with me that we may not die, neither we nor our little ones. I will be surety for him, and if I bring him not back to thee let me bear the blame for ever."

To this Jacob replied, "If it must be, it must. Take your brother and go; but, if I am bereaved of my children, I am bereaved."

On hearing of the return of the ten brothers to Egypt, Joseph ordered that they should be taken into his own house, and at his noontide meal he joined them.

"Is your father well—the old man ye spoke about?" he asked, and the brothers answered that he was well. Then he saw Benjamin, his mother's son, and said, "Is this your younger brother of whom ye spoke to me?" and they answered that it was. And then, seeing, perhaps, in his brother's eyes the eyes of their mother who was dead, he was overcome with emotion and hurried into his chamber and wept.

This is the first mark of humanity which Joseph's historians have allowed to him, but its life was not long. After washing his face, he ordered his servants to put his silver drinking cup, which he also used for divination (for since coming into Egypt he had acquired the superstitions of a pagan), into the corn-sack of his brother Benjamin, in readiness for the next turn in his intentions.

On the following morning, the brothers, with full sacks and cheerful hearts, set out on their homeward journey. But hardly were they yet gone from the city, when Joseph said to his steward, "Up, follow the men; charge them with stealing the governor's drinking cup; and ask them wherefore they have rewarded evil for good."

The steward did as he was bidden, and then followed a scene which, according to the Bible story, is almost identical in its essentials with that which befell Jacob when he was pursued across the Syrian Desert by Laban. On being accused by the steward of the theft of the cup the brothers replied, "God forbid that thy servants should do such a thing. Examine our sacks, and with whomsoever of thy servants the cup be found, let him die."

The cup was found with Benjamin, and the brothers were overwhelmed with confusion. They were brought back to Joseph, who said, "Did ye not know that such a man as I am could certainly divine?"

There seemed to be nothing before them now except that Benjamin should die, or be kept as a slave in Egypt. But Judah, a rugged countryman with a quivering voice, stepped out and spoke to Joseph in words that are among the noblest in Scripture, telling him how he had asked them if they had a father or a brother and they had answered that they had a father who was old, and a younger brother who was the child of his old age, being the only one left of the two children of his mother, how when he had said, "Except ye bring your youngest brother down with ye, ye shall never see my face again," they had returned to fetch him; but how when they had come face to face with their father, he had answered them that the lad's mother had borne him two sons only and one of them was dead, therefore, if they took this one also, and mischief befell him, they would bring his grey hairs with sorrow to the grave; and how, finally, when the famine had been sore in the land of Canaan, he, Judah himself, had become surety for his younger brother to his father, knowing well that if the lad did not return with him his father would die.

"Now therefore I pray thee," said Judah, "Let thy servant abide in Egypt as bondman to my lord instead of the lad, and let the lad go home with his brethren."

Moved by this appeal, Joseph ordered his Egyptian servants out of his room and then revealed himself to his brothers.

"I am Joseph, your brother, whom ye sold into Egypt."

At this, the brothers became afraid, thinking Joseph's vengeance would now fall upon them for what they had done to him in the past. But Joseph added, "Be not angry or grieved with yourselves. It was not you that sent me here before you, but God, that I might preserve you a posterity on the earth and save your lives by a great deliverance."

After this astonishing declaration, Joseph changed his intention of keeping Benjamin in Egypt and decided to send for his father.

"Tarry not," he said, "tell my father of all my glory in Egypt, and make haste, bring him down to me; for, by the life of Pharaoh, the good of all the land shall be yours."

The brothers returned with joy to Canaan, and when they had told their father that Joseph was still alive, that he was governor over all the land of Egypt, and what message they had brought from him, he first fainted from the shock of their story and then, recovering himself, he said, "It is enough. Joseph, my son, is yet alive. I will go and see him before I die."

It was a natural and perhaps beautiful impulse—that of a father to answer the call of a long-lost son, however shamefully he had forgotten and cruelly he had neglected him. But in yielding to it Jacob was turning back the clock of Israel's hope by more than four hundred years. Apparently he did not think of that until, well on his way to Egypt, he came to a sanctuary at Beersheba, where, as he believed, God told him in a dream not to be afraid to go into the pagan country, for He would be with him and bring him back a great nation.

With this solace to his soul, Jacob left the Land of Promise, with his sons and his sons' sons and his menservants and his maidservants, not one of the chosen people remaining. They were sixty-six persons in all, therefore 252 fewer than Abraham had brought in with him from the Syrian Desert 200 years before.

Thus, the promise given by God to the father of the Hebrew people—that Canaan was to be his home and He would give it to him and to his children as an everlasting possession, that they

might become a light to the world and a blessing to all the nations
—had, down to that hour, most pitifully and woefully failed.

XII.   The Death of Jacob

Jacob appears to have entered Egypt (probably about the sixteenth or seventeenth century before Christ) at a point not far
from what is now called Port Said. Joseph came in his chariot to
meet him at Heliopolis, and after embracing and kissing him he
took him up to the royal city and presented him to Pharaoh.

What is reported of the interview between the Hebrew patriarch
and the Egyptian king is sufficient to show that the priestly writers
of a later age had little help from Egyptian historians. Pharaoh,
like all other kings of Egypt, was a deity to whom his people
addressed their prayers, yet we read that the old Hebrew herdman
blessed him. Then Pharaoh asked Jacob what occupation he followed, and being told that both he and his family were shepherds,
he gave them a well-watered corner of Goshen, now identified as
the north-east of the delta, a thing he could only have done by
evicting his Egyptian tenants at the time of their sorest need.

On that fertile land, the best in the country of the pharaohs,
Jacob and his following lived and worked during the remaining
five years of the famine, growing rich in cattle and sheep and
other possessions. The famine came to an end, but the Israelites
did not return home. Neither did Jacob think it necessary to obey
the implied command of God at Beersheba that, after the days of
privation had passed, he should go back to the Promised Land. He
remained in Egypt for another twelve years, making seventeen
years in all. Then, growing old and feeling the approach of death,
he gathered his sons about him and gave them the blessing that was
to determine their destiny through future generations.

"Gather yourselves," he said, "that I may tell you what will
befall you in the last days."

It is a strange spectacle to think of—Jacob, who had stolen
from Isaac the promise to Abraham (which was understood to be
the promise of God), in his house, or perhaps his palace, in Goshen,
surrounded by his ten sons, and dividing among them, as the heads
of ten tribes, a land that did not belong to him.

Of Judah, he predicted that the sceptre should not depart from
him until Shiloh (presumably the Messiah) should come, "unto

whom the gathering of the people should be"; and of Joseph, he foretold that the blessings of his father should be upon him to the ends of the earth and to the utmost bounds of the everlasting hills—privileges which have never, to our knowledge, been fulfilled. Finally, he caused Joseph to put his hand under his thigh (where God had touched him in the wrestling at Bethel), and made him swear that he would not bury him in Egypt but with his fathers in his own country, although he had spent at least thirty-seven years of his life outside of it. And then, having made an end of his blessings and commandments, he gathered up his feet in his bed and died.

They gave him a gorgeous funeral. After his body had been embalmed by Egyptian physicians, and the Egyptians (or more probably the Egyptian court) had mourned forty days for him, Joseph asked permission of Pharaoh to go up to Canaan to bury his father according to the oath he had made to him. Pharaoh agreed, and gave Joseph chariots and horsemen and a great company of his own people to go with him. So Jacob, who had come into Egypt as a wandering shepherd on his camel, with his family of sixty-eight men, women and children behind him, went out of it in his coffin like a king.

They buried him in Canaan in the cave over which Ephron the Hittite had haggled with Abraham. It is a still stranger spectacle that comes to the eye of the mind with the thought of that funeral —the bare Vale of Hebron and the bleak hill-country of Beersheba, going down to the deep declivity of the gaunt wasteland of the Dead Sea; the great multitude of blue-coated Egyptians and of black-hooded Israelites gathered together in the field by the gate of Hebron, under the grey walls of the sanctuary of the chief of the Canaanite gods; and then the Canaanites themselves in their sheepskin coats, looking on and wondering what great mourning there could be in Egypt—for few of them would remember Jacob and only the oldest would know anything of Joseph.

After the burial of his father, Joseph, in his oriental garments, went back to Egypt with the horsemen and chariots of Pharaoh. His brethren went with him, for the Land of Promise was nothing to them now, and their only wish was to get back from the bleak moorlands of Beersheba to the fat pastureland of the country of their adoption.

Joseph lived about fifty years after his father's death, but what he did thereafter we do not know, beyond the tradition favoured by old Arabic writers that he constructed waterworks and canals in a western depression of the Nile Valley called the Fayum.

The pharaoh of Joseph's earlier days died and another of the pharaohs succeeded him. Whether the second was as favourable to Joseph as the first had been we are not told, but it is hardly likely that a governor would be lightly superseded who had gained all the land of Egypt for Pharaoh by buying it from the people at an unfair price in their hour of sorest need. All we learn is that the Israelites became rich and numerous, and from this we conclude that Joseph remained in power for many years longer.

What the Egyptians thought of their alien governor is not recorded. That they would fear him is certain. That they would hate him is possible. But at length, and at a great old age, he also felt death clutching at his heartstrings, and calling together his two children by the daughter of the Egyptian priest and also their children, as well as the children and children's children of his brethren, he said, "I die, but God will bring you back into the land of Abraham and Isaac and Jacob."

And then he, too, exercised the right of determining or predicting the destiny of future generations (which may be assumed to belong to God alone), and made them swear that on leaving Egypt (it had been good enough for him for nearly a hundred years) they would take his bones back for burial in the land of his fathers. Apparently, they forgot to do this. His body was embalmed and put into a mummy-case, but we are told that it was not taken to Canaan until three or four centuries afterwards, when it was buried not at Hebron but, for reasons unknown to us (unless it be true that Jacob had bought or won territory there), at Shechem.

XIII. Birth of the Messianic Idea

Such is the history of the children of Abraham. It is impossible not to see that in spite of passages of great beauty, tenderness and humanity, it is a sorry and often a sordid story. That it is literally true is by no means sure; that it is substantially so (apart from its pagan fables) is beyond possibility of question. Although it is now something like 4,000 years since they lived and died, Isaac, Jacob and Joseph as historical persons make as strong appeal to our sense of reality as many who lived and died only yesterday. That in nearly all their doings they represent a deep decline in the purity and power of the Hebrew faith is certain. But this need not too deeply depress us. The flow and ebb, followed by the increasing flow of the rising tide, is not more certainly a law of the physical world than of the spiritual one, and the backward wash of belief which came after the pure and simple faith of Abraham, was, as we shall see, succeeded by a mighty onrush of true religion.

Learned writers, not lacking in belief, tell us in these days that the culminating incident in the lives of Abraham's children is enough of itself to discredit a fundamental part of them as actual happenings. They say that what we call the blessing of Jacob was not in any sense an utterance of Jacob at all; that it was a poem; that internal evidence is sufficient to show that it was written by another (perhaps by several others) who lived in the times of two kings coming more than a thousand years later; that it pretends to foresee the establishment of institutions which were not created until centuries afterwards; that it assumes the existence of tribes whose origin is described, as a contemporary occurrence, in a song (the Song of Deborah) which is known to have been written long after Jacob was dead and buried, and, above all, that the reference to Shiloh was not to a sacred person but a sacred shrine, and therefore the passage foretelling the coming of the Messiah, who was to hold dominion over the nations, must be a manifest anachronism, since the Messianic idea did not come to the Hebrew mind until, more than a thousand years later, it was borne down by political troubles.

The writer of the present book dissents from this sweeping condemnation. He thinks much of such criticism is feeble in thought and necessarily conjectural. Some of it, such as the objection to Shiloh, makes nonsense of the sentence in which the name appears and folly of its prophecy.

To the learned men of our own age, and of preceding ages, who, rejecting the doctrine of the direct divine inspiration of the Bible, which makes God the chief author of some of man's wickedest doings, have looked for the truth of the history of religion in the internal evidence of the Bible itself, the world owes a debt it can never repay. But if the writers of early ages wrote with a liberty which often made fact hardly distinguishable from fiction, the tendency of the writers of our own day is to approach the traditions of the past without vision, without heart, and too often, without brain. Tradition is a marsh-fire lighted by memory and imagination combined, and it reveals its secret only to those who approach it with equal courage and respect.

It is true, as we shall see, that when in later times the Hebrew people were broken and hopeless, in poverty and want, in captivity and slavery, when they were crushed by hard taskmasters and wasted by anarchy and war, the cry was loudest which their prophets sent up, through the courts of kings and the councils of statesmen, for a great being akin to God, yet vested in human form, who would establish a golden age on the earth which should compensate poor human creatures for their miseries.

But to declare that the Messianic idea came into existence only a few centuries before Christ, to meet the hard necessities of the Jews in their most trying time, is to reduce its value to mankind to the most pitiful proportions. To say that when Abraham, from the gate of Ur, crossed to the Syrian Desert to look for a land he knew nothing of, he was merely thinking of a little shelf of territory on the eastern shores of the Mediterranean which, though neither fertile nor beautiful, was yet to be the central home of humanity in all ages, is to rob his faith of much of its credibility and nearly all its nobility. To say that when thinking of the Promised Land, he was not also thinking of a promised leader who was to save man from himself, from his sins, and from the wrath of God, is to reduce the Messiah to the position of a tribal chieftain who was only intended to rescue his people from the tyranny of their fellowmen.

The idea of the Messiah was older and greater than that—older than Abraham himself, older than any faith we have any knowledge of, and perhaps as old as man himself. Therefore, to say that Jacob came too soon to know anything about it, or that having lived a life that was often unworthy and impure he could not give expression, on his death-bed, under the hallowing wings of death, to the hope which, throughout the ages, has kept the soul of man alive—the hope of a Deliverer, a Redeemer, a Saviour, who should come some day and to whom "the gathering of the nations would be"—this is to be deficient in the light by which all the religions of the world have lived.

Of Joseph the same is true. Earnest believers of the Scriptures as a whole have said that he never existed; and, indeed, the story of his life presents many difficulties. That a seven years' famine over all the world should be unknown outside the Bible is a disturbing circumstance. Only less bewildering are some of the lesser incidents of Joseph's record, such as that he was the child of his father's old age when he had several younger brothers, and that Benjamin is spoken of as a lad in the second year of the famine when he must have been at least twenty-five years of age. But, taken altogether, and making allowance for records which are manifestly unhistorical, and even of pagan origin, it is impossible to question Joseph's reality. Only such a man as he was could have carried the story of the Israelitish people to the lamentable point at which we afterwards find it.

If Joseph had been the last of the children of Abraham, the Hebrew soul would now be dead. That it still lives and fights on every battlefield of human thought is due to the fact that four centuries after him (and perhaps largely as a consequence of his tyrannies and transgressions) a mighty man of God, a greater than Joseph, a greater than Jacob, perhaps a greater than Abraham himself, arose in Egypt itself to save his people not only from the slavery of their bodies but also from the corruption of their souls.

He was a Hebrew by parentage, but an Egyptian by birth. His name was Moses.

CHAPTER VI

Moses

I. Egypt Before Moses

To know Moses aright we must know something of his country. Egypt, the birthland of Moses, was in his time a little land of some 3,000 square miles, on the north-east extremity of Africa. Its first name was Kimet—the Black Country. In modern times it has been described as the paradise of the world, the valley of the Nile, in particular, being called a place of unequalled beauty and enchantment.

As it came from the hand of nature, Egypt is, however, a place of almost unequalled desolation. The Nile for many miles is a long stretch of turbid water with scarcely more beauty than a common canal. It has a belt of cultivable land on either side of it, which is generally flat and featureless. Beyond this, to east and west, are lifeless deserts of sand, broken at intervals by scraggy hills that are often gaunt and ugly. Apart from three cities of noble proportions and great activity, it is now a country of decay and death, of ruined temples, dead races and dead creeds.

Nevertheless, there is something to explain the rapture which Egypt excites. Seen under a grey sky it is forbidding and repellent, but the sky is usually bright and brilliant. Morning and evening, at the rising and setting of the sun, Egypt lies in a blaze of glory which almost persuades us that the Gates of Heaven have opened on the world. At such time, too, the deserts on either side of the long ribbon of water are often lit up by the magic of the mirage, which seems to create cities of dream in the sky, with temples and towers and emerald lakes of celestial beauty.

The climate is variable, sometimes treacherously cold and boisterous, but generally equable and calm. The land is liable to plagues of locusts, scorpions and other reptiles that destroy life with frightful rapidity. But it has the one great advantage over the countries surrounding it of the river that runs through it from south to

north, making its banks wondrously fruitful, and therefore favourable to the welfare of human life. This natural enrichment made
Egypt from the earliest ages the centre of civilization. It also
determined for good and bad the character of its inhabitants.

II. Who Were the Egyptians?

Who the Egyptian people were at the beginning we do not know.
Students of the Bible, who cling to the belief that the human family
had its origin in a first man, have done their best to prove that,
coming from Ararat, the Egyptians were a branch of the descendants of Noah. Less trustful minds think they were an indigenous
people intermingled with Hittites, Syrians, Libyans, bedouins and
even negroes.

In early ages they were fierce and cruel, and made conquest of
the nations to the north of them. Afterwards they became peaceful and placid, and more interested in the triumphs of the mind and
of the skilled hand than of the sword. They built cities of incomparable magnificence and manufactured articles which have never
been surpassed in beauty.

All this appears to carry us back as far as 4,000 to 5,000 years
ago, and therefore earlier than anything we yet know of Ur of the
Chaldees. The intervening years have seen nearly all the works
of the early Egyptians disappear. The surrounding deserts, swept
by overwhelming winds, have hidden them in the earth. Deep
under the sands of Egypt lie the bones of a buried nation.

The early Egyptians were by no means without literature. They
left behind them books which were written on a perishable paper
made of bulrushes, and called papyrus. They are chiefly collections of proverbs and songs, with some romances, which are mainly
interesting as crude creations of primitive intellects. They left
also a Book of the Dead, which shows that they were early occupied with thoughts of death.

But our principal knowledge of their character, life and thought
we have found for ourselves in recent years from the amazing
discoveries of archæology. Digging into the sands of Egypt and
learning to read the inscriptions on its tombs and temples, we have
come to know many of the secrets of the buried Egyptians.

One such monument, earlier than the time of Moses, and therefore almost certainly familiar to his eyes, is associated with

Cheops, a king of accursed memory, who kept a hundred thousand men twenty years at work building the Pyramid that was to be his tomb. It was, on the whole, a miserable people who inhabited this land in which the living were subordinated to the dead, and the masses were slaves to the kingly and priestly classes.

In very early times the Egyptians called themselves "the people," which meant, perhaps, that they thought they were the only town-dwelling inhabitants of the East—all others being merely nomads and desert folk. Their government recognized two classes only, the ruling class and the slaves. They traded by caravan over the earliest highways, and acquired great natural wealth. Their staple produce was corn, and they were the grain growers of the world.

III. The Religion of the Egyptians

But their chief interest was in their religion. This was at first of a low African, and afterwards of a high Asiatic, type. It is here that they come into closest touch with the modern world, and if a summary of their beliefs shows that they anticipated much that has a disquieting resemblance to later faiths, we must face it without fear.

They believed in miracles and magic and attributed their effects to the intervention of their gods. They believed in sacrifice, which was often human sacrifice. They believed in a scapegoat—sometimes a divine man, sometimes a divine animal, a bull, upon whose head could be invoked all the evils that would otherwise befall the people themselves for their sins.

They had highly organized religious sects, with a priesthood that was paid and hereditary. They clothed their priests in gorgeous vestments, which were understood to be necessary to the solemnity of their office, when, after a series of prostrations and adorations, they approached their altar and entered into their holy of holies. They believed in ablutions and anointings as well as in feasts of consecrated bread and beer, which had to be consumed by the priests, or reserved and adored and eaten and drunk by the faithful, as a medium of intercourse with their deities.

They thought disease was a penalty of sin and could be healed by incantations. They believed in demons and were convinced that they could be expelled from a man or from a temple by magical words of command pronounced by their priests. They believed in a kind of hell, which was a vast cavern under the earth inhabited by the prince of devils and his victims. They believed in prayers for the dead, but this was probably suggested to them not by the thought of speeding on their departed to a blessed hereafter, but by frequent pillaging of their tombs.

They believed in a day of judgment, and held annual feasts of atonement for sin. After each of such feasts the sinners were required to pay two fees, the one to the god, the other to the sanctuary, both of which meant the priests. As a result the priests were rich and powerful. They were the only interpreters to the people of the mysteries of their sacred writings in faith and morals, and without them there could be no communion with their gods—a claim not unknown to the priests of modern religions.

IV. The King-God of the Egyptians

In early ages the Egyptians believed in many deities, including the sun, the moon, the stars and the sea, but they also believed in the efficacy of wooden and golden images of animals and reptiles, which they made for themselves and kept in their homes and carried before their armies in war. Some of these images were hideous and others were grossly obscene—especially such as were images of the gods of fecundity. In later ages they believed in a trinity of gods, consisting of a male god, a female god and their son. Still later they believed in one supreme god who was the creator of the world. The first of these sovereign gods was the first king of Egypt.

His name was Osiris, and he had a wife named Isis. Osiris was a god of goodness and mercy, but he had a brother named Seth, who was a god of evil and injustice. Seth tempted Osiris to his downfall by offering him all the pleasures and kingdoms of the world. With seventy conspirators he invited him to a banquet, induced him to enter a coffin, then shut down the lid of it and flung it into the Nile.

But Isis, the faithful wife, set out in search of her husband's body, and after long wanderings she found it. Then Seth got possession of it again, cut it into pieces and scattered them over all Egypt. Isis collected the fragments and finally Osiris, risen from the dead, ascended into the higher world of the sky. Thereafter, the kings remained the representatives of the King-God, and therefore gods in themselves.

V. *Egyptian Belief in Immortality*

The Egyptians believed in a kind of immortality. Towards 3,000 B.C., their conception of the hereafter took a crude but definite form. Unlike Abraham, the Hebrew, who came at least a thousand years later, and was content with the stern but grand thought that after he had lived his life on earth he would descend into soundless death, leaving his people, his children, to inherit the golden age in which Shiloh would come, the Egyptian could not reconcile himself to the idea of annihilation.

Recent explorations in the sands of Egypt show that the Egyptian, like the Chaldean, refused to believed that his body would see corruption. It would almost appear that he honestly believed there was no such thing as absolute death. In an inner chamber of his tomb, when age or war or disease had taken him, his body, if he was a king, lay encased in gold and sealed down in a sarcophagus, while in the corridors outside lay his chariots and dead charioteers, his jeweled chairs and golden drinking vessels and all else that had belonged to his royal state.

He appears to have known that while there his body would be practically dead. But he believed that in the meantime his soul would pass into the sky and become a star in the firmament, and that after a universal judgment of all mankind, it would come down and re-inhabit his embalmed body (which would now be deathless) and restore his servants to life also. Then he would go forth as a king with his slaves behind him (for king would still be king and slave would still be slave) to a second existence on the earth, which would not differ from the first except that it would be everlasting.

With this hope of immortality, the Egyptian, if he was a king, comforted himself in the grim consciousness of his mortality. With such fumbling after another existence he reconciled himself to the brevity of the present one. How pitiful his thought was, we see for ourselves when we look at his resurrected remains now lying in our museums, with his frayed and rotting grave-wrappings torn back from his shrivelled and sunken face.

With what hope the Egyptian comforted himself in temporary

death, if he was one of the slaves who died (in numbers greater than ever fell on any battlefield) to build the pyramid that was to be the tomb of his king, we do not know. Perhaps it was not the hope of everlasting life but of eternal rest. Or perhaps it was a hope of a future which would compensate him for the miseries of the past—such a hope as we catch a thrilling echo of when we ride in remote parts of the deserts of Egypt to-day and come upon a circle of sinking stones which surround the burial-places of the Egyptian dead, and see, at the sun-rising or the sun-setting, a company of travelling bedouins (their descendants in blood, perhaps, if not in faith) riding round and round them on their camels and calling to them by what they believe, in their ignorance of religions, to have been their names in life, "Achmed! Mohammed! Arise! Arise!"

VI. Egyptian Belief in a Messiah

Above all, as we see from certain of his inscriptions, the Egyptian from remote antiquity believed in a Messiah, a being who was to save him from his sins and become the king of an earthly but eternal kingdom. Among the inscriptions of Rameses the Great there is a dialogue between the great god Amon-Re and the king, which shows that the Egyptian theory of kingship had been founded on a Messianic idea.

"I am thy father: I have begotten thee like a god," says Amon-Re; and the king replies, "I am thy son and thou hast given me the power of a god."

The Egyptian also believed himself to be deeply versed in astronomy, and appears to have thought that when this begotten son of the sovereign father came to earth his advent would be signalized to the faithful by a star, and that he would be born into the world as a babe. Nevertheless, all this high religious development among the ancient Egyptians (which bears a creeping resemblance to still higher religious developments that came later) was joined with deep moral depravity, as the pictures on their national monuments sufficiently prove.

Such, then, as far as we know, were the Egyptians, their social state, their system of government, their national aspirations and their religious beliefs before the Hebrew people came to live in their midst. What happened, then, during the two, three or four hundred years of almost total darkness which followed the death of Joseph?

VII.　*The Pharaoh Who Knew Not Joseph*

The Hebrews had been about seventy years in Egypt before their powerful kinsman died. It is reasonable to assume that during those years he had not only increased their material prosperity, but elevated their social status and enlarged their education. Three generations had arisen in the meantime, therefore it is safe to conclude that at his death his peasant-born people were both rich and powerful.

On the other hand, the Egyptians must have been miserably poor, for all the land of Egypt belonged to Pharaoh, and they were his tenants under a heavy rental. Yet they came, as we have seen, by long descent of a highly cultured people and were the natives of the soil, the builders of great cities and the makers of matchless works of art, while the Hebrews were aliens whose fathers had lived in tents in a thirsty land, and had never yet, down to that time, built or made anything.

It is easy to see what sooner or later must have been the result of that unequal condition—a clash of race with race, a rebellion, perhaps a revolution. It might be long in coming, for the Egyptians were then a crushed and enervated people, enfeebled by moral corruption, while the Hebrews were a vigorous and ambitious nation, quick to see their opportunity and far from slow to benefit by it.

It is not necessary to accept the unsupported traditions that the Hebrews attempted to take possession of the country of their adoption; or that Hebrews from Jerusalem (there was probably no Jerusalem then, and if there had been there were no Hebrews to live in it) came down from Canaan and wrecked and burnt the cities of Egypt, robbing its temples and insulting the images of its gods; or that the Hebrews, having made money out of the Egyptians by extortionate trade, reduced them still further by usury. The natural sequel is sufficient. Being the only freeholders in Egypt, and the descendants of the governor who had saved it from starvation, the Hebrews were wealthy, and their wealth was their power, and they used it to their own advantage.

Time passed—how long a time we do not know. The Bible

indicates more than 400 years, modern historians say much less. But at length arose a pharaoh who "knew not Joseph." The words have more than their obvious significance. They are intended to say that a new king of Egypt rebelled against the policy of Joseph and set himself to undo the effects of it. He was apparently a brute, and his brutality knew no measure. There is a widespread Egyptian tradition that many of the Hebrews were leprous and scabby and that, to cleanse the country of their impurity one of the Egyptian kings drove some of them into the desert to starve, and cast others, with lead tied to their legs, into the Nile.

What is certain is that the pharaoh who "knew not Joseph" robbed the Hebrews of Goshen of their possessions, and reduced them by the rigour of his tyranny to the meanest servitude, making them work like galley-slaves in his canals, in his quarries, his granaries and his brick-kilns. The earth sleeps full of forgotten history. Some day, perhaps, when archæologists have more fully explored the upper delta of Egypt, the remains of Hebrew cities will be found there, and then a new and yet more appalling page may be added to the story of man's martyrdom of man.

Yet, terrible as were the miseries of the Hebrews in Egypt under the pharaoh who "knew not Joseph," the effects of them were not altogether bad. Suffering is the seed of the soul, and the miseries of the Hebrews may have recalled some of them to their neglected religion. It is clear that during the time of their prosperity a vast number had reverted to paganism. That they kept images of pagan gods in their houses, and exhaled the poisonous atmosphere of heathenism around them, is shown by their subsequent conduct.

In the long period of their prosperity they had probably forgotten Canaan as the Land of Promise. Only once, and then in limited numbers, had they even set foot in it. But now, in the time of their adversity, by the mysterious power with which rumour sweeps over the desert, there came back through the centuries the memory of the greatest of their ancestors and the hope of a deliverer, a liberator, a redeemer.

There is an Egyptian story which points in this direction. A magician or sacred scribe of Egypt told Pharaoh of a dream in which it had been revealed to him that a marvellous and divine child would be born of a Hebrew woman and grow to such wisdom and virtue that not only Egypt but all the world would fall at his feet, and he would be remembered throughout the ages.

This was probably no more than a disguised version of something which certain of the Hebrews themselves had said in their secret meeting-places about their slavery and the only way out of it. But Pharaoh, being a coward as well as a bully, appears to have taken fright at a thought which fell into line with the Egyptian belief in a son of God, as shown in the dialogue between the great god Amon-Re and the king. So, to avoid the danger of being supplanted, he attempted to do what (if we accept the first chapters of the first book of the New Testament) a half-Jewish king accomplished many centuries later in Bethlehem—to strike at the coming of the Messiah by slaughtering the children.

Under the pretence of preventing the Hebrews from outnumbering the Egyptians and, by joining with their enemies, taking possession of the country, Pharaoh charged the Hebrew midwives that when they did their office with the Hebrew women they should kill the children as often as they were sons. The midwives, out of pity or patriotism, evaded his command, and then he told the Egyptians in general to cast all male Hebrew infants into the river.

It is hard to believe that any king could be so insane as to aim at annihilating the manhood of the people who slaved for him. But, if the story is true, the sequel to it is only one more proof that a touch from the hand of nature is enough to make foolishness of the schemes of the mighty. It is the shallow stream that makes most noise; the deep one is silent, but it finds its way to the sea. In this case, the deep water that rolled over the murderous design of a terrified and tyrannous pharaoh was a very simple matter—the love of a mother for her child.

VIII. The Birth of Moses

Somewhere about 1200 to 1300 B.C.—a great date in the world's history—in the royal city of Egypt (no longer on the site of Alexandria, but now on the margin of the Nile), lived a Hebrew named Amram with his wife named Jochebed. Both were of the tribe of Levi, which had been specially charged by Jacob to keep alive the hope of Abraham. They had two children, a son named Aaron, about three years of age, and a daughter named Miriam, probably between six and seven.

At the time of Pharaoh's edict, the woman bore a second son. It is described as a goodly child, uncommonly large and beautiful, and out of the mother's love for it, and the father's belief that it was intended by God to be a blessing to Israel, they tried to hide it from the Egyptian authorities. But a healthy child was hard to conceal from the prying eyes and listening ears of their Egyptian neighbours, and when, after three months, they could hide the infant no longer, the mother conceived of a scheme to save it.

According to tradition, which is not history, but the shadow of history touched by the light of imagination, the pharaoh of that time had no son. He had one daughter, and she was childless. It was the habit of the princess to go down every day with her women to the river to wash, and in this the Hebrew woman built her hope of saving the life of her boy.

With the pride of every mother yet born into the world, she told herself that no woman with a heart who had once looked upon the face of her beautiful son would dream of destroying it. So she persuaded her husband to make a little boat or ark of bulrushes and daub it with slime and pitch, and, this being done, she put her child into it, probably asleep, and gave it to her daughter to carry it to the river and commit it to the water, so that it might float down with the tide to where the princess would be, while she herself, with a beating pulse, followed at a distance and hid behind a tree-trunk to see what would happen.

What happened was what she had expected. The Nile, which gallops like the Rhone in some places, ambles like the Saône in others, and the little boat with its precious freight sailed safely down the river until it came to a clump of flags near the place where the princess and her women were washing. There the princess saw it, and she sent one of her maids to bring it ashore.

The babe took her heart immediately. It was crying, and she called for Egyptian wet nurses to comfort it, but the child would not take the breast of any of them. On seeing this, Miriam, the sister, stepped up and said it was a Hebrew child, as the princess must see, and therefore it would only allow itself to be suckled by a Hebrew woman. Hearing this, the princess sent Miriam to find one, and the girl ran off to the hiding-place of her mother, who came with a palpitating heart and offered her breast to the child, and he took it.

After that, the princess decided to adopt the child (giving him the name Moses, which was not Hebrew, but derived from an Egyptian word meaning that she had taken him out of the water), and said to the mother, "Take this child away and nurse it for me, and I will pay you wages."

The mother returned home in joy and triumph, no longer fearing the prying eyes and listening ears of her neighbours. And thus, out of the love of a mother for her child, the crafty scheme of a king came to naught, and a life was saved to the human family which was to direct for nearly a thousand years the destiny of nations.

What happened to Moses during the next succeeding period we need no books to tell us, although tradition steps in with still another story. It says that while he was an infant his real mother brought him at intervals to his foster-mother, and that on one of these visits, the princess, in pride of his beauty and size, took him in to Pharaoh, her father, and said, "Look! Why should you not adopt him as your son and make him the heir to your kingdom?"

The king, notwithstanding his inhumanity, is said to have been in the act of taking the child in his arms when the magician or scribe who had told him of his vision of a Hebrew Messiah who was to wipe out the Egyptian king and nation, cried, "Stop! That is the child I saw in my dream. Kill him." Upon this the princess snatched the child from her father's arms and hurried away with him.

It is not unlikely that Moses as a boy played in the royal palace and saw much of the royal barbarian. His later life shows that he knew how little divinity belonged to a king, and his bearing towards another and later pharaoh is proof enough that in the presence of trucklers and time-servers he feared the face of no man.

IX. The Flight of Moses

We are told that Moses was educated for the priesthood at Heliopolis, which was the oldest university in the world, so it is probable that he learned all that Egyptian letters, philosophy and religion had to teach him.

We are also told that on reaching manhood he became a general in the Egyptian army (soldier and priest were often one), and on the occasion of a rising of the Ethiopians drove the rebels out of Egypt. Further, we are told that he grew to be a man of commanding stature and attractive personality, that an Ethiopian princess fell in love with him on seeing him returning in victory from the war against her own people, and that he married her.

What is more natural and certain is that, brought up at the knees of a Hebrew mother, he absorbed (perhaps in secret) the spirit of his race, and that in common with others of the youth of his race dreamed the grandiose dream of his great ancestor, Abraham, of a promised land in which his children would increase and multiply and become a blessing to all the nations.

It is said that after the death of his foster-mother, the princess, which appears to have occurred during his early manhood, Moses ceased to frequent the court of Pharaoh. But that may have been due less to the loss of his royal protector than to the fact that by this time he had thrown in his lot with the youth of his own people, who were perhaps forming themselves into an active revolutionary force, and that he had become a marked man in the eyes of the Egyptian authorities. This is partly borne out by a story in the Bible.

We read that, walking in a desert place, he saw an Egyptian smiting a Hebrew, and that in anger at the brutal outrage on one of his brethren he killed the Egyptian, and, after looking about him to see that he was not being observed, he buried the man's body in the sand. What the Hebrew did we are not told, but the next event in the history of Moses appears to show that he circulated the story of his deliverance, and that out of his innocent gratitude came the first disaster in the life of his deliverer.

Next day, Moses saw two Hebrews striving together, and hoping to make peace between them, he said to him that was in the wrong, "Why do you strive with your brother?"

Upon this, the fellow turned on him and replied, "Who made you a judge over us? Would you kill me as you killed the Egyptian yesterday?"

At that, Moses, realizing that his crime was known, left everything behind and fled across the frontier of Egypt into Asia.

X. Moses in the Wilderness of Sin

Finding himself on the eastern side of the Red Sea, Moses may have thought of taking the direct course north into Canaan, but he could not have done so. It was Canaanite country down to the borderland of Egypt, in the hands, it is said, of the Philistines, who had been driven back by the inhabitants when they had tried to force the gates of Goshen. Therefore, that way to the Land of Promise was forbidden to Moses as a Hebrew.

Besides, he was a fugitive, flying for his life, so he took the safer caravan route which ran along the western shore of the Red Sea to what was called the Wilderness of Sin. There he had another encounter. Coming upon the seven daughters of a Midianite priest who were trying to water their flocks at a well and being driven away from it by the male servants of another master, he drove off the shepherds and assisted the girls, who thereupon ran to the tent of their father, who was a shepherd as well as a priest, to tell him of their powerful protector.

The end of the romantic adventure was that the shepherd-priest, prompted perhaps by the motive which made Laban give Rebekah to Jacob (that of securing a son-in-law to help him to feed his sheep), gave one of his daughters to Moses, who although married already to the Ethiopian princess, married the Midianite girl and had two sons by her.

Years passed—perhaps many years. The Pharaoh "who knew not Joseph" died, yet Moses remained with his father-in-law and family in the Wilderness of Sin. He was a miserable man. As the consequence of one rash act, he had cut himself off from his people and deprived them of his help in their time of bondage.

Every year of his exile deepened his despair. The Egyptian caravans that came south from Succoth brought reports of the increased sufferings of the Hebrews—their abject slavery, their bitter poverty, their helplessness, their humiliation, and above all, their shameful submission to the gods of Egypt.

Moses was like an eagle in a cage. To return to Egypt would be to walk into the arms of death, and perhaps to make yet more slave-like the bondage of his people. In his groanings his sleep would be broken; he would see visions and hear voices. He would think God's hand was upon him.

Near the southern extremity of the Wilderness of Sin there is a mountain called Sinai, 7,000 feet high and covered by a scraggy growth. From ancient times it had been called the Mountain of God, because God was thought to dwell there. Leading his flock up this sacred hill from the south side of the desert, Moses came upon a bush that was burning. Perhaps it had been set afire by the scorching sun at noon, which sometimes kindles the whole southern side of Sinai into a blaze. But Moses thought the bush, although living, was not being consumed, and he told himself that an angel must have lighted it. Then through the crackling of the branches he heard a voice which seemed to speak to him. It told him to return to Egypt, to deliver his people from the hand of Pharaoh, and take them back to the land which had been promised to the children of Abraham.

Perhaps this voice was an echo of what he had heard in the secret meetings of his people in Egypt; perhaps it was a distempered interpretation of his dreams by night, but he believed it to be the voice of God.

Moses answered that he was slow of speech and slow of tongue, and neither Pharaoh nor his people would listen to him—a flash that so lights up the stalwart man that we seem to see him before our eyes. But the voice replied that his brother, Aaron, could speak well, and he would go with him and be his spokesman. And lo! Aaron was even then on his way to him.

Soon afterwards Aaron arrived in the Wilderness of Sin on a visit to Moses in his exile, and taking this as the last proof that it was God who had spoken to him from the burning bush, Moses left his father-in-law, his wife and two sons behind him, and with his brother set out for Egypt.

Looked at in whatever light we please, this is a fact of unquestionable history. It is also a fact of almost unequalled sublimity. More than 600 years had passed since the great fore-father of the Hebrew race had by faith crossed the Syrian Desert to look for a land he knew nothing of. During more than 400 of these years that faith had been lost to his children by duplicity, by greed, by the quarrels of brother with brother, by idolatry and their legacy of suffering and shame. And now, a mighty son of Abraham had caught it back by the power of the Spirit, and was returning to the most powerful and tyrannical empire on the earth to free his people from their afflictions and to purify them of their corruptions; believing he had been appointed by God to be their liberator and redeemer.

Thus Moses became the first of the pre-Messiahs.

XI. *The Return of Moses to Egypt*

The task which Moses had undertaken when he returned to Egypt was one of apparently insuperable difficulty.

We read that during their 300 or 400 years in Egypt the Hebrews had increased from sixty-six persons to 600,000—an almost incredible number. If we had to understand that they were all living, with many Egyptians, in a single place (the only one mentioned in the four narratives in the Bible), we should have to believe that Rameses was a larger city than existed in the world at that time or during many centuries later. Clearly, they occupied the whole of the territory of at least sixty square miles which is now called the Delta, and stretches from the north-east corner of Goshen to the near neighbourhood of Succoth, a city or village on the neck of the Red Sea.

Over this wide area Moses had to carry on his mission, mainly in secret, for, though the king who had sought his life was dead, he must have been still a marked man, having been brought up in the palace and fled from it to join forces with his own people. He could carry on no public propaganda. He could make no open appearances. He must have travelled, probably afoot, from village to village, wherever the Hebrews were living in their miserable habitations, their hovels and, perhaps, their holes in the ground.

His mission was twofold. The first part of it was to awaken the national spirit in his people, to make them feel that they were a greater nation than their masters who held them in bondage, and though condemned to the hardest and meanest of tasks, they were the heirs of a land, not far away, which flowed with milk and honey.

His story was bitterly wrong, but Moses believed it. Later facts show that he knew little or nothing of Canaan. The barrier of a hostile race had shut him off from it. He had accepted the traditional belief that had come down through the ages, and been accepted by nearly all the Semitic nations, that from the borderlands of Philistia to those of Lebanon there was a country of unparalleled fertility, a garden planned on earth by Heaven. And then it was *their* garden, *their* country, promised to them by God as an everlasting inheritance.

It is pitiful to see how hard the Hebrews found it to accept this part of the story of Moses. What they said to him in Egypt is all written down in later chapters of the Bible. Even in the misery of their souls and the thraldom of their bodies, they cried, "Let us alone that we may serve the Egyptians."

The second part of the mission of Moses was the far greater one of awakening the religious spirit in his people, of calling them back from the corrupt worship of idols to the faith of Abraham in a universal and invisible God of righteousness and mercy, who had chosen them out of all the nations of the world to be a light to all the earth.

It was a stupendous task to make the majority of the Hebrews, in their anguish of spirit and cruel bondage, believe that this exalted destiny was to be theirs by right of a covenant which God had made centuries before with the greatest of their fore-fathers. Whether he ever brought them to a right understanding of the service, as well as the inheritance involved in the covenant with Abraham, is lamentably uncertain in the light of subsequent happenings. But though Moses was slow of speech and tongue, there was fire on his lips, for the time came at length when his people seemed to be as one man behind him, believing him to be a man-god, a saviour and a deliverer, whom they were intended to follow through the perils of life and death.

And now we come to a part of the story of Moses which is almost more difficult to the modern mind than anything else in Scripture. It is not only "soaked in the supernatural," it seems to be steeped in the impossible. If we have to accept it as the literal or even as the figurative word of God, we must abandon our faith in Him as a God of love and mercy. To believe that, for any good purpose whatever, He told his people to lie and to steal; that He slaughtered a vast multitude of His children to punish their king, that, being all-powerful, He hardened the heart of their pharaoh to a long period of suffering for his subjects merely to show that He could lay His hand on Egypt and that He was a God above all other gods—this is enough to tempt us to go back from the God of Abraham to the gods of Ur, and that we cannot do.

Happily, it is not necessary. Neither is it required of us to accept as miracles a series of natural incidents which make havoc of Bible history as a record of actual happenings, and rob religion of its purity and sublimity.

Eight out of ten of these incidents are extraordinary calamities of a kind that might have occurred in almost any country, and most easily of all in the swampy lands of northern Egypt. We have only to recognize the possibility that Aaron, the brother of Moses, may have been an Egyptian priest before he became a Hebrew one, and that the strength of the pagan priest lay in his power of creating the belief that events of natural occurrence had a spiritual significance and were always foretold by the gods, and more than half of the miraculous in what follows disappears.

XII. Moses and the Pharaoh

When Moses turned from his persuaded and repentant people to their king to demand their liberation, he was meeting a man he had never seen before.

During the 200 to 400 years of the sojourn of the Hebrews in Egypt there must have been many pharaohs, but we hear of three only. The first was the simpleton who encouraged an alien governor to enrich his own race and impoverish the native inhabitants. The second was the zany who attempted to destroy the manhood of the whole body of his slaves and servants. The third was a sceptic, who in his stubborn pride thought he could withstand the power of God and man.

Who this man was we do not know—perhaps the last pharaoh of the eighteenth dynasty, whose withered remains now lie, for every idler to look upon, in a glass case in the Cairo Museum. He had his prophets and magicians to appease the superstitions of his subjects, but he believed in himself only. Nevertheless, he could not refuse to receive Moses in audience. There was no door in Egypt that dare be closed against the spokesman of 600,000 despairing men.

It is a grotesque picture that presents itself to the mind when we try to see those two face to face—the little pigeon-breasted being with a raucous voice who believed himself divine, and the big-limbed man who may have been no orator but had a heart of fire and a head that might have been modelled by Michelangelo. We think of him as a stalwart creature with no fear about him, no sanctimoniousness, no sickly or mawkish sentimentality, capable of the highest flights of the spirit when it was alone with God, capable, too, of turning his talk to the common lingua vulgaris whatever conventions might be made to blood, full of natural delight in all that came up from the depths of his big heart, but a man above all, and a great one.

"Let my people go that they may worship their own God's command," said Moses. And the strutting mannikin, boiling with rage, replied, "Who is your God that *I* should obey him? I know not your God, neither will I let your people go."

When Moses had gone out after that first encounter, the king did what such puny souls, in the fury of their suicidal insanity, always do under like conditions—laid heavier burdens upon the people represented by their spokesman.

Manifestly, it was a time of great natural convulsions, such as Egypt, notwithstanding its generally equable temperature, has frequently suffered from. The first sign of these convulsions came with the flooding of the Nile, which, breaking from its springs in the snow-capped mountains of a neighbouring country, had carried the clay of the river banks along with it. By the time it reached the royal city of Egypt, the river seemed to be turned into blood, and, dig as they would, the people could find no water fit to drink.

To Moses, in his frenzy at the king's refusal, this was the work of God, and returning to Pharaoh he said, "Let my people go, or other afflictions will fall on your country." Pharaoh answered as before, and then Egypt, in the prolonged convulsions of nature, was smitten by a succession of plagues—a plague of frogs, of flies, of locusts and of black darkness by day as well as night. After each of these plagues Moses returned to Pharaoh with the same demand but Pharaoh "hardened his heart" again and refused to liberate the Hebrews.

It is impossible to think that even for a moment Pharaoh believed the calamities his country was suffering from were at the hand of the Hebrew God. All the rationalists have not been born within the past two centuries in Europe; and across the magic-making sands of Egypt we can hear the echo of the explanations with which this one justified his conduct.

"Blood? Who does not know that the blood of the Nile is only a mixture of the snow-water and the red soil of Abyssinia?" "Locusts? Who has not seen the black blight that crosses the desert and falls on our fields and eats up every green leaf that springs from them?" "Darkness? Who has not felt the chill of the dark cloud that comes up from the sea and turns day into night?"

But at length, when his pride could brook no longer the importunity of Moses, Pharaoh cried in his rage, "Get thee from me; take heed to see my face no more; for on the day when thou seest my face thou shalt die." And then Moses, bridling his wrath in the strength of his faith, replied, "Thou hast spoken well. I will see thy face no more."

XIII. The Exodus from Egypt

It was the beginning of the end. If there is one thing more sure than another about Moses it is that he shared with the prophets of all ages the power of looking deeper than other men into natural events. At this moment Moses saw, what speedily came to pass, that a terrific tempest was about to break over Egypt. It would carry death on its wings and mow down life as with a scythe, especially the life of the young and the feeble. This did not disturb his belief that God would be behind it, therefore he told his people that at the dead of night the Invisible God with his Destroyer by his side, would pass through the land and cut down the first-born of the Egyptians, from the first-born of Pharaoh on his throne to the first-born of the captive in the dungeon and the first-born of the maid behind the mill—the most servile of servants.

It was impossible to think of another calamity so fearful. Ten thousand battlefields could not leave such a furnace of bitter suffering. But from this affliction the Hebrews were to be saved. They were to be ransomed by an act of sacrifice—not the sacrifice that dated back to the early belief of primitive man, but the sacrifice of redemption, the sacrifice of a father to redeem his children.

To bring about this new and nobler redemption, Moses told the Hebrews what they were to do. He took risks—prophets always take risks. Moses foretold the exact time of the coming of the catastrophe. That was the first month of the year. On the fourth day of the first month every man was to take a lamb; he was to keep it alive until the fourteenth, then kill and eat it, with peculiar rites, and with his loins girded and his shoes on his feet and his staff in his hand ready for flight, for on the midnight of that day the Destroyer of God would pass through the land and smite the first-born of the Egyptians, both of man and beast.

But in order that He might spare the Hebrews, they were to dip a bunch of hyssop in the blood of the lamb and sprinkle the blood on their lintels, so that seeing it God might not suffer His Destroyer to go into their houses and kill their children, but pass on and spare them.

It was a terrible scene that followed, and none the less awful if it is understood to be founded not on a mracle but on natural causes, a death-dealing wind such as has frequently swept over Egypt, leaving a swathe of dead behind it.

On the fourteenth midnight of the first month Pharaoh was sporting in his palace, and the Egyptians were sleeping in their beds, but the Hebrews were watching and waiting, with the young mothers clutching their babes to their breasts, and listening with throbbing hearts to what they believed to be the deadened step of the Destroyer as He passed down the street. Suddenly there came a great cry throughout the land. There was not a house in which there was not one dead. And the Hebrews, taking advantage of the dismay and confusion of the Egyptians, took to headlong flight—a terrified and disordered multitude with their little ones on their backs.

We read that there were 600,000 of the Hebrew men, not counting the women and children; that in the wild sky of the stormy night a pillar of fire went before to show them their way; and that in three days they had crossed the Goshen marshes and reached the shores of the Red Sea.

There they trenched in the hope of rest. But Pharaoh, who, in the meantime, had recovered from the first shock of the loss of his own first-born and from the disaster that had befallen his nation, had begun to look upon all that had happened as a natural occurrence. He had said to his people, "Why should we let the Hebrews go from serving us?" Therefore, he had made ready his bodyguard of 600 chosen chariots with their captains and horsemen and pursued them. Before he had overtaken them the night had fallen, and the two "armies" lay within a short space of each other till morning.

The night was a tempestuous one. The wild winds of that desolate region were shrieking through clouds of blinding sand. The Hebrews, foreseeing certain destruction, were saying to Moses, "Were there no graves in Egypt that you brought us here to die?"

At dawn it was seen that a north wind (not an east one) had driven back the shallow water of the gulf at the narrow point at which the modern canal has deepened it, so the Hebrews passed over the bed of the Red Sea as over dry land. But when the 600 chariots of the Egyptians followed them, they were first stuck in the mud, thereby losing their wheels, and then overwhelmed by a returning tide from the south which swept back the waters and swallowed up their captains and horsemen.

It was a triumphant rescue, a nation's springtime of glory. The Israelites saw the dead bodies of their oppressors lying on the seashore with their jewelled swords in their belts, and according to eastern custom Miriam, the sister of Moses, with her women, took her timbrel and danced, singing, perhaps, the words of her brother; "The Lord shall reign for ever and ever."

XIV.   Moses and the Passover

Thus, after centuries of bondage, the Hebrews escaped from Egypt. They had gone into it as a family, and they came out of it with a strong hand as a nation. To keep in remembrance the pain and travail, the glory and triumph of their deliverance, they established a rite.

It was not in itself a new rite. Perhaps it had come down to them from pagan religions of remote antiquity, wherein it had probably stood as a sacrifice to the god of the spring. But, as the sacrifice of their redemption from the winter of slavery and sin through the blood of the lamb, it has been continued at the same time of the year, with changes of form and of meaning, to this day. It is called by some of us the Passover; by others, in a deeper sense, the Eucharist.

When Moses landed his 600,000 men (henceforward to be called Israelites) on the northern shore of the Red Sea, he was within a few days' march of the Promised Land.

Making allowance for the slow travelling of his women and children, and perhaps for their flocks and herds, he was then within a fortnight's journey of the home of Jacob at Beersheba, and little more than that from the grave of Abraham at Hebron, or yet the Canaanite city on the Judæn hills, which, in a time to come, was to be the central home of their religion.

That he did not take that course is sufficient of itself to answer the writers who say that the Hebrews left Egypt as an organized army. The Philistines (or some other wild tribe) to the number of perhaps 20,000 were now entrenched on the narrow strip of Canaan by the sea, and Moses said, looking at the dispirited multitude of his unarmed and unmanned refugees, "Let us not take them that way, lest peradventure at the sight of war they repent and return to Egypt."

Yet he was still in a foreign land. It was a desolate peninsula, hardly larger than a third of Italy and scarcely 120 miles across its broadest base. But it was surrounded by enemies who might wish to make his people their slaves. Besides the wild Philistine raiders on the west, there were the Babylonian battalions on the north, as well as the Egyptian garrisons on the southern side of the Red Sea and the marauding tribes that roved about the peninsula itself. It says something for the Egyptian tradition that Moses was brought up as a soldier, that he evaded the worst of his perils with masterly strategy. But it took him a long time to do so. The Bible says years—forty years, an almost incredible period.

To follow the wanderings of the Israelites in the wilderness from the records of the four biblical historians is impossible. Many have tried to harmonize the narratives; none have succeeded in doing so; probably none will ever succeed, so conflicting are they in time, place and fact, so confusing in motive, so obviously written in a later age by writers who had another interest to serve than that of telling the simple and human story of Moses and his fugitive people flying from a land of tyranny to what they expected to be a haven of peace. But it needs little light from imagination, and nearly none from tradition, to look into the long night that preceded what they believed, only too pitifully, to be their dawn.

In the hope of giving his tired people safety and repose after their bondage in Egypt and the exhaustion of their escape, Moses first turned south, as he had done before when he was flying alone. In the third month of his journey he encamped in the Wilderness of Sin. There his father-in-law met him, bringing his wife and sons.

It does not appear that the Israelites ever thought of settling, even temporarily, in the land then occupied by the Midianites. We have reason to think that its soil was better than it is now, but they never attempted to cultivate it. It does not appear that during their long wanderings they ever did any productive work anywhere. They had been so long a slave race that it is possible there was nothing they could do.

Never has there been a concourse of more helpless emigrants. After they had eaten up the unleavened bread which they had made of the dough they had brought out of Egypt on their shoulders and baked in the sun on their backs, they were content to live from first to last on the only fruit of the unproductive desert, the "manna"—probably an Egyptian corianda seed which, like the mushroom, rose from the earth before sunrise and rotted after sunset.

A long period of impotent idleness will destroy the muscles of the soul as surely as those of the body. Only a people of great spirit can survive the corroding effects of it, and the Israelites at that time, crushed by centuries of bondage, were a people of rags and tatters.

There is much to say for them. They found themselves in a wilderness. The land of inexhaustible fertility, the garden planned for them on earth by Heaven, seemed as far away as ever. The leader they had followed appeared thus far to have failed them. They had nothing they could call their own except the earth and sky. In gloomy moments their hearts turned back to Egypt. They hungered for a visible god to worship, to come close to them and comfort them, even if it were only such an image of a god as in their darkest days in Egypt they had kept in their houses. They began to tell themselves that the God of Moses was nothing but a phantom who lived, if at all, in the vague reaches of the unsearchable skies, and did not see or hear or care. "Did we not tell you when we were in Egypt," they said, "to let us alone that we might serve the Egyptians?"

It was the cry of the paganized soul, which, after ages of polluted slavery, was drifting back to the condition of primitive man. Moses heard it and called on God to show him how to save his people from idolatry. He thought God showed him a way.

It was then the height of summer, when storms of thunder and lightning fell with appalling suddenness and intensity on the Wilderness of Sin. One such storm came in this first heavy hour of the exodus of the Israelites. The thunder roared and echoed in the mountain, the lightning leapt from peak to peak, the air quivered and the earth trembled. This was like nothing the

Israelites had heard or seen on the plains of Egypt. It could only be the voice of God—the God of Moses, of Abraham, Isaac and Jacob; and he was a God above all gods.

But the end was not yet. Mount Sinai, which (as we see from a song which was written later) was volcanic, burst into eruption. A thick darkness of smoke covered the top of the mountain and fire as from a furnace descended from it. The people quaked with fear. They thought God was speaking to them in the thunder. They dared not listen, so they cried to Moses, "Speak thou to us and we will hear; but let not God speak to us, lest we die."

XV.   The Ten Commandments

Moses went up into the thick darkness where God was, leaving his brother Aaron as governor and high priest over the people. He remained many days and nights on the mountain to think out what he was to do if he were to carry his tempted and benighted followers in purity of faith to their journey's end.

It is possible that he fasted, and that, as the strength of his body failed, his mind became confused. He came to believe that God spoke to him, giving him ten commandments for the guidance of His people, and telling him to write them down on two stones that they might serve as an everlasting remembrance of His will. It is even possible that in the clouding of his senses he thought God wrote the commandments with His own hand, and that in the sincerity of belief he afterwards said so.

That they were the work of Moses himself is beyond question; they make war upon every error and vice of the Egyptian people whom he had left behind him. The first five of them were declarations of God's sole divinity; and the second five were laws concerned with social duties, the relation of man to woman, of man to man, of master to servant and slave. That the Ten Commandments were divinely inspired it is not difficult to believe, for they have been the groundwork of nearly all law that has existed in the world from that day to this.

With the two stones under his arm and joy in his heart, Moses turned back to the valley. But while he had been on Mount Sinai struggling with his soul for their salvation, his people on the plain had been returning to their idolatry. The thunders of the living

God of the universe being no longer in their ears, they were turning back in thought to the fat faces of the dead gods of Egypt. "Up, make us gods that will go before us," they had said to Aaron, "for as for this Moses, the man that brought us out of the land of Egypt, we wot not what has become of him."

Aaron had done as such priestly parasites always do—submitted to the will of the people. "Break off the earrings which are in the ears of your wives and your sons and daughters and bring them to me," he had said.

When the people had done so, he had made the gold into a molten calf, just as he might have done if he had been back in Egypt; he had set it up on an altar and proclaimed a feast to it.

Early next morning the people had built a fire about the Golden Calf and made offerings to it, had sat down to eat and drink, and then, rising up, they stripped themselves naked and danced and sang around the idol, exactly as they had been wont to do on feast days in the country of their exile, saying, in the confused delirium of their new-born liberty, "These be thy gods, O Israel, which brought thee out of the land of Egypt."

Moses, with the two stones under his arms, heard the shouting of the people as he descended the mountain. He thought at first it was the noise of war in the camp. But when he came nearer and saw the dancing of the naked people, and heard their singing, his anger became uncontrollable. Hastening down, he cast the Golden Calf into the fire and fell upon Aaron with bitter reproaches.

Aaron (once more according to the manner of his kind) threw the blame upon the people, but the wrath of Moses was not to be so easily appeased. What he did to Aaron as a chief author of the idolatry we are told later on, but now he took up his place at the gate of the camp and cried, "Who is on the Lord's side, let him come to me."

The Levites came to him, and he said, "Put every man to the sword who has been guilty of this sin, even if he is your own brother."

The Levites did as they were commanded, and 3,000 men fell that day. But next day the iron judge of his people was on his knees before the Judge of all men. "Thy people have sinned a great sin," he said, "but if Thou canst forgive them, forgive them. If not, let *me* be blotted out of Thy book for ever."

XVI. The Ark of the Covenant

What happened next is not easy to follow. Moses left the Wilderness of Sin and set his face towards the Promised Land. Tradition paints vivid pictures on the background of reality, and we see the vast camp travelling northward with Moses at the head of it; 600,000 men, besides women and children, moving on and on over the uncultivated waste; old women with a string of half-naked children dragging behind them; old men with the remnants of their miserable belongings on their backs; children born and dying on the way. Still the mass of indistinguishable humanity moving on. Floods, droughts, the ravages of roving tribes, the extortions of settled armies. Is it possible that the world has witnessed anything like it?

Then, worse than the starvation of the bodies of the wanderers, the increasing starvation of their souls. Moses saw it. Clearly he began, after a while, to feel pity for the weakness of his helpless people, which forbade them to realize the existence of a God whose form they could not see constantly among them. A symbol of the real presence of the Deity seemed necessary to the feebleness of their intellects and to the poverty of their souls. Therefore, Moses ordered that an ark should be made, and the stones of the Commandments put into it, with rings at either side for staves by which it could be carried on the shoulders of the priests.

The Ark can have been no bigger than the chest which a sailor pushes under his bunk at sea, but probably it opened at the side, and as often as the camp halted the side was thrown back so that everybody might look upon the words which they could not read but believed to be written by the hand of God.

It is a moving thing to think of, the immense company of fugitives, now a chastened and humbled people, with the Ark of the Covenant going before them, and (however we understand it) in the skies ahead of them an awful guide of flame and smoke, a pillar of cloud by day and a pillar of fire by night—the only visible manifestation of the presence of God.

Months passed, probably years, in irregular wanderings. The wanderers slept in tents, ate only the fruit of the desert and drank only the water of such wells as they passed on the way. The ills of mortality were certainly with them. Sometimes they had to carry their sick on their backs, and oftentimes to bury their dead in the lonely wastelands and push on without them.

But they had their cheerful times also. Always, in later days, the Hebrews sang during their sojournings, and none of us need be ashamed of the tears in our eyes when we think of this multitude of children out of the land of bondage singing together to comfort their torn hearts as they tramped through the wilderness on their way to their father's home:

> Behind the howling desert with its sand,
> There waits beneath the stars the Promised Land.

XVII.   The Tabernacle

Unhappily, Moses went one step farther. At the beginning of the second year of their wanderings he ordered the building of a tabernacle.

The Tabernacle was a wooden structure about sixty feet long, twenty-five feet wide and twenty feet high. Apparently it was no more than a tent among the many tents of a migratory people, hardly differing in appearance from the headquarters of a general in the midst of the tents of an army. It was never used as a tent. In the eyes of the wanderers it became the residence of God, in short, an Egyptian temple such as Moses had seen in his youth (and perhaps Aaron had ministered in) adapted to the needs of a nomad people.

An altar of wood, covered with gold, was put up in it. The Ark of the Commandments was set on the altar. On the top of the Ark there was a seat, called the mercy-seat, which was understood to be occupied by God. On the horns (or side) of the altar there were images of two cherubs, called the cherubim and seraphim. Their faces were turned towards the occupant of the mercy-seat and their outspread wings were over him. A table stood in front of the altar. On this table there were dishes for flat cakes called shewbread, and flagons for wine. These cakes and wine were consecrated and perpetually reserved as the food and drink of the priests. A veil was hung in front of the altar, and this was the boundary of a sanctuary, a holy of holies, and beyond it none but the priests might go.

After the Tabernacle was built Moses appointed Aaron, his brother, and his brother's sons, to a perpetual priesthood to minister to it. That the high priest might do so with a solemnity becoming to his sacred office, Moses ordered that, like his pagan predecessors, he should be clothed in special vestments. These vestments were of the utmost splendour, and probably of the pattern used by the Egyptian priests. They were of purple, scarlet and gold, with a chain and breastplate studded with jewels of emerald, sapphire, topaz, amethyst, beryl and jasper. They also consisted of a linen ephod, a robe and a brocaded coat and mitre.

The people were called upon to provide the material for these vestments, and we read that they did so in such abundance that at length they had to be told to bring no more. But whether the picture this presents of a settled people abounding in wealth accords with our sense of the condition of a wandering horde of impoverished pilgrims, passing through a barren wilderness, with few possessions beyond the clothes on their backs and the sandals on their feet, and with no food except that which sprang from the desert ground, is a question which each of us must ask and answer for himself.

XVIII. *The High Priest*

The first duty of the high priest in the tabernacle was to act as an intermediary with God. With prostration and adoration we see him approaching the altar, presenting the petitions of the people to God and receiving God's replies. In return for this priestly service the people were required to make sacrifices. One of these sacrifices was the sacrifice of the redemption, which consisted of the sprinkling of blood on the horns of the altar, and of eating and drinking bread and water (never blood, under pain of being cut off from the congregation) after they had been consecrated by the high priest or his sons.

Once a year the people were required to make an atonement for their sins by paying two fees of equal amount, whether they were poor or rich, one to the priest and the other to the sanctuary. Once a year, too, they were to make a sin-offering to God, by offering a live lamb to the priest, who, after laying both his hands on it, and confessing over it the iniquities of the nation, was to drive it out into the wilderness with their transgressions on its head.

Who first among the wanderers conceived this rhodomontade of ritual it is not easy to say. That, in the books which we call the

Books of Moses, God Himself is made responsible both for the ritual of the Tabernacle and for all else that pertains to it, no longer satisfies the modern conscience. Whether the ritual had its origin in the memory of Aaron, the creator of the Golden Calf, or was invented hundreds of years later by priests who, living in a fully-developed religious state, were seeking divine authority and security for their own position and profession, is a matter for divided opinion.

That it had its origin in Moses it is hard to believe. But it is impossible to deny that if he did not create the ritual of the Tabernacle, he tolerated it. Nor is it difficult to see why he did so. He had to meet the spiritual hunger of his homeless wanderers in an alien land. They were a vast, and, for a time, an increasing multitude. It is more than probable that they were wholly illiterate. After so many years of slavery, scarcely one of them in a thousand would be able to read or write. They had no sacred book, no scriptures, and only two tables of stone. Besides these there was nothing and nobody but Moses himself to speak to their souls, and not in a hundred years could he make a hundredth part of them hear the sound of his voice. Clearly, the great leader in his loneliness told himself that if the souls of his people were to be kept alive they must have symbols. Pitiable spectacle! By the eye of the mind we see what happened. The Tabernacle, like the Ark, was made in parts, with rings and staves at their sides, so that it might be taken from place to place. We read that during the long period of the wanderings it was carried to forty-two different resting-places. At each of these resting-places we see it seated on elevated ground, with its broad side open to show what was within—not only the Ark, but also the altar and the mercy-seat and the cherubim and seraphim, and the table bearing the consecrated elements of bread and wine. We see thousands, perhaps hundreds of thousands of the people, on their day of rest, their Sabbath, sitting or kneeling on the ground in front, looking with eyes of ecstasy into the open Tabernacle as into Heaven itself, and singing with rapturous voice the hymns which Moses had written for them and they had committed to memory. We hear the rolling of their voices, like the voice of an inland sea, over the stark desert lands; "The Lord is my strength and my song and He is become my salvation. Who is like unto Thee, O Lord, glorious in Holiness, fearful in praises, doing wonders?"

Grand, majestic, but not unpitiable man! That Moses thought

of this as idolatry is not to be believed for a moment. Had he not said, "Cursed be the man that maketh any graven or molten image, an abomination to the Lord." But that while denouncing such idolatries he was encouraging them is hardly to be denied. Both then and later, when he set up a fiery serpent in the wilderness, so that such of his people as had been bitten by serpents (looking up to it and adoring it) might live, he was manifestly going back to his early memories of the visible gods of Egypt—to what he had seen as a boy of the symbols of pagan religions of the remotest antiquity.

But if so, bitter was the price he was to pay for it.

XIX. Seditions against Moses

Meantime, Moses had his troubles as a leader. One of the worst of them was war. Nothing is clearer in the history of the Israelites than that Moses was a man of peace. Again and again he tried to fix it in the minds of his people that neither sword nor sling but God alone was their true defence.

Nevertheless, in his passage through the wilderness he encountered the armed resistance of native kings, who refused water to his people and tried to prevent their progress. Sometimes he made long detours to avoid conflicts (hence, in part, the length of his wanderings), but sometimes he was compelled to yield to the will of the young bloods among his followers (born in the wilderness) to meet resistance by wars of defence. In such wars the Israelites (who were dexterous in the use of the stone and sling) won notable victories, and, in spite of their leader, followed them up with barbaric atrocities. This led to an effort on the part of certain of the native kings to subdue the Israelites by subtler methods than war.

One such method was that of Balak, the king of the Moabites. Attributing the success in battle of the wandering horde of the Israelites to the favour of their God, this person is said to have conceived (at the instigation of a soothsayer named Balaam) the device of alienating their allegiance by an appeal to their passions.

Balak sent into the Israelite camp the handsomest of the daughters of his people, decked in their most beautiful garments, to seduce its young men. The girls were to go all the way to this end, but as soon as they saw that the young Israelites were so enamoured of them that they could not let them go, they were to say they must leave unless the young men were prepared to abandon the worship of their God and worship the god of the Moabites.

At first this plot seemed likely to fulfil Balak's expectations. On hearing the maidens say they must return to their people, the young Israelites called God to witness how miserable they would be without them. Upon this, the girls agreed to remain with the young men, and to become their wives, on condition that they worshipped the same gods as themselves. The young men, in the fire of their passion, consented to do this, thus breaking the law of their race and religion. But Balak had counted without Moses, who demanded that the young men should send away the foreign women, or be sent away themselves. This put an end to the rebellion, but not until 14,000 of the rebels had perished.

Moses had also to deal with seditions against himself. One of these was created by a rich Hebrew named Korah, who had the advantage over Moses of being an eloquent speaker. He told the Israelites that Moses had been so long their leader that he was giving himself the airs of a prince; that, contrary to the law of the Hebrew religion, he had presumed to bestow the dignity of an everlasting hereditary high-priesthood on his brother and his brother's sons on his own authority alone, and not by the common suffrage of the people. Moses crushed Korah in spite of his eloquent blather, by showing the Israelites what God had done for them through him, and by saying that it was only by God's will that he stood where he did.

Later, Moses had trouble within his own family. His sister, Miriam, who had watched by the ark when it took him as a child down the Nile, raked up out of jealousy the story of his marriage to the Ethiopian woman. She became leprous. Moses put her out into the desert for seven days, and when she returned to the camp, disgraced and degraded, she died.

Aaron, also, became envious of the supremacy of his brother as a prophet, and perhaps for this reason or, more probably, for further relapses into idolatry, like that at Sinai, Moses treated him to the same iron discipline. Calling together the congregation, he placed Aaron in the midst of it, and then publicly stripped his high-priest's garments off his back and put them on to his son Eleazar. Dejected and disgraced, Aaron died soon afterwards.

It would be surprising, indeed, if we found that Moses escaped the slanders which disfigured the record of Abraham. According to the scribes of low spiritual development, who wrote centuries later and put words into his mouth and even into the mouth of God, he did not. Although never accused of sexual immorality, he is again and again charged (apparently to his glory) with the toleration of atrocities which in our day would disgrace a naked savage.

One case of such toleration follows a murder committed by Phineas, the son of the second high priest, Eleazar. Late in their wanderings in the wilderness, the Israelites, tiring of the manna which was their only food, lusted for flesh. In his wrath God, for their punishment, gave them flesh in the form of quails. The quails produced a plague whereof 24,000 persons died. Disease or sudden death was attributed to sin, and in this case the sin was said to have been that of certain of the younger Israelites who were going after the daughters of the Midianites.

At length one of them became so bold that he brought a Midianite woman into the camp in the very sight of Moses. Upon this Phineas rose up from the congregation, followed the man and the woman into a tent, killed the man with his javelin and then ripped up the woman through her stomach. After that barbaric act, the plague, it is said, was stayed; and God, the God of Abraham, is said to have rewarded Phineas with an everlasting priesthood.

We are no longer required to believe this atrocious story as the record of an actual happening, first, because Moses himself had married a Midianite woman and had two Midianite sons then in the camp; and, next, because Phineas was already heir to an hereditary priesthood through that which had been conferred on his grandfather.

XX. *Moses on the Borders of Canaan*

Thirty-eight or more years had passed by this time, and the Israelites had come near to the borders of Canaan. They were eager to enter their Promised Land; but Moses, who still knew little or nothing about it, had begun to have doubt of its security. Therefore he sent twelve spies into the country to find out its strength and its weakness. Apparently, the men entered by the low-lying lands on the south of the Salt Sea; went up to Abraham's city, Hebron (ruled by giants who were called sons of Anak), followed the line of the coast through Joppa to Lebanon, and then turned back by the foot of Hermon, through the valleys of Galilee and Jordan, until they came to the grape-growing country of Jericho. There they cut a forked bough from a well laden vine, hung it across a pole, and climbing the Moabite hills by the site of the fortress, wherein many centuries later the untamable soul of a fiery ascetic was to end his tumultuous life, returned to the camp.

Their report of Canaan was a bad one. They said they had found mountains which their people could not climb; wide rivers they could not cross, and a race of giants they could not encounter. Such of us as have lived in the country know that the report of the spies was, in large part, untrue, but it threw the leaders of the people into a panic. Was this what they had wandered so far for, suffering hunger and thirst, heat and cold, disease and death? Was this the land promised by God to their fathers as an inheritance to their children for ever?

We read that Moses flung himself face down on the ground and wept. Could God ever forgive this people who had forgotten all He had done for them? But then a strong-hearted man, Joshua, who had been one of the spies himself, arose and said, "If God has promised the land to His own He will give us possession of it."

That was like a trumpet-call to the souls of the wanderers. Moses rose, and his people with him. Their wanderings were near to an end, and they turned their faces to the last stage of their journey.

XXI. *The Sin of Moses*

But a black cloud was hovering over them. Moses was soon to die. The heaviness of years was upon him. We read that, although he had reached the great age of a hundred and twenty, his eye was not dim and his natural force was not abated. But his spirit was like the frayed edge of a blown-out cloud. He was never to set foot in the Promised Land. He had sinned and, therefore, the consummation of the hope of his life was to be denied to him.

Too long the world has permitted itself to believe the dishonouring story of the chroniclers of the seventh century that the sin for which Moses was to be so sorely punished was that, in his anger at the impatience of his people, he had struck the rock at the waters of Meribah in the Wilderness of Sin after the Lord had told him merely to speak to it. Such of us as have a higher reverence for the majesty and justice of God will look for a deeper reason, and in this case we shall easily find it.

Moses had spent eighty years of his life in proclaiming the faith of Abraham, that God was the invisible Spirit of the Universe; that He was the Maker of Heaven and earth; that there was nothing supernatural in the world except God; that God had no symbols and that He could not be worshipped and adored through images. Every word which Moses can be believed by instructed persons to have said had been intended to teach that doctrine. And yet he had practised the reverse of it.

He had boxed up God in an ark and housed him in a tabernacle. He had permitted his people to adore Him in things made by hands, in cherubim and seraphim and in a fiery serpent. He had allowed them to worship Him in rites and ceremonies, which had always obscured and often obliterated Him, in feasting and fasting, in washing and anointing, in putting on vestments and taking them off again, and in making sacrifices of the blood of living creatures.

All this he may have done as a concession to the hardness of their hearts, to the feebleness of their intellects, and to the poverty of their souls. But that way lay idolatry and the return of humanity to the paganism of primitive man. And in the future it would lead to the division of faiths, the division of nations and to bitter wars between the children of one father.

Moses saw that in committing this sin, however innocently intended, he had cut himself off from the heritage of God. Hitherto, he had believed himself to be the God-man, who, when the children of Israel had reached the land promised to their fathers, was to bring in the Golden Age, the Kingdom of Heaven on earth, that was to make them a blessing to all the nations.

If Moses thought this of himself, it was no more than others in later ages thought about him. One Jewish philosopher of a thousand years later called him the Viceregent of God. Another, writing in an apocryphal book, put it into the mouth of Moses himself that, born and dying as a man, he was of divine origin, a great angel of God, hardly distinguishable from the Christ who had been foretold and was expected.

It was all wrong. He was not the Messiah—he was a sinful man. And now, for violating the first commandment of God, he was to part company with his people on the very threshold of the Promised Land, and they were to go on without him. This was to be his punishment.

XXII. *The Death of Moses*

From the place at which Moses received the report of the spies, he made his last march with his people. It must have been along the ragged western boundary of the Arabian Desert and the jagged eastern backs of the Moabite mountains. It was early morning. Behind them lay the wilderness they had passed through. During the forty years of their wanderings vast numbers of the 600,000 who had escaped from Egypt had died there. They had perished in the torrid heat and arctic cold of that desolate region—sleeping by night in their tents, or more often on the open ground, and going on by day as long as life allowed, because their leader had told them they were returning home. It is an awesome thing to think about—that long trail of indistinguishable graves in the thousand miles of desert grass which stretched by circuitous routes as far back as Sinai.

Moses was going towards Pisgah, the highest peak of the mountain range which divided the desert from Canaan. When he reached the breast of Nebo, perhaps in the mist of morning, he turned about and waved his hand to the people behind him. They stopped and he spoke to them.

What he said is reported at too much length in the fifth book of what we call the Books of Moses, as well as in the book of the Jewish historian Josephus, who may have had other and more ancient authorities. We can no longer believe that all that is attributed to Moses in either of these was his. Much of it was based on a seventh century tradition of a farewell speech, and some of it was copied from Babylonian writers of an earlier date. But the substance of what Moses said to his people in that hour of their parting is easily seen and as easily summarized.

Standing on the mountain breast with the vast multitude of his followers before him, he told them how he had found them in the bitterness of their bondage in Egypt and had brought them out of it, as God had directed, and how they and their fathers had wandered with him in the wilderness, and God had fed and protected them. Behind the hills on the west lay the goodly land which God had sworn to give to the father of their people when he had entered into the covenant with them whereby they would become a blessing to all the nations. They were about to enter it and possess it, and it was to be a heritage of their children and their children's children. But they must be diligent to keep God's commandments, especially that one which said that they should serve no other gods, the work of men's hands, of wood and stone, who could neither see nor hear nor smell. If they did keep His commandments God would go with them and prolong their days. If they did not, they would perish off the land and the Lord would scatter them among the nations. Nevertheless, their God was a merciful God, and if, in their outcast state, they sought Him with all their hearts and souls they would find Him, and He would restore them to their inheritance.

As for himself, he had offended against God, and he was not to go with them. He was to die in the wilderness of their wanderings. Soon, very soon, he would leave them, and they would see him no more.

At this, according to the Jewish historian, the people, even the women and children, fell into tears, remembering the dangers they had passed through with Moses, begging his forgiveness for the murmurings they had made against him, and asking him to intercede for them with God for their sins against Him.

He promised to do so, and then they wept the more. He told them not to weep for him, because a still greater glory was awaiting them. From the grave of a prophet a still greater prophet arose, and it was to be so in this case.

"The Lord your God will raise up to you a prophet from the midst of your brethren, like unto me. Him you will hear."

Last of all Moses blessed his people and parted from them with the tremendous words:

"The eternal God be your refuge and underneath you the everlasting arms."

When he had finished speaking he turned to go. The people followed him, still weeping. He told those who were nearest to him not to add to his grief by giving way to tears, and then he beckoned to those who were remote from him to stay behind. Only the high priest and Joshua accompanied him farther. It is said that his two sons attempted to attend him to the place of his death, but he waved them back. A little later he laid his hands on Joshua as a sign, it is said, that God had appointed him to be his successor, and then he sent both Joshua and the priest away also. In the hour of death, and under the mighty hand that was over him, he was to meet God alone.

For the story of what follows we need no authority. As Moses had ascended Sinai amid the thunders of the storm to plead for his people, so he went up Nebo with the burden of his own sins upon him. The multitude of his followers at the foot of it watched him go until a cloud came down and covered him. Climbing the mountain through the cloud he came to its highest peak. It was the summit of Pisgah. Then the cloud cleared, and he saw the land below him. It was the Land of Promise.

The prospect from this point, even as we see it to-day with the grandeur of that moment gone from it, is one of the most impressive in the world. It covers a space of 100 miles wide by 80 deep. On the south lies the glassy eye of the Dead Sea, with its four doomed cities buried in its bosom. On the north rises the height of Hermon, with its white cap of sunlit snow on its broad forehead. Beneath and between runs the Jordan, and in front is the palm-covered city of Jericho, with a stony old road going up to the Mount of Olives. Beyond are the pinnacles of Jerusalem, and, on the outer edge of the green plain of Jaffa, there is the blue bar of the Mediterranean —"the utmost sea" and the boundary of the known world to Moses.

This was the last sight he was to look upon—the goodly land he had tried through forty years to reach. And now he was never to set foot in it.

Great liberator! Not without sin, but sublime in your remorse, your renunciation and your repentance! Mourn not too much that you are not to go down into the place of your dreams. No great leader of men has ever yet entered his promised land. But with his dying eyes he has sometimes had visions of its future. What were yours?

Did you see the prophet who was to come after you as an earthly King of Kings, a greater than Pharaoh, a mightier than Cæsar, going out from this land promised to Abraham, with his chariots and horsemen, in the vain thought that he could conquer the world by the sword? Or did you see him, perhaps, as a poor sojourner on life's highway, toiling up that stony road from Jericho to Jerusalem with bleeding feet, yet firm and unafraid, because he believes with all his soul that he is to be the last sacrifice for the sins of his fellow-men, and by the will of his God he is to die for them?

"How small is Pisgah," although it parleys with the sky, "when Moses stands on the top of it!"

CHAPTER VII

The Promised Land

I. *The Return of the Israelites*

THE STORY of the return of the Israelites to their Promised Land, as recorded in the Book of *Joshua,* is one of the most painful in history. It is worse than painful; it is horrible. It is the story of a reign of terror lasting from forty to sixty-five years.

In view of this fact a Jewish philosopher at the time of Christ described it as an allegory. A Christian Father three centuries later gave it a similar description. Historians of a later age have gone further.

A critical examination of the Book of *Joshua,* with its medley of contradictions, its tangle of myth, legend and tradition, its maelstrom of inhumanity and atrocity, added to the evidence of recent excavations in Palestine and of a series of tablets discovered in Egypt, has led some modern writers so far as to say that no such thing as an organized conquest of Canaan ever occurred at all. The utmost they believe to have happened is that, about the time of Moses, a few Hebrew groups from the east of the Euphrates crossed the Moabite mountains, made sporadic raids over the Jordan and contracted peaceful alliances with the Canaanite people.

But we cannot so easily elude the admitted difficulties of the settlement of the Israelites in Canaan. It is one of two things. If there was no organized conquest of Canaan by the Israelites there could have been no wandering in the wilderness; if there was no wandering in the wilderness, there could have been no exodus from Egypt; if there was no exodus there could have been no bondage; if there was no bondage no such man as Moses could ever have existed. Yet Moses, the bondage, the exodus and the wanderings are so veined through and through the Bible, almost from the beginning to the end, that to remove them would be to destroy it as an historical document.

We cannot remove them. It is impossible to construct the history

137

of the Hebrew people during the next 200 years after Moses on the evidence of a few old walls in Jericho, a few old bones in Gezer and a few tablets from Tel-el-Amarna. Apart from well-known facts in external history, we can only construct it from the Book of *Joshua,* however brutal and barbaric it may be.

At what date the conquest of Canaan took place we do not know. Some say as early as 1450 B.C. Others say as late as 1250 to 1100 B.C. The Book of *Joshua* is believed to have been first cast into form by a prophet living in Judah in the ninth century, but internal evidence seems to show that important parts of it cannot have been written until two or three centuries later. By that time the writers were too far away from the events they were recording to have personal knowledge of them. But this does not require that we should think that the leading events of the early residence of the Israelites in Canaan, as recorded in *Joshua,* are not substantially and fundamentally true.

We read the Bible carelessly if we do not see that immediately after the death of Moses an almost complete change took place in the Israelite cosmogony. The prophet gave way to the priest. Behind Joshua was Eleazar. Like his father, Aaron, Eleazar was essentially a pagan. His god was no longer the God of Moses, still less the God of Abraham, the invisible and universal Father of mankind, who had chosen the Hebrew people to be a light to the world and a blessing to all the nations. He had become a god of Egypt, a god of Chaldea, a god of vengeance who had laid on one family of His children the bloody task of exterminating all other families and destroying all other gods.

This new cosmogony required that the Israelite priest, as the sole representative of God, should be the real ruler of the people, however the military ruler might be made his spokesman. As a sign of his supremacy his priestly power and prestige must stand, whatever else might fall. Individual liberty must be submerged in priestly government. Personal possessions must cease. Henceforward no man must have anything of his own. There must be no more Korahs to resist, by the influence of their wealth, the will of the man of God. The spoils of war must fall into the priestly treasury. It must be called the treasury of the Lord.

Such was the new order which followed the death of Moses, and it accounts for nine-tenths of the myth and legend as well as the inhumanity and barbarity that attach to the conquest of Canaan by the Israelites. Therefore, in the great epic of Hebrew history, and in the story of the development of the human soul as a seeker after God and a searcher for a saviour, it is impossible that the Book of *Joshua,* notwithstanding its horrors, should not have a place.

II. *The Entry of the Israelites into Canaan*

According to early tradition the vast army of Israelites went down the slopes of the eastern hills into the valley of the Jordan, shouting "Hosanna to the Lord God of Israel!" We can well believe it. After the long night of their bondage in Egypt, and the heartbreaking sufferings and disillusionments of their pilgrimage in the wilderness, they must have thought they were returning home. At the great moment of their entrance into Canaan, they believed the land was to be theirs, and theirs alone, by the free gift of God.

But there was much they did not know. They did not know that the Canaan they were coming to was not the Canaan their ancestors had left behind them. During the 400 years of their sojourn in Egypt the land and its people had changed. Not long after Jacob had settled in Goshen a trio of shepherd kings (perhaps the Hyksos kings) had left the eastern side of the Egyptian delta and passed into Canaan with an army of 200,000. They had established an organized government there, with courts, fortresses, temples, priests and judges. They had also conscripted the native inhabitants to help them to conquer two larger countries on the north—Syria and Phœnicia.

As a result the Canaanites had ceased to be the peace-loving and sluggish race who had welcomed Abraham 600 years before. They lived no longer in dirty mud-built camps which sprawled over the face of the unclean earth, but in walled-in cities that were centres of commerce. They tilled the soil and cultivated their vineyards, but they had nevertheless become an active and even a warlike race, fighting with spears and swords and chariots of iron and battle-axes. They were prosperous and many of them were rich, and they were ready in times of danger to fight in defence of their families and possessions.

About three centuries later the shepherd kings had been driven out of Canaan and Phœnicia by powerful nations on the north-east, and then a new chapter had begun in the history of the native inhabitants. No longer held together by an alien master, they had broken into war among themselves.

Canaan, in particular, had become a province of many principalities. Every city, every village and every hamlet elected its head, and called him its king. Some of us who know the country feel, when we read the Bible, that at the time of the Israelite invasion, there must have been a Canaanite king in certain districts to every 100 acres. Many of these kings were farmers, some shepherds, some traders, and some were brigands, for the country swarmed with them. The consequence was perpetual conflict.

The Canaanite kings were all of the same family, and therefore they fought the fiercer. Only one passion united them—love of what they believed to be their native land. They had then been something like 1,000 years in it, and were bound to it by what they believed to be sacred ties. At the call of their pagan religion they had made human sacrifices of the first-born of their children that their bones might become foundations for the corner-stones of their sanctuaries.

Such was Canaan when the hosts of Israel appeared on the horizon. The reputation of the Israelites had gone before them. In the eyes of the Canaanite tribes it was not a good one. They were a wandering race of wild-eyed fanatics akin in character to the Ishmaelites, who lived in tents and wore big gold earrings. They believed they were under the special protection of supernatural powers. Their God was, in their view, the only true God, and all other gods were false ones. He lived in the skies and was the Maker of Heaven and earth. He had chosen the Israelites out of all the peoples of the earth to be His peculiar people. He had destroyed their enemies; He had helped them to vanquish the great king of Egypt; He had divided the waters of the Red Sea to permit them to pass through on dry land; He had wiped out two of the most powerful of the kings of the wilderness of Sinai when they had denied them water to drink and attempted to impede their progress. Above all, He had told them, as they believed, that about 600 years before He had made a covenant with the first of their ancestors, Abraham the Hebrew, who lay buried in "the field of Abraham" at Hebron, to give the land of Canaan to them as an everlasting inheritance.

The terror of these reports had probably been reaching the Canaanites for years by the caravans that came from the south and west. The Israelites were coming on and on over the desert by circuitous courses, and as often as the Canaanites heard of them their hearts failed and melted. But the common danger united the divided tribes, and when at length the Israelites appeared on the top of the eastern hills—a vast horde as of human locusts blackening the breast of the mountains—the Canaanites bolted the gates of their cities and shut up their women and children in their homes.

Clearly, it was to be war. But if it was to be war it should be war to extermination. Canaan or Israel—which was it to be?

III. The Conquest of Canaan

As far as we can judge, the Israelites entered their Promised Land by the ravine north of the Dead Sea which faces the city of Jericho.

They were then on the eastern side of the valley of the Jordan. That is a long stretch of land of irregular width extending from the north of the Dead Sea to the south of Galilee, and, by the "fault" in the crust of the earth, lying 1200 feet below the level of the Mediterranean. It is now a sparsely populated and indifferently cultivated region, with certain tablelands of good pasturage, but covered in great part by a rank growth of semi-tropical vegetation. It was then the site of several cities, called "the cities of the hills," of some farms and many sheepcotes. By reason of its isolation from the main current of life, it was also the refuge of exiles and outlaws. The Israelites called it the country of the sun-rising. In later ages the Jews called it Peræa. We now call it Trans-Jordania.

It would take the Israelites one long day's march to reach this place, and hence they must have carried one day's food with them. More they could not have taken, inasmuch as their only bread, the manna of the desert, sprang up at dawn and perished at nightfall. Therefore, on the morning after the day of their coming into Canaan, they were confronted by the first of human necessities— were they to starve or to steal?

Apparently, the Israelites had little compunction. Since the land itself was theirs, everything that it contained was theirs. We read that manna ceased, and they "ate of the fruit of the land of Canaan all that year." This can only mean that they rifled the barns of the Canaanite farmers, and took the corn of previous years which the farmers had sown, reaped, threshed and stored for themselves and their families. The result would not have been resistance, with bloodshed on both sides. The Canaanites might be men of war, but overwhelmed by immeasurably superior numbers they would perish, or else fly, perhaps to the neighbouring stronghold of Jericho.

Such, then, was the first event in the conquest of Canaan, and it called for a new conception in the minds of the Israelites of the Covenant of God with His people. God had indeed given this land to His own, but only in the sense that He would stand by them while they conquered it—wiping out its present inhabitants, root and branch, men, women and children. The priests told them it was so, and in proof of it they produced a book of Commandments by Moses, which nobody had ever seen before, or as far as we know, has ever seen since.

From this time forward war became a sacred act, attended by rites of purification, by divine mysteries, and by ceremonies of sanctification. Thus, in the history of the Hebrew people, warfare, aggressive warfare, with all its horrors, was the creation of the priests. Yet they were the descendants of the children of Abraham!

IV. Crossing the Jordan

It is impossible to follow with certainty the chronology of the early chapters of *Joshua,* but it would appear that ten days after the Israelites entered Canaan they crossed the Jordan.

What is the Jordan? Notwithstanding an age-long impression, born of its divine associations, the Jordan is one of the least beautiful rivers in the world. Apart from its source at the foot of Hermon, where it sparkles in the sunshine over many-coloured stones, and its sharp descent into a steep and winding channel where it leaves the Lake of Galilee, it is for many miles no more than a zigzag stream, fringed and overshadowed by reeds and canes, and flowing sluggishly for a great part of the year without loveliness or life under a temperature of stifling heat.

The usual width of its natural bed is not greater than that of a wide street in a modern city. Its average depth is no more than three to five feet. But in the late spring and early summer, when the rains fall on the mountains to the east and the snow melts on the heights of Hermon to the north, it overflows its banks in a thin sheet of water on to the flat lands on either side.

At the bottom of the ravine facing Jericho it is a turgid trench, never transparent, often discoloured by the clay it has passed through, sometimes odorous from the mineral deposits which back up from the Dead Sea, rarely wider than two to three miles, or deeper on an average than a few feet or even a few inches. This, then, was the Jordan the Israelites had to cross over, a river which a grown man might wade without the water rising above his waist.

We are told that it was the time of Passover, which usually falls towards the end of March. We are also told that it was the time of harvest, which even in the valley of the Jordan is rarely earlier than the middle of May. The Jewish calendar may have changed since the days of Joshua, but the priests were undisturbed by difficulties of nature. To enforce their new conception of the Covenant, and magnify themselves and their leader, they gave it out that the crossing of the Jordan was to be a miracle like that of crossing the Red Sea.

How the miracle came to pass is told in conflicting stories. We read that the waters of the Jordan were cut off from the waters which came down from the mountains and stood up in a heap, so that the bed of the river became bare; that the Ark of the Covenant of the Lord was carried on the shoulders of the priests to stones in the middle of the stream; that the priests remained there with the Ark until 40,000 of the fighting men of Israel had marched through on dry land shouting hosannas and then, the hallowed Ark of the Covenant having followed them, the cloven waters returned from the mountains and flowed as before.

That this puerile story, so dishonouring to God, so degrading to religion, is the record of an actual happening is not to be believed by instructed persons. But that it may have had its origin in some natural occurrence (such as the temporary damming up of the waters by an earthquake on the mountains) is possible of belief.

If such an event was used by Joshua's priests to operate as a miracle on the superstitious minds of the Israelites, that fact is sufficient of itself to account for the atrocities which their benighted people afterwards committed. The living God was with them. He was leading them, in the visible presence of the Commandments written by His own Hand, into the land that had been promised to their forefathers. They were to enter it and possess it, even if, in doing so, they had to cut off every living thing that breathed.

V. The Israelites in Gilgal.

After the Israelites had crossed the Jordan, they settled on the western plain in front of Jericho—a desolate spot, with sulphurous and salt-laden soil and a sparse and scraggy undergrowth. Their place of settlement was a circle of stones such as we now call a cromlech, with the Ark, and perhaps the tabernacle of Moses, inside of it, and the tents of the 40,000 men of war outside. Joshua called it Gilgal, which means liberty, a name that was probably intended to remind his people of the bondage they had left behind them.

How long the Israelites remained in Gilgal we have not been told, although there is an impossible mention of three days. It is probable that they stayed until the wives and children of the 40,000 had followed them, without a miracle; possibly until the whole body of the Israelites remaining alive after the frightful mortality in the wilderness had also crossed the Jordan; certainly until Joshua had prepared his men of arms for war.

About a mile away from the camp was the city of Jericho. Except Hebron, it was the oldest and strongest of the Canaanite fortresses, and almost certainly the richest. Therefore, it must have been, in Joshua's view, the first to be conquered.

In preparing to conquer it he adopted the simplest of military expedients. We read that he sent two young men as spies into Jericho to find out which parts of it were strong and which were weak. How they got inside the city we do not know, since it is written that the walls were strongly shut up against the children of Israel, and none went in and none went out. Nevertheless, they visited a house which was built partly on the city walls and over-looked by a window the country outside of them.

It was probably an inn. There were many inns in eastern countries crossed by caravans. They were usually kept by women of notoriously bad character for the unworthy convenience of the men whose business required that they should be long from home. This house was kept by such a woman. She is called a harlot. Her name was Rahab.

Rahab must have known the race and occupation of her visitors, 500,000 of them being encamped on the plain outside her eastern window. She must also have thought that if so vast a multitude besieged Jericho they would assuredly conquer it, and perhaps enslave or even slaughter its inhabitants. Therefore, it is probable that from no higher impulse than that of self-protection she received the spies and entertained them.

According to the Jewish historian, the king of Jericho was that night at supper in a neighbouring inn, and hearing that two men from the Hebrew camp were lodging with Rahab, he sent messengers to command her to give them up to him that he might examine them by torture.

Before the messengers arrived Rahab, hearing that they were coming, hid the men under the flax she kept to ripen on the roof of her house, and when the king's messengers came she told them a plausible story. It was true that two men had been there, but she had not known whence they came; and now they were gone, and she did not know where they had gone to.

Deluded by this explanation the messengers went away travelling, by the harlot's advice, in a wrong direction. Then Rahab went up to the Hebrews on the roof and (speaking in monotheistic language which nobody in the world, except Abraham, had ever yet spoken down to that day) told them she knew their God was the only God, the God of Heaven and earth, and then begged them to requite the kindness she had shown them by delivering her life from death when the Israelites came into the city to destroy it. The spies promised to do so.

"Our lives for yours," they said, and then added in obvious remembrance of the night when the Destroyer of God had walked through the streets of Egypt, "hang a scarlet thread before your windows that the commander of the Hebrew army may know whose house it is and spare you."

After that, the woman lowered the men by a cord from the window overlooking the outside of the walls, and they escaped. When they returned to Joshua they told him what had happened to them in the harlot's house, and said the Lord had delivered Jericho and its inhabitants into his hands, but how they knew this is not clear, unless the harlot had agreed to open the gates to them.

VI. The Destruction of Jericho

Then came the conquest of Jericho. The account of it, in its various forms, is full of contradictions. The Jericho of to-day is an open and rather miserable hamlet built on volcanic ground. In

Joshua's time the earlier Jericho, which stood on a neighbouring site, was apparently a well-fortified city, surrounded by strong walls, almost hidden by palm trees and impossible of assault by such wooden battering-rams as were used in later ages to make breaches in the walls of still greater Palestinian cities. The priestly story says it was taken by supernatural agencies.

God Himself became the commander-in-chief of His hosts. Through Joshua He gave command that the Israelites should march on seven consecutive days round the walls of Jericho. The armed men were to go first, then the company of priests carrying the Ark; then another company of priests bearing rams' horns for trumpets, and finally the vast body of the people. On six days the trumpets were to be blown, but no more was to be done, and the Israelites were to return at night to the camp at Gilgal. But on the seventh day at dawn, at the sound of the trumpet and at a signal from Joshua, the whole multitude were to shout with a great shout, and then the walls were to fall down flat and the Israelites were to enter and possess the city.

This, according to the priestly narrators, was done, with the result that had been expected. On breaking into Jericho the Israelites destroyed all who were in it, both men and women, young and old; took possession of the gold and silver and vessels of brass and iron it contained, and put them into the "treasury of the Lord," and then burned the city itself with fire, including, apparently, the human remains they had left unburied in it.

Only one person (with her family) was saved alive, and that was Rahab, the harlot, who was brought into the camp of Israel and promoted to honour and immortality. Then a curse of long antiquity was pronounced by Joshua on any man who should rebuild Jericho, that the foundations of it should be laid in the body of his first-born and the gates of it in the bones of his younger son—a curse, never fulfilled, which shows that the muddy imperfection of paganism was still clinging to Joshua himself.

Such is the story of the first of the atrocities committed by the Israelites in the conquest of Canaan. To think of it as the record of an actual occurrence is impossible to the modern intelligence. That the method and motive of the destruction of Jericho, as described by Joshua, had historical foundation is not to be believed for a moment by anyone who has attained to a right understanding of the sublime promise made to Abraham. Apart from the injury to the soul of man which the belief would imply (that God the invisible and merciful maker of the universe was the slaughterer of creatures of His own creation and the receiver of their stolen goods), there is the material fact that no one who has seen the recent excavations in Jericho will accept the statement that the walls of the city ever collapsed at all.

But this is not to say that Jericho did not fall by some natural happening such as frequently occurs in that volcanic region to this day—as recently as yesterday at Shechem. Hence it only remains to us to conclude that in their ignorance, their avarice or their lust of power, the priestly classes immediately after Moses distorted a simple historical event out of all recognition, and by playing upon the belief of their half savage people (that none of their enemies or the enemies of their paganized gods were to be saved, but all were to be put to death) led them to perpetrate further atrocities which were false to the religion of Abraham and a disgrace to their humanity.

VII. The Attack on Ai

After the destruction of Jericho came the attack on Ai. This was a small Amorite city only ten miles north of Jericho and three miles east of Bethel, with a shallow valley between. Joshua knew nothing of the place, so he sent spies to view it. When the spies returned they told him it was unnecessary to send a large part of the army to conquer Ai, for its fighting men were few.

Joshua sent 3,000 only. But when the 3,000 approached Ai, 12,000 of the Amorites burst out on them and chased them away. So fast was the flight of the Israelites that they lost only thirty-six men. But small as the loss was, the Israelites, who had expected to sweep over the land as conquerors, were overwhelmed with confusion.

Joshua himself, crushed with disappointment, threw the blame upon God. In a spirit akin to that of the Hebrews in the earliest days of their murmurings in the wilderness, he rent his clothes, fell on his face before the Ark, put dust on his head, and cried, "Alas, O Lord God, wherefore hast Thou at all brought this people over Jordan, to deliver us into the hands of the Amorites to destroy us?"

Apparently, his priests knew better. They knew that, according to the faith of their time, if disaster befell the hosts of Israel it was by the act of God and in punishment of a sin committed against

Him. Therefore, they caused God to say through Joshua, that an accursed thing was among them, and until they put it away He could no longer be with them, and they would be unable to stand before their enemies.

The accursed thing was theft. Something had been stolen from "the treasury of the Lord." How the priests came by this thought, whether by rumour or suspicion or divine revelation, we are not told, but as the treasury of the Lord was the treasury of the priests it touched them closely. Therefore, they required that Joshua should call the tribes together, tribe by tribe, family by family, man by man, so that the stolen property might be reclaimed and the thief discovered.

Joshua did so, choosing the customary ordeal of the lot. The lot fell first to the tribe of Judah. On subdividing Judah into families the lot fell next on a family called the Zarhites. On dividing the family of the Zarhites man by man the lot fell finally on an Israelite named Achan, or Achar.

But Achan was still master of his secret, so Joshua played the part of the procurator. Adopting a paternal tone, and calling Achan "my son," he appealed to him to give glory to God and make confession of his sin, saying what he had stolen and where he had hidden it.

Either from remorse or fear of detection Achan confessed. During the sacking of Jericho he had come upon a goodly Babylonian garment and some silver and gold, and being tempted he had hidden them in the earth under his tent.

Joshua sent messengers to Achan's tent, and they found the stolen goods and put them in the treasury of the priests. But the guilty man gained nothing by his confession. After loading him with bitter reproaches as a troubler of Israel, Joshua ordered that both he and his sons and daughters should be stoned with stones and then burned with fire.

This being done, the Lord, we are told, turned from the fierceness of His anger against Israel, and ordered Joshua to go up to Ai again, promising to give the king and his people and city into his hands, so that he might do to them as he had done to the king and people and city of Jericho.

Thus, according to the priestly chronicles, the God of Joshua, who had once been the merciful God of Abraham, allowed thirty-six innocent Israelites to be slaughtered for the sin of one man, and one man and his family to be put to death for stealing from the treasury of the priests what had already been stolen from the Amorites.

In making his second attack on Ai, Joshua did not rely on the promise of God, but on superiority in numbers and on his skill in that art of mutual deception which is still a first principle in war.

Choosing 30,000 Israelites (nearly three to one of the inhabitants of Ai), he sent them by night to lie in ambush in the valley between Ai and Bethel; and in the morning he led 5,000 more up to the gates of the city, expecting the Amorites to believe that the second attack would be the same as the first and could be defeated in the same way.

The ruse justified Joshua's expectations. When the king saw the 5,000 approaching, he sent out all his men of war to battle with them, whereupon the Israelites, making pretence of being beaten, fled back towards the wilderness. Thus the city, with its old men, its sick and infirm and its women and children was left open, and when the fighting men of Ai were too far away in their pursuit of the Israelites to return and save their city and its helpless inhabitants, Joshua signalled with his spear to his 30,000 in ambush to rise up and destroy it.

They did so, sacking the defenceless place, taking possession of its cattle and other spoil, slaying its inhabitants and then setting the city afire, with the dead remaining unburied in it. On this the 5,000 Israelites, in their pretended flight, seeing the smoke of the burning city, turned on their pursuers and annihilated them, so that not one soul of the people of Ai remained alive.

After that, according to the priestly narrators, Joshua celebrated his victory by building an altar, making burnt-offerings and peace-offerings, and reading aloud the blessings and cursings which he told his followers had been written by Moses at the command of God.

VIII. The Killing of the Five Kings

The sequel was speedy. Rumour of Joshua's reign of terror having spread over Canaan, a tribe of the Canaanites, called Gibeonites, decided to save themselves from extermination by an act of deception. They lived near to Joshua's headquarters, but, going wilily to work, they sent ambassadors with old garments on their backs and clouted shoes on their feet to Gilgal, to give themselves the appearance of having travelled from a far country, to ask Joshua to make a league with their people.

Joshua did so (contrary to the supposed command of God that he should exterminate all the Canaanites), and he swore an oath of peace with them. But finding after a few days that their people were his neighbours, and thinking, perhaps, that they had come to betray them, he had first the intention of slaying them, but remembering his oath and (like a more tragic blunderer who came later) thinking himself bound by it although he had made it in ignorance, he spared their lives, saying, "Wherefore have ye beguiled us? . . . . Now therefore ye are cursed, and there shall none of you be freed from being bondmen, and hewers of wood and drawers of water for the house of my God."

As there was no house of God in Canaan at that time, and no such occupations as that of hewer of wood and drawer of water until centuries later, it is probable that the incident is unhistorical. It is also probable that Joshua was in no way deceived by the smooth story of the ambassadors, but, needing guides and spies for the conquest of a country in which he was a stranger, he took this means of securing them.

The natural result came quickly. Five of the kings of the uplands of Canaan, including the king of Hebron, and the king of Shalim (now called Jerusalem), hearing that one of their own tribes had become spies and slaves of the Hebrews, set out to punish them. Upon this the Gibeonites cried to Joshua, "Come up and save us."

Joshua ascended from his headquarters at Gilgal, and in the midst of a hailstorm in which Heaven assisted with its stones as much as Joshua by his sword, he drove off the Canaanite armies. The five kings themselves, in their flight, took refuge in a cave, but Joshua found them, ordered that great stones should be rolled against the mouth of their hiding-place and a guard set in front of it to prevent their escape, while he pursued and annihilated their subjects.

It is here, we are told (not in the language of poetry, as unpoetical people suppose, but in the plain words of circumstantial narrative), that Joshua called on God to let the sun stand still and the moon be stayed that he might have light to finish his slaughter. They stood still for a whole day and night while Joshua avenged the Gibeonites of their enemies by exterminating every soul of them.

How long a time was occupied in these appalling atrocities we cannot be sure—perhaps five years, perhaps more. Apparently, they were followed by some twenty other years in which Joshua, with an army of about 330,000 swept over a great part of the uplands in the middle of Canaan, from the eastern border of the Maritime Plains to the Dead Sea and from Hebron to Lebanon and Sidon. During this period thirty-one of the Canaanite and kindred kings had been overcome, their possessions looted, their lands confiscated, their cities destroyed, and all their inhabitants slaughtered (including the women and children, the old and the infirm) except such as escaped into fortified places or fled in terror to the mountains.

IX. *The Land Divided among the Tribes*

The last chapters of the Book of *Joshua* are now generally admitted to possess little historic value, and to have been written at least two centuries later by another group of priests as free of hand as the first. But if we are to have any regard for their records, we must conclude that even after this prolonged reign of terror there were other lands to be possessed, and that twenty to twenty-five further years were spent by Joshua in conquering an incredible number of kingdoms to the south and west of the uplands, in butchering their people in such numbers as could not be believed by those who heard of it, after pilaging their cattle, their gold and silver, and even their clothes.

By this time Joshua was old and stricken in years, and removing his headquarters from Gilgal by Jericho he gathered the congregation at Shiloh in the vicinity of Bethel, set up the Tabernacle there and began to divide the land of Canaan among certain of the tribes who had helped him to conquer it. Later, he settled at Shechem, appointed cities of refuge for the man-slayers ("until they could stand before the congregation"), and made further distribution of the land among his leaders as a whole—excepting the Levites who, having the priesthood and therefore "the treasury of the Lord," were already in possession of the largest inheritance of all. Then he dismissed them to their new homes, saying "Return with much riches to your tents, and with very much cattle, with silver, and with gold, and with brass, and with iron, and with very much raiment, divide the spoil of your enemies with your brethren. . . . To your tents, O Israel!"

Joshua himself went to his own inheritance, which was at Ephraim. How long he remained there we do not know, but when he was 110 years old he returned to Shechem, gathered the leaders of the tribes about him again, made them his last speech and gave them his blessing.

His last speech was a feeble echo of the last speech of Moses, beginning with an account of the forefathers of Abraham, in the Land beyond the Flood, where they had served other gods; of the leading of the Hebrew people by Abraham into Canaan; of the going by Jacob and his children into Egypt; of their coming out of it under Moses, and concluding with a beautiful if terrible account of the conquering of the Promised Land under himself.

> Thus saith the Lord God of Israel. . . . I have given you a land for which ye did not labour, and cities which ye built not, and ye dwell in them; of the vineyards and olive-yards which ye planted not do ye eat.

Therefore, they were to choose whom they would serve, whether the false gods their fathers had worshipped in Egypt and on the other side of the Euphrates or the Lord God of Israel who had done such signs and wonders in their sight.

The congregation cried, "God forbid that we should forsake the Lord to serve other gods." After writing this witness in a book and setting it under a stone in an oak, Joshua dismissed them again to their tents with a last word of farewell, "I am going the way of all the earth" he said; and then he saluted them, and they him, not without tears, and they went their way.

X. *Joshua and Eleazar Die*

Not long afterwards Joshua died, and to our infinite relief, Eleazar, the high priest, died also. It is not easy to say anything good about either. Nothing, or next to nothing, they did had not been better undone. Joshua has been described, both by writers of the past and of the present, as the first after Moses of the warriors of freedom. But he was a merciless despot, and of freedom he knew nothing at all. Not incapable of hypocrisy, he used the harlot and the thief for his purpose, and was himself used in turn by the priests and the Levites.

Poor shadow of Moses in his passionate moods—of the strength, the sincerity and the simple faith of the liberator of the Hebrew people without a trace. Dying in the fullness of his days on his bed at Ephraim and being buried at Timnath-Serah, with the lands about him bestrewn with the bones of a martyred nation, he left a long record of inhumanity to the shame of Israel, and the horror of a scandalized world.

Of Eleazar, the black night-bird of the conquest, with his acidulous face half hidden behind Joshua, what is there to say except that he was the son of Aaron, the maker of the Golden Calf, and that he carried the priesthood farther back than his father himself towards the place it had occupied in the religions known to him in his boyhood, without having a leader strong enough to strip his priestly robes off his back.

Apparently, his last act, according to the chroniclers, was to bury the bones of Joseph at Shechem in the parcel of ground which Jacob had bought from Hamor, the Hittite. This is an astonishing record. It requires that we should believe that three to four centuries after the death of Joseph, Moses had carried his mummy-case through the terror of the disordered flight by midnight from Rameses to Succoth, through the wild alarm of the crossing of the Red Sea and through the toil of the forty years' wandering in the wilderness, followed by the mystical passage of the Jordan and the unrecorded trail of sixty odd years at the tail of the armies in Canaan.

Great must have been the credulity or great the faith of the Hebrew people of the seventh century B.C.

Such is the story of the conquest of Canaan as we extract it from the medley of myth and legend which we call the Book of *Joshua*. That it is history in the modern sense we cannot believe; but that it is based on ancient tradition, and that its principal incidents were of actual occurrence, we can scarcely question.

XI.   *Was This the Promised Land?*

Was this, then, the Promised Land—the land promised to Abraham at the gates of Ur when, rising from his tent in the sunrise, with the free air of the desert about him, he was told by God to leave the Babylonian plains that were the hotbed of corrupt and sensual religion and go to a country he knew not of—a country He would give to him and his children for an everlasting possession, to become a light to the world and a blessing to all the nations? Six centuries had passed since then—centuries of bondage and slavery in an alien land, followed by forty years of wandering in the wilderness in hunger and thirst and the constant presence of death. Was this their home? The land flowing with milk and honey? The gift of God they had tried to win by war—this narrow bridge between the desert and the sea, whose soil, after sixty further years of fighting, was unclean from corruption, whose streets were running with blood, whose cities (such of them as had not been burnt to the ground) were evil-smelling charnel-houses, foul with the decaying remains of unburied dead—this sulphurous scar on the face of a barren earth?

Had Abraham deceived himself at Ur of the Chaldees? And again at Shechem, where he thought God appeared to him and said, "Unto your seed I give this land?" Had the hope of Israel been a dream?

The Land of Promise! Better the wandering in the wilderness! Better the bondage in Egypt! Better the corruptions of Ur of the Chaldees!

Churchmen of all creeds have tried to reconcile themselves to the enormities perpetrated in the conquest of Canaan by arguments that do as little credit to their intellects as to their hearts. God, they say, had His hidden purpose, and before His divine wisdom man can only bury his head in the sand—it is the resource of the ostrich. On entering Canaan the Israelites had to kill or be killed—it is the excuse of the criminal. In order to fulfil His promise, God had to teach the Israelites the arts of war—it is a blasphemous denial of His omnipotence. In wiping out the Canaanites, the Israelites were but cleansing the Promised Land of an impure people who worshipped idols to make place for a pure one that worshipped Jehovah—it is a travesty of the plain truth of history that there was no immorality of the Canaanites which the Israelites did not presently copy, and no pagan religion they did not revive.

It will not do. If we are to reconcile the story of the conquest of Canaan with the history of religion, we must look in other directions. When we read that story first, it is the horror of it that oppresses us. When we read it again, it is the pity of it that lies heaviest on our hearts.

First, there is the pity of the Canaanites. They were idolators, practising some of the mad rituals of the religions of antiquity, but nothing has come down to us which forbids us to believe that, according to the standard of their time, they were not a civilized people. They had become warlike, yet still, as in the days of Abraham, they lived human lives in cities and villages, cultivating their olive-grounds, planting their vineyards, and carrying on commerce with the nations about them. For no other reason that could have been apparent to themselves than that they did not worship a God they had never heard about, they were fallen on by a fanatical enemy out of the wilderness who lived in tents and did no work, yet claimed their country for their own.

As a consequence, their land was laid waste; their vineyards and olive-grounds were destroyed; their harvests, ripe for the gathering, were either stolen or trodden into the earth; their sanctuaries were violated; their cities and villages were given up to the flames; and death was made to take toll not only of their men of war, but also of the helpless among their people, including the very young, the very old and the very poor. No more awful spectacle of a country in utter desolation had ever before come of earthquake or other convulsion of nature in her wrath than was wrought on Canaan by the hands of the Israelites.

Next, there was the still greater pity of the Israelites themselves. With few exceptions they were an illiterate people, most of them born in the desert, of fathers who had been slaves in a land in which liberty was unknown, where they had worked in the ditches of Fayum, and on the tombs of their kings, until they had fallen in tens of thousands and been huddled underground. By the inspiration of a leader with divine fire on his lips they had come to believe that notwithstanding their misery and degradation they were the chosen people of a God who was the God of all the earth, and that He had given them the coveted land of Canaan as an everlasting inheritance, and as a light that was to be a light to all the world. What wonder that when they escaped from their slavery and came to claim their home, and were told by their priests that by the command of Moses they were to take possession of it, no matter at what cost, they did so by slaughtering, without mercy or remorse, every living thing that breathed?

But what a penalty they paid for it—in their bodies, their lives and their souls! As a consequence of the barbaric warfare they waged, vast numbers of them perished by plagues. In hundreds of thousands they must also have died by the sword of an enemy immeasurably better armed and trained in war than themselves.

In listening to the priestly voices that told them that their God was hardening the hearts of their enemies in order that they might attack them and thus throw themselves on their destruction, they were descending to the worship of a deity of the remotest antiquity who was less of a god than a fiend.

Miserable men! Conquered and conquering, equally pitiable. But let us not think the future cannot be bright because the past has been base. The God of Abraham was not dead. The hope of a Saviour, a Redeemer, a Messiah, was not extinct. Through this dark night of horror the pillar of fire was still leading on.

CHAPTER VIII

The Hebrew Anarchy

I. The Levite and His Concubine

AFTER THE REIGN OF TERROR came a rule of anarchy. It was the natural sequence. Anarchy does not usually begin with rapine and the lust of blood. Generally, it has its origin in a dim sense of man's right to his manhood and a desire to be master of his own soul. Deep in the heart of men, especially after periods of physical suffering and spiritual tyranny, there is a desire to cast off authority and stand in the full liberty of the individual spirit before God alone. It was so in the case of the Israelites. After Joshua there were to be no more Joshuas. After Eleazar there were to be no more Eleazars. "In those days there was no king in Israel, every man did that which was right in his own eyes." These are the last words in the Book of *Judges*. In a right chronology they would have been the first.

But the most imperative law of human life is the law of life in community—the necessity of living in human fellowship, in mutual dependence. Set that aside, under any provocation, and human society falls to a welter of chaos and barbarity. This, too, was the case with the Israelites. Responsible writers have said that the Book of *Judges* is, both to the historian and to the student of life and character, the most interesting and moving of the books of the Jewish Bible. "What food for heart and mind in its mingled comedy and tragedy!" "What wild justice!" "What supreme righteousness!" "What heroic submission to the will of God!" "What lovely touches of ancient manners, what beauty and what charm!"

It is difficult to regard such rhapsodies with anything but contempt. The Book of *Judges* is in reality a horror of great darkness, a long series of impure, chaotic and often barbaric stories, with scarcely more than one redeeming incident or inspiring emotion. That, indeed, is its only apparent use in the history of religion—to carry the soul of man from the black midnight of despair to the light and hope of a spiritual morning.

The events it records appear to have occurred in the twelfth and eleventh centuries B.C. But, so far as we can see, they were not written out until nearly five centuries later. In the meantime, they had become tainted by the low morality of the period of their authorship. But clearly they were founded on ancient tradition, and therefore they are, so far as we can see, substantially true. What happened, then, to the Israelites during the next succeeding 100 years, or thereabouts, after the death of Joshua?

Putting aside the first chapter and a half of *Judges* (which is obviously the work of a later writer, who gives the lie to much of the earlier story of the conquest), we see the Israelites, dismissed from Shechem to their inheritances, making their way to various parts of their Promised Land. Worn out by their homeless wanderings in the wilderness, and sick to their souls of the butcheries of the wars into which they had been led by bad prophets and worse priests, they set themselves to the industries of peace—to the tilling of their soil and the cultivation of their vineyards.

In this they were not successful. It is almost certain that the Israelites made bad farmers. It is probable that having fought their way to their Promised Land they thought their work was done, and it was for God to do the rest, a mood of mind not unknown to modern history. As a consequence they fell a prey to idleness and sloth, and, as far as the spoils of their enemies would permit, to luxury and sensuality.

II. Inter-Tribal War

Before long there were wars among themselves. They were generally about women. One of the worst of them was a war between the tribes of Ephraim and Benjamin. The cause of it was an event of peculiar atrocity.

A Levite of Ephraim took his concubine (Josephus says his wife) and set out on a journey. In the evening of the day he reached a Benjamite city, intending to lodge there. At first no one offered him hospitality, according to eastern custom, and with his concubine he sat down in the street to wait. At length an old man, returning from his work in the fields, took both of them into his house. "Peace be with thee," he said. "Let all thy wants lie upon me; only lodge not in the street."

What followed reads like a repetition of the story of the visit of the angels to Lot on the eve of the destruction of Sodom, but with a more gruesome and horrible ending. Darkness had fallen, and the old man and his only daughter were eating and drinking and making merry with the Levite and his concubine, when a number of evil men of the city (they were called "sons of Belial," meaning brutes and blackguards) beset the house, beat at the door and demanded that the man-guest should be given up to them for the basest of uses. The old man beseeched the brutes not to act so wickedly, and when they persisted in the demand he, like Lot, offered them his virgin daughter. The rabble refused the girl and continued to call for the man. Then the Levite thrust his concubine out to them and they carried her away and abused her. At dawn of the following day they let her go, and then the outraged woman, in her misery and shame, stumbled back to the house where her lord was lodged, and (afraid perhaps to knock) fell down at the door of it.

Meantime, the Levite, having saved himself at the cost of his concubine, had slept peacefully in his bed. Early in the morning he rose to go his way, and opening the door he found the tragic figure of the dishonoured woman lying along the doorstep with her outstretched hand on the threshold.

"Up, let us be going," he said, but the woman in her abasement made no reply. An attempt has been made to excuse the Levite's conduct by saying that the woman was already dead. There is not a particle of ground for the statement. Setting the woman on an ass, the Levite turned his face towards home. What he did when he got there was such a deed as had never been seen since the children of Israel came out of Egypt. We can well believe it.

Taking his knife, he killed the woman, divided her body into twelve parts and sent one part to each of the twelve tribes, perhaps as a witness to the wrong he thought he had suffered at the hands of the Benjamites, perhaps as a call for vengeance.

There was a loud outcry among the Israelites. An assembly was called at Mizpeh (the meeting-place of the tribes before the establishment of Jerusalem) to consider the rights and wrongs of the appalling atrocity. The Levite pleaded his own cause and palliated, not without falsehood, his cowardly conduct. The result was sufficiently astonishing.

In thrusting the woman out in the dark the miserable man had been as guilty as the rabble to whom he had surrendered her, but he was vindicated by the assembly, perhaps on the ground that the woman was his possession and he had a right to do as he pleased with her; perhaps because it was believed that his own life had, as he declared, been in danger; perhaps, as his apologists still say, because he was thought to have asserted the purity and sanctity of marriage—God save it!

Brutal as was the verdict of the tribes, the conduct of the Benjamites was still more barbaric. Being asked to deliver up for punishment the men who had committed the original offence, they refused to do so. And since they did not punish the men themselves, the Ephraimites concluded they had condoned the crime of their sons of Belial, and even made themselves a part to it.

The result was a long and bloody war between the men of Ephraim and the men of Benjamin. Many thousands were killed on both sides, chiefly by the exercise of the deceitful arts employed by Joshua in his attack on Ai. Victory fell finally to the Ephraimites, but neither they nor the general body of the Israelites were satisfied. After they had slaughtered all the women of the tribe of Benjamin, they swore an oath that no man of any other tribe should give his daughter in marriage to a Benjamite.

III. The Capture of the Maidens

Time passed, and it was seen that for the want of women the tribe of Benjamin was in danger of being exterminated. What was to be done? The Israelites had sworn an oath to God, and they believed it to be inviolable. At length, unknown to the Ephraimites, a "certain man" of the Hebrews (an identity only too obvious), claiming to act according to the dictates of God, told the leaders of the people that he could show them a way whereby they could keep their oath and yet let the Benjamites take their women. His way was a sufficiently dastardly one.

Thrice a year a feast was held between Shiloh and Shechem. That is a pleasant place still, with its low hills and shallow dales, its blossoming trees and sweet-smelling groves, perhaps the most pleasant in Palestine. There, after the religious ceremonies at

Shiloh (the place of the Tabernacle) were done for the day, it was the custom of the Ephraimites, who being near to their homes were accompanied by their wives and daughters, to allow their young maidens to go together in pairs, singing and dancing and playing in the fullness of their girlish joy.

The scheme of the "certain person" (Phineas) was that on such an occasion the men of Benjamin should lie in ambush among the trees until the girls, in their innocent happiness, came near, and then burst out on them, capture them, carry them away and make them their wives. And if, afterwards, the bereaved parents complained to the leaders of the tribes (meaning the priests) they were to be told that since they had neglected to protect their daughters they had no right to be angry with the Benjamites.

The dastardly scheme of cheating both God and man was carried out with the result that had been expected. The tribe of Benjamin was saved from extermination, but the soul of Israel was degraded. And this was the first-fruit of the anarchist principle that every man should do what was right in his own eyes.

After the war between the tribes of Ephraim and Benjamin, the morality of the Israelites went down headlong. They, too, had lost their women in the wanderings and the wars, and they began to take toll of the Canaanite women about them.

It was not difficult to do so. The Canaanites had been captured but not exterminated. Many of them were living in the near neighbourhood of the Maritime Plains, never having been seriously assailed; others were permitted to inhabit some of the cities of Canaan itself on condition that they paid tribute to their conquerors; others, again, driven across the Jordan, had taken refuge in the eastern hills and the deserts beyond them, and still others in the highlands that lay north of Upper Galilee. To the Israelites in the middle ridge of Canaan (all they possessed of the Promised Land) that was an environment which tempted them to the capture of the Canaanite women.

Possibly they were helped in that transgression against the law or custom of their religion by the Canaanites themselves. The conquered people had succumbed to superior numbers, but they had not yet given up hope of recovering possession of what they believed to be their native land. It is conceivable that during the time of their temporary weakness they thought the easiest and subtlest way to that end was through their women. It is also conceivable that they resorted to the device of Balak, the king of the Moabites, who, in the time of Moses, sent the handsomest of the daughters of his people, decked in their most beautiful garments to the tents of the Israelites to seduce them from their allegiance to the God who gave them victory, even at the cost of becoming their wives. Apparently, the Israelites were nothing loth to fall a prey to this temptation. In the absence of a strong leader, the result was the inevitable one—the women had their way. We read that the Israelites forsook the God of Israel, married the daughters of Canaan and worshipped in their groves the gods who inhabited them.

In that hour of anarchy this was a natural if not pardonable transgression. Chief among the Canaanite gods was Baal. He had local deities called Baalim in every part of the country. There were the Baalim of the wells and rivers who, being supplicated, brought water to their thirsty land, and the Baalim of the flocks and herds who increased their harvests and multiplied their sheep and oxen. The Canaanite women knew them all, having been brought up among them and accustomed to pray to them. Thus, added to the call of their human passions, the Israelites were besieged by the demands of their material interests.

In like manner human passions and material interests were at work with the Canaanite women also. It is not necessary to think that in marrying their alien husbands they were deliberately betraying them. If the Israelites had lost their women in the wanderings and the wars, the Canaanites had lost their men. Then the Israelites were in possession of the lands in which the Canaanite women had been born, and without them they had no inheritance.

Furthermore, it is reasonable to assume that in their mixed marriages both husbands and wives justified themselves in their hours of tenderness in their own eyes by the thought that after all they were one people, coming of the same old stock and speaking practically the same language, having lived together in the far-off days of their ancestors in the grey-green country beyond the flood.

Nevertheless, the consequences to the Israelites were fatal. Remembering their broken oath to God, who had brought them out of the land of bondage; conscious of their loss of inheritance as a separated people and their heirs of the promise; degraded by their apostasy; demoralized by the grosser abominations of their worship of idols (such as the burning of their first-born children in the fires of Baal)—they became still more slothful, effeminate and sensual, incapable of war, and therefore of defending themselves from the enemy nations around them.

There were many of these on every side, and they fell on the Israelites one by one, generation after generation, almost year after year, raiding, pillaging and burning their Hebrew settlements, carrying off their spoils of war and their women—always their women.

IV.   Othniel

One of the first of the enemy nations to fall on the Israelites was a branch of the Assyrians. These were then a semi-savage people who lived on the north-east coast of the Arabian Desert. We are told that the king of Mesopotamia, seeing his opportunity in the weakness of the Israelites, came down to Canaan and carried away a number of its new inhabitants to his own country, where for years he made them slaves.

It is a pitiful thing to think of, that, not a great way from the place in which these degenerate descendants of Abraham slaved for a heathen king, a little company of their ancestors, 700 years before, had passed over the desert in the proud hope, which they believed they had received in a message from the sky, that they should inherit the earth, bring in the Golden Age, and become a blessing to all the nations.

But the faith of Abraham was not dead. At length a deliverer arose in Israel. His name was Othniel. He gathered an army of Israelites, crossed the desert, drove the king of Mesopotamia over the Euphrates (probably an error for the Tigris), and brought back the Hebrews who had been held in captivity.

For this proof of valour and patriotism he was made commander of Israel, the Israelites having, in the face of their enemies, abandoned by this time the anarchist principle of every man doing what was right in his own eyes, and established a kind of mixed military and legal democracy, and called their commanders their judges.

V.   The Judges

The origin and meaning of the name judge is uncertain. Probably it comes from the Phœnicians, who entrusted the supreme power to chief magistrates. Certainly it meant more to the Israelites than it now means to modern races. A judge of Israel had legislative as well as administrative power. He was not infallible and his rank was not hereditary, but he was nominated for life and his judgments were not to be disputed. Probably he was chosen for his physical strength, without regard to his wisdom or his knowledge of law.

Apparently, the theory of the Israelites was that the man to whom God gave victory was God's man, and therefore the most proper to rule over them. Thus he led them into the field against their enemies in times of war, and in times of peace he sat in his tent, in the market-place, or at the gate of the city to hear the disputes among themselves and to judge between them; perhaps according to the laws, now lost, which are supposed to have descended from Moses, perhaps according to the laws afterwards called "breast-laws," which had their origin in the judge's own breast—the laws of his heart and conscience.

Othniel appears to have been the first of the Israelite judges. It is probable that after his victorious return from Mesopotamia, with the liberated slaves behind him, he cleansed for as long as he lived the Hebrew settlements of their idolatries and corruptions. But after his death his people fell back to their former condition. Again the Canaanite wives and the groves inhabited by the gods! Again the barbarities of pagan worship with the burning of the first-born children in the fires of Baal! And again the sloth, the effeminacy and sensuality which enfeebled and debased them, and left them at the mercy of their surrounding enemies.

VI.   Deborah

The next but one of the enemies to fall on the Israelites were a section of the Canaanites themselves, the section which had been driven back into the highlands to the north of Upper Galilee. Having renewed their strength, they had returned to reconquer what they believed to be their native country. By this time they had established a kingdom, with its capital at an ancient city called Hazor, under a king named Jabin, who styled himself the king of Canaan. Jabin's commander-in-chief was Sisera, who is sometimes described as his captain and sometimes as his son, and was probably both.

Of Sisera we know little except that he was young, that his mother was alive, that he lived in Harosheth (opposite the lofty north-eastern end of Carmel), where he kept a splendid court, independent of his sovereign, and that, according to words afterwards put into the mouth of another, he counted among the rewards of reconquest of Canaan that of capturing some of the beautiful Israelite women. Twenty years, it is said, he harassed the Hebrew settlements, reducing the inhabitants to such a condition of subjection that they fled from their villages, forsook their highways and only walked in their byways.

Then another liberator arose in Israel. This time it was a woman. She was believed to be a prophetess, a reader of the will of God, and she lived with her husband under a palm tree between Ramah and Bethel. There the Israelites came to her for judgment. Her name was Deborah.

Criticism, both Jewish and Christian, has for ages exhausted itself in Deborah's praise. She has been said to have been a woman of leonine courage, burning with a sense of intolerable wrong, a patriot of unparalleled purity, a poet whose words of fire and flame aroused a slumbering people as by a heavenly trumpet, a minister of God's justice, before whose religious fervour we can do nothing but hold our breath and be silent.

When Sisera's tyranny had reached its extremity, it came to Deborah's knowledge that he contemplated a general attack on the whole country, and that he was waiting in the highlands for the most favourable moment to make it. Seeing in this an opportunity of drawing Sisera to his destruction, Deborah made a treaty with Barak, a chieftain of the Galilean highlands who lived unseen in Mount Tabor, the dome-shaped hill which stands on the north-east of the plain of Esdraelon. "Up," she said, "take 10,000 men and hide thee in Mount Tabor and the Lord God of Israel will deliver this captain of Jabin's army into thy hands."

At first Barak demurred. He would only go up if Deborah went with him. This was probably a precautionary measure, which meant that he counted on the influence of the prophetess to bring the whole of the Israelite tribes to his assistance. Apparently,

Deborah attempted to bring them, and partly succeeded and partly failed. Some came at her call; others, soul-sick of war, refused to do so. In the end, Barak and Deborah went up the mountain with 10,000 men and two of the northern tribes behind them.

Then Sisera, being told that Barak and his army had disappeared, and seeing from his headquarters in the hills that the great plain below him was clear, went down to it with 900 chariots of iron, a large army of fighting men and a multitude of Canaanite tribesmen, expecting to sweep over the land without serious resistance. He was met by the 10,000 Israelites who had been lying in ambush, as well as by many of the other tribes and utterly routed.

VII. Battle between Canaanites and Israelites

We learn that the battle took place in what was afterwards called the valley of Jezreel, which was between the Jordan and the plain of Esdraelon, that 40,000 Israelites in all were engaged in it; that during the fight a great storm raged; that the wind blew in the faces of the Canaanites, whose eyes were thereby so darkened that their tribesmen could not see to use their arrows and slings, while the coldness of the air would not permit the soldiers to use their swords; that the Israelites took courage at this, thinking Heaven was fighting on their side; that falling on the Canaanites in their confusion they destroyed vast numbers by the sword, filling the neighbouring river, the Kishon, then at its highest, with their dead and driving the living beyond it.

Of those who escaped we hear of one only—Sisera himself. The impartial historian need not fear the reproach of holding a brief for this miserable man when he says that his ultimate fate, in its atrocity and horror, makes his own enormities, so far as we know them, seem human by comparison.

Apparently, it was spring, when the land of that region is sodden by rain and the overflow of the rivers. Sisera's chariot stuck in the soft ground, and to escape death or arrest he leapt out of it and "fled away on his feet." Perhaps the course of his flight was towards his palace in the highlands on the north-east. It is equally probable that it was towards the south-west, and that he was trying to reach his countrymen who were living in the security of the Maritime Plains. Barak and his soldiers went in hot pursuit of him.

Being young, and alone, and in peril of his life, Sisera outran his pursuers, and in a lonely part of the great plain (used sometimes as the mustering-place of the Galilean traders) he came upon the tent of a woman. Her name was Jael, and she was the wife of a Kenite. This was another name for a part of the tribe of the Midianites in which Moses had married in the Wilderness of Sin. After that event, the Kenites, although at peace with the Canaanites, had been friendly with the Israelites, and it is hinted that Heber, the husband of Jael, was a descendant of the father-in-law of Moses.

Knowing nothing of this, and only seeing that the woman was not an Israelite, the wretched fugitive took refuge at her house. She pretended to welcome him. "Turn in, my lord," she said. "Turn in to me and fear not."

He was thirsty and asked for a drink of water. She gave him milk from her leather bottle. He was weary and lay down. She covered him with a mantle. His strength was spent after his long flight, and she encouraged him to sleep. As drowsiness overcame him, he bethought himself of his enemies who were close behind, and said, "Stand in the door, and if anybody should come and ask 'Is there a man here?' answer 'No'." She said she would do so.

Then the beaten and broken, but far from unpitiable man, suspecting no harm and trusting to the humanity and tenderness of the woman, fell asleep.

Meantime, Jael stood by her door as if to throw the pursuers of Sisera off the scent. But as soon as she knew he was helpless and at her mercy, she took a nail of the tent and, going softly to the side of the sleeping man, she drove it through his temples and brain and transfixed him to the ground. After that act of treachery and barbarity (than which the skies have perhaps never looked down on a more dastardly outrage), the woman returned to her door, and seeing Barak going by in his pursuit of Sisera, she went out to him and cried, "Come, and I will show thee the man whom thou seekest."

VIII. *The Song of Deborah*

There were loud rejoicings in the camp of the Israelites when this appalling atrocity became known. In due time a festival was made to celebrate the victory and to divide the spoils of it. At this festival a song was sung which has become immortal. For centuries the Song of Deborah has been belauded in language that has known no measure. "An inspired utterance!" "A work of genius!" "The greatest war-song of any age or country!" But what in reality is it? To realize this we have to reconstruct. By the eye of history let us reconstruct the scene that inspired it.

What a scene it must have been! Probably at Shiloh, and in one of the abandoned and whitewashed temples of a Canaanite Baalim. Gone were the fat cheeks of the gods of the wells and the rivers. In their places were the swords and spears and shields, and even the personal garments stripped from the enemies whose naked bodies had then been cast into the river to be swept to the sea. Around the temple, where the hideous images of animal gods had stood, were the huddled mass of what remained of the 900 iron-bound chariots of Sisera. Inside, were some fifty to a hundred of the Israelite leaders (improperly called kings and princes, since there was none such in Israel at that time) squatting on the cushions on the ground and eating and drinking from early morning until late at night, and, like Laban's guests at Jacob's marriage in the Syrian Desert, all "drunk and in the dark." At one side of the gathering was Deborah; at the other side Barak. Then the stifling and sickening air, full of vain boasting of what had been done in the battle; tales of bloody adventures; perhaps of hair-breadth escapes, certainly of merciless slaughter of the enemy that had been blinded by the beating of the elements. High talk and loud laughter. Proud predictions of a triumphant future. Then a cry for a song from Deborah.

"Awake, awake, Deborah, awake, awake, utter a song!"

Then Deborah, probably a middle-aged, masterful, mastiff-faced woman, perhaps with a voice of a man and the eye of a hawk, sitting as she sings.

First a word of praise to the Lord God for the avenging of Israel. When they marched out into the field the earth trembled, the heavens dropped, the clouds also dropped water, the stars in their courses fought against Sisera. Then praises of the kings (there were none such) who had done battle for Israel. They came and they fought. They took no money. They fought for Heaven. Then a loud glorification of Deborah herself. The villages had ceased to exist, the highways had been unoccupied; travellers had walked in the byways, and the people had worshipped false gods, yet there had not been a shield or a sword among 40,000 to fight for God until she, Deborah, arose, a "Mother in Israel."

Then with merry jest and bitter sarcasm, perhaps amid gusts of derisive laughter, the cursing of the leaders of Israel who had not answered the call of the prophetess and were not with them that day—the children of Reuben who had remained in their sheepfolds to hear the bleating of their flocks; the children of Gilead who had continued in their farmsteads beyond Jordan with their wooden ploughs and hay forks, and the children of Dan who had stayed in their puny ships on the sea—perhaps the Sea of Galilee. "Curse ye," cries the angel of the Lord, "curse ye bitterly the people who came not to help of the Lord!"

Next, the blessing of those who had helped the Lord against his enemies, jeopardizing their lives unto death in the high places of the field—glory to them all, including the children of Benjamin, who had so lately been guilty of the grossest brutality. Then (in a louder note of triumph) blessings on Jael, the cowardly and treacherous woman who had killed their fallen enemy in his sleep while he trusted his life to her womanly keeping. "Blessed above all women shall Jael be! Blessed shall she be above all women of the tent!"

Then an impossible description of the act of Jael's crime which belies the previous account of it. Not while he was lying unconscious in sleep did she kill him by driving a nail with a hammer into his temples and through his brain, but while he was standing on his feet and drinking. "At her feet he bowed, he fell, he lay down; at her feet he bowed, he fell; where he bowed, there he fell down dead."

Finally, a scene in the dead man's palace in the high mountains at home. The mother of Sisera is awaiting his return from battle. She is in his harem surrounded by his women. The time is long and her anxiety is feverish. When she can endure it no more, she looks out of the window at the lattice and cries, "Why is his chariot so long in coming?" Has he not conquered? Have not his fighting men divided the spoils of the Israelites, to every man a maiden or two and to Sisera rich needlework of divers colours as well?

The women of the harem try to comfort her. "Comfort ye, mother, he will soon be here. Soon we shall hear the thundering of his chariots down the street." But she cannot be comforted, and the last we see of the mother of Sisera is her pale face at the window looking out for the son who will return to her no more.

Thrilling, barbaric, magnificent! Transcendent in its simplicity and vivid in its reality! Worthy to rank with the greatest pictures in literature, if only it had been touched with one note of human pity and pathos. But Deborah has no tears for it. A scream of derisive laughter, of soured and inflammatory humour runs through her burning words, tempting us to say that no woman in the world, certainly no mother, could possibly have written them, and that they were not the product of the eleventh century at all, but probably of the barbaric writer of the fourth.

Such is the Song of Deborah, of which it has been asked, "Whose heart has not been thrilled by its burning words, which seize the memory and ring in it for ever?" And of the fiendish atrocity it celebrates, "Who will blame her? Who will not be ready to applaud the wild justice of Jael?"

Such, if it is indeed the Song of Deborah, is the warwhoop of an enraged monster. And to think that the fixed stars now look down on the desolate scene of it!

IX. Gideon

It is a relief to pass from these narratives of tyranny, sin and shame, in which it is difficult to distinguish by their conduct between the worshippers of God and the worshippers of Baal, to the brief history of a great Israelite, who had the spirit of the first of the Hebrew patriarchs.

Not long after the deaths of Deborah and Barak, the Israelites fell back to their former idolatry, their sloth, effeminacy and sensuality, and became once more a prey to their surrounding enemies. This time it was to the Midianites, previously described as peaceful shepherds, but now a horde of nomads like the Ishmaelites, roving over the eastern deserts, doing no work, carrying on no trade and living solely on plunder. They fell on the Israelites like grasshoppers in multitude, riding camels without number, and swept over the country from the east to Gaza, eating up its substance, taking possession of its women, compelling its men to plough the lands while they reaped the harvests, and imposing their Baal upon them as a protection against the Hebrew God.

Seven years the barbarians are said to have continued this tyranny. As a result, a famine fell upon the Israelites. A large part of the poorer and weaker of them fled to the mountains, and took refuge in caves in the rocks and in holes in the ground. No such spectacle of a people in utter subjection had been seen on the earth since the Israelites themselves under Joshua had dealt as hardly with the Canaanites, reaping where they had not sown, inhabiting houses they had not built and eating of vineyards they had not planted.

The history of man on this planet has few scenes more abject in their irony. The heirs of the Covenant who had come out of Egypt with a high hand, crossed the Red Sea with shouts of triumph, sung their psalms of praise in the wilderness, and descended to the Jordan with hosannas, thinking they were about to enter a country which God had given to them as an everlasting possession, were now living in the uttermost depths of debasement like vermin under the earth of their Promised Land, while a base-born swarm of half-savage marauders were sweeping over it like princes.

But at length a great man arose in Israel. His name was Gideon. He was no more than a farmer and the son of a farmer, but he had the spirit of Abraham. He lived at Ophrah, a village or homestead not yet identified, but believed to have lain a little to the west of Shechem. His father had raised an altar to Baal in the city itself, probably as a means of conciliating his enemies, possibly of hoodwinking them. Gideon was less tractable. His heart was hungering for an opportunity of liberating his people. Tradition says that certain of his brothers had been murdered by the raiders, and hence he had the further object of avenging their deaths.

It was harvest time. Gideon had reaped his harvest and was about to thresh it. In Palestine the usual threshing-floor was then, as it is now, in the open, on a piece of ground worn bare and hard by long usage. The farmer lifted on his wooden fork as much of a sheaf as it would carry, held it high in the air and shook it above his head until the corn fell to the ground and the chaff was carried away by the wind.

This was a process impossible to Gideon. The Midianites lay

encamped on the great plain in front of him, 120,000 strong, with their camels around them. At sight of the threshing they would sweep up like the waves of a black sea and take possession of the produce. To avoid this danger Gideon threshed in the winepress, a hidden quarter at the back of the house. There an event of great moment occurred to him.

X. God Appears to Gideon

The story in the Bible is that God in His own person appeared to him face to face, in the form of a man, and told him to go out against the Midianites and deliver himself and his people. Legend says the day was hot, and Gideon lay down to rest and an angel appeared to him in a dream. The modern world is content to believe that within his own mind, as he worked in the winepress, and as the result of a struggle between his higher and lower natures, the first whisper of the divine will came to him.

His higher nature said, "Up, drive out these heathen usurpers, for the Lord is with you." His lower nature answered, "If the Lord be with me why am I here? Why has all this evil befallen us? Where are the miracles our fathers told us of? No, the Lord has forsaken us and delivered us into the hands of the Midianites." But again his higher nature said to him, "Go out in your might and save Israel." And once more his lower nature replied, "Who am I that I should save Israel? My family is poor, I am the least in my father's house, and our enemies are a great multitude." Still his higher nature insisted, "Go out and I will be with you, and you shall smite the Midianites as one man."

Whether this was an actual occurrence, or a dream, or the feverish operation of his tormented mind, Gideon told it to a company of his friends, and they said, "It is the voice of the Lord."

That night, believing that the God of Israel had called him to the high task of delivering his people from the Midianites, Gideon, with ten of his servants (his followers), went down to the city, Shechem perhaps, and in the darkness and silence of eastern streets, threw down the altar to Baal which his father had set up.

On the following morning the inhabitants, mainly Israelites, were astonished and terrified, probably from fear of the penalty they would have to pay at the hands of their oppressors. "Who has done this?" they asked. Their suspicion fell upon Gideon, and they went up to his father's house and demanded that he should be brought out to them and killed, for it was better that one man should die than that a whole nation should perish. The answer of the father of Gideon was significant. Approving in secret, perhaps, of what his son had done, he said; "Will *you* plead for Baal? If Baal be a god let him plead for himself."

XI. *Gideon Fearless*

From this time forward Gideon was named Jerubbaal, which is said to mean the adversary of Baal. The overpowering might of a great thought had taken possession of the man who had thought himself weak, and from that hour forward he knew no fear. He blew a trumpet, as a chieftain might do in calling his clansmen. Also, he sent messengers, north, south, east and west to summon the tribes of Israel, and 32,000 came to his call.

The number was small compared with the 600,000 who are said to have come out of Egypt, showing that the apostasy among the Israelites must have been pitiful since they came into the Promised Land, or else their mortality appalling during the wanderings and the wars.

But small as the voluntary army was, it was too large for Gideon, who shared with Moses the belief that on the field of battle it was not stones and slings nor swords and battle-axes, but God alone who was the giver of victory. Therefore, for the first time in the history of military commanders, and probably for the last, he set himself to reduce the number of his combatants without regard to the multitude of their adversaries.

His method of doing so was twofold. First, he told his people plainly the perils they would have to encounter in doing battle with so vast a force, and of the atrocities they might suffer if they fell into the hands of an enemy so barbarous. As a result 22,000 of the feeble-hearted became fearful and hastened home immediately. But 10,000 were left and even this number was larger than Gideon desired.

His second device for reducing the number of his army was more subtle than the first, but no less effective. The time was summer, the weather was hot and the men were thirsty, so to test their manhood he sent them down to the river to drink, with others to watch them. As many of them as knelt by the river's brink and lapped with their tongues like dogs were to be told to go home, as persons wanting in courage; but as many as, though kneeling like the rest, lifted the water in their hands and drank it from their palms were men and they were to remain.

Only 300 withstood this second of the tests, but they were enough for Gideon, since God could conquer as easily with few as with many. How he concealed his 300 and where he trained them we are not told; probably it was in the shelter of the low hills and shallow dells between Shiloh and Shechem (where the maidens of Ephraim were captured), for certainly the Midianites can have known nothing about them.

XII.　Gideon's Strategy

Gideon's strategy was simple. Dividing his little army of yeomen into three companies, he decided to charge the vast horde of the Midianites on three sides at the same moment and so produce uproar and panic. Every man, besides the sword in his hand, was to carry a trumpet hung about his neck, and a lantern enclosed in an earthenware jar strapped about his waist.

"Look on me and do as I do," he said, and, when the time came for the attack, he led his 300 by night, each to his proper place, in the highlands overlooking Jezreel. Below, the 120,000 Midianites lay asleep in the open with their camels in a wide circle about them. Then the Israelites crashed down on their enemies with the most thrilling of war-cries, "The sword of the Lord and of Gideon!" At the same time they blew their horns, smashed their earthenware jars and flashed the light of their lanterns into the faces of their sleeping foes.

The result on the Midianites was overwhelming. Thinking, in the confusion of their sudden awakening, that the attack which had fallen on them from every side was a supernatural visitation by the angels of the God of Israel, they arose in the darkness and fled in terror, killing more of their own in their flight than fell by the swords of the Israelites.

Thus Gideon, with his handful of 300, drove the mighty host of the enemy before him like sheep, some say to the desert of Judæa, others to the eastern mountains and as far along to the lands above them as Jabbok, the traditional place of the wrestling of Jacob with the angel. The Midianites were utterly destroyed, and they lifted up their heads no more.

When Gideon returned home his people who had remained behind, delirious with joy at their deliverance, offered him an hereditary judgeship. "Rule over us," they cried, "both thou and thy son, for thou hast delivered us from the hand of the Midian."

Gideon refused. Even in the flush of victory his religion, like that of the greatest of his ancestors, had no room for human sovereignty. "I will not rule over you," he said, "neither shall my son rule over you. The Lord shall rule over you."

After 700 years it was the voice of Abraham again! Gideon went back to his farm and his farming, but he lost nothing by his great renunciation. To the last hour of his life he was in reality the greatest of the judges. No more living sacrifices! No more pagan sensualities! No more Baalim! His mere presence among his people purged them of their idolatries and impurities, and their land had rest.

Great is the soul of man, than which nothing can be greater, since it partakes of the soul of God himself!

XIII. Samson

The sequence of twelve judges, or high priests, ended with Samson. The narrative of his herculean adventures (*Judges* XIII–XVI) does not represent him in the capacity of a ruler in Israel, or even as a leader of his own tribe, either in war or in peace; his action is always that of a private individual, although as the supreme official, taking the place of king, he possessed the sole right to offer the Temple sacrifices, offering on behalf of the whole nation what he was believed to embody in his sacred person. The circumstances of his birth were similar to those of Gideon, with the addition that he came under the Nazarite vow, for the unshorn head and abstinence from wine was observed by the Arabs also when they were engaged in war or pursuing revenge.

The story of Samson's exploits owes much to popular legend; but there is no reason to disbelieve that there underlies it an authentic tradition of a strong, childlike, patriotic hero, who on various occasions in the days of Israel's oppression had wrought havoc among the Philistines.

XIV. Eli

After Samson, Eli became governor of the Israelites. His name is not in the genealogy of the high priests descended from Aaron, yet the visit of the man of God to him seems to indicate that he was the only substitute for a high priest. The office of chief priest inaugurated by Moses had evidently fallen into disuse, only to return in the time of Samuel. There was no temple in Shiloh at this time. There was the Tabernacle, in which the sacred Ark was kept, and we hear already of two posts which were in front of it. The priests used to sit by the posts of the Tabernacle to be consulted by the people.

Eli was a good man. He had two bad sons, who had hereditary rights as judges. They abused their position, were guilty of great injustice towards men and impiety towards God, robbers with violence, guilty of impurity with the women who came to worship at the Tabernacle, obliging them to submit to their lusts by force, or enticing them by bribes. They are called sons of Belial. Eli remonstrated with his sons, but they did not listen to him. "A man of God" came to Eli and warned him that for his sons' transgressions God would punish him by cutting him off from his office in the next generation, and raise up a faithful priest.

At this time there lived Elkanah, a man of the tribe of Ephraim, who had married two wives. He had children by one of his wives, Peninnah, but none by the other, Hannah. He loved Hannah as Abraham loved Sarah, as Jacob loved Rachel, but the Lord had shut up her womb. The mothers of the great men of the Bible are at first nearly all barren. The object of this is clear. It is to show that the birth of the great Hebrews was usually supernatural. They were born, not according to the ordinary laws of nature, but by direct intervention of God. It was in this case.

Elkanah went with his wives to Shiloh to offer sacrifice at the yearly vintage festival. An ox or sheep was slain. Portions were given to the priest. The rest was eaten by the offerer of the sacrifice and his family. It was a happy occasion, but Hannah was sad. Seeing the other wife's children sitting with their mother, she fell to tears, lamenting her loneliness. In the bitterness of her soul she went into the Tabernacle to beseech God to give her children, and in doing so she vowed to consecrate her first son to the service of God, that his way of life should not be like that of other men. He should be a Nazarite, never to drink strong drink or to have his hair shaven. Eli blessed her and told her that God would grant her petition.

After that she returned home with her husband full of hope, and in due time Hannah bore a son, and she called his name Samuel.

CHAPTER IX

The Kings of Israel

I. Samuel

IN HANNAH'S SONG of rejoicing occur the prophetic words "The Lord shall judge the ends of the earth; and he shall give strength unto his king and exalt the horn of his anointed." Their authenticity has been doubted. They speak of an anointed king. There had not yet been any such king in Israel. Is she speaking out of the tradition of a Messianic king, the traditional idea of a divine king? If not must we conclude that Hannah's song of thanksgiving is merely an interpolated forgery.

After Samuel was weaned, his mother fulfilled her vow of consecrating the child to the service of God. She took him up to the house of Eli and "lent him to the Lord," leaving him in the Tabernacle and visiting him yearly to bring him priestly garments. The boy grew up in the house of Eli and was a joy to him. He ministered to the aged priest. He used to open the doors of the house of God and light the lamp. Eli became very old and blind.

One night, when the light had gone out, and Samuel was in bed, asleep, he heard, we are told, a voice calling to him. He thought it was the voice of the old priest, and rose up and went to him. "Here I am. You called me," said the boy.

"I called not, my son, lie down again," said Eli.

Again, and yet again, the voice called and the boy answered as before. At length Eli perceived that God was calling to the boy, so he said, "Go, lie down again, and if the voice calls a fourth time say 'Speak, Lord, for thy servant heareth!'"

The boy did so; the voice called again, and God said (what the man of God had said already) that He would punish Eli for the iniquity of his sons, and because he had not restrained them. Next morning, when Eli asked what had been said to him, the boy told him, and Eli said, "It is the Lord. Let Him do what seemeth good."

Time passed. Samuel grew to manhood. The Lord was with him. His fame as a prophet spread through all Israel. He made his home at Ramah.

The prediction that disaster would fall upon the house of Eli because of the iniquities of his two sons was soon fulfilled. The Philistines came up from the south and made war on Israel. They were not a Semitic people. They had not come from the desert of Arabia, but in ships from the islands of the Mediterranean. They had been among the pirate bands that reached Egypt. It was inevitable that the Hebrews should meet the Philistines and clash. Both were trying to conquer the land at the same time.

The Philistines made a great attack. They were the conquerors, and slew 4,000 of the Hebrews. The Hebrews appealed to Eli, desiring him to send out the Ark of God. So the Ark of God came out and the sons of the high priest with it, charged by their father that if they failed to save it they were to return no more to his presence. Again the Hebrews suffered a crushing defeat, and in escaping they lost the Holy Ark to the Philistines, who carried it off to their own stronghold in the city of Aphek.

When the news came to Shiloh the whole city was in lamentation. Eli, now a man of ninety-eight, was sitting on a high throne at one of the gates. He heard the mournful cries of the people, and sending down for the messenger who had brought the news, being uneasy about his sons, he was overwhelmed with grief, fell down from his throne and died.

II. The Philistines

Now, although the Ark of the Hebrews was in the hands of the Philistines it proved no blessing to them. God sent a destructive disease upon them, and they died in great numbers of dysentery. The Philistines conceived that they suffered their misfortunes by reason of the Ark, so they sent the Ark back to the Hebrews on a cart drawn by a yoke of kine without drivers to a village of the tribe of Judah of the name of Bethshemesh.

The people of the village saw the cart approaching, and, leaving their work in the fields, ran to the cart and took the Ark down, and then offered the cart and the kine as a burnt-offering to God.

Samuel, the prophet, now grown to manhood, but nevertheless a soldier, a governor and a judge, told his people, the Hebrews, that the Ark had been allowed by God to be taken from them as punishment for their sins, and if they wished to retain it they were to worship God, as the only way to gain victory over their enemies, since God had not promised them victory and freedom from slavery by weapons of war, but by being good and righteous men, and only by being so could they hope for the fulfilment of God's promise to their fathers.

The people applauded his discourses, and betook themselves to their prayers. And at the next encounter with their enemies the Philistines were beaten.

After that the Philistines made no more expeditions against the Hebrews for many years; but Samuel made expeditions upon them, humbled them, and took back the country which they had formerly taken from the Jews.

So it passed until Samuel became infirm with old age. He then committed the governorship to his two sons, Joel and Abiah. These two lived and judged, one at the city of Bethel and the other at Beersheba. They were not of the disposition of their father, Samuel; they perverted justice for money and gifts and bribes, lived in costly luxury, violated the laws and generally assumed the character of kings.

This greatly afflicted Samuel, who loved justice and hated tyranny and all forms of kingly government.

God appeared to him and comforted him, saying that it was not he (Samuel) whom his sons and the people had so wickedly despised, but God Himself, as the Israelites had done from the very day that they came out of Egypt, and therefore he (Samuel) had been told to ordain them a king.

But in telling them this, Samuel pointed out what they would suffer from a king. He would take away their sons from them, for purposes of war, their lands also, and make them merely the husbandmen of their own possessions, their vineyards, and do likewise.

But the people were so foolish as to be deaf to all these warnings, and desired Samuel to procure them a king, for it was necessary to have a king to fight their battles and avenge themselves on their enemies, and it was in no way absurd that while their neighbours had kingly government they should have it also.

To this Samuel answered, "Very well, go home for the present, until I shall have learned from God who it is that He will give you for your king."

III. Saul

At that time was living a Benjamite of good family, of the name of Kish. He had a son, good-looking, tall of body and of good understanding. His name was Saul. He was a farmer. He had three sons, Jonathan, the eldest, Ishui and Melchishua, and two daughters, Merab and Michal.

This was the man Samuel accepted as the appointed of God. The prophet took a vessel of oil and poured it on the head of this young man, and kissed him and said, "Be thou a king, by the ordination of God, against the Philistines, and for avenging the Hebrews for what they have suffered from them."

Later Samuel called the people together at Mizpeh, and, without telling them that he had already anointed Saul to be king, told them that they had been unmindful of God and had rejected God as their king, and wished to have a man for their king. God had consented to give them the liberty of nominating their own king, and therefore they were to cast lots as to whom it should be.

Election was first taken upon the tribe from which the king was to come, and when it fell upon the tribe of Benjamin the lot was again taken for the family of that tribe, and finally for the single person of the family. The result of this form of election was that Saul, the son of Kish, was taken for king.

Then Samuel said, "God gives you this young man to be your king. See how he is higher than any of the people [probably meaning taller], and worthy of this dominion."

So Samuel anointed Saul with the holy oil and the people cried "God save the king," and the prophet wrote it down in a book. Thus the Hebrews changed their form of government into a regal government, for in the days of Moses and his disciple Joshua it had been an aristocracy, and after that, for many years an anarchy, and after that they had permitted themselves to be governed by him who appeared to be the best warrior—whence it was that they called this interval of their government the Judges.

After this scene at Mizpeh, Samuel went back to his own city,

Ramah, thinking his life's work done, and Saul returned to his own country Gibeah, where he was born.

After this the Philistines made another attack upon the Hebrews, and were beaten by Saul. The people were pleased that they had appointed Saul king. Other victories for Saul followed.

But later the tide of Saul's popularity turned. It was the old story over again. God became angry with Saul for showing mercy to his enemies, for sparing the Amalekites whom He had commanded him to destroy, because they had done great mischief to the Israelites while they were in the wilderness on the way to the country out of Egypt, to make war upon them, to leave none of them alive, but to pursue them through every age and to slay them, beginning with the women and the infants, and to do this for the mischief they had done to their forefathers, and so blot out their names for ever.

Saul promised to do this, "for God hated" the nation of the Amalekites, and commanded Saul to have no pity even on the infants, but to wipe out the very memory of the nation.

Saul obeyed only up to a point. He destroyed the Amalekite cities, but he preserved their king and governor, and his soldiers carried off their riches and their cattle.

On this Saul returned home with joy, thinking he had done glorious things, but God was grieved that the king of the Amalekites had been preserved alive.

God therefore told Samuel that He repented of having made Saul king, and Samuel told Saul, falling upon him with bitter reproaches. He had made him head of the tribes of Israel and the Lord had anointed him king. But what had he done? He had disobeyed God by not utterly destroying the Amalekites. He had thereby rebelled against God. Rebellion was as the sin of witchcraft and stubbornness as an iniquity and idolatry. Therefore, because Saul had not destroyed everything, the Lord had rejected him from being king of Israel.

Saul begged to be forgiven, but Samuel would not forgive him. And when Agag, the king of the Amalekites, came "delicately" to Samuel, saying, "Surely the bitterness of death is passed," Samuel answered, "As thy sword hath made women childless, so shall thy mother be made childless." And he hewed Agag in pieces.

After that Samuel returned to his home at Ramah, and went up to Saul at Gilgal no more to the day of his death.

In the meantime Samuel was told by God to look for another king to take the place of Saul. We read that God led him to the right one. He was to go to Bethlehem to the house of a man named Jesse, and there he would find him.

It would seem marvellous indeed if Samuel were not directed by divine ordinance that he should go with such confidence to the home of an obscure shepherd in Bethlehem to choose the future king of Israel—marvellous if without divine guidance he should so easily discover the one who was to become the greatest of the Hebrews. There was nothing about the father of David to distinguish him from other men. He was a simple shepherd living in Bethlehem and grazing his flocks in the meadow-lands beneath. But his descent associates Jesse with the beautiful story of Ruth.

When, after the death of Samson, Eli, the high priest, was also governor of the Israelites, and the country was stricken with famine, a man of Bethlehem, in the tribe of Judah, by name Elimelech of Bethlehem, took his wife, named Naomi, and their two children (sons) born to them, Chilion and Mahlon, and moved into the land of Moab, which was on the other side of the valley in which lay the Salt Sea (Dead Sea).

He prospered there and married his sons to daughters of Moabites, Orpah for Chilion and Ruth for Mahlon. Elimelech died, and after ten years of health, his two sons died. Only Naomi, his widow, was left, and with her her sons' two widows. Finding herself very lonesome now that she had lost husband and sons (those that were dearest to her were dead), she decided to return to her own country, Bethlehem, and gave her daughters-in-law liberty to leave her, saying she wished them a more happy and prosperous wedlock than with her poor sons who were gone.

But Ruth said, "Intreat me not to leave thee, or to return from following after thee; for whither thou goest, I will go; and where thou lodgest, I will lodge: thy people shall be my people, and thy God my God."

In the end Orpah stayed behind in her native country of Moab, but Ruth went along with Naomi, her mother-in-law.

When Naomi came to Bethlehem, Boaz, a near kinsman of Elimelech, entertained her. Her fellow citizens received her kindly and called her by her true name, Naomi, which in the Hebrew means happiness, but she said "Call me Mara," which means sorrow.

IV. Boaz and Ruth

It was harvest time, and Ruth by leave of her mother-in-law went out to glean for food behind the reapers on a part of the field belonging to Boaz. Boaz came from Bethlehem and said to the reapers, "The Lord be with you," and they answered him, "The Lord bless thee."

Boaz saw the Moabitish girl (although a widow she is called a damsel), asked who she was, and, being told, embraced her as a relation and gave his servants orders to allow her to glean, and let her eat and drink with his reapers.

Ruth told her mother-in-law, Naomi, how Boaz had treated her.

Now Boaz, after the manner of his country and time, slept in his threshing-floor during the harvest, and when Naomi heard of this she told Ruth to go to the threshing-floor by night and lie down by Boaz, as a kind of expression of gratitude to him for what he had done for them, and also thinking that if Boaz companied with the girl he might continue to be good to them.

So Ruth went and lay down secretly by the feet of Boaz while he slept. When he awoke about midnight, he saw that a woman was lying by his feet and he asked who she was, and she told him. He said no more, but in the morning he awakened her, gave her as much barley as she could carry, and told her to return home to her mother-in-law unseen, saying, at the same time, that, according to the custom of the Hebrews, he who was nearest of kin to her should marry her, but if he refused to do so then he, Boaz, would marry her himself.

At noon Boaz went up to the city of Bethlehem, gathered the local senate together, and sent for Ruth and for her nearest kinsman. He asked the kinsman if he wished to retain the inheritance of Elimelech and his sons. The kinsman answered that he did. "In that case," said Boaz, "you must not remember the law by half, but do everything required of you, the widow of Mahlon is here, and you must marry her if you want to retain her husband's field." This the kinsman refused, being unwilling to marry the Moabite damsel, whereupon he was required to give up with Ruth her dead husband's field.

V. The Birth of David

Then Ruth, being free, Boaz married her, and within a year they had a son. Their son was called Obed, and Obed was the father of Jesse, the shepherd, to whom Samuel the prophet was sent by God to choose the future king of Israel. Thus it came to pass that Jesse's son David, who was to become the greatest of the Hebrews, was by this ordinance of God "born of mean parents." He was descended from a Moabite woman, not a Hebrew.

By the advent of David, the hope of a Messiah was brought nearer to fulfilment than ever it had been before. Many sceptical historians of modern times think that the Messianic idea had a pagan origin. They say it came from the cult of Mithras, a Persian god, whose history goes far back. The Mithraic legend is lost, but it is thought that Mithras had a supernatural birth, which was associated with shepherds watching their flocks by night, and angels singing psalms in the sky, and wise men bringing gifts to the divine child and adoring him. Mithraism had a Messiah also. After death the virtuous were sent to a place of blessedness and the vicious to a place of torment; but one day the struggle between good and evil was to cease, and then the Divine Bull was to be sacrificed to Mithras, who was to call all men from their tombs, separate the good from the bad, and establish a divine government in the world.

If all this bears a chilling resemblance to Christianity, with its doctrines of the atoning sacrifice, the immortality of the soul, the resurrection of the flesh, the last Judgment and the reign of the Messiah, we have no reason to be afraid. My own theory is that the dream is older than Christianity, older than any form of paganism, and as old as man himself. It is the dream of the Deliverer who is to save man from the burden of his sin, to make his peace with God and to rescue him from the hardships of his earthly condition.

This Deliverer, sometimes called the Messiah, sometimes Immanuel, sometimes the Wonderful, appears to have a place in all ages and all religions. It seems as if humanity has never been able to bear its hard lot without the hope of a Messiah. The Christian dream sprang from an oriental people, who had sinned deeply and suffered much, and hence it has the warmth, the colour, the beauty, the humanity, the simplicity, and perhaps the superstition of the East.

The Messianic hope in the Jewish people probably began to live in the days when Abraham turned his face towards Canaan. Certainly it was strong in the hard times when Moses fled with his afflicted people from Egypt towards the Promised Land, which, after long wandering, he was permitted to see from the mountain top but not to enter. It became stronger still from the day when Jehovah took a young lad from the sheepcote, a shepherd boy, and made him ruler over Israel. It is hard to think of any less likely sovereign for a nation surrounded by enemies; but David, the son of Jesse, the grandson of Ruth, became a great warrior, a great poet, and a great king. He was a very human creature, who sinned miserably and suffered terribly. But in spite of this God loved him, and finally promised him—and his people—that his children and his children's children should continue to reign over his kingdom, and that his throne should be established for ever.

VI.   Samuel Visits Jesse

We are not told what Jesse, the shepherd, supposed to be the occasion of Samuel's unexpected visit to him. But he had many sons. There were eight of them. The seer asked for them to be brought before him. The first to be presented to him was the eldest, very tall and handsome. But Samuel thought he heard the voice of God saying to him, "Look not on his countenance, or the height of his stature . . . Man looketh on the outward appearance, but the Lord looketh on the heart."

Samuel therefore rejected the eldest son. Others were presented in like manner and rejected. "The Lord hath not chosen these," said Samuel. "Are these all your children?"

Jesse answered that there was another, his youngest, and he was out keeping his sheep. "Send for him," said Samuel, and he sat down until the youngest son came, perhaps carrying his harp under his arm, for David loved music and had skill in improvising song and in dancing, leading a joyous life. He was ruddy, powerful of build and goodly to look upon. It was told of him that he had once killed a lion and a bear that had taken the lambs in the fold.

Samuel was pleased with him. He thought God said to him, "Arise, anoint him, for this is he."

Samuel anointed David. We do not gather that either he or his father or his brothers thought David had been anointed king, but that he had been anointed successor to the king. We read that from that day the Spirit of God came upon David, and departed from Saul.

VII.   David and Goliath

Another and simpler story is told of the introduction of David to Saul.

The Philistines had gathered their armies together against Israel. Saul sent his armies to meet them. They met at a place with a valley between them. On the hill on one side of the valley were the Philistines and on the hill on the other side were the Israelites. Sometimes armies settled their wars by single combat. The Philistines selected a giant named Goliath of Gath. He was over nine feet tall and wore protective armour from head to foot.

Goliath came down into the valley every day, morning and evening, for forty days and challenged Saul to send a man down to fight him. If their man killed him, the Philistines were willing to become their slaves. But if he killed the Israelite, then the Israelites would become the slaves of the Philistines.

Saul heard the challenge and was dismayed. There was no man in the Israelite camp who could meet and defeat the Philistine giant. But during the time in which Goliath was defying Saul and his people, the seven elder sons of Jesse were with Saul in the field.

They were clearly a conscripted army, keeping themselves on their own provisions. Jesse called David from the sheepcote near Bethlehem and sent him to the camp with food for his brothers.

When David arrived in the camp, the Philistines and the Israelites were making ready for battle. But first came the Philistine champion with his customary challenge. David heard it. He asked what it was about, and was told that Goliath was defying Israel, and that Saul would enrich any man who could meet him, give him his daughter and free his family from taxation.

David, speaking contemptuously of this "uncircumcised Philistine," his elder brothers heard and reproved him. They had not the Spirit of God. But Saul heard what David had said and sent for him.

David said to Saul, "Let no man's heart fail because of him; thy servant will fight the Philistine."

Saul said, "Thou art but a youth, and he is a man of war."

David told Saul how he had killed the lion and the bear that had taken the lambs from the fold. Could he not do the same by this uncircumcised Philistine, who had defied the armies of the living God?

At length Saul consented.

"Go, and the Lord be with thee," he said.

When Goliath saw David, the stripling, coming down to meet him, wearing no body armour, carrying neither sword nor spear, he laughed in disdain.

"Come to me, and I will give thy flesh to the fowls of the air," he declared.

To this David replied, "Thou comest to me with a sword and a spear and a shield; but I come to thee in the name of the Lord of Hosts!"

With that, he put his hand in his bag, took out a sling, ran to a brook for smooth stones, and slung one of them at the giant. The stone struck the giant's forehead and sank into it, and he fell on his face—dead. Then David cut off the head of Goliath with his own sword.

The Philistines fled in terror, and the armies of Saul shouted with joy.

"Whose son is this?" said Saul to one of his officers.

"On my soul, I cannot tell," said the officer.

"Inquire and bring him to me," said the king.

So David, carrying the head of Goliath, was brought to Saul. "Who art thou, young man?" said Saul.

"I am the son of thy servant Jesse, the Bethlehemite," David answered.

VIII.   David and Saul

David found favour in the king's eyes. Whenever the evil spirit took possession of Saul, David would take his harp and play to him, perhaps also chanting some of his own early psalms, and the king was refreshed and the evil spirit left him. He made David his armour-bearer, living in the Israelite camp. The duty of an armour-bearer was not that of a warrior, but of a sort of apprentice in arms, whose most warlike function was to kill outright those whom his master had struck down in battle. But David became a valiant soldier and went into war with Saul. He had great victories. When he returned with the king from battle, the women of the cities used to dance and sing, saying, "Saul hath slain his thousands, but David his tens of thousands."

David must have been a man of charming and magnetic personality, one of the rare souls that win all hearts. Everybody felt it. All Israel and Judah loved him. King Saul's affection was tinged at first with envy, and later with bitter jealousy. Saul's daughter Michal loved him. We are told that he was good to look upon, tall and graceful, with long red hair and beautiful dark eyes. He may have inherited his good looks from Ruth, his Moabite grandmother. Saul's son Jonathan loved him "with his whole soul." Jonathan might have been jealous of David, the obscure, untaught shepherd-lad who was supplanting him; but his chivalrous spirit united him to David in a covenant of closest friendship which is one of the beautiful stories of the Old Testament.

David increased his reputation as a soldier and became a general favourite. He was chief of the guard at court, so that Saul's jealous fears of him were constantly exasperated by personal association. It is revealed that Saul regarded David as a rival of his dynasty, and Jonathan is seen by his father as little better than a fellow conspirator.

One day, when the evil spirit was in Saul and David played to him, Saul cast a javelin at him, intending to kill him. Twice this occurred. David avoided the king; but the king conceived a scheme to destroy him. Hearing that his daughter Michal loved David, Saul offered her to David as a snare to him, thinking thereby to provoke the Philistines still more strongly against David, as the son-in-law of the Israelite king. Not Jonathan, but David would be the next king. The Philistines would say, "Let us kill David."

David excused himself from marrying Michal, saying, "Who am I, and what is my father's family in Israel that I should be son-in-law to the king?"

But Saul insisted, married David to his daughter, and then sent out David to fight the Philistines, expecting that he would be killed.

But David returned victorious, and Saul's jealousy increased. He gave commands to assassinate his son-in-law, but Jonathan defended David against his father and went out to warn David to fly. "Fear not," said Jonathan, "for thou shalt be king over Israel, and I shall be next to thee. That my father knows." They kissed one another and parted. Saul then sent to his daughter's house to have David watched. Michal helped David to escape from her father, by letting him down through a window and putting an image into his bed, saying David was sick. Clearly, she was a pagan. Saul was furious with his daughter. He took Michal away and married her to another man, proof enough that the law of Moses on marriage and divorce was unknown in Palestine at that time—about 1000 B.C.

David attempted to find a place of refuge in the prophetic circle of Samuel at Ramah. But Saul's enmity followed him there.

Deprived of the protection of religion, as well as of justice, David next tried his fortunes among the Philistines at Gath. He was recognized and suspected as a redoubtable foe, but made his escape by feigning madness which, in the East, has inviolable privileges. It is hardly probable that the slayer of Goliath fled to the Philistines with their dead hero's sword.

David turned to the wilds of Judah and was joined at Adullam, traditionally placed two hours' journey south of Bethlehem, by a small band of outlaws, of whom he became the head. From this time forward he may be said to have been a robber chieftain, and to have taken up the life of a guerilla captain. Apparently, he demanded payment from the people whom he protected. Yet his magnanimity is manifested during the king's continual pursuit of him as an outlaw. Saul had pursued David to Gibeah and pitched his tent there. David, who had found out Saul's resting-place, went to it by night. Saul lay sleeping in his tent in the trench of his camp, with his spear stuck in the ground by his bolster.

One of David's officers said, "God hath given thine enemy into thy hands. Smite him." David made reply, "Who shall stretch forth his hand against the Lord's anointed?" But he took the spear and a cruse of water by the bolster and went to the other side of the hill. Nobody saw him, so deep was their sleep. Then he cried aloud.

Saul heard David's voice, and said, "Is this thy voice, my son David?" "It is my voice, O king," said David. "Why do ye pursue thy servant? What have I done?"

Saul said, "I have sinned; return my son David, for I will no more harm thee. . . . Blessed be thou, my son David; thou shalt do great things." So they parted.

But Saul struggled with his evil spirit in vain. Again and again it came back to him.

So David concluded at length that the only way left to him to escape from Saul was to join the Philistines. This is hard to understand, except on the ground of his defiance. But the Philistines received him and his 600 men joyfully.

David remained with the Philistines one year and four months. During this period the prophet Samuel died.

IX. The Woman of En-dor

In those days the Philistines gathered their armies together for war against Saul. They pitched their camp near to the Israelites. Saul, who was degenerating rapidly, was in fear of them. He had no one to give him counsel now that Samuel was dead. Being unable to get any oracle from God, he said to his servants, "Seek me a woman that hath a familiar spirit, that I may go to her and inquire of her." And they told him of a woman at En-dor, who claimed to have the power of calling the dead back to earth.

Belief in the resurrection of the dead appeared late in Judaism; any worship of the dead was banned, and it was thought an outrage to God to declare men immortal. The practice of dealing with spirits was punished. But Saul disguised himself and went by night to the woman at En-dor, and asked her to bring him one whom he should name. The woman at first refused, objecting that the king had cut off all wizards. Saul swore that no punishment should come to her. Then Samuel appeared. She alone saw the spirit. When Saul asked her who it was, the woman answered, "I see a god coming up out of the earth. An old man cometh up; and he is covered in a mantle."

Saul recognized the prophet by the description. Samuel was dead, a spirit of the grave, but that did not hinder him from coming back as he had lived. And his first words were the complaint, "Why hast thou disquieted me to bring me up?" Saul answered that he was sore distressed, for the Philistines were making war upon him, and he had no one to tell him what to do.

Samuel told him that he could do nothing, since God had departed from him (Saul) for not executing his fierce wrath upon Amalek, and therefore He had given his kingdom to David. Moreover, the Lord would give his kingdom into the hands of the Philistines.

X. *The Death of Saul*

It is obvious that when the people called for Saul they were calling for a Saviour. The priest Eli and the seer Samuel, dare not rescue them from their surrounding enemies. Thus, Saul stood to them in some manner as a Messiah, and it was not until after his own sin in his failure to carry out God's commands to the letter that he lost the royal favour and therefore lost the kingdom, before he had accomplished the task to which he had been called.

Already, David had taken the first step to the throne. No longer an outlaw with a band of wandering companions, he was the head of a small colony of men and on friendly footing with the city south of Hebron. At thirty years of age he was anointed king of Hebron, the first ruler of the southern kingdom.

No sooner was he crowned than the Philistines became troublesome again. Rigorously, they followed him, but he defeated them. Luring them into a most unfavourable strategic position, he turned to attack. In utter bewilderment they fled back to their own land. In one of the many battles, the Israelites were beaten by the Philistines, Jonathan was slain and Saul struck by arrows. Saul called upon his armour-bearer to kill him. His armour-bearer refused to kill the Lord's anointed, and Saul fell on his sword and died.

Next day the Philistines found Saul and his three sons lying dead on the battlefield, and sent up their bodies to the house of their idols.

David was returning from a battle with the Amalekites when a man came running into his camp with the news of the death of Saul and Jonathan. He told a false story, thinking it would please David, that at Saul's request he had killed the king.

David said to the young man, "How wast thou not afraid to stretch forth thine hand to destroy the Lord's anointed?" Then he ordered one of his young men to kill the messenger, and this was done.

David lamented the death of Saul and Jonathan in a lament which was full of wild sorrow and passion:

How are the mighty fallen! Tell it not in Gath, publish it not in the streets of Askelon, lest the daughters of the Philistines rejoice.

. . . Saul and Jonathan were lovely and pleasant in their lives, and in their death they were not divided. . . . Ye daughters of Israel, weep over Saul. . . . How are the mighty fallen in the midst of battle! O Jonathan, thou wast slain in thine high places; I am distressed for thee, my brother Jonathan; very pleasant hast thou been unto me; thy love to me was wonderful, passing the love of women. How are the mighty fallen!

It was the cry of a great heart, over the enemy who had sought his life as well as over the brother who had protected it. Such was the spirit of the Lord's anointed!

David caused his people to learn the lament by heart, and to teach it to their children. It is probably the oldest of the writings of Scripture, and it is still among the best. Little is he to be envied who can read it without tears.

After the death of Saul and Jonathan at Gilboa, David reigned seven and a half years in Hebron over the tribe of Judah, while Ishbosheth, Saul's son, ruled the rest of Israel. On the death of Ishbosheth, all Israel chose David as king, and he reigned for forty years.

David found, in the midst of Palestine, a certain little fortress which, even from the beginning of the invasion of Canaan, had withstood all the attacks of the soldiers. This little fortress was called Jerusalem, which may have meant "city of peace" or perhaps "city of Shalim," who was a Canaanite god. It was built up on a spur of rock and almost unconquerable by ordinary methods, and this city David made his capital. From there he attacked the Philistines. The Holy Ark of God was removed from the house of Abinadab, in Kiriathjearim, and brought by David in triumph to Jerusalem. His recovered wife, Michal (separated from her second husband and perhaps suffering from the pain of being torn away from him whom she had come to love), was there before him.

As he entered, leading the procession, there was shouting and the blowing of trumpets. And, according to the custom of the time, David leapt and danced about the Ark. His wife, Michal, looking through her window, saw him doing so, and she despised him. The general opinion is with her. David was doing something unworthy of his kingly dignity. Nothing of the kind. His dancing was a religious ritual. He was visibly enacting the story of Israel from the days of its flight from Egypt, when, following the Ark, and with the pillar of cloud by day and the pillar of fire by night, it was journeying to the Promised Land. This was the climax and end of that journey, the fulfilment of the journey of Moses.

But the foolish woman saw nothing of this. So, a little later, when David returned to his household, she fell on him with reproaches and contempt. How glorious was the king of Israel to uncover himself by day in the eyes of the handmaidens and his servants as one of the vain fellows shamelessly uncovered himself! David replied to her with dignity. It was before the Lord he had uncovered himself. Yet he would be more vile than that, he would be base in his own eyes. Michal should be punished with the basest punishment a woman could bear. She would have no child to the day of her death.

David then undertook the task of beautifying his capital, for his victorious wars had filled his storehouses to overflowing with all manner of precious booty. He had a vast supply of gold, silver, and brass and precious wood. He had many captives to slave in his labour gangs, even as his own forefathers had slaved in the labour gangs of the Egyptians. Hitherto, his people had lived in tents, and eaten and slept and worshipped as barbarians. He wanted to erect and establish a great temple, and to show the world of his time that he was no longer a robber chieftain to a rich and mighty monarch, but he had to turn to the Phœnicians for help in his building. They claimed to know all about architecture, and were glad to sell their services.

Jerusalem, when David took it, must have been like almost any other Canaanite town. All we know is that it was surrounded by a tremendously high stone wall, and that it had two massive doors, with a narrow entrance closed by a wooden portcullis. The houses were flat-roofed, one-storied huts of stone, plastered with mud. There was no furniture inside them. The people ate and slept on the ground like animals. Horrid smells filled every corner. Savage, half-starved pariah dogs prowled about among dirty children, naked, but for the good-luck charms strung about their necks, their faces covered with sores and scars from drinking foul water.

Such was probably Jerusalem when it became the capital of David's empire. He began to make himself a tyrant like the kings of the other peoples of the Orient. Once, he even stole away the wife of one of his soldiers, and afterwards had the man killed to get him out of sight.

XI. David and Bathsheba

David was no longer young by this time. He was probably approaching fifty years of age. He arose from his bed at eventide and walked on the roof of his royal house, and from the roof he saw a woman washing. She was very beautiful to look upon. He asked who she was, and was told she was Bathsheba, the wife of a Hittite named Uriah, who was away at the war fighting his battles. He sent messengers for her and she came to him. It is wrong to assume that she was compelled (instances of women consenting to the will of the king were not wanting). He lay with her, and she returned to her house. It is equally wrong to assume that she was not a consenting party. The woman conceived and sent word to David that she was with child.

Upon this David sent to Joab, his commander at the front, telling him to send Uriah back to him. Joab did so. David had no particular duty to impose. He asked Uriah how the war prospered.

Then he told him to go down to his house and rest. Why David did this, we hardly dare to ask ourselves. Uriah left the king's house, and there followed him a "mess of meat" from the king. But Uriah did not return to his home, and when David asked him why, Uriah answered that his comrades were encamped in the open field on the bare ground, and he could not go to his house and sleep in his bed, remembering their hardships. David then told Uriah to remain in Jerusalem two days longer, and then he would send him back to the battlefield. There is no suggestion that Uriah had any suspicion of what had happened between his wife and the king. In the morning David wrote a letter to his commander in the field, telling him to put the bearer of his letter into the forefront of the hottest battle, and then retire from him that he might be smitten and die. This letter he gave into Uriah's hand and sent him away.

There is no possible way of excusing this act. It was one of the foulest. When the commander received the letter brought by Uriah he did as the king had ordered, with the result the king must have expected. Uriah was put at the forefront of the battle and was deserted and killed.

Then Joab sent the king report of the war, and told the messenger to say, "Thy servant, Uriah, is dead." When the wife of

Uriah heard that her husband was dead, she mourned for him. And when the time of her mourning was past, David sent for her, and she became his wife and in due time bore him a son. There is little excuse for this, except that in that age the love passion was held to forgive nearly every offence. There are many proofs of this fact, some of them as late as the time of Josephus. The man who committed a crime for love was acquitted with those who avenged the circumstances of the crime. Further, it may be remembered, for whatever it may be worth, that, if the law of Moses had then been in operation in Israel, Bathsheba would have been stoned to death if her husband had returned home and been able to prove her infidelity, while the king would have escaped punishment.

We read that what David had done displeased God and that He sent Nathan, a prophet or seer, to rebuke and punish David. The prophets of those days were called seers, not spokesmen for God, but foreseers of future events. They probably came from the East.

Until Nathan arrived David does not seem to have been conscious of the enormity of his offence. Nathan was to make him so. He told the king a parable. There was a rich man who had many flocks and herds. And there was a poor man who had nothing save an ewe lamb. The lamb had grown up with him and with his children, and ate of his own meat and drank of his own cup. There came a traveller to the rich man, and he spared his own flock, but took the ewe lamb of the poor man and dressed it for his guest.

Nathan, having told this story, asked what should be done to the man who had done this wicked thing. David's anger was greatly kindled by the story, and he said, "As the Lord liveth, the man who hath done this thing shall surely die." Whereupon Nathan said to David, "Thou art the man." He had taken the wife of Uriah, and put Uriah to the sword. Therefore the sword should never depart from his house.

The king was overwhelmed with remorse, and said, "I have sinned against the Lord."

The punishment of David came quickly. He had given the enemies of the Lord occasion to blaspheme, and soon his punishment began. Bathsheba's child was born, unnamed. David became very fond of it. It grew sick and he was overwhelmed with grief, both for his own sake and Bathsheba's. He prayed to God to spare the child's life. He fasted; lay all night on the earth and would not eat.

The members of his household tried to comfort him, but he could not be comforted.

Seven days passed and the child died. David's servants were afraid to tell him so, but he guessed it from the whispering of the servants, and he said, "Is the child dead?" They answered, "He is dead."

Then David arose and washed and ate, saying, "While the child was alive I fasted and wept; but now that he is dead wherefore should I fast? Can I bring him back again? No, I shall go to him, but he shall not return to me."

He comforted Bathsheba, and after a time she bore him another son, and called his name Solomon.

But this was only the beginning of David's punishment. The misconduct of the king had broken the sanctity of marriage and gone far to destroy family chastity. As a result came a very gross offence which was closely linked with David's. Amnon, his eldest son, conceived an impure passion for his virgin half-sister, Tamar, who was own sister to Absalom. He became sick of his love and one of his friends observed this, and learning the cause suggested an evil expedient. Amnon was to feign sickness, lie in bed, and when the king, his father, came to see him, he was to beg that his sister, Tamar, should be sent to nurse and cook for him. This was agreed to by the king. Tamar, in her innocence, came at his father's command, and Amnon, taking advantage of his opportunity, forced her. Then she, in her shame, begged him to ask the king to give her to him as his wife. But Amnon, by a law that is the cruellest in nature, having no further use for her, turned her out of his house, calling his servant and saying, "Put this woman out from me, and bolt the door after her."

The hatred with which he hated was greater than the love with which he had loved her. The best that can be said for Amnon was that he hated himself for yielding to the temptation of her beauty. Tamar put ashes on her head, rent her garments and went on crying. Absalom, her brother, met her, and asked the cause of her distress, and, being told, he begged his sister to say nothing, but leave matters to him. Tamar remained disconsolate in her brother Absalom's house.

The king heard what had happened. As none but Absalom knew, it was probably from Absalom that the king heard the story. He was wroth, but that was all. He did nothing to Amnon. Probably, almost certainly, Absalom thought he ought to have punished Amnon. He did not. Was his own offence present to his mind? Was he asking himself who was he to punish such an offence? Who am I, O Lord, that I should punish an offence I committed myself?

Absalom said nothing to Amnon, either good or bad.

Two years passed. Then Absalom had a sheep-shearing feast, and he invited the king also, but David excused himself, wherefore Absalom asked that his brother, Amnon, should go with him, and all the king's sons. The king, suspecting something, said, "Why should he go with them?" But Absalom pressed the king and he consented.

Absalom had arranged his plan with his servants. They were to observe his brother Amnon, and when he was merry with wine they were to kill him. "Be courageous, be valiant," he said.

The servants carried out their orders. Amnon was slain. The other sons got on their mules and fled.

When the king heard the news, he tore his garments and threw himself on the ground. Clearly, the king was now wroth with Absalom. This was a crime he could and must punish, though he could not punish the crime committed on Absalom's sister. Absalom had to fly from his father.

For three years David mourned for Amnon every day. Absalom was three years at Geshur, in Syria. Meantime, the heart of the people was with Absalom. He was young and comely. He had a cheerful face, long hair. He was the son of his father, the handsomest man of his age. "From the sole of his foot even to the crown of his head there was no blemish on him."

David's heart began to relent towards Absalom and he would go and comfort him, having ceased to mourn for Amnon, seeing he was dead, as in the case of the child of Bathsheba. He sent a messenger to bring Absalom to Jerusalem. Absalom came. But the king never called for him. He lived two years in Jerusalem without once seeing the king's face. Absalom complained. If the king had any cause of offence in him let him kill him or send him away. At length, public opinion compelled David to call Absalom. They met. The king kissed Absalom, but that was all.

Absalom was now the king's eldest son, and the natural heir to the throne. And the people loved him. Presently he began to be hostile to his father, and assumed rights that did not entirely belong to him, although claimed by king's sons and sons' sons for ages.

When people went to the gate of the city for judgment he judged them. The people accepted his judgments. Thus Absalom is said to have stolen the hearts of the men of Israel from David his father.

Absalom, discontented, went to Hebron with 200 men from Jerusalem. Messengers came to David, saying, "The hearts of Israel are after Absalom."

At length Absalom, with his advisers (conspirators against David, egging him on to revolt) conceived the idea of displacing their king. Evil grew by what it fed on. They thought of invading Jerusalem and proclaiming Absalom king. Absalom had now become a traitor—to his own father.

From this moment our hearts go back to David. He hears that his son is coming up with an army against him. He could not fight his own son. He had an army infinitely greater than Absalom's and could easily have destroyed him. But he would neither kill Absalom nor let Absalom kill him.

David decided to fly before Absalom. He left Jerusalem and went up Mount Olivet, and wept as he went, his head covered and barefoot.

The people followed him, every man covering his head and weeping as he went, saying, "Wherever the king shall be, whether in life or death, there we shall be." But David said, "Pass over." And so they passed over the brook Kidron on the way to the wilderness.

On the way a member of the family of Saul came and cursed David, and threw stones at him, crying, "Come out, come out, thou bloody man, and thou man of Belial."

David said to his officer, "My son seeketh my life. How much can this Benjamite do? Let him alone; let him curse." So David left Jerusalem—the great warrior, running away from battle with his own son. To such of us as know the road it is a pitiful picture. His last words to the commander were, "Deal gently with the young man, with Absalom."

Meantime, Absalom had entered Jerusalem amid the acclamations of the enemies of the king, who cried, "God save the king."

Then came the battle between the forces of the king and of his son, Absalom. It took place in the wood of Ephraim, and 20,000 men fell. Absalom, whose army was defeated, fled on a mule, but the mule galloped under the thick boughs of an oak, and Absalom's flying hair was caught in the boughs of the oak and the mule rode away from under him.

Then Joab, a kinsman of David, came up and killed Absalom, and his armour-bearers threw his body into a pit in the wood.

Two of the soldiers of David, who was beyond Jordan, ran to tell him of the victory. They found him sitting between two gates. As the first man came up the king said, "Is all well?" The man answered, "Blessed be the Lord thy God which hath delivered up the man who helped against my lord the king."

"Is the young man safe?" asked the king.

The man answered, "I saw a great tumult, but I do not know what it was."

Then the second man arrived, crying, "Tidings, my lord the king. The Lord hath avenged to-day all them that rose up against thee."

David asked, "Is the young man, Absalom, safe?"

"May all that rise up against thee to do thee hurt be as that young man is," was the answer.

The king was overwhelmed. He went up to his chamber over the gate and wept, saying, "O my son, Absalom, my son, my son, Absalom. Would God I had died for thee, O Absalom, my son, my son!"

It is one of the great moments of the human soul.

David had a great welcome when he returned to Jerusalem and set himself to watch over the children of Israel. But he was old, and his active life was finished. He was probably about sixty-six years of age. He fainted in a battle with the Philistines. The time had come for him to go.

But now came Nathan the seer, who had charged David with his sin against Uriah, and he prompted Bathsheba to appeal to David for the succession for her son, Solomon. Bathsheba did so, going to the king's chamber and reminding him that he had promised that her son should reign after him.

David assented. "Assuredly Solomon thy son shall reign after me," he decided. Thus, he was faithful to Bathsheba to the last.

He ordered that Solomon should be anointed king that very day. This was done, the trumpets were blown and the people cried, "God save Solomon."

XII. Solomon

David occupied his last years in composing psalms in honour of God, in making a census of the people (numbering them) and in preparing to build a temple. His own people were of little use for this purpose. They had no skill in handicraft. David first gathered up the strangers and set them to work as masons to hew stones, to build a house of God. Then he sent to Tyre and Sidon for timber from Lebanon. He meant the temple to be magnificent, such as would bring glory in all the countries round about.

Then he called his son, Solomon, who was of tender years (perhaps twelve years of age), and told him it had been in his mind to build a home to God. But God had said to him, "Thou has shed blood and has made great wars; therefore thou shalt not build a house to My name."

But his son, who would be a man of peace, should build it. Then he adjured Solomon to build a temple. "Arise, therefore, and build the sanctuary of the Lord God, to bring the Ark of the Covenant of the Lord and all the holy vessels into it."

Thus David, like Moses, was not to enter his promised land. David's last charge to Solomon was, "I go the way of all the earth; be thou strong therefore, and show thyself a man."

It is reasonable at this juncture to conclude,

(1) That the anointing of Saul as king by Samuel was a Messianic anointing.

(2) That Saul's sin was the reason why Samuel was told to anoint the son of Jesse of Bethlehem.

(3) That David's career as king, first at Hebron and afterwards at Jerusalem, unified the Israelite people and raised them to a point of power and splendour they had never had before and can never have had since, not even in the time of Solomon.

(4) That nevertheless David's sins, both as a military leader and as a man (especially in the case of Bathsheba) were thought to cause God to divert the fulfilment of His promise, and to cast forward the Messianic hope to a descendant of David in some time to come.

I do not see any indication of when that Messianic descendant is to arise. But every incident in the story of David radiates towards it, and culminates with the final promise that the Messiah must come from the loins of David.

On this the Messianic hope of the Jewish people was built, through all the 1,000 years that followed David, down to the period immediately before the birth of Jesus of Nazareth. That it may have continued for some time after the fall of Jerusalem is possible, but not certain, inasmuch as the fall of Jerusalem would seem to the Jews to put an end to the possibility of the restoration of David's throne and dynasty.

The Messianic hope, therefore, was only put back while a new life was given to it for the future. That life has never failed. It still lives. Every Sabbath day in the synagogue is heard the prayer for the coming of the son of David who is to establish the kingdom of God on earth—to re-establish the throne of David at Jerusalem.

The great, the grandiose dream of the Jew for another thousand years.

XIII. Solomon as King

David was succeeded by his favourite son, Solomon, a boy of fourteen when he came to the throne. Solomon is usually spoken of as a person of surpassing wisdom, but he was rather a person of unrestrained cruelty, looseness and self-indulgence. He was clever, he could coin smart proverbs and solve riddles. Nevertheless, he was far from wise, for his rule in Israel brought little to his people except corruption, idolatry, misery and debt. He tried to imitate the extravagant, loose-living oriental monarchs around him. To his dying day he was never able to act the grand oriental emperor.

One of the first things Solomon did when he came to responsible manhood was to build a splendid palace. Tens of thousands of slaves were at work felling trees far north in Lebanon and quarrying limestone for Jerusalem. Phœnicians were called in to serve as architects. Everywhere, slaves were writhing beneath Solomon's task-masters and free men were muttering against Solomon's tax-gatherers. The subject people on the borders seized their opportunities and rebelled. The Edomites, the Moabites, and the Aramæans broke away and proclaimed their independence. Solomon let them go. Later, he compelled even the Hebrew freemen to become his slaves for one month out of every three. A rich portion of every crop was taxed away to fill the coffers of the imperious king. After many years he completed his palace. Compared with the palaces of the emperors of Egypt and Babylon it was a paltry thing. But to the children of a primitive desert folk, who had lived in goat-skin tents, the palace seemed the most wondrous thing ever built by men.

Having built his palace, which was large enough to house his hundreds of wives and concubines, Solomon remembered that he had promised his father that he would build a temple in which the sacred Ark should be sheltered for all time. It was to be the home of God. Sacrifices thereafter were to be made only in the Temple. Solomon is chiefly remembered in history for the magnificence of this building on Mount Moriah in Jerusalem. Some few stones of it still stand and are kissed every Sabbath by the lips of the devout.

The Temple proved, in after years, to be the salvation of Solomon's dynasty—perhaps it did more to perpetuate Israel on earth than any other material thing; but it was a poor little place, as the descriptions in the Bible sufficiently show. It was small, probably smaller than many thousands of city synagogues throughout the world to-day.

The size of Solomon's Temple is indicated by Josephus. It was erected of white polished stone, 200 feet in length and the same in height, and seventy feet wide, the front porch facing east. It was encompassed by a double row of cloisters, with marble pillars and roofs of cedar wood ornamented with slabs of beaten gold. Some of the doors of the thirty rooms were of solid silver, others were of cedar inlaid with gold. The floor of the inner and more sacred temple was laid with plates of gold. Solomon covered the building inside and outside with gold. One gets the general impression of a small and rather vulgar gilt box, without architectural design, without shape, without beauty, with nothing but gew-gaw and glitter. The altar, thirty-five feet broad and seventeen and a half feet high, is recorded to have been furnished with 10,000 golden candlesticks, according to the command of Moses. How so many candlesticks could stand on so small an altar is a mystery. The Ark contained nothing but the two tables of stone that preserved the Ten Commandments which God spoke to Moses on Mount Sinai.

Viewed from our modern standpoint, it was indeed almost an insignificant building. Nevertheless, it cost a great deal of money, and to find this Solomon imposed still heavier taxation on his people. When taxation failed he began piracy, and sent out a fleet of ships in search of gold and silver. After that he had to resort to borrowing from the king of Tyre, who lent him large sums which he never got back. So by tyranny and oppression, by piracy and fraud, Solomon carried out his ambitious scheme.

Solomon became something of a pagan, having married many foreign princesses. He found that they had taken their strange gods and priests into his harem. Yahweh was no longer the sole God of Israel, and the Temple on Mount Moriah had to share with the foreign idols. The religious practices of Solomon's time were often low, lewd and unclean. The people became very poor, but Solomon ruled and revelled in peace, and in peace he died. But after he had reigned forty years it was peace more terrible than war.

XIV.   The Captivity

After Solomon came Rehoboam, one of his sons, who straightway told his people that his little finger was stronger than his father's thigh, and that, while his father had scourged them with whips, he would scourge them with scorpions. The result was that the Hebrew kingdom broke up, and from that time forward there were two kingdoms in Palestine—Israel on the north and Judah on the south, Israel being three times as large as Judah and containing rich valleys and high roads while Judah was rocky, dry and arid as the desert. The people of the south, however, were far less corrupt in their worship.

Two hundred years passed and the divided nations of the Hebrews spent much of their time anointing and assassinating their kings. Finally, the two little Hebrew kingdoms went down to their doom.

Then came the outside powers to take possession of Palestine. Palestine was a tiny land, with few natural resources, but strategically it was of great importance, and that is why it was so incessantly the victim of invasion. It was a narrow bridge between Asia and Africa, and every great empire-builder, every imperious trading king had to thunder his way across it, if he wished to go from east to west or from south to north.

While David lived these covetous neighbours could be kept off. Palestine was a difficult country for the stranger to conquer, and the great guerilla warrior, who knew its hills and valleys and was skilled in military art, could beat them off. He had beaten them off repeatedly and thus preserved the independence of Israel, keeping alive at the same time the enthusiasm of his people for the worship of the God of Israel. But Solomon had adopted other ways with his heathen neighbours. He had conciliated them. After the division of the two Israelite nations, Judah and Israel, Solomon's way was for a long time the settled policy of the Israelite kings. One after another married the daughters of the kings and nobles of the surrounding nations. As a result, they became more and more pagan, and the influence of the women of the harems was powerful.

This suited the policy and the religion of the kings of the surrounding nations. They wished to possess themselves of the gate to the west and at the same time to promulgate their faiths, and no way looked so easy as to marry their daughters to the Israelite kings.

Thus was the land promised to Abraham going back to heathenism, at least, as far as the kings and their courts could make them go.

Egypt was the first to take advantage of the civil war in Palestine, and so came the Egyptian dominion. After Egypt came Assyria from the north. The Assyrian invasion fell first upon the Israelite kingdom. The Israelites fought for three long and ghastly years. At length, in 722 B.C. they fell before the Assyrians and all the wealthy and the learned, and 27,000 of the best of the ten northern tribes were carried off into captivity in Assyria. There they became mixed up with the people around them. To this day we speak of them as the lost ten tribes. No one knows what eventually became of them. No explorer has ever found them. They faded out of history, and so ended the northern kingdom.

The southern kingdom, Judah, was spared for a while. Then, when Assyria went to destruction, Egypt laid its hold on Palestine. When Egypt was overthrown Babylon seized the little land. Then, in 597 B.C. Judah, also, came to an end.

In the eighth year of the reign of Jehoiakim as king of the Hebrews, Nebuchadnezzar, king of Babylon, conquered Palestine, despoiled Jerusalem of its temples and utterly wrecked the city. The conqueror carried off a large number of the rich and powerful classes back with him to Babylon, leaving behind the poorer people (chiefly in Samaria and parts of Galilee). The people carried off into captivity were the more luxurious and corrupt. Those remaining were the cleaner, the more religious. This was about 586 years before Christ.

The story of the survival of the Hebrew people is largely the story of the men dragged off to Babylon. Babylon was a mighty city at the time of the captivity. Nebuchadnezzar had succeeded his father on the Babylonian throne in 606 B.C. He had annexed Syria to the empire. He continued the restoration of Babylon which his father had begun, and made it one of the wonders of the world. Its outer wall was fifty miles in length, and so thick that four chariots could drive on it abreast. It contained mighty temples adorned with jewels and precious metals and vast palaces brilliant with coloured bricks and tiles.

What its size was we do not know, nor the extent of its population, but abroad to the very horizon stretched its vineyards and meadow lands. It had the reputation of great wickedness. But to the miserable destitute wanderers from a little backward hill country, the sight of Babylon's magnificence must have been overwhelming. This possibly disturbed their faith. How could one still believe Jerusalem to be the Holy City or Yahweh the mightiest of the gods? No, Babylon was the true Zion, and Bel, the sun god, was the real Lord of Hosts. So, to many of the exiles, the God of their fathers died. Their old religion perished. But nevertheless Judaism, a new religion, was born. For not all the exiles were swept off their feet by the grandeur of Babylon and its gods. A heroic minority refused to be stampeded. That minority turned to the dead prophets of Judah, and out of the teaching of the dead prophets the minority fashioned the younger and nobler faith.

Meantime, King Nebuchadnezzar of Babylon put no obstacle in the way of his Jewish captives. All he had wanted was to destroy the kingdom of Judah, merely because its independent existence made his hold on Palestine an uncertain one. He needed Palestine, because it was the bridge between his empire and the rest of the world. Now that he had secured that bridge, he wished the defeated and exiled men of Judah all the goodwill in the world.

But it cannot be supposed that the captives in Babylon suffered nothing from the Babylonians. There were many who could not be at ease in the strange land, so they sat by the waters of Babylon and wept. They hated the new land, for it was not their own. In their minds they looked back to the little hills of Palestine. Like beggars around a fire, the exiled warmed their hearts with tales of past glories, with glowing stories, which they elaborated, about Moses, David and Solomon. They could not dismiss entirely the great Israelite idea of the promise given to Abraham, repeated to Jacob and again to David, that through them the Messiah should come whose throne should be the throne of David, whose city was to be Jerusalem, which was to be the centre to which the peoples of all the earth should come.

Many of the exiles grew rich and powerful within the court of Babylon and forgot the humble land from which they had come. The rest plodded on in aching home-sickness, living in their own wretched quarters outside the city, the prisoners and slaves of the profligate pagans within—they, the chosen people who, in the days of their pride, had received God's promise that there should never be wanting a man to sit on the throne of David. Why had God forsaken them? Was it because of their sins that He had taken back His word?

They could not sacrifice to God, for sacrifice in Babylon would have been a violation of their Deuteronomic code of laws revealed to them fifty years before. Jerusalem was the only proper place to sacrifice. Nevertheless, they devoted one day of the week (the Sabbath) to undivided thought of God. They prayed and they feasted in their little synagogues (synagogue really means meeting-house), always with their faces turned towards Jerusalem, and piteously begged for the coming of the day of their redemption.

CHAPTER X

The Hebrew Prophets

I. The Message of the Prophets

WHEN in the uttermost depths of their distress, a new race of prophets appeared among the Children of Israel, bringing a new message of hope to keep their starved souls alive. These prophets were not the direct mouthpiece of God; if they spoke divinely inspired words it was no more than did the famous poets and seers of all ages throughout the world.

The message the Hebrew prophets sent forth was born of practical wisdom; the prophets were ordinary men, but they had the power of being able to see farther and deeper than other people into the meaning and trend of everyday events. They declared that God would remember His penitent children; that He would fulfil the promise made to them; that He would guide their footsteps back to the land He had bestowed on them as an heritage and in due time would give them a great ruler, a glorious king of the line of David, who would sit proudly on the throne and use their humbler enemies as his footstool. The newcomer would establish a Kingdom of God on earth; he would rule the whole of the world in the awe-inspiring name of God. It was, indeed, a revival of the Messianic hope, in accordance with the spirit of the Babylonian captives, and at one moment this comforting message of the prophets seemed on the threshold of fulfilment.

Some forty years after the beginning of their bondage, Babylon was conquered by Cyrus, king of Persia, and he gave forth that the Israelites were free to return to their own country. With hearts overflowing with rejoicing at their deliverance, 40,000 of them shook the dust of Babylon off their feet and went home; the rest stayed where they were and perished in the bitterness of their shame.

The faithful remnant believed at first that Cyrus was indeed the Messiah who was to bring them salvation, and one of their prophets, not remembering the necessary descent from King David, so acclaimed him. After a time they began to consider themselves Babylonians—they wished no longer to be identified as Judæans. They turned their backs on their birthright. Some of them had given money to those who had returned, to help them on their way, but that was as far as they had been prepared to go. Their feet were set firmly in the land of their adoption.

The march of the 40,000 across the desert from Babylonia to Palestine took three months. And their homecoming was sorrowful. Palestine, the land flowing with milk and honey, was a dreary waste. The houses were fallen to ruin. Jerusalem was a heap of stones. The fields about it were strangling in the grip of weeds.

The despairing Israelites set up a rough stone altar on Mount Moriah as a substitute for their destroyed Temple. And for twelve bitter years they struggled on. Is it not conceivable that at times they cursed the day they had set forth rejoicing from the prosperous land of their captivity?

II. The Courage of the Prophets

When Solomon had completed the building of his Temple, the prophets did not figure conspicuously in its services. They were too fond of freedom to allow their worship to be confined within the four walls of such a prison, however stately. Accustomed to living in a state of wildness, almost lawlessness, their idea of true worship was that calling for no other setting than a primitive tent in the valleys or a rough stone in the heart of the forest. They desired to hold commune with their God in the open, where they could feel His presence and see above their heads the very floor of Heaven. They desired to feel on their cheeks the sharpness of the wind, the lash of the rain and the soft kiss of the sun, the strong forces held in leash by the omnipotent hand of their God. They could not understand the worship of the people who dwelt in the city; they resented it, and with stern voices called out for a return to the simple life—the life of the nomad of the desert. They were filled with loathing for the Baal worshipped by the Canaanites, and their one purpose was to keep the eyes of the Hebrews fixed firmly on the covenant which their fathers had made at the holy mountain in the heart of the wilderness. They were true patriots, frenzied with zeal, who persistently set before the people the fact that they belonged not to Baal but to the great Jahweh.

These prophets were fearless men. Even kings could not daunt them. When David lusted after another man's wife and stole her, Nathan the prophet charged him to his face with being an accursed breaker of the law. When Ahab, king of Israel, took to wife Jezebel, the Phœnician princess, it was the prophet Elijah who prevented her from destroying her husband's race. Courageous in the purpose of his God, Elijah, a wild man with uncut hair and naught but a sheepskin to cover his nakedness, rushed forth with flaming tongue to denounce her wickedness and that of the king. A stern, merciless figure, the whole of his life was devoted to passionate protests against the deadly vice, luxury and corruption which stalked throughout the land.

The term "prophet" denotes one who announces or speaks the Divine Will. Before the coming of the prophets of the Old Testament there were the seers. Before he was called "the prophet of God," Samuel was a seer. But the function of the seer was completely distinct from that of the prophet; the former was closely connected with divination by sacrifice, the latter was quite otherwise. Again, unlike the seers, the prophets appeared, not individually, but in companies; when they prophesied they did so to the accompaniment of music, rhythmic dance music, and such was the strong excitement produced thereby that he who was seized by it was incapable of standing. In the Scriptures we read that Saul was thus affected.

We may assume, then, that the character of the seer may be traced to a kind of dervish derivation. Even today in the East we can recognize external forms of the seer phenomenon in the practices of the dervishes. In *Samuel* we read of gay processions with hand-drum and pipe, processions which were customary features of religious feasts. True, their basic origin was the demand for an outlet for natural joy, but sometimes they took on a deeper meaning, changing their character to express serious emotions, feelings of a deeper intensity. It happened sometimes that the seers or prophets, under the powerful influence of the divine afflatus, surrendered their personality and appeared to be actually possessed by a supernatural power. They were swayed and ruled by a divine spirit. Occasionally they were possessed by a frenzy of an evil nature.

The seers and prophets, however, were not peculiar to the Hebrew nation. We find reports of them in the histories of other peoples. They may be recognized as a wakening element of sacredness in a carnal society. The prophets, fearful of the loss of divine righteousness in all matters pertaining to religion, felt compelled to warn the backsliders of the doom which awaited them. And in this respect they especially criticized the conduct of kings, who, seated on their thrones, were above all power of human authority. Hence, the condemnation of David by Nathan in the matter of Uriah, and of Ahab by Elijah after the murder of Naboth.

III. Elijah

The figure of Elijah, the sternest of the Hebrew prophets, is one of the most noble encountered in the pages of the Old Testament. A man of God, like Moses and Samuel, he holds communion with the Most High. He walks through life alone but unafraid. He has very little in common with the other prophets of whom we read in Hebrew writings and elsewhere. He is solitary, sublime. On his shoulders are the spiritual mantles of both prophet and priest.

Elijah first appeared in the Bible in I *Kings* XVII, 1. A native of Tishbite, or Thesbon, in Gilead, he is described as Elijah the Tishbite. He lived in the reign of Ahab in the first half of the ninth century B.C., 100 years after David. He predicted that a drought would fall on the land, and the prediction was fulfilled. During part of the years of drought and famine he lived by a brook near Sidon. He drank of the brook and was fed by ravens night and morning—the ravens brought him bread and flesh.

Then the word of the Lord came unto Elijah, saying, "Arise, get thee to Zarephath . . . behold I have commanded a widow woman there to sustain thee."

He comes upon the woman gathering sticks, and says, "Fetch me a drink." As she is going to fetch it he says, "Bring a little bread also." The widow answers that she has only a handful of meal in a bowl and a little cruse of oil, that she is going in to make a cake for herself and her son that they may eat of it before they die of the famine.

"Fear not," says Elijah, "do as I tell you, for the Lord God of Israel says, 'The barrel of meal shall not waste, neither shall the cruse of oil fail.'"

The woman obeys Elijah, and she and he and her household eat many days, and the barrel of meal wastes not, and the cruse of oil does not fail.

This is the clear forerunner of the story of the feeding of the five thousand by Jesus.

The son of the woman falls sick. He dies. The woman thinks the prophet has brought evil upon her. "Art thou come to bring my sin to remembrance?" she asks, suggesting that the child had no known father. Yet she is called a widow.

Elijah takes the dead child out of her arms, carries it up to a loft, stretches himself over it three times, calls on God to let the child's soul come back to him.

The child returns to life, and Elijah gives him to his mother, who says, "Now I know thou art a man of God."

In the third year of the drought Elijah demanded to see King Ahab.

"What do you want with me, thou troubler of Israel?" asked Ahab, meaning that Elijah had caused the famine that had followed the drought. Elijah answered that Ahab had given himself up to the worship of Baal, and hence the drought and famine. He proposed a test—the priests of Baal to sacrifice to Baal while he (Elijah) sacrificed to Yahweh. At the trial the prophets of Baal failed—Elijah succeeded. Ahab killed the false prophets.

Elijah tells Ahab to go in and eat, for the famine will soon be over. Himself, he goes up to Carmel, sits with his head in his hands waiting for sign of rain, sends his servant to look at the sky and the sea. At length (after being sent seven times) the servant returns to say there is a cloud in the sky of the size of a man's hand. Elijah sends to Ahab to tell him to make haste to escape the rain that is coming.

And it came to pass . . . that the heaven was black with clouds and wind, and there was a great rain.

While Ahab is still alive, Elijah is told to go to Damascus and anoint Hazael the king of Syria to be king of Israel in Ahab's place, and Elisha in his own place. This, also Elijah does. He finds Elisha ploughing in the fields in the valley of the Jordan and casts his mantle over him. And Elisha leaves his oxen and plough and runs after Elijah, saying, however, "Let me kiss my father and mother and then I will follow thee."

Elijah agrees to this and Elisha goes back. Elisha then follows Elijah and ministers to him.

This incident bears a chilling resemblance to Jesus's call of certain of his disciples.

Later, there is the incident of Naboth's vineyard. Ahab asks for it. Naboth refuses to give or sell it. Jezebel, the wife of Ahab, brings about the death of Naboth on a charge of blasphemy. Ahab then takes Naboth's vineyard. Then Elijah comes down with "the word of the Lord" and denounces the king, predicting that for his wickedness the dogs shall lick his blood and that of his wife. This fate befalls Ahab and Jezebel. It is a shocking story, one of the most shocking in the Old Testament.

In II *Chronicles* XXI, 12–15, we have a glimpse of Elijah, and in II *Kings* 2 we get a last sight of him before his death. Elijah is living with Elisha at Gilgal. (Elijah's appearance is described in II *Kings*, I, 8. He was a hairy man, and girt with a girdle of leather about his loins.)

It was here that the last scene of Elijah's life occurred. When they reached the banks of the Jordan, Elijah wrapped his prophet's mantle together and with it smote the waters. By a last miracle the waters parted and the two walked across dryshod. After Elijah had blessed Elisha, we read:

> And it came to pass, as they still went on, and talked, that, behold, there appeared a chariot of fire, and horses of fire, and parted them both asunder, and Elijah went up by a whirlwind into Heaven.

Such is the fitting supernatural close to an earthly life which is all supernatural.

A great, stern, vindictive, merciless figure. It is difficult to think of such a life in the history of actual happenings. Some of the early Rabbinical traditions were that Elijah was not really a man, but an angel in human form. Also, that he was "without father, without mother, without descent, having neither beginning of days nor end of life; but made like unto the Son of God"—as in the case of Melchisedec, king of Salem, in the days of Abraham, as described in *Hebrews* VII, 3.

Elijah's position after his translation to Heaven (obviously in his earthly body) is made just as miraculous. He is to be the forerunner of the Messiah. Jesus sees him on the Mount of Transfiguration. To this day he takes part in the Jewish feast of the Passover, when the door is open to receive him after the glass of wine has been poured out and stands waiting for him.

The story of Elijah also reads like a parable, a poem, an apocalyptic narrative. It is difficult to see that it has any historical importance.

IV.　Elisha and Elijah

The story of Elisha is in great part a repetition of that of Elijah, with the Shunammite woman and her son taking the place of the widow.

It certainly may be said that these two prophets stand as the spokesmen of God against the worship of false gods. But the God for whom they speak and act seems often to shock the moral sense. It is sometimes difficult to see in what way he is superior, except in power, to the false gods. He is certainly no more merciful, and it is hard to realize that he is always more moral.

There is an undoubted foundation in history for certain of the scenes at the background of the Bible story of Elijah.

Meander says the drought in Phœnicia lasted one whole year; Jesus (Luke IV, 25) says (in Nazareth) the drought covered the whole land for three years and six months (the "heaven was shut up" and "great famine was throughout all the land"); and James says (V, 17) that Elijah was "a man subject to like passions as we are, and he prayed earnestly that it might not rain; and it rained not on the earth by the space of three years and six months."

Thus it is clear that a belief in a long drought and consequent famine (in Kings seven years, in the mouths of Jesus and James three and a half years) did actually survive from the time of Elijah in the ninth century until after the time of Christ.

After careful thought I conclude, (a) that such general incidents as are described in the Elijah story did actually occur; (b) that some such man as Elijah did exist, that he was a very real person to Jesus, and to James and to John the Apostle when they ask Jesus to command them to call down fire from Heaven on the Samaritan who refused to receive their Master (Luke IX, 54); also, that Elijah's supernatural power was generally accepted, as shown by what John says, (c) but this does not compel me to accept the long series of supernatural incidents which are attached to Elijah's story; they may very well have grown with the centuries as other such stories grew.

Finally, I do see a very distinct Messianic character in the whole story of Elijah. He is made the mouthpiece of God. He is endowed with power from God to bring down fire from Heaven. He is able to increase the meal and oil, as Jesus increased the loaves and fishes. He is able to raise from the dead the widow's son as Jesus raised the widow's son at Nain, and precisely in the way he raised the daughter of Jairus. He is supernaturally born, has no descent, no beginning and no end. He ascends to Heaven in his earthly body from the country of the Jordan as Jesus ascends from the Mount of Olives.

All these are points of resemblance to the story of Jesus, which almost suggest that, when the story of Jesus came to be written about thirty years after his death, it may have owed something to the story of Elijah.

On the other hand there are wide differences. Jesus is born of a mother, though not of a father. This is more in harmony with certain of the Messiahs of the mystical religions. He actually dies as a man, while Elijah never dies. His death is of the essence of his life and mission, the redemption of the world.

The after-existence of Elijah is not given in the story in *Kings*. But it is obvious that during the ten centuries between Elijah's time and Christ's there had grown up a legend concerning him. He was to come again. His second coming was to foretell the end of the world, and the approach of the Messiah.

Jesus accepted this belief, but it is difficult to see what form it took in his mind. Did he believe that the appearance of Elias (Elijah) on the Mount of Transfiguration was his appearance in the body in which he had ascended in the chariot of fire? If so, what about the body of Moses, who appeared with him? Was that also an actual body? Moses had actually died and been buried by the angels of God in the plains of Moab. His earthly body had gone to corruption. Was it his spiritual body in which he appeared to Jesus and the disciples?

Again Jesus said, in effect, that Elijah had come in the person of John the Baptist. But John had been born of a father and mother, and he had been beheaded by Herod Antipas, and his body had been buried by his disciples. What, then, was the exact idea about Elijah in the mind of Jesus? Was it Elijah's spirit which appeared to him? Was it the soul of Elijah which had come in the person of John the Baptist?

I see nothing to wonder at in the Rabbinical tradition that Elijah had not been a man at all, but an angel from God. Yet if he had not been a man, liable to be put to death, why did he fly from Jezebel when she threatened to take his life?

I conclude that the story of Elijah, as it has come down to us, is the effort of humanity in the ninth century to express the idea of the Christ. What was the idea then?

1. That the Christ would not be born of father or mother.
2. That he would not suffer hunger, but be fed by God (?the ravens).
3. That he would not suffer death.
4. That while he lived he would exercise the powers of God on earth—to destroy God's enemies, to defend the weak and oppressed, to work miracles of mercy.

Beyond this the idea of the God-man did not yet go. He was not yet of the seed of David. He was not yet to establish a kingdom of God on earth, which would last for ever. Humanity (in Elijah's time and down to the days when his story was written) had not yet reached to this height. But I cannot doubt that the idea of Elijah was for a long time the Hebrew idea of the Son of God, the intermediary through whom God expressed Himself to man. Elijah was the immature and very imperfect idea of the God-man, the Messiah.

V. Amos

Amos, an Israelite prophet of the eighth century B.C., was a native of the country a few miles south of Bethlehem. He was a shepherd, but also a trader of sycamore figs. Of himself, Amos said:

I was no prophet, neither was I a prophet's son, but I was an herdman, and a gatherer of sycamore fruit. And the Lord took me as I followed the flock, and the Lord said unto me, go, prophesy unto my people Israel.

For some time Amos sojourned in the northern kingdom, prophesying with a loud voice the fall of the kingdom of Israel. When, however, his fiery words reached the ears of the head priest of the royal sanctuary at Bethel, his zealous activity was at once suppressed.

The tenor of the prophesies of Amos was that Jeroboam, the

king of Israel, should find death by the sword, and that Israel should be led away captive out of their own land. Amos does not clearly state why these terrible afflictions are to be visited upon the chosen of God, but we are led to believe that there is a definite moral and religious backsliding in Israel. The poor are being unmercifully oppressed; the brute head of injustice is reared throughout the land; and so-called religious rites are being practised which to Jahweh have no moral meaning and are, therefore, abhorrent. To Amos, these rites are actually immoral. The children of Israel must gather the warning to their hearts in time or else suffer the dread captivity. But the prophet does not give a full description of this threatened bondage.

The literary quality of his prophecy in the Old Testament is undeniably great. And yet this master poet was, on his own admission, merely a shepherd and a gatherer of sycamore fruits. I believe that certain portions of the text of his prophecy may have been altered by others who came later and that certain passages may have been interpolated, but I greatly doubt whether the concluding passage, foretelling the restoration of Israel, is an interpolation, although many eminent scholars held this view. To my view, it breathes the very spirit of the man. Moreover, faith in the restoration of Israel is the unfailing characteristic of all the Hebrew predictions of God's vengeance on His people for their sins. The Hebrew people never seem to have doubted that a Messianic age was coming.

VI. Hosea

Hosea flourished between 789 and 693 B.C. Of the man himself we know nothing, except those facts which can be gleaned from his prophecies. He dwelt in the northern kingdom, and Uzziah and other kings of Judah heard his voice as did Jeroboam, king of Israel.

The Book of *Hosea,* apparently, dates from a period prior to 734 B.C. It is divided into two parts. The entire work portrays vividly the richness and prosperity marking the reign of King Jeroboam, but it also throws many sidelights on the anarchy and social disorder which followed after. It is like a mirror held up before the face of the kingdom. The latter portion of the work may be described as a general survey or summary of prophetic teaching. Hosea condemns the priests in no uncertain tone and calls down fire upon the heads of wayward kings and princes. Neither class is spared the lash of his tongue. His condemnation is all-embracing. And so familiar does he appear to be with the trickeries and intrigues of those who hold temporal power and the habits of those who hold spiritual power that it has led to the belief that perhaps Hosea, himself, was a member of the priestly class.

Hosea tells us that he began prophesying when, obeying the command of God, he contracted a union with a certain woman called Gomer, a woman of loose morals, a profligate. She leaves him, and gradually falls into the depths of degradation, but the affection of her husband is not dimmed thereby. Then, in accordance with a divine behest, he brings back the wanderer to the shelter of his house and enshrines her in seclusion. For a long time he watches over her patiently, kindly, but he does not give back to her the privileged status of a wife.

In these personal experiences, Hosea observes a direct parallel to the long-suffering love of God for the wayward children of Israel; he observes how the backsliders will be brought again into the way of righteousness by discipline of soul and body, and a discipline marked by the overthrow of all their institutions, both temporal and spiritual.

A stranger among his own kin, Hosea could not, like Amos, enjoy the comfort of friends on the fulfillment of his mission. His return home was filled with bitterness, with sorrow and shame.

The prophecy contained in the Book of *Hosea* may be divided into two sections. The first appertains to the widespread growth of immorality and its attendant social disorder, a state of affairs which had come to pass because of Israel's alliance with either Egypt or Assyria. Hosea explains the nature of the punishment which will be visited on Israel for this. The forthcoming judgment will be the absolute destruction of the nation which, in its blindness and pride, has turned its face from God and hungered after the ways of the unrighteous. The foundations of the nation were crumbling even then, though the noise of the destruction was deadened by the licentious mirth and laughter of those who offered up sacrifices to idols of stone and wood on the lofty heights of Ephraim. The day of reckoning was at hand. In the land of Israel no truth or mercy could be found. There was no knowledge of God the omnipotent. The fair land lay under a black cloak of lies, thefts, murders, adulteries and blasphemies. The king of Samaria would vanish as foam upon the water. The pitiless Assyrian was at hand, and both fortress and city would fall before him.

Yet, in spite of their backslidings, Jahweh would forgive Israel, as Hosea had forgiven his erring wife Gomer. For the people of Israel were the children of God, and He would have compassion on them.

The deep, emotional temperament of the prophet Hosea reminds us strikingly of Jeremiah. But how much more so does it remind us of Christ himself?

VII. Micah

A prophet of the time of Jotham, Ahaz and Hezekiah—739 to 693 B.C. Therefore, Micah belonged to the time of the first Isaiah, of whom he is believed to have been a friend. Micah, like Amos, was probably of humble origin; perhaps a husbandman. He was the last of the great prophets of the eighth century B.C.

Of the three main parts of his book, the second consists of prophecies of the Messiah. It is thought that these chapters cannot be ascribed to Micah himself, because they presuppose the historic outlook of the exile or even of one who lived during a still later period. There is internal evidence of later authorship of the Messianic portion, in which it is suggested that Israel will be united once more with their kindred Hebrew nations, in the establishment of the kingdom of peace and righteousness—a kingdom whose foundations will be based on the knowledge and fear of the Lord.

Micah also looked forward to the kingship of a Messiah of the house of David, who, like his great ancestor, should come forth from the city of Bethlehem. There was hope for Zion—a hope of future restoration; but she must first bear with patience the rightful chastisement of her sins.

There are passages in *Micah* which appear to have their parallels in the New Testament, and there is an almost literal resemblance between *Micah* IV, 1–3 and *Isaiah* II, 2–6, prophesying the rebuilding of the Temple. These verses, in both cases, predict the last days when the House of the Lord shall be established on the top of the mountains, when many nations shall come to it, when the law shall go forth from Zion and the word of the Lord from Jerusalem. And the Lord shall judge among many people, and rebuke strong nations afar off, and they shall beat their swords into ploughshares and their spears into pruning-hooks, when nation shall not lift up a sword against nation, neither shall they learn war any more.

Read the great chapter *Isaiah* II, 1–22. Mark that the words are often the same. Was Micah quoting Isaiah? Very unlikely. But if the fourth chapter of *Micah* was by a later hand, it is extremely probable that the writer was directly copying Isaiah word for word. Mark, also, that the writer of the fourth chapter of *Micah* is either foreseeing the captivity in Babylon or he is writing after it.

. . . for pangs have taken thee as a woman in travail. Be in pain, and labour to bring forth, O daughter of Zion, like a woman in travail; for now shalt thou go forth out of the city, and thou shalt dwell in the field, and thou shalt go even to Babylon; there shalt thou be delivered; there the Lord shall redeem thee from the hand of thine enemies.

Mark, further, that in *Micah* (V, 2) a ruler is promised *and that he is to come from Bethlehem*.

But thou, Beth-lehem Ephratah, though thou be little among the thousands of Judah, yet out of thee shall he come forth unto me that is to be ruler in Israel; whose goings forth have been from of old, from everlasting.

This is the prophetic authority which (in the nativity stories in the Gospels) is supposed to have been given to Herod the Great by his wise men when he asked them where the Christ was to be born.

In Chapter V, verse 5, it is written:

And this man shall be the peace, when the Assyrian shall come into our land.

Thus in *Isaiah,* the ruler whose goings forth have been from of old, "from everlasting," who is to come from Bethlehem, is to be there when the Assyrian comes and is to deliver his people from the Assyrians.

Obviously, therefore, the ruler out of Bethlehem is God Himself, who has existed from the beginning.

Observe, that if the prophecy is read as referring to Jesus of Nazareth, it is all false prophecy, for none of the things foretold has come to pass.

The magnificent closing passages of *Micah* are undoubtedly a prophecy of the coming of a great ruler, a Messiah, who is to subdue all the enemies of God, who will punish the people of God, *but* in the end he will have mercy. He will turn again and have compassion on his people; he will subdue their iniquities and cast their sins into the depths of the sea. Then he will perform the truth of Jacob, and the mercy he promised to Abraham in the days of old he will fulfil.

VIII. Isaiah

In the time of Isaiah, when the fortunes of the Hebrew people were low, the Messianic hope began with the admission of sin. Their sufferings were due to their sins. Those sins offended God. They must be atoned for before God could take the Hebrew people back to His favour. Therefore, the Messiah to come would be a king indeed, but a suffering king, who would make peace for his people with God by going through great affliction:

> He is despised and rejected of men; . . . and we hid as it were our faces from him; he was despised, and we esteemed him not. Surely he hath borne our griefs, and carried our sorrows; yet we did esteem him stricken, smitten of God, and afflicted.

Isaiah dwelt in Jerusalem, and at one period seems to have exerted a great influence in the circles of the court. His tongue knew no fear. He could, without permission, address a king, and speak the truth without hiding its unpleasantness. The place he held in society was evidently far higher than that held by Amos the shepherd. Unlike Jeremiah he was married. He had at least two sons.

Isaiah had certainly great rhetorical skill and literary discipline. The invasion of Sennacherib in 701 B.C. gave rise to some of his greatest prophecies; tradition tells that he saw the inevitable triumph of the Assyrian invasion, and that he would go about the streets of Jerusalem naked, calling upon the people to submit rather than to resist the invader.

The burden of his message to the captive Jews was a warning of the dread things to come, but he did not neglect to console them and put heart into them. Believers, semi-believers and unbelievers, were they not all the children of God? Some had strayed, strayed far; but their feet could be led back into the paths of holiness.

After the return from bondage we find the prophet recognizing Cyrus, the Persian king, as, in fact, the Messiah or Anointed One.

But was the whole of the so-called Book of *Isaiah* really written by that prophet? The accepted opinion now is that there was a second Isaiah who wrote much later, and that the work of the second Isaiah starts with the chapter (XL) which begins: "Comfort ye, comfort ye, my people."

It is worth observation that the most characteristic religious peculiarities of the disputed prophecies in *Isaiah* laid stress on doctrines whose conception is supposed to date from the time of the writing of the Book of *Daniel*—such doctrines as the influence of angelic powers, the resurrection of the body, the eternal punishment of the wicked and vicarious atonement.

All this leads to the conclusion that the second Isaiah was probably as late as the author of the Book of *Daniel,* while the first Isaiah may have been written about the time of the Assyrian conquest.

IX. *Zechariah*

Zechariah appeared in Jerusalem in the second year of Darius, 520 B.C., that is, about the time of the Captivity. His prophecies have many objects closely related to what he conceived to be the needs of his own time.

1. The restoration of the Temple, destroyed by Nebuchadnezzar in 586 B.C. Cyrus permitted the Jews to return to Palestine in 538, eighteen years earlier than Zechariah's prophecy. The Temple was not completed until 516, about four years after Zechariah's prophecy.

2. Seventy years have passed since the beginning of the conquest of Palestine by Nebuchadnezzar, and the prophet is waiting for signs of the Messianic coming and finds none. The cities are still mourning, and "all the earth sitteth still, and is at rest." Apparently this means that Zechariah is waiting for the turmoil which is to precede the coming of the Messiah.

3. The prophet is asking whether the fast days which arose in the Captivity are still to be observed.

4. The scene of Zechariah's prophetic visions is Jerusalem. The restoration of the Temple is the chief hope and dream, but be-

hind this is the hope of the greater restoration of David's kingdom.

5. This kingdom is to be the Messianic kingdom. It is a purely Israelite kingdom that is to come. The lordship of Assyria and Egypt is to end; foreign tyrants are to fall, and the autonomy and martial power of Israel are to be restored. The scattered exiles are to return from all lands.

6. Then comes a difficult passage about the shepherds who are to rule the nation. A struggle between these shepherds appears to be an allegory of past events, a figurative report, not a prophecy.

7. Towards the close of the prophecy comes a variation in the Messianic promise. All heathendom is gathered together against Jerusalem and perishes here. God gives the victory to the country folk of Judah and they march on Jerusalem. There is great lamentation concerning a martyr "whom they have pierced."

8. Finally, comes a fourth variation of the Messianic deliverance. The heathens take the city (Jerusalem), but do not wholly destroy the inhabitants.

The God (Yahweh), at a time known only to himself, is to appear with all his saints on Mount Olivet, destroy the inhabitants of Jerusalem, and the new era begins.

Much of this is very confusing. Zechariah's prophecy leaves the impression of having been written at various periods. Some of it conveys the impression that it was written during the Captivity; some of it in post-exilic times. Some of it seems to belong to as late as the overthrow of the Persian empire in 330 B.C.

Many of the most important of the passages quoted from the prophets in the New Testament and made to apply to Christ are gathered from *Zechariah*. Of these are the following:

Behold, I will bring forth my servant the BRANCH. [III, 8]
For who hath despised the day of small things? [IV, 10]
Behold the man whose name is the BRANCH; and he shall grow up out of his place, and he shall build the temple of the Lord. [VI, 12]
Thus said the Lord of Hosts; In those days it shall come to pass, that ten men shall take hold out of all languages of the nations, even shall take hold of the skirt of him that is a Jew, saying, We will go with you, for we have heard that God is with you. [VIII, 23]
Rejoice greatly, O daughter of Zion; shout, O daughter of Jerusalem; behold, thy King cometh unto thee; he is just, and having salvation; lowly, and riding upon an ass, and upon a colt the foal of an ass. [IX, 9]

Did Jesus know, when riding into Jerusalem, that he was in a sense realizing this prophecy? It would seem that he did. *"Thy King."*

> And I said unto them, If ye think good, give me my price; and if not, forbear. So they weighed for my price thirty pieces of silver. And the Lord said unto me, Cast it unto the potter; a goodly price that I was prised at of them. And I took the thirty pieces of silver, and cast them to the potter in the house of the Lord. [XI, 12, 13]

The parallel here goes no farther than the words "thirty pieces of silver," and "cast them to the potter in the house of the Lord." It is merely verbal. The incident is a totally different one from that of Judas throwing the thirty pieces back in the Temple. The incident described in *Zechariah* has nothing to do with Jesus, and nothing whatever to do with Judas. Try to fit verse 13 into the incident of the Gospel, of Judas casting the thirty pieces back at the high priests and the high priests buying a potter's field with them, and we see that there is no relation whatever between it and the incidents prophesied in *Zechariah*.

> And one shall say unto him, What are these wounds in thine hands? Then he shall answer, Those with which I was wounded in the house of my friends. [XIII, 6]

Again, put this parallel to the incident of Jesus risen from the dead and appearing to the disciples in the room in Jerusalem, and we see that it has no possible relation to the incident of Zechariah.

> And his feet shall stand in that day [the day when Jerusalem will be taken captive] upon the Mount of Olives, which is before Jerusalem on the east . . .

Observe that Jerusalem faced the east—the Temple faced the rising sun.

> . . . and the Mount of Olives shall cleave in the midst thereof toward the east and toward the west, and there shall be a very great valley; and half of the mountain shall remove toward the north, and half of it toward the south. [XIV, 4]

This is apparently an unfulfilled prophecy.

My conclusion is that Zechariah was writing about events that took place during his time or after his time. I think it almost certain that the prophecies of the Book of *Zechariah* were written at different periods, and that they were not all written by the same prophet. I think a great deal that is prophecy is due to this cause. The prophecies are dealing in the mystic apocalyptic way with incidents of which we have lost definite knowledge. The parallels (such as they are) between *Zechariah* and the Gospel narratives are mainly verbal, and in no case do the incidents associated with the words seem to be the same, but quite different. I think Zechariah was looking forward to a Messianic age, and that he thought it would come soon.

Incidentally, Zechariah casts a light on the life of the prophets. He says:

> I will cause the prophets and the unclean spirit to pass out of the land. [XIII, 2]
> The prophets shall be ashamed every one of his vision . . . . neither shall they wear a rough garment to deceive. [XIII, 4]

See the reference in *Zechariah* III, 1—Satan standing at the right hand of the high priest Joshua. My inference is that *Zechariah* (or this portion of it) was written after the Hebrew captives had brought back from Babylon the Persian idea of Satan, of the Devil as the author of evil. Against this theory of Satan, see *Isaiah* XLV, 6–7: "I am the Lord, and there is none else. I form the light, and create darkness; I make peace, and create evil."

X. *Jeremiah*

The last of the prophets before the Exile, Jeremiah belongs to the period 626 to 586 B.C. By birth he was a countryman, coming of a priestly stock whose estate lay in the land of Benjamin. He began to prophesy in the thirteenth year of Josiah, when he was still young. He had foresight. He could see the storm clouds gathering over Israel, and could read their portent while the statesmen still went about their political affairs wrapped in a cloak of false security.

In 621 B.C., a few years after he began to prophesy, the "Book of the Law"—*Deuteronomy*—was discovered in the Temple. This discovery led to a reform movement, and Jeremiah was one of those who supported the movement in Jerusalem and elsewhere. There is, however, an uncertainty about this, because it becomes difficult to think that a sanguine preacher, as Jeremiah was in his youth, should have become a complete pessimist later.

An important point is that the Book of *Deuteronomy*, hitherto thought to be dealing with the earliest period in the history of the Israelite people, belongs, according to modern scholars, to a late period.*

But in this book there is also a spirit more priestly than prophetic. Great stress is laid on the edict that in no sanctuary save the Temple built by Solomon may God be worshipped. That means that all the little village shrines of God must be destroyed. As a result, all their priests had to go to Jerusalem to find work as helpers in the Temple. This may have been partly good. The priests at that time were ignorant and superstitious. But there was another side to the reform. The code of laws, especially, was priestly. It required that sacrifices should be brought and handed over to the priests. It tried to box up God in a tiny little house of stone and mortar. It took the mighty spirit called religion and tried to limit it within a comparatively feeble thing called the Church.

But was not all this done when the Ark was made, or at least when it was put into the Temple of Solomon?

There are various stages in the development of Jeremiah. At first, he was certainly not a pessimist. His aim was to drive into the better minds the conviction that the only hope of salvation for Israel lay in a universal return to the true God—a God who, unlike other gods, was omnipotent, not a mere national god and one whose favour could be purchased by the offering up of costly sacrifices.

At one period Jeremiah apparently believed that consequent judgment could be averted by this means. Afterwards, a closer acquaintance with Jerusalem disillusioned him. The result of his observation there, in the streets of Jerusalem, was that there could not be a single just and honest man, high or low, rich or poor. He calls the people of Jerusalem "a people of Gomorrah." This pessimistic tone of mind in Jeremiah has caused to enter into the language of most nations the word "jeremiad" as an equivalent for a gloomy denunciation.

For prophesying against Jerusalem he was accused by priests,

---

*It is a fact of great significance to observe that a great deal of the Mosaic laws, as given in the so-called Mosaic books, has its counterpart in the Babylonian laws, but whether the Mosaic laws preceded or succeeded the Babylonian laws is not altogether clear. These laws concern the land and its cultivation; the landlord and tenant; the neglect of the land; the relations of husband and wife; the laws of marriage; the laws of purchase; the bride price; the bridegroom's father providing the bride price; the marriage contract; the contract for divorce; the rights of a widow, of a concubine, and so on.

prophets, and all the people of high treason. No king is mentioned at that period, the period of Jeremiah's denunciation. In the fourth year of Jehoiakim, 605 B.C. (which was the first year of Nebuchadnezzar), Jeremiah was bidden to write down all the words that the Lord had spoken to him concerning Jerusalem, Judah, and all the nations from the days of Josiah onward. In the following year, Jeremiah's scribe, a man called Baruch, read the prophecies of Jeremiah, first to the people assembled in the Temple, then to the princes, then to the king. The king threw Baruch's roll into a brazier. The burden of the prophecy of Jeremiah was that the king of Babylon would come and destroy the land. The burden of his preaching was that God Himself would destroy the Temple, even though it had been built to His glory. Jeremiah held that God did not demand sacrifices, but only demanded faith in the human heart.

When Jeremiah had the courage to express these ideas in the Temple courts, there was a great clamour for his death, and only with difficulty did he escape. Later, he was seized, beaten, flung into prison, lowered into a miry pit and left to die. A scroll of his sermons was torn to pieces and burned by the king of the time. When all the people were madly clamouring for war, he, alone, stood for peace. His God was not the possession of one little tribe and did not dwell in one little shrine. He was not Yahweh merely: He was God.

When Jerusalem was destroyed by the Babylonian host in 586 B.C. Jeremiah was left behind to keep peace among the rabble who had not been carried off into exile. But the mad desire of the rabble to break away from the Babylonian empire led a band of fanatics first to murder the ruler of their land and then to fly off into Egypt. When they fled they dragged Jeremiah with them.

In far-off Egypt the prophet could not be silenced. Jeremiah began once more to speak his mind, but this time he did not escape. According to tradition the infuriated mob stoned him to death. Such was the end of Jeremiah, a true man of God.

Such, at least, is the narrative as it comes down to us. The fathers Jerome and Epiphanius say that Jeremiah was stoned to death at Daphnæ, but this is uncertain. Was Jeremiah really a patriot? He did counsel submission to the Babylonian king, but this may have been only because his clearness of vision showed him how hopeless was resistance. After his death, the popular belief in

Jeremiah rose, and other prophecies were added to his book—notably those regarding the new Covenant and the restoration of the people after a lapse of seventy years.

XI. *The Epistle of Jeremy*

This apocryphal book of the Old Testament purports to have been written by Jeremiah to the exiles in Babylon. The author was probably a Jew of Alexandria. He holds up to derision both the idol gods of Egypt and the idolatry of Babylon. It is possible that it was written in the first century B.C. or a little earlier.

According to this apocryphal book the writer warns those in captivity that they were not to set eyes on their own land for the space of seven generations; that they were to see men bow down to idols, but they themselves were not to bow the knee. For idols were the work of men's hands; they had not tongues to speak or ears to hear, neither were they possessed of the power of self-preservation. They could not send down blessings upon the heads of their worshippers—even the most trivial of blessings. They were without life; they were of less value then the commonest articles of domestic use. The writer compares an idol to a scarecrow, an object capable of deluding the imagination but powerless to protect.

It is significant that both the writer of the epistle and St. Paul, as well as St. Clement of Alexandria, described idolatry as the worship of a thing made by hand totally without any invisible spirit behind or within it. It is clear, however, that the more enlightened heathen minds, almost in all ages, but certainly from Plato downwards, thought of the idols as the mere physical representations of the invisible gods, but the idols themselves were not gods. Against this, however, St. Paul, in his address on Mars' Hill, Clement of Alexandria, and, apparently, the writer of the Epistle of *Jeremy* takes the view that, in the eyes of the unenlightened pagans, who would be by far the largest number of them, the idols of wood and stone were, themselves, the gods.

XII. *Ezekiel*

One of the prophets in exile, was the son of a priest. His name was Ezekiel. He had strange visions, and afterwards wrote them in frenzied words. Like every other ancient prophet, he was what we call a mystic. His influence on the future of his people proved tremendous. The children of the exiles did not outlive Ezekiel's priestly ideas for at least 400 years. Indeed, many have not outlived them to this day.

Ezekiel was a priest of the Jerusalem Temple. He almost certainly had the training of the cultivated priesthood of his time. Presumably he was born about thirty years before 597 B.C., the time when Nebuchadnezzar carried off the Israelites to Babylonia. In Babylonia, apparently, Ezekiel spent the rest of his life. His prophecies are dated from "the year of our captivity." He dwelt, with his fellow-exiles, on one of the mounds caused by the waters of the great flood which lay waste the country and formed a big canal not far south of the city of Babylon. Here, with his fellow-exiles (who had a form of local government by elders and were for the most part prosperous and contented, with no demand made on them by the Babylonian government, save the payment of taxes, Ezekiel lived in his own house, quietly, as a Babylonian subject. Nevertheless, his exile had bitten deep into his soul, and he deplored political denseness of the government at Jerusalem under King Zedekiah, and the lack of morals and depth of religious belief of the people.

Ezekiel, like Jeremiah, did not regard Nebuchadnezzar in an unfriendly light. He looked on him as God's instrument for the chastisement of His wayward people. He regarded opposition to the rule of the Babylonians as being suicidal, and looked upon the political downfall of the nation as being proof of God's anger at the widespread depravity undermining the moral and religious life of the nation. Jerusalem he considered as being a sink of iniquity, and said it must be destroyed. And yet, like Hosea and Amos, in spite of the vision of punishment to come, his eyes were not blinded to the glorious fact that God out of His great love for His people, would not suffer them to perish utterly. He told of a remnant, a little brand plucked from the burning, and how it would be cherished safely in the fallow land until the thunder of God's wrath had faded away and a new day had dawned.

The political creed of the prophet Ezekiel may be summed up thus: the complete destruction of Jerusalem and the people who dwelt therein, immediate submission to Babylon and the restoration of those in exile. And this he identified with the will of God. He then paints a happy picture of the returned Israel, and outlines a new constitution—a form of government in which the control of public religion is left solely in the hands of the priesthood. Probably this is the outcome of his priestly upbringing and education.

XIII. Daniel

The Book of *Daniel* is now generally regarded as a work dating from the time of Antiochus Epiphanes (175–164 B.C.). There are no means of determining anything definite regarding the alleged author of the book. The Old Testament makes mention of four people of the name of Daniel.

The Jewish historian Josephus accepted without doubt the reality of Daniel as an historical personage. He stated that the prophet was a relative of Zedekiah, but this is now a conclusion long abandoned. It was thought that Daniel was a Jew of noble birth born at Upper Beth-horon, a village in the neighbourhood of Jerusalem, but we can find no evidence of this in the Bible. According to Rabbinical authorities, Daniel returned to Jerusalem with the other exiles. This, therefore, places his date in the period of the Captivity. Other traditions, however, say that he did not leave Babylonia, but that he died and was buried there.

The Book of *Daniel* does not contain a biographical sketch of the prophet. The writer merely makes him the central figure. But it is quite probable that there was a man of the name of Daniel who was a spiritual leader of the Jews held captive in Babylon. It is believed that the fame of this great leader was handed down to the time of Antiochus Epiphanes, when some gifted writer among the Jews, realizing the great need of the people for consolation in their affliction under the cruel persecution of that tyrant king, took the character of the seer, Daniel, who flourished during a period of similar persecution, and enshrined him as the central figure of his writings.

The account of Daniel himself is that he was an interpreter of dreams, and that his reward for a correct interpretation of Nebuchadnezzar's dream of the writing on the wall was the first step towards his political advancement. It is quite possible that this is a repetition of the story of Joseph in *Genesis*. There are, indeed, certain points which bear a striking resemblance. In both stories we read of a young Hebrew on whom is bestowed political preferment because he possesses the divine ability to interpret dreams of a heathen king. In both stories we read how the astrologers at the court of the king fail in their attempts at interpretation, and of how, when the young Israelite is summoned, he clears up the mystery entirely to the king's satisfaction.

Another incident in the life of Daniel describes God's care of him when he is cast into the den of the lions.

The book was written in two languages—Hebrew and a dialect of Aramaic. The first part is obviously written for the purpose of conveying to the minds of the Israelites the essential necessity that they shall have faith in their own God who, in His own time, will deliver them from the hands of their heathen oppressor. The second part of the book is apocalyptic, and some of the beliefs contained therein rule out the possibility of the writer having dwelt in the courts of Nebuchadnezzar.

Among the many doctrines propounded perhaps the most outstanding is the complete system of angelology, whereby entire control of the affairs affecting human beings is left to a hierarchy of commanding angels, among whom are Gabriel and Michael. From whom the Israelites borrowed this idea is not certain, for it is quite distinct and foreign to the primitive Israelite idea of God. It is certain that it was not borrowed from Babylonia. It might, however, have been taken from Persian doctrines, for the religion of that people contained a most complicated system of angelology. We may assume, therefore, that the doctrine of the angels set forth in *Daniel* points to the fact of prolonged Persian influence in Israel. Moreover, it is in *Daniel* that for the first time in the Old Testament the doctrine of the resurrection of the dead is set forth, and this doctrine is also generally believed to have had its origin in Persia.

These evidences are internal, but they appear to prove conclusively that the book belongs to a late period. They have value also in proving the date at which beliefs of great importance to the Christian faith made their first appearance in the Jewish religion.

The prophecies in the Book of *Daniel* appear to centre in the period in which it was apparently written—the period of Antiochus Epiphanes, when that monarch was endeavouring to overthrow the worship of Jahweh and establish in its place the religion of Greece.

In regard to their general style, the prophecies in *Daniel* differ fundamentally from all other prophetic writings of the Old Testament. The earlier prophets confined themselves to general predictions, but not so the author of *Daniel*. He paid particular regard to details, and they usually refer to the period in which he flourished. In the place of the prophesies concerning the freeing of the Israelites and their return home to Jerusalem, as is set forth in *Jeremiah, Ezekiel,* and *Isaiah, Daniel* foretells the coming of an ideal Messianic kingdom. The development of the Christian faith owed much to his prophetic work, in so far as the writer of the book never once lost sight of the sublime idea of a future deliverance—a hope which became the very keystone of Christianity:

The whole latter half of *Daniel* seems designed as a message of comfort to the children of God in their deep sorrow and distress from its prediction of the complete overthrow of their enemies and the coming of a Messiah or anointed one.

Several notable additions were made to the Book of *Daniel*. The first of them relates the story of Susanna. We are told how, early in the period of the Captivity, the beautiful and pious Susanna, wife of Joachim, was walking alone in her garden and was there observed by two elders, who were also judges. The beauty of Susanna inflamed their hearts with lustful desires, and they made infamous suggestions to her. Susanna, the pure of heart, remonstrated with them and repulsed them, and the two elders, mortified by her attitude and seeking vengeance, brought a false accusation of adultery against her. She was found guilty of the charge, but on her way to the place of execution the prophet Daniel interposed. By skilful cross-questioning of the two elders, apart, he convinced the people of the innocence of Susanna.

It is possible that this story may have its origin in a Babylonian legend, which is to be found also in the Koran. The first part of it is founded on a tradition contained in the Talmud and Midrash of two elders, who, during Israel's captivity in Babylonia, seduced some of the women on the pretext that by so surrendering themselves they should be honoured above all women by being the mother of the anointed one, the Messiah.

It is very interesting to observe how this idea of the human birth of the Messiah through a woman goes through the history of religions. Later on, we find it in Josephus, as taking place in Rome. In the Talmud it is the means whereby the so-called supernatural birth of Jesus himself is accounted for.

XIV. Folk Stories

Early in the years of the Captivity the exiles of high spirits in Babylon had begun to rewrite the legends of their people. If they could not be allowed to preach at least they could write. The writing was on scrolls by Hebrew scribes. They patched together the ancient traditions that had come down to them on old, worn scraps of parchment or by word of mouth. Much of the substance of the Old Testament, as we have it, is the work of the exiles of the Captivity. The prophets, though they thundered against the iniquities of Israel and preached woe, woe, also foretold comfort when the period of captivity and contempt should be over. The Messiah should come to gather his people from the far corners of the earth, the Temple should be rebuilt in Jerusalem, and all the nations should worship the God who had given this law to the Jews on Mount Sinai.

The theory of the writers was that the reason why the chosen people had been crushed was because of their sins. Yahweh had not been defeated when Israel and Judah were destroyed. On the contrary, Yahweh, himself, the God of Israel, had destroyed his people to punish them for their idolatrous ways. Yahweh could not be punished by other gods. He was Lord of Heaven and all the earth. He, alone, was God, and it was to establish this belief that the unhappy souls in exile wrote their new history.

But the history they wrote was not of the past alone. The Hebrews in exile believed that their story was not ended, but only beginning. God would, of course, take pity on them once more and restore them to their own land. God's "anointed one" would himself then be king. From that time onward joy and peace would reign throughout the land. All would be well with God's children for ever.

XV. The Temple Rebuilt

At length the returned exiles laboured on the rebuilding of the Sanctuary. In less than five years their work was done. The new Temple was much like that of Solomon, but it lacked all Solomon's splendour. The old men wept with disappointment when they looked on the second Temple. Some of the exiles remaining in Babylonia sent a heavy golden crown to Jerusalem for the coronation of the

Messiah. In the meantime, Cyrus, who had been selected as the Messiah himself, had died. His empire was about to crumble to pieces. The returned exiles thought that in a moment all the kings of the world would be swept away, and God's anointed one alone would reign at last.

Years passed. Nothing happened. The Messiah did not arise. The hearts of the Jews in Jerusalem turned to Galilee. They lost faith in God and His prophets. God had failed them. The prophets had promised glories if His Temple were rebuilt, and God had not kept His word. The prophets were liars. God was a deceiver. The Messiah would never come.

The fifty years of neglect during the Exile had left the land a wilderness. Enemies now came plundering and raiding. The Philistine from the west; the Samaritan from the north. Judah was a very little country. Only twenty miles from end to end.

But still a tiny remnant of the minority of this little country clung to God and His promise.

XVI. Nehemiah

Then came Nehemiah, a Jew, who had been a high official in a Persian court. He was full of faith. He set about building a high wall around the broken half-ruined Jerusalem. Many of those who had remained in exile in Babylonia began to throng back to the homeland. But the old yearning for the coming of the reign of peace was now despised. The new race of prophets looked forward to the establishment of a physically powerful empire. The old dream of a Messiah, who would bring justice and freedom to all men, was converted into a craving for a war lord who would demand atonement in blood from every heathen who refused to bring sacrifices to Jerusalem three times a year. The Jews alone were considered blessed. The Gentiles were all accursed.

But back in their own land things did not go as they had expected. The divine kingdom did not come. There were ages of further sin and suffering, with adversaries and oppressors without and within, and the early faith which Abraham brought out of Arabia had repeatedly degenerated into paganism. Each of the foreign peoples in turn had left their impressions on the Hebrew religion. It had taken something from its Assyrian masters, something from its Babylonian masters, something from its Persian masters, something from its Greek, Egyptian and Syrian masters.

These influences can be traced both in their good effects and bad. The marvel is that anything of its original faith remained. That the essential soul of it survived all the tumultuous fight for material existence is, I think, due to the Messianic hope. The Jew never lost his confidence in the promise given to Abraham and renewed in David. The little line of Hebrew prophets never became extinct. They kept alive the soul of their hope—that God would work out their salvation, that some day and somehow He would rescue them from their conquerors, He would cleanse them of their sins and forgive their transgressions, and make them, as He had said, His own people, and through them, and by them, would come the redemption of the world.

It was a long travail, and perhaps the bitterest part of it was not the loss of their Ten Tribes to the Assyrians, or their captivity to the Babylonians, but their sufferings under their own rulers—or what seemed to be, and claimed to be, their own rulers.

CHAPTER XI

The Coming of the Romans

I. Troublous Times in Jerusalem

THE REBUILDING of the Temple was completed in the second year of Darius Hystaspes (520 B.C.). The waste cities were also rebuilt and repeopled. During the long reign of Darius the Jews were blessed with a high degree of material prosperity. The supreme spiritual authority was vested in a society of pious and pre-eminently learned men, founded by Ezra, out of which grew "the Great Synagogue." During the life of Nehemiah the breach between the Jews and Samaritans became final, by the erection on Mount Gerizim of a rival temple to that of Jerusalem and the creation of a new priesthood.

For five centuries after this, Jerusalem knew not a single generation of peace. Internal factions tore it to pieces; the city was the possession in turn of Persian, Macedonian, Syrian, Egyptian, and Roman; it was never wholly independent.

Alexander the Great, on his way to conquer the whole East, did not deem it necessary to storm Jerusalem. The inhabitants submitted (332 B.C), and he even deigned to have sacrifices offered on his behalf to the national god of his new subjects, a great number of whom he carried away to Egypt to people his newly founded city of Alexandria. Thirty years later Ptolemy Soter, who had become king of Egypt, invaded Syria, took Jerusalem and carried off 100,000 of the inhabitants. For a hundred years Judæa remained under Egyptian rule, and to force the Jews into the Greek religion the temple of Jerusalem was dedicated to Jupiter Olympus; idol temples were built in every village; pigs were sacrificed on the altars; the Jewish rites and ceremonies—the observance of the Sabbath, the sacrifices enjoined by law, the rite of circumcision—were forbidden. Had it not been for one family of illustrious rebels—the Maccabees—the religion of the Jews would have been abandoned and their nationality lost.

During the rule of Antiochus, or about the year 165 B.C., there lived at Modin (a small place between Jerusalem and Joppa), a priest named Mattathias. He had five sons: John, Simeon, Judas, Eleazar and Jonathan. Mattathias, lamenting the condition of his people, called upon them not to obey the command of Antiochus. He took sword and slew both the man who sacrificed as Antiochus had commanded and the king's general who compelled him to sacrifice, overthrew the altar to Jupiter, and cried, "If any one be zealous for the laws of his country and for the worship of God, let him follow me."

He then went into the desert with his sons. Many followed them. The king's general went in pursuit of them in the desert, and fought them on the Sabbath Day. The Jews would not defend themselves on the Sabbath Day. But Mattathias and his sons taught them to defend their lives even on the Sabbath, or they would all perish. They were persuaded and fought in self-defence, and this rule prevailed thereafter among the Jews.

Mattathias now gathered a great army about him, overthrew the altars and slew all that broke the laws of Moses.

Thus he ruled for one year. Then he fell into a distemper, and calling his sons, said, "O my sons, I am going the way of all earth; but I beseech you to be mindful of the desires of your father. Recover your ancient form of government, dispose your souls to die for your laws and God will not forget you. Your bodies are mortal, but they receive a sort of immortality by the remembrance of what actions they have done. Therefore, scruple not to lose your lives. Take Maccabæus for your general because of his courage and strength."

Then Mattathias died, and was buried at Modin.

II. Judas Maccabæus

After the death of Mattathias, his son, Judas Maccabæus, took upon himself the administration of affairs, and cast their enemies out of the country. Thereupon the general of the Samaritan forces took up arms against Judas. But Judas beat him.

Then Antiochus himself got together his army, with many mercenaries, and sent them into Judæa to destroy Jerusalem.

Judas met the great army and addressed his own soldiers, saying, "O, my fellow soldiers, this is the time for courage and contempt of danger. Either you conquer now or your seed will be wiped out if you lose this battle. Fight manfully, believing that besides the glorious reward of liberty you shall obtain everlasting glory."

At break of day the battle began. The forces of Antiochus were utterly routed, and Judas achieved his first great victory.

Not long after King Antiochus Epiphanes died in Persia, after an attempt to capture and plunder a rich temple of Diana.

Meantime, Judas made his way to Jerusalem and at once cleansed the Temple by throwing out the pagan idols introduced by the pagan king who had tried to impose his paganism on the Jews in their Sanctuary. This was in the year 165 B.C. He established the feast of "Lights" and other ceremonies with the singing of psalms and hymns, and he did much to keep alive the hope of a Messiah. But for him it might have been extinguished. He became the Messiah of the Jewish people.

Quite clearly during the time of Judas Maccabæus the belief in the resurrection of the just was universal. It is exemplified in the following incident.

When the pagan king is torturing her sons, a mother says to them, "I know not how ye came into my womb, neither was it that I bestowed upon thee thy spirit and thy life, and it is not I that brought into order the first elements of each one of thee. Therefore, the Creator of the world, who fashioned the generation of man, in mercy give back to thee again both thy spirit and thy life as ye now continue thine own selves for the Lord's sake."

The king appeals to the mother to save the last of her sons. She laughs the cruel tyrant to scorn, and says to her son, "My son, have pity on me that carried thee nine months in my womb, and gave thee suck three years, I beseech thee, child, lift up thine eyes to the heavens, and recognize that God made them. . . . Fear not this butcher, but prove thyself worthy of thy brethren, accept thy death, that in the mercy of God I may receive thee again with thy brethren."

This is a significant illustration of the belief in the resurrection of the just. The idea at the back of it is that those who do great and noble deeds shall not go down to extinction, but shall live again, everlastingly. But there is nothing yet about the resurrection of the unjust—the eternal punishment.

Always a great soldier, Judas at length fell fighting with 1,000 men against 20,000 in Judæa; 200 of these fled and deserted him.

The remaining 800 wanted him to retire and fight another day, but he said, "Let not the sun see such a thing that I should shew my back to the enemy." The enemy encompassed Judæa. He stood, the last to stand, and fell with his face to the enemy.

Seeing their general fallen, the others fled. Two of his brothers received his body by a treaty with the enemy, carried it to the village of Modin and buried it in the tomb of his father, Mattathias. This was in 160 B.C.

So fell the greatest of the Jewish warriors since David. A man of great heart and great valour.

Judas had been high priest in Jerusalem for three years. After his death his brother Jonathan became high priest and general of the Jewish army. The Maccabæan revolt lasted altogether about forty years, the government being a theocracy—a Jewish theocracy ruled by high priests.

III.   The Sanhedrin

It was at this period that the Sanhedrin was established as the supreme national tribunal. It consisted of seventy-one members, and was presided over by the Nasi, at whose side stood the Ab-Beth-Din, or father of the tribunal. Its members were of different classes of society—priests, elders, scribes, doctors of the law and others exalted by eminent learning. The limits of its jurisdiction are not known with certainty; but there is no doubt that the supreme decision over life and death, the ordeal of a suspected wife, and the like criminal matters were exclusively in its hands. By degrees, the whole internal administration of the commonwealth was vested in this body, and it became necessary to establish minor courts, similarly composed, all over the country.

IV.   The Dream of the Messiah

Amid all the disturbing changes brought by the passing centuries, the dream of the Messiah lived on. It had two aspects, that of the city of the promised Kingdom of God and that of the man who was to preside over it. The city remained the same (it was always Jerusalem), but the man changed with the changing conditions of the people. When they had heard of him first he was indeed a great king, but he was also a great saint, a suffering saint, the despised and rejected of men, who was to sacrifice himself and all his worldly honour and glory to save his people from the consequences of their sins and to make their peace with God. But now he was a conquering hero, a mighty man, an essentially human creature, a fighting champion, who, by God's help, and the strength of His out-stretched arm, was to scatter their enemies, to gather all the Gentile nations about him as his willing subjects, and to rule them from the throne of David according to the law of Moses, with Jerusalem as the centre of the world.

But the centuries passed, and the grandiose dream had not been fulfilled. Abuses and corruption continued. Great reformers arose among the Hebrews, who fought for the purification of their faith, triumphed and fell. Then sixty-three years before the beginning of the Christian era a great new power, the Roman empire, took possession of Palestine. The law of the Roman empire was force, and it knew no other law. It was out to conquer all the countries of the earth, and Palestine was worth conquering—a hundredfold better worth conquering than ancient Britain (which Rome was besieging about the same time), although it was less than a fifth as big. The narrow strip of territory along the east coast of the Mediterranean was perhaps the richest trade route of the world—the route north from Egypt to Damascus, and west from Mesopotamia to Tyre, which was one of the greatest of ancient seaports.

The Roman way of governing its subject states was to send governors and procurators, with armies of occupation, to look after its rights of possession, to make a frequent census and to gather tribute, but to leave the native kings to reign as vassal princes. Their principle of government was to conciliate the conquered people if they could, and, if they could not, to crush them. The pagan Romans could not conciliate the Hebrews, therefore they crushed them. When they set up their standards in the synagogues, proclaiming the divinity of their Roman emperors, the Hebrews flung them out, as insults to their religion, which knew no god but God. The result was war, and the blood of the Hebrews was mingled with their sacrifices.

Strange as it may seem to modern Christians, the Jews before Christ were a warlike people, particularly the Galileans. To read the earliest of Jewish historians is to realize that, for many years before the beginning of the Christian era and at least seventy years after it, Palestine was a scene of almost perpetual warfare, with thousands, tens of thousands, sometimes hundreds of thousands of persons left dead on the battlefields. More than once during the reign of the only Roman procurator whose infamy perpetuated his name, the streets of Jerusalem were strewn with the slain.

When the Jewish people turned for help to their native kings, they found them bought and sold and in the pockets of their Roman masters, the adulterous and incestuous house of the Herods, currying their favour, imitating their sexual vices and living before the eyes of all in flagrant violation of the laws of Moses. Worse still, when they turned to their high priests to protect them in the rights of their religion, they found that the powerful heads of their religious courts, their Sanhedrin, who should have been the independent successors of Aaron, were the lackeys and slaves of the pagan procurators, appointed by them and subject to dismissal at their pleasure.

Among the Essenes, the law of the Sabbath was so strict that they would not raise a hand to defend their lives on that day. When the Romans entered Jerusalem they did so on the Jewish Sabbath, and it is said that many of the priests continued to worship at their altars, and were slaughtered as they poured libation and burned incense.

According to their usual plan the Roman conquerors left native rulers behind them. Antipater, of an Idumæan family, a half-Jew, was made procurator of Judæa. Later, the Roman senate, at the instance of Mark Antony, made the son of Antipater, Herod, afterwards called Herod the Great, king of Judæa. Still later, Herod the Great became king of all Palestine. This was about the year 37 B.C.

V.   Herod the Great

As king of the Jews Herod was completely subject to his Roman masters. He was formally an orthodox Jew, but he broke the laws of Moses repeatedly. At one moment he plundered the treasury of the Temple. He nominated the high priests, and compelled them to dispense the sacred law according to his wishes. He put his own profit above the law always. A corrupt king makes a corrupt people. Palestine, during Herod's time, was often lawless. There were brigands and burglars in great numbers in the inland towns. The seaports were haunted by pirates. In the great trading route from north to south, the caravans were often robbed by brigands, who found it easy to escape into the mountains on the southern side bordering on the sea, and into the deserts on the east beyond Jordan.

Herod paid tribute to Rome, farming the taxes. In these he laid heavy burdens on the people.

He built temples and palaces, amphitheatres and cities all over Palestine with the money he took from the people. His effort was to imitate the Greek civilization, which distinguished the Roman empire from barbarous lands.

He was from first to last a sedulous courtier of the Roman empire, and was, for a time, rewarded with the confidence of Augustus.

In his personal morals he was a low creature. Apparently his political power was strictly limited. It is not certain that he had power over life and death. At an important moment he had to appeal to the Emperor for authority to execute two prisoners whom he had condemned.

VI. A Great Spiritual Awakening

The hope of the Messiah had seemed to die down during these hard times, but it was not dead. Perhaps the great religious sects, the Pharisees in their formalism, and the Sadducees in their rationalism, had lost faith in it, and begun to talk of it as a prophet's vision, a poet's dream, that would come to nothing. It is difficult to see much sign of it in the life of the Jews immediately before Christ, but it was there, a slumbering fire in a hidden place. That hidden place was the heart of the common people, the poor and the oppressed. They had had enough of war; they were crushed to the earth with taxation, direct and indirect (tributes to Rome and to the Temple, plus two per cent on everything they ate and drank and clothed themselves with), and they were looking to Heaven for their salvation. They found it there. It was the old Messianic hope in a new form. The Redeemer was to be a spiritual messenger from God. He was to be both human and divine, a Son of Man as well as a Son of God, and above all, a Prince of Peace. When he came it might be in the clouds, surrounded by a great company of angels, or from the hills like David, newly anointed by God, or he might be born of a virgin in some home of the house of David. But he would come soon, and then the poor would be made rich and the wronged would be righted, and the sick would be healed and the broken-hearted would be comforted, and there would be peace in all the world.

This revived and yet more grandiose dream, which gathered up the threads of old prophecy and assembled them afresh, first found expression in a small religious sect called the Essenes. They made little figure in history, being at the utmost some 6,000 out of a total population of perhaps 6,000,000. A few hundreds of them lived in religious houses on the plains by the Dead Sea, practising the utmost austerities, having all things in common, never marrying or begetting children, only waiting and watching for the Kingdom of Heaven that was soon to be established, and the spiritual King who was to come. The rest were scattered over the country, chiefly in humble homes or among people who had no homes at all—friendless old men and widowed old women who gathered about the Temple, thinking the Messiah must surely first appear in that sacred place, and praying they might not die until they had seen the glory of their Lord.

VII. Heathen Religions

Assuredly, the Messianic idea—that of a divine being who was to save the world from its sufferings—began very early in the history of religion. It displayed itself in heathen religions long before Christ. The divine king, in the character of a redeemer of his people, is to be found in Egyptian religions of the remotest antiquity. The Brahm-Hindu religion includes a god who is to die to save his worshippers from the consequences of their sins, and Jesus himself was a mediator before he became the Supreme God of all. And then the Mithraic religion, which survived to the time of Christ, contained a profoundly moving belief in a king who had paid the price of his life to save his people.

Shall we, then, deny that among the silences of Scripture in certain of the first chapters of *Genesis* there is not the foreshadowing of the Messianic hope, or that this exalted conception did not have its slow development through gross and barbaric rites, before it found its perfection in the spirit of Christ?

If so, what were the highest of the rites in the religion of primitive man? And shall we not be compelled to admit that idolatry itself, in its apparently most barbaric form, played its part in the making of the religion of the Cross? Among the Hebrews, as well as among the heathens, its first form was allied to that of kingship. The kingship idea had earlier forms, such as those of the priest and the judge. The idea of the anointed king was essentially the same as that of the Messiah. The earlier forms failed, as the persons representing the Messianic idea failed, to save the people.

Moses was, in a sense, the Messiah. David was, in a sense, the Messiah of the Hebrew people until by sin he fell. Nevertheless, he was so beloved of God, that God promised him that although he should not himself establish the kingdom of God on earth, yet the Messiah should be born of his loins.

The Hebrew Messianic idea down to the death of David was a political idea. The kingdom of God to be established by the son of David was to be an earthly kingdom, to belong to the Hebrew people to the exclusion of all other peoples, and it was to govern the world. The descendants of David, however, fell into idolatry and sin, and God punished them by delaying the advent of the Messiah. The dynasty of David was broken up, the Hebrew people were taken captive and the throne of David was occupied by heathen kings.

The prophets then arose to speak in the name of God. They claimed that God had spoken to them and told them what to say. The substance of what God told His prophets to say was that they were being punished by captivity (first at the hands of Assyrian kings and afterwards at the hands of Babylonian kings) because they had been unfaithful to their own God, Jehovah. But that God's anger would yet be lifted away, and He would forgive His people and fulfil the promise He had made to David —in short, the Messiah should arise in spite of all.

Some of these promises were in fact fulfilled. But the sins and idolatries of the Hebrew people continued. Then the prophets changed the character of the Messianic idea. It was no longer a personal Messiah who was to arise, and no longer was the Messiah to be a conquering Messiah. The Hebrew people themselves were to be the Messiah of all mankind, and this world Messiah was to suffer and to die, and to rise again and to overcome the world for God. The Jewish nation was to die and rise again.

Again, this form of the Messianic idea failed, owing to the continued faithlessness of the Hebrew people. God allowed the

Egyptians and then the Greeks to possess the Promised Land of the Hebrews, and the Messianic idea lost heart and almost died out, except among the faithful, who were chiefly the common people.

Then arose the Maccabæan revolt, the purging of Israel, the reconquest of the Temple from the idolatrous foreign kings, the re-establishment of the supremacy of the laws of Moses, and the restoration in the hearts of the people of the early Messianic idea of a son of David. Simultaneous with the re-establishment of the political Messianic idea came the rise of the sect of the Pharisees, and the development of a semi-spiritual Messianic idea. When the Messiah came he would come as a spiritual son of David. He would come in the clouds surrounded by legions of angels. He would hold a great assize of the living and the dead, who would rise from their graves, or come from Sheol. Then, after the great judgment, the new kingdom of God would be established on earth by the Messiah, and he would reign over it for ever.

VIII. Pharisees and Sadducees

But once more the Hebrew Messianic idea underwent a change. The Hebrews were divided into two chief sects—the Pharisees, who believed in the resurrection as an essential part of this Messianic scheme, and the Sadducees, who did not believe in the resurrection, and totally rejected the Messianic idea, because they disbelieved in the idea of kingship. The Sadducees were the priests, and they wished to go back to the idea of the time of Samuel.

On the top of this religious squabble among the Hebrew people about the Messianic idea came a political fact of great importance. The new and great empire of Rome took possession of Palestine, and established a kind of self-government under Roman control.

The effect of this on the two sects was that the Pharisees (the ruling Pharisees) lost their old fervour and degenerated into formalists in their observance of the law, while the Sadducees, who had been placed by the Romans in the position of high priests, had thrown in their lot with their masters and desired nothing so little as the fulfilment of the old Davidic dream, except the Daniel idea of a half-Davidic, half-spiritual Messiah.

This condition nearly killed the ancient Messianic hope among the ruling classes. But not among the humbler people, who were the pious people, suffering under the tyrannies of their Roman rulers and smarting under the cruelties of their religious chiefs, the Sadducees, who taxed them heavily for the Temple, its priests, and its upkeep, while starving the synagogues and the little country rabbis. As a consequence there grew up underground, as it were, another deep Messianic hope.

This was immediately before the time of Jesus of Nazareth, and what exactly were to be the means whereby the new Messianic hope could attain to fulfilment is by no means clear. For instance, we do not know that the Messianic hope, immediately before Jesus, centred in a suffering and dying Messiah. Almost certainly it did not. The disciples had no conception of it. The idea bewildered them. Nothing was said then, or in Christ's time, that justifies the thought. On the contrary, much is said (by Simeon in the Nativity story and by the disciples at various moments) which justifies the opinion that, under the tyrannies of their masters in Church and State and the manifest demoralization of their country, the Jews immediately before Jesus had swung back to the earliest form of the Davidic Messianic idea— that somewhere and somehow God would send a great king of the Jews who (perhaps by the help of angels) would drive out the Romans, expel from the Temple the corrupt Jewish rulers of it, cleanse their religion, and establish a new kingdom on earth.

This was chiefly a political aspiration, although religion entered into it. It was transcendent only in a sort of secret sense. It was a kind of hidden and secret hope. It was to find its fulfilment soon, but how and when nobody knew.

IX. When Jesus Came

Then came Jesus of Nazareth. Born in humble circumstances in Galilee. Place unknown. Precise date unknown. Some time round about the period of the death of Herod the Great. Possibly (not probably) before that event. Possibly a few years after it. Before he appeared on the stage of the world John the Baptist had arisen. The Messianic hope of the Baptist was not political. The kingdom he foretold was religious. It recognized the existing condition of Jewish suffering as God's punishment for the sins of the Jews. In this he was another witness. He called for repentance of sin and baptism as a sign of repentance. He called for a righteous conduct as a means of escaping the doom that was to come to the sinner on the establishment of a new kingdom. That kingdom was to be presided over by a Messiah, a son of God. He was to come soon. He (the Baptist) was his forerunner.

Clearly, John believed that the kingdom that was to come was to be an earthly kingdom founded on righteousness, not on force of arms, on military power. Hence, John makes no reference to the expulsion of the Romans. He never got into trouble with Rome. But he does very clearly indicate the downfall of the corrupt Jewish hierarchy. He condemns the Pharisees. In short, to John, the kingdom to come, in which the righteous should be saved, and from which the unrighteous should be excluded, was to be a kingdom of the soul, *working on earth.*

The Messianic idea apparently went through developments. In its first expression it was akin to that of the later Isaiah. It was a great spiritual regeneration. The broken-hearted were to be healed, the captives were to be delivered. And the Messiah himself was to be the medium whereby this was to be brought to pass. In short, the prophecy of the moral regeneration of mankind and the liberation of the people from their bondage were to be brought about by him.

Later, and towards the end of his life, the Messianic idea of Jesus separated itself entirely from life in this world. The welfare of the body no longer mattered to him. What the Romans could do did not matter. What the religious leaders of the Jews could do did not matter. Nothing mattered to him except the welfare of the soul. Therefore, the kingdom he looked for was no longer in any sense a kingdom of this world. He cared nothing for the restoration of the kingdom of David. If he were the Messiah, he did not claim to be the son of David. Rather, he renounced it.

Jesus made the much higher claim of being the Son of God. Therefore, the kingdom he looked for was a kingdom of Heaven, a kingdom of God. In a word, he centred his Messianic hope on the salvation of his people from their sins and their inheritance of a kingdom of Heaven.

Did this mean after death? I think it did. It meant everlasting life. He had left behind him the teaching of his earlier years. That was good, but not all. To win the right to this kingdom of Heaven, of God, something was necessary. First, complete repentance. Next, a sacrifice to God for the sins of man. What was that sacrifice? The sacrifice of the Messiah, the Son of God, himself. In short, his own life, his death on the Cross, in suffering, in degradation, in shame. God would accept this as a means of atonement for man's sin.

If this bears a chilling resemblance to the pagan idea of the sacrifice of the God-man to make reconciliation with the supreme deity for the transgression of mankind it must be so. I cannot escape from it. I think it a far greater thought than that of the Jewish Messianic idea that is associated with the restoration of the dynasty of David. That is of the earth earthy. This is of the Heaven heavenly.

I think Jesus went to his death with that hope. He passed through the agony of Gethsemane, the shame and suffering of the Cross with that thought—not that as a son of David he was helping to drive out the Romans and expel the corrupters of the law from the Temple, but that, as the Son of God, he was laying down his life to ransom the souls of men from the burden and the penalty, the everlasting damnation of sin.

Beyond this last phase of the Messianic hope, the idea of the Messiah has never since gone. For hundreds of years, perhaps thousands, the Messianic idea had been struggling to fulfil the needs of man—the needs of his soul as well as of his body. In Christ (Jesus of Nazareth) it did fulfil that need. And during the 2,000 years since Jesus, the Messianic idea has remained. It has not developed. Perhaps it is impossible that it should develop.

Observe that Jesus alone in his time understood the theory of the Messiah in this sense. His disciples never understood it so during his lifetime. They never grasped the thought that the kingdom he foretold was not a kingdom of this world. Down to the day of his death, they continued to think of the kingdom as of this world. Even after his death they thought of it so. They never grasped the idea that in order to bring about the kingdom he looked for he must first die. When he talked about the necessity of his dying they did not understand him. They only saw him beset by his enemies, who wished to take his life. They were so far from reconciling themselves to his death that they took swords to Gethsemane to protect him from death. They never, for one moment, understood what he said (if he did say it) about rising from the dead after three days. They were bewildered by such talking. It conflicted with every expectation, every idea of the Christ who, when he came, was to establish his earthly kingdom and reign over it for ever. They never understood what he meant by coming again to them.

END OF BOOK I

BOOK II

Jesus Christ

CHAPTER I

The Nativity

I. A Personal Study

THE MOST MOVING, effective and popular form to give to a Life of Jesus would be, perhaps, to make it a *personal study* —to make every incident illustrate and develop his character; to heighten and deepen the impression of his personality; to show his humanity, his pity, his love, his indignation at wrong, his eagerness to help the weak; to protect the oppressed; to be the champion of the poor, the heavily-laden, even the sinful. This would reach the hearts of readers, as no account of his divine and supernatural power would do. Not to separate him from humanity, but to unite him to it—in his temptations, in his momentary failures, in his ultimate triumphs.

If this could be done, without injuring the divine side, it would bring him very close to humanity in its sorrows and sins.

To read into every incident the human creature, to show the great but always human impulses that move him. And to carry that on to the last moment on the Cross, the last cry in the hour of death, and to the last appearance after the Resurrection, the final moment of parting with his disciples before his Ascension.

It would be a great thing to show, first, his love of his little group of disciples, and then their corresponding love of him— even when he seemed to fail them at the end, or when they had failed him.

If all this could be done without sacrificing his higher qualities, it could hardly fail to have an immense and worldwide appeal. It would speak not only to those who wish to bend the knee to him as a transcendent genius, as one who is scarcely distinguishable from God, as one who is, perhaps, one with God, but to the humbler and vaster multitude of those who want him as a friend, a helper, a guide, a protector, a brother and yet a saviour, a redeemer, the being who has ransomed them from sin, has borne the burden of their sins and wiped them out, and, above all, has made their peace with the Father.

II.   Did Jesus Ever Exist?

But let us, without irreverence, begin with a fundamental question. Did Jesus of Nazareth ever exist? This is a question which was first asked in Alexandria in the third century of the Christian era by the pagan philosopher Celsus. It has been asked since by thousands, not of rationalists only, but of devout believers all over the world. Was he an historical person, a physical being of flesh and blood, or only a sublime myth, a divine idea? There is not a little to justify the question. We have no such knowledge of his life as we have of almost any other person of world importance. Renan, a French historian of high distinction, has said that if we had to write all we know of Jesus beyond possible contradiction we should have to limit ourselves to a few lines. And Strauss, a German theologian of no less eminence, has said that all that can be recorded with certainty about Jesus could be written on the shortest piece of paper.

Yet how near we are to the age in which Jesus is believed to have lived. His life as it has come down to us is almost a contemporary story. Julius Cæsar was assassinated only about fifty years before the birth of Christ. Those middle-aged lovers, Antony and Cleopatra, died only some twenty-five years earlier. Livy, the Roman aristocratic yet republican philosopher, was still living when Jesus, according to our chronology, was twenty years of age. Virgil was then writing his *Æneid* and Horace his *Odes*. Ovid was still alive. Augustus and Tiberius were his contemporaries.

Thus Jesus was, according to tradition, only a little way back in our tale of time. He was still in his twenties when the Roman armies were on the borders of the Rhine, and fourteen years of age when the first Roman governor was appointed to Britain. It was not more than forty years after Christ that the British revolted against the Romans and there was a bloody battle at Sunbury-on-Thames.

How does it come to pass that the history of his own age has little or nothing to say about him? Josephus, a fellow-Jew, born in Jerusalem only six years after the Crucifixion, and becoming governor of Galilee, wrote a long History of the Jews, mentioning

Jesus only once, and even this was probably an interpolation by a later writer. Plutarch makes no reference to Jesus. Tacitus has no more to say of him than could be put into two or three short sentences. Philo, although he is said to have been a friend of Luke, to have met Peter or Paul in Rome, and to have been still alive when the early converts were reading the Gospels in Alexandria, never alludes to him. The same may be said of Pliny the Younger, of the many authorities of the Talmud, and nearly every writer coming fifty years after him. Jesus may be said to have passed practically unnoticed through a world in which some 600,000,000 persons now owe him civil, political, and spiritual significance. He was ringed round with the world's greatest activities without appearing to take any part in them. What a parody is the life of Jesus if we are to take it as a record of fact!

III. Written Testimony

When and where was he born? We have only the most meagre authorities. The earliest Christian authorities are four little books, each about the size of a modern pamphlet. They are said to be *according* to four men who were his followers and disciples. They were all persons of humble birth and limited education—fishermen, tax-gatherers, tent-makers, and such like. Whether they actually wrote the books in question, or dictated them, is uncertain. They are said to be *according* to St. Matthew, St. Mark, St. Luke and St. John, apparently meaning by that they were not actually penned by the persons whose names they bore, but were intended to represent their preaching, their recollections and their spirit.

It is probable that in their first form they were written in the tongue of their native province—Aramaic—long ago a dead language and now read by few. This appears to have been about twenty to thirty years after the death of their Master, and when, thirty to forty years after that, the Faith he had founded took on new aspects, the little books were rewritten in another and more widely read language, the Greek, and this, no doubt, meant serious textual changes. Of Jesus himself it may safely be said that although we know he was widely and deeply read in the Hebrew Scriptures, and although he went through a trial under a Roman governor who could possibly speak to him only in Greek, and there is no mention of a translator, yet it is not certain (except for the record of one pregnant moment) that he could write.

Only one of them is unquestionably the record of an eye-witness. One other is believed to have been written under the inspiration of another eye-witness, a boy who musthave lived with his mother in Jerusalem in his teens, at the time when Jesus was put to death there. A third is clearly the writing (perhaps directly into Greek) of a person of another race, who wrote under the influence of a learned half-Jewish, half-Roman proselyte. And the fourth, coming long after the earlier three, is probably from the pen of a Greek scholar, possibly a priest who was educated at Alexandria.

The four small books were for the better part of 2,000 years our chief authorities on the life of Jesus. They were often called biographies, but they were not biographies in the modern sense of the word. The utmost that can be said of them is that they are, in some cases, collections of moving anecdotes about Jesus, and sometimes passages from the best-remembered of his sublime discourses. Nevertheless, they claimed to tell the story of Jesus from his birth to his death, and as such they give us all that we actually know of him with any certainty as an historical being.

It is very little, and often very contradictory. In none of the four Gospels, and certainly not in the supplementary book called the *Acts of the Apostles,* is even the date and place of the birth of Jesus exactly stated. At first, it appears to have been believed that he was born in the year of the beginning of the Christian era, and even Luther, down to his day, clung to that opinion.

IV. The Story of the Gospels

The Gospels belong to the second half of the first century of the Christian era. They are of the highest value because they take us back to the period which followed the death of Jesus, and sometimes to eye-witnesses of his acts. Presumably they were written late in the second half of that first century. Why was this? Because the early Christian Church, represented by the disciples, did not expect that any succeeding ages would require such knowledge. It did not believe that there would be any succeeding ages. The idea of a world 2,000 years after the death of Jesus hungering to know every intimate fact of his life, and the least thing he did and said, and all that happened to him on his earthly pilgrimage was the remotest thing from the thoughts of the early Christians. Assuredly, the immediate friends, followers and disciples of Jesus believed that the end of the world was near, that some of them would not see death until Jesus had come again and established a new world in which everybody would know him. Seeing that the world was so soon to come to an end, why write books for the future?

The apostles were solely concerned in preserving in the heart of their followers the living image of him whom they expected to see so soon returning in the clouds.

There is another explanation, a more obvious one, namely, that the disciples were ignorant and uneducated men, that by far the larger number of them were probably unable to write long, consecutive stories, that only one or two or three could make any attempt to do so, and that the Gospels bearing their names, which came later, were written, perhaps under their inspiration, by other hands.

Later, as the younger generation of followers arose who had not known Jesus, had not sat at meat with him or heard him speak or seen him do his mighty works, it seemed to become necessary that some record should be made for temporary use. This is evidently the limited use made of the earliest Christian writings.

Apparently, the earliest Christian writings circulated were the letters of St. Paul. But it is possible that before the first of St. Paul's letters there was a Gospel written, perhaps by Matthew, who, being a tax-gatherer, may be presumed to have had, to some extent, the pen of a ready writer. This Gospel is now known as the Gospel according to the Hebrews, and was almost certainly written in Aramaic. It is now lost, except in so far as passages have been incorporated in the Gospels that come later. It is probable that this Gospel was of the nature of Sibylline Leaves, that it was passed from hand to hand among the disciples, and that if anybody remembered anything not included in it, he either inserted his recollection or mentioned it to Matthew for inclusion.

It is obvious that the Gospel according to the Hebrews concerned itself mainly with the sayings of Jesus. It was intended to keep in memory his discourses. It would not appear that this Aramaic Gospel contained many episodes or facts of the life of Jesus. The Gospel was probably written for the disciples and their followers in Palestine. Such were probably the conditions under which the Gospel was composed, and the purpose it was intended to serve.

The Gospels we now call canonical were written later for all Christians. They bear the mark of their origin, and, to some extent, indications of the place and time at which they were written.

The first, in order of time, was probably *Mark*. St. Mark is understood to have been the interpreter of the apostle Peter. Papias says that Mark wrote down the words and deeds of Jesus from Peter's recollection. He gave a lifelike impression of being an eye-witness. The Gospel of St. Mark was probably written in Rome, and was intended for the Roman converts who may have been asking for a sign as a proof of the Messianic character of Jesus. Hence, his Gospel is full of the supernatural, and concerns itself largely with miracles. It confines itself almost exclusively to a very simple purpose, namely that of narrating the actual facts of the life of Jesus. To Mark, therefore, the chief facts were the miracles which Jesus performed. The miracles are by much the most important element in Mark's story of the life of Jesus. The Gospel of St. Mark was probably written about thirty-four years after the death of Jesus—that is to say about A.D. 64. This was the year of Peter's martyrdom, to which Mark does not refer. Hence, the conclusion would be that it was completed before the martyrdom.

The second of the Gospels in the order of writing was probably *Matthew*. It was, perhaps, written a year or two after *Mark*. The main object of St. Matthew was to compile the sayings of Jesus, to give an account of his sermons, which included his parables—the stories he invented to enforce his doctrines. Therefore, *Matthew* contains less than *Mark* about the miracles and more about the doctrines, particularly the doctrine of the coming of the Kingdom of Heaven. It is obvious that the Gospel of St. Matthew appropriates some of the incidents of *Mark,* just as the Gospel of St. Mark had appropriated some of the discourses of *Matthew* in the earlier Aramaic Gospel according to the Hebrews. *Matthew* tells us little of the external history of Jesus.

The third of the Gospels in the order of time of writing was probably *Luke*. St. Luke was a companion and pupil of St. Paul. He is believed to have been an educated Greek, though this is doubted. He is said to have been a heathen by birth and education, who became first a Jew and afterwards a Christian. This, again, is uncertain. In a prologue to his Gospel, Luke says that his work is a studied composition, founded upon anterior documents—a kind of Gospel anthology based on what the writer conceived to be authentic documents of the record of eye-witnesses. The writer claims to know all previous writers, to have perfect understanding of them, and to be able to give a sure account of what is true to their narratives. Therefore, Luke's Gospel is a combination of Mark's and Matthew's, rejecting some of the one and some of the other, and adding some that is new. The date of *Luke* is uncertain, but it is believed to have come shortly after the two earlier Gospels.

These three Gospels—*Mark, Matthew* and *Luke*—are called the Synoptic Gospels, because they are supposed to give the story of Jesus without serious variations.

The fourth of the Gospels in the order of writing was probably *John.* A gigantic mass of modern literature discusses this Gospel as to points of authenticity, authorship and date. The generally accepted opinion is that it was written under the inspiration of John, the son of Zebedee, after his return from Patmos, and when he must have been approaching ninety years of age. On the other hand, it is held that it was perhaps the work of another John, namely, John the Presbyter, who had been educated by the rabbis of Jerusalem.

The Gospel of St. John does not contain a parable or an exorcism. It presents an allegorical method of interpreting the facts and meaning of the life of Jesus. It is presumed to have been written partly under the inspiration of Hellenic Christianity. It differs from its predecessors in the important facts of life, and in the significance of these important facts. It also differs in the addition of a new spirit, a new interpretation of the life, death and religion of Jesus. In this Gospel, Jesus makes an explicit statement of his divinity: "He that hath sinned against me hath sinned against the Father," and so on.

There are those who hold that this Gospel was actually written by the apostle John, the son of Zebedee; those who hold that it was inspired by John, but written, revised or altered by his disciples; those who deny that it was the work of John, and assert that it is fictitious as a history; those who hold that it is a work of allegorical inspiration, produced about the year A.D. 150. There is a dogmatic interest in *John,* not always present in other Gospels. We feel it vibrate. It is impossible to deny the enormous contribution of the last chapters of *John* to Christian faith.

The fifth historical document in order of writing was the *Acts of the Apostles.* This was probably written about forty years after the death of Jesus. It is believed to be the work of St. Luke, and therefore a kind of continuation of Luke's Gospel. It narrates the events which followed the death of Jesus; his Resurrection, his appearance to the disciples, and his Ascension. It is thought to have been written before the destruction of Jerusalem and of the Temple. Otherwise, it would not have been made a charge against Stephen that he said the Temple would fall. This may be a confusion of thought. Stephen was stoned before the destruction of the Temple, but the historian may have written after the event.

V. The Apocryphal Gospels

Besides these four Gospels and the supplementary *Acts* there appear to have been a large number of other Gospels. St. Luke, in his opening passage, indicates Gospels that no longer exist. The dates of these are necessarily quite uncertain. Their value is equally uncertain. They are obviously of a lower grade of authenticity.

At a later period, extending far into the second century, a number of apocryphal Gospels were written. Many of these are tiresome and puerile amplifications of the four Gospels.

The Church finally grew tired of the thousands of manuscripts, Gospels, and Epistles which gathered about the name of Jesus, and in the fourth century it made a rigid sorting of them, casting out all except the four Gospels and the *Acts.* In doing so, it appears to have been moved by the desire to retain only such documents as experience showed were most nourishing and elevating to the mind and soul of man. Apparently, this was the main test, and, as a result, the sceptical critics have since said that in the fourth century man created Jesus Christ as in the Old Testament man created God.

Thus, the story of Jesus of Nazareth came down to us solely in the four Gospels and the supplementary *Acts* with the letters of St. Paul as accessory witnesses. These together constitute all we know about Jesus of Nazareth. They are the whole sum of our knowledge. All else is inference, deduction and conjecture.

But in casting out all other Gospels and letters and apocrypha, the early Christian Church gave an absolute authority to what was left. In fact, it pronounced what remained to be divinely inspired —the absolute Word of God, not in spirit merely but also in letter. The contents of the New Testament became, therefore, the declared Word of God. Nothing in it was to be questioned. The writers were to be understood to have written under God's direct inspiration. Christians were asked to look upon the Gospels as works written under direct divine guidance. What the writers had written was what God had directed them to write. There was no possibility of error. It was blasphemy to question any chapter, verse or word of what was there set down.

All this was in serious opposition to the conclusions of some of the early fathers of the Church. Origen and Augustine, in particular, who had questioned or even disbelieved certain passages which were contained in the Gospels, doubted the possibility of a literary interpretation of various other chapters as a record of events that actually happened.

But the absolute literary inspiration of the books of the New Testament was maintained by the Church for centuries, and generally acknowledged by the Christian world. Then, little by little came the consciousness that the Gospels could not properly be regarded as divinely inspired, because they contained irreconcilable elements and apparently manifest errors; that the Gospels did not always agree with each other; that their stories often excluded each other, and that it would be possible for religious minds without irreverence to believe that, while God may indeed have inspired the authors of the Gospels to write what they knew about Jesus, He was not to be charged with responsibilities for what they wrote—that their writings were marked by the natural limitations of their personal knowledge, by the limitations of the knowledge of the age in which they lived, of their civilization, their country and their religion.

VI. Perplexing Differences

To this stage, after age-long struggle, the thought of man had reached. The efforts of modern minds to harmonize apparently conflicting stories were failing lamentably. It was not possible to harmonize the whole of the Gospels.

Looking at the Gospels as a whole, they do not always give the impression of being the record of eye-witnesses. They contain much that could not be known to the writers; much that could have been known only to Jesus himself; much that he was extremely unlikely to reveal to anybody. How was the modern mind to account for this? It began to see the influence of earlier writings on the Gospel. These earlier writings were mainly the prophetic writings of the Old Testament.

Prophecies were constantly quoted as having their fulfilment in the facts of the Gospel story. This, in the end, suggested that the prophecy sometimes inspired the Gospel, and that the Gospel fulfilled the prophecy. Little by little the Gospel story had accommodated itself to prophecy, but this was different in different minds—the prophecy which lived most vividly in the mind of St. Matthew lived less vividly in the mind of St. Luke, and hardly at all in the mind of St. Mark. Thus the modern mind accounts for many of the divergencies of the Gospels.

In spite, however, of all differences, there is a miraculous harmony on the central point. The four Gospels differ from each other in minor facts and agree in salient facts. Their chronology is irreconcilable. It is impossible, for instance, to say with certainty on the authority of the Gospels whether the ministry of Jesus was confined to one year or was extended to three years or more. It is impossible to say with certainty on the authority of the Gospels whether Jesus made only one visit to Jerusalem or many. There are countless other differences in the Gospel stories, some of them important, some not important.

But this is a condition which applies to all biography. Set any four authors to write the story of any man who is only ten years dead, and although each of the four may have known their subject intimately, how different is the result! Often it seems as if it were in each case a totally different person who has been described. Such is the result when the writers were the actual intimates of the subject; the constant eye-witness of his actions; and when they were writing only ten years after his death. And yet Jesus was from thirty to sixty years dead when the Gospels were being written, and then they were written not always by eye-witnesses, but by friends of eye-witnesses.

But through it all, almost miraculously, in spite of great perplexing differences, the supreme personality behind the Gospels is fundamentally the same.

In the external incidents, the external parallels, the anxious soul perceives the finger of God.

VII. *The Parentage of Jesus*

The precise date of the birth of Jesus is not known. The Gospel of St. Luke alone gives the definite idea that it was in the region of Cæsar Augustus, and during the taking of the first imperial census, when Cyrenius (Quirinius) was the governor of Syria. And this is doubtful. There are undeniable contradictions between the Gospels and history. Luke's account is irreconcilable with history. The first effort to redate the world for all civilized nations from the birth of Jesus (in the year 752 of the Roman calendar) was soon given up. Later criticism set back the birth of Jesus by two, four, six and even ten years.

The accepted opinion now is that Jesus must have been born within two years before the death of Herod the Great, which took place in the spring of 4 B.C. It is generally believed that Jesus was born at the end of 5 B.C. There has been no agreement as to the month, date or day of his birth. Before the fifth century it is placed in the calendar at periods variously assigned to January 6th, March 25th, April 19th and May 20th. The date now adopted is December 25th.* In the Roman calendar December 25th was the day of the winter solstice, when the sun, reaching its apparent farthest point from the equator, seems to stand still and then to turn back wheel-like in its path through the heavens. It is extremely improbable that it is the absolute historical date.

The name Jesus is supposed to be derived from Joshua, and in every act of the life of Jesus it came to acquire a mystic significance. It was believed to be determined by divine command, and to contain an allusion to his character as the saviour of mankind. But Jesus is a common name in the East, where it is accepted as the Greek form of Joshua, and where there were many thousands of persons named Jesus before, during and after Jesus of Nazareth. Therefore, it is difficult to believe that in the case of

---

*The first certain mention of December 25th is made by a Latin chronographer of A.D. 354 and it runs in English as follows: "The Lord Jesus Christ was born on December 25th—a Friday—and the fifteenth day of the New Moon."

Jesus of Nazareth it bore any special significance that did not apply to countless persons who were certainly not marked out by God for a particular mission.

The father of Jesus, according to common report during his lifetime, was a carpenter, living in Nazareth of Galilee, and called Joseph. We know little about Joseph. Tradition tells us that at the time of the birth of Jesus he was an old man. There was no contemporary evidence of this. It is said that he had been married before he married the mother of Jesus, and had had a considerable family by his first wife. Again, there is not a particle of proof. Both of these statements belong to a period long after Joseph's death, and have the appearance of being devised to account for and support the theory that Jesus came into the world by supernatural means and not as an ordinary man.

Nobody, during the lifetime of Joseph, claimed for him any higher rank than that of a son of the people; but after the death of Jesus it was said that Joseph was of royal descent. Two of the Gospels, *Matthew* and *Luke,* traced his descent from King David. There is a clash of opinions and explanations. Two genealogies given in *Matthew* and *Luke* differ from each other and their historical records. They may be said to exclude each other. Both cannot be true. The only point they have in common is the fundamental claim that Joseph the Carpenter of Galilee was of royal descent, and that, therefore, Jesus, his son, was a son of David.

But then came a serious difficulty. Joseph is said to have been only supposed to be the father of Jesus, having had no part in him as a parent. Therefore, the genealogies of Joseph are on different ground. It is of little consequence whether Joseph was or was not descended from David if he was not the natural father of Jesus.

The way of escape from the gaps and inconsistencies of the genealogies is to say that they formed no part of the original Gospel but were inserted afterwards, perhaps by another hand. This seems highly probable. Modern theologians have attempted to harmonize the genealogies. In *Matthew* it is said that the father of Joseph was Jacob, the son of Matthan. In *Luke* he is said to have been the son of Heli, the son of Matthat, who was the son of Levi. The explanation of the harmonist is that Jacob and Heli were both sons of Matthan, or Matthat, one of them being the actual father of Joseph, the other brought up by him. What wriggling!

The persons who composed the two genealogies of Joseph must have known quite well that the lists were not of any great authenticity. Joseph was a poor carpenter of Nazareth, and to claim that his descent, as far back as David in one case and God in the other, would be known to anybody is to ask too much.

Joseph is described as a carpenter, which is probably what we now, in country towns, call a builder, combining a variety of trades. Clearly, he was widely known and generally respected, and it is possible that in the busy times that followed, when there was much building in Galilee, he became a man of certain substance. We do not know where he died and was buried. We do not know whether he lived long enough to see his son become a great man—the greatest the world has ever seen, although it took it centuries to realize that. We feel that he was an upright and honourable person, who kept his own counsel and knew how to do well by a woman. Tradition says he was an old man when he became betrothed to Mary, a widower with a family of sons and daughters by an earlier marriage, but there is no authority for this in the Bible, and one prefers to think of him as a young man, and that he first saw Mary when he was resting in the market-place of Nazareth after his day's work, and she came in a line of other girls for the household water to the town well, in her long, seamless blue gown, with her brown pitcher on her shoulder, and the golden light of the eastern sunset over her.

We known very little about the Virgin Mary, who her parents were and whether she had any blood brothers and sisters. We do not even know what her condition of life was, although a little incident coming later seems to show that she was poor. At the great moment of her life, with one doubtful exception, she does not seem to have had any of her own about her. She was very quiet and silent. Putting aside the rapturous anthem which we sing in church, all the words recorded as coming from her lips could be written in a single sentence. She was the last and most beloved of the sisterhood of beautiful young women in the Bible who became faithful wives and tender mothers.* The women of Nazareth had a reputation for beauty. It was beauty of the Syrian type, dark-eyed full of languorous grace. Christian

*In the Old Testament we find the name Mary (its Hebrew form Miriam) only once, in the sister of Moses. According to its derivation, the name Miriam means "the beautiful," or "the Perfect One."

art has always represented the Holy Mother as beautiful. It is probable that she was sixteen or seventeen years of age when we hear of her first as being betrothed to Joseph the carpenter.

We do not know from what social class she came, although the inference is that she belonged to the same class as Joseph, and we know that after the birth of Jesus she was poor. Who her father —Joachim—was we are not told, but, according to a tradition of the fourth century, her mother was St. Anne, recognized as the patron saint of carpenters. A relative we hear about is Mary's elderly cousin, Elisabeth, the wife of Zacharias, a priest, living in Hebron; and there is mention of a sister, also named Mary, married to a Galilean named Cleopas, by whom she had several sons. After the death of Jesus, these sons were sometimes referred to as his brothers. But the terms brother and sister were so freely used among eastern peoples that it is possible that Mary Cleopas was not the blood-sister of Mary the mother of Jesus, and that her sons were only figuratively her relatives.

We have no genealogy of Mary; the claim that Luke's genealogy is Mary's being hardly worth consideration inasmuch as it breaks down at sight. In the East, at that period, it was not of the first consequence who a man's mother was. It was only at a later age and with another race that the mother of a great man was also of great importance, and with the formal establishment of a Church to whom motherhood made a strong appeal, Mary, the mother of Jesus, became supremely important, whereas Joseph was entirely obscured by her. Tradition says that Mary died in Jerusalem at fifty-nine years of age. Therefore, if she were, say, seventeen years of age at the birth of Jesus, she died about nine years after her son.

The one outstanding fact which has placed Mary in the position of the first among women is not merely the fact that she was the mother of Jesus, but the belief in how she became so. The birth is ascribed to the miraculous act of God—that Jesus was begotten, not of a natural father but of the Holy Ghost.

VIII. The Virgin Birth

Mary is said by two of the Gospels to have given birth to her child by a miraculous conception. There is no indication that anything of this was known during her lifetime to anybody except herself and her husband.

All we know about the parents of Jesus, apart from the story of the Virgin Birth, is that they lived, that they died, and were probably buried where they lived in the obscurity from which they never emerged during the lifetime of their son. But long after the death of both of them the story gathered about them relating to the birth of Jesus. Joseph and Mary were not merely humble people as had been supposed, they were, in fact, descended from a line of kings, particularly from the greatest of all Jewish kings, David. The objection to this is that John (assuming that he is the writer of the Gospel bearing his name), who knew most about Mary, says nothing concerning her. It is urged, in answer to this, that, knowing the story of the Virgin Birth was in circulation, John says nothing to discredit it.

The two forms of the story of the Virgin Birth may be briefly described. In *Matthew,* Mary was found with child. Joseph wished to put her away privately, without shaming her. But an angel appeared to him in a dream and told him that Mary had conceived of the Holy Ghost, and that she would bring forth a child whose name should be Jesus, and that he should save the people from their sins. Joseph then married Mary, and when the child was born he called his name Jesus.

The story of Mary's miraculous conception, as told by St. Luke, differs from this in some particulars. In *Luke,* an angel, who is named Gabriel, appears to Mary in Galilee. Mary is a virgin, betrothed to a man named Joseph. The angel announces to Mary that she is to become the mother of a son, that she is to call his name Jesus, that the Lord God would give him the throne of his father, David, and that he should reign over the house of Jacob for ever. Mary is astonished and asks how can this be. But the angel answers that the Holy Ghost shall come upon her, and that the Holy One born of her shall be called the Son of God. Further, the angel tells Mary that her cousin, Elisabeth, has also conceived a son in her old age, and Mary says, "Behold the handmaid of the Lord; be it unto me according to thy word."

St. Luke tells us that the Maid of Nazareth went up with haste into the hill country to her cousin, who lived sixty-five miles away, and she entered the house of Zacharias and saluted Elisabeth. And it came to pass that when Elisabeth heard the salutation of Mary, the infant (the unborn John the Baptist) leaped in her womb; and Elisabeth was filled with the Holy Ghost. And she cried out with a loud voice and said, "Blessed art thou among women, and blessed is the fruit of thy womb. And whence is this to me, that the mother of my Lord should come to me? . . . And blessed is she that believed, for there shall be a performance of those things which were told her from the Lord." And Mary said, "My soul doth magnify the Lord . . . for He hath regarded the low estate of his handmaiden: for behold, from henceforth all generations shall call me blessed."

Here is a most definite prophecy, recorded in the first generation, before it could be fulfilled. There is nothing in all history comparable with it. If Mary of Nazareth was not what the Christian faith claims that she is—the specially chosen mother of the incarnate God—then she was only a very humble and uncultured village girl suffering most unaccountably from an amazing delusion.

Nothing is said here about Joseph and what he thinks. Joseph marries Mary and the child is born to him in Bethlehem.

Both stories of the miraculous conception require that Mary should, in later years, have ceased to think about what was predicted by the angel. Her subsequent conduct betrays very little consciousness that Jesus was in any way different from any other son of any other mother.

My conclusion is that, as in the case of the genealogies, the accounts of the Virgin Birth were separate documents put into the Gospels after they were written. The Gospels would be more conclusive without them. They do not harmonize with the rest of the Gospels. On the contrary, they disagree with them. The singing of the psalms between Mary and her cousin, Elisabeth, seems obviously interpolated by a much later hand. It must, nevertheless, be said that Christianity has gained immeasurably by the idea of the miraculous birth of Jesus. It has thrown him high in a plane above humanity and nearly approaching to God. In recent years Christianity seems to be losing by it. The supernatural birth of Jesus drags him away from humanity.

It is clear that St. Paul, for example, has no knowledge of the doctrine of the Virgin Birth. He says that Jesus, being made of a woman and descended from David, according to the flesh, is the son of God according to the spirit of holiness. Taken altogether, the evidence is that Jesus was subject to the ordinary laws of nature in his birth. He was the son of Joseph, the carpenter of Nazareth, and of Mary, his wife. The divinity of Jesus rests on other grounds than those of the miraculous conception, an idea which is not peculiar to Jesus, but belongs also to pagan faiths and to the infancy of the human mind.

The most noteworthy parallel to the Christian legend is the legend of Buddhism. The historical founder is said to have been of virgin birth. A legendary biography of Buddha, which was certainly pre-Christian, begins with a story of Buddha's former life in Heaven. He then announces his intention of descending into the womb of an earthly woman and being born as a man that he may bring salvation to the world. The story of the earthly birth of the Buddha is interesting in the light of the nativity stories of Christ, both in point of resemblance and difference.

The primitive races require that their great men should be born of gods. Christianity does not require it. The Church believes in the Virgin Birth as necessary to the doctrine that all mankind were born in sin. Hence it excludes the participation of a sinful father in order to sever Jesus from all connection with original sin. Not until our own time did the Church find it possible to exclude the mother of Jesus also.

All the same it is impossible to over-estimate the value of the cult of the Virgin Mary to the Catholic Church. Impossible to say how much devotion to Our Lady has done in the history of Christendom.

IX. *Joseph and Mary in Bethlehem*

Mary remained three summer months with her cousin, Elisabeth, in Hebron and then returned to Nazareth.

Some few months later a decree was issued by the Roman emperor, Cæsar Augustus, that "all the world"—the Roman world—should be taxed, and for this purpose (so we are told) it was necessary that everyone should go up to his own city. Bethlehem was, according to the genealogy, the city of Joseph (being the city of David), so Joseph had to go there for his taxing and he took his young wife with him. Why he did this, Mary being by this time far advanced in pregnancy, has been the subject of scores of conjectures, some of them rather foolish and none of them of serious significance. The only thing of importance is that the journey was long, seventy miles at least, taking two nights and three days, passing through Samaria, where the half-Semitic people were hostile and inhospitable to Jews, and that it was probably the middle of winter, when the weather of Palestine can be most bitterly cold.

Coming to Bethlehem they found that many Bethlehemites from the outlying towns had arrived before them, that the inns were full and that the only accommodation they could secure was in the quarters provided for cattle. This was probably what is now called the *fundak* in certain eastern towns, a square space like a farmyard enclosed by high walls, with the middle of it open to the sky for the camels to lie out upon, and rough log-built loose boxes leaning against the walls, each with its broad, open-mouthed wooden manger from which cattle can feed on either side. And in one of these mangers for her bed, Mary, her time being fulfilled, gave birth to her child, and they called him Jesus.

If these were simple and naturalistic happenings to usher into the world what millions believe to be the most tremendous event in human history, there was enough of the supernatural to follow them. The city of Jerusalem sits on the crest of a cone-like rock, which is surrounded by a stony waste of unequalled desolation, but the six-miles road going south to Bethlehem runs into scenes of charming pastoral beauty. Bethlehem stands on a ledge, with broad meadow-lands below it to the east, which die off into a desert of boulders that go down by a steep declivity to the lonesome region of the Dead Sea.

In these meadows, on the day of the birth of Mary's child, a company of shepherds were keeping watch over their flocks by night. "Watch" is the only word for it, for the desert was infested by wolves, jackals and hyenas, who prowled after dark in search of prey. As a consequence, the good shepherd could neither slumber nor sleep, but at the first call of his sheep or bark of his dogs he had to be up with his strong staff, to follow the wild beasts to their lair, to beat them until they dropped their victim and then to carry it back, maimed and bleeding and perhaps dead. As this was an adventure not unattended by danger to the shepherd himself, it was literally true that the good shepherd sometimes gave his life for his sheep.

The life of the Palestinian shepherd is often a hard and always a lonely one. During the summer he feeds his sheep on the mountains, and at the beginning of winter he brings them down to the lowlands, and keeps them there until the lambs have come in March, when he leads his bleating flock back to the hills, with the youngest and weakest in his arms. As a consequence he rarely has a home or wife or children, and he has little company except his visions and dreams.

These must have been many in the days of Joseph and Mary, and perhaps the shepherds of Bethlehem found the chief of them in the sky. Nowhere in the world does the sky seem so wonderful as in Palestine, and at night it is sometimes like a miracle. Often there are depths upon depths of clear blue air, with innumerable stars, which seem to throb and pulse, to form into flowing silvery robes and almost to utter sounds as they trail through the sky. It is little wonder that untaught shepherds of the East think Heaven must be in the sky, for nowhere else in the universe is there anything so celestial.

Whether the shepherds of the first Christmas Day were Essenes (as their condition might have made them) we do not know, but we are told that as they sat together in the night, in the meadows below Bethlehem, a great light shone over them, and the voice of an angel came out of it, telling them not to be afraid, for he brought them good tidings of great joy—that in the city of David there had been born that day a saviour who was Christ the Lord, and they would find the babe lying in a manger in swaddling clothes. Then it seemed to the shepherds that with the angel there was a heavenly host who sang an anthem, which perhaps they had heard in their hearts before: "Glory to God in the highest, and on earth peace toward men of good will." After the angels had gone, and perhaps daylight had come and their flocks were safe, the shepherds went up to Bethlehem and there found the young mother and her child in the place to which they had been directed. And then they went away, telling everybody of the wonderful things they had seen and heard.

X. *The Divine Infant*

At eight days old the infant was circumcised, and after forty days, the period of her purification being fulfilled, Mary, with her child in her arms and a pair of young doves and a pigeon for sacrifice in her hand, went up to Jerusalem for her purification and to present her first born in the Temple, according to the law of Moses.

At the Temple she came upon a religious old man, who had been waiting for the advent of the Messiah. His name was Simeon. It had been promised him by the Holy Ghost that he should not die until he had seen the Christ.

When Mary entered the Temple with her child, it was revealed to Simeon that the child Jesus was the Christ he had been waiting to see. The old man took the child in his arms and blessed God that he had been allowed to see the fulfilment of his hope—the coming of the Christ and the glory of Israel—saying, *"Lord, now lettest Thou Thy servant depart in peace."*

Mary and Joseph marvelled at the things that were spoken of their child.

At the same moment a widow named Anna, eighty-four years of age, who, in expectation of the Prince of Peace, had lived in the precincts of the Temple, waiting and watching and fasting and praying, made the same testimony to the divinity of the child Jesus. And then, the customs of the law being fulfilled, the young mother, with her child in her arms and her husband by her side, returned to her home in Nazareth, pondering all these things in her heart.

One is constrained to ask why Mary should have been required to go to the Temple for her purification. If she were a virgin, where lay the essential impurity in her as a mother that she needed this ceremony and period of purification? If she was not sullied by the fact of her miraculous motherhood, no purification was necessary. If the child was divine, of Virgin Birth, if the mother had conceived of the Holy Ghost, she was without taint and needed no purifying. If she needed it, then she was tainted like all other women.

The Virgin Birth story would seem to have originated in the very ancient idea of impurity attaching to the marriage relation, the notion that superior purity lay in virginity. Man was the vehicle of impurity; the sex passion in man was impure. But Judaism regarded marriage as a divine institution, and children as a blessing of God. The Ebionites subsequently rejected the supernatural conception of Jesus. Belief in the Virgin Birth of Jesus of Nazareth was probably inculcated in the myth-forming epoch when the Jewish world (perhaps also the pagan Gentile world) outside Palestine wanted proof of the divinity of Jesus—that he was the Messiah.

Nowhere in the New Testament is the sinlessness of Jesus connected with the idea of his miraculous, sinless birth. The sinlessness of Christ does not stand or fall by the hypothesis of his sinless birth. The greatness of Jesus and the value of his revelation to mankind are in no way assisted or diminished by the manner of his entry into the world. Every birth is just as wonderful as a virgin birth could possibly be, and just as much a direct act of God.

The story of the birth of Jesus may be steeped in supernaturalism and saturated with superstition; the two sources from which it comes may contradict and eliminate each other, linking the origin of Christ with prophecies which were nothing but predictions of earlier historical happenings; but the Nativity is something far other than a fable, a myth, and the poor shepherds with their singing angels, the Wise Men with their strange presents, the star of Bethlehem and the old man and old widow cannot be dismissed. Heavy-handed critics who, however learned, think that reason is the only channel of knowledge, who do not know the East and have never drawn one breath of its golden air of vision and dream, do not realize that there is something truer than the material truth, and that is the essential soul of it.

The Nativity, in its childlike simplicity, has probably done more to perpetuate the life of Christianity than any other single incident in the life of Christ, even more perhaps than the immeasurably greater and more tremendous incidents of the trial, the death and the resurrection.

XI. *The Mother and Child*

The early Fathers may have been long in seeing the value of the Christmas festival, but, when they did see it, they saw it by the light of inspiration. Only inspiration could have revealed to the Church the value of the figures of the Mother and Child. If Christ had, like Mithras, been born out of a rock, how remote from humanity he would have been! He might have been worshipped as a god; he could never have been loved as a man. That he was born of a woman; that he passed through her body and became flesh of her flesh; that in his birth the eternal miracle was repeated which comes with every child that is born into the world—this brought Christ into the closest chamber of the human heart and made him a member of the human family. And then how close it brought the mother!

Perhaps races of the East may have felt this more than the races of the West, and women more than men, for twice during the life of Christ, when people were moved by the tenderness of his words, woman cried out to him that the breasts that had suckled him were blessed. And deep under the mother-pride was the mother-sorrow, all the sorrow the mother-heart can know. And, finally, the mother-right of intercession for afflicted sisters with him who had been hers on earth and was now sitting at God's right hand in Heaven! The Blessed Virgin! The Sacred Heart! The Mother of all Mothers! We should be blind not to see what a mighty force for Christianity the Catholic Church has made out of the figure of the simple Galilean girl of whom we know almost nothing at all.

And then the child—could inspiration go farther than to take the babe out of the manger in Bethlehem and make it the central figure of the Faith? If we had to remember Christ solely as the mighty supernatural being who rebuked the storm on the sea and bade Death stand back, we should think of him with awe, perhaps with fear. But when we remember him as a helpless child, we think of him with love. Only a sapless cynicism or an arid imagination can fail to see the importance of the cradle in the history of Christianity. In some inexpressible way, which none of us can comprehend, it makes every child the representative of Christ, whether it is born in the palace or the stable.

And think of this—there is no authentic portrait of Jesus of Nazareth in the world, and while the most learned theologian could not tell you whether he was tall or short, or dark or fair, and the two prophecies which are supposed to describe his physical appearance contradict each other, and while there is nobody on earth who knows what he was like to look upon as a man, every young mother in the world knows what he was like as a child—her own baby.

XII.   The Star of Bethlehem

It would appear that Joseph and Mary did not return at once to their home in Nazareth, as stated by St. Luke, but that they remained and lived together in Bethlehem for nearly two years after the birth of Jesus.

At the end of that time, according to St. Matthew's account, a group of strange men, who are called the Wise Men of the East, came to Jerusalem, saying "Where is he who is called king of the Jews? We have seen his star in the East and have come to worship him." Perhaps they have come from Babylon, and are descendants of the faithless Jews who remained in the alien land after the end of the Captivity, when their fellow-Jews returned home. Perhaps they have lost their faith and yet retained the memory of the hope of Israel. Certainly they are astrologers, and therefore they think that God speaks to His children by the stars, warning them of what is to come and of what is happening in distant places. And perhaps, sitting together at night, two years before in the East, they had seen a star in the sky that had never before swum into their ken, indicating Judæa and denoting a birth, and they had said, "That is the king of the Jews who is to regain the throne of his father David, and rule the world in righteousness." And, perhaps then, at the call of the faith of their forefathers, which was not dead in them but rose in their hearts again, they gathered together presents fit for the King of Kings and set out to worship him, going afoot across the wide Syrian Desert, through the old pagan city of Petra and up to the heights of Moab, where, in sight of the Promised Land and the utmost sea, Moses died and God buried him.

The people of Jerusalem hear their question, and have no doubt of its meaning—the king who is to redeem Israel has been born among them.

Herod hears it also, and he has no uncertainty about its significance. He knows he is only a half-Jew, and no better than a usurper on the throne of David, and that if a true descendant has been born in his dominions there will soon be an end of his dynasty. To meet that danger he determines to destroy the Messiah while he is still a child. First he calls his high priests and demands to be told where the Christ is to be born. They answer in Bethlehem, for has not the Lord said by the mouth of His prophet that out of Bethlehem shall come a governor who shall rule His people Israel—a reference which is gleaned from one verse of one of the prophets only? Next, Herod calls the Wise Men and questions them closely about the time at which they saw the star in the East. Then, masking his purpose, he tells them to go to Bethlehem to search diligently for the child, and when they have found him to return, so that he, too, may go to worship him.

Bethlehem lies a short six miles south of Jerusalem, but the Wise Men set out by night, as if it were the middle of summer and they were going on a long journey. The star they had seen in the East appears to them again and goes before them, but travelling from north to south now, not from east to west, according to the order of nature. It stops over a house in Bethlehem, and by that they know they have reached their destination. Going into the house, they find the young child, with Mary his mother, and, falling down before him, they worship him. Then opening their treasures, they present the strange gifts they have brought with them for the poor woman's child—gold, and frankincense and myrrh.

This story of the star of Bethlehem has some slight support from the fact that a combination of bright stars did actually occur about the time when the Wise Men said they saw the star of the king of the Jews in the eastern sky. Kepler, the German astronomer, in the sixteenth and seventeenth centuries, attached a mystical significance to the coincidence in time and place of a triple conjunction of Mars, Jupiter and Saturn, five years earlier than the commonly accepted date of the birth of Christ. This, he declared, was the light seen by the Wise Men as recorded in *Matthew,* and perhaps the light seen by the shepherds in St. Luke's story. But if Kepler's date for the star was 7 B.C. it cannot agree with Matthew's story according to which it must have appeared some two years earlier than the date at which the Wise Men reported what they had seen to Herod in Jerusalem.* But in point of fact Herod was in Jericho almost the whole period between 6 B.C. and his death there in 4 B.C. Before that he was in Jerusalem.

*The varying opinions of the early Fathers and the school men as to the year of the birth of Christ are as follows:

7 B.C.   According to Benedictine authors of *L'Art de Vérifier les dates.*
6 B.C.   According to Kepler.
5 B.C.   According to Chrysostom.
4 B.C.   According to Sulpicius.
3 B.C.   According to Clement of Alexandria, Irenæus, and others.
2 B.C.   According to Eusebius, Jerome, and others.
1 B.C.   According to Tertullian, Luther, and others.
A.D. 1.   According to Norisius; later than A.D. 1.
A.D. 2.   According to Paul of Middelburg.
A.D. 3.   According to Lydiat.
The accepted date is the latter end of 5 B.C.

Matthew's story requires also that we should believe that during the interval which divided the birth of Christ from the arrival of the Wise Men in Jerusalem, the shepherds said nothing about the supernatural appearance, that Simeon and Anna and others said nothing, and that for two or more years (in spite of the supernatural appearance) the birth of Christ was unknown in Jerusalem.

Apparently the Wise Men rest at Bethlehem that day, for they are warned in a dream not to return to Herod; so they go back to their own country by another way. After they have gone, Joseph also has a dream, in which an angel of the Lord tells him to take the young child and his mother and flee into Egypt and remain there until word is brought to him again, for Herod is seeking to take the child's life.

Joseph does as he is directed, and husband, wife and child leave Bethlehem by night.

When Herod finds that the Wise Men do not return to Jerusalem, and concludes that they have deceived him, he resolves to remove all possibility of danger from the new-born descendant of David by giving an order that all the male children in Bethlehem and in the country round about it, up to two years of age, shall be destroyed. His command is carried out, with the result that there is great lamentation among the mothers of Bethlehem.

Then death lays its hand on the tyrant himself. A loathsome and incurable distemper takes possession of him, and (as one learns from another authority) he goes down to his palace at Jericho, to bathe in the hot springs of Callirrhoe, beyond Jordan. And there, a year or two later, he dies.

Then the angel of the Lord appears to Joseph in Egypt, telling him to take the young child and the mother, and return to his own country. Joseph does so, but before he reaches his home in Bethlehem he hears that Archelaus, a son of Herod, and as ruthless as Herod himself, is ruling in his father's room. Therefore, warned by yet another dream, Joseph goes on to Galilee, which is in the tetrarchy of another of Herod's sons, Herod Antipas, and makes a new home in a city called Nazareth. This is the first time mention is made in *Matthew* of Nazareth as the home of Joseph and Mary.

Such are the two stories of the birth of Jesus as they have come down to us in the Gospels. Undoubtedly, they are beautiful. But their beauty is that of the mirage in the desert which dissolves at the next movement of the setting sun. Are they the stories that were in the mind of St. Paul when, about the time when they first became current in Palestine, he warned his foreign converts against "foolish fables and endless genealogies?" Sceptical critics have dismissed them as pernicious inventions, steeped in the supernatural and saturated in superstition. Therefore, it is the duty of believers to look at them steadily and to judge of them fearlessly. Only so can we penetrate to the heart of them, comprehend the meaning of them, and understand the important events which came of them.

XIII.　*Supernatural Birth Stories*

Miraculous events relating to the birth of Jesus appear to have been quite unknown at Nazareth, either then or at any later period of the life of Jesus. We have no reason to think that Jesus himself knew anything about the miraculous circumstances which are said to have attended his birth. Nothing in Mary's later life gives any betrayal of her consciousness that her son was king of the Jews, the Saviour who was to come—the Messiah. Nothing in the subsequent life of Joseph conveys any indication of his knowledge of the fact. The astonishment with which Joseph and Mary appear to have received the words of Simeon and Anna is not reconcilable with the dream of Joseph or with the prediction of the angel who appeared to Mary, inasmuch as it requires that both of them should have forgotten these incidents.

The story of the massacre of the male children of Bethlehem is quite unknown to history, and has no existence in any authenticated document of the first century outside *Matthew*. Josephus, who records in detail the atrocities of Herod and gives a circumstantial account of his later days, says nothing about the massacre of the children. In like manner, St. Luke knows nothing either of the massacre or of the flight into Egypt, although he wrote, as he says, in full knowledge of all that was known and had been written by eye-witnesses.

The accepted theory now is that in the interval of, perhaps, thirty years after the death of Jesus the idea of his supernatural birth had been developed out of the thought which had begun to exist towards the end of his life, that he was the Messiah. Being the Messiah, he must be the son of David, and, as the son of David, he must fulfil the prophetic condition of being born in the city of David, namely, Bethlehem. The prophecy in *Hosea* (XI, 1) says

"I have called my son out of Egypt." The prophecy in *Isaiah* (VII, 14) says that "a virgin shall conceive and bear a son, and shall call his name Immanuel"—*God with us.*

The beautiful words of Isaiah are commonly referred to as being among the prophecies that were believed to have been fulfilled:—

> For unto us a child is born, unto us a son is given; and the government shall be upon his shoulder; and his name shall be called Wonderful, Counsellor, the Mighty God, the Everlasting Father, the Prince of Peace. Of the increase of his government and peace there shall be no end, upon the throne of David, and upon his kingdom, to order it, and to establish it with judgment and with justice from henceforth even for ever. The zeal of the Lord of Hosts will perform this. [*Isaiah* IX, 6–7]

This is said to be a prophecy of the birth of Jesus. Obviously it is not so. Historically it was not fulfilled. Jesus did not establish the throne of David, and the kingdom was not established for ever.

The fulfilment of this prophecy is assumed to be recounted in *Luke* II, 1–15, and especially verse 11. "For unto you is born this day in the city of David a Saviour, which is Christ the Lord."

There is nothing whatever in the birth story in *Luke* which corresponds with the alleged prophecy in *Isaiah,* except that Jesus was the son of a man "of the house and lineage of David; nothing about establishing the throne of David, or about the kingdom of David lasting for ever.

In *Isaiah* it is not even said that the promised one is to be born in the city of David—Bethlehem.

XIV. *His Messiahship*

It would seem that the accounts of the visits of the Wise Men and the murder of the innocents at Bethlehem harmonized with the Jewish Messianic notion respecting the star which was to come out of Jacob.

Against the prophetic theory there is the fact that, throughout his life, Jesus was spoken of as a Galilean from Nazareth; that his parents were so spoken of. That Jesus was never spoken of as a Bethlehemite; that we do not know that he ever visited Bethlehem; and that on the last day of his life no attempt was made to represent him as a Judæan. On the contrary, a marked attempt was made to establish the fact that he was a Galilean.

Nowhere else in the Gospels is Bethlehem referred to as his birthplace.

The fact that he was called the son of David is only applicable to dogmatic and historic accounts. He was the son of David, not because he was born in Bethlehem, but because he was, dogmatically, the follower of David.

The prophetic theory of the Messiah as the son of David was necessary to the current Jewish faith. If it had succeeded with the Jews it might have made Jesus the leader of the Jewish sect. But it failed with the Jews, and is of no account to Christianity.

Christianity does not rest on the fact that Jesus was descended from David. His Messiahship is entirely independent of this. Neither does Christianity require that as an evidence of Messiahship a Christ should be born in Bethlehem. What does it matter to Christianity that Jesus was the son of David if he was the Son of God? Taken altogether, the story that Jesus was born in Bethlehem is a stumbling-block to Christianity. The conclusion would be that, in the case of the genealogies, to show in this case the story of the supernatural birth the chapters in *Matthew* and *Mark* were interpolated after the Gospels were written.

But can we disturb the idea that Jesus was born in Bethlehem without also disturbing the theory of the Incarnation? Consider what the Incarnation has been to Christianity. Could Christianity have lived without it? If it could be proved that Jesus was not born in Bethlehem, would not the sentiment associated with Christianity lose much? Remember the beautiful story of the Nativity as it has come down through the ages. How this has constituted Christmas. Above all, the Christmas of children. If we uproot all this and prove that it belongs to the world of myth, the Christmas of the ages becomes an empty observance instead of the heart-warming re-assertion of a living truth.

We know that, except in the two Nativity stories in *Matthew* and *Luke,* he is always spoken of as a Galilean, as Jesus of Nazareth. He bore that name from the beginning of his ministry. He was apparently arrested, tried, condemned, and executed under that name. That name was written at the head of the Cross. He was sent to Herod Antipas by Pontius Pilate because his accusers spoke of him as a Galilean. (His accusers never recognized his

Judæan origin or descent.) He was accepted as a Galilean by Herod Antipas, and sent back (quite obviously) to Pilate, because the offence with which he was charged, on which he had been arrested, had been committed in Judæa. There is not the slightest reason to suppose that Herod Antipas sent him back to Pilate because he knew, or had suddenly found out, that Jesus had been born in Bethlehem, and therefore was a Judæan, and as such came under the direct jurisdiction of the Roman governor.

After his death Jesus was spoken of by Peter as Jesus of Nazareth. Among his apostles and disciples he never ceased to be known as Jesus of Nazareth, until he became (as in the mouth of Paul) "Jesus Christ the Lord."

It was not until thirty or more years after his death that the idea that he had been born in Bethlehem of a Judæa-born father (by law) began to be promulgated.

XV. The Nativity Stories

When were the Gospel Nativity stories written?

We do not know. We have good reason to believe that Matthew's Nativity story did not exist in the earliest form of Matthew's Gospel. Whether Luke's Gospel story, as it has come down to us, existed in the earliest form of Luke's Gospel we do not know. We have various reasons for thinking it did not. It seems quite clear that the writers of *Matthew* and *Luke* did not know the Nativity stories which are found at the beginning of their Gospels when they wrote the body of their Gospels. They frequently use language which eliminates their Nativity stories. They never, by any chance, use language which supports the Nativity stories.

What, then, is the conclusion we have come to? I think it is that Jesus was a Galilean, probably (though not certainly) born in Bethlehem. If Jesus was a Galilean, Joseph was probably a Galilean also. If Joseph was a Judæan, his son could not have been born in Judæa without becoming also a Judæan. Jesus was never, during his lifetime, accounted a Judæan. The conclusion, therefore, is that both Joseph and Jesus were Galileans, and probably both were of Nazareth.

Joseph (only less than Jesus) was associated in the popular memory with Nazareth—never with Bethlehem. He was known (apparently widely) in the Nazareth country. There is no evidence that he was known in Bethlehem. He had to take his wife not to the house of friends, but to a common stable.

There is no evidence that Mary the mother of Jesus had any connection with Bethlehem. She is never (outside the Nativity stories and the few, very few, passages connected therewith), mentioned in relation to Bethlehem.

But there is the fact that he is frequently addressed as the Son of David. The blind man and the demoniacs so addressed him. What does this mean? Does it mean that they had acquired some mysterious knowledge of his descent from David, which he was hiding from others? The title "Son of David" had a dogmatic meaning. Obviously it was generally used to denote anybody with the Davidic spirit; or anybody likely to bring the Davidic blessing to the long suffering Jewish people.

It was the title of honour—not to be taken literally, as if meaning that Jesus was actually descended by blood from David.

It is impossible not to see that this and this only is meant by the salutation which Jesus receives (notably from the blind beggar) in the earlier part of his ministry.

Whether the same salutations on his entrance to Jerusalem mean something more is not so certain. It is probable that by that time the Jewish people who accepted Jesus were prepared to believe that he fulfilled all the conditions of the prophets concerning the Messiah.

Later, much later, St. Paul accepted the idea that Jesus was the son of David according to the flesh. This was when, years after the death of Jesus, his friends were finding the prophecies applying to him. Thus, St. Paul indicates two things (1) his belief that Jesus was physically descended through Joseph from David; (2) that his descent from David was only part of his claim to be the Christ, but that he was also the Son of God, according to the spirit.

Moreover, St. Peter on the Day of Pentecost claims for Jesus that he is the son of David in fulfilment of the oath sworn by God that as the fruit of David's line, according to the flesh, He would raise up Christ to sit on His throne.

That Jesus (although he sometimes permitted himself to be called the son of David) did not favour the idea that the Messiah was the son of David is shown by the passage in which Jesus refers to the Christ as Lord, and asks how then could he be at the same time the son of him who called him Lord. Not even when he is taunted with his lowly origin does he retort by announcing his descent from David, and therefore his eligibility for recognition as the Messiah.

But never before the Birth stories does the idea find expression that being the son of David he was anything more than man. The idea of a being half human and half divine had not occurred to his contemporaries.

St. Paul does indeed speak of *Jesus as descended from David.* St. Peter also does so, but says nothing of his Virgin Birth. The single eye-witness among the evangelists says nothing about his birth, which he surely must have done if he had known it to be miraculous. The other Gospels (and *Matthew* and *Luke* later) not only do not speak of the miraculous birth, but they give currency to popular theories which appear to exclude it.

The genealogical tables in *Matthew* and *Luke* are framed on the assumption that Jesus was actually descended by flesh from David. Yet they say he is not, on his father's side. And they say nothing whatever about his mother's side, and all inference that one of the genealogies is his mother's genealogy is pure conjecture. It also leaves the other incidents as utterly useless.

My inference from all this is:

1. That the contemporaries of Jesus believed he was descended from the house of David, through Joseph.

2. That they believed he was the son of Joseph and therefore the son of David.

3. That the genealogies existed earlier than the Virgin Birth story and are no part of it.

4. That when the Virgin Birth story was added to the genealogies, the latter had to be altered by the addition of the parenthetical words "as was supposed."

This is the plain sense of the matter. Anything else makes the genealogies superfluous. Nothing makes them reliable or luminous. They are utterly irreconcilable.

It is urged that Jesus's mother and family "had a high and holy interest" in guarding the secret of his miraculous birth. But this is not reasonable. Neither his mother, his family, nor Jesus himself had the slightest interest in keeping the fact secret. It would have helped towards his recognition as the Messiah if they could have proved or even asserted it (as the mother of the emperor Augustus in her case did). That there could be no witness to it except the mother herself is not true. There would be Joseph, as long as he lived, and Elisabeth the mother of John the Baptist.

But the idea is that the story of the miraculous birth was not made until after Mary's death.

None of them bears any testimony to the truth of it.

1. If this witness of Elisabeth was intended to bear testimony to the divinity of Jesus, it failed. There is nothing to show that anything she said influenced anybody, even her own son.

2. If the witness of the angels who sang over the meadows of Bethlehem was intended to bear testimony, it failed—nobody except a group of shepherds appeared to have heard anything about it.

3. If the witness of the shepherds was intended to bear testimony, it failed—there is nothing to show their "praising God and glorifying" was heard by anybody else.

4. If the witness of the Wise Men of the East is intended to bear testimony, it failed—there is nothing to show that anybody in their own country came to hear of the coming of the king of the Jews. This coming did no good whatever, but much harm, since it led to the slaughter of the children of Bethlehem.

5. If the slaughter of the children of Bethlehem was intended to make a bloody stamp on history of the advent of the Christ and the opposition of the evil powers of this world, it failed—for it has never been mentioned in history, and it produced no effect on its time.

Furthermore, Herod the Great had no power to condemn to death until the Sanhedrin had condemned to death.

What twenty-three sane men could have condemned the innocent children of Bethlehem, under two years of age, to death on no charge whatever? Would not such an outrage of humanity have awakened the indignation of Rome, as well as Jerusalem, and led to the disclosure of Herod's motive?

What evidence is there that anybody ever heard that Herod committed this bestial act out of fear of the birth of the Messiah?

The whole incident of the miraculous birth of Jesus is apparently useless for any purposes of truth that Jesus of Nazareth was the Christ. It leaves the real life of Jesus in the world untouched. He gets no help from it at any moment. It comes after his life is over and finished and his victory is won.

Again, what is the divine purpose of the supernatural birth of Jesus?

To establish Christ's sinlessness, through a sinless mother. The theory falls within itself both as to son and mother, concerning whom the natural objection is that if Jesus was sinless why was he circumcised? If Mary was a pure virgin, and the birth of Jesus did not disturb her purity, why did she require purification?

Further, if the sinlessness of Jesus is to be established by the purity of Mary, his mother, from taint of human contamination in the conception of her child, the sinlessness of Mary herself from taint of human impurity in her own conception must also, in logic, be established.

The Church has, after an effort of many centuries, established the Immaculate Conception of the Virgin, as well as of her child, but that is not enough.

It should, in logic, establish the Immaculate Conception of Mary's mother, and so on and on back through the ages, to the hand of God, or the taint of impurity comes down to Jesus.

What then is the conclusion?

If the story of the Virgin Birth is contradictory, deficient in evidence, what remains?

If the descent of Jesus from David is refused by Christianity on the ground that Joseph was *not* the human father, and therefore Jesus had no line of connection with David, it follows that Jesus does not fulfil the prophecy which required that the Messiah should come of the house and lineage of David.

If it were accepted that Joseph *was* the human father of Jesus, and therefore descended from David, and also that he was born of a virgin, and accepted as the Promised One by the angels, the shepherds, the Wise Men, and others, what more is shown than that Jesus is the Messiah of Jewish prophecy—a Jewish Messiah, intended to sit on the throne of David, and to rule his Jewish kingdom according to the law of Moses?

If Christianity refuses this limited role for the founder of the universal religion, the Messiah of all the peoples of all the world, what is left?

Very little that is beyond question is left except a bald, realistic story.

But are we to put aside the stories of the birth of Jesus in *Matthew* and *Luke* because of their contradictions and inconsistencies? By no means. We cannot. Because, however imperfect in their letter, their spirit is true. To understand them aright we have to go farther back—farther perhaps than the Hebrew prophecy that a virgin is to bear a child. Far back, to the call of the heart of man for the purity of a Saviour that shall be both God and man.

Before the knowledge of an after-existence came to the consciousness of mankind it seems to have been there. Man could not conceive of God apart from humanity. Can he even yet do so? If we trace this back through time, what do we find? First, we find religion taking forms of nature worship that were attended by licentiousness. There were persistent and gross forms of idolatry. The power of procreation was worshipped. Every physical power of man was deified. Even Jerusalem has ominous heathen associations of this gross kind. Religion expressed itself in sensuality. It was natural. But to the modern sense it was horrible. Then, as man's religious sense arose, there was a recoil from all this. Women, in particular, recoiled from it. Absolute sinlessness then became a supreme attribute of the expected Messiah.

The story of the divine birth of Jesus has become the pulse of the world. Strip the divine element away and perhaps the heart of the world would stop.

There is, however, not the slightest evidence that during the lifetime of Jesus anybody knew anything about his supernatural birth. It would be wrong to say that belief in the Virgin Birth existed from the earlier days of the Christian faith. It is not mentioned in *Mark,* probably the earliest account of the life and death of Jesus. It is not mentioned in the early Aramaic book of *Matthew.* There is no satisfying proof that it existed in the earliest form of *Luke.*

Never was there a more obvious legend.

It is fair and reasonable to say that it came into existence only when the early Church (about the time of Ignatius) thought it had need of it—to separate Jesus from all sin, to distinguish him from all other prophets.

It did not do that, for supernatural birth had already been claimed for the founders of other faiths—particularly Mithras. The cult of Mithraism existed side by side with Christianity, and down to the beginning of the second century hotly contested with it for supremacy.

Nevertheless, the doctrine of the Virgin Birth has had a vitalizing effect on Christianity. It has led to the deepening of the religious spirit. It seemed necessary to the Church which was struggling hard to account to itself for the Resurrection and all that it implied. It has played a great part in sustaining the soul of the Church, and it was a main force in making the Christmas festival, which for many centuries has played a beautiful part in the history of Christianity.

My conclusions in regard to the birth story are that Jesus was born in Bethlehem in the last days of the reign of Herod, the King of Judæa. Herod died in the middle of March, 4 B.C. Jesus was born at the beginning of that year, or perhaps at the end of 5 B.C. say in December. I do not think he was born on December 25th. That day was chosen many years later because it was an established holy day—the birthday of the sun. The birth in Bethlehem no doubt came about by the necessity that the parents of Jesus should go at intervals to the native town of the husband for enrolment. Joseph took Mary with him, and she gave birth to her child while there. I see no reason to question that she gave birth to Jesus in a cave or a stable. Mary's espousal to Joseph was in every respect the same as marriage in its responsibilities, and in the rights of the child to be born within wedlock. Espousal in the East has always been a recognized form of marriage—generally adopted in the case of a very young bride and followed by a period of a year or more in which the husband does not claim marital rights.

It was commonly believed that Joseph, the father of Jesus, came of the family of David; but I see no reason to accept either of the genealogies of Joseph. They were honestly put forth by Matthew and Luke, but they broke down from the utter impossibility of tracing any man's lineage through something like 4,000 years—least of all a working man's. The effort to account for the difference in the genealogies by saying that one is the legal genealogy and the other the natural genealogy is, in relation to a working man's family tree, too weak to waste words upon. The attempt to separate Joseph from Jesus by saying that he was only "supposed" to have begotten Jesus is the interpolation of later Christian writers who had doctrinal purposes to serve.

I see no evidence in the Gospels to show Mary's descent. Neither of the genealogies of Joseph can be thought to have anything to do with Mary. We know nothing about Mary's family, who her parents were or whether she had any brothers and sisters. The mention of a sister of her own name is dubious, inasmuch as such a thing would be impossible unless her father or her mother married a second time, and we hear nothing of this.

The mention of John the Baptist's mother, Elisabeth, as the cousin of the mother of Jesus is hardly believable, though not absolutely impossible. Mary was clearly a very young girl, Elisabeth was past the usual age of child-bearing, say forty-eight years.

We never hear of this relationship again, and it was not until long after the death of Jesus that anything was said (outside *Luke*) of his being the second cousin of John the Baptist. Beyond this Mary stands without family connections of any kind.

The accepted idea that Joseph was an old man has no authority in the Gospels, where nothing of the kind is even vaguely hinted at.

It was not until the second century that the idea that Joseph was an old man was heard of.

This was an after guess of Epiphanius, one of the early Fathers, who were always guessing. It was intended to buttress the idea that Joseph could not have been the human father of Jesus, that he was not the father of any other child by Mary. In short, that he was not Mary's husband at all, but merely the man in the house. It is mentioned in certain of the apocryphal gospels which were cast out by the Church in the fourth century.

In like manner there is no authority in the gospels for the statement that they had no other children. On the contrary, it is clearly indicated that Mary had other sons and at least more than two daughters.*

*The brothers and sisters of Jesus: James, Joses, Simon and Judas. The sisters are not named (*Matthew* XIII, 55, 56. *Mark* VI, 3). His mother and his brethren come to Jesus (*Luke* VIII, 19; *Mark* III, 31). Jesus journeys with his mother and his brethren to Capernaum (*John* II, 12). The brothers mentioned with the mother after the death of Jesus (*Acts* I, 14).

CHAPTER II

His Childhood

I. *The Silence of the Gospels*

IT IS ONE of the most astounding facts of history that after giving so detailed an account of the birth of Jesus, and of every circumstance attending it, the Gospels should be silent about the first twelve years of his life. No word of his infancy and boyhood has come down to us. The incident of the flight into Egypt to escape the wrath of King Herod would seem to have been referred to by St. Matthew solely to justify the prophecy "Out of Egypt have I called my son"; and St. Luke considers it enough to record that, after he was taken by his mother to Nazareth, the child grew and waxed strong in spirit, filled with wisdom, and that the grace of God was upon him. Beyond this we are left to conclude that from his infancy onward he lived in Galilee, and that Nazareth came to be recognized as his native town.

Facts as to the colour of his hair and eyes, whether he was fair or dark of complexion, are matters of pure conjecture. We know nothing with certainty, and can only surmise that he was good to look upon from the circumstance that the women and children of Nazareth have always been famous for their beauty, usually of the dark Syrian type, but often distinguished by fair hair and blue eyes.

If either Mary or Joseph inspired Luke or Matthew in the writing of the story of the birth, it is sufficiently astonishing that they said nothing of the boyhood of Jesus. The silence of the Gospels is significant. After the death of a famous man, rumour is nearly always busy, among his friends and within his family, about the events of his early life, particularly his child life. Many things are recalled which in the cases of ordinary men who never emerge from obscurity are permitted to be forgotten. The brothers, the sisters, the parents, particularly the mother of such a man, recall little incidents which seem (after the event) to have presaged and prepared for the future.

The harmless efforts usually made by mothers to find in their memories incidents of childhood which foretold future greatness are conspicuously absent in the case of Jesus. There is nothing of this in the Gospels. All we hear about the infancy of Jesus comes to us from the apocryphal Gospels. They are almost always puerile stories—the very babyhood of the human intellect—such as that Jesus preached sermons in his cradle, telling of his Messianic mission; that he worked miracles in his play with other children. It is said, for example, that they shaped models of animals and birds in clay and sand, and that Jesus had only to touch them with his finger and blow upon them to cause them to walk or fly away.

That he was fondly interested in animals, birds and flowers is amply proved by his many intimate references to them in the discourses and parables. In his young days in and about Nazareth he had many opportunities of observing the lambs in the pastures, the young camels in the passing caravans, the nesting birds and the lilies of the field; and it is only reasonable to suppose that, like most children, he cherished his particular animal pets. No doubt he had a boy's love of sailing-boats from what he must frequently have seen of them on the neighbouring Lake of Galilee, and it is hardly questionable that at an early age he learned to make practical use of the carpenter's tools accessible to him in his father's workshop. He may have made his own toys.

There is a legend of his helping his father with his work, and that when Joseph cut his timber too long or too short Jesus had only to touch the wood and it became exactly the right size.

All this is a continuation of the effort which began soon after his death to convey the thought that Jesus knew throughout his life on earth, and perhaps before it, of his supernatural power, his Messianic mission, and all that was to happen to him. There is nothing in the New Testament to justify this. When, centuries after the death of Jesus, the early Christians came to separate the Gospels deserving of reverence from those that were unworthy of credence, they naturally cut out all such fantastic legends.

II. Nazareth

Nazareth was quite unknown to the writers of the Old Testament, who never once mention it. There is no reference to it in the Talmud. It is not mentioned by Josephus, although he was governor of Galilee and his official home was Tiberias, only six miles away on the near shore of Galilee. But no other place name in history stands in relation to it in importance. All that appears to have been known of Nazareth in the time of Herod the Great was its bad character. The common saying "Can any good thing come out of Nazareth?" was a question which perhaps had a hostile rather than a negative significance.

The little Galilean town lay in the hollow of the hills which enclose the green plain of Esdraelon. It was near to the great road for land traffic between Egypt and the interior of Asia; it was the nearest point from the inland to the sea. The caravan roads from Tyre and Sidon passed to the north of Nazareth near Capernaum, and it is possible that the neighbourhood had acquired an evil reputation for smuggling. Robbers who fell upon the traders halting their camel trains in the valley at night may have had their secret lurking-places in the vacant tombs on the stony hills behind Nazareth. We do not know. All we know is that Jesus was brought up in a town that bore a bad character. The one thing we definitely know about the people of Nazareth is that they stoned Jesus and tried to kill him by violence.

The natural surroundings of Nazareth as they are to-day would be familiar to Jesus. The town commands one of the finest prospects in Palestine. Built on a height, it overlooks a vast region—to the northward the verdant plain of Esdraelon, with the white houses of Safed and Cana, the silver gleam of the Lake of Galilee and distant stretches of the Jordan; on the east the plains of Peræa, which form a continuous line broken by the far-off snow-capped mountain of Hermon; on the south a clear view of the hills of Samaria and the dome of Mount Tabor with the dreariness of Judæa beyond, parched as by a scorching wind of desolation and death; and on the west the fine outline of Mount Carmel, with a gap giving a clear glimpse of the Mediterranean.

Within this circle, the cradle of the Kingdom of God, was the world of Jesus from his childhood onward.

There has long been much ignorance concerning Nazareth. The impression that it was a secluded little village is false. Renan describes it as a small town of scattered and irregular houses, with stony streets and crossings and perhaps 4,000 inhabitants. He thinks that Nazareth did not perhaps differ from this in the time of Jesus, and that its population has not much varied. This is almost certainly wrong. It takes no sufficient account of the degrading changes which Nazareth, in common with all Galilee, has undergone under Islam since Jesus. The three Gospel authorities always call it a city. It was almost certainly one of the 240 towns mentioned by Josephus whereof none had fewer than 15,000 inhabitants. There is reason to think that there were as many as 20,000 inhabitants in the time of Jesus. It is common to speak of it as a very primitive little place. This is probably quite wrong.

Nazareth was a Jewish city, and, like the towns about it, had for many years been under the transforming influence of Herod the Great. It was probably semi-Roman. It was certainly semi-Jewish. It may have resembled the old Jewish towns of the "Russian Pale." Certainly the streets were narrow and crooked, with side alleys that in winter time were turned into water-courses. The tenements, mostly of stone and mud, were lofty. We hear that the houses throughout Galilee were of many stories in height, and that, as a consequence of the loss of life from fires and earthquakes (there were hot streams as near to it as Tiberias), an order came from Rome that they were to be reduced from seven stories to four, five and six.

The inhabitants of Nazareth in the time of Jesus may have been mainly Jews, but there were among them many people of nearly all eastern races—Phœnicians, Syrian Arabs and Greeks—a mixed and perhaps incongruous population.

Nazareth was only a few miles off the trade route north and south, probably four or five. This may have determined its trade and the character of its inhabitants. Many of these may have been brigands, the country being overrun by them.

The best that can be said for the Nazarenes is that, being cast off from the commercial advantages of the trade route, they carried on some of the native industries. It was too far from the lake for fishermen or boat-builders, but there were the many occupations of husbandry and stock-raising, and there would be people of the better class in Nazareth, Cana, and the other little towns about, with their vineyards and olive plantations and prosperous pasturages.

Much building was going on within a few miles of Nazareth during the reign of Herod the Great, and a little later Antipas was building his palace in the new capital of Tiberias on the western shore of the Lake of Galilee, where there were hot springs. These activities would give abundant occupation to the Galileans, and it is not necessary to suppose that the Nazarenes did not enjoy a life of comfort.

III. The Home of Jesus

The accepted idea is that the home of Jesus was a little mud-built dwelling of two rooms, with the workshop adjoining, containing for furniture a few cushions to sit and sleep upon, a few earthenware jars for food, and one or two wooden chests for clothes. This is almost certainly wrong; it is a description of an Arab house. Mary's home would be a Jewish home; we read of tables, chairs and other substantial furniture, and the structure itself would be of stone and timber. Christian art has fostered the error. Painters who knew nothing of Palestine have persisted in depicting the joiner's shed by the side of a rustic cottage with the branches of the vine trailing over it.

Much harder and sterner was the reality. The idea that Joseph was a maker of ploughs, yokes and arrows is probably a mistake. He had better work to do. The country in his time was full of better work. He was probably a building carpenter, perhaps brought to Galilee (if he was a native of Bethlehem) by the building which Herod was doing there. Joseph's trade as a carpenter does not necessarily imply that he worked solely with the adze and saw. One of the apocryphal Gospels causes a carpenter to explain that he makes not only ploughs and yokes and ox-goads, but that he also builds temples. In such small communities a carpenter was a skilled and versatile craftsman, a wheelwright, a blacksmith, a mason and something of an architect. Joseph may have come to Nazareth as a young man, and met his wife there. If so, he did not do his work in a shed at home, but travelled, it may be, miles every day to it, or, when working at a distance, stayed all the week at the place of his work and returned home for the Sabbath. On the other hand, he may have engaged himself wholly in Nazareth, and have employed journeymen and apprentices. There is no reason to suppose that he was not a man of considerable financial substance.

That Mary's home may have been humble is not improbable. There is nothing in the Gospels to indicate the condition in which the early life of Jesus was passed. On this point, however, there is an illuminating passage in one of the letters of St. Paul:

> For ye know the grace of our Lord Jesus Christ, that, though he was rich, yet for your sakes he became poor, that ye through his poverty might be rich. [II *Corinthians* VIII, 9]

Has this a material significance? If so, it is important. The gentle refinement of Jesus in all circumstances of his life precludes the idea that he was brought up in anything like sordid poverty.

It is quite safe to conjecture that Jesus was nurtured with loving tenderness. How otherwise could it have been when he was blessed with such a mother—the one mother who has been exalted above all others in all the world and in all time? The incidents of his childhood may not have been very different from those attending the lives of other children who were his contemporaries in Nazareth. Very certainly he would receive his earliest education in the synagogue, which was the only school.

The synagogue was the chief centre of Jewish life. Every town had its synagogue, generally a small, unadorned, rectangular building, with a large porch outside and a double row of columns within on either side, leaving a broad nave and two narrow aisles. The interior was rather rude—benches, a reading-desk, a kind of railed dais, the cupboard in the wall for the Scroll of the Law.

The synagogue was the heart of the community—its church, club, meeting-house, court-house, university, school. Always open. The officials were the rabbi and the reader, or chazzan. The rabbi was ill paid—the chief priests in Jerusalem lavishly paid—according to the practice in all churches. The reader was generally a miserably paid old man, often beyond other work.

IV. His Early Education

In towns of large size there were several schools for children. The primary school, called the *beth ha-sepher* was for children under thirteen. Each of the 480 synagogues of Jerusalem had one such school. Then came the *beth ha-Talmud* in the Temple hall. It was the great high school. The highest school of biblical learning. But these schools would not be found in towns of the size of Nazareth.

The synagogue of Nazareth would be the first school of Jesus.

His teacher would be the old reader to the synagogue, whose method of instruction would be to seat his children in a circle on the floor, and then set them to chant passages (in a rhythmical singsong) from the Bible, as he read aloud to them, until they knew the words by heart. This method of instruction would probably be the earliest form of education which Jesus would have as a child.

Later, he would learn to read and write, and still later he would be taught by the rabbi—a kind of substitute for the *beth ha-Talmud*.

He would speak the language of his own people. This would be a dialect of Hebrew and Syriac, called Aramaic. Clearly, it was a marked dialect, or else it could acquire a marked accent from the broadening of the vowels. Later, as we shall see, the Galilean dialect of Aramaic was a means of identification at a critical moment. It "bewrayed" the speaker of it. Aramaic was, no doubt, the language spoken in the home of Jesus. It was his mother-tongue, and probably it carried him everywhere in Palestine, for it seems to have been universally spoken.

But pure Hebrew must have been read in the synagogues. The books of law were written in Hebrew, and after reading from them on the Sabbath the reader would roughly translate what he had read. Thus Jesus almost certainly learnt Hebrew. Moreover, we have the word of St. Paul that Jesus spoke to him in the Hebrew tongue.

Then the Greeks were the pedlars and wholesale dealers. The Jewish people would certainly learn something of Greek. Thus it is very likely that Jesus, from his childhood up, learned to speak not only Aramaic, but also Hebrew and some Greek, the languages of the home, the synagogue and the market-place.

Such was life in the native town of Jesus. But outside of it, there would be the interest of the great trade route a few miles away—the coming and going of the caravans from north and south; the mules and camels raising the dust in the summer, trapsing through the mud in the winter. Then the daily incidents of the trade route—the quarrels, fights, murders perhaps.

All this going on, almost within sight, day by day, during the most impressionable period of a boy's life.

The only other education in the early boyhood of Jesus would probably centre round his father's workshop. This was almost certainly adjoining his dwelling-house. The adze and the saw and their uses would become known to him. He would have permission to use them, as children do.

It is reasonable to assume that if his father's work took him to the little towns in the near neighbourhood (Cana and even Capernaum) as it almost certainly would, Jesus would sometimes go with him. It is only a natural inference.

He would also learn something of the country and its constitution—the plough, the harrow, seed-time and harvest, the habits of animals and birds, the varieties of the wild flowers and the cultivated produce of the garden. His familiarity with the garden (as seen in his sayings later) was of a kind that comes of association in childhood. The man born in the heart of a great town hardly ever shows such intimacy as the man born and brought up in close touch with the country. So strong is this in Jesus as almost to suggest that he was himself a gardener rather than a carpenter.

And then the still greater events in the world outside, of which breathless news would constantly be brought in to Nazareth. Some of these were important events, which were to make a great impression on his later life—to colour it, and to put words into his mouth which we shall better understand when we see the occasion of them.

We are accustomed to think of the infancy of Jesus as if spent in a little forgotten valley, where men like Joseph the carpenter lived and died in complete obscurity and ignorance of what was going on in the world. This is utterly wrong.

Let us see what occurred within a day's journey of Nazareth, during the first ten years of the life of Jesus. It may cast a light back on his life, and show what was happening to him in those dark years of which the Gospels are silent.

V. *The Death of Herod the Great*

Jesus was only a few months old when Herod the Great died. Herod had lived a bad life and came to a bad end. Some years before his death he was smitten with an incurable and loathsome malady, not difficult to recognize from the description given of it in Josephus as the result of an evil life. This hideous fact appears to dispose of the legend that, when Herod ordered the slaughter of the children of Bethlehem, he killed one of his own illegitimate children in the massacre.

Apparently, Herod's disease at length reached his brain. He conceived the idea that two of his elder sons (Alexander and Aristobulus) were conspiring against him. After putting them to torture on the evidence of his servants, he condemned them to death, and then applied to the Roman emperor for permission to execute them.

Augustus granted this permission, apparently reluctantly, and afterwards said, with an untranslatable play upon words, "It is better to be Herod's swine than his son."

About the same time Herod, acting under the mistaken impression that he had the power to will away his kingdom without the ratification of the Roman emperor, made his seventh son, Antipas, by his Samaritan wife, heir to his kingdom. Near to his end he altered this will and made his son, Archelaus (by the same Samaritan wife) king of Judæa.

A few days after the execution of his sons, Alexander and Aristobulus, Herod himself died miserably.

After his father's death, Archelaus made a speech in his honour (in the Roman manner), extolling the dead king and promising to follow in his footsteps.

But knowing the idea was abroad that Herod had not been sane when he altered his will in his favour, and probably knowing, also, that his right to the kingdom of Judæa was not valid until it received the ratification of the Roman emperor, Archelaus declared his intention of going to Rome for it.

He went. His father's friend, Nicholas of Damascus (not a Jew), went with him to plead his cause. Antipas, his brother, followed him to oppose him. Another Archelaus, the son of his sister, Salome, therefore his nephew, with a reputation as a public speaker, also followed Archelaus to Rome to plead against his uncle, on the ground that he had slaughtered the people about the Temple.

While Archelaus was in Rome, pleading his cause with Cæsar, there was an insurrection in Palestine, and much blood was shed in Jerusalem. The emperor's decision was to put aside the last will of Herod the Great and alter the status of all the sons. Archelaus was made ethnarch of Judæa and a great part of Samaria. Antipas was made tetrarch of Galilee and Peræa. Philip was made tetrarch of the country north of Galilee. Thus the Roman empire was strengthened by the removal of all rights to kingship.

Jesus was then a young child in Nazareth.

VI. Herod Antipas

Antipas, afterwards called Herod Antipas, returned to Galilee. His palace at that time was a few miles north of Nazareth.

He was the sovereign under whom Jesus lived all his life. He was twenty years older than Jesus, and had been educated with his brother, Archelaus, in Rome. A cunning, foxy person, he constantly visited Rome to curry favour with the emperor.

In the manner of his father, he built cities all over Galilee. He built a wall about a city and called the city Livias, after the emperor's wife, and he built other cities in Galilee in imitation of the Roman example. All this, of course, he did with the money extorted from the people in taxes. For a time he was rewarded with the confidence of Augustus, but later Augustus openly expressed his contempt for Antipas.

Philip, called Herod Philip, his brother, acted similarly. He enlarged and beautified Paneas, a city at the fount of the Jordan, and called it Cæsarea-Philippi. Thus we witness two of the sons of Herod currying favour with Augustus Cæsar.

Meantime, Archelaus, going from bad to worse, was at least a sincere ruffian. In violation of the law, he married the widow of his brother Alexander, although she had children by her former husband, and another husband still living. Archelaus oppressed his people to such an extent that the Emperor Augustus counselled him to deal gently with his subjects. But he continued to show himself so fierce and tyrannical that at length the Jews accused him before the emperor. Archelaus was summoned to Rome and banished to Vienne, Gaul, the Siberia of the Roman Empire.

This was when Jesus was about ten years of age.

The territory of Archelaus was then taken over by Rome itself. It was put under the governor of Syria, with a procurator in Judæa. The governor was Cyrenius; the procurator was Coponius. Their first act was to organize a census and taxing.

The census was to be taken after the Roman method, not the Jewish method.

For this reason and other reasons, the Jewish people were affronted. The high priest, Joazar, tried, without much success, to persuade them to submit to the census, showing them the uselessness of resistance. Joazar was a Pharisee, a believer in the Resurrection, and presumably he held the hope of a Messiah. He had been nominated by the people.

Eventually, Cyrenius found this out and deposed him, and appointed Annas, who was a Sadducee, therefore not a believer in the Resurrection, and probably held the Messianic hope in contempt. This is the first appearance in history of the man who was to play the major part in the last hours of Jesus.

VII. Judas the Galilean

The leader of the revolt was one Judas, the Galilean. He is sometimes described as a Gaulonite of the city of Gamala. It is doubtful where he was born, whether in Galilee or on the eastern side of the Jordan. He was a Pharisee.

The accepted theory is that he objected to the Roman taxation on the ground that it was no better than slavery. Therefore, he exhorted his nation to assert their liberty. The people are said to have been infected with this doctrine to an incredible degree. A violent war followed.

Josephus, who is hostile to Judas, speaks of the revolt as seditious, and that while waged under the pretence of public welfare it was really done in the hope of personal gain. Famines followed, and reduced the people to the last degree of despair. Cities were demolished. Josephus says that Judas was the author of a seditious doctrine which brought the whole Jewish nation to destruction.

All this is worse than false.

If it were true, it would mean that not Judas only, but the whole of the Jewish people were destitute of the first sense of the duties and obligations of civil life—namely that a nation could not live under any government without paying the expense of it.

But this was not the first time the Jewish people had paid taxes. They had paid taxes to Archelaus and to his father, Herod the Great. The true ground of revolt was partly national and partly religious.

It meant that the Hebrew kingship had gone. The throne of David was usurped. Therefore, all national aspirations must be considered dead. While Herod the Great sat on David's throne, the Jews did not realize that already the Jewish kingship was dead, and that only the ghost of it remained.

Now they realized that instead of being the subjects of a monarch of mighty David's line they had only a Roman governor and a Roman procurator to rule over them. And their Roman masters not only taxed them, but practically wiped out the authority of their cherished religion.

The Roman procurator in Judæa stood for Cæsar, not for David. The Sanhedrin might have its police and prisons to safeguard the Jewish religion, but the Roman procurator appointed the high priest (the head of the Sanhedrin), and capital sentence could not be executed without his sanction.

Thus the Roman emperor was really (and for the first time) the master of the Jews. More, the Roman emperor himself was a ruler in whose name everything that was done was accounted divine.

His standards were put up for adoration. The Romans wished to put them up in the Temple. To pay tribute through Herod had been one thing; to pay tribute to the roman procurator who came under the standard of the "divine" Cæsar was quite another. The Jews had only one God. They would not recognize a god in Cæsar.

But there was one deeper ground of revolt. By crushing the monarchs of the Jews the Romans had dealt a blow at the central life of the Jewish heart—the life of the Messiah, who was to re-establish the throne of David.

Thus the revolt was, in its heart, a Messianic revolt. That is why it infected the people so greatly.

The revolt of Judas the Galilean ended in great suffering and great slaughter. It began in Jerusalem, but apparently passed all over Palestine.

It is almost certain that Galilee suffered from it, although Herod Antipas, in his anxiety to stand well with Rome, would do his utmost to keep it out of his dominions. It would be impossible to keep it out. Refugees would fly wounded across the border from Samaria to Galilee. Wounded men would be taken in and sheltered by the Galileans who sympathized with them.

Finally, Judas was conquered and killed, and the revolt was suppressed.

But though Judas himself was crushed, his spirit was not wiped out. It survived in two movements—one of them representing the national sect, the other the Messianic side. The followers of the first were called Herodians; the followers of the other were called

Zealots. Their influence lived on for many years. They reappear in the later life of Jesus.

All this occurred when Jesus was between ten and twelve years of age. It took place within a few miles of the home of his childhood. Is it possible that it can have made no impression upon him?

Every day there would be news of the war coming in by the caravans. During the war there would be the sympathy of the synagogue. The synagogue (particularly the little country synagogue) would certainly be on the side of Judas—whatever side Jerusalem, the chief priest and the Sanhedrin might take.

In Galilee, Judas would be personally known. It is probable that within their closed doors (if Herod's spies could be kept out) they prayed every Sabbath for Judas and the success of his armies. It was a secret, subterranean wave of emotion. It would pass through every house, too.

The subjects of Herod Antipas might not be affected by the taxing of the Roman procurators, but they must have been deeply moved by the quenching of the hope of Israel. When Judas fell it would be a crushing blow to the Jewish spirit, especially the spirit of the poorer Jews.

The blow would be felt in the house of Joseph the Carpenter also. Perhaps Joseph knew Judas. Perhaps Jesus had seen him and been patted on the head by him. What more likely? The likeliest thing in a life of which we have no actual knowledge—the patriot, the fanatic, and the big-eyed, spiritual-looking boy.

Thus the first great experience in the early life of Jesus was that of the struggle of his people for the life of the Messianic hope.

Do we know nothing of the dark years in the life of Jesus whereof the Gospels are silent when we know with certainty that this tremendous upheaval—the destroying of cities, the bringing of famine—was going on for nearly two years under his eyes? Did he not see all this?

His sermons and addresses give abundant proof of his knowledge of life in nearly all its phases. Only a teacher who knew life through and through could have preached the Sermon on the Mount.

To think that the lofty wisdom of that sermon came out of the air, and not out of direct contact with the sternest realities of the earth, is to imagine a foolish and stupid thing.

VIII. The Feasts of the Jewish Year

When he was twelve years of age, Jesus was taken for his first visit to Jerusalem to attend the festival of the Passover. This is the only incident which breaks the silence of the Gospels in the life of Jesus in the thirty years from his birth until the beginning of his ministry. It is recorded in *Luke* alone of the four synoptic Gospels. We therefore know nothing positive concerning his boyhood in Nazareth.

During his infancy and childhood Jesus no doubt joined in the ordinary games and exercises of the neighbouring children; he may often have accompanied older boys on excursions over the hills, perhaps as far as the Lake of Galilee. In the springtime there would always be interest in the varying activities of the fields and vineyards; in the autumn the harvesting of the fruit, the grapes, the olives, the figs and dates. In the town there were the open bazaars, the life of the streets and the market-place, and he may have added to his store of knowledge and wisdom by talking with the camel drivers and travelling pedlars gathered round the fountain in the evening when the women came down to draw water. The domestic interests of his home must have formed an important part of his education.

Almost certainly Jesus spent a considerable portion of his young days in the synagogue, attending the feasts and festivals as a silent onlooker, if not as an actual participant in the ceremonies. The synagogue was a school of piety and virtue, and however much of secular education there may have been, the teaching was mainly religious.

The feasts of the Jewish year had their origin in the procession of the seasons and crops. Thus, the Passover is the festival of spring, and Pentecost is the feast of the harvest. Tabernacles is the feast of the gathering of the grapes and fruits. The Feast of Unleavened Bread was formerly distinct from the Feast of the Paschal Lamb (Passover).

Many of these occasions were joyous festivals, in which the young people of the town could take an understanding delight. In the Feast of Pentecost, for example, the synagogue was dressed with flowers; pillars and balconies were entwined with roses, lilies of the field, narcissi lilies, pansies and evergreens. In the Feast of

Tabernacles wooden booths were erected in the square or the courtyards of the synagogues in commemoration of the days when the children of Israel lived in tents in the wilderness. Each child's father had a booth to himself, thatched with green boughs, and hung with fruit—apples, grapes and figs. During this beautiful festival they ate under the boughs. The synagogue rustled with palm branches (as commanded in *Leviticus*). One could not breakfast before blessing the branches.

On the seventh day of Tabernacles the child had a little bundle of leafy boughs styled "hosannas," which he whipped on the synagogue bench, his sins falling away with the leaves that flew to the ground as he cried, "Hosanna, save us now."

The ninth day of Tabernacles was best, the Rejoicing of the Law, when the fifty-second portion of the Pentateuch was read.

The Scrolls of the Law were carried round and round the synagogues seven times, and the boys took part in the procession carrying flags and wax tapers, and joining lustily with their elders in the alternative phrases, "Save us, we pray thee" and "Prosper us, we pray thee." In the more important synagogues the last night of the Feast of Tabernacles was celebrated by torch-light dances in the large space called the Court of the Women. This was apparently the climax of rejoicing. Jesus would possibly see this in Nazareth.

An important event in the life of every Jewish boy was the ceremony of Dedication, a feast in celebration of a Jewish redemption —in memory of the miracle of the oil that kept the perpetual light burning in the Temple when Judas Maccabæus reconquered it— one lamp being lighted on the first night, another on the second, and so on until there were eight lamps burning in a row.

IX. Confirmation

The Confirmation ceremony of becoming a "son of the Commandment" did not take place before the age of thirteen. It made the child a man, his sins (the responsibility for which had hitherto been upon his father's shoulders) now resting on himself. Counting hitherto for as little as a woman in the congregation, he now became a full unit in himself, with, perhaps, his blue-striped praying-shawl to wrap himself in at the synagogue, and his phylacteries—winding the first leather strap round his left arm and its fingers, so that the little cubical case containing the holy words sat upon the fleshy part of the upper arm; and binding the second strap round his forehead, with the black cube in the centre; and thinking the while of God's Unity and the Exodus from Egypt, according to the words of *Deuteronomy*, XI, 18:

> Therefore shall ye lay up these my words in your heart and in your soul, and bind them for a sign upon your hand, that they may be as frontlets before your eyes. And ye shall teach them to your children . . . and thou shalt write them upon the door posts of thine house, and upon thy gates.

Then the boy saying his portion, or Posher. On the first Sabbath of his thirteenth year he would be summoned as a man to the recitation of the Second Scroll, intoning a section of it from the parchment manuscript.

His fears, his shyness, appearing on the platform before the whole congregation. In his Sabbath clothes. Preparing for this act at night in bed. Learning it by heart. Then the great moment. After a few timid notes his voice soaring triumphantly, the people listening. After the service his parents being congratulated on the way he had said the Posher.

It is possible, however, that this ceremony of so making a boy a son of the Commandment is of somewhat later date than the time of Jesus.

Among the sacred festivals in which Jesus must have taken interest was the celebration of the Day of Atonement, which was preceded by a long month of prayer, ushering in the New Year, and made terrible by loud peals on the ram's horn.

The sinner was warned to repent, for the New Year marked the Day of Atonement.

On the tenth day, in every house a gigantic wax taper burned. Many of the worshippers in the synagogue were clad in their grave clothes; the extreme zealots, standing all the time, swayed to and fro and beat their breasts at the confession of sin. Many sat on the floor against the walls.

The custom of scapegoat was often included in the ceremonies of the Day of Atonement. The Jewish high priest laid both his hands on the head of a live goat, confessing over it all the iniquities of the children of Israel, and having thereby transferred the sins of the people to the beast, sent it away into the wilderness.

And so, the boy lived and grew, his vision turning back towards the ancient Palestine, and forward towards some vague Restoration, his days engirdled with prayer and ceremony.

Having in view his necessary familiarity with these ceremonies as they were conducted in the little synagogue of Nazareth, one can well apprehend that Jesus, even at twelve years of age, was spiritually attuned to their significance, and that his experience had prepared him with a full knowledge of the purpose of his first visit to Jerusalem. Very surely he regarded it as a most important event. It may be that already he was conscious that he was going about his Father's business. Joseph and Mary must also have considered it important, or they would not have taken him with them on so long a pilgrimage. It was their religious duty to take him. In his twelfth year, according to Jewish usage, a boy becomes capable of an independent participation in the sacred rites.

For non-Jews the incident of Jesus going up to the Temple had another and perhaps more moving significance. It occurred a few months after the end of the Judas revolt. We have no right to say there is any connection between the two events, but to the Christians who come nearly 2,000 years later they present a striking contrast.

On the one side the violent suppression of the national and theocratic spirit of the Jewish people by the new power of Rome. On the other hand, the festival which celebrated the liberation of their race from the thraldom of Egypt.

Hebrew tradition connects the Passover with the Exodus, the beginning of the theocratic life of the Jewish nation.

According to tradition, the Passover of Egypt was preordained by Moses at the command of God to commemorate the exodus of the Jewish people from Egypt, where they had been held in bondage, and the hope of their race suppressed. It consisted of the eating of unleavened bread and bitter herbs in memory of their pilgrimage. It is thought that it was originally a pilgrimage feast to Jerusalem. There were three great festivals in Jerusalem which the Jews were expected to attend. To the poor Jews, living at long distances from Jerusalem, attendance at all three might be difficult or impossible.

But it is clear that to go up to Jerusalem for the Passover was a duty which every orthodox Jew in Palestine considered it incumbent upon him to fulfil.

It represented above all the discharge of a religious obligation, but it may have had other and less solemn uses. The seven days of Passover at Jerusalem may have had their social, domestic and even commercial uses also. To see friends once a year, to buy the necessaries, such as clothing not obtainable in the smaller towns, and working tools, even perhaps to sell some of their own produce.

The scene of it at ordinary times could not have failed to be one of great interest. A whole nation going up to its central Temple to make sacrifice in memory of the deliverance of their race.

But it is not unreasonable to assume that so soon after the failure of the revolt of Judas against the pagan power it had a deeper and sadder note.

On the face of it the journey was reasonable and natural. Jerusalem was the centre of the religious life of the Jewish people of Palestine. The Temple was the heart of it. The little synagogues scattered over the land were like mission churches. Their congregations held it to be their duty to go up to Jerusalem once a year for the greatest of the Jewish feasts. The Passover, which fell at the end of what we now call Easter (spring), began in the evening of the fourteenth day of the first month—that is April 14th, a fixed date apparently—and it continued for seven days.

Even without historical records, it is not difficult to imagine the scenes in the little towns of Galilee, the days of preparation, the arrangements for the members of the family who were to go, the part of those who were to remain at home, the new clothing that was provided, new hooded gabardines for the boys and strong new sandals for all, the food to be taken, and the tents. The paschal lambs to be offered in sacrifice, the gathering up of the pack mules, the grooming and bridling of the asses on which the women were to ride with the young children who could not be left behind. There would be camels, too, for the richer pilgrims. The men and boys would be expected to walk all the way, a distance of about eighty miles, including three or four days' journey through the bleak stony land of Judæa. The days might be dry and even bright, but the nights would be cold, especially in the exposed parts of Peræa, where it would be necessary to encamp under the brilliant Palestinian sky.

At early dawn, on the morning of the starting out from Nazareth, everything would be ready. Probably there would be many people from Cana, or from as far north as Magdala, joining the Nazarenes; all Galilee going up to Jerusalem. The caravan would grow longer as it passed through the towns and villages on the way, other people being added to it at each halt. Then, at the sun's rising above the heights of Mount Tabor, the procession would move off.

It is appropriate to emphasise the drawn-out length of the slowly moving procession. The boys and girls who formed a part of the company would not always remain with their kinsfolk. They would be free to run about from end to end of the line of march, lingering here and there to make new friends, to share their food and to rest in their separate camps at eventide. There need have been no anxiety concerning their temporary absence from their own people. This circumstance explains, and affords an excuse for, the seeming indifference of Joseph and Mary on the return journey when, as recorded by St. Luke, the child Jesus tarried behind in Jerusalem, and was not to be found among their kinsfolk and acquaintances in the company. They would appear to have been accustomed to such an act of truancy.

X.   *The Pilgrimage to Jerusalem*

The first thing to remember about these festival pilgrimages from Galilee at Passover is that they were pilgrimages of rejoicing. Passover was a time of thanksgiving and rejoicing. Consequently, the whole spirit of the pilgrimage would be a spirit of gaiety and rapturous joy. The anniversary of the escape of the children of Israel from their bondage in Egypt. It was the annual holiday, corresponding in some measure with Christmas in Christian countries.

It took place in the spring of the year, when nature is kind, the sun shining in a clear sky after the gloom of winter, the wild flowers, the lilies of the field, giving colour to the plains, the lower slopes of the hills showing their fresh green.

As the long procession marched on its way the people would join in singing hymns, anthems and songs. Chanting the psalms of David and reciting little catches similar in character to that which comes at the end of the Passover service—a sort of "House that Jack Built."

We can picture them (as long as they are on orthodox Jewish

territory, as in Galilee and the greater part of Peræa, south of Gadara, which was largely pagan) looking up their friends in villages, towns and farms on the way; calling out the inhabitants to come along with them, and carrying them off, the increasing joy of the company growing larger. The arrival at the ford over the Jordan, facing Jericho; crossing the ford; going up to the great old city. Buying and perhaps selling on their way. The children, the boys and girls, the babes in arms. The young mothers riding on asses, the men marching beside them. The little hospitalities on the way, the dates, the figs, the grapes.

Then the ascent from Jericho to the top of the hill beyond Bethany, after passing by the old Jericho road with its great gorges and deep valley.

Then coming in sight of Jerusalem. The drawing up in a vast multitude as they looked down on the Holy City—with its white Temple, its marble palaces, their green gardens, after the desert path or the bare plains.

Josephus says the usual course of the Galileans going up from Galilee to Jerusalem was through Samaria.

This is plainly incorrect, as a general practice. That the Galileans did sometimes go up by that direct course, being by many miles the shortest, is beyond doubt. But it was a course attended by great discomfort, often by open quarrels, sometimes by fierce fights. The Samaritans had no love to lose for people with their faces set towards Jerusalem (which stood to them for nearly every thing they hated), and hence they denied them help. I see them trying to prevent them from using the wells—not only the many general wells about cities like Shechem, but even the well sacred to them by association with the Fathers of their Faith, such as Jacob's well. I see them refusing to allow the Galileans to approach these wells when they were half dying of thirst; refusing shelter to young mothers and little children on wet and cold or stormy nights.

What happened we know. In their wrath the vast multitudes of the pilgrims sometimes set fire to the Samaritan villages and burnt them to the ground.

After such reprisals, the Galileans would find themselves in state quarrels. The Samaritans would appeal to the Roman procurator at Cæsarea (Samaria). The Roman procurator would protest to Herod Antipas, the tetrarch of Galilee. Antipas, as a kind of Jew, would be compelled to side with his subjects, the Galileans, hence perpetual friction between the tetrarch Antipas and the Roman procurator.

The reflection of all this is plainly seen in the Gospels. We need not go far to find the cause of the disagreement between Pilate and Herod Antipas. There must have been an almost perpetual state of feud between them. The procurator would send his soldiers to defend the Samaritans. The soldiers (almost without being conscious of it) would sometimes pursue the Galileans over the Galilean frontier—on their way home from Jerusalem after Passover. This would be a grievous offence to Antipas—the procurator assuming rights over the territory of Antipas.

It is clear, therefore, that the ordinary way up to Jerusalem from Galilee was across the south end of the lake into the Peræan territory, sometimes called Galilee, skirting, but not generally entering, the city of Gadara, which, besides being a few miles too far east and up the hill to be the direct way to the Jordan road—the road along the side of the river—was open to the objection of being only partly and by no means predominantly Jewish, and therefore not the most suitable for a joyous and perhaps rather tumultuous concourse of Galilean people.

But there was still a third way from Galilee to Jerusalem, and St. Luke seems to have had it in mind in his later account of the journey of Jesus from Galilee to one of the feasts at Jerusalem.

This would be through part of Samaria, perhaps the least hostile part, and then down to the western side of the Jordan and along the road by the river, under the wilderness of Jericho until the plain of Jericho is reached, and then westward through Jericho and thus up the Mount of Olives road to Bethany and thence into Jerusalem.

The last night of the journey would probably be spent at Bethabara or Jericho. The enthusiasm which had been flagging from physical weariness would be revived by the thought that in the morning they would be within sight of the Holy City, and the religious scenes under the sky, throbbing with stars, would be deeply moving. With the dawn there would be a lifting up of the people's hearts, and a new energy would hasten the last lap of the pilgrimage. Then from the slopes of the Mount of Olives would come the first view of Jerusalem, with its white buildings and surrounding wall, and the vast throngs of people crowding round the gates where the camels were being relieved of their burdens.

The Galileans would enter by the Damascus Gate and stream through the tortuous streets overshadowed by very lofty houses. Vast numbers of strangers would be received there. Josephus says as many as 3,000,000. He also says that in one year there were more than 250,000 paschal lambs filling the air with their bleating on the side of the Mount of Olives. But Josephus is never to be trusted for accuracy when it is a question of figures. Jerusalem in those days could not possibly have accommodated as many as 3,000,000 visitors, even with the help of outside encampments. Such numbers represent half the population of Palestine at that time.

Finally, the outer court of the Temple was reached. It had been robbed of the glories of King Solomon, but it was still splendid to look upon. On three sides ran a double and on the fourth side a triple colonnade of brilliantly white marble with ornate cedar roofs, while various coloured stone slabs covered the broad level floor. Here, in three spaces, was the Temple market, the taverns or booths with the tables of the money-changers, the benches of the traders in objects of sacrifice, the sacrificial cattle, wine, oil, corn, salt and incense. Provisions also for the animals for slaughter—oxen, lambs, doves (the poor man's sacrifice). The lambs were offered by thousands.

There was noise in the cries of men and beasts, of sellers and buyers, a clinking of money. To a great extent the occasion was in the nature of a fair, and though secular work was prohibited, yet in the intervals of ceremonial the bazaars were open, and there was buying and selling and chaffering, with shrill cries from the vendors of goods which the people from the far-off towns wished to take home with them.

XI. The Passover Celebration

The celebration of the Passover had public and official aspects which were invested occasionally with pomp and ceremony; but it also had its private and domestic side. On the day before the Passover, in every dwelling, the last crumbs of leavened bread were solemnly burnt, for no one might eat bread for eight days, only Passover cakes—large biscuits without yeast, full of holes, speckled and spotted—which took the place of bread.

The streets were deserted, the people being all indoors. The evening table was precisely laid for the Seder service. There were cups and strange dishes. First the cup of consecration, over which the master of the house had pronounced a blessing, was drunk. Then hands were washed and the meal was served. This consisted of the roasted shank-bone of a lamb, bitter herbs, sweet spices, cakes of unleavened bread, a sauce called harôseth, made from dates, raisins and vinegar, the paschal lamb and the flesh of subsidiary sacrifices. The master of the household dipped a morsel of unleavened bread into the harôseth and ate it, and a similar sop was given to each one present. Afterwards the paschal lamb was eaten and three other cups of wine were drunk at intervals, with thanksgivings and singing of the Hallel (*Psalms* CXIII–CXVIII). A large cup of wine was reserved for the prophet Elijah, betokening the certainty of God, that He would send His Messiah to deliver His people and raise them to the sovereignty of the world.

During the feast the youngest child asked the head of the household, "Wherein doth this night differ from all other nights? For on other nights we may eat leavened and unleavened bread, but tonight only unleavened." The father's reply in Hebrew lasted an hour or two, explaining the meaning of the Passover.

There was a certain note of rejoicing, even of merriment, in the proceedings, laughter mingling with the chorus of the *Chad Gadya*.

Chad Gadya! Chad Gadya! One only kid of the goat! And a cat came and devoured the kid which my father bought for two zuzim. *Chad Gadya! Chad Gadya!* And a dog came and bit the cat which had devoured the kid which my father bought for two zuzim. *Chad Gadya!*

The commentators of an after time explained the meaning of this jingle as typifying the procession of the ages, the passing of the ancient empires—Egypt, Assyria, Persia, Greece, Rome—the ultimate triumph of the people of God when the Messiah should come.

XII. In the Temple

It is more than probable that during the sojourn in Jerusalem Jesus became familiar with the sights of the city and its surroundings which were afterwards to be universally associated with his name—the Garden of Gethsemane, the Mount of Olives, the Mount of Calvary, the Pool of Siloam, all that remained of the splendour of Solomon's palace and the city of David. In the Temple, where the sacred Ark was an object of devotion, he would find many interests to linger over, and no doubt he attended most of the ceremonies and listened to the discourses of the doctors. Possibly some of the priests took more than passing notice of the Galilean boy with the large wondering eyes, and spoke with him. On such points, St. Luke, our only informant, is silent.

The story told in the Gospel of St. Luke states briefly that at the end of the Feast of Passover the parents of Jesus bent their way homeward to Nazareth, that they started on the journey not knowing that Jesus had tarried behind. They supposed him to have been among their travelling companions. His absence from their side gave them no immediate anxiety, because they believed that perhaps he was with other boys of his own age—not improbably his so-called cousins, the sons of Mary Cleopas. But after they had accomplished a day's journey they missed him. They sought for him in vain among their friends and acquaintances of the caravan, and when they found him not they turned back again to Jerusalem, seeking him. They sought him for three days.

Then at length they found him, probably in one of the outer halls of the Temple sitting in the midst of an assembly of the doctors, both listening to them and asking them questions. And all who heard him were astonished at his understanding and answers. And when Mary his mother saw him she was amazed and reproached him, saying, "Son, why hast thou thus dealt with us? Behold, thy father and I have sought thee sorrowing."

Whereupon Jesus is reported to have replied, "How is it that ye sought me? Wist ye not that I must be about my Father's business?"

It is said that the mother of Jesus did not understand his answer. Finally, it is said that Jesus returned to Nazareth with his parents and was subject to them, and that he increased in stature and wisdom and in favour with God and man, but that his mother kept all these sayings in her heart.

XIII. Jesus and the Divine Mission

Such is the story of the visit of Jesus to Jerusalem in his twelfth year.*

*The significance of the twelfth year is diminished by its frequent use in scripture and tradition for kindred purposes, as that at twelve years of age Moses had outlearned his teachers, that Samuel prophesied in his twelfth year, that Solo-

It presents many difficulties. Obviously the object of the story is to show that Jesus, as early as his twelfth year, was conscious of his divine mission, of his special relation to God, perhaps of his Messiahship. It has no obvious relation to what goes before or comes after it. It stands alone as a break in the scheme of the Gospels on the life of Jesus during the thirty odd years from his birth to the beginning of his Ministry. It presents a picture of scholastic life that is obviously not Jewish as we see it in various references in the Bible, and with our own eyes still in the East, and therefore is presumably the conception of a foreigner.

The only possible authority for the story is the mother of Jesus, and it requires that we should eliminate many things we have been told in her name in earlier parts of the same Gospel. It requires us to believe that when Mary spoke of Joseph as the father of Jesus she must have known that, according to her earlier story (if it was hers), he was not so, and that for personal reasons she was concealing his true origin.

It requires us to believe that when she is described as not understanding what Jesus has said about his relation to God she must have forgotten the incidents relating to the Virgin Birth, the visit of the angel and the announcement of the divine character and mission of her unborn son, the message of the shepherds, the prophecies of Simeon and Anna, the presents of the Wise Men, the flight into Egypt and the massacre of the children of Bethlehem.

It requires us to believe that when Jesus answered his mother that God was the only Father whose business he had to think about he was openly avowing what she was attempting to conceal. It requires us to believe that if this was the first statement by Jesus of his divine mission, it failed to produce effect, since the doctors were totally unaffected by it in that character. It requires us to believe that not only had Mary and Joseph been so unmindful of the welfare of the child who, according to the angel, was the Son of God, as to set out on their long journey home in a large company of perhaps hundreds of persons, without assuring themselves that he was with them, and so heedless of their sacred charge as to lose sight for a whole day, in a tumultuous throng, of the son

mon's wise judgments began when he was twelve, and Daniel's when he was twelve, and that, if a man was a divinely appointed seer, he manifested the fact from his twelfth year onwards.

who was to be the Saviour of the world; but also that Jesus himself had been so indifferent to the anxiety and pain and sorrow of his parents about his absence from their side that he had remained three days and two nights in Jerusalem after he must have known that they were gone.

It requires us to believe that after he was gently, tenderly and affectionately reminded of this failure of duty in this regard he replied in terms which in any other child of twelve years of age would have deserved serious reproof.

But are we required to believe all this? Is it necessary to our faith in Jesus as the Messiah?

For my own part, remembering the stories of the apocalyptic Gospels (scarcely less inhuman, less degrading to Jesus, less humiliating to his mother) which the Church wisely rejected as far back as the third century, I humbly but reverently say of the contradictory story of the visit of Jesus with his parents to the Temple, as told in *Luke,* that I simply cannot believe one word of it.

Not on such pitiful and painful grounds can our faith in Jesus as the Messiah be founded.

But are we, therefore, to reject the spirit as well as the letter of the story of the visit of Jesus to the Temple? By no means.

That Jesus, a sensitive child, would be under the influence of the recent Messianic revolt, is to me probable, almost certain. That on the morning of the departure of his parents from Jerusalem he should be missed by his parents is no less probable. That he should be found in the Temple corridors among the doctors asking questions is easy to believe.

Is not this enough? Does it not carry us far? All the rest is probably myth.

CHAPTER III

His Environment and Education

I. *The Country of Jesus*

IN ORDER TO FOLLOW the life of Jesus we must know something about the land in which he lived. It is a very small country. We may describe Palestine as a strip of territory extending along the eastern shore of the Mediterranean. Its total length is about 140 miles. Its breadth varies from about twenty-five miles in the north to nearly eighty miles in the south. Its total area is about 9,000 square miles, the country west of the Jordan being about 6,000 square miles. It is, therefore, about one-fifth the size of England, or not much bigger than Wales.

It is divided into two sections, eastern and western, and between them runs the River Jordan, which stretches from the Lake of Galilee on the north to the Dead Sea on the south. Its physical features are various. It has high lands and mountains rising to 3900 feet (Mount Hermon, 9,150 feet, is not within the boundaries of Palestine, although visible from Nazareth), but a considerable part of the land lies below sea level, the Lake of Galilee being about 1,292 feet below the level of the Mediterranean Sea, and the Dead Sea even below this. The city of Hebron, a city of refuge in Abraham's time, south of Jerusalem, was 3,040 feet above sea level.

The climate, as a consequence, is equally variable. It belongs to the sub-tropical zone. In midsummer it is very hot, often sultry. In winter it is often intensely cold, although snow rarely lies for more than a day or two, except on the high mountains. The rainfall is scanty, but there are periods of heavy rains with thunderstorms, usually continuing from November to March. The Christian art which represents Jesus and his disciples, in nearly all circumstances, bareheaded, barefooted and clothed in the lightest of garments, is the work of persons of limited knowledge of the country and its climate. Thick hooded gabardines were worn in the winter. Sandals were the usual footgear, but we have John the Baptist's authority for saying that the men also wore laced shoes.

Moses described Canaan as "a land full with the blessings of Jehovah." But by no modern standards could Palestine be called "a land flowing with milk and honey," though it may have seemed so to the Israelites, while crossing the desert under Sinai. The plain which extends along the Mediterranean coast is fruitful, and so is a large part of Galilee, but a great part of southern Palestine is stony and barren, and much of it is arid desert fringed with a feeble vegetation that has an expression about it of being sorrowful and desponding. On the whole, it is a hopeless, dreary, heartbroken land. In the early spring there is the vivid green of grass and rank weeds, with splashes of scarlet and white where the lilies of the field yet grow, as beautiful as in the time of Jesus. But with the passing of spring the colour on the hills fades, the flowers of the field die, there are no scarlet poppies and the grass seems to wither to a dull grey, hardly distinguishable from the stones.

There are, and always have been, great numbers of vertebrate animals in Palestine. There are large flocks of sheep and goats, and, if we are to credit the Gadarene story, swine also were kept in considerable numbers. There was a small native breed of oxen, and a sturdier kind used in the work of the plough. The camel, the horse, the mule, and the tall oriental ass were the draught animals. There were, and always have been, large numbers of dogs, most of them pariahs, uncared for and despised; but among the richer classes the Arabian gazelle hound (Saluki) was no doubt favoured. King Solomon observed (*Proverbs* XXXI–29) that there were three things which go well and are comely in going; a lion, who is the strongest among beasts, a greyhound, and a he-goat.

The names of many of the animals mentioned in the Bible have been so translated as to give a wrong impression. The "lion," now extinct in Palestine, was the puma; the "hart" is the gazelle or fallow deer; the "coney" is not the rabbit, but the Syrian hyrax; the "leopard" is the cheetah; the "fox" is the jackal; the "leviathan" is probably the crocodile, still occasionally to be found. There were large herds of wild goats (ibexes) in the southern wilderness, preyed upon by the hyena, the jackal and the wolf. The desert country in Judæa going down to the Dead Sea, and beyond the Jordan in Peræa, was infested by wolves in the time of Jesus. Snakes were not uncommon. Scorpions of the deadly species and poison spiders were a universal pest, and there are frequent references in the Bible to plagues of locusts and ants. There were great numbers of birds, many of them singing birds, including the nightingale. The eagle, vulture, stork, owl, partridge and quail are mentioned, and references to many of these are to be found in the recorded sayings of Jesus.

The flora of Palestine has great variety; the oleander, the magnolia and mimosa still flourish, and may have been known to Jesus. In the mountain regions there are many wild flowers of much beauty. In the valley of the Jordan, the vegetation is semi-tropical, consonant with the great heat in summer. The distinctive trees of the country are the terebinth, the cedar, the sycamore, the plane, the acacia and the date palm. Olive trees are abundant. The rose can hardly have been cultivated to anything like perfection in the time of Jesus. The flowers to which he refers are mostly the wildlings, the lily of the field, the rose of Sharon.

The population of Palestine has varied greatly at different periods. Josephus says that in his time (less than half a century after Jesus) there were 204 cities and villages in Galilee alone, and that not many of them contained fewer than 15,000 inhabitants. If we accept the calculation of Josephus, the population during the Jewish wars must have been out of all proportion to the area of the country. The armies he mentions and the dead he numbers almost pass belief to those who know the capacity of the country. Jesus himself speaks of cities which no longer exist. The remains of many towns are still to be seen in all parts of the country.

Capernaum, by the lake side, is now a mass of masonry, lying amidst a tangled confusion of thistles, nettles and wild mustard. Jericho, the accursed, lies a mouldering ruin to-day; Bethlehem and Bethany, in their poverty and humiliation, have nothing now to remind one that they once knew the high honor of the Saviour's presence. Where Sodom and Gomorrah reared their domes and towers is the solemn silence of the Dead Sea over whose waveless surface the blistering air hangs motionless, about whose borders nothing grows but weeds and scattered tufts of cane. Nazareth is forlorn. Renowned Jerusalem itself, the stateliest name in history, has lost its ancient grandeur and has become a pauper village.

The account of Jerusalem by Tacitus is meagre, but he mentions that the walls with towers were 120 feet high. We think of it as a great oriental city, but one can walk round its entire walls in a couple of hours. It was hardly more than half as big in the time of

Jesus, yet at the time of the Passover it is said to have housed 3,000,000 of persons. We think of the Temple as one of the great buildings of the world, yet we could have put the Temple of Herod (which was larger than the Temple of Solomon) inside the transept of more than one of the great cathedrals of the modern world. Solomon's Temple was not larger than an average-sized chapel of the present day. It had, however, a tall tower, which was 240 feet high.

Jerusalem, apparently, had a magnificent appearance in the eyes of the people of the time of Christ.

We think of the Jordan as a great river, yet, except in the rainy season, it is not as wide as Pall Mall, in London, or the Champs Elysées, in Paris.

We think of the Lake of Galilee as a great sea with a fleet of ships. The size of the lake is thirteen miles by eight at its greatest. The area of water is, therefore, less than that of Loch Lomond in Scotland. In the Gospels the ships are described as small, although the passage in which Jesus is described as sleeping indicates a cabin. Josephus writes of "climbing up" into ships, and says that there were as many as 230 vessels on the lake, each with four mariners. To call them "ships" is an exaggeration. They would better answer to the description of fishing-boats. There appears to have been a considerable fishing trade in Galilee.

In reading the story of Herod and the Wise Men we think of the distance of Jerusalem from Bethlehem as great. Even Strauss says it is a three hours' journey. It is less than six miles, and this fact of itself makes much of the story incredible.

All these popular misconceptions becloud the story of Jesus and often falsify it. They are due to two causes. First, that Jesus in his discourses and parables described simple, homely scenes. In reading them we forget that this is the way of all men of genius—to bring the general down to the particular. Next, the world does not remember that since the time of Jesus, Palestine has undergone three devastating changes which have altered it in every respect but one—the Roman conquest, the Arab conquest, and the Crusades.

As a result the Palestine of the present time bears nearly no resemblance to the country of Jesus. The natural conditions alone are the same. What nature made remains—nothing else whatever. Judæa remains with its temple rock; the Mount of Olives remains; the Jordan remains; the Lake of Galilee remains.

II. The Education of Jesus

What happened to Jesus during the five years that followed upon his first visit to the Temple? What was the nature of his education? It is sufficient that the orthodox and the unorthodox biographies of Jesus, however they may differ in other respects, are strangely in agreement about his higher education.

According to both he had none.

But there is an outstanding difference between their view of this fact. The orthodox claim that he had all knowledge and wisdom, but that he was taught of God. It needed that no man should tell him anything, for he had known everything from the beginning. The orthodox still fortify themselves in this view by the question of the people who asked where Jesus acquired his learning, seeing he had never been taught. The unorthodox, on the other hand, hold that he knew very little.

It is characteristic of the sceptical critics, particularly in France and Germany, down to the middle of the nineteenth century (Strauss, an entirely conscientious student, almost alone excepted) that they thought of Jesus as a kind of divine ignoramus. He had no scholastic training. It is not likely that he knew Greek. He had no Greek culture. No element of any other profound culture reached him. Born in the bosom of Judaism, he remained a stranger to the Hellenic developments which were going on in his own time, in Jerusalem, perhaps, and certainly in Alexandria.

That he was even ignorant of the scholasticism which was soon afterwards to form the Talmud, although some of the Pharisees had already brought it into Galilee.

That he was ignorant of the theory of Lucretius which, a century earlier, had established the unchangeable system of nature.

That, although born at a time when the principles of positive science had already begun to be proclaimed in the enlightened parts of the world, when even Babylon and Persia were not strangers to it, Jesus was so behind his age that he lived entirely in the supernatural—that he believed in miracles, in prayer, in angels, in the Devil, in demoniacal possession, in sin as a cause of disease, and that his influence with the multitude was largely due to the childish and charming simplicity and sincerity with which he presented these outworn beliefs.

Further, the sceptics claim that he was not only not a theologian, but he was not a politician and had no acquaintance with the condition of the world. That he had no apparent knowledge of the Roman power. That the name of Cæsar was nearly all that had reached him. That he had no intelligent knowledge of the imperial system he lived under, or of the empire of which he was a subject. That when he talked of kings and courts he spoke as one who was utterly and almost childishly unfamiliar with them, and had never seen anything of them.

How the sceptical biographers come to the knowledge of all this, which is put down with so much gay certainty, it may be a little difficult to understand. There is nothing in the only authorities (the Gospels) which, read with whatever attention, would justify one tenth of all this.

We are compelled to conclude that nine-tenths of these sweeping statements are derived from the fact that Jesus of Nazareth was a native of a little town of 3,000 or 4,000 inhabitants (as they think or once thought) in an unimportant province of an obscure country which lay entirely outside the tide of the great world.

How could this charming young villager acquire any scholarship or any true conception of the world?

It needs no courage in these times to refuse to accept the conclusions of either the orthodox or the unorthodox.

To the former, the orthodox, it may be replied that if the manhood of Jesus means anything in the scheme of God, it means that he went through a man's way of acquiring knowledge, and that any teaching by God apart from the duty and task of learning from life reduces the manhood to foolishness. Not by the poor shift of saying "God taught him" are we to account for the fact that after the thirty odd years of the life of Jesus of which we are told nothing in the Gospels, he suddenly appears and speaks with a tongue greater than that of Marcus Aurelius. That is not the way of God with man, and the manhood of Jesus forbids us to believe it.

To the unorthodox it may be replied that the internal evidence of the reported words of Jesus afford proof that he was a man of deep and lofty education, in the highest and best sense; that the developments of modern thought, of modern science, are day by day supporting with fresh proofs his so-called "backward" beliefs, rightly interpreted.

Furthermore, that the conditions of his life in Galilee, and in Palestine generally, were the best for producing in his clear intelligence that knowledge of the world, and of the scheme of the universe, in which later ages are still toiling far behind him.

Let it be admitted at once that of general book knowledge, of what are called profane subjects, it is extremely improbable that Jesus knew much. Certainly Jesus could not attend universities. There were schools of some sort, and the words "not having been taught" show that in the time of Jesus there was some kind of scholastic tuition. But there was the tuition of vivid life open to him.

It will perhaps come as a surprise, but it must be realized that Jesus of Nazareth lived in an age of great events, and the period of some of the world's greatest intellectual achievements.

Virgil wrote the fourth book of his *Georgics* within twenty years of the birth of Jesus, and died within fifteen years of that event. Horace died within three years of the birth of Jesus, and Livy and Ovid lived until Jesus was about twenty-five years of age.

All this was going on at the period of Jesus, and only a few hundred miles away from him.

It is probably quite impossible for internal evidence of the spoken words of Jesus, and certainly impossible for external historical evidence, to show that Jesus had any knowledge of all this. But it is quite possible to show that of other activities no less important he had opportunities of acquiring the most intimate personal knowledge.

Therefore, to assume that he was an uninstructed young villager outside the current of the world, and ignorant to the last of its main activity, is of a par with the other examples of irresponsible and unconscientious assurance which has for ages clogged the history of Jesus with statements for which there is no authority.

What, then, do we rightly know of the education of Jesus? There are many things which we do not know, but there is one thing that we do know.

We know one fact of supreme importance—that during the period of his youth and young manhood, the whole of Palestine (and perhaps Galilee in particular) was passing through a period of intense political, religious, social and literary excitement. How did this affect Jesus?

In the silence of the Gospels we are justified in reading the unrecorded facts by our knowledge of the condition of his parents at the time of his birth, and by his own condition when, after a lapse of thirty dark years, he reappears in the eyes of the world.

In an attempt to bridge that period, without departing from any known facts, let us at once dismiss the idea that the son of the Carpenter of Nazareth must, by reason of poverty, have been denied all kinds of educational opportunities.

Beyond a very limited period, we do not know that Joseph was a poor man. That he began life as a poor man there is good reason to believe. That Mary was poor when Jesus was born is sufficiently shown by the fact that she had only two doves and a pigeon to offer to the Lord for the gift of her son.

Beyond that, we know nothing of the material condition of Joseph except that he was well known to the people in various parts of Galilee, that his wife and children were well known and that he was obviously held in esteem among his own people.

There is, therefore, nothing incongruous in the supposition that during the period of building activity in Galilee, which began with Herod the Great and was continued by his son, Herod Antipas, Joseph became a man of a certain standing in his business, a certain substance, that he became a master-carpenter.

There is certainly no reason for thinking that Joseph remained a poor man.

It is, therefore, not unreasonable to think that he gave his children every educational advantage that Galilee could afford.

What the educational opportunities of Nazareth were we do not know. That they were not merely those of a small village we can be entirely sure. Money appears to have been abundant in Galilee. The taxes were readily paid. The instruction of the young seems to have been faithfully attended to.

We do not know that there was any rabbinical school, either in Nazareth or in any of the neighbouring cities, or indeed, nearer than Jerusalem. But we do know that the scholarship (particularly the biblical scholarship) of the Jewish masters was not limited to Jerusalem. We know that in the time of Jesus, as in later times, including our own, the greatest scholars do not usually gather to the capital, that, on the contrary, they usually escape from it. We know that some of the greatest Jewish scholars of the time of Jesus lived in what we should describe as the provinces. We know that some of them supported themselves in poverty on the small stipends of rabbis in small cities.

We know that in the time of Jesus, Galilee had its learned men, its missionaries, scholars, poets, patriots.

Is there anything improbable in the thought that, after Jesus had passed through the elementary schooling (up to thirteen years of age) of the reader in the synagogue, he studied under some such learned rabbi, either in Nazareth or some neighbouring town?

Next, let it be remembered that the Chief cause of the intense intellectual activity in Palestine during the youth of Jesus (say from his twelfth to his eighteenth year) was the Roman occupation of Judæa and Samaria, and the consequent subjection of the territory of the Roman time-server, Herod Antipas.

After being crushed in their revolt under Judas the Galilean, they were constantly assaulted by the paganism of their Roman masters. The central doctrine of their religion was being assailed in the claim of the Roman emperor to be "divine," and by the effort of his procurators to compel devotion to his personal divinity. It would have been astonishing if this condition had not given rise to an intense religious activity.

It did.

The synagogue during the youth of Jesus was manifestly a powerful if secret force.

III. Hillel

Two great Jewish teachers had arisen, and their influence extended to the farthest ends of the country. The first of these, in point of popularity, was Hillel.

Hillel was a rabbi of Babylonian origin who lived at Jerusalem in the time of Herod the Great. Where he lived after Herod's death appears to be unknown. His ancestry was traced back to David, therefore he had the prestige of birth. He had the further prestige of wide learning. He was numbered among the recognized leaders of the Pharisaic sect. He was also one of the leaders of the Sanhedrin, and filled a leading post in it for forty years. He died when Jesus was about fourteen years of age, leaving behind him a school which was called the "School of Hillel."

If he advanced no novel interpretation of the Law, he produced a deep effect by enjoining and practising the virtues of charity, heredity and purity. He might be described as a catholic Jew. His chief tenet was the Fatherhood of God.

If this brought, as an inevitable sequel, the brotherhood of men, Hillel did not shrink from it. He wrote a great number of proverbs and maxims which, during his life and especially after his death, were in common circulation through the synagogues of the country. Some of these are controversial; many were on the highest plane of thought and feeling.

He was an apostle of peace, and in many of his maxims he recommends equally the love of peace and the love of mankind. "What is unpleasant to thyself that do not to thy neighbour; that is the whole Law, all else is but exposition." To love one's neighbour as oneself was a fundamental law of religious morals. "Judge not thy neighbour until thou art in his place."

The mystical profundity of Hillel's consciousness of God is indicated in the words he puts into the mouth of God himself. "If I am here everyone is here; if I am not here nobody is here."

There is nothing derogatory to Jesus in the thought that some of his noblest sayings may have been partly borrowed from the rabbinical schools. But he borrowed nothing that he did not improve in the process.

What Hillel's view of the Messianic hope was is not quite sure. A descendant of the same name, in the fourth century, declared that Israel did not expect a Messiah, because the promise of a Messiah had already been fulfilled in the days of King Hezekiah. There seems to be some reason for thinking that the greater Hillel took this view.

But it should be obvious that during the Roman occupation in Judæa, and the reign of Herod Antipas in Galilee, the too frequent insistence in the Messianic hope was not a path of personal safety with the powers in control. Quite the contrary.

Such, then, was almost certainly, one of the first of the teachers of Jesus. It is difficult to believe that through his synagogue and the rabbi under whom he studied the proverbs and maxims of Hillel were not among the chief text-books.

If anything in Hillel's maxims bears resemblance to the sayings of Jesus we shall do no wrong to the great Being who came later to say that Hillel was in some senses his first master—"if one should speak of a master at all in connection with such a lofty genius as his."

IV. Philo

But Hillel was not the only fire that was feeding the soul of the Jewish people during the years of the youth of Jesus, about which the Gospels are silent. There was Philo, the Alexandrian Jew.

Philo survived Jesus by about ten years, and was at the height of his activity during the period of the young manhood of Jesus.

In spirit he was perhaps more nearly akin to Jesus than Hillel had been. A fiery spirit, who did not hesitate to challenge his adversaries both within his race and outside of it, and did not hesitate at a later date to challenge Cæsar himself face to face.

On one side he was Greek, on the other side Jewish—a cosmopolitan Jew. He believed the law of Moses to be divine. The true sage who follows the law of Moses is, in Philo's view, a citizen not of a particular state but of the world.

Philo held that man is a twofold being. On one side he is a creature of sense, and so has in him the fountain of sin and all evil. The body, according to Philo, is a prison, a coffin or a grave for the soul which seeks to rise again to God. He thought the logos the highest mediator between God and the world, *the first-born son of God,* the high priest who stands before God on behalf of the world—a strangely significant anticipation of the cardinal doctrine of Christianity.

Philo wrote an exposition of the Mosaic law for the Gentiles. It was circulated, studied and discussed not only in Alexandria, but in the synagogues of Palestine also. It dealt with the Ten Commandments and discussed priesthood and sacrifice, the Sabbath and its observances, the matrimonial laws, adultery and murder.

Here, again, was another master of Jesus, if we can speak of anybody as his master.

Certainly, both of these great Jewish teachers must have been constantly discussed in the synagogues during the youth of Jesus. The synagogue was a kind of debating forum. It is not necessary to think of Jesus as taking part in discussions. Indeed, it is difficult to do so. He was probably a silent listener. But it is impossible to think of Jesus as a "divine ignoramus" if he was in constant touch with the teachings of Hillel and Philo.

But Hillel and Philo were not the only masters of Jesus.

Within the close security of the little synagogue of Nazareth, and perhaps under the guidance of the old rabbi who was attached to it—perhaps a scholar who may have given up Jerusalem for the sake of his studies, or his devotion to the higher call of his faith—it is not difficult to see Jesus going back from Hillel and Philo to the prophets. What a temptation! To go back to the story of the old captivity in the midst of the new captivity. The captivity to the Babylonians, and the captivity to the Romans—the last as real and dangerous to body and soul. Captivity for the Jewish people, not in a foreign country but in their own.

V. Prophecies and Psalms

And then there were the prophecies of Daniel. The book written, perhaps, by some enthusiastic Jew of the time of Antiochus Epiphanes, and headed by the name of an ancient sage.

The hope with which their fathers had kept their souls alive.

I will lift up mine eyes to the hills from whence cometh my strength.

Go and cry in the ears of Jerusalem, saying, "Thus saith the Lord . . ."

What iniquity have your fathers found in me that they have gone far from me?

How they express the spirit of the modern time! They might have been written for this very day!

The moving and uplifting predictions of a day when God would remember His people and fulfil His promise to David.

It is clear enough that Jesus was familiar with these prophecies. He knew them all, with their glories and terrors, their pictures of the nations falling to pieces one after the other, of the cataclysm of Heaven and earth, and then of the advent of the Messiah, of his coming in the clouds attended by legions of angels, to save his people.

Nor is that all.

In the little synagogue at Nazareth, within closed doors perhaps, it is easy to see the Jewish people going back to the Psalms of David—for comfort, to uplift their crushed and torn hearts with David's note of hope and joy.

Jesus knew the Psalms.

O give thanks to the Lord, for He is good; for His mercy endureth for ever.

Hear my prayer, O Lord, give ear to my supplications: in Thy faithfulness answer me, and in Thy righteousness.

The religious poetry of the Psalms had entered in his soul. The sweet words of the Psalms remain on his lips to the end. They help him to face the worst that life can bring. Who knows if they were not the hymns he sang on the last night of his life?

The pathos of it all. The thrill of it all!

Such, then, was the education of Jesus; and the place of his education.

A Jew? The son of a carpenter?

Yes, but the clearest, finest, most exalted brain that was then living in the world, or has ever since lived.

Jesus was a man of genius.

Nazareth? A little town of 4,000 inhabitants, or yet 20,000 as we now know it to have been? The despised city? The obscure corner of an unimportant province?

Yes, but for Jesus of Nazareth the greatest university in the world.

VI. The Death of Augustus

It is just as easy to answer the objection of the sceptical biographers that Jesus had no acquaintance with the condition of the world; that he knew little or nothing of the Roman empire; that the name of Cæsar was nearly all that had reached him.

Jesus of Nazareth passed his early life under conditions in which ignorance of these things was practically impossible to any intelligent being. Only an ignoramus—and Jesus was no ignoramus—could have lived in Galilee, particularly in southern Galilee, and perhaps especially in Nazareth, in the years between A.D. 6 and A.D 18 without acquiring a very intimate knowledge of such subjects.

To realize how much Jesus knew of the condition of the world (not in Palestine only) during this period, it is only necessary to say what was going on in the world and in what way the chief events of the period were affecting the people in Galilee.

When Jesus was about eighteen years of age the emperor Augustus died, the emperor in whose time Jesus had been born.

He had lived, on the whole, a good life. Although often unscrupulous in early life as to the means by which he rose to power, and although it might be said of him (as Voltaire said) that he had extinguished political liberty, his life as a whole gave him the right to rank as one of the world's great men. The hostility of the historians who came immediately after him (Tacitus particularly) who described him as an accomplished political actor, is obliterated by our knowledge of the magnitude of what he accomplished.

It cannot be said that he had been a friend of the Jewish people. He had supported Herod the Great when he oppressed them. And when Archelaus appealed to him on the death of Herod, he made a good bargain for the Roman empire. Again, in dispossessing Archelaus he relieved the Jews of an oppressor, but he made another good bargain for Rome by taking possession of Judæa and thus robbing the Jews of that province of the last vestige of nationality.

But whatever his faults, and they were not too few, they were partly atoned for by the sufferings of his last years, which were clouded by many sorrows.

The story of his end is deeply moving. Relinquishing the responsibilities of empire to his stepson, Tiberius, the old man, then approaching his seventy-seventh year, with his old wife, Livia (she had been his wife for nearly fifty-two years), left Rome on his last journey. Travelling by road to Astura (Torre Astura) at the southern point of the little bay of Antium, he sailed thence to Capri and to Naples.

At Puteoli the pasengers and crew of a ship just come from Alexandria cheered the old man by declaring, as they poured libations, that to him they owed their life, safe passage on the seas, freedom and fortune. Although he was not yet the "Divine Augustus" doubtless the sailors had prayed to him in a storm.

At Naples, in spite of increasing weakness, he struggled to be brave, and sat out a gymnastic contest which was held in his honour. But he was forced by continued illness to set out again on his journey. Finally, he was forced to stop at Nola, his father's old home.

It was afterwards said that his stepson, Tiberius, was with him, and that they had some final talk about state affairs, but this is uncertain, the probability being that Tiberius was not there, but elsewhere, indulging his pleasures.

But his old wife was with him, and he died quietly in her arms (his faithful counsellor throughout so many years), exhorting her to live mindful of their wedded life. He died on August 19th, A.D. 14, in his father's house, in the same room in which his father had died, and on the anniversary of his first consulship fifty-seven years before.

They took his body back to Rome and carried it in slow procession along the Appian Way, on the shoulders of senators to Campus Martius and there burnt it. His ashes were placed in a mausoleum on the Tiber, and the senate, by formal decree, added his name to the number of the gods recognized by the Roman state.

Tiberius, his stepson, succeeded him. He ascended the throne at fifty-six years of age. A very different man.

Certainly he ran no risk of being described as a political actor. A silent or sullen man. During his early years of utter impenetrability he was said to have had no faults. It was a question of whom he liked, or if he was liked by any single being.

The elder Pliny describes him as the gloomiest of mankind. It is believed that he brooded on the mysterious and was the victim of superstition. He had lived, in early years, an active and vigorous life, and done great service as a soldier. Then a great change came over him. This was not long before he was adopted by Augustus as his successor.

Earlier, his domestic life had been darkened by a great shame. He had a daughter named Julia, of wit and beauty but a disgraceful huzzy, whose dissolute character and reckless disposition had given rise to scandal. Nevertheless, she was the leader of Roman society. For a time Tiberius had shut his eyes to her conduct, but at length he inflicted the severest punishment upon his daughter. He banished and disinherited her, and punished her many lovers. The Roman world awoke for a while from its fool's paradise of pleasure.

But Tiberius was crushed. His position in Rome became intolerable to him, and he left for Rhodes, remaining away for several years.

On his accession to the position of emperor, another change took place in him. He, too, indulged in the lowest sensual pleasures. He fell into the hands of unworthy instruments. The chief of these was Sejanus, an astute statesman, but an unscrupulous and disloyal scoundrel. Sejanus nursed the darker side of Tiberius's character. As a result, the imperial household began to be disgraced by hideous debauchery. Tiberius, tempted by Sejanus, was always suspecting treachery. Historians of Rome remember Tiberius at this stage as the sovereign who was always trying his subjects for treason, sometimes on the slightest pretext.

Such was Rome and the Roman court during the years immediately following the death of Augustus.

VII.   The Influence of Rome

Is it conceivable that Palestine alone was unaffected by what was happening in Rome?

Remember, first, that there was constant intercourse between Rome and the Palestinian dependency. Hundreds, perhaps thousands, of Romans were in Palestine, as officials, as tax-gatherers, as legionaries. They usually came into Palestine by Cæsarea, the seaport on the western coast which Herod the Great had rebuilt and renamed. Sometimes they came by Tyre, the seaport farther north—it had ports for larger vessels, Cæsarea being probably an open roadstead.

In the former case the main body of Roman soldiers would remain in Cæsarea, the central seat of Roman authority and its garrison. In the latter case they would travel south to Cæsarea through Galilee.

Is it conceivable that they would not bring with them the atmosphere of the court they had left behind them—that what was happening in Rome remained unknown in Palestine?

Another point. Almost immediately after the accession of Tiberius the leading Roman officials in Judæa were changed. Coponius, the procurator, had (perhaps before) been succeeded by Marcus Ambivius, and afterwards by Annius Rufus. Now Rufus was deposed and Valerius Gratus came. Certainly Gratus became procurator of Judæa about a year after Tiberius became emperor. The condition of the Jewish people did not improve under Gratus. He deposed Annas from the position of high priest, probably at the appeal of the Jewish people. Within two and a half years three high priests followed in quick succession—Ishmael, Eleazar (a son of Annas) and Simon.

Then came Joseph Caiaphas, the son-in-law of Annas. This is

the first time this man, who played so large a part in the life of Jesus, appears in history.

VIII.   The Building of Tiberias

The Jewish people in Judæa began to be yet more heavily taxed by their Roman masters. We hear of a two per cent tax on all they ate and drank. It is probable that their religious liberties were less respected than before.

But the effect of the new order in Rome had a still more direct effect, on Galilee in particular. It had one very direct channel of communication. This was through Herod Antipas, the tetrarch of Galilee and Peræa. This time-server and cunning sycophant was always in close touch with Rome.

He was always running off to Rome, probably spending as much of his time and money (the money of the people of Galilee) in Rome as in his own dominion. He was there in the year of the accession of Tiberius.

When he returned to Galilee, he repeated for the new emperor what he had done for the old one. He began to build a city in honour of Tiberius. The date of the building of Tiberias is uncertain. Some place the beginning as early as A.D. 15; some as late as A.D. 28. The latter is clearly wrong. I have, myself, little doubt that it was begun in the year after the accession of the new emperor.

Antipas selected the finest site for it—the west side of the Lake of Galilee. This would give it the best view. Also, it had one other advantage. Near by, a little to the south, ran hot streams with medicinal waters. The idea of Herod Antipas was to build a great city as a health resort. The rich of Jerusalem (of all Palestine) would resort to it—perhaps of all the countries round about. Herod Antipas determined to call the new city after the name of the new emperor. It was to be Tiberias.

Who shall say but that deep in Herod's secret heart was the hope that the emperor himself would visit the new city (Tiberias) some day? The emperor was known to be in low health, why should not he?

And then behind the obvious prestige that would come to him as the host of the Roman emperor, who shall say he was not cherishing the hope that he (Antipas) might regain the kingship of Judæa (perhaps of all Palestine), which had been lost under

Augustus, first on the death of his father, Herod the Great, and afterwards on the degradation of his brother Archelaus?

But there was one difficulty. The site selected for the new city to be called Tiberias was that of an old Hebrew city. There were few traces of the old city of Sepphoris remaining, but the cemetery was still there, and the veneration of the Jews for the place of their dead excited serious opposition to its disturbance.

The burial-places of their fathers were to be left untouched. But Herod Antipas (only half a Jew by blood, and only outwardly so by faith) was not troubled by the Jewish reverence for the old cemetery. He began to plough it up and scatter what was left of the bones of the dead.

This was abominable outrage in the eyes of his Jewish people. We hear of troubles in Galilee. But they could only be settled one way. When Herod Antipas was resisted by his own people, or by outside people, he did not hesitate to call for Roman help. We know that he did so on at least two occasions later. It is reasonable to think he did so now.

It is easy to see what happened. Tiberias had to be built in hot haste, to bring the sick emperor to Galilee. Is it not probable that the city was built largely by forced labour? If so, is it not also probable that Joseph, the carpenter of Nazareth, worked at the building of it? Nazareth was only some fourteen miles away. Is it conceivable that, at such a time, Herod Antipas permitted him to work at the making of ploughs and harrows and yokes?

Jesus was then about nineteen years of age. Did he not see all this? It was going on under his eyes. In the light of these plain facts of history, is it possible to talk of him as an untaught young Galilean villager, who knew nothing of the world, nothing of the Roman empire, and to say that the name of Cæsar was nearly all that reached him? Rome was brought to his door. His sovereign, the miserable sycophant, had brought it there.

Jesus was precisely in the place of all others in the world in which it was impossible that he should not know all about the nations of the world, the kings, their courts.

But that was not all.

CHAPTER IV

Visits to Jerusalem

I. The Trade of Jesus

NOT THE LEAST UNWORTHY of the charges against Jesus made by the sceptical biographers is that he never worked, but that during the years of his ministry, unlike St. Paul, he lived on the benevolence of a group of well-to-do people, mostly women, who had come under his influence. But there are few things of which we can be more satisfied than that Jesus worked for at least fifteen years. And that he worked with his hands.

It was the common practice of the people of that age and country, whatever their social condition, to bring up their sons to manual labour. The most eminent teachers worked with their hands. To do so was an honour. Not to be able to do so was a disgrace. Whatever the condition of Joseph of Nazareth at the period of the youth and young manhood of Jesus, we may, therefore, be sure that he was brought up to a definite occupation.

What was the trade of Jesus?

Was he a carpenter? That is the commonly accepted view; always has been. Legend and Christian art have accustomed us to that idea. We have never thought of Jesus as anything but a carpenter.

The apocryphal story of his childhood that, going about with Joseph he would touch the timber and it would become longer or shorter according to the carpenter's needs is only another exercise of the feeble intellects who wished to prove the possession by Jesus of supernatural powers from his earliest years.

So deeply grounded is the idea that Jesus was a carpenter, yet the evidence is of the slightest. Only once in the Gospels (in *Mark*) is Jesus described as a carpenter, and the passage is of doubtful authority—"Is not this the carpenter?" More frequently he is called "the son of the carpenter," a description which gives further grounds for thinking that Joseph was widely known as a master-carpenter, working, perhaps not only in Nazareth, but in many of the towns of Galilee. Otherwise it is strange that Jesus, in his full manhood, is known by his father's name and trade—not for himself and by his own trade.

If we had, however, to judge by the internal evidence of his sermons, sayings and parables, we should say Jesus was more probably a gardener. His references to the building of houses are very few. "I will liken him unto a wise man, which built his house upon a rock." His references to the fields, the flowers, the vines, the fruit, the wheat, are many, as for example, "Every tree is known by his own fruit. For of thorns men do not gather figs, nor of a bramble bush gather they grapes." "Consider the lilies of the field." "I am the true vine."

Nevertheless, it is probable that tradition is well founded—that Jesus followed the trade of his father. It was usual for sons to do so. The son of the rabbi became a rabbi; of the farmer a farmer, a fisherman a fisher. The adze and the saw must have been familiar to Jesus; children learn to use their father's tools.

Furthermore, there is the fact, as already stated, that there was great building activity in Galilee during the years of the young manhood of Jesus. Therefore, everything contributed to make him a carpenter.

Thus we are led, without any strain of probability, to the conjecture that Jesus, as well as Joseph, worked as a carpenter at the building of Tiberias, the city in the Roman manner that was being built over the desecrated graves of the Jews, and rushed up, perhaps, to meet the needs of Tiberius.

This would give him opportunities of close observation of Herod Antipas, of the life lived in his palace by the tetrarch, his courtiers and soldiers. It would also explain many things—the name by which Jesus afterwards called him ("the fox") and the way he bore himself towards the great moment, later on, when they met face to face and the life of Jesus was in Herod's hands.

II. The City of Tiberias

The city of Tiberias appears to have been completed in about three years. It is certain that the emperor did not visit it. Herod's expectations were assuredly not fulfilled. But strangers came and inhabited it. A number of Galileans also came. The Galileans were compelled to live in the new city.

Some of them appear to have been rich people, but the majority were poor, and, where Herod had not forced them to live in Tiberias, he tempted them to remain by building houses for them at his own expense and giving them land also, on condition that they should not forsake it. Some of them, not being freemen, Herod made free, but obliged them not to leave the city. All this was in transgression of the ancient Jewish laws, and Herod knew it.

Tiberias was a pitiful failure. It had been built on sepulchres (or by the taking away of sepulchres), and that was contrary to Jewish law.

Being a city of slaves (there was no legal slavery among the Jews, but Herod Antipas appears to have made slaves, or perhaps to have bought Roman slaves from the Romans of the occupation), Tiberias speedily developed the vices of its inhabitants.

It became notorious for its licentiousness. Rich persons from Jerusalem and important Roman officials from Cæsarea came to it on the pretence of seeking the benefit of its curative waters; but really for baser reasons. Herod Antipas added to its evil reputation by making an irregular marriage there. In A.D. 23 or thereabouts (the date is uncertain) he married the daughter of Aretas the king of the Nabatæans, a warlike people who lived at Petra in Arabia, whose territory made boundary with his own on the east. Aretas was also king of Damascus, and is mentioned in connection with St. Paul's escape by night from that city.

He was a vassal of Rome, therefore the marriage of his daughter to Herod Antipas would give no offence to his Roman masters. Aretas, who was a true Arab, appears to have been in every way a better man than Herod Antipas, who was a sensualist and the son of a sensualist. The marriage, too, was a cleaner marriage than nine-tenths of the marriages of the Herod dynasty, which seem to have been a long succession of incestuous unions. But it must have been against Jewish law, and therefore it cannot have failed to give offence to Herod's Jewish subjects.

Such was the moral atmosphere in which Jesus of Nazareth lived as a young man. It is impossible that he should not have been witness to what was going on within a few miles of his home, perhaps on the very scene of his daily occupation.

He saw his people oppressed by the half-Jew, half-Philistine, who had been appointed by their Roman masters to rule over them. He knew all about his "king" and his court. To speak of Jesus in such an environment as an untaught villager, who knew nothing of Cæsar beyond his name, is to talk folly.

To think of him as ignorant of the way of kings and courts is stupidity. He had them constantly under his eyes.

I claim no authority for such a scene, but it pleases me to think of the young Galilean, with his carpenter's kit over his shoulder, passing the time-server of Rome, the sycophant, the sensualist, the corrupter, the oppressor of his own people in the streets of his new city, with uplifted head and the silence of disdain.

III. Portraits of Jesus

Jesus must have been in his early manhood when Tiberias was completed.

What manner of man was he? What was he like to look upon? We do not know. There is no authentic portrait of him either at that or any later period of his life. It was against Jewish law to make a portrait. The portraits of him are all imaginary. The earliest were beardless.

It was not until the time of Constantine that the conventional portrait existed. It does not rest on any authentic tradition. Perhaps all this is a fortunate dispensation. It has left every age and race to create its own ideal, to satisfy the call of its own soul, perhaps not the least of the reasons for the universality of Christianity.

In the fourth century, a bishop of the orthodox Church in Palestine stated that he saw many kinds of old paintings and images of Jesus and of his first apostles. But in the East all this making of pictures of Jesus was regarded as a revival of heathendom, and the bringing down of God to the level of a picture. Yet images came more and more into use from the sixth century, with the theory of the miraculous impressions which Jesus himself made on his garments and particularly on the handkerchief with which he wiped his face on the way to Golgotha, and on the linen in which Nicodemus had buried his body, and which was left in the tomb, and finally, by pretended primitive pictures by Luke, who was supposed to be a painter as well as a doctor.

In the eighth century certain ideal pen-pictures of Jesus were made under the name of the great writer on dogma, John of Damascus. And in the fourteenth century the last of the Greek ecclesiastical historians, Nicephorus, made others. The best known of the latter is one by a pretended Publius Lentulus in a letter to the Roman senate. This, however, was not written earlier than the twelfth century.

The portrait by Nicephorus, the Greek historian, is a composite picture, based partly on *Isaiah* and partly on the old artistic ideals of Byzantium. According to this picture (in words) Jesus was very fair to behold, his stature was fully seven spans (a span was approximately nine inches; therefore Jesus was seven times nine inches, or five feet three inches tall. Thus Jesus, by present standards, was a very short man. But clearly he was a tall man according to the standards of height in his own time.

His hair was fair and not very thick, slightly tending to curl; his eyebrows, however, were black and curved; his eyes bright and with a dash of yellow; his nose was prominent, the beard yellow and not reaching far down. He wore the hair of his head long, for neither scissors nor the hand of man had ever been upon his head, except only the hand of his mother when he was a child. He stooped somewhat in his gait, and his walking was not quite erect.

His complexion was the hue of wheat; his face not round but oval, like that of his mother, and only slightly ruddy. Dignity and intelligence, gentleness and freedom from all passion are therein expressed. He was altogether like his blessed and immaculate mother.

So much for the portrait of the Greek historian, Nicephorus.

The picture of Lentulus differs.

In this Jesus is a man of lofty stature, of much presence and of venerable countenance. He who looks on him may either love or fear him. His hair is curled and crisp; very dark coloured and of a brilliant sheen, falling from his shoulders in waves, parted in the middle of the head after the manner of the Nazarites. His forehead is open and altogether clear; his face without a wrinkle or a spot, of moderate redness. His nose and mouth are blameless, his eyes are bluish-grey; his beard is strong and dark, not long, but parted in twain. In rebuke he is awful; in exhortation mild and amiable, dignified. None ever saw him laugh, but often weep. His carriage straight and upright. Hands and arms "glorious to behold." Speech short and modest, the fairest of the children of men.

Such is the picture originating with the supposed letter of Lentulus, probably written in the twelfth century, which is the foundation for the portrait of Jesus that has descended to the present day.

It has been preserved through the Middle Ages and still survives.

Keim says we find no passage in history which proves that his outward form had been a subject of eulogy. "On the other hand, it is plain that his was a manly, commanding, prophetic figure. The people, so much at the mercy of outward impressions, could not otherwise have greeted him as a prophet, nay, as the son of David. The reproach of his foes would have attacked his bodily defects. . . . Besides, we have the fact lying before us that his appearance on the scene, his word, his voice, his eye, seized and shook the hearer and beholder, and that men, women, children, the sick and poor felt happy at his feet and in his presence."

There is truth in Keim's conclusion that "we cannot easily think of the even balance and harmony of the spirit that rests in God as united to a repellent physiognomy. We think of Jesus as healthy, vigorous, of expressive countenance, with characteristic features, as if of a spirit and a will that must create what was full of character. Perhaps he was not especially beautiful; but at any rate noble; with whole heart in his features.

"His vigour of health is proved by his ruthlessness of life, and by the daily expenditure of strength, both of body and mind, demanded by the stormy importunity of the mental and physical misery of Israel."

His disciples were working-men, accustomed to long hours of labour, but again and again he seems to wear them out. They sleep while he is awake—only once is he asleep while they are awake. He sends them to quiet places to rest, while he goes on working.

He was assuredly of commanding presence. Clearly he inspired a certain awe. The most noticeable examples are:

Where the officers of the Temple sent to arrest him return home and excuse themselves as best they can, by saying, "Never man spake like this man."

The various attempts to take him, to stone him, and his removing himself from their midst unharmed—only to be understood as the result of their fear of him.

The moment of his arrest in Gethsemane, when the soldiers fell to their faces as he said, "I am he."

Going up to Jerusalem on his last journey. "He went before, ascending up to Jerusalem" (Luke XIX, 28).

I see this as characteristic of his manner. In all probability it was so that he walked to Cæsarea Philippi—walking ahead of his disciples, alone, deep in thought.

Some of the early pictorial representations of Christ are undeniably painful, almost offensive. Among the earliest "portraits" is the fair, beardless shepherd in the mosaics of the catacombs of Rome.

The central figure of Leonardo's *Last Supper* represents him as very different from Michelangelo's "wrathful Saviour driving the damned to the abyss." Guido's *Ecce Homo* is generally satisfying. Albrecht Dürer's *Christ* was painted for himself. The imaginary portraiture is so various that, as a consequence, we do not know with any certainty whether Jesus was dark or fair, tall or short, or what the habitual expression of his face may have been.

He was a Jew, but it is not even sure that his features were of the Jewish type. It is thought by some that the Galileans, although confessing the Jewish faith, were not of unmixed Jewish blood, although this is denied by others. A dark complexion with black hair was not invariable. There was certainly a fair type in the people of early Palestine. David is described as having golden locks, and Samuel was fair haired.

Each of us may draw the picture of Jesus for ourself according to our own reading of his words and our interpretation of his life. Speaking for myself he is never at any period (least of all towards the end of his life) the gentle and mild personality usually imagined.

IV. The Humanity of Jesus

On the side of his human nature I feel no wrong done to my faith in his divinity to think of him as in every way a man. There is no indication whatever of the submission to human passions. Yet there are reasons to think they were strong in him. But if his human passions were strong, there was something stronger—his spiritual passions.

Historians tell us (on what authority we do not know) that the women of Nazareth had a wide reputation for a kind of languorous loveliness. It is not to be said that Jesus was at that time or at any other time indifferent to the society of women. Superficial and sceptical critics have declared that he was deficient in manhood.

Quite the contrary. It is clear that to the end of his short life he loved to have women about him. It is equally clear that he had an immense appeal to women. But their behaviour to him, as humble, devoted and worshipful followers, is the most unmistakable witness at once to the strength of his masculinity and to its purity. Only to powerful masculine natures, not to the meek and feeble and even saintly ones, do women behave as the women who surrounded Jesus behaved towards him.

He seems to have been a man of men; and women always seemed to know it. Men knew it, too, and always behaved as if they knew it. There is not a moment, down to the last morning of his life, when any man dared to take the smallest liberty with him.

Men marry early in eastern countries. Certainly Jesus did not marry. It is impossible to think of him as devoting himself to one woman. His devotion to *all* women seems to have forbidden it.

Among the causes to which he was to devote his life was the cause of women.

Jesus is often described as looking at people and things—"looking round about." It is probable that his eyes were large and steady, softly expressive with kindness, perhaps searching and possibly dark in colour, thereby attracting attention.

We do not know the tone of his voice, but we know that it was gentle and persuasive, yet capable of reaching vast multitudes in the open air. Clearly it was loud and deep and resonant. A German commentator declares that he had the Jewish defects—that he never observed beauty, that he never laughed, but taught by tears, threats and reproofs. But it is impossible to believe that he did not appreciate beauty. Did not his admiring description of the lily imply that the flower was more beautiful than Solomon in all his glory? We are not told that he ever laughed; but his smile must have been in the nature of a beatitude.

Nothing is more notable in the personality of Jesus than his desire to be loved—not as a teacher merely, but as a man.

He desired, above all, that his disciples should love him. There are moments when he seems to me to ask nothing of his disciples but that they should love him. I may doubt (as I do) the story of the appearance of Jesus to his disciples on the shores of Tiberias (which in little things as big betrays a later origin than the days immediately after the Resurrection), but I cannot doubt that the writer had fastened on one of the outstanding characteristics of Jesus—his desire to be loved, which includes his love to be trusted and therefore to be followed.

At every stage of his life with his disciples his desire to be loved by them appears—at his first call of them, at various trying moments in his life with them, even when he must have found their misunderstanding of him very trying, at the period of his going to Jerusalem, of his arrest (when he answers the question of the soldiers, and others, by saying, "I have told you that I am he [Jesus of Nazareth]. If therefore ye seek me, let these go their way.") Earlier, also, in his prayer for his disciples at the Last Supper, when he says, "I pray for them . . . And now I am no more in the world, but these are in the world. . . ." Again, when he says of his disciples that they have continued with him in his temptations.

I do not see that he ever betrays real anger with his disciples, not even when he retorts on Peter at Cæsarea Philippi. And not even when Judas betrays him, or is about to betray him.

"That thou doest, do quickly."

"Judas, betrayest thou the Son of Man with a kiss?"

And the disciples never fail in returning the love of Jesus. Their personal love for the man is even more noticeable than their devotion to him as the spiritual Master. They contend as to which shall be most to him, nearest to him in his hour of glory, in his hours of trial. If they fly from him in fear at the moment of his arrest, one of them at least quickly repents and follows him to the high priest's house.

If in the high priest's house Peter's fear takes hold of him again, and he denies knowledge of him, his remorse is awakened and he goes away weeping bitterly.

If the disciples are hiding in Jerusalem in terror in the moment of his crucifixion, and again on the third day (Sunday) after his death, they are not reproaching him with deceiving them, or having led them into peril, but weeping for him.

Earlier, when, against their importunities, he determines to go up to Jerusalem and face the death that awaits him there, (as the disciples believe), one of them (and that one Thomas) says, "Let us go up and die with him."

If Judas betrays him (from whatever motive), his remorse is so deep that he goes out and hangs himself.

Always and everywhere, during his life and after his death, and during his reappearance in the Resurrection and down to the moment of his Ascension, their love of their Master never fails them or him.

It continues when he is gone. They go to their own deaths not only for the Saviour, but for the friend. He is their beloved Master to the last.

And what applies to the disciples applies no less to the women followers. From first to last the love of women is conspicuous in his story. A few of them minister to him. Many follow him up to Jerusalem. Some stand about his Cross. Some witness his burial. One at least is the first to visit his grave in the dawn (or before it) of Sunday morning. Mary Magdalene is the first to announce his Resurrection. All through his life as a teacher and healer the faith of women in him never fails. A woman kneels in the crowd and touches the border of his garment, believing that to be enough to heal her. Another cries through the crowd, "Blessed is the womb that bare thee, and the paps which thou hast sucked." Still another, a heathen, believing his love to be greater than the calls of his race, is reported to have said, so great is her faith in his love (in reply to words which I cannot believe to have been spoken by him—that it was not meet to take the children's bread and cast it to the dogs), "Yea, lord, yet the dogs under the table eat of the children's crumbs."

Everywhere and always, the love he asked and the love that was given to him by those who lived with him, who came closest to him, who knew him best, is the dominating fact.

Clearly, the personality of Jesus was, above all, a personality which inspired love—an immense and deeply moving devotion. He was the great friend. On his human side he never for one moment failed anybody who came near to him. Everybody he knew was ready to die for him. Even Judas at the last was ready to die for him—and *did* die for him. As far as one knows, so did they all.

V. His Visits to Jerusalem

How often was Jesus in Jerusalem?

Once during his ministry as the Gospels of Matthew and Mark indicate? Twice as the Gospel of Luke indicates? Or four times as the Gospel of John indicates? My view is that he visited Jerusalem repeatedly, that he knew it thoroughly—every phase of its life, every class of its inhabitants. As a devout Jew it was his duty to go up once a year at least—to the Passover.

Only by realizing that during the dark years not recorded by the Gospels Jesus was frequently in Jerusalem can we follow his spiritual development, or fully understand what, during his ministry, he saw and did.

If from twenty to twenty-five years of age he went up to Jerusalem once a year at least, what did he see?

First he saw the effect of the Roman occupation. Almost certainly he saw Gratus, the procurator of Judæa. Possibly Cyrenius, the governor of Syria.

We know enough to see that many of the governors and procurators who ruled Judæa from A.D. 6 to A.D. 76 were unprincipled and cruel men, hating, robbing, oppressing and insulting the Jews and their religion.

Jesus saw their officials, centurions, legionaries, auxiliaries, perhaps their eunuchs and slaves. He saw their official life as it made itself manifest in relation to the Jewish people. He saw the Roman soldiery parading the streets to preserve order, especially at the times of the feasts, when great multitudes of Jews crowded into the city. He saw their arrogance, their contempt for the Jewish people. These upstarts of an empire of yesterday, ruling with whips the people who counted their descent from Moses.

Jesus must have seen their way of amusing themselves. Their pagan sports in the amphitheatre (built by Herod the Great), almost under the shadow of the Temple. Jesus saw (must have seen) the demoralization of the life of Jerusalem by the Roman governors, procurators, soldiers and their attendant women. They reproduced in Jerusalem the society they came from—that of Rome.

Rome was then honeycombed with sensuality. The profligacy of imperial Rome (in the time of Tiberius) had never before been surpassed for gross and obscene sensuality. We get glimpses of the immorality of the Roman soldiery in the repellent legends of the first and second centuries to account for the story of the Virgin Birth.

The Roman soldiery were frequently sent over the country (of Judæa) to put down revolts. How they did so and what a trail of corruption they left behind them we also know. We get glimpses of the brutality of the Roman soldiery in Jerusalem in many records of the time. The moral atmosphere of Jerusalem during the early years of the manhood of Jesus was certainly corrupt. Indeed, the whole country was corrupt, Galilee no less than Judæa; Shechem no less than Jerusalem. The presence of the Romans was almost certainly responsible for much of this.

We know that some of the Romans brought their wives with them, but more brought their mistresses and many found their harlots in Palestine itself. We know that prostitution was very prevalent in Palestine during the lifetime of Jesus. For this the leaders of the Jewish people were not without blame. The prostitute was supposed to be held in contempt in Palestine, especially by the Pharisees, who adopted an uncharitable, almost an inhuman attitude towards her, due to a certain hypocrisy.

Prostitutes were shut out by the religious classes. The law of Moses was hard on the harlot. The object of the Mosaic law was to preserve the purity of the Jewish race. The prohibition against prostitutes was confined to Jewish women, it did not cover foreign women. The daughter of Israel was forbidden to become a prostitute; but no penalty attached to disobedience, except in the case of a priest's daughter, who was condemned to be burnt, a betrothed damsel, who was to be stoned, and a wife, who was to be put to death. Prostitutes were forbidden to enter Jerusalem, but we learn that they infested the streets, the roads and the gardens.

Much of this was due to the Roman occupation—the presence of the Roman garrison. The Jewish religious authorities turned a blind eye to it.

Incidentally, they did thereby no worse than the Christian religious authorities of a later age, when in the Middle Ages in London the "bordels" or "stews" near London Bridge were licensed by the bishop of Winchester, and (in one case) owned by a lord mayor of London; and when in France (at Avignon, for a time the home of the popes in exile) the profits of the trade of prostitution were shared by the city and helped the upkeep of the university.

Jesus must have seen all this—his soul sick at the sight of it; perhaps a certain pity for the prostitute mingling with his indignation at the licentiousness of the Roman and the hypocrisy of the leaders of his own people.

Jesus saw, also, the economic corruption which the Roman occupation brought with it. The Jews no longer, as in the time of Herod, went up to their own cities to be taxed. Tax-gatherers visited them at their homes, in the Roman manner, where the amount of their possessions could not be hidden. The tax-gatherers under the Romans were chiefly Jews. The Romans appointed Jews to gather the tribute, because it was less easy for Jew to deceive Jew. The Jewish tax-gatherer generally bettered his instructions. He often demanded more than was due, using intimidation for the purpose. The difference he kept for himself, and thus he frequently became rich by his ill-got gains.

But his riches were his only consolation. He was hated by the Jewish people, becoming an outcast among them—a pariah. He had sold himself to their Roman master, thereby doing the work which (a few years earlier) their brothers under Judas the Galilean had bled and died to prevent.

The Jews would not associate with or sit at meat with the publican. He could not be denied access to the Temple, but socially he was cut off from his people. Jesus saw all this. He saw the sufferings of the publicans as well as the economic corruption of the Roman system. Later, we shall see what view he took of them. They served him for at least one of his most moving parables.

When he turned to the Church of his race he found no consolation. There were two classes—the Pharisees and the Sadducees. The Pharisees had degenerated into formalists. The soul of their faith had gone out of them. The form of their religion had taken the place of the spirit. Great sticklers for the sanctity of the Sabbath. Great sticklers for the shadow of moral purity. Often great and manifest hypocrites. Jesus saw them (must have seen them) in the streets, praying in the places in which they could be seen. He saw them going up (at the time of the feast) to the Temple, with musicians blowing trumpets before them. Grotesque spectacle! The man with his eyes shut, the musicians going before him!

Jesus must have looked on this empty and blazing hypocrisy. The sickening sham of it. How he afterwards scarified it!

He must have seen the ways of the Sadducees. They were the rationalists of the Jewish faith, believers in the law of Moses, but rejecting the Resurrection, and therefore the hope of a Messiah.

The Sadducees were the wealthy class; perhaps, also, the intellectual class. The huge landowners, the large property-owners in Jerusalem, perhaps the greater traders. It is not improbable that the Sadducees made terms with the Roman occupation, and stood in relations of friendship with the governors and procurators. Perhaps even bought privileges and exemptions with bribes. The dinners at night at the rich men's houses. Houses lit up. The flares. Lazarus lying at the gate in the half darkness. The procurator drawing up. The musicians in the courtyards. Such of us who know the East can fill in the picture. Jesus saw all this (must have seen it) to his bitter shame. How he afterwards used it!

VI. The Sanhedrin

Then the Jewish courts. When he looked to the Jewish courts Jesus saw the utter subjugation of his people. The terms of the Roman occupation were that the Romans should control public security, while the Jews were to retain their religious courts and all that pertained to them—all violations of the law of Moses. But this covered wide ground, and the Romans had put their hands on it. The Sanhedrin had (theoretically) the duty of safeguarding the Jewish religion. But in reality it had lost this authority.

The Sanhedrin consisted of two councils—the great Sanhedrin of seventy-one members; the lesser council of twenty-three members. Apparently, the Sanhedrin was practically self-elected. It consisted of both sects. In the time of Jesus the sect of the Sadducees predominated. The Roman power appointed the chief priest —the origin and history of the high priesthood. The high priest was a judge. Had formerly stood in the position of the king. He was the priest-king. The supreme official in the Church-nation. The sons of Aaron alone possessed the right to offer sacrifices in the Temple. On the great Day of Atonement the high priest appeared in a representative capacity, and offered on behalf of the whole nation, which he was believed to embody in his sacred person.

Aaron, the brother of Moses, was the first incumbent of the office. He was believed to have been appointed by God and to have been consecrated by Moses.

His successors were all to be through his line. This order was broken. Solomon first broke it. After the Exile the civil authorities arrogated the right of appointment, and from that time onward Judaism became that monstrous abortion, a political religion.

Then Herod appointed six high priests in succession. The control of the high priesthood by the Roman power was contrary to the Jewish religious law, yet some of his high priests acquiesced in it, probably for their own advantage. It must have been a gross offence to Jesus.

At first the high priest was appointed for life. Afterwards he was dismissed at will. The age of eligibility was twenty years. But high priests were appointed at a much younger age. One was a young boy, appointed by Herod the Great, and then straightway drowned in the Jordan by his order. The great Sanhedrin alone was supposed to nominate the high priest. The high priest had a house connected with the Temple, and another in the city of Jerusalem. If he committed a crime he could be tried by the great Sanhedrin. He must be married. The high priest was to be superior to all other men, in physique, in wisdom, in dignity and in health. If he were poor he was to be made rich. By the time of Jesus all this was dust and ashes.

Joseph Caiaphas was now high priest. Annas probably and Joseph Caiaphas certainly had no blood right of succession to the high priesthood. Annas had one daughter, who was married to Joseph Caiaphas.

Jesus must have seen the operation of the high priesthood under the Roman occupation. If Annas had ceased to be high priest, and therefore president of the Sanhedrin, he was still the chief power in the Sanhedrin. St. Luke is in error in speaking of Annas and Caiaphas as the "high priests" of that year. There was an assistant high priest for the lesser Sanhedrin. This was the blunder of a non-Jew. There could be only one high priest. Perhaps Annas presided over the lesser Sanhedrin—after he ceased to be high priest. Perhaps he remained an associate high priest. Perhaps he was a kind of high priest emeritus. In any case he carried on a profitable business.

VII. The Sights of Jerusalem

According to the Talmud, Annas kept a kind of bazaar on the Mount of Olives. According to Josephus he kept a poultry farm there. We know that Annas had a house on the Mount of Olives as well as a house inside the city. It is almost certain that his farm was for the sale of fowls, doves, sheep, and other animals, to be sold for the sacrifices. It was difficult or impossible for the multitudes who came to the Passover from long distances to bring their sacrifices with them. It was convenient to buy them in Jerusalem. Thus Annas probably carried on a great and highly lucrative trade in beasts for sacrifice.

Jesus saw this—must have seen it—the activities of Annas in his farm which was near to the traditional site of the Garden of Gethsemane. The trade in religion. The ex-high priest Annas growing rich on the law of Moses.

Jesus saw the activities of Caiaphas also.

On the eastern side of the Temple there was a broad space, partly open to the sky and partly under cover as the colonnade to the Temple. At the time of the Passover this was turned into a public mart. The Jews who came to the Passover came from many countries, bringing their foreign money with them. The money used in Jerusalem during the Roman occupation was, clearly, the Roman coinage.

Therefore, the need of money-changers, to change the foreign money into the Roman money for the purchase of the creatures for the sacrifice.

The colonnade of the Temple was the mart of these money-changers. There would be as many of them as the space would permit, each sitting, in eastern manner, at his little improvised table. The space open to the sky would be occupied by the pens and cages of Annas's farm servants. On another side of the Temple (probably the northern side) would be the place for the butchers who sold the meat after it had been on the altar and then wheeled out again—for sale to all comers. This mart was the perquisite of the high priest, probably his largest source of personal revenue.

Think, then, of Jesus of Nazareth going up to the Passover in Jerusalem during the time between his twentieth and twenty-fifth years. What sights! The dense masses of people crowding into the little city—Josephus says that in A.D. 65 there were as many as 3,000,000 in Jerusalem at the Passover, and that the sacrifices included 256,500 paschal lambs.

The thronged and noisome streets; the Jews from all districts, all provinces; the rabbis and readers from country towns; the tax-gatherers; perhaps the prostitutes; the Pharisees going up to the Temple, with the musicians walking before them—not looking up, pretending not to see, stopping to pray at street corners; the rich

Sadducees in their carriages; the poor elbowing their way; the blind beggar led by a boy or dog, rattling his can as he stumbles along; the clamour of many tongues.

On the great days of the feast Jesus would see Joseph Caiaphas going up to the Temple in his robes and with his retinue. He would see Annas coming in (perhaps by the Damascus Gate), also with his retinue from his house on the Mount of Olives. He would also see Herod Antipas with his Galilean soldiery, crossing the space from his house against the western walls to the Temple. Antipas made it a rule to come up for Passover—as a Jewish ruler he could not do less.

And then the scene on the eastern side of the Temple—Jesus would see that also. The money-changers and merchants, under the colonnade; the jabbering, nagging, perhaps swearing and quarrelling over the changing. The shouting at the beasts, the whipping of them into the Temple through the gate nearest to the sacrificial altar of unhewn stone.

There were places for the slaughtering of the beasts—beasts probably slaughtered before being wheeled into the Temple—the air rent with their cries.

Inside there were galleries for women, also courts for Gentiles. There were places for the priests to wash their hands from the blood after the sacrifices. The Roman soldiery keeping order among the quarrelling Jewish crowd; perhaps marching through them and scattering them with whips and sticks. The reek from within; then the carcasses being wheeled out to the butchers' benches. The chief servant of the high priest walking first along the benches after the carcasses had been laid out, and touching with his stick the pieces which were to be reserved for the high priest's table.

What a spectacle! The senses of Jesus of Nazareth must have been revolted by it. This gross mockery of the spirit of sacrifice! The spirit which led Abraham to offer up Isaac (as his dearest possession) descended to this! All the soul gone out of sacrifice. Sacrifice become a degrading and revolting business, a gross and shameless trade. The blood, the roasting, the reek, the buying and selling, the money-changing—all this in the name of God, and in the city of David!

The soul of Jesus sick at the sight of Jerusalem and all that was being done in it, both by Romans and Jews. The God-man walking through scenes like these. What is he going to do? And when?

Such was the metropolis of Palestine at the time of Passover in the early manhood of Jesus.

Jesus was not alone in deploring it. Perhaps members of the Sanhedrin itself—rich Pharisees like Nicodemus—secretly deplored it. Poor people, also, like Lazarus, who, with his sisters Mary and Martha, lived at Bethany, a few miles beyond the walls, over the Mount of Olives.

Probably Jesus made these friendships first during his early visits to Jerusalem. Probably he lodged at their house during the Passover. Jesus escaping from the pestilential atmosphere of the Passover at night to Bethany.

CHAPTER V

Back in Galilee

I. What Jesus Saw

RENAN DESCRIBES the return of Jesus from Jerusalem to Galilee as an escape from the turmoil of the metropolis of Palestine to the joyous life of the northern province, his peaceful home country.

Four or five little villages, the beautiful vine groves and olive plantations, the hills covered with wild flowers, the warbling of the birds, the songs of the vine-dressers—what a relief to him to return from his sojourns in Jerusalem to his beloved Galilee; to find there his heavenly Father in the midst of the green hills and clear fountains, among the crowds of women and children who, with joyous souls and the song of the angels in their hearts, waited for the salvation of Israel!

A charming pastoral, but, like much else from the same source, utterly unhistorical. Almost the reverse of history.

When Jesus returned to Galilee it was to a densely populated and deeply agitated and embarrassed country, full of trouble. Three millions of persons huddled together and suffering many injustices. Two hundred and forty towns and villages making (according to more than one writer) an almost continuous city from south to north. Tiberias becoming year by year a more and more pagan and licentious city. A writer speaks of it as a heathen city which would not have been tolerated in Judæa. Tiberias had not only its amphitheatre, like Jerusalem, but all the most brutal games known to Greek and Roman were played in it. It had also a stadium and racecourse, where cruelties, unknown elsewhere in Palestine, were frequently practised. Herod Antipas had transferred his palace from Sepphoris, the ancient capital of Galilee, to Tiberias.

There, with a council of nobles, he lived in lavish luxury at the expense of his people. Antipas had squandered great sums on

Tiberias. We read that his palace was adorned with marble statues of the emperor, and that much gold was expended on its decoration. He imitated every vice of Rome, which was just then at the height of its extravagance.

The little towns round about (and throughout Galilee) paid the price of this excess. They were heavily taxed to keep up the extravagances of Herod Antipas.

Galilee had not before suffered from poverty. During the first years of the life of Jesus it had been a place of property and even wealth. Capernaum, in particular, being "the way to the sea" for the rich fabrics and spices and other products of Babylon to the western world through Tyre, had been a centre of wealth and luxury. It used to be said, "Go south for learning; go north for wealth."

But Galilee could not live against the crushing burden of the taxation of Herod Antipas for the building and upkeep of his heathen city. The Galileans were a high-spirited people, trained to war from their infancy to protect themselves from the robbers, brigands and burglars, who were drawn to their territory in the wake of the trade caravans.

A writer tells that it was not at first that they submitted to the burden of crushing taxation. On one occasion they made an attack upon the royal palace at Tiberias, dragged out the royal furniture and broke it up in the streets. Josephus, a servant of Rome, and often a traducer of his own people, describes this incident as an act of brigandage. It was clearly a protest on the part of the Galileans against the heathen life being lived by their half-Philistine ruler at their expense.

But Antipas, who was a coward in himself, had always at hand the Roman legionaries to protect him and enforce his will on his subjects. The Galileans were crushed, and had to submit. Several times (probably by way of punishment for revolt) Galilee had to support a portion of the Roman army in winter quarters, an illegal and monstrous outrage.

This was the first thing Jesus would see on returning from Jerusalem to Galilee. Year after year such scenes occurred, and each year the oppression became greater. Jesus saw other and still worse aspects of rule by Rome through the medium of Herod Antipas.

Going to his work in the other cities of Galilee—Chorazin,

Capernaum, Nain, Cana, Bethsaida, Nazareth, Magdala—Jesus must have seen not only the poverty of the poor through the heavy burden of taxation, but the ruins of homes by the moral corruption of Tiberias and Jerusalem. The houses in sorrow for the daughters debauched in these cities. "The bunch of feathers where the hawk has been." The old fathers and old mothers in their empty homes.

Jesus saw all this, must have seen it. He must have seen, also, the physical effects of this condition.

One of the first of such effects was a large increase of mental and nervous diseases among the people. There appears to have been a great increase in the number of the paralysed. Galilee began to swarm with the paralysed and demoniacal.

I think Jesus, during these years, saw much of the poor in the little towns of Galilee. It was then that he first came to know the fishermen of the Lake of Galilee. I think his heart was bleeding for the poor and oppressed. I see him turning to the synagogue. What was there to do or say?

The little synagogues in the 200 or 300 towns of Galilee—how were they meeting the crushing affliction? They were probably helpless, dumbfounded, unable to see the hand of God in what was going on. The poor little ill-paid, faithful country rabbis, hardly daring to open their lips. Others silent from fear of spies among themselves. The remnant of the Galilee "Zealots" (followers of Judas the Galilean) huddled away in corners, not daring to say more of their Messianic hope.

One thing was almost certain, the hope of the Messiah was subsiding. The grandiose thought which had haunted their dreams for hundreds of years was dying down, or being concealed. Against this mighty, overwhelming pagan power of Rome and its lackey, Antipas, what could the people of Galilee do? What hope could there be of the fulfilment of the promise given to David?

I see Jesus going from the intimidated little synagogues of Galilee into the mountains. He loved the mountains. He liked nothing better than to sit and meditate on the hills about Nazareth, which were probably covered then, as now, with fig and olive trees and wells and tombs, and had a far view of the sea—the utmost sea, the Mediterranean.

It has been well said that these hills of Peræa became the birthplace of Christianity.

I think a new light came to him there, a new and far greater thought, destined to become the germ of a universal religion. I picture Jesus going back to the prophets; to the story of the Captivity; to the miserable doings outside Babylon. And then to the words of Isaiah, "He was led like a lamb to the slaughter."

What, after all, did this Roman tyranny amount to? What did it matter to be poor? To be oppressed? Nothing mattered to man in the long run except the welfare of his soul. Why trouble about the doings of those who could injure the body only, but had no power over the soul? It was better for the welfare of the soul to be poor than to be rich, to be the ruled rather than the ruler, to be the oppressed rather than the oppressor. To be rich was to provoke violence, war, outrage. To be poor was to live in peace with God and man. To pile up wealth was to separate the soul from God. Riches were a danger because they tempted the rich man to set up a barrier between himself and God, thus withering and destroying his soul.

To be dependent on God for the daily bread was to be very close to God. Therefore poverty, if it was not want, was a blessing in so far as it brought man into closer dependence on God, from season to season, from day to day, thus enlarging his soul. Therefore, blessed were the poor! Therefore, it was hard for the rich to enter Heaven.

What exquisite and touching parables were to come out of all this later!

Out of this, too, came quite another conception of the Messiah. The Messiah was no longer to be a conquering Messiah, but a prince of peace, coming from the throne of God. And the kingdom of Heaven when it came would be above all a kingdom of peace. It would come, not by a change of masters, but by a change of heart. People should be told that the treasures of the world were worthless to the soul. Let them lay up their treasures in Heaven.

Who was to go out and say this, to dedicate his life to saying it?

I see Jesus, realizing that this was his own task, his own duty. It was quite a different task from the one he had thought of before. Nobody must be able to mistake him for another Judas the Galilean. Still less for one of the agitators who used religious propaganda for personal gain. He must ask nothing, take nothing. He must go out with bare feet and empty hands. He must renounce all, leaving everything behind him. He must sacrifice the world in the service of the world. He must go to the crushed and suffering with this word of consolation, to the poor and afflicted above all others.

Do not be afraid to be poor. To be poor is to be rich. Why fear those who injure the body and have no power over the soul?

This, I think, was the second stage in the spiritual development of Jesus. The Messiah was to be the Great Comforter. A Jew, probably, whose call was to be his own people, but not necessarily a son of the house of David.

I see Jesus burning with the desire to begin on this mission.

II.   The Death of Joseph

Then I see him confronted and stopped by a great impediment. His father dies at this time. We hear nothing of Joseph after Jesus begins on his ministry. Only once during the ministry is he mentioned, and then it is not said that he is alive. It is practically certain that he died between the twelfth year of Jesus and the beginning of his ministry.

What effect would the death of Joseph have on the life of Jesus? A very sensible effect. If the plain words of the Gospels, several times repeated, are to be accepted in their simple and natural sense, Joseph left four sons and perhaps three daughters behind him— his own children and Mary's.

That Joseph died before Jesus seems certain. If he died when Jesus was still a young man, some of these seven would still be children. Jesus was the eldest. He was, therefore, when his father died, the head of the family—the breadwinner, responsible for the welfare of his mother and brothers and sisters—charged with the duty of keeping the home together.

If this (the date of Joseph's death) is conjecture, it is at least more human and reasonable than nine-tenths of the fantastic conjectures which have been associated with his name. I count the death of Joseph, and the domestic duties which thereby fell upon Jesus as the head of his family, as not the least among the conditions that delayed the beginning of his ministry. I think of the postponement as a bitter thing to him. But it was the hand of God.

III. Pontius Pilate

When Jesus was about twenty-nine years of age two events occurred which were of the utmost consequence in his career.

The first was the arrival in Palestine of the man who was to play the largest part in the events which culminated in his death. Valerius Gratus, after eleven years' service, was dismissed from the procuratorship, and Pontius Pilate was made procurator of Judæa and Samaria.

Pilate was the fifth Roman procurator of Judæa, Samaria and Idumæa. We know little of Pilate's previous life. He was probably a minor aristocrat, a Roman knight of the equestrian order, an order not considered (by Tacitus) worthy to take part in the administration of the empire. The date of his birth appears to be unknown, but he was probably in early middle life when he arrived in Palestine. His subsequent career is fully known.

His character may be easily summed up—he was in every act, down to the last, a coward and a bully. Philo, the Jewish philosopher of Alexandria, who makes no mention of Jesus, has much to say of Pontius Pilate. Philo says that Pilate was "inflexible, merciless and obstinate," that his administration was characterized throughout by corruption, violence, robbery, ill-treatment of the people he was sent to govern, and continuous executions without even the form of a trial. It is difficult to make any kind of reasonable defence of any act he is known to have performed. Everything he did had been better not done. He had little understanding of the people he ruled, and he was constantly quarrelling with them.

Apparently, he arrived late in the year A.D. 26. His first act on establishing himself at Cæsarea (the headquarters of the Roman army of occupation) was to order a portion of the army to winter quarters in Jerusalem, and to send the imperial standards and votive shields with them.

As the standards which Pilate sent bore upon their field the image of Tiberius, represented as a god, they therefore constituted a breach of Jewish law. Pilate knew that they would be offensive to the Jews, who would probably resist them. Such emblems of the Roman rulers had hitherto been kept aloof from the Holy City. Therefore, he sent them into Jerusalem by night, under the cover of darkness, and probably (almost certainly) had them set up in the prominent places, at the corners of the streets, in the public squares, at the very places where the Pharisees were accustomed to stand and pray. My conjecture would be that Pilate did all this, as "a new broom sweeps clean," to commend himself to the emperor.

In the morning, when the Jews saw what had been done—that Jerusalem had been given the appearance of a pagan city—they hastened in great numbers to Cæsarea, and besought Pilate to order that the standards should be taken away, as their presence was an insult to the Jewish faith, which recognized one God only—the invisible God.

Pilate, like the fool he was, refused, although he must have known that the Jews had a right to control their religious worship, saying that he could not so insult his emperor as to remove his standards. The Jews then said they would not go home until Pilate had consented.

Every day they persisted in their request that Pilate should remove the images. Everyday Pilate refused.

On the sixth day of their importunities, Pilate secretly ordered his soldiers to take up ambush behind him when he came out to sit on the judgment seat. When the Jews petitioned him again he would give a sign to the soldiers to surround them, and, this being done, he threatened the Jews with speedy death if they did not desist.

The Jews thereupon threw themselves on the ground and declared that they would welcome death rather than acquiesce in a transgression which required that they should recognize the divinity of a man. This awakened the cowardice in Pilate, and he ordered that the images should be sent back from Jerusalem to Cæsarea.

Shortly afterwards, Pilate conceived the idea (probably not without cause) that Jerusalem was insufficiently supplied with good water. Therefore, he set about the construction of an aqueduct to bring water to Jerusalem in the Roman manner, from a distance of about twenty-five miles (200 furlongs), perhaps from the pools of Siloam, south of Bethlehem. This would have been quite justified if Pilate had discharged the expense out of the tribute paid by the Jews to the Roman power. But, instead, he pillaged for the purpose the money of the treasury of the Temple.

Herod the Great had done so before him, and even then it had been a grievous offence. But for a totally heathen ruler to lay hands on the sacred money of the Temple was a barbaric outrage. How he could have done so except by secret collusion with the high priest (with Caiaphas or with Annas), or else by open violence, it is difficult to see. The Roman soldiers were forbidden to enter the Temple. Would they not be forbidden to enter the treasury of the Temple?

The Jewish people rebelled, and once more Pilate resorted to a cunning and cruel device to defeat them. He clothed a number of his Roman soldiers in the habit of the Jews, and, with daggers in their garments, he sent them out among the Jews to surround them. When the Jews importuned him afresh he gave a signal to his soldiers, whereupon they fell upon the Jews, who were unarmed, and a great number of them were slain.

Thus Pilate put an end to the opposition.

Jesus must have seen or heard of these acts of barbarity.

Another act of brutality which Jesus must have seen or heard of is mentioned by St. Luke. He speaks of the Galileans whose blood Pilate "mingled with their sacrifices."

We have no historical record of this incident, but it is not difficult to reconstruct it. I read this to refer to a renewed effort on Pilate's part to set up the imperial standards. Probably it occurred at the first Passover after Pilate's coming, that of A.D. 27.

The Galileans came in large numbers to the Passover. Herod Antipas, as we have seen, although a bad Jew, came with them— had to come. The Galileans were almost the only survivors of the sect of the "Zealots." Zealot and Galilean had become almost synonymous terms.

My conjecture would be that at this first Passover after his coming to Judæa, Pilate (who was stubborn and stupid enough for any madness, and was almost certainly still smarting under his previous rebuff) caused the imperial standards, with the image of the emperor, to be set up in the Temple itself under the cover of the night. Further, the next morning, the Galileans, going to sacrifice, found the images there and flung them out. Finally, that Pilate ordered his soldiers to do what the first of the Roman conquerors did years earlier—kill the Galileans at the very foot of the altar. Hence Pilate mingled the blood of the Galileans with their sacrifices.

Herod Antipas must have been there. To stand idly by when Pilate had slain some of his subjects was impossible. Apparently, he protested to Pilate. He could not have done less and remain the ruler of Galilee. This may have been the beginning of his quarrel with Pilate, a quarrel only composed on the last day of the life of Jesus.

The clear duty of Herod Antipas was to complain of this outrage to the governor of Syria, who was Pilate's superior. I think it probable that he did so. Counting on the high favour in which he had hitherto stood with the emperor (had he not built a city in the emperor's honour?), he went to Rome to make his protest to Tiberius himself.

We know that Herod Antipas was in Rome in A.D. 28. And out of that visit to Rome came an event which had an important although indirect effect on the life of Jesus.

Strange irony of fate that such an incident should contribute to lead Jesus to his death!

For some time before, things had been going badly with the emperor Tiberius. He had suffered from a long succession of calamities. Under the influence of Sejanus, he had allowed himself to leave Rome and go into retirement in the Campagnia for the free and unobserved indulgence of his pleasures.

This was in A.D. 21. Two years later, Sejanus poisoned the son of Tiberius, yet he continued to hold his place of power, as a kind of regent. Four years after that Sejanus persuaded Tiberius to hide himself away in the island of Capri.

In A.D. 28 Julia, the dissolute stepdaughter of Tiberius (as dissolute as her mother), who had been banished twenty years before, died miserably in exile. And a year later (A.D. 29) Livia, the mother of Tiberius, who had been for fifty-two years the wife of the emperor Augustus, died.

Thus Tiberius had for ten or twelve years been hard beaten by fate.

IV. The Morality of Rome

The effect of all this on the morality of Rome was terrible. Stories of the lamentable state of the imperial household, tales of the hideous debaucheries practised in the deepest retirement of Capri, poisoned the air of half the world. As a consequence of the tyrannies which Sejanus, the plotter, was permitted to exercise in his master's name, there was frequent and open rebellion.

Once Tiberius returned to Rome in an effort to regain command of himself, to put an end to plots against himself and his family, to resume control and to purify Rome and his court. But very soon he returned to his former way of life. Much of this terrible story comes from the *Annals* of Tacitus (which were not published until eighty years after the death of Tiberius), and it is all under the suspicion of being derived from a poisoned source, possibly the mother of Nero, who was trying to prepare the way for her infamous son; but there can be little doubt that it is substantially true.

This was the condition in Rome when Herod Antipas arrived there after his quarrel with Pontius Pilate. It is little likely that he got any serious hearing for what, at that time, would look like a petty quarrel. But his visit was not fruitless, although its only result was evil.

He met in Rome at this time (as far as it is possible to judge of the date) the woman with whose name his own is chiefly associated. This was Herodias.

She was his niece, the daughter of his half-brother, Aristobulus, whom his father, Herod the Great, had put to death. She had married another of his half-brothers, Philip, also called Herod, not the tetrarch, but a disinherited son of Herod the Great. Thus the marriage had been incestuous.

As her father died early in 4 B.C. Herodias in A.D. 28, when she met Antipas, could not have been less than thirty-two years of age. She was probably some few years older, in the period of her full womanhood. She had one child by Philip, a girl named Salome, probably about ten or twelve.

Herod Antipas and Herodias fell in love with each other. He proposed to Herodias to take her back with him to Galilee. She objected that he had a wife there already. Herod thereupon undertook to divorce his Arab wife, and Herodias promised to join him at Tiberias as soon as he had done so. On this understanding Herod Antipas returned to Galilee.

We read that he returned home about midsummer A.D. 29, which corresponds with St. Luke's reckoning, "about the fifteenth year of the reign of Tiberius."

But rumour of his plot to divorce his Arab wife had reached Tiberias before him. Somebody had come back to Tiberias with the tale. Spies had brought it to his Arab wife, and in her anger and shame she contrived a means to defeat the intention of Herod

Antipas to put her to shame, without revealing her knowledge of his plot.

When Antipas arrived at the royal palace she was in bed, and she said she was sick. She asked her husband to send her for a change of air, back to a place in the territories of her father. This seemed to the slow-witted Antipas to jump with his desires. Not seeing through his wife's purpose, he agreed to do as she proposed, and she was forthwith sent with an escort of soldiers into her father's territory.

Then he sent messengers to Rome for Herodias, and she came. Abandoning her husband Philip, she joined Antipas bringing her daughter, Salome, with her. They were married and lived in the palace at Tiberias, already notorious for many excesses. Thus both Herod and Herodias committed offences against the law of Moses, as given in the Book of Leviticus. Herodias had married a second time while her husband was still alive, and after she had a child by him—Salome. She had married her husband's half-brother, who was also her uncle. Thus they had both contracted an unlawful and incestuous marriage, according to the law of Moses.

Such was the state of things, at the period indicated in the first verse of the third chapter of *Luke*. What followed was natural, and it led to events of the greatest consequence in the life of Jesus.

It has sometimes been referred to a later period (as late as eight years afterwards), but to do so is not only to set aside the circumstantial story in the Gospels, but to make chaos of all subsequent dates.

V. *Aretas*

When the father of Herod Antipas's Arab wife, Aretas, the Arabian king, came to the knowledge of what had been done to his daughter, he determined to avenge her. Gathering a large army he made war upon Herod, and crossed into his territory with the intention of destroying him. Aretas was a great soldier, and his people were great soldiers. Herod Antipas had to go out to meet him, or Galilee would be overrun. In order to do so he had to enlist or conscript a large number of his Galilean subjects. He succeeded in doing so. It would appear that the young men of Galilee permitted themselves to be bribed by higher wages to become the soldiers of Herod Antipas, the flagrant law-breaker.

For what purpose?

To fight for this incestuous adulterer, this breaker of the law of Moses.

Herod Antipas's army (led perhaps by Herod himself) went out to meet the army of his outraged father-in-law, the Arab king. Apparently, they crossed the Jordan into Peræa, and went down towards the region of the Dead Sea. In the light of later events it would appear probable that Herodias and her young daughter Salome went with Herod Antipas, or followed him.

Jesus was in Galilee at this time. He must have been witness to all this iniquity. Did it colour some of his judgments on marriage and divorce?

VI. Spiritual Development

It may be a hazardous adventure to follow that part of the spiritual development of Jesus whereof we have no historical record. But it is an adventure which, in the long silence of the Gospels over the years of the formative period of the life of Jesus, must always have an immense fascination.

Like every other man who has lived in the world, Jesus of Nazareth must have been in some measure a creature of circumstance. If he was not like other men in this he cannot be regarded as a man. Through certain years of the world, and certain events, he lived. We know what those years and events were. We conclude that he could not escape from the effects of them. Knowing what manner of man he was, and having seen what events he lived through, let us ask ourselves how his spiritual development was affected by them.

From his twenty-first to his thirtieth year Jesus of Nazareth had lived in the midst of scenes of perhaps the most appalling wickedness the world had yet witnessed. He had seen the demoralization of the holy city of Jerusalem under the Roman occupation. He had seen the corruption of the Jewish religion under its time-serving high priests. He had heard of the demoralization of Rome under the rule of Tiberius and his favourite, the arch-schemer Sejanus, of the plots, and counter-plots, of the extortions of provincial governors. He had seen the arrival of Pontius Pilate in Galilee and his brutal tyrannies. Finally, he had seen the outrageous transgression of the law of Moses by Herod Antipas in his marriage with Herodias, and the submission of the Galileans to the enlistment of the army with which Antipas was to meet his father-in-law.

It was the abomination of iniquity. Not his own country only, but all the world, as never before, was full of wickedness. Incest, persecution, barbarous cruelties, abominations of all kinds.

The enormity of all this must have carried Jesus of Nazareth beyond the thought of his own people and country. I picture him returning to the mountains to think out this shocking condition of the world. He has to make up accounts with himself. He has to think things out. What does it mean?

The spirit of Daniel takes possession of him. The calamities that were falling on the world were the punishment inflicted by God upon man for his sin. Sin was at the root of all the troubles of the world, and the heart of sin was selfishness. Out of selfishness comes covetousness, avarice, violence.

This leads him to the third stage of his spiritual development. The Messiah who is to come is not to be merely a worldly king, a man of the house of David, an avenger of the Jewish people who was to re-establish the throne of David, nor yet merely the comforter who was to reconcile man (the descendant of David) to his hard lot, to his poverty, to his sufferings of various kinds, to disease of body and mind.

The Messiah who was to come was to be the Universal Judge— a divine being to be sent from God, himself a God, a Son of God, who was to come in the clouds, attended by legions of angels, and judge all the peoples of the earth, casting the evil into everlasting punishment, the gehenna of Jerusalem, establishing the righteous in a Kingdom of Heaven, which would last on the earth for ever.

This Messiah, this Judge to whom all the powers of the world would be as chaff, would come soon. The signs of his coming, as foretold by the prophets, were all present at that time. War, rebellions, earthquakes, the falling of towers (like the Tower of Siloam) and the destruction of life—all these things were taking place.

An earthquake had just then occurred in the neighbourhood of the hot springs south of Tiberias. An earthquake had lately taken place in Rome, and there had been great loss of life. An amphitheatre at Fidenæ had broken down and many thousands had been buried in the ruins. The armies of Rome, striding over the unknown countries of the western world (including Gaul and Britain), were causing unutterable slaughter. Never before had the world looked upon any such iniquities.

The messenger from God, the Judge of all the earth, would not only come soon, but very soon. No one knew when. At a moment, at the twinkling of an eye, when man did not expect him, he would appear. Let man be prepared. To be prepared was to repent—repent of the sins and wickedness which had brought the world to this pass. To repent before it was too late, and the Judge was here, to avenge God, who had been outraged by His creatures. To repent and so to become children of the new world—the new Kingdom.

This, as I see it, was the final spiritual development of Jesus before he began his ministry. Having reached this point he could wait no longer; he must go out and preach the Gospel of repentance. The souls of men were in peril; at all costs he must go out to save them. A great crusade against sin. His soul ablaze with this errand of warning.

If this is fantasy, surely no fantasy was ever more reasonable. In the silences of those eighteen dark years in the Gospels, who will say such scenes did not occur? At some time, under some conditions, Jesus must have left his home at Nazareth. We know that it was in this year he left it, when, according to *Luke,* he was about thirty years of age.

It is not difficult to see him at this time in his relations with his family. His "brothers and sisters" were now grown up, and could take care of themselves and his mother. He was no longer necessary as the head of the family. He could go. He must go. He could resist the call no longer. God was calling him.

And what of the feelings of his family? In the light of later events, it is not difficult to reconstruct the scenes in the home at Nazareth. His brethren are against him. Perhaps they need his help still, or think they would be the better for it. Perhaps they have no sympathy with his mission, looking upon it as a dream. Judging by their conduct a little later we may assume that they are contemptuous of it. They were almost afraid for his sanity. This wild thought of the speedy coming of the end of the world— what does it mean? He has studied too much, read too much; spent too much time alone—among the tombs, on the mountains.

And then his mother. Perhaps his mother, siding with his brothers out of pity for him, out of thought of the wandering, friendless life he is about to live, the derision, perhaps contempt, he is to face, the persecution, perhaps the suffering, the martyrdom. If she had any recollection of the Virgin Birth, of the visit and prediction of the angel, of the scenes in Bethlehem, and all that is recorded in the Gospels, she would have thought of this moment in the life of Jesus as the beginning of the divine mission fore-ordained.

We are not told that she did. We only know that she remained with the other members of the family and sided with them, apparently against Jesus. Nevertheless, Jesus held to his purpose. A painful, perhaps a tragic parting. The exalted spirit of the elder brother whom they could not comprehend.

And then the last moment. The early morning, perhaps Sabbath morning. Going off without purse and scrip or a second coat—homeless—without a place to lay his head—leaving everything behind him—relying on his heavenly Father (to whose work he was to dedicate the future of his life) to provide for him. Outside the house—on the road or street—going off with strong step—hardly daring to look back—the mother looking after him from the open door. A great, pathetic, yet exalted human moment. Is it to take too great a liberty with the silences of Scripture to reproduce this hour which, one way or other, as surely took place nearly 2,000 years ago in the little town of Nazareth in Galilee as that the sun that day rose over the world?

This would be in the spring of A.D. 29. Probably about April, when Jesus was about thirty-three or thirty-four years of age.

What manner of man was he, at this beginning of his ministry? Jesus is usually spoken of as a gentle teacher at the beginning of his ministry, a tender spirit bringing a message of peace and love to a little province of an obscure country, hidden away from the busy world among its olive fields and vineyards, and with its little shining lake in the midst of it.

Christian art from the earliest ages has so painted Jesus and his surroundings. A soft, sensitive angelic creature, full of sweetness and charm, sitting on the shores of the lake, or among the wild flowers on the hillside, with a company consisting chiefly of women and children about him, teaching them in gentle accents, by means of parables, the story of God's love and forgiveness.

It is difficult for me to think of anything less likely to have been done. Neither the tumultuous scenes he had lived through for thirty-three years, the wild chaos of the world's condition, nor (particularly) the anarchy of his own country and the condition of his own people at that moment in the world's history would appear to justify such a picture.

On the contrary, they seem to make it a grotesque impossibility. The Jesus who left Nazareth was a different man altogether; his scene was different and his mission was different. He had left his home as a homeless wanderer for the sake of a mission. A fiery soul. A fanatic, perhaps. Assuredly no milksop. All this would express itself in his person. I think of him as a man of dominating personality; of immense power; of masterful character, forced out into the world by a divine urge.

I have no historical authority for any kind of personal portrait. But in my own eye, he is a man of more than common stature, with a deep, penetrating, resonant and far-reaching voice, capable of reaching vast multitudes, and swaying them to great outbursts of emotion. When he commands, people obey—they cannot help but obey. He has gentleness, but he is certainly no weakling. He has charm, but above all he has strength. His face is capable of the sweetest of smiles, but it is usually solemn and even severe. He has tenderness, but above all passion. He is a fiery spirit, a flaming sword, a living soul, with a terrible message, a warning, almost a threat.

What was his warning? That the world was coming to an end. That for its sins and wickedness the existing order was soon to be destroyed. That God was about to send a heavenly messenger with a legion of angels to establish a new dispensation. That when this heavenly messenger should come his first work would be to judge mankind, to separate the righteous from the evil.

VII. *Jesus in Capernaum*

Where did Jesus first take his message? I think (contrary to the general opinion) he took it first to Capernaum, and the little towns of northern Galilee. For reasons that will afterwards appear, I think it was there, and at that time, that Jesus began his ministry. Why not Tiberias, the centre of the iniquity he was about to denounce? Why not Jerusalem, the heart of the political tyranny and the religious hypocrisy he had witnessed? The reason is clear. If Jesus had gone first to either of these places his mission would never have been allowed to begin. In Tiberias Herod Antipas (or his officials in his absence) would speedily have disposed of him. If he had gone to Jerusalem, Pontius Pilate would have arrested him as a disturber of the peace, and the high priest must have destroyed his mission before it was born, because it cut at the foundations of the edifice of their religion, as they practised it.

He took it first to the common people of his own race and country, the poor, the oppressed, the downtrodden of Galilee, because, if they had sinned, they had suffered most.

I see Jesus of Nazareth going into the little synagogues of Capernaum, taking the book from the reader, reading a passage from the prophet Daniel and then applying it to the present time. What the prophet had foretold was coming to pass—now. Did they not see the signs of it?

We have no record of the first sermons of Jesus. There were no disciples yet to remember and report them. But the substance of the first message of Jesus has come down to us: *"Repent, for the kingdom of Heaven is at hand."*

The preaching of Jesus attracted wide attention. The man who foretells the speedy coming of the end of the world always attracts attention. Largely from fear or from remorse, people come in crowds to hear him. A kind of hysteria takes hold of them. He is always sure of followers, wherever he may appear or whatever he may be.

But Jesus was speaking with authority and knowledge. His knowledge astonished his hearers. They knew him, and they were at a loss to know where he had come by his learning.

I see the synagogues crowded as often as Jesus entered them. I see the congregations becoming so great that the little rectangular buildings are no longer able to contain them, and Jesus speaks in the market-place, and perhaps in the fields or on the hillsides outside the towns. Vast multitudes following him.

We read that people thronged to hear him—from Tyre, Sidon, all the country on the north of Galilee. Fear, terror, thought of the pains and penalties of the life hereafter, dread of the great Judge who was to come, brought people about Jesus in thousands. His message was true. Their prophets had foretold it. Such was the fiery cross Jesus carried into Capernaum at the beginning of his ministry.

Many were convinced by Jesus, repented of their sins, and looked with joy for the coming of the Kingdom of God which he predicted. Others openly reviled him.

Some of the latter were probably the broken nervous wrecks who had been driven insane by the tyrannies they had been subjected to—the robbery, over-taxation, confiscation and general corruption of the government they had lived under, the general downfall of their nation, race and religion. Why talk to them of the coming of a Kingdom of God? What had God ever done for them? A beneficent Providence was a mockery. God did nothing.

Such people, broken in body and brain were, in the view of Jesus, possessed of devils. He believed disease was one of the ways in which the devil tempted and destroyed man. The devils took possession of man in the form of disease. It might be a man's own sin which had brought about his disease, or it might be his father's sin, or it might be the sin of others, the sin of the society he was compelled to live in. But disease was to Jesus the expression of sin. To get rid of sin it was necessary to cast out the devils that created disease.

Such was the demonology of Jesus, not greatly differing except in manner from the theory of modern science about disease. When a man understood to be "possessed of devils" reviled Jesus in the synagogues, in the fields, Jesus adopted the attitude of a master over the devils. By the strength of his will and mind and heart he overcame them. With a loud voice he commanded the devils to come out of the man. The evil spirits in the man obeyed his imperative command, the command of their master. The man became sane and calm.

What was Jesus doing? He was adopting an attitude towards a kind of mental malady which is familiar to modern science. But he was none the less performing miracles—miracles of the spirit of good over the spirit of evil.

The people of Capernaum were astonished. They had seen nothing like this before. Such miracles were proof of the divine mission of Jesus.

Although it was not strictly in accordance with prophecy that the Messiah should work miracles, it appears to have been the common expectation that he would do so. People began to ask themselves, "Is this the Christ?" or "Is it Elias?" I see the people following him about in ever-increasing multitudes, especially the diseased, the insane, the sick, the poor, the oppressed, the downtrodden. He was casting out devils. He was healing the paralytic. By sheer power of will he was doing this. But above all he was crying, *"Repent, for the kingdom of Heaven is at hand."*

The fame of Jesus passed over all Galilee. It went down to Judæa. The daily caravans carried it south. At this point the life of Jesus was crossed by an event of great importance. The spirit stirring in Jesus and his followers was at the same time stirring in others. After a time the same caravans returned north with a similar story.

While Jesus of Nazareth, on the shores of the Lake of Galilee, was crying, "Repent, for the kingdom of Heaven is at hand," another, on the banks of the Jordan, was delivering the same message. This was John the Baptist.

CHAPTER VI

The Baptism

I. *John the Baptist*

O F John the Baptist, as an historical personage, we know almost as little as of Jesus of Nazareth.

It is true that Josephus has more to say about him, and that what he says is more certainly authentic, in the sense of coming from his own pen. But whether the source of his information was Agrippa II or Banus (the old teacher of Josephus who, it is believed, had seen John), it is clear that neither he nor they know anything for themselves. Everything said about John clearly derives from the Gospels, although a different interpretation is given to events according to the religious bias or political needs of the historians.

What do the Gospels say about this astonishing man?

All four Gospels mention him. Three of them give no personal facts of importance. *Luke* alone tells the story of his birth—that he was born in one of the cities of Judæa, assumed to be Hebron, that his parents were both descended from the priestly class, Zacharias, his father, being himself a priest (of the section of Abia), and his mother, Elisabeth, a daughter of the house of Aaron; that they were old and had prayed for a son; that, while Zacharias stood at the altar in the Temple of Jerusalem offering incense, the angel Gabriel appeared to him and announced the forthcoming birth of a son, told him that his child would be a Nazarite all his life, that he would be filled with the Holy Ghost from his mother's womb, that he would convert the children of Israel, and that, with the power of Elijah, he would prepare the people for the coming of the Messiah; that Zacharias, hesitating to believe this, had been struck dumb; that his mouth had been opened again when, at the circumcision of the child, a name had to be given to him; and that the child (according to the instructions of the angel) had been called John.

370

We do not know the exact date of John's birth. But again the Gospel (*Luke*) gives the only indication. We are told that the mother of Jesus was the cousin of Elisabeth, notwithstanding the disparity of probably thirty years in their ages. Mary, being newly with child, visited her cousin Elisabeth when she was in her sixth month.

Therefore John was about six months older than Jesus, and, if Jesus was born on December 25th, 5 B.C., John must have been born in the previous summer. This is all we know. The last we hear of the infancy of John is that "the child grew and waxed strong in spirit and was in the desert till the day of his showing in Israel." Observe the resemblance to the last words in *Luke* (I, 80) about the infancy of Jesus.

What happened to John during the many succeeding years until he reached manhood is quite unknown. He may have continued to live in complete obscurity in his father's house at Hebron, the mountain city on the fringe of the Judæan desert, with few trees and little vegetation about it; being brought up, according to the prediction of the angel, as a Nazarite, never joining a rabbinical school and never going up to Jerusalem. Or it may be that in gratitude to God for the gift of his son in answer to his prayer, Zacharias (like the mother of Samuel) dedicated him to God by committing him to one of the religious houses which existed at that time in the heart of the desert, on the shores of the Dead Sea. The Essenes lived there—a large confraternity of monks, not strictly Jewish, but following the law of Moses.

It may be that John was brought up by the Essene monks and remained with them until manhood, when, differing from them in some of their tenets, and particularly in their way of life, he left them for the more active work of seeking the salvation of the outside world.

It is not impossible to account for John as one who, coming out of a long seclusion in which he had contemplated the religion of Moses in its purity into a society which violated the religion of Moses by many transgressions, was so shocked by the hypocrisy of the Church and the tyrannies and iniquities of the world that he broke into wild denunciation.

But apart from the circumstantial statement of the evangelist, it would be easier to account for John by assuming that the same conditions which produced Jesus of Nazareth had produced John

—the constant spectacle of the world under his eyes, the tyrannies of the Roman occupation, the perpetual shedding of blood, the crushing taxation, the frequent violation of the Jewish religion by the representatives of paganism, the time-serving and corruption of the Jewish priesthood, and, finally, the incestuous adultery of the Jewish king or tetrarch.

What had brought about the spiritual development of the son of the carpenter in Nazareth might equally have brought about the spiritual development of the son of the priest at Hebron. The clear knowledge of existing conditions shown by John forbids the thought that he had learned them at sight. If we had no escape from that conclusion we should be compelled to believe that John was either a myth or that he was taught of God. But it is not necessary to think either.

II. His Ministry

The next time we hear of John is specially dated. We are told that in the fifteenth year of the reign of Tiberius (which, if plain figures bear their plain meaning, was A.D. 29) there spread through Judæa and all Palestine the fame of a young reformer—John, the son of Zacharias.

Whether this was the beginning of John's ministry is uncertain. It is thought that the date in *Luke* is intended to indicate the beginning of the ministry of Jesus, not of John. Vast commentaries have been written on the pros and cons of this detail. Christianity is entirely unaffected by the issue. It is sufficient to accept the statement of the evangelist at its face value. According to that, John began to preach when he was about thirty-four years of age. "The word of God" says Luke, "came unto John in the wilderness, and he came into all the country about Jordan, preaching the baptism of repentance for the remission of sins."

He had cut himself off from human relationships, and departed from all dependence on human society. He was practising extreme austerities. Clad in a camel's skin, and girt about with a leather belt, he was living on the only food of the desert—locusts and wild honey. Apparently, he fasted for long periods, and for that reason some said he was possessed of a devil.

We do not hear that he ever went up to Jerusalem. Presumably he confined himself to the people of the desert and of the country north of it on the banks of the Jordan. Almost certainly he was preaching to those who came and went, north and south, by the trade route that passed from Jerusalem, and the countries south of it, through Peræa to Cæsarea Philippi and Damascus.

Clearly John the Baptist was, like Jesus, deeply imbued with the spirit of the prophecies of Isaiah.

He describes himself as, "the voice of one crying in the wilderness, 'Prepare ye the way of the Lord, make his paths straight,' " thereby taking almost literally the words of Isaiah, "The voice of him that crieth in the wilderness, Prepare ye the way of the Lord, make straight in the desert a highway for our God" (*Isaiah* XL, 3). The burden of his message was that the end of the world was coming, that it was near, that the Messiah, who had been foretold by the prophets, was shortly to be expected, that he would bring a great wrath on the wicked and establish a kingdom of Heaven in a cleansed and purified world. "Repent, for the kingdom of Heaven is at hand." This was his watchword.

Clearly, he was a man of commanding personality, certainly a powerful and perhaps a violent preacher. It is certain that he was stirring the conscience of the people. Whatever their conduct had been, however they had silently acquiesced in the conduct of their leaders, they had been secretly conscious of wrongdoing.

John made a profound impression. We read that multitudes from Jerusalem and all Judæa went out to hear him. The effect of his preaching was overwhelming. The time was near when God would put an end to a world which had sinned against Him. When that time came God would send His messenger, His Messiah, who would thoroughly purge His floor, exterminate the unrighteous, both great and small, rich and mighty.

John was no respecter of persons. He hated the priestly class. When, perhaps out of curiosity, more probably out of fear, a number of scribes and Pharisees came out to him, he fell upon them with bitter reproaches. "O generation of vipers, who hath warned you to flee from the wrath to come? Bring forth therefore fruits meet for repentance."

Particularly he denounced transgressions in high places. That was the time when Herod Antipas, having dealt badly by his Arab wife, had brought Herodias, his half-brother's wife, from Rome, and married her. John openly denounced this marriage as adultery and incest, and called upon the tetrarch of Galilee to send the woman back to her home.

It is probable that, at this time, he was preaching on the western side of the Jordan, in Judæa, which was in the territory controlled by Pontius Pilate, the Roman procurator.

Pilate appears to have taken no notice of him. At least, he did not interfere with him. Although John was gathering vast multitudes about him, Pilate did not suspect him of a political purpose. Pilate had not yet reached that condition of nervous panic which led him, a few years later, in the case of another such person in Samaria, to mistake religious delusion for political rebellion—to his own utter destruction. Pilate probably looked upon John as an impossible religious fanatic, one of the many who were always prophesying a new Heaven and a new earth.

At all events, John's preaching was harmless to the Roman occupation. If John was insulting Herod Antipas by his denunciation of his marriage with his niece, that was Herod's own affair. Herod had insulted Pilate by making representations against him to Rome —let him look after his own reputation.

Therefore, Pilate left John alone. The priestly class also left him alone. Annas and Caiaphas paid no heed to him. It is more than probable that they did not like this everlasting prophesying, this constant reminding of the people of the old hope of the advent of a Messiah. They had possibly lost all interest in a Messiah, perhaps persuaded themselves (as many did) that the Messiah had already come. Even Hillel is sometimes credited with that opinion.

But, in any case, John was harmless, although he shouted so loud. He did not attempt to interfere with their actual work at the Temple. Probably he never set his foot in it. He never said anything contrary to the law of Moses. He never blasphemed. He never (unlike Jesus later) said anything which they could fasten upon to report to their friends of Rome. Besides, John had an immense influence with the people. The priestly class was afraid to interfere with him. Therefore, the best course was to ignore him.

III. The Rite of Baptism

John went on from strength to strength. He gathered a group of disciples about him. They practised one rite which appears to have attracted great attention. This was the rite of baptism.

How did John come to think of baptism?

Baptism was not entirely new to the Judaic religion. It is an error to think of it as the ceremony used for the initiation of proselytes into the Jewish religion; this was a rite of much later origin. But a form of baptism is referred to both in *Isaiah* and in *Ezekiel*. Obviously baptism was not a rite peculiar to Judaism. It had been practised by pagans, particularly, perhaps, by the Persian cult of Mithras. Therefore, if John had been brought up among the Essenes in the religious houses on the eastern side of the Dead Sea he would be familiar with baptism. The Essenes probably came from the country east of Peræa. Certainly they baptized.

What did John's baptism mean?

It meant, what baptism had always meant, the renunciation and remission of sin. Converts were baptized into "regeneration and exemption from their guilt." According to Tertullian, even if a man had stained himself with homicide, and he went in search of water, he could purge himself from his sin. According to Josephus, baptism was a bathing for the purification of the body after the soul had already been purified by repentance.

Clearly the baptism of John was for the sinner, and for the sinner only. It cleansed him from his past. After his baptism his sins were forgiven him, and he became a sinless man. If he sinned again, he was restored to his sinless state not by a second baptism, but by a supplementary rite. Further, the baptism of John was closely united to the Messianic hope. The sinful man, becoming sinless, became an inheritor of the kingdom of Heaven, which the Messiah, when he came to earth, was to establish.

Therefore, the mission of John was to call as many as possible to this sinless state, whereof baptism was the symbol. John's baptism was at once relevant to the remission of sin and to the inheritance of God's kingdom. It is evident that John's ceremony of baptism was by total immersion. The whole man must be cleansed of sin, if he is to be fit for the Kingdom. Hence John went in search of deep water. He probably began in Judæa in the early spring of A.D. 29, and when, as the summer came on, water became scarce on the western side of the Jordan he went over to the eastern side, to the deep pools about the town of Bethabara (on the opposite side of Jordan from Jericho, not the more northern town of the same name). He was then in Peræa, the territory of Herod Antipas, whose incestuous marriage with Herodias he had openly denounced. It is improbable that John gave a thought to this, or that he would have concerned himself for a moment about the risk he ran in going over to the country of the tetrarch whose conduct he had condemned.

John's popularity increased rapidly. He was not far from Jerusalem, about twenty-two miles away. People could come to him and return in a day; they walked so far, or they rode on asses. Vast numbers gathered about him. Great multitudes, smitten by fear or conscience, were baptized by him. Baptism gave his ministry an added solemnity. He came to be called the Baptist.

IV. The Memory of Elijah

John performed no miracles. He did not claim to forgive sins. He made no pretension to supernatural powers. Yet multitudes continued to flock to him from all parts. In a little while his fame had passed all over his small country. Clearly, he was a powerful personality—a preacher of immense force and authority. He reminded the people of their old Jewish prophets. The idea began to be entertained that he *was* one of the old prophets, the prophet Elijah. They remembered the prophecy which said, "Behold, I will send Elijah the Tishbite before the coming of the day of the Lord."

Among the Jewish people there had always been a certain hope, a certain fear, that Elijah would come back to earth. The memory of that sublime, awesome and solitary figure still haunted the Jewish mind. Nearly 1,000 years before that time Elijah had come from the land east of the Jordan to wage war in the name of the God of their fathers against the worship of Baal. He was the foe of the rich and mighty. God spoke to him in "the still small voice."

Clad in his mantle of skins, girt about the loins with a leather belt, he had gone up into the hidden places of Mount Carmel. There he had been admitted to strange and awful intimacy with the Most High, and when he came down to the valleys it had been as God's spokesman. Living apart from men he had come down from the mountains in the great crisis in the life of the people to rebuke the kings themselves in their courts, to sound the note of righteousness and to threaten the awful judgments of God against the sinners who transgressed His law. He worked many miracles, including, apparently, raising the dead.

Nobody knew how Elijah lived. When the people suffered from famine they were told that God sent ravens into Elijah's hidden place on Carmel to feed him. Nobody knew how he died. The accepted belief was that he did not die at all, but was translated from earth to Heaven, carried up in a whirlwind, by a chariot of fire and horses of fire, and that he was now among the heavenly inhabitants recording the deeds of men.

But he would come back to earth some day. God would send him again before the great and dreadful day. Nobody knew when that would be. But it would be shortly before the coming of the Messiah. Elijah would be the precursor of the Messiah. Three days (mark, three) before the Messiah, Elijah would again appear.

And after the archangel Michael had blown his trumpet, Elijah would come with the Messiah, whom he would present to the Jews. Then Elijah would work seven miracles. Among them was that of raising the dead before men's eyes. After that would come the Messianic reign. During the Messianic reign Elijah would be one of the Messiah's princes, to help him to judge mankind. And he would finish his course on earth by killing the evil spirit of the world at the command of God.

Such was the awful figure which had long haunted the imagination of the Jewish people.

And now, pricked in their conscience by the searching denunciation of John, and perhaps inflamed by his resemblance to Elijah, they began to think that John was Elijah himself returned to earth. After a while they went further than that, and sent messengers to ask him if he were not the Christ. John denied this. But he said, in effect, that he was the forerunner of the Christ, that one was coming after him who was mightier than he, whose shoe latchets he was not worthy to unloose, whose fan was in his hand, who would gather the wheat into his garner and burn up the chaff in unquenchable fire.

It was the figurative language of the oriental, but his hearers were orientals also, and they knew what he meant. Such was the astonishing man who had appeared on the banks of the Jordan about the same time as Jesus on the shores of Galilee.

The Gospels begin the story of Jesus with that of John, thus leaving the impression that John was in some sort the master of Jesus. Some commentators go so far as to declare this to mean that John's attestation to Jesus was the foundation of his ministry.

It is not impossible that the evangelists, writing at a time when John's name was still potent, may have thought so. But there is no other reason either in profane history or in the Gospels for the inference that Jesus owed anything to John. If John began before Jesus, it was, as far as we actually know, only a few months earlier. In that small country a few months were sufficient for all he is reported to have done before Jesus appeared. I think, for reasons presently to be explained, that Jesus had already begun on his ministry before he heard of John's.

Jesus probably first heard of John when he was in Capernaum on his first (unreported) mission. Jesus owed nothing to John except the sympathy he took and gave—two ardent young souls inflamed with the same mission. It is my belief that Jesus went up to John's baptism immediately he heard of it.

Why did Jesus go up to the baptism of John? I consider this one of the main questions of a Life of Jesus.

V. Revelation of the Divine Purpose

More than once in the Gospels it is said that Jesus knew all that was to happen; that when he asked questions of men it was only to try them; that, in particular, he knew that Judas was to betray him.

But this claim cannot be upheld. More than once or twice he says that in the greatest of matters he does not know all, that only the Father knows when the end will come. The utmost claim he makes is to say that the coming of the Kingdom will be in the time of the living generation, that some of them who are standing with him will not taste of death until they have seen the Kingdom come with power. Farther than this he himself never goes. Only his disciples and the evangelists claim for him all pre-knowledge. It is always, throughout his life, as if he knew that God revealed to him stage by stage as the need arose what was to happen in the near future. At his baptism it was revealed to him that he was to die for the salvation of the world.

He claimed to be one with God, but never the equal of God. He said, "the Father is greater than I." He was the Son of God, and no one could know the Father except through the Son. No more than this.

If he had known all that was to happen to him during his sojourn on earth, would he always have done what he did? Would he, for example, have gone, just at the time that he did go, across Jordan to meet John the Baptist? Did he know beforehand that the occasion was to be one of stupendous destiny? Or was his intention in going merely casual?

In this connection we are not to forget the family relationship between the two men. If Mary, the mother of Jesus, was the cousin of Elisabeth, the mother of John, then Jesus of Nazareth and John the Baptist were second cousins. Had they ever met before? If John had ever gone up to Jerusalem, had he never seen Jesus at the Passover? Or had the possible seclusion of John in the religious houses of the Essenes on the east of the Dead Sea been sufficient to account for the fact that the cousins knew nothing of each other? Masses of commentary, pro and con, have been written in answer to these and similar questions.

With all respect I say that it has been, for the most part, energy utterly thrown away. Whether the cousins met, or did not meet, until they became men does not matter in the very least to Christianity. What does matter is whether they knew of the predictions of the angels before their births—that the one should be the Messiah and the other the forerunner of the Messiah.

We are told that the Jews were baptized of John confessing their sins. Did Jesus go up to make such confession? One of the apocryphal writings does indeed attribute to Jesus a confession of his sins at his baptism, but the canonical Gospels indicate no such thing. The fact that Jesus was going up to the baptism of John shows that the idea of his sinlessness had not yet suggested itself to him.

Why, then, did Jesus cross the Jordan to receive baptism from John. That is the question of importance to Christianity. To make even a conjectural answer it is necessary to trace the spiritual development of Jesus through the silences of the Gospels by the facts which they state, before and after.

VI.   The Supernaturalism of Jesus

I think it probable (contrary to the accepted opinion which has no apparent foundation) that Jesus went up from Galilee to the baptism of John, alone. He had not yet chosen his disciples. He probably went afoot from Capernaum to the borders of Samaria, and then took the road usually followed by Galileans to the junction of Peræa, and so down by the rugged Peræan caravan track to Bethabara, where he knew John to be. It is more than probable that through Galilee his fame had gone before him, and that at every mile his mission and his miracles were being talked about. It is not improbable that, as he passed by, the people came out to speak to him, to bring their sick to him, particularly their possessed, their demented (of whom, as we know, the country, thanks to its evil government, was then full) to be healed by him. It is reasonable to assume that, where he found faith, he did as he had done at Capernaum. It is probable that, as he went on, people looked after him in awe, and said among themselves, "Is this Elias?" or "Is this the Christ?"

The Messiah! Always the Messiah! Deep in his own heart, and deep in the hearts of the common people, was the old hope. His mission at Capernaum had probably had as great an effect upon Jesus himself as upon the people, perhaps a greater effect. He remembered what had been called his miracles. His casting out of devils. His raising of the paralytic.

It is possible that the power to do this had come upon him with surprise. He believed God had given him this power. Not of himself, but by God's power he had done these wonders. He began to see the world, and the physical laws of the world, by a new light. God was the power that presided over the laws of nature. He had divided the sea from the land, the night from the day, the summer from the winter. The wind blew and the storm raged because God had willed it so. But the mighty laws of nature which seemed so inexorable were subject to God's will. God who had the power to create physical law had the power to change, control and arrest it.

Thus there came to Jesus, out of his thrilling experiences at Capernaum, that knowledge which the sceptical critics have denied him, knowledge of the theory which, a century earlier, had established the unchangeable system of nature. And with the knowledge of that theory came his reply to it, that God was over all.

Jesus was now more than ever a supernaturalist. How far his supernaturalism went we shall partly see later. It is certain that he believed in the omnipotence of the Spirit of God over the life of man—the Spirit was God. God could do, or undo, everything. And he whom God ordained to act in His name could do anything.

This brought Jesus back to the thought of the Messiah. Contrary to much prophecy, the people of the time of Jesus believed that when the Messiah came he would work miracles, give signs and wonders.

Jesus appears to have held the same opinion. When the Messiah came he would come as a great physician, to heal the wounds of the people inflicted by the evil powers they lived under. The world was more full of suffering than ever before since the beginning of man. The Messiah would be the great healer, physical as well as spiritual.

The Messiah! Always the Messiah!

VII. The Journey to Bethabara

It would be a three or four days walk from Capernaum to Bethabara. On that long and lonely journey the memory of Jesus would go back to other things that had happened to him at Capernaum. Perhaps he had expected opposition, contempt, derision. But what a response! The poor, the weak, the sick, the down-trodden, the broken-hearted—how they had looked up at him with yearning eyes when he had spoken of the coming of the kingdom of Heaven, and of the Divine King whom God would send to rule over it!

When will he come? Where? The infinite pity of it! How it had torn at his heart!

As he went on his way he saw many things. The soldiers of the army of Herod Antipas had passed over this road only a little while before him, on their way to meet the oncoming army of his father-in-law, Aretas, the Arabian king, who was invading his territory to avenge the wrong done by Antipas to his daughter. They were going up to the great fortress at Machærus on the east of the Dead Sea, the southern border of Peræa, the place at which the dominions of Antipas and Aretas touched.

Jesus saw that the army of Antipas had left their trail behind them. Every town, every village they had passed through had been stripped of its food to feed the soldiers. It was as if the locust had passed over the land, leaving a long trail of desolation behind. The people were hungry and helpless. Their early spring harvest had been taken away, even their reserves of seed carried off; their young cattle slaughtered; no hope for next year's sowing.

The suffering and despair of the people. Their cry to Jesus. When would the Messiah come? Was it certain that he would be an angel, coming in the clouds? What if he were on the earth now, a man to be chosen and ordained by God! Man had waited age after age for God to send His Messiah, and in the midst of suffering and oppression had never ceased to cry, "How long, O Lord, how long?" Could mankind wait any longer?

Who shall say that in the spiritual exaltation of the long journey along the desert road through Peræa and Bethabara such thoughts did not come to Jesus? Who shall say that half-consciously the idea did not come to him that perhaps he himself would be the chosen of God?

Who will say that he did not think of the baptism he was going up to as a consecration to his work, a kind of anointing, such as Samuel had given, in the name of God, to David? There would be glory in the thought. To be the sovereign of souls, greater than any temporal sovereign. A king, not of one nation, one race, but of an invisible kingdom which had no limits but the limits of humanity.

But there would be terror in the thought also. To be the chosen of God, to preside over the invisible kingdom of the soul, was to be the ordained to a sovereignty a hundredfold more perilous than that of any king who sat on a throne. Such a one would carry strife into the very heart of the family. He would set father against son, and mother against daughter. He would have to put away the world and call upon all men to put it away. And, then, becoming the master of the world, he would be the servant of all mankind. The great scapegoat, the great sin-bearer, the great sufferer, the great martyr.

If Jesus saw things so he could not have been over-eager to claim the place of the Messiah. On the contrary, he would dread the thought of it. Yet if God chose him for that task he must go on with it. "Not my will, but Thine, be done."

On the third or perhaps fourth morning after setting out on his journey from Capernaum, Jesus would come within sight of Bethabara. To one who knows the country the scene is not difficult to imagine. The white desert city with the early sunlight over it. The blue thread of the Jordan running through a green jungle. The grey glassy waters of the Dead Sea, lying like a blind eye, ten miles farther south, with a bare stretch of barren wilderness between.

Perhaps the little city is almost empty as Jesus passes through it; nearly all the inhabitants gone down to the shingly shores of the river, where a large company has gathered in the neighbourhood of the pools of Salim. A throng of all kinds of people, from Judæa and the country round about; rich, poor, tax-gatherers, notorious sinners, and some of the soldiers of the army of Herod

Antipas, who have come stealing back from the fortress of Machærus to listen to the prophet. They are kneeling on the ground about him. I see the Baptist in the midst of them. A powerful man in camel's skin and leather girdle, with sandals and bare head.

In a voice that thunders over their heads he is denouncing the iniquities of the world and foretelling the judgment of the wicked. He is sparing none. "O generation of vipers!" he cries.

If any have come to his baptism in mere terror of the wrath to come, let them first bring forth fruits meet for repentance; let them know that the axe is now laid to the root of the tree, and every tree that has not brought forth good fruit will be hewn down and cast into the fire. They may be Israelites, and they may be saying to themselves they have Abraham as their father, but God is able out of the very stones under their feet to raise up children to Abraham and so fulfil His promise to their father.

He denounces the rich, the rulers, the priests, and, above all the people in high places, who have openly broken the laws of Moses and are living in incest and adultery. The wrath of God will fall on them. It is coming. It will be soon. "Repent, for the kingdom of Heaven is at hand."

He knows all of them, and he lashes the sinners to the bone. The rich come forward and question him. "What shall we do then?" "He that hath two coats let him impart to him that hath none, and he that hath meat, let him do likewise."

The tax-gatherers come next. "What shall we do?" "Exact no more than that which is appointed you." Then follow the soldiers —the men who had been bought by the wages of Herod Antipas, perhaps demanded higher wages that they might help him to break the law of Moses. "And what shall we do?" "Do violence to no man, neither accuse any falsely; and be content with your wages."

He knows all their doings. "Repent and be baptized for remission of your sins," he cries, or "beware of the wrath to come," for one is coming who "will thoroughly purge his floor, and will gather his wheat into the garner; but he will burn up the chaff with unquenchable fire."

It is a scene of great emotion, half fear, half ecstasy—a wild, almost intoxicating scene.

At intervals the sinners fling themselves on their faces before the Baptist and confess their sins. Then he lifts them up and leads them down into the river and baptizes them.

The others look on in breathless silence until the Baptist and his regenerated penitents come up out of the water, and then, almost beside themselves, they break, perhaps, into loud hymns, hosannas, psalms of David, the joyful ones about God's mercy and forgiveness.

Is this an imagined scene? The essential part of it is all in the Gospels.

VIII.   Jesus and John

At length, when the people about him had all been baptized, John saw Jesus, a majestic white figure on the dark road coming towards them, and went forward to meet him.

What happened next is told differently by the four evangelists. Matthew's story is as follows:

> Then cometh Jesus from Galilee to Jordan unto John, to be baptized of him. But John forbad him, saying, I have need to be baptized of thee, and comest thou to me? And Jesus answering said unto him, Suffer it to be so now: for thus it becometh us to fulfil all righteousness. Then he suffered him. And Jesus, when he was baptized, went up straightway out of the water: and, lo, the heavens were opened unto him, and he saw the Spirit of God descending like a dove, and lighting upon him. And lo, a voice from Heaven saying, This is my beloved Son, in whom I am well pleased.

This, according to modern students, was written about thirty-five years after the event it records. According to the early Fathers of the Church (Justin, Clement, Augustine) the words of God in the first version of the Gospel of St. Matthew, the so-called Gospel of the Hebrews, were, "Thou art my Son. This day have I begotten thee."

Thirty years later than the Gospel of St. Matthew, the Gospel of St. John, written when the disciple was about ninety years of age, gives the following version of what occurred sixty to seventy years earlier, that is to say, when he was between twenty and twenty-five years of age.

> These things were done in Bethabara beyond Jordan, where John was baptizing. The next day John seeth Jesus coming unto him, and saith, Behold the Lamb of God, which taketh away the sin of the world. This is he of whom I said, After me cometh a man which is preferred before me; for he was before me. And I knew him not; but that he should be made manifest to Israel, therefore am I come baptizing with water. And John bare record saying, "I saw the Spirit descending from Heaven like a dove, and it abode upon him.

And I knew him not; but he that sent me to baptize with water, the same said unto me; Upon whom thou shalt see the Spirit descending, and remaining on him, the same is he which baptizeth with the Holy Ghost. And I saw, and bare record that this is the Son of God."

Here are two widely different stories. Did the incidents recorded actually take place? Did the heavens open and something resembling a bird of the dove species descend from them and alight upon Jesus? Did the voice of God really speak? Was it heard by Jesus only? Or did John also hear it? And was it heard by the other persons present? On the answer to these questions much depends. There is nothing more important to Christianity than to find out whether Jesus of Nazareth was ever proclaimed by God to be the Messiah. And if so, when and where and how?

The evidence of the Gospels as to what took place at the baptism of Jesus is perplexing. Did the voice of God say, "Thou art my beloved Son; this day have I begotten thee"? These are almost literally the words which God is said to have addressed to the psalmist in *Psalm* II, 7. "Thou art my son; this day have I begotten thee."

Alternatively, the words suggest a spiritual not a physical relation—meaning that Jesus has been begotten spiritually by God, after he has been begotten physically by his human father.

By this interpretation it would seem that the story of the Virgin Birth is unhistorical, since it involves a contradiction to say that Jesus was the Messiah from his mother's womb and that he only became so at his baptism thirty-three or thirty-four years later.

If the Baptist said "I knew him not," did he mean that as a man Jesus was a total stranger to him? If so, it is difficult to believe (except on the assumption of the Baptist's lifelong monastic seclusion) that they were cousins, and that in a small country like Palestine, a distance of sixty-five miles (which the mother of Jesus is said to have travelled when she was an unmarried girl of perhaps sixteen) had been sufficient to keep them apart.

Did the Baptist mean that, while knowing Jesus as a man, he did not know him as the Messiah? If so, the supernatural revelations attending his own birth and that of Jesus had not been made known to him by his parents, and the Virgin Birth (as far as it concerns the visit of Mary, the mother of Jesus, to his own mother, Elisabeth) had probably not been historical.

If the Baptist said, in saluting Jesus, "I have need to be baptized of thee, and comest thou to me?" did he mean that it had been suddenly revealed to him by the Holy Ghost (as to Simeon at the Temple) that Jesus was the Messiah? If so, why did he consent to baptize Jesus, who, being the Lamb of God who was to take away the sins of the world, had no need of the baptism of repentance for the remission of sins?

The Messiahship presupposed sinlessness; baptism presupposed sinfulness.

Did the Baptist actually receive assurance of God's own voice that Jesus was the Messiah? If so, why did he go on with his mission, what he had been foretelling being fulfilled; the One he had promised having arisen; the kingdom of Heaven being not only at hand but having come?

And how did it come to pass that he had ever afterwards any uncertainty about the Messiahship of Jesus (such as we shall hear of later) since he *knew?*

If the Baptist heard the voice of God proclaiming the Messiahship of Jesus, did not the other persons present at the baptism also hear it? If so, how did it occur that they did not make the fact generally known, in Jerusalem and throughout Judæa, and not leave it in doubt (even among some of the disciples of both masters) down to the last days of the life of Jesus, to his great peril and suffering?

IX. *Opinions Concerning the Baptism*

But the evidence of the Gospels as to what took place at the baptism of Jesus is not more perplexing than the evidence of historical interpretation. Clearly the evangelists, writing about thirty-five years after Jesus, believed the incidents to be of actual physical occurrence—that the heavens did actually open, that a dove did actually descend and remain on Jesus, and that the voice of God did actually proclaim him to be His beloved Son.

Equally clearly, the Apostolic Fathers were so far from doubting the physical reality of the incidents that they added to them— the old and lost Gospel of Justin giving also a heavenly light and a flame bursting out of the Jordan.

No less clearly the early Fathers of the Church, without questioning the physical reality of the incidents, gave them a dogmatic intention, that of being the first witness to the Trinity—all three elements of the Godhead being there, God the Father in Heaven, God the Son on earth, and God the Holy Ghost in the dove which descended from the sky. Still later, some of the Fathers, unable to carry any further the supernaturalistic interpretation, gave a mystic view of the incidents—Origen (who had dealt faithfully, sanely and humanly with the impossibilities and absurdities of the first chapter of *Genesis,* taken as literal accounts of actual happenings) giving it as his opinion that only the simplest and most ignorant of minds would believe that a solid mass like the heavens did actually break open and that a bird of the dove species did actually descend out of the riven sky.

Before the end of the second century a sceptical view of the incidents had been put forward by Celsus and others, who declared the whole story to be delusion. Nothing had happened at the baptism of Jesus except the baptism itself, the supernatural incidents being clumsy and unbelievable imposture. But in the third century came the making of the Canon, and after that the literal interpretation of the incidents of the baptism was insisted upon.

Many centuries passed and then came attempts at a naturalistic interpretation. This was that some physical manifestation had really happened; that at the moment when Jesus went down into the waters of Jordan with the Baptist a thunderstorm broke; that as he was coming up out of the water there was a flash of lightning out of the dark clouds which preceded thunder, and it seemed to the onlookers to fall on the head of Jesus. Hence the disciples of the Baptist, who were looking on, mistook the appearance of light for a dove, and a roll of thunder, which immediately followed, as a voice from Heaven. And that to these sounds somebody, probably John himself, in his excited state at that moment, gave the words reported, "Thou art my Beloved Son. This day have I begotten thee."

Such, according to the naturalistic biographers of Jesus, was the natural origin of the story of what happened at his baptism.

It is difficult to think of anything more puerile. It requires that we should believe that John and his disciples at the moment of the baptism were looking for a divine revelation of the Messianic character of Jesus (they were plainly looking for no such thing, and their subsequent conduct shows that if they received any such revelation of the Messianic character of Jesus they never afterwards paid any attention to it); that, in a country in which thunderstorms are of common occurrence (in some seasons of almost daily occurrence), they were so carried away by religious frenzy that they could not distinguish between a dove and a flash of lightning, or a clap of thunder and the voice of God; and that Jesus of Nazareth himself was so lost to all self-control that not then, merely, at that moment of excitement, but to the end of his life (assuming the story of the baptism to be current during his lifetime), he continued to countenance this childish interpretation.

Surely it is time we had done with all this dishonouring foolishness. Permit me, in all humility and reverence, to offer an explanation that shall be in harmony with the spirit of our own age.

I think that the sole authority for the story of what happened at the baptism of Jesus is not John or his disciples, but Jesus himself. That he told the story to his disciples in the language of metaphor, which he nearly always afterwards employed in speaking to his own immediate followers. That this was the usual language of the prophet, the poet, the seer, in which everything becomes figurative, concrete, and is personified. I do not think that when Jesus came to the Baptist he had any distinct consciousness that he was the Messiah. It was a Jewish notion of great antiquity that the Messiah would be unknown even to himself until Elias, his forerunner, announced him. I do not think that when he went up to the Baptist he had any idea that he was sinless.

I do not think that when the Baptist saluted him with the words, "I have need to be baptized of thee and comest thou to me?" he was thinking of Jesus as the Messiah, but only as the young Galilean prophet of whom report reached him daily, perhaps by that mysterious wave of rumour which passes over the desert with the swiftness of the wind, or perhaps by the caravans which came down from Galilee—bringing stories of the purity of his life, the nobility of his thought, the sublimity of his ideals, and perhaps, after all, of the miracles he had wrought in casting devils out of persons possessed by them, in changing bad men into good men, in turning scoffers and blasphemers into faithful and devoted followers.

I do not think that the Baptist was witness to any of the supernatural incidents recorded by John, or he could not possibly have acted as he acted, either then or afterwards. If the Baptist's disciples were witness to them, they, also, must have acted differently. I think Jesus, when he reached the Baptist, after the moving scenes he had passed through, after his sudden and unexpected consciousness of his power over evil spirits (the casting out of devils), after the wonder and worship of the people of Capernaum, of Galilee and of Peræa, was in a state of deep religious emotion, amounting almost to ecstasy, which trembled upon the verge of a consciousness which he hesitated to think of; that in the existing troubled state of the world he might, perhaps, be called upon to take up the heavy burden of the messenger of God on earth.

It is probable that he approached the Baptist in this condition of spiritual exaltation, and that the salutation of the Baptist (whom he recognized as a man of God, a greater than Elias) startled him and perhaps moved him deeply. The scenes he witnessed on the shores of the Jordan must have increased this emotion—the preaching of the Baptist, the confessions of the penitents, the psalms and hosannas of the converts.

I think this was the mood in which he went down into the Jordan, and that everything which happened after he met John happened to Jesus only. If there was a voice, Jesus alone heard it. If there was a light, it was seen only in the soul of Jesus. The effect produced was on the mind and soul of Jesus only.

It is not incredible that when Jesus came up out of the water, perhaps with the psalms of David ringing in his ears, he believed he heard the voice of God speaking to him; that (like Stephen at his martyrdom) he believed he saw the heavens open to him. What happened was not a vision or dream (Jesus alone of the prophets did not attach importance to dreams), but a revelation from the unseen. Great souls in all the ages at great crises in their lives have received such revelations, and it is presumptuous of lesser creatures to question their reality—their spiritual reality.

I think Jesus believed he heard the voice of God calling him to be the Messiah. And who, looking at what happened afterwards during the remainder of his life, and what has happened in the world since, will say that he was not right?

It was a tremendous, overwhelming moment, that moment on the banks of the Jordan, when, coming up out of the waters with the hand of the man of the desert in his hand, Jesus realized that he was chosen of God to be His Messiah, His servant, His beloved Son! Perhaps the greatest spiritual crisis in the history of man. Compared with it the material crises of the rise and fall of empires have been but as noise and vapour, dust and ashes.

CHAPTER VII

The Temptation

I. The Forty Days

WHAT HAPPENED to Jesus immediately after the baptism is a question attended by difficulty as to both time and place.

The three synoptic Gospels say that he was led by the Spirit into the wilderness to be tempted of the Devil, and that he remained there for forty days. The fourth Gospel says nothing of the Temptation, and so accounts for the whereabouts and doings of Jesus during many ensuing days as to make the six weeks' sojourn in the wilderness at this, or any other period, an impossibility.

According to the synoptics it would appear probable, from the next movements of Jesus, that his forty days' temptation were passed in the wilderness of Peræa. What are we to understand about his going to Nazareth?

According to St. John's Gospel the six weeks following the baptism were passed (except for a few days in Galilee) in Jerusalem, and in the neighbourhood of the places where the Baptist was baptizing—Bethabara, Salim and the Jordan generally.

Not only is the Temptation attended by difficulties as to time and place, it is beset by problems concerning its reality and its significance in the life of Jesus. The Gospel of Mark attaches little importance to it. Beyond recording the fact of the Temptation in three or four lines, and saying that the wilderness in which it took place was infested by wild beasts, the Gospel of Mark says nothing about it. On the other hand the Gospels of Matthew and Luke give full and detailed accounts of it, and clearly assign to it an important place in the life of Jesus.

According to *Matthew* and *Luke* the story of the Temptation is as follows:

Immediately after the baptism, Jesus, being full of the Holy Ghost, returned from the Jordan and was led by the Spirit into the wilderness, to be tempted of the Devil. There he fasted forty days and forty nights; and after that he became hungry. Then the Tempter appeared to him, apparently in the most barren part of the wilderness, and said (taunting him with his newly declared divinity), "If thou be the Son of God, command that these stones be made bread."

To this Jesus answered, "Man shall not live by bread alone, but by every word that proceedeth out of the mouth of God."

The Devil took him from the desert to Jerusalem, and setting him on the pinnacle of the Temple, said (again taunting him), "If thou be the Son of God, cast thyself down; for it is written, He shall give His angels charge concerning thee; and in their hands they shall bear thee up, lest at any time thou dash thy foot against a stone."

To this Jesus answered, "It is written again, Thou shalt not tempt the Lord thy God."

After that the Devil took Jesus up into an exceedingly high mountain, and showed him all the kingdoms of the world and the glory of them, and said, "All these things will I give thee, if thou wilt fall down and worship me."

Jesus answered, "Get thee hence Satan, for it is written, Thou shalt worship the Lord thy God, and him only shalt thou serve."

Then the Devil left Jesus and angels came and ministered to him, and afterwards he returned in the power of the Spirit into Galilee.

Such is the literal story of the Temptation as recorded in the Gospels. How is it to be understood? As the record of an actual occurrence? As an allegory? As a vision, carrying perhaps a spiritual message? Let us see.

II. *Various Interpretations*

When it was first circulated (who knows how long afterwards?) in the two Gospels of Matthew and Luke, it was probably accepted by the early Christians as the record of an actual occurrence. That the divine Spirit should permit Jesus to be tempted of the Devil (revolting as it is to the modern mind) would come as no unfamiliar idea to the Jews at that period. They were familiar with the idea that God put His favourites to the test. He had put Abraham to the test—to sacrifice his son. He had given up Job to Satan to the test of plagues and misfortunes —to curse God and die. The Devil had been permitted to tempt the Israelites in the wilderness during the absence of Moses.

That God should lead Jesus into the wilderness for the Temptation (however incongruous to us) would be no unfamiliar thought to the people of that time. To all the peoples of the eastern world the wilderness was associated with the idea of the lurking-place of the infernal powers.

That God should assign to Jesus the self-discipline of fasting would also be no unfamiliar idea. Moses had fasted on Mount Sinai. It was an old idea of the Jews that the Spirit tested God's favourites by the holy discipline of fasting. It was by such means that the men of God purified themselves—proved themselves.

The fast was to weaken Jesus and thus to tempt him to forsake his mission as Messiah, or to show that no suffering would henceforth ever make him forsake it. That the fast should last forty days was also a familiar idea. Moses had fasted forty days. Forty was a number held sacred in Jewish antiquity.

Finally, that God should commit Jesus to the Temptation of Satan was no unfamiliar idea. Satan was an evil deity borrowed, perhaps, from the Persian religion, but accepted by Judaism. Satan had long been the Jewish incarnation of evil. He was the enemy of mankind. He was, to the Jewish people, the special enemy of the Messiah.

Jesus, as the Messiah, the Son of God, was about to destroy the works of Satan—the kingdom of Satan. Therefore Jesus was above all others the being to assail. Satan must destroy Jesus, the Messiah, or be himself destroyed.

But after the early Christians, among whom the Gospels of Matthew and Luke were first circulated, came the early sceptics of the latter half of the second century (the time of Marcus Aurelius) declaring the story of the Temptation to be unworthy of the consideration of intellectual people.

What was the *use* of the Temptation? they asked. If Jesus was the Messiah, the begotten Son of God, it was not necessary for God to put him to a trial. God must have known, before He chose Jesus, that he was strong enough to go through the trials of the Messiahship. To say that the Devil should show Jesus all the kingdoms of the world from the summit of any mountain, how-

ever high, was to talk the language of foolishness. That the Devil
took Jesus into Jerusalem and placed him (to the astonishment of
the Jews) among the pinnacles of Solomon's Porch, in near proximity to the roof of the Holy of Holies, which no layman was
permitted to approach, was childish nonsense.

To all this the early Fathers of the Church (always the most
literal of the commentators) made many reasonable replies. Origen
answered that it was unnecessary and impossible to make a
strictly literal interpretation of the story of the Temptation, and
showed very plainly how absurd was the attempt to accept it as a
record of actual facts. To Origen the Temptation was an allegory.
To Theodore of Mopsuestia it was a record of events which Jesus
did actually experience (Jesus did really go from the desert to
the Temple and to the high mountains, as Ezekiel did from the
River Chebar to Jerusalem), but only in the Spirit. Therefore,
the Temptation was not a thing that happened to Jesus corporeally
and externally, but merely in a vision, a dream.

But after all this came the rationalistic critics, with their many
shafts of ridicule. The incongruous idea of Jesus being carried
about from place to place through the air to three distinct places
(which could not have been less distant from each other than
forty miles in one case and a hundred miles in another), like Faust
by Mephistopheles on a broomstick to the Brocken, was too ridiculous even to laugh at.

The incongruous idea that angels came to minister to Jesus after
the Devil had departed from him, bringing, presumably, material
food, although themselves ethereal beings, was ridiculous, as
ridiculous as that angels brought material food to Elijah during the
great famine.

Finally, and most illogical of all, that Satan, knowing Jesus
to be the Messiah, to be God, should dare to ask him, in return
for any worldly possessions whatever, to fall down and worship
him, was to confuse the fundamental ideas of God and the Devil
and to outrage all common sense.

The orthodox made many shifts to meet such ridicule. When
Julian asked, "How could the Devil hope to deceive Jesus, knowing he was God?" Theodore replied that the divinity of Jesus was
not yet known to the Devil, although such knowledge on the part
of the Devil is of the essence of the Temptation. When asked how
Satan could show Jesus all the kingdoms of the world from any

mountain in Palestine, the orthodox answered that probably he showed them on a map!

But the shifts of the old supernaturalists to interpret the Temptation did not descend to such depths of unimaginative puerility as those of the naturalists of a time not very remote from our own.

When required to account for the impossibility of the story of the Temptation according to natural laws, the orthodox of a later age offered the solution that, deeply exhausted by all he had gone through before and during the baptism, Jesus, on reaching the wilderness, had dropped down and fallen asleep among the stones and remained sleeping for several days, during which he dreamt the incidents of the Temptation, and upon awakening a few days later, with the vividness of the dream still upon him, he had firmly believed that they had actually taken place.

To this, the obvious answer is that Jesus was not subject to dreams; that he never attaches importance to dreams, and that nowhere is he known to report one. But perhaps the crowning puerility of the naturalists came when, feeling compelled to admit that the Temptation could not be accounted for as purely a dream, they set themselves to account for it as a real event of some kind by saying that after a period of fasting, and therefore exhaustion of body and mind, Jesus had been visited in the wilderness by an artful Pharisee, who, personating the Devil, put him to the test (nobody knows how) of the three temptations in the interests of the Jewish priesthood, either to win Jesus over to their side, or perhaps to give countenance to a rising against the Romans.

Such are some of the many interpretations of the reputed Temptation which have masqueraded through theological, sceptical and rationalistic criticism during so many centuries. They reduce the Temptation to a thing that is not only not useful to man, but the reverse of useful. Thus, they degrade Jesus by showing him, at the bidding of the Devil, going here and there on foolish and impossible errands; they present a picture of incidents in his life which could never occur in the life of any man. Hence the Temptation does not bring Jesus nearer to humanity, but removes him farther away. It has no recorded effect on his later life on earth, and therefore is a useless excrescence.

In a word, the Temptation, as a record of events of real occurrence in the life of Jesus, becomes a superfluous folly. If we had to take the story literally, in our day, we should be compelled to think of it as a myth.

Meantime, while the world has been groping after a literal interpretation which, if ever found would never be of any value to any human creature—the spiritual interpretation which would have had immense value to all mankind in all ages has been missed. What is this spiritual interpretation? What actually happened to Jesus during the forty days and forty nights he spent in the wilderness?

Obviously, Jesus himself was the only authority as to what took place. Did he report it to his followers, at some later moment in the concrete, imaginative and figurative language which he frequently employed in speaking to his own people about the experiences of his soul? And did they repeat it to the scribes who wrote the Gospels under their inspiration as the actual experiences of his body? What, translated into language of our own time, does the Temptation of Jesus in the wilderness mean? A very simple, very natural, very tragic and exalted thing. Perhaps there is nothing which it is more important to the modern world to know. What is it?

III. An Experience of the Soul

As in the case of the baptism, so now in the case of the Temptation I take the view that what happened to Jesus took place, solely and only in the innermost recesses of his soul. The three incidents of the Temptation had no actual occurrence, but were strictly confined to the soul of Jesus—his excited, suffering soul.

When he left the place of the baptism in an excited state of body and soul, I think he escaped as speedily as possible from the people who were surrounding, following and saluting him. It had always been his habit to go into solitary places to meditate and pray, and now, under the spell of the most overwhelming emotion that had ever yet come to him, he hastened away to a lonely place, to be alone, to think out what had happened and to take account of himself.

I think it almost certain (from what comes later) that he went back into the wilderness of Peræa, not forward into the wilderness of Judæa, which, at Bethabara, he had hardly yet touched.

I think he probably went up to the wilderness east of Mount

Gilead—a god-forsaken waste of bare, black, volcanic stones unbroken by bush or trees or grass, the resort in those days, as it still is, of wild beasts.

There I think he fasted for many days, not with any thought of self-discipline, but because his mind was too much occupied with the concerns of his soul to give any thought to the needs of his body. In that desolate place he heard constantly in his heart the voice he is believed to have heard from the sky on the banks of the Jordan—"Thou art my beloved Son. This day have I begotten thee."

What was to be his Messianic plan, and how was he to carry it into effect? He was still a man. He had not ceased to be the Son of Man in becoming the Son of God. The human and the divine in him were struggling for mastery, and that is why what happened to him in the wilderness is called his Temptation. They continued to struggle, as we shall see, to the last hours, almost to the last moment, of his life, and that is what is meant when it is said, at the close of the Temptation, that the Devil "departed from him for a season."

He comes close to all other men in that; but with this difference, that while we, out of our weakness, are constantly falling under the temptations of our lower nature, the tempting thoughts which assailed him from his humanity never for more than a short period quelled the force and purity of his unconquerable soul. Perhaps that is one principal reason why of all human beings that have ever lived on this earth he is the most beloved.

The struggle between the man and the God in Jesus was never stronger, perhaps, than in those days, when he was alone in the wilderness of Peræa. A great temptation came to him. If he were the Son of God, why should he not fulfil all that had been foretold of the Messiah by the prophets—recover the throne of David, re-establish the fallen kingdom of Israel, and rule both his own people and the Gentile world from Jerusalem according to the law of Moses?

That was what his people were waiting for, it was all they were waiting for. He had read it in the Scriptures; he had heard it at Capernaum, on the journey through to Peræa—everywhere. In their sufferings under their hard taskmasters, this was the Messiah whom the Israelite people, from the Babylonian captivity downward, had prayed for. To see such a Messiah arise had been the grandiose dream which for centuries had haunted the Jewish soul.

If he were the Son of God, as the voice from Heaven had told him, why should he not bring it to pass? He had the power now; if he were the Son of God, should he not use it?

He thought, perhaps, of the poverty of the people as he had so long witnessed it; if he were the Son of God, should he not command the very stones to be made bread for them?

He thought, perhaps, of the corruption of the Temple as he had seen it; if he were the Son of God, should he not cast himself down from it, or destroy or cleanse it?

He thought, perhaps of the incestuous adulteries of the Jewish rulers against whom (although the common people had condemned them) the high priests had made no protest, although they might have charged the persons committing such open and shameless violations of the law of Moses before the Sanhedrin, and thereby cast them out of the number of those who had Abraham for their father; if he were the Son of God, should he not destroy such rulers and wipe out such judges?

He thought, perhaps, of the tyrannies and cruelties of the Roman occupation, its frequent, almost continual, wars and murders, and the brutal attacks within the Temple itself, in which the blood of the Galileans had been mingled with their sacrifices; if he were the Son of God, should he not banish this Pilate, this brutal and cowardly assassin, and drive him for ever out of the company of living men?

And then, he thought, perhaps, of the weak and bereaved, the downtrodden and disinherited, the people in the little houses of the little towns on the shores of the Lake of Galilee, who had been robbed (as he had seen them) of their sons, who had gone off to Peræa as soldiers to protect the iniquities of the violators of the sacred law, and of their daughters, who had been carried off to Tiberias as harlots, to satisfy their lusts; if he were the Son of God, should he not protect them and save them?

Was it not all written, as the Baptist had said, in the Books of the Prophets, that when the Messiah came, consecrated and anointed by God, he would purge his floor, gather the wheat into his garner and burn the chaff in fire unquenchable?

Is it not possible that, in those first half-delirious days after his baptism, while he walked through the desolate wilderness of

Peræa, hungry, athirst, in his excited state of body and soul, remembering at once the wickedness and sufferings he had witnessed and the predictions of the prophets he had been taught to hold sacred, and, above all, the voice he had heard from the sky, when coming up out of the waters of the Jordan ("Thou art my beloved Son. This day have I begotten thee"), Jesus saw himself, like the Messiah who, according to Daniel, was to come down from the clouds of Heaven, descending from the heights of Mount Gilead, going through Peræa, Galilee, Samaria and Judæa, gathering together the outcast people of Israel and leading them up to Jerusalem to claim the throne of their father, David?

Is it not also possible that he saw the gates of Jerusalem falling (as the walls of Jericho fell) before the hosts of God, the Roman legions taking flight before the legions of angels that God sent with him?

Why not? The mighty Roman army had indeed crushed Judas the Galilean, and driven his surviving followers, the Zealots, into the secrecy of the closed synagogues, but he was the Messiah, the chosen of God, and God would send legions of angels with him if he asked for them, before whom the legions of Rome would fly as chaff before the wind.

More, is it not possible that in his vision of the future, standing as it were on an exceedingly high mountain and seeing all the kingdoms of the world stretched out before him, Jesus, in those hours of exaltation, saw himself establishing the kingdom of Heaven on earth, as the Messiah-king, ruling the whole world in the name of God?

IV. What It Meant to Jesus

Then came a great moment.

Jesus began to see that all this was, after all, nothing but a temptation out of his human nature. It was not God's way to save His people by setting up temporal kings and kingdoms. The kingdom of Heaven was not to be established on earth by creating another stronger temporal king and kingdom. That was the Devil's way, and if he attempted to follow it he would not be the instrument of God but the promoter of the plans of the Devil.

Jesus believed in the Devil, as millions in all ages have believed in him, as millions believe in him still, although they call him by other names. The Devil was the master of the world. The world was the kingdom of the Devil, with all its principalities and powers.

No man ever believed this as Jesus believed it, or proclaimed it as Jesus proclaimed it. If a man were rich and powerful, if he held the welfare and even the lives of his fellow-men in the palms of his hands, he was the servant of the Devil and had bent the knee to him. And now, on the very threshold of his Messianic mission, the Devil was tempting him with power and dominion, tempting him in the name of God, but still tempting him, telling him that if it were true that he was the Son of God he could do anything —he could command the very stones under his feet to be made bread, and become the master of the world.

But Jesus saw that he could only do this by becoming the slave of Satan, by bending the knee to him. Jesus turned his back on his temptations, "Thou shalt not tempt the Lord thy God . . . Get thee behind me, Satan."

What then?

Had the prophets been wrong? Was the age-long hope of a kingdom of Heaven to be established on earth only a vain dream, a delusion? Was it not time that the promise given to David should be fulfilled, that a greater than David should arise and sit on David's throne, and gather the world about his footstool?

It was a bitter struggle. It seemed as if the hope of the ages had fallen to dust and ashes. Then came the divine whisper. We are told that the Devil, failing to overcome the unconquerable will of Jesus, left him for a season (he came again to him, as we shall see), and that angels came and ministered to him.

I think what is meant by this is that the angels brought him a new thought, a blessed thought, a greater and loftier thought than had ever come to any of the prophets. What if temporal power and possessions were of no account to man's salvation? What if all real power and all real salvation lay within the soul of man? What if nothing mattered to man except the salvation of his soul? Hitherto he had been thinking (humanity had always been thinking) of the kingdom of Heaven that was to come on earth as a temporal and visible kingdom—what if it were a spiritual and invisible one? What if the only kingdom to come on earth was the invisible one which every man might carry in his heart, the kingdom within, the kingdom of love and of the peace that love brings with it? And what if this invisible kingdom was not for the sons of David only, but for the sons of God throughout the world?

And then, the Messiah?

What if he were not to be a temporal king of a temporal kingdom, but a spiritual king of a spiritual kingdom? Not a king of the Jews only, but a king of all the peoples of the world—all the children of the universal Father?

There was glory in the thought.

To be the sovereign of souls, not of one nation only but of all nations, not of one race, but of all races; the king of a kingdom which had no limits except the limits of humanity, which knew no difference between Jew and Gentile, between bond and free—the kingdom of the children of God throughout the world!

But there was terror in the thought also.

To be the chosen of God, to preside over the invisible and universal kingdom of souls was to be ordained to a sovereignty which was a thousandfold more perilous than that of any earthly king whatever.

Such a sovereign must needs carry not peace, but a sword. He must take strife into the very bosom of every family. He must set father against son, and mother against daughter. He must call on all men to put away the world, and the things of the world.

Renunciation! Self-sacrifice! Service! Suffering! These must be his watchwords.

And he himself? He must prepare to be, not a king in the sense in which David was a king, but the servant of all men, despised and rejected, the great sufferer, the great martyr.

I see Jesus confronting the future with this thought at once divine and terrible. I see him telling himself what his Messianic plan was to be—to go back to the little towns of Galilee, to Judæa, to Jerusalem, to preach the Gospel to the poor, to heal the brokenhearted, to preach deliverance to the captives, and the recovery of sight to the blind, to tell men that if they are to be saved from their sins, they must separate themselves from the world, they must live in the spirit, that the kingdom of Heaven was within them.

And then—what then?

God would tell him what then. His fate was in God's hands, for God was over all. Whatever it might be he would go through with it.

"Not my will, but thine, O Lord!"

Meantime, he knew what he had to be and to do. He, the ordained of God, had to be the lowliest among the sons of men. He had to be a wanderer, without a place to lay his head. He had triumphed over his temptation. His soul was at peace.

Having established this spiritual and moral view of his mission as the Messiah, Jesus returned to the company of men. He was no longer a follower of Moses, yet he was the greatest of all the followers of Moses; he was no longer a Jew, yet he was the greatest Jew that had ever lived on the earth. He was the founder of the universal religion. He went up to the wilderness of Mount Gilead as Jesus of Nazareth.

He came down as the Christ!

V. John the Baptist and Herod Antipas

We have two leading accounts of the relation of John the Baptist and Herod Antipas, those of Josephus and the Gospels.

Josephus says that Herod Antipas was jealous of the influence of John the Baptist with the people, and therefore he first imprisoned him and afterwards executed him.

The objections to this are: (1) that John was a Judæan and would naturally fall into the jurisdiction of the Romans who then held direct control of Judæa—Pontius Pilate being governor or procurator at the time of the death of John—and the Romans would not be likely to tolerate the execution of one of their subjects without good cause being shown; (2) that jealousy of the popularity of a prophet would not of itself explain punishment by death, whatever ordinary interpretations were put upon his methods of securing popularity. Herod Antipas was merely tetrarch, and though he held (almost certainly) the power of life and death, he was not allowed by Rome to do what he liked with his subjects, as his ultimate downfall shows.

The Gospel story is that Herod Antipas had broken the law of Moses by marrying his brother's wife under conditions of great provocation (1) when his brother had a child by his wife, (2) when he (Herod) had a wife living.

According to the Gospels, John the Baptist denounced this union as incestuous, and called upon Herod to send the woman away. The woman thereupon contrived John's death by means of her daughter, Salome, who, having pleased Herod Antipas by dancing for him and for his friends at the festival of his birthday, and being promised any present she cared to request, asked, under the instigation of her mother, for the head of John the Baptist.*

Herod is said to have been sorry to yield to this demand, but in order not to be shamed before his other guests he consented, and so John was beheaded.

On the whole, the Gospel story is the more credible. Herod had probably arrested John as a turbulent person who had alienated the allegiance of his soldiers by denouncing their master as a breaker of the law of Moses and by his general counsel to the soldiers, which was certainly contrary to what Herod required of them.

This would be quite within his power and right to do, and he might have kept John in prison for life on that ground alone. But to execute John for no other reason was a judicial crime, in short, a murder. Herod's conduct after John's death (as indicated in the Gospels) seems to show that he knew he had murdered John, for he imagined that Jesus was John come back from the dead, perhaps to punish him, and he was very clearly anxious to see Jesus in order to make sure that he was not John.

There is not a word to say for Herod Antipas, whether in the light of the story according to Josephus, or the story according to the Gospels.

VI.   Herod Antipas and Jesus

I do not think, however, that the motive apparently ascribed to Herod Antipas in *Luke* IX, 7–9, for desiring to see Jesus is at all the true one. I think that "fox" had quite obviously another motive, and that Jesus knew it and acted accordingly.

My view is as follows:

When the Arabian wife of Herod Antipas reached the country of her father, he, Aretas, the Arabian king, declared his inten-

---

*John the Baptist-Salome incident anticipated in the Book of *Esther*.

The story of Herod's promise to Salome leads me to question the veracity of this incident, since the same was said to Esther by King Ahasuerus (*Esther* V, 3) : "Then said the king unto her: What wilt thou, Queen Esther? and what is thy request? it shall be even given thee to the half of the kingdom."

And later (VII, 2) : "And the king said again unto Esther on the second day at the banquet of wine: What is thy petition, Queen Esther? and it shall be granted thee; and what is thy request? and it shall be performed, even to the half of the kingdom."

tion of avenging his daughter by invading the territory of Herod Antipas. He set out from his capital, Petra, for that purpose, intending, probably to take Herod's fortress on the north-east of the Dead Sea, Herod Antipas's nearest stronghold.

Herod thereupon set out to meet and drive back Aretas, taking his new wife, Herodias, and her daughter with him. He had difficulty in enlisting a sufficient army in Galilee, because the Galileans knew that he was going out to defend a condemned cause—his breaking of the law of Moses by marrying his brother's wife. In order to procure a sufficient army he had to pay the larger wages which the worst elements among the Galileans demanded. He travelled by the Peræan road through Bethabara beyond Jordan where John the Baptist was then preaching and baptizing.

John had been denouncing the conduct of Herod Antipas in marrying Herodias. He counselled the soldiers against doing violence and demanding more than their wages, in short, against fighting for Herod, the profligate and law-breaker. Herodias heard of this, and saw that if John the Baptist alienated the allegiance of the soldiers Herod Antipas would be beaten by Aretas.

The army of Herod Antipas had reached the fortress on the north-east of the Dead Sea, and were entrenched there when the army of Aretas was daily expected to attack it. So the idea then came to Herodias to protect Herod, and therefore herself (who would have short shrift if Herod were taken), by persuading her husband to execute John the Baptist and so put an end to his hostile propaganda among the soldiers.

Her proposals to that effect were publicly rejected by Herod Antipas, not out of any love of John the Baptist, but out of fear of his great popularity in Peræa and perhaps in Galilee.

John had great influence with the people; he had a powerful personality and was a speaker of immense force and authority. He reminded his hearers forcibly of Elijah. He stationed himself near some water fountain, as at Bethabara, to baptize the people. Herod arrested and imprisoned John in order to silence him. The place of John's imprisonment was the Castle of Machærus, or fortress, on the southern boundary of Peræa.

The narrative of the beheading of John the Baptist implies that Herod Antipas was staying at the castle. Herod's birthday probably fell on the eve of the expected attack of Aretas. He gave a feast, at which his captains and chief men-at-arms were present.

At this feast, Salome, the young daughter of Herodias (apparently about fourteen or fifteen years of age, judging by later events in her history) danced. Herod was delighted, and in his cups he asked the girl what present he could make her, offering anything (no matter what) up to half of his kingdom. Salome asked her mother what request she should make, and Herodias, trembling for her own safety (which was perhaps in imminent peril from Aretas), and thinking the best way to protect herself was to put an end to John the Baptist, told her to ask for his head.

Herod Antipas was shocked by this (not necessarily from motives of humanity, but for fear of its effect on his subjects, who held John in reverence as a prophet), but in dread of betraying his fear before his captains, he ordered that John the Baptist should be beheaded. Accordingly he was executed. But the result proved to be the reverse of what Herodias had expected. The soldiers of Herod (full of the spirit of John) were overcome by terror at the part they had played in protecting the breaker of the law of Moses and so bringing about the death of the prophet of God.

Consequently, they fled before the army of Aretas, when he came down upon them, and were utterly routed. Aretas drove Herod out of his fortress, and took possession of it.

Returning to Tiberias after his defeat, Herod Antipas found another prophet condemning his adulterous marriage even more severely than John the Baptist had done.

This was Jesus of Nazareth.

While John the Baptist had condemned Herod as a breaker of the law of Moses, Jesus had gone farther, and condemned him as a breaker of the fundamental law of God. John had said that Herod had committed adultery by marrying his brother's wife; but Jesus was saying that all divorce was adulterous.

Herod Antipas (now back at Tiberias) heard that this propaganda was going on almost under his very walls—along the coast of the Lake of Galilee.

When he said, in effect "This is John the Baptist, whom I beheaded, risen from the dead, let me see him," he was not revealing his mind. There was nothing in the thought of his time to support the idea that a man who was dead and had been buried could rise from his grave and walk the world again. It is highly improbable that he ever said any such thing, or, if he did say it, that there was anybody in Galilee who would understand such language.

If he himself had seriously thought of it as possible that John, whom he had beheaded, and whose body he had permitted the disciples to take away and bury in a tomb, had risen from the tomb,* he could have set his mind at rest on the subject by having the tomb opened that he might see if the body of the prophet had gone. If he had done so, and found that the body had disappeared, he must still have encountered the opposition of the Galileans, who would have told him that Jesus was a Galilean, whose father, mother and brothers they knew, and that he had been living and preaching in Galilee while John was still alive.

Even if Herod had convinced himself that Jesus was John risen from the dead, he must have remembered that there was no purpose to be served by arresting and executing him afresh, since the prophet who had risen from the dead once would be able to rise again, and that to do anything else was impossible. The theory of Herod Antipas that Jesus was John the Baptist risen from the dead was a palpable and shallow fiction to hide a sinister design— that of getting hold of Jesus (who was perhaps not easy to lay hands upon, being even more than John, protected by the reverence of the people) and putting an end to him as he had put an end to John.

Jesus perfectly understood the secret notion of the "fox," and acted according to his knowledge. He left the territory of Herod Antipas immediately, and sailed (apparently from the coast near to Tiberias) to Bethsaida (Julias), which was in the territory of Herod Philip.

It was at Bethsaida that occurred the incidents which we call the feeding of the multitudes.

After these incidents, whatever they were, the multitudes were so sure that Jesus was the Messiah that was to come that they wished to claim for him the kingdom that belonged to the Messiah according to the prophets, the kingdom of his father David.

The people tried to take him by force (clearly against his wish) and proclaim him king—the king of the Jews. To escape from this Jesus disappeared into the mountains behind Bethabara, his

---

*Tradition says they buried it in Samaria not far from the traditional site of Jacob's Well, on a knoll which catches a far view of the Mediterranean through a cleft in the hills.

disciples and the people returning to the western shore of Galilee. From there, Jesus went on to Tyre and Sidon. Then he returned from Tyre and Sidon to Galilee, followed by another great multitude.

This is my reading of the Herod Antipas incident, and the link I think it makes in the chronology of the life of Jesus.

CHAPTER VIII

The Disciples

I. Where Jesus Began His Ministry

THE Gospels of Matthew, Mark and Luke all agree that after the Temptation in the wilderness Jesus returned to Galilee. *Matthew* and *Luke* say he returned to his own town of Nazareth. *Luke* (IV, 16) leaves the inference that he may have taught in the synagogues south of Nazareth before reaching Nazareth. *Matthew* (IV, 13) states that "after leaving Nazareth" he came to Capernaum. *Mark* mentions Capernaum, but does not mention Nazareth until later. It is obvious from *Matthew* (IX) that the miracle of the man sick of the palsy took place not at Capernaum but at Nazareth, or in the country about Nazareth.

That it did not occur at Capernaum is also shown by *Mark* (II, 13) which speaks of his returning to the seaside—Capernaum was on the sea, Nazareth was inland. John, who does not refer to the Temptation, says that Jesus went up from Judæa to Galilee. That on the third day after reaching Galilee he went with his disciples to the marriage at Cana of Galilee, and that after the feast at Cana he went onward to Capernaum.

It is commonly understood that the period of the Temptation occupied forty days; and it is probable that Jesus returned from the wilderness to Peræa, in the neighborhood of Bethabara, about the end of March (A.D. 29). It was during his absence in the wilderness that John the Baptist was arrested by order of Herod Antipas and carried off to the fortress of Machærus, ten miles farther south. Jesus, on hearing of the arrest, no doubt returned with new ardour to Galilee.

I do not, for one moment, believe that the first appearance in Galilee was at a marriage feast in Cana, or that his first miracle after his baptism and temptation was that of turning water into wine. I think that he would not pass Nazareth to reach Cana without entering into it (a thing he would have to do if John's story is right). Nor do I believe that after the exalted scenes of his baptism and temptation he would perform a miracle of mere power, and add to the drinking of a merry company who were already "well drunken."

I reject the miracle of turning water into wine as false and wrong to the spirit of Jesus, and incapable of any rational spiritual interpretation. This questionable event is recorded in only one of the Gospels (*John*). It is claimed for it that as it concerns the mother of Jesus only less than Jesus himself, and that she (who was then living in John's family) may be in some sort the first authority for it. How did it come to Mary at the feast of Cana of Galilee that Jesus could provide wine? Had she any thought that he would perform a miracle? If so, how did she come by that knowledge? Had he performed miracles before his baptism? Is the taunt of his brother about doing in Jerusalem what he had done in Capernaum a reference to his pre-ministerial experience of miraculous power?

But if Mary knew the divine power of Jesus at the feast of Cana, how did it come to pass that after he had cast out devils, and so on, she, thinking he was himself possessed of a devil, and beside himself, went with his brethren to take possession of him?

John definitely dates the occurrence three days after the baptism of Jesus. He gives specific mention of witnesses—four of the disciples. Nevertheless, the story of the first miracle is so entirely out of harmony with other events of a like nature that it is difficult to assign it to the place given by John, whose chronology is often widely at variance with that of the other evangelists. But whatever the date, and whomsoever the witness to it, I ask permission to place it at this stage of the development of Jesus.

The story of the first miracle is as follows. The third day Jesus was at a marriage in Cana of Galilee. His disciples had also been invited. The mother of Jesus was also there. The wine ran short. The mother of Jesus told him so. "They have no wine," she said. He thought she was asking him to work a miracle and make some wine. He answered, brusquely, "Woman, what have I to do with thee? Mine hour is not yet come." That is to say his time had not come to work miracles. Nevertheless, his mother said to the servants, "Whatsoever he saith unto you, do it." So seeing six stone waterpots partly filled, Jesus told the servants to fill the waterpots, and the servants filled them to the brim. Then he told them to draw out the contents and take them to the governor of the feast, probably the father of the bride. They did so.

The governor of the feast tasted the water and found it to be wine—good wine—the best. And turning to the bridegroom (who apparently had provided the wine for the feast) he said, "Usually, a man gives his guests good wine at the beginning of the feast, and when the guests have well drunk he gives them worse wine, but thou hast kept the good wine until now" (otherwise when their palates are vitiated or they are drunken and do not know good wine from bad).

And then the writer of the Gospel says, "This beginning of miracles did Jesus in Cana of Galilee, and manifested forth his glory; and his disciples believed on him."

A perfectly shocking story; I simply do not believe it.

It is impossible not to see it is totally out of harmony with the other miracles, which are generally of healing; impossible not to realize that it belongs to the category of the visit of the boy Jesus to the doctors in the Temple. Both are intended to show that Jesus was conscious of his special powers. The second story is intended to show that his mother was conscious of them also.

It has been urged both in remote and modern times that it was unworthy of Jesus that he should not only remain in the society of drunkards but even further their intemperance by an exercise of his miraculous power. By this miracle, Jesus did not, as was usual with him, relieve any want, any real need, but only furnished an additional incitement to pleasure, and performed a miracle of luxury rather than one of true benevolence. Unless the story of the turning the water into wine has an allegorical significance (which has never satisfied the conscience of humanity) it is unlike Jesus and unworthy of him.

And then, what of its effect? Did it establish faith in his supernatural powers among the worldly guests? We are not given a hint of that. Did it confirm the faith of his disciples? We are not told so. In either case, it fails. What, then, does it do—what purpose does this story of the turning of water into wine serve? It serves no other purpose whatever than to show to Jesus himself that he possessed the supernatural power which by this time he knew belonged to the Messiah, and that Mary his mother was aware that he possessed this supernatural power, since the direction she gives to the servants shows that she had a preconception of the fact that Jesus was about to perform a miracle and even of the manner in which he was about to perform it. If this is all, it is impossible not to reject the story. An immeasurably greater miracle was at that moment going on in the soul of Jesus—the miracle of the great thought that God is not a vengeful master but *Our Father.* There lies the heart of the universal religion. That was the real miracle of that moment in the life of Jesus.

II. *His Second Temptation*

Great in the spirit, mighty of purpose, Jesus returned from the wilderness to the ways of men, and began to preach in the towns by the Lake of Galilee, saying, "Repent, for the kingdom of Heaven is at hand." This was one-half of John's message. Soon afterwards Jesus returned to his own country, and to his own city, Nazareth.

Here comes the first of the great silences in the Gospel narrative; but it is easy to see what happened to Jesus in his own place and among his own people. First, he went back to his mother's home. He had been absent some months. His absence had given rise first to uneasiness, then to vexation and finally to downright wrath. His kindred were incapable of understanding him. Why should he set up as a prophet? Why should he sow discord where there had been peace? Why should he set father against son, mother against daughter, brother against brother? What was he that he should try to rise above his station? Why could not he be content to live and die a carpenter like his father before him?

To all these, he made answer that God had called him. In the Jordan, the Holy Spirit of God had spoken to him. He was there heralded as the beloved Son of God. In the desert, God had been with him. Angels had followed and ministered to him. He had been tempted of the Devil and had conquered him. Now he was come forth strong in the spirit to call on them to repent, for the kingdom of Heaven was at hand. His kindred thought him a man carried away by vanity and by much brooding upon himself. His mother thought him possessed. She had only pity for his madness. He struggled to show her that there was no madness in him. She struggled to restrain him from his purpose of going about from town to town to preach his gospel of the Kingdom. He loved her, and he had to make choice of his natural affection for her and his love of the work to which God had called him.

This was the second great temptation of Jesus. He conquered

his natural affection, and gave himself up to his mission. But the conquest was won at a great price. The scar of that warfare remained upon his spirit to the last. He had listened to the calls of his heavenly Father. He had no longer a mother, no longer brethren or sisters. He had been compelled to choose between them and God. The Holy Ghost grew stronger in him. The God in him increased. The man in him became less. But the wound of his humanity was left upon him.

III.   The First Sermon in Nazareth

After this scene with his own kin, he went into the synagogue of Nazareth on the Sabbath Day, and stood up to read. The words he read were from *Isaiah* (LXI, 1), which *Luke* records as:

> The Spirit of the Lord is upon me: because He hath anointed me to preach the gospel to the poor; He hath sent me to heal the brokenhearted, to preach deliverance to the captives, and recovering of sight to the blind, to set at liberty them that are bruised, to preach the acceptable year of the Lord.

Then, rolling up the book (it would be a scroll), he went on to say that this prophecy was that day fulfilled in him. The Holy Ghost, the Spirit of the Lord, was upon him. He was sent to preach the Gospel to the poor. He was sent to heal the brokenhearted. He was sent to say that the year of the Lord, the coming of the Kingdom, was near upon them. Now was the time! A time when the rich were grinding the faces of the poor, when the followers of the princes of the world were pretending to be followers of God. But all this must come to an end. Did they suppose he had come to bring peace? No, but dissension.

Then the people of Nazareth began to say to themselves "Is not this Joseph's son?" And Jesus answered, "No prophet is accepted in his own country" (implying that Nazareth was his own country). And all they in the synagogue rose up in wrath. This carpenter was glorifying himself and degrading them. So with one accord they drove him out of the synagogue and out of the city, hounding him, taunting him, mocking him, following and surrounding him and pushing him forward to the brow of the hill on which their city stood, there to hurl him headlong over the precipice and kill him. (Nazareth did not exactly stand on a hill, only partly so; the brow of the hill is far away.)

IV. Choosing the Disciples

Jesus escaped from Nazareth and went into Capernaum, and Magdala, Bethsaida, Chorazin and the other cities of Galilee. He found disciples among those who believed in him. They were twelve poor men like himself. He had no rich followers, no rich friends. There were fishermen among them, and publicans, and no doubt notorious sinners. These promptly yielded to his extraordinary personal magnetism, left all they had and followed him.

The first two evangelists, Matthew and Mark, say that Jesus, walking by the Lake of Galilee, saw two brothers, Simon called Peter and Andrew, casting a net into the sea, for they were fishers. He said to them, "Follow me, and I will make you fishers of men." Straightway they abandoned their nets and followed him. Going a little farther he came upon two other brothers, James and John, the sons of Zebedee, mending their nets. He called them and they immediately left their ship and their father and followed him.

In his own country he saw a man named Matthew, sitting at the receipt of custom; and he said to him, "Follow me." And the man arose and followed him. This was the beginning of his calling of his disciples. John tells a quite different story in which the scene is not Galilee, as in *Matthew* and *Mark,* but the vicinity of the Jordan. There, after John the Baptist, standing with two of his own disciples, had proclaimed Jesus to be the Son of God, the two disciples who heard this left John and followed Jesus. One of the two was Andrew, the other is not named. Andrew found his brother, Simon (afterwards called Peter), and called him, and brought him to Jesus. The following day Jesus went into Galilee and there he found Philip. Philip found Nathanael.

The call of Nathanael and his reasons for accepting Jesus as the Son of God are given—that inasmuch as Jesus by divine intuition had seen Nathanael with the eyes of the soul before his physical eyes had seen him, therefore Jesus must be the Son of God, and the king of Israel. When Philip speaks of Jesus as a Messiah coming from Nazareth, Nathanael asks, "Can any good thing come out of Nazareth?" Nathanael was probably of the city of Cana, a neighbouring city to Nazareth. It is therefore reasonable to think that he knew better than anybody, except Jesus and his family, what reputation Nazareth had.

Luke's account of the vocation of Peter and his companions differs.

In *Luke*, Jesus has appeared in Nazareth, and preached in Capernaum and "in the cities of Galilee," and gathered a great multitude of followers, when, in order to avoid the crowd on the shores of the lake, he enters into one of two empty ships (or fishing-boats) and speaks to the people on the shore. After he has finished speaking the owner of one of the boats, a man named Simon, comes back from where he had been washing his nets, and Jesus tells him to launch out into the lake and let down his nets for a draught. Simon objects that he and his companions, James and John (Andrew is not mentioned), had been fishing all night and taken nothing. Nevertheless, at the word of Jesus he consents. The result is a great catch of fish, and Simon is so astonished that he falls down at the feet of Jesus, and says, "Depart from me, for I am a sinful man, O Lord." Upon this, Jesus said, prophetically, "Fear not, from henceforth thou shalt catch men." And when the fishermen have brought the boats to land they forsake all and follow him.

It would not be fair to say, as the rationalistic commentators do, that the mere happy fortuity that Jesus had brought them a large catch of fish had caused Simon and his partners to believe in Jesus. They had obviously heard him speaking to the people, and their act in giving up all and following him was probably the culminating point of their convictions with respect to him.

The sceptical critics refer the whole incident to natural causes by saying that Jesus probably knew that a storm was approaching and that therefore deeper water, farther from the shore, was the most promising fishing ground. But this lame effort of the sceptics breaks down, as nearly all their other efforts do. Peter and his companions were lifelong fishermen and might be assumed to know the habits of the fish and the Lake of Galilee better than an inland carpenter. Yet they are astonished. To them, it was clearly a miracle that Jesus should know where, and under what conditions, the fish could be found. It might be a miracle of power or of knowledge. Either Jesus *caused* the fish to congregate, or he knew, by supernatural means, where they congregated.

Did Jesus interrupt the chain of natural phenomena? Did it serve any apparent object to do so? Was the use of his miraculous powers extravagant? Was this the way he engrafted the faith in his Messiahship on his chief disciples? Was it thus that he won his disciples?

Or was it not rather by his preaching, by that power of word which afterwards made Peter ask to whom else they should go (when Jesus asked if they, too, were going to leave him) since he had the words of eternal life? My conclusion is that the disciples were called after they had heard Jesus preach, after they had, perhaps, seen some of his miracles. There is no resisting the conclusion that from the first they believed him to be the Christ. Vaguely, perhaps, but under their uncertainty the thought was there. This is the Promised One. This is the One foretold. This is the Saviour we have looked for.

Nothing less than this accounts for what they did. They are to be the inheritors of the kingdom of God with him. They are to be nearer to him than other men. When the Kingdom comes they are to sit on higher seats. This is their hope. And Jesus, in talking to them, never discouraged this idea. Quite the contrary.

For this great future they were willing to be, like him, homeless wanderers, who had nowhere to lay their heads.

Assuming that Jesus had been exercising his ministry for a considerable time before he called his disciples, I see no reason for thinking that the disciples acted as if under a hypnotic spell, or that they showed themselves rash in following Jesus.

In the first Gospel (IX, 9) mention is made of a man named Matthew, who was sitting at the receipt of custom, to whom Jesus said "Follow me."

In *Mark* and *Luke,* this man is called Levi.

Jesus was at that time in his own country. The inference is that Matthew was a tax-gatherer, or publican, and that the district in which he gathered taxes was that of the upper country about Nazareth. Levi and Matthew were obviously the same person.

It is the accepted opinion that in the Gospel of St. Matthew the evangelist was narrating his own call. The fact that Matthew speaks of himself in the third person has suggested to certain critics that the apostle was not the author of the first Gospel.

Against this it can be urged that many historians (Josephus particularly) do the same—speak of themselves in the third person. The author of the *Acts of the Apostles* (if he were Luke) also does so. That Matthew was the original author of the Gospel bearing his name is not to be questioned on that ground alone, if at all.

The fundamental idea of the New Testament writers concerning the twelve is that Jesus chose them all. But according to *John* certain of the disciples called each other. *Matthew* does not give the choice of the whole twelve.

Luke narrates how after a night spent in the mountains in prayer, Jesus called his disciples to him, and out of the number of them he chose twelve whom he called also apostles. These twelve (*Luke* VI, 14) were:

Simon (Peter)
Andrew (Simon's brother)
James
John
Philip
Bartholomew
Matthew
Thomas
James (son of Alphæus—name otherwise unknown)
Simon (called Zelotes)
Judas (brother of James) and
Judas Iscariot

After choosing these Jesus comes down to the plain, and delivers what is called, in *Matthew,* his Sermon on the Mount.

Mark III, 13: Jesus goes up into a mountain and calls to him whom he would and they come to him. And he ordained twelve, that they might be with him, and that he might send them forth to preach, to have power to heal sicknesses and to cast out devils.

The twelve disciples, according to *Mark* are:

Simon (Peter)
James
John
Andrew
Philip
Bartholomew
Matthew
Thomas
James, the son of Alphæus
Thaddæus
Simon
Judas Iscariot

In *Matthew* (XIX, 28) Jesus promises the disciples that they shall sit on the twelve thrones judging the twelve tribes of Israel. It is probable that the number of the disciples had been suggested to Jesus by the number of tribes of Israel. Why did he choose them? *Mark* says he chose the twelve to be with him that he might have their companionship on his journeys.

They were, according to *Matthew* (XIII, 52), to become scribes, well instructed unto the kingdom of Heaven.

Another motive of Jesus in choosing the twelve was that he might send them forth to preach. He did this, and it is interesting to reflect that Judas must have been among the twelve thus sent forth.

V. The Disciples Individually

We have, in the New Testament, four catalogues of apostles— in *Matthew, Mark, Luke* and *Acts* (not *John*). In each list the first name is the same—Peter. According to the fourth Gospel Peter was of Bethsaida. According to the Synoptics he lived in Capernaum. Peter, according to the Synoptics, was the first to be called. Not so according to *John*.

Peter has a priority throughout the story of Jesus. "Ardent by nature," always beforehand with the rest of the apostles, whether in speech or act. His denial was quickly repented of. He was faulty, but prompt in courage. The first, according to *Matthew*, to express a conviction of the Messiahship of Jesus. This pre-eminence of Peter among the apostles is conceded also in the Epistles of St. Paul.

James and John are usually named together, as brothers, the sons of Zebedee (otherwise unknown). These two are the only disciples who rival Peter. They stand high in the esteem of their Master—John in his affections. John, probably the younger of the brothers, was almost certainly the youngest of the apostles.

Thus Peter, James and John form the inner circle of the disciples of Jesus. They are with him at the great moments of his life, at the great scenes, and most prominent in the scenes in which all the other apostles are present.

But in John's Gospel, Peter and John are supreme. James is not even named in the fourth Gospel. In John's Gospel, Peter is made one of the first in the society of Jesus at the beginning. But as the story proceeds Peter steps back and gives place to

John. John is called "the beloved disciple"—"the disciple whom Jesus loved."

The fourth Gospel gives the birthplace of Philip as Bethsaida (the city of Andrew and Peter). Nathanael (although called by Philip and described by Jesus as an Israelite without guile) never becomes an apostle, unless he is hidden under one of the other names, when he may have been Bartholomew.

In the fourth Gospel Thomas appears in the "guise of mournful fidelity" (*John* XI, 16) and in another place as noted for incredulity (XX, 24, 25) and once again in the appendix (XXI, 2). Against everything to be said in disfavour of Thomas it must be mentioned that when Jesus was going up to Jerusalem for the last time, and the other disciples were apparently trying to dissuade him from going, Thomas alone says, "Let us also go, that we may die with him."

The rest of the disciples are inconspicuous: James, the son of Alphæus, Simon the Canaanite, or the Zealot, a name which seems to indicate that he belonged to the few survivors of the sect of Judas the Galilean, a sect of zealots, for religion; Matthew, the publican; Judas, the second Judas; and Thaddæus. Finally, Judas Iscariot, who is afterwards conspicuous.

Besides these twelve there were a mass of partisans of Jesus unnamed. In *Luke,* we are told that besides the twelve Jesus chose seventy, and sent them out two and two to the districts he intended to visit, that they might be forerunners, proclaiming the approach of the kingdom of Heaven. These seventy are not mentioned in any of the other Gospels, nor in *Acts.* What was the significance of the numbers twelve and seventy? Critics say that the twelve stood for the twelve tribes of the people of Israel. The seventy were representatives of the seventy-two peoples with as many tongues which, according to the Jewish and early Christian view, formed the sum of the earth's inhabitants. If so, this denoted the universal distribution of Jesus and his kingdom, and ought to have shown the early Church (if it had understood the symbolism of the numbers) that Jesus intended his Gospel for all mankind.

Moreover, as Strauss points out, seventy was a sacred number with the Jewish nation. Moses deputed seventy elders. The Sanhedrin had seventy members. Thus Jesus fixed a number which was "signification of the distribution of the Gospel for all kindreds of the earth."

Acts I, 21 indicates that Jesus had more than twelve as his constant companions. Peter, in asking for the choice of a disciple to take the place of Judas, says, "Wherefore of these men which have companied with us all the time that the Lord Jesus went in and out among us."

Why did he not select men of higher education, of great influence, persons less likely to misunderstand his own aims and mission?

It is important, since one betrayed him, one denied him. All misunderstood him. All fled away from him and hid themselves when they found their hopes of the immediate coming of the kingdom (as they knew it) had collapsed at his arrest, execution and death.

CHAPTER IX

The Ministry
(A General Survey)

I. The Four Gospels

THE POINTS IN COMMON between the four Gospels are many,
and the chief of them is that they leave the impression of
presenting the portrait of the same man and of telling the story of
the same life. It is true that the Gospel of St. John differs widely
from the earlier three in portraiture and in fact. But the points
of difference as to time and movements in all four are very many
and very serious. *Matthew* and *Mark* are nearest alike in chronology and order. *Luke* differs from both at important moments.
John departs widely in matters of both time and place.

In *Mark* the ministry begins with the return of Jesus to Galilee
after his temptation in the wilderness. He goes to Capernaum.
From Capernaum he goes into "a solitary place." He preaches in
various unnamed places in Galilee. He goes again into a desert
place. From the desert he returns to Capernaum. From Capernaum he goes into the mountains. He goes to the country of the
Gadarenes, on the south-east of the Lake of Galilee. In Galilee he
visits his own city of Nazareth. From somewhere in Galilee he
crosses the lake to Bethsaida, in the territory of Philip. From
Bethsaida he walks on the sea, and returns to the land of Gennesaret, which lies between Capernaum and Magdala. From the
plains of Gennesaret he goes up to the borders of Tyre and Sidon.
From the borders of Tyre and Sidon he returns to the Lake of
Galilee. From the western side of the lake he again goes over to
the eastern side—Bethsaida.

From Bethsaida he goes on to Cæsarea Philippi. From Cæsarea
Philippi he goes into a high mountain—presumably Mount Her-
mon. Coming down from Mount Hermon he passes through
Galilee on his way to Jerusalem. From Galilee he goes over to
Peræa and follows the road on the eastern side of Jordan to the

neighborhood of Bethsaida. From Bethsaida he crosses the Jordan and goes up to Jericho. From Jericho he goes up to Bethany. From Bethany he enters Jerusalem.

Altogether the ministry, according to *Mark,* takes place in Galilee alone, down to the final visit to Jerusalem, and occupies a little over a year.

In *Matthew* the history of the ministry is practically the same as in *Mark.* Returning from the wilderness, after his baptism, Jesus goes into Nazareth on his way to Capernaum. From Capernaum he goes up into the mountain—probably a mountain above the plains of Gennesaret. From Gennesaret he crosses to the country beyond Jordan, or to Galilee of the Gentiles. From here he goes down by sea to the land of the Gergesenes. Thence he goes into his own city—Nazareth. From Nazareth (or the country about it) he goes into the desert place. From the desert place he returns by ship to Gennesaret. From Gennesaret he goes up to Tyre and Sidon. From Tyre and Sidon he returns to the Lake of Galilee. From the plains of Gennesaret he goes up to the coasts of Cæsarea Philippi. From Cæsarea Philippi he goes up into a high mountain —apparently Mount Hermon. From Mount Hermon he returns through Galilee and the road beyond Jordan through Jericho to Bethany. From Bethany, or Bethphage, he enters Jerusalem.

This is essentially the same itinerary as in *Mark,* and occupies apparently about the same time—a little over a year. Jesus is never in Jerusalem until he goes up to his crucifixion.

In *Luke* the movements of Jesus are much less easy to follow than in *Mark* and *Matthew,* and towards the end they become confused, apparently out of Luke's ignorance of the geography of Palestine, and partly out of his indifference to, or his ignorance of, the lapse of time. After his return from the Temptation, Jesus goes directly to Nazareth, where he reads and delivers important passages and utterances, as set forth by the writer. In the Nazareth story as given by Luke is a reference to Capernaum, which satisfies me that Jesus had had a ministry both in Nazareth and in Capernaum before his baptism. From Nazareth Jesus goes to Capernaum. From Capernaum he goes through Galilee. While having his central home in Capernaum, he goes into the wilderness, and returns to Capernaum. He goes to Nain. He passes through every city and village of Galilee. He crosses from the Galilee side of the lake to the country of the Gadarenes, which was on the southeast of the lake. He returns to the western side of the lake and crosses to Bethsaida, which is on the north-east side of the lake. I see no reason to believe there ever was any other Bethsaida.

From Bethsaida Jesus goes up into a mountain—probably Mount Hermon. He returns to Galilee on his way to Jerusalem. He travels through Samaria. The journey to Jerusalem through Samaria is confused. At one moment he is in the house of Mary and Martha, which was in Bethany (Judæa). At the next he is back in Samaria. By some zigzag course (if the journey is authentic) he comes to Bethany (thereby going twenty miles out of his direct road to Jerusalem). From Jericho he comes naturally to Bethany. From Bethany he comes to the Mount of Olives. From the Mount of Olives he descends into Jerusalem.

How long the ministry lasts, in *Luke*, it is difficult to say. Obviously, the journey to Jerusalem is a confused account of two journeys to Jerusalem, the first of them through Samaria, and so direct to Jerusalem (of which nothing is said), and the second by the road on the eastern side of the Jordan and so up through Jericho.

John's account of the movements of Jesus is even more confusing than Luke's. After the baptism, Jesus remains two days in Judæa. On the next day (the third day) he returns to Galilee. The first place he visits is Cana of Galilee, thus going past (if not through) Nazareth without stopping there. From Cana he goes to Capernaum. From Capernaum he goes up to Jerusalem for the Passover. Thus, if the baptism took place in March or early April, Jesus went up to Jerusalem almost immediately after his return from Bethabara, which is about twenty-two miles from Jerusalem. From Jerusalem Jesus goes through Samaria back to Galilee. In Galilee he again visits Cana. After the visit to Cana he goes again to Jerusalem for a feast of the Jews.

If this is the Feast of Tabernacles it takes place in October. Therefore, Jesus has done nothing that is reported since Passover in April until October, except pay a short visit to Cana. Here is another gap. We hear next that Jesus is back in Galilee and is crossing the lake—presumably to the north-east, where he feeds the five thousand. From there he goes up into the mountain to escape from the people who would take him by force and make him a king. After his disciples have gone into a boat to return towards the western side of the lake, Jesus, in the fourth watch of the night (about three o'clock to six o'clock in the morning), walks to them on the water.

Hereabouts, there is a big gap in *John,* and when we next hear of Jesus he is in Jerusalem. He goes up to the Mount of Olives, and preaches in the treasury of the Temple. He gives sight to a blind man in Jerusalem, and preaches in Solomon's Porch. He is stoned out of Jerusalem. He goes to Jordan, where John used to baptize. There he hears that his friend Lazarus is ill. After some days he goes up to Bethany and raises Lazarus from the dead. He goes from Bethany into Ephraim, a city near the wilderness. He returns from Ephraim to Bethany and sups at the house of (apparently) Martha and Lazarus, and there Mary (who is confused with the woman who was a sinner) anoints his feet with oil.

John either accepts the idea that Mary did this same act twice or else the second verse of Chapter XI is an unnecessary anticipation of the full story told in verse three of Chapter XII. From Bethany Jesus rides into Jerusalem.

Thus, according to *John,* Jesus was at least twice in Jerusalem before his final visit—three times altogether. Therefore the ministry must have lasted something more than two years—say from March, A.D. 28 to April, 30, or from March, A.D. 29 to 31.

II.   Harmonizing the Accounts

It is when we come to the efforts to harmonize these conflicting accounts of the movements of Jesus that the utter impossibility of their existing together becomes most apparent. Separately, they may live—collectively they die—for they produce nothing but confusion. The student who thinks the whole of the four Gospels inspired by God feels compelled to fit one into another. This is, I am sure, absolutely impossible.

Having carefully considered some dozens of such attempts to harmonize the four Gospels in this elementary matter of the movements of Jesus during his ministry and the length of time occupied by his ministry, I find the result a chaos. It leaves gaps of three months in one and nine months in another in which Jesus is doing nothing—in which he is in "retirement." But the idea of rest and retirement for long periods is beyond the limits of common sense.

Again, the attempt to harmonize time in the stories of the life of Jesus leads to impossibilities. For example, Sir William Ramsay attempts to explain the manifest conflict of chronology in *Luke* III, 1, and *Luke* III, 23. "Now in the fifteenth year of the reign of Tiberius Cæsar, Pontius Pilate being governor of Judæa and Herod being tetrarch of Galilee . . ." "And Jesus himself began to be about thirty years of age . . ."

If Jesus was born "in the days of Herod the King of Judæa" he must have been born before March 4 B.C. when (beyond doubt) Herod died. Ramsay's belief appears to be that the birth of Jesus occurred in 6 B.C. The death of Augustus occurred in A.D. 14, and this was, therefore, the year in which Tiberius became emperor. The fifteenth year of Tiberius's *reign* would therefore be A.D. 29. In that year, Jesus would not be about thirty years of age but about thirty-four or thirty-five.

To escape from this dilemma Ramsay says that the word *reign* in *Luke* ought to be *authority*, which corresponds more nearly with the original Greek word used by Luke. Further, that for three years before the death of Augustus, Tiberius had been the *authority*, the acting emperor, and that his period would therefore be counted from A.D. 11. All this is totally contrary to the practice of historians (except in one or two of the rarest cases); but what does it lead to?

It leads to the statement that the year in which John the Baptist began to baptize, and Jesus began to preach was A.D. 26, when Jesus would be about thirty-one years of age. By this calculation Ramsay thinks he has harmonized *Luke* III, 1, and *Luke* III, 23. But what he has actually done is to deprive *Luke* III, 1, of any trace of historical authority. It says, Pontius Pilate being governor of Judæa. But Pontius Pilate was (in A.D. 26) in Jericho, and did not arrive in Judæa until A.D. 27. Again Ramsay, in common with other commentators, endeavours to explain *Luke* II, 2: ("And this taxing was first made when Cyrenius was governor of Syria"). The event about to be recorded by Luke is the journey of Joseph with Mary to Bethlehem, to be taxed. As this occurred before the death of Herod, the king of Judæa, it must have occurred before 4 B.C. But Cyrenius did not become governor of Syria until A.D. 6. Ramsay and countless others think it necessary to prove that Cyrenius was governor twice, the first time being during the last years of Herod. There is no historical authority for this statement.

The obvious truth is that the verse in parenthesis in *Luke* II, 2, is an interpolation by a later writer than the apostle. Also, that the line in *Luke* III, 23, "And Jesus himself began to be about thirty years of age" is simply a mistake. Most obviously he was then between thirty-three and thirty-four, if Jesus was born in the time of Herod the Great, which we have no reason to disbelieve.

Such are the mazes into which we are led by attempts to harmonize dates in the Gospels, whether they are considered separately or together. The truth is that the final verses of the Gospels were probably written about thirty years after the events recorded, when exact dates were no longer remembered and perhaps no longer considered important.

I conclude from all this, and much more of the same kind on which theologians have spent (and I think wasted) years of their lives, that what is left to the biographer of Jesus is the duty of fixing clearly in his mind the character of Jesus as revealed by the Gospels taken together, and then to reject whatever they contain which conflicts with that clear conception. Also, to judge of the movements of Jesus during his ministry by the closest examination he can make of the four witnesses, accepting nothing that does not agree with the whole. This will require that he should reject obvious repetitions of incidents, and obvious impossibilities in date or geography. In short, he must bring to bear on the four Gospel narratives precisely the same liberty of judgment in determining the course of Jesus's life, as the synod of the fourth century brought to bear on the Gospels in making the Canon.

In the long run, the call of the human spirit is the ultimate test to which the movements of the life of Jesus as well as his teaching, his character and his mission, must be brought. In obedience to this spirit, I approach the Gospels as the only authorities for the facts of the life of Jesus, but as authorities whose evidence often conflicts, and must therefore be weighed on its credibility, exactly as any other literary evidence would be weighed by the biographer of any other person.

CHAPTER X

The Ministry
(According to St. Matthew)

IN THE Gospel of St. Matthew Jesus first appears as coming from Galilee to Jordan, to be baptized of John. This was probably at the eastern side of Jordan, in Peræa, which was in the territory of Herod Antipas. John is at first unwilling to baptize him, saying he, himself, had need to be baptized by Jesus, but Jesus prevails upon John to baptize him. Coming out of the water Jesus sees the Spirit of God descending on him like a dove, and hears a voice saying, "This is my beloved Son, in whom I am well pleased." The voice is clearly not addressed to Jesus, but to the onlookers, yet the onlookers cannot have heard it, or, having heard, they cannot have understood it to mean that in any special sense Jesus was the Son of God.

From his baptism Jesus is led up by the Spirit into the wilderness to be tempted by the Devil. The wilderness is obviously the wilderness near to Jordan—the Judæan wilderness. The temptations are given in detail. The Devil leaves Jesus, having failed to conquer him, and angels come to minister to him.

At some time hereabout John the Baptist is arrested and cast into prison—for what reason is not yet stated by Matthew. On hearing of John's arrest, Jesus departs into Galilee.

If John's arrest was by Herod, it was obviously not to avoid Herod that Jesus left Judæa and went into Jerusalem, as he was thereby passing out of the Roman territory of Judæa into the Galilean territory of Herod—in short, was running into Herod's arms, if Herod had any designs against him.

Clearly, he went to Nazareth. On leaving Nazareth he went to Capernaum and dwelt there. He began to preach and to say, "Repent, for the kingdom of Heaven is at hand."

425

Walking by the Lake of Galilee (probably by Capernaum) he asked Simon and Andrew to be his disciples. Not much farther away he called the two other brothers, James and John, the sons of Zebedee, who is otherwise unknown to the Gospel story. Jesus went about Galilee preaching the gospel of the Kingdom, and healing all manner of diseases.

His fame went through all Syria. People followed him in great multitudes from Galilee (where he was), from Decapolis, from Jerusalem, from Judæa and from beyond Jordan (eastern side). On the side of a mountain (not named or indicated, but presumably near to Capernaum) Jesus delivered to his disciples (there are only four actually chosen disciples thus far, so the term here must refer to all that followed him) what is known as the Sermon on the Mount.

Jesus comes down from the mountain and great multitudes follow him. He heals a leper.

He re-enters Capernaum and there a centurion (Roman) asks him to heal his servant who is at home. Jesus offers to go. The subsequent incidents lead up to a statement by Jesus which indicates his belief that the Kingdom will contain many that are not Jews and will not contain many that are Jews. Jesus goes into Peter's house (apparently in Capernaum) and heals his wife's mother who lay sick of a fever. He touches her hand and the fever leaves her. People possessed of devils are brought to him and he cures them. There is a significant quotation of prophecy here, spoken by Esaias: "Himself took our infirmities, and bare our sicknesses."

Jesus, seeing that great multitudes are crowding about him, decides to go to the other side of Galilee. A scribe comes and says, "Master, I will follow thee whithersoever thou goest." Jesus answers the scribe that in that case he must be prepared to be homeless. He, himself, has no home. "The foxes have holes and the birds of the air have nests; but the Son of Man hath not where to lay his head." Another disciple also expresses a desire to follow Jesus, but asks first to go and bury his father. Jesus says, "Follow me, and let the dead bury their dead."

He goes into the ship with his disciples, and falls asleep. A great storm rises. His disciples awaken him. He rebukes them for their want of faith. Then he rebukes the waves and the sea, and then there follows a great calm. The disciples marvel and ask themselves what manner of man is this that the winds and the sea obey him.

He lands in the country of the Gergesenes. This is on the eastern side of Galilee, almost due east from Capernaum. There he meets two men who are possessed of devils. He casts the devils out of the men, and allows them to enter a herd of swine which are grazing near. The swine run violently down a steep place and leap into the sea and perish. The keepers of the swine go back to their city (not named, perhaps Gamala) and tell what has happened. The "whole city" come out to meet Jesus, and beg him to depart from their coasts. The obvious meaning of this is that Jesus is acting by the power of the master of evil spirits, Beelzebub. Therefore, they fear him and beseech him to go away. This is the beginning of the demonizing of Jesus, and the effect of it is bad. Jesus re-enters the ship and returns to the western side of the lake, coming to his own city, Nazareth.

This is his second visit to Nazareth since his baptism. Sick people are brought out to him. It is noted that in curing them he forgives their sins, indicating that sin is the cause of their sickness. The scribes object to his claim to forgive sins, and call it blasphemy. But the multitude looking on are with Jesus.

He sees (presumably in or near Nazareth) a tax-gatherer sitting in his custom house, and calls him to be his disciple. The man forsakes his work and follows him. His name is Matthew. Jesus sits at meat in the house of a publican—presumably Matthew. The Pharisees of the place see this, and say to the immediate disciples of Jesus, "Why eateth your Master with publicans and sinners?" Jesus answers them that they who are sick need a physician, not they that are well. "I am not come to call the righteous, but sinners to repentance."

Then the disciples of John the Baptist come to him (apparently in Galilee), and ask how it comes to pass that "We and the Pharisees fast oft, but thy disciples fast not?" Jesus answers by an Eastern question, "Can the children of the bridechamber mourn as long as the bridegroom is with them?"

A certain ruler comes to Jesus and says his daughter is dead, but if Jesus will come and lay his hands on her she will live. Jesus rises to go to the ruler's house. On the way a woman who has been sick for twelve years comes behind him and touches his garment. Jesus sees her, and says, "Daughter, be of good comfort; thy faith hath made thee whole." And the woman is cured from that hour.

Jesus reaches the ruler's house, and sees the usual minstrels about it, singing the dirge for the dead. He says, "Give place; for the maid is not dead, but sleepeth." The people are said to laugh him to scorn. But he has them all turned away, and then he takes the maid by the hand, and she rises. The fame of this passes all over the land. Apparently, he is still in his own country—about Nazareth.

As Jesus turns to depart, two blind men follow him, saying, "Thou Son of David, have mercy on us."

The salutation *may* have been expressive of a universally held belief that Jesus was descended from the house of David: but, more probably it is the usual form of salutation applied to all men of divine gifts.

Jesus asks the blind men if they believe that he can cure their blindness. They say they do. Whereupon he touches their eyes, saying, "According to your faith be it unto you." And straightway the blind men see. It is significant that Jesus makes faith in the victim a first essential of their cure. The sick person *must* believe he can be cured, and that Jesus can cure him. He commands the blind men to tell nobody what he has done, but they spread it abroad over all the country. They bring him a dumb man. The dumbness is believed to be due to a devil. The devil is cast out, and the dumb man speaks.

Again the Pharisees say, "He casteth out devils through the prince of the devils." This was what was said when he caused the devils to enter the swine, and the people begged him to go away.

Jesus goes about the cities and the villages (presumably of lower Galilee) teaching in the synagogues, preaching the gospel of the Kingdom, and healing every sickness and disease. Seeing the multitudes who follow him, he is moved with compassion for them because they were as sheep without a shepherd.

Changing the figure, he said that the harvest was plenteous but the labourers were few. So he called twelve disciples and gave them power to cure diseases, and sent them out to preach the kingdom of Heaven, to say, "The kingdom of Heaven is at hand," to heal the sick, to cleanse the lepers, raise the dead, and cast out devils.

The twelve disciples so chosen and sent out were:

Simon, whom he renamed Peter
Andrew, his brother
James
John
Philip
Bartholomew
Thomas
Matthew
James (called Jonas)
Lebbæus, otherwise Thaddæus
Simon the Canaanite
Judas Iscariot

Hitherto, we have heard of only five of these twelve. Of two others we shall hear again. Of the remaining five we shall never hear anything more in the Gospels. Having called his disciples, he proceeds to send them out to preach and to teach (X, 5).

He tells the twelve that they are to take neither gold nor silver nor brass in their purses; neither two coats, nor shoes, nor staves. The workman was to be worthy of his meat. They were not to go into the way of the Gentiles, nor into any city of Samaria. They were to go to the lost sheep of the house of Israel.

This last clause is in complete opposition to the teaching of Jesus, *both before and after,* except at one moment. Jesus, himself, went to the Gentiles and cured the Gentiles, preached to the Samaritans and made converts of the Samaritans, and foretold the admission of the Gentiles to the kingdom of Heaven. Is it here that at this period Jesus did not think his work went beyond the Jews?

Jesus warns his twelve that they will be brought before governors and kings for his sake, for a testimony against them and the Gentiles. He gives further warnings covering a wide scope—that brother shall be against brother and father against child, and so on. "Ye shall not have gone over the cities of Israel, till the Son of man be come."

And fear not them which kill the body, but are not able to kill the soul, but rather fear him which is able to destroy both soul and body in hell. [X, 28]
Think not that I am come to send peace on earth; I came not to

send peace, but a sword. For I am come to set a man at variance against his father . . . [X, 34, 35]

If all this is to be read as the instructions given by Jesus in view of the immediate missionary errand of the twelve, it is, as we shall see, far beyond the necessities of the case. All is greatly exaggerated as a forecast of anything the disciples are likely to suffer in Galilee, on their short missionary journey. The disciples encounter no such terrors, and return to Jesus totally unscathed either by governors or kings. But if it is to be read as general instructions to apply to all missionary errands after his death, it is justified by the subsequent events. In the latter case, however, the issuing of such instructions is obviously unnecessary at this period. The whole of Chapter X of *Matthew* is a great message, if it can be read as the last message of Jesus to his disciples before he finally leaves them. It resembles what he says at the Last Supper in *John*. Clearly, Jesus is at the time in the neighbourhood of his own country—Nazareth. But now he goes into the bigger cities.

John the Baptist has heard in the prison of the works of Jesus, and he sends two of his disciples to ask, "Art thou he that should come, or do we look for another?"

Obviously, John, down to this time, did not know Jesus for the one who was to come—the one he had foretold. If he had known him to be so at the baptism of Jesus he must have ceased foretelling the coming of the Lord. He must have altered his message. That he did not know that Jesus was the Messiah down to the moment of sending the two disciples from his prison is proved by the terms of his message. Either this incident is true or it is not true. If it is true the statement put into the mouth of John the Baptist by the writer of the Gospel of John is false. If this incident of sending the disciples is false the words put into the mouth of John may be true. It is one of two things. *It cannot be both.*

Jesus answers by showing John's disciples what kind of miracles he works, and commands them to go and tell John what they have seen and heard.

The disciples of John go back with the message, and Jesus pronounces a great eulogy of John the Baptist, declaring that he is more than a prophet, that among them that are born of women there has not risen a greater than John the Baptist. John has prophesied. He is the Elias that was to come—before the Messiah. Thus Jesus points directly to himself as the Messiah, foretold by all the prophets down to John, and says, excusing his ambiguity, "He that hath ears to hear, let him hear."

Jesus thereupon pronounces a vehement denunciation upon his generation (XI, 16). He begins to upbraid the cities in which his mighty works had been done. Evidently they had not repented. They had run after him to heal their sick, but that was all. They had not listened to his warning—they had not repented. He names three unrepentant cities. They are Chorazin, Bethsaida and Capernaum. If the mighty works done in this land had been done in Tyre and Sidon they would have repented long ago in sackcloth and ashes, and Tyre and Sidon were notoriously wicked cities. Yet it will be more tolerable for Tyre and Sidon on the day of judgment than for those cities which think themselves so much better. Capernaum, in particular, which is exalted to Heaven (thinks so highly of itself or is so highly thought of) will be brought down to hell. If the mighty works done in Capernaum had been done in Sodom it would have remained to this day. Therefore, in the day of Judgment it will be more tolerable for Sodom than for Capernaum. Here, in Chapter XI, 24, comes a break.

Then come three beautiful passages, not obviously relevant, which seem to me to belong certainly to the first Galilean period, when the people were receiving him gladly (XI, 25–30).

At that time Jesus answered and said,
"I thank thee, O Father, Lord of Heaven and earth, because thou hast hid these things from the wise and prudent, and hast revealed them unto babes. Even so, Father: for so it seemeth good in thy sight. All things are delivered unto me of my Father: and no man knoweth the Son, but the Father: neither knoweth any man the Father, save the Son, and he to whomsoever the Son will reveal him. Come unto me, all ye that labour and are heavy laden, and I will give you rest. Take my yoke upon you, and learn of me; for I am meek and lowly in heart: and ye shall find rest unto your souls. For my yoke is easy, and my burden is light."

These beautiful and pathetic appeals come immediately after the fierce denunciation of the cities who have not accepted him and have not repented. They appear to have been spoken in or near his own city (Nazareth) shortly after he had sent out his disciples.

Then comes an indication of the time of the year. "At that time Jesus went on the Sabbath Day through the corn; and his disciples were an hungred, and began to pluck the ears of corn, and to eat." The corn would be ripe for plucking and eating about May in that country. (The twelve disciples whom he had just before sent away are with him again. Has there been an unrecorded interval of time here? It seems to be so. Where has Jesus been?) The Pharisees protest to him that by doing so the disciples are breaking the Sabbath. He answers them by saying that David was permitted to break the Sabbath. Also, that the priests in the Temple are permitted to do so.

The Son of Man (obviously himself) is Lord of the Sabbath Day. Then (still on the Sabbath) he goes into the synagogue, and heals a man with a withered hand. The Pharisees thereupon hold a council against him, how they may destroy him. I am uncertain whether destroy means to kill him, assassinate him, or by legal means to cast him out of the synagogue and so destroy him as a teaching power. It seems in this case that it means physical destruction. And if so, it is a shocking feature of a condition of religion in which for Sabbath-breaking a man may be assassinated.

Jesus withdraws himself from the Pharisees who are trying to destroy him. Great multitudes follow him and he heals them of their diseases. Strangely, he tells the great multitudes not to make him known. The only intelligible meaning of this is that he asks the multitudes not to let the people lying in wait to destroy him know where he is, and thus be taken (as he was finally taken) when he is practically alone and unprotected by his followers.

Whence he has gone is not stated. The people bring him one possessed of a devil—blind and dumb. He heals the man, who sees and hears. They are amazed and say, "Is not this the Son of David?" Two points. This must have been in a new place, or the people would not have been amazed at what he had done to dumb and blind men before. The use of the words, "Is not this the Son of David?" shows that the common use of the term "Son of David" was doctrinal. They do not ask, "Is this man of the lineage of David?" They said, in effect: "The Messiah, who is to come, is the Son of David. He is to work many miracles. This man works wonderful miracles such as we have never seen before. Surely this must be the Messiah, the Son of David." If this is the common use of the term all the subsequent salutations of Jesus as the Son of David are to be read in the same light. The blind men are not saluting Jesus as one who is known to be of the lineage of David, but as the Messiah—proved to be the Messiah by the marvellous miracles he works. He may or may not be descended from David by blood, but that does not matter to them in the least. They may neither know nor care anything about it. There are isolated cases only in which the blood kinship is either meant or cared for. The reference by Jesus himself to the relation of the Messiah to David is a clear indication of his desire to separate the blood relationship from the spiritual relationship. The Messiah is the *Lord* to David. Therefore, he is not the son of David.

The Pharisees (on seeing the healing of the blind and dumb man possessed of a devil) say especially what they said before in another place: "This fellow doth not cast out devils, but by Beelzebub the prince of the devils." It is the old double idea: disease is of the devil; to cast out the devil one must be the master of devils. Therefore, the people were afraid of the master of devils. In a former case (east of the Jordan), when Jesus cast the devils out of two men and allowed the devils to enter the swine, the people begged him to go away.

In this case, Jesus answers the Pharisees very easily, by saying that Satan would not cast out his own. If he, himself, is casting out devils, and thus preventing them from doing harm to men, it is because he is acting by the Spirit of God, in order that the kingdom of God may come.

Here he says a significant thing, although the application is not altogether apparent: "He that is not with me is against me; and he that gathereth not with me scattereth abroad." Does he mean that the people must not be indifferent to the difference between him and the Pharisees? If they are not with him they are against him.

Then again he pronounces a scorching denunciation of his generation. "O generation of vipers, how can ye, being evil, speak good things, for out of the abundance of the heart the mouth speaketh!" (XII, 34).

Then certain of the scribes and Pharisees ask him for a sign. What can they mean? A sign of his supernatural power? He has given them many signs.

He cries that "an evil and adulterous generation seeketh after a sign, and there shall no sign be given to it, but the sign of the prophet, Jonas. For as Jonas was three days and three nights in the whale's belly; so shall the Son of Man be three days and three nights in the heart of the earth."

Then comes another warning. The men of Nineveh repented at the preaching of Jonas. Therefore they will condemn this generation which has not repented at the preaching of a greater than Jonas.

Then Jesus denounces with flaming words this "wicked generation" which does not heed his words.

It is at this time, when he is denouncing his generation in language without measure in fierceness, that his mother and brethren come to look for him. They want to speak to him (perhaps to take him away, thinking he is losing himself, though this is not said in *Matthew*), and somebody goes in to him (in some house) and tells him they are asking for him. But the exaltation of his spirit has by this time so separated him from earthly and human ties that he answers:

"Who is my mother? And who are my brethren?"

He stretches out his hand towards his disciples and says, "Behold, my mother and my brethren! For whosoever shall do the will of my Father which is in Heaven, the same is my brother, and sister and mother."

Has the sense of his mission taken him out of the range of ordinary human emotions?

He goes out of the house and sits by the sea side. Clearly, he is still in Galilee, and not far from the Lake of Galilee. There he goes into a ship, and a multitude stand on the shore in one of the little natural amphitheatres which may still be seen along the coast from Magdala to Capernaum. He speaks many parables to the people. These parables are all intended to illustrate the mysteries of the kingdom of Heaven.

His reason for speaking parables is that people's hearts have waxed gross, and their ears are dull of hearing and they hear not, their eyes have been closed, and they see not. Hence, he must speak to them in parables—the parable of the sower; the parable of the tares, of the grain of mustard seed, and the parable of leaven.

Jesus sends the multitude away, and coming out of the ship he goes "into the house." This phrase "into the house" refers not to any particular house, least of all to any house of his own, but to whatever house he enters. Clearly houses were open to him wherever he went. The disciples come to him and ask him to explain his parables to them. He does so, and he speaks other parables—in the house. The parable of the treasure hid in the field; the parable of the merchant and the costly pearl and the parable of the net cast into the sea. Comparing the kingdom of Heaven with a fishing net from which the good is gathered and the bad cast away, he explains that so shall it be at the end of the world. The angels shall come forth and sever the wicked from the just. And shall cast them in the furnace of fire. There shall be wailing and gnashing of teeth. Clearly the intensity of the spirit of Jesus is increasing. He sees everlasting punishment to the wailing and gnashing of teeth in a furnace of fire.

After finishing these parables Jesus departs thence. He comes again into his own country—only to be understood as the neighbourhood of Nazareth. There he teaches in the synagogue. The people are astonished at his wisdom and say, "Whence hath this man this wisdom, and these mighty works? Is not this the carpenter's son? Is not his mother called Mary? Are not his brethren, James, and Joses, and Simon, and Judas? And his sisters, are they not all with us? Whence then hath this man all these things?" And they were offended in him. And Jesus said unto them, "A prophet is not without honour, save in his own country, and in his own house."

He did not do many works in his own country, Nazareth, because of the people's unbelief.

Herod Antipas, then living at Tiberias, hears of the fame of Jesus, and thinks he must be John the Baptist risen from the dead. This sounds like nonsense, for what, at that time, could have suggested to Herod the possibility of such a miracle? Then follows the story of Herod and his treatment of John the Baptist—the reason why he had arrested him (for the sake of Herodias, his brother Philip's wife); his desire to put him to death; his fear of doing so, because the people thought John a prophet; the incidents of his birthday, when the daughter of Herodias danced before him and his company, and he is so pleased with her that he promises, with an oath, to give her whatsoever she may ask; how she (instructed by her mother) asks for the head of John the Baptist in a charger, and the "king" is sorry, but for "his oath's sake and them which sat with him at meat" he ordered that the head should be given to her; how he sent and beheaded John in the prison; how the head was brought in a charger to the damsel, and she brought it to her mother, and how, finally, the disciples of John took up his body and buried it and then went and told Jesus.

All this occurs, according to *Matthew* (XIV) when Jesus was in Nazareth or the neighbourhood at that time, or shortly before it while he was still in Galilee, perhaps preaching from the ship to the multitudes on the shore. The time of the year is not indicated. When Jesus hears of the death of John he departs by ship into a desert place. Where did he go to? Why? Clearly he thought that what had befallen John might befall himself.

There were only two directions in which he could go. He could not have gone to a desert place on the western side of the Lake of Galilee. There was no such desert place on the western side of Galilee. The entire western coast was (according to history) a continuous and almost unbroken line of cities and villages. Moreover, it was impossible to get out of the territory of Herod Antipas (the obvious object of going away) by travelling west of the lake only, instead of going as far north as Syria or Phœnicia—an impossible supposition. If he went south by ship he would come to territory no safer, being still Herod's territory. If he went due west he would come to the coast of Ituræa, which was the territory of Herod's brother, Philip. If he went north-east he would come to the desert country south of Cæsarea Philippi, also in the territory of Philip.

Almost certainly it was to the last-mentioned that he went. But we are told that when the people heard thereof (that is, that he had gone, and where he had gone to) they followed him on foot out of the cities. This means that either they walked across to Ituræa by crossing the Jordan at the south of Galilee, or they walked north past Capernaum and so on to Cæsarea Philippi. In either case they would be at least three days making the journey, carrying their sick.

Jesus, seeing the great multitude, was moved with compassion towards them, and he healed their sick. There were about 5,000 men, besides women and children. In the evening his disciples came to him and said, "This is a desert place, and the time is now past; send the multitude away, that they may go into the villages, and and buy themselves victuals." Jesus said, "They need not depart; give ye them to eat." The disciples answered, "We have here but five loaves, and two fishes." Jesus said, "Bring them hither to me." Then he commanded the multitude to sit down on the grass. (It is described as a desert place, but it was not without grass.)

He took the five loaves and two fishes, blessed them, looking up to Heaven, and then gave the loaves to his disciples, who, in turn, gave them to the multitude. And after they had all eaten the disciples took up twelve baskets full of fragments.

It is apparently a circumstantial story. All the surrounding facts are intensely real. The one outstanding thing is that five loaves and two fishes are made to feed 5,000 men, besides women and children —who knows how many more?

Then (it is late in the evening by this time) Jesus tells his disciples to get into a ship, and go before him to the other side of the sea. They do so, and he remains, sending the multitude away. And when the multitude are gone, he goes up into a mountain alone to pray. Then comes a difficulty. In verse twenty-three we are next told that "when the evening was come" he was in the mountain alone. But in verse fifteen we are told that it was evening when the disciples first came to him and asked him to send the people away. Meantime, he has fed them and sent them and his disciples away and gone into a mountain to pray. The storyteller has forgotten his story, or else there has been an interpolation here by another hand than that of the writer of the original Gospel. If we pass from the end of verse fourteen to the beginning of verse twenty-two we have a perfectly harmonious and consistent story, in which the events are logically linked together. Were verses fifteen to twenty-one interpolated? It looks as if they were.

By this time (evening) the ship in which the disciples had set sail was in the middle of the Lake of Galilee. The wind was high and contrary, and they were being tossed on the waves. In the fourth watch of the night Jesus went to them, walking on the sea. The disciples saw him and thought he was a spirit, and cried out for fear. He answered, "It is I, be not afraid." Peter cried, "Lord, if it be thou, bid me come unto thee on the water." Jesus said, "Come." Peter got down on to the water, but when he saw the wind boisterous, he was afraid; he began to sink, and cried, "Lord, save me."

Jesus stretched out his hand and caught him, and, when they had entered the ship, he reproved Peter for his want of faith. Then the wind ceased, and the disciples said to Jesus, "Of a truth thou art the Son of God." They tell him that he is the Son of God. Later, when Peter says the same, Jesus speaks as if he had never heard it from them before. Then we are told that "when they were gone over, they came in to the land of Gennesaret."

Not the least of my reasons for thinking that the miracle of the walking on the water never occurred is based on the fact that in the ship the disciples tell him he is the Son of God, and that when the same is said later (at Cæsarea Philippi) by Peter, he hails the name as having been revealed by God, and rewards Peter for saying it by promising him the keys of Heaven. It is one of two things. Either Jesus received the name Son of God first on the Lake of Galilee (where he took no notice of it), or at Cæsarea Philippi, when he attached great importance to it. I choose the latter and reject the former. Further, the two miracles are contrary to the clear laws of nature, and Jesus in his clearly attested miracles went beyond nature (carried nature farther), but did not go in the face of nature, contradict and subvert nature. Moreover, it does not in any way enhance my sense of the power of Jesus to think that he could walk on the water, or that he could make five loaves and two fishes feed 5,000 men, besides women and children.

The men of Gennesaret, as soon as they knew Jesus had arrived in their midst, sent out into all their country round about and brought to him all that were diseased, and besought him that they might only touch the hem of his garment; and as many as touched were made perfectly whole.

Here we are back out of the land of a legendary world into a world of reality. Jesus is now in Ituræa (Gennesaret), the territory of Philip, the brother of Herod, with whom Herod was not on good terms.

Scribes and Pharisees come to him. They ask him why his disciples transgressed the tradition of the elders by not washing their hands before eating. Jesus answers them, in his usual way, by asking another question: "Why do ye also transgress the commandments of God by your tradition?" He gives them an example of their practice (XV, 4), and, having answered, he denounces them, "Ye hypocrites, well did Esaias prophesy of you, saying, 'This people draweth nigh unto me with their mouth, and honoureth me with their lips, but their heart is far from me.'" More he says (see verses 16, 17).

Then he departs from Gennesaret into the coasts of Tyre and Sidon. How he goes, whether partly by ship, is not said. His fame has gone before him.

A woman of Canaan comes out of the coasts of Tyre and Sidon, and cries, "Have mercy on me, O Lord, thou Son of David; my daughter is grievously vexed with a devil." Thus a Gentile calls him "Lord" and "Son of David." Jesus does not answer the woman. The disciples try to get him to send her away. He answers strangely, "I am not sent but unto the lost sheep of the house of Israel." Is it meant that the disciples asked him to cure the woman's daughter and let her go, because she was continuing to follow the way after them?

Then the woman comes to Jesus and says, "Lord, help me." He answers the woman, "It is not meet to take the children's bread, and to cast it to dogs."

Is this possible? Is it in any harmony with the teaching of Jesus at any other authenticated moment? Most assuredly it is not. That he should call the Gentile woman's daughter a dog is incredible. I simply will not believe it. How, then, is this amazing and monstrous passage to be understood? My explanation is that whether written by Matthew in the original Gospel or not, it was the work of a writer who took the side of the early Christians in Jerusalem during the first years after the Crucifixion. If it was Matthew, then Matthew believed the Gospel was for the children of Abraham only. Paul resisted this theory and destroyed it. But it may have got into the original version of the sayings of Jesus by Matthew before that, and so become perpetuated. I reject it absolutely. It is an outrage on all that Jesus afterwards taught.

The woman answers beautifully. "Truth, Lord, yet the dogs eat of the crumbs which fall from their masters' table." Enough to make Jesus ashamed of himself if he ever said the hateful words attributed to him. Then Jesus said, "O woman, great is thy faith: be it unto thee even as thou wilt." And her daughter was made whole from that very hour.

Then Jesus left the outskirts of Tyre and Sidon (we do not hear that he ever entered the wicked cities), and came nigh to the Lake of Galilee, and went up into a mountain, and sat down there. Then follows an almost exact reproduction of the feeding of the five thousand. Only the number of the people and of the loaves differs. In this case there are "four thousand men, beside women and children." The loaves are seven and the fishes are described as "a few little fishes." The same words are used as in the case of the telling of the earlier miracle. The disciples who had witnessed the feeding of the five thousand, besides women and children, only a little while before, are still unable to understand how so many are to be fed on so little.

Palpably it is the same story. But the second story is written by somebody who has read the first story. He is probably writing from memory, and so gives different numbers. Or, perhaps, he has oral tradition that the numbers in the first story were not right. Then, after the Gospel was written, the second story was inserted into the original manuscript by some clumsy hand—somebody who did not observe that it was there already. The scene is practically the same. In the case of the feeding of the five thousand the miracle takes place, apparently, on the east coast of the lake. In the case of the feeding of the four thousand the miracle takes place, apparently, on the north-east side of the lake, because Jesus, returning from the neighbourhood of Tyre and Sidon, is drawing nigh to Galilee.

Comparing the scenes of the two stories, the balance of probability is that, if the miracle occurred, it was on the east side, inasmuch as there are no such mountains "nigh unto the Sea of Galilee" on the north-east coast, and the road leading to Tyre and Sidon. The mountains at least are not "nigh."

After the feeding of the four thousand, Jesus takes ship and comes into the coasts of Magdala—that is to say he sails down the western shore of the Lake of Galilee. At Magdala, apparently, the Pharisees with the Sadducees come to Jesus and desire a sign from Heaven. What exactly do they mean by a sign if the miracles are not a sign? Jesus answers, by a striking figure, that the sign is present to their eyes if they could only see it.

> When it is evening, ye say, "It will be fair weather, for the sky is red. And in the morning, it will be foul weather to-day, for the sky is red and lowring." O ye hypocrites, ye can discern the face of the sky; but can ye not discern the signs of the times?

Nevertheless, he answers that to that wicked and adulterous generation which seeks a sign no sign shall be given except the sign of the prophet Jonas. He has said that to them before (XII, 38–41), apparently at or near Capernaum. This also occurs at or near Capernaum, near Magdala. Is it the same incident repeated? Is only the time different? This second demand for a sign is obviously the same as the first—the one near Capernaum, the other near Magdala. Capernaum and Magdala are adjoining and almost connecting towns. Almost the same words are used—*Matthew* is a little fuller, that is all.

In Chapter XVI there is clearly something omitted. Jesus and his disciples cross from Magdala, on the west coast of the lake, to the other side. They have forgotten to take bread with them. Jesus says, "Take heed and beware of the leaven of the Pharisees and of the Sadducees." The simple and rather stupid men who were his disciples think this (which has an obvious reference to the foregoing clash with the Pharisees and Sadducees) is a kind of reproach for their carelessness in forgetting the bread. Jesus says:

> O ye of little faith . . . do ye not yet understand, neither remember the five loaves of the five thousand, and how many baskets ye took up? How is it that ye do not understand that I spake it not to you concerning bread, that ye should beware of the leaven of the Pharisees and of the Sadducees?

Then they understood. Does this in any way strengthen the miracle of the feeding of the thousands? I do not think so.

Then Jesus comes to the borders (coasts) of Cæsarea Philippi. This was far north. The ship could not take them beyond the neighbourhood of Bethabara.

There, at Cæsarea Philippi, occurs a memorable scene. Jesus asks his disciples, "Whom do men say that I the Son of Man am?" "Son of Man" is not in itself a definite description. Clearly, it does not mean Messiah, Christ, King. It has some quite simple meaning. It is a kind of synonym for "I." Or it denotes the Son of Man as a species. The disciples answer Jesus that some say he is John the Baptist; some Elias; others Jeremias, or one of the other prophets. Jesus follows the disciples up. "But whom say ye that I am?" Peter answers, "Thou art the Christ, the Son of the living God."

This is the first time, assuming that the miracle of walking on the water did not occur, that any of the disciples has clearly said that Jesus is the Son of God. Several of them have been hovering on the verge of it—asking questions which show that the idea had suggested itself to their consciousness.

It is an argument against the miracle of the walking on the water that the disciples say to him, "Of a truth thou art the Son of God" (XIV, 33). If they had already said this to him in the ship he would not have asked the question at Cæsarea Philippi. He would have known what their answer would be. He would have known that they thought him the Son of God, and his answer, like his question, would have been superfluous.

He says to Peter: "Blessed art thou, Simon Bar-jona: for flesh and blood hath not revealed it unto thee, but my Father which is in Heaven."

Then follow two verses of much moment:

And I say also unto thee, that thou art Peter, and upon this rock I will build my church; and the gates of hell shall not prevail against it. And I will give unto thee the keys of the kingdom of Heaven: and whatsoever thou shalt bind on earth shall be bound in Heaven: and whatsoever thou shalt loose on earth shall be loosed in Heaven.

Here is a passage of vast consequence. Is it to be understood that because Peter has been told by revelation (flesh and blood not having told him) that Jesus was the Christ, the Son of God, therefore on Peter Jesus would build his Church, putting all power on earth into his hands, all salvation into his hands, placing it within his power to give or to deny Heaven, giving him the keys of Heaven?

Why?

Is it because, the revelation having been given to Peter, God has chosen Peter for this task? Put him above all his fellow disciples? Left the keys of Heaven for them in his hands? Is it in harmony with what he says elsewhere of the apostles? It is most certainly not. The language used to Peter seems definite and specific, but the soul of man revolts at the thought that into the hands of any mortal man God, through Jesus, gives the keys of Heaven. My soul revolts utterly against it. I cannot believe it. *It is not like Jesus.* He needs no human intermediary, and nowhere else demands one. I believe this passage to be falsely rendered.

Jesus then charges his disciples that they should tell no man that he was Jesus the Christ.

From that time (presumably during the next six days in which they remain in the neighbourhood of Cæsarea Philippi) Jesus shows his disciples how he must go up to Jerusalem and die there. He will suffer many things of the elders and chief priests and scribes, and be killed—and on the third day he will be raised to life again.

Peter rebukes him for this, saying, "Be it far from thee, Lord: this shall not be unto thee." He rebukes Peter, saying, "Get thee behind me, Satan."

Peter, who does not understand Christ's duty to God, is tempting Jesus to hold on to life when he knows he must die, to fulfil his mission. Peter is like the Satan who tempted him in the wilderness immediately after his baptism, and he used the same language to him as to Satan: "Get thee hence, Satan."

Then Jesus makes clearer than ever before that not only is he to die, but any who follow him must be prepared to die also. He uses the language applicable only to the punishment of the Roman powers for the worst of criminals, thus anticipating his own manner of death. He says:

> If any man will come after me, let him deny himself, and take up his cross and follow me. For whosoever will save his life shall lose it; and whosoever will lose his life for my sake shall find it. For what is a man profited, if he shall gain the whole world, and lose his own soul? Or what shall a man give in exchange for his soul? For the Son of Man shall come in the glory of his Father with his angels; and then he shall reward every man according to his works.

Then he seems to answer the unrecorded question of his excited disciples—when shall this be? "Verily I say unto you, there be some standing here, which shall not taste of death, till they see the Son of Man coming in his kingdom."

To this exalted mood he has now risen, and carried his disciples with him. Six days afterwards comes the great moment of the Transfiguration. What is it? And what does it mean?

General Comments

I

1. That the sayings directly attributed by Matthew to Jesus are in the main of the very highest value—that they are of the essence of his teaching.

2. That a few of the sayings in *Matthew* are utterly out of

harmony with the character of Jesus as revealed in the book, and with the holy teachings of Jesus as reported in the book.

3. That two or three incidents are repeated, with little change of scene or words.

4. That some passages (such as the long passage on sending out the disciples) are clearly out of place and time.

5. That there is a manifest omission between the sending out of the disciples and their coming back. Nothing is said about their return. The next time anything occurs the disciples whom he has just sent out are with him. Obviously, there is some unrecorded lapse of time. Where was Jesus during that time? And where had the disciples been? How had they fared, and had any of the troubles he foretold occurred to them? *Matthew* does not say.

6. The two miracles of the feeding of the thousands of men, beside women and children, are clearly the same miracle, only differing as to scene and number of persons fed, and quantity of food used to feed them. But the geographical statements of where the miracle occurred, what the movements of Jesus were before the miracle and after it, the time at which it occurred and the time at which subsequent incidents occurred, convince me that there is not reasonable evidence to justify the belief that the miracles of feeding ever occurred at all. I reject these on other grounds than those of time and geography. Further, I reject the miracle of the walking on the water on grounds of time, what happened before, when it happened and what happened after. Further, the words spoken by the disciples in the ship, "Of a truth thou art the Son of God," make the same words and their implication at Cæsarea Philippi, and the promise made to Peter, impossible.

I do not believe that either the miracle of the walking on the water or that of the feeding of the thousands ever occurred. I think they were interpolated into the narrative of Matthew by a much later writer.

7. Further, I think the passage addressed to Peter at Cæsarea Philippi is open to grave suspicion of interpolation, or of interpretation.

8. I think the scene of the Canaanite woman and her daughter assigns words to Jesus which he could not have spoken without being false to anything he ever said or did. I do not believe he said them. And, if Matthew wrote them, I think it must have been in Jerusalem about the period of the conflict between the Mother

Church at Jerusalem and St. Paul about the inclusion of the Gentiles.

II

1. The whole of the ministry of Jesus from his baptism to the Transfiguration takes place, according to *Matthew*, in the towns of Galilee; in Ituræa, from the due east side of Jordan up to Mount Hermon; in the borders (coasts) of Tyre and Sidon.

2. Jesus is repeatedly in his own country (the neighbourhood of Nazareth) and repeatedly in Capernaum. He is never in Tiberias or Sepphoris (if it still existed). He is once in Nain. He is never in Cana of Galilee. He is never as far south as Samaria. He never goes to Jerusalem.

3. The time occupied by this part of the ministry is not clearly indicated. We do not hear of the Feast of the Passover. Therefore, I conclude that the ministry begins after the Passover of that year. I think it probable that the baptism of Jesus occurred in April; that John the Baptist was arrested not long after the return of Jesus to Galilee—probably end of May. I think the scene of the disciples walking in the ripe corn could not have taken place later than the early part of June, when the harvest in Palestine is reaped.

I think the disciples of John came to Jesus to ask whether he was the one who was to come when he was in Galilee and in the neighbourhood of his own country. There was probably a long interval between the arrest of John the Baptist and his execution. This interval is not, apparently, accounted for in *Matthew*. It was probably during this interval that the disciples of Jesus were going about on the missionary errands on which he had sent them. I do not think *Matthew* gives any account of where Jesus was during that period. He may have been in Judæa, Samaria, and above all in Jerusalem while his disciples were away; one of the other Gospels will show this. They may have rejoined him on his return from Judæa to Galilee.

I think it was then, and when he was again in his own country, that he heard of the death of John the Baptist, and of Herod's inquiries about himself, and that he then went up to the territory of Herod Philip. I think the visit to Cæsarea Philippi and to Mount Hermon took place at this period—this climax of the second great period of his ministry.

I think, therefore, that (according to *Matthew*) the chronology of the ministry may perhaps be this:

Baptism about end of April, A.D. 29.
Arrest of John the Baptist about end of May, 29.
Preaching, teaching throughout Galilee, working of miracles in Galilee down to the autumn of 29.

	A.D.
Sending out the twelve disciples	Autumn 29
Going (himself) into Judæa	Autumn 29
Returning (himself) from Judæa to Galilee probably early part of	30
Disciples rejoining him in Galilee, probably early part of	30
News of the death of John the Baptist, probably about	February 30
At Cæsarea Philippi, probably about	March 30
Journey to Jerusalem, probably from	March 30
In Jerusalem, probably from	April 30
Death	April 30

I see no reason in *Matthew* for thinking that the ministry lasted longer than one year—indeed a little less.

General Summary of the Effect of the Ministry

1. I think Jesus was sure, from the time of his baptism, that he was the Messiah, the messenger of God, who had been foretold by the prophets. But, inasmuch as the people looked for a very different Messiah (not a spiritual Messiah, but a temporal one) that he concealed, as far as he could, his Messianic character for the time being, telling everybody to "tell no man" of his miracles, and so on. The people of Galilee were at first deeply astonished by the daring and authority with which Jesus taught a gospel that seemed to supersede the law of Moses, to go further than the law of Moses, and, in some instances, almost to abrogate it.

2. I think the people were more concerned with the power of Jesus to work miracles than with his teaching, although it is clear that his teaching had a great fascination for great multitudes.

3. It is obvious that the people were less disposed to obey the

call of Jesus to Repent, for the kingdom of Heaven was at hand, than to take advantage of his gifts of healing.

4. That Jesus was deeply disappointed at this, and that it finally brought a deep feeling of resentment, which led him to predict woes to the cities which had not repented although they had seen the mighty works he had wrought, and must have realized (if they had known their scriptures) that the prophesied Messiah had come.

5. I think he was angered by the constant nagging of the Pharisees, who fastened on to his transgression of certain of the minor Mosaic laws (such as the rigid observance of the Sabbath, the washing before meat, and so on), and that this led to the fierce denunciation of the formalism and hypocrisy of those who put the letter of the law above the spirit of it.

6. Evidently he believed that disease was the product of sin, and that the way to cast out diseases (devils) was to forgive sins. And that when he claimed the power to forgive sins the Pharisees (and others) thought he was committing blasphemy.

7. I think his pity for the people was very deep (living under the peril of the judgment), and that he sent out his disciples to teach and to heal in a world full of hypocrisy and sin, and therefore disease-giving.

8. I think this sending out of his disciples on their missionary errand was the end of the first period of his ministry; the end also of the first of the two periods of his ministry in Galilee.

9. I think that throughout this period, from his baptism, until he parts from his disciples, he is convinced that he is the Messiah, the messenger whom God had promised to send to bring in the kingdom of Heaven.

10. I think this was the climax of his first phase. He, himself, the Messiah, was now going up to Jerusalem.

CHAPTER XI

The Ministry
(According to St. Mark and St. Luke)

I. According to St. Mark

THE Gospel of Mark begins by announcing that it is the Gospel (or good news) of Jesus Christ, the Son of God.

Then the book quotes the prophets who foretell, "As it is written . . . Behold I send my messenger before thy face, which shall prepare thy way before thee. The voice of one crying in the wilderness, Prepare ye the way of the Lord, make his paths straight." Is this the prophecy? Then comes the fulfilment. "John did baptize in the wilderness, and preach the baptism of repentance for the remission of sins." All the land of Judæa and they of Jerusalem went out to him, and he baptized them in the Jordan, confessing their sins. John was clothed in camel's hair and did eat locusts and wild honey. He said: "There cometh one mightier than I after me, the latchet of whose shoes I am not worthy to stoop down and unloose. I indeed have baptized you with water, but he shall baptize you with the Holy Ghost."

It came to pass in those days that Jesus came from Nazareth of Galilee and was baptized by John. As he was coming out of the water he saw the heavens opened, and the Spirit (clearly the Holy Ghost) like a dove descending upon him. And he heard a voice from heaven saying, "Thou art my beloved Son, in whom I am well pleased."

Then the Spirit (still the Holy Ghost) drove him into the wilderness. He was in the wilderness forty days tempted of Satan. He was with the wild beasts, and the angels ministered to him. The wilderness, as will be seen later, must have been the wilderness of Judæa, about the Jordan.

Here there is a break, and then we are told that John was put in prison—*Mark* does not here say by whom or why. After this (perhaps by reason of it) Jesus comes into Galilee and preaches

448

the Gospel of the kingdom of God. This may be an extension of the message of John.

The message of Jesus is, "The time is fulfilled, and the kingdom of God is at hand; repent ye and believe the gospel" (the good news). This is something more than John said.

Jesus, walking by the Lake of Galilee, saw Simon and Andrew, his brother, fishing, for they were fishers. He called to them to follow him, saying they shall be "fishers of men." Straightway they forsook their nets and followed him.

A little further (presumably on the shore of the Lake of Galilee) Jesus sees James and John, the sons of one Zebedee (of whom we know nothing), also fishermen, mending their nets. Jesus calls to them also, and, in like manner, straightway they leave their father in the ship with his hired servants and go after Jesus. Evidently all this occurs on the southwest coast of Galilee. They go together into Capernaum. And there Jesus enters into the synagogue on the Sabbath Day and teaches. Presumably he repeats the message above, that the time is fulfilled and the kingdom of God is at hand, and they must repent and believe the Gospel. The people are astonished at his doctrine. He preaches with authority.

Then comes the first of his recorded miracles. A man with an unclean spirit comes out, saying, "Let us alone; what have we to do with thee, thou Jesus of Nazareth? Art thou come to destroy us? I know thee who thou art, the Holy One of God." Jesus rebukes this unclean spirit, telling it to hold its peace and come out of the man. The unclean spirit cries with a loud voice and tears the man, but comes out of him. The onlookers are amazed. "What thing is this?" they say, "what new doctrine is this? For with authority commandeth he even the unclean spirits, and they do obey him."

Immediately the fame of Jesus spreads through all the region round about Galilee. The foregoing looks like an interpolated passage. The story is continued in the next verse. Jesus comes out of the synagogue and goes with James and John into the house of Simon and Andrew. Simon is a married man, and his wife's mother is lying sick of a fever. They tell Jesus about her, whereupon he takes her by the hand and lifts her up, and immediately the fever leaves her, and she ministers to them.

In the evening of that day (apparently) the people bring all their diseased and all that are possessed of devils (clearly a different malady) to Jesus. So that all the city seemed to be gathered at the door. He heals many of divers diseases, and casts out many devils. It is said that he forbade the devils to speak, because they knew him. Evidently he did not wish the people to know him as "the holy one of God."

Next morning, rising up a great while before day, he leaves Capernaum and goes into a solitary place to pray. Simon and others follow him. And when they find him they say, "All men seek thee." He answers, "Let us go into the next towns, that I may preach there also." The next towns would be Magdala on the south, Chorazin on the north.

Apparently, they go (where to is not said), and Jesus preaches in the synagogues throughout all Galilee, and he works miracles as he goes through. A leper comes to him on the way, a leper kneeling to him and beseeching him to make him clean. Moved with compassion, Jesus touches the man and he is made clean, and the leprosy leaves the man immediately. And sending the man away he charges him strictly not to say anything about his case to any one. But he is to show himself and fulfil the requirements of the law of Moses. But the man publishes the story of his curing, with the result that Jesus can no more walk openly in the city. So he stays outside in the desert places. But all the same the people come to him from every quarter.

He goes again to Capernaum, perhaps to the house of Simon. It is noised about that he is there, and many gather to hear him and he preaches there. There is some hiatus here. The following miracle cannot have been worked in Capernaum.

Again the people bring one sick of the palsy, who has to be carried by four others. They cannot get near to Jesus by reason of the crowd, so they uncover the roof where he was, and having broken it up they let down the bed on which the man sick of the palsy lay.

It is difficult to follow this. If Jesus was in the house, and the crowd was dense about the door, they must have climbed to the roof from the back (there are sometimes steps at the back of eastern houses), to get at the opening in the roof, for the coming and going of the people who live in it and use the roof. But finding the opening not sufficient for the sick man on his mattress, they broke open the roof until the space was large enough to admit of the lowering of the mattress.

When Jesus sees how great is their faith, he says to the sick man, "Son, thy sins be forgiven thee." Certain scribes are sitting there, and they say to each other, "Why doth this man thus speak blasphemies? Who can forgive sins but God only?"

Jesus answers them strangely. He says, "Whether is it easier to say to the sick of the palsy, Thy sins be forgiven thee; or to say, Arise, and take up thy bed, and walk? But that ye may know that the Son of Man hath power on earth to forgive sins, I say unto thee [the sick man] Arise, and take up thy bed, and go thy way into thine house." And immediately the man rises and takes up his bed and goes before them all. Wherefore, they are all amazed and glorify God, saying, "We never saw it on this fashion."

Here is the fact that Jesus attributes the man's sickness to his sin. When the sin is forgiven the sickness leaves the man. Jesus claims the right to forgive sins. Then Jesus goes again to the seaside. The people follow him in multitudes and he teaches them. Previously (it was said) he returned to Capernaum, and the "house" referred to is presumably that of Simon. But Capernaum is on the seaside, therefore the house in which Jesus cured the palsy was not on the seaside. The story is a jumble. He was now by the seaside (position not given—presumably it is near Capernaum). As he passed by he saw Levi, sitting at the receipt of custom, and said to him, "Follow me." And Levi rose and followed him. It came to pass that Jesus sat at meat at his house. Whose house—Levi's? Or is it the house of Jesus in Capernaum? It has never been said that Jesus had a house. On the contrary it has been said that he had not where to lay his head. My conclusion is that Levi's house is meant. The disciples are at meat there also. The scribes and Pharisees seeing Jesus eat with publicans and sinners mention this to the disciples. Jesus hears this and says, "They that are whole have no need of the physician, but they that are sick. I came not to call the righteous, but sinners to repentance." To explain why he and his disciples do not fast he uses the figure given in *Matthew:* "Can the children of the bridechamber fast while the bridegroom is with them?"

He passes through the cornfields on the Sabbath Day, and the disciples pluck the ears of corn. The Pharisees call it unlawful on the Sabbath Day. He answers by telling them what David did, when he went into the house of God and did eat the showbread, also what the priests do in the Temple. Jesus obviously knows the land better than his critics. "Therefore the Son of Man is lord also of the Sabbath."

He enters into the synagogue. Clearly, he is still in Capernaum. He cures the man with the withered hand. It is on the Sabbath Day. The scribes are standing by watching him with suspicion. He looks round on them with anger, "being grieved for the hardness of their hearts," and says to the man with the withered hand, "Stretch forth thine hand." The man does so and he is healed.

The Pharisees straightway take council with the Herodians how they may destroy him. Who and what are the Herodians? The sole offence of Jesus, down to this time, is that he does good on the Sabbath Day, when by the strict letter of the law he should do nothing. His enemies want to destroy him for that. Does this mean that they want to kill him? Jesus withdraws himself to the sea.

Here again it is difficult to follow the geography. If, all this time, Jesus is at Capernaum (there is nothing to the contrary) he is already on the margin of the sea.

> Jesus withdrew himself with his disciples to the sea; and a great multitude from Galilee followed him, and from Judæa, and from Jerusalem, and from Idumæa, and from beyond Jordan, and they about Tyre and Sidon, a great multitude.

Here is a complete jumble from which there is no way out but one—that Jesus went into Samaria, all other places being covered by the foregoing. And it was impossible for people to "follow" him from north and south at the same time. My inference is that the writer meant to say that from all parts of Palestine people came to him when they heard what great miracles he was working. Either this, or else the writer of the Gospel as it has come down to us did not know the country, and was using names without knowledge.

Jesus tells his disciples to keep a small ship waiting for him so that he might escape at will from the multitudes that thronged here. Meantime, people who had plagues and unclean spirits fell down before him, crying "Thou art the Son of God." He charges such people "not to make him known."

Jesus went up into the mountain and he called unto him whom he would, and they came. That is to say that he had only to call and anybody came to him. There he ordained twelve "that they should be with him, and that he might send them forth to preach, and to have power to heal sicknesses, and to cast out devils." The names of the twelve are given—as in *Matthew*.

They must have come down from the mountain, for we hear next that they go into a house, and a multitude crowds about it.

Then the friends of Jesus hear of all this, and they say, "He is beside himself," and they try to lay hold of him. Obviously these friends include his family and they conclude that he has become insane.

Here (III, 22) comes a break, which probably means the interpolation of a passage. Verses 22 to 30 describe how scribes come down from Jerusalem and say: "He hath Beelzebub, and by the prince of devils casteth he out devils." He answers them by asking (his usual method of argument), "How can Satan cast out Satan?" Either this goes before the reference to the friends or it was put in to account for it.

Then his brothers and his mother come, and standing outside the house send in for him. He replies, "Who is my mother, or my brethren?" Looking round about him on his disciples he says, "Behold my mother and my brethren! For whosoever shall do the will of God, the same is my brother, and my sister, and mother."

The exaltation of his spirit is fast separating him from all human ties. He has reached a great stage of religious frenzy to make this reply possible.

He begins again to teach by the seaside. Obviously, he has not yet left the neighbourhood of the Lake of Galilee, for there is no hint that he goes west to the sea by Haifa—the Mediterranean. Here he sits in a ship and teaches the great multitude on the shore. He teaches them by parables, all intended to define and describe the kingdom of God which is soon to come, as in the parable of the sower and the parable of the mustard seed. It is observable that Jesus nearly always uses the similes of the husbandman, rarely of the builder, which almost suggests that he was not a carpenter.

In the evening after speaking these parables he takes ship and passes over to the other side. Plainly this means he sails from the western coast of Galilee to the eastern coast. A storm of wind comes, the ship fills with water. He lies asleep on the hinder part of the ship. The disciples awake him, saying, "Master, carest thou not that we perish?"

Jesus rises, rebukes the wind, and says to the sea, "Peace, be still." And the wind ceases and there is a great calm. Then he says to the disciples, "Why are ye so fearful? How is it that ye have no faith?" The disciples fear exceedingly and say among themselves, "What manner of man is this, that even the wind and the sea obey him?"

They come, in the ship, to the eastern side of the Lake of Galilee, the country of the Gadarenes. It is the south-east and south. Does this correspond with the country called Gennesaret? I think not. Or is it Gadara, to the south-east of Galilee? In *Matthew* (VIII, 28) it is said to be "the country of the Gergesenes." Jesus (in *Matthew*) was apparently in Capernaum, and he "gave commandment to depart unto the other side"—from north-west to south-east—if the country of the Gergesenes is Gadara. The incident of the swine occurs in both Gospels.

On leaving the ship he comes upon a man with an unclean spirit, who had his dwelling among the tombs. No man could bind him, not even with chains, for as often as he was fettered he broke his fetters in pieces, and no man could tame him. Always by day and night he was in the mountains, and in the tombs, crying and cutting himself with stones. When he sees Jesus afar off he runs to him and cries, "What have I to do with thee, Jesus, thou Son of the most high God? I adjure thee by God that thou torment me not." For Jesus had said to him, "Come out of the man, thou unclean spirit." Then Jesus asks, "What is thy name?" "My name is Legion, for we are many," says the evil spirit, and beseeches Jesus that he will not send them away out of the country. A great herd of swine is feeding near at hand, and the devils implore Jesus to allow them to enter the swine. Jesus gives them leave to do this. Then the unclean spirits come out of the man and enter into the swine, and the swine (numbering about two thousand) run violently down a steep place into the sea and are drowned.

The latter part of the story is extremely difficult. First, a minor point. If the miracle took place on the eastern side there is a "steep place" down which the swine might run. If it took place on the south-east there is no such steep place, the country of the Gadarenes being flat to the water's edge for miles inland. In *Matthew* the miracle takes place in the country of the Gergesenes. There is no "steep place" in the country of the Gadarenes near to the sea. In *Matthew*, unlike *Mark*, there are two men possessed of devils. The rest of the story is the same in *Matthew* as in *Mark*.

I confess that I intensely dislike this miracle, so far as it concerns the swine. It serves no apparent purpose. It almost looks as if Jesus were making terms with the evil spirits, or was encouraging the destruction of the swine. Also, it is impossible to understand the demonology which merely requires the destruction of the swine. In short, it is an expression of the demon spirit that is utterly unintelligible to humanity. It can scarcely be assumed that the vengeance of the devils is against the owners of the swine (destroying their property), not against the swine themselves. This alleged miracle stands alone among the miracles concerning devils in its apparent uselessness.

The swineherds fly back to their city (not named) and the people come out to see what has been done. They see Jesus, and the man who was possessed with the devil. The violent man is now sitting clothed and in his right mind. The people from the city are afraid and pray Jesus to depart out of their country. This means that they believed he cast out devils by the power of devils, therefore he was himself a devil.

I find it difficult to reconcile these conflicting stories, namely that the people ask Jesus to go away and that they crowd about him and follow him; that they believe him to be a master of the devils and yet that they call him the son of David and ask him to heal them. I feel unable to accept this miracle so far as it concerns the swine. I think verses 9–14 of Chapter V ought to be omitted.

Jesus passed over by ship to the other side. If he was in the country of the Gadarenes (on the south-east side) he probably returned to the western side. Later, we heard of the going back to his own country.

He is near the coast when one of the rulers of the synagogue, Jairus by name, comes, falls at his feet and beseeches him to lay his hands on and heal his little daughter, who is on the point of death. Jesus goes with him towards his house. A great multitude follow him, and throng about him. A woman who has had an issue of blood for twelve years, tried many physicians and suffered from them, getting no better but becoming worse, comes behind him in the press and touches his garment, saying, "If I may touch but his clothes, I shall be whole." Straightway she is cured; she is healed of her plague. Jesus immediately knows that virtue has gone out of him, turns and says, "Who touched my clothes?" The disciples say, "Thou seest the multitude thronging thee, and sayest thou 'Who touched me?'" But Jesus sees the woman, and she, fearing and trembling, falls at his feet and tells him the truth. "Daughter," he says, "thy faith hath made thee whole."

People come and tell the ruler of the synagogue his little daughter is dead, and say, "Why troublest thou the Master any further?"

But Jesus says to the father, "Be not afraid, only believe." Then coming to the house of the ruler of the synagogue and seeing a multitude about it, weeping and wailing, he goes into the house, and says, "Why make ye this ado, and weep? The damsel is not dead, but sleepeth." The people laugh him to scorn. He puts them all out, takes the father and mother of the child, and with three of his disciples, Peter, James and John, he goes into the room in which the child lies. He takes the child by the hand and says, "Damsel I say unto thee, arise." And straightway the child rises and walks, and Jesus orders that food should be given her. She was twelve years of age.

II.　According to St. Luke

According to the Gospel of Luke the ministry of Jesus began when he was "about thirty years of age." This is the time fixed by Luke as that of his baptism. Luke fixes the period of the baptism by the period in which John baptized.

This, he says, was the fifteenth year of the reign of Tiberius Cæsar, when Pontius Pilate was governor of Judæa and Herod (Antipas) was tetrarch of Galilee, and Annas and Caiaphas were high priests.

These dates are confusing. The reign of Tiberius began in A.D. 14. Therefore, fifteen years after that date would be A.D. 29. If Jesus was about thirty years of age at that time he must have been born either in the first year of the Christian era or the year before it. But in that case he was not born, as we are told in the Gospels (*Matthew* and *Luke*), in the time of Herod the Great, because Herod died in 4 B.C. In order to explain away the difficulty it is said the years of Tiberius's reign would date from the year in which he became acting emperor, not the year of the death of Augustus. (It would be as reasonable to reckon the reign of George IV from the year in which he became regent to George III.) But if we date back to the year at which Tiberius became regent to Augustus we are back at A.D. 12, perhaps A.D. 11, and in the latter year Pontius Pilate was not yet governor of Judæa.

After the baptism Jesus "returned from Jordan, and was led by the Spirit into the wilderness."

"Returned" forbids the idea that Jesus (who presumably came to the baptism from Galilee) went on to the wilderness south-east of Jerusalem. It points to the country which lies north of Jericho. The Temptation is essentially the same in *Luke* as in *Mark* and *Matthew*. After the Temptation the Devil "departed from him for a season."

> And Jesus returned in the power of the Spirit into Galilee; and there went out a fame of him through all the region round about. And he taught in their synagogues, being glorified of all.

Why his fame should go about before he had yet done anything that is recorded is not explained. Did he begin his ministry before his baptism?

> And he came to Nazareth, where he had been brought up; and as his custom was, he went into the synagogue on the Sabbath Day, and stood up for to read.

This is very significant. He had been accustomed to do this before he went to Jordan to be baptized by John. We see a little later in *Luke* that his first appearance in Nazareth after the baptism was on the first Sabbath after his return to Galilee. Therefore the words "as his custom was" *must* refer to the period previous to the baptism. We begin to see why his fame passed through the region round about. He was already known as a teacher before he went to John.

> And there was delivered unto him the book of the prophet Esaias. And when he had opened the book, he found the place where it was written.

This is to say, he deliberately looked for and found the passage he read. He rises and reads:

> The Spirit of the Lord is upon me, because He hath anointed me to preach the Gospel to the poor; He hath sent me to heal the broken-hearted, to preach deliverance to the captives, and recovering of sight to the blind, to set at liberty them that are bruised, to preach the acceptable year of the Lord.

This is not literally exact from *Isaiah*. But it is of the essence and heart of the manner of Jesus as the Messiah.

He closes the book and sits down. All eyes in the synagogue are fastened on him. What does he mean by this? He tells them: "This day is this scripture fulfilled in your ears." Implying that to-day I fulfil this scripture. This is what I, Jesus of Nazareth, have come to do. The Spirit of the Lord is upon me, and it has anointed me to do these things.

The people wonder. They say, "Is not this Joseph's son?" Jesus sees what they think. Then follows a strange passage. He says, "Ye will surely say unto me this proverb, Physician, heal thyself; whatsoever we have heard done in Capernaum, do also here in thy country."

Clearly, he had already worked miracles in Capernaum. When? Not since his baptism. Capernaum, which is farther north, he has clearly, according to *Luke,* not yet reached. "Verily I say unto you, No prophet is accepted in his own country." Then he tells them in effect that they are not to pride themselves upon being the chosen people.

Many widows were in Israel in the days of Elias, when the heaven was shut up three years and six months, when great famine was throughout all the land; but unto none of them was Elias sent, save unto Sarepta, a city of Sidon, unto a woman that was a widow. And many lepers were in Israel in the time of Eliseus the prophet; and none of them was cleansed, saving Naaman the Syrian.

This seems to say, the Gentiles may be preferred before you when the great day of the Kingdom comes. The people of Nazareth are filled with wrath at this. They rise up and thrust Jesus out of the city, and lead him to the brow of the hill whereon their city was built that they might cast him down headlong. But he passed through the midst of them and went his way. Jesus then leaves Nazareth and comes to Capernaum. Luke states that Capernaum is a city of Galilee, thus showing that he is not writing for Jews. At Capernaum Jesus teaches on the Sabbath Day. The people are astonished at his doctrine, for his word is with power. *Power* was the distinctive note of Jesus, both in word and act.

In the synagogue there was a man who had an unclean devil, and cried with a loud voice, "Let us alone; what have we to do with thee, thou Jesus of Nazareth? Art thou come to destroy us? I know thee who thou art; the Holy One of God." This incident is, according to *Mark,* but in *Matthew* and *Mark* no mention is made of Nazareth at this point. Jesus cast the unclean spirit out of the man. And the fame of Jesus went out into every place of the country round about.

He went into Simon's house (this is the first time Luke has spoken of Simon) and cured his wife's mother of her fever. When the sun was set the people brought their sick to him, and he laid his hands on them and cured them. And he cast out other devils, who cried out, saying "Thou art Christ, the Son of God." But he rebuked them, telling them not to speak, for they knew that he was Christ.

Did he not want to be known as the Christ?

When it was day (next day clearly) he departed and went into a desert place. But the people sought him out, and found him and stayed with him, and besought him not to depart from them. Jesus replied that he must preach the Gospel of the Kingdom to other cities (beside Capernaum). And he preached in the synagogues of Galilee.

The people pressed upon him to hear the word of God as he stood by the Lake of Galilee, so he entered into one of the ships, which was Simon's, and asked him to thrust a little out from the shore. Then he sat down and taught the people from the ship. His sermon is not given here, however.

After he has finished speaking, he tells Simon to go out into the deep and let down the nets. Simon answers that they have toiled all night and taken nothing. Nevertheless, at his word they will let down their nets again.

They do so and bring up a great quantity of fish. Their nets break and they beckon to their partners in another ship to come and help, and both ships become so full that they begin to sink. Simon (now called Peter), seeing this, falls down at Jesus's knee, saying, "Depart from me, for I am a sinful man, O Lord." Jesus answers, "Fear not; from henceforth thou shalt catch men." And when they had brought their ships to land, they forsook all and followed him.

This is not a very inspiring story. Apparently, the sole reason that Simon and his partners —James and John—become the disciples of Jesus is that he brings them a great catch of fish! I assume they recognize his supernatural power.

Jesus is in a "certain city . . ." (Luke is very uncertain about place names in Palestine, concerning which he knows little). A man full of leprosy comes and falls at his feet saying, "Lord, if thou wilt, thou canst make me clean." Jesus puts forth his hand and touches the man, saying, "I will: be thou clean." And immediately the leprosy leaves him. In *Luke,* as in *Mark* and *Matthew,* Jesus is constantly charging the people on whom he works such miracles to tell no man. This man is to show himself to the priest and offer for cleansing, according as Moses commanded. But so much the more his fame goes abroad, and great multitudes come together to hear and be healed. Jesus withdraws himself into the wilderness to pray.

A break occurs here (V, 16). Then on a certain day, as he was teaching, and there were Pharisees and doctors of the law sitting by "which were come out of every town of Galilee and Judæa and Jerusalem [the repeated reference to Jerusalem, as distinct from Judæa, is as marked in *Luke* as in the other Synoptic Gospels], and the power of the Lord was present to heal them," a man who had a palsy was brought to him. But his friends could not get at Jesus by reason of the crowd about the doorway, so they let the bed of the sick man down into the room where Jesus was in the house by removing the tiling on the roof. Jesus said to the man, "Man, thy sins are forgiven thee."

At this the scribes and Pharisees said among themselves, "Who is this which speaketh blasphemies? Who can forgive sins, but God alone?" Jesus answered them as in *Mark,* and then said to the sick man, "Arise, and take up thy couch, and go into thine house." And the man went home, glorifying God. The people were amazed and filled with fear, and said, "We have seen strange things to-day."

Jesus sees a publican, named Levi, sitting at the receipt of custom. Jesus says, "Follow me." The publican does so. Levi makes a great feast for Jesus, at which there is a great company of publicans and others. The same scene occurs as in *Mark.* Jesus says, "I came not to call the righteous, but sinners to repentance."

They say to him, "Why do the disciples of John fast often . . . likewise the disciples of the Pharisees; but thine eat and drink?" Jesus makes the same answer as in *Mark:* "Can ye make the children of the bridechamber fast, while the bridegroom is with them?" All this seems to be copied by Luke from *Mark* (Chapter II). This for Luke, on the whole, is less remarkable than Mark.

And it came to pass on the second Sabbath after the first, that he went through the corn-fields; and his disciples plucked the ears of corn, and did eat, rubbing them in their hands.

This verse is important. It shows the time of the passing through the corn-fields and thereby the time of the baptism. The corn is ripe about the middle of May. This was about a fortnight later than the arrival of Jesus in Galilee; before that Jesus had been forty days in the wilderness during the Temptation. Thus the baptism took place about fifty-five days before the middle of May —about the middle of March. The year was probably A.D. 29. This is the clearest date for chronological purposes in the Gospels.

Certain of the Pharisees objected that to pluck the corn was not lawful on the Sabbath Day. (These nagging old nobodies, who could think of nothing but the little things when they were in the presence of the big things!) Jesus answered as in the other Gospels, concluding with, "The Son of Man is Lord also of the Sabbath."

He enters into the synagogue and cures the man with the withered hand, encountering once more the accusation of the scribes and Pharisees about the breaking of the Sabbath. The foregoing is transcribed almost literally from *Mark*. The scribes and Pharisees now commune one with another what they may do to Jesus.

There is an obvious break at verse twelve of Chapter VI.

> And it came to pass in those days [two or three weeks after the return from the Baptism] that he went out into a mountain to pray, and continued all night in prayer to God.

It is repeatedly said of Jesus that he goes into the mountains to pray. He is generally alone.

> And when it was day, he called unto him his disciples, and of them he chose twelve, whom also he named apostles. [VI, 13]

Jesus then came down with them and stood in the plain below the mountains, and in the presence of the company of other disciples and of a great multitude of people out of Judæa, and Jerusalem and from the sea coast of Tyre and Sidon, which came to hear him, and to be healed of their diseases. Then follows a fine scene of the ordination of his apostles (VI, 20–49). He is not sending them out at this point. The place ("the plain") was probably between Capernaum and Magdala on the lowland at the foot of the mountain land—the Lake of Galilee glistening in front. The time probably about June of the year 29. Warm sunshine, perhaps hot. Early morning. The few boats on the sea. The patrol from Tiberias passing by on the road between them and the sea.

After this ordination of the apostles Jesus re-enters Capernaum.

A certain centurion sends the elders of the Jews to Jesus to ask him to come and heal his servant who was ready to die. The elders of the Jews (evidently not yet unfriendly towards Jesus) urge that the centurion was a good friend of their nation who had built a synagogue for them, so he was worthy that Jesus should do this for him. Jesus goes with the elders of the Jews towards the house of the centurion. Before he reaches the house the centurion sends friends, saying, "Lord, trouble not thyself, for I am not worthy that thou shouldest enter under my roof . . . but say in a word, and my servant shall be healed."

Jesus is astonished at this instance of faith in a Gentile (probably a Roman) and says, "I have not found so great faith, no, not in Israel."

The friends of the centurion return to his house and find the servant healed.

This story has points of resemblance to the story in *Mark* of Jairus, one of the rulers of the synagogue, whose little daughter lay near to death. This occurs in Capernaum.

The day after Jesus goes into a city called Nain, and many of his disciples and much people go with him. It is a long journey and a very steep one, up a mountain side, but perhaps not impossible. The position of Nain is high up on the hills, south of Nazareth. As they come nigh to the gate of the city, a dead man is being carried out. He is the only son of his mother, and she is a widow. Many people of the city are with her. When Jesus sees her, he is touched with compassion and says to her, "Weep not." Then he approaches the bier and touches it, and the bearers stand still.

Then Jesus addresses the man on the bier. "Young man, I say unto thee, Arise." And he that was dead sat up, and began to speak. And Jesus delivered him to his mother.

This is a very touching and beautiful scene. Jesus and his following going up the hillside to Nain. The little procession coming out of the gate on the way to the cemetery. The widow. Jesus. The bier stopped. Was the young man dead? I do not think so. The effect of the miracle is that "There came a fear on all; and they glorified God, saying that a great prophet is risen up among us; and that God has visited His people. And this rumour of him went forth throughout all Judæa, and throughout all the region round about." Round about Nain would mean Galilee, particularly the country of Jesus.

Clearly, the standards by which the people of that time judged a prophet to be great was his power of working great miracles, not by what he said, what his power might be of foretelling future events or of speaking as from God.

The rumour of Jesus that went through Judæa reached John the Baptist through his disciples. John was lying in prison in the fortress east of the Jordan, but his disciples were probably in Judæa, and hearing these stories from Galilee about Jesus they repeated them to John in Peræa. Whereupon John sent two of his disciples to Jesus to ask, "Art thou he that should come? Or look we for another?"

This shows that, at the baptism of Jesus, John did not know that he was baptizing the Messiah. This is also made clear by the fact that while the forerunner of the Messiah, John the Baptist went on preaching the forerunner's message after the baptism, just as before it. But now, hearing of the astonishing things Jesus is doing, he thinks Jesus must be the Messiah himself already come. Nobody can know better than Jesus whether this is so. Therefore, John sends two disciples to ask him.

Where the following scene takes place we do not know. Jesus was last heard of in Nain. This was probably somewhere near Nain. At least in Galilee. When the disciples of John the Baptist come to Jesus with John's question, Jesus is healing sick people. Jesus goes on with his healing. Then he turns to the disciples and says, "Go your way, and tell John what things ye have seen and heard . . . and blessed is he, whosoever shall not be offended in me."

This scene also has points of beauty. The crowds pressing upon Jesus, the healed going away with shouts of thanksgiving. Then a moment's pause—the crowds dispersing—and then Jesus speaking to John's disciples standing open-mouthed by his side. The disciples of John go back, speechless, perhaps. And then Jesus turns to his own people who remain, and speaks about John. Not a note of jealousy on John's side, and of course none on the side of Jesus. Jesus says:

What went ye out into the wilderness for to see? A reed shaken with the wind? But what went ye out for to see? A man clothed in soft raiment? Behold, they which are gorgeously apparelled, and live delicately, are in kings' courts. But what went ye out for to see? A prophet? Yea, I say unto you, and much more than a prophet. This is he, of whom it is written, Behold I send my messenger before thy face, which shall prepare thy way before thee. For I say unto you, Among those that are born of woman there is not a greater prophet than John the Baptist; but he that is least in the kingdom of God is greater than he.

All the people that heard him, including the publicans, "justified God" and were baptized. But the Pharisees and lawyers "rejected the counsel of God," and Jesus denounced them (see Chapter VII, 31–35).

Then came a touching and beautiful incident. Where it takes place we are not told. Almost certainly in Galilee.

One of the Pharisees asks Jesus into his house to eat. He goes and sits down to meat. Then a woman in the city, "which was a sinner," when she knew that Jesus sat at meat in the Pharisee's house, brought an alabaster box of ointment, and standing at his feet behind him weeping began to wash his feet with her tears and wipe them with the hair of her head, kissing them and anointing them with the ointment.

When the Pharisee who had invited Jesus to his house saw this he said, "within himself" (not openly), "This man, if he were a prophet, would have known who and what manner of woman this is that touches him, for she is a sinner."

The answer of Jesus is given in Chapter VII, 40–47. Then he says to the woman, "Thy sins are forgiven." And those who sat at meat with him began to say within themselves, "Who is this that forgiveth sins also?" Then to the woman Jesus says, "Thy faith hath saved thee; go in peace."

This is clearly a different story from that of the woman at Bethany. The moral drawn from it is also entirely different. It is not hinted that the woman at Bethany is a sinner. Here the alabaster box is said to indicate that she was a prostitute. I doubt this very much. The fact that the woman in the Bethany story *breaks* the box is said to indicate that she was a sinner. This is nonsense. Here in *Luke,* where she is plainly described as a sinner, she is not said to break the alabaster box.

After this Jesus goes throughout "every city and village, preaching and showing the glad tidings of the Kingdom of God."

The twelve were with him. Certain women were also with him, out of whom he had cast evil spirits and infirmities—Mary Magdalene (out of whom he is afterwards said to have cast seven devils), Joanna, the wife of one of Herod's stewards, named Chuza, and Susanna, of whom we are told nothing. These women are said to minister to him.

Who were these women, what were they, and is it meant that they helped to maintain Jesus? I confess I do not like the verse, and the implication that a group of well-to-do women kept him. It is true that the consideration is not one that would disturb Jesus. It disturbs me.

The women came, no doubt, out of Tiberias. Mary Magdalene one of the prostitutes from Herod's court. Tradition has always assigned the character of a prostitute to her. And her name has come down through the ages as the generic name of the prostitute.

Joanna, the wife of one of Herod's stewards, may very reasonably be understood to be a woman whose soul revolted against what she looked upon at Herod's court. So she leaves it, and her husband in it, and follows Jesus, whom she sees and hears perhaps at Magdala, as she drives through. Mary Magdalene, with many lovers, perhaps, looking out at her window, hears the preacher in the street. Or more probably sees some act of divine tenderness to one of her class.

Then follows the parable of the sower, as given in *Mark* and *Matthew*, but without the relevancy it has there. Then comes the incident of the mother of Jesus and his brothers coming to see him. But again without the reason assigned in *Matthew* for their visit. There is nothing in *Luke* to explain the visit. The incident has little or no value, however.

On a certain day (time not recorded) Jesus went into a ship with his disciples, and says, "Let us go over unto the other side of the lake."

It is not stated where he is then, but he appears to be on the western side of Galilee. As they sail he falls asleep; a storm comes, the ship fills with water, the disciples are in jeopardy, and they awaken him and say, "Master, Master, we perish!" Jesus rises, rebukes the wind and the raging of the water, and they cease, and there is a calm.

Then he reproaches them with their want of faith. And they say one to another, "What manner of man is this? For he commandeth even the winds and water, and they obey him."

It is a poor story, without the slightest value except to indicate the power of Jesus. It suggests another interpolation. We can read the story better by omitting verses 23, 24 and 25, thus passing directly from verse 22 ("And they launched forth") to verse 26 ("And they arrived at the country of the Gadarenes"). All between is needless and to me unbelievable. Jesus does not work miracles without purpose.

Having arrived at the country of the Gadarenes, he meets the demoniac, as described in *Mark*. The incident of the swine is the same. It is the same, also, in the particular that when the swine-herds return with the people of the city, the only interest is apparently in this man who is now clothed and in his right mind, *except* that "the whole multitude of the country of the Gadarenes round about besought him to depart from them, for they were taken with great fear." Thus they thought Jesus was casting out devils by collusion with devils—the old superstition.

Jesus returns to his ship and sails to the western side, the side from which he came. The man who has been a demoniac wishes to go with him, but Jesus tells him to return home and show what great things God has done for him. The man goes his way and publishes throughout the city what great things Jesus has done for him.

When Jesus reaches the other side of the Lake the people receive him gladly, having been waiting for him. Then comes the incident of the man Jairus, precisely as given in the earlier Gospels, and also of the woman who touched the border of his garment. This is copied almost literally from *Mark*. The order of incidents is the same also, showing that Luke here was merely translating from the earlier Gospel.

Then Jesus calls his twelve disciples together, gives them power and authority over all devils and to cure diseases, and sends them to preach the kingdom of God and to heal the sick.

There is no escaping from the conclusion that demonology plays a great part in the life of Jesus on earth, that he constantly associates disease with the presence of devils in the sick, and that he thinks disease is usually the result of sin.

Jesus gives the same commands to his disciples before sending them away—that they are to take nothing for their journey, neither staves, nor scrip, bread nor money, nor a second coat. If a city will not receive them they are to leave it, and shake its dust off their feet as a testimony against it. And with this command the twelve disciples leave Jesus and go out preaching the Gospel and healing everywhere.

Next comes the story of Herod Antipas. He has heard of Jesus and is perplexed about him, because some are saying he is John risen from the dead. Herod says, "John have I beheaded; but who is this, of whom I hear such things?" And Herod desires to see

Jesus. Nothing is said in *Luke* of the murder of John by Herod, as told in *Mark*.

Then, suddenly, and apparently with no recorded lapse of time, the apostles who are sent away return to Jesus. They tell him what they have done. It is abundantly clear that there has been an interval of time. Luke clearly knows nothing of what happened during that interval. Or, if he knows it, puts it later, and in the wrong place.

Jesus takes the disciples aside into a desert place belonging to the city called Bethsaida. This takes up the story of *Mark* after omitting the long digression about the murder of John the Baptist. The object is clear. Jesus distrusts Herod, and intends to give him no opportunity of seeing him. When the news comes to him of Herod's desire to see him Jesus is probably in Herod's territory. So he goes (probably by land) to Philip's territory on the northeast coast of the Lake of Galilee. The people on the west of the Lake follow Jesus, and he receives them and speaks to them of the kingdom of God, and heals those in need of healing. It is frequently said that he speaks of the kingdom of God, but what he said is not always recorded. His parables on the Kingdom are all bunched together later. When the day begins to wear away the disciples come and say, "Send the multitude away. . . ."

Then follows the miracle of the feeding of the five thousand taken from *Mark;* and in the same place as in *Mark*. It is much more briefly told in *Luke,* and suggests even more strongly that it is an interpolation.

The whole story of the feeding of the five thousand in *Luke* is magnificent, and almost, if not quite, superfluous.

There is a clear break at the beginning of Chapter IX, 18. Nothing accounts for this sudden change. We do not know what becomes of the multitude, or that Jesus sends the disciples back by ship, or that he goes into the mountains to pray (only that he is alone praying when the next event begins), or that he walks on the water, or that Peter comes to him as in *Matthew*.

All this in *Luke* disappears and we come immediately to a scene which corresponds in substance to the scene in Cæsarea Philippi, recorded in *Mark* as coming much later.

Between the feeding of the five thousand and the scene in *Luke,* we lose many incidents recorded in *Mark:* (1) the walking on the water; (2) the scene with the Pharisees about the washing of hands before eating; (3) the sayings of Jesus about the hypocrisy of the Pharisees; (4) the going into the borders of Tyre and Sidon and meeting the Greek woman (called a Canaanite in *Matthew*); (5) the return to the Lake of Galilee and the coming of the man with the impediment in his speech (the deaf man); (6) the feeding of the four thousand.

Why all these omissions in *Luke?* That Luke had *Mark* before him (or an original version of *Mark*) is clear by the transcriptions previously made. Why did he omit these scenes? Is it not probably (1) that he did not accept them; (2) that they did not exist in the *Mark* he knew; (3) that, therefore, they were interpolations? That is to say that Luke knew nothing of the walking on the water, the feeding of the four thousand, and the other incidents.

And it came to pass, as Jesus was alone praying (IX, 18) his disciples were with him; and he asked them, "Whom say the people that I am?" They answered "John the Baptist." Jesus said, "But whom say ye that I am?" Peter answered, "The Christ of God." And Jesus straitly charged them to tell no man that thing. He went on to say that the Son of Man was to suffer many things, and be rejected of the elders and chief priests and scribes, and be slain, and be raised again the third day.

The foregoing about his fate is reproduced from *Mark*. But there is nothing in *Luke* of the prediction of Peter's supremacy, as in *Matthew,* about building his Church on the rock of Peter, and of giving him the keys of the kingdom of Heaven. Neither is there anything of this (about Peter's supremacy) in *Mark*. Only in *Matthew* does this appear. In the narrative of the same event in *Mark* and *Luke* it is conspicuously absent. In *Mark* Peter is sharply rebuked and by no means glorified.

In *Luke* Jesus warns his disciples of the suffering that must fall on all who follow him, and of the ultimate salvation they shall have. Further, he tells them that the Kingdom shall come so soon that some of them will not taste of death till they have seen it. We are not told in *Luke* where this occurred. Eight days after this Jesus takes Peter and James and John into a mountain to pray. Then follows the scene of the Transfiguration.

It will be noted that incidents recorded in the earlier Gospels as having occurred before the Transfiguration are in *Luke* made to follow it. Also fresh incidents occur in Luke after the Transfiguration.

Again, *Luke* differs from the earlier Gospels in that after recording (IX, 51) "when the time was come that he [Jesus] should be received up, he steadfastly set his face to go to Jerusalem," we are told that Jesus enters a village of the Samaritans, and, a little later, that he sends out seventy disciples "before his face into every city and place, whither he himself would come," giving them essentially the same warnings as when he sent out the twelve. And he then pronounces the "woe" on Chorazin and Bethsaida and Capernaum.

Also, when the seventy return as at the next breath telling of their success, of how the devils have been subject to them, Jesus says:

> I beheld Satan as lightning fall from Heaven. Behold, I give unto you power to tread on serpents and scorpions, and over all the power of the enemy; and nothing shall by any means hurt you. Notwithstanding in this rejoice not, that the spirits are subject unto you; but rather rejoice, because your names are written in Heaven. [X, 18–20]

The last sentence (verse 20) sounds like Jesus, the earlier part of the passage most certainly *does not*.

In *Luke* the last journey to Jerusalem is a prodigiously long one. The journey through Samaria (according to *Luke*) was at the most a three or four day journey. Yet enough occurs in it in *Luke* to occupy at least a month.

We do not pick up the actual movement of Jesus until we reach Chapter XVIII, 35, when, having reached Jericho (a strange way round to Jerusalem if the journey was through Samaria) he sees the blind man by the wayside.

Thus from Chapter IX, 51 to Chapter XVIII, 35 *Luke* is occupied with the last journey to Jerusalem. My inference would be that some of the incidents in these nine chapters occurred before the setting out for Jerusalem on the last journey.

General Comments

I find *Luke* deficient in order. What, in his introduction, he claims to do (to set out the events in order), is, in my judgment, precisely what he does not do.

I find him deficient in motive. It is difficult for me to follow the development of the spirit of Jesus as he passes through life. This is not so in *Matthew*. From that fact alone I should conclude that

Luke did not know the Gospel of Matthew as it has come down to us. If he had known it he could not have preferred his own disordered and often motiveless story to Matthew's. Also, he could not have omitted some of Matthew's incidents.

On the other hand, it is clear that he knew *Mark,* but not, I think, in the form in which *Mark* has come down to us. I think he knew *Mark* in some earlier form. It was a *Mark* without the feeding of the five thousand (as *Mark* tells it) and without the feeding of the four thousand. It is also clear that he did not know any previous Gospel which contained the miracle of the walking on the water. Or, alternatively, that he rejected that miracle.

My impression is that the feeding of the thousands and the walking on the water were all of much later date, and were put in part into *Mark* first, and afterwards altogether into *Matthew,* after *Luke* was written. In like manner I think *Luke* had interpositions at a later day. It does not seem to me possible that the original *Luke* can have contained the story of the Virgin Birth, or it would not also have contained references to the natural birth of Jesus which conflict with it—such as the story of the visit to the Temple at twelve years of age, the coming of the mother and brothers, and so on. Even the story within itself conflicts with the idea of a supernatural birth, as in the account of the purification of Mary and the circumcision of Jesus.

The sending out of the twelve disciples and their immediate return suggests a break. Something occurred while the twelve were away. What was it? Jesus himself was alone. Where was he? I think he was probably in Jerusalem. Some of the incidents, afterwards given in *Luke,* indicate a sojourn in Jerusalem before his final visit.

The sending out of the seventy is peculiar to *Luke,* I think, and has nearly no value. The words put into the mouth of Jesus on their return (about the power he gives them over poisonous creatures) are very dishonouring. It resembles the humiliating and dishonouring words put into his mouth after the Resurrection in *Mark* XVI, 18, "They shall take up serpents; and if they drink any deadly thing, it shall not hurt them." Those pitiful people who came later and mauled the Gospels have in their gross ignorance of his spirit degraded him woefully. Finally, I find *Luke* much less intelligible and infinitely less inspiring than *Matthew* down to the period of the Transfiguration.

CHAPTER XII

The Ministry
(According to St. John)

THE Gospel of John begins by saying that the Word (Christ) was from the beginning. Christ was at the beginning with God. Christ was God. All things were made by "Him." Without him nothing was made that was made. *Christ* was the light of man. Then *John* leaps forward to John the Baptist. John the Baptist was a man sent from God. He came to bear witness of the Light, that all men through him might believe. John was not himself that Light, but the witness of the Light. The Light was in the world, and the world was made by him, but the world knew him not. He came to his own and his own received him not. But to as many as received him he gave power to become the sons of God. The sons of God were born, not of the blood, nor of the will of the flesh, nor of the will of men, but of God.

Is it possible that this is to be read as a witness to the immaculate conception? It does not refer to Christ, but to all who receive him and become thereby the sons of God. The Word (Christ) was made flesh, and dwelt among us. John the Baptist bore witness of him, saying, "This was he of whom I spake, He that cometh after me is preferred before me . . . And of his fulness have all we received, and grace for grace. For the law was given by Moses, but grace and truth came by Jesus Christ. No man hath seen God at any time; the only begotten Son, which is in the bosom of the Father, he hath declared him."

When the Levites from Jerusalem went to John and asked him, "Who art thou?" John answered, "I am not the Christ." Then they asked him, "What then? Art thou Elias?" "I am not," he answered. "Art thou that prophet?" "No." "Who art thou?" "I am the voice of one crying in the wilderness, Make straight the way of the Lord, as said the prophet Esaias."

They that were sent to ask him these questions were Pharisees.

They asked, "Why baptizeth thou then, if thou be not that Christ, nor Elias, neither that prophet?" John the Baptist answered:

I baptize with water, but there standeth one among you, whom ye know not. He it is, who coming after me is preferred before me, whose shoe's latchet I am not worthy to unloose.

All this was at Bethabara, beyond Jordan, where John was baptizing.

The next day, after this visit of the Pharisees, John the Baptist saw Jesus coming to him, and he said:

Behold the Lamb of God, which taketh away the sin of the world. This is he of whom I said, After me cometh a man which is preferred before me; for he was before me. And I knew him not; but that he should be made manifest to Israel, therefore am I come baptizing with water.

Does John mean that he baptized Jesus to make him manifest as the Light that was to come?

John then bears this record:

I saw the Spirit descending from Heaven like a dove, and it abode upon him. And I knew him not; but he that sent me to baptize with water, the same said unto me, Upon whom thou shalt see the Spirit descending, and remaining on him, the same is he which baptizeth with the Holy Ghost. And I saw, and bare record that this is the Son of God.

And the next day after John stood, and two of his disciples (apparently with him) and looking upon Jesus as he walked he said, "Behold the Lamb of God!" And the two disciples who heard John the Baptist say this left John and followed Jesus.

Jesus turned and saw them following and asked, "What seek ye?" They answered, "Where dwellest thou?" Jesus replied, "Come and see." They went with him and saw where he dwelt and abode with him that day, for it was about the tenth hour (four o'clock in the afternoon). Apparently then, Jesus had a house near to Bethabara. And the two disciples stayed with him there one day.

One of the two disciples was Andrew. Andrew found his brother Simon and said, "We have found the Messiah, the Christ." Andrew brought Simon to Jesus. Jesus received Simon and renamed him Cephas, a stone.

All this disposes of the narrative of the Synoptic Gospels, about the Temptation, the return to Galilee and the finding of Simon near Capernaum. The day following, Jesus would go forth to Galilee.

Galilee at its nearest point is a long day's walk from Bethabara. He finds Philip and says to him, "Follow me." Philip belongs to Bethsaida, a town on the extreme north-east of the Lake of Galilee. Philip finds Nathanael, who belongs to Cana, to whom he says, "We have found him, of whom Moses in the law, and the prophets, did write, Jesus of Nazareth, the son of Joseph."

Nathanael does not become an apostle. Nathanael asks, "Can there any good thing come out of Nazareth?" "Come and see" says Philip. As a native of the neighbouring city of Cana, Nathanael knows the reputation of Nazareth.

Jesus sees Nathanael coming and says, "Behold an Israelite indeed, in whom is no guile." Nathanael asks Jesus how he knows him. Jesus answers that before Philip called Nathanael when he (Nathanael) was under a fig tree he saw him. Nathanael says, "Rabbi, thou art the Son of God; thou art the King of Israel."

Later, Jesus tells Nathanael that he shall see Heaven open, and the angels of God ascending and descending upon the Son of Man (himself). Nathanael belonged to Cana of Galilee, the scene of the miracle of turning water into wine.

Such is the beginning of *John*. It is a completely different story from that of the Synoptics. Nearly all the humanity of Jesus is put aside. He is God walking the world in the form of a man. He knows himself to be the Son of God from the first. John the Baptist knows him to be the Son of God. Nathanael knows him to be the Son of God. Philip knows him to be him of whom the prophets wrote. Andrew knows him to be the Christ. There is no uncertainty as to who and what he is.

From this high realm we now come down to the earth.

On the third day (that is, apparently, the third day after John the Baptist saw Jesus at Bethabara), Jesus is at a marriage in Cana of Galilee. This is possible, but highly improbable. It takes no reasonable account of the distance. On the second day John sees Jesus at (apparently) Bethabara. On the night of the second day Jesus returns to his home or lodgings with two of John's disciples, who have now become his. It is then the tenth hour—four o'clock in the afternoon. Cana of Galilee cannot be less than seventy miles from that place—Bethabara. Yet Jesus is at Cana the next day—the third day!

The mother of Jesus is there. Jesus and his disciples are called. Observe the difficulty, if not impossibility, of all this story. Jesus and his disciples could not have been called until they arrived in Cana on the same day and at an inevitably later hour. Then follows the story of the turning of water into wine (*John* II, 3–11).

Is there any good reason why I should not say that from the beginning to the end the story of the miracle is degrading to Jesus? It serves no purpose except to display the powers of Jesus. It is the story of water being turned into wine to help men who have already "well drunk" to drink more. And this is the first act of Jesus after his baptism and his Temptation! I simply will not believe it.

If I am asked for an explanation of how this miracle came into John's Gospel I reply that it came in at a period in the history of the Church when (the immaculate conception being accepted) it was necessary to find some evidence that Mary the mother of Jesus was conscious of his supernatural powers—the result of his supernatural origin. Down to this moment there is not, in any of the Gospels, the faintest indication that the mother of Jesus knew anything about his supernatural powers or origin. And if John's Gospel was not published until say A.D. 90 the Christian world had to wait sixty years after the Crucifixion for this revelation. It is all, to me, unbelievable, and extremely belittling to Jesus.

This beginning of miracles did Jesus in Cana of Galilee, and manifested forth his glory; and his disciples believed on him.

The only disciples we know of yet had already accepted the word of John the Baptist that Jesus was the Son of God foretold by Moses. Did it require this turning water into wine to convince them?

After this, according to *John,* Jesus went down to Capernaum and his mother and brethren went with him.

And they [Jesus, his mother, his brethren, and his disciples, only three thus far] continue in Capernaum not many days. And the Jews' Passover was at hand, and Jesus went up to Jerusalem.

If this is true, the baptism of Jesus took place only a few days before the Passover. Assuming there was no Temptation of forty days in the wilderness (John says nothing about the Temptation) the baptism (John does not distinctly say that the Baptist baptized Jesus, although he may be said to imply it) must have taken place in March or early April. This agrees roughly with the Synoptic Gospels. But in order to harmonize *John* and the Synoptics it is necessary to date the baptism earlier in the Synoptics than in *John*, and to assume that Jesus went from the Temptation to Jerusalem, instead of going directly to Nazareth. Or that after his first visit to Nazareth he must have returned south to Jerusalem.

On the whole I regard John's story as improbable. It makes Jesus go 100 miles north, and then return to Jerusalem in "not many days." It is possible, but improbable.

At this first Passover in the ministry of Jesus he goes into the Temple at Jerusalem and casts out the money-changers, making a scourge of small cords and driving them out like sheep. The incident is the same in the Synoptics where, however, it occurs not at the beginning of the ministry of Jesus, but at the end of it, after his entrance into Jerusalem on the ass.

Here, as in the Synoptics, the Jews ask him for a sign to show why he does this. Whereupon Jesus (not apparently relevantly) says, "Destroy this temple, and in three days I will raise it up." The Jews answer, "Forty and six years was this temple in building* and wilt thou rear it up in three days? . . . But he spake of the temple of his body," and the disciples remembered what he had said after he had risen from the dead.

It is said that while Jesus was in Jerusalem at the Passover many believed in him when they saw the miracles which he did. What miracles? He had done none, recorded by John, except that of turning the water into wine seventy odd miles away. If he worked miracles in Jerusalem during this first Passover we know nothing about them from John.

Here is introduced a Pharisee named Nicodemus (this is apparently in Jerusalem). He is called a ruler of the Jews. He comes to Jesus by night, saying, "Thou art a teacher come from God, for no man can do these miracles [what miracles?] that thou doest except God be with him." The reply of Jesus presupposes a question by Nicodemus which is not given, "Except a man be born of water and of the Spirit, he cannot enter into the kingdom of God," says Jesus.

Then follows a conversation between Jesus and Nicodemus (*John* III, 6–13). Then Jesus says, "As Moses lifted up the

---

*The Temple of Herod was begun about 25 B.C. It was therefore finished about A.D. 21. At this time it was about A.D. 29.

serpent in the wilderness, even so must the Son of Man be lifted up; That whosoever believeth in him should not perish, but have eternal life."

The lifting up of the serpent in the wilderness by Moses is described in *Numbers* XXI, 5–9. It tells of how the people of Israel spoke against God and against Moses for bringing them out of Egypt into the wilderness, where there was no bread; but the Lord sent fiery serpents among the people and they bit the people, so that many died; how the people came to Moses, confessed their sins and begged him to ask the Lord to take away the serpents and how Moses prayed to the Lord for the people; and how the Lord told Moses to make a fiery serpent of brass and set it on a pole, and when a man who had been bitten by a serpent looked up upon the serpent of brass he lived.

This is the figure to which Jesus likens himself. They that look up to him will have eternal life. Those who do not will perish.

> For God so loved the world, that he gave His only begotten Son, that whosoever believeth in Him should not perish, but have everlasting life. For God sent not His Son into the world to condemn the world; but that the world through him might be saved.

After this conversation with Nicodemus by night, Jesus and his disciples come into the land of Judæa. I am not certain that this means that Jesus came from outside into Judæa. He was already in Jerusalem, apparently, when Nicodemus came to him. But Jerusalem and Judæa are separately mentioned in many cases. In Judæa he tarried with his disciples and baptized. Later, it is said that Jesus himself did not baptize, but that his disciples baptized.

At the same time John, also, was baptizing in Ænon, near to Salim, because there was much water there. Salim was nearer to the Dead Sea than Bethabara. It is at a bend of the Jordan. The river is deep, and rather grey and muddy with the soil from the banks. Trees border the banks on both sides. It is rather a beautiful spot, about four miles from the Dead Sea and four or five from Jericho, a little south of Bethabara, and on the western side of Jordan.

Here (Chapter III, 25–26) is the record of a kind of complaint by the disciples of John about Jesus. The substance of the complaint is that Jesus who was with him beyond Jordan and to whom he (John) had borne witness, was baptizing and "all men come to him." John's reply is a defence of Jesus, and a depreciation of himself. He says that he (John) has never claimed to have been the Christ, but (as he implies) Jesus is the Christ, being the one who was sent from God, the Son of God.

When Jesus hears that the Pharisees are saying that he (Jesus) is baptizing more disciples than John, he leaves Judæa and goes back to Galilee, through Samaria. At Sychar, near the well called Jacob's he sits down. It is noon. His disciples go into the neighbouring city to buy food. A woman comes to draw water. Jesus asks her to give him a drink. The woman is surprised that he, being a Jew, asks her, a woman of Samaria. "For the Jews have no dealings with the Samaritans," says the writer of the Gospel of John, which shows that either he was not a Jew himself or, being a Jew, he was writing for non-Jews—all Jews knowing this. Jesus answers her. "If thou knewest the Gift of God, and who it is that saith to thee, Give me to drink; thou wouldest have asked of him, and he would have given thee living water." The woman says "Sir, thou hast nothing to draw with, and the well is deep; from whence then hast thou that living water? Art thou greater than our father Jacob, which gave us the well, and drank thereof himself and his children?"

Jesus answers, "Whosoever drinketh of this water shall thirst again; but whosoever drinketh of the water that I shall give him shall never thirst." "Sir," says the woman, "give me this water, that I thirst not, neither come hither to draw." Jesus then tells her to call her husband. "I have no husband," she answers.

"Thou hast well said, I have no husband, for thou hast had five husbands and he whom thou now hast is not thy husband." "I perceive that thou art a prophet," says the woman. Then, breaking off from this, she says, "Our fathers worshipped in this mountain, and ye say, that in Jerusalem is the place where men ought to worship."

Jesus answers, "Woman, believe me, the hour cometh when ye shall neither in this mountain, nor yet at Jerusalem, worship the Father . . . God is a Spirit, and they that worship him must worship him in spirit and in truth." The woman says, "I know that Messiah cometh, which is called Christ; when he is come, he will tell us all things." Jesus answers, "I that speak unto thee am he."

Then his disciples come from the city and marvel that he condescends to talk with the Samaritan woman, but they say nothing. Nobody says, "Why do you talk with her?"

Meantime, the woman leaves her water-pot at the well, returns to the city, and says to the men, "Come, see a man, which told me all things that ever I did; is not this the Christ?" The men come and see Jesus. But the Gospel does not record what they said to him or he to them. It goes on with a discussion between Jesus and his disciples, in which the fact appears that it is harvest time. "Lift up your eyes and look on the fields; for they are white already to harvest."

This is quite natural. It was not long after Passover. John's Gospel indicates that Jesus was at the Passover almost immediately after his baptism—if he was baptized, according to *John*.

We are told that many of the Samaritans of the city believed on Jesus on the report of the woman. They ask him to stay with them. He stays two days. And many more believed on him for his own words. And these said to the woman, "Now we believe, not because of the saying, for we have heard him ourselves, and know that this is indeed the Christ, the Saviour of the world." And after the two days Jesus goes on from Samaria to Galilee.

This vivid story is full of difficulties. Part of the conversation between Jesus and the woman of Samaria is very real, the remainder is very mystical. It requires that we believe that Jesus had a supernatural power of reading the thoughts of another. Only so could he have known the woman's true story through her apparent falsehood. It requires that he should have told her that he was the Christ, although in none of the Synoptic Gospels has he said this to anybody (not even to his closest disciples) until the scene in Cæsarea Philippi, and then only as one who admits what has been said by another. If Jesus told the woman of Samaria that he was the Christ, it is not conceivable that he had not told his disciples. And if he had told his disciples, all their conduct afterwards (and especially at the end) is not only cowardly and contemptible, but totally beyond explanation. I think important sections of the story suggest that it was written to meet a need of the Church towards the end of the first century. I also think that it contains one of the greatest of the utterances of Jesus (IV, 20–24):

> Our fathers worshipped in this mountain; and ye say, that in Jerusalem is the place where men ought to worship.

Jesus saith unto her, Woman, believe me, the hour cometh, when ye shall neither in this mountain, nor yet at Jerusalem, worship the Father.

Ye worship ye know not what; we know what we worship; for salvation is of the Jews.

But the hour cometh, and now is, when the true worshippers shall worship the Father in spirit and in truth; for the Father seeketh such to worship him.

God is a Spirit; and they that worship him must worship him in spirit and in truth.

But it is my feeling that verses 22 and 23 ought to be omitted. The verse 22, which says "salvation is of the Jews" is out of harmony with Jesus, and the gospel he preached. And verse 23 is only a less perfect version of verse 24.

The importance of the passage in which Jesus says that neither in the mountain nor in Jerusalem shall ye worship the Father, because God is a spirit and they that worship Him must worship Him in spirit and in truth must not be overlooked. I think this is of the very soul of Christ's teaching, the essence of the eternal religion, requiring no temples, no priesthood, no ritual, nothing but the soul of man in communion with the spirit of God.

Jesus, after his two days in Samaria, is now in Galilee. John's Gospel does not say he goes into Nazareth, but it quotes the words he used in Nazareth, according to *Luke:* "For a prophet hath no honour in his own country." In John's Gospel these words have no relevance, they are without motive. One asks why they are there. Moreover, they are out of harmony with the next succeeding words.

The Galileans receive him, having seen all the things which he did in Jerusalem, for they also went up to the feast (the Passover). Observe that we have not been told of anything he did at the feast; only of certain things he said.

Jesus comes again to Cana of Galilee. There a certain nobleman (a ruler) of Capernaum comes to him and beseeches him to heal his son who is at the point of death. In *Luke* (VII, 2) the nobleman (who is called a centurion) sends the elders of the Jews, and the sick man is his servant, not his son. The subsequent incidents are the same as in *John.*

And here comes a sudden break in John's Gospel. It is now, by John's story, at the utmost, a very short time after the Passover. Jesus has seen Nicodemus. He has been in Jordan, baptizing. He has returned to Galilee by way of Samaria. Arriving in Galilee he has been to Cana. And now, no other act being recorded, it is said that there was a feast at Jerusalem, and that he went up to it.

What feast was it? When did it take place? This is all he has seen of Galilee on his second visit since the beginning of the ministry. Galilee sees little of him. Jesus goes up to Jerusalem again. At Jerusalem there is a pool called in the Hebrew tongue Bethesda. [That the Gospel explains what the pool is called in Hebrew shows that the writer is not writing for the Jews.]

In one of the five porches to the pool of Bethesda a multitude of impotent people are lying: the blind, the halt, the withered, waiting for the moving of the water. An angel goes down at a certain season to the pool and troubles the pool. Whosoever first after the troubling of the water steps in is cured of his disease.

When Jesus arrives at the pool he finds a man lying there who has had an infirmity for thirty-eight years. Jesus says to the man, "Wilt thou be made whole?" The impotent man answers, "Sir, I have no man, when the water is troubled, to put me into the pool; but while I am coming, another steppeth before me."

Jesus says to the man, "Rise, take up thy bed, and walk." The man is immediately made whole, rises, takes up his bed and walks. A striking picture. The disappointed man year after year remaining on. Going down day by day, watching, hoping. Another chance lost. Still hoping on.

The day was the Sabbath. The Jews say to the man who was cured, "It is the Sabbath Day; it is not lawful for thee to carry thy bed." The man answers, "He that made me whole, the same said unto me, Take up thy bed and walk." The Jews ask who it was who told him that. The man does not know, for Jesus has gone.

Later, Jesus sees the man in the Temple and says to him, "Thou art made whole; sin no more, lest a worse thing come unto thee." The man then knew who it was that had cured him (presumably everybody in the Temple knew Jesus), and he goes out and tells the Jews it was Jesus. "Therefore did the Jews persecute Jesus and sought to slay him, because he had done these things on the Sabbath Day." Jesus answers them, "My Father worketh hitherto, and I work." Therefore the Jews sought the more to kill him, because he had not only broken the Sabbath, but had said that God was his Father, thus making himself the equal of God.

Hereafter follows the long dispute between Jesus and the Jews about his relation to God, in which Jesus claims the witness not only of John, but of the Scriptures, who testify of him—especially of Moses—"for he wrote of me."

Here comes (Chapter VI) a strange break in John's narrative. All the foregoing takes place, apparently, in Jerusalem. But now without a word we are switched back to Galilee. "After these things Jesus went over the Sea of Galilee, which is the Sea of Tiberias." Obviously, John was writing for a foreign public. The Jews did not, at that period, call the lake the Sea of Tiberias. The city of Tiberias was begun to be built about fourteen years earlier. To the Jews it would be the Sea of Galilee.

A great multitude followed him, because they saw the miracles which he did on them that were diseased. It is clear that the chief interest of the people in Jesus was not in his teaching but in his cures. Jesus went up into a mountain and sat there with his disciples. Jesus saw a great multitude come to him, and he asked Philip, "Whence shall we buy bread, that these may eat?"

If they are on the north-east side of the lake it is natural that he should ask Philip, for Bethsaida was Philip's native place. Philip answered that two hundred pennyworth of bread was not sufficient for them.

Why this mention of two hundred pennyworth? Did that chance to be the whole sum in their treasury? Andrew then said, "There is a lad here, which hath five barley loaves and two small fishes; but what are they among so many?" Jesus said, "Make the men sit down." It is mentioned that there was much grass in the place— an indication of locality and time of the year. Probably early summer.

The men sit down in number about five thousand. Jesus takes the loaves, gives thanks, distributes to the disciples, who give to the people. The same with the fishes, "as much as they would."

When they were filled Jesus told the disciples to gather up the fragments that remain, that nothing might be lost. They gathered the fragments and filled twelve baskets with what was left of the five loaves.

When the people saw this miracle they said, "This is of a truth that Prophet that should come into the world." The expectation of the Messiah was that he would work vast miracles.

The people were so sure that Jesus must be the prophet who

was foretold that they wished to take him by force, and make him a king. The Messiah was to be a temporal king. The people wished to make Jesus such a king.

Jesus "departed into a mountain himself alone." Does this mean that Jesus had the power of dematerializing—of disappearing in the midst of a crowd? Several stories seem to indicate this, as his disappearance at Nazareth, when the people of his native town wished to cast him over a cliff, and his disappearance in the Temple, when the people were about to stone him.

When even was now come the disciples went down to the sea, entered into a ship and went over the sea towards Capernaum. Thus the feeding was in the north-east, and they had sailed from the west. The sea arose by reason of a great wind. The disciples, who were rowing (it was a row boat), were about four miles out, when Jesus, walking on the sea, drew nigh to the ship. The disciples were afraid. But he said, "It is I; be not afraid."

They willingly received him into the ship, and immediately the ship reached the land on the western side—the Capernaum side.

This story of the feeding differs in important particulars from the narratives in the Synoptic Gospels. There is no mention of Peter walking on the sea to Jesus. Altogether the story seems to be transcribed from the Synoptics, or perhaps written from memory of what the Synoptics contained.

The following day when the people stood on the other side of the sea and saw there was no other boat that could have brought Jesus across they said to him, "Rabbi, when camest thou hither?" Jesus answered, "Ye seek me, not because ye saw the miracles, but because ye did eat of the loaves, and were filled." Then he told them not to labour for the meat which perishes, but for the meat which endureth unto everlasting life, which the Son of Man shall give you.

They ask him what shall they do that they may work the works of God. [Do they mean work similar miracles?] Jesus tells them to believe on him whom God hath sent.

Then they ask an astounding thing—if they had witnessed the feeding of the five thousand: "What sign showeth thou then, that we may see, and believe thee? What dost thou work? Our fathers did eat manna in the desert; as it is written, He gave them bread from Heaven to eat." Jesus answers, "Moses gave you not that bread from Heaven; but my Father giveth you the true bread from Heaven. For the bread of God is he which cometh down from Heaven, and giveth life unto the world."

"Lord, evermore give us this bread," the people say, and Jesus answers, "I am the bread of life; he that cometh to me shall never hunger; and he that believeth on me shall never thirst." The Jews then murmur at him because he said, "I am the bread which came down from Heaven." They (the Jews) say, "Is not this Jesus, the son of Joseph, whose father and mother we know? How is it, too, that he saith, I came down from Heaven?" Jesus answers:

Murmur not among yourselves. No man can come to me, except the Father which hath sent me draw him. . . . Verily, verily, I say unto you, He that believeth on me hath everlasting life. I am that bread of life. Your fathers did eat manna in the wilderness, and are dead. This is the bread which cometh down from Heaven, that a man may eat thereof, and not die. I am the living bread which came down from Heaven; if any man eat of his bread, he shall live for ever; and the bread that I will give is my flesh, which I will give for the life of the world.

The Jews, hearing this, say among themselves, "How can this man give us his flesh to eat?" and Jesus answers, "Except ye eat the flesh of the Son of Man, and drink his blood, ye have no life in you. Whoso eateth my flesh, and drinketh my blood, hath eternal life, and I will raise him up at the last day."

We hear next that all this was said in the synagogue at Capernaum. Many of the disciples (meaning this time the followers of Jesus) say, "This is an hard saying; who can hear it?" Jesus knows what they are murmuring and says, "Doth this offend you? It is the spirit that quickeneth; the flesh profiteth nothing; the words that I speak unto you, they are the spirit, and they are the life."

From that time many of his disciples went back and walked no more with him. Jesus said to the twelve, "Will ye also go away?"

Peter answered, "Lord, to whom shall we go? Thou hast the words of eternal life. And we believe and are sure that thou art that Christ, the Son of the living God."

All this is deeply instructive. Incidentally, it presents a picture to the eye of Jesus with his disciples (in the general sense) walking with him. Next, it gives a clear enough idea of what he means by eating his flesh and drinking his blood. His *words* are the spirit. The flesh is nothing; it is the bread of the world, like the manna given them in the wilderness. Finally, coming immediately after the story of the feeding of the five thousand it suggests that the miracle was suggested by and had its origin in the teaching, not the teaching in the miracle. People heard the strange teaching about the bread he could give them, and by and by it took the concrete form of a miracle by which he fed thousands with a few loaves and fishes.

A final point, Peter's declaration, "Thou art that Christ," is the same that he made at Cæsarea Philippi, according to the other Gospels.

Another break comes here (Chapter VII, 1). We are in Capernaum, and yet the Gospel says, "After these things Jesus walked in Galilee; for he would not walk in Jewry, because the Jews sought to kill him."

But the next verse says:

Now the Jews' Feast of Tabernacles was at hand. His brethren [the alleged brothers of Jesus, the other sons of Joseph and Mary] therefore said unto him, "Depart hence, and go into Judæa, that thy disciples also may see the works that thou doest. For there is no man that doeth anything in secret, and he himself seeketh to be known openly. If thou do these things, show thyself to the world." For neither did his brethren believe in him.

Jesus answers, "My time is not yet come; but your time is alway ready. . . . Go ye up unto this feast. I go not up yet."

Having said this he remained in Galilee. But when his brethren had gone up to Judæa he also went, but not openly—in secret. The Jews at the feast looked for him and asked, "Where is he?"

There was much discussion among them as to whether he was a good man or a deceiver.

About the middle of the period of the feast Jesus appeared in Jerusalem and went into the Temple and taught. Whereupon the Jews marvelled and said, "How knoweth this man letters, having never learned?"

Jesus answered:

My doctrine is not mine, but His that sent me. If any man will do His will, he shall know of the doctrine, whether it be of God, or whether I speak of myself. He that speaketh of himself seeketh his own glory; but he that seeketh His glory that sent him, the same is true, and no unrighteousness is in him.

First, the people in the Temple knew the condition of life in which Jesus was brought up—that he had had no rabbinical teaching in the sense of having passed through a rabbinical school. Obviously, they were not prepared for the astonishing learning in the law which Jesus displayed. Therefore, this question. And the answer of Jesus appears to say "It is true I have not been taught by man, but God has taught me. Moreover God has taught me because I have done His Will." Thus Jesus claims divine inspiration.

Jesus says further, "Did not Moses give you the law, and yet none of you keepeth the law. Why go ye about to kill me?" The people answer, "Thou hast a devil. Who goeth about to kill thee?" Jesus replies:

> I have done one work, and ye all marvel.
> Moses therefore gave unto you circumcision . . . and ye on the Sabbath Day circumcise a man. If a man on the Sabbath Day receive circumcision that the law of Moses should not be broken, are ye angry at me, because I have made a man every whit whole on the Sabbath Day?

The first thing to observe here is that, although nothing is said about it in this part of John's narrative, it is clear that between the time of the arrival of Jesus in Jerusalem and his going into the Temple to teach he had performed a miracle (that of making a sick man whole) on the Sabbath Day. This miracle may very well be one of the miracles recorded in some places in *John,* or in one of the Synoptic Gospels. It can, therefore, quite properly be put in this place in order to make a true and consecutive narrative.

The next thing to notice is that the Jews were trying to assassinate Jesus, to kill him, not by the legal means of bringing him to trial before the council as a breaker of the law of Moses, but by deliberate murder. Nothing else can be meant by Jesus when he reproaches the Jews with having the law of Moses, and yet not keeping it, otherwise they would not go about to kill him. And the Jews, on their part, recognize the idea of Jesus that they are murderers, by saying, "Thou art a devil. Who goeth about to kill thee?"

Then said some (evidently other Jews who knew of the intention of certain of the fellow Jews to assassinate Jesus) "Is not this he, whom they seek to kill? But lo, he speaketh boldly, and they say nothing unto him. Do the rulers know indeed that this is the very Christ?"

Then we see the attitude of these others. Clearly, they think the rulers are trying to kill Jesus, probably because they know (or fear) that he is the very Christ, and they have no use for the Christ any more. But they (the others) do not at all believe Jesus is the Christ. How do they come to that view? Because they know all about Jesus, where he comes from and who he is. Whereas, when Christ comes no man will know where he comes from.

This was obviously a form of belief in the Messiah—that he would appear from nobody knew where, at a time nobody knew. Because they knew all about Jesus they could not believe him to be the Christ.

Then Jesus, knowing what was being said by this group outside the ruling classes, rose in the Temple and cried, saying in effect, "Ye both know me, and ye know whence I came; and I am not come of myself, but he that sent me is true, and whom ye know not. But I know him, and he hath sent me."

Then, it would appear, that Jesus antagonized nearly all classes of the Jews. They sought to take him, yet nobody laid hands on him. Probably each wanted somebody else to lay hands on him. On the other hand, many of the people believed in him by reason of his miracles (they are not recorded here in *John*), saying, "When Christ cometh will he do more miracles than these which this man hath done?" meaning, apparently, that more is impossible. Also meaning that to work miracles was the prime test and sign of the Messiah.

The Pharisees and the chief priests, thinking apparently that the majority of the people were against Jesus, sent officers (soldiers of the Temple) to take him. But the officers came back without him, and when asked by the chief priests and the Pharisees why they had not brought him, they answered, "Never man spake like this man."

Upon this the Pharisees were angry and said to the officers, "Are ye also deceived? Have any of the rulers or of the Pharisees believed in him? Only the people who knew not the law are cursed with belief in this man."

Then Nicodemus (the Pharisee who came to Jesus by night) said, "Does our law judge any man, before it hears him, and knows what he has done?"

The chief priests and Pharisees retort, "Art thou also of Galilee? Search and look; for out of Galilee ariseth no prophet."

What was it that Jesus had said, which caused the officers of the Temple to return to their masters the chief priests and Pharisees without arresting him. He had said this: That he would be with his people for a little while and then he would go away to him that had sent him; that they should seek him and not find him, and that where he went they could not come.

The Jews asked themselves, Whither is he going that we cannot find him? Is he to go to the dispersed among the Gentiles (meaning, apparently, the Jews dispersed among the Gentiles)? And what does he mean by saying they should seek him and not find him, and where he was going they could not come?

Then on the last day (the great day) of the Feast (of Tabernacles) Jesus stood up (apparently in the Temple) and cried, "If any man thirst, let him come unto me, and drink. He that believeth on me, as the scripture hath said, out of his belly shall flow rivers of living water." Observe that here, in parenthesis, it is said, "But this spake he of the Spirit, which they that believe on him should receive, for the Holy Ghost was not yet given; because Jesus was not yet glorified."

Is this an interpolation? Was it thought necessary to say that Jesus did not really mean that rivers of water should flow out of the bellies of those who believed on him?

Assuredly, these bold words of Jesus made a deep division among those who heard him. Some said, "Of a truth this is the Prophet," obviously the Messiah; others said, "This is the Christ." But still others clung to the old story, "Shall Christ come out of Galilee. Hath not the Scripture said that Christ cometh of the seed of David, and out of the town of Bethlehem, where David was?"

Manifestly, the people who urged the latter objection had no idea that Jesus was descended from David, or that he was born in Bethlehem. So there was division among the people. Some wanted to take him. But no man did so. The officers did not take him, although sent to do so. But went back without him. They were obviously afraid to touch one who, judging by his words and acts, *might* be the Christ.

Jesus, at this time of the Feast of Tabernacles, went up into the Mount of Olives. I judge that he was probably accustomed to do so on his visits to Jerusalem. Thus he may have stayed at Bethany in the house of Mary and Martha. And either then, or at some similar time, the incident recorded in *Luke* (X, 38–42) may have occurred.

In the early morning he went again to the Temple. All the people came to him, and he sat down and taught them.

The scribes and the Pharisees brought to him a woman taken in adultery, and when they had set her in the midst they said, "Master, this woman was taken in adultery, in the very act. Now Moses in the law commanded us that such should be stoned: but what sayest thou?"

This they said to tempt him. He was the friend of harlots. They were always about him. If he defended or excused the woman they had him in their power and could accuse him before the council.

Jesus made no reply. He stooped down and with his finger wrote on the ground, as though he heard them not. So they continued asking him, "What sayest thou?" Then Jesus rose up and said, "He that is without sin among you, let him first cast a stone at her." And again he stooped down and wrote on the ground.

The scribes and Pharisees, being convicted by their conscience, went out one by one, beginning at the eldest, and Jesus was left alone with the woman. Then Jesus raised himself up again, and seeing none but the woman, he said, "Woman, where are thine accusers? Hath no man condemned thee?" "No man, Lord," said the woman. "Neither do I condemn thee; go, and sin no more."

This story is said to have been interpolated. The earliest manuscripts do not contain it. No story of Jesus rings more true to his character. In every particular it is like Jesus.

At verse 12 of Chapter VIII there appears to be another break. It may be immediately after the festival, or it may be on the last day.

Jesus speaks again, apparently in the Temple (it was in the treasury), saying, "I am the light of the world; he that followeth me shall not walk in darkness, but shall have the light of life."

To this the Pharisees reply, "Thou bearest record of thyself; thy record is not true."

Jesus answers, "Though I bear record of myself, yet my record is true; for I know whence I came and whither I go; ye cannot tell whence I come or whither I go. Ye judge after the flesh; I judge no man. . . . I am one that bear witness of myself, and the Father that sent me beareth witness of me."

The Jews then say, "Where is thy Father?" and Jesus answers,

"Ye neither know me, nor my Father; if ye had known me, ye should have known my Father also."

No man laid hands on him for his time was not yet come. Jesus further said, "Ye are from beneath. I am from above. . . . I am not of this world." The Jews said to him, "Who art thou?" Jesus answered, "Even the same that I said unto you from the beginning. . . . He that sent me is with me; the Father hath not left me alone."

After these bold words many believed on him. Jesus said to those that believed, "If ye continue in my word, then are ye my disciples indeed. And ye shall know the truth, and the truth shall make you free."

Later, Jesus accuses the Jews of breaking the law of their father Abraham by trying to kill him. Therefore, they are no children of Abraham. They answer that they are not born of fornication. They have one Father, even God, and Jesus answers, "If God were your Father, ye would love me, for I proceeded forth and came from God. . . . Ye are of your father the Devil, and the lusts of your father ye will do. He was a murderer from the beginning."

The Jews reply, "Say we not well that thou art a Samaritan, and hast a devil?" Which Jesus answers, "I have not a devil; but I honour my Father, and ye do dishonour me. . . . I say unto you, If a man keep my saying, he shall never see death."

The Jews answer, "Now we know that thou hast a devil. Abraham is dead, and the prophets; and thou sayest, If a man keep my saying, he shall never taste of death. Art thou greater than our father Abraham, which is dead? And the prophets are dead; Whom makest thou thyself?"

Jesus then declares, "If I honour myself, my honour is nothing; it is my Father that honoureth me, of whom ye say, that he is your God. Yet ye have not known him; but I know him, and if I should say, I know him not, I shall be a liar like unto you. . . . Your Father Abraham rejoiced to see my day, and he saw it, and was glad."

The Jews said to him, "Thou art not fifty years old, and hast thou seen Abraham?" Jesus answers in the pregnant words, "Before Abraham was, I am."

Then the Jews take up stones to cast at him; "but Jesus hid himself and went out of the Temple, going through the midst of them, and so passed out."

Does this mean, as would appear, that Jesus dematerialized himself?

After this comes the miracle of the giving of sight to the man born blind. I cannot believe that the record of the miracle in *John* (IX) is anything more than another version of the miracle of the giving of sight to the blind man in the Synoptic Gospels (*Luke* XVIII, 35; *Mark* X, 46; and *Matthew* XX, 30—two blind men). The difference is that in *John* the miracle occurred chiefly in Jerusalem, whereas in *Mark, Matthew,* and *Luke,* it occurred in or near Jericho. In the Synoptic Gospels it is a clear and natural story. In *John* it is obviously a "made" story, to illustrate dogmatic ideas.

I accept the story of the miracle as told in the Synoptics. I regret it as it appears in *John.* At the time indicated in *John* (not long before the raising of Lazarus), Jesus could not have been in Jerusalem. But he could very well have been near Jericho, on his way up to Jerusalem by the Peræa road from Galilee. Therefore, I would strip the narrative in *John* of the visit of Jesus to Jerusalem (the visit preceding the last) at the end of the dispute with the scribes and Pharisees, and their stoning him out of the Temple, and out of Jerusalem.

I should omit the miracle (as being out of place) but include the passages from Chapter X, 22–33, going on from the first part of the account of his visit to Jerusalem at the Feast of the Tabernacles to the second part of the same account. This does not mean that I see any reason to doubt the intervening parables, but only that I find them wrongly placed. The parables were probably told during the visit in question. Thus for the last part of the visit:

And it was at Jerusalem the Feast of the Dedication. . . . And Jesus walked in the Temple in Solomon's porch. Then came the Jews round about him, and said unto him, How long dost thou make us to doubt? If thou be the Christ, tell us plainly.

Jesus answered them:

I told you, and ye believed not. The works that I do in my Father's name, they bear witness of me. But ye believe not, because ye are not of my sheep, as I said unto you. . . . And I give unto them eternal life; and they shall never perish, neither shall any man pluck them out of my hand. My Father, which gave them to me, is greater than all; and no man is able to pluck them out of my Father's hand. I and my Father are one.

Then, again, the Jews took up stones to stone him. And Jesus said, "Many good works have I shewed you from my Father; for which of those works do ye stone me?"

The Jews replied, "For a good work we stone thee not, but for blasphemy; and because that thou, being a man, makest thyself God."

This is the close of the ministry of Jesus in Jerusalem down to his last visit. John goes on from this point to the raising of Lazarus.

Jesus, according to John, removed himself to the neighbourhood of Bethabara, where John used to baptize. While there he received the message from Martha and Mary telling him that their brother Lazarus was sick. Incidentally the presence of another hand than that of the original writer of *John* is proved by the unnecessary second verse of Chapter XI, which could only have been interpolated by some believer who did not see (1) that John had not yet said anything about Mary anointing the feet of Jesus, and (2) that he tells it at full length, and in its proper place later on in his Gospel, namely in Chapter XII, 1–6.

I am sure as I can be of anything, when the Gospel narrative is so confused and out of order (almost deliberately defying order), that the whole of the visit of Jesus to Jerusalem preceding the last took place several months before the final visit, namely, at the time of the Feast of Tabernacles, while the last visit took place at the time of the Passover of the following year. The interval covered several months. In the meantime, Jesus had, I conclude, returned to Galilee, going back, probably, through Samaria.

On reaching Galilee, he was rejoined by his disciples (apparently they were not with him during his visit to Jerusalem at the Feast of Tabernacles). Also, not long after his return to Galilee and his being rejoined by his disciples (who had come back to him after their mission), he received news of the death of John the Baptist. His disciples then urged him to get out of the territory of Herod Antipas, lest Herod should do to him as he had done to John. Jesus accepted this advice and went north through Galilee to Peræa, the territory of Philip. Therefore, we find him at Cæsarea Philippi, and on the mountain, probably Hermon.

After the Transfiguration, I think Jesus determined to go up to Jerusalem with the deliberate intention of meeting his death, having become convinced that he must die, and die in Jerusalem, for the fulfilment of the task God had laid upon him. He went up to Jerusalem through Galilee.

As he was passing through Galilee, he' was told that Herod Antipas was asking about him and wished to see him, and his disciples again urged him to get out of Herod's territory.

He refused to do so, spoke contemptuously of "that fox" (showing full knowledge of Herod's character from first to last), saying that in spite of Herod he would go straight on to Jerusalem, and also that he had no fear of dying at Herod's hands, inasmuch as a prophet must die in Jerusalem.

I think he there, at the extreme south of Galilee, turned eastward, to take the usual road of the Galileans, beyond Jordan. This brought him to Bethabara, and here the narrative of the Synoptic Gospels and John's narrative come together. I think that at Bethabara he received the message from Martha and Mary about Lazarus. He then crossed Jordan and came near to Jericho. Before reaching Jericho he came upon blind Bartimæus and gave him sight. After passing through Jericho he came upon the publican Zacchæus and gave him *moral* sight. Then he climbed the hill towards Jerusalem with his following behind him—his disciples, the man who had been blind and now could see, the publican who was now converted, and the company of women who had come down with him from Galilee. As he came near to Bethany, Martha, hearing that he was coming, had run out to meet him, to say that her brother Lazarus was dead and they had buried him. This is, in my view, the only intelligible order of events.

General Comments

Unlike the Synoptics, which confine the ministry of Jesus to about one year, all of it (except an undefined part of it in *Luke*) taking place in Galilee, John causes almost the entire ministry of Jesus to take place in Judæa, and most of it in Jerusalem.

That John, the fisherman of Capernaum, can have forgotten (or not dwelt lovingly upon) that part of the ministry which took place in Galilee, is very difficult to believe. That John, the fisherman, should have focused his eyes on the ministry in Jerusalem is very difficult to believe. That it should have been John, the fisherman who reported that part of the ministry which concerns the visit to Jerusalem at the time of the Feast of Tabernacles, when there appears to be no indication that either he or any other of the twelve was with Jesus, is an added difficulty.

On the other hand, if the Gospel were written by John the Presbyter, who apparently lived in Jerusalem, and may have known nothing of the ministry in Galilee, the disproportion in the Jerusalem narrative becomes intelligible. Further, it becomes yet more intelligible in the light of the fact that nearly all in the Gospel of John which concerns the ministry in Galilee is taken, often literally, from the Synoptic Gospels. Again, the whole spirit of the Gospel of John makes it difficult to believe that it is the work, either directly or indirectly, of the fisherman of Capernaum.

The Gospel of John is not Jewish. It does not rest, as do the Gospels of Mark and Matthew, on the Jewish view of the Messiah, or on the paramount authority of the law and prophets. It is grounded on a new interpretation of the Godhead of Jesus, which makes him one with God from the beginning, the creator of the world with God.

All this may have been very true to the mind of John the Presbyter, who lived in the heart of the new religious movement which came from Greek sources—from Alexandria. But nothing in the world can be less like the probable and natural evolution of the mind of the fisherman of Galilee.

As to minor points in John's narrative which appear to prove that the writer was an actual eye-witness of the events he records (such as that it was very cold on the night when Jesus was taken to the house of the high priest), it is equally possible that the eye-witness was the Presbyter John. Also, it is more probable, inasmuch as John, the fisherman, could not have been present at the high priest's house without exciting as much suspicion as Peter did, and furthermore John, the fisherman, could not have had any privileges at the high priest's house such as gained him admission and gave him the power to introduce Peter.

Finally, I do not yet see any sufficient ground for believing that the Gospel according to John was written by John, the son of Zebedee.

Incidentally, I find very few references to John, the fisherman, in any of the Gospels. And the references to him in John's Gospel only indicate the possibility that the actual writer of the Gospel *knew* John, the fisherman, and put him into the Gospel story wherever possible, sometimes in apparently impossible places, as at the Cross, when the disciples, who had *all fled* on the arrest of Jesus in Gethsemane, were almost certainly in hiding. They were still in hiding, and behind locked doors, on the first day of the week, when Jesus appeared to them after his Resurrection.

General Chronology of the Ministry of Jesus According to the Gospel of St. John

1. That when John the Baptist was baptizing at Bethabara beyond Jordan, Jesus was there.
2. That two of John's disciples forsook John and followed Jesus to his abode somewhere near.
3. The day following Jesus went up to Galilee.
4. That on the third day he was at Cana of Galilee.
5. That he went to Capernaum.
6. That the Passover being then at hand Jesus went up to Jerusalem.
7. That after this he and his disciples "came into the land of Judæa," whatever that may mean, seeing that Jerusalem is in Judæa, and baptized there.
8. That he then left Judæa and went again into Galilee, passing the night in Samaria, and meeting the Samaritan woman at Jacob's well.
9. That he went on from Samaria into Galilee and a second time visited Cana of Galilee.
10. That a feast of the Jews came again, and once more Jesus went up to Jerusalem, having just come from Jerusalem.
11. That he was again "after these things" back in Galilee.
12. That again the Passover of the Jews was nigh.
13. That he went by ship to Capernaum and crossed the Lake of Galilee to an undefined place (probably Bethsaida) and returned to Capernaum.
14. Apparently Jesus now returned to Judæa and then came back to Galilee, "for he would not walk in Jewry because the Jews sought to kill him."
15. The Feast of Tabernacles was at hand, so he went up to Jerusalem.
16. He remained in Jerusalem until the end of the Feast of Tabernacles and then he was stoned by the Jews, and "went

away again beyond Jordan" to the place where John had baptized.

17. He came up from beyond Jordan to Bethany and raised Lazarus.

18. He left Bethany and went to Ephraim, a city in the wilderness.

19. Six days before the Passover he returned from Ephraim to Bethany.

20. Next day he entered Jerusalem.

21. "Before the feast of the Passover" he gave his last supper to his disciples, and several chapters report what he said at it, comforting his disciples.

22. From the supper he crosses the brook, Cedron, to a garden, and there he is arrested.

23. He is taken first to the house of Annas.

24. From the house of Annas he is taken to the palace of Caiaphas.

25. From the palace of Caiaphas he is taken to the palace of Pilate.

26. John does not say anything about Pilate sending Jesus to Herod (this appears in *Luke* XXIII, 6–12), but he condemns Jesus.

27. From Pilate's palace he is taken to Golgotha and there crucified.

28. After his death Joseph of Arimathæa asks permission of Pilate to bury Jesus, and he does so, Nicodemus also being present, nobody else being mentioned.

29. On the first day of the week Mary Magdalene, "when it was yet dark," came to the sepulchre, and found the stone rolled away from the foot of it. She ran back for Peter, and he and John returned with her, and found the sepulchre empty, and the grave clothes lying in it.

30. The disciples therefore returned home, but Mary remained, and looking into the sepulchre she saw two angels who spoke to her. A moment later she saw Jesus standing by her side. He said "Mary!" She cried, "Master!" He told her to go and tell the disciples that he had risen.

31. Mary returned to the disciples, and told them she had seen Jesus and he had spoken to her.

32. In the evening within closed doors, "where they had assembled for fear of the Jews," Jesus himself appeared to them.

33. He breathed on them and blessed them and disappeared.

34. After eight days he appeared again to his disciples under like conditions, and gave them proof of his physical reality.

35. After this he appeared to his disciples again at the Lake of Galilee, eating with them, and giving special instructions to Peter.

36. The Gospel does not say how or when Jesus ascends to Heaven.

37. The Gospel concludes with two very feeble and almost incredibly stupid verses, written by another hand than that of the main body of the Gospel.

While it must be admitted that the chronology of *John* is incapable of being harmonized with the chronology of any of the Synoptic Gospels, it must also be said that the closing chapters of John's Gospel reach the greatest heights to which the Spirit of Christ attains.

In those chapters, and in some that precede them, Jesus is an immeasurably greater being than in any of the three Synoptic Gospels. He is beyond doubt, in his own mind, or in the minds of the chief among his disciples, the Son of God; his is the Light of the World; he is the Resurrection and the Life; by him alone can man reach God; by his death alone can man be redeemed from the burden of his sin; by him alone can man be ransomed and gain everlasting life.

It is impossible not to realize that this is the highest note in Christianity; that it is this note which has made Christianity live; this claim that speaks to the human heart, through all the ages, with its universal consciousness of sin. And it is because Jesus is the Saviour, the Redeemer, that he is loved and worshipped, not because he is good and wise, and his moral teaching is the purest and highest the world has known.

The moral teaching of Jesus, exalted as it is, would not have made a religion. It would only have made a morality.

The religion of Jesus rests on his divinity and on nothing else whatever; that he, being God (the Son of God) came to earth as a man, suffered as a man, died as a man, rose again as a God, and that God the Father has accepted this sacrifice as a redemption of man's sin. True or not true *this* is Christianity, and in John it is expressed as nowhere else.

CHAPTER XIII

The Teaching of Jesus During the First Galilean Period

I. *The System of Democritus*

EITHER Jesus knew nothing of the system whereby Democritus had accounted for God and the universe nearly 500 years before him, or he rejected it.

The theory of Democritus was that the universe was created by the collision of atoms in infinite space. In this theory there was no place for a Providence or an intelligent Personal Cause, working to an end.

Democritus admitted the existence of a soul in the human body but he regarded it as material, and consequently it perished when the body perished. He thought there existed a class of beings greater than men and dwelling unseen in the upper regions of the air. Some of them were benevolent and others malignant. Thus, the system of Democritus was not so much a religious system as a physical system. It had hardly any morality or religion in it.

By Democritus the soul was regarded as a material part of the human body, and almost divine. It rejected the notion of a Deity having a part in the creation and government of the universe. It accepted (as a kind of concession to popular superstition) the idea that there were beings, not men, who manifested themselves to man by means of images in dreams.

It probably recognized one God as the soul of the world, "the perpetual flux," the eternal ever-changing force; but it attributed the popular belief in many gods to the effort to explain phenomena such as thunder and lightning. Obviously, the belief of Jesus had little to say to all this.

Either Jesus knew nothing of the theory of the Stoic school, whereby Zeno accounted for God and the universe about 300 years before him, or he rejected that also.

The Socratic theory of the universe may be said to have been

497

built on the divinity of natural law. Natural law was unchangeable, consequently, no such thing as miracle or the supernatural had any place in it. The world was faultless. Therefore it must have been produced by a faultless artificer. The artificer must be self-conscious and personal. This personal creator must be greater than the thing he creates. *This is God.*

The Stoic God is the soul of the *unwise,* which holds together all things in one fixed law. Such was the scheme of the universe according to the Stoics. Man was the creature of God. The soul of man was a part of God. It was the divine spark. He came from God, and at death returned to Him. All men are brothers because all partake of the divine spirit.

II. What Is Stoicism?

It is not certain that the Stoics believed in any life after death. The individual soul must be absorbed into the universal soul. In any case, the soul must return at death to the deity from which it came. What, then, is Stoicism? It is a rule of conduct, a morality. Virtue, alone, is admirable. Neither sickness nor adversity can harm a man. The Stoic ethic is the "Gospel of those who do not believe in the supernatural." The natural law is divine.

Stoicism, according to its followers, would lead us to pity and forgive our enemies. Of course, prayer would be impious, an offence against law. Miracle would be impossible, nature being unchangeable. Death is a mystery, like generation, and no more to be feared. "Toss me into what climate or state you please, I will keep my divine part content, if it but exists and acts according to the laws of nature."

Of this system Marcus Aurelius, nearly two centuries after Jesus, was the highest exponent. But the tragic fact remains that in him it broke utterly to pieces as a guide to life. Nobody was so eloquent or wise in propounding the doctrine of passive resistance to the evils of life, the doctrine of brotherly love, of not resisting evil; yet he permitted the most cruel and barbaric of all the persecutions of the Christians. Justin Martyr and Polycarp fell under his cruel rule even more brutally than Peter and Paul under the rule of Nero.

Knowing little of the teaching of Jesus, Marcus Aurelius destroyed his followers because they refused to include the emperors of Rome among their gods—a bewildering number that was being constantly added to by vote of the senate; because they declared the worship of such gods to be idolatry, and were accused of gross immoralities and unnatural vices; because they held their services in secret; and for other reasons not difficult to explain.

To answer this accusation against Marcus Aurelius and Stoicism that Christian emperors acted still more brutally is to say nothing against Christianity—Stoicism was at its highest expression in Marcus Aurelius. Christianity was not expressed at all by the emperors who persecuted in the name of Jesus. They bore the name of Christ, but had no other conceivable relation to Christianity. They were pagans in every essential of belief. They violated the first precepts of Christianity. Jesus condemned them in advance again and again. He exposed them and warned his disciples against them. He said, in effect, "These people have nothing to do with me."

Further, Marcus Aurelius, the wisest of Roman emperors was *grossly ignorant* of the Christians. The advocate of mercy wrote contemptuously of the wretched creatures torn to pieces by the lions in the amphitheatre, who begged and prayed for a day's further life.

What then? The systems of Democritus and of Zeno were not religions. What is true in them has lived, as science, not as religion. What they had to say to the soul of man is dead and forgotten. The theories of Democritus and Zeno were like the breath of the South Pole on humanity, leaving it an icicle. They never, for so much as a moment, touched the soul of humanity—the highest thing in man.

III. The Consciousness of Sin

Jesus may not have known of the systems of Democritus and the Stoics. If he had known of them he must certainly have rejected them as an explanation of man in the universe. The religion of Jesus begins and centres itself on man in his relation to God. It has its origin not (as generally supposed) in man's consciousness of the existence of a God, but in man's sense of sin. That man is conscious of sin—this is the central thing in the religion of Jesus.

The next thing is that man fears the penalty of sin. That penalty is death. I think this leads to the idea of God. There is only one

God. He is the great controlling power over all. God is not a material power in the infinity of the universe. He is a spirit above and beyond and outside the universe. Man is the Son of God. Man is composed of two elements—body and soul. The soul is from God, it is a part of God. God has His angels and one of their functions is to guide and guard men.

But there is another power in the universe—the power of evil. This power is Satan. Satan also has his angels. Their chief function is to betray and deceive man, and lead him to forsake God. What we call "the world" is Satan's. Its riches, its treasures, its glory, its shows are for Satan to bestow. Satan gives them to those who forsake God and worship him. Satan is for ever struggling for the soul of man. For man to yield his soul to Satan is sin.

All this lies at the root of the religion of Jesus. He did not invent it. And neither did he invent what followed upon it. He was a Jew, and all this came to him from before the days of Abraham.

Thereafter came many other developments. The essence of the teaching of Jesus is that man has sinned against God. Man must repent of his sin and be forgiven by God, or he will be everlastingly lost.

Jesus follows the Hebrew prophets of hundreds of years before him in thinking that a day is coming when God will destroy the kingdom of the world, which is now controlled by Satan, and set up on earth another kingdom. This will be the kingdom of God. God will send His own messenger to preside over this kingdom. This messenger will be the Messiah, the Christ.

Before he comes a forerunner will come to warn people to repent of their sins, and so escape the wrath to come. When the messenger of God, the Messiah, the Christ, comes, he will judge men, dead and living, and divide the good from the evil, giving life everlasting to the good, and condemning the bad to eternal death—perhaps to eternal torment.

Thus, I think the religion of Jesus is the religion of forgiveness of sins. He touched humanity more closely than any before him, because he brought more strongly than Democratus or Zeno or Marcus Aurelius the thought that God was man's Father, that He loved man as His son, His beloved son and was waiting and watching for an opportunity to forgive man's sin—to wipe it out. This, in my judgment, is the essence of the religion of Jesus—

makes it aflame with fire, while Stoicism remains dead as ice. This is why Christianity has had its immense effect.

IV. Possession by Demons

Does Jesus in this early period of his ministry believe in possession by demons? I think he does. He speaks of it too frequently to be misunderstood. I think he believes that Satan has his bad angels, just as God has His good angels, and that the bad angels are sometimes permitted by man to enter into and possess him, so that without help from outside he cannot cast them out. I believe Jesus thinks of this possession by demons just as we think of the control of evil passions, such as drink, avarice and lust, which a man first allows to enter into him, and which then become so strongly entrenched in him that he cannot cast them out without help from outside.

I think Jesus believes that by prayer and fasting, and the development of the highest forms of the spiritual nature, a man may acquire such mastery over the evil powers in another man that he can cast them out of him. He can command them to come out, and they *must* come. Imperfectly understood in the past, the possession by demons and the expulsion of demons has been taught to be mere superstition; but modern science is seeing things differently. I think this is a perfectly established fact at the present time.

V. Did Jesus Believe in Miracles?

I think Jesus did works for which we have no other name than miracles. I think it probable that he worked many miracles that are not recorded, but only generally mentioned in the Gospels. On the other hand I cannot accept all the stories in the Gospels of the miracles worked by Jesus. I distinguish between those that agree with themselves and those that do not. I reject those of which the evidence is contradictory and incapable of being harmonized. I reject those that are merely indications of power, believing that Jesus never exercised his power merely for its own sake. I reject those that are in deliberate violation of the laws of nature.

On the other hand, I accept some that are the intensified action of nature. Therefore, I cannot accept such miracles as the feeding of the five thousand with five loaves and two fishes. The law of

God is that man should live by the sweat of his brow. To give food to five thousand when nothing has been done to earn that food is to outrage God's law—Jesus never outrages God's law. I do not accept the miracle of Jesus walking on the water. It is at best a miracle of supernatural power, without a recognizable or worthy object. On the other hand, I accept the raising of the widow's son, of Jairus's daughter and even of Lazarus, but I put an interpretation upon these that does not strip the inexorable law of Death of its majesty and solemnity and unchangeableness.

VI.   Did Jesus Believe in Prayer?

Undoubtedly, Jesus believed in prayer. In the systems that had gone before him in the pagan Greek world there was really no place for prayer—Stoicism had no place for it. If natural law was entirely unchangeable, if everything had been preordained and must happen, then why prayer? It was an offence. If God was no more than a fiery power to which all life must return, why try to speak to it, to influence it, to make it alter its plan?

In Jesus, as a Jew, inheriting the principles of his people from before the time when they came out of the East with Abraham, all this was different. God was a spirit holding complete control over the physical universe. Whatever He had made He could alter. Just as the forefathers of Jesus had prayed to God for victory in battle, and sung psalms of thanks to Him, so Jesus taught his disciples to pray. "Ask, and it shall be given you." Clearly Jesus believed God answered prayer. But what they were to ask was little—nothing more than daily bread. Only this and the spiritual things—the forgiveness of their sins, as they forgave them that owed debts to them; to be kept from temptation, and so on.

VII.   Sin as the Cause of Disease

Did Jesus believe that disease was caused by sin? In spite of some difficult passages, I do not think so. I believe he thought that disease was often the result of sin. This is so obvious a fact that we all know it. In some cases of miracles, where he says, "Sin no more . . . lest a worse come unto thee," he is speaking directly to the sinner in language such as any doctor might use to-day.

I do not think that Jesus shared to the full the belief of his people about sin as the first cause of disease. That belief of the Jews finds frequent expression in the Gospels, as when the Pharisees told the man born blind that he was "altogether born in sins." The origin of this Jewish belief in sin as the cause of disease, and suffering of other kinds, dates far back in Jewish history.

Certainly it is clear, and perhaps natural, that during the Babylonian exile this idea existed. It is seen in the fact (1) that having accepted the idea that God was in an especial sense the God of the Jews; (2) that God had distinctly promised Abraham first and David afterwards that His chosen people should inherit the earth, and (3) that finding themselves taken captive and their country gone from them, they should conclude not that God's promise had failed, or they must have lost all faith in God, but that God had permitted these evils to fall on them by reason of their sins.

In like manner, it is clear that the Jews adopted the same attitude towards disease, (1) that the God of Israel, having chosen them as His people, could not have intended that they should be afflicted with diseases; (2) that they were so afflicted with diseases because they had sinned against Him; (3) that the general form of their sin was following after other gods; (4) that these gods were the demons, the servants and evil agents of Satan.

Further the Jews of the time of Jesus clearly believed that it was given to man, by the power of an evil spirit (Beelzebub), to cast out an evil spirit. Whether they believed that by power of God a man might cast out an evil spirit is not so certain.

This was the general belief of the Jewish people at the time of Jesus. It was a belief in demonology. That Jesus at the beginning of his ministry shared, in some sense, some part of this belief in demoniacal possession can hardly be doubted. In his miracles he is constantly commanding the evil spirits to come out of the persons possessed. When he ordains his disciples and sends them out, he always gives them power to cast out evil spirits. He refers to such power of casting out demons as coming to those who have obtained it by prayer and fasting.

Therefore, it is difficult not to recognize that (1) he believed in the possession by evil spirits; (2) he believed in the spiritual power of the good spirits to cast out and destroy the evil or unclean spirits. Huxley declared that if Jesus believed in demonology (the badge of the primitive tribes in all countries) he could not believe in Jesus. But later and perhaps greater scientists are not so sure that the belief in demons is without foundation. Conduct among men leaves no escape from the theory of demoniacal possession. The complete conquest of the evil tendencies in men leaves no escape from the thought that *evil* powers can be expelled by *good* powers. To call these evil and good powers evil and good angels is only a change of words.

Thus the belief of Jesus differs from the belief of Democritus and of the Stoics in saying there are two forces in the world (not one only), a force for good and a force for evil. *And the contention between these two for the soul of man is of the essence of the religion of Christ.*

Did Jesus believe that disease itself was the expression of the personal sin of the sufferer? Apparently, the Jews did so. I do not think Jesus did. It is true that in working his miracles of healing he sometimes says, "Thy sins are forgiven thee" and "Go and sin no more."

But, first, it must be remembered that in certain cases of disease cured by Jesus, the disease may have been most certainly the result of sin, and, next, the injunction about sin and forgiveness may have been due to the basic theory of Jesus that *all* men had sinned and all *deserved to suffer.* In by far the larger number of his miracles of healing nothing is said of the sin of the sufferer as the cause of the malady, and in the one outstanding case of the reference to the people whose blood had been shed by Pilate between the Temple and the altar, and of the sixteen on whom the tower of Siloam fell, it is explicitly stated that their misfortunes had fallen on them not because they had sinned or because their parents had sinned, but that *all men having sinned* all men might likewise perish.

What, then, was the belief of Jesus about sin? That all men had sinned. That it was necessary for every man to repent of his sin against God before he could enter the kingdom of God. That the sin of man lay chiefly, if not entirely, in submitting to the temptation of Satan, the temptation of the world and its honours, glory and possessions, the desire to become rich and powerful, to control the will and lives and labour of other men.

That the way to repent of such sin was to renounce the world, and the rewards of the world, to become poor, to become meek, to trust absolutely in God, not to make any vain attempt to do without God, but to rely on Him day by day for daily bread; not to fight for the possession of the good things of this world, but to put them aside, to think only of the spiritual things, to consider the welfare of the soul above the welfare of the body, to resist no man, to fight no man, because the only temptation to fight, the only reason any man can have to fight, is for the possession of the things of this world. The things of this world are of no use in the kingdom of God.

It will be observed that the persons possessed of devils, and the devils by whom they are possessed, nearly always address Jesus as the son of David and the Holy One of God. There was an ancient belief among eastern peoples generally that lunatics whose wits were lost to earthly affairs had their wits in Heaven, and were thereby possessed of knowledge denied to the mortals who had all their natural faculties in this life. But believing this, how did it come to pass that the people of Galilee did not take heed of these cries of the possessed ones, if they heard them, and accept Jesus in the character the possessed ones gave him?

Jesus, as will be seen, is constantly warning the people he cures, and demanding of the demons he expels, that they shall "tell no man" of him. This obviously means that if he were commonly reported to work these miracles, which no other man had ever before worked, but which had been foretold of the Messiah in the Scriptures, the whole world would know him for what he was —the Christ—or, failing that, would accuse him of masquerading in the character of the Messiah, as others had done before him, and so bring him to his death for blasphemy.

This he did not yet wish, because his time was not yet come.

VIII.   The Law of Moses

The attitude of Jesus to the law of Moses was absolute acceptance of it. But did he not rescind it in the matter of divorce? I think he saw clearly that the spirit of the law of Moses was being smothered by the body of it. His early teaching was not intended to undo or abrogate or otherwise disturb the law of Moses. But only to carry it farther. To go through the form of it to the soul of it. To get at the essence of it. To express the essence of the law in vivid terms. This led to language that seemed to be at war with the possibilities of human nature—such as "love your enemies."

I think this was deliberately done to get at the heart of the intention of the law, to break away the crust of formalism, of sophistry, of casuistry, of imposture and of hypocrisy by which it had been so long encrusted.

IX.   *The Messiah*

Did Jesus think he was the Messiah? I cannot have a doubt of it. From the first moment of his ministry he believed he was the Messiah—that God had laid on him the burden of being His messenger to call humanity to repentance, back from the service of Satan to the service of God. The time of the coming of the Kingdom was near. Men must repent, or they would be lost in everlasting death. If they repented they would gain everlasting life.

The Messiahship of Jesus at this period was a spiritual kingship, not a temporal kingship. It was natural that when the people saw Jesus working the miracles expected of the Messiah, the King, they should wish to carry him off *by force and make him a king*. But Jesus had fought that temptation before and conquered it. His was to be no earthly kingship, only a spiritual kingship.

Further, Jesus had already gone as far as the Israelite prophets, farther than most of them, perhaps farther than all. They had thought first of a conquering Messiah. Next, of a suffering Messiah—a Messiah who was to suffer *with* his people, the Jews. I doubt if any of the prophets thought of the Messiah as the Saviour of the Gentiles. This was, I think, in this early period of the Galilean ministry, the thought of Jesus—that he was the Messiah who was not to rule over, but to suffer *with* his people—with *all mankind*. I do not think Jesus had yet attained to the idea (of which the Hebrew prophets seem to have known nothing) of a Messiah who was to suffer *for* his people. This is questionable in the light of *Isaiah* LIII. But it may not have been an *individual* man as the Messiah. I see no trace of that thought in these early days of his Galilean ministry.

CHAPTER XIV

The Transfiguration

I. The Universal Religion

THE ANSWER to the woman of Samaria (*John* IV, 21–24), may be accepted as the first expression of the Universal Religion: the moment at which Jesus ceased to be a Jew, and became at the same time the greatest of Jews. On reaching Galilee he received news of the death of John the Baptist, and fearing the same fate for himself, before his time was yet come for it, he went up quickly through Galilee out of the territory and jurisdiction of Herod Antipas (whom he evidently distrusted) into the territory of Herod Philip on the north-east. It was at Cæsarea Philippi that he first put to the disciples the test question, "Whom say ye that I am?" and received for the first time the definite assurance of their belief that he was the Christ.

According to *Matthew*, Jesus comes into the coasts of Cæsarea Philippi. There he asks his disciples, "Whom do men say that I the Son of Man am?" This use of "Son of Man" shows it was not in the mouth of Jesus synonymous with "Son of God." The disciples answer variously: "Some say that thou art John the Baptist; some Elias; and others Jeremias, or one of the prophets." Jesus says, "But whom say ye that I am?" and Peter answers, "Thou art the Christ, the Son of the living God."

Jesus then says, "Blessed art thou, Simon Bar-jona, for flesh and blood hath not revealed it unto thee, but my Father which is in Heaven." This shows that Jesus himself had never told Peter that he was the Christ, but that God had revealed it to Peter. Then Jesus charges his disciples that they should tell no man that he was Jesus the Christ. I think his warning, as of old, that they should tell no man was not intended to discountenance their belief that he was the Messiah—he could have done that more simply, more directly and more effectually by denying it once for all—but to indicate that he had something yet to do before he put it in the power of his enemies to destroy him as a blasphemer.

507

From that time forward Jesus began to show his disciples a new thing—that he must go up to Jerusalem, suffer many things of the elders and chief priests, be killed and raised again the third day.

II.　*Jesus Transfigured—According to Matthew*

Six days later Jesus takes Peter, James and John and goes up into a high mountain, probably Mount Hermon, in the neighbourhood of Cæsarea Philippi, as it is not until later that *Matthew* says that Jesus and his disciples were come to Capernaum, and that leaving Galilee they came into the coasts of Judæa beyond Jordan.

In the mountain Jesus was transfigured before his disciples. His face shone as the sun, and his raiment was white as the light. And there appeared to them Moses and Elias, talking with him. There is a manifest break here, and then (*Matthew* XVII, 4) Peter says, "Lord, it is good for us to be here: if thou wilt, let us make here three tabernacles; one for thee, and one for Moses, and one for Elias."

While Peter speaks a bright cloud overshadows them, and a voice out of the cloud says, "This is my beloved Son, in whom I am well pleased; hear ye him." When the disciples hear this voice they fall on their faces and are afraid. Jesus touches them and says, "Arise, and be not afraid."

When they lift their eyes they see no man, but Jesus only. And as they come down the mountain, Jesus charges them that they tell no man of the vision until he has risen again from the dead.

Such is the story of the Transfiguration according to *Matthew*. I find:

1. That it is a version from the disciples' point of view. They alone (Peter in particular) can have reported it.

2. That it carries no message of any kind whatsoever, inasmuch as the voice from the clouds says nothing that the disciples do not know. They are already aware that Jesus is the Christ and they hear him.

3. That something is obviously missing to give meaning to the scene.

I think that the Transfiguration of Jesus was not a tangible thing, such as is described, with his face and garments white and the presence of Moses and Elias, talking with him. All this is a legendary story which does not bear examination as reality, and is attended by impossible and even foolish incidents, such as Peter's suggestion that he and his fellow disciples should build tabernacles on the mountain top.

III. Jesus Transfigured: According to Mark

In *Mark*, as in *Matthew*, Jesus and his disciples are at Cæsarea Philippi. The same questions are asked by Christ and answered by Peter and the other apostles. Peter remonstrates against the statement by Jesus that he must die. Whereupon Jesus rebukes Peter, saying, "Get thee behind me, Satan."

The meaning of this is that Peter does not know that it is according to God's plan that he, Jesus, should go up to Jerusalem, be killed, and rise again, after three days.

Jesus then calls the people and says to them, including his disciples:

> Whosoever will come after me, let him deny himself, and take up his cross, and follow me. For whosoever will save his life shall lose it; but whosoever shall lose his life for my sake and the gospel's, the same shall save it. For what shall it profit a man, if he shall gain the whole world, and lose his own soul? Or what shall a man give in exchange for his soul?

The last verse of Chapter VIII and the first of Chapter IX (which ought to be the end of Chapter VIII) say that his followers must not be ashamed of him and his teaching in "this adulterous and sinful generation," or he will be ashamed of them when he returns to establish his Kingdom. Also that the Kingdom will come before death comes to all of them.

Then comes the Transfiguration. Again the same difficulties in *Mark* as in *Matthew*. Who could have reported it? Only the disciples. To whom was the voice from Heaven speaking? Only the disciples. What did the voice tell them that they did not know already? Nothing!

Then six days later he goes up into a high mountain with Peter, James and John. The description of the Transfiguration scene is almost verbally the same as that which is given in *Matthew*. Elias and Moses are said to be "talking with Jesus." Again we find the same thing at the verse beginning "And Peter answered and said . . ." He had nothing to answer. Something seems to

be omitted. The substance of Peter's answer is the same as in
Matthew. "For he wist not what to say; for they were sore
afraid." The cloud is the same and the voice and message are the
same. The passing of the cloud is the same, and the after effect.

Again the same charge from Jesus that they should tell no man
what things they had seen till the Son of Man were risen from the
dead. "And they kept that saying with themselves, questioning
one with another what the rising from the dead should mean." In
other words, did Jesus mean the rising from the dead at the judgment day? If so they all believed in that. But he seemed to mean
rising from the dead before the judgment day—in short, three
days after his death. What did this mean? It was a new thing. They
had no understanding of it. Abraham and David were dead and
buried, and they would rise at the Judgment. But they had not
risen yet. What did Jesus mean by saying that he would rise in
three days?

The disciples could not understand it. They never did understand it, until it actually happened—until they believed it had
actually happened. Then it changed everything. Jesus from that
moment was a different being to them.

IV. Jesus Transfigured: According to Luke

In *Luke* the Transfiguration appears in an earlier period of the
ministry. But the scenes of it are the same. Herod Antipas has
heard of Jesus, and he is reported to be asking, "Who is this, of
whom I hear such things?" They told him of the things which
Jesus said—things which John the Baptist might have said. They
are not the things John the Baptist did, for John wrought no
miracles, whereas Jesus is described mainly as a miracle worker.

But Jesus is preaching a gospel which, if it prevailed, would
speedily put an end to men like Herod Antipas. So the "fox"
desires to see Jesus.

Jesus hears of Herod's desire, but he knows his man, and gives
Herod no chance of seeing him. He goes away out of Herod's
territory to a desert place belonging to the city called Bethsaida.
Bethsaida was obviously in the territory of Herod Philip, brother
of Herod Antipas. Bethsaida was not far from Cæsarea Philippi.
But Luke does not mention the latter. Probably being a stranger to
the country he does not know it. But thereabouts occur the scenes

of the feeding of the five thousand. Thereabouts also occurs the questioning of his disciples, as in *Matthew* and *Mark*: "Whom say the people that I am?" He receives the same answers, and it is Peter again who answers that Jesus is "the Christ of God."

Again, as before, Jesus "straitly charged them, and commanded them to tell no man." Further, he goes on, as in *Mark,* to predict his end. That he is to suffer many things, be rejected of the elders and chief priests and scribes, be slain and be raised again from the dead. Again, he says that if any man wishes to come after him he must deny himself, take up his cross and follow him. Again, he tells them that to save their lives would be to lose them, and to lose their lives would be to save them. That it is of no use to a man to gain the whole world if he is to lose himself or be cast away. Again, he warns his disciples that if they should be ashamed of him, and his death, and so on, he will be ashamed of them when his hour of glory comes, and the kingdom of God is established. And again he tells them that his Kingdom will come before all of them have died.

Then comes the Transfiguration. It is eight days, according to *Luke,* after this conversation. The same scene is reported by the disciples.

Who told the writer that the two men who talked with Jesus were Moses and Elias? Are we to assume that Jesus told him? Or that he knew it by divine intuition (as Simeon knew the babe Christ at the Temple)?

Then comes (IX, 31, 32), an important addition to the story as told in *Matthew* and *Mark:*

[Moses and Elias] who appeared in glory, and spake of his decease which he should accomplish at Jerusalem. But Peter and they that were with him [James and John] were heavy with sleep; and when they were awake, they saw his glory, and the two men that stood with him.

Does this mean that they had dreamt the earlier part of the scene and then awoke to find it true?

The succeeding scene is practically the same as in *Matthew* and *Mark*. It is open to the same objection. The voice from the cloud tells the disciples nothing they do not know. "And they kept it close, and told no man in those days any of those things which they had seen."

Does this mean that they did not tell the other disciples?

The important addition in *Luke* is that the prophets who appeared to Jesus in his Transfiguration spoke of his death which should come to pass in Jerusalem. Is this the substance of the scene, the meaning of the Transfiguration? Is it intended to say that at the Transfiguration it became known to Jesus that he was going to die—to die in Jerusalem—at the charge of the Jews, but at the hands of the Romans?

The objection to this interpretation of the motive of the Transfiguration is that Jesus appears to have known all this before—as is shown in his interview with his disciples at Cæsarea Philippi. It seems as if the two scenes had got themselves transposed—ought the scene on the mountain to come before the scene in Cæsarea Philippi? Or did the supernatural visitors on the mountain tell Jesus more than that he should die at Jerusalem?

V. The Meaning of the Transfiguration

I am satisfied that the story of the Transfiguration in the Synoptic Gospels is a very imperfect one. Clearly the writers kept their word to "keep it close." They never ceased to "keep it close" —if they ever understood the meaning of it. I doubt if they ever *did* understand it.

My view is that the Transfiguration in the Gospels is an unread secret—that it marks the hour when Jesus realized the full meaning of the task before him. Hitherto, he had known only part of the burden laid on him by God. He had known that he was the Christ. He had realized that he was the spiritual Christ, the Christ of Isaiah's prophecy, the suffering Christ—not the Christ who was to sit on the throne of David and re-establish the Jewish kingdom.

I think that the Transfiguration (whatever form it took in reality) was intended to tell Jesus that he was not only the Christ of God, but also the Son of God. That as the Christ he might fulfil the Jewish conception of the Christ, which made him a King-Christ, a man who ruled in the name of God, who never died, least of all on the tree (cross), which was an accursed death. But that as the Son of God he undertook responsibilities to God for the sins of men, and had to atone to God for them and thus wipe them out. That he was to do this by becoming in the highest sense the Son of Man, and representing man, and taking, as man's representative, the burden of man's sin and making his peace with God.

I think this message which came to Jesus in the Transfiguration told him that he was a Christ who had to die in his character as man, to go through terrible human and spiritual sufferings, to be given up by his own people to the punishment imposed by the Roman Gentiles; that this punishment (as he knew) would be the punishment of death for claiming to be king; and that the punishment of the Romans would be crucifixion.

Further, I think he was told that according to the scheme of God, whereby his suffering and death as a man who stood as the representative of humanity, all men were to suffer death through him, though not in their own persons; that the salvation of men from the penalty of their sins was to be won through this suffering and death of Jesus, who was to die for them, in their name, as their representative, as the human son of man who stood for humanity, but that man had to contribute his own part to his salvation. That part was to accept Jesus, his teaching, his representation, in a word to *believe* him, and the power of his word and death. Those who so believed were thereby ransomed, saved from the burden and punishment of their sin, entitled to the resurrection and the enjoyment of the kingdom of God—to life everlasting.

But those who did not accept and believe in this remedial and sacrificial work of Jesus remained dead in their sins, had no resurrection, did not become heirs to the kingdom of God. Further, that there were unmistakable indications of punishment after death, of a condition called hell—everlasting suffering.

This was the meaning and outcome of the Transfiguration. That Jesus, realizing now the full burden of his Christ nature, saw that in his human character he was to suffer and die. He was to suffer and die in Jerusalem at the hands of his own people, the Jews, and of their masters, the Romans.

He saw also that everybody who followed him and took his name must in like manner suffer and die. Therefore he forewarned his disciples. But he also saw that his suffering and death were not to be everlasting. Unlike the scapegoat of Israel, he was to rise out of death, he was to conquer death, he was to inherit eternal life.

He placed his period of death at three days. Why three days I do not know—why not one day, one hour or one moment of death I do not know. Where he was to be, and what he was to do, during those three days of death I do not know. Whether he was to descend into hell and suffer (as the representative of humanity) all the tortures of the damned, being himself innocent, I do not know. I only know that he said he was to rise from death after three days.

He told his disciples so, but they did not understand him. In spite of all he said, most of them appear to have continued to believe that as the Christ of the Scriptures he would not die. John and James believed so. Only Thomas, and perhaps Judas Iscariot, believed in the material fact that he would die, that on going to Jerusalem he was deliberately walking into the arms of death.

Jesus's own attitude towards his death is clear. He realized that as the Son of God he was to die in his person as a man instead of humanity. It would be terrible. Not merely so many hours of physical suffering. Countless martyrs and prophets had gone through that. The suffering of the death of all men was to be borne by him. Only so could he redeem humanity from the authority of the law by which it was condemned.

He thought he could bear all this, that his Father would not forsake him, that he would be supported by the Divine Spirit. That his death as a ransom for many would be his glory. That after his three days of death as the scapegoat of man he would rise to his glory.

Then the disciples again. After the death of Jesus they understood what he had said to them during his life. They understood, too, what he said to them at his resurrection. They were saved from the penalty of their sins by death. God had accepted his death as a propitiating sacrifice.

What now was before them? To go out into all the world with the glad news that by the death of the Christ all men would be saved from the burden of their sin who accepted him as their representative. He had died for them. They died in him. But they also rose in him to everlasting life—to the inheritance of the kingdom of God.

In going through the world with this good news they knew they would share his fate, they would suffer as he had suffered. They would be killed as he had been killed. But what matter? They would only die in the flesh. Only the bodily part of them would die.

The spirit in them would live, because he had died to save it from death.

Then came the Day of Pentecost. It was then that the full realization of their position and their work came upon them. Think where they stood! Each in his character as a human creature, with father, mother, wife, sons, daughters. They must share this salvation, this everlasting life. It was impossible to think of life everlasting for themselves without their sharing it.

Then think of the general body of their fellow men, and the thought of the eternal death, perhaps eternal punishment, everlasting torment that awaited them! The apostles told themselves that they must draw them into the great kingdom of God; make them sharers in the Atonement; make them acceptors of the belief in Christ, which would ransom them and make them at one with God. So they hurried away. They were aflame with a desire to make all the world accept the God-Christ.

They would suffer in doing so. Humanity would fight against its own salvation. In its blindness and sin it would fight against itself, its own eternal welfare. It would kill them. But what matter? They would no sooner die than they would be with the God-Christ. He was waiting for his people to come to him. The quicker they came to him the sooner his kingdom would be established. The more they suffered in his name the more their glory, the higher their place in his kingdom.

So Stephen, being stoned, looks up into Heaven and sees his Saviour and says, "Lord Jesus, receive my spirit."

Even as Jesus himself had not run away from suffering and death, so they (his followers) did not run away from it. They, like him, did not ask for it. They did not commit any kind of spiritual suicide. They were like the soldier in battle who knows he must die if he goes forward at a terrible moment, and yet goes, because he *must*.

Then came the death of the Christians in Rome at the hand of Nero. They might have escaped death by blaspheming the name of Christ, by swearing allegiance to the name of Cæsar as divine. They refused to do so, and died, bound up to stakes and being burnt alive in the grounds of the palace of the emperor, for the joy of his friends. They did not shrink. Why? Because the death of the body had no terrors now that the everlasting death of the soul was impossible, now that life everlasting lay behind death.

CHAPTER XV

The Atonement

I. The Religion of Christianity

THE ACCEPTED IDEA of Christianity among, perhaps, the majority of mankind down to the present day is, apparently, that it is a faith built on the teachings of Jesus, his moral teachings on the relations of man to man, on the condition of the poor, the perils of the rich, on marriage, divorce, war, peace, the duty of forgiveness, the beauty of mercy, on humility before God, on sincerity of worship. This, of itself, is obviously only a part of Christianity. It is the morality of Jesus, not the religion of Christianity. If Jesus had stood to the world for no more than this, Christianity would not have been a religion, but only a system of morals. And Jesus would have differed from many teachers who had gone before him only by the greater purity and nobility of his system of morals.

The spirit of this moral teaching was not new. The great rabbis of his own race had taught much the same morality for at least 200 years. The prophets of his own people had delivered the same message. The law of Moses was not essentially different. Where Jesus differed from these was in the greater purity of his moral conception, in getting down to the spirit that lay beneath the letter, in stripping away the outer crust that had gathered about the law and getting at the heart of its spirit.

If Christianity had meant no more it might have become a new sect of the Jewish faith, and by slow degrees it might have made its way over the world. It would never have conquered the world. It would never have taken the heart of the world by storm. Jesus would never have stood alone among the spiritual guides. And the so-called Christians who have denied the supernatural element in Christianity would for ever (as they have hitherto) have left the world cold.

From the beginning of his ministry Jesus claimed to be more

than a moral teacher. He claimed first to be a messenger of God—the Messiah, the Christ. If he did not do so in set words it was for the obvious reason that such a claim, in his age, in his country, amid such conditions as existed, would have brought his life to a swifter termination before his work was done. At this first stage of his life he gave witness of his Messianic claim by performing miracles such as man had never before performed. He foretold the coming of a kingdom of Heaven (or of God) on earth in which the morality he taught would be fulfilled. To his disciples he spoke of himself as the head of that kingdom, the King, the Christ. He allowed others to call him so.

II. The Attitude of the Disciples

And what, during his lifetime, was the view his disciples and apostles took of him? They believed that he was the Christ. They believed that he would, within their lifetime, establish the divine kingdom on earth. They believed it would be everlasting. They thought it would be a temporal kingdom, with Jerusalem as the centre, the Jews (as the chosen people of God) as its chief subjects, and the Gentile world, in an outer part, admitted by the grace of God on accepting the Jewish faith, adopting the law of Moses, becoming Jews in all essentials, and having Jerusalem as the centre of their spiritual world.

I think they were established in this view of Jesus and his character and mission by the miracles he performed even more than by his teaching, his parables, his words of truth which no other man had. I think this remained their attitude to their Master down to the day of his last entrance into Jerusalem. From that day forward their faith began to fail. They were puzzled, depressed and bewildered by a new development in Jesus—by his constant allusions to his sufferings at the hands of the Jewish rulers, to his forthcoming death amid ignominy and shame. All this conflicted with the Jewish Messianic hope in which they had been brought up —that Jesus, when he came, would come for ever, that he would never die, above all that he would not die "on a tree" (an accursed condition). Above all, they were puzzled by his talk of resurrection, of his appearing to them again, of the sufferings they were themselves to go through.

Such was the state of the disciples down to the arrest, trial, condemnation, death and burial of Jesus. All this crushed them. They behaved like men who thought they had deceived themselves. Apparently, they never for a moment accused Jesus of deceiving them. Their love for him as a man never failed them. Three days after his death they were gathered together in secret weeping over the loss of him. But their belief in him as the Messiah had gone— must have gone. If they had still believed that he was the Christ they could not have behaved as they did behave. They had gone through an awful disillusionment. Perhaps they thought he also had done so. If they had suffered, he had suffered more. They had lost a beloved master. But they had seen him die in humiliation, and their faith in him as the Messiah was dead.

Their hopes were annihilated, as is seen by the words of the disciples on the road to Emmaus: "The chief priests and our rulers . . . have crucified him. But we trusted that it had been he which should have redeemed Israel."

Not at first could they realize that he who had been dead and buried had risen from the grave. But at length they were compelled to believe it. He appeared to them, spoke to them, counselled them, comforted them, reassured them. Then they remembered what he had said while he lived, that all these things were to happen to him, that he *was* to die and that after three days he was to rise again from the dead.

From that hour everything was changed for them. They began to see Jesus (now ascended to Heaven) from a new point of view. He had died in degradation, but he had conquered death and risen from the grave, and was now in Heaven, sitting on the right hand of God the Father. He was still the Messiah as they had always believed. More, he would come again to establish the kingdom of God on earth. He would come soon; within the lifetime of the present generation; some of them would not die before he came again. And when he came it would be in clouds of glory, in the rays of the sunrise, perhaps, surrounded by his holy angels.

But that was not all. If Jesus had so far departed from the accepted expectations of the Jews about the Messiah, if he had gone through death, why was it? It was because he was not merely the messenger of God, he was the Son of God, a part of God, and he had come to earth and lived and died for a great purpose. What was that purpose? To give his life as a ransom for the sins of men. To ransom sinful men. To lift off the head of man the sins for which God must otherwise punish him, perhaps cast him out.

This, then, was the meaning of that degrading death on the Cross—to save the world by the sacrifice of his own blood as the God-man. He had said so while he was with them, but they had not understood him. Now they understood him. So the Cross ceased to be the sign of his shame to them. It was the sign of his glory. Those who had brought him to that shameful death were indeed guilty before God, and would be brought to a fearful accounting, but none the less they had acted as God permitted, foresaw, perhaps intended. Through his death on the Cross, Christ, the God-man, had by his acceptance of death which he might have avoided made atonement to the Father for the sins of as many as were willing to repent their ill deeds and accept his blood as a sacrifice.

Through his death he had made a new covenant with God, which was to supersede the covenant made by God with Moses—to lift away all the sin of man, to make man's peace with God. All that remained to man was to accept this new covenant, and this they could do by accepting Jesus. Jesus crucified, risen from the dead, ascended into Heaven, to come again in glory and establish the kingdom of God on earth—this was the Christianity of the first apostles. It found full expression first in Peter on the Day of Pentecost; afterwards in Paul, then in the author of the Epistles to the Hebrews. It was the Christianity of the primitive Church.

At whatever other points they differed among themselves, on this one point they were agreed—that Jesus of Nazareth was the Son of God. He came to earth to wipe out the sins of the world. He did so by dying an agonizing yet glorious death on the Cross. "Christ and his crucifixion" became their text and watchword. "There is none other name under Heaven given among men, whereby we must be saved." Such was the transfiguring change which came upon the apostles within seven weeks from the death of Jesus, transforming the untaught fishermen of Galilee into inspired persons, ready to die for the faith that was in them.

How did they come by it? Did they derive it from the prophets? What had Jesus said to them during his life that justified the central doctrine of Christianity (the thing that lifts it above a morality and makes it a religion) that he (who had been with God from the beginning) had come to earth from God to give his life as a ransom for many?

III.   The Meaning of the Atonement

The first thing we realize as we pass through the three first narratives of the life of Jesus is that this idea of atonement for the sins of men by his death as sin-bearer does not appear until death seems to him to be within sight. Next, we see that from the time of the Transfiguration onward the declarations of Jesus concerning his approaching fate concern chiefly the suffering and death that await him. Next, that he has no wish to escape from that suffering and death; on the contrary that he regards it as part of a great divine scheme which he is to fulfil. Next, that he seeks to console his disciples by telling them that three days after his death he will rise again, and that the object of his death is to give his life as a ransom for many.

What does he mean by this? Has he by supernatural means arrived at the conclusion that he must die? Or has he merely, in a natural way, adduced the general thought that having made the hierarchy of his nation his implacable enemies, he had put them, and they had put themselves, in a position in which they must kill him, or be killed themselves. He does not "swerve from the path of his destination," yet on going up to Jerusalem, knowing he will die there, he may not be said to be committing suicide. Grant that he sees that he has something to do which only his death will bring about, and we see that he is in the position of the soldier on the battlefield who does not shrink from "going over the top" although he knows he will surely die in doing so.

The disciples did not understand the discourses of Jesus about his coming death, because they could not "make them tally with their preconceived ideas concerning the Messiah." Peter protests. Jesus rebukes Peter. Whether the idea of a dying and suffering Messiah was widely diffused among the Jews in the time of Jesus may be a point for discussion, but that the disciples of Jesus knew everything about it may be confidently denied. Their conduct and their expressions during his life, and for two days after his death, show clearly that such an idea had never entered into their minds.

And now comes the question did Jesus know anything about it? And did he associate with the idea of a suffering and dying Messiah the doctrine of the expiation of the sins of the people by his death? If he did, did he find this idea in the Old Testament?

Strauss says, "The Old Testament does, indeed, contain the doctrine of an expiation of the sins of the people to take place *after* the Messianic era, (*Ezekiel* XXXVI, 25, XXXVII, 23, *Daniel* IX, 24), but there is no trace of this expectation being effected by the suffering and death of the Messiah." Again, of Philo and Josephus, the two authors who wrote soonest after the period in question, the latter is silent as to the Messianic hope of his nation, and the former though he speaks of a Messiah, says nothing of his sufferings and death. Strauss remarks, "Thus nothing remains as evidence except the New Testament and later Jewish writings,"— but may not the passage in *Isaiah* (XLIII, 3) be so interpreted?

In the Gospels there are few passages which justify the thought that the friends of Jesus had the least idea either of a suffering and dying Messiah, or of a Messiah who could ransom man by his death. On the contrary, there are many indications which show them to be incapable of understanding Jesus in his repeated announcements of his death. *John* (XII, 34) puts into the mouth of the multitude the statement, which they had found in the law, that "Christ abideth for ever."

It is true that there are a few passages which by inference may be thought to refer to a suffering Messiah. In *Luke* the address of Simeon to Mary at the Temple, "Yea, a sword shall pierce through thy own soul also," may possibly be interpreted to mean that she was to suffer a mother's agony at the violent death of her son. Again, John the Baptist's exclamation on seeing Jesus approach him, "Behold the Lamb of God, which taketh away the sin of the world." "This, too, might be understood," says Strauss, "to prove that the idea of expiatory suffering on the part of the Messiah was current in Christ's time. But both these passages have been shown to be unhistorical." And assuredly they are totally out of keeping with all we know of the subsequent life of Mary (except her presence at the Cross according to *John* only), or of the subsequent behaviour of John the Baptist, who was the forerunner of the Messiah, and yet after he has been told, as by God, that Jesus was the Messiah, goes on with his former work of foretelling the coming of the Messiah (instead of helping him in his Messianic work), and afterwards of sending his disciples from his presence to Jesus to ask whether he is the Messiah or not.

Thus the opinion that the Messiah was to suffer and die in expiation of the sins of the world had no existence among the disciples and friends of Jesus during his lifetime. It was only after his death that the idea became current among them. Thereafter it is to be found in Peter, in Paul, in Philip, in the author of *Hebrews* and elsewhere. It becomes suddenly the cardinal doctrine of the primitive Church.

Whence was it derived? Does Peter refer it to the teaching of Jesus? Does Paul? They refer it chiefly to the Old Testament prophets, to Moses above all. Philip, in his interview with the Ethiopian eunuch on his way from Jerusalem to Gaza, refers it to Isaiah in the well-known passage: "He was led as a sheep to the slaughter and like a lamb . . ."

But even Philip refers to Isaiah chiefly to prove that the Messiah must suffer and die. He does not by data go on to prove that by his death he must redeem the world for its sins. He does not quote the verse from *Isaiah* LIII, 5:

> He was wounded for our transgressions, he was bruised for our iniquities; the chastisement of our peace was upon him; and with his stripes we are healed.

It is probably true that many ancient writers (among them a pupil of Hillel the elder) discover in the chapter in *Isaiah* a suffering and dying Messiah. "It would appear," says Strauss, "that they referred the prophecies to a totally different subject, namely the people of Israel as a whole." Clearly, however, the apostles of Jesus, after his death, had no uncertainty that the passage referred to the Messiah, that the Messiah was Jesus, and that the prophecies foretold not only a violent death, but the expiatory power of that death in wiping out the sins of man.

And now how much of this idea can the early apostles be supposed to have obtained from Jesus himself? I am afraid the answer is very little, so far as we know from the reported words of Jesus in the Gospels. It is true that after the Transfiguration he says that his blood will be shed for many for the remission of sins (*Matthew* XXVI, 28). Further, he says, he must give his life a ransom for many (*Matthew* XX, 28). Again he believes himself to be the true shepherd who lays down his life for the sheep (*John* X, 11–15). And once more he says, by an apparently mistaken metaphor, that "except a corn of wheat fall into the ground and die, it abideth alone, but if it die, it bringeth forth much fruit" (*John* XII, 24).

Once more, at the Last Supper, he presents in the second Gospel the cup as "the blood of the new testament," and in the third Gospel as "the new testament in my blood," and this may, as Strauss says, be meant to signify that as by the bloody sacrifice at Sinai God sealed His old covenant with His ancient people, so now, by the Messiah's blood, He seals the new covenant which centred in Christ—the pledge of His forgiveness—and that this may be the true meaning of the bread and wine at the Last Supper. But that the death of the servant of God is to have a propitiatory relation to the sins of the rest of mankind is an idea which Jesus during his lifetime rarely dwelt upon. And when he spoke of it his disciples did not understand it.

The idea that the Messiah should suffer and die, and that his death should wipe out the sins of man had, as far as we can see, no place in the consciousness of the people with whom Jesus lived on earth. But that it had a place in his mind, and was the inspiring force that led him to his death, seems to be beyond question. Where did Jesus get this idea of a sacrificial death? Was it from Old Testament prophecy? Was it from direct inspiration of God? Was it that, being God, he knew it to be the scheme of his mission, what he came down from Heaven to earth to do? Or was it by a combination of these means that the thought came to him, took possession of him and led him on to the Cross?

My conclusion is that the last mentioned is right. I think the spiritual development of Jesus of Nazareth was gradual. I think it was little by little, as he passed through his life as a man, God revealed to him His great purpose with respect to him. It was not at first that he realized his divine mission. It is probable that he reached his Messiahship about the time of his baptism and that his ministry, the opposition he encountered, the persecution he suffered, culminating in his being stoned out of Jerusalem, and being dogged by the ruler classes of his own people and hunted by Herod Antipas, added to the exalted sense of the power given to him to work miracles, led to the conviction that he was not only the messenger of God, the Messiah, but the Son of God.

I think everything that happened to him after he left Jerusalem and made his way through Samaria to Galilee, and went up from there to Cæsarea Philippi, strengthened this sense of his Sonship to God. When at Cæsarea Philippi he asked his disciples, "Whom do men say that I the Son of man, am?" and Peter answered,

"Thou art the Christ, the Son of the living God," Jesus was startled and thrilled by the unexpected reproduction of his own thought.

His Transfiguration, six days later, in the presence of three of his disciples is a concrete rendering of the results of the struggle of his own soul—to know what he, the Son of God had to do, what was his mission in life, what he was sent on to the earth to do. Under the figurative form of Moses and Elias he believed he received the divine command—to go up to Jerusalem, to suffer and die at the hands of his enemies—and his assurance that he would rise from the grave, reappear to his disciples, ascend to Heaven and reappear at the end of the world to judge men and establish the kingdom of Heaven on earth. I apprehend that he believed that the object of his death was to atone to God for man's sin (even the sins of his enemies in killing him) ; to atone to God for man's transgressions from the beginning of the world. It is not improbable that he derived some part of this idea from Old Testament prophecy (particularly from *Isaiah*), but that he believed he received it directly from the prophets themselves—from Moses and Elias.

I think the story of the Transfiguration came from him, and from him only. That his three disciples may, indeed, have gone up into the mountain with him, but that they were heavy with sleep ; that on coming down from the mountain in the brilliant eastern light of morning Jesus told them what they kept first to themselves (by his command) and afterwards revealed to the writers of the Gospels—that he had talked with the prophets during his sleepless night about his death, which he should accomplish at Jerusalem, and what the results of his death would be. I think that from that time forward this overpowering idea of an expiatory death to wipe out the sins of the world possessed Jesus every day and hour.

I find it infinitely moving to think of that great soul going up to Jerusalem to his death, and his predestined fate as the Redeemer (who was to die in absolute degradation, alone, forsaken), surrounded by a company of followers who believed he was going up to a great worldly conquest. That they did not, could not, understand him, that they found such a fate for the Messiah contrary, as they believed, to all the teaching of the ages, is deeply affecting. His last struggles in his retreat to Ephraim before his last entrance into Jerusalem ; his last appearance in the Temple ;

his last view of Jerusalem from the Mount of Olives; his last supper, with the breaking of the bread and the drinking of the wine of what he believed to be the new covenant which God was about to make with man by the shedding of his own blood; all this is profoundly moving.

Does the foregoing require that we should believe that coming to the idea of a suffering and dying Messiah, and of an expiatory sacrifice by natural means, Jesus was in any sense a self-deceived man in concluding that all this had been taught him by God—that it was by God's own direction he was told to do what he did?

I think not.

On the contrary, I think this was all the way of the development of the spirit of Jesus, as ordained by God. I hesitate to say that Moses and Elias did actually appear to Jesus on the mountain of the Transfiguration. To say they did appear to him and speak to him was his characteristic and concrete way of explaining to his disciples that a great and transfiguring change had taken place in his soul, that he *now* knew what he had to do—to die in shame, in order to wipe out the sins of man, to ascend to Heaven and to come again in glory and judge mankind, and to establish the kingdom of God on earth as it was in Heaven.

But now comes the great and final question on which the Christian religion rests: Was it true? Did God make this new covenant with man by virtue of the sacrifice of Jesus? Christianity answers *Yes*. It cannot live and remain Christianity without giving this affirmative answer.

The test of Christianity is to-day precisely what it was to Peter, to Paul, to the author of *Hebrews*. Christ and his Cross and what his Cross stood for. This, not his morality (however lofty and inspired), is the secret of Jesus. The appeal of Jesus to humanity is that he answers the cry of the human heart, borne down by the sense of sin, for salvation from the consequences of sin (which, on his own merits by his own repentance, no man can achieve). Life everlasting. Reconciliation with God the Father. Forgiveness. Mercy. All won by the sacrifice of the God-man to God the Father. This is Christianity. Nothing else can be.

IV. Punishment for Sin

No man escapes from the sense of sin. If a man were proved to be destitute of this sense we should be compelled to regard him as insane. He would be a moral idiot, or a madman. All history testifies to the unhappiness which comes to the conscience of man as a consequence of the sense of sin. The root and cause of the discordance of life is sin. Sin is the darkening of the light which lighteth every man that cometh into the world. When man is brought face to face with sin and tries to get away from it, and to cast off the burden of it, his attempt is called repentance. What is repentance? Is it merely a change of ethical standpoint? Is it remorse? Is it a sense of degradation, of having lost either self-respect or the respect of others in whose esteem we could wish to stand well? Is it fear of punishment?

It must be admitted that fear of punishment plays a large part in repentance. John the Baptist addresses himself mainly to the fear of punishment. He says, "Repent! Flee from the wrath to come." He accuses the Pharisees of a mere attempt to escape from the consequences of their sins, and tells them to go back and bring forth fruits meet for repentance; in short, prove their sincerity, and that they deserve to escape punishment.

But Jesus goes farther than this, although he includes this. He calls for repentance as a way of wiping out the consequence of sin —punishment. His theory of atonement undoubtedly covers the idea that by suffering for sinful man he exempts sinful man from the penalty which in divine justice would otherwise be imposed. He does, indeed, mean that he ransoms many by taking their stripes. The idea of a suffering Messiah in *Isaiah* (LIII) is mainly based on this idea. The Messiah is wounded for our transgressions, and with his stripes we are healed.

But there is more in the theory of atonement according to Jesus than the wiping out of punishment. There is more in penitence than shame, more than fear. There is hope—hope of reconciliation with God.

Jesus sees that the deepest part of sin is the wrong that is done to God. The divine goodness has been wronged by the evil in sinful men. God has been good to us; He has given us a thousand blessings; He has given us our sight, our hearing and all the senses that have made life beautiful. He has been merciful. He has forgiven us again, every day and always. His love to us has been that of a father. And yet we have wronged that love. Our sin being that we have offended the eternal and everlasting spirit of justice without which life and the world cannot live.

But, above all, sin has separated us from God. Sin is above all an offence against the all-merciful Father. Therefore, repentance according to Jesus is the effort to reconcile God to us in spite of our sins. And the Atonement of Jesus is based above all on the theory that he by his death has made for man a new covenant of union—an at-one-ment with God.

Thus, there are two great impulses in the heart of sinful man to which Christ's sacrifice appeals: (1) the desire to escape from the burden and punishment of sin in the life hereafter (this means Christ takes our chastisement, and therefore calls for our eternal gratitude and love); (2) that Christ brings us who are God's prodigal children back to the arms of the merciful Father, who is waiting to receive us (this means that Christ reawakens the divinest part of us, and so wins our eternal devotion).

No true spiritual work in human life was ever attained except by co-operation with God. When a man finds not simply that he has done wrong, but that he has done wrong to one who has always loved him, the penitence begins in his heart.

Something of this is expressed in the parable of the prodigal son. The prodigal says, "I have sinned against Heaven and before thee, and am no more worthy to be called thy son." And when the father sees him, while he is yet a long way off, he has compassion on him and runs and falls on his neck and kisses him.

And hence, the highest and noblest part of the Atonement is this reconciliation of man to God, not the wiping out of the penalty of sin. Hence the love of Jesus, which is at the heart of Christianity.

Sin is rebellion against God. When we sin against our fellow-men we offend God, for He is the author of all righteousness, and sin in every form is rebellion against His will. The psalmist who declared, "Against thee, thee only, have I sinned," may have inflicted grievous wrong on his neighbour, yet he saw clearly that what he had done was ultimately sin against God. In the final reckoning of life the sinner must deal with Him. We cannot accept the Christian doctrine of sin until we hold its conception of God, and of man's relation to Him. Sin is an offence against God. God desires to forgive. Sin to Him is no call for punishment, but a signal for forgiveness. God regards sin with a view to forget sinners. This is not to say that God forgives sin without demanding any conditions from the sinner. There must be the temper of heart which we call repentance. Forgiveness of sin is not the same thing as remission of punishment. The failure to recognize this distinction often leads to serious confusion.

By the laws of God man must suffer for his evil doings. But his punishment may itself be the means by which he is roused to penitence. On the other hand, the man who apparently escapes the arm of justice may be confirmed in his evil courses, and when he needs must face the awful challenge of his conscience, as it is quickened in the presence of God, he finds himself held in the power of sin. Freedom of sin is freedom from its power. Forgiveness is described in many ways in the New Testament. It is too great a fact to be described in human language. It is described as redemption, reconciliation, atonement and salvation. Each term stands for a truth which has had the assent of Christian experience throughout the ages.

It is difficult for us, to whom the social conditions in which these terms had their origin are so remote, to appreciate their full force, but this is a reason for a careful study of their historical significance. The forgiven man is a regenerated man. Formerly, he lived in sin, now he is freed from it and has attained a new life—a new knowledge of the Divine Will. He has passed from death unto life, from slavery to freedom, from darkness to the light of God's presence.

The sinful man is born into a new order—the spiritual—out of the old order—the physical—wherein he is a new creature, for the old things are past and gone and all things have become new. It is plain that forgiveness is the divine Will for all of us.*

My own general conclusions on the teaching of Jesus in relation to sin are as follows:

I think Jesus thought of sin as rebellion against God. Sin is to him the name of the offence man commits against God when he resists His will. The offence a man commits against his fellow-man is not sin. It is wrong, injustice. For such wrong, such injustice, there must always be punishment. But sin against God (although it may and *does* demand punishment, hence the belief of Jesus in a hereafter in which the evil and unrepentant suffer) is something far higher and deeper than anything that can be wiped out by punishment.

A man commits a crime against his fellow-man, and after the law has punished him according to its code, his crime is, in the eyes of the law, wiped out. He is free of that crime. It can no more be brought against him. But the sin the sinful man has committed against God cannot be wiped out by punishment. It can only be

*From an article in "The Times" (London).

wiped out by repentance, by the acceptance of this repentance which we call redemption, by atonement—the making of the sinful man once more at-one with God. Thus the psalmist means that the sin he has committed is against God. God the merciful and loving Father, whose will has been outraged.

The reconciliation with God of the sinful man must begin with repentance, and repentance must begin with faith. The sinful man must believe in the mercy of God the Father and his willingness and eagerness to forgive. So the central theory of the Christian religion is that Christ, the Son of God, calls the sinful man to repentance, promises him forgiveness by the mercy of God, and by the Atonement made for his wrongdoing against God (not against man) by God's only begotten son—the sinless being who comes to earth and dies for as many as accept his sacrifice.

We may accept or reject that sacrifice. There is atonement for all of us. If we accept we are saved, redeemed, made one with God. Jesus illustrates this theory of sin again and again. He does so in the exquisite parable of the prodigal son. The father is willing to forgive. As soon as the prodigal repents of his evil life and turns homeward to his father's home, the father, seeing him a long way off, *runs* to meet him. The prodigal may have done grievous wrong to his fellow-men, and he has suffered the inevitable punishment of his wrongdoing. But the greatest crime he has committed is his sin against his father. He is forgiven at sight, by the mere fact of coming home (no more than that).

Again, observe the attitude of Jesus towards sin in the people (often cured of diseases) in whom he announces the forgiveness of sin. When he tells such people to go in peace for their sins are forgiven, he clearly means that they have been reconciled to God. Their act in coming to him he accepts as an act of faith, otherwise of repentance, and speaking as if in the Divine Name he says, "Thy sins are forgiven thee." Here is a fact of immense importance. Chiefly from the beginning of his ministry (after his baptism) he speaks as one with divine power, as a representative of God, as one with God, as in a position to forgive the sin which has been committed against God.

It is difficult, in the light of this fact, to comprehend the arguments upon which writers like Martineau deny that Jesus ever claimed to be the Messiah. By promising the forgiveness of sin he was distinctly claiming to speak with the voice of God, as the representative of God on earth. It was unnecessary for him to say, "I am the Messiah." He was speaking as the Messiah alone could speak, as no other man who had ever lived on the earth (or has ever since lived on the earth) had a right to speak.

In doing so he appeared to outrage the Mosaic law, which recognized in sin an offence which could only be forgiven by God Himself. The chief priest could not forgive it, the Sanhedrin could not forgive it, the prophets could not forgive it, Moses himself could not forgive it; only God Himself could forgive sin, because sin was committed against Him alone. What wonder, then, when Jesus pronounced the forgiveness of sins, the orthodox Jews accused him of blasphemy? It *was* blasphemy in any man to claim to speak in God's name, to forgive sin. Only One could do it, and that was God. Therefore, to claim to do it was to claim to be God, or one with God. And as there was only one God, Jesus, by doing so, offended against the central doctrine of the Jewish faith, according to the view of the Jews, who saw him as a man only. One thing alone could remove the blasphemy from the account of Jesus, and that was the recognition of Jesus as the Messiah, as the representative of God, the messenger of God, the spokesman of God (as man had never before him).

This the Jews could not do. Hence Jesus was a pretender who was aiming a deadly blow against the very heart of the Jewish faith. And as such he had to be destroyed. The law of Moses required, demanded, that he should be destroyed. Such was the first stage in the great drama. It began in the second period of the ministry of Jesus in Galilee; it developed during the period of the visit to Jerusalem between the Feasts of Tabernacles and Dedication, culminating in Jesus being stoned out of Jerusalem. And it reached its climax when, after the raising of Lazarus, and the entrance up to Jerusalem, the casting out of the money-changers, the denunciation of the Temple and what it had been made to stand for, there was danger that this new claimant to partnership with God would carry off the whole nation after him as the Messiah foretold by the prophets.

Thus regarded, the story of Jesus acquires a new and tremendous force. It is lifted out of the little things, the small greatness, into a mighty conflict of principles. It elevates the motives of the chief priests in some degree. They are sufficiently degraded by their false position and by their trickery, including their commerce with Judas, but even if they had been a high class of man, instead of (as I think) a low class, they could hardly have acted otherwise than they did in bringing Jesus to book, to judgment and even to his death, except by frankly recognizing him for what he claimed to be—the Son of God. It was hard or impossible for them to recognize him as the Son of God. They (being what they were) wanted no Messiah, no fulfilment of the prophecies, no coming of the son of David. All that would have cast them out. There was no room in Palestine for Jesus Christ and Joseph Caiaphas at the same time. So Caiaphas had to settle accounts with Jesus. And hence his speech to the Sanhedrin, defending the destruction of Jesus.

CHAPTER XVI

The Later Ministry

I. *The Seventy Disciples*

AFTER Jesus and the disciples come down from the mountain of the Transfiguration, there follow in *Luke* about nine chapters before we come to his arrival at Jericho, where he sees and cures the blind man. It is difficult to believe that these nine chapters deal with the journey from northern Galilee to Judæa on the way to Jerusalem, as Luke seems to intend them to do. What happened in these chapters? "And it came to pass, when the time was come that he should be received up, he steadfastly set his face to go to Jerusalem."

This is in Chapter IX, 51, immediately after Jesus and the disciples have come down from the mountain, probably Mount Hermon, on the extreme north. He sends messengers before him into a village in Samaria. Thus the whole length of Galilee is for the time being skipped.

The Samaritans, seeing that he is going towards Jerusalem, receive him badly, whereupon James and John seem to wish to call down fire from Heaven to consume the Samaritans; but Jesus says, rebuking them, "Ye know not what manner of spirit ye are of." He has not come to destroy men's lives but to save them.

They pass on to another city. A man wished to follow him. Jesus warns him, saying, "foxes have holes, and the birds of the air have nests; but the Son of Man hath not where to lay his head." Another man wants to follow him, but wishes first to go and bury his father. Jesus, in his almost dehumanized exaltation of spirit, says, "Let the dead bury their dead." Yet another wishes to follow him, but asks to go home first and say farewell to his family. Again Jesus says, "No man, having put his hand to the plough, and looking back, is fit for the kingdom of God."

After this, Jesus appoints other seventy disciples, and sends them out two and two to every city and place to which he is himself going.

"The harvest truly is great, but the labourers are few," he says (*Luke* X, 2). He gives the seventy his instructions. He is deeply disappointed at the failure of his mission thus far, and pronounces woe on Chorazin, Bethsaida and Capernaum (X, 13–15). Then the seventy come back to him and he says, "I beheld Satan as lightning fall from Heaven." Satan falling from Heaven. What did Heaven mean to Jesus? What did Satan mean?

Then Jesus gives the seventy power to tread on serpents and scorpions, so that nothing shall hurt them. This reads very trivially—serpents! scorpions! A lawyer comes to tempt him, asking "What shall I do to inherit eternal life?" In answer to the lawyer's question, "Who is my neighbour?" Jesus speaks the parable about the man who went down from Jerusalem and fell among thieves (X, 30–37).

Where Jesus is at that time is not clear. In the next verse he is in Bethany of Judæa. "Now it came to pass . . . that he entered into a certain village; and a certain woman named Martha received him into her house." We know that Martha's house was in Bethany. And it came to pass that, as he was praying in a certain place, his disciples asked him to teach them to pray, and he taught them what we call the Lord's Prayer. Where was he when he taught the disciples the Lord's Prayer? Luke does not tell.

Afterwards comes the incident of dining with the Pharisee, who marvels that he does not wash his hands before dinner. To this he pronounced the woe on the Pharisees who make clean the outside of the platter. There follows a long denunciation of lawyers also (XI, 39–54). Where is Jesus now? There is nothing in *Luke* to show.

An innumerable multitude of people gather about him, and he preaches a great sermon against hypocrisy and the leaven of the Pharisees (XII, 1–40). This is one of the greatest, if fiercest, of his discourses, and when Peter asks him if he has spoken one of his parables—the parable of the watchful servants—to his disciples or to all, he answers vehemently, and concludes with a great passage: "Suppose ye that I am come to give peace on earth? I tell you, Nay; but rather division. . . ." (XII, 51–53.) Then come two other apparently disconnected passages of great power (XII, 54–57).

Luke then goes on to say (XIII, 1–5), "There were present at that season some that told him of the Galileans, whose blood Pilate had mingled with their sacrifices." (This historical incident must have occurred shortly before; probably about A.D. 27 or 28.) Jesus says, "Suppose ye that these Galileans were sinners above all the Galileans, because they suffered such things? I tell you, Nay; but, except ye repent, ye shall all likewise perish."

It was the Jewish belief that when disaster befalls a man or a nation God permits it to do so because the man or the nation had sinned. Not that Pilate was any the less a tyrant. "Or those eighteen, upon whom the tower in Siloam fell. . . ." Clearly, the tower of Siloam had lately fallen, killing eighteen.

II. Towards Jerusalem

"And he went through the cities and villages, teaching, and journeying toward Jerusalem" (XIII, 22). But it is clear that he has for a long time been within two miles of Jerusalem.

"The same day there came certain of the Pharisees, saying unto him, Get thee out and depart hence, for Herod will kill thee." But according to *Luke* he is no longer in the territory of Herod, having passed through Galilee and into Samaria, and then into Judæa. Then comes the lamentation over Jerusalem (XIII, 34):

O Jerusalem, Jerusalem, which killest the prophets, and stonest them that are sent unto thee; how often would I have gathered thy children together, as a hen doth gather her brood under her wings, and ye would not!

Surely, this is spoken just as he comes in sight of Jerusalem. The preceding passage, "Go ye and tell that fox," was almost certainly spoken in Galilee. Thus there is no kind of recognizable geography in *Luke*. The writer does not know the country.

And there went great multitudes with him; and he turned and said unto them, If any man come to me, and hate not his father, and mother, and wife, and children, and brethren, and sisters, yea, and his own life also, he cannot be my disciple. [XIV, 25, 26]

Then come three beautiful parables. 1. The lost sheep; 2. The piece of silver; 3. The prodigal son.

Next comes a parable which no person of ordinary intelligence can call beautiful, as it has come down to us in *Luke*. It is the parable of the unjust steward. A rich man has a steward who has wasted his goods. He dismisses the steward, but in doing so calls him to account for his stewardship, as one might do if one dismissed one's agent, but intended to prosecute him by law if necessary. The steward sees nothing but poverty before him, and asks himself how he is going to escape it. An idea comes to him. He will escape poverty by making base terms with the people who owe his master money. To the man who owes a hundred measures of oil he says, "Write out an acknowledgment of fifty." To another who owes a hundred measures of wheat he says, "Write out an acknowledgment of eighty." Clearly, he intends to pass these off in the accounts he is to present to his master of the indebtedness of his debtors. And his expectation is that having, by this deceit, this conspiracy with the debtors, saved one debtor fifty measures and another twenty, the debtors will house and feed him when his master turns him out of doors.

And now comes the weakness of the parable. The lord commends the unjust steward, because he has done wisely, and the writer of the Gospel, or Jesus, adds the reason for the lord's commendation, that "the children of this world are in their generation wiser than the children of light." Thus the steward, who has first robbed or wasted the goods of his master, and has now carried out a conspiracy with his debtors to cheat him again, is "commended" by the lord for his cleverness. This presupposes that the lord has come to know of the conspiracy. If he had done so, what would have been his action as a natural man? Surely to punish the steward by law, with all that conspired to cheat him. The lord might forgive the conspiracy against him, but to "commend" it, and to call the conduct of the steward that of one who had "acted wisely," is to stamp himself a contemptible weakling.

The commentators who do not accept the obvious interpretation that the "lord" of the verse 8 is the "lord" of verses 3 and 5, and who say the "lord" of the verse 8 is Jesus himself, make the predicament still more serious. If Jesus commends the conduct of the unjust steward; if he goes on (as in Verse 9) to advise his disciples to make themselves friends of the mammon of unrighteousness that when they fail they (the representatives of the mammon of unrighteousness) may take them into everlasting habitations, the parable puts Jesus in the position of one who is recommending a piece of palpable theft, gross conspiracy and wicked treachery, as conduct worthy of imitation!

The whole parable, as it has come down to us, is a piece of

stupidity, its application is utter wickedness, and to attach it to Jesus is impossible. The commentators have wriggled for ages to account for it. It is not to be accounted for. The best that can be done with it is to stop the parable at the end of verse 7 (not verse 8, as some of the commentators suggest) and then to go on to verse 10, or perhaps even to verse 13: "No servant can serve two masters . . ." Here is Jesus speaking in his natural and recognizable character. In verses 8 and 9, it is not Jesus who is speaking, but a very stupid and wicked person.

In some of the early manuscripts of *Luke* the parable stops at the end of verse 8. But that does not satisfy me. Verse 8 is false whether the "lord" is the real man, as he most certainly is, in which case he is a fool, or Jesus, which I refuse to believe.

In Chapter XVI, 16, there is a significant statement. "The law and the prophets were until John; since that time the kingdom of God is preached, and every man presseth into it." If this means that the law and the prophets end with John the Baptist, it conflicts with the next following verse and with countless sayings of Jesus that he was not come to destroy the law, but to fulfil it—to carry it to yet higher development, to uncover the soul of it, to vivify the spirit of it, which has been almost crushed out of life by the formalism of the Pharisees. "And it is easier for Heaven and earth to pass, than one tittle of the law to fail."

After this there comes, as out of the blue, a verse which has no apparent relation to what goes before or comes after it. It is an abbreviated version of what Jesus had said elsewhere on marriage and divorce:

Whosoever putteth away his wife, and marrieth another, committeth adultery; and whosoever marrieth her that is put away from her husband committeth adultery. [XVI, 18]

Then follows the parable of Lazarus the beggar, who lay at the rich man's gate, died, and was carried by angels to Heaven, while the rich man also died and was carried off to hell. There is the clear belief in a place of torment. It is impossible to escape from the certainty that Jesus believed that rewards came to those who had suffered in this life, and punishment to those who had not suffered, and had lived in (apparent) disregard of suffering. Lazarus is poor, he inherits Heaven. The rich man has been indifferent to the poverty of Lazarus, leaving to him at the most the crumbs that fell from his table, and pitying him less than the dogs did who came and licked his sores—therefore, he is in hell.

The paradise of Lazarus is being in the bosom of Abraham. The hell of the rich man is being in flames, suffering the agony of thirst. There is no escape from these flames and this agony. Apparently, it goes on everlastingly. This torment comes, apparently, to one who has not looked to Moses and the prophets. There are people in life so eaten up by selfishness that they would not be persuaded if one rose from the dead.

III.   Jesus and His Resurrection

Where all the foregoing occurred is not certain. But verse 11 of Chapter XVII suggests that it was while Jesus and his disciples were on their way to Jerusalem, passing "through the midst of Samaria and Galilee." The words of this verse suggest that the writer of *Luke* either did not know the geography of Palestine or was indifferent to it. Remember that since he said that Jesus had set his face towards Jerusalem, and since he had entered certain villages in Samaria, he had been staying in the house of Martha and Mary in Bethany on the Mount of Olives. It is impossible to follow Luke's itinerary. It is all a muddle.

"As he entered into a certain village, there met him ten men that were lepers." We are not told what village. Jesus tells them to go and show themselves to the priests, and on the way they are cleansed. One of them returns to thank Jesus. He is a Samaritan. Is Jesus now in Judæa? I think so. Otherwise Luke would not make a point of saying that the leper was a Samaritan, unless he meant that the only grateful one among the lepers was a kind of Gentile.

The Pharisees question him here. "When will the kingdom of God come?" they ask. "The kingdom of God cometh not with observation," he answers. "Neither shall they say, Lo here! or Lo there! For behold, the kingdom of God is within you." This is a saying of the greatest importance.

Then follow his warnings about the coming of the great day when the Kingdom is to be established. Again, he speaks of his second coming, and what is to come before it. He is to be rejected of his generation. His second coming is to be when his people least suspect it. When the day of his return comes it will be sudden.

They must then make a swift choice. They must be prepared to sacrifice everything that they may gain eternal life:

> Whosoever shall seek to save his life shall lose it; and whosoever shall lose his life shall preserve it. I tell you, in that night there shall be two men in one bed; the one shall be taken, and the other shall be left. Two women shall be grinding together; the one shall be taken, and the other left.

To all this the disciples ask, "Where, Lord?" and Jesus answers, "Wheresoever the body is, thither will the eagles be gathered together" (XVII, 33–37). I do not quite see the relevance of the reply.

Jesus tells the parable of the importunate widow and the judge (XVIII, 6–8):

> Hear what the unjust judge saith. And shall not God avenge His own elect . . . ? . . . Nevertheless when the Son of Man cometh, shall he find faith on the earth?

Then he speaks the parable of the Pharisee and the publican who go up to the Temple to pray (XVIII, 10–14). A beautiful parable. I should say that it was spoken in Jerusalem, perhaps in the Temple quarters, within sight of such scenes as it describes.

People bring their children to him that he would touch them. His disciples rebuke the mothers. Jesus calls the children to him, and says, "Suffer little children to come unto me, and forbid them not, for of such is the kingdom of God." Again I see this happening in the Temple courts—a beautiful scene.

IV. The Rich Man

Then comes a "certain ruler," asking Jesus what he shall do to inherit eternal life. Jesus says, "Why callest thou me good? None is good, save one, and that is God." In reply to the man's question he tells him not to commit adultery, not to kill, not to steal, not to bear false witness, and to honour his father and mother.

"All these [commandments] have I kept from my youth up," says the man. "Yet lackest thou one thing," says Jesus. "Sell all that thou hast, and distribute unto the poor, and thou shalt have treasure in Heaven; and come, follow me." The man is sorrowful. He cannot do it. He is rich. He goes.

Jesus looks after him and says to his disciples, "How hardly shall they that have riches enter into the kingdom of God. For it is easier for a camel to go through a needle's eye, than for a rich man to enter into the kingdom of God." "Who then can be saved?" says someone. "The things which are impossible with men are possible with God," he answers. Peter says, "We have left all, and followed thee." And Jesus says, "There is no man that hath left house, or parents, or brethren, or wife, or children, for the kingdom of God's sake, who shall not receive manifold more in this present time, and in the world to come life everlasting."

> Then he took unto him the twelve and said unto them, Behold we go up to Jerusalem, and all things that are written by the prophets concerning the Son of Man shall be accomplished. For he shall be delivered unto the Gentiles, and shall be mocked, and spitefully entreated, and spitted on. And they shall scourge him, and put him to death; and the third day he shall rise again. And they understood none of these things, and this saying was hid from them, neither knew they the things which were spoken.

V. Nearing Jericho

After this Jesus is nigh unto Jericho, and a certain blind man sits by the wayside. Here we link on to the story in *John*. If we take the foregoing passages as rightly following what goes immediately before, then we have to think that the preceding scenes did not take place in the Temple quarter, but on the way up from Galilee through Samaria to Jerusalem. I do not think that need be so. Luke's chronology is again at obvious fault. Much of the foregoing took place at an earlier period, I think on an earlier visit to Jerusalem, but these latter passages clearly relate to the last visit to Jerusalem.

VI. General View of Luke's Chronology

From the baptism to the Transfiguration Luke assigns the ministry entirely to Galilee. From the Transfiguration to the arrival in Jericho he assigns all the ministry to the journey from Galilee to Jerusalem. The journey on which all these incidents are assumed to occur is of about 100 miles at most, and might occupy one week if taken directly. It is difficult to think that it occupied months.

My view is that *Luke* records the events of two journeys to Jerusalem in these chapters. The first of the visits was at the time of the Feast of Tabernacles. On this journey Jesus went (with his twelve disciples) through Samaria to Jerusalem. What occurred in Jerusalem on this visit is partly recorded by *Luke* and partly by *John*. I think he lodged with Martha and Mary outside Jerusalem —at Bethany on the Mount of Olives. It would be in the Temple court that he told certain of the most beautiful of his parables, and it was there he had some of the most passionate of his scenes with the scribes and Pharisees. It is probable that it was from there that he was stoned out of Jerusalem—driven out, perhaps, through the Golden Gate.

I think Jesus with his twelve apostles then returned to Galilee, passing back through Samaria. On returning to Galilee the seventy, whom he had sent out, came back to him. It was then the disciples of John the Baptist came again, this time with the story of the execution of John. Or, perhaps, others brought that story to him from the farther side of Jordan, the caravan companies coming up from the eastern side of the Dead Sea. Then he goes north through Capernaum to the territory of Philip—Cæsarea Philippi.

VII. *The Gospel of the Kingdom Preached to the Poor*

In the course of these journeys Jesus preached among the poor, the blind and the sick, the gospel of the Kingdom. He told the poor, who groaned under the double burden of the Roman rule and of the rich and mighty among their own people, that they were to wait patiently and hope on, for great things were coming. The kingdom of Heaven was near; the temporal powers of the earth were soon to be swept away, and God was to rule the world in His own person. All their wrongs would then be righted; all their bruises would be healed. If they were blind they would regain their sight; if they were heavy-laden they should find rest.

What matter if they were under the Roman heel? The time was near when they should bruise the Roman head. Then let them raise no rebellions. Let them do no man violence. Let them not resist evil. Rather let them love their enemies. And as for the things of this world, let them look to God for raiment like the lilies of the field, and for food like the sparrows of the air. More than this, when God's kingdom came on earth all things would be the exact opposite of what they then were, and the order of the world would be reversed. What was now first should then be last. The people great in the world now should be least then; the rich should be the poor; the poor should be as the rich; the publicans and sinners, being repentant, should enter before the Pharisee, who was righteous in his own eyes and an abomination in the eyes of God.

More and still more, when the kingdom of God came on earth, the poor, the halt, the blind, the heavy-laden, the beggars at the rich man's gates, the lepers covered with sores, all these would sit on thrones to judge the rich, the great, the mighty, the Pharisees, the scribes, the rulers of the synagogues, the priests and the chief priests. So blessed were the poor, for theirs was the kingdom of Heaven; blessed were they that were hungry then, for they should be filled; blessed were they that wept for they should laugh. Let them rejoice in the day that was coming to them when they should inherit the earth and see God. But woe unto the rich, for they had already had their reward. Woe unto them that laughed for they should mourn and weep.

This was the gospel that Jesus preached to the poor of Galilee, and the common people heard it gladly. They drank it in like living water. Other men had offered them consolation, but no man had given them water like this. Judas the Galilean had promised them the overthrow of the powers of Rome, but Judas was dead, and their hope in him was gone. They saw no hope in resistance. But here was deliverance that God Himself was to work out for them. Here was a kingdom that would heal all their pains. So the voice of Jesus went over the country round about, and men came from near and far to listen to him. He was indeed fulfilling the prophecy; he was preaching the gospel to the poor; he was preaching deliverance to the captives; the giving of sight to the blind, the acceptable year of the Lord.

The poor followed him three days without food. One woman lifted up her voice in a crowd and said, "Blessed is the womb that bare thee, and the paps which thou hast sucked." And Jesus answered, "Yea rather, blessed are they that hear the word of God, and keep it." Did he remember the home at Nazareth? Could he forget that his mother had rejected his gospel?

VIII. *Jesus Heals the Sick*

In another sense Jesus, going up and down among the poor and blind and lame and outcast of Galilee, was bringing healing to the broken-hearted. He began to work miracles. It was found that the touch of the hand of Jesus cured the sick of their diseases. Such things had been heard of before. Holy men strong in the Spirit of the Lord had healed the sick. Jesus was strong in the Spirit. He spent his days preaching to the poor, and his nights alone in prayer on the mountains. The lepers came to him and he cleansed them of their leprosy; the blind beggars called upon him and they regained their sight. He spoke to the dumb and they spake; he spoke to the mad and they recovered their senses.

All these diseases he called devils, just as he called his temptations devils. He believed they came of outraging the laws of God. Therefore, the man sick of a disease was a man of sin. It might not be his own sin, but the sin of his fathers, or the sin of his people, but whosoever it was, the man who bore it was the embodiment of sin. And as Jesus cured these sick people he said "Your sins are forgiven you" that is, the sins whose penalty you are suffering are forgiven in you; go and sin no more. The way to be free of disease was to fear God from generation to generation.

Thus with the double gospel of the glad tidings of the Kingdom, and of the healing of the sick by power of the Holy Ghost, Jesus went through Galilee. And all the poor folk followed him, saying, "Blessed is he that shall eat bread in the Kingdom" and again, "Surely this man is the Christ that was to come." At one moment the people of Galilee, in view of his miraculous powers, tried to carry him away and make him king, but he fled from them to the mountains. The temptation of worldly power he put under his feet.

Jesus accepted the name of the Christ, but laid on his disciples an obligation to conceal it, from fear that the people would rise to hail him as the Messiah who was to turn out the Roman and sit on the throne of David. He had gone through that temptation already and triumphed over it.

IX. The Rich and Great Are Offended

Meantime, the rich and great had heard what Jesus was doing, that he was promising the Kingdom to the poor and the outcast. Many of the Pharisees and scribes came down from Jerusalem to Galilee to see and hear him. At first they derided him. Then they tried to trip him. They set men to pretend to be his disciples that they might the more easily betray him. His gospel levelled a blow at their sect, for it denied them the Kingdom. One Pharisee asked Jesus to eat with him, and expressed horror when he sat down without first washing his hands. Jesus told him that it was of more consequence that his heart should be clean than that his hands should be so. You are rich, he seemed to say, you give tithe, and make prayers in public, and love the top seats in the synagogue. If you had more of the love of God and less love of the praise of men, you would give alms of all you have, and not think so much about your ceremonies.

Hearing what answer Jesus had given to the disciples of John the Baptist, learning who the common people took Jesus to be, and what the disciples of Jesus called him, the Pharisees thought to bring to a vital test the claims of Jesus to be the Christ. If Jesus put forth that he was the Christ, he must accept himself as king of the Jews, and if king of the Jews, he could not acknowledge the powers of Rome. So they came to him and said, "Master, we know that thou art true, and teachest the way of God in truth, neither carest thou for any man; for thou regardest not the person of men. . . . Is it lawful to give tribute unto Cæsar?" He saw their drift. They had no desire to accept him as the Christ. Already they were his enemies even as he was their enemy. Their sole aim was his downfall. If he said "It is not lawful" they must report his treason to Pilate as that of a man (like Judas the Galilean) designing the downfall of the Roman power, perverting and deceiving the people. But he betrayed nothing. Asking for a coin, he pointed to the head of Cæsar and said, "Render therefore unto Cæsar the things which are Cæsar's; and unto God the things that are God's." The Pharisees were silenced.

Failing to catch him on grounds of Roman law, the Pharisees tried to do so on their own law. They asked him which was the chief commandment, thinking that he would betray himself by putting forward that which concerned his own mission, but he answered, "Thou shalt love the Lord thy God with all thy heart . . . and thy neighbour as thyself." It was the law of Moses. Jesus had come to fulfil the law. The law was always the essence of his gospel.

Again they tried to trip him by asking if it was lawful to break the Sabbath Day, and he showed by instances from David that the Sabbath was made for man, not man for the Sabbath.

And having failed to catch him in treason either to the law of the Romans, or the law of Moses, they tried to catch him by his own law, the law of that gospel which promised the Kingdom to the poor and to the outcast. So they brought him a woman taken in adultery and said, "Moses in the law commanded us that such should be stoned; but what sayest thou?" If he acquitted this woman, whose guilt was clear, he set aside the law of Moses, and they would turn to the people and say, "This man is an enemy of God, for he is against the law and the prophets." If he convicted her, they would say, "Of such is the kingdom of Heaven."

Jesus tried to escape the test, and, to avoid the eyes of the woman, he stooped down and with his finger he wrote on the ground as if he heard them not. But they pressed him for his answer, feeling that now at length they had caught and could openly dishonour him. Then he rose up, looked into their faces and said, "He that is without sin among you, let him first cast a stone at her." They were crushed, they were convicted, and they slunk away, leaving Jesus with the woman alone. Then he said to her, "Where are those thine accusers? Hath no man condemned thee?" "No man, Lord," the woman answered. "Neither do I condemn thee; go, and sin no more."

X. Mary Magdalene

On yet another occasion a Pharisee, named Simon, asked Jesus into his house to eat with him, and while they sat at meat together a woman of the city, who was a sinner, came in and knelt behind him weeping, washing his feet with her tears, wiping them with the hair of her head, and anointing them with ointment. At that the Pharisee said to himself, "If this man had been a prophet he would have known what manner of woman this was, and knowing that he would have reproved and stopped her."

Jesus, however, reproved and stopped the Pharisee and not the woman. He spoke a parable which meant this: "Simon, to me there is no difference between men, except in the love they bear me, and this woman loves me more than you do. You have asked me into your house to eat, but she has washed my feet with her tears. She loves me most, because she has most cause to love me."

Never for an instant does he allow that any human creature, however befouled by sin, is unclean. He is very gentle with sins of sense. The Pharisee, if he was a convert, or half-convert, must have been ashamed; if one of those who had been set to catch Jesus he must have known that Jesus had seen through him.

Why should not this same woman have been Mary Magdalene? The earlier translators appear to have had no doubt of her identity. The evidence is of equal weight for and against it.

XI. *The Gospel Preached to the Profligate*

At this point in the life of Jesus we recognize the meeting of two ways. Hitherto, his mission had lain chiefly with the poor; henceforward, it lay equally with the outcast and downtrodden. He drew them to him with parables, and one of these was the parable of the prodigal son. A certain man had two sons, and the younger of them asked his father for the portion of goods that would fall to him, and the father gave it to him, and he went away into a far country, and wasted his substance in riotous living. And when he had spent all he hungered, and while feeding swine he would fain have filled his belly with the husks that the swine did eat.

Then coming to himself, he resolved to return home to his father's house and say, "Father, I have sinned against Heaven, and before thee, and am no more worthy to be called thy son; make me as one of thy hired servants." And he arose and came to his father. But when he was yet a long way off his father saw him, and ran to him, and fell on his neck and kissed him, and ordered the best robe to be put on him and the fatted calf to be killed for him, saying, "For this my son was dead, and is alive again; he was lost and is found."

The publicans and sinners were the prodigal sons; the world had only fed them on husks after all; and if they but returned home their Father would run to meet them and fall on their necks and kiss them, and put the best robes on them and kill the fatted calf. The outcasts were moved by these appeals.

Some time later, in another province, a publican named Zacchæus, being a little man and seeing the throng that came with the prophet of Nazareth, climbed into the boughs of a fig-tree that he might look upon him as he passed. And there Jesus saw him and called him, saying he meant to rest in his house. And Zacchæus came down and approached Jesus, and led him to his home, and believed upon him and received his gospel, and joined the number of those who looked for his Kingdom. Then straightway, in earnest of that hope, he resolved to give half of all he had to the poor, and if he had extorted anything from any man to restore to him fourfold. Zacchæus knew well the gospel of Jesus.

XII. Why the Rich and Great Were Offended

Now the coming to Jesus of men and women of evil life became from this time onward the chief ground of his offence to the Pharisees. It was their great accusation that he consorted with sinners. But when they came to him with this complaint he did not spare them.

He told them that they would neither go into the Kingdom themselves nor suffer others that were entering to go into it. They sat in the seat of Moses and told men what to do, but did it not themselves; they read the commandment "Love thy neighbour as yourself" and yet they destroyed widows' houses and for a pretence made long prayers; they compassed sea and land to make one proselyte, and when he was made they made him twofold more the child of hell than themselves; they made believe to reverence the Temple, but really reverenced only the gold of the Temple; they pretended to swear by the altar, but really were thinking only of the gift on the altar; they were careful to pay tithe, but forgot to be merciful to the poor; they washed their hands, but not their hearts; they were blind guides; they were grinders of the faces of the poor, they were like whited sepulchres; they were serpents; they were a generation of vipers.

Woe to them, because they knew the way to the Kingdom and yet entered it not, but tried rather to keep out the outcasts, the lepers, the publicans and sinners that would enter it. Theirs would be one day the greater damnation.

In illustration of this Jesus told the Pharisees a parable. Two men went up to the Temple to pray, and one was a Pharisee and the other was a publican. And as they prayed the Pharisee lifted up his eyes and said, "Lord, I thank thee that I am not as this sinner here." But the publican fell on his knees and cried in his anguish, "Lord, have mercy on me, a sinner." And God listened to the publican and sent him home forgiven, but the Pharisee he did not hear.

He told them another parable. A certain man planted a vineyard and filled it with good things, and let it out to husbandmen and went into a far country. And when the season came he sent a servant that he might receive from the husbandmen the fruit of the vineyard. But they caught him and beat him and sent him away empty. Then he sent another servant, but they treated him likewise. And again he sent a third servant, and him they killed. Then having one only son, his well-beloved, he sent him also, saying, "They will reverence my son." But when the husbandmen saw the son they said among themselves, "This is the heir; come, let us kill him, and the inheritance will be ours." And so they killed the son and cast him out of the vineyard. Now what, said Jesus, will the lord of that vineyard do? He will come and destroy the husbandmen, and give the vineyard to others.

The Pharisees knew what Jesus meant by this parable, and they knew that he had spoken it against themselves. God was the lord of the vineyard, the vineyard was the world, they were the husbandmen, the servants were the prophets that had been slain, the son was Jesus himself. They had tried to take the inheritance from God, but God would turn them out of the world and give the world to the poor, the distressed, the downtrodden, the meek. That would be when the Kingdom should come. The Pharisees were wroth and would have lain hands on Jesus, but for fear of the people.

Nevertheless, some of the Pharisees were convinced by his words and arrested by his works, and among them were two that came to him in secret. One was Nicodemus, a ruler of the Jews. Nicodemus came by night, and to him Jesus said, "Except a man be born again, he cannot see the kingdom of God." That which is born of the flesh is flesh. You must be born of the Spirit of God. Every man born of woman is born of sin. God's Spirit alone can save him, and God's Spirit is written in the law. Obey God's law and you will be born again of God's Spirit. "Art thou a master of Israel, and knowest not these things?" Such the simple doctrine of Jesus concerning the new birth, and it means no more than it says. But it deals a hard blow at the supernatural birth and the sinlessness of Jesus himself.

The second to come was a young rich man, perhaps Joseph of Arimathæa, and Jesus tells him to keep the commandments, and go and sell all he has and give it to the poor. He says, in effect, your riches are an inheritance stolen from God. They are fruits of the vineyard that should belong to God. Though you did not make them yet you inherited them. They are the sign of commandments broken. You cannot hold this stolen wealth and still be God's servant. That would be serving God and being served of the devil. Give up your riches to the poor.

When the young man heard this he went away sorrowful, for he had great possessions. And seeing him go Jesus said to his disciples "How hardly shall they that have riches enter into the kingdom of God." To make riches is to break God's commandments, and to keep them when made is to try to serve God and mammon. Therefore, it is easier for a camel to go through the eye of a needle than for a rich man to enter into the kingdom of God. Nevertheless, with God all things are possible.

XIII.   Denunciation of Wealth

Jesus gave the Sadducees and Pharisees no quarter in his denunciation of wealth. He painted them a picture of the great judgment in which he who had not sold all and given to the poor was cast down into hell, and he who had done so was taken up into Heaven. On either hand of the judge the people should stand, and to those on the right hand he should say, "Come, ye blessed of my Father, inherit the Kingdom prepared for you from the foundation of the world. For I was an hungred, and ye gave me meat; I was thirsty, and ye gave me drink . . . for inasmuch as ye have done it unto one of the least of these my brethren, ye have done it unto me."

The Sadducees and Pharisees were not slow to see that such teaching levelled a blow at the foundations of their sects. There was no making peace with such doctrine. Here was no mere matter of dogma, no mere question of idle belief. It was the vital question of their actual social condition as a people. Jesus said that they had no right to exist as a class. They had usurped the world which belonged equally to all men. Therefore, their worship of God was vain, for they taught for doctrine the commandments of men. There was but one cure, they must sell all and give to the poor. They must serve and trust God henceforward, and serve and trust mammon no more.

The Pharisees rose in anger, and failing to laugh Jesus down they would have laid hands on him. They got at his mother and brethren and tried to persuade them that Jesus was mad. His mother and brethren came in pursuit of him, believing the lie, and thinking to restrain him. But Jesus turned his back on them. "My mother and my brethren," he said "are those who believe on me and on God who sent me."

XIV. *The Poor Man's Prayer*

Thus, Jesus went on to live among the poor and the sinners. His following grew day by day, and he sent batches of his disciples to the towns to preach his gospel. The time was short, the labourers were few, the harvest was near. They were to go as he went, without money in their purse, or a second coat to their back, trusting to God to clothe them as he clothed the lilies of the field and to feed them as he fed the sparrows of the air. He taught them a prayer which they were, themselves, to use and to teach to the children of the Kingdom, to the poor and the downtrodden, the publicans and sinners:—"Our Father, who art in Heaven, hallowed be Thy name. Thy Kingdom come. Thy Will be done in earth as it is in Heaven. Give us this day our daily bread. And forgive us our trespasses, as we forgive them that trespass against us. And lead us not into temptation, but deliver us from evil."

No rich man could pray, "Give us this day our daily bread." He had taken care to secure the thing prayed for. It was a prayer for the poor only, and one full half of the gospel of Jesus. The other half was "Thy Will be done."

The disciples went away, but still the crowds about Jesus became greater and still they were the outcast, the women who had been sinners and the men whom the world despised. And wherever he went the sick and lame were brought out in beds into the street for him to heal them. And as he passed by the blind beggars at the wayside called upon him, for they could not see to reach him.

CHAPTER XVII

Events in the Life of Jesus

I. The Flights of Jesus

THE TRACES of Jesus's various flights from his enemies are almost obliterated from the fourth Gospel. In *Luke* and *Mark* they can with difficulty be distinguished. Only in *Matthew* are they plainly indicated. But Matthew has no apparent intention of representing Jesus as a poor fugitive. It is reserved for Celsus to do this. Elijah repeatedly fled from his enemies, but as repeatedly he presented himself before the face of royalty and defied them.

Jesus's escape into the mountains appears to be after the people have tried to make him a king. He sought seclusion not merely because he wished to preserve his life, but certainly for the sake of his vocation. It was not yet his steadfast conviction that the Messiah must die. On the contrary, up to this time he was convinced that he had to live and rule.

Immediately after he heard of the death of John the Baptist, he went by ship in a north-easterly direction to the point at which the Jordan enters Galilee. This was the plain of El-Bateiha, at the foot of Et-Tell, or The Hill, near to Bethsaida (also called Julias).

This country was a part of the district of Lower Gaulanitis, in the tetrarchy of Philip. But Philip had died either in A.D. 33 or 34, and since then it had been a dependency of the Roman province of Syria—Bethsaida being Philip's place of sepulchre. Jesus would have been safe there against Antipas, even if the half-brother of Antipas had been alive, because Philip was no friend of his cunning and intriguing half-brother. But he was still more secure in this place of refuge under Roman dominion, because while Antipas was compelled doubly to respect this district, it was as yet scarcely incorporated and was left comparatively free and to itself. The journey to Bethsaida before the feeding of the five thousand cannot be called a flight.

How long he stayed in that district we do not know. The Gospels place in this period the great miracles of the feeding of the multitudes and the walking on the sea. The return of Jesus to Capernaum is a return to the territory of Antipas, and therefore makes the flight from Galilee (after the news of John's death) an absurdity.

Why did Jesus go to Gadara? Was this a flight? The excursion to the south-eastern shore of the lake and thence to Gadara is narrated by the Gospels as occurring entirely before the death of the Baptist. There is not the faintest reason given why Jesus should undertake this journey of more than three leagues, first to the south-east of the lake and thence farther into the country, if his purpose was not that of hiding himself from his enemies.

The reason given in *Luke* is the simple one that he "went throughout every city and village preaching and showing the glad tidings of the kingdom of God." It will be remembered that at this stage of his ministry Jesus did not think it his duty to take the glad tidings of the Kingdom to the Gentiles, and that in going to this country of the Gadarenes he was going to the country of the Gentiles. Nor was it necessary for Jesus to go so far to rest. He was not driven there by the storm, so why, after landing, did he proceed to Gadara, the city being some miles inland?

Keim's view is that on retreating to Gadara Jesus was making a retreat into Roman territory. But was Gadara in Roman territory? If it was the capital of Peræa it was in the territory of Herod Antipas. From whom then, is it assumed by Keim, that Jesus was flying away when he went to Gadara? Gadara refused an asylum to Jesus. But the reverse is plainly given in the Gospels, and it has nothing to do with political interests, nothing to do with his Messianic claims. Nor is the argument of Keim (based on the idea that inasmuch as in going to Gadara Jesus was going to the country of the Galileans he must have been flying for shelter and safety) at all valid in the light of the fact that Jesus went to the coasts of Tyre and Sidon about the same time, having no reason to do so then—unless the journey followed the murder of John the Baptist and was part of the escape from Antipas.

Again, the flight after the death of John the Baptist (as given in *Matthew*) is extremely unsatisfying. Jesus goes by ship "to a desert place apart." This is (according to other Gospels) Bethsaida (or Julias). There he feeds the five thousand. From there he walks on the sea back to the land of Gennesaret—the coast of Capernaum—thus returning to the territory of Antipas. From there he goes to the coasts of Tyre and Sidon, once more the land of the Gentiles, outside the territory of Antipas. After a short stay near Tyre, he comes back to the Lake of Galilee and finally takes ship to Magdala.

All this seems but a short period while Jesus is assumed to be flying away from Antipas. It is all feeble supposition. The only way Keim escapes from its absurdity is to deny part of the fact, as when he says that *Mark* VII, 31, is "untenable." Gadara was about nine miles from Tiberias. Many Jews dwelt there, but it was reckoned a Greek town in the time of Augustus. It was a considerable Romanized city of perhaps 30,000 population, and possessed many rich inhabitants. It contained many sepulchral caves.

The Græco-Roman territory excluded all the operations not only of Antipas, but also of the Pharisees, more completely even than the district of Julias. The thought would never occur to his opponents that Jesus, the Jew, with Jewish principles, would have withdrawn into the country of the Gentiles. Moreover, there is not a hint of any danger to Jesus in Galilee from the religious leaders until after the death of the Baptist. Why should he fly for shelter to Gadara? And, being in Gadara, how has he escaped from Antipas and his friends?

The third flight of Jesus (according to Keim) followed the deputation from Jerusalem (perhaps the Sanhedrin) to ask him why he did not observe the ordinance about the washing of hands (see *Mark* VII, 24).

> And from thence he arose, and went into the borders of Tyre and Sidon, and entered into an house, and would have no man know it; but he could not be hid.

Keim says:

> Jesus had reason for retiring to a greater distance than necessary. His principles prevented him from setting foot in purely Gentile ground. The road from Capernaum to the region of Tyre would represent a journey of twelve to fifteen leagues—thirty-six to forty-five miles; and that from Tyre to Sidon another eight to ten leagues —twenty-four to thirty miles.
>
> The district of the maritime city of Tyre—the city itself was still prosperous after all the storms of conquest had swept over it, and luxuriously splendid in spite of its narrow, crooked lanes, of inconveniently high houses, and its disagreeable factory odours—extended far inland towards Galilee. He now trod (in the district

north-east of Galilee) for the first time the hill country of upper Galilee, which begins north-east of the Lake of Galilee. He went along the Damascus road through the hills of Joseph's Grove, which lay about nine miles from the head of the lake. Vine-clad hills by the road, alternately rugged and pleasant, rich in fine prospects, the Jebel Safed rising to a height of 3,000 feet on the right and Jebel Jermak to 4,000 on the left.

Either here or there Jesus would be in perfect security. This is the country of Phœnicia. Jesus is not reported by the Gospels as carrying on any missionary work here. Accident causes him to meet the Phœnician (or Canaanite) woman, but that is all. See however the scene of his return and the feeding of the four thousand, which seems to indicate large numbers following him, and his sending them back. None of these journeys seems to me to indicate a flight.

After his return from Tyre, Jesus is said to return to Magdala, the Shady Place (Dalmanutha). Here the indefatigable Pharisees present themselves to him, and demand a sign, obviously a Messianic sign.

Speaking of the flight to Tyre and Sidon, Keim says, "Since, according to *Matthew*, the journey to Jerusalem (to the Feast of the Tabernacles?) soon followed this retreat to Tyre, the latter must be placed with the beginning of the spring." I think not. I think it was in the early autumn. I think the flight to Cæsarea was in the early spring. "In Palestine," continues Keim, "winter lasts from November to January as a rainy season, and snow also occurs towards the end of this season. But the snow does not lie long, and it is mentioned by Josephus as something remarkable. As spring weather does not begin until February and March, and even then the roads are impassable or in very bad condition the time in the text is the earliest that can be fixed upon."

In *Matthew* XVI, 6 we read that after the feeding of the four thousand and the return to Magdala, and after the surprising demand of the Pharisees and Sadducees for a sign from Heaven, Jesus refused a sign, spoke about the sign of the prophet Jonas, and left them and departed. Where to? Clearly he returned by ship to some other place on the Lake of Galilee.

And when his disciples were come to the other side, they had forgotten to take bread. Then Jesus said unto them [obviously thinking of the Pharisees and their demand for a sign], Take heed and beware of the leaven of the Pharisees and the Sadducees. And they reasoned among themselves, saying, It is because we have taken no bread.

What possible connexion has the "leaven of the Pharisees" with the fact that they had come to a somewhat desolate part of the east side of Galilee without having brought bread? The disciples were surely not without common intelligence? A gross and inconceivable misunderstanding. Jesus was, according to *Matthew* and *Luke,* speaking to them of the *doctrine* of the Pharisees. According to *Mark* Jesus was thinking of the *matza* of the Pharisees.

We know nothing of Jesus's last flight except its goal—Cæsarea Philippi. *Mark* says Jesus went into the town of Bethsaida (or Julias). There happens the incident of the blind man of Bethsaida, and the striking scene of Jesus leading the blind man out of the town by the hand.

Then they come to Cæsarea Philippi, and there follows the great interview with the disciples and the answer of Peter, "Thou art the Christ" (*Mark* VIII, 27–38), and then the Transfiguration (*Mark* IX, 2).

Then the coming down from the mountain and the cure of the boy with the dumb and deaf spirit. "And he said unto them, This kind can come forth by nothing, but by prayer and fasting." Thereafter they depart and pass through Galilee, and, according to *Mark,* into the coasts of Judæa by the farther side of Jordan, perhaps by the Wady Fa'ar, followed by the coming to Jericho and the incident of blind Bartimæus. Then the coming to Bethany, the sending out of the two disciples for the colt, and the entry into Jerusalem. Jesus returns to Bethany at eventide. In the morning he returns to Jerusalem.

II. The Author's Conclusions

My conclusions are that some of these "flights" have no appearance of being running away. They are not consistent with any definite intention on the part of Jesus of escaping from anybody. What power had the Pharisees over his personal movements? When the members of the Sanhedrin came to him, had they got it within their power to bring with them their Temple police, and arrest a man found guilty of offences against the religious laws of the Jews?

Apparently they had this power. It was the power they exercised at Gethsemane when they finally arrested Jesus. Therefore, it *is* possible that Jesus had reason to escape from them, lest they should take him unawares.

Against this they would naturally be restrained by his popularity. The people thought Jesus a prophet, and they would try to save him from being arrested and carried off to Jerusalem to be tried. It *is* conceivable that, after he had dishonoured the Pharisees and scribes who came with members of the Sanhedrin to ask him why his disciples did not obey the laws of their elders in the washing of hands before food (the important scene described in *Matthew* XV, 1–20), his departure into Tyre and Sidon may have been to avoid these powerful persons of whom the disciples of Jesus appear to have been afraid. "Knowest thou that the Pharisees were offended?" Jesus is asked. And he answered, "Let them alone; they be blind leaders of the blind; and if the blind lead the blind, both shall fall into the ditch."

The second and last flight of Jesus was undoubtedly the flight to Cæsarea Philippi after the news came of the murder of John. There Jesus had to take reckoning with his own soul. There he went through the mystic Transfiguration, and came to the conclusion that he had to go up to Jerusalem and to die. If anything had remained with him of the old prophetic conception of the Messiah, it died here. Daniel fell back to the second advent. Jesus returned to Isaiah's idea of the suffering, dying and sacrificing Messiah; or, rather, Son of God. After that came his revived courage. He must go through to Jerusalem, whatever the ruling religious classes or "that fox" might do.

> The road to Cæsarea might lead through Bethsaida, [declares Keim]; Jesus might here make his first halt, and then returning to the right bank of the Jordan pass on for a distance of about three leagues to the basaltic Jacob's bridge. The plain of Merom, particularly in inclement seasons, is a swamp.

Jesus was going north in the early spring. The scene—the snow deep on Hermon. The glistening of the snow in the moonlight on the night of the Transfiguration, and the million stars on the dry snow on the morning after as Jesus and his disciples came down from the mountain.

> Here [at Jacob's bridge] he would again take first the Damascus road, the left bank of the Jordan, and scale the heights by the side

of the little lake of Merom. Going round the plain of Merom, at
this time of the year converted into a part of the lake and therefore quite impassable, a journey of six leagues (eighteen miles)
would bring him to the village district which bounded Cæsarea
Philippi on the south. Here he stood on the border-line of the
ancient land of Israel, the measure of whose length, from Dan,
near Cæsarea, to Beersheba, is something like 110 miles, and in a
district which was one of the most splendid and luxurious in the
country.

Countless of the early Christians, the early Fathers came there
in the first centuries of Christianity. In a sense, it was the birthplace of their faith. Here were the numerous sources of what
Josephus calls the "lesser Jordan." Many branches of the Jordan
come down from far beyond Cæsarea. Some of the sources apparently run underground.

The crystalline, copious springs of the Jordan, gushing from
the perpendicular rocks. Tracts of fertile marshland, where, as early
as the days of the Judges, the Danites migrating from the south
found everything the earth could produce. Fields of wheat, barley,
maize, rice, hedges of olives and stretches of luxuriant pasturage;
while in the summer the whole district is a sea of flowers, whence
the bees gather a rich harvest.

The Jordan is here only twenty paces wide. Many nameless
brooks flow over the stones, which shine in the sunlight—a thin,
sparkling, moving veil. Thickets of trees, alive with birds, surround the foot-hills of Hermon. On its head, its cap of snow.
Beyond, Cæsarea, and before one reaches the foot of Hermon,
there were many towns and villages, including the castle and tower
of Lebanon, which looks towards Damascus, with the splendid
marble temple of Augustus, built in 19 B.C. by Herod. Cæsarea,
itself, the ancient Paneas, exists to this day, among a quantity of
ruins, near a handful of houses, bearing the name Banias, lying
in an angle formed by two arms of the Jordan.

This city, Cæsarea, was a creation of Philip, Herod the Great's
son, who built it about 3 B.C. and called it Cæsar Augustus. It was
mainly Gentile, although it had numerous Jewish inhabitants. It
had a temple of Augustus (who was deified while living). Thirty
years after the death of Jesus it was (by Agrippa II) renamed
Neronias in honour of Nero, and a year or two later it participated
in the festivities of Titus in celebration of the subjugation of Galilee and the destruction of Jerusalem.

How much Jesus saw of Cæsarea we do not know (says Keim). He did not enter the city itself, but merely visited the city about it. Here, in this Roman country, he was quite safe from his Jewish and semi-Jewish foes, but he was as good as completely out of Israel. . . . The feeling that he was driven out from among the people whom he wished to serve must have weighed heavily on his mind during this journey. Perhaps he had no eyes for the glories of nature, which would have wooed him here with the first balmy breath of spring.

Here he became the subject of a heavy presentiment. . . . What remained to him if he merely saved himself and not Israel, whom he would have to renounce if he set forth alone? Oppressed by insupportableness of this existence, he resolved to bow to his destiny, nay, to the will of God, who was afresh showing him his path, the path of the Jordan from its source to its mouth, the long, mysterious, dangerous, but great path to Jerusalem.

These closing words of Keim are very fine, yet not quite fine enough. Is it too much to imagine Jesus flying from Galilee, after the death of John, with no thought but that of escaping? He goes on and on until he comes into the pagan world at the gates of the pagan city, surrounded by the temples of Rome and her emperor, surrounded by her pagan people.

Should he go on?

No; from that spot of all others he was to send out into the world the word that was to destroy the pagan civilization. The great struggle engaged him. And then came the final and absolute abandonment of the idea of the Messiah.

The Messiah, the Son of God, must die. The sacrifice to God, for the sin of the world. He decided to go back. He must die in Jerusalem. He will come back for the establishment of the kingdom of Heaven on earth. Here is born the great thought of redemption by the sacrifice of himself. The Transfiguration is only the visible picture of this thought. Moses, Elias, the new covenant. After that, all is clear. No dark clouds, until the very last days. He will go straight on.

III. *Escaping Unseen through Crowds*

There are several incidents in the Gospels of Jesus passing unharmed through crowds of his enemies who are trying to take his life, or to lead him on to his death.

In the fourth Gospel we are continually being told that the Jews tried to kill him; that the Pharisees wished to take him and sent officers to seize him; that stones were cast at him. We are told that all these efforts failed because the hour of Jesus was not come. In one case, the emissaries sent out to take him were overwhelmed by the force of his words—"never man spake like this man" (*John* VII, 46)—or the dignity of his person, and returned without fulfilling their errand. Again we read that Jesus passed unharmed through the midst of an exasperated crowd "Then took they up stones to cast at him; but Jesus hid himself, and went out of the Temple, going through the midst of them, and so passed by" (*John* VIII, 59).

Strauss says that the writer of the fourth Gospel does not intend us to think of a natural escape, but of one in which the higher nature of Jesus, his invulnerability, so long as he did not choose to lay down his life, was his protection. But I take the view that the words "Jesus hid himself," followed by the words "going through the midst of them," were intended to imply that Jesus had the power of dematerializing himself at will, and leaving the crowds staring into vacancy, having lost him whom they wished to kill.

John is not alone in indicating this power of dematerialization. We find it in *Luke* IV, 30 where, after his first visit to Nazareth following his baptism, his fellow townsmen (indignant at his discourse in the city) tried to cast him headlong from the brow of a high hill, and he passed through the midst of them and went his way. Again, the power of dematerializing himself appears in the account of his first appearance to the disciples after his resurrection, when the doors being closed he "stood in the midst of them" (*John* XX, 19).

It is obvious that the belief in the power of Jesus to dematerialize himself would rob him of his humanity. He would cease to be a man if he could make himself a phantom. Nothing else in the story of his life justifies it. He was born of a woman; he was a child; he grew to be a man. He was sometimes tired and had to take rest. On the Cross he suffered physical pain. He knew hunger and had to eat. He knew thirst and had to drink. He died.

If his body was not liable to all the laws of a man's body he was not a man. If he could dematerialize himself, become invisible and pass through crowds like a spirit, his body was not a man's body. If he could walk on the sea his body was not subject to the laws of man's body. If he defied the laws of gravitation and rose into the sky, his body was not a man's. If he carried into another realm the law of digestion proper only (as far as we know) to life of man in this world, his body was not a man's body. If his body was not a man's body he was not the Son of Man.

That he should have been the Son of Man was as much of the essence of his mission in this world as that he should be the Son of God. Therefore, I interpret the scenes of his passing unharmed through crowds that set out to kill him to the dignity, majesty and power of his human personality—not to any supernatural power of turning himself into a ghost, which would degrade and lower him.

IV. Casting Out Devils

Jesus was said to cast out devils by a league with Beelzebub. The first time this charge was made was after Jesus had cured a dumb demoniac (*Matthew* IX, 34). The people marvelled and the Pharisees said, "he casteth out devils through the prince of the devils." Again (*Matthew* XII, 22) they brought him one possessed with a devil, being blind and dumb, whom he healed, and the people said, "Is not this the son of David?" But the Pharisees said, "This fellow doth not cast out devils, but by Beelzebub the prince of devils."

Strauss says it is suspicious that the demoniac who gives occasion to the assertion of the Pharisees is in both cases dumb. Demoniacs were of many kinds, every variety of malady being ascribed to the influence of evil spirits.

The answer of Jesus to the charge of acting in concert with the prince of devils is the obvious and convincing one, that to say that the prince of evil will empower anyone to cast out the instruments of evil is to talk foolishness. Why should the prince of evil wish so to undo his work?

An outstanding evidence of the prevailing idea, that demons would only obey the representative of the master of devils, is given in the incident of the curing of the demoniac whose devils, being expelled from him, went into the Gadarene swine. After the swineherd had been in the city, presumably to acquaint his master, the owner of the swine, of the destruction of his property in the swine, the people who came out of the city to see Jesus pray of him to leave their shores. "Then the whole multitude of the country of the Gadarenes round about besought him to depart from them; for they were taken with great fear" (*Luke* VIII, 37).

Apparently, they were afraid of him, on the same ground as that alleged against him by the Pharisees, that he was in league with the evil powers. It is curious that the people of Galilee, knowing nothing of the incident, received Jesus gladly on his return to the Galilean shore.

V. Calling for a Sign

The Messiah, according to the Jews, was to be a sign giver. Frequently, especially in the early part of the ministry, the people ask for a sign. The only explanation of this is that they want some kind of proof of the supernatural or divine power of Jesus, in order that they may be sure that he is the Messiah. Clearly, too, the prevailing question is, Is this man the son of David, therefore the Christ?

It is remarkable and extraordinary, however, that on several occasions the demand for a sign comes immediately after the performance of some great miracle, such as the second feeding of the multitude. One asks, What better sign could men wish for than what the people had just witnessed? One way of reconciling the events is to say that the demands for a sign came from people who had not witnessed great miracles, or perhaps before great miracles had yet been worked. The answer of Jesus is usually to refuse to give a sign.

In one case the Pharisees come to Jesus ("in the unlikely companionship of the Sadducees," says Strauss), and tempt him by asking him for a sign from Heaven. Jesus answers that a wicked and adulterous generation seeketh after a sign; and there shall no sign be given to it, but the sign of the prophet Jonas—an enigmatical reference to the period of three days which originated later. Twice Jesus responded to the request with the same enigmatical reference to Jonas.

VI. The Visit of His Mother and Brothers

All the Synoptics mention the visit of the mother and brethren to Jesus. And in all Jesus answers that they who do the will of God are his mother and brethren (*Matthew* XII, 46; *Mark* III, 31; *Luke* VIII, 19). Matthew and Luke do not tell us the object of their visit, nor give any special reason for the reply of Jesus. But Mark says it occurred after he had, as the Pharisees thought, broken the Sabbath; after the Pharisees were taking counsel with the Herodians to destroy him; after great multitudes were following him, and people with unclean spirits were falling down before him and calling him the Son of God; after he had ordained the twelve and given them the power to cast out devils, and when his friends (having heard of all this) thought he was beside himself. Therefore, they were trying to lay hold of him, perhaps to protect his life, perhaps to keep him from further madnesses (as they may have thought).

It is then that he answers, "How can Satan cast out Satan?" and says that if Satan rises up against himself he must come to an end. There is an obvious break between verses 29 and 30 of *Mark* III, for verse 30 gives an obvious reason for the visit of his mother and brothers. "Because they [his enemies] said, He hath an unclean spirit." That is to say common report said that Jesus himself was possessed of a devil. There and then his brethren and his mother come to see him, hoping no doubt to take him away.

He is at the time obviously in a house, and a multitude of people are sitting outside of it, and his mother and brethren call him. Then the people tell him that his mother and brethren are without and seek for him. Whereupon he answers, "Who is my mother, or my brethren?" He looks round on his disciples, who do not believe that he is possessed of a devil, and says, "Behold my mother and my brethren! Whosoever shall do the will of God, the same is my brother, and my sister, and mother." Surely this explains the apparent severity of the answer of Jesus.

It has been said that after the accepted accounts of the birth and childhood of Jesus (in *Matthew* and *Luke,* not in *Mark*) it is questionable whether we ought to accept the explanation of Mark. But it would be more than reasonable to urge that after this explanation of the visit of his mother (with his brethren) revealed by all the Synoptics, it is questionable whether we ought to accept the accounts of the birth given by two of them.

Jesus apparently knew that his family had accepted the view of the Pharisees, and he was naturally offended and resented it. Hence he said that only those who believed in him as God's messenger (not the Devil's) were his (spiritual) brethren. He said, in effect, that he preferred his spiritual to his bodily relatives.

VII.   Contentions among the Disciples

The three first evangelists, says Strauss, narrate several contentions for pre-eminence among the disciples. Matthew and Mark mention a dispute which was excited by the two sons of Zebedee. These disciples (according to *Mark*), or their mother (according to *Matthew*), petition for the two first places next to Jesus in the Messianic kingdom. *Luke* contains no mention of such a contention.

At the Last Supper Luke makes the disciples fall into a dispute which among them shall be greatest. Jesus had often to suppress such disputes, which clearly originated in a worldly Messianic hope of the disciples. The answer of Jesus is always the same in spirit: "Whosoever will be greatest among you let him be the servant of all." Jesus sets a child in the midst as an example of humility. "Except ye be converted, and become as little children, ye shall not enter into the kingdom of Heaven. Whosoever therefore shall humble himself as this little child, the same is greatest in the kingdom of Heaven." At the Last Supper he washes the feet of the disciples. John, however, who gives the scene of the washing of the feet, mentions no dispute.

VIII.   The Love of Jesus for Children

Children are brought to Jesus that he may bless them. The disciples wish to prevent it. But Jesus says, "Suffer little children, and forbid them not, to come unto me, for of such is the kingdom of Heaven." And he lays his hands on them.

An incident of this kind occurs in all the Synoptics (*Matthew* XIX, 13; *Mark* X, 13; *Luke* XVIII, 15). In *Matthew* it occurs on the coast of Judæa beyond Jordan, after one of his discourses (on marriage) and before the visit of the young man who had great possessions. In *Mark* it occurs in the same place and after the same discourse on marriage. The words are practically the same, with the addition, "Verily I say unto you, Whosoever shall not receive the kingdom of God as a little child, he shall not enter therein"; and Mark presents the beautiful picture of Christ taking the little children up in his arms and putting his hands upon them and blessing them. One can imagine him seated with a child on his knee, with its head in the crook of his arm, being tenderly caressed as he speaks.

In *Luke,* it occurs when he is on his way to Jerusalem, and is said, by an apparent error of geography, to be "passing through the midst of Samaria and Galilee," and not among the same circumstances. In essence it is the same incident. Were there two such scenes? It is hardly likely that the disciples would try to turn the children away from the Master who loved children. Had it any relation of sequence to the dispute about superiority in the kingdom of Heaven?

IX. *The Anointing of Jesus*

An occasion of the anointing of Jesus by a woman as he sat at meat is mentioned by all the evangelists (*Matthew* XXVI, 6; *Mark* XIV, 3; *Luke* VII, 36; *John* XII, 1). The chronology differs. Luke places the incident early in the ministry of Jesus, before his departure from Galilee, while he was in the country near Nain, after he had raised the widow's son; after John's disciples had visited him and returned to their Master, and when Jesus was sitting at meat in the house of one of the Pharisees. In Luke's story the place is not indicated, the city is not named; the woman is described as a sinner; her name is not given; she brings an alabaster box of ointment and washes the feet of Jesus with her tears and wipes them with her hair, and kisses his feet and anoints them with ointment. The Pharisee is shocked by this, and thinks that if Jesus had been a prophet he would have known that the woman was a sinner, and would certainly (according to custom) have forbidden her. Jesus answers as in *Luke* VII, 40–43; and the scene ends by Jesus saying to the sinner, "Thy sins are forgiven . . . go in peace."

In *Matthew* it is the same story, yet different. It is at the end of Jesus's life, after he has entered Jerusalem, and returned to Bethany. Jesus is in the house of one Simon the Leper, when a woman comes with an alabaster box of ointment while he is at meat and pours it on his head, not his feet. The disciples are indignant at the waste, and say that the ointment might have been sold and given to the poor. Jesus reproves them, and defends the woman, saying she had poured the ointment on his body for his burial.

No particular disciple is mentioned as expressing the indignation at the waste, but it is said (immediately after the record of the incident) that Judas Iscariot went to the chief priests and bargained to betray Jesus.

In *Mark* the same story is told as occurring in the house of Simon the Leper in the same circumstances, with the addition of the prophetic words of Jesus, "She hath done what she could: she is come aforehand to anoint my body to the burying. Verily I say unto you Wheresoever this gospel shall be preached throughout the whole world, this also that she hath done shall be spoken of for a memorial of her."

But in *John* the story is different in some particulars. The time is practically the same as in *Matthew* and *Mark,* and the scene is at Bethany six days before the Passover. But it follows the raising of Lazarus, and the absence in Ephraim, and precedes the entrance into Jerusalem.

It is doubtless in the house of Lazarus and his sisters, for we are told that Martha is serving out the meal and that Lazarus was one of them that sat at the table with him. Then Mary comes with a pound of ointment of spikenard and anoints the feet of Jesus. Judas Iscariot protests and says that the ointment might have been sold for 300 pence and given to the poor. Jesus makes the same reply as in *Matthew* and *Mark.* But nothing is said then about Judas going to the priests to betray Jesus.

Are we to conclude that there were two anointings? If Luke's is the true story, the woman was probably not Mary of Bethany, because she was in Galilee, near Nain, and perhaps near Magdala. Was the woman of Luke's story Mary of Magdala, otherwise Mary Magdalene? If not, was the conversion of Mary Magdalene another incident, not otherwise described than as the casting out from her of seven devils.

The house in *Matthew* and *Mark* is the house of Simon the Leper, the father of Judas Iscariot. In *John* it is evidently the house of Lazarus, Martha and Mary. Were these the same house? Who was Simon the Leper? As Simon the Leper takes no part in the story in *Matthew, Mark* and *John,* it is possible that Simon was dead; that the house had formerly been his, and was still so called; but he had been, perhaps, the father of the house? On the other hand, the Pharisee in Luke's story is almost the central person in the incident. Out of his objection the moral of the story comes. In the story in *Matthew* and *Mark,* only the woman is the central figure. In the story in *John* both the woman and Jesus are central figures.

The difference of time between the story in *John* and in *Matthew* and *Mark* is not important—the one *before* the entrance into Jerusalem, the other *after*. There is the difference that in *Luke* the sinful woman anoints the feet of Jesus—a sign of her shame only —whereas in *Matthew* and *Mark* she anoints the head, which might be taken to be a sign of her desire to anoint him to his enthronement as the Messiah, which they all believed to be near. Does this give any colour to the idea that Judas's objection to the anointing was not merely that the valuable ointment had been wasted, but that he was secretly rebelling against the Messianic expectations which the anointing foreshadowed?

There is no other indication of Judas's rebellion against the Messianic hope, unless it is the fact of the betrayal itself. If Judas had really believed that Jesus was on the point of establishing a worldly kingdom, would he have betrayed his master for thirty pieces of silver, or for any bribe whatever? Had he not the right of the others to a place of high power if his Master came into his Kingdom.

But in *John,* Mary anoints the *feet* of Jesus. Therefore Judas has no right to think she is anointing him in advance to his Messianic position. On the other hand, Jesus seems to be answering the unspoken thoughts of the disciple when he says the woman had kept this against the day of his burying. It was *not* the day of his burying, but many days before it.

Origen held that there were three separate anointings. This requires us to believe that on three occasions Jesus was expressly anointed, each time after a meal, each time by a woman, each time by a different woman, and that in one of the cases Jesus should have defended the woman by saying she was doing this to his burying. But this is too much to believe.

Some of the commentators tried to establish the occurrence of two different anointings from the fact that the feet are anointed in *Luke* and *John* and the head in *Matthew* and *Mark*. I think this trifling.

The differences of time between *Matthew* and *Mark* and *John* is one of a few days, and this also is unimportant. The only thing that seems to be of real consequence is the difference of motive and the lesson in the narratives of *Luke* and of the other Gospels. It is *Luke* against all three.

My conclusion is that there were two anointings, not one or three—that Luke's story stands as the anointing perhaps of Mary Magdalene, and the story of Matthew, Mark and John as the story of Mary of Bethany.

It is worthy of mention that in *Mark* and *John* the value of the ointment is given as 300 pence. It would be strange indeed if the value of the ointment were the same in two entirely different incidents. John gives the name of the woman (Mary) and the name of the dissenting apostle (Judas). This is given by some critics as a further proof that John was an eye-witness. On the other hand, Strauss regards the story in *Matthew* and *Mark* as the parent item out of which the stories in *Luke* and *John* were created. In *Matthew* and *Mark* the anointing has no specific object. In *Luke* it is the tribute of a repentant sinner. In *John* it may reasonably be considered the expression of a sister's devotion and gratitude to Jesus for raising her brother from the dead.

X. The Woman Taken in Adultery

This incident occurs in *John* VIII, 1 to 11. It occurred in the Temple (or temple area) in Jerusalem, but when and on which visit is uncertain.

The Pharisees and scribes bring a woman taken in adultery to Jesus, and obtain his opinion as to the procedure to be adopted against her. Jesus appeals to the conscience of the accusers and dismisses her with an admonition. This is a shapeless version. The scribes say, "Moses in the law commanded us, that such should be stoned; but what sayest thou?"

Strauss says that in no part of the Pentateuch is this punishment prescribed for adultery, but simply death (*Leviticus* XX, 10; *Deuteronomy* XXII, 22). Nor, he says, was stoning for this offence appointed in the *Talmud*. It was strangulation. Also, he fails to see what there was to annoy Jesus in the question put to him.

What there was came of the constant tenderness shown by him to sinful women, as in the case of the woman who was a sinner, whose sins he forgave. This seems a sufficient answer to Strauss on that head. Again, Strauss says the scribes could not expect

Christ to decide otherwise than according to law. This is, I think, a shallow objection. The scribes thought he superseded the law (in respect of Sabbath breaking and so on), and that he dared to forgive the sins of a sinful woman. What would he dare to do in this extreme and palpable case of violation of the law?

Strauss says the circumstance of Jesus writing on the ground has a legendary and mystical air, for it seems to imply something more mysterious than a mere manifestation of contempt for the accusers. Again, I say no. It is a mark of the shame he feels at the whole shameful incident—shame in the presence of the guilty woman.

Once more Strauss finds it scarcely conceivable that every one of the men who had dragged the woman before Jesus, zealous of the law, should have so tender a conscience as to leave the woman behind them uninjured.

My answer is that they were themselves convicted of sin before the law, and must therefore have been afraid to go farther against another transgressor—particularly against a weak and helpless woman; and, being convicted by their own conscience, they went out one by one, and when Jesus saw none but the woman and said to her, "Woman, where are those thine accusers? Hath no man condemned thee? She said, No man, Lord. And Jesus said unto her, Neither do I condemn thee; go, and sin no more."

The incident was long held to be apocryphal. It did not find a place in early versions of the fourth Gospel. But a narrative of one interview between Jesus and an adulteress is very ancient, since, according to Eusebius, it was found in the Gospel of the Hebrews.

It used to be thought that the woman in the Gospel of the Hebrews was the adulteress in *John,* although there were points of difference in the measure of their sins. Strauss wonders that the woman in the Gospel of the Hebrews has not been united with the woman who was a sinner in *Luke.*

CHAPTER XVIII

Mary Magdalene

I. Who Was Mary Magdalene?

THE NATURAL FOES of Jesus had gathered themselves together, the rich, the Pharisees, the scribes, the chief priests and rulers of the Jews. They mocked at his sorry retinue. They made his immediate company a ground of offence. This was a company of women who ministered to him. Joanna, the wife of Chuza, Herod's steward, Susanna and many others. Some who had been healed of infirmities and others whose sins he had asked God to forgive.

A certain family of two sisters and a brother were a group beloved by Jesus, and he frequented their house. It is by no means impossible that they were at first residents of Magdala, where, as neighbours of the people of Nazareth, they may have been friends of Jesus in his youth. In Magdala the household during the youth of Jesus may have consisted of Martha and Lazarus, brother and sister near of an age, and Mary a younger child. Mary suffered from infirmities which were known as devils. At the beginning of his ministry, or before it began, Jesus may have healed her of these infirmities. Then with her new birth into the world she may have fallen into the temptation of some wicked rich man, been abandoned by him, have sunk to lower depths of life, and finally drifted into the ways of a woman of the city, a woman of the streets, a harlot. While this was going on, Lazarus, who loved her, may have tried in vain to rescue her. He may have become a follower of Jesus, and as such taken her the glad tidings of pardon. All may have been useless for a time. With her lovers she may have gone her way in wickedness.

Among the women who ministered to Jesus was Mary Magdalene. Who was she? What was she? Old Bible scholarship identified her with Mary of Bethany, the sister of Lazarus and of Martha, with the woman who was a sinner, and perhaps also with the woman taken in adultery. But modern Bible scholarship objects to this identification. Mary Magdalene is merely Mary of Magdala, probably a rich woman who ministered to Jesus of her substance, certainly one whom he had cured of nervous and mysterious maladies, known to the language of the time as seven devils. The older theory was based partly on inference from the evidence of the written word, and partly on tradition. Mary of Bethany repeats the act of the woman of the city. To be a woman of the city is to be called by the city's name. The newer theory refuses to invade the silences of Scripture and turns its back on tradition. What the word says it says, and no more and no less may be accepted.

Thus the tradition of the Magdalene is swept away by realistic criticism. But is it not to count for something? It is old; so old that none can say where it began. It has even found its place in the headlines of our Bible. It may be a false tradition, but the probabilities are on its side. And there is some direct scriptural evidence in its favour.

II. *The Two Marys*

But to accept the old theory of the Fathers that Mary Magdalene was Mary of Bethany and Mary of Bethany the woman who was a sinner is to get rid of some baffling difficulties. The two Marys cannot be followed separately with any feeling of rightness and probability. Viewed apart, they are only as episodes in the life of Jesus, without beginning or end. Taken together, they are a thread of interest that runs by the side of his own. Mary of Magdala begins nowhere and Mary of Bethany ends nowhere. There is no continuity in their stories if they are two; but if they are one, and if they are identical with the sinful woman, and if she is identical with the woman taken in adultery, the story of all is sweet and clear and continuous, beginning where we see it in a great redemption and ending only at the Cross.

Some difficulties there are in accepting the old monkish theory of the identity of the two Marys and of the tradition of the Magdalene, but they are chiefly material ones of time and place and condition. Thus, the adulterous woman is brought before Jesus at Jerusalem and the sinful woman washes his feet with her tears at Nain. Mary the sinner is Mary of Magdala, but Mary the sister of Lazarus and Martha had her home at Bethany. These difficulties are not of much moment. They yield before a little whole-some imagination, and a desire to illuminate the truth in the dark places of the world by the light of love and worship.

But to give a license to our imaginations to invade those silences wherein the truth lies hidden, let us see if the humblest effort to find a cause for effects to combine characters that bewilder by their similarity of name will not enable us to make a simple, sweet and probable story of what is only a multitude of disconnected epi-sodes without some such thread of connexion.

Let us say that the woman who had been taken in adultery was the same who washed the feet of Jesus in the house of Simon the Pharisee, that she was Mary Magdalene, and that Mary Mag-dalene was Mary the sister of Lazarus and of Martha.

Thus, lower and lower, Mary may have sunk. Meantime, Martha, a girl of other nature, may have married a rich Pharisee of Nain. This man may have had one sore feeling about his union, the relation of his wife to the shameless Mary. By and by the enemies of Jesus, thinking to bring his gospel of repentance to the test of an awful case, take Mary and bring her before him (at Jerusalem) charged with adultery. Jesus may have recognized her as the girl possessed of devils long ago. Then might follow the story as it is told in the Gospels of how he shamed her accusers, and pardoned the woman herself.

On returning to Galilee Jesus may have gone into the house of a Pharisee in Nain to eat, and this Pharisee may have been he who married Martha. And while they sat at meat together, Mary, now repentant, having come back in contrition to her own country, may have entered the house of her sister and begun to wash the feet of Jesus. At that Simon, seeing her, and knowing her too well, but perhaps unwilling for his own wife's sake to turn her out of doors, said within himself, "If this man had been a prophet he must have known what manner of woman it was that touched him." Then follows the rebuke of Jesus, showing Simon that the only difference he sees between men is the difference of love, and that Mary loved more and had been forgiven more than himself.

Martha may have been a follower of Jesus, but Simon an unbe-liever, perhaps one of those who were set to catch Jesus by their pretended belief. And in due course this Pharisee may have taken the leprosy and Simon the Pharisee become Simon the Leper. Then Martha, his wife, may have called on him to believe upon the prophet of Nazareth. He may have refused, may have resolved to go up to Jerusalem to present himself to the chief priests, and wash in the Jordan. Thus the family may have come to remove from Nain to Bethany. Simon may have grown worse, and been compelled to separate from his wife. They may have parted at Bethany, and Lazarus may have gone to live in the house of his sister, Martha.

Does this wrong the silences of Scripture so grievously that it may not be allowed as a possible explanation of many bewildering difficulties? If the word is against it, then it must fall; but if it is opposed to no clear truth, and attempts to overlap no insurmountable fact, then the probabilities of the story are enormously in its favour. It makes a sequence of incidents, it provides motives for action, it prepares the way for the catastrophe with which this mighty tragedy must close.

And this brings us to matters of more consequence than the identity of Mary Magdalene with Mary of Bethany. Whoever this woman was, whether Mary of Magdala simply, or also Mary of Bethany, her devotion to Jesus was full and complete. It was more absolute than that of any other disciple. Not Simon Peter or even John followed Jesus with such brave loyalty, such tender strength, such forgetfulness of self. If she were the woman taken in adultery she owed Jesus much. If she were the woman who was a sinner she repaid him by washing his feet with her tears and wiping them with the hair of her head. If she were Mary of Bethany she anointed him with ointment. Though she were no more than Mary of Magdala she followed him to the Cross, stood by him when he died, was present at his funeral, paid honour to his tomb and was the first to whom he appeared after he had risen from the dead.

Can we resist the inference that whosoever and whatsoever Mary Magdalene may have been, her devotion to Jesus was partly personal? The inference is not mine to begin with; it was started fifteen centuries ago. For putting it forth with other so-called heresies, an earnest man was excommunicated from the Church and his books were burned. But why need we shrink from it? What wrong can it do to Mary Magdalene? What dishonour to Jesus? Let us state it plainly. Whether Mary Magdalene was merely Mary of Magdala, out of whom Jesus cast seven devils of nervous and apparently inexplicable maladies, or also Mary of Bethany, whose brother Lazarus he raised from the dead, as well as the woman taken in adultery for whom he shamed the hypocrites, and the woman who was a sinner who washed his feet with her tears, her devotion to his person has at every stage the outward marks of the devotion of a woman to a man.

As a woman she followed him from Galilee to Golgotha, as a woman she ministered to him, as a woman she knelt at his feet, as a woman she wept at his Cross, as a woman she followed his body to the tomb, and as a woman she brought spices to honour the place of his rest. Not only the fidelity of the devotee, but the love of the woman appears in every act of Mary Magdalene. She may not have been conscious of it as a thing apart from the allegiance of a disciple, for it was a love as spiritual as an angel's, though as warm as a woman's. Never once may she have awakened to the sense of it, or, if ever, only as she stood at the door of the tomb when the stone had been rolled away, and she wept for the beloved body that had gone. And even if then she knew the secret of her heart, that under the worship of the disciple lay the love of the woman, the moment of consciousness must have been brief. When the risen Jesus had appeared to her and spoken her name, he had ceased to live as a man in her heart and had become as a god.

III. The Humanity of Jesus

Mary Magdalene is a saint of the Church, and no name of any follower of Jesus, save only the name of the other Mary, his mother, comes closer than her name to the innermost shrine of belief. Does it smudge that shrine as with an unholy hand to say that the devotion of Mary Magdalene to Jesus was partly personal, that it went on from the mission to the Master, that it began with the prophet and ended with the man? Wherefore should it? What stain does it impose on Mary Magdalene? Surely none, whoever she was, and whatever she was, whether the repentant courtesan of Magdala or the sister of Lazarus. Then what deduction does it make from the purity of her faith? Surely less than none, for whether her seven devils were merely the mysterious maladies which Jesus cast out of her, or the madness of a base life from which he had rescued her, the fullness, depth and sincerity of her devotion to him as a saviour, apart from her love for him as a man, are clear and untroubled by doubt.

I repeat that the idea is not mine. It dates back to the third century of the Church. Hounded out of all hearing by monkish fanaticism, it has never since dared to raise its voice in Christendom. Only once, so far as I know, has its echo been heard, and it was heard but faintly. Yet it spoke clearly enough, if very meekly in the Life of Jesus which stirred all Christendom some fifty years ago.

But there is a more important question than whether this old idea of Mary's devotion dishonours Mary. Does it dishonour Jesus? Certainly it accentuates his humanity. It strips him of a character in which he has walked during fifteen centuries through evangelical Christianity; the character of a god who is not merely a god but a man, of a man, who is not merely a man but a god. He ceases to be a non-natural man, and becomes a real man; he is no longer a god masquerading in man's body but without man's nature, and becomes a god with man's passions. Perhaps the loss is a gain.

The humanity of Jesus must have been absolute. If he was God, his manhood meant nothing if it was not complete. If he was man, he must have had man's passions. If he had not man's passions, he was not a man. Either way his manhood must have been real to be anything. He must have been born like a man, nurtured like a man, must have grown up like a man, loved like a man, sorrowed like a man, and died like a man. Whether God or not, on no other terms could he be human. Let him be born by miracle and die by miracle and rule his life by miracle and he ceases to belong to humanity. If he were God assuming man's body for man's redemption he must have been a natural man, or he was not man at all, but still God only. If his mission was to fulfil the law, to lead men to love God and his neighbour as himself, he must have had the limitations of humanity, or his example was worth nothing. Thus he must have been tempted like other men. At all points he must have been like those whom he came to teach, save only that he never sinned.

We do not deny some of men's passions to Jesus. Indeed, we think of him as subject to every noble impulse of man save one. If that one passion were base we should dishonour him by thought of it. But the passion of love is the noblest whereof the heart of man is capable. It lifts up the fallen, it purifies the befouled, it sweetens the soured. Where love is, there no evil thing can live. If corrupt passions seem to exist beside it, the thing we take for love is not love but lust.

Now, if Jesus was a man, with a man's passions, whether God or not, wherefore should it dishonour him to think of him as subject to that noblest passion of all? How he ruled it, how he guided his life through it, is another thing, in no wise affected by the first consideration of his subjection as a man to the mightiest, worthiest, purest, most Godlike passion of men.

That Jesus of Nazareth loved Mary Magdalene was the astounding theory for which a good man suffered a kind of martyrdom. I do not espouse it. There is no direct evidence in the world for it. Without such evidence no mere man would be so bold as to countenance it. It might do much harm, and it could do little good. But that the human heart of Jesus must have been subject to the passion of human love I do confidently believe. Moreover, to show the absolute humanity of Jesus is the sufficient and only answer to unbelief in his divinity. That Jesus, the incarnation of the Christian faith, was a man, yet without man's passions, a non-natural man with the powers of a god, is the doctrine which makes the chief bulwark of atheism. The mind rejects it as incredible; the heart rejects it as worthless. But both mind and heart are open to a god that is a man at all points, subject to all man's temptations.

Allow to Jesus the human passions and he becomes for the first time our elder brother. Shut him off from the one mighty and noble passion that walks with us through life, wrecking us where it is wrongly directed, making us strong where its direction is right, and we close our hearts to him. How is he our elder brother if he has not an elder brother's knowledge and sympathy born of similar passions? But if he has all these, then he comes close to us. We can tell him our sorrows, our joys, our expectations in this life, our longings for the life to come. He goes into our hearts. We believe in him. He is our Saviour.

For a human Christ the world is very hungry. Pressed harder by life than ever our fathers were, we hunger and thirst for the man-god that Jesus is and was, and should always be. The world to-day is crying out for Jesus of Nazareth, for Jesus the man. It wants the Redeemer in the elder brother.

Though this idea of the subjection of Jesus to all noble human passions is not my idea, yet it is with fear and many misgivings that I put it forth. It has long possessed me, and I have held it back. If I know my own heart, I advance it with no unworthy motive. I have found it a reply to unbelief in the personal divinity of Jesus, and without that divinity Christianity cannot live. It has broken down the hardest scepticism I have yet encountered. The idea of the elder brother has found its way where that of the non-natural man-god could not go.

I realize its perils, and they are great. If some of their reverence and more of their lip-service find offence in it, and a stumbling-block, let all remember how he whom God has sworn to raise up of the fruit of the loins of David to be Lord and Christ should be in all things whatsoever a man of like passions with ourselves. But in the face of all dangers he who is confident of a pure intent has but to make his account with God. It is for Him to see to the result. If this thing is true, it will live, and if false, and a wrong to whom it would honour, may the Lord with a finger of fire blot it out of man's memories for ever, even as he will blot out of the book of life the name of him that adds to the book of the revelation of God.

What the attitude of Jesus was to Mary we know only by the indirect references of Scripture. If she was the woman taken in adultery, he would not lift his eyes upon her shame, and he silenced her accusers. If she was the woman who was a sinner, he defended her against the self-righteous Pharisee. If she was Mary of Bethany he supported her against the complaint of her sister; he wept at sight of her sorrow for her brother, he accepted her offering of ointment and reproved the anger she provoked in Judas. Being no more than Mary of Magdala, she was suffered to follow him and minister to him. Whatever she was, he must have read the secret unknown to herself. He did not drive her from him. Yet the band of devoted women who surrounded Jesus must have seen his reproach. The Pharisees did not hold back their hands from any weapons of persecution. They openly charged Jesus with making his friends of men who were publicans, and his familiars of women who were sinners.

When Jesus entered Jerusalem (about the year 32), Mary was still with him. We gather this from the conversation in the house at Bethany. Martha complained that while she was cumbered with much serving her sister helped her not at all. Was it nothing to Jesus that Mary had left her to serve alone? And Jesus answered, "Martha, Martha, thou art careful and troubled about many things, but one thing is needful, and Mary hath chosen that good part which shall not be taken away from her." We know that Mary Magdalene had been following at the feet of Jesus. Clearly, Mary of Bethany was in his train. Can we resist the inference that the two were one?

It would appear that Jesus used this opportunity to leave Mary behind him, for she was in Bethany at the death of Lazarus. Does it wrong his sacred character to conclude that this parting from the devoted woman who has followed him was another triumph over temptation? Say that he had known when the fidelity of Mary to the Master had deepened and strengthened into love of the man. Say that he had seen this change first with fear and then with pain. Admit that he, on his part, had believed himself too deeply immersed in God's work to be touched by human love, that his mission had so consumed him that his human impulses were as quiescent as if they did not exist. Say that bit by bit the presence of Mary, her half-conscious affection, her pure devotion had taken hold of him, that equally for her sake and for his own he may have thought of sending her away, and that at that moment the Pharisees reproached him with her company, the sinner, the notorious woman of the city. Assume that she may have wished to leave him that he might suffer nothing from her unforgotten infamy, and that he may have restrained her, being resolved to let the world see that he was on the side of the outcast and down-trodden. Say that he parted from her at length at the more homely plea of Martha. Is there any dishonour to his sanctity in a chain of facts like that?

If there is none, and if the facts are credible, if they are even possible, Jesus, having left Mary at Bethany, may have known for the first time the full depth of the trial he had gone through. It must have been a temptation greater than any that the Devil put before him in the wilderness when he offered him the king-doms of the world; a temptation like to that which drew him to his mother at the hour of their parting at Nazareth. But fiercer and more terrible, for it was a temptation coming from the noblest side of his nature as a man. Nevertheless, he triumphed even over that. It was his first principle that for the kingdom of Heaven's sake the world and all that was in it should be renounced.

So once more his spirit conquered. Once more he put his human longings beneath his feet. But it must have been at an awful price.

It had been needful, and it had been done, but the penalty must have been terrible. That the heart of Jesus was sore as he entered Jerusalem we know, and many wild words and sane words that sound harsh and cruel seem only explicable by the light of such a chain of facts as are here supposed.

IV. The Gospel of Renunciation

Perhaps it was at this moment of agony that two new disciples came to him, and one said, "Lord, suffer me first to go and bury my father." And Jesus answered, "Let the dead bury their dead." In other words: If you follow me you have a cross to bear. You must reckon on the cost, lest when you have gone half-way you should have to turn back. Your natural affections will try you, but you must crush them down. If you are children of the Kingdom you will be tempted to make terms with the world. Do not do it. Cut the world away from you, with all its loves and ties whatsoever.

And another disciple came to him and said, "Master, I will follow thee whithersoever thou goest." And he seemed to answer, Come, but first think well what you are doing, I can promise you nothing, for I have nothing myself; no father, no mother, no brethren, no sisters, no ties of heart or blood. As for the things of this world, "the foxes have holes, and the birds of the air have nests, but the Son of Man hath not where to lay his head." And to all he said, "Think not that I am come to send peace on earth; I came not to send peace, but a sword. For I am come to set a man at variance against his father, and the daughter against her mother, and the daughter-in-law against her mother-in-law. And a man's foes shall be they of his own household."

Thus did Jesus tread down another temptation of his human nature, and thus did he pay the penalty of his divinity. The man in him had become less, and the god in him had grown greater.

CHAPTER XIX

The Discourses of Jesus

I. The Gospel of St. John

IN THE FOLLOWING Summary I have not extracted the sermons that are in the Gospel of St. John. This for two reasons:

(1) That the teaching of Jesus about the kingdom of Heaven does not seem to be the same in *John* as in the three earlier Gospels.

(2) Because there is a mass of mysticism and eastern imagery in *John* that does not read like the words of Jesus as they are given in the other Gospels.

On the first of these points I should say that John's Gospel was written when the disciples had ceased to hope for the near coming of the kingdom, and had begun to think that Jesus meant a spiritual kingdom in the heavens, not a material kingdom on the earth. And on the second I should say as a student of mere style that the language of Jesus as reported by John is John's own version of the meaning Jesus conveyed to his mind, or the meaning that he had by the thought of years extracted out of the words of Jesus. There is hardly any mystic speech in the sermons of Jesus given here. All are concrete, dramatic and human, while there is hardly any concrete, dramatic and human speech in *John* at all. There is nearly the same difference between Jesus in *John* and Jesus in *Matthew* as between St. Paul's Epistle to the Romans and the Gospel of Luke. *John* should agree with the other Gospels in all essentials, but it must be interpreted (if it needs interpretation) by *Matthew, Mark* and *Luke:* not *Matthew, Mark* and *Luke* by *John.*

II. Sermons of the First Three Gospels

The sermons of the first three Gospels are as simple in teaching as a child's story, and their meaning is this:

578

1. The kingdom of Heaven is at hand.

2. When that kingdom comes all the orders of the world will be reversed, the rich and great will be cast down, the poor and meek and the repentant will inherit the earth. The heavy-laden will find rest, the sick will be healed.

3. More than this, the poor shall judge the rich. The publicans and sinners shall judge the self-righteous hypocrites.

4. The first in this world shall be the last in the Kingdom, and this shall apply not only to mankind in general but also to the chosen children themselves.

5. Therefore repent, and become fit for the Kingdom. If you are rich, sell all you have. If you are poor, do not try to be rich. If you are heavy-laden, remember that rest is coming to you. If you mourn, remember that you shall yet be glad.

6. That Jesus himself was the Son of God who was to be at the head of the Kingdom.

This is the simple teaching of the sermons of Jesus, but much is said besides.

III.   The Teaching of Jesus

1. When God sent man into the world He permitted him to be tempted of devils. These devils were man's passions, as represented by his eye, his hand, his feet. If man yielded to these he rebelled against God. He set himself up as God's enemy. He tried to possess the earth, to build farms, to stand on himself and the earth. All this stood to Jesus for Satan. This tendency to sin becomes greater in every generation. Adam fell, his children were more liable to fall, and so on. Thus men were *evil* by natural bias—original sin.

2. That, foreseeing this rebellion, God has given man a law which he should obey. If he obeyed this law he must resist all the devils. The law said, in effect, "Thou shalt love the Lord thy God with all thy heart and soul and strength and thy neighbour as thyself." If man loved God with all his heart, and loved his neighbour as himself, he could not become rich and great and set up an empire against God.

3. That nevertheless men yielded to Satan, and set up this empire of the world.

4. That certain of the rich and great, knowing that they were violating God's law yet unwilling to yield up the empire of Satan,

made hypocrites of themselves, robbed the poor, destroyed widows' houses, yet said long prayers before men.

5. That for this they must be utterly destroyed.

6. Yet there was a way of salvation, for such of them as would fly from the wrath to come; they must be born again, back from the ways of the flesh to the ways of the spirit; that the course was clear—obey the law which said, "Thou shalt love the Lord thy God and thy neighbour as thyself." This would require that they should start life afresh, renouncing the empire of the world, giving up the world's wealth, living and labouring as the poor live and labour, trusting God as the lilies trust Him for raiment, as the sparrows trust Him for food.

Then, besides this, there were the more personal references to Jesus, telling what he thought of himself and his mission.

1. He was the Son of God in a special sense, for God had sent him to tell the story which even the prophets had not told, and to work miracles such as the prophets had not worked. All men who followed the law of God were God's, but he was God's especial son, because, as his works showed, God was in him and he was in God, and God and he were as one.

2. That he was the Son of Man also, and as such could possess himself of the kingdoms of the earth if he but listened to the temptations of Satan, the temptations of his eye, his hand, his foot —of his people and disciples waiting for a Messiah, his mother and brethren who loved him and thought him mad, of women who would have laid down their lives for him, followed him through all troubles, ministered to him, stood at his cross, buried him, wept at his grave, wept when his body was lost.

3. That as Son of God and Son of Man he had chosen his part, and it was this: Never to yield to Satan, never to have part or lot in the empire of the world; never to possess kingdoms, to be rich, to have money, or to have a second coat, never to let even natural affections draw him off from God. Rather than this, to pluck out his eye if it tempted, and to cut off his hand if it offended him. Thus to go on to the end, and thus to call on all men to go on, each in the degree in which he could do it, well knowing that the full measure of this baptism of renunciation was not possible to all men.

4. That this renunciation of the world would lead him through

awful trials, and at every step in life's path he should be beset, and become the most tempted of all men that had ever lived on the earth, because his natural emotions were strongest and his chances of empire in the world were greatest.

5. That in the end this renunciation and the mission coming of it must lead him to his death. But that he must go on to his death with eyes open, because his death would crown all, because then the world would hear him, because then his gospel would be realized as a possible thing completed, finished, and thus his death would ransom men (as many as believed in him) from the curse of sin, and bring men (as many as accepted him) into atonement with God. If men cannot be ransomed by his words his death must ransom them. He will die for his gospel, and then men will believe in him.

Further, that for himself, death would be welcome; it would be the end and goal. Sin and Satan, the eye, the hand, the foot, would no more tempt him. Life would be over for the great Son of Man and God, and being over (without fault found in him by the world itself) the ways of God would be justified before men, every tittle of the law would be fulfilled, man would see that it was no impossible law that God had given, but a law that man could keep.

6. Finally, that there was a great reward for all men coming and very near, the kingdom of Heaven on earth, and that he, Jesus of Nazareth, Son of God, elder brother of Man, should sit on the throne of that kingdom surrounded by the little ones of the world, the poor, the downtrodden, the sick, the harlots, the publicans (with all their sorrows and sins gone), to judge the rich, the great, the hypocrites, the whited sepulchres, the destroyers of widows' houses, the tyrants who had been sitting at the head of Satan's kingdoms.

This is the Gospel of Jesus as told in the Sermons.

IV. The Principal Discourses of Jesus

The Sermon on the Mount   *Matthew* V, 1–48
                                      Luke VI, 20–49

Woe to the cities which have not believed.

"Come unto me, all ye that labour and are heavy laden, and I will give you rest."   *Matthew* XI, 20–30

The sinful woman in the Pharisee's house.	*Luke* VII, 36–50
Seeking a sign and the answer.	*Matthew* XII, 38–45
Foretelling his death and resurrection.	*Matthew* XVI, 21–28
	Matthew XVII, 22, 23
	Matthew XX, 17–19
Disciples striving which shall be greatest.	*Matthew* XVIII, 1–35
Jesus's reply.	*Matthew* XX, 20–28
Warning against the Pharisees.	*Matthew* XXIII, 1–39
In the Temple declaring himself the Light of the World.	*John* VIII, 12–59
Calling himself the good shepherd.	*John* X, 11–21
Important discourses on many subjects.	*Luke* XII, 1–59
On the report of the Galileans whose blood Pilate had mingled with their sacrifices.	*Luke* XIII, 1–3
Jesus answering the report of the eighteen on whom the Tower in Siloam fell, with the moral that all men are sinners, illustrated by the parable of the fig-tree.	*Luke* XIII, 4–9
Warning the people to count the cost of discipleship.	*Luke* XIV, 25–35
On the kingdom of Heaven : when shall it come ?	*Luke* XVII, 20–37
Answering his disciples, when they think the Kingdom will immediately appear.	*Luke* XIX, 11–27
Answering the Pharisees on the subject of divorce.	*Matthew* XIX, 3–12
About Cæsar's coin.	*Matthew* XXII, 15–22
On the Resurrection.	*Matthew* XXII, 23–33
Is Christ the son of David?	*Matthew* XXII, 41–46
Woe to the scribes.	*Mark* XII, 38–40
	Luke XX, 45–47

His answer to Nicodemus.
The essence of it is :

"For God so loved the world, that
He gave His only begotten Son, that
whosoever believeth in him should
not perish, but have everlasting life.
For God sent not His Son into the
world to condemn the world; but that
the world through him might be
saved."   *John* III, 1–21

On fasting (with illustrative para-
bles).   *Matthew* IX, 14–17

On the Sabbath:
Disciples plucking ears of corn on the
Sabbath.   *Matthew* XII, 1–8
Jesus healing a man's hand on the
Sabbath.   *Matthew* XII, 9–14
Jesus replying about the Sabbath.   *Luke* XIII, 14–17
Commending the Widow's offering.   *Luke* XXI, 1–4
Jesus reproving the ambitions of
the disciples, yet promises them the
Kingdom.   *Luke* XXII, 24–30
Teaching love and humility by
washing the disciples' feet.   *John* XIII, 1–20
Foretelling Peter's denial and the
scattering of the Twelve.   *Matthew* XXVI, 31–35
Farewell address and intercessory
prayer.   *John* XIV–XVII

The Synoptic Gospels differ from *John,* both in form and in
matter. *Matthew* contains long discourses. *Luke* short ones. *Mark*
has four. There is no Sermon on the Mount in *Mark.*

In *Matthew* Jesus delivers the Sermon on the Mount immediately
on his return from the Baptism. He ascended a mountain and
delivered the discourse from there. Luke presents a much shorter
discourse which begins and ends in the same way, the whole tenor
being the same. Luke says he *came down* from the mountain to
deliver it. In both *Luke* and *Matthew* the sermon is followed by his
going into Capernaum* and healing the centurion's servant.

In *Luke* (VI) the *blessings* are followed by corresponding

*The only existing remains of a synagogue in Capernaum are said to be that
of the centurion.

curses. It was a principle of the Ebionites that he who had his fortune in this present age would be destitute in the age to come. Jesus is supposed to have applied this to the present life and the life in the kingdom of Heaven.

The Sermon on the Mount is regarded as a counterpart of the law, delivered on Mount Sinai. It is unimportant whether (as Matthew says) he *ascended* the mountain to deliver this discourse, or *descended* from the mountain to the plain, as Luke says. All that concerns us is whether there were two discourses or one only; or whether the discourse given in full in *Matthew* contains also the discourses as given in *Luke*. I think the latter is the true explanation.

The Sermon on the Mount in *Matthew* is obviously made up of many discourses, and it is difficult to believe that they can all have been delivered at the same time. They deal with subjects which cannot easily be connected. Many of the passages may be said with reason to have a certain relation to each other. But I take the view that this is so mainly by virtue of careful compilation. In general they deal with different subjects, and the whole sermon would, I think, gain greatly if they were presented as separate discourses.

Do these discourses describe the condition which is to come with the kingdom of Heaven? Or are they intended to be practical counsel for the conduct of life in this world before the Kingdom comes and while men are preparing for it, and making themselves ready for it?

It is a difficult question to answer, because some of the counsel given seems to be a counsel of perfection only possible of realization in a heavenly kingdom that shall be under divine government. Some thinkers (Tolstoy for example) take them as practical laws for life in the world as it is. In applying them to the personal life of the world they abrogate government, human law, human justice, and seem to lay humanity open to the attacks of its lowest elements —as in the counsel, "Resist not evil." The whole theory of human justice is to resist evil, to root it out, to destroy it—by force if absolutely necessary. The theory of Tolstoy is, however, that when evil is resisted (by violence of government) it grows and increases; that violence creates violence, resistance makes for counter resistance; whereas submission to evil eventually roots it out.

Are these discourses not on the lines of the advice John the Baptist gives to the people who ask him what they are to do to escape the wrath to come, only immeasurably deeper in thought and broader in range?

I take the view that Jesus was answering the same questions as those put to John—that he was preparing mankind for the coming of the kingdom of Heaven.

V. Adultery and Divorce

The passages in *Luke* XVI, 18 and in *Matthew* XIX, 9–12 on marriage, adultery and divorce are thought by certain critics to have reference to the adulterous Herod Antipas.

Strauss thinks this interpretation is purely visionary, and there is no direct connexion between the passages and Herod's adultery and false marriage. But it is clear that it must have been spoken about the time when Herod Antipas imprisoned John the Baptist for denouncing his adultery, his putting away of his Arab wife. Therefore, I see little ground for the charge of its being a visionary explanation. In short I take the view that the denunciation of second marriage by Jesus was almost certainly provoked by the fact of Herod's adultery, which (in relation to John) must have been a subject of vivid interest to all the people surrounding Jesus.

Further (and very important) I think it reasonable to connect this denunciation of the adulterous marriage with Herod's first reference to Jesus, when he is convinced that Jesus is John the Baptist raised from the dead.

The four or five events link themselves very closely together and should be told consecutively:

(1) John's denunciation of Herod for his adulterous and incestuous marriage, following his putting away of his Arabian wife.

(2) Herod's imprisonment of John.

(3) Herod's execution of John.

(4) The denunciation of divorce by Jesus.

(5) Herod's thinking that Jesus was John come back from the dead.

(6) Herod's desire to see Jesus, whom he naturally regards as a thorn in his side, a living danger, another popular preacher who is telling the people of Galilee that their sovereign lord has broken the law of Moses in relation to marriage and is living in open disregard of the law of God.

(7) Herod's desire to kill Jesus as he killed John—to get him out of the way; hence the disciples of Jesus twice urging him to leave Herod's territory.

The complete prohibition of divorce is thought, by some critics, to be intended to refer not to the present time, but the coming time, the time of the kingdom of Heaven which was to come on earth. But there was to be no marriage *then*.

VI. *The Lord's Prayer*

When was the Lord's Prayer given? According to *Matthew* it was given during the Sermon on the Mount; therefore, at the beginning of the ministry. According to *Luke* it was given at the close of the ministry. Strauss thinks it is anything but natural to suppose that the disciples of Jesus should have remained until the last journey without any direction to pray, or how to pray. "He had doubtless often prayed in their circle," although only once is he so recorded.

Is there anything original in the thought or terms of the prayer? This can hardly be belied. But, while the elements of the prayer may be found in earlier rabbinical writings (often in similar phraseology), the selection and combination is original. Jesus clearly believed in the duty of prayer and in the efficacy of prayer.

In *Mark* XI, 24–26 Jesus says that whatever things we desire when we pray, and believe that we shall receive, we shall receive. But there is one condition—that God will grant us forgiveness only if we, on our part, grant to our fellow-men forgiveness.

VII. *On the Messiah, the Resurrection and Immortality*

Jesus asks how can the same personage be at once the Lord of David and the son of David. The majority of commentators apply the psalm in which David speaks of the Lord to the Messiah. The apostles use it as a prophecy concerning Christ (*Acts* II, 34; I *Corinthians* XV, 25). Jesus plainly means that it is David who speaks and that the Messiah is his subject. Jesus believed the psalm to be a Messianic one. This was also the idea of his time. Did he mean that according to his higher nature the Messiah was the Lord of David, while according to his human nature he was his son? Was Jesus merely trying to embarrass the Pharisees? Or did he mean (what the words imply) that the Messiah was not the physical son of David, in short that it was not necessary to be born of the line and lineage of David to be the Messiah?

Was Jesus voicing the objections of those who, knowing nothing of the descent of Jesus from David, but thinking him merely the son of an obscure carpenter of whose descent nothing was known, were therefore unwilling to believe that he could be the Christ?

In short was Jesus speaking of himself when he said, "I who am not descended from David am nevertheless the Messiah." David did not expect that the Messiah would be his son.

Jesus tries to convince the Sadducees that there will be a resurrection from the dead by showing that Abraham, Isaac and Jacob are dead and buried (*Matthew* XXII, 31). This is a very difficult point, needing careful consideration. Is it his object to prove that the idea of the Resurrection and the idea of immortality is contained in the law? Is he saying that Abraham, Isaac and Jacob are dead and buried, but that nevertheless God is the Lord of Abraham, Isaac and Jacob. Can one imagine that he is the Lord of dead men? If he is the Lord of these three, it follows that they are living. *Therefore there must be immortality.* The dead must survive. Also there must be resurrection from the dead. Jesus asks, "Why should it seem so wonderful that the dead shall rise?" Then he shows that their fathers were alive, otherwise their faith was dead.

What does he mean by his references in the sermons to the resurrection from the dead? Does he ever indicate in his discourses any belief that the bodies of the dead shall rise? I do not think so. It is the spirit he thinks and speaks of as surviving. The Sadducees did not believe in any survival after death. Jesus certainly did, and defended his belief by the Scriptures.

Then look at St. Paul's view of the Resurrection. Does he anywhere say that the body rises *as it was buried?* He does speak of a *spiritualized* body that will rise. Jesus is alive to him at his conversion, although he has not seen or touched him but only heard a voice speaking in the Hebrew tongue. Moreover (very important) St. Paul's faith is built on the Resurrection of Jesus as the *first* that rose from the dead.

It follows that St. Paul knew nothing of anybody having risen from the dead before Jesus. Therefore St. Paul knew nothing of the raising of Lazarus.

Moreover, it is not certain that St. Paul believed in the actual physical resurrection of Jesus, although he speaks of the many evidences of his Resurrection—that he was seen of this person, that and the other, including the 500 in Galilee. St. Paul indicates plainly a spiritualized body.

St. Peter, on the other hand, is made to declare that he ate and drank with Jesus after he was raised from the dead.

Thus, it is clear, either that the early disciples did actually believe that Jesus rose from the dead in the body in which he was buried, that he exercised all the functions of that body for forty days, and rose to Heaven in that body, after eating a meal, or else that all this found its place in the Gospels long afterwards by virtue of oral tradition, and perhaps in answer to the scoffers and wranglers who were saying that Jesus (after his death at all events, and perhaps during his so-called life on earth) had been merely a phantom, not a real flesh and blood man, refusing meat and drink.

VIII. The Greatest Commandment

After the Pharisees and Sadducees (they are represented as being friendly sects in their opposition to Jesus) have been put to silence (or rather the Sadducees) on the subject of the Resurrection, a lawyer comes to tempt Jesus with a question:

"Master, which is the great commandment in the law?" Jesus answers, "Thou shalt love the Lord thy God with all thy heart, and with all thy soul, and with all thy mind . . . And the second is like unto it, Thou shalt love thy neighbour as thyself. On these two commandments hang all the law and the Prophets."

Mark and Luke differ from this in the form. And Luke appends to this the parable of the good Samaritan. The lawyer in Mark says, "Well, Master, thou hast said the truth." Jesus tells him that he is not far from the kingdom of God. The fundamental fact is that out of the Mosaic code Jesus selects the two commandments concerning the love of God and of our neighbour as the most important.

But are we to understand that in the view of Jesus this was all that was necessary to inherit the kingdom of God?

What, then, of the Messiah, the Atonement, the new covenant, of all that is of the essence of Christianity? Are we to understand that in the opinion of Jesus the law of Moses contained all that was necessary?

IX. *The Messiah in Relation to the Law*

In *Matthew* V, 17 Jesus says he did not come to destroy the law but to fulfil it. Also that until Heaven and earth passed away, not one jot or tittle of the law should pass away. Thus it follows either that he has not then realized that he was the Messiah charged with the duty of changing the law, or else that the Messiah would never change the law.

I arrive at the conclusion that he knew he was the Messiah from the moment of the baptism, and that he did not at this period think the Messiah had to supersede the law. Did he ever think the law had to be put aside? On the other hand *Luke* (XVI, 16) seems to present a contradiction by causing Jesus to say that the law and the prophets were in force until John came, leaving the inference that thereafter, that is, during his own life and after it, they came to an end.

So little was it according to the design of Jesus at the beginning of his ministry to disregard the law that he is constantly calling for a far stricter observance of the law than the custom and precepts of the scribes and Pharisees required.

He presents a series of Mosaic commandments, and so presents them and comments upon them and illustrates them by parables as to indicate a desire to penetrate to the spirit of the law instead of cleaving to the mere letter, as the Pharisees were doing. *Matthew,* as distinguished from *Luke,* is constantly presenting this aspect of the mind of Jesus. And from that fact (among others) we may deduce the conclusion that *Matthew* was written later than *Luke.*

The denunciation of those who say *Lord, Lord,* but who, by reason of their evil deeds, will be rejected by him on the day of judgment, decidedly presupposes the Messiahship of Jesus. Did this come at a later stage than the Sermon on the Mount? I do not think this follows.

X. *Jesus and the Law*

In his teaching, the meaning of the Mosaic Law was deepened by Jesus. For instance, there was the precept, "Thou shalt love thy neighbour, and hate thine enemy." Jesus regarded this as a perversion of the Mosaic injunction to love one's neighbour. According to him, the duty of loving your neighbour did not carry permission to hate your enemy.

XI. *The Synoptic Gospels and the Fourth Gospel*

The teaching of Jesus in the Synoptic Gospels goes farther and wider than Strauss indicates.

Not only did Jesus commend poverty in itself and as a condition blessed by God (blessed are the poor *in spirit* is a manifest and rather impudent interpolation which robs the word of Jesus of its significance and reduces it to foolishness), he also blessed the oppressed, the heavy-laden, the downtrodden, and promised them a great reversal of their condition in the kingdom of Heaven that was to come. He promised comfort to the unhappy, the drying of the tears of the sorrowing, health and happiness to the sick, and, above all, mercy and forgiveness to the sinful. He was tender and full of charity to fallen women.

In short, he was on the side of the unfortunate and the despised always. He did not ask himself what merit they possessed to entitle them to the blessed future. It was enough for him that they were sorrowful to be, in his view, certain of a blessed condition in the world that was to come, whether it was a reconstructed world of the present life, or a life hereafter.

The central doctrine on which all this was based by Jesus was that this world was under the government and control of Satan, of one evil power, and therefore all the good things of this life were given to those who were the servants of Satan, whereas the world to come (whether the kingdom of God on earth or the kingdom of God in Heaven) was under the government of God, and therefore everything would be reversed—the poor of this world would become the rich, the downtrodden of this world would sit on thrones and live in mansions, the despised and sinful who repented would come into the inheritance of God's mercy and forgiveness.

I think this, stated roughly, is the heart and essence of the teaching of Jesus in the Synoptic Gospels. Therefore, in his discourses and in his parables he is often answering the question put to John the Baptist: "What shall I do to be saved?" In the Sermon on the Mount he answers it first one and then another way to fit the varying conditions of life. Later, he goes farther, and deals with the great problem of man's relation to God, and the necessity of man's redemption.

This, towards the end of his ministry, leads him up to the reason of his death, the object of his death and the work to be achieved by it. But not until near the end does he openly dwell on his own share in the redemption of the world, on his own position as the Son of God.

In the fourth Gospel nearly all this is changed. Here, instead of holding back the revelation of his divinity, Jesus openly avows it. From the beginning he asserts it. What, in the Synoptics, he has half hidden from his closest friends and disciples, he states plainly to strangers. Rarely in the Synoptics does he avow his divinity, does he admit that he is the Christ, does he say (however indirectly) that he is the Messiah, that he is the Son of God.

On the contrary, when he is saluted in towns which indicate belief in his divinity, his succession from David, his Messianic character, he restrains the people who so salute him and warns them to tell no man. Only at what seems to be the very verge of the end (at Cæsarea Philippi) does he tolerate the declaration of his divinity, and thereafter talks openly of the character of the Son of God, whose mission it was to die for the redemption of the world.

But in *John* he *begins* by declaring his divinity, and goes on declaring it, never wearying of declaring it, and so on to the end. Look at the teaching of Jesus as it is given in the fourth Gospel.

XII.   Jesus and Nicodemus

The conversation of Jesus with Nicodemus in the third chapter of *John* is the first considerable specimen of Christ's teaching. Apparently, it takes place in Jerusalem, after the first Passover following the baptism. Nicodemus is described as "a ruler of the Jews." He comes to Jesus by night, calls him Rabbi, and says they know that he is a teacher come from God because he does miracles which nobody could do unless God were with him.

What further he says, what counsel he asks, we are not told, but Jesus appears to answer an unrecorded question when he says, "Except a man be born again, he cannot see the kingdom of Heaven." Nicodemus asks, "How can a man be born when he is old? Can he enter the second time into his mother's womb, and be born?" And to this Jesus replies by a statement which implies that the birth he has spoken of is a spiritual birth: "Except a man be born of water and of the Spirit, he cannot enter into the kingdom of God."

Jesus further explains the meaning of the new birth by saying that what is "born of the flesh is flesh; and that which is born of the Spirit is spirit." In other words, he had not said that a man was to re-enter his mother's womb, but that his spirit should change and undergo a new birth. Why, then, should Nicodemus marvel when he is told that he must be born again? To this Nicodemus asks, "How can these things be?" And Jesus replies, "Art thou a master of Israel, and knowest not these things?"

The obvious fact is that Nicodemus had betrayed lamentable ignorance of things which were of common knowledge among persons of his position and education. It had, perhaps, been pardonable of illiterate fishermen in Galilee to be unfamiliar with such thoughts and language, but that a ruler of the Jews (almost certainly a member of the Sanhedrin) should not understand them in their only true sense, and apply a physical interpretation to the words of Jesus, was astonishing and unpardonable.

But the conversation in *John* between Jesus and Nicodemus does not end at this. Jesus is described as going on from a proposition which Nicodemus ought to have found no difficulty in understanding to a declaration of his own character, mission and ultimate end, and the object of his life in this world, which (it is not unreasonable to say) no man living could at that time have understood.

He tells Nicodemus, who could not understand a very ordinary earthly thing, a very extraordinary heavenly thing, namely, that he (whom he plainly indicates under the title of the Son of Man) is to be "lifted up" as Moses lifted up the serpent in the wilderness. In other words, that he is to be crucified. Further, that whosoever believes in him shall not perish, but have eternal life.

Still further, although partly by repetition, that all this is to come to pass because God so loved the world that He had given him (His only begotten Son) that whosoever believed in him should not perish but have everlasting life. Finally, and again by repetition, that God had not sent His Son into the world to condemn the world, but that the world through him should be saved.

More in the same spirit Jesus says to Nicodemus. The final words of Nicodemus are not given. If at the last moment he had said, "How can these things be?" it would have been a natural question to ask. Nobody had ever before heard such doctrine.

Did Jesus say this to Nicodemus? Did he say it at the beginning of his ministry? Did he reveal to this strange Jew at this early time what he had not yet revealed to his nearest disciples? If he did, which of them recorded it?

Was it never recorded by anybody until the writer of the fourth Gospel reported it? If this writer was John the Apostle, are we to assume that he alone was present when Nicodemus came to Jesus by night? If Matthew was present, why did he not report this tremendous revelation of the divinity and mission of Jesus?

If the first Gospel does not contain this conversation of Jesus with Nicodemus, and as we are compelled to conclude that Matthew the apostle must have known of it, are we forced to the conclusion that the writer of the first Gospel was not the apostle Matthew? If Peter was present when Nicodemus came to Jesus by night, why did he not report it to Mark, whose Gospel he is supposed to have inspired? Why was it said to be a virtue in Peter to have said the same thing in answer to the question Jesus put to him long afterwards ("Whom say ye that I am?") at Cæsarea Philippi? And, above all, why did Jesus say at Cæsarea Philippi that flesh and blood had not revealed to Peter the fact that Jesus was the Son of God, if he himself had said the same to Nicodemus, and Peter had heard of it?

Or, are we to conclude that none of the disciples heard the conversation between Jesus and Nicodemus, and that it was given to the writer of the fourth Gospel by revelation of God long after the event?

On the other hand, are we compelled to come to quite opposite conclusions, namely that the conversation between Jesus and Nicodemus did not take place at the beginning of the ministry but at the end of it, or that it did not occur at all?

The latter, a very serious interpretation of the incident, is favoured by certain facts, (1) that we never hear of Nicodemus except in the fourth Gospel; (2) that we never hear of him again even in the fourth Gospel, except twice, first when the Pharisees and chief priests (Chapter VII) are conspiring to lay hands on Jesus to assassinate him and Nicodemus pleads for a fair trial ("Doth our law judge any man before it hear him?"), and, second, at the hour of the burial when he comes to the tomb with a hundred-weight of myrrh and aloes; (3) that no sensible effect seems to have been produced on the mind of Nicodemus by the most astounding declaration that was ever made to a man.

XIII. Jesus and the Woman of Samaria

Immediately following the report of the astonishing conversation between Jesus and Nicodemus comes in the fourth Gospel the equally astonishing conversation between Jesus and the woman of Samaria. Jesus, early in his ministry, has left Judæa, after his first Passover following the baptism and the conversation with Nicodemus, and is going through Samaria towards Galilee (*John* IV). In Samaria he comes to a city where there is a well. It is the well in the parcel of ground which Jacob gave to his son Joseph. Jesus rests at the well about midday, while his disciples go into the city to buy food. While he is resting a woman of Samaria comes to draw water, and he asks her to give him water to drink.

She is astonished that Jesus, being obviously a Jew, should ask a woman of Samaria to give him a drink, because the Jews have no dealings with the Samaritans, and perhaps also (although the Gospel does not say so) because she is a woman. Jesus answers strangely. He says that if she had known who it is that asks her to give him a drink, she would have asked drink of him, and he would have given her living water.

The woman cannot understand this language, and after saying the obvious matter-of-fact thing that the well is deep and Jesus has nothing with which to draw water, she asks him whence he has this living water. Is he greater than their father Jacob who gave them the well?

To this Jesus replies that those who drink of the water of this well will thirst again, but those who drink of the water he can give them will never thirst, for the water he will give will be a well of everlasting water springing up into everlasting life.

The woman says, "Sir, give me this water that I may never thirst again, and never have need to come here any more to draw water."

Upon this Jesus changes the course of the conversation and tells her to go away and call her husband. The woman answers that she has no husband, whereupon Jesus astonishes her by revealing knowledge of her life. When he asked her to call her husband he had known she had none, and also that she had had five husbands in the past and that the man she was then living with was not her husband.

At this the woman (who presumably has never seen Jesus before or he her) says, "I perceive thou art a prophet."

Again the course of the conversation is changed, this time by the woman, who says that her people worship in this mountain (the mountain by the well) but the Jews say that in Jerusalem is the place where men ought to worship.

Upon this Jesus says what is, perhaps, one of the greatest things he ever said: "Woman, believe me, the hour cometh, when ye shall neither in this mountain, nor yet at Jerusalem, worship the Father." And then, after a manifest and impudent interpolation totally irrelevant to the line of thought Jesus is pursuing and totally unlike him in spirit, Jesus says, "But the hour cometh, and now is, when the true worshippers shall worship the Father in spirit and in truth."

Upon this the woman, who appears to be struggling to reach the high thought of Jesus, and only catching on to his vision of a divine future, says she knows that the Messiah is to come, and that when he comes he is to tell them all things. And then Jesus makes to this strange woman of Samaria this astonishing revelation, not yet made to the disciples, who presently return and ask him commonplace questions.

"I that speak unto thee am he."

Did Jesus reveal his Messiahship to the strange woman by the well? To what purpose did he reveal it? What was the effect of his having revealed it?

Later, we are told that the Samaritans (who were first arrested by the woman's story that the unknown Jew had told her all about her many husbands) prevail upon Jesus to remain with them for two days, and then they say they believe and know that he is indeed the Christ, the Saviour of the world, not because of what he had said to the woman about her husbands, but because they had heard him for themselves.

Did all this happen? If so, who recorded it? Was the writer of the fourth Gospel present when the Samaritans made their declaration of belief in the Messiahship of Jesus? Who told him that Jesus had said he was the Christ? Had the woman told him? If so, had she not told the other disciples? If she had why had not Matthew told this story for himself and Mark for Peter? Why was it reserved for John to tell it thirty years after the Synoptic Gospels had been written?

If Jesus, who knew all things (and nobody had need to tell him anything), was aware that the disciples knew what the woman said he had told her, where was the merit of their saying what Peter said at Cæsarea Philippi? Flesh and blood *had* told Peter that Jesus was the Christ. Jesus himself had told them, through the medium of the woman of Samaria, just as he had told them (less plainly perhaps) through the medium of Nicodemus.

What is the explanation of these two outstanding incidents in the life of Jesus? Are we to conclude that neither of them happened? Or that if both happened the writer of the fourth Gospel put into them much more than the disciples understood them to contain?

Strauss apparently rejects both as unhistorical and totally out of harmony with the facts of the life of Jesus as elsewhere recorded. I prefer to accept the essential part of both, but with modifications. First, I think that the coming of Nicodemus by night occurred in Jerusalem on the occasion of the first visit of Jesus after the baptism, namely, about the time of the Feast of Tabernacles. I think it concerned the new birth, but probably did not go farther than that. The second mention of Nicodemus comes properly in Jerusalem about the time of the Feast of Dedication, when the chief priests were attempting to assassinate Jesus, without the law.

I think the conversation with the woman of Samaria came shortly after these two scenes with Nicodemus, on the journey of Jesus out of Jerusalem (when he was probably stoned out) through Galilee to Samaria. I think the conversation with the woman concerned her own life, and that it included the great passage in which Jesus lifts up religion to the condition of the universal faith.

The story was told by the woman to the disciples, or in their hearing, but I do not think it went the length of making Jesus declare his Messianic character to the woman. All this was, I think, kept back from the disciples until the culminating scene in Cæsarea Philippi.

XIV. *Who Wrote the Fourth Gospel?*

What, then, is to be made of the fourth Gospel? Is it the work of the apostle John? Or is it the work of another, coming much later, writing under the influence of the disputes current towards the end of the century in Alexandria, and filling out the bare lines of incidents which the earlier evangelists had not considered important with the theology of a much later time?

I strongly incline to the latter opinion. I think there are a great many other reasons for believing that the fourth Gospel was not written by John the apostle.

It is through the Gospel of John alone that we know anything of Nicodemus. He appears first as coming to Jesus by night. Next, as the advocate of Jesus so far as to protest against his being killed without a hearing. Finally, as partaking with Joseph of Arimathæa in his burial. It is astonishing that the other evangelists know nothing of the latter incident.

Mary Magdalene must have seen Nicodemus with Joseph of Arimathæa at the sepulchre, if he was there. She could hardly have failed to tell the disciples. Matthew was one of the disciples who must have known of the presence of Nicodemus as well as of Joseph, yet he speaks of Joseph and does not mention Nicodemus. Peter must have known from Mary Magdalene of the presence of Nicodemus as well as of Joseph, yet Mark (his scribe) mentions Joseph and omits Nicodemus.

Further, Nicodemus is described in the fourth Gospel as having for his first duty to bring a hundred-weight of a mixture of myrrh and aloes for the preservation of the body; and yet Mary Magdalene, according to *Mark* and *Luke,* on the first day of the week (the day of the Resurrection) brought the sweet spices which they had prepared to anoint the body of Jesus, when if they had seen Nicodemus (as the Synoptics show they ought to have done) they must have known that their work had been anticipated and the spices were unnecessary.

Had the sweet spices any other function than that of the myrrh and aloes of Nicodemus? Was the one a fragrant and the other a bitter thing? Even if so, was it possible for the sweet spices of Mary to be used after the body had been wrapped with linen clothes? All this may be deferred until the Resurrection has to be discussed.

But the conclusion to be arrived at now is that either Mary Magdalene was not present at the burial of Jesus or Nicodemus was not present. John says Nicodemus was present, but he knew nothing of Mary having been there. The other three Gospels say that Mary Magdalene was present when Jesus was laid in the grave, but they knew nothing about Nicodemus being there. The balance of evidence, and of probability, is that Mary Magdalene was there and Nicodemus was not there.

There are other reasons against the Nicodemus incident. "With touching piety," says Strauss, "the Christian legend has recorded on the tablets of her memory the names of all the others who were present to do honour to their murdered Master; but they omit Nicodemus."

It might be said with equal truth that the piety of the Christian legend has recorded all except Mary the mother, and left it to John only to mention her presence at the Cross. Therefore, we can equally question Mary the mother's presence at the Cross as Nicodemus's presence at the grave.

Was the relation between Jesus and Nicodemus fabricated by tradition during the years between the writing of the Synoptic Gospels and the writing of the fourth Gospel, between, say, about A.D. 60 and about A.D. 90?

I think this probable. It may have had its birth in the gibe of the enemies of Christianity towards the end of the century that Jesus did not convert the educated classes, the rulers of his own people, but only the upstart classes, the riff-raff. By the time of the writing of the fourth Gospel, Christianity was making claim to a class of intellectual adherents. Already, it must have been felt to be necessary to prove (what is said in the Synoptics) that among the upper classes there were many who secretly believed in him, but were afraid to avow their belief from fear of being cast out of the synagogues—of social ostracism.

Joseph of Arimathæa is the only member of the upper classes named in the Synoptic Gospels as an adherent. And even in *John* (VII) the Pharisees try to disparage Jesus by saying that none of the rulers or the Pharisees, but only the ignorant populace believe on him. And he himself thanks God that his teaching is made clear to babes and sucklings and hidden from the wise.

This reproach of appealing only to the ignorant was clearly a thorn in the side of the early Church. Hence, thinks Strauss, a new personage was devised, whose Greek name seems to point to his origin in the minds in which he was created.

Again, the conversation with Nicodemus strikes Strauss as immaterial or impossible as a conversation with an educated Jew. The language used by Jesus about the necessity of a *new birth* was the common language of the educated Jew about a conversion from idolatry. Therefore, Nicodemus would not talk about it in its physical character as an impossibility, but in its spiritual character as unnecessary. He would not have said, How can a man enter a second time into his mother's womb? But Why should I, a Jew, a son of Abraham, be born again, since I have been born again in the faith of being a Jew?

Thus Nicodemus by his reply to Jesus shows that he was either not a Jew or that he was not an educated Jew, and thereby merits the rebuke of Jesus, "Art thou a master of Israel, and knowest not these things?" Nicodemus, if he had really been what he is described as being, could not have understood the words of Jesus in their corporeal sense, but in their spiritual sense; and in their spiritual sense he must have deeply resented them, not been bewildered by them.

But he took literally what Jesus meant figuratively, and this, according to Strauss, makes his language and behaviour utterly inconceivable. Again Strauss argues that in verses 11–13 of Chapter III the evangelist is making Jesus restate the theory of the prologue to *John*.

The idea of the pre-existence of the Messiah which is propounded in verse 13 is not foreign to Paul, however. Once more, Strauss takes the view that verse 14 is out of keeping with the position of Jesus at the time. It is not conceivable that at the beginning of his ministry Jesus talked of his crucifixion. Is it credible that already he foresaw his death and the specific form of his crucifixion? And that long before he instructed his disciples on this point he communicated it to an unknown Pharisee?

Again, to talk of himself as the Messiah and yet to say he was to be crucified, and to couple his death with a reference to the brazen serpent in the wilderness, was to present a picture that was quite incongruous with Jewish ideals. Nicodemus could not possibly have accepted such a Christ as Jesus was representing himself to be, with such a fate awaiting him as death on the tree.

From all this, Strauss concludes that the whole incident belongs to the evangelist's point of view at the time when he wrote, not at the beginning of the ministry of Jesus, the threshold of his ministry.

My conclusion is that nearly all the difficulties about the incident of Nicodemus (except his presence at the grave) can be removed by altering the chronology of the incident, by putting it at the period of the Feast of Dedication or thereabouts. Even then the closing part of the conversation from verse 11 onwards must be under the suspicion of being the work of the evangelist himself, written about A.D. 90, and expressing the theory of Christianity which by that time had established itself in the world.

To say that Jesus himself spoke like this within the hearing or with the knowledge of his disciples at the beginning of his ministry is to make the behaviour of the disciples a mystery. It is sufficiently difficult to believe that he ever himself spoke like this to his disciples, or within the hearing or with the knowledge of the disciples.

Think of it! That after he had told them he was the Son of God, that he was sent by God to save mankind, that in doing so he would be crucified, they should run away when these things came to pass! It seems incredible.

XV. *Jesus in Defence of His Sabbath Breaking*

Jesus, in *John* and in *Mark,* defends his activity on the Sabbath against the charge of Sabbath breaking, by three arguments: (1) The example of David, who ate the show-bread; (2) the practice of the priests in the Temple on the Sabbath Day; (3) the course to be pursued when an ox, sheep, or ass falls into a pit.

These arguments are strictly in accordance with the Jewish theory that the Sabbath may be broken to save life or to preserve it, plus the rights of the priesthood and the Temple which supersede the law or supplement it.

But in the fourth Gospel Jesus is made to argue from the uninterrupted activity of God. "My Father worketh hitherto and I work," that is to say that "God never ceases to work, and neither do I." "This was a principle in Alexandrian metaphysics," says Strauss, "with which the author of the fourth Gospel was more likely to be familiar than Jesus."

In the Synoptic Gospels, miracles of healing on the Sabbath are followed up by declarations of the nature and design of the Sabbath institution; but in the foregoing a direct claim is made for Christ in his relation to God. It is as much as to say, "Since God never ceases to work, I also do not cease to work, because I am the Son of God." This theme is of perpetual recurrence in John's Gospel. It treats, Strauss thinks, of things which the Jews expected of the Messiah, and which Jesus claimed for himself—a right to work on the Sabbath because God works always.

Into this category of things, in the fourth Gospel, which Jesus does because God does them, Strauss includes the raising of the dead (particularly the raising of Lazarus) and the effect of judging the world.

Strauss concludes that if Jesus spoke as he is said by John to have done, the manner of speaking attributed to him in the other Gospels is fictitious. In the Synoptics Jesus ordinarily speaks of himself as less than God, as unable to do anything except by the will and power of God, whereas in the fourth Gospel he constantly claims a power that is the same as that of God.

XVI. What Jesus Says about Himself

Jesus represents himself in the fourth Gospel as the giver of the spiritual manna. He says the equivalent of this to the woman of Samaria about the water. He says he is the bread of life that cometh down from Heaven. This has its analogy in the idea of Philo that "the divine word is that which nourishes the soul."

Jesus goes further. Strauss says, "He represents his *flesh* as the bread from Heaven, which he will give for the life of the world. To eat the flesh of the body of the Son of Man, and to drink his blood he described as the only means of attaining eternal life. The similarity of these expressions to the words which the synoptists and Paul attribute to Jesus at the institution of the Lord's Supper led the old commentators to understand the passage as bearing reference to the Sacramental Supper to be appointed by Jesus."

There is certainly an analogy between the expressions used. But John knew nothing of the institution of the Lord's Supper. He says nothing about it as a sacrament. The Last Supper does not appear in *John* as a sacrament.

Remember that when Jesus in the synagogue at Capernaum calls himself the "bread from Heaven" the Jews murmur that he is one whose father and mother they knew. They cannot understand how he can arrogate to himself a descent from Heaven. It was a *hard* saying. It caused many of his disciples to fall away from him. The further we read in the fourth Gospel the more striking is the repetition of the same ideas and expressions. Strauss regards this as positive proof that the discourses of Jesus in the fourth Gospel are to a great extent the free compositions of the evangelist.

Among Strauss's reasons for doubting if the discourses of Jesus in the fourth Gospel are the actual words of Jesus himself, and not merely words put into his mouth by the evangelist, is the clear fact that in the Synoptic Gospels Jesus's method of speaking is by parable, whereas the method in *John* is allegorical, and it might be fairly said that in the strict and exact sense there are no parables in *John*. It is another man speaking in another way. The parabolic form was not the form of the writer of the fourth Gospel, while it was very clearly the way of Jesus. His method of speaking was always to resolve the abstract into the concrete. John's method was exactly the reverse—to resolve the concrete into the abstract.

In *John* (XII, 23–36), after the supper at Bethany and the entrance into Jerusalem, Jesus is reported as giving a long address touching his forthcoming death, and then it is said that having finished "he departed, and did hide himself."

Then, in verses 37–43, the evangelist speaks for himself, and then, without any break or introduction, Jesus is reported in verse 44 to have spoken again, beginning, "Jesus cried and said, He that believeth on me . . ." and so on to verse 50.

That Jesus withdrew himself from the public eye is a fact supported by the other evangelists, although they represent his retirement (to Ephraim) as preceding, not succeeding, his entrance into Jerusalem.

John claims that the speech in verses 44–50 is an actual discourse direct from the lips of Jesus. And it is argued by some critics that he returned, after his departure, to speak these last words. But this is an explanation which fails to convince. It is a clear case of the fourth evangelist summing up for himself the teaching of Jesus as he understands it, and putting it into the mouth of Jesus even when he is not present to speak it.

XVII.   Maxims Attributed to Jesus in the Fourth Gospel

"For Jesus himself testified, that a prophet hath no honour in his own country." This is given in *John* (IV, 44) after he has said that Jesus departed from Samaria, where he had been staying two days, into Galilee. Here it is obviously out of place—Galilee was the country of Jesus and he was going into it. And when he arrived in it the Galileans received him well. Can it be possible that the writer of the fourth Gospel thought Samaria or perhaps Judæa, was the country of Jesus? Had the story of his birth in Bethlehem begun to be accepted before the fourth Gospel was written in about A.D. 90?

This is possible, but improbable. Jesus was going into Galilee from Samaria. It cannot be supposed that the writer of the fourth Gospel thought Samaria was the country of Jesus. And if he thought Jesus was a Judæan by virtue of his parentage and his birth in Bethlehem, his chronology was wrong, for nothing had down to that time (according to his record) happened in Judæa to provoke the word of Jesus that a prophet has no honour in his own country.

The same idea is in *Matthew* XIII, 57, *Mark* VI, 4, and *Luke* IV, 24. "A prophet is not without honour save in his own country, and his own house." But there it is highly appropriate, because it refers to the unfavourable reception of Jesus in Nazareth. Clearly John knew nothing about the birth of Jesus in Bethlehem, *in any other passage,* but constantly presupposes that Jesus is a Galilean and a Nazarene.

According to *Matthew* and *Luke* Bethlehem was the birthplace of Jesus and the home of his legal father, Joseph; therefore, Jesus was a Judæan. Nevertheless, it is of the utmost significance that both Matthew and Luke make Jesus refer to Nazareth as his native city, while they, also, speak of the country about Nazareth as his own country.

XVIII.   The Last Supper and Gethsemane

"Arise, let us go hence" (*John* XIV, 31).

This is apparently the end of the Last Supper in *John*. But it is immediately followed, without a break, by Chapters XV, XVI and

XVII. All of these chapters are very beautiful. But were they spoken by Jesus? Or were they the direct writing of the evangelist, although put into the mouth of Jesus? Are we to assume that Jesus spoke these beautiful passages on his way to the garden of Gethsemane? Or that he spoke them in the supper room after rising, and when remembering that he had more to say? The former explanation is favoured by the opening of Chapter XVIII.

"When Jesus had spoken these words, he went forth with his disciples over the brook Cedron, where was a garden, into which he entered. . . ." Thus they might, after a considerable walk in which he was speaking all the time, have crossed the Cedron.

Strauss argues that the position of the words in *John* is perplexing, and he leaves the inference that the passage "I am the true vine" may have been words of the author of *John*. In *Matthew* (XXVI, 46) Jesus says, "Rise, let us be going"; in *Mark* (XIV, 42), "Rise up, let us go." But in both these cases the words are spoken, not after the Last Supper and before going to the garden, but in the garden itself and after the agony.

This also presents difficulties. Why does Jesus say, "Let us go?" Does he mean, "Let us fly away," as the disciples afterwards did? Or does he mean, "Let us go out to meet my doom—the traitor is coming." The former interpretation is incredible. The latter agrees with his conduct both before and after.

XIX. The Authority of the Fourth Gospel

Modern criticism views the discourses of Jesus in *John* as suspicious, partly because they do not agree with historical probability, and partly on account of their external relation to other discourses and narratives. In *John* the most educated Pharisee has, on the lips of Jesus, no advantage over a Samaritan woman of the lowest grade. Jesus speaks the same language to everybody. There is no verisimilitude in the mind of those who ascribe it to the discourses of Jesus in the Gospel of John.

When were John's many discourses of Jesus committed to writing? They were not published until at least sixty years after they had been delivered. Where were they in the meantime? Is it conceivable that the three earlier evangelists knew nothing of this vast treasury of the speech of Jesus? Some say that the evangelist (assuming John the son of Zebedee to be he) took down the discourses of Jesus in the Aramaic language as they were delivered. Is it likely? A young Capernaum fisherman? Is it possible? All this is clearly unhistorical.

Again others attributed the reports to the outpouring of the Holy Spirit, which gave all these discourses to John when, at ninety-two years of age, he sat down to write.

Is that likely? If so, we have to assume that Jesus in A.D. 30 foresaw nearly all the objections that were going to be urged against his teaching in the intervening sixty years before John took up the pen. Is that sensible? The general argument, so often advanced, founded on what a good memory might achieve among men of simple lives, unused to writing, lies in the region of abstract possibility. But John, who remembers so much, also forgets so much and puts so much in the wrong places. Are we then to charge the author of the fourth Gospel with a great deal of free invention?

"Critics are agreed," says Strauss, "that the tendency of the fourth Gospel is to spiritualize the common faith of the Christians into the Gnostic," and thus to crush many errors that had arisen during the first sixty years of the Church.

Finally, the champions of John bring forward the supernatural assistance of the Paraclete which was promised to the disciples, to recover the memory of all Jesus had said—the aid of the Holy Spirit. But this compels the conclusion that the Holy Spirit not rarely contradicted the writers of the earlier Gospels.

In the first three Gospels Jesus (1) adapted his teaching to the necessities of his shepherdless people; (2) contrasted the corrupt institutions of the Pharisees with the pure moral and religious precepts of the Mosaic law; (3) corrected the carnal Messianic hope of the age by a purely spiritual hope of a spiritual kingdom. In the fourth Gospel he dwells almost entirely on the doctrine of his own relation to God. This is not entirely peculiar to John, but in his Gospel it is almost the sole thing.

In answer to this the defenders of John say that it is intended to furnish a supplement to the first three Gospels, to supply their omissions, to go deeper than in the earlier Gospels it was safe and wise to go.

Strauss points out that the style of the fourth Gospel is everywhere the evangelist's own, not that of Jesus. From this, and more, Strauss holds it to be established that the discourses of Jesus in

John are free compositions of the evangelist, founded on what he understood to be the teaching of Jesus, and then put into the mouth of Jesus.

If so, who was the writer of the Gospel of John? I should most certainly say, not the apostle, although the old apostle's recollections may have been used (almost certainly *were* used) by the writer in his record of events.

The eye of the eye-witness is more than once clearly indicated. But I should confidently say that the hand that held the pen was not that of the old apostle of ninety-two years of age at the time the fourth Gospel was written.

XX. *Discourses Often Wrongly Placed in the Gospels*

It is important to note that sometimes the discourses of Jesus are quite wrongly placed in the Gospels. For example, in *Mark* (IX, 41) there is a beautiful discourse which has no apparent connexion with what goes immediately before it—the report of John that he had seen a man casting out devils in the name of Jesus.

XXI. *The Parables*

Many of the discourses already referred to are in themselves very brief, and several of the most vital lessons of Jesus take the form of illustrative comparisons or similitudes to which the Greek rhetoricians gave the name of parables, meaning a fictitious narrative or allegory of circumstances which might naturally occur. The parable is of eastern origin. There are some beautiful examples in the Old Testament, such as Nathan's parable, told to King David, of the rich man who had many flocks and herds, yet (when he wished to entertain his guest) took the poor man's lamb.

But by far the most beautiful parables are those of Jesus, some of which (such as that of the prodigal son) have no equal in the literature of the world, whether in the quality of incident or in spiritual significance. Jesus carried the art of the parable to its highest pitch. He had one clearly defined object in the majority of them—to illustrate the character of the kingdom of Heaven which was to come. And he does this without diminishing the human value and reality of his story by so much as one incident untrue to real life in this world.

In *Matthew* XIII, 34, 35 it is written, "All these things spake Jesus unto the multitude in parable; and without a parable spake he not unto them. That it might be fulfilled which was spoken by the prophet, saying, I will open my mouth in parables; I will utter things which have been kept secret from the foundation of the world." Thus, to some of his disciples the parable was a kind of cipher, a hidden way of speaking to those who could understand, concealed from others. "Who hath ears to hear, let him hear." This was one view of the Parables. By no means the only view, or the best.

An analysis of the four Gospels reveals that forty-three parables of Jesus are the whole sum recorded. They are distributed as follows:

Parables peculiar to *Matthew* (eleven):
The Tares, XIII, 24
The Hidden Treasure, XIII, 44
The Pearl of Great Price, XIII, 45
The Draw-net, XIII, 47
The Unmerciful Servant, XVIII, 23
The Labourers in the Vineyard, XX, 1
The Father and Two Sons, XXI, 28
The Marriage of the King's Son, XXII, 2
The Ten Virgins, XXV, 1
The Talents, XXV, 14
The Sheep and Goats, XXV, 31

Parables peculiar to *Mark* (two):
The Seed Growing Secretly, IV, 26
The Householder, XIII, 34

Parables peculiar to *Luke* (seventeen):
The Two Debtors, VII, 41
The Good Samaritan, X, 30
The Importunate Friend, XI, 5
The Rich Fool, XII, 16
The Servants Watching, XII, 35
The Wise Steward, XII, 42
The Barren Fig-tree, XIII, 6
The Great Supper, XIV, 16
The Tower and Warring King, XIV, 28

The Piece of Money, XV, 8
The Prodigal Son, XV, 11
The Unjust Steward, XVI, 1
The Rich Man and Lazarus, XVI, 19
The Unprofitable Servants, XVII, 7
The Unjust Judge, XVIII, 2
The Pharisee and the Publican, XVIII, 10
The Ten Pieces of Money, XIX, 12

Parables peculiar to *John* (three) :
The Bread of Life, VI, 32
The Shepherd and the Sheep, X, 1
The Vine and the Branches, XV, 1

Parables common to *Matthew* and *Luke* (three) :
The Houses Built on Rock and on Sand, *Matthew* VII, 24;
Luke VI, 47
The Leaven, *Matthew* XII, 33; *Luke* XIII, 20
The Lost Sheep, *Matthew* XVIII, 12; *Luke* XV, 4

Parables common to the Synoptics (seven) :
The Candle under a Bushel, *Matthew* V, 15; *Mark* IV, 21;
Luke VIII, 16
The New Cloth and the Old Garment, *Matthew* IX, 16; *Mark*
II, 21; *Luke* V, 36
The New Wine in Old Bottles, *Matthew* IX, 17; *Mark* II,
22; *Luke* V, 37
The Sower, *Matthew* XIII, 3; *Mark* IV, 3; *Luke* VIII, 5
The Mustard Seed, *Matthew* XIII, 31; *Mark* IV, 30; *Luke*
XIII, 18
The Vineyard and the Wicked Husbandmen, *Matthew* XXI,
33; *Mark* XII, 1; *Luke* XX, 9
The Young Leaves of the Fig-tree, *Matthew* XXIV, 32;
Mark XIII, 28; *Luke* XXI, 29

Therefore
John omits forty of the parables of Jesus,
Mark omits thirty-four,
Matthew omits twenty-two,
Luke omits sixteen.

The large proportion of parables recorded exclusively in *Luke*
(seventeen) shows clearly that Luke had access to sources un-

known to Matthew and John, and equally unknown to Mark. The contention that Mark and Matthew were indifferent to some of the parables recorded by Luke cannot be accepted, and that John was indifferent to all the forty-three parables of Jesus except three is unthinkable. The only inference is that he knew nothing whatever about them.

Finally, it is to be concluded that the four Gospels were not only not the writings of eye-witnesses, but that they were not even the writings of persons who had been inspired by eye-witnesses. This may be a hard saying, but I see no escape from it. Are we then to surmise that some of the parables are fictitious? Not necessarily. Only that four later writers gathered together what information they could collect. Or, that a group of eye-witnesses set down just the parables which they could remember. The last theory agrees generally with my own.

The parables which are intended to illustrate the kingdom of Heaven are the parables of the Tares, the Hidden Treasure, the Pearl of Great Price, the Draw-net, the Unmerciful Servant, the Labourers in the Vineyard, the Marriage of the King's Son, the Ten Virgins, the Talents, the Seed Growing Secretly, the Leaven, and the Sower.

Great multitudes gather about Jesus, so that he has to go into a ship that is anchored near the shore. From there he tells the parable of the Sower. It is a parable of the kingdom of Heaven. A man sows good seed in his field. While he is asleep his enemy sows tares among the wheat. When the seeds grow, and the wheat and the tares are together, the man's servants ask if they should root up the tares. He says, in effect, "No, lest you should root up the wheat with them. Let both grow together until the harvest. Then when they are both out, I will tell the reaper to gather together the tares, bind them into bundles and burn them, but take the wheat into my barn."

The interpretation of this, as given by Jesus, is that the man who sows the seed is the Son of Man (himself), the field is the world, the tares are the wicked, the good seed are the children of the Kingdom; the enemy who sows the tares is the Devil; the harvest is the end of the world, the reapers are the angels. As the tares are burned in the fire so shall it be to the wicked at the end of the world. The Son of Man shall send his angels to gather them that do offend and cast them "into the furnace of fire."

Whether this is authentic as the explanation of Jesus, I feel uncertain. It reads much like the doctrine of the later Church. It is the only strong declaration of the belief of Jesus in a physical hell. Nevertheless, it must be admitted that it is in keeping with the intense ardour of the spirit of Jesus during the second Galilean period.

Jesus tells another parable. The kingdom of Heaven is like a grain of mustard seed, which a man sows in his field. It is the least of all the seeds, yet when it is grown it is the greatest among the herbs and becomes a tree, so that the birds lodge in its branches.

Still another parable of the Kingdom. The kingdom of Heaven is like leaven which a woman hides in three measures of meal until the whole is leavened. Again, the kingdom of Heaven is like a treasure hid in a field. When a man finds it, he conceals his find and goes and sells all he has and buys the field. Or, again, the kingdom of Heaven is like a merchant seeking goodly pearls. When he has found one pearl of great price he sells all he has and buys the pearl. And once more, the kingdom of Heaven is like a net, which being cast into the sea gathers any kind of fish. And when it is full and drawn ashore the good fish are gathered into pots and the bad fish are cast away. So shall it be at the end of the world. The angels will come, separate the wicked from the just, and cast them into the furnace of fire, where there shall be wailing and gnashing of teeth.

There are twelve of the parables which directly illustrate the kingdom of Heaven. But many others have side references to the Kingdom. Many deal with the time of the coming of the Kingdom. But a good number deal with the life of man in the present world, before the coming of the Kingdom, inculcating the higher virtues of justice, mercy, righteousness.

Much of the value of the parables lies in the fact that their teachings on conduct are universally applicable, although in some instances their lessons may be only vaguely adaptable to modern times. In the parable of the rich man and Lazarus, for example, there is no indication of any conduct on the part of the rich man which excludes him from Paradise, and no indication of any conduct on the part of the poor man which entitles him to Paradise. It may be said that the rich man was indifferent to the needs of the poor man, and so merited punishment; that he was wanting

in compassion to the poor. His sumptuous life is simply presented
as a contrast to the misery of the beggar. Jesus concerns himself
with none of this. To Jesus, the fact of a man being rich was an
indication that it was difficult for him to be good. Hence, *"Blessed
be ye poor, for yours is the kingdom of God. . . . Woe to you
that are rich, for ye have received your consolation."* A similar
estimate of the effect of poverty and riches is given in the narrative
of the rich young man and in the aphorism concerning the camel
and the needle's eye.

This was of the essence of the teaching of Jesus. To be rich
was to live in a condition not favourable to the growth of virtue.
To be poor was to live in a condition highly favourable to virtue.
Such was clearly the opinion of Jesus, although nothing was impossible to God.

These are obvious divergencies and repetitions in the parables,
the explanation being that Jesus delivered some of them (apparently) more than once. In the first telling they appear to have
been simple; in the next telling more emphasized.

Collectively, the parables have clear reference to himself and to
his mission on earth. In their different ways all the parables of
Jesus were intended to explain the kingdom of Heaven. Its coming. What it would be like. What relation this world bore to the
Kingdom. The position of Jesus himself. The conduct of man in
relation to him. The aim of God in relation to man. There are
various other aspects of the teaching of Jesus in relation to the
Kingdom embodied in the parables.

XXII.   Prayer

Jesus repeatedly held out the prospect of answer to prayer without fail, a hearing of prayer without exception. "Ask, and it shall
be given you; seek, and ye shall find; knock, and it shall be opened
unto you."

It was his own habit to pray in seclusion, in the wilderness, in
solitary places, in the mountains. Only once is he shown praying
publicly with his disciples—when he is teaching them what is
known as the Lord's Prayer. But he is frequently referred to as
praying in secret. Thus, in *Mark* I, 35, "And in the morning, rising
up a great while before day, he went out, and departed into a
solitary place, and there prayed." Again, "And he withdrew him-

self into the wilderness, and prayed" (*Luke* V, 16). "He went out into a mountain to pray, and continued all night in prayer to God" (*Luke* VI, 12). "He was alone praying" (*Luke* IX, 18).

"And it came to pass, that, as he was praying in a certain place, when he ceased, one of his disciples said unto him, Lord, teach us to pray, as John also taught his disciples" (*Luke* XI, 1).

After this, Jesus gives them the Lord's Prayer. Then he puts a case to them of a friend coming to a man at midnight to ask for the loan of three loaves, because a friend has come to him and he has nothing to set before him. The man refuses on the ground that he is in bed with his children, and he cannot be troubled. But the asker importunes, giving him no peace until he does rise and give the loaves. Jesus then adds the moral, "I say unto you; Ask, and it shall be given you; seek, and ye shall find; knock, and it shall be opened unto you. . . . If ye then, being evil, know how to give good gifts unto your children, how much more shall your heavenly Father give the Holy Spirit to them that ask him?"

Jesus insists that prayer should be in secret. He nowhere teaches public prayer. When his disciples wished to pray they should go into their closet, shut the door, and God would hear their secret prayer. But does not Jesus say that God knows better than man what he needs and therefore imply that prayer is not necessary? Or is it not rather that although God knows best what is good for man's needs yet He requires that man should ask? This would imply that there is virtue in the act of supplication, and that it is God's will that a direct appeal should be made to Him.

XXIII. Blasphemy

The Jews stoned Jesus out of Jerusalem because they said he had been guilty of blasphemy. They justified his Crucifixion by saying he was a blasphemer. What did Jesus himself say? "Wherefore I say unto you, All manner of sin and blasphemy shall be forgiven unto men; but the blasphemy against the Holy Ghost shall not be forgiven unto men. And whosoever speaketh a word against the Son of Man, it shall be forgiven him, but whosoever speaketh against the Holy Ghost, it shall not be forgiven him, neither in this world, neither in the world to come" (*Matthew* XII, 31, 32). This curse does not apply to blasphemy against the Son of Man.

XXIV. The World's Greatest Man

Jesus taught the coming of the kingdom of God, but this included also a new national morality for the kingdom of this world also. He condensed the law into two sentences: "Love God" and "Love your neighbour." He denounced the spirit of conceit in the words: "Hypocrite, cast out first the beam out of thine own eye, and then shalt thou see clearly to pull out the mote that is in thy brother's eye." His preaching was convincing. His sermons, including the composite Sermon on the Mount, give a vivid picture of Jesus preaching. We hear him clearly. We can almost distinguish his voice. It is a persuasive voice, but it is also an imperative one. He speaks with authority. It is not the preaching of Paul. Yet it has resemblances. Paul comes nearer to the manner of Jesus in some of his epistles. Paul's address at the end of the first Epistle to the Thessalonians has something of the ring of Jesus's farewell to his disciples in the fourth Gospel after the Last Supper; also his farewell in the last chapter of the Epistle to the Philippians.

Jesus himself, his own personality, was always much greater than anything he said or did, and his every act rose out of his personality as nothing more than an imperfect expression of his inner world. If we had no other means of judging Jesus than the records of the effect produced by his personality, we should be compelled to conclude that he was *the world's greatest man*.

The strongest impartial sceptic, who has taken the trouble to read the Gospels carefully, will not attempt to deny this. But to see the personality of Jesus ought we not to put away all the commonplace phrases by which he has been known—the meek and mild, and gentle Jesus? He was no prudist. His manner of life was laid by no rules. No gloomy fastings, as among the Pharisees, although he did fast during the Temptation. No washing and purifying of hands and vessels to avoid defilement. No systematic praying. No public praying. His speaking was emphatic, strong and commanding. He had no uncertainties. He spoke as one who knew, and he left on his hearers the impression that he knew. His voice was full and resonant. Sometimes he spoke to 5,000 and was heard. On the last day of the feast in Jerusalem he rose and cried above the mumbling of prayers. He silenced all other voices.

CHAPTER XX

The Miracles

I. The Attitude of the Scientist

THE ATTITUDE of the modern scientist, down to quite recent years, towards the miracles of Jesus seems to me most unsatisfactory. The naturalists of the first half of the nineteenth century made some attempt to reconstruct the miracles, to give a new turn to events which they could not entirely deny. The results were a series of deadly imaginings which made the first mystery of the miracle look plain, simple and intelligible by comparison. Often, the versions of the miracles made by the rationalists descended to the lowest level of puerility.

The modern scientist has taken up a different attitude. He has either entirely denied the miracles, or anything akin to the miracles, referring the accounts of them to sheer imposture, or sheer stupidity; or he has tried to dispose of well-authenticated incidents of cure by saying they were the result of "suggestion," "imagination."

The former method was that which Huxley adopted in his controversy with Gladstone on the subject of the miracle of the casting out of devils into the Gadarene swine. Of the second method a typical example occurs in "Jesus of Nazareth," by Edward Clodd, the most uninspiring, arid example of dry-as-dust literature I have lately read.

In treating of the miracles of the casting out of devils, Clodd says "that we now know that the disease spoken of as 'possession' was madness of a more or less severe type, which prevailed largely among the Jews, being fostered by the state of excitement in which they lived" (all of which is true); and that the "exquisite feeling of Jesus for every form of suffering, joined to the look and tone of authority which marked him, would make him very skilful in using his gentleness and strength with soothing yet unmistakable power to bring the possessed to his right mind."

This, again, is true, and it is true, too, that the belief current in Jesus's time that he was the Messiah would largely account for the cures while he lived, and magnify them after his death into tales of the marvels he had wrought, even to the raising of the dead.

Clodd, then, cites a story of the famous chemist, Sir Humphry Davy. A man suffering from paralysis came to him to be treated by electricity. On his sitting down, Davy placed a small glass thermometer under the man's tongue to take his temperature before beginning. The patient thought this was the instrument to be used for curing him, and he said he felt it running through his system. Davy was curious to see what lasting influence the imagination alone would exert, and without undeceiving the man he sent him away and told him to come every day to have the operation repeated. The man did so, with the result that (without anything more being done for him than placing the thermometer in his mouth) he was, after a short time, cured. Clodd thinks this accounts for many of the stories in the Bible of the cures of the possessed.

It accounts for nothing. It leaves the miracle exactly where it was. A startling event took place whereof the causes are entirely outside human knowledge. There is no natural means of accounting for such a cure. The cure may be called "suggestion" or "imagination" or what you will, but it is still entirely outside explanation. Science cannot account for it. It only knows, what anybody may see, that the cure has occurred. It could not repeat it at all. No law can be brought to bear upon it. What, then, was the incident in the life of Sir Humphry Davy? It was a miracle, an absolute miracle, being entirely outside human understanding or the power of man to perform. Sir Humphry Davy could not have guaranteed the power of performing it on his next patient similarly affected. An entirely unknown force had been at work, the patient's absolute faith that Davy had the knowledge and the instrument to cure him. It was this faith (call it what you will) that cured him, added, perhaps, to Davy's tacit admission to the patient that his thermometer was curing him, although it was doing nothing.

So the miracle stands. And in the case of Jesus it is intensified by his undoubted power of creating in his patients the faith necessary to cure. Of course, Clodd goes on to say that we (the scientists) are not called upon to account for each and all of the miracles of Jesus.

This was also the attitude taken by Huxley. Thus he rejects the stories of the cures of blindness in the blind man who touched the bones of the two saints in a basilica, etc. But the cures of blindness are no less well attested, although Huxley rejects them as impostures. The truth is that down to this hour it is impossible for science to say what limit there is to the inner spirit (suggestion, imagination) to cure anything. The strengthened hope, the revived courage, these and other psychical powers which are entirely outside human knowledge are fully known by any physician to be the best and greatest agents of cure. And what does he know about these? About how they are created? How they operate? What can be done to create them or bring them into activity? Nothing, or next to nothing. These mighty forces, beyond medicine, beyond all that science through all the ages has learned, beyond all the mechanical devices which have been invented to promote cure, are the greatest of all the powers in healing, and the physician knows nothing about them, except that they are there. Then why deny to them the name of miracle?

The boundaries of the natural and the supernatural are constantly changing, and have changed more during the past century than at any period of the world before. A hundred years ago it was a fact of which the world could offer no supernatural theory that men should converse across thousands of miles of ocean. Now it is a natural fact. Yet the natural fact has within itself the element of the supernatural. We know that such and such things happen. But we do not even yet know *why* they happen. In the unknown and apparently unknowable lies the miracle, the supernatural. Above all is this so in the realm of spirit. That the spirit of Jesus acts in such and such ways we know. Why it so acts we do not know. Therein lies the miracle.

Are there any limits to miracle? Obviously, there must be. No miracle worker can give a new leg to the man who has lost his leg. Therefore, the story in Luke's Gospel about one of the disciples (in Gethsemane) cutting off the right ear of a servant of the high priest and of Jesus touching it and healing it (if that means causing the ear to return to its place or a new ear to come) is palpably unhistorical.

Several other stories of miracles by Jesus are just as palpably unhistorical. But within the limits of what may be called natural law no unexplainable cure ought to be called impossible, or brushed aside to give room for "suggestion" and so on. It is miracle, and should be frankly recognized as such.

The words from *Isaiah* (XXXV) to which Jesus referred in his message to John the Baptist are regarded as the chief foundation of the narratives of miracles worked by Jesus:

> Say to them that are of a fearful heart, Be strong, fear not; behold, your God will come with vengeance, even God with a recompence; He will come and save you.
>
> Then the eyes of the blind shall be opened, and the ears of the deaf shall be unstopped.
>
> Then shall the lame man leap as an hart, and the tongue of the dumb sing; for in the wilderness shall waters break out, and streams in the desert.
>
> And the parched ground shall become a pool, and the thirsty land springs of water; in the habitation of dragons, where each lay, shall be grass with reeds and rushes.
>
> And an highway shall be there, and a way, and it shall be called The way of holiness; the unclean shall not pass over it; but it shall be for those; the wayfaring men, though fools, shall not err therein.
>
> No lion shall be there, nor any ravenous beast shall go up thereon, it shall not be found there; but the redeemed shall walk there;
>
> And the ransomed of the Lord shall return, and come to Zion with songs and everlasting joy upon their heads; they shall obtain joy and gladness, and sorrow and sighing shall flee away.

It is difficult to decide whether miracles of the kind attributed to Jesus were expected of the Christ among the Jews of the Christian era. Rabbinical writings, apart from the fact of their late date, did not prove this. The miracles which the Messiah was to work were to correspond to those of Moses, which did not at all resemble those of Jesus.

The words of the Jews in *John* do indeed show that miracles were expected of the Christ. "When the Christ shall come," they ask, "will he do more than this man hath done?" But we have no definite indication of what miracles Christ was expected by the Jews to perform. The evidence for the general fact that Jesus did work miracles is as strong as it is possible for historical evidence to be.

II. Jesus as a Miracle-Worker

The Jewish people expected miracles from the Messiah. Moses and the prophets had performed miracles. Moses dispensed meat and drink to the people in the Wilderness of Sin. Jesus fed the five thousand in the desert place about Bethsaida. Elisha opened the eyes of the blind. Jesus opened the eyes of the blind. Elisha raised from the dead the widow's son. Jesus raised the son of the widow of Nain. The Messiah, when he came, was to have power over life and death.

Jesus, as the Messiah, had to meet the expectation that he was to be a miracle worker. He was constantly challenged by those who doubted his Messiahship to give a sign that he was the Messiah. This was a vindication of their faith. He repeatedly refused to give a sign "to this perverse and adulterous generation," saying that no sign should be given except the sign of his own Resurrection from the dead. Yet according to the Gospels he worked many miracles. At certain moments when he worked miracles people asked, "Is not this the son of David?" At other moments they asked themselves whether, when the Christ came, he would work more miracles than Jesus had worked, clearly meaning that he had worked enough to convince them that he was the Messiah.

Thus the test of ability to work miracles was the greatest test which the people applied. Jesus, according to the Gospels, more than satisfied the demand made by the people of his time. Many people believed on him as the Messiah solely because of his miracles. Some (and among them the Samaritans) believed he was the Christ, not so much by reason of what he *did* as by reason of what he *said*. But the astonishing fact remains that some of the cities which witnessed his greatest miracles did not believe on him and remained unrepentant.

What other signs did they require? Apparently, some required a sign from Heaven, some supernatural manifestation. Such signs from Heaven were not entirely wanting. One occurred at his baptism—the dove and the voice—yet nobody appears to have seen or heard it, except Jesus himself, unless John the Baptist saw and heard it, as he said he did.

The enemies of Jesus certainly did not see his Resurrection, and clearly they did not believe in it. On the contrary, they accepted natural explanations of it. How can we reconcile the declaration of Jesus that no sign should be given to his generation except the sign of his Resurrection with the many signs of the miracles recorded in the Gospels? Did the miracles actually happen? Or were they modernized versions, adapted to Gentile and Judæan senses, of the events (perhaps fabulous) recorded in the Old Testament?

There is the fact that in the preaching and the epistles of the apostles (excepting two general notices in *Acts* II, 22 and X, 38) the miracles of Jesus appear to be unknown. Peter never refers to them in detail; hardly refers to them at all. Everything appears to be built on his Resurrection. In the Gospels Jesus is reported to have raised at least three persons from the dead. Yet Paul speaks of him as "the first fruits of them that slept," thus showing, apparently, that either he knew nothing of, or disbelieved, the stories of the raising of the son of the widow of Nain, the daughter of Jairus, and of Lazarus.

The Gospels say that he performed the most transcendent miracles. How does it come to pass that the apostles of the early Church say nothing of these miracles, that they do not base their faith upon them, that nevertheless he was the Messiah or the Son of God? Was it only during the lifetime of Jesus himself that these signs of his Messiahship were necessary to faith in him? After he had himself risen from the dead was that fact alone necessary to the apostles as a means of conversion, of establishing faith in him, of building up his Church? Can it be possible that the circumstantial stories of the miracles performed by Jesus are fables? Or it is impossible to account for the other facts of the life of Jesus without believing that his miracles actually happened, that they were real historical occurrences?

III. *List of the Miracles*

The miracles recorded in the Gospels are of many kinds, but may be classified, roughly, as follows: (1) Miracles of healing; (2) miracles of power; (3) miracles that have no general denomination.

The following is a complete list of the Miracles of Jesus:

Two Blind Men Cured	*Matthew* IX, 27
Dumb Spirit Cast Out	*Matthew* IX, 32
Tribute Money Provided	*Matthew* XVII, 24
Deaf and Dumb Man Cured	*Mark* VII, 31
Blind Man Cured	*Mark* VIII, 22
Jesus Passing Unseen through the Crowd at Nazareth	*Luke* IV, 30

Draught of Fishes	*Luke* V, 1
Widow's Son Raised to Life at Nain	*Luke* VII, 11
Healing the Infirm Woman	*Luke* XIII, 11
Healing the Man with the Dropsy	*Luke* XIV, 1
Healing the Ten Lepers	*Luke* XVII, 11
Healing the Ear of Malchus	*Luke* XXII, 50
Turning Water into Wine	*John* II, 1
Healing of the Nobleman's Son	*John* IV, 46
Healing the Impotent Man at Bethesda	*John* V, 1
Jesus Passing Unseen through the Crowd in the Temple	*John* VIII, 59
Healing of the Man Born Blind	*John* IX, 1
Raising of Lazarus	*John* XI, 43
Officers Falling to the Ground	*John* XVIII, 6
Draught of 153 Fishes	*John* XXI, 1

Miracles common to *Matthew* and *Mark:*

Healing the Syrophœnician's Daughter	*Matthew* XV, 2
	Mark VII, 24
Feeding the Four Thousand	*Matthew* XV, 32
	Mark VIII, 1
Cursing the Fig-tree	*Matthew* XXI, 8
	Mark XI, 12

Miracles common to *Matthew* and *Luke:*

Healing the Centurion's Servant	*Matthew* VIII, 5
	Luke VII, 1
Healing the Blind and Dumb Demoniac	*Matthew* XII, 22
	Luke XI, 14

Miracles common to *Mark* and *Luke:*

Healing the Demoniac in Synagogue	*Mark* I, 23
	Luke IV, 33

Miracles common to *Matthew, Mark* and *Luke:*

Healing the Leper	*Matthew* VIII, 2
	Mark I, 40
	Luke V, 12

Healing Peter's Mother-in-law	*Matthew* VIII, 14
	Mark I, 30
	Luke IV, 38
Stilling the Tempest	*Matthew* VIII, 26
	Mark IV, 37
	Luke VIII, 22
Casting Out the Legion of Devils	*Matthew* VIII, 28
	Mark V, 1
	Luke VIII, 27
Healing the Man Sick of the Palsy	*Matthew* IX, 2
	Mark II, 3
	Luke V, 18
Healing the Woman with the Issue of Blood	*Matthew* IX, 20
	Mark V, 25
	Luke VIII, 43
Raising Jairus's Daughter	*Matthew* IX, 23
	Mark V, 38
	Luke VIII, 49
Healing the Man with the Withered Hand	*Matthew* XII, 10
	Mark III, 1
	Luke VI, 6
Casting a Devil out of a Child	*Matthew* XVII, 14
	Mark IX, 17
	Luke IX, 38
Healing Blind Bartimæus (Two Blind Men)	*Matthew* XX, 30
	Mark X, 46
	Luke XVIII, 35

Miracles common to *Matthew, Mark* and *John:*

Walking on the Sea	*Matthew* XIV, 25
	Mark VI, 48
	John VI, 19

Common to all the Four Evangelists:

Feeding the Five Thousand	*Matthew* XIV, 15
	Mark VI, 35
	Luke IX, 12
	John VI, 5

IV. A General Analysis

1. That there is only one miracle which the whole of the four evangelists record.

2. That there are only eleven miracles which any three of the Gospels record.

3. That there are only six miracles which any two of the Gospels record.

4. That three of the miracles are recorded by *Matthew* only. That two of the miracles are recorded by *Mark* only. That seven of the miracles are recorded by *Luke* only. That there are eight of the miracles which *John* alone records.

5. That there are thirty-eight miracles by Jesus recorded altogether by the Gospels as a whole.

Of these

Matthew records twenty

Mark records eighteen

Luke records twenty-one

John records ten.

This analysis is something of a surprise in that *Luke* records most of the miracles; that *Matthew* records more than *Mark;* and that *John* records less than half of the miracles recorded by *Luke*.

It is of interest to note that *Luke* alone records the raising of the widow's son at Nain. That *John* alone records the raising of Lazarus, and that *John* alone records the turning of water into wine at Cana. *Matthew* alone records the miracle of the tribute money being found by Peter in the mouth of the fish, and *Luke* alone records the healing of the ear of Malchus in Gethsemane. Only *Matthew* and *Mark* record the feeding of the four thousand. Only *Matthew* and *Mark* record the cursing of the fig-tree. The only miracle of Jesus which the Gospels unanimously record is that of the feeding of the five thousand. Three of the Gospels (*Mark, Matthew* and *John,* but not *Luke*) record the miracle of the walking on the sea.

There is no unanimity of testimony about the thirty-eight miracles of Jesus. Accordingly, the records cannot have come from men who were all eye-witnesses. Even *Matthew* omits sixteen which the others taken together record, while *John* omits twenty-eight which the others record. The conclusion is that none of the writers of the Gospels, as they have come down to us, were eye-witnesses. Nor, in view of serious omissions, can it be thought that the writers were inspired by eye-witnesses.

Do the miracles, as recorded in the four Gospels, bear evidence within themselves of their own authenticity? Do they appear to come of the Jewish expectation that the Messiah must perform miracles? Are they therefore created by the Old Testament stories? Are any of them without parallel in the fifty or sixty miracles recorded in the Old Testament? The early Christians, according to Strauss, transferred to Jesus as the actual Messiah the miraculous legends of the Old Testament, out of which the Jews were supposed to have composed the miraculous portrait of their expected Messiah.

Undoubtedly, many of the miraculous stories of the New Testament do come from the Old Testament, but not all. There is nothing in the Old Testament to account for the birth of Jesus, his baptism, his transfiguration, resurrection, the changing of water into wine at Cana, the stilling of the storm and the walking on the sea. But it cannot escape observation that many of these miraculous stories of the New Testament which have no counterpart in the Old Testament are precisely the miracles which the reason of the modern man finds it most difficult to accept as realistic representations of actual events.

In order to accept them, the mind has to take up a new attitude, adopt a different method of explanation. It has to point to many of them as expressions of the Christian spirit in symbolic and allegorical forms. Not that these narratives are intended by their narrators to be merely allegories, the symbolical elaborations of spiritual truths, but that the religious imagination gave birth to these illustrations without distinguishing between the poetic form and the absolute truth of the event recorded. In short, it "conceived history and idea in combination and conferred on each equal truth and certainty."

But this way of explaining the miracles which refuse to be explained on grounds of reality is full of danger. It is subject to violent changes, according to the mind looking at it. It destroys the reality of all the surrounding incidents. If one thing is not real other things about it lose reality. The changing of the water into wine is an impossible and perhaps repellent event as a thing that actually happened. Attaching a symbolic meaning to it, it may cease to be that, but it thereby destroys the reality of everything about it, it becomes a thing of much less than naught as an historical happening.

V. The Casting out of Devils: According to Matthew

After the Temptation Jesus went about Galilee and Syria preaching and healing the sick of diseases and torments and those which were possessed of devils and those that were lame (*Matthew* IV, 23).

At Capernaum they brought to him many that were possessed of devils and he cast the spirits out with his word (*Matthew* VIII, 16).

In the country of the Gergesenes on the other side (of Galilee) he met two that were possessed of devils, coming out of the tombs, so exceeding fierce that no man might pass that way. They cried out to Jesus, calling him the Son of God, and asking why he came to torture them "before the time" (*Matthew* VIII, 28).

Was it the devils who were crying out or the men? And what did the men or the devils mean by saying that Jesus had come to torture them *before the time?*

A good way off from them was a herd of swine feeding, and the devils besought Jesus that if he must cast them out of the men he would let them go into the swine. Jesus consented to this, and the devils came out of the men (presumably at the command of Jesus) and entered into the swine, whereupon the swine ran down a steep place and perished in the waters. The swineherds then ran off to the city and told what had happened, and the whole city came out to meet Jesus and they besought him that he would depart out of their coasts.

[Note: This is, to me, an incredibly fantastic story, belonging to the very infancy of the human intellect.]

Back in his own country, after his visit to the country of the Gergesenes, they brought to him a dumb man possessed of a devil (*Matthew* IX, 32). When the devil was cast out, the dumb man spoke. The people marvelled, and the Pharisees said, "He casteth out devils through the prince of the devils."

We are told (*Matthew* X) that Jesus called his disciples and gave them power against unclean spirits to cast them out. He sent out his twelve apostles, giving them power to heal the sick, cleanse the lepers, raise the dead and to cast out devils.

It is to be observed that at this period the disciples had seen one person raised from the dead—the daughter of Jairus, "a certain ruler." When Jesus (still in Galilee) is sending back the disciples of John the Baptist, telling them to say what miracles they have seen, he mentions the giving of sight to the blind, the making of the lame to walk, the cleansing of lepers and making the deaf to hear, the raising of the dead and the preaching to the poor, *but he says nothing about casting out devils.*

"At that time" (when and where? Obviously in Galilee, in the harvest time) they "brought unto him one possessed with a devil, blind, and dumb" (*Matthew* XII, 22). He healed him, so that the blind and dumb spoke and saw. And then the people said, "Is not this the son of David?" Obviously, the son of David was expected to cast out devils. Again, the Pharisees said Jesus cast out devils by Beelzebub the prince of the devils. Thus there were two ideas current among the Jews at the time of Jesus, (1) that the Messiah would come with power to cast out devils, (2) that only the prince of devils could cast out his own. The common people held to the first, the Pharisees to the latter view.

Jesus rejected the views of the Pharisees, and rejected it by asking why Satan should cast out Satan. He said that he cast out devils by the Spirit of God in order that the kingdom of Heaven might come.

In answering the Pharisees about a sign Jesus, still in Galilee, says that when the unclean spirit is gone out of a man it walks through dry places, seeking rest and finding none. Then it says to itself, "I will return into my house." And when it returns it finds it empty, swept, and garnished. Therefore, it goes, takes to itself seven other spirits more wicked than itself, and they enter into the man and dwell there, and the last state of that man is worse than the first (*Matthew* XII, 43–45).

The meaning of this appears to be that the evil spirit that is cast out of a man may return to him, and possess him and bring other evil spirits back with him, and thus the condition of the man is worse than before the first evil spirit was cast out.

Jesus, who has been in the land of Gennesaret (after flying from Herod to the "desert place apart") goes up to the coasts of Tyre and Sidon (*Matthew* XV, 21). This is perplexing. Why did he return to the near neighbourhood of Herod just after flying away from him? In the neighbourhood of Tyre and Sidon a woman of Canaan comes to him, calls him Lord, and the son of David, tells him that her daughter is grievously vexed with a devil and clearly asks him to heal her.

Jesus at first refuses, saying the incredible and unbelievable thing, "It is not meet to take the children's bread, and to cast it to dogs." He is reported to say this hard thing *after* he has commended the faith of the pagan centurion and said (*Matthew* VIII, 11) "that many shall come from the east and west, and shall sit down with Abraham, and Isaac, and Jacob in the kingdom of Heaven [clearly indicating the Gentiles] but the children of the Kingdom shall be cast out into outer darkness; there shall be weeping and gnashing of teeth."

The poor Canaanite mother accepts this and pleads that even the dogs eat of the crumbs which fall from their master's table, and thereupon Jesus, by reason of her great faith, fulfils the woman's prayer, and the woman's daughter is made whole that same hour. Observe that here the cure is performed in the absence of the patient. But, indeed, nowhere yet has the faith of the possessed one in the power of Jesus to cast out the devil been necessary.

After coming down from his Transfiguration Jesus is met by "a certain man" who kneels down to him, calls him Lord, and asks him to have mercy on his son who is a lunatic (*Matthew* XVII, 14). The son is sore vexed, and falls into the fire and often into the water. The father had brought the son to the disciples of Jesus (such of them as had remained behind when Jesus with Peter, James and John had gone up into the mountain) but they could not cure him. Jesus rebukes the devil in the child, and the devil departs from him, and he is cured from that hour.

The disciples then ask Jesus "apart," why they could not cast the devil out (remember, they had been given power to cast out devils), and Jesus answers, "Because of your unbelief . . . Howbeit, this kind goeth not out but by prayer and fasting." All this, on the surface, is mysterious, and very hard to understand, but the answer of Jesus, "Because of your unbelief" makes the meaning clear. Jesus means that the psychical power was too weak in the disciples. They did not really believe that they could cure this extreme case. If they had believed, they could have done it.

But in order to believe so great a thing it was necessary to fast and pray. Only by such spiritual austerities were such spiritual powers given. There was no limit to the spiritual power that came by faith. If one's faith was only as large as a grain of mustard seed one could say to a mountain, "Remove hence," and the mountain would be removed. *Nothing was impossible to faith.* But Jesus here was not thinking of the physical power of faith.

After his Temptation in the wilderness and after he had called four of his disciples, Jesus went into Capernaum, and entered the synagogue and taught. The people were astonished at his doctrines, for he taught as one having authority and not as a scribe. There was a man in the synagogue who had an unclean spirit, and he cried to Jesus, "Let us alone; what have we to do with thee, thou Jesus of Nazareth? Art thou come to destroy us? I know thee who thou art, the Holy One of God" (*Mark* I, 23).

Who was speaking? The man or the devil within him? Obviously, the devil, not the man, for Jesus rebuked him, saying, "Hold thy peace, and come out of him." And when the unclean spirit had torn the man and cried with a loud voice, it came out of him. The onlookers were amazed and said, "For with authority commandeth he even the unclean spirits, and they do obey him." The fame of this miracle went all over Galilee.

He went down to the sea (obviously Galilee) and great multitudes followed him, and he healed many. And unclean spirits when they saw him, fell down before him and cried, "Thou art the Son of God." And he charged them that they should not make him known.

Two things here are worthy of note. First, that the man possessed of the devil and the devil by which he is possessed are not distinguished one from the other. Next that the devils have a supernatural knowledge of Jesus as the Son of God. Further, that Jesus tells them not to make his identity known.

VI. *The Casting out of Devils: According to Mark*

In ordaining the twelve, while still in Galilee, Jesus gave them (as in *Matthew*) power to cast out devils (*Mark* III, 15). The scribes came down from Jerusalem and said that Jesus cast out devils by Beelzebub, the prince of devils. Jesus answered (as in *Matthew*), "How can Satan cast out Satan?" (*Mark* III, 22).

There is an obvious omission between verses 29 and 30. "Because they said, He hath an unclean spirit" (*Mark* III, 30).

Immediately after this the mother and brothers of Jesus came calling him. Previously in verse 21, it is said that when his friends heard of it they went out to lay hold on him, for they said he was beside himself. This verse is obviously out of its proper order. It has no relation to what goes before it, but is clearly related to verse 30. My conclusion is that after Jesus had cast out devils the idea became current that he was possessed himself of a devil, and that the devil in him commanded and controlled the devil in other people. Therefore, his friends tried to lay hold of him, and his mother and brothers came to take him away, to take care of him, lest he should fall into the hands of the authorities, who might imprison him or otherwise dispose of him. Naturally, he deeply resented this and hence his answer, that those who believed on him or followed him were his (spiritual) brethren.

Jesus goes (apparently) from the plains of Gennesaret on the eastern side of Galilee to the other side of the lake, into the country of the Gadarenes. Then follows the same story as in *Matthew* IX, 32, with certain differences (*Mark* V, 1–17).

Coming out of the ship he met out of the tombs a man (one man, not two) with an unclean spirit. He lived in the tombs, was very violent, no man could bind him. When he was bound with chains he broke them asunder. Nobody could tame him. Night and day he lived in the mountains, crying and cutting himself with stones.

When he saw Jesus he cried, "What have I to do with thee, Jesus, thou Son of the Most High? I adjure thee by God, that thou torment me not." Jesus had said, "Come out of the man, thou unclean spirit." He had also asked the spirit what was his name, and the spirit had said his name was Legion, for they were many.

There is the usual confusion between the man possessed of the spirits and the spirits in the man. Then the spirits beseech Jesus that he will not send them out of the country, but into a herd of swine which are feeding on the mountains. Jesus consents to this request, whereupon the unclean spirits go out of the man, and enter into the swine (there are about 2,000 swine), and the swine run violently down a steep place and plunge into the sea. Then the people who have fed the swine fly off to the city, and the people of the city come back to see what has been done. And they find

Jesus and see the man that was possessed with the devil (we have just before been told there were many unclean spirits), and the man who had had the legion was sitting, clothed and in his right mind. Clearly, the man had before been naked.

The people were afraid when they saw this and heard how it had befallen the man possessed with the devil, and also what had happened to the swine, and they prayed Jesus to depart out of their coasts. Jesus went back to his ship, whereupon the man who had been possessed of the devil prayed to be permitted to follow him. But Jesus forbade him to do so, and told him to go home to his friends and tell them what great things the Lord in his compassion had done for him.

Is there any good reason why I should not say that this, as told in *Mark,* is a silly story, utterly degrading to Jesus, except so far as concerns the beautiful closing part of it? Omit the conversation of the unclean spirits with Jesus, and omit the swine, and the story is natural and even beautiful. It is the demonological part of it that makes it foolish and degrading. And this probably comes entirely out of the current Jewish ideas of demonology.

We are told at the close of the story that the man published the facts of his cure in Decapolis; but we do not hear that anything came of it. Nobody believed in Jesus on account of what he had done. Men simply "marvelled." Now, the country of the Gadarenes was strictly on the south of Galilee, a flat country without mountains or "steep" places, and although the country is said to have extended to the mountainous district of the north-east of the lake, there is no record or trace of a city nearer than the city in the south.

After Jesus had visited his own country and been rejected there, he sent out his twelve disciples, by two and two, and gave them "power over unclean spirits," and "they cast out many devils" (*Mark* VI, 7, 13).

Again, here, as in *Matthew,* Herod Antipas hears of Jesus and says that he is John the Baptist risen from the dead (*Mark* VI, 14).

Once more I connect Herod's declaration with the activities of Jesus in casting out evil spirits.

Mark (VII, 24–30) tells the story of the Canaanite woman and her young daughter with an unclean spirit. Jesus has gone up to the borders of Tyre and Sidon. The woman behaves exactly as recorded in *Matthew*. So does Jesus. The first answer of Jesus is equally mysterious. It is incredible that he was merely trying the faith of the woman, as some commentators think.

In *Mark* (IX, 14–39) we have the same story as in *Matthew*. Coming down after his Transfiguration Jesus finds a man whose son has "a dumb spirit." All the details are similar. Jesus rebukes the foul spirit, saying, "Thou dumb and deaf spirit, I charge thee, come out of him, and enter no more into him." Whereupon "the spirit cried, and rent him sore, and came out of him; and he was as one dead, insomuch that many said, He is dead. But Jesus took him by the hand and lifted him up." The subsequent scene with the disciples is the same. "This kind [of devil] can come forth by nothing, but by prayer and fasting." Just as mysterious as before.

Jesus goes back to Capernaum (he often comes and goes to and from Capernaum) and John says to Jesus, "Master, we saw one casting out devils in thy name, and he followeth not us; and we forbad him, because he followeth not us." Jesus answered, "Forbid him not; for there is no man which shall do a miracle in my name, that can lightly speak evil of me. For he that is not against us is on our part." Apparently, others could cast out devils by the name of Jesus.

VII. The Casting out of Devils: According to Luke

After Jesus had been baptized, tempted, visited Nazareth and been cast out of it, he came to Capernaum and taught on the Sabbath Day. Then (*Luke* IV, 32) follows the story of the man in the synagogue with an unclean spirit. The story is essentially the same as in the two earlier Gospels.

When the sun was setting the people brought their sick to him, and he laid his hands on them and healed them. And devils came out of many, crying out, "Thou art Christ the Son of God." Jesus rebuked the devils and suffered them not to speak because they knew he was the Christ (*Luke* IV, 40).

Repeatedly the Gospels couple the name Christ with Son of God. But this conflicts with the fundamental Jewish doctrine— God was one; He could have no Son, even in Christ. Did the evanglists not know this? If they did not know it, were the evangelists Jews? Or had their Christianity altered their view?

After Jesus, from the plains of Galilee, had been up into the mountains to pray, and continued all night, and had come down again, and a great multitude of people out of all Judæa and Jerusalem, and from the sea coast of Tyre and Sidon, had come to see and hear him (clearly his fame had gone very far), there came with the sick many who were vexed with unclean spirits (this is one of the few occasions on which the demoniacs come of themselves), and they were healed (*Luke* VI, 17).

In sending back a message to John the Baptist, Jesus says nothing about casting out devils (*Luke* VII, 22). While he was journeying to and fro among the cities and villages of Galilee, there went with him "certain women which had been healed of evil spirits and infirmities, Mary, called Magdalene, out of whom went seven devils, and Joanna the wife of Chuza, Herod's steward, and Susanna and many others which ministered unto him of their substance" (*Luke* VIII, 2).

This is significant. Mary Magdalene and many others had had evil spirits cast out of them. These were the women who followed him during the remainder of his ministry, and remained with him to the end. What were the evil spirits? Were they (like the rest) unclean spirits? Is it meant that they were women of sensual life? Is Mary the woman who was a sinner mentioned in the previous chapter (*Luke* VII)? It certainly seems so. And what is meant by "ministered unto him of their substance?" Is it meant that they, being well off, contributed to his maintenance? If so, the beauty of the story is seriously impaired.

Observe that in *Luke* (VIII, 20) the visit of his mother and brethren has not got the vivid connexion of the story as related in *Matthew* and *Mark*. It has lost its reason for existence. It is of little value. It has no relation to the idea that he is possessed of a devil, and has to be cared for and protected.

On a certain day Jesus, who has been travelling to and fro in the cities of Galilee apparently on the eastern side of the lake, crosses with his disciples to the other side of it. They arrive at the country of the Gadarenes, "which is over against Galilee" (*Luke* VIII, 26). This description indicates a country due east, of, say, the plains of Magdala. Then follows the story of the man possessed of devils. It differs in detail from the story in the two earlier Gospels. The man had been possessed of devils for a long time. He wore no clothes. He cried out at the sight of Jesus as before. Jesus asked him (obviously the devil), "What is thy name?" The devil answered, "Legion."

Legion then besought Jesus "that he would not command them to go out into the deep," a variation on go out of the country. They asked to go into the swine who were feeding on the mountain. When the devils entered into the swine, the same happened as in *Matthew* and *Mark*. The swineherds behaved as before. The people came from the city to see. "Then the whole multitude of the country of Gadarenes round about besought him [Jesus] to depart from them, for they were taken with great fear." The man wished to follow Jesus, but Jesus sent him away as before. There is no essential difference in the two accounts.

Jesus calls his disciples together, and sends them out, giving them power and authority over all devils, and to cure diseases (*Luke* IX, 1).

Herod the tetrarch hears what is being done by Jesus, and concludes that he is John the Baptist, "risen from the dead."

Jesus departs privately to a desert place, which according to *Luke* belongs to the city called Bethsaida. It is not said in *Luke* that he takes ship and crosses the lake to this place. In *Matthew* (after the same account of Herod) it is said that Jesus departed thence *by ship* into a desert place apart. *Luke* calls the desert place Bethsaida.

On the next day (*Luke* IX, 37), when Jesus with the three disciples were come down from the mountain of Transfiguration, they met the man who prayed of Jesus to heal his son, his only child, who had an evil spirit. Then follows the same story of Jesus rebuking the evil spirit. But *Luke* says nothing of the conversation between Jesus and the disciples about the reason why they could not cast the evil spirit out of the child.

In *Luke* (IX, 49) is the same question as in *Mark* by John about the man who was casting out devils in the name of Jesus. And the same answer by Jesus: "Forbid him not; for he that is not against us is for us."

Jesus appoints seventy disciples and sends them out two and two, to every city and place to which he himself will come, a sort of advance guard. But he says nothing about their casting out devils (*Luke* X, 1).

Somewhere (not clearly indicated in *Luke* X, 17) the seventy return to Jesus and say, "Lord, even the devils are subject unto us through thy name." Whereupon Jesus says, "I beheld Satan as lightning fall from Heaven. Behold, I give you power to tread on serpents and scorpions . . ."

All this seems to me rather trivial stuff, totally out of character with Jesus. But then comes something that sounds worthy of him.

"Notwithstanding in this rejoice not, that the spirits are subject unto you; but rather rejoice, because your names are written in Heaven." This verse 20 is very noble, and seems to come as an immediate rejoinder to verse 17—"Lord, even the devils are subject unto us through thy name." Is it possible that verses 18 and 19 are interpolations? They certainly look as if they were.

Jesus was in "a certain place" (*Luke* XI, 1). It is not otherwise indicated by *Luke*. But the reference to it comes immediately after the description of a scene in the house of Mary and Martha, whose home was in *Bethany*.

After Jesus has taught his disciples the Lord's Prayer "he was casting out a devil, and it was dumb. And it came to pass, when the devil was gone out, the dumb spake; and the people wondered" (*Luke* XI, 14). But some of them said, "He casteth out devils through Beelzebub, the chief of the devils." Jesus makes the same reply as before, but he finishes up by using stronger words than he spoke in answer to John, when told that another was casting out devils in his name. It is no longer now, "He that is not against me is with me," but, "He that is not with me is against me, and he that gathereth not with me scattereth."

Here (*Luke* XI, 24) comes the passage describing an unclean spirit going out of a man, and then coming back bringing seven other evil spirits with him, "and the last state of that man is worse than the first." This (*Luke* XI, 27) is the place in which "a certain woman of the company" (perhaps one of the Galilean women out of whom he cast evil spirits) cried out, "Blessed is the womb that bare thee, and the paps which thou hast sucked."

VIII. The Silences of John

John's Gospel contains no reference to the casting out of devils. The whole of the stories of possession are omitted. Why is this? Were the miracles of this kind unknown to John? Or did he omit them because the other evangelists had told them? If so, why did he tell so many others stories that had previously been told by his predecessors?

Or was it because, though he knew of the alleged miracles of casting out devils, he did not believe them? Remember that he says nothing of the Temptation of Jesus himself by Satan. In writing at the end of the first century, probably about thirty years after the synoptists, perhaps in Alexandria, or at least outside Palestine, was he avoiding the mention of a group of miracles which he knew well the Gentile world of his age would utterly reject?

Some of the cases of possession resembled cases of natural disease, like epilepsy—did John exclude these cases from the number of his miracles because he knew that the knowledge of the time and place in which he was attributed such ailments to the operation of purely natural laws which had nothing whatever to do with demoniacal possession.

Julius Cæsar suffered from epilepsy, and his attacks were practically identical with the attacks of some of the persons in the Synoptics out of whom Jesus was said to cast devils. How could John pretend to the public of his age that men like Julius Cæsar were possessed of devils? Would not the great Roman world have laughed such stories to scorn? And if told that John believed that Jesus cured persons suffering as Julius Cæsar suffered and that he cured them by exorcising the devils in them, would not they reject him as a charlatan?

Does this account for the fact that John's Gospel says nothing about the story of the lunatic and the Gadarene swine, for example? Does it account for his silence about the temptation of Jesus by Satan? Or is there yet another explanation?

What may that other explanation have been? John's conception of Jesus was that he was of God, a priest of God, and that he was with God from the beginning. How Jesus became flesh John does not explain. He says nothing about his birth by a virgin. He only says that Jesus "was born, not of blood, nor of the will of the flesh, nor of the will of man, but of God," and that "the Word was made flesh, and dwelt among us."

This might mean that Jesus had neither father nor mother, nor childhood nor growth to manhood, but that he simply appeared —descended perhaps from the sky in the earthly body of a man. *But for two passages.* Twice only John mentions the mother of

Jesus—once at the marriage at Cana of Galilee and again at the foot of the Cross. I do not think he ever mentions Joseph. Once only he speaks of the brethren of Jesus, saying that they were not in sympathy with him, and that at a certain moment they taunted him. He says nothing (that I can recall) about the mother and brothers of Jesus coming to him during his ministry— whether for the reason assigned by Mark and pictured by Matthew, or in the way indicated by Luke.

What, then, may have been John's reason for omitting the temptation of Jesus by Satan? Is it not that the idea of the Holy One of God, the Messiah, the Christ, the Son of God, the part of God, being tempted by Satan was outside John's conception of his character? If Jesus was what John thought him, the idea that Satan could tempt him at all was inconceivable. Above all inconceivable that Satan could tempt him (the God of all the earth) by offering him all the kingdoms of the world as a reward for going down on his knees and worshipping Satan.

Such an idea must have been not merely incredible to John, it must have been preposterous. So John did not mention the temptation of Jesus by Satan because he did not believe it. Did he believe in demoniacal possession? Does the fact that John says nothing about the miracles of the casting out of devils reflect any grave doubt on their reality? Did they ever occur at all? Is there evidence within themselves, as related by the Synoptics, to cast grave doubts upon their historical reality as actual events? Is not the case of the Gadarene swine an outstanding case that breaks down on its own evidence, that the scene makes it practically impossible of occurrence, and some of the facts make it foolish and therefore degrading to Jesus?

My own conclusion is that the silence of John (the mere silence) is not enough to throw the stories in the Synoptics out of court. The stories in the Synoptics are many and very circumstantial. Can we allow ourselves to believe that they are all myths? Allowing that the three records are closely related to each other, are there not sufficient differences to justify the belief that we have three reporters of the events, all sufficiently independent and all believing in the miracles?

Against these three can we put one, and accept his *silence* as sufficient proof that the miracles did not occur? I think we cannot. Assuming that John rejected the miracles, or that, without rejecting them, he was silent about them for fear of antagonizing the intelligence of his time, I think we are compelled to conclude that there was a foundation of truth in these stories—*that something did occur*. What *was* that basis of truth? What *did* occur?

IX. *An Analysis of the Cases of Casting out Devils*

1. We see that these miracles of the casting out of devils all come at the beginning of the ministry of Jesus and closely follow the temptation of Jesus by Satan, and are apparently related to it in some way.

2. That there are a great many of them. That they are the largest class of the miracles. That they leave the impression that more people in Galilee in the time of Jesus suffered from possession by devils (or what was considered so) than from any other malady—almost more than from all other maladies.

3. That the sufferers from possession, unlike the sufferers from diseases, did not of themselves come to Jesus to be cured, and that their cure was therefore never in response to any expression of faith on their part, although two or three times the cure may be thought to have been worked as a reward for the faith of their friends or relations.

4. That the only occasion on which faith is mentioned as a condition of the cure of a demoniac (the case of the son of the man who is waiting for Jesus when he comes down from the mountain of Transfiguration) is when the want of faith in the disciples make their efforts at cure fail.

5. That on this occasion the principle of cure for extreme cases of possession is attributed to prayer and fasting not on the part of the sufferer, but on the part of the person casting out the devil.

6. That the possession of devils is never spoken of as a sin, or the consequence of a sin, and no cured demoniac is told to go and sin no more.

7. That the victim of the devils is always represented as a great sufferer from the devils which possess him, and that the act of casting out the devil is often described as tearing him, rending him, and in the final result leaving him prostrate and as one who is dead.

Did the three evangelists believe in the possession by devils?

There can be no doubt at all that they did. They probably took their belief from the accepted Jewish view of demoniacal possession which was:

1. That into the living bodies of wicked persons the evil spirits who were the servants of Satan entered; that the evil spirits were *unclean,* and tortured and killed their victims by unclean sensualities; that the effect of this was that the wicked persons suffered horribly; that in the end the wicked persons died miserably and in great torture.

2. That this Jewish belief was probably an early stage of the theory of divine punishment, that God gave Satan permission to send his devils into the bodies of very wicked persons to torment and destroy them in this life—there being at first no idea of a future and everlasting hell for the wicked. After the devils had tortured the wicked person to death, they were punished for his sins and exterminated.

3. That there was, nevertheless, salvation for the wicked persons possessed of devils, and this came by the casting out of the devils. The devils could be cast out by God's great messengers, particularly by the Messiah, or in the name of the Messiah.

4. Therefore, if a man had great success in casting out devils, he was thought to be either the representative of the Messiah or perhaps the Messiah himself.

Thus, read in the light of the Jewish view of demoniacal possession and its cure, we see (1) that the devils whom Jesus cast out nearly always recognized him as the Messiah, and addressed him as the Christ, the Son of God; (2) that they were afraid of Jesus because they knew he had the power to cast them out; (3) that they loved to be in possession of a human body, and to torture it to death; (4) that when they were cast out they had to wander about in the wilderness without corporeal form, and without power to exercise their evil nature, until they could find another body to inhabit and to torture.

Such was, apparently, the belief of the first three evangelists. Did Jesus share this Jewish belief in demoniacal possession? Or did he merely accommodate himself to the belief of his time and race in order to work the cure? In order to answer this question it is necessary to look at the various cases to see what they were. Judged by modern scientific knowledge the cases described in the three first Gospels divide themselves into three classes at least, as follows:

1. Cases of what we should call acute nervous attack, accompanied by hypochondria and melancholia. To this class would probably belong most of the cases of the women, like Mary Magdalene, Joanna, the wife of Herod's steward, Susanna and many other women out of whom Jesus is said to have cast devils, and who followed him on his ministry down to his death at Jerusalem. The precise nature of their sufferings is not given, and that of itself assumes the absence of the violence and bestiality described in other cases.

2. Cases of what we should call epilepsy. To this class would belong the cases of the people who fell into the water and into the fire, and suchlike.

3. Cases of sheer madness, such as that of the naked man in the country of the Gadarenes, who lived in the tombs, was very violent, no man being able to hold him, who, as often as he was bound by chains, broke them, so that nobody dare go near him, and who day and night lived in the mountains, crying and cutting himself with stones.

Most of these cases modern science would claim to understand, to know the conditions which caused them, to point to methods of cure for many of them, and to attribute them to the operation of natural laws. Are we to understand that Jesus believed that these were cases of possession by devils? If he did so believe, and if modern science can account for them otherwise, on the grounds of natural laws, Jesus was obviously deluded. And if he was deluded, how can we think he knew everything, that nobody had need to tell him anything, that he was all-wise, that he was divine, that he was the Christ, that he was the Son of God? Was he two thousand years behind our time and our knowledge? If so, of what use is he to our time? How can we reverence and worship him?

The answer to this may be that Jesus may not have believed in demoniacal possession, yet he may have appeared to believe in it, and acted as if he did believe in it, in order to produce the effect he desired, that of liberating the sufferers from their sufferings. Assume that a Jew in his day actually believed he was possessed of a devil as a punishment of his sin, would it not help him to get rid of his malady to address him (or his devils) according to such belief? Remember that Jesus always addressed the unclean spirit in the man until he had expelled it, and only then addressed the man, the sufferer.

But is it honouring Jesus to say that he adopted this artifice to rid the deluded victim of his sufferings? Are we not compelled to conclude that Jesus himself did actually believe in demoniacal possession? I think we are compelled to believe this, and I do not feel that this belief in Jesus puts him outside the pale of recognition by modern science as a person of divine claims to universal knowledge. How much does science yet know of madness in many of its forms? Is there not a limit to its knowledge? Do we not still recognize that insanity is a dark realm in which science often walks in the dark? Is it by any means absolutely sure that satanic agencies do not exist, and that they do not take possession of man against his will and perhaps as a result of his wickedness. In short, is there not something still to be said, within limits, for the ancient Jewish theory?

Has science utterly banished it? Is not science confronted by cases in which the madness cannot be explained except on the ground that a spirit of evil takes control of a man and compels him (often against his will and in opposition to his intelligence) to commit acts which he knows to be wrong? Is not the effect of this to tear the victim to pieces, and to make him suffer most when he most resists the evil impulses which, coming from without, have taken possession of him and mastered him?

If this is so, is there anything lowering to Jesus in the idea that he believed in such forms of demonism, and that he used the means said by the evangelists to be employed by him to cast out devils?

What was the theory of good and evil taught by Jesus?

1. That there were two powers in the world, a power for good and a power for evil.

2. That the power for good was God, and He was the maker and controller of all the universe.

3. That the power for evil was Satan, and he was the prince of this world.

4. That God sent His angels to strengthen good men.

5. That Satan sent his devils to torment and destroy all wicked men.

6. That he (Jesus), as the Son of God, had control over the

devils of Satan and could cast them out of men; that he could give others (such as his disciples) the power to cast them out; that the disciples could only exercise this power in his name, and in the measure of their faith in him and by the power derived from prayer and fasting.

7. That the work of John the Baptist had been to call the afflicted—the wicked, the persons possessed of the spirits of evil—to cast out their wickedness, to repent, because the end of the world was coming and the new order was near, the kingdom of Heaven, when men should be judged according to their acts, when those who remained in the possession of evil should be destroyed and those who were supported by the angels of God would be given everlasting life.

8. Finally, that Jesus himself, as the Son of God, had come in the flesh to atone to God for the transgressions of those who had permitted the spirits of evil to take possession of them, and had not cast them out, and were doomed to everlasting destruction.

9. That by his death he would redeem these tortured sinners, and make their atonement with God.

X. General Summary

Regarded from this psychical standpoint, are the miracles of the casting out of devils contrary to science as we know it in our own day? And was not the method of Jesus in casting out devils very closely akin to the methods approved by science now in the cure of melancholia, epilepsy, madness? Does not the physician *command* the patient to control himself; in a word, to expel, not to indulge the evil impulse within? And is not the process of expulsion essentially the same now as it was with the victims cured by Jesus? A mighty struggle on the part of the sufferer, followed by great prostration, a kind of rending and tearing and then—peace, quiet, serenity, "clothed and in his right mind."

Thus, stripped of the language of the earlier time and of the East, is there so much difference between the way in which Jesus cast out the evil and the way in which the evil is cast out by the modern physician? The chief difference is that the grandest of modern physicians can only do this in some cases, whereas Jesus (according to the evangelists) could always do it. Was this by virtue of his greater power, and is there any ground for objecting to the theory that he could always do it because he had divine power? There remains the difference that while the old Jewish theory of demoniacal possession held that it was inflicted only on the wicked and as a punishment of wickedness, modern science does not attribute madness, or any form of epilepsy or nervous disorders, to wickedness on the part of the victim of it.

But neither does Jesus. Nowhere does he speak of the person possessed of devils as a wicked person. Nowhere does he conclude his cure by telling the sufferer to go and sin no more. In the case of the naked lunatic in the country of the Gadarenes he says quite a different and much more human, beautiful and sympathetic thing. When the grateful man wishes to follow him he tells him to go back home to his friends and tell them what great things the Lord in his compassion has done for him. No. I do not think it necessary, in honour to Jesus, totally to reject the miracles of the casting out of devils. I only ask that they should be interpreted spiritually and in the light of modern science.

CHAPTER XXI

The Miracles
(Continued)

I. Cures of Paralytics

MANY CURES by Jesus of paralysis are recorded in the Gospels. The condition is known as palsy, a word which has been applied to it since ancient times. There is a loss of muscular power, with wasting of the muscles, due to disease or injury to the spinal cord. In extreme cases the muscles of the hands or the feet are atrophied and a claw-like hand or a clubbed foot is the result. A feature of this form of the disease is the twitching of the wasting muscles. Heredity plays an important part in the incidence of this malady. In the time of Jesus bad government, tyranny, robbery by the Roman and Jewish rulers, licentiousness and corruption among the ruling classes had led to many kinds of nervous diseases, and paralysis, or palsy, was in many cases the direct result.

Jesus has come down from the mountain, (*Matthew* VIII, 5–13) after preaching the Sermon on the Mount and has entered into Capernaum when a centurion (a Roman) comes to say that his servant at home is sick of the palsy and is grievously tormented. Jesus says, "I will come and heal him." The centurion objects that he is not worthy that Jesus should come under his roof, but if he will only speak the word his servant will be healed. Jesus marvels at this exhibition of faith and says, "I have not found so great faith, no, not in Israel."

After saying, further, that in the kingdom of Heaven many will come from the east and west (meaning, obviously, many Gentiles) and sit down with Abraham, Isaac and Jacob, and that the children of the kingdom (meaning the chosen people) will be cast out, he says to the centurion, "Go thy way; and as thou hast believed, so be it done unto thee." And his servant, says the Gospel, "was healed that self-same hour."

The same story is told in *Luke* (VII, 1–7) with certain
additional circumstances. Jesus had lately delivered a discourse
akin to that of the Sermon on the Mount, and had entered into
Capernaum, when people came to him to say that a certain centurion's servant who was dear to him was sick and ready to die.
When the centurion heard of Jesus (and probably of his miracles)
he sent to the elders of the Jews entreating them to ask Jesus to
come and heal his servant.

The Jews entreat Jesus to do this for the centurion, saying he
is a worthy man, who loves their nation and has built a synagogue for them. Jesus goes with them, but when he is still far
from the centurion's house, the centurion sends friends to him,
saying that he is not worthy that Jesus should come under his
roof, and neither had he thought himself worthy to come to Jesus
himself, but if Jesus will only say the word his servant will be
healed. Jesus marvels (as in *Matthew*) at this display of faith in a
Gentile, and then the friends who were sent return to the centurion and find the sick man is well.

After Jesus had been in the country of the Gergesenes and
cured the man possessed of devils and sent the devils into the
swine, he crosses the lake in a ship and comes into his own city
(*Matthew* IX, 1–8). This is Nazareth, and apparently his second
visit to Nazareth, for *Matthew* also (IV, 13) shows that immediately after the Temptation Jesus returns to his home in Nazareth.
In Nazareth they bring him a man sick of the palsy lying on a bed.
He says to the sick man, "Son, be of good cheer; thy sins be forgiven thee."

Two things are here noticeable: (1) that although Nazareth
had rejected him a very short while before, and had tried to throw
him over a cliff, some Nazarenes by this time believed in him; and
(2) that thus early Jesus claimed the power to forgive sins, or
the authority to say that sins were forgiven.

Upon hearing the words of Jesus certain of the scribes say within themselves, "This man is blaspheming," meaning that he is
claiming the power of forgiving sins, a power which God alone
possesses, therefore he is claiming to be God. Jesus knows what
they are thinking, and answers their thought strangely, by asking
them which it is easier to say to the sick man, "Thy sins be forgiven thee," or to say, "Arise and walk." Then in order that
they may know that he, the Son of Man, has power on earth to

forgive sins, he says to the sick man, "Arise, take up thy bed and go unto thine house." No more is said of the blasphemy, but the people of Nazareth marvel and glorify God that such power has been given to men.

In *Mark* (II, 3) the same story is told, but the scene is different. It occurs not in Nazareth, but in Capernaum. And the incidents are different, or at least enlarged. Mark describes Jesus as being in the house. It is noised about that he is there, and a great crowd of people gather in and about the house. Jesus is preaching the word to them, when some come bringing a man sick of the palsy. Four are bearing him, but they cannot get near to Jesus by reason of the throng, so they uncover the roof of the house where Jesus is, and when they have "broken it up," they let down the bed wherein the sick man lay. Observing their faith, and consequently the sick man's faith (seeing that he permits all this to be done to him), Jesus says to the sick man, "Son, thy sins be forgiven thee."

Certain of the scribes are sitting there, and they say to themselves, "Why doth this man thus speak blasphemies? Who can forgive sins but God only?"

From this point onwards the scene is the same as in *Matthew*, and is succeeded by the same incident, the calling of Levi (*Matthew*).

The scene in *Luke* is as follows. Jesus, early in his ministry, has been out in the wilderness, and has returned, and is in a house when men bring a man who is taken with the palsy (V, 17). And (as in *Mark*) the multitude in and about the house is so great that they cannot get at Jesus, so they go up on the roof of the house, and let the sick man down through the tiling with his couch into the room where Jesus sits. From this point onwards the scene is the same.

In *John* (V, 1) occurs the incident of the impotent man of Bethesda. This may reasonably be assumed to be a case of paralysis, one of the many types of palsy, not, perhaps, recognized as such by the people of the time. Jesus is in Jerusalem at a feast which is not named, but probably it was during his visit at the time of the Feast of Tabernacles or between that and the Feast of Dedication.

In Jerusalem there is a sheep-market. Near by the sheep-market there is a pool which is called in the Hebrew tongue Bethesda.

It is described as having five porches—presumably it is surrounded by a wall that has five porches or entrances. In these
porches lay a great multitude of impotent folk, as well as of the
blind, halt, withered. They were waiting for the moving of the
waters. The belief of the multitude was that an angel went down
at a certain season into the pool and troubled the waters. Whoever, then, stepped into the water after it was troubled was cured
of whatsoever disease he had.

It is not said at what intervals the angel came down and troubled
the waters. Apparently, nobody knew; the angel came at irregular
intervals, and hence the infirm people waited and watched from
day to day. Among those who waited was a certain man who had
had an infirmity for thirty-eight years. He was lying in a bed, a
mattress.

Jesus visited this place, Bethesda, and saw this man lying, and
knew (it is not said how, whether by natural communication or
divine revelation) that he had been a long time in that condition.
So Jesus selected this man for the use of his curative power. He
said to him, "Wilt thou be made whole?"

The impotent man answered that when the water was troubled,
he, being impotent, could not get into it himself, and he had
nobody to put him into the pool, and that while he was struggling
to get into the water another stepped down before him. Jesus then
said to the man, "Rise, take up thy bed, and walk." Immediately
the man was made whole, and took up his bed and walked.

It is not said that the impotent man asked Jesus to cure him.

This occurred on the Sabbath Day. The Jews saw the man carrying his bed on the Sabbath (that is to say *working* on the Sabbath)
and protested, "It is the Sabbath Day; it is not lawful for thee to
carry thy bed." The cured man answered that he (clearly he does
not know Jesus) who had cured him had told him to take up his
bed and walk. The Jews asked who the man was, but he could not
tell them, for Jesus had removed himself from the place, a multitude being there.

I understand this to mean that after Jesus had cured the impotent
man many of the other infirm, lame, blind, and otherwise afflicted
had crowded about him, so that he had been compelled to escape.

After this Jesus found the healed man in the Temple and said
to him, "Thou art made whole; sin no more, lest a worse thing
come unto thee."

Then the man left the Temple, and having by this time discovered who his healer was, he told the Jews it was Jesus. Whereupon the Jews persecuted Jesus and sought to slay him, because he had done these things on the Sabbath Day. Jesus had not in this case broken the Sabbath himself. He had done no work. But he had told the man to work (to carry his bed) so he had been the cause why the Sabbath had been broken. But when Jesus heard the charge of the Jews he answered them, "My Father worketh hitherto, and I work."

Does this mean that God works on the Sabbath, and therefore Jesus feels justified in working, such good works? I think this is the meaning. *"Therefore* the Jews sought the more to kill him, because he had not only broken the Sabbath, but said also that God was his Father, making himself equal with God." Thereafter follows a long discourse by Jesus on his relation to God.

As usual, the miracle here is not the chief thing with John, certainly not the only thing. The chief thing in this, as in all the other accounts of miracles in John's Gospel, is the doctrine that is linked on to it—the doctrine of Jesus about the Sabbath, about his power to forgive sins, his relation to God, and so on. The story is imperfectly told. The narrator is not thinking of the miracle first and last. Therefore, he tells the story imperfectly, probably omitting essential things—the man's faith in Jesus to cure him.

In considering these cases of the curing of palsy it is well to realize that modern medical science agrees that, while the processes of cure are being carried out, the will of the patient is of the highest help as contributing to re-establish the connexion of the brain with the muscles.

I suggest that the cures of paralytics by Jesus were in all cases due to the exercise of his will on the will of his patients. In every case of which the facts are stated (except the case of the man at the pool of Bethesda) the *will* of the patient to cure at the hands of Jesus, and faith in his power to cure, are clearly indicated. It is so in the case of the servant of the centurion, for, though the servant himself does not appear, the profound faith of the centurion is such as leaves no doubt (in any of the varying narratives) that before he came to Jesus himself, or sent his friends to Jesus, he must have communicated his complete confidence in the power of Jesus to cure to the servant himself.

Jesus was deeply moved by the profound faith of the centurion, who was so certain of the power of Jesus that he did not think it necessary that he should come to his servant, being confident that he had only to say the word and his servant would be healed. At this unparalleled evidence of faith all the psychical power of Jesus was called out, and who shall say that his distance from the patient detracted in the slightest from the exercise of his psychical power?

In the case of the man sick of the palsy in Nazareth there is no direct reference to the operation of the will of the man, and although the friends of the sick man show their faith by bringing him to Jesus (by carrying him on his bed), and the sick man shows his faith by permitting himself to be carried, it is necessary to read Matthew's story in conjunction with the story in *Mark*, which is more full.

In *Mark* the zeal of the sick man is reflected in the zeal of the four men who, carrying him on his bed, go so far as to overcome the difficulty of getting at Jesus that they ascend to the roof of the house (when the throng forbids their getting in through the door), and let the sick man down through the roof. In their laborious conveyance of the sick man, Jesus sees their faith and the faith of the sick man who is brought. Hence the will of Jesus operates in response to the call of faith in the sick man, and in turn this reacts on the man. Thus the miracle is a miracle of the soul of Jesus. As such it is strictly in accordance with modern science, which says that the patients suffering from certain forms of paralysis and undergoing passive treatment as means of cure should be told by the operator to *will* the movement which he is performing, and thus contribute to re-establish the connexion of the brain with the muscles.

The cure of the paralytic by Jesus was therefore strictly in accordance with modern science. But was it any the less a miracle on that account? No, because modern science knows that the will of the patient will re-establish the connexion of the brain with the muscles and thus contribute to cure paralysis. Modern science does not know how the will operates; it does not know what mysterious force is at play within the patient, or how or why it works. That is the unfathomable mystery of God, which the wise physician knows to exist, but does not know how to bring into operation.

The theory of those who believe in the miracles of Jesus is that he above all beings that have ever lived on the earth had been endowed with the power of acting on the will of diseased persons, inspiring them with absolute confidence in his power to cure them, and thereby performing the cure. The first cause of that cure is faith—faith within himself in the power conferred upon him by God, faith in the patient in Jesus as the possessor of that power.

It is a miracle of the soul, a psychical mystery, therefore an infinitely greater miracle than the material miracle of science, of medicine, of treatment.

In the case of the impotent man at the pool of Bethesda I find the evangelist too much occupied with dogmas which are related to the miracle to give a clear account of the miracle itself. It is an imperfect story. Only one clear indication is given of the man's faith, of his response to the faith of Jesus, of his will to be cured. That is when Jesus tells him to rise, and he rises, and when he tells him to take up his bed, he does so.

Is this less than an act of faith? Remember that the man has been helpless for thirty-eight years. A man of whom he knows nothing comes and say to him in effect, "You have no need to wait for the angel to trouble the waters. I say to you get up now, lift up your bed and carry it home."

And without a word of dissent the man does it. What might have been expected of him if any ordinary man had said to him what Jesus said? He might have been expected to say. "Don't talk foolishness. I have been lying helpless for thirty-eight years unable to stand on my feet and unable to carry anything. Why should you insult my intelligence by telling me now to rise up and walk and carry my bed?"

This would have been the answer of a man in whom Jesus had not inspired faith. But that the man obeyed Jesus without a word, that he rose, apparently instantly, and stood and walked, shows that (although he says nothing about faith) his faith was instantly awakened. He believed, Jesus made him believe, that even after thirty-eight years of lying helpless in a bed, he *could* rise and walk and carry his bed. *And he did.*

What, then, is the miracle? It is a miracle performed on the *will* of the patient, in other words on his mind, on his soul. This, then, is the miracle performed by Jesus on the impotent man at the pool of Bethesda. He, by his vast store of will, of soul, of faith, called on the will and soul and faith of the sufferer, and it thereby worked his cure. That this is a miracle is clear, for though it is known to medical science it is outside the power of medical practice.

II. *The Messianic Hope and the Curing of Disease*

How far were the miracles of Jesus performed on the paralytic (as on the blind and those otherwise afflicted) due to the Messianic hope? I think materially. The Old Testament shows in various passages that the cures of the lame and paralytic were in accordance with Messianic expectation. In *Isaiah* XXXV, 6 it is promised in obvious reference to the Messianic time, "Then shall the lame man leap as an hart," and after the description of further cures it is said that they "the ransomed of the Lord . . . shall obtain joy and gladness, and sorrow and sighing shall flee away."

Therefore, I find that in nearly every case of miracle performed by Jesus faith is the first necessity and the presence of the Messianic hope is clearly indicated, or may reasonably be presupposed. In the cases in *Matthew, Mark* and *Luke* the paralytics are brought to Jesus after he has preached the gospel of the Kingdom, inspired the hope of the Messiah, and after, as would certainly appear, the people had begun to believe that Jesus was himself the Messiah. In the case of the infirm man at the pool of Bethesda the whole atmosphere may be said to be impregnated with the Messianic hope. It is believed that at certain times an angel comes down and troubles the waters, and that the first to step into the water after it has been troubled is cured. It is pure supernaturalism such as the Messianic hope alone can keep alive. Some day the Messiah himself will come. Meantime, his angel comes at intervals with foretastes of the blessed relief he will bring.

The pool of Bethesda could only have existed in a society that was waiting for the Messiah. Therefore every sick person was waiting for divine aid. So when Jesus spoke to the infirm man he was speaking to one who was waiting and watching for the miracle that would make him whole. Thus the Messianic hope lies at the root of the faith that is the first necessity of the miracles of Jesus. Where the Messianic hope was strongest there faith was strongest, and there Jesus could work more miracles. Hence, the numerous miracles of Galilee, outside Nazareth, where faith was least, owing to the fact that they knew Jesus as a man whose mother and brothers were with them.

Where the Messianic hope was lowest, as in Jerusalem, the faith was weakest, and the miracles of Jesus fewest.

III. The Nature of Leprosy

Among the sufferers whom Jesus healed were people afflicted with leprosy, the greatest disease of mediæval Christendom, identified, on the one hand, with a disease endemic from the earliest historical times (1500 B.C.) in the delta and valley of the Nile, and, on the other hand, with a disease now common in Asia, Africa and the West Indies. Mediæval leprosy is authentically represented in a picture of the sixteenth century by Holbein; St. Elizabeth gives bread and wine to a prostrate group of lepers, including a bearded man whose face is covered with large round reddish knobs, an old woman whose arms are covered with brown blotches, and whose leg is swathed in bandages through which matter oozes. This agrees with descriptions of leprosy given by the ancients. The cause is believed to be infection by a microbe.

Three types of the disease are usually discovered. In the first the skin is chiefly affected. In the second the nerves. In the third both skin and nerves. The eruption differs according to the type of the disease. As the disease progresses open sores are developed. The patient whose condition is extremely wretched gradually becomes weaker and eventually succumbs to exhaustion. A severe case may end probably in two years, but usually the illness lasts several years. It may last twenty to thirty years. Complete recovery from the severer forms of leprosy rarely if ever occurs.

The white leprosy of the Old Testament, the type most frequently referred to in the Bible, is distinguished by nerve degeneration. It still exists in Palestine.

IV. Cures of Lepers: In Matthew

Jesus was coming down from the mountain after preaching the Sermon on the Mount (VIII, 2), and great multitudes were following him, when a leper came and worshipped him, saying, "Lord, if thou wilt, thou canst make me clean." Upon this, Jesus put forth his hand and touched the leper, saying, "I will; be thou clean." And immediately the leprosy left the man. And Jesus said to him, "See thou tell no man, but go thy way, show thyself to the priest, and offer the gift that Moses commanded, for a testimony unto them."

Unto whom? Also note that Jesus cured the leper (apparently) in the presence of a great multitude, yet he told the man to say nothing about it!

When Jesus calls together his twelve disciples, and sends them out to preach, he includes the power of cleansing lepers among the gifts he gives them (X, 8).

V. Cures of Lepers: In Mark

Jesus, soon after his arrival in Capernaum, leaves it to go into "the next town," and there he meets a leper (I, 40), who says to him (as the leper says in *Matthew*) "If thou wilt, thou canst make me clean." Jesus is moved with compassion, and touches the leper and says, "I will; be thou clean." And, as soon as Jesus has spoken, the leprosy leaves the man and he is cleansed.

Then Jesus charged the man, as in *Matthew,* to tell no man, to show himself to the priest, and so on. But the man went about to publish it much and to blazen the matter, so that Jesus could no more enter the city, but had to go into desert places, apparently to avoid the multitude.

VI. Cures of Lepers: In Luke

Some short time after Jesus had preached from Peter's ship, it came to pass that "in a certain city" there was a man full of leprosy, and seeing Jesus he fell on his face and besought him saying, "Lord, if thou wilt, thou canst make me clean."

This is clearly the same case as the one recorded in *Matthew* and *Mark*. Jesus does the same thing, with the same result, and utters the same warning, gives the same instruction about going to the priest, and so on. The man in the same way publishes his case abroad, with the result that great multitudes come to Jesus to be healed of their infirmities and Jesus withdraws himself into the wilderness.

Jesus was on the way through Samaria and Galilee to Jerusalem (apparently when going up to the Feast of Tabernacles) when, as he was entering into a certain village ten lepers met him (XVII, 11). They stood afar off and cried, "Jesus, Master, have mercy on us." Jesus told them to go and show themselves to the priests. And it came to pass that as they went they were cleansed. And one of them, when he was healed, turned back, fell down on his face at the feet of Jesus, giving him thanks. He was a Samaritan. Jesus asked, "Were there not ten cleansed? But where are the nine?" Was this stranger the only one to give glory to God? Then Jesus said to the Samaritan leper, "Arise, go thy way; thy faith hath made thee whole."

VII. A General Summary

In *John* there does not seem to be any cure of a leper.

But when John the Baptist sends his messengers to Jesus, and Jesus directs their attention to the actual proofs of his Messiahship, he adduces among them the cleansing of lepers. And (as seen above), when Jesus empowers his disciples to perform all kinds of miracles, the cleansing of lepers is numbered among the first. Yet, so far as I can see, Jesus cured only *one* leper, in addition to the ten, if the story of the ten is a separate case of cure and not merely the same cure so told as to serve a dogmatic purpose.

Whether there is only one case of the cure of a leper or eleven cases, there is no difference in the descriptions of the cure. It is the same cure under the same conditions at different times, and in different places, with the same words addressed to Jesus, the same replies from Jesus, the same instruction about going to the priest in obedience to the law, and against publishing the cure, and the same violation of his wish.

The rationalistic critics endeavour to dispose of the supernatural character of this miracle. They assume that the patient was at the crisis of healing, and hence the command to go to the priest, who only received lepers when they were cured or on the point of being cured. All this is feeble and futile. There is no indication of the stage of the disease when Jesus cures the leper. Jesus touches the leper, and the leprosy immediately disappears. After that he orders certain Jewish observances, which were intended to re-admit the unclean man into the company of the clean, and that, so far as the disease is concerned, is all.

The question is the fundamental one: Are we to believe that by the exercise of supernatural power Jesus cured instantaneously and by the touch of his hand, an obstinate, probably long-standing and almost incurable disease? Strauss says, "Leprosy, from the thorough derangement of the arterial fluids of which it is the symptom, is the most obstinate and malignant of cutaneous diseases."

Are we to understand that without any of the aids now employed to cure it, without the lapse of any time, without any help from long-continued cleansing and the building up of a better condition of body and of nervous system, Jesus should instantaneously cure it, by the touch of his hand, or by the psychical power behind the touch, so the skin corroded by the malady should instantly become pure and healthy? Or are we to say that such a story of supernatural cure comes from the realms of fancy?

In oriental and in Jewish legends the sudden appearance and reappearance of leprosy is not uncommon. Referring to this fact Strauss says:

> When Jehovah endued Moses (who was about to go into Egypt) with power to work all kinds of miracles, he gave him a token of his power to cure leprosy by commanding him to put his hand into his bosom, and when he drew it out again it was covered with leprosy. Again he was commanded to put it into his bosom, and when he drew it out a second time it was once more clean. [*Exodus* IV, 6]
>
> Above all, among the miracles of the prophet Elisha, the cure of a leper always plays an important part, and to this event Jesus himself refers in *Luke* IV, 27.
>
> The Syrian general, Naaman, who suffered from leprosy, applied to the Israelite prophet for his aid; the latter sent to him the direction to wash seven times in the Jordan, and on Naaman doing so the leprosy disappeared, but was subsequently transferred by the prophet to his deceitful servant Gehazi. [See II *Kings* V]
>
> I know now that we ought to read behind these Old Testament stories to account for the origin of the narratives in the Gospels.
>
> If then, the cure of leprosy was, without doubt, included in the Jewish idea of the Messiah, the Christians of the early Churches, who believed that the Messiah had really appeared in the person of Jesus, had a yet more decided inducement to glorify his history by such traits taken from the Mosaic and prophetic legends, with the single difference that, in accordance with the mild spirit of the New Covenant they dropped the primitive side of the old miracles.

In short, Strauss infers that the cases of leprosy cured by Jesus were not said to be diseases inflicted by way of punishment.

In *Luke* (IX, 55) Jesus rebuked James and John for asking him to call down fire from Heaven to consume the Samaritans who would not receive him "because his face was as though he would go to Jerusalem," by saying, "Ye know not what manner of spirit ye are of; for the Son of Man is not come to destroy men's lives, but to save them."

But Strauss's theory of the cures of leprosy by Jesus requires that we should believe that the evangelists deliberately invented incidents which never happened; therefore it would seem that they lied, and that the stories of cures are false.

The cure of the ten lepers in *Luke* (XVII, 12) is in every respect similar to that of the single leper, with the exception that the leper who returns is described as a Samaritan. Strauss thinks this injures the credibility of the narrative, in so far as it points to a dozen other reasons for the miracle.

"That the cured leper," he declares, "who is presented as a model of thankfulness happens to be a Samaritan cannot pass without remark by the evangelist who alone tells the parable of the Good Samaritan. The fact that in the Good Samaritan story two Jews, a priest and a Levite, show themselves pitiless, while a Samaritan proves himself compassionate, so here, nine unthankful Jews stand contrasted with one thankful Samaritan."

Strauss concludes from this that the cure of the ten lepers cannot be historical and that Jesus was here, as well as in the other case, pronouncing a *parable,* and not working a cure.

But it is the evangelist who tells the story of the cure of the ten, while it is Jesus who tells the parable of the Good Samaritan. It may be true that something parabolic is intended by the evangelist (or his informant) in a miracle which holds up one of the members of the hated race of Samaritans as a model of virtue. "This narrative," suggests Strauss, "may therefore be partly an account of a miracle and partly a parable."

VIII. Conclusions

I think there may have been two cases of cure of leprosy in the life of Jesus, and two only. The first (as recorded in *Matthew* and *Mark*) occurred at the beginning of the ministry and very shortly after the return of Jesus to Galilee from his baptism in Jordan. The second occurred at the end of the first part of the ministry, when Jesus was going up to Jerusalem for the Feast of Tabernacles. But clearly it occurred in Galilee. And therein lies its improbability. That after Jesus had cured a leper in the neighbourhood of Capernaum ten other lepers should be living in Galilee (however far south) within say ten miles, without having heard of the cure of their fellow-leper, or, having heard of it, without making an effort to reach Jesus, when he was rarely more than that distance away from their city, and was often not more than half that distance away from it, makes the story look incredible.

That, by an act of will, by a single touch of the hand, Jesus arrested a disease, restored decayed flesh, healed suppurating wounds, built up again wasted tissues, degenerated nerves, can only be credited by those who are prepared to accept wholly and unquestionably the idea that he exercised supernatural powers, powers as absolute as those of recreation. We have no record of this having ever been done before, except in the stories of Moses and Elisha. We have no record that it was ever done again, by Jesus or by another. Although we are told that the cures of the lepers were widely published, we do not gather that they contributed to establish faith in the Messiahship of Jesus.

This substantial proof that Jesus was the Messiah left the world about him still in doubt. It is not certain that it was enough to convince even his own disciples, who did not believe or declare their faith in him until months afterwards at Cæsarea Philippi. One asks how such unquestionable proof of the divinity of Jesus did not sweep down all unbelief.

Then the fact that John's Gospel says nothing of these cures seems to show that either the writer knew nothing about them or did not credit them. To say that he did not narrate them because they had been narrated by *Matthew, Mark* and *Luke* is not satisfying. He told other stories over again, stories less wonderful.

Again, the Epistles of Peter and Paul say nothing about them. Why? Was everything miraculous swallowed up for them by the one great miracle of the Resurrection of Jesus? Were these and like evidences of the Messiahship of Jesus quite unnecessary to them? Or did they know nothing about them?

The social position of the leper was a very pitiful one. In the time of Jesus lepers were not forbidden to go about the country, to move from house to house; but they were cut off from intercourse with the healthy. They were unclean, and they must not come near the clean. The clean must not touch them. The lepers, therefore, knew nothing of a caress. The sweetest expressions of affection were denied them. In the public roads they were compelled to announce their condition, to cry out "Leper! Leper!" The pitiful condition! The awful isolation from the family of man!

Next, think of these persons in relation to the synagogue. They could not enter the synagogue for fear of contaminating the clean. Places were assigned to them outside, where they could hear the word of the law, its promises.

Think of the Messianic hope. The Divine Being who was to come, who would cleanse them from their impurity. Think of this in relation to the cures by Jesus. Jesus stretched out his hand and touched the leper. That of itself would be almost enough to awaken all the forces of the soul of the afflicted.

I think the miracles performed by Jesus in the cure of lepers were (like the cure of demoniacs) *psychical* miracles, the miracles of the mind and will of Jesus acting in co-operation with the mind and will of the sufferers. My reasons for this are:

1. That nowhere in the Gospel narratives do we see any indication of the extreme leprosy depicted in Holbein's picture.

2. That nowhere (as far as I can see) in the Old Testament stories of leprosy is there any indication of such extreme forms of leprosy.

3. That the story of the cure of Naaman's leprosy (II *Kings* V) to which Jesus himself refers, indicates a kind of leprosy that is not malignant and incurable.

4. That the description of the leprosy which falls upon Gehazi, in the same chapter, "The leprosy therefore of Naaman shall cleave unto thee, and unto thy seed for ever; and he went out from his presence a leper as white as snow," indicates the same less malignant and curable type. That in like manner the leprosy of Moses' hand (*Exodus* IV, 6, 7) and of Miriam (*Numbers* XII, 10) is not, as Strauss says it is, the worst, but the least malignant type of leprosy, akin to psoriasis.

5. That in this type it is clear lepers did not suffer from hideous disfigurement, from eruptions, from loathsome discharge. They were able to live in society, to keep their own houses, to be married and live with their wives, to hold offices of state, to be captains in the army, even to continue to be kings.

The leprosy common in Palestine was generally a cutaneous disease produced by the climate of that country. It made the skin white, and perhaps scaly. To be "white as snow" is the phrase nearly always used to describe it. But it was curable, and was sometimes of short duration. The Mosaic ritual for the reception of the cleansed leper back into society, and into the use of the Temple and the synagogue, is proof enough that the leprosy was not only not virulent but was often cured. It ran its course and was then gone, and the cured leper was then received back into the company and the worship of his fellow-men.

The Mosaic ritual consisted chiefly of a process of cleansing. In Naaman's case it was brought about by washing seven times in the Jordan. In this ritual the leper, on reaching the stage of cure, was told to present himself to the priest and obey the commands (generally intended to cultivate cleanliness) which he would give him.

The lepers whom Jesus cured are never described as suffering from loathsome forms of leprosy. They were certainly suffering from a contagious skin disease which made them look "white as snow." Modern science tells us that this is a stage far from incapable of cure, by cleansing, by better nutrition and by the development of a better nervous condition.

My view is that this is the type of leprosy indicated in all of the few cases referred to in the New Testament. Whether there was only one leper cured by Jesus, or eleven, the type was the same in all cases.

What, then, was the nature of the miracle performed by Jesus? It was, in my opinion, a psychical miracle. Jesus inspired in the leper (both by word and act) confidence that he could be cured.

He *touched* the leper, thus leaving the impression on the leper that he was not afraid of contagion, that, in fact, there was no danger of infection. Then he sent him to show himself to the priest, thus inspiring in the leper the sense that he was cured, or on the point of being cured, that his leprosy was leaving him. The reaction upon the leper in that stage of leprosy worked the cure.

It was a miracle of the will, first of Jesus, who inspired the leper with confidence in the possibility of cure, and then of the leper himself, who exercised all his will (his faith) to call into play the curative forces within himself that would expel the disease, thereby releasing the man from a fixed idea, that he was incurable, and possibly permanently invigorating him with the impression that he could be, and was being, cured. Thus we read that not instantly in some cases, but on their way to the priests, the lepers found themselves cured—lepers no longer. Their skin which had been white as snow began to take on a healthy colour.

Therefore, I do not feel it necessary to take either the entirely supernatural view that Jesus by a touch of the hand banished from the diseased body a virulent malady, and did in a moment what would now require years of treatment, or to say that the whole story of the cure of lepers by Jesus is a fable from the realms of fancy.

I think Jesus actually performed a miracle upon the man's spirit, which, reacting upon his body, worked his cure. And the cures of the lepers were closely interlocked with faith, faith in Jesus as the Messiah. This applies to all the miracles of Jesus.

IX.   *The Great Physician*

Notwithstanding the long and patient perusal of the means whereby the armies of death may be withstood—a plague, perhaps typhoid, smallpox, paralysis; the long search for the causes of disease, for the invisible germs; the discovery and invention of means to detect the first causes, the combination of powers to defeat them—all the efforts through the long ages to promote cures of apparently incurable evils—the wise physician will agree that, above and beyond everything that his science and research have done, and continue to do, to heal, the great power whereby disease is conquered and death kept back *lies within the spirit of the stricken person himself,* and that the mightiest force in bringing the sick back to health, the dying back to life, has been one *reviving within the soul of the patient his lost hope, the lost courage, the lost faith.*

And is it not just this mightiest of all the forces that the Great Physician, Jesus, brought to bear in the miracles of healing which are narrated in the Gospels? Modern science may say that to cure this or that disease of long standing is an achievement outside all experience; that science has no means of accounting for it even yet, nearly two thousand years after Christ; but if science allows that the spiritual forces within the sick man are the most powerful in bringing about cure, and if it agrees that these forces are beyond its comprehension, and probably always will and must be beyond its comprehension, not to be measured, not to be followed in their operation, but nevertheless certain and not to be disputed, then science cannot say that what we call miracle is impossible, that it does not happen. *It is happening every day under the eyes of the scientific physician,* who knows that far as his knowledge and research have gone (and thank God they have gone very far) the last and greatest factor in cure lies hidden and incalculable in the human spirit itself.

X. *Cures of the Blind*

Among the sufferers cured by Jesus the blind were more numerous than those afflicted by any other malady. The blind in an eastern country in the time of Jesus can have had few opportunities of acquiring knowledge. As a consequence, many of the persons among the poor born blind became beggars by the roadside. Their only channel of education would be through the synagogue.

Sitting in the synagogue they would hear the law and the prophets read. It is a pathetic fact that deeper into their minds than into the minds of persons with sight would fall the blessed hope of the Messiah. When the Messiah came they would see, they would be no longer poor. It is an impressive thought that on regaining their powers of vision the first thing they would look upon would be the sunlit face of their Christ, their Redeemer. The Redeemer to the blind in Palestine would be the son of David. Therefore, their minds were always busy with the thought of the son of David who was to come. When they heard of a miracle worker who gave sight to the blind they instantly thought of him as the son of David.

XI. *Cures of the Blind: In Matthew*

During the early part of his Galilean ministry, not long after his visit to the country of the Gergesenes, and the raising of the daughter of Jairus, Jesus was leaving Jairus's house when two blind men followed him, crying, "Thou son of David, have mercy on us" (IX, 27). And when he was come into the house (his own house, apparently) the blind men followed him, and Jesus said, "Believe ye that I am able to do this?" meaning to cure their blindness. And the blind men answered, "Yea, Lord."

Jesus then touched their eyes and said, "According to your faith be it unto you." And straightway their eyes were opened. Then he charged them, "See that no man know it." But they, going away from him, spread the news over all the country.

In verse 22 of Chapter XII we learn that there was brought to Jesus a demoniac who was blind and dumb. Jesus healed the man and "the blind and dumb both spake and saw." This occurred, according to Matthew, after the disciples of John the Baptist had visited Jesus. On his way to Jerusalem Jesus passed through Jericho. As he departed from Jericho (XX, 30) two blind men sitting by the wayside, when they heard that Jesus passed by, cried out, saying, "Have mercy on us, O Lord, thou son of David."

The multitude by whom Jesus was surrounded rebuked the two blind men, telling them to hold their peace; but they cried the more, "Have mercy on us, O Lord, thou son of David!"

Jesus stood still, and called them, and said, "What will ye that I shall do unto you?" and the blind men answered, "Lord, that our eyes may be opened." So Jesus had compassion on them and touched their eyes, and immediately their eyes received sight, and they followed him.

XII. Cures of the Blind: In Mark

Jesus had been to the coasts of Tyre and Sidon, and returned to the Lake of Galilee, through the midst of the coasts of Decapolis. After feeding the four thousand he sailed with his disciples to Dalmanutha. Then he went to Bethsaida.

At Bethsaida (VIII, 22) they brought a blind man to him, and besought him to touch the man. Jesus took the blind man by the hand and led him out of the town, and when he had spit on his eyes, and put his hands on him, and asked him if he saw anything, the blind man looked up and said, "I see men as trees, walking." Then Jesus put his hands again upon the blind man's eyes. And then the blind man's sight was restored, and he saw every man clearly. Then Jesus sent the blind man to his home, saying, "Neither go into the town, nor tell it to any in the town."

This is not the story of a man born blind, otherwise, when partly restored, he would not have identified what he saw as trees or as men.

There is a very human appeal in the incident of Jesus leading the blind man out of the town, apparently leaving all the others behind him. The fact that sight is not immediately restored and needs a second touch of the hands of Jesus on the blind man's eyes seems to suggest physical cure, not psychical. The touch of the hands on the eyes seems also to suggest physical agency in the restoration of the blind man's sight.

On the other hand Jesus had to deal in the case of the blind with precisely the same mental condition in the patient as he had to deal with in the case of the leper. The blind also believed that their cure came from a touch. They did reach to the height of the psychical effect of the will of Jesus. Therefore, though the touching of the eyes may not have been necessary to Jesus, it may have been necessary to carry the conviction of being cured to the mind of the blind man.

But why did the first touch succeed only partially, and the second completely? Again, this may have been necessary to bring conviction to the man that he was being cured. That the touching of the blind man's eyes twice cured him I do not think it necessary to believe. But it was a physical aid to the psychical cure—the power and will of Jesus setting up faith in the sufferer, and the faith setting up the cure.

Thus faith is the root of all the cures of Jesus. He himself repeatedly says so. *Faith* can do anything. It can work any miracle in man. At one moment Jesus goes so far as to say it can work any miracle in nature. It can even remove mountains. But we feel that this is the language of the East, not to be taken literally. Faith is to Jesus the great healer of all diseases.

Has modern science ever said anything against that? Is it not always saying that *Faith* in the sufferer (the spirit of hope, believing in recovery, certainty of cure) is the first force in effecting the cure of disease?

Jesus was on his way to Jerusalem, his last visit to Jerusalem. He came to Jericho. As he went out of Jericho with his disciples and a great number of people, blind Bartimæus, the son of Timæus, sat by the highway side begging (X, 46). When Bartimæus heard that it was Jesus of Nazareth who passed by he cried out, "Jesus, thou son of David, have mercy on me."

Many of the people told him to hold his peace, but he cried the more, "Thou son of David, have mercy on me." Jesus heard him and stood still, and commanded that the blind man should be called.

They called the blind man, saying to him, "Be of good comfort, rise; he calleth thee." Then the blind man, casting away his garment, rose and came to Jesus. And Jesus said, "What wilt thou that I should do unto thee?" The blind man answered, "Lord, that I might receive my sight." Jesus said, "Go thy way; thy faith hath made thee whole." And immediately the blind man received his sight and followed Jesus.

This is the same story as in *Matthew* (XX, 30) with the difference that it is one blind man, not two, and that Jesus does not touch the eyes of the blind man, as in *Matthew,* and he does not attribute his cure to faith. Further, Mark's account differs in giving a name, and a father's name, to the blind man. The story in *Mark* gives a greater sense of reality to the incident. Further, it expresses more clearly the fundamental cause of the cure—not the touch of the hand of Jesus on the eyes of the blind man, but the faith in the mind of the blind man. Bartimæus has absolute faith in the power of Jesus to make him see. All that remains to set that faith in motion upon the body of the blind man is the word of Jesus, the will of Jesus, the soul of Jesus, saying to the blind man, "Go thy way; thy *faith* hath made thee whole."

Another psychical miracle, the miracle of the soul of Jesus reacting on the soul of the blind man, and thereby on his body. Does this require belief in the instantaneous and complete cure of the blindness of the blind man? I do not think that follows. It only follows that the processes of cure have begun; that he was blind, and now sees.

Nor does it require that we should believe that the blindness of Bartimæus was the worst form of blindness, that it was incurable blindness, the blindness in which the nerves of the eye are dead. Palestine was full of blind people. Every tenth person was more or less blind. Yet cures of blindness reported are few. And the blindness caused by the climate of Palestine was rarely the worst blindness.

XIII.   Cures of the Blind: In Luke

In the indefinite period in *Luke* when Jesus is said to be passing to Jerusalem "through the midst of Samaria and Galilee" as he came nigh to Jericho a certain blind man sat by the wayside beg-

ging (XVIII, 35). This is clearly the same incident as in *Matthew*
and *Mark*, except that it is not two blind men as in *Matthew*, but
one blind man as in *Mark*, and he does not come upon him on
departing from Jericho, as in *Matthew* and *Mark*, but on approaching Jericho. The difference is unimportant. The rest of the story
is identical with the story in *Mark*. Jesus said to the blind man,
"Receive thy sight; thy faith hath saved thee." And immediately
the blind man received his sight and followed Jesus, glorifying
God. And all the people, when they saw it, gave praise to God.

My conclusions are the same as in the case of the story told in
Mark. Jesus performed a psychical miracle on the blind man. He
called to the man's faith, and the man's faith responded, and by
the reaction of his faith on his physical body the blind man was
cured of his blindness.

We do not know the exact character and condition of the man's
blindness. And who shall say, what oculist of our own time dare
say, that if a blind man had absolute faith that he, the oculist,
could cure his blindness instantaneously (not merely by the long
processes of treatment) the powers of man's physical nature reacting upon his faith would not bring about his cure? We have no
test to which to put this. Since the time of Jesus the world has had
no test. Jesus, alone, is reputed to have possessed psychical power.
Who shall say, who can possibly say, that he did not possess and
exercise it?

One thing above all is clear—that in all cases of the cure of disease thus far, the first condition, in the view of Jesus, is faith—
faith on his own part and that of his disciples working miracles,
and in most cases a faith in the sufferer which answers to his own
faith.

XIV.   *Cures of the Blind: In John*

Jesus is in Jerusalem. It is after the last day of the Feast of
Tabernacles. The Jews have attempted to stone him, apparently
in the Temple, or in one of the courts of the Temple. Jesus has
passed out of the Temple; he is said to have hidden himself to
escape from those who had taken up stones to stone him.

As he passed by he saw a man who had been blind from his
birth (IX, 1). It is not said *here* that the man was *born* blind. His

disciples asked Jesus, "Who did sin, this man, or his parents, that he was born blind?" They certainly believed that somebody had sinned. Perhaps they thought Jesus believed somebody must have sinned that the man should be born blind. Jesus answered, "Neither hath this man sinned, nor his parents, but that the works of God should be made manifest in him." What did Jesus mean? Did he mean that the man had been blind from his birth solely in order that he (Jesus) coming long years after (the man having suffered blindness from infancy to manhood) may be cured of his blindness by him, so that the faith of his disciples in his character as the Messiah may be established?

This is incredible. That God should inflict blindness on the man to establish the belief of the twelve disciples is incredible. But the faith of the disciples in Jesus as the Messiah did not then need to be established. They already believed him to be the Messiah. They had repeatedly pronounced him the Christ. The cure of the man's blindness was totally unnecessary to establish their faith. They had seen blind men cured before.

But Jesus goes on to say that he must work the works of Him that sent him while it is day; the night cometh wherein no man can work. Further, he says that as long as he is in the world he is the light of the world.

Observe that all this from verse 2 to verse 5 suggests a dogmatic purpose. The eye of the evangelist is not (as in *Mark*) on the blind man. It is on some dogma which he is trying to establish.

Then we return to reality. Jesus spits on the ground and makes clay of the spittle, and anoints the eyes of the blind man with the clay. Then he says to the blind man, "Go, wash in the pool of Siloam." The man goes and does so, and comes back seeing. All this happens on the Sabbath Day.

The neighbours of the blind man say, "Is not this he that sat and begged?" Some answer, "This is he." Others say, "He is like him." The man who had been blind says, "I am he." The neighbours ask how his eyes were opened, and he answers that a man called Jesus made clay and anointed his eyes and then told him to go to the pool of Siloam, and wash; and he went and washed and recovered his sight.

The neighbours ask him where is this man, and he answers that he does not know. Then the neighbours bring the once-blind man to the Pharisees, and the Pharisees ask the man how he received his sight, and he answers, "He put clay upon mine eyes, and I washed, and do see."

Then the Pharisees say, "This man is not of God, because he keepeth not the Sabbath Day." They mean by this that by making the clay on the Sabbath Day Jesus did *work* on the Sabbath, and thereby broke the Sabbath.

But others among the people ask, "How can a man that is a sinner [as a breaker of the Sabbath must be] do such miracles." So there is division among them. They ask the once-blind man what *he* thinks of the man who opened his eyes. The once-blind man says, "He is a prophet."

But the Jews were not prepared to believe that the man had been blind until they had inquired of his parents, and asked, "Is this your son, who ye say was born blind? How then doth he now see?" The man's parents answered that they know the man to be their son and that he was born blind. But by what means he sees they do not know; or who opened his eyes. "He is of age," they say; "ask him, he shall speak for himself."

The parents talked like this because, according to the evangelist, they feared the Jews, who had agreed among themselves that if any man confessed that Jesus was Christ he should be put out of the synagogue. The Jews call the once-blind man again and say, "Give God the praise, not this man, because we know this man to be a sinner." To that the cured man replies, "Whether he be a sinner or not I do not know. I know only one thing, that whereas I was blind, now I see."

The Jews then crossquestion the man more exactly as to what Jesus did to him, evidently intending to get more precise evidence of his working on the Sabbath. The man answers rather impatiently that he has told them already what Jesus did. The Jews then turn on the man and revile him, saying, "Thou art his disciple, but we are Moses' disciples. We know that God spoke to Moses, but as for this fellow we do not know whence he is—where he comes from." The man replies in effect, "Well, here is a marvellous thing, that you do not know whence he is, and yet he has opened my eyes. We know that God does not hear sinners, but if a man be a worshipper of God and doeth His work, God hears him. Since the world began it has never been heard before that any man opened the eyes of one that was born blind. If this man were not of God, he could do nothing."

This answer of the once-blind man seems to imply (1) that God only gives power to do good deeds to his own good people; (2) that Jesus had done a good thing in giving him sight, therefore Jesus was from God; (3) that never before had it been known that the eyes had been opened of one born blind.

The Jews reply boldly, "Thou wast altogether born in sins, and dost thou teach us?" And then they cast him out, presumably out of the synagogue. It is clear that the Jews think the man was born blind because he was born in sin.

Then comes a sequel to the story. Jesus hears that the Jews have cast (out of the synagogue) the man he had cured, and he goes in search of him. When he finds him he says, "Dost thou believe on the Son of God?" And the man answers, "Who is he, Lord, that I might believe on him?" Jesus replies, "Thou hast both seen him, and it is he that talketh with thee." The man replies, "Lord, I believe."

Jesus says, "For judgment I am come into this world, that they which see not might see; and that they which see might be made blind." Then some of the Pharisees who hear this say, "Are we blind also?" And Jesus replies, "If ye were blind, ye should have no sin; but now ye say, We see; therefore your sin remaineth."

This is the last of the stories of the cures of blindness as recorded in the Gospels. I confess that it leaves a deep sense of unreality upon me. It is not a simple story of how a man born blind was restored to sight. That fact is almost ignored in the theological discussion which follows.

This discussion turns on the following points, (1) whether Jesus *worked* on the Sabbath Day in the action of giving sight to the blind man, in which case he is a sinner, and not a prophet, not Christ; (2) the proof that Jesus must be from God because he gave sight to a man born blind (as his parents testify) and no man before Jesus had ever done so; (3) that Jesus was the Son of God; (4) that Jesus came into the world to give (spiritual) sight to those who had been blind, and to make blind those who thought they had spiritual sight but had not.

Was the incident of giving sight to the man born blind historical? Did it occur in Jerusalem before Jesus was stoned out of it? Or is it the same incident as that of the blind man Bartimæus at Jericho? I think it a different incident. I think it occurred in Jerusalem shortly after the Feast of the Dedication and before the stoning out of Jerusalem. And I can see no ground for doubting that something occurred in relation to it which led up to the stoning.

But the story differs from the other stories of the cure of the blind in some important particulars; (1) the man does not call on Jesus to cure him, or at least he is not reported to have called on him; (2) Jesus nowhere tells him that he is cured by reason of his faith.

On the other hand the man's faith is implied by what he does. When he is told to go to the pool of Siloam and wash, he goes and does so. In spite of the danger of being cast out, he declares his belief that Jesus is a prophet, that he is from God. He permits himself to be cast out, and when Jesus finds him he worships Jesus.

Thus I see no external fact which differs from the facts in the cures of other cases of blindness. Jesus performs a psychical miracle on the man. He uses the clay for the same reason that he used the spittle—to appeal to the man's imagination, his belief. Or perhaps there is a physical reason attending the use both of the spittle and the clay.

Modern science tells us that infantile blindness (the earlier blind man may not have been blind from his birth, but blind from his infancy or boyhood) is caused most frequently by inoculation of the eyes with hurtful material at the time of birth. That the ophthalmia of infancy is an infectious germ disease. In the majority of cases the disease is curable if proper treatment is employed at an early period. If the treatment is too long delayed, cure is more difficult, in some cases impossible.

But cure of diseases of the eye from this cause are not always impossible. The treatment required above all is cleanliness. It requires washing. Is it beyond reason to say that Jesus added to the psychical appeal the cleansing effect of the clay and of the washing, and that together they effected the cure, helped, stimulated by the call to faith? The man's absolute faith, in spite of all dangers, stands out clearly.

XV. A General Summary

Considering the prevalence of eye disease in Palestine, it is remarkable how few are the cures of blindness recorded in the Gospels.

In *Matthew* they are three only:
1. The two blind men in Galilee (IX, 27).
2. The blind and dumb demoniac (XII, 22).
3. The two blind men at Jericho (XX, 30).

In *Mark* there are two only:
1. The man at Bethsaida (VIII, 22).
2. Blind Bartimæus at Jericho (X, 46). (The same as No. 3 in *Matthew*.)

In *Luke* there is only one:
1. The blind man at Jericho (XVIII, 35). (The same as in *Matthew* and *Mark*.)

In *John* there is only one:
1. The blind man in Jerusalem (IX, 1).

Thus there seem to be only three distinct and different cases and the case of the blind and dumb demoniac. In *Matthew* there are two blind men at Jericho. The cases are few and not dissimilar. In all cases (except *John's*) they profess their faith in the power of Jesus to open their eyes. In all cases (except *John's*) Jesus says their faith has cured them. In all cases the miracles appear to be psychical miracles, helped out by cleansing.

With the miracles of Jesus the ordinary natural explanation (based on physical science alone) will not serve us, to account for the cure of a man who is congenitally sightless. Not one of the first three evangelists mentions the case of the man *born* blind. It appears in *John* only. In *John* it is connected with a dogmatic discourse. This is characteristic of John, it applies to nearly everything he narrates.

John rarely or never tells a story in "day-light." He nearly always tells it with a kind of commentary attached. It is not the incident that first of all interests John, as the incident interests the earlier evangelists. It is the thought he derives from it. Therefore, John is not a pure historian, first and last. He is a theologian, using history to prove the tenets of his theology. This is very specially the case with the incident of the man born blind. All the problems attending the position of a man thus born are introduced into it.

It is difficult to see why the three evangelists omitted this specially powerful miracle of a man *born* blind, if it occurred. The evidences are against it. The magnitude of the miracle might have been expected to attract Mark, who loved the most dramatic best. He says nothing about it, while he tells stories of cures of the blind which are immeasurably less important. Hence, the suspicion arises that the cure of the man born blind never did occur. Looked at again, it seems to be compounded of two or more other stories— the story of blind Bartimæus as told in *Mark* and the blind and dumb man instanced by Matthew.

Next, John gives to Siloam (which is by interpretation Sent) a Greek interpretation, whereas, by the more probable interpretation, it means a waterfall. John's interpretation (Sent) is apparently intended to indicate that by a special providence the pool received the name Siloam because at a future time the Messiah, as a manifestation of his glory (or, to use John's language, "that the works of God should be made manifest in him"), would be "sent" of the Father. This is a play upon words by a writer (not a native of Palestine) probably unacquainted with Hebrew.

Again, the reason given for the cure of the blind man (quoted above) is identical in *spirit* with the reason given by John for the raising of Lazarus. After the disciples had replied to Jesus that if Lazarus were sleeping he was doing well, and Jesus had said plainly, "Lazarus is dead," he goes on to say that he is glad for the disciples' sakes that he was not there (in Bethany), to the intent that they might believe in him.

Finally, the cure of the man born blind occurs in *John* about the same time as the cure of the blind men in *Mark,* immediately before the entrance of Jesus into Jerusalem. On the whole, the evidence goes to show that the incident did not occur as described in the fourth Gospel, that it is another version (with dogma attached after the manner of *John*) of the cure of the blind man at Jericho, and furthermore (and consequently) the fourth Gospel had not an apostolic origin. John the fisherman must have been an eye-witness.

The fourth Gospel has fewer miracles than the three first Gospels, but they are nearly all of greater magnitude. The Synoptics have simple cures of paralytics cured by Jesus, but the fourth Gospel has the case of one who has been lame thirty-eight years. The Synoptics have two cases of raising from the dead of persons who have lately died, but the fourth Gospel has the raising of a man who has been four days in the grave, and in whose body, it is believed, corruption has begun. The Synoptics have simple cases of the cure of blindness that might have been of short duration. The fourth Gospel has the case of a man born blind.

Observe the close analogy of the case of the man born blind with that of the leper Naaman. Both are told to go and wash— Naaman in Jordan, the blind man in the pool of Siloam.

Some of the foregoing appears to be contradictory. Although the time in *John* is almost the same as in the three earlier evangelists, between the time of this incident as in *John* and the incident as in the Synoptics I place some months. In *John* the cure of the man born blind would be in the winter of A.D. 29. Jesus would then (being soon afterwards stoned out of Jerusalem) go up through Samaria to Galilee and thus on to Cæsarea Philippi, and then come down through Galilee (partly through Samaria, as far as the Wady Fa'ar) to Jericho, and there meet Bartimæus.

I find an added value and probability in the fact that Bartimæus must have heard of the cure of the man born blind, which had occurred not long before not far away from Jericho, in Jerusalem.

XVI.   *Other Miracles of Healing*

In the early part of his Galilean ministry sick people crowded about Jesus, being carried into the streets, and so placed that they might touch him as he passed. Sick people had such faith in his power to cure them that they only sought to touch him, to lay hold of the hem of his garments in order to be healed. Thus Jesus operated on the sick not by direct appeal to their faith, but as if possessed within himself of such healing power that it needed only the faith of the sufferer and his slight contact with Jesus to effect an instant cure. His power of healing does not of its own voluntary act dispense its virtues, but is subject to being drawn from him without his assent.

There is the case of the woman who had an issue of blood. This incident occurs in *Matthew* IX, 20, *Mark* V, 25, and *Luke* VIII, 43. In all three Synoptic Gospels it is the same story, told in the same narration and in the same way, but with certain unimportant details of environment. It is fullest in *Mark*. It comes into the middle of his story of the cure of the daughter of the ruler of the synagogue. In two of the Gospels Jesus is on his way to the house of the ruler of the synagogue, and is surrounded by multitudes of people, when a woman who had an issue of blood for twelve years came behind him and touched the border of his garment, and immediately was healed.

Jesus had not seen the woman, but he is represented as conscious that he had been touched and that virtue had gone out of him. He asked who had touched him. And then the woman, fearing and trembling, fell down before him and confessed that it was she who had done so.

Jesus then said to the trembling woman, "Daughter, be of good comfort; thy faith hath made thee whole; go in peace." Jesus did not say, "Thy sins are forgiven thee, go and sin no more"; only that the woman's faith had healed her. Once more a psychical miracle originating in the sufferer. In this miracle, simply to touch the clothes of Jesus had a healing efficacy. It exhibits the healing power of Jesus apart from his volition.

Some rationalistic critics argue from this that the story reduces Jesus from a psychical miracleworker to the position of a human magnetizer, who is conscious of a diminution of strength just as an electrical battery, after being drawn upon, has less power left to be drawn upon.

Such an idea of Jesus is said to be repugnant to the Christian consciousness, which requires that Jesus should act only under governance of his will. No previous knowledge on his part of the person touching him, not a word from her to him or from him to her, nothing but a touch—this, they think, degrades Jesus. An involuntary exercise of curative power.

Is there any warrant for the historical reality of the narrative? My conclusion is that there is. The woman's own forces of recuperation were called into full play the moment she succeeded in pushing through the throng and touching Jesus, having persuaded herself in advance that that would be enough to effect her cure.

Strauss gives many incidents from *Acts* to show that sick persons were cured by the involuntary acts of the apostles. We are told, for example, that the handkerchief of Paul cured all kinds of sick people, and that the very shadow of Peter had the same efficacy, while the apocryphal Gospels represent a mass of cures to have been brought about by means of the swaddling clothes of the infant Jesus and the water in which he was washed.

Are we to understand all this as true, or as self-deception? I think neither. They all presuppose the awakening of psychical powers in the persons cured, and modern science does not deny the great curative power that lies in faith. Not the handkerchief, not the shadow of Peter, not the swaddling clothes of Jesus, or the water in which he was washed, but the *belief* of the sufferer that these are enough—this is the origin of this miracle.

"Natural science," says Strauss, "is not able to accredit such cures on grounds of natural law. Hence, these cures are driven from the objective to the subjective, and receive their explanation from psychology. Now psychology, taking into account that without a real curative power in the reputed miracleworker, solely by the strong confidence of the sick person that he possesses this power, maladies which have a close connexion with the nervous system may be cured."

This is all the miracles claim—led by strong faith in the healing power of anything that came in contact with Jesus many sick persons became well.

Therefore, I do not regard these stories as legendary. I think they have their origin in the Messianic hope—the firm belief that the Messiah when he came would work miracles by the exercise of his will, by his mere presence, by the sufferers touching him or his garments, that everything about him would be charged with the power of healing. And, also, I think they are proof that the multitudes were accepting Jesus as the divine messenger who was bringing this power.

It all presupposes that the people are looking upon Jesus as a supernatural being.

XVII. Cures on the Sabbath

"In the great theatre of disease, crowded with all kinds of sufferers, Jesus, the exalted and miraculously gifted physician, appears and selects one who is afflicted with the most obstinate malady, that by his restoration he may present the most brilliant proof of his miraculous power." So says Strauss in dealing with the miracle of the impotent man at the pool of Bethesda.

Jesus might have cured others at the pool, but he did not. He chose the worst perhaps. Why? Were not the others as worthy of being cured? Or was Jesus thinking only of himself, or displaying the highest curative power by taking the worst case?

"For the rest," says Strauss, "this highly embellished history of a miraculous 'cure' was represented as happening on the Sabbath, probably because the command to take up the bed offered the most suitable, and spectacular, occasion for the reproach of violating the Sabbath." Strauss is deliberately bent on dishonouring the miracle by showing that it could only have occurred if it had an unworthy motive.

Jesus gave great scandal to the Jews by occasionally performing his miracles on the Sabbath. The two leading cases of the supposed desecration of the Sabbath are the plucking of the ears of corn by the disciples (*Matthew* XII, 1) and the cure of the man with the withered hand (*Mark* III, 3). The plucking took place in the fields. According to *Matthew* and *Mark,* Jesus went from this scene immediately into the synagogue of the same district (not named) and there defended himself against his accusers, calling on the man to stand forth in the midst and then casting reproving glances around. "Only such cures, it is said, were prohibited on the Sabbath as were attended by labour," says Strauss. "But there was a controversy between the schools of Hillel and Shammai whether it was permitted to administer consolation to the sick on the Sabbath."

The objection of the Jews to the cures of Jesus on the Sabbath appears to be that he used natural means of cure which involved labour, however slight. Therefore, they were violations of the Sabbath to the strict Jews. The miracle of the outstretching of the hand is thought to have its parallel in the Old Testament (I *Kings* XIII, 1). The point of the story is that (in *Luke* and *Mark*) Jesus's defence lies in the question, "Is it lawful to do good on the Sabbath or to do evil, to save life or to destroy it?"

"Further," according to Strauss, "it cannot have been cures in general with which that saying of Jesus was connected, but any service performed by him or his disciples which might be regarded as rescuing or preserving life, and which was accompanied by external labour."

Apparently the Pharisees of the time of Jesus rigidly excluded such acts, but Jesus held them to be justified even in the strictest observance of the Sabbath—to save life or to preserve it—and the balance of rabbinical opinion to this day is in his favour.

In the porches of the pool of Bethesda in Jerusalem, Jesus found a man who had been lame for thirty-eight years. It was the Sabbath, yet Jesus told him to get up and carry his bed. Therefore, he told him to labour on the Sabbath. Incidentally, it has been held by Woolston, an English critic of some notoriety in his day for denying and even ridiculing the miracles of Jesus, that all that Jesus did in this case was to expose a hypocrite. There is not the faintest justification for this in the Gospel story. Moreover, the sequel disperses it. That the man had a real infirmity is shown by what Jesus says to him when he meets him later, "Behold, thou art made whole; sin no more, lest a worse thing come unto thee." Here is an undoubted miracle.

XVIII.   Jesus and Disease

Did Jesus regard disease as the punishment of sin? On the face of the records it would appear that he did. In curing the paralytic in Nazareth, Jesus says to the sick man, "Son, be of good cheer, thy sins be forgiven thee."

This was in accordance with the Jewish opinion that an evil befalling an individual, especially disease, was a punishment of his sins. This opinion was held by the Hebrews of the Old Testament also. As in *Leviticus* (XXVI, 14), where it is said as by God that if His people will not hearken unto Him and do His commandments; if they despise His statutes and abhor His judgments, He will appoint over them terror, consumption, and the burning ague that shall consume their eyes and cause sorrow of the heart. Further, that God will bring seven times more plagues upon them according to their sins. Again, in *Deuteronomy* (XXVIII) it is said that if the people hearken not to the voice of God He will smite them with consumption and with a fever and with an inflammation (verse 22). He will also smite them with madness and blindness (verse 28).

Strauss says that if we had the Synoptic narratives only we should be compelled to believe that Jesus shared the opinion of his fellow-countrymen and contemporaries, that disease was the result of sin. "But it is said, there are other passages where Jesus directly contradicts this Jewish opinion," and that when he uses the language, "Son, be of good cheer, thy sins be forgiven thee," he is making merely an accommodation to the sick man, who must have believed he was stricken for his sins, and therefore the forgiveness of his sins was intended to promote his cure.

The principal passage quoted in support of this is the reply of

Jesus (*John* IX, 13) to his disciples when they find the man born blind, and they ask him whether his blindness was the consequence of his own sins or the sins of his parents. This was a very difficult question in Jewish theology, because that theology recognized that the consequences of sins could descend to the third and fourth generations.

It may here be observed that there have been early Christian theologians who have held the shocking opinion that children could commit sin before birth, while they were yet in the womb.

Jesus's answer to the question of the disciples was that neither for his own sins nor the sins of his parents was the man born blind, but that the cure which he was about to perform upon him might be an instrument in manifesting the miraculous power of God.

But what an appalling exhibition of cruelty on the part of Jesus! To think that, by the will of God, this innocent man and his innocent parents must endure all the terrible sufferings involved in his blindness from the time of his birth up to the time of his madness (bringing him down to begging by the high roads) in order that Christ might prove his Messiahship in the eyes of a group of disciples and a little throng (perhaps) of onlookers by curing his blindness!

Then think with what folly the explanation charges Jesus—that this clear-minded man of genius does not know that the same effect precisely would have been made upon the disciples and onlookers if the blind man had brought his blindness on himself by his misdeeds. The fact of the blind man being innocent or being guilty did not matter one straw in the reckoning of the miraculous power of his cure. The cure was the cure equally the same whether the man was innocent or guilty.

What, then, is the reason the evangelist gives for this explanation? Obviously, he had a theory in theology to support, an objection of the enemies of Christianity, or of Jesus, to answer. Surely that is the beginning and end of the explanation, which is utterly unworthy of Jesus as given in the fourth Gospel.

Again, Jesus says to the man at Bethesda who was lame for thirty-eight years, "Sin no more, lest a worse thing come unto thee." "This," says Strauss, "is equivalent to saying to the paralytic, 'Thy sins are forgiven thee' and that if he sins again a worse disease than paralysis will be inflicted upon him by God."

What did Jesus mean? Did he mean that the disease of the man was the direct and natural cause of certain excesses in his earlier life? Or was the idea of certain natural excesses and certain diseases outside the mode of thinking in the time of Jesus? Did the Jews think that there was a positive connexion between disease and sin, so that the one could not exist without the other? And did Jesus share this view?

The fact is that in the Gospel stories there is no hint of natural excesses causing the diseases. Sin is the only thing spoken of, and we are compelled to believe that Jesus was thinking of sin only. So says Strauss. But what does sin mean to Jesus? Merely an operation of the mind? If a man commits an act which leads on to disease is not that act sin? If so, who is to forbid Jesus from using the language of his time (the only language his people understand), and saying that if a man who has, one way or other, violated and outraged the laws of nature, the laws of health, and thereby become diseased, that he has sinned? *He has sinned*. He has committed a crime against God, who, if He is the Creator of man, desires his well-being, his health, not his destruction by disease.

But now comes the question, "Did Jesus mean that all disease and suffering was sin?" If so, is it sin in a man to suffer from the operation of natural forces which he could not in any way control? Say he was struck blind by lightning, has he therefore sinned? Is an innocent child who has fallen from his nurse's arms, injured his spine and become a paralytic for life, a sinner?

It is monstrous to think so. We have no reason to say Jesus ever thought so. Where he uses the words, "Sin no more," "Thy sins are forgiven thee," he applies them, we are compelled to believe, to distinct cases of disease brought on by sin—sin in the sufferer, or, it may be, in the parents of the sufferer on the principle of the terrible law relating to the third and fourth generations.

Again, there is the passage in *Luke* (XIII, 1) where Jesus is told of the Galileans whom Pilate had caused to be slain while they were in the act of sacrificing, and of others who were killed by the falling of a tower. "There were present at that season some that told him of the Galileans, whose blood Pilate had mingled with their sacrifices." And Jesus answering said, "Suppose ye that these Galileans were sinners above all Galileans, because they suffered such things? I tell you, Nay; but, except ye repent, ye shall all likewise perish." He says the same about the eighteen who were killed by the fall of the tower in Siloam. Obviously, these were two historical incidents of recent occurrence.

What did Jesus mean?

The informants clearly meant that the Galileans and the eighteen had died as a divine visitation for their wickedness. Jesus did not believe these men were especially sinful. But that all men were sinners, and that unless all sinful men repented all men would perish.

Strauss does not see how in these expressions Jesus is repudiating the popular Jewish notion. The sense of the words of Jesus is this: that these men met with their calamities is no evidence of their *special* wickedness, any more than that the fact that you have been spared is evidence of your special virtue. On the contrary, earlier or later evil will befall all men unless they repent.

This vulgar Hebrew opinion (of the supposed law of connexion between disease and sin) is in contradiction to the view we find in the Sermon on the Mount, in the parable of the rich man, and elsewhere, and according to which the righteous in this world are the suffering, the poor and the sick. Both of these views are, in Strauss's opinion, to be found in the discourses of Jesus.

How did he solve for himself the opposition between two ideas of the world, presented by the two different sides of the culture of his age?

XIX. *Conclusions*

My own conclusion is that Jesus did not think disease was always the punishment of sin; that in the cases in which he speaks of sin in relation to cure he cannot be accused of attributing *all* disease to sin; that he may reasonably be understood in all such cases to speak of diseases that have been the natural punishment of the transgressions of nature, of excesses, therefore of sins against nature and consequently against God, the author of nature; that it is not in every case of the cure of diseases that he says "Go and sin no more," and therefore it is reasonable to think the words apply only to the cases in which the disease was due to sin (in the foregoing sense); that there is no other reason to assume that he accepted the Jewish idea that all disease was due to sin, any more than to assume that he thought good health was always the reward of virtue; and, finally, that his general theory of the blessing that awaits the sufferings by poverty and disease forbids utterly the belief that he thought disease the consequence of sin.

In proof of the last point I advance, as to me unanswerable, the spirit of the opening passages of the Sermon on the Mount in which blessings and the reward of the kingdom of Heaven are promised to sufferers of all kinds, and also the parable of the rich man and Lazarus.

In this parable (*Luke* XVI, 20) Lazarus is described as being full of sores, yet he is carried at his death into Abraham's bosom. There is no mention of his repentance; there is only the fact of his disease and poverty, and that during his lifetime he received evil things. On the other hand, the rich man is described as receiving good things during his lifetime, and there is no indication that he suffered from disease. The obvious and reasonable inference is that he did not suffer from disease, yet at his death he is condemned to hell. Lazarus, the diseased man, receives the reward of Heaven at his death. The rich man, who had every earthly blessing, receives the punishment of eternal torment. Against this, I see no reply. Jesus did not think all disease the punishment of sin.

But how do I account for the theory of Jesus in the cases of the Galileans who were slain by Pilate and the eighteen who were killed by the fall of the tower of Siloam? Jesus says they were no more guilty than other people, and that unless all repent all shall likewise perish. Does he mean that all men are sinful by nature? That this sin in nature must be wiped out by repentance or else evil will befall? Does he mean that the evil that will befall is evil in this life—death by Pilate or by the fall of a tower?

I think he means:

1. That all men are sinful.

2. That punishment of man's sin must come if he does not repent.

3. That the punishment he predicts is not necessarily punishment in this life, or that it has any necessary relation to disease.

4. That he does indeed think that some specific cases of disease cured by him were due to sin, and therefore he told the persons he cured to sin no more lest the sins, or perhaps worse, should fall on them. This is indicated in his parable of the leper out of whom came a devil, which returned with seven other devils, thus making the latter end of the man worse than the first.

Jesus does not mean or ever say that all disease is the punishment of sin, but in one specific and outstanding parable he shows that disease was followed by a blessed reward and therefore had no relation to sin. Consequently, I conclude that Jesus did not accept the old Jewish notion that disease and sin were one.

CHAPTER XXII

The Miracles
(Continued)

I. Jesus Rendering Himself Invisible

THERE ARE at least three, perhaps four, occasions during his lifetime in which Jesus renders himself invisible in the midst of crowds. There are also several occasions after his Resurrection on which he disappears as if he had become, or was, a spectre.

Take the incidents during his lifetime. The first is recorded in *Luke* IV, 28–30. After his baptism in Jordan and his Temptation in the wilderness, Jesus returned "in the power of the Spirit" into Galilee. There he taught in two synagogues.

He came to Nazareth. This might have been early after his return to Galilee, because Nazareth is on the southern side of Galilee, the side from which he was entering it. It was the city in which he had been brought up, and "as his custom was [showing plainly that he had done the same before he went up to his baptism, during that unrecorded period of his young manhood of which the Gospels give us no direct record but only this and two other indications] he went into the synagogue on the Sabbath Day and stood up for to read."

The minister of the synagogue, the *Chazan,* also according to custom, gave him the book of the prophet Esaias (*Isaiah*) and when he had opened it he read aloud the following passage which, though not literally quoted in the Gospel of Luke, is essentially right in substance:

> The Spirit of the Lord is upon me, because He hath anointed me to preach the Gospel to the poor; He hath sent me to heal the brokenhearted, to preach deliverance to the captives, and recovering of sight to the blind, to set at liberty them that are bruised, to preach the acceptable year of the Lord.

After Jesus had read this passage he closed the book, gave it back to the minister of the synagogue and sat down. There was an

obvious silence, during which the eyes of all who were in the synagogue were fastened on him, as if they were wondering what he
had read that passage for, and what was the message he wished
them to take from it.

Then, reading their thoughts, Jesus said, "This day is this scripture fulfilled in your ears." Clearly, he meant his people to understand that the prophecy of Isaiah was that day fulfilled in his own
person—that God had that day anointed him to "preach the acceptable year of the Lord."

In other words, Jesus was asking them to understand that he
(Jesus) was the Messiah foretold by Isaiah.

The people were amazed, and said to each other, "Is not this
Joseph's son?" Jesus read their minds again and said, "Ye will
surely say unto me this proverb, Physician, heal thyself. Whatsoever we have heard done in Capernaum, do also here in thy country."

By this it becomes clear that as he could not since his baptism
have visited Capernaum before coming to Nazareth (Capernaum
being nearly twenty miles farther on) he must have said and done
things (miracles probably) at Capernaum before his baptism, in
that unrecorded period of which the Gospels give no account.

Jesus then explained why he had done in Capernaum what he
had not yet done in Nazareth—things which were understood to
be proofs of his Messiahship. "Verily I say unto you, No prophet
is accepted in his own country."

After that Jesus carried the attack on his native city a stage
further—to the point of an attack on the scepticism of his own
race—and showed that God accepts the Gentile in preference to
His chosen people, where the faith of His chosen people fails.

He told two stories from the Old Testament. The first was of
the three years and six months of famine in the land. There were
many widows in Israel in those days of Elijah, but unto none of
them was Elijah sent save to a widow of Sidon, a pagan in a pagan
city. The second was of the leprosy that was rife in Israel in the
time of Eliseus the prophet, but none of the lepers was cleansed
save Naaman, a Syrian, not a Jew. Thus would God do with the
children of Abraham, if they rejected the Messiah.

What was the result of these scorching words? The people of
the synagogue of Nazareth heard these things, and, filled with
wrath, they rose up and thrust Jesus out of the city, and led him to

the brow of the hill whereon the city was built, intending to cast him down headlong. But, we are told, *passing through the midst of them* he went his way. Are we to understand that the evangelist meant that Jesus rendered himself invisible—dematerialized himself, so that they could not see him—that they lost him? He went on to Capernaum.

The second occasion on which it is, apparently, recorded that Jesus rendered himself invisible in a crowd is in *John* VIII, 59. Jesus was in Jerusalem. It was shortly after one of the Jewish feasts. He had his lodgings on the Mount of Olives, and, coming down in the early morning to the Temple, he had shamed the scribes and Pharisees who had brought before him a woman who had been taken in adultery. Thereafter, there had followed an angry interview between Jesus and the Pharisees, turning first on Jesus's denunciation of them as the sons of the Devil, and next on the claim of Jesus to come from God. "Ye are of your father the Devil, and the lusts of your father ye will do. . . . He that is of God heareth God's words. Ye therefore hear them not, because ye are not of God." To this the Jews replied, "Say we not well that thou art a Samaritan, and hast a devil?" and Jesus answered, "I have not a devil. If a man keep my saying, he shall never see death." Then the Jews retorted, "Now we know that thou hast a devil. Abraham is dead, and the prophets; and thou sayest If a man keep my saying, he shall never taste of death. Art thou greater than our father Abraham . . . ?" Jesus answered, "Your father Abraham rejoiced to see my day: and he saw it, and was glad." The Jews laughed at this, replying "Thou art not yet fifty years old, and hast thou seen Abraham?" and to this Jesus made answer, "Before Abraham was, I am."

Clearly the Jews took this to be a distinct claim to divinity, to be the Son of God. That was an unforgivable offence. They took stones to stone Jesus, apparently intending to kill him as he came out of the Temple. But "Jesus *hid himself* and went out of the Temple, going through the midst of them, and so passed by."

From this last passage it can hardly be questioned that the evangelist meant to say that by the exercise of supernatural power Jesus rendered himself invisible, and so passed through the midst of the infuriated crowd of Jews and out of the Temple.

Later, Jesus escaped out of the hands of the Jews again, in

circumstances so nearly akin that they leave the same impression, namely, that he rendered himself invisible, dematerialized himself, and so left Jerusalem to avoid being stoned out of it (*John* IX and X). Jesus had heard that the Pharisees had cast out the man who had been born blind, and the result was an angry encounter between himself and the Pharisees. Jesus began it by saying that he came into the world that those that were blind might see, and those that thought they saw might be made blind.

"Are we blind also?" asked the Pharisees, and Jesus answered, "If ye were blind ye should have no sin, but now ye say, We see, therefore your sin remaineth."

Taking his illustration from the Palestinian shepherd, beautifully and perfectly rendered, Jesus spoke of himself as a good shepherd, who lays down his life for the sheep. At this there was further division among the Jews, some saying, "He has a devil and is mad." Others saying, "These are not the words of one who has a devil. Can a devil open the eyes of the blind?"

It was the time of the Feast of the Dedication. It was winter. Jesus was walking in the Temple in Solomon's Porch when some of the Jews came about him and said, "If you are the Christ, tell us plainly."

Jesus answered, "I and my Father are one."

That was enough. It was blasphemy to the Jews, and once again they took up stones to stone him.

Jesus said, "Many good works have I showed you from my Father; for which of those works do ye stone me?" The Jews replied, "For a good work we stone thee not; but for blasphemy; and because that thou, being a man, makest thyself God."

John records, *"But he escaped out of their hand."*

Is it meant by the evangelist that, as before, he "hid himself," made himself invisible?

Was Jesus stoned out of Jerusalem? I think it not improbable that he was.

Such are the reports in the Gospels of the occasions on which Jesus escaped from hostile crowds who were seeking to take his life.

Do the evangelists intend in all cases to convey the impression that he rendered himself invisible—in some way dematerialized himself—so as to save his life? I think this is undoubtedly their intention—to suggest that among the miraculous powers of Jesus was that of making his own body invisible in a crowd by a sudden exercise of his will.

But if Jesus did actually possess this power, and if he exercised it on three, or perhaps four, separate occasions during his lifetime, how does it come to pass that the people of Palestine did not realize that he was a divine person? There was no record in the world, outside the region of magic, of any other man ever having done so. Why did not this fact alone make a great impression?

We do not hear that if it happened it made any impression upon anybody. After it had occurred in Nazareth his fellow-citizens gave no indication of fear of him. After it had occurred in the Temple, the people did not show fear that it might occur again when he walked in Solomon's Porch.

In short, his known power of dematerializing himself—if he ever exercised it—produced no impression whatever upon anybody. It might have been the commonest event of life instead of the rarest—within the reach of every man instead of beyond the reach of any man who had before lived on earth.

This, therefore, is, in my judgment, outside belief as an explanation of what occurred on these occasions. What *is* the explanation which commends itself to reason and to Faith?

The natural explanation of these incidents is that Jesus overawed and mastered the crowds by the sheer force of his commanding personality—the hostile crowds in all cases simply fell back before the majesty of his person. We have endless evidences in the Gospels of the power of the personality of Jesus. Nearly every dscription of his relation to others gives an idea of his power. He was a commanding, masterful man. He compelled obedience. Nearly every adjective used about him, every phrase describing him, gives proof of this. It passes through and through the story of his life. So strongly do I feel this that if I were to meet with any phrase which indicated weakness of will on his part, feebleness of character, I should instantly suspect it as spurious. No imaginative writer could possibly use more emphatic words to describe a powerful character than the Gospels use about Jesus.

It is only in the prophecies, in one of them in particular (*Isaiah* LIII, 1–12), that a different personality is indicated.

> He was oppressed and he was afflicted, yet he opened not his mouth. He is brought as a lamb to the slaughter, and as a sheep before her shearers is dumb, so he opened not his mouth.

This passage (*Isaiah* LIII, 7), accepted by Christians as prophetic of Jesus, is perhaps the *chief* (not the only) foundation for the commonly accepted idea of the character of Jesus as "meek and mild."

But it is not supported by the Gospels' portrait. In the Gospels Jesus is not chiefly distinguished for meekness and mildness. On the contrary, the Gospel portrait of him is of a man of quite opposite characteristics. His first characteristic is strength. He "commands" the people to sit down in the miracle of the feeding of the multitudes. When he calls his disciples he commands them, "Follow me." When John asks him to call down fire from Heaven on the inhospitable Samaritans, he tells him sharply that he does not know what spirit he is of. When Peter tempts him he says, "Get thee behind me, Satan." He denounces the Pharisees to their faces. He whips the money-changers out of the Temple. When the soldiers come by night to arrest him—in Gethsemane—he steps forward and demands to know whom they want, and says, "I am he," and they fall to the ground before him.

He asks them again whom they seek, and when they say "Jesus of Nazareth," he answers, "I have told you that I am he." This is the conduct of a resolute man, a man accustomed to command. He had almost to command the soldiers to arrest him. All through his life this personality shows itself. He is a master of men. Men are constantly falling back before him. Power and strength are his chief human qualities. He has the qualities of his strength and power.

Like nearly all strong men he is gentle with the weak. Like nearly all powerful men he is slow to anger, but when roused to wrath he is overwhelming. Like nearly all manly men he is tender to women and gentle with children. Like nearly all virile men he is pure towards women. Being a sinless man, he is merciful to sinners. But his strength and power and control over men is in evidence all through his life.

Even his silence at his trial is strong—the silence of contempt (as when before Herod)—and his defiance at the challenge of Caiaphas is that of one who does not know the name of fear. His answers to Pilate are the answers of one whose strength is superior to Pilate's power. Pilate feels this and bursts into a flare of passion, but his anger makes no impression upon Jesus.

In lesser points of personal manner and, perhaps, of personal appearance, Jesus showed all through the Gospels this masterfulness of character. He is frequently described as "looking," showing apparently that his eyes were large and his gaze was steady and often long. We know that he sometimes spoke in public to vast multitudes in the open air, and from this we know that his voice was deep and clear and resonant. What Luther said of Paul was yet more true of Jesus—"He spoke pure flame."

The crowd of women who followed him from Galilee to Jerusalem, and who stood, although afar off, at his crucifixion, after the disciples had fled, testify not to the womanly side of his nature but to the manly side.

What he was like to look upon we do not know. But I am convinced that tradition and what is called Christian art have belied him. The painters—most of whom clearly and palpably knew as nearly as possible nothing of the Gospels, or they would never have used scenes and incidents that have no place in them—have through all the ages pictured Jesus as a dreamer, a long-haired, sleepy, abstract person, whose eyes are always looking inward. I am convinced that this is wrong. What a contrast we find in the energy of Jesus, his straight, powerful, commanding language, his hard blows, his fighting spirit!

For my own part I think of him as a big man, a powerful man, a man whom no ordinary man, or even crowd of men, would molest or even attempt to browbeat. I think that men were drawn to him by his power, and that they fell back from him as a result of his anger. From all this, and much more of the same kind that can easily be deduced from his memoirs, I conclude that the reasonable explanation of the escape of Jesus from the crowds that attempted to kill him, or stone him—at Nazareth, in the Temple, and elsewhere—was that he overawed them by his personality, his commanding presence, above all by his sense of being in the right.

This simple natural explanation is sufficient for me. Why then these incidents in the Gospels in which the evangelists appear to desire to indicate the exercise of supernatural powers by Jesus to enable him to escape danger, if not death?

I think those explanations came afterwards—not from eye-witnesses of the life of Jesus, not from the apostles who were with him from day to day, but from the writers who came later and wrote the Gospels as we now have them on the foundations of their memoirs or, as in the cases of Mark, Peter and John, from their recollections.

The moral of all the foregoing is that I believe in the absolute *manhood* of Jesus, in his humanity from first to last, and that I see no reason whatever for accepting any story which removes him from his humanity. *Jesus was a man*—none the less because he was also a god. Without his humanity his mission in the world, his life in the world, became meaningless—a spectral foolishness.

II. Raising of the Dead

There are three instances in the Gospels in which Jesus raises the dead. One is common to the three Synoptic Gospels; a second is peculiar to *Luke;* a third is peculiar to *John.*

The Widow's Son of Nain.

According to the chronology of *Luke* the earliest of these instances was that of the raising of the widow's son of Nain (*Luke* VII, 11–18).

Soon after the beginning of his ministry in Galilee, apparently about harvest time (say, May, A.D. 29) Jesus, while preaching in the cities and villages of Galilee, came to the city of Nain. This city is on the extreme southern side of Mount Tabor. Nain is not far from Nazareth. It is high up the mountain country above the Lake of Galilee, almost due west from Tiberias, which lies at the foot of the lake. Jesus had been in Capernaum the day before. There he had cured the servant of the centurion. He had gone up to Nain and many of his disciples were with him, and a multitude of people were following him.

As he approached the gate of the city a dead man was being carried out to burial, probably in a graveyard outside the gate. He was borne on a bier. Apparently, there was no sort of coffin. He was the only son of his mother and she was a widow. His mother was following him to his burial, and a number of the people of the city were going with her. She was in deep distress, and weeping. This was the funeral cortège Jesus came upon.

It was coming down the hills through the gate of Nain, while Jesus, his disciples and his followers were going up. Jesus had compassion on the woman and spoke to her.

"Weep not," he said, and then he stepped to the bier and touched it, and the bearers stood still. Then Jesus spoke to the dead man, saying, "Young man, I say unto thee, Arise."

Upon this the dead man sat up and began to speak, and Jesus delivered him to his mother.

This miracle made a profound impression upon the spectators. They glorified God, declaring that a great prophet had risen among them, and that God had visited His people. The rumour of this incident went forth through all Judæa, as well as all the region round about Nain—Galilee, with its countless cities and villages.

The natural explanation of the foregoing incident is discussed by Strauss, who says that Jesus *"speaks* to the young man lying on the coffin." But there is no mention of a coffin, and in an eastern country in the time of Jesus there would be no coffin. The dead would be wrapped in grave clothes, with the face open, until the last moment, and then covered at the instant of placing it in the grave.

Now, say the rationalists, no one would speak to a dead person, but only to one who would be capable of hearing. A miracle-worker, they say, capable of raising the actual dead, would go to work without calling on the co-operation of his subject. But, according to Strauss, the argument of the rationalists would require us to believe that all the dead whom Christ will raise at the last day are not dead at all, as otherwise they would not hear his voice, which it is expressly said they *will* do. ("Marvel not at this, for the hour is coming in the which all that are in the graves shall hear his voice, and shall come forth"—*John* V, 28.)

"Certainly one who is spoken to must be supposed to hear, and in a certain sense to be living. But this presupposes that he who raises the dead can penetrate even the ears of those from whom life has departed." Strauss suggests that it is "a tissue of fiction."

Is it?

Strauss says, "What an empty, presuming comforter would be he who, when a mother was about to consign her only son to the grave, should forbid her even the relief of tears, unless he could offer her some ground of consolation."

The idea of the rationalists is that Jesus saw some signs of life in the youth, and so spoke the words which completely awakened him. The words of Jesus, "Young man, I say unto thee, Arise," are the authoritative command of the miracleworker. They are not like the encouraging words of the physician on recalling his patient from the unconsciousness produced by an anæsthetic, "You are all right," and so on. The evangelist clearly regards the incident as a miraculous resurrection of the dead. It is also explicitly said that "Jesus regarded his deed as a miracle."

In forming my own conclusion I begin by calling attention to the custom in the East of burying the dead a few hours after their decease. This is forced upon them by the heat of the climate. The incident of the raising of the only son of the widow of Nain took place in summer. It was at, or perhaps about, the time of the corn harvest—the incident is, at least, narrated after that of the disciples plucking the ears of corn on the Sabbath. It was, therefore, not earlier than the middle to the end of May, and might have been in June. At that time it would have been very hot in Palestine. To keep a dead body overnight would be perilous even in country districts. In a little town like Nain, perched upon the rocks, probably with narrow streets into which the air would enter little—so built to protect the inhabitants from the storms of wind in winter—it would be extremely dangerous.

To bury early after death was not a bad practice of the Jews, as Strauss says, but a condition forced upon them. The consequence would be the growth of the practice of premature burial. Remember that, as everybody knows who has lived in the East, the Oriental has frequently only one serious illness during his life and that when he becomes seriously ill he prepares to die, and generally does die. This effect on the sick man has its effect on his family. They never doubt that actual death has taken place when the usual signs of life are gone. The pulse fails, the heart is not felt to beat, consciousness is gone, there is no movement—the man is dead.

Modern science knows that this is not always so. A man may appear to be dead hours before he is actually dead. *He may be dead in the sense that he has lost all powers within himself to call himself back to active life.* In that condition, unrecognizable to the people of Palestine in the time of Jesus, the Jews hurried their dead to the grave to save themselves from infection, or perhaps from contagion. They had no uncertainty or misgiving in doing so. And they were generally justified. Particularly were they justified in the case of an epidemic. And it is precisely in such a case that death, in the sense I have described, is most deceptive.

In cholera, for example, especially in eastern countries, there is a condition that is not distinguishable from death. It may last for hours and then end in absolute death. Only the great physician knows that recovery is possible. He himself cannot bring it to pass. Only nature operating by itself can do so. Therefore he waits and sometimes the spirit of life, which hovers somewhere about the dead, reanimates him.

Now come to the case of Jesus and the widow's son of Nain. He may have died of cholera. His family may be compelled to hurry him into his grave. He is dead to all purposes. If he is buried, he will never know, nobody will ever know, that the power of life was about him still. But Jesus knew this. He possessed the power of penetrating to the living power that still hovers round the dead. Jesus called to that spirit. It answered him. He penetrated the dead ears. The dead heard. He rose and spoke.

This is a miracle, but it is not an outrage of the laws of nature. It is an effort of super-nature—the super-nature that was in Jesus above all men.

Such is my interpretation of the raising of the widow's son of Nain.

The Daughter of Jairus

There are three records of this miracle.

1. In *Matthew* (IX, 23-26). Immediately after the first visit of the disciples of John the Baptist (the visit in which they asked why the disciples of Jesus did not fast) a certain ruler (not otherwise named or described), possibly a civil ruler, came to Jesus and said that his daughter was dead, but if he would come to her she would live.

Jesus followed him, and so did his disciples. When he came to the ruler's house he saw the usual crowd of people and the usual minstrels in it, who, in Eastern manner at a death, were moaning and wailing and singing and playing and otherwise making a noise. Jesus said to these people, "Give place, for the maid is not dead but sleepeth."

At these words the people laughed him to scorn, so sure were they that the girl *was* dead. It does not appear that down to this moment he had seen the girl or entered the death chamber. But now, having caused the noisy mourners to be turned out of, or away from, the house, he went into the death room, took the maid by the hand, and at that touch she arose. The narrative in *Matthew* concludes by saying that the fame of this event went abroad into all the land.

2. In *Mark* (V, 22–43). Shortly after the return of Jesus from the country of the Gadarenes, when he passed over the sea to the other side (probably to the western coast of Galilee between Tiberias and Magdala), one of the rulers of the synagogue, Jairus by name, fell at the feet of Jesus and told him that his daughter lay near to death, and prayed of him to come and lay hands on her that she might be healed and live.

Jesus went with him, followed by a crowd of people. Before he reached the house of Jairus messengers came to Jairus to tell him that his daughter was dead, and therefore there was no reason to trouble the Master any further. Jesus heard the message and said to Jairus, "Be not afraid; only believe." Then coming to Jairus's home, having brought with him only Peter, James and John, and seeing a tumult about it or in it of people who wept and wailed greatly, he said, "Why make ye this ado and weep? The damsel is not dead, but sleepeth."

The people laughed him to scorn for this. He put them all out, and then, taking the father and mother of the girl with him, he entered into the room where the girl was and found her lying on her bed or couch. She was twelve years of age. Then he took the young girl by the hand and, speaking to her in the Aramaic tongue (her own tongue, the tongue of her country), he said, "Damsel, I say unto thee, Arise." And straightway the girl arose and walked. The parents who saw this miracle were greatly astonished, but Jesus charged them to say nothing about it to anyone. Also he ordered that something should be given to the girl to eat.

3. In *Luke* (VIII, 41–56). After, as in *Mark,* the return of Jesus from the country of the Gadarenes to the western side of Galilee, a man named Jairus, who was a ruler of the synagogue, fell at his feet and besought him to come to his house to see his only daughter, about twelve years of age, who lay dying. Jesus went with him, but, before he reached the ruler's house, somebody came from it to Jairus and told him not to trouble the man as his daughter was dead. Jesus heard this and said to Jairus, "Fear not; believe only, and she shall be made whole."

When he reached the house he would not allow anybody to go in with him, except Peter, James and John, and the father and mother of the young girl. All the people were weeping, but Jesus said, "Weep not; she is not dead, but sleepeth." The people laughed him to scorn, knowing that she was dead.

The story is here badly told, for we read next that he put them all out, and took the girl by the hand and called to her, saying, "Maid, arise." And the spirit came again to the girl, and straightway she arose, and Jesus commanded them to give her meat.

The parents of the child were astonished, but Jesus charged them that they were to tell no man what had been done. Thus, the story in *Luke* is the same as in *Mark,* except that it is confused in one particular and badly told.

Such are the three narratives of this miracle. The divergencies are not material, but some critics have concluded that they are important enough to justify the conclusion that there were two events, not one. I think such criticism is foolishness. Clearly, there is only one event narrated, but with slight variations of time and minor incidents. Strauss says that the exclusion of the minstrels is an argument against this being a miracle. The only reason for the exclusion can be that such persons were unfit, from want of faith, to be present, but surely, says Strauss, the sight of such a miracle would have been the very means of removing their unbelief. Again, he says that Mark and Luke regard the miracle as a mystery, known only to the three disciples and the parents of the girl. He quotes other critics who argue that the fact that Jesus, if he said anything to the girl on recalling her to life, addressed her in her native language is proof that the narrator (Mark) or his informant (Peter) was actually present at the event.

Then again, Strauss thinks that the *natural* interpretation of the incident speaks for itself in the fact (vouched for by all three evangelists) that Jesus said the girl was not dead, but merely in a sleeplike swoon. Therefore, both he and the rationalists and semi-rationalists, as well as some decided supernaturalists, believe, on the strength of the declaration of Jesus, that this was no case of raising from the dead at all, and therefore no miracle. Jesus does not in any of the narratives admit that the girl is dead or say that he has raised her to life. He speaks to her as one who can hear, to whose brain his voice and command can penetrate, and she answers by obeying him.

Against this, it is argued by the supernaturalists that Jesus does undoubtedly claim to have raised the dead, either in this case or the case of the widow's son of Nain, for, when a little later he sends back his answer to John to the question of whether he is, or is not, the Messiah, he distinctly commands John's disciples to tell their master that the dead are raised up.

Strauss argues that there are many conditions, especially in the illness of a young girl, which have a deceptive resemblance to death; that, in the indifferent state of medical science among the Jews in the time of Jesus, a swoon might be mistaken for death.

One other critic says that the life-giving word of Jesus, added to the touch of his hand, furnished with divine power, was the means of restoring the girl to life.

III. Conclusions

1. I can have no doubt that all three evangelists believe they are recording a miracle—that Jesus did actually raise to life one who had been actually dead. That they did undoubtedly think they were narrating an account of a resuscitation of the dead.

2. That Jesus actually behaved as one who believed he had raised the girl from the dead.

3. That to raise dead persons to life was expected of the Messiah, and that Jesus was thinking of this expectation when he told John's disciples that the dead were being raised to life.

4. That the girl *was* dead—in the sense that she might never have returned to life but for the life-giving power of Jesus in calling to the spirit, which returned to her.

5. That in this case, as in the case of the widow's son of Nain, but more naturally because death (or what stood for it) had obviously occurred within a few minutes (perhaps half an hour at the utmost) of the arrival of Jesus at the house of Jairus, all the arguments which apply to the case of the widow's son of Nain apply to the case of the daughter of Jairus.

6. That in these cases, as in all cases of resuscitation of the dead, there is this difference from the cases of the healing of diseases and the casting out of devils—that all the power exercised in the miracle is exercised by the miracle worker; that everything came from Jesus, that the dead did nothing to help him. The miracles of the raising of the dead, therefore, were the greatest of the miracles of Jesus, being the strongest exercise of his power.

7. That in this connexion it is well to remember a belief which has prevailed in many countries and in many ages, namely, that the life-spirit hovers round the body of the dead for a sensible time, sometimes counted in minutes, sometimes in hours, after the patient is beyond all uses of life, or when he is really dead. From this have come many practices of primitive but deeply religious people, such as the practice in remote parts of Ireland of throwing open the window of the death-chamber at the moment of death, and leaving it open for a considerable time so that the soul which still hovers about the dead may go forth when it wills to do so.

In other countries, in early times, it was usual to keep silence during a sensible period after death, because of the belief that the soul was still present in the death-room.

Elsewhere, particularly in Eastern countries, it was usual for numbers of persons, with musical instruments, to gather about the house, and make loud cries to the dead to come back to life. "Oh, why did ye die? Come back to your own," they would wail.

8. That something akin to the belief was in the evangelist Luke when he wrote of the daughter of Jairus, "And her spirit came again," as if the life-spirit had been out of her body, but was not yet gone, and Jesus called to it, and it came again to the girl.

9. That this explanation does not deny the miracle, or diminish the marvel of it, but recognizes and increases it. The girl was dead; the spirit was called back to the girl by Jesus; that it *came* back to her.

In the case of the raising of the son of the widow of Nain, it is clear that the chronology of Luke requires us to believe that all the disciples were called before the incident at Nain; also that the disciples were present with Jesus when he raised the widow's son. Therefore, Matthew was with him and saw the miracle. And Peter was with him and saw the miracle. And John, the son of Zebedee, was with him and saw the miracle. Yet Matthew does not mention it, although he gives accounts of miracles of less power and importance. Mark does not mention it, although he, too, tells of lesser miracles, and Mark, according to general belief, was instructed by Peter. And John does not mention it.

What are we to conclude? Either that Matthew and John did not write the gospels that bear their names, and that Mark was not inspired by Peter, or that Luke obtained his information from a non-apostolic and therefore less reliable source.

A certain concession is claimed for John. It is said that he did not retell the miracles told in the three Synoptic Gospels because he had still more startling stories to tell of miracles which they do not relate. But that leaves us on the horns of a great dilemma, as we shall see in the next case of the raising of the dead—the raising of Lazarus.

IV. The Raising of Lazarus

The miracle peculiar to the Gospel of *John* is that of the raising of Lazarus.

This is not only by far the most important of the miracles of its kind, but it is the only one which has a direct bearing on the fate of Jesus, being, as we shall see, connected by a sequence of incidents with his death.

The story—not at all well told—is in *John* XI, 1–46. Jesus is in the place where John the Baptist used to baptize—"Bethabara beyond Jordan" (see *John* I, 28), that is, Peræa. Many persons were with him, including his disciples, presumably all of them. A message came to him there from the two women Martha and Mary, whom we have heard of once before, through Luke, as living in a "certain village" not named by him. We now hear that they live at Bethany, a village nigh unto Jerusalem, about two miles off.

They send a message to Jesus at Bethabara to tell him of the illness of their brother Lazarus, of whom we have not heard before, although it appears that he was a friend both of Jesus and of his disciples. He is described, indeed, as an intimate friend of Jesus, whom Jesus loved as he also loved Martha and her sister. Obviously, the sisters were anxious that Jesus should come to their brother, believing that if he came their brother would not die.

But on receiving the message Jesus said, "This sickness is not unto death." And then he added that the illness of Lazarus was "for the glory of God, that the Son of God might be glorified thereby." Later he said, "Our friend Lazarus sleepeth, but I go that I may awake him out of sleep."

To this the disciples reply, "If he sleep, he shall do well."

The evangelist then tells us that Jesus had spoken of the death of Lazarus, whereas the disciples had supposed that he had spoken merely of Lazarus taking his rest in sleep. Jesus perceived this misunderstanding, and said plainly, "Lazarus is dead." He added that he was glad for their sakes that he had not been at Bethany, at the time of the illness of Lazarus, "to the intent ye may believe. Nevertheless, let us go unto him."

Jesus, with his disciples, then went up towards Bethany, and when he came near to it he heard that Lazarus had been four days dead and buried. Meantime, many of the Jews, including, apparently, some from Jerusalem, had come to comfort the sisters on the death of their brother. Martha heard that Jesus was coming towards Bethany and she went out to meet him, leaving Mary, with her friends, at home.

When Martha met Jesus she said, "Lord, if thou hadst been here, my brother had not died. But I know that even now, whatsoever thou wilt ask of God, God will give it thee." Jesus answered, "Thy brother shall rise again." Martha then said, "I know that he shall rise again in the resurrection at the last day." Whereupon Jesus answered, "I am the resurrection and the life; he that believeth in me, though he were dead, yet shall he live. And whosoever liveth and believeth in me shall never die. Believest thou this?"

To this Martha replied, "Yea, Lord; I believe that thou art the Christ, the Son of God, which should come into the world," and having said this she returned to her house and said secretly to Mary, her sister (why secretly is not apparent) : "The master is come and calleth for thee."

When Mary heard this she arose quickly and hurried out to meet Jesus, and the friends who had been comforting her went out with her, thinking she was going to the grave to weep. Mary met Jesus where Martha had left him, outside the town, and fell at his feet, saying, what her sister had said, "Lord, if thou hadst been here, my brother had not died."

When Jesus saw Mary weeping, and the friends who had followed her weeping, he was troubled and asked, "Where have ye laid him?" They answered, "Lord, come and see."

The evangelist tells us that Jesus wept, and that the people said, "Behold how he loved him!" But some of them said, "Could not this man, which opened the eyes of the blind, have caused that even this man should not have died?"

They came to the grave. We are told it was a cave, and that a stone lay upon it—not *against* it. Jesus said, "Take ye away the stone." Then Martha said to Jesus, "Lord, by this time he stinketh; for he hath been dead four days." Jesus answered, "Said I not unto thee, that, if thou wouldest believe thou shouldest see the glory of God?" Observe that he had not, according to *John,* said this to Martha, but had said something like it to the disciples at Bethabara.

The people took away the stone from the cave in which Lazarus was buried. And Jesus lifted up his eyes and prayed, saying, "Father, I thank Thee that Thou hast heard me. And I know that Thou hearest me always; but because of the people which stand by I said it, that they may believe that Thou hast sent me."

Having said thus, he cried with a loud voice, "Lazarus, come forth." And he that was dead came forth, bound hand and foot with grave clothes, and with his face bound about with a napkin. And Jesus said unto them, "Loose him, and let him go."

Such is the story of the raising of Lazarus as told in the Gospel of John. It is told nowhere else.

Although all the other disciples appear to have been present, only John mentions it. Matthew must have seen it, yet his Gospel, which gives the far less important and remarkable incident of the raising of the daughter of Jairus, says nothing about it. In like manner, Peter must have witnessed the raising of Lazarus, yet he said nothing about it to Mark, or else Mark did not believe it. And Luke, who heard from some non-apostolic authority the story of the raising of the widow's son of Nain, heard nothing of this far more important incident of the raising of Lazarus. John alone, of all the disciples who witnessed it, recorded it—if John the apostle was indeed the writer of the Gospel.

Again, none of the apostolic Epistles contain any reference to it—although it was this miracle, above all others, which led the chief priests and the Pharisees to seek the death of Jesus. Furthermore, John recorded it perhaps thirty years after the other evangelists had written. For thirty years the Gospels were without this story. Is it possible that the raising of Lazarus actually took place if only one of three inevitable witnesses says anything about it? Is it possible that it can be true if nobody either in the Gospels or the Epistles knew anything about it until sixty years after the death of Jesus?

Also, is it not possible that the writer of John's Gospel was not the apostle. If we look at the story as told in *John* we see that it is not told simply for itself, as the stories in *Mark* are told. It is obviously told for a dogmatic purpose. That purpose is to show

(1) that Jesus actually raised the dead after corruption had set in; therefore, there could be no question of a psychical miracle only, but of an actual corporeal miracle; and (2) that Jesus did this to establish the faith of his disciples first, and afterwards of the spectators, in the fact that he was the Son of God, who, when he came to earth, according to Jewish belief and tradition, was to raise the dead to life—no matter if corruption had set in and their bodies had gone to dust.

But this interpretation of the doctrinal purpose is beset with difficulties. It requires us to believe firstly that Lazarus had fallen sick and died, and his two sisters had been immersed in sorrow solely in order that Jesus might manifest his Messianic power in the most remarkable manner, and secondly that the miracle was performed in order that the disciples and the spectators should have further proof that Jesus was indeed the Son of God. But the first reason is almost barbaric and outrages human sensibilities, and the second is foolish, inasmuch as the disciples did not require any further proof that Jesus was the Son of God; they had already proclaimed him as such.

What am I to conclude? That the incident did not occur at all? This is not a necessary conclusion. That something else occurred which carried conviction to the mind of the evangelist that the dead had actually been raised? I think this is unquestionable. I also think that Jesus and nearly everybody who witnessed it regarded the event as a miraculous concurrence. I think some of those who witnessed the incident did not believe in it as a genuine resucitation, or that, if they did, they believed it was a miracle wrought by the help of Beelzebub, as in the case of the casting out of devils.

In *John* (XI, 45-47) we have the statement that while some believed on Jesus as the Son of God by reason of the raising of Lazarus, others went away and told the Pharisees and the chief priests; and the Pharisees, gathered together at a council, probably (almost certainly) believing that the whole incident of the raising of Lazarus was either an imposture or a miracle performed by evil agencies, decided to bring about the destruction of Jesus for fear that great numbers of the Jewish people would believe that he was what he claimed to be—the Son of God. No *man* could be the Son of God, therefore this man who claimed to be such must be destroyed.

I believe the incident of the raising of Lazarus to be an historical occurrence because:

(1) I find it difficult or impossible to account for the arrest, trial and crucifixion of Jesus except on the basis of this incident.

(2) The enormous number of people in Jerusalem at the Passover were believing that beyond the Mount of Olives, at Bethany, was a man who had raised a dead man to life; that this was by old prophecy and long tradition the last, highest and surest mark of the Messiah, the Christ, the King of the Jews; that therefore, Caiaphas, the high priest, said, "If we let him thus alone all men will believe on him; and the Romans shall come and take away both our place and nation." Therefore, he decided that Jesus must die, for "it is expedient for us that one man should die for the people and that the whole nation perish not."

Caiaphas was not prophesying when he said this. He was warning his council against a certain happening.

Now I connect all this sequence of incidents (from *John* XI, 45–50) and see them as the beginning of the definite plan to compass the death of Jesus.

Thus the story in *John* directly connects the miracle with the first positive act of the Sanhedrin. After that everything comes in order. It is then near to the time of the Passover. An attempt is made to take Jesus immediately, in order to dispose of him before the vast multitudes who come to Jerusalem for the Passover (many of them Galileans) arrive.

Jesus goes from Bethany to Ephraim. While he is away the chief priests put something like a price on his head. They also try to entrap Lazarus, because he was a reason why the people were believing in Jesus as the Son of God.

Six days before the Passover Jesus returns to Bethany. Next day, that is, five days before Passover, Jesus enters Jerusalem. People are now gathering into Jerusalem for the Passover in great numbers. Time is short. The chief priests and the Pharisees must do something speedily if they are to take him before the vast multitudes arrive—multitudes consisting mostly of believers in Jesus.

Hence the temptation offered to Judas; the hurried midnight arrest; the hurried morning trial; the hurried crucifixion and hasty burial.

So much for the historical aspect of the incident of the raising of Lazarus. It is necessary to make the subsequent incidents plausible—believable. Why it was not recorded before I do not know. Why it was wrapped in a cloud of dogma I do not know, except that Christianity had, by the time of the last year of the first century, lost its primitive simplicity and become saturated in Christian gnosticism.

Now about the miracle as miracle.

The first thing I see is that the story is not told realistically as are the other stories of the raising of the dead in the synoptic Gospels. Is there any good reason why I should not say that as a story it is badly told? From the first verse of *John* XI to the eleventh verse of *John* XII the writer shows that he knew little or nothing of the art of telling a story. To say, as some theologians do, that it is a great story, greatly told, is to talk utter nonsense.

Next, that we are made to feel throughout that we are not merely listening to a story of something that had happened, but to a statement of belief. The story does not give the impression of a real happening. The stone is on the top of the cave, yet Lazarus is told to come forth. Lazarus is bound hand and foot, yet he immediately rises and comes forth. The eye of the narrator is not on the event. It is on the thoughts behind the event. More than once he goes in fear that it is not an actual occurrence.

This puts me on my guard against certain incidents in it. I think the dogma smothers the actual occurrence. I think the four days dead and buried do not synchronize with the other parts of the story and the geography of the locality. Bethany is not more than twenty miles from Bethabara. The journey would not take more than five hours. Having regard to the incidents in Bethany it might be a six hours' journey. But taking the geographical facts into account, it will be seen that if Jesus stayed only two days at Bethabara, after receiving the message from the sisters, and if Lazarus was four days in his grave before Jesus reached Bethany, Lazarus must have been dead and buried *before the sisters sent their message.*

What do I conclude from it? That Lazarus was not four days dead and buried. That he was perhaps only a few hours dead and buried. That the "four days" and the words of Martha about corruption were probably put into the story to answer the objection of the Greek critics of the earlier synoptic Gospels, that Jesus had merely restored the apparently dead, not the actual dead.

So Lazarus was to be so completely and assuredly dead that

corruption had set in. But this warning of Martha which indicates her disbelief in a miracle of raising her brother from the dead is put in after words from her which indicate her belief that Jesus had only to ask God and Lazarus would still live.

This convinces me that the first words of Martha, not the last words, are historical—that the words about the four days and the corruption were later interpolations—or that they were put in to meet the objections of the sceptical critics. Thus I place the raising of Lazarus in a position exactly equivalent to that of the widow's son of Nain.

Lazarus had probably died that day and had just been buried when Jesus arrived in Bethany. Jesus had called for the opening of Lazarus's tomb for precisely the same reason which impelled him to call for the setting down of the bier outside the gate of Nain. Then the incidents had been the same as are recorded. His humanity had been really moved. The inhumanity of the motive and the foolishness of the weeping disappear. The calling back of the spirit of Lazarus becomes thereby a deeply moving incident.

It is a miracle precisely as the incident of the raising of the widow's son is a miracle—and it is inspired by the same human pity, added in this case to Jesus's love of Lazarus and his sisters. Its effect went farther because of the time and place, and the eagerness of the enemies of Jesus to stamp it as an imposture.

Some rationalistic critics say that Jesus had obtained from the messenger sent by the sisters such information of the circumstances of their brother's illness as led him to conclude that it was not likely to prove fatal, and therefore he said, "This sickness is not unto death."

This would account for Jesus remaining two days longer in Peræa, but it would not explain why he also said (at the same time) "but for the glory of God, that the Son of God might be glorified thereby."

The latter part of this statement becomes meaningless if it is assumed that Jesus was convinced that his friend was merely suffering from a temporary illness. But how comes it, says Strauss, that after two days Jesus alters his explanation, and says plainly that Lazarus is dead? To say that he had a second message is to go entirely beyond the Gospel. When Jesus announces his intention of going up to Bethany he says, "Our friend Lazarus sleepeth; but I go that I may awake him out of sleep."

The rationalists say that this means only that some second messenger had told Jesus that Lazarus was in a state of coma. But the absurdity of this explanation is shown by the further words of Jesus, "I am glad for your sakes that I was not there, to the intent ye may believe." To this the obvious answer is that Jesus had no reason to raise Lazarus from the dead to the intent that his disciples might believe, because they already believed, and knew, that he could raise the dead. Therefore, the raising of Lazarus, so far as they were concerned, was useless.

From the arrival of Jesus in Bethany the evangelistic narrative is, says Strauss, more favourable to a rational explanation. If it is true Martha had said, "Lord, if thou hadst been here, my brother had not died; but I know, that even now, whatsoever thou wilt ask of God, God will give it thee," it is impossible to believe that she could have said (apparently a few minutes later, when Jesus also had replied, "Thy brother shall rise again," and had continued his interpretation of this as a reference to the general resurrection at the last day by saying, "I am the resurrection and the life," and had then gone to the tomb and called for the stone on top to be removed), "Lord, by this time he stinketh, for he hath been dead four days."

The first declaration of Martha plainly means that Jesus, being in her view the Messiah who was to come, and the Messiah being by ancient Jewish belief endowed with the power of raising the dead, Jesus could, by asking God, raise Lazarus from the dead; while the second declaration of Martha as clearly means that it was impossible that Lazarus could be raised from the dead because of the length of time since his death, and the fact that his body was already within the grasp of decay.

Again the rationalistic critics say that the fact that after the stone was removed from before the grave and before Jesus said to Lazarus, "Come forth," he thanked God for having heard his prayer, proving that Jesus did not recall Lazarus to life by the words "Come forth," but that on looking at him in the grave he saw that he was still alive.

The answer to this, however, is that if Jesus saw that Lazarus still lived the disciples and spectators must have seen it also, the grave being open, and they would, therefore, never have thought of it as a miracle that at the call "Come forth" Lazarus should arise and leave his burial-place. But clearly the spectators believed that a miracle had been performed, the sisters and disciples believed it, and some of the Jews took the story back to the chief priests, who also believed it.

We must therefore, either reduce the event to the supernatural, as the evangelical narrative does, or regard it as false and unhistorical. "We have hitherto," says Strauss, "been ascending a ladler of miracles, mental disorders, all kinds of bodily maladies in which the sufferer was never so injured as to lose consciousness and life. In all three cases it is not difficult to conceive that Jesus in a purely psychical manner, by word, look and influence, may have penetrated the entire corporeal system. But this is more difficult in cases of insane persons who were distracted to the extent of raging madness, or in the cases of diseases which have no immediate connexion with the mind, as in leprosy, blindness and lameness."

"But now," argues Strauss, "we have to deal with the dead. The corpse from whom all life and consciousness have flown has lost the last fulcrum for the power of the miracle-worker. It does not see him, hear him, feel him. It receives no impression from him. How, then, can it be said that he can call it back to life?"

Such is Strauss's argument. He quotes Woolston that each of the three narratives of raising from the dead is intended to supply what was wanting in the preceding. The daughter is still on the bed on which she died. The widow's son is on his bier being carried to burial. Lazarus is four days in his grave.

So Lazarus had been some time in the nether world, and the reality of his death could not be doubted.

Then as to the motive of the three miracles. The motive of Jesus in raising the daughter of Jairus was to reward the faith of the father. The motive of Jesus in raising the widow's son at Nain was compassion for the mother. The motive for the raising of Lazarus was love of him and of his sisters. But this does not satisfy.

There are orthodox theologians who argue that the raising of the dead would be attended by a spiritual awakening. But we have no knowledge of this. We never hear any more of Jairus's daughter, or of the widow's son, or (except once) of Lazarus. Woolston pertinently asks, why did not Jesus, instead of raising these apparently useless people, raise John the Baptist?

Is it said that Jesus knew it to be the will of God that men being dead should remain dead? There is the motive ascribed by John to Jesus for letting Lazarus die and then raising him from the dead. Can it be supposed that Jesus designedly allowed Lazarus to die so that by restoring him to life he might procure more faith for himself, or that he might perfect the spiritual condition of the little family at Bethany? Or was the motive the more general one of spreading faith in himself as the Son of God? Here, an eminent critic says, "By no means! Never did the Saviour of the needy, the noblest friend of man, act so arbitrarily and needlessly."

If Jesus was not prompted by the motives assigned to him by John, then the story in the fourth Gospel is unhistorical.

Again, other explanations. That in the thirty years or thereabouts after the writing of the synoptic Gospels and the writing of *John,* amateurs and collectors of anecdotes were at work, who went about gleaning stories of Jesus. One such person was Papias.

Next, that these anecdotes fluttered about like the light winged inhabitants of the air, from the place that gave him birth, flying everywhere, and not seldom losing all association with their original locality. The fact remains that this incident of the raising of Lazarus was unknown to the author of the first Gospel, or being known, was rejected by him gives rise to a suspicion that it did not really happen. "Of all the miracles performed by Jesus, the raising of Lazarus, if not the most wonderful, is yet the most marvellous," says Strauss. "Therefore, if its reality could be established, it would be the most pre-eminent proof that Jesus was a divine messenger, indeed, that he was the Messiah expected by the Jews."

Again, the resurrection of Lazarus had, according to John, a direct influence on the fate of Jesus, and assuredly led up to his death. To say it had not is not to know, or not to believe, John's Gospel. Thus, the event had a double significance—pragmatical as well as dogmatic.

Nevertheless, the orthodox theologians have discovered all sorts of reasons why the synoptic writers should have said nothing about it.

(1) That it was necessary to say as little about it as possible during the life of Lazarus lest the Jewish authorities should compass his death—a precaution unnecessary, when John wrote, as Lazarus was probably dead by that time.

(2) That the story was in everybody's mouth when the synoptic

Gospels were written. Therefore it was unnecessary to write it down.

All this is sheer conjecture; there is not the slightest justification for it in the Gospel stories. The orthodox theologians prove too much; according to their reasoning, three-quarters of the Gospels would probably never have been written at all, and assuredly the greatest fact in the Life of Jesus, his crucifixion, would have been unknown apart from doubtful references to it in Josephus and Tacitus, as would his Resurrection have been unknown, apart from mention of it in the Epistles of *Paul* and *Peter*.

How, then, is this neglect for sixty years of the raising of Lazarus, to be explained? It occurred in the very gate of Jerusalem. If it happened, thousands must have known of it. Is it agreed that the synoptic Gospels are Galilean histories, written by Galileans for Galileans, and that the writers were not present at the raising of Lazarus? In that case, we must conclude that none of the Synoptics is written or inspired by the apostles, because *all* the apostles, including Judas, were present at the raising of Lazarus, and were witnesses of the subsequent happenings linked to it. Therefore, the apostolic authority of the three first Gospels is materially weakened.

"We nevertheless," says Strauss, "distinctly declare that we regard the history of the resurrection of Lazarus, not only in the highest degree impossible in itself, but also destitute of external evidence. Consequently, theologians have long declared that the resurrections in the New Testament are nothing more than myths, which have their origin in the tendency of the early Church to make her Messiah agree with the type of the prophets, and of the Messianic idea."

So far Strauss. But in spite of the absence of external evidence I hold to the historical verity of the fundamental part of the story of Lazarus, because I cannot account for the fate of Jesus without it.

V. Influence of the Old Testament

In attempting to explain how the writers of the Gospels came by these stories, Strauss says that they adapted them from the Old Testament, and he points out that Elijah raised the son of a widow, as Jesus did at Nain (I *Kings* XVII, 17). The circumstances are almost identical. And there is also the incident of

Elisha raising the son of the Shunammite woman (II *Kings* IV, 18).

Elijah and the Widow of Zarephath

In the *First Book of Kings* (XVII, 2–24) Elijah is told by God to hide himself by the brook Cherith before Jordan. He was to drink of the brook and the ravens were to feed him. But the brook dried up, and he is told to go to Zarephath, where a widow woman would sustain him. At the gate of the city he comes upon the widow woman gathering sticks, and he calls to her, "Fetch me, I pray thee, a little water in a vessel, that I may drink." She is going to fetch it when the prophet calls again, saying, "Bring me, I pray thee, a morsel of bread in thine hand." She answers that she has only a handful of meal in a barrel and a little oil in a cruse, and she is gathering sticks that she may make a little food that she and her son may eat before they die. Elijah says, "Fear not. Go and do as thou hast said, but make me thereof a little cake first, and bring it unto me, and after make for thee and for thy son. For thus saith the Lord God of Israel, the barrel of meal shall not waste, neither shall the cruse of oil fail. . . ." The woman does as the prophet tells her, and what he has promised her comes to pass.

But after a time the son of the widow falls sick and dies, and the woman says, "What have I to do with thee, O thou Man of God? Art thou come unto me to call my sin to remembrance, and to slay my son?"

Evidently she had sinned in relation to her son, or believed the death of her son was punishment for her sin, and Elijah had led to God's remembrance of it—an old Jewish belief.

Elijah took the son (evidently a child), carried him up to a loft where he slept, and laid him on his bed. "And he stretched himself upon the child three times, and cried unto the Lord, and said, O Lord my God, I pray thee, let this child's soul come into him again." And the Lord heard the prayer of Elijah, and the soul of the child came into him again and he revived. And Elijah delivered him to his mother.

Elisha and the Shunammite Woman

The prophet Elisha lodges at intervals with a Shunammite woman, and she keeps a room for him, believing him to be a man of God, (II *Kings* IV, 8–37). The prophet promises the Shunammite a son. The promise is fulfilled. In the harvest time the son goes out into the fields, and is apparently sunstricken. The father of the boy carries him home to his mother, and she rests him on her knees till noon and he then dies. So the woman now carries her dead son up to the prophet's room, and, laying him on his bed, shuts the door on him and goes out. Then she hurries away to Mount Carmel, where the prophet has his permanent home. The prophet sees her coming and says to his servant, "Behold yonder is that Shunammite. Run now, I pray thee, to meet her and say unto her 'Is it well with thee? Is it well with thy husband? Is it well with the child?' "

The servant does so, and the woman answers, "It is well." But when she comes to the prophet she throws herself at his feet and tells him what has befallen her son, reproaching him for giving her a son and then taking him away. The prophet then tells his servant to take his staff and hurry away to the woman's house, not stopping to speak to anybody he may meet on the way, and lay his staff on the face of the child. His servant does this, and then he and the mother wait for the coming of the prophet.

The prophet, an older man, comes later, but the child is still dead. Elisha then turns his servant, and even the mother of the child, out of the room, and he is alone with the dead. Then the prophet prays to God, and then lies upon the child, putting his mouth upon the child's mouth, his eyes upon his eyes and his hands upon his hands.

After a time the child opens his eyes. Then Elisha calls to his servant, "Call this Shunammite." She comes, and Elisha says to her, "Take up thy son."

My conclusion is that these are fundamentally the same stories. It is possible that they suggest the stories of the raising of the daughter of Jairus and of the widow's son of Nain. But there are essential differences. The New Testament stories have a much greater reality. Only the prayer is the same, and in the second story the fact of turning the others out—with the difference that Jesus turns out only the musicians who are laughing him to scorn for saying that the daughter only sleeps, while Elisha turns out both his servant and the mother of the child.

On the other hand, it does not appear that the Shunammite went to Elisha with any hope that he would raise her son from the dead, but only to reproach him. He had promised her a son. She had not wanted one. Had he given her a son and then taken him away merely to punish her?

To quote Strauss: "Even one already dead and laid in his grave, like Lazarus, was restored to life by the prophet Elisha—with the difference that the prophet himself had been long dead, and that the contact of his bones reanimated the corpse (II *Kings* XIII, 21). A strange resemblance to the story of the raising of Lazarus."

Elisha is dead and buried and bands of Moabites are invading the land.

And it came to pass as they were burying a man that, behold, they spied a band of men; and they cast the man into the sepulchre of Elisha; and when the man was let down, and touched the bones of Elisha, he revived and stood up on his feet. [II *Kings* XIII, 21]

Altogether, I accept only that part of Strauss's theory which suggests that when the evangelists were *narrating* the actual incidents of the miracles of Jesus they bethought them of the prophetic miracles and gave them the same colouring.

VI. *Prophecies Concerning the Resurrection*

For the hour is coming, in the which all that are in the graves shall hear his voice, and shall come forth. [*John* V, 28–29]

No man can come to me, except the Father which hath sent me draw him; and I will raise him up at the last day. [*John* VI, 44]

For the Lord himself shall descend from Heaven with a shout, with the voice of the archangel, and with the trump of God; and the dead in Christ shall rise first. Then we which are alive and remain shall be caught up together with them in the clouds, to meet the Lord in the air, and so shall we ever be with the Lord. [I *Thessalonians* IV, 16, 17]

My inference from these extracts is:

1. That beyond doubt or question the passage in *Thessalonians* is intended by Paul for a literal description of the second coming of Christ. The dead who believe in Christ are to rise out of their graves, and the living who believe in him are to be caught up in the clouds to meet him in the air, and all together are to be with him—but whether in a kingdom in the air or in the earth we are not told.

2. That this prophecy takes no account of a change of body from the temporal to the spiritual. If the dead are to rise with spiritual bodies (as suggested by Paul) the living are to be caught

up into clouds with their physical bodies and in spite of all natural laws to the contrary.

3. That Jesus is made in *John* to promise the resurrection of the dead from their graves in the last days.

4. That there is nothing in the New Testament to indicate the belief among the Jews (or in the mind of Jesus or his disciples) that resurrection from the dead was to take place during the earlier human life of Jesus, but only at his second advent. Therefore, there is nothing to encourage in the minds of the Jews the belief in the miracle of the resurrection of Lazarus, except the concurrent belief that the days of Jesus *were* the last days—that he was about to establish the kingdom of Heaven then and there.

5. Therefore that the miracle and the belief that those were the last days operated on each other—the dead were being raised, therefore those were the last days, and the Messiah had come; the Messiah had come and those were the last days, therefore the dead were being raised.

CHAPTER XXIII

The Miracles
(Continued)

I. *Another Class of Miracle*

THE GREATER MIRACLES of Jesus are miracles of belief, and may, in all cases, be said to have their motive in compassion, simple, human compassion for the sick and suffering, and for the sorrowing relations of the dead. All these miracles are, in my judgment, closely related to the Messianic hope. They were expected of the Messiah. It had long been believed that the Messiah, when he came, would perform such miracles.

There is, however, a smaller group of incidents which do not belong to this class. The motive for them is not compassion in any strict sense. They have no relation that we know of to the Messianic hope. It was not the current Jewish belief that the Messiah, when he came, would perform these miracles. They have no relation, that I can see, in the coming of the kingdom of Heaven. They serve no useful purpose (and never did) that I can see, except to show the supernatural power of Jesus—to establish faith in his divinity by showing that he did what man had never before done.

The chief of the miracles of this class are:

1. The Turning of Water into Wine.
2. The Feeding of the Five Thousand.
3. The Feeding of the Four Thousand.
4. The Walking on the Sea.

Let us examine the Gospel records of each of these in sequence.

II. *The Turning of Water into Wine*

This miracle is recorded in one of the Gospels only (*John* II, 1–11). John the Baptist was baptizing in Bethabara beyond Jordan. When the Jews sent priests and Levites of the sect of the

Pharisees from Jerusalem to ask him whom he claimed to be, John answered that he was not the Christ. When they asked him if he was Elias, the forerunner of the Christ, he answered that he was not.

They said, "Art thou the prophet?" He answered, "No." They then said, "Who art thou?" He replied that he was a forerunner, "the voice of one crying in the wilderness. Make straight the way of the Lord"—as the prophet Esias had said. Then they asked, "Why, then, do you baptize, if you are not Christ, nor Elias, nor the prophet?"

He replied, "I baptize with water; but there standeth one among you, whom ye know not; he it is, who coming after me is preferred before me, whose shoe's latchet I am not worthy to unloose."

The next day after this conversation John, seeing Jesus of Nazareth coming towards him, said, "Behold the Lamb of God, which taketh away the sin of the world. This is he of whom I said, After me cometh a man which is preferred before me."

Later, presumably, while he was baptizing Jesus (although *John* says nothing about the baptizing), the Baptist says, "I saw the Spirit descending from Heaven like a dove, and it abode upon him." Then he says, "I knew him not, but he that sent me to baptize with water, the same said unto me, Upon whom thou shalt see the Spirit descending, and remaining on him, the same is he which baptizeth with the Holy Ghost. And I saw, and bare record that this is the Son of God."

The next day after that (the day after the baptism) John was standing with two of his disciples when he saw Jesus walking, and he said (as he had said at first sight of him), "Behold the Lamb of God!" Whereupon the two disciples of John left him and followed Jesus, believing him to be the Messiah, who, according to John and the prophets, was to come. One of the two was Andrew of Bethsaida. Jesus saw them following him and asked them why. They said "Master, where dwellest thou?" He answered, "Come and see."

They went with Jesus and saw where he dwelt, and as it was then about the tenth hour (four in the afternoon) they stayed with him that second day. Andrew then (apparently the same day) went in search of his brother, Simon Peter, also of Bethsaida, and said to him, "We have found the Messias."

On the next day following (that is to say the third day) Jesus went back to Galilee. On the way, apparently, he found Philip, who was of the same city as Andrew and Peter—Bethsaida. Jesus said to Philip, "Follow me." Philip did so, and (still apparently on the way to Galilee) Philip found Nathanael (of Cana, or Nain, as we hear elsewhere) under a fig-tree, probably at some distance, and said to him, "We have found him, of whom Moses in the law, and the prophets, did write, Jesus of Nazareth, the son of Joseph." Nathanael then asked, "Can there be any good thing come out of Nazareth?" and Philip answered, "Come and see."

Jesus saw Nathanael coming towards him and said, "Behold an Israelite indeed, in whom is no guile." Nathanael questioned how Jesus knew him, and Jesus replied, "Before that Philip called thee, when thou wast under the fig-tree, I saw thee." Nathanael answered, "Master, thou art the Son of God, thou art the King of Israel." Whereupon Jesus said, "Because I said unto thee, I saw thee under the fig-tree, believest thou? Thou shalt see greater things than these. . . . Hereafter ye shall see Heaven open, and the angels of God ascending and descending upon the Son of Man."

Such are the conditions preceding the miracle, and necessary to its appreciation.

We are now told that in this third day (the day on which Jesus set out from the vicinity of Bethabara beyond Jordan, although possibly a little farther north) Jesus, with his five followers (the unnamed one, Andrew, Peter, Philip and Nathanael), arrives at Cana of Galilee. Cana is about six miles beyond Nazareth on the road towards Tiberias on the way to the Lake of Galilee.

There is a marriage that day in Cana. If Nathanael was of Cana it is possible that he was on his way to it when Philip found him.

The mother of Jesus is at the marriage, and both Jesus and his five disciples are invited to it. In the course of the marriage festivities the mother of Jesus comes to him and tells him, "They have no wine," meaning that the wine (provided by the bridegroom, according to the Jewish custom of that time) has run out. Jesus answers his mother brusquely. According to the Gospel story he says, "Woman, what have I to do with thee? mine hour is not yet come."

Nevertheless, his mother says to the servants of the house, "Whatsoever he saith unto you [asks you to do] do it."

There were six stone waterpots, such as were in every Jewish house, with taps from which to draw off the contents, used for the purification before food, and these waterpots were capable of holding two or three firkins apiece.

Jesus said to the servants, "Fill the waterpots with water," and the servants filled them to the brim.

What, if anything, Jesus did then is not recorded, but it is clear that the water at that moment became wine. Jesus said to the servants, "Draw out now, and bear unto the governor of the feast."

The servants did so. And when the governor of the feast tasted the water that had been made wine (without knowing that it came from the waterpots, though of course the servants knew) he called for the bridegroom, saying, "Every man at the beginning doth set forth good wine; and when men have well drunk, then that which is worse; but thou hast kept the good wine until now." And the evangelist closes the story by saying, "This beginning of miracles did Jesus in Cana of Galilee, and manifested forth his glory; and his disciples believed on him."

Such is the miracle of the turning of water into wine, according to the Gospel of John, who alone records it. It is with the deepest distress that I attempt to analyse it, feeling it to be, from first to last, deeply dishonouring to Jesus. It is a trivial and even an unworthy incident in itself, and it comes at a time which makes lower the narrative of his life and mission.

When does it come?—Three days after John the Baptist has recognized Jesus as the Messiah whose coming had been foretold by the prophets—the Lamb of God who was to take away the sins of the world. Two days after three of John's disciples had forsaken him for Jesus because they believed that Jesus was the Christ. And this was his first act at the beginning of his mission as the Messiah!

What was the Miracle?—The providing, by means of supernatural power, of more wine for the guests at a marriage feast after the wine already provided had been exhausted. More, the providing of an enormous quantity of good wine for guests who had already "well drunk" and had reached that stage in which the palate is so demoralized as to be unable to distinguish good wine from inferior wine.

What object is it said to serve?—That of manifesting the glory of Jesus, and (apparently) of causing his disciples to believe on him. How the glory of Jesus, who had three days before been recognized by John the Baptist, under the direct revelation of God, to be the Messiah, should be made manifest by the display of his power to turn water into wine is beyond comprehension.

How the disciples who had left John because they believed Jesus to be the Christ, and had already proclaimed him to each other, as the Messiah of whom Moses in the law and the prophets wrote, were made to believe on him, or were even strengthened in their belief, by seeing him perform this miracle, in these circumstances, is also beyond comprehension.

But the story of the miracle fails of the appearance of reality at almost every point. As an historical record it is open to the objection that, as told, it could not have occurred. It was physically impossible that Jesus and his new disciples could have been at the feast at all if it was held in Cana of Galilee on the third day after his baptism at Bethabara beyond Jordan.

I know the ground. Bethabara is at least a hundred miles from Cana by either of the two roads connecting them. This is a foot journey of at least three days. Yet, according to John, at four o'clock in the afternoon of the day after his baptism at Bethabara (and the second day after John's conversation with the Jews) he was at this house, or lodging perhaps, in or near Bethabara, and on the next day he was at the marriage at Cana of Galilee.

- Or even assuming that the place at which Jesus and the disciples slept was on the road back towards Galilee, and they made a day's journey before four o'clock in the afternoon of the second day, there would still be two days' journey from there to Cana.

Making allowance for the fact that a Jewish marriage might take place at any hour of the day or night, and that marriages in eastern countries generally take place in the evening, and omitting the fact that the Jewish day begins at sundown, and that at that time of the year (probably the middle of February) sundown would be about five o'clock in the afternoon, it is plainly impossible that on foot or by any method of locomotion used in his time he could have been present at the marriage at all.

The part taken by the mother of Jesus is not consistent with anything else the Gospel tells of her. That she should have told him that there was no more wine has no other significance than that she thought that in some manner he would supply the want. If she thought he would supply the want, she can only have thought he would do so by supernatural means. We are not told of any incident in his earlier life which gave his mother reason to think he possessed supernatural power, except the apocryphal stories of the miracles performed in his childhood, which the Christian Church has long discarded as false and dishonouring.

On the contrary, she had borne herself towards him in earlier years, and she bore herself towards him after this event, as if she had never known that he possessed supernatural powers. Even if it is to be believed that the promises to her before his birth and after it must have prepared her for the exhibition of his divine power, it is inconceivable that she should think that his first exercise of it as the Messiah, the "God with us," would be to make wine at a wedding feast.

The terms of his rebuke of his mother leave the inference that she knew that he was to prove his Messiahship by miracles, and that he told her brusquely that the time had not come for him to do so. Yet that, nevertheless, he belied his own word, and *did* perform a miracle as if his time for manifesting his power *had* come. That his mother, notwithstanding his rebuke, continued to believe that he would work a miracle, and that in requesting the servants to do whatever he told them to do she showed that she believed that he would perform the expected miracle. That he did provide in plentiful measure the wine that was wanted.

Against this, the apologists urge their various arguments in an effort to give dignity and reality to this miracle.

They say that the miracle was a mystical exposition between the baptism of John and the baptism of Jesus; that as the one baptized with water, the other, by turning water into wine, indicated the altered direction of the life and teaching of Jesus.

It is a feeble apology without any authority. Such apologists claim to know more than the evangelist, who assigned one reason for the miracle, and one result of it—that Jesus thereby manifested his glory and that his disciples believed on him.

Again, this miracle is false to the character of all but a few of the miracles of Jesus. The turning of water into wine differs from all the other important miracles of Jesus (except the feeding of the multitudes and the walking on the sea) in being a miracle performed in direct opposition to natural law. The miracles of healing the sick, the blind, the lame, even of the casting out of devils and the calling back of the dead to life, may reasonably be said to be miracles in harmony with nature. They may be said to carry the powers of nature farther than our experience has given us knowledge of, but they are never in opposition to nature.

We may *know* how the blind can be made to see, but sight is natural, and it is not to oppose natural law but to call for a stronger exercise of it than science may yet have attained to, to make a blind man see.

The same can be said of all the other miracles of healing, and even of the raisings of the dead. But this miracle is wrought *against* nature. Water is water, and if it lay by itself it would not change its nature in a thousand years. To say that Jesus turned water instantaneously into wine is to say that he merely made an exhibition of supernatural power. It was a miracle of mere power, without motive and without result.

The disciples did not need that he should exercise this power in order that they should believe in him, and we are not told whether or not the governor of the feast, the bridegroom and the guests at the wedding believed in him as a result of the miracle. For all we know to the contrary, this miracle of mere power failed.

Against this the apologists urge that it was not a miracle against nature, but only an acceleration of nature; that Jesus did not thereby abrogate the processes of nature; that wine comes from the water that nourishes the vine plant in the ground; that without water the wine could not come; therefore, what Jesus did in turning the water into wine was miraculously to make nature go farther, to do the work of say a year in a moment.

The answer to that is clear—that the water alone was in the waterpots, and water alone can do nothing to make wine. It has to nourish the vine plant in the soil. Therefore, it is water, plus soil, plus all the processes of pressing and fermenting by which wine is made. Consequently, the miracle attributed to Jesus was not an acceleration of a natural process, but a complete denial of natural law.

Jesus never did this. None of his authenticated miracles are unnatural, in the sense of abrogating or wiping out the laws of nature. They are only miraculous in carrying the laws of nature farther by the addition of the powers not given to nature.

Again, this miracle of turning water into wine differs from the authenticated miracles in having no relation to his claim as the Messiah, or to his mission in establishing the kingdom of Heaven.

Some of the prophets, Moses, for example, are said in the Old Testament to have exercised power over water (as turning water into blood), but nowhere known to me is it said to be expected of the Messiah that when he came he would be able to turn water into something else. Nowhere is this power said to be a sign of the Messiah. In sending back the disciples of John with the tangible answer to his question, "Art thou he that should come?" Jesus covers the whole ground of his authenticated miracles, but he says nothing about turning water into wine.

Such a miracle was not necessary. It was useless. It was degrading. How, then, did it come into the story of his life?

The story of this miracle is not to be found in any of the other three Gospels. It is not referred to (few of the miracles of Jesus are) in any of the Epistles. Yet two of the disciples appear to have been present at the wedding feast in Cana of Galilee. Peter must have been there, yet, if it is true that he inspired Mark (as Papias says), either he said nothing to Mark about the miracle of turning water into wine, or Mark thought nothing of it, although it must have been the first of the miracles of Jesus witnessed by Peter, and therefore the most likely to make an impression upon him.

One of the two disciples of John the Baptist who deserted him for Jesus is left unnamed by John. There is no apparent reason why he should not be named, except that he was the disciple under whose name the Gospel was being written.

Therefore, I conclude that the unnamed disciple was probably John. Thus John is the only witness of the miracle who makes record of it. This does not necessarily mean that with John the apostle's own hand the Gospel bearing his name was written. But, nevertheless, it gives a certain measure of authority to the miracle as an historical incident. There the historical authority for the miracle ends.

If the three Synoptic Gospels were written and published between A.D. 60 and 70, and John's Gospel was not written or published until about A.D. 90–92, it follows that the story of the miracle either came into currency in the twenty to thirty years between, or that if it was current before the Synoptic Gospels were written it was generally rejected by them.

I take the former view—that the miracle of the turning of water into wine was unknown to the writers of *Matthew, Mark* and *Luke,* and that it first came to be known either during the intervening twenty to thirty years, or on the publication of John's Gospel itself.

I ask myself what could have suggested and created it during that period. I think it was created by the Christian-Gnostic movement within the Church, which hungered for (1) all indications of the supernatural power of Jesus, and did not discriminate between what was in harmony with his mind and what was out of harmony; (2) all indications that his supernatural power existed from his birth, even before his birth, during his childhood and youth and at the beginning of his ministry, and in the first acts of it. Also, that Jesus himself and everybody close to him, his parents above all, and his mother pre-eminently, were from the beginning, and right through his life, conscious that he possessed divine power, including the power of working miracles.

This hunger for evidence of the inborn miraculous power of Jesus gave rise to the multitudinous apocryphal Gospels (generally very crude and foolish), which were produced apparently and particularly during the latter part of the first century to the end of the second century. Most of the apocryphal Gospels have disappeared, having been cast aside as utterly unworthy and mischievous when the Canon was made in the fourth century.

But before their destruction some incidents from them found their way into the Gospels which afterwards became canonical, and these were not taken out when the Gospels became the Canon.

I think the Nativity stories in *Matthew* and *Luke* belong to these apocryphal Gospels. Also the story (as now found in *Luke*) of Jesus at twelve years of age in the Temple.

The clear object of this story (as of many stories of his infancy, childhood and early boyhood) was to prove that from the beginning Jesus was conscious of his divinity, of his position as the Son of God, of his work and mission.

In like manner, I think this story of the miracle of the turning of water into wine was meant primarily not as an evidence of the supernatural power of Jesus, but of his mother's knowledge of his supernatural power.

It is the first indication of his mother's knowledge that her son differs from the son of any other mother. Not one word in the three earlier Gospels (outside the two Nativity stories) gives the slightest indication that she knew that her son was the Messiah, that he had any special powers of any kind whatever.

On the contrary, there are incidents (the incident in the Temple being one of them) when she behaves to Jesus as if no such idea had ever entered her mind, rather the contrary. I think it reasonable to conjecture that the Christian-Gnostics were encountering towards the end of the first century the objection that if Jesus was supernaturally born, and if he possessed divine powers from the moment of his birth, how did it come to pass that his mother knew nothing about it?

To answer this objection, this legend of the feast at Cana of Galilee grew. I am compelled to reject it altogether. It breaks itself to pieces under the eyes of any impartial inquirer, at every rock of historical possibility. It is chronologically false. It could not occur at the time given for it. It is morally unworthy of Jesus, and especially unworthy of the period of his life at which it is alleged to have taken place. It is out of all harmony with the spirit of his more important miracles, being in violation of natural law (which the chief miracles of Jesus never are). It is incapable of any mystical interpretation that appeals to common sense and does not conflict with the plain intention assigned to it.

It has no motive that will bear examination, and the motive assigned to it shows that it was unnecessary and that it failed. In a word, it is unworthy of Jesus, and I refuse to allow any apocryphal story of a degrading kind to lower his credibility as an historical personage.

III. The Feeding of the Five Thousand

The miracle of the feeding of the five thousand with a few loaves and fishes is reported in all four of the Gospels. Let us examine each of these reports in succession.

In *Matthew* (XIV) we are told that immediately after Jesus heard of the execution of John the Baptist by order of Herod Antipas, he "departed thence by ship into a desert place apart." The people followed him on foot out of the cities. Jesus saw a great multitude consisting of about 5,000 men, besides women and children. He had compassion upon them and healed their sick. "When it was evening" his disciples came to him, saying, "This is a desert place, and the time is now past [Probably this means merely that a considerable time has passed for the people without food]; send the multitude away, that they may go into the villages, and buy themselves victuals." But Jesus said to his disciples, "They need not depart; give ye them to eat." The disciples demurred, "We have here but five loaves and two fishes," they explained. Jesus told the disciples to bring the people to him, and when they came he commanded them to sit down on the grass. Then he took the five loaves and the two fishes, and looking up to Heaven, he blessed and brake, and gave the loaves to his disciples, who gave them to the multitude. And all the 5,000 men, besides women and children, ate and were filled. And when the meal was over, the fragments which remained were twelve baskets full. He sent the multitudes away, and "went up into a mountain apart to pray," and "when the evening was come he was there alone."

According to *Mark* (VI) Jesus had been into his own country, probably including Nazareth, and his disciples had followed him. His own country people had rejected him, and he had gone round the other villages preaching. He had then called to him the twelve and had sent them out by two and two to preach his Gospel, giving them power to work miracles. They had gone out and preached the Gospel of repentance, casting out many devils and healing the sick.

The story of the execution of John the Baptist is here interpolated, but it is not given as a reason for what follows. The apostles returned and told Jesus what they had done.

Jesus said to them, "Come ye yourselves apart into a desert place and rest a while," for there were many coming and going, and they had no leisure so much as to eat. So Jesus and his disciples took ship and sailed to a desert place privately.

The people saw them sail, and many ran afoot out of the cities and were waiting for him again at the place to which the ship had sailed. When Jesus came out of the ship and saw so many people, he was moved with compassion towards them, as sheep not having a shepherd, and he began to teach them. And "when the day was now far spent his disciples came unto him, and said, This is a desert place, and now the time is far passed. Send them away, that they may go into the country round about, and into the villages, and buy themselves bread, for they have nothing to eat."

Jesus answered, "Give ye them to eat." The disciples replied, "Shall we go and buy two hundred pennyworth of bread?" probably meaning that no less would do.

Jesus said, "How many loaves have you?" They went to look, and returned saying they had five loaves and two fishes.

Jesus commanded the disciples to make all the people sit down by companies upon the grass. So they sat down in ranks, by hundreds and by fifties. They were in all about 5,000 men. Then Jesus took the five loaves and two fishes, and looking up to Heaven he blessed and brake the loaves, and he divided the two fishes, and gave the bread and the fish to the disciples to set before the people. They all ate and were filled, and the disciples took up twelve baskets full of the fragments that were left. Then he sent his disciples back to the ship, telling them to go to the other side, while he sent the people away. When he had sent the people away he departed into a mountain to pray.

Thus *Matthew* and *Mark,* with unimportant differences, tell the same story. The motive given is different. In *Mark* they go to the desert place for *rest.* The subsequent incidents (the walking on the sea) show that the scene of the miracle of the feeding of the five thousand was the eastern side of the lake. On the return of the ship Jesus came to the western shore in the land of Gennesaret.

According to *Luke* (IX, 7), after Jesus had sent out his twelve disciples, Herod the Tetrarch heard of all that was being done by him and concluded that he was John risen from the dead. Herod desired to see Jesus, but this is not given as the reason for what follows. The disciples return and tell Jesus what they have done, and he takes them aside privately into a desert place. This desert place is here, for the first time, said to belong to a city called Bethsaida. But it is not said in *Luke* that Jesus and his disciples took ship to get to it.

When the people knew that Jesus had gone they followed him, and he received them and spoke to them of the kingdom of God, and healed such of them as had need of healing.

"When the day began to wear away" the twelve disciples of Jesus said to him, "Send the multitude away, that they may go into the towns and country round about, and lodge, and get victuals, for we are here in a desert place." To this Jesus replied, "Give ye them to eat." The disciples answered, "We have no more but five loaves and two fishes; except we should go and buy meat for all this people." The people were about 5,000 men.

Jesus said, "Make them sit down by fifties in a company," and the disciples did so. Then Jesus took the five loaves and the two fishes and looking up to Heaven he blessed them, and brake, and gave to the disciples to set before the multitude. And the people were all filled, and there was taken up of the fragments that remained twelve baskets.

Once more the same story. The only important difference is that the name of the desert place is given—Bethsaida. Clearly, Bethsaida was far away from the homes of the people, for it is suggested by the disciples that they should (at the close of the day) be sent away to the neighbouring villages, not only to buy victuals, but also to lodge. This suggests that Bethsaida may have been on the eastern side of the lake. If so, it would be in the territory of Herod Philip. Bethsaida could not have been on the western side, which from north to south was thickly populated and has no desert place near it. A possible explanation is that Luke knew of one Bethsaida only—the Bethsaida on the coast of Gennesaret.

In the three other Gospels the scene is clearly on the extreme eastern side of the lake, not (as Luke indicates) on the western side. Against Luke is the fact that there could have been no desert place on the western side, and therefore no need for the miracle, which is further evidence that Luke did not know the country. Another point is that the succeeding incidents in *Luke* are not the same as in *Matthew* and *Mark* (see the miracle of the walking on the sea).

According to *John* (V, 1), Jesus had been in Jerusalem at the time of a feast of the Jews, which is not named. While there he had visited a pool in the sheep-market called the pool of Bethesda, where a great multitude of impotent people lay waiting to be cured. He had cured on the Sabbath Day a man who had had an infirmity for thirty-eight years. He had then returned to Galilee and crossed over the lake, apparently from the coast near to Tiberias. There he had gone up into a mountain and sat there with his disciples. A great company of people had followed him, some of them by boats from Tiberias, and he said to Philip, one of his disciples, "Where shall we buy bread that these may eat?" The evangelist says that Jesus only said this to prove Philip, for he, himself, knew what he would do.

Philip answered, "Two hundred pennyworth of bread is not sufficient for them, that every one of them may take a little." Then another of the disciples, Andrew, said, "There is a lad, which hath five barley loaves, and two small fishes. But what are they among so many?" Jesus said, "Make the men sit down."

There was much grass in the place. From this it is concluded that it was spring or early summer. In verse 4 (VI) it is said that it was nigh to Passover, say the middle of April. According to John's chronology it must have been the second April (second Passover) after the baptism of Jesus.

The people sat down. There were about 5,000 of them. Jesus then took the loaves, and when he had given thanks he gave them to the disciples, and the disciples to the people. In the same way he distributed the fishes.

When the people had eaten, Jesus said to his disciples, "Gather up the fragments that remain, that nothing be lost." Therefore, the disciples gathered the fragments of the five barley loaves which remained, and they filled twelve baskets.

When the men (apparently the five thousand) saw the miracle which Jesus had performed, they said, "This is of a truth that prophet that should come into the world."

The evangelist goes on to say that the people, thus persuaded that he was the Messiah, wished to take him by force, and make him a king. But he departed again into a mountain alone. And when "even was now come" the disciples took ship and went over the sea towards Capernaum.

The subsequent incident (the walking on the sea) shows that the scene of the miracle was the opposite side of the lake from Capernaum. Also, that the five thousand had come to Jesus from the coast about Tiberias on the western side. Therefore, if (as Luke says) the place was Bethsaida, it follows that Bethsaida was on the north-east side of the lake and in the territory of Herod Philip.

IV. The Feeding of the Four Thousand

Two of the Gospels have the miracle of the feeding of the four thousand as well as the miracle of feeding the five thousand. Shortly, apparently very shortly, after the feeding of the five thousand, Jesus went to the near neighbourhood of Tyre and Sidon. There he cured the daughter of the Canaanite woman (*Matthew* XV, 22). It would appear from an earlier reference to Tyre and Sidon (*Matthew* XI, 22) that Jesus had either been in Tyre and Sidon before, or that he knew of their bad character. My inference is that he had *not* been there before, or that he had not worked miracles there before. Hastening to Galilee, and coming near to the lake, he went up into a mountain, and sat down there.

Great multitudes came to him, bringing their lame, blind, dumb and maimed, and he healed the sick. The multitude wondered when they saw the dumb to speak, the maimed to be whole, the lame to walk, the blind to see, and they glorified the God of Israel.

Then Jesus called his disciples to him and said, "I have compassion on the multitude, because they continue with me now three days and have nothing to eat; and I will not send them away fasting." His disciples asked, "Whence should we have so much bread in the wilderness, as to fill so great a multitude?" Jesus asked, "How many loaves have you?" They answered, "Seven, and a few little fishes."

Jesus commanded the people to sit down on the ground. And he took the seven loaves and the fishes, and gave thanks and brake them and gave to the disciples, and the disciples to the multitude. And they all ate and were filled, and they took up of the broken meat that was left seven baskets full. There had been 4,000 men, besides women and children.

And then Jesus sent away the multitude and came into the coasts of Magdala. Observe that the concluding verses are almost verbally the same as in the account of the feeding of the five thousand, that the order of ideas is the same.

In the Gospel of *Mark* (VIII, 1) Jesus had returned from the neighbourhood of Tyre and Sidon, had come to the sea of Galilee, "through the midst of the coast of Decapolis."

This would seem improbable. Decapolis is on the extreme south of Galilee, and consequently Jesus could not have come to Galilee by the coasts of Decapolis without making a long and unnecessary circuit, crossing the Jordan at the south end of the lake.

There were great multitudes following him and remaining with him, and as they had nothing to eat Jesus called his disciples and said, "I have compassion on the multitude, because they have now been with me three days, and have nothing to eat; and if I send them away fasting to their own houses they will faint by the way, for divers of them came from far." Upon this the disciples said to Jesus, "From whence can a man satisfy these men with bread here in the wilderness?" Jesus asked them, "How many loaves have ye?" They answered, "Seven."

He commanded the people to sit down on the ground. Then he

took the seven loaves and gave thanks, and brake and gave to his disciples to set before the people. The disciples did so. In like manner he blessed the few small fishes which they had and set these also before the people. So the people ate, and were filled, and they took up of the broken meat that was left seven baskets. The people who had eaten were about 4,000.

Jesus then sent them away, and straightway he entered into a ship with his disciples and came into the parts of Dalmanutha, that is, Magdala.

Such are the stories of the feeding of the multitudes—three stories of the feeding of 5,000; one story of the feeding of 5,000 besides women and children, and two stories of the feeding of 4,000. The stories seem at first sight very circumstantial. The details appear to be highly realistic. But on close examination they do not bear the test of reality. Take, first, the natural facts relating to the feeding of the five thousand. Clearly, the scene is the desert behind Bethsaida (Julias) in the territory of Herod Philip. The multitude followed Jesus partly by ship from the coasts of Tiberias. According to all the Synoptics, it was evening when Jesus began the miracle. There were, according to *Matthew,* 5,000 men, besides women and children. According to *Mark, Luke* and *John,* 5,000 men. They were told to sit down in groups of fifty and one hundred.

They were fed by bread and fish broken by Jesus, and delivered by him to the disciples, who delivered the pieces to the multitude. Thus Jesus alone broke bread for 5,000. Twelve disciples carried the food to 5,000. This, in any reasonable computation, must have been the work of several hours. On a rough computation three hours. Yet when it was all done and over, and twelve baskets of fragments had been gathered up, and Jesus had sent the multitude away and had himself gone up into a mountain to pray, and the disciples had taken ship to go over the sea towards Capernaum, it was still the same time.

Before the beginning of the miracle *Matthew* says "it was evening." At the end of it, "when the evening was come," Jesus was, says *Matthew,* alone on the mountain. "When the day was far spent," says *Mark,* the disciples spoke to Jesus before he performed the miracle. Yet "when the evening was come," he had fed the five thousand, sent the disciples back to the ship, and had departed into a mountain to pray.

"When the day began to wear away," says *Luke,* the disciples spoke to Jesus about the people. *Luke* says nothing about when the miracle was over.

On the other hand, *John* does not say when the miracle was begun, but he says it was so, and the people had tried to take Jesus by force and make him a king, and he had escaped from them into a mountain, the disciples taking ship from Capernaum, "when the even was now come."

Thus the miracle, according to the reports, took little or no time. It was practically, if not quite, timeless. Time stood still for it. This is not a little matter. It shows that the narrator was not recording a reality. He was inventing, and in the process of invention his memory had failed him, that he was thinking of something else.

Next, as to place. The country east of Bethsaida (Julias) does indeed answer to the description of a "desert place" and probably always has done so, being a flat place for at least eight miles on three sides. But if the miracle took place near to the lake, there is the fact that Jesus would have far to go to reach the mountain. There is no mountain nearer to Bethsaida (Julias) on the northeast than Tell Faras, and that is between sixteen and twenty miles away. This renders the statement of *Matthew* absurd that "when the evening was come" he was there alone. If the miracle was performed near to Bethsaida (Julias) "when it was evening" he could not have been in the mountain much before midnight. If it was performed near to Tell Faras, the disciples could not, as *John* says, have taken ship for Capernaum "when the even was now come." It must have been night before they could reach the coast.

Take next the feeding of the four thousand. It is not easy to determine the scene of this miracle. Jesus, according to *Mark,* was returning from the coasts of Tyre and Sidon to the Lake of Galilee through the midst of the coasts of Decapolis. This is impossible. It is like returning to London from Manchester by way of Cornwall.

Later, after the miracle, *Mark* says Jesus "straightway" entered with his disciples into a ship and came into the parts of Dalmanutha, which, if Magdala, is quite natural. In *Matthew* the miracle was performed near to the Lake of Galilee, but it is also said that it was on, or perhaps near, a mountain. There are no mountains nearer to the lake on the north-west road from Tyre than Hazor, which is about sixteen miles to the north-west; Kadesh-

Naphtali, which is from eighteen to twenty miles north, and Beth Anath, which is about twenty-five miles north.

It is true that the city of Safed (about 2,000 feet) sat on a hill, but it was about six miles from the lake, while the city of Chorazin, which was about a mile from the lake, was 500 feet below sea level. Thus the scene of the feeding of the four thousand is impossible to determine.

This is also not immaterial. It shows that the narrator's eye was not on a reality, and that his want of knowledge of the geography of the country was leading him astray, that he was thinking of something else.

If anything occurred on the way back from Tyre (and I confidently think something did occur), I should conclude that it was with the crowds who had followed him on his way back to Galilee. The Canaanites, the Gentiles, the pagans who came from the west, from as far back as the coasts of Tyre and Sidon, and were sent back home, before Jesus took ship for Magdala.

Take, next, the resemblance of the two miracles. It will be seen that they resemble each other in every particular except as to scene, the number of loaves and fishes, and the number of baskets of fragments remaining. The same motive is given for each—compassion for the people who have not eaten, are far from villages where they can procure food, and liable to faint before they reach home. This is natural, but it is not natural that almost precisely the same methods should be used and the same words employed to describe the two distinct occasions. Still more strange that the disciples who had seen precisely the same miracle performed a few days (or, it may be, a few weeks) before, make precisely the same answers to Jesus, as if they had never seen the exercise of his power to multiply food, and are answered in precisely the same way.

This suggests that the two miracles are one, and have somehow not been united. I do not think so. Whatever happened at Bethsaida (Julias), and whatever happened on the north-west road from Tyre, I am convinced that two entirely distinct incidents occurred. My only criticism, as will be seen later, will be as to what it was that occurred at both.

The unanimity of the stories of the feeding of the multitudes does not strengthen my belief in them. On the contrary, it sensibly weakens my belief. Not only are the facts the same, but the order in which the facts are stated and the words in which they are stated are the same. From this I conclude that, notwithstanding minor differences, we have not four distinct and independent authorities for the miracle, but only one authority.

We have to take the miracle of the feeding of the multitudes on the authority of *one reporter only,* and that reporter a crude one.

Finally, the character of the miracles of the multiplying of prepared articles of food. These miracles do not labour under the disadvantage of the miracle of turning water into wine, of having an insufficient or unworthy motive.

The motive of compassion for the multitudes who had followed him and remained with him for many hours, in one case, as he says, for three days, without food, is entirely worthy of Jesus.

But the character of the miracle is no less contrary to nature, although the opposition to nature is not altogether so violent.

What was the origin of the legend? I think the origin of the legend was in the Christian-Gnostic movement, which sought to prove that the power of Jesus was entirely without limit, but did not reflect that Jesus never exercised his limitless power against nature or without some relation to the main mission of his life— the preparation of the world for the kingdom of Heaven.

The motive of compassion which is said to have inspired the miracle may be freely admitted, but that the miracle only produced the effects which might naturally be expected of it may as easily be denied. The five thousand who saw themselves fed by one who had nothing with which to feed them but a few loaves and fishes would certainly never have forgotten the miraculous event, or ceased to believe that the miracle could only have been performed by a divine person, with powers far surpassing those of a man.

Yet they *did* forget it. They were the people of the cities lying on the west and north of Galilee, and these are precisely the cities which Jesus shortly afterwards (as I think a true chronology shows) condemned for their unbelief, saying that if the mighty works they had witnessed had been done in Tyre and Sidon they would have repented long ago.

In like manner it was the people of Chorazin who must have witnessed the miracle of the feeding of the four thousand, and the people of Magdala who must have followed Jesus when he returned after performing that miracle; and yet Chorazin shares with Bethsaida and Capernaum the denunciation of Jesus, and

Magdala is precisely the city which, immediately after these astounding miracles, was the first to ask for a sign that he was the Messiah.

> Woe unto thee, Chorazin! woe unto thee, Bethsaida! for if the mighty works, which were done in you, had been done in Tyre and Sidon, they would have repented long ago in sackcloth and ashes. . . . And thou, Capernaum, which art exalted unto Heaven, shalt be brought down to hell; for if the mighty works, which have been done in thee, had been done in Sodom, it would have remained until this day. [*Matthew* XI, 21, 23]

> And he sent away the multitude, and took ship, and came into the coasts of Magdala. The Pharisees also with the Sadducees came, and tempting desired him that he would show them a sign from Heaven. [*Matthew* XV, 39; XVI, 1]

My conclusion must be that the miracles of the feeding of the multitude is a legendary growth from the fact that vast multitudes followed Jesus about, thinking nothing of hunger and thirst, in their eagerness to hear him as he told them of the coming of the kingdom of God. But that nothing was done except to fill them with so great a joy, so great a spirit, such a frenzy that they were carried away by it.

I think this frenzy ebbed away when Jesus left them; and that in a few days it was gone, and that no tangible faith in him remained, such as *must* have remained if they had had the memory of miraculous meals which he (like Elisha at the widow's house) made for them while they followed him for long hours and even for three days in desert places where there was no food.

I think the unbelief that followed this ebbing away of faith was the cause of Jesus's reproof and denunciation.

Therefore, I deny the miraculous multiplication of prepared food by Jesus, and think the story paltry and partaking of the outward appearance of mere jugglery. But I believe in the far greater and more spiritual miracle of so filling vast numbers of persons with spiritual rapture that the calls of their animal nature were utterly forgotten.

For my belief in the miracle of the feeding of the multitudes I do not need a few little loaves and a few little fishes, but I do need the sense of a mighty triumph of the spirit over the body. *That,* in my view, is the miracle both at Bethsaida and near Chorazin, on the road back from Tyre.

I think, as time went on, it became difficult, or impossible, for the people of a later age, who were outside the range of the magnetic power of Jesus, to account for the fact that vast multitudes followed him about for days without food, or (when in desert places) the possibility of procuring food. And out of this (in colder natures and less imaginative minds) grew little by little the story of the multiplication of prepared food.

That this story derived something from the story of Elijah and the widow's meal and oil in the Old Testament is to me clear. But that it was a creation is shown by its materialization and the atmosphere of unreality about it.

Strauss argues that the legend may have had its origin in Old Testament history and Jewish popular belief that the discourses of the prophet as much as of Jesus on bread and leaven were always figurative, not realistic. Thus the bread of life which Jesus gives (*John* VI, 27) and the false leaven of the Pharisees and Sadducees.

Jesus sometimes spoke of himself as one who was able to give the true bread of life to wandering and hungering people. He also spoke of himself as the bread of life, and said, not at the Last Supper merely but where there was no natural bread present, that his people must eat of the bread of his body and drink of the wine of his blood.

On the other hand Strauss holds that this cannot alone account for the origin of the history of the miracle, because the Gospel of John stands alone in the above method of derivation.

In the fourth Gospel reference is made to that bread from Heaven which Moses gave to their [the people's] fathers in the wilderness (*John* VI, 31). Then a passage in *Exodus* XVI (the story of the giving of the quails and manna to the people of Israel in the wilderness), is, thinks Strauss, perfectly adapted to engender the expectation that its antitype would occur in the Messianic times, and we learn, he says, from rabbinical writings that among the functions of the first Goël which were to be revived in the second, a chief place was to be given to the importation of bread from Heaven.

But I see no Messianic reference in the story of the quails and manna.

Strauss says that on comparing the stories in the Old Testament with the stories of the feeding of the multitudes in the New Testament we see a striking resemblance. The locality is in both cases the wilderness. The indication is that the people should perish of hunger. I see no resemblance beyond this. The rest is totally different. The people in the New Testament are not murmuring against God; in the Old Testament they are murmuring.

More nearly related is the Old Testament story of Elijah (I *Kings* XVII, 8–16) of how the store of meal and oil in the possession of the widow of Zarephath was miraculously replenished. Again, as Strauss says, the prophet Elisha (II *Kings,* IV, 42) fed a hundred men with twenty loaves, *barley* loaves as in the case of Jesus, according to *John.*

All this clearly suggests that when the story took shape the early Christians fell back upon the Old Testament for the *form* of their story, but the object of the story in the New Testament was different.

V. *The Walking on the Sea*

Three of the Gospels narrate the story of how Jesus walked on the sea—*Matthew, Mark* and *John. Luke* does not give the story, but rather obviously avoids it, by switching the history of Jesus on to another event after the feeding of the five thousand.

In *Matthew* (XIV, 23) we are told that after Jesus at Bethsaida (Julias) has sent his disciples back to the ship, telling them to go before him to the other side of the lake, and after he has sent the multitudes away and gone up into a mountain alone to pray, it is *evening.* The ship is then in the midst of the sea, tossed with waves, for the wind has risen.

In the fourth watch of the night (that is between three and six) Jesus goes to his disciples, walking on the sea.

When the disciples see him walking on the sea they are troubled and (clearly not knowing him) say, "It is a spirit," and they cry out for fear. But Jesus speaks to them, saying, "Be of good cheer; it is I; be not afraid."

Upon this Peter answers, "Lord, if it be thou, bid me come unto thee on the water." Why Peter should wish to go to Jesus is not clear. Jesus says, "Come."

When Peter came down out of the ship he walked on the water to go to Jesus. But when he saw that the wind was boisterous he was afraid and, beginning to sink, he cried, "Lord, save me." Jesus immediately stretched out his hand and caught Peter, and said to him, "O thou of little faith, wherefore didst thou doubt?"

Then they went into the ship, and the wind ceased, and the other disciples came to Jesus, and said, "Of a truth thou art the Son of God."

Mark's version of the miracle (VI, 47) is as follows:

Jesus was in the mountain. Evening had come. The ship containing his disciples was in the midst of the sea, and he was alone on the land. Jesus saw the disciples toiling in their rowing, for the wind was contrary to them. About the fourth watch of the night (three to six in the morning) he went out to them, walking on the sea. He would have passed them by. Why? If he had not gone out to help them, what *had* he gone out for? When the disciples saw him walking on the sea they supposed he was a spirit. They all saw him and were troubled.

Immediately he spoke to them saying, "Be of good cheer; it is I; be not afraid." Then he went up to them and into the ship, and the wind ceased.

The disciples were amazed beyond measure. The evangelist explains their amazement by saying that they had considered not the miracle of the loaves, for their hearts were hardened. In other words they had forgotten the miracle, although it had occurred less than twelve hours before, or it had made no impression upon their hearts, had created or nourished no belief in Jesus as a supernatural being.

They landed on the coast of Gennesaret. And when they stepped out of the ship they knew Jesus.

This story differs from Matthew's. First it omits the incident of Peter calling to Jesus, and stepping out on to the waters to walk to him, sinking, and being caught up and taken back to the ship. Next, it says that although Jesus had saluted them with the words, "It is I; be not afraid," they did not know him until they had landed at Gennesaret.

The absence of the incident regarding Peter is significant. If (as Papias said) Mark wrote down what Peter remembered, the fact that he did not include Peter's attempt to walk on the sea seems to argue that it did not happen. Peter must have been a better authority than Matthew.

According to *John* (VI, 19) Jesus had escaped from the multitudes who wished to take him by force and make him a king, and had gone up into a mountain alone. When even was come his disciples went down to the sea and took ship, intending to go over to Capernaum. It was then dark, and Jesus had not returned to them. The sea rose, by reason of a great wind that blew. When they had rowed twenty-five to thirty furlongs, they saw Jesus walking on the sea and drawing near the ship. They were afraid, and Jesus said, "It is I; be not afraid."

Thereupon they gladly received him into the ship, and immediately the ship reached the land to which they were going.

Next day (presumably the day of the morning on which they landed) the people who had been on the eastern side of the sea and seen that Jesus had not sailed with his disciples, and that the disciples had sailed away without him, were astonished to find him at Capernaum. Some others who had followed Jesus by boat from Tiberias and had, apparently, returned home after the miracle, and had not found either Jesus or his disciples at Tiberias, had sailed again next morning to Capernaum, seeking Jesus. And they said, "Rabbi, when camest thou hither?"

Such are the three stories of the miracle of walking on the sea. Is there any good and sufficient reason why I should not say it is a worthless and even stupid story, without dishonouring the divinity of Jesus?

1. It has no object. It serves no purpose. Jesus does not go out to save his disciples in their hour of peril, for in Mark's story he is said to be passing them by.

2. If, it is argued, that from the moment Jesus enters into the ship the wind ceases, and therefore his presence in the ship causes the wind to cease and that was the object of his walking on the sea, the answer is that never elsewhere is the actual bodily presence of Jesus made a necessity of the exercise of his divine power; that frequently he is described as exercising his power at a distance, consequently that it was not necessary to the powers assigned to him in the reports of other miracles that he should wait from the evening of the day upon which he sees his disciples being tossed about in a stormy sea until three to six o'clock next morning to save them from the tempestuous sea.

3. That the distance from the shores of Galilee by Bethsaida (Julias) to Capernaum is (as anybody may see on the spot) little over four miles (thirty-two furlongs), and that if the disciples were twenty-five to thirty furlongs (as *John* says) from the eastern shore when they saw Jesus coming towards them, and if the wind

was contrary to their course to Capernaum, they were already within the shelter of the higher lands on the north-west coast and must have come into calm water soon, whether Jesus had entered the ship or not.

4. That the necessity of believing that the human body of Jesus was exempt from the law which governs all other human bodies whatsoever, "namely the law of gravitation, that he does not sink in the water, but walks erect on it as on firm land," has no value whatever in the story of his life and mission, just as all similar stories which exempt him bodily from natural law have no value for him, and are of no use to the religion he founded.

It requires, as Strauss says, that we should conceive the body of Jesus as an ethereal phantom. This was the opinion of the Docetae, but the fathers of the Church condemned it as irreligious, for the obvious reason that it destroyed his humanity, and hence they are at pains to prove that he was a real man, who ate and drank.

But if Jesus ate and drank, the food he took was material and must have obeyed the laws of matter, and the first of the laws of matter was that it could not maintain itself on the surface of the water, but must sink.

It has been argued that the "spiritual activity of Jesus" which refined and perfected his corporeal nature completely emancipated his body from physical laws; the answer to this is that in the real things of his life it never did so. That he was born with a natural body, that he was baptized a natural body, which sank in the water and then came out of it, that he died a material body and was buried a material body, and to say that at this moment he made himself a spectre or that he had by faith the power of sustaining himself on the surface of the water, and thus reduce his specific gravity by an act of his will—to say all this is to provoke the question of why he did so, and to that question there is no answer.

It cannot be held that he did so to establish the faith of his disciples in his divine power, for had they not, only a few hours before (if the miracle is to be accepted), witnessed the miraculous multiplication of a few loaves and fishes into food sufficient to satisfy 5,000 persons?

Then the explanation given by Mark of the amazement of the disciples at the appearance of Jesus walking on the sea, that they had forgotten the miracles of the loaves, is humiliating in the last degree to Jesus, while the immediate reason given by Matthew for the cry of the disciples, "Of a truth thou art the Son of God," that when Jesus stepped from the sea into the ship the wind ceased and thus their lives were saved, is degrading to their character, having regard to the far greater works which they had witnessed in the saving of other people's lives.

And, finally, the account in *John* of the demand, "Rabbi, when camest thou hither?" made by the people who followed from Tiberias next morning after the day on which they had witnessed the miracle at Bethsaida (Julias) that Jesus should give them a sign, so that they might see and therefore believe on him, is proof of one of two things; that they had never seen the feeding of the five thousand or believed (what they must have heard from the disciples) that he had walked on the sea to the place and where they found him; or that nothing of either kind had ever occurred at all.

The question asked by the people from Tiberias of Jesus at Capernaum, "Rabbi, when camest thou hither?" is nonsense, since Jesus might easily in the time have walked back to Capernaum by land, the distance being at the utmost seven or eight miles.

Clearly, the writer of *John* did not know the geography of the Lake of Galilee.

Again the subtilization of the body of Jesus is not consistent with itself in the story as told in *Matthew* and *Mark*. Assumed that the body of Jesus had been suddenly dematerialized into a shadow while he walked on the sea, it must have been as suddenly materialized when Peter makes his experiment to dispense with the law of gravitation and Jesus has to catch him from sinking and lend him a helping hand—the hand must have been a real hand, not a phantom hand.

And in all the stories it is obvious that if Jesus was a spectre, as his disciples thought him, while he was walking on the sea, he must have become a material creature when he stepped into the ship. Therefore, the body of Jesus in this story is neither one thing nor another—neither spirit nor matter—but at one moment spirit and at the next moment matter. In short, an absurdity. The whole story "approaches very near to the exaggerations and follies of the apocryphal Gospels."

Now look at the attempt to read this story in the light of a parable on the power of faith.

The theory is that, according to the doctrine of Jesus, the believer who, having faith, may "remove mountains," may also, if necessary, walk on the sea, and that in proportion as faith falters power ceases.

Strauss finds that the account of the fourth Gospel has features which betray an unhistorical character.

John (in the parenthetical verse 23, Chapter VI) leaves the impression that the people from the unknown coast who were present at the miracle of the feeding of the five thousand on the plain behind Bethsaida came and returned in boats. This leaves the reasonable inference that they were a considerable part of the five thousand. Now all the references to the "ship" in which the disciples sailed to Capernaum (they probably sailed from the neighbourhood of Tiberias) show that it was a row boat, and the largest row boat on the Lake of Galilee might hold twenty persons. Therefore, if half the five thousand were from Tiberias, it would require that the "other boats" which returned to Tiberias were a vast number—not fewer than 120!

The idea becomes ludicrous. What was Herod Antipas doing if he wanted to arrest Jesus, and if from the battlements of his castle (on a rock that was less than a mile south of Tiberias) he saw a fleet of 120 boats leaving his coasts under his very nose, to follow Jesus to the opposite side of the lake, where he would be outside Herod's territory, and therefore free from his jurisdiction?

"This passage of the multitude, therefore," says Strauss, "appears only to have been invented to confirm by their evidence the walking of Jesus on the sea."

But it fails to do so, because Jesus might so easily have returned to Capernaum during the evening or night by land. "After pruning away these offshoots of the miraculous," continues Strauss, "the main stem is left, namely the miracle of Jesus walking on the sea." The Jewish mind was familiar with the idea of God's power over the sea. Among the miracles of Elisha is that of dividing the Jordan by a stroke of his mantle, so that he could walk over it dryshod (II *Kings* II, 14), and also that he caused a piece of iron which had fallen into it to float. In the book of Job (IX, 8) we are told that Jehovah walked on the sea as on a pavement. In the time of Jesus miracle workers claimed to be able to walk on the water. Popular superstition in many countries attributed to wonderworkers the power of walking on the water. "Hence," concludes Strauss, "it is natural that to certain of the followers of Jesus it seemed impossible that he did not possess this power."

But here they made the usual cardinal error of mistaking the attitude of the mind of Jesus towards miracle. He was always against working any miracle merely as an exhibition of his power. Again and again he refused to give a sign when the wish for the sign came of a desire to prove his power. He would not allow his divinity to be put to the proof. He only exercised it from motives that were far higher and fewer than the proof of his divinity.

It is in my own view the crucial test of a miracle by Jesus that it is *not* performed to prove his divinity, but from motives of love and compassion.

The moment I see the motive of the exhibition of power at play I suspect the story, and nearly always find myself compelled (on other grounds) to reject it.

In conclusion, therefore, I am compelled to reject the miracle of the walking on the sea, because:

1. It is inconsistent with itself.

2. It serves no purpose.

3. It is in violation of natural law that the body of Jesus should not be corporeal at all times, as it was at all the great moments of his life, from his birth to his burial. (The life after the Resurrection is another matter.)

4. It is dishonouring to the memory of Jesus and hurtful to the religion he founded.

According to *John* (VI, 23), it is one of two things—either the men from Tiberias who came to Capernaum the following morning looking for Jesus, having been at Bethsaida (Julias) the previous afternoon, saw the miracle of the feeding of the five thousand and believed that Jesus walked on the sea during the night, and did not a few hours later call upon Jesus to show them a sign that they might see and believe on him, or they called upon him to show them a sign that they might believe on him and did not see the miracle of the feeding of the five thousand, and knew nothing of his walking on the sea. Both *cannot* be true. Which is true? I think the large balance of truth lies on the side that they called for a sign and had not seen or heard of the miracles.

No fact is more obvious (and few facts are more difficult and painful to one who wishes to accept the Gospel stories as nearly as possible in the form in which they come down to us) than that all the critics seem to make a special point of *spiritualizing* away the humanity of Jesus during his lifetime so far as to make him supernaturally born, fast for long periods, be carried through the air by Satan, disappear in crowds, walk on the sea, and then of *materializing* him after his death and resurrection so far as to make him exhibit the wounds of the Cross, apparently healed, although only some thirty-six hours have passed since they were inflicted upon him, call for bread to appease apparent hunger, eat solid food, light fires and begin to cook a meal.

CHAPTER XXIV

Towards Jerusalem

I. *The Knowledge of Jesus*

IT IS IMPOSSIBLE to believe that Jesus never visited Jerusalem after his twelfth year until he went up finally to his death. It was his duty as a Jew to go to the feasts. He ate of the Passover on the night before his death. Those of the evangelists who appear to exclude Jesus and to confine his life and ministry to Galilee are obviously wrong. John indicates many visits to the feasts at Jerusalem during his ministry, but it is reasonable to assume that Jesus went up to Jerusalem again and again before his ministry. He betrays a most intimate acquaintance with the Holy City and the life there, the doctrinal traditions of the rabbis, the hypocrisies of the Pharisees, the disputes of the various rabbinical schools.

Unless we accept the Christian legend that Jesus was independent of human teachers, it is reasonable to believe that by these means he became familiar with the learned culture of his age and nation. During the last days in Jerusalem, and after his Resurrection, Jesus told his disciples to go out into all the world to preach his gospel. How much did he know of the world? Renan and others say he knew nothing. He was a Galilean, and, as far as the Gospels explicitly state, he knew little of the world beyond Galilee, except Jerusalem, parts of Judæa and Samaria. How utterly stupid is this —that he knew no more of his own country than the Gospels make mention of!

It is true that we have no record that he ever travelled outside his own country. We have no record that he knew more than about half of Palestine. If we are to judge by the Gospels he did not know Tiberias, although his home was within nine miles of it. He did not know Sepphoris, the capital of his native Galilee, only a few miles to the north and within sight of the hills above it. He did not know Joppa, although Peter, a Galilean fisherman, knew it; or Cæsarea, the capital of Judæa, although Philip, the evangelist, knew it. Nor did he know Antioch, although it was a great centre of Christian life a few years after his death.

He had no knowledge of Damascus, although Paul knew it, nor of Hebron, although it had been the first home of the father of his people, Abraham, and the first capital of David, who was later believed to be the king from whose loins Jesus had descended. He did not even know Bethlehem, although it was apparently prophesied that the Messiah should come from that city, while a few years after his death it was supposed that he himself was born there, and his father had been born there, and it was only six miles from Jerusalem, which he frequently visited.

He knew nothing of Mesopotamia, from which his race had sprung, or of the Assyrian and Babylonian country, which was closely wrapped up with the history of his people. Or Persia from which much of the faith of his people came. In like manner, he did not know Asia Minor, although Peter and John, the fishermen of Galilee knew it; or Italy, although a few years after his death Peter sailed to Naples, and Paul (as well as Peter) went to Rome. He did not know Rome, although Pontius Pilate came from there and returned to it, and Antipas, his own sovereign, was constantly going and coming from there.

In short, if we must judge of the knowledge of Jesus from the Gospels, he knew nothing of the world outside the country north of Galilee as far as Hermon, on the west as far as the coasts of Tyre and Sidon, as far east as the Peræan road on the other side of the Jordan.

But is it conceivable that this was the limit of his knowledge of the world into which he was sending his disciples? It does not require that we should believe that he actually travelled beyond the narrow circle of about 100 miles by thirty miles of Palestine to see that he had a very wide knowledge of the world. He knew the history of his people as told in the Scriptures. He knew the significance of prophecy better than the prophets themselves appear to have known it, for he put an interpretation upon some of the prophecies which was immeasurably truer to later history than the literal interpretation of the men who spoke and wrote. He saw farther and deeper into the future than any other speaker or writer of his own age. He knew that within measurable time Jerusalem would fall, and the Roman power would possess Palestine, or if he did not know and foretell this the Gospels are impudent fiction, and false story.

And what was his knowledge of the mind of the world into which he was sending his apostles? Did he know nothing of the religions of the pagan world? Paul knew the religion of Greece; did Jesus know nothing of it? Paul knew Æschylus and the teaching of the Greek poets; did Jesus know nothing of these? Peter knew that he and his fellow-evangelists were to suffer not alone from their own religious rulers but also from rulers in foreign lands; did Jesus, notwithstanding his specific warnings, know nothing of the reason for such persecutions?

Was he, in short, as nearly as possible, an ignoramus, utterly ignorant of conditions outside Palestine, when he was telling his followers to go out into all the world to preach his Gospel? It is almost too childish a proposition to discuss. Admit that Jesus never left a certain small section of his small country. Admit that we have no record that he attended rabbinical or other schools. Admit that he makes no mention of the philosophical teaching going on in the world during his time. Admit that he never mentions the great men of his own and foreign countries who lived in his time, or had died only a few years before his birth. But recognize in his reported words a wisdom which transcends that of any of the philosophers of the outside world; that he gave a gospel to his early followers which has transcended in depth and has lasted longer and exercised a deeper and wider influence than any of the philosophies of his age, and previous ages.

What then?

Are we to say he was a transcendent genius who knew things without being taught, that he was a prophet taught of God?

If we are forced to this conclusion we get very near to an admission of his divinity. We cannot account for him on any other grounds. A prophet of Galilee, born probably and brought up in the little mountain town of Nazareth, yet sending his disciples out to conquer the world by a new and eternal religion. And they did conquer it.

His visits to Jerusalem must have formed the foundation of his knowledge of the conditions of human society which became the subject of his most poignant teaching. There he saw the poor— Lazarus at the gate; the rich man enjoying all the good things of life. There he saw the fallen woman whose condition touched him deeply. There he saw the hypocrisy of the Pharisee which awakened his wrath. His view of the iniquities of the human condition appears to have come to him chiefly in Jerusalem. I think Jerusalem drew him like a magnet, yet it is clear that he hated it. His soul revolted against Jerusalem, although the most moving of his passages refer to it. "O Jerusalem, Jerusalem."

Then he saw the Roman power there, its arrogance. He saw the Jewish restiveness under Roman power, also the futile efforts made to overthrow it. He saw the corruption of the official classes and contrasted the luxury in which they lived (Annas had apparently three houses and Caiaphas two) with the poverty of the poor rabbi in Galilee who, like Hillel, was often on the verge of starvation. When would all this end? The god he found in Jerusalem was not his God. The effect of all this on Jesus cannot fail to have been very deep, and to have enforced his rebellion against the existing order.

II. His Way of Life

There must have been moments—perhaps many moments— when his strength of will and character were such as left the impression of a wild-eyed fanatic. By his passionate exhibition of his force of will in the presence of the possessed, Jesus may have produced the suspicion that he was beside himself, suggesting the thought of powers of darkness. This gives a very marked indication of the personality of Jesus—his compelling manliness is always apparent. His dauntless courage is evident in his attacks upon the Pharisees, and in his relentlessness to his own country people, his sharp rebukes to his disciples.

He stands in the line of the great minds whose inner confidence is never shaken by the storm. But he also stands in the line of the world's great men in his utter loneliness at his grandest moments, as in the lonely hour when many of his disciples leave him and he asks the twelve, "Will ye also leave me?" And in his lonely hour in Jerusalem, in Gethsemane, when the disciples cannot watch with him, when he knows that it is to be his last with them, and after he has told them that he must leave them very soon. He did not lose confidence in himself, but, encompassed by enemies, he felt himself alone. It was when the human brotherhood was failing, showing itself unregenerate, that his inner genius strengthened and his declarations of his kinship with God became most emphatic. "Night it must be ere Freedland's star will shine."

Thus he met the sceptical, cold, derisive question of the Pharisees, "When comes the kingdom of God?" by saying in effect, "The kingdom of God comes not with the observation of material things. Men shall not say, Lo here! Lo there! For, behold, the kingdom of God is in your midst."

How can anybody doubt that Jesus proclaimed himself the Messiah! This alone is proof of it. If the Kingdom was there, then must the Messiah have been there also.

> I thank thee, O Father, Lord of Heaven and earth, because thou hast hid these things from the wise and prudent, and has revealed them unto babes.

And then, later, the uncommon beauty and profound sublimity of the pearl of sayings that rings like the Old Testament:

> Come unto me, all ye that labour and are heavy laden, and I will give you rest. Take my yoke upon you, and learn of me; for I am meek and lowly in heart, and ye shall find rest unto your souls. For my yoke is easy, and my burden is light. [*Matthew* XI, 28–30]

The foregoing saying may have belonged to the earlier and more successful Galilean period, or yet to the later Galilean period, when the spiritual rulers of the nation, the scribes and the Pharisees, have rejected him, while the unlearned and childlike people, in their simplicity and good nature, have understood and accepted him.

This may have been the height of his Galilean period. "In the place of the scribes," says Keim, "he promises an easy yoke, and a burden which will bring rest to the soul. The rulership of the nation, the regeneration or the judgment of the world, healing or miraculous power—all are secondary to the principal fact that he led mankind to the knowledge of and communion with God."

It is a plausible opinion that before he made his final entry into Jerusalem Jesus had resolved upon preaching the gospel to the poor; heading a great poor man's agitation in Palestine. In entering upon a new campaign against the ruling classes he made an appeal to the oppressed and downhearted. Remember that when Jesus was taken to Calvary he had no money. The Roman soldiers divided his clothes, but we hear nothing of dividing money. He never sought or obtained wealth. He lived and died a poor man. It is idle to say that asceticism, which includes poverty, was never a part of Christian teaching. It was so from the first.

Jesus spoke approvingly of John the Baptist for having nothing effeminate about his habit and dress. He said of himself that he had not where to lay his head, but not as any kind of self-pity. He enjoined upon his apostles the simplest apparel and equipments. From this it is difficult to suppose that he wore anything better himself, unless it was the coat without seam which the women who followed him may have woven for him, and which was found on him when he was stripped for his death. Jesus as little despised the anointing of his face and hair as the washing of his feet. At table he permitted wine and delicate food, such as bread and honey, flesh, fish and fowl. Dwelling in a large and well-to-do household, he brought others to table with him, and he was also fond of being a guest at hospitable tables. At meals he clearly assumed the position of the head of his family. He took the bread, gave thanks, broke it and handed it round.

These meals (probably in the evenings), were in a sense his training ground for his disciples. When he ate with them last and took leave of them, he showed how much he had loved their company and how reluctantly he was parting from them. It was very simple, very human and very touching.

In his private intercourse with his disciples there was the lofty tone of a fellowship which was consecrated to the service of God and mankind. There was no sign of communism. This came after his death. The disciples had left their property when they joined him, but we are not told that they sold it for the benefit of the little commonwealth. They had a purse, presumably a common purse, but this may have been for the gifts they received on the way. They used the common purse for their common needs, as is shown by the Last Supper, and also for gifts to the poor, as is implied from the complaint of Judas at Bethany. But only the supply of daily wants seems to have been thought of. Jesus paid taxes for himself and for certain of his disciples, therefore, presumably, for all. Yet we are not told that he owned property, and it does not appear that, like Paul, he ever had need to resume from time to time his former calling.

We do not hear, except once, that Jesus ever took gifts from the people to whom he ministered. Once it is said that the women who followed him ministered to him of their substance. How far this went it is impossible to say. It is perfectly clear that Jesus never permitted it to go far. He lived plainly the life of a poor man. It is utterly against any reasonable conception of his character that he tolerated any collecting of money. It is incredible that he could have said what he did about the lilies of the field, and then allowed his disciples to go round with a collecting box. He trusted to God from day to day for his daily bread. And in that country and climate it was easy to do so. Dates grew by the wayside; figs and grapes were plentiful. Starvation was practically impossible. It was (to him) God being "mindful of him."

If the miracle of the feeding of the multitudes has to be rejected, yet the atmosphere of it may be true. When the disciples reflected that it would cost 200 pence (denarii) to feed so many, they were not saying they possessed so much, but merely hoping that such an expenditure was impossible to him.

It seems certain that Jesus himself never carried any money with him. Yet he distinguished himself always from the poor. He frequently wished to be alone, sometimes in a room, oftener in the open air, generally on the mountains. It is not true to say that he never prayed with his disciples, but he loved to pray alone. He always ruled his little company. Whenever they moved from one place to another it was he who gave the command.

He travelled, apparently, always afoot, except when he entered Jerusalem on his last visit. Renan's statement that he was accustomed to ride a mule while his disciples walked, thus surrounding himself with a sort of sovereign state, is (like more than one other statement from the same quarter) without so much as a vestige of authority. Indeed, all the evidences are against it. He was clearly a strong man, capable of long continued exertion. When the crowds pressed upon him, so that he had no time even to take food, he escaped to solitary places to rest and sleep. He was grateful for a drink of water. On his journeys he sometimes walked side by side with his disciples. On other occasions, particularly on going up to Jerusalem for the last time, he walked ahead of them.

This is a striking picture—Jesus walking ahead of the ever-increasing multitude which followed him up from Jericho to Bethany. At that moment he had great things to think about, and his disciples were full of great, although vain, hopes. Sometimes he would stay with a rich Pharisee while his disciples distributed themselves among the poorer people of the town or village. Sometimes the reception of Jesus was not hospitable, and occasionally he severely condemned it. But when John, the disciple, asked him to call down lightning from Heaven on the Samaritans who had denied him hospitality (because they saw that he was going up to Jerusalem, which they loathed), he reproved him strongly.

We may get a good idea of the sort of chamber he would occupy from the account of the room provided for the prophet Elisha by the Shunammite woman, who said to her husband, "Let us make a little chamber, I pray thee, on the wall; and let us set for him there a bed, and a table, and a stool, and a candlestick; and it shall be, when he cometh to us, that he shall turn in thither. And it fell on a day, that he came thither, and he turned into the chamber, and lay there."

We read in *Luke* that Jesus was to visit at the home of Martha and Mary. This was in Bethany. Probably he had made frequent visits, during the preministerial days, and again at the time of the Feast of Tabernacles and of Lights, as well as on the last journey. At these times, Martha would be busy with the work of the house, while Mary would sit at his feet, listening to him.

III. The Message from Bethany

After coming down from Mount Hermon, Jesus had set his face towards Jerusalem in the settled conviction that he was to die there, and that his death was to be the climax and crown of his life. Surrounded by enemies, he saw that for the fulfilment of the work assigned to him it was ordained that he should die in Jerusalem. For Jerusalem killed all the prophets and must kill him also some day.

It was now nigh to the Passover of A.D. 30, and people were going up to Jerusalem by the road on the east of Jordan and by the oasis of Jericho. Jesus and his disciples went with them, the usual way of the Galileans. Many of the incidents recorded in the Synoptic Gospels, particularly *Luke,* occurred on this journey; some of the parables, chiefly those relating to the hereafter, were spoken, and some of the miracles were worked.

In Jericho he did many wondrous works. It was there that he met Zacchæus, chief of the publicans, and was hailed by blind

Bartimæus. One can see Jesus as he was in those days, grown wearier, heavier, older, giving the very essence of his life to the sick and the blind who cast themselves in the road before him to be healed, and crying "Come unto me, all ye that labour and are heavy laden, and I will give you rest."

And while he was there a message came to him from Bethany that his friend, Lazarus, was ill. What should he do? Return to the region of Jerusalem at the peril of his life? He knew that the Pharisees must surely take him if opportunity served. Or should he turn a deaf ear to the cry of Mary and the voice of Martha? He could see them in their trouble. He knew their faith in him. If he were with Lazarus they believed that Lazarus could not die. He must go back to Bethany at all risk to himself. But then there were his disciples to think of also. He would be leading them to their deaths. In the midst of this a second message came from Bethany saying that Lazarus was dead. Then Jesus resolved that go back he must. "Let us go unto him," he said, obviously meaning, "Let us go to Bethany," which was practically Jerusalem. But his disciples said, "Master, the Jews of late sought to stone thee, and goest thou to Judæa again?" He answered them that he was going back with his eyes open. He was not stumbling. After that he spoke of Lazarus as one who slept, and of himself as one who was going to awake him out of his sleep. Thereupon Thomas said to his fellow disciples, "Let us also go, that we may die with him."

It is inconceivable that Thomas meant that they should die with Lazarus. What he obviously meant was that if Jesus went up to Jerusalem he would die, his enemies would kill him. Therefore Thomas meant, "Let us also go up to Jerusalem that we may die with Jesus."

Now, assume that others of the disciples shared Thomas's fear that if Jesus went up to Jerusalem he would be killed, and we have a motive for Judas's betrayal. He, with the other disciples, would die with Jesus. He (Judas) did not, like Thomas, wish to die with Jesus. Probably, almost certainly, he did not want Jesus to die. How was he to save his own skin and the life of Jesus at the same time?

Then came to Judas the idea which is dealt with later.

The disciples resolved that whither their Master went they also must follow, even if it was to death itself. So they set out for Judæa, followed by a great multitude with wild eyes full of the joy of expectancy. Bartimæus, with eyes that were seeing now for the first time. And walking ahead of them, alone, silent, speaking to none, Jesus.

The road from Jericho is very impressive, especially the first part of it. The oasis of Jericho and the sandy waste, going down to the south-east to the Dead Sea; the dark hills like unbroken upright walls beyond; the running water at the foot of the road upwards, with the fig-trees with their feet in or near the stream; the old Jericho road of huge round stones, not one of them sharp, suggesting the running of water over them for endless ages; the difficult ascent, the vast valley on the right, going up, an immense fissure in the face of the earth, the largest and most awesome thing in Palestine. Not a sign of life. The stony road beyond the fort through the walls of rock. Then, the scene behind being shut out little by little until it is gone; the Dead Sea, with its blind, scaly grey surface; the blue streak of the Jordan. The wild flowers in the spring are most plentiful where the ground is most stony.

Finally, the sight of Jerusalem. It is seen from the plains below, and is then obscured, but again, beyond the Mount of Olives, it reappears spread out in the spring sunshine with its white Temple, its marble palaces, their green gardens and shining domes, shining edifices from the height of Zion to the steep slope of Moriah; and in the nearer ground the grey-white village of Bethany, lying close against the hillside just under the heights of Jerusalem.

IV.   First Foreshadowing of the Betrayal

After the raising of Lazarus—the full story of which has been told elsewhere in this work—the report of the miracle spreading rapidly, people came from near and far to look upon the man who had been raised from the dead. In the house of Simon the leper there was a supper. Jesus sat at meat with the restored and now apparently healthy Lazarus, and with his disciples. Martha served. And while they ate, Mary came and anointed the feet of Jesus with ointment and wiped them with the hair of her head. It was the same act over again that she had done in the house of Simon, the Pharisee, save only that she had then washed the feet of Jesus with her tears.

And here we come upon an incident that would be perplexing but for one natural explanation. As Mary did this, and all the house was full of the odour of the ointment, one of the disciples, Judas Iscariot, began to grumble and to ask why this waste? The ointment was worth 300 pence. It could have been sold for that much. And the money could have been given to the poor. Was Judas thinking of the poor? Was he thinking that if the ointment had been sold he would have had the selling of it? Was he a thief? Beyond the one word of John, there is nothing to show that Judas was angry at the loss of an opportunity for theft. The grounds of conjecture are against John. Judas may have been a thief, but, if so, Jesus cannot have known it, or he would have replied, "Are you sure that you are thinking of the poor?" Even if Judas was angry at a lost opportunity for theft, what reason had he to think that the 300 pence would have been his to handle? He kept the purse for Jesus and his disciples, but the ointment belonged to Mary. Was all that belonged to Mary cast into the treasury of Jesus?

Is it not clear that, whatever the feeling of Judas, it concerned Mary in the first instance? Was he wroth at her constant devotion to Jesus?

I seem to feel a great gap in the Gospel narrative here, which, probably, none of the Gospel writers could fill. It seems to supply one of the several possible motives for the betrayal of Jesus by Judas. There is no hint of opposition before this. It is the first shadow of a feeling contrary to Jesus. Nothing occurs later that suggests a more adequate motive for the betrayal. Is it possible that the betrayal dates in the heart of Judas from this moment?

The motives usually assigned for the betrayal are few and unsatisfying. First, there is the motive of avarice, based on the character of thief which is fixed on Judas by *John* (XII, 6). Is this enough to account for the act? For thirty pieces of silver Judas sold his Master. The sum was a small one. Would Judas have taken so little if money had been the sole gain that he promised himself? The chief priests and elders were eager to lay hands on Jesus. To do so at night without danger from the people was worth more to them than thirty pieces of silver. They must have paid ten times as much if money alone had stood between them and their end.

Was Judas a fool as well as a thief? The probabilities are against the inference. He knew the value of money, for he kept the purse of Jesus and for his disciples. In that fact, also, lies a second objection to the motive of avarice. As keeper of the purse of the little company, a thief might hope to gain more than thirty pieces of silver for himself. To say that Judas was prompted to the betrayal of Jesus by desire of a sum so small is to imply that he was a thief who robbed himself. In a word, the motive of avarice is an absurdity.

Next, there is the motive of pride. Judas was weary of long endurance of the despiteful character of a follower of the man of Nazareth. He was waiting for the Kingdom. Jesus had promised it, and Judas believed that, being the Christ, he had power to make it come quickly. For reasons of his own, Jesus was holding back; but if evil chance could force his hand the Kingdom must needs come straightway. Let Jesus fall into the toils of his enemies, and stand in danger of death, and then he must assert his sovereignty and establish in Israel the throne of his father, David.

So Judas resolved to become in himself the instrument of that evil circumstance, and thrust upon Jesus the tardy honour which his spirit shrank from, and encompass, at the same time, his patient followers in the glory of his miraculous triumph. For this motive of pride there is not a shred of scriptural evidence, and hardly the rag of tradition. It gives a semblance of probability to the act of Judas by lifting it into the region of pure romance.

Again, there is the motive of envy. Judas was of a masterful spirit. He had joined Jesus in all loyalty, but grown daily more envious of his power. Thus, in a blind spasm of malice, at last he betrayed to his death the Master whom his heart could follow no more. For this explanation there is at least one shadowy piece of evidence, the behaviour of Judas in the house of Simon, the Pharisee. But, unlike the motives of avarice and of pride, this motive of envy is belied by the one other great act of Judas, his death by his own hand. No remorse would in the course of nature follow a betrayal springing from such a cause. The end desired would be the destruction of Jesus. Envy is the only passion with which remorse cannot live.

Nevertheless, is it not possible that envy comes by one angle into closer contact than avarice or pride with the only motive that is at once consistent and human for so base and mysterious a betrayal? The earlier record of Judas contains only a single passage wherein his individuality is distinct from that of his fellow-disciples. It is the passage already mentioned, telling what occurred in the house of Simon. There Judas is in partial antagonism to Jesus. Never before has he been so, and never afterwards is there a hint of conflict.

What does that passage mean? The fearless early commentators who did not shrink, to their great cost, from saying that the devotion of Mary Magdalene to Jesus was partly personal to the man, leapt to the conclusion that the rebellion of Judas against Jesus was partly personal to Mary. For this inference there was no other scriptural authority than the indirect evidence of the scene in the house of the leper. Was it enough? The Church answered no, with much emphasis and indignation.

Nevertheless, in the absence of direct evidence to establish any other motive whatever, whether that of avarice, which is an absurdity, or that of pride, which is pure romance, or that of envy, which is inconsistent with the later facts, a motive which is in harmony with the stronger impulses of human nature is surely worthy of credence, though the positive evidence supporting it is slight.

That Judas loved Mary Magdalene; that he witnessed with agony her devotion to Jesus; that once the pangs of his unregulated passion mastered him and he girded at Mary; that again he succumbed to the tortures of his secret love and revenged himself on Jesus.

This is a blunt statement of the motive of personal jealousy which has been assigned for the betrayal. Strange and bewildering it surely is that to nearly all Christians the idea of jealousy as an impulse to the act of Judas is something of a shock. By long use and familiarity they can accept without a quiver the more sordid idea of paltry avarice looking to a gain of thirty poor pieces of silver. But that he whom they look to in love and reverence and hope of the Kingdom should have been betrayed out of the baser promptings of that great passion which in its noblest impulses may have animated him, is a humiliation and disgrace.

Yet they have but to think of it, and they must see that it touches Jesus with no stain, while it raises Judas for the first time to the level of a man with a human soul. There was no humanity in the betrayer if he sold his Master for a paltry bribe; there was no intelligence in him if he thought to force his Christ to stride to his earthly throne in the mock regal robes of Herod;

there was no pity or remorse in him if he tried to destroy his prophet because he envied him. But all these are his, though so sadly distorted, if his awful act came of the madness of unrequited love.

We know nothing of the story of Judas before the betrayal save that he came from Kerioth, a town lying a day's journey beyond Hebron at the south of the tribe of Judah, and that he was the son of one Simon. What Simon this was we cannot say. If we might once more invade the silences of scripture, we might easily fill the gap in the Gospel narrative, and make credible the motive of jealousy by bridging over the little difficulties of material fact. Let us try to fill the gap.

Simon may have been Simon, the Pharisee, who married Martha, and became Simon, the leper. Judas may have been known to Mary of Magdala in the days of her infirmity. He may have loved her. When she fell away into base life Judas may have turned his back upon her. But when she returned to the feet of Jesus his old affection for her may have revived. He may have struggled against it, but it may have tormented him. It may be that Judas helped to induce Jesus to leave Mary behind at Bethany. It may be that he tried to dissuade Jesus from returning to Bethany when the news came of the death of Lazarus. And it may be that after the miracle, seeing Mary at the feet of Jesus, worshipping him, all the gall in the heart of Judas rose to his throat, and he blurted out his subterfuge about the waste of the ointment.

If this was so, did Jesus understand him, though to all the other disciples the words of Judas meant nothing? "Let her alone; against the day of my burying hath she kept this. For the poor always ye have with you; but me ye have not always." This was no answer to one whom Jesus knew to be a thief. Did it not say, "Let her alone. This is only for a little longer. It will be all over very soon."

Can it be that on that Judas rose up and, in the tumult of his emotions, went off to betray Jesus to the chief priests? He knew that the chief priests and rulers were waiting for an opportunity to take Jesus. Perhaps he thought that having taken him they would banish him. If all this is probable, the reply of Jesus to Judas was full of tender insight into the secret of his heart.

V. *Jesus in Ephraim*

The visit of Jesus to Ephraim is indicated only in John's Gospel, and is there attributed to the poorest of all motives—the desire of Jesus to save himself from the Jewish ruling authorities, who, after they had received news of the raising of Lazarus, concluded that it was necessary to put Jesus to death if they were to save the nation.

> Then from that day forth they took counsel together for to put him to death. Jesus therefore walked no more openly among the Jews; but went thence unto a country near the wilderness, into a city called Ephraim, and there continued with his disciples. [*John* XI, 47–54]

The three earlier Gospels say nothing of this going to Ephraim, but caused Jesus to go directly into Jerusalem after coming up from Jericho (thereby omitting the story at Bethany and also the raising of Lazarus).

John's story shows Jesus returning to Bethany six days before the Passover, and then occurs the supper at which Mary anoints his feet.

Many critics reject the Ephraim journey, with the incident of the raising of Lazarus, and place the supper after the entry into Jerusalem. I see no reason to do so, but also I see no reason to accept John's account of the reason for the flight to Ephraim. That, at that stage of his life, Jesus should fly from the danger of death, having sought death and being on the point of walking to his death (for surely this is of the essence of Christianity), is utterly unbelievable. And if it were credible that he escaped from the Jews to save his life immediately after the miracle at Bethany, it is inconceivable that he should return to it six days later, thus putting himself into the same danger. What, then, is the meaning of the flight into Ephraim?

My conclusion is that Jesus (being six to ten days too early for the Passover) went into the wilderness which had been, as I think, the scene of his first temptation (after his baptism) to strengthen his soul for the trial that was to come. This, and not fear of the Jews, was the object of the journey to Ephraim.

Nor do I think he took *all* his disciples with him into the wilderness. I think it probable that he took only the three who had been with him on the mountain of the Transfiguration, and were afterwards to be nearest to him in Gethsemane.

Judas, I feel, was left behind in Bethany. And it is impossible to believe that the multitudes who had followed him up towards Jerusalem (including the women who had followed him from Galilee) were not also left behind in Bethany.

Remember, that the disciples and followers of Jesus were accustomed to such disappearances. He had often disappeared and then reappeared. It was characteristic of him. He went into the mountains, across the Lake of Galilee, into the desert places, to be alone—to pray—to be with God—to make up his reckoning with his soul.

CHAPTER XXV

Cleansing of the Temple

I. The Entry into Jerusalem

ACCORDING TO the Gospel of John it was on the next day following the supper at Bethany that Jesus entered Jerusalem. It was certainly after his sojourn in the wilderness of Ephraim. The material fact is unimportant. Many people had, by this time, come to the Holy City for the Feast of the Passover, and, hearing that Jesus was coming, they went up to Bethpage, on the Mount of Olives, to meet him. They carried branches of palm and went forth crying "Hosanna: Blessed is the King of Israel that cometh in the name of the Lord." All Jerusalem was astir and the streets were thronged. People asked: "Who is this?" And the crowd answered, "This is Jesus, the prophet of Nazareth in Galilee."

A deep melancholy filled the soul of Jesus. No longer serene and satisfied, but silent and perturbed and occasionally lit up with defiance. His heart was sore, but his eye did not flinch. The Spirit was strong upon him. He was entering Jerusalem in God's name. He was making a direct challenge to the rulers of the Jews, an effort to assert his Messianic authority. But while the people understood it to be the assertion of a political Messianic authority, Jesus intended it for a spiritual authority.

He entered the city riding upon an ass. This is said to be according to the prophecy in *Zechariah* (IX, 9): "Rejoice greatly, O daughter of Zion; shout, O daughter of Jerusalem; behold, thy king cometh unto thee; he is just, and having salvation; lowly, and riding upon an ass, and upon a colt the foal of an ass."

Not a few modern writers (chiefly among the Germans) have said that the fact that Jesus chose to ride into Jerusalem on an ass is proof of his desire to make his entry into Jerusalem a Messianic entry, as of a king. This is said in ignorance of the spirit of the time and country of Jesus and of the East generally. The ass was indeed then, as it is now, the animal constantly ridden by the people going about on their ordinary business. But to put a pretender to a dignity on an ass in a procession was to show contempt for him. It was the sign of the people's contempt for his pretensions. On the occasion of the suppression of a rebellion in Parthia, about six years after the Crucifixion, the head of it was set on an ass which, among the Parthians, was considered the greatest reproach possible.

This custom in Syria of setting a man on an ass by way of disgrace is still kept up in Damascus, and during the Turkish rule the Turks showed their despite against the Christians by not suffering them to ride horses on any occasion, but asses only. Jesus must have known this eastern custom perfectly. It is, therefore, inconceivable that in riding into Jerusalem on an ass, instead of walking or riding on any other animal, he was about to impress the Jews of Jerusalem that their king was coming.

If he had any thought about it at all, as I think he certainly had, it was to indicate that he was *not* coming as a temporal king—the king of the house of David—but as the suffering Messiah, the spiritual Christ, who made no pretensions to temporal sovereignty, but quite the reverse. That the disciples and the children did not understand this, but cried, Hosanna, was their mistake, not his. Later, at the trial before Caiaphas, nobody ever mentions that Jesus rode into Jerusalem on an ass. The Jews knew better than to mention a fact which told against their accusation.

John says that the disciples did not understand this at the first, but when Jesus was glorified (as he ascended into Heaven) they remembered that these things were written of him, and that they had done these things unto him. Therefore, the people who had been with him when he raised Lazarus out of the grave bore record.

In other words, the people of Bethany and of Jerusalem, who had seen Lazarus raised from the dead, joined the crowd about Jesus and testified to what they had seen. The Pharisees saw all this and said among themselves, "Perceive ye how ye prevail nothing? Behold, the world is gone after him."

It is not until after the entry into Jerusalem that it is said, in *Mark,* that the scribes and chief priests sought that they might destroy Jesus. The spirit of the multitude is that of an expectant army coming into Jerusalem to take possession of it. Some of the Pharisees among them protest against his being acclaimed the

Messiah. They say, "Master, rebuke thy disciples." To which Jesus answers, "I tell you that, if these should hold their peace, the stones would immediately cry out."

Does he mean that the fact (that he is the Christ) is so manifest that the very stones would cry out if men were silent? If so, is Jesus accepting the salutations of the multitude who are taking him into Jerusalem? That he is a king, and that he is coming in the name of God—that he is a divinely appointed king? And if he is accepting their salutations, is he sharing their hope—that the kingdom of David is about to be established? If this is a true reading of *Luke,* and if Jesus answered the Pharisees so, it is small matter for surprise that, not believing in him as the Christ, they should set about to have him arrested for blasphemy. They could do nothing else and remain Jews.

Whatever part Jesus may have taken, it must be judged of in the speech of his age, his race and the mood of his followers. In that age, in those conditions, some visible demonstration may have seemed to Jesus to be necessary. To our modern sense of what befits a great man, it would seem immeasurably a greater and nobler thing that he should enter Jerusalem afoot, simply, in the dignity of his splendid manhood. But this might not have made so deep a Messianic impression. It is possible that here lies the key.

Jesus had again and again, on the journey south, tried to make his disciples see his errand to Jerusalem in its right light. He was the king of the Jews, the Christ, the son of the living God. But his kingship had nothing to do with this world. It would have nothing to do with triumphal entry into Jerusalem, such as the procurators made when they came up at the time of Passover with their guards from Cæsarea Philippi in chariots, riding magnificently caparisoned horses, in glittering helmets, and with the blare of trumpets. How should he tell that truth to his disciples? He selected the humblest animal, the creature the humblest man or woman rode upon any day of any year. *This* was the symbol of his kingship—nothing more. On a general view of the four narratives of the entry into Jerusalem it is abundantly clear,

1. That the people (fresh from the raising of Lazarus, a miracle such as no other man had ever done, yet they believed him to have done) thought Jesus was the Christ, and that he was making a Messianic entry into the city of David, to take possession of his

throne, and to establish his Kingdom, and that as king, by the divine right, he would never die, and his Kingdom would never end.

2. That the chief priests and Pharisees thought all this a lie, an ignorant pretence on the part of the populace; that Jesus knew perfectly well that he had not performed the miracle of raising the dead which, above all else, had carried the people away; that he knew he was not the Christ, yet permitted himself to be called the Christ, the king appointed by God to take possession of the throne of David.

3. That Jesus knew he was not going up, as the multitude thought, to glory, but to death. He believed he was the Christ in a much higher sense than the people believed it. The Christ to them was no more than the Messiah, the messenger of God, who was to bring in the thousand years of peace.

To Jesus, the Christ was the Son of God. As the Son of God he was not (like the Messiah) to live on. He was to die. By his death he was to ransom the world. This was the sacrificial work God the Father had laid upon him. "For this cause came I into the world." In his humanity he was to go through death. All who followed him had to go through it. They were to lose their lives that they might gain it.

It was at once a humble and a triumphant entry. Great numbers of the Jews gathered in Jerusalem for the feast came out to meet him. The people of the villages on the Mount of Olives went down with him. There were numbers of children. There was a great scene as he entered by the Golden Gate. He was hailed as the son of David, who came in the name of the Lord. He accepted that name and character.

According to a calculation made from the fourth Gospel, Jesus entered Jerusalem on Sunday, the first day of the Passover week. Thus (*John* XII, 1) he returned from Ephraim to Bethany six days before Passover. Passover was either on Friday, or it was on the Sabbath, Saturday—apparently it was on Friday. Six days before Friday (counting from Thursday) would be Saturday. In the evening of Saturday (after the close of the Sabbath) they made the supper at Bethany. On the next day after the supper (Sunday, the first day of the week, see *John* XII, 12), Jesus entered Jerusalem. The intervening days from Sunday until Thursday morning are not indicated in *John*. On the night of the beginning of Passover (after 6 P.M. on Thursday, if Passover was on Friday) he held his Passover Supper.

Nothing in *Luke* indicates the day of Jesus's entry into Jerusalem. Nothing more than "one of these days" to indicate the passage of time while in Jerusalem. Nothing more than "Then came the day of unleavened bread" to indicate the day of the Last Suppper. There is nothing in *Matthew* or in *Mark* to indicate the day of the week of Jesus's entry into Jerusalem. According to *Mark* (XIV, 1) the feast at Bethany was held two days before Passover—therefore on the Thursday. On the first day of unleavened bread (Thursday morning) Jesus sent his disciples to prepare the Passover. After 6 o'clock on Thursday he celebrated the Passover. That night he was arrested. The following morning (Friday) he was tried and condemned. On the evening of that day (before 6 P.M.) he was buried.

Some critics say Jesus entered Jerusalem from Bethany early on the morning of the Sabbath. This would be Saturday, April 9th. The objection to this is (1) that the casting out of the money-changers could not have occurred (as the Synoptics indicate) on the Sabbath; (2) that in travelling from Bethany to Jerusalem on the Sabbath Jesus and all his followers would be breaking the law —they would be breaking the Jewish Sabbatic law which, according to *Exodus* XVI, 29, forbade a longer journey on the Sabbath than six stadia, about one Roman mile. But according to *Acts* (I, 12) and Josephus, the Mount of Olives was a Sabbath Day's journey from Jerusalem, or six stadia, but Bethany was fifteen stadia, a stadium being about a furlong (*John* XI, 18).

II. The Traders Driven out of the Temple

Thus Jesus entered the Holy City and came to the Temple, and in its outer courts he found traders in doves and sheep and goats, and money-changers, and the Pharisees and chief people who came to buy sacrifices. There were the rich Pharisees buying doves and goats for sacrifices—the richer the worshipper the costlier his sacrifice, the more his display, his rivalry. There were the traders bartering and haggling over the prices of the sacrifices, with pious words on their lips, but cheating when they could. And the priests permitting it for their own gain. No room there for the poor, the widow, the publican, the harlot, however repentant.

Jesus saw all this at a glance. These people were serving mammon, and yet trying to make a show of serving God. With the Devil's money they were trying to bribe God. And that was the Temple of God, built for a house of prayer, and outside of it were the blind lying begging at the gate, and the poor who could not buy doves and goats, and the heavy-laden who were waiting for their masters when they should have made an end of their mock worship.

Such was the scene Jesus came upon after that entry into Jerusalem. He had fled from Herod, and from yet more terrible devils within himself. He had been renouncing human joys, and the passions of man that God's kingdom might come, that the poor might have the Gospel preached to them, that the outcast might hear the glad tidings, that he might live his own doctrine of self-sacrifice. And here in Jerusalem, in the heart of the Temple, were the chief men and rulers openly flaunting the worship of the Devil in the name of the worship of God.

At thought of this the heart of Jesus rose in wrath. He overturned the tables of the money-changers; he took a whip and whipped the traders out of the place, crying, "It is written My house shall be called the house of prayer, but ye have made it a den of thieves." And the traders went out before him, and the Pharisees and chief people slunk away. Not because they feared the arm of one man, or the light of wrath that flashed in his face, but because he was in the right; because they were thieves and they knew it, hypocrites and were ashamed of it in their hearts. No gentle Jesus here, no meek and patient Jesus, but the Jesus of stern and mighty soul, the Jesus who had denounced the scribes and Pharisees.

Then, when the rich hypocrites and the traders were gone from the Temple and it was clean, the blind and the lame and the poor that had lain outside came in to Jesus, and he healed and taught them. On the last day of the festival, when the fasts were over and the wine cups were filled, he stood up and cried, "If any man thirst, let him come unto me, and drink." The poor understood him.

Going out of the Temple the disciples of Jesus drew his attention to its grandeur and to the goodly stones it contained. Then he prophesied that the time was coming when not one stone should be left upon another. That was because men had thought more of the gold that was upon the Temple than of the Temple itself, more of the gift than of the altar, more of the house than of the prayer. In the time to come men would not worship in buildings made with hands. That which is born of the Spirit is Spirit.

In *John* (II, 14) the incident of the purification of the Temple occurs during the first residence of Jesus in Jerusalem, immediately after the visit to Cana of Galilee, therefore within a short time after his baptism. In *Matthew* (XXI, 12) it occurs during the last visit of Jesus to Jerusalem, and immediately after his entry into the Holy City. The ancient commentators thought, as many modern ones still think, that these were separate events.

There are slight differences in the narrations; also slight differences in the language used by Jesus. In the Synoptic Gospels Jesus uses an exact quotation from the Old Testament. In *John* he gives a free version. In *John* he is immediately called to account by the Jews. In the Synoptics nothing occurs until next day, when a question is put to him which is thought (I consider wrongly) to have no reference to the purification of the Temple.

On which side lies the error? It is difficult to believe that the same incident (as it is substantially) occurred twice. Therefore we have to decide when it most probably occurred.

I take the view of the Synoptics that it occurred during the last visit to Jerusalem, and that it led on to the end. If such an assertion of authority, such an outrage on the rights (or perquisites) of the Temple authorities (particularly Annas), had occurred at the beginning of the ministry, the ministry would probably have come to a quicker close. The synoptists evidently knew nothing of any earlier visit to Jerusalem, and nothing of an earlier purification of the Temple. The upholders of John say that the added details in his story (the scourge, the different treatment of different classes of traders, the more indirect allusion to the Old Testament passage) are so many proofs that he was eye-and-ear witness of the scene.

Mark (XI, 16) has a dramatic reference, "And would not suffer that any man should carry any vessel through the temple," which has the support of Jewish custom, that did not permit the court of the Temple to be made a thoroughfare. This justifies Jesus, and partly explains why the money-changers did not resist, but it does not prove that Mark was an eye-witness. It was the writer's memory, not his eye, that was at work in making that reference.

The fourth Gospel antedates the acknowledgment of Jesus by the disciples. It is impossible to show any reason why the scene should occur at the beginning of the ministry. There are strong grounds for the opposite opinion. It is no inconsiderable argument against John's position of the event that Jesus (who frequently avoided collision with the authorities, because his time had not yet come) should from the outset have courted it by this violent act. At this time (John's time) he had not given himself out as the Messiah (and had not been generally or largely recognized as the Messiah) and only Messianic authority would have given safety to such an act.

The rulers of the Temple (at the period indicated by John) would have had nothing to fear from arresting Jesus and punishing him for such summary conduct. Jesus, also, had then no following to protect him. But to the last week of his life such a scene is perfectly suited. He was followed by a great crowd. He was protected by an immense recognition as a prophet. He was safe from any open opposition from the rulers of the Temple upon doing what Jewish law and custom justified him in doing.

After his Messianic entrance into Jerusalem, it was his direct aim in all he said and did to assert his Messiahship, in defiance of his enemies. And he was not alone. He had a multitude behind him. He had Jewish law and custom behind him. He had the force of might by his side. Then there was the irresistible impression of the commanding personality of Jesus, which was always powerful even when gentle. Such a group of usurers (they were breaking the law by practising usury within the Temple, or at all with Jews) and cattle-dealers, who had no right there and knew it, would find no protection from the corrupt priesthood, who had taken their money.

Then there is the probability that many of the Jewish onlookers (long scandalized by the sacrilegious traffic which they had never dared to resist) made common cause with Jesus.

We must realize what exactly the Temple stood for to the Jew of the time of Jesus. When it became, and in what sense and to what extent it became, "this holy place." What was the sin of predicting its downfall? This knowledge is necessary to realize the enormity of the offence of Jesus when, as the false witness declared, he said he could cast it down. It had become a thing in itself. God *dwelt* in the Temple. It was His house, His central abode. Christ took the view that the central abode of God was in the heart of man, therefore God could not truly be worshipped except in the spirit, not in houses made by hands. It was the house of the Ark of the Covenant. The Temple was sacred because it was the house of God's Ark. Sacrifices could only be made in the Temple, and when the Temple fell sacrifices ceased.

The Temple was the place which the invisible Spirit of God entered, and made His place of residence. Hence it became God's house, and God had no other house. Jesus broke all this to pieces by his words to the woman of Samaria, and by what he said about destroying the Temple and building it again in three days.

But it is argued that this supposition that many of the Jewish onlookers were in sympathy is fatal to the entire incident, since it makes Jesus the cause of an open tumult, and therefore it is difficult to reconcile his conduct with his usual aversion to everything revolutionary, and with his direct command to "resist not evil."

The extraordinary sensation made by this event is at once seen by the stupefied and unresisting retreat of the money-changers, the reverent quietness of the people, and the speechlessness and inactivity of the Temple guard.

One can reconstruct the scene of sudden interruption. The many traders, the great numbers of beasts for sacrifice, the tables covered with coins; the Temple guard walking to and fro, and the chief inspector sitting on a high seat from which he overlooked the whole market. Then the buyers, the Jew clients, the foreign festival guests. And then this Galilean, followed no doubt by a great number of the people who had come up with him from Galilee, as well as many of the people of Jerusalem. They are all swept out by one man with a whip of light rushes in his hand, or perhaps no whip whatever. They go. They make no kind of resistance. The Pharisees make no protest then. The priests are called, but either stay away or, coming, say not a word. The soldiers of the Temple are at hand, but not called. Nothing done. The Temple swept clean. Not a word is said that day.

What did it mean? Fear of one man? Fear of his followers? One thing it certainly meant—the conviction in the minds of all that Jesus was in the right, that this trading, however countenanced by the ruling powers, was a violation of the law of Moses, a profanity of the sanctity of the Temple, a breach of the law of God.

More than that, one cannot resist the conclusion that at that moment at least the conviction (or the fear) had taken hold of everybody that this prophet of Nazareth was what his followers declared him to be—the Messiah. To contend against the servant of God would be like contending against God Himself. So they submitted; they allowed themselves to be swept out like sheep, before the force of one man—and the right.

III. The Day of Triumph

This was the day of greatest power and triumph for Jesus. If he had really been minded to claim the throne of David, it was *then* he could have done it with most chance of at least a temporary success. The Roman garrison of Pilate had probably already arrived in Jerusalem from Cæsarea. It was the custom of the Roman procurator to come from Cæsarea (where he kept his army of occupation) to Jerusalem (where he kept constantly only a small force) at the Passover.

This was obviously in order to keep the peace, to protect the sovereignty of Rome, at the time when the subject race, the Jews, were celebrating the festival which recalled the most triumphant fact in their history—their liberation from their thraldom in Egypt. Their passions were then at their highest and might break out into any wild rebellion. Pilate, the procurator, would come from the west. It would be a true Roman coming, as of the representative of the Roman conquerors—chariots, war-horses, shining helmets and fluttering banners. Pilate would no doubt take up his residence in the old palace of Herod the Great—the castle.

They were accustomed to make the journey in twenty-four hours. And the Galilean bodyguard of Herod Antipas (his mercenaries) were, perhaps, also there. Herod Antipas was in the habit of coming to Jerusalem at Passover. This was required of him as a Jewish ruler, although he was a bad Jew. He would come to safeguard his own people, the people of Galilee and the people of Peræa. He had reason to do so—Pilate had done great wrong to them already. But the people of Jerusalem would have been with Jesus. The bodyguard of Antipas (being Jews) would have been afraid to fight against him; they had had a bitter experience a few months before, in fighting for their ruler (who had violated the law of Moses) against Aretas; and it is at least arguable that against three millions of Jews when gathered in Jerusalem for the Passover (according to Josephus) the soldiers of Pilate might have had more than enough to do. They might have fled.

It is true that the victory (if the attempt had been made) must have been temporary only. The Roman governor was near with his cohorts. An insurrection under Jesus of Nazareth must surely have been crushed with limitless bloodshed. But at that moment it looked possible.

Jesus had no such designs. His disciples may have wondered why. Judas in particular may have wondered why. They had still much to learn; that all this was a religious revolt and not, in any sense, a political revolt.

In dealing with the scene of the cleansing of the Temple, Origen regarded it as incredible that so great a multitude should have unresistingly submitted to one man, a man whose claims had ever been obstinately contested. Therefore, Origen appeals to the supernatural powers of Jesus to extinguish the wrath of his enemies, and to render their opposition impotent. Hence, Origen ranks the incident among the greatest of the miracles of Jesus, and seems to cast a measure of doubt on the historical value of the Gospel narrative. But in order to make a myth of the entire scene, it is necessary to show how it could have originated, and there is nothing to suggest this except that, according to the synoptists, Isaiah and Jeremiah prophesied that the Temple should be made a den of robbers.

But here we have in the incident a necessary link in the chain which led Jesus to his death. It is a clear necessity of the story of the end. In all probability the person chiefly offended by it was old Annas, who was hit in his pocket. It is reasonable to think he was the instrument that carried out the betrayal by Judas. Thus it leads on to the Crucifixion. We cannot sacrifice the purification of the Temple as an integral part of the story of the Cross.

IV. *The Last Days in Jerusalem*

Jesus made no terms with the chief priests and rich men, the rulers and the Pharisees, and they made no terms with him. They protested, but he did not mind them. While his enemies were tempting him in an effort to destroy him, either before the Sanhedrin or before Pontius Pilate, and to dishonour him and make him impotent among the people, Jesus moved unmolested about the Temple, teaching. One of his favourite halting places was Solomon's Porch, a crumbling relic of colossal marble blocks in the eastern wall. Here he spoke to the people, sometimes in the presence of his enemies, sometimes to his disciples in the presence of the people only.

The priests and Pharisees were determined, if they could, to weaken his authority with the people, for "they feared the people." Much as they hated Jesus, much as they were resolved to have his life if they were able, in the midst of the enthusiasm they were afraid to touch him. Instead, they came upon him and plied him with subtle questions. By this means they hoped, either that they would set him a problem he could not solve, or that he would give them an answer which they could turn against him.

But Jesus met them all. He gave them replies which only turned against themselves; and in turn he asked them questions which compelled them to silence. He spoke parable after parable, all telling them plainly, if they were willing to hear, how grievously they were rejecting the grace that was being offered, and how terrible in consequence would be their retribution. Last of all, when nothing that he said would move them, he turned upon them with the tremendous invective: "Woe unto you, scribes and Pharisees, hypocrites, because ye are like unto whited sepulchres," and walked out of the gate.

John concludes the events of those two days in Jerusalem with the words:

These things spake Jesus, and departed, and did hide himself from them. But though he had done so many miracles before them, yet they believed not on him; that the saying of Esaias the prophet might be fulfilled, which he spake, Lord, who hath believed our report, and to whom hath the arm of the Lord been revealed? Therefore, they could not believe, because that Esaias said again, He hath blinded their eyes, and hardened their heart, that they should not see with their eyes, nor understand with their heart, and be converted, and I should heal them. These things said Esaias, when he saw his glory, and spoke of him. Nevertheless, among the chief rulers also many believed on him; but because of the Pharisees they did not confess him, lest they should be put out of the synagogue. For they loved the praise of men more than the praise of God.

That the chief priests were actively at work to bring about the destruction of Jesus after the raising of Lazarus is obvious. For a poor ray of comfort to their consciences, hiding from themselves, if they could, the true ground of their hatred, they pointed to the fact that the law said that no prophet could come out of Galilee. These crowds that followed Jesus were ignorant of the law, and they would not know this. No chief man or Pharisee followed this prophet of Nazareth. Therefore, they declared, he was a false prophet and they should take him. They were clearly for assassination without trial when one of their number, Nicodemus, rose and said, "Does our law, by which you would justify this execution, sanction the taking of a man's life without first hearing him?" At that they were ashamed and went off each man to his house.

V. The Flight from Jerusalem

All the same, they held to their secret resolve to kill Jesus, if opportunity offered, and rumour of this conspiracy reaching Jesus he left Jerusalem and retired again to Bethany. He had always prepared for great events by prayer; and for this greatest event in the world's history he prepared himself by two days of retirement. And going off, at the bend of the road on the summit of the Mount of Olives he saw the city spread out behind him, with its domes and roofs, a gorgeous spectacle, and wept over it, saying,

> O Jerusalem, Jerusalem, thou that killeth the prophets and stonest them which are sent unto thee, how often would I have gathered thy children together, even as a hen gathereth her chickens under her wings, and ye would not!
> If thou hadst known, even thou, at least in this thy day, the things which belong unto thy peace! But now they are hid from thine eyes. For the days shall come upon thee that thine enemies shall not leave in thee one stone upon another, because thou knowest not the time of thy visitation.

From the raising of Lazarus onwards Jesus knew full well the hostility of the chief priests. He thought it part of a preordained plan. Therefore, his personal hostility to the enemies who brought about his death was never bitter. Even his anger against Judas Iscariot was never great.

It is abundantly clear that the chief priests and Pharisees did not believe in the miracle of the raising of Lazarus. But they saw that the people believed in it, and that it would therefore lead to grievous consequences. They held councils to consider what was to be done. Was there any reason to do anything? There was none. But each man in his heart believed that his class was in danger from this new prophet. Jesus taught that they had no right to exist.

Many people believed in Jesus, partly for the sake of his gospel of the Kingdom, and partly for the sake of the miracles he wrought. If the multitudes of the poor believed that the Pharisees and rulers and priests had no rights to the place and power and wealth they held, the multitudes of the poor would try to pull them down. This was the secret terror in the hearts of the great people. But they could not confess this even to one another. What they adopted was an excuse. If the people believed Jesus to be the Christ, they would accept him as king of the Jews. If he was given out as an aspirant to the throne of David, the Romans would come and suppress the insurrection. In suppressing it they might take away even such privileges as left them still a nation. More than this, the priests wished to uphold the Roman yoke, because it was the source of their riches and honours. Therefore, they could not stand by and let Jesus prevail alone.

Then one of their number, Caiaphas, the high priest that year (for the office of high priest under the Romans changed often) said, "It is expedient that one man should die for the people, that the whole nation perish not." And from that time they took definite counsel together to put Jesus to death.

VI. *The Divinity of Jesus*

But before they could put him to death they must have something with which to accuse him before the powers of Rome. The nearest accusation was that which they had thought of—the accusation of a claim on the part of Jesus to be king of the Jews. So they lay in wait for him, and later, after his two days of prayer and meditation, as he walked in the Temple in Solomon's Porch they came to him and said, "How long will you keep us in doubt? If thou be the Christ tell us plainly."

To this Jesus answered, "The works that I do in my Father's name, they bear witness of me. . . . I and my Father are one."

Now when the Pharisees heard this they thought they had entrapped him. Being a man, he made himself God. This, in their view, was blasphemy and deserving of death by Jewish law. But

Jesus answered them, in effect, "Is it not written in the law that all men were called Gods to whom the word of God came? Why, then, do I blaspheme if I call myself the Son of God, seeing that I am doing God's works, and speaking God's words? Am I not showing you that the Father is in me, and I in Him?"

Perhaps this incident occurred during the first visit of Jesus to Jerusalem. The occasion of it is of less consequence than its doctrine. It is the one plain word of Jesus himself on the point of his divinity.

Such was the situation. *One more serious aspect.* Jesus was threatening the very existence of the Jewish high priesthood and the Sanhedrin. The high priesthood was corrupt, if only because it was based on a wrong foundation. The high priest ought to have succeeded by direct descent from Aaron. For a long time past he had been appointed by Rome. Herod the Great had made his own high priests. Pontius Pilate's predecessor had appointed Caiaphas. Another Roman procurator had appointed Annas, the father-in-law of Caiaphas.

It was impossible that Jesus of Nazareth and Caiaphas could exist side by side in the same country. Jesus of Nazareth must be destroyed. But how? The people were on his side, and the chief priest was afraid of the people.

Jesus had made his last reckoning with himself before taking the final step of re-entering Jerusalem to meet, as he well knew it must be, his death. How did he know it must be? First, because, like all prophets, he saw deeper into the future than the ordinary man, and therefore knew what the high priests and Sanhedrin would do, must do—give him up to the Gentile power, the Roman power. Also, he knew what the Roman power must do in self-defence—execute him, which he knew would mean crucify him as a man who was (or would be, in their eyes, instructed by the Jewish authorities) trying to alienate the people from their allegiance to the Roman emperor.

In the meantime, the Jewish authorities had been trying to bring about the destruction of Lazarus who, in their view, was a party to the deception which was leading the people away to belief in Jesus, who by virtue of false and sham miracles was assuming the character of the Son of God, the Christ, as foretold by the prophets. It is not unlikely (*John* XI, 57) that the chief priests were tempting the people by bribes to betray and arrest Jesus.

The supper at Bethany was six days before the Passover. Others than the disciples were present on this occasion. And when the scene with Judas Iscariot came these others witnessed the clash between Judas and Jesus.

It is possible that some of these were among the unbelievers referred to in *John* (XI, 46) who "went their ways to the Pharisees and told them what things Jesus had done." Probably some of these went to the chief priests with the story of the rebellion of Judas, and so led to the first step towards the betrayal.

Judas was in a mood that prepared him for overtures, and I think Annas found a means of getting at him. It is not unreasonable to assume that he offered a bribe to Judas through an intermediary, and that Judas yielded to the first overtures. I think it probable that the overtures came from Annas, the arch conspirator and organizer and chief agent in all high priestly corruption.

VII.   In Jerusalem Again

Jesus knew what was before him, and made no attempt to avoid it. On the contrary, he seemed to provoke it, as in the scene of the casting out of the money-changers, and the denunciation of the hypocrisy of some of the ruling classes.

Then came the near approach of the Sabbath. I think Jesus knew (whether by intuition, his natural power of seeing deeper and more clearly than other men, so that no man needed to tell him anything, or by direct information given to him) what was going on in the councils of the high priests—the intercourse with Judas, the scheme for arresting him and disposing of him before the Passover.

In the latter case, there was at least one obvious source of information. Through these scenes in Jerusalem there passes an unnamed person—the young disciple in the garden who fled, leaving his linen clothes behind him, the disciple who followed Jesus into the house of the high priest and who had influence enough there to bring Peter in also—possibly the person who actually held the pen long afterwards in the writing of the Gospel of John.

I think this unnamed person was perhaps John the Presbyter. He was known to the high priest, and, if secretly a disciple of Jesus, he may have been the natural source of the knowledge of Jesus about what was going on in the camp of his enemies. However this may be, I feel that Jesus knew he was to be arrested on the night of the day before the Friday that was (in the evening) the beginning of the Passover, and also (that year) of the Sabbath.

I feel that he knew that it was expected to arrest him at night when the multitudes, who might protect him from the soldiers of the Temple, were not present, and in a garden in which he was accustomed at that season of the year, when the nights were often (not always) warm, to spend his nights.

I think this was the reason he held his Passover supper one night earlier than Passover night.

When Jesus returned from Bethany into Jerusalem, and had reached the Temple, the chief priests and the elders of the people came to him and asked, "By what authority doest thou these things?" By this question they obviously meant by what authority he had cast the scribes and money-changers out of the Temple. Jesus answered them by asking another question, according to his custom, and so silenced them. Jesus said, "The baptism of John, whence was it? From Heaven, or of men?"

Then he told the parable of the man and his two sons, the moral being in its application to the chief priests. It had a close relation to his question about John.

Again he told another parable (*Matthew* XXI, 33–44), the parable of the householder whose son was killed by his husbandmen, with its intensely close application to himself and the Jewish hierarchy who were scheming to destroy him. The result of these direct attacks on the religious powers was significant (XXI, 45), "And when the chief priests and the Pharisees had heard his parables, they perceived that he spake of them." Therefore, they tried to ensnare him by other means. "But when they sought to lay hands on him, they feared the multitude, because they took him for a prophet." Nothing can be clearer than that down to this moment (Monday of Passover week) Jesus had an immense hold on the people of Jerusalem.

After this, the Pharisees took renewed counsel how they might entangle him on points of law. First, with some of their own scholars, they sent some Herodians to ask whether it was lawful to give tribute to Cæsar. Their object was obvious—to get him to say something which they could use to his injury with the Roman authorities. They got their answer. It silenced them.

The Herodians were a political party, adherents of Herod, certainly not partisans of Rome. Neither were the Pharisees. But both had an interest in destroying Jesus. The interest of the Herodians came of their resentment of the Messianic claims of Jesus, or the Messianic claims made for him. The family of the Herods expected the Messiah to come through themselves. This is indicated by the birth story in *Matthew*, where Herod the Great massacres the children of Bethlehem in the effort to destroy "the king of the Jews."

The incident may be unhistorical, yet the story denotes the popular opinion that the Herod family were jealous of the Messianic claims of Jesus as indicated by the story of the Wise Men from the East.

That the killing of the children (while it might wipe out the Messiah of the Wise Men and the Star) could establish the Messiah of the Herod dynasty is one of the illogical hopes which attach to nearly all myths.

Antipas, the Sadducee, was then the only remaining son of Herod the Great. But he was old. Could they have hoped that a Messiah would still be born of him and Heriodias? Could that have been a ground for their joining with the Pharisees to destroy Jesus?

The Pharisees and the Herodians being routed, the Sadducees tried their hand. They did not believe in the Resurrection (even at the last day), and they asked of Jesus the perplexing question, whose wife was the woman to be who had been married to seven brothers?

The Sadducees got their answer, and they, too, were silenced.

Then came the Pharisees to the attack again. They got one of their number, who was a lawyer, to ask Jesus which was the greatest commandment in law.

Jesus said unto him, Thou shalt love the Lord thy God with all thy heart, and with all thy soul, and with all thy mind. This is the first and great commandment. And the second is like unto it, Thou shalt love thy neighbour as thyself. On these two commandments hang all the law and the prophets.

Then Jesus turned the fire on them. He knew they believed that the Christ must be the son of David, and he asked, "What think ye of the Christ? Whose son is he?" They answered, of course, "The son of David." Jesus replied in effect, "Then how did it come to pass that David in spirit called Christ the Lord? . . . If David called Christ the Lord, how is Christ David's son?"

Nobody was able to answer him, and from that hour forth they did not ask him any more questions.

I see no escape from the conclusion that here Jesus shows that he knew nothing about his being descended from David, nothing about the nativity story, nothing about his birth in Bethlehem, of an adopted father who was descended from David; and that if he had accepted the acclamations of the possessed and the blind as the son of David, he had thought of such acclamations only in their dogmatic sense, and not their historic sense.

After this Jesus speaks to the multitudes. He warns the people against the scribes and Pharisees, who sat in Moses' seat, and tells the people to do as the scribes and Pharisees say, but not as they do. They bind men with heavy burdens. All their good works are done that they may be seen of men. They make broad their phylacteries, and enlarge the borders of their garments; they love the uppermost rooms at feasts, and the chief seats in the synagogues, and greetings in the marketplaces, and to be called "Rabbi."

He warns the people not to allow themselves to be called Rabbis, for only one is their master and that is Christ. They are only brethren. He also warns the people to call no man their father upon earth, because only one is their Father and he is in Heaven. Also, they are not to allow themselves to be called Master, for there is only one Master and that is Christ. Then he shows that the man who wishes to be the *greatest* among them must be the *servant* of all.

Then follows his accusation of the scribes and Pharisees who act in complete defiance of all this—"But woe unto you, scribes and Pharisees, hypocrites!" (*Matthew* XXIII, 13–15). After this terrific denunciation he denounces the ceremonial worship of the Temple, and describes those who follow it as blind guides.

Whosoever shall swear by the temple, it is nothing; but whosoever shall swear by the gold of the temple, he is a debtor!

Ye fools and blind: for whether is greater, the gold, or the temple that sanctifieth the gold?

And whosoever shall swear by the altar, it is nothing; but whosoever sweareth by the gift that is upon it, he is guilty.

Ye fools and blind; for whether is greater, the gift, or the altar that sanctifieth the gift?

Whoso therefore shall swear by the altar, sweareth by it, and by all things thereon.

And whoso shall swear by the temple, sweareth by it, and by him that dwelleth therein.

And he that shall swear by Heaven, sweareth by the throne of God, and by him that sitteth thereon.

Woe unto you, scribes and Pharisees, hypocrites! for ye pay tithe of mint and anise and cummin, and have omitted the weightier matters of the law, judgment, mercy, and faith; these ought ye to have done, and not to leave the other undone.

Ye blind guides, which strain at a gnat, and swallow a camel.

Woe unto you, scribes and Pharisees, hypocrites! for ye make clean the outside of the cup and of the platter, but within they are full of extortion and excess.

Thou blind Pharisee, cleanse first that which is within the cup and platter, that the outside of them may be clean also.

Woe unto you, scribes and Pharisees, hypocrites! for ye are like unto whited sepulchres, which indeed appear beautiful outward, but are within full of dead men's bones, and of all uncleanness.

Even so ye also outwardly appear righteous unto men, but within ye are full of hypocrisy and iniquity.

Woe unto you, scribes and Pharisees, hypocrites! because ye build the tombs of the prophets, and garnish the sepulchres of the righteous.

And say, If we had been in the days of our fathers, we would not have been partakers with them in the blood of the prophets. Wherefore ye be witnesses unto yourselves, that ye are the children of them which killed the prophets.

Fill ye up then the measure of your fathers.

Ye serpents, ye generation of vipers, how can ye escape the damnation of hell?

Wherefore, behold, I send unto you prophets, and wise men, and scribes; and some of them ye shall kill and crucify; and some of them shall ye scourge in your synagogues, and persecute them from city to city.

That upon you may come all the righteous blood shed upon the earth, from the blood of righteous Abel unto the blood of Zacharias son of Barachias, whom ye slew between the temple and the altar.

Verily I say unto you, All these things shall come upon this generation.

O Jerusalem, Jerusalem, thou that killest the prophets, and stonest them which are sent unto thee, how often would I have gathered thy children together, even as a hen gathered her chickens under her wings, and ye would not!

Behold, your house is left unto you desolate.

For I say unto you, Ye shall not see me henceforth, till ye shall say, Blessed is he that cometh in the name of the Lord.

This is perhaps the greatest of all the discourses of Jesus. A wild, almost ferocious denunciation, every word blasting, of the sham and hypocrisy of the religion of the time. Perhaps the most violent, passionate and crushing invective ever spoken. Great in itself, great in its teaching, great even in the majesty of its words —a supreme passage.

VIII. Jesus or Caiaphas

Is it wonderful that from the moment this great denunciation was delivered there could be nothing between Jesus and the ruling powers of Jerusalem but war to the death? There could no longer be any room in the Holy City for Jesus and the Pharisees and the high priests together. Jesus or Caiaphas, and all that Caiaphas stood for—which was it to be?

It is to be realized that all the foregoing was delivered within the precincts of the Temple (see *Matthew* XXI, 23). Think of it, in the Temple! Think of the effect of it, the scribes and Pharisees present—and shamed into silence. The people present—and their rulers afraid of them!

Clearly, Jesus left the Temple after this great discourse, and (according to *Matthew*), never returned to it. All that he says later, in *Matthew,* appears to be said, not to the people or to the ruling classes, but to his disciples.

The fact then recorded is that on leaving the precincts his disciples came to him to show him the buildings of the Temple.

What can this mean? Jesus had seen the buildings of the Temple before, and knew them as well as his disciples. Can it be possible that they were showing him some additions to the buildings? Or some new carvings on the buildings, making them more gorgeous? The reply of Jesus makes me incline to the latter opinion. Luke says that some spoke of the Temple, how it was adorned with goodly stones and gifts.

Jesus said unto them, "See ye not all these things? Verily I say unto you, There shall not be left here one stone upon another, that shall not be thrown down." Probably he said more to indicate the destruction of the Temple. The other Gospels show that he did say more.

IX. On the Mount of Olives

Jesus and his disciples went out to the Mount of Olives and sat looking westward on Jerusalem and the Temple beyond the Kidron and the burial-place.

Here four of the disciples (Peter, James, John and Andrew, the two pairs of brothers) ask him privately when the destruction he has foretold will come to pass. "Tell us, when shall these things be? And what shall be the sign of thy *coming,* and of the end of the world."

Clearly, the disciples understood the closing part of Jesus's speech on the Temple to be foretelling the coming of the Christ after Jerusalem had become desolate, and when the people would hail him with the cry, "Blessed is he that cometh in the name of the Lord."

The people in the Temple clearly knew now that Jesus was in effect claiming to be the Christ. Or at least the disciples knew that Jesus was so claiming.

Jesus told them that the time was not far off when it would all be destroyed; it had rejected him and it in turn would be rejected. He said:

Take heed that no man deceive you; for many shall come in my name, saying, I am Christ; and shall deceive many. And ye shall hear of wars and rumours of wars; see that ye be not troubled: for all these things must come to pass, but the end is not yet. . . . But he that shall endure unto the end, the same shall be saved.

And this gospel of the Kingdom shall be preached in all the world for a witness unto all nations; and then shall the end come.

He went further. He told them that the day would come when the Son of Man would return to the world, not, as now, as a pleading friend, but as a judge. He would come in the clouds of Heaven with power and great glory, "And he shall send his angels with a great sound of a trumpet, and they shall gather his elect from the four winds, from one end of Heaven to the other."

Then he says, "Verily I say unto you, this generation shall not pass, till all things be fulfilled. . . . Watch, therefore, for ye know not what hour your Lord doth come."

He tells the beautiful parable of the ten virgins and the parable of the talents, both of which have a direct bearing on what he has been saying. Finally, at the close of this talk on the Mount of Olives, he says to his disciples, "Ye know that after two days is the Feast of the Passover, and the Son of Man is betrayed to be crucified."

The foregoing is the whole story, as told in *Matthew*, of what takes place in Jerusalem from the cleansing of the Temple down to the preparation for the Last Supper.

Meanwhile, in the city, the determination to get rid of Jesus grew stronger than ever. On the evening of Tuesday, after he had left, a special council was held to plot his capture. After their first defeat the Pharisees changed their strategy. They had employed guile in such a way that by question and answer they might, in a pacific and argumentative way, arrive at the employment of force, which meant legal apprehension, indictment and condemnation. The passages which indicate a resort to brute force are not always to be taken as meaning lynching, murder, assassination, but as the employment of a means to bring Jesus within the power of the law—either the Jewish law of the Sanhedrin or, if they were not powerful enough to crush and destroy him, the Roman law of the governor. This intention is plainly indicated in the Gospel of Luke.

The three factions went to work at first separately, then two parties joined, and finally all three joined as confederates to crush Jesus.

1. The Pharisees, because they believed him to be a blasphemer who claimed to be the Son of God.

2. The Herodians, because Jesus claimed to be the Messiah, or his followers claimed it for him.

3. The Sadducees, because, claiming to be either the Son of God or the Messiah, he claimed to be the king of the Jews and so endangered their position with the Roman authorities.

When they put to him the question, "What thinkest thou, is it lawful to give tribute to Cæsar?" the Herodians naturally expected that Jesus would give a negative answer, "No, pay no tribute to Cæsar." If Jesus had done so he would have committed himself irretrievably to his ruin. Repudiation of the tribute was repudiation of the Roman rule. It was high treason against emperor and empire; it was the first principle of revolution. What would the Roman procurator do? He would instantly punish the new Galilean with the cross. But what then? The odium of the execution of the prophet would, in the eyes of the people of Jerusalem, lie not with them, the Jewish rulers, but with the Romans.

A religious trial was full of risk. It would expose the rulers to the popular hatred. They were suffering enough already from acquiescence in the execution of John the Baptist. Even if they had not contributed to John's death, and popular opinion seems to have thought they had, they had not attempted to punish Antipas, to bring him to book either before the Sanhedrin or the procurator.

And then there was no certain prospect of the co-operation of the Roman procurator in any religious trial. Pontius Pilate would probably say, "What have I got to do with your religious disputes? You have your own law. Judge him for yourselves."

But Jesus, with his searching intellect, saw through the whole wretched scheme.

"Why tempt ye me, ye hypocrites?" he asks. "Show me a penny." That is, he asked for the coin of the *census,* the money in which it was customary to pay tribute.

They give him the Roman coin called a denarius—the coin which represented the moderate but hated capitation tax, the symbol of the Jews' slavery to the Gentile power above them. This coin (in other countries) bore the image and the legend of the reigning emperor, Tiberius. But the emperor in the time of Jesus, and down to the time of Flavius, struck a special coin for Judæa in deference to the Jewish faith. This special coin did not contain a portrait of Tiberius, but it contained his name, and a full expression of the Roman domination. Perhaps at the festival-time, when the image-impressed coins were flowing into the money-market at Jerusalem, it was this coin which was handed to Jesus. This was the distinctively Gentile coin, and perhaps it was secretly hoped that his anti-Roman indignation would be roused to one of the flaming outbursts of wrath which were known to come from him. But no, quite the contrary. Jesus, unlike the Jews, did not take offence at the heathen image.

"Whose is the image and superscription?" he asked. "Cæsar's," they answered. "Then render unto Cæsar the things which are Cæsar's, and unto God the things that are God's."

"This," says Keim, "was an utterance worthy of Solomon, and more than that." I should prefer to say that Jesus was giving his own disciples and the people generally yet one more lesson —that he did not aim at terrestrial power; that he had not come as a temporal king of the Jews; that his Kingdom was not of this world.

His reply was a crushing humiliation to the people sent to catch him out, and who knew they could no longer truthfully denounce him as a rebel and enemy to Rome. But it must also have been a crushing disappointment to his disciples, and that large body of his followers who were eagerly waiting from hour to hour for the moment when Jesus would establish his Kingdom.

Therefore, I put this temptation last, and if not last, then on a late day of his stay in Jerusalem. And from that moment forward I would see the enthusiasm excited by his entry into Jerusalem subside, both within his own circle and without.

CHAPTER XXVI

The Betrayal

I. *The Galilean Movement*

IN CHAPTER XXII, verses 1–6, Luke records in his Gospel:

> Now the feast of unleavened bread drew nigh, which is called the Passover. And the chief priests and scribes sought how they might kill him; for they feared the people. Then entered Satan into Judas surnamed Iscariot, being of the number of the twelve. And he went his way, and communed with the chief priests and captains, how he might betray him unto them. And they were glad, and covenanted to give him money. And he promised, and sought opportunity to betray him unto them in the absence of the multitude.

Meantime, it is evident that the disciples were in perplexity at the exalted mood of the Master, and that Judas, who was present on the Mount of Olives, was secretly in great alarm.

One thing Judas sees clearly—that the Master will now fall into the hands of the Jewish authorities. He has thrown himself into their hands. If they do not take action against him now they will lose all power with the people. They must arrest him. And, arresting Jesus, they will arrest his immediate followers also. The disciples of Jesus will be his accomplices in the eyes of the Jewish authorities.

The idea of saving his own skin comes back to Judas. He understands the situation of the Jewish authorities—that they are afraid of taking Jesus because he has the people behind him. If they could only take him when the people are not present to defend him!

He decides to go to them to-night, now. It would be doing the chief priests a good turn. They would absolve him from all blame as an informer. And then they might even pay him.

Meantime, what has been happening that day in Jerusalem?

Pontius Pilate, the Roman procurator, has arrived from Cæsarea, his official home. His Roman auxiliaries have come with him on his journey from Cæsarea, with his chariots, his captains, his centurions. Arriving at sunset, he enters the Holy City by David's Gate. His official residence in Jerusalem is believed to have been the palace of the former King of Judæa—Herod the Great. Pilate has established himself there. His soldiers are garrisoned in the various towers which Herod built for his soldiers.

It has always been the practice of the Roman procurator to come into Jerusalem at the time of the Passover. It is necessary to do so; necessary to watch these tumultuous Jews. Especially at this festival above all others, when all their fanaticism is at full play. Some of them, the chief priests, the Sadducees and their sympathisers may have given up the hope of a political Messiah. The ruling classes among the Jews have certainly given up all thought of the political Messiah of the prophets. They are well enough off as they are. But the common Jew prays every Sabbath in the synagogue for the coming of the day of the Messiah, as foretold by Isaiah.

Pilate has heard all this during his three years in Judæa. He has had bitter experience to teach him. He is amused by it, or thinks of it with contempt on ordinary days. But on the day of Passover (symbol to the ignorant and superstitious Jew of his deliverance from another power, Egypt) he is compelled to consider it seriously. He fears that, excited by religious frenzy—a sort of religious intoxication—the Jews may rebel. They have done so before, both in his own time and in the time of his predecessors. Accordingly, it is necessary to bring his soldiers from Cæsarea.

Therefore, on that Wednesday night, the Roman power is present in Jerusalem.

Herod Antipas has also arrived in Jerusalem from Tiberias, the corrupt city he has built on the shores of the Lake of Galilee. We can picture the arrival of the half-Semitic, half-oriental potentate from the direction of Samaria, with his captains and their attendants. He comes in by the Damascus Gate. Herod Antipas is a kind of Jewish sovereign, as his father, Herod the Great, had been. A very bad Jew, a pagan in heart and in life, but a Jew of political necessity.

As a Jewish sovereign he had to make an appearance at the chief Jewish feast. He had to bring his soldiers, too. This would be expected of him by his Galilean subjects, who would be in Jerusalem for the Passover in hundreds of thousands. He had to safeguard them against the Roman governor of Judæa.

Pilate and he had had differences before. The Roman had interfered with his (Herod's) subjects on a previous occasion. They had had a bitter quarrel over that. It had never been healed, perhaps never could be. The like must never happen again. Herod Antipas was in Jerusalem, partly to watch Pilate and to take care that he did not encroach on his rights as the nominal king of the Galileans.

Herod and his soldiers establish themselves in another palace, not far from the Temple.

Then the Jews, themselves. Vast multitudes of them from all countries in which Jews live are now in Jerusalem or encamped in the immediate neighbourhood. Josephus says there would be incredible numbers at such a time—even three millions. They are crowded then in a mass. The whole city densely packed with the Jews from all parts. All excited, more excited than ever before. They have heard of this new prophet of Galilee. He gave sight to the blind. He raised the dead. People are saying that he is the promised son of David. He will proclaim himself. This is their expectation.

Then the chief priests and the officials and their soldiery of the Temple. The Jewish authorities with their own temporal power, going out of the city to meet Pilate, or receiving him at the gate of David. Everything that day is humming with excitement.

Then, in the Temple, Jesus of Nazareth, the prophet of Galilee, surrounded by a vast multitude of the people. For once the crowds of Jews have been there—not at David's Gate to meet Pilate; not at the Damascus Gate to look on at the magnificent arrival of Herod Antipas. The streets are deserted; but about the Temple, where the Galilean is teaching, there are dense crowds expecting at any moment to see a miracle, while the soldiers of the Temple are walking to and fro on the outskirts of the throng—helpless, afraid.

Such is the state of Jerusalem that day.

Evening comes. The Galilean goes out at the Golden Gate, facing the Mount of Olives, and so on to his resting-place at the other side of the valley, telling the people who would follow him to go back.

Then the night of that same day—Wednesday. I see the chief priests, with certain members of the council, gathering (informally, not as a Sanhedrin) at the palace of Caiaphas.

The most urgent subject is what they are to do about the prophet of Galilee. First of all, Jesus is a corruptor of the faith. They (the high priests) are the supporters of the faith. Therefore, it is their duty to put him down. He is a peril to them, personally and officially, most of all now, at the time of the Passover, with these three millions of frenzied Jews in Jerusalem, with Pilate here.

He has insulted the Jewish authorities, held them up to contempt; poured scorn upon them, exposing their corruptions, their ignorance of the law, their violation of the law. He has even spoken doubtfully of the Mosaic law. They know this. Secretly, they know that he has impaled them on the spike of their self-interest—the casting of the money-changers out of the Temple.

But this concerns one of them chiefly, and although Annas is a person of consequence, they cannot speak of that. They have other and higher things to think about—the safety of their race and nation.

There was that story of the raising of Lazarus. They had never believed it. There was the flight of the Galilean. They had hoped he would not come for the Passover. He had come. The populace had received him as a king, as the King Messiah. He had accepted that character, accepted their acclamations. He had spoken parables against the Jewish authority. He had humiliated and degraded the Jewish authority. He had violently resisted the Jewish rule in one instance at least.

Finally, he had told parables which could have no meaning but that (1) the promises given by God to their father Abraham would be given to other peoples—even those they thought of as the publicans and harlots; and (2) he was the Son of God, and that they were trying to kill him, as the evil husbandmen killed the heir.

Such a man was a danger, a great danger. What would be the result if he were allowed to go on? The people were with him. They would follow him, perhaps fight for him. They might even attempt to re-establish the monarchy of David in his person, to place him on the throne as King Messiah.

At this time of the Passover, when the fanatical passions were at full play, what more likely? All these millions of ignorant Jews, who knew nothing except their Scriptures and the prayers they made in the synagogue on the Sabbath.

The result would be bloodshed, insurrection. Their poor little soldiery of the Temple would not be able to withstand it. What then? The Roman power would step in. What more likely? They were there in Jerusalem at the moment. Pilate was there in Jerusalem. They knew him. Never since he came to Judæa as procurator three years ago had he let slip any opportunity of offending the Jews.

He had thus antagonized the people he had been sent to govern. Once they had complained of him to his Roman masters, would he not jump at this chance of squaring accounts with them? What would he say?

He would tell them that their Jewish law and Jewish courts had been left to them by Rome in the expectation that they knew best how to govern their own people. But if they permitted insurrection they were incapable of self-government, and were no longer to be trusted with the protection of the public peace.

What next?

They (the Roman power) must take matters into their own hands. They must do what they had done before, put down the rising of this rabbi as they had put down the rising of the other Galilean rabbi—Judas the Galilean.

This time there was more reason. Judas the Galilean had only protested against the Roman taxation. This man (Jesus) protested against the rule of Cæsar. What else was it, if he claimed Cæsar's throne, saying that he, not Cæsar, was the rightful king of the Jews?

The Romans would say, "We cannot tolerate any pretender to the throne in Judæa. He must be put down. We will do this."

But that would not be all. The Roman procurator would tell them that inasmuch as they (the Jewish authority) had been helpless to control this rising, and were useless for the protection of the peace, he must report them to the emperor.

"If he does that, what will be the consequence?" they ask.

The consequence will be that the Roman emperor will take away their place and nation. He will take away their home rule. Pilate will make his representations to Rome. We are on bad terms with Pilate. Always have been. He has never forgiven us. He will say we are not fit to govern.

Well, what is the outcome?

We must lay this man by the heels. How? And on what charge? As a subverter of the law of Moses? But there is one great difficulty—the people. They believe in this man, are following him like sheep.

"Perceive ye how ye prevail nothing? Behold, the world is gone after him."

The chief priests and the Pharisees gathered in a council and said, "What do we?" Otherwise, "What are we to do? This man performs many miracles. If we let him alone, all men will believe in him. Believe what? That he is the Messiah, the Christ, the Son of God, the king of the Jews, foretold by the prophets and long expected? What will be the result? That the Romans will come and take away our place and nation? The Romans, unlike our Jewish people, do not expect a Messiah, a Son of God, a Christ. If they hear that a great multitude of the Jewish people believe that this man is the Christ, the king of the Jews, they will say 'We must crush this. And the only sure way to crush it is to take away from these Jews their privilege of self-government. They have no excuse for setting up a king of their own, for establishing any power that shall be at war with the sovereign power of Rome.'"

Therefore, Caiaphas, who was the high priest *that year* (a mistaken touch which suggests that the writer was not a Jew), said to the Pharisees, "Ye know nothing at all. Now consider that it is expedient for us, that one man should die for the people, and that the whole nation perish not."

There is a certain confusion of thought here. The writer of the Gospel says that Caiaphas spoke this not of himself, but being high priest that year, he was compelled to prophesy that Jesus should die for the nation, "and not for that nation only, but that also he should gather together in one the children of God that were scattered abroad."

This passage of explanation of Caiaphas's words (*John* XI, 51, 52) seems to me a manifest interpolation. It breaks the flow of thought and words. The passage should go from "unto them" (verse 49) to "Nor consider that it is expedient" (verse 50) omitting verses 51 and 52, and continuing with verse 53. Nothing else seems to make sense of the passage. If verses 51 and 52 are really meant to say that Caiaphas was divinely inspired, then both Caiaphas and all his friends were stone deaf and stone blind not to take warning and leave Jesus alone. To touch him would be to fight against God.

According to *Matthew,* two days before the Passover the chief priests and elders assemble in the palace of Caiaphas and consult together as to how they may secretly take Jesus and kill him. Can they be thinking of assassination? It is difficult to believe it. But they decide that it cannot be done on the feast day, lest there should be an uproar among the people.

A vast number of their people do believe that he had raised the dead. They are saying openly that the Galilean must be the Messiah. This suits him. Rumour says he has said the same about himself, and that his disciples are constantly saying it.

Some of the members of their council have been saying that the best way to crush this Galilean movement is to ignore it, the best way to destroy this Jesus of Nazareth is not to know him. But how fatal that is! So the others say, "Perceive ye how ye prevail nothing?"—by your passive policy. "Behold the world is gone after him."

What are they to do?

The man must be put down, but *they* cannot put him down for two reasons: (1) because there are people who would side with him; (2) because they have no legal right to take life.

What, then, is going to happen?

The Romans will soon take note of this man and his movement. If he and they claim for him a sovereignty such as is implied in the Messiahship, the Romans will step in and stop the pretender, as a traitor to Cæsar, who is the only legal king of the Jews, and punish his followers as breeders of disorder.

But the Romans will not be likely to stop there. Particularly, the present Roman governor will not stop there. They know this man Pilate of old. He is no friend of the Jews. On the contrary, he has, from the first day of his coming, been their bitter enemy. They have had to complain to Rome against him. He will jump at an opportunity of squaring accounts with them. He will tell them that it was first of all their business to put down this impudent pretender, whatever he calls himself or is called. But since they have not done so, and since they are obviously afraid of doing so, for fear of the religious sentiment of the people, it has become necessary for the Roman governor to do so.

And if he does so, and is resisted, what will be the end? He will make such representations to Rome as will put them (the authorities of the Jewish courts) in the wrong. And the end of that will be that the Jewish courts will be abolished by the Roman emperor, and their right of self-government will be wiped out. And with it, they themselves will go. There will be no high priests, no Sanhedrin. The Jewish rights will be abolished. The Jewish courts put down as well. The Temple will cease to exist. In a word, the semblance of the Jewish state will be abolished. The whole Jewish nation will cease to exist.

If this is not to happen, what must they do? They must put down this man Jesus of Nazareth. Why not?

"Consider," says Caiaphas, the high priest, "is it not more expedient for us that one man should die for the people (the Jewish people) than that the whole nation should perish?"

The Gospel states that he says this as a sort of unconscious prophecy, being "the high priest for that year." Nothing of the kind. He says it as a man who sees the plain facts before his face.

The others agree. But how is the Galilean to be put down, since the people are going after him? Particularly the Galileans. There are vast numbers of Galileans in Jerusalem for the feast. The Galileans will fight for their prophet. Are they not always fighting, these Galileans? Did they not fight for Judas the Galilean? What trouble they give to the Romans! They will fight more and longer for this Jesus of Nazareth, this Messiah, this Christ, as they believe him to be.

It is a terrible difficulty. The priestly class find themselves between two fires—the Roman authorities on the one side and their own people on the other.

They are perplexed.

II. Judas

At that moment, as we know, Judas Iscariot came to them. It was late on the Wednesday night, perhaps very late. He had left Jesus and his fellow-disciples asleep on the Mount of Olives, perhaps in Gethsemane.

It is no great liberty of imagination to picture Judas, creeping through the dark streets, a passing wayfarer with his lamp, and arriving at the door of the palace of Caiaphas, the high priest, at the very close of such a conference.

Word comes in that a man is asking for the high priest.

"Who is he?"

"Judas, a disciple of the Galilean."

It is easy to imagine the old man, Annas, former high priest, alone with Judas in a room, under the flickering light of an oil lamp, bargaining over the earthly fate of the greatest Being that ever lived among men.

According to *Matthew*, Judas is very crude. He says to the chief priests, "What will ye give me if I deliver him to you?" And they covenant to give him thirty pieces of silver. And from that time Judas sought opportunity to betray him.

A very crude story.

"I am told that you wish to take this man, but fear to do so, because of the people."

"Well?"

"I can show you how to take him, when he is alone, practically alone, and the people are not there to defend him. I know his comings and goings. I know where he will be at a convenient moment. I can take you to where he will be in the quiet of the night."

To Annas this is like a voice from Heaven. If this man can do what he says, and, being a disciple of the Galilean, he obviously can, what a good thing for everybody! There will be no tumult among the people, no bloodshed, no uproar, no trouble of any kind. The Galilean can be arrested by night when the people are in their beds and asleep; the council can be summoned to try him in the night; he can be dealt with in any way that seems best; and before the people are awake in the morning he and his disciples also, since it would be folly to leave them free, at liberty to make further rebellion, to run round the city, raising rebellion, will be arrested, tried and dispatched to—nobody knows where.

The prophet of Galilee, the charlatan, the pretended Messiah, the false King Messiah, the trickster supposed to give sight to the blind, to raise the dead, will have gone.

What a relief! This dangerous person, with his dangerous and dishonouring movement will be at an end. The Passover will go on in peace. The Jewish rulers will be safe. The high priests will be safe. *He* will be safe.

Annas thanks Judas for his information and agrees. But Judas makes one condition. If he delivers his Master into the hands of the chief priests, he himself must be exempt from arrest.

"Certainly. It is always so. That is understood." Annas thanks Judas again. Perhaps flatters him. He is doing a great service to his race and nation. It is true he will be giving away his Master, but . . .

That suggests thoughts of motive. Annas does not inquire too closely into the motive of Judas. To his mind, in the mood of that moment, there can be only one motive for Judas's conduct. He wants something for himself. That is the only motive for the common informer at any time. Perhaps he may also be moved by pique, jealousy, anger, but that does not concern Annas. He asks Judas how the council is to repay him for what he is doing for his people. It is a great service. The council could wish to reward him.

The idea of money has indeed occurred to the mind of Judas, even if only as a secondary consideration. Perhaps there is a momentary hesitation. Annas comes to the relief of Judas. Suggests thirty pieces of silver.

It looks like a great sum to Judas. It *is* a great sum. If a husbandman's wages are only one penny a day, and there are ten Roman pennies to the smallest piece of Roman silver, here are the wages of a year.

Remember that Joseph was sold to the Ishmaelites, who took him into Egypt, for twenty pieces of silver. Herod the Great left a legacy of fifteen pieces of silver to each of his bodyguard. The thirty pieces of silver afterwards bought a field large enough to be a cemetery for the strangers in Jerusalem (where there were many Romans and Greeks) for about thirty years.

And then remember the fascination of a large sum (a year's income) to a poor man like Judas. Remember, also, that the keeping of the purse for the company is a poor thing; very little in the purse, always living on the verge of poverty; the daily bread for the day, no more; all above that, by command of the Master, to be given to the poor.

Judas agrees. Annas promises that the money shall be paid to Judas whenever he comes back with information which enables the Jewish authorities to arrest Jesus.

It is arranged that Judas is to watch for a favourable opportunity in which Jesus can be taken without fear of the people.

Judas leaves the palace of Caiaphas, and goes back to the Mount of Olives.

Is this too free an exercise of imagination? It is all in the Gospels—as plain as words can make it. "Two days before the Passover the chief priests and the scribes sought how they might take him by craft and put him to death."

Who reported the scene?

Who, indeed, reported any of the scenes of the betrayal of Jesus by Judas?

III.   Motives for the Betrayal

I do not think the story of Judas Iscariot can possibly be complete without a thorough inquiry into his character and motives from first to last.

1. He was probably not a Galilean fisherman. Only about four of the disciples were so—Peter, his brother Andrew, and the two sons of Zebedee, John and James. If Judas Iscariot came from Hebron, in the south, he was almost certainly not a fisherman. He may have been a trader, travelling in Galilee, when he came upon Jesus.

2. He was deeply and sincerely impressed by the prophet of Nazareth, who was preaching in wonderful words and doing wonderful works. This probably spoke to the Jewish soul in Judas, which was looking for the deliverance of his people from the tyrannical yoke of the Roman master.

3. He probably joined Jesus in all sincerity, renouncing all his material aims to do so.

4. If he had been a trader, he had probably some knowledge of money and how to use it, of buying and selling, and some knowledge of human nature; so that he was easily duped by the imposters who would certainly gather about the Master. I think this might naturally have led to his becoming the treasurer of his little company, the keeper of the bag, or purse.

5. He may have sincerely shared in the development of feeling in all the disciples towards Jesus, until, at the source of the Jordan (Cæsarea Philippi), he, like Peter and the other disciples, became convinced that he was the Messiah, the Christ, the Son of God.

6. I think Judas, like the others, cherished the worldly side of the prospect of being the immediate follower of him who was to redeem Israel, to deliver the Jewish nation from the bondage of the Romans.

7. This expectation in his case, as in the case of others, was constantly being depressed by Jesus's repeated assurances that he must first die at the hands of the Jewish rulers, and then come to them again in some undefined future, which only God knew of.

8. This uneasy feeling may have been stronger in Judas than in any of his fellow-disciples, Thomas excepted, so that, unlike

Thomas, he found it hard to reconcile himself to the idea of going up to Jerusalem to die with Jesus.

9. The events at Bethany would deepen this feeling in Judas. I do not know what he thought of the incident which we know as the raising of Lazarus. But it is clear to me that when he came within sight of Jerusalem his soul underwent a serious ordeal.

10. He may have begun to doubt the Messiahship of one who, contrary to all Jewish teaching, had to die to establish his Messiahship—the firm Jewish belief having been that the Messiah when he came would live for ever.

11. I suggest that the sight of the preparations for the Passover awakened the old Jew in Judas, making him feel afresh the power and the majesty of the great faith of his fathers, and at the same time the powerlessness and impotence of the Galilean peasant, who had seemed so great in Galilee and now looked so feeble and small in Judæa.

12. I think this, and many meaner emotions, began to make play with him. Satan may quite properly be said to have entered into him, causing him to see Jesus with different eyes, as one of the many self-deceived fanatical prophets who had led his followers on to destruction.

13. He may have remembered Judas the Galilean and the welter of blood into which he led his followers, and he may have thought of Jesus as about to do the same.

14. It was impossible that this should not lead him to think of himself also, and the ruin, perhaps death, which awaited him if he entered Jerusalem with this man who was deliberately, quite sincerely, but quite madly heading on to his destruction.

15. This was probably the moment when, left behind in Bethany, perhaps, while Jesus and the favoured few were at Ephraim, he came into touch with Annas, the high priest, in his house on the Mount of Olives, only a few furlongs away.

16. I think the old serpent, Annas, read Judas through and through; that he spoke tenderly, and perhaps almost pityingly, of Judas's master as a self-deceived man who was threatening to destroy himself and his followers. I think this broke down the last bulwark of Judas's resistance to the impulse that had come over him—to save Jesus from the consequence of the one mistaken intention, and at the same time to save his disciples.

17. I do not believe that when Judas yielded to Annas, and took

his money, he intended to betray Jesus to *his death*. I am sure he did not, or the story of his last act would not be for me historical. I think he expected that Jesus would be dealt with by the Jewish authority, the Jewish council, perhaps the Sanhedrin; and Judas knew that the utmost punishment it could inflict would be banishment and excommunication. Not for Judas's sake, but for the sake of Jesus, I revolt against the idea that anything worse than this formed any part of Judas's original design.

18. Once having yielded to the Satan that had taken possession of him, he was carried farther—into any deceptions, into continued intercourse with Jesus in his most sacred hours, even into the room of the Last Supper. All this he justified to himself as necessary to his plan of saving himself, and even of saving Jesus, from the worst consequences of his forthcoming scheme.

19. I think the language of Jesus at the Last Supper finally convinced Judas that Jesus was (as the high priest had told him) on the eve of a revolutionary movement; that probably on the following day (the first day of unleavened bread), when the ancient spirit of the Jewish people was at its highest, or perhaps that very night, after the festival feast, when the streets, and particularly the Temple courts, would be full of excited and even delirious crowds, Jesus would proclaim the downfall of the old order, the coming of the Messiah. I think it possible that Judas saw Jesus and all his followers slaughtered that night (it is not an unreasonable imagining), and that this was to be the way of the death which Jesus had foretold for himself again and again from the time of Cæsarea Philippi.

20. I think this determined for Judas the time to act, and caused him to rise from the table and go. I think Jesus's last words to him (I cannot reconcile myself to any other words spoken by Jesus either to Judas or about him) showed Judas that by some means Jesus *knew*.

But it was too late to think of that now. He must go on. He then went for the first time to the Temple, obtained the guard, and led it to Gethsemane, the place he well knew to be the nightly resort of Jesus and his disciples.

Thus far down to this stage.

Later, I see Judas, realizing that he has been deceived by the high priests; that they have sent Jesus on to the Roman procurator to be tried on the capital charge, with the certainty that he would be found guilty and put to death. I see him wandering, like a lost soul, about the house of Annas, during the inquiry there; about the palace of Caiaphas, during the examination of the high priest. He was in no danger of being called as a witness against Jesus, for (beyond doubt) it would be part of the bargain with Annas that he should not be called.

Finally, I see his remorse overwhelming him. I see him forcing his way into the Temple after the guards have taken his Master to the Judgment Hall of Pilate, throwing down the money which he has taken to betray the innocent blood, and going out to hang himself.

It is likely, almost certain, that the two high priests did not themselves go to Pilate's Judgment Hall. I think it conceivable that Judas, like a lost soul, wandered outside Pilate's castle; followed the crowd that took Jesus to Herod Antipas, and then brought him back to Pilate; heard the frantic cries from within, "Crucify him! Crucify him!" and *then* returned to the Temple and the high priests, perhaps in the midst of their satisfaction at reports which had just reached them, that Pilate had at last yielded and Jesus was condemned.

I recognize a certain inevitableness, as of Greek tragedy, in all this. It takes no liberty with history. I see Judas, tempted by Satan, struggling with himself, revolting against Satan, deceived by Satan, and, thinking he had committed the unpardonable sin, and was for ever a lost and damned soul, killing himself.

But I see also, afar off, the spirit of Jesus saying to this lost soul, at his last moment of repentance, "This day shalt thou be with me in Paradise."

Judas had fully exercised his free will, but he had been the means by which a predetermined plan had been carried out. An almighty power had led him on. A greater than Satan. The Greeks would have called it the Furies. May we, without irreverence, call it God?

The foregoing is my way out of the vulgar, crude, unnatural, barbaric story of the character and activities of Judas Iscariot, which has for ages degraded not only human nature, but Jesus himself.

CHAPTER XXVII

The Last Supper

I. *According to Matthew*

JESUS AND HIS DISCIPLES were on the Mount of Olives, and after Jesus had finished "all these sayings," he said to his disciples, "Ye know that after two days is the Feast of the Passover, and the Son of Man is betrayed to be crucified."

Apparently, this means that Jesus expected to be crucified at the time of the Passover.

We are then told that the chief priests and elders gathered together at the house of the high priest, who was Caiaphas, and consulted how they might take Jesus by subtlety and kill him.

Earlier than this, Jesus was at Bethany; the meal at the house of Simon the leper was over. "Now the first day of the Feast of Unleavened Bread," that is to say on the fifteenth day of Nisan (April), the disciples came to Jesus and asked him where he wished them to prepare for him to eat the Passover (*Matthew* XXVI, 17).

This cannot be strictly accurate. The disciples must have come to Jesus on the day of preparation (the 14th, if that was the day of preparation), not the actual day of the eating of the Passover, because the Passover service was on the evening of the day of preparation, the beginning of the first day of the Feast of Unleavened Bread. The fourteenth day of Nisan, after sunset, was the beginning of the first day of unleavened bread. If that is wrong they must have come to him on the morning of the thirteenth, the evening of the fourteenth being (according to *Leviticus*) the beginning of the Passover, and the Passover festival supper being on the first day of unleavened bread.

Jesus answered the question of his disciples by telling them to go into the city to such a man, and say to the man, "The Master saith, My time is at hand; I will keep the Passover at thy house with my disciples."

Clearly, the man was one of his adherents, in the confidence of

Jesus, and knew perfectly what he meant by saying, "My time is at hand." He meant the time of his death. But the astonishing thing is that the twelve disciples did not know. Who, then, was this man? Tradition says it was Joseph of Aramathæa, who is said to have had a house in Jerusalem, as well as a farm (in the hands of a factor) at Bethpage, on the Mount of Olives. Also, clearly, the man knew something in advance, as though Jesus had told him he might wish to eat at his house when his time came.

The house was in the noblest quarter of Jerusalem. Never before had Jesus been known to choose for himself the houses of the great; but for what he was about to do that night no place was too magnificent. He chose two of his twelve, Simon Peter and John, and with the authority of an overlord he sent them into the city, where they made ready the Passover.

That is to say they arranged for the cleansing of the house of all leavened bread, the killing of the beast, the baking of the unleavened bread, the bringing of the bitter herbs, the wine, and so on. And in the evening he went into the city and sat down with the twelve at the supper table.

The first thing Jesus talked of was his forthcoming betrayal. As they ate, Jesus said, "One of you shall betray me."

This made them exceedingly sorrowful, and every one of them asked, "Lord, is it I?" And Jesus answered, "He that dippeth his hand with me in the dish, the same shall betray me."

No doubt the method of eating was the ancient oriental one of putting the dish with the bread and meat and bitter herbs, perhaps the bread and the meat mixed together like a kind of hash, into a common dish which was placed in the middle of the table, and from this they all ate as they sat about the table, by reaching forward and dipping their hands into the dish.

Jesus also said, "The Son of Man goeth as it is written of him; but woe unto that man by whom the Son of Man is betrayed. It had been good for that man if he had not been born."

The theory of this is that Jesus was to be betrayed, according as God had foreseen and known, but none the less the man who betrayed him to his death would suffer and be damned.

Then Judas asked, "Master, is it I?" And Jesus answered, "Thou hast said."

So Judas knew that Jesus had divined that he was to be betrayed by Judas, and all the other disciples must have heard and known it.

Here the subject changes. Then, as they were eating, Jesus took bread and blessed it and brake it and gave it to the disciples and said, "Take, eat; this is my body."

After that he took the cup, and in like manner gave thanks, and gave it to the disciples, saying, "Drink ye all of it. For this is my blood of the new testament, which is shed for many for the remission of sins."

The disciples must have eaten the bread and drunk the wine. There is no indication that they found any reason for not doing so, any difficulty in apprehending the description Jesus had given of the bread and wine. It is therefore apparent that unlike the disciples referred to in an earlier chapter and at another place (*John* VI, 50–69) they did not attach the physical meaning which had so disturbed the earlier disciples that they had left Jesus on account of it.

What, then, did the disciples understand by the words of Jesus? Clearly, the meaning they attached to them was the same in kind as the meaning they had always, as Jews, attached to the bread and wine and meat and bitter herbs of the ordinary Passover they had eaten and drunk throughout their lives—that they were the symbols of the bread and meat and wine and bitter herbs which their forefathers had eaten of during their flight from Egypt; not the same, but the representation or symbol of it. But there was this difference, that in giving them the bread and wine Jesus was substituting himself as the vehicle of sacrifice—not physically, because there he sat eating with them at the same time, and to say that he was offering them his physical body to eat and his physical blood to drink, while his body and blood were there in the flesh before them at the table, would be unintelligible. Not physically, but spiritually, was the offering made.

And what did this offering of his spiritual body and blood mean? It meant that by anticipation (not as a memorial and a memory, as in the case of the ordinary Passover) he was indicating that he was giving his life for them, for mankind, for the remission of their sins.

That it was a difficult thought is obvious, and how far the disciples understood it we do not know; there is nothing to tell us. Probably the symbol only became intelligible to them after the death of their Master and the coming of the Holy Spirit to them at Pentecost.

Nothing more is said after this in *Matthew* except that Jesus said he would not drink henceforth of the fruit of the vine until that day when he drank it with them in his Father's kingdom. Nothing is said about the duty of the disciples to eat and drink this again as a memorial of Jesus. Jesus does not establish a custom like that of the Passover.

After that they sang a hymn, and went out into the Mount of Olives.

The first thing that strikes me in Matthew's account of the Last Supper of Jesus is that nothing is recorded which bears any real resemblance to the Passover feast of the Jews. Having eaten the Passover feast with Jews in Jerusalem, I am not reminded of it by anything in Matthew's story.

The outstanding features of the Passover feast—the youngest (child) asking why they are eating unleavened bread, on that night in particular, the telling of the long story of the flight of the children of Israel from Egypt, the eating of the bitter herbs to typify the bitter sufferings of the Israelites in Egypt, the wine poured out four times, the Messianic hope indicated, the cup of wine poured out for Elijah (Heb. Alianovah: the Messiah), the door of the room flung open as for the Messiah or his forerunner to enter—none of these is even remotely suggested in Matthew's account of the Last Supper of Jesus.

It may be urged that it all goes before, and therefore, being the customary ritual, is not reported. On the other hand, it may be averred that, inasmuch as Jesus and the disciples are described as *still eating,* it can be concluded that the customary ceremony of the Jewish Passover feast had not taken place at all, and that Jesus had substituted something else, something quite different.

Was the something quite different the giving of the bread and the wine, *as his body and blood?* And was Jesus therein establishing an entirely new and different Passover feast? Not a Passover feast at all, but a sacramental ordinance signifying a new covenant which man was making with God, or God with man, on the eve of the sacrifice which Jesus was about to make of his life for the remission of mankind's sins? There is not a hint of this in *Matthew.*

Houtin says:

The early Christians gathered often for brotherly meals. St. Paul adapted to those love-feasts notions resembling those found in cults in which the god was eaten. From this came the Communion, together with the Catholic Mass and the Lord's Supper of the Protestants. The primitive liturgy was celebrated in Greek, the common language of the Mediterranean shores. . . . As late as about the year 300, Arnobius, the apologist, said that the Christians would consider it as an insult to their deity were they to imprison Him within walls and to imagine He needed a material dwelling-place, "just as do human beings, cats and ants."

The passage had special reference to the building of temples for the worship of God (the earlier practice of the Christians being to hold their meetings for worship in private houses), but it applied especially to the Sacrament, the elements that were the body and blood of Christ being shut up in a box or cupboard in a temple built specially for the worship of God.

For myself, I can only repeat that never, at any celebration of the Passover held in any country (Palestine included), have I been conscious of anything that recalled to me the Lord's Supper as recorded in the Gospels. *Quite the contrary.* Is it true that the uniting of the Lord's Supper was an afterthought of the Jewish Christians, intended (like the appeal to the Jewish prophets) to make Jewish Christians?

II. *According to Mark*

Jesus is apparently still in Bethany, and it is the next day after the meal at the house of Simon the leper.

The story in *Mark* (XIV) differs in essential features. In telling his disciples where he wishes to eat the Passover, Jesus says that they are to go into the city, and there they will meet a man carrying a pitcher of water. They are to follow this man, and when he enters a house they are to follow him in, and say to the goodman of the house, "The Master saith, Where is the guestchamber, where I shall eat the Passover with my disciples?" And the man will show them a large upper room *furnished and prepared,* and there they (the disciples) will make ready for supper.

The disciples do as Jesus bids them, find things as he says and make ready for the Passover.

It may be noted that there was no ceremonial reason why Jesus should eat the Passover in Jerusalem. Being in Bethany, he might have done so there, according to Jewish custom, but it was the Jewish custom to eat the Passover in Jerusalem, and people came from long distances and from far-off countries to do so. Again, note that the man at whose house they were to eat the Passover was to show them a room *furnished and prepared*. This clearly indicates a previous arrangement between him and Jesus.

In the evening Jesus came to the place he had indicated, and sat down with his twelve disciples, Judas being still with him.

Again, as they sat and ate, Jesus spoke about his betrayal, and what follows is almost identical with the story in *Matthew*, except that Judas does not ask, "Is it I?" and Jesus does not reply, "Thou hast said."

After that Jesus breaks the bread and gives the cup as in *Matthew*, saying the same words—that this was his body and this was his blood of the new testament which is shed for many. Also, Jesus says, as in *Matthew*, that he will drink no more "until that day that I drink it new in the kingdom of God." Clearly, according to *Mark*, Jesus also had drunk of the cup which he called his blood, thus making it yet more impossible that he can have attached a physical meaning to his own words—that the wine was his actual blood. After they had sung a hymn, they went out into the Mount of Olives.

III. *According to Luke*

Jesus is in the Mount of Olives, where, exactly, *Luke* does not say. There is no meal in the house of Simon the leper.

Luke (XXII, 1) states that as the Feast of Unleavened Bread drew near the scribes and elders sought how they might kill Jesus, but how they feared the people (chiefly because the people held Jesus to be a prophet, perhaps the Messiah, and would protect him), and how at that crisis Satan entered into Judas, and he found a way to betray his Master, by going to the chief priests and captains (clearly captains of the Temple, the Jewish soldiery) and offering to deliver Jesus into their hands, and how the chief priests and captains were glad of the help proffered by Judas and covenanted to give him money, and how Judas thereafter sought opportunity to betray Jesus in the absence of the people—the multitude.

Then came the day of unleavened bread when the Passover must be kept, and Jesus sent Peter and John to prepare the Passover. They asked where, and he gave practically the same answer as in *Mark*, that when they entered the city a man would meet them bearing a pitcher of water; they were to follow him into the house, and say to the goodman of the house, "The Master saith unto thee, Where is the guestchamber, where I shall eat the Passover with my disciples?"

The mystery in *Matthew, Mark* and *Luke* about the man and the place has been subject to various conjectures. Some critics say it was a prearranged plan made by Jesus with some man in Jerusalem, in order that his whereabouts, while eating the Passover, should not be known to the chief priests, who might fall on him there and take him by subtlety while the people themselves were all indoors at their own Passover feasts.

Clearly, he wished to eat the Passover with his disciples in peace before he was arrested.

But it is difficult to see why Jesus should have made all this cloud of mystery before his disciples, unless it is assumed that he was speaking before Judas, and, knowing Judas to be the disciple who was waiting to betray him, he did not wish to put him into possession of a fact which, between then and the time of the supper, he might communicate to the chief priests and captains. But what was the good of throwing dust in the eyes of Judas if Judas was to go with him to the supper? Sooner or later he would know where it was to take place.

Other critics say the house was probably that of the mother of Mark (John Mark), although there is not the slightest evidence for this.

Again, other critics say that all this mystery is merely intended to indicate the supernatural or clairvoyant knowledge of Jesus, and is reported merely to give evidence of his possession of this power. But was it necessary that after so many miracles Jesus should prove that he was a clairvoyant? It is a little matter, probably unworthy of further discussion.

The disciples, Peter and John, did as they were told, and when the hour was come, Jesus sat down, and the twelve with him. It is thought that some of the followers from Galilee, particularly some of the women, were present at the supper, but there is no authority for that either.

Jesus then said, "With desire I have desired to eat this Passover with you before I suffer."

Clearly, he had not concealed from his disciples his belief that his end was to come during the time of the present Passover.

For I say unto you, I will not any more eat thereof, until it be fulfilled in the kingdom of God. And he took the cup, and gave thanks, and said, Take this, and divide it among yourselves. For I say unto you, I will not drink of the fruit of the vine, until the kingdom of God shall come.

Here is a passage full of meaning and intention. First, he had eaten, or was about to eat; then he said he would eat *no more* and drink *no more* until the kingdom of God should come. Thus he meant first that this was his last meal on earth before his death and his return to earth to establish the kingdom of God on earth. It was therefore an announcement of the very near approach of his end. No more.

Sceptical critics, seeing that Jesus had eaten of the bread, object that it outrages common sense to say that he could have meant that he was eating of his own body, who sat there under the eyes of the disciples. The answer of believers is that he only said the bread was his body after he had consecrated it by giving thanks. I confess I find this to be a sort of shuffling with the fact.

Then comes his announcement of the reason of his death. He breaks the bread, gives thanks, gives to the disciples, and says, "This is my body which is given for you." And to this he adds, "This do in remembrance of me."

It is the first time he has said so—the only time he says so. Here is a new thought. The disciples are to have other feasts like the present (perhaps at Passover only, or in particular) and to break bread and *perhaps* repeat his words, so as to keep them in remembrance of the fact that he had given his body in death for them.

After that, after supper, he did the same with the wine (the cup) saying, "This cup is the new testament in my blood which is shed for you." Was Jesus instituting a Sacrament, a custom for the Churches, such as the Passover for the Jews? Clearly, the early disciples (Peter and Paul) thought he was.

Then comes another subject. After that, Jesus begins to speak of his betrayer, saying the hand of the man who is betraying him is with him on the table; that the Son of Man will go as it was foretold, but woe to the man by whom he is betrayed. As in the two earlier Gospels the disciples inquire among themselves which of them it is to be. This does not, in *Luke,* appear to trouble them much, for immediately they begin to quarrel as to which of them will be the greatest in the new Kingdom when Jesus has established it. Jesus stops the quarrelling by telling them that, unlike the way of the Gentiles, the youngest of them will be the greatest, and the chief of them shall serve.

Then he cheers them by saying that they are those who have continued with him in his temptations. Clearly, he has had other temptations than the temptation in the wilderness after his baptism. Therefore, he will appoint them a Kingdom as his Father has appointed a Kingdom to him. They will eat and drink at his table in his Kingdom, and sit on thrones, judging the twelve tribes of Israel. Note that there are *twelve* of them without him, and all twelve will hold these places of great honour. But one of the twelve sitting with him is Judas!

Again a break and another subject. Then, for some reason not apparent, Jesus proceeds to warn Peter, telling him that Satan has desired to have him that he might sift him as wheat. But he (Jesus) has prayed for Peter that his faith shall not fail, and that when he is converted he should strengthen his brethren.

I find it hard to follow all this. Jesus is sure of his disciples. Peter is converted already. Jesus promises his disciples seats at his table in the kingdom of God. He says they are to judge the twelve tribes of Israel. Yet he says that he has prayed for Peter that when he is *converted* he may strengthen his brethren. Not a word about praying for Judas, the disciple who is just about to betray him. Peter answers Jesus, "Lord, I am ready to go with you, both into prison, and to death"; and Jesus answers, "Peter, the cock shall not crow this day before that thou shalt thrice deny that thou knowest me." (It is late at night, but nevertheless the beginning of a new day.)

Then comes an utterly incredible incident. Jesus, who has, throughout his ministry, taught the gospel of non-resistance, that violence is wrong, even in self-defence, that the moral law alone triumphs, says now, "When I sent you without purse, and scrip, and shoes, lacked ye anything?" They answer, "Nothing!" Then he says to them, without any logical connexion with either question or answer:

> But now, he that hath a purse, let him take it, and likewise his scrip; and he that hath no sword, let him sell his garment, and buy one. For I say unto you that this that is written must yet be accomplished in me, And he was reckoned among the transgressors; for

the things concerning me have an end. And they said, Lord, behold, here are two swords. And he said unto them, It is enough.

Is there any good and sufficient reason why I should not say that I believe that the whole of this passage (*Luke* XXII, 36–38) is a most impudent and degrading interpolation, probably written in the second century and put into Luke's Gospel to meet the much better needs of the Church at that time, in utter and flagrant defiance of the whole spirit of Jesus? The Jesus in those verses is not Jesus of Nazareth in any line or word. Worse, he is little better than a simpleton. Remember, there were three armies in Jerusalem at that moment, all hostile to him—the army of the Temple guard and police; the army of Herod Antipas, and the army of Pontius Pilate. All fully equipped. Are we to assume that Jesus was warning his disciples that his end was near; that it would come to him (and perhaps to them) in the form of the force of armed men; that it was necessary to withstand that force, although he had said, only just before, that his end was predetermined and could not be withstood, yet they *were* to withstand it, with two poor little swords, buckled about the jerkins of two fishermen, who had probably never handled a sword in their lives? The assumption is ridiculous. Two swords would be "enough" against the soldiery of the Temple or perhaps of Herod and even of the legionaries of Rome? Impossible!

I feel ashamed to think that this statement has been palmed off on Jesus by men of little brain and bad heart, and that it is still accepted (perhaps tacitly) as having come direct from his mouth. What Jesus has suffered from his own!

After the supper Jesus went out, "as he was wont, to the Mount of Olives," and his disciples also followed him.

It should be observed, first, that nothing is said about Judas. We are left to assume that he was present all through the supper, for all the twelve were there, and that when Jesus went to the Mount of Olives Judas was among those who followed him. The ensuing verses show that he did not—another evidence of the bad narrating constantly encountered in *Luke*.

Next, there is nothing in any of the reports of the Last Supper in the three Synoptic Gospels which is in any way worthy of the event. The proceedings concern chiefly Jesus's announcement that he is to be betrayed; that his betrayer is to be one of his own people;

and (in *Luke*) that when the time comes for his arrest by his enemies an effort is to be made to resist his arrest.

No hint, except in one incident, of the solemnity of the Jewish Passover service; of the majesty of the ritual which keeps alive that great memory; of the great hope of the Messiah. Against the above, however, there is the fact of the breaking of bread, and the promise of a new testament in his blood, which is to be shed for the sins of many. It is true that this is the still grander idea, but the Synoptic Gospels do not seem to me to bring it out. It is as if the writers never understood it.

IV. *According to John*

In *John* it is not recorded where the Last Supper took place. Chapter XIII begins with a general statement that *before the Feast of the Passover,* when Jesus knew that his hour was come, and that he should depart out of the world unto the Father (in other words, that his death was near), he loved his own unto the end. The first verse is obviously a broken verse, the end apparently being lost.

Further, it is clear that between verse 1 and verse 2 there is a gap. Something was written in this space which told of the preparations for the supper. There is no indication of the time of the supper, nor of the day.

John's Gospel takes up the story after the Last Supper is ended, the Devil having now put it into the heart of Judas Iscariot to betray Jesus. Thus, the second verse is also a broken fragment, having no end and no apparent connexion with verse 3, which goes on to say that Jesus, knowing that the Father had given all things into his hands, and that he was come from God and went to God. . . .

Once more a break, and verse 4 begins with a matter that has no apparent relation to what had been said in verses 1, 2 and 3. Then in verse 4 (the supper being ended) the real story of the proceedings, according to John, begins. There is no hint that this is the Passover supper. Jesus rises from supper, lays aside his garments, takes a towel, girds it about him, pours water into a basin, and begins to wash the feet of his disciples and to wipe them with the towel. Peter, when his turn comes, protests, saying, "Thou shalt never wash my feet." Jesus answers that if he does not wash him, Peter has no part with him. At this Peter answers that if so, he wishes that not his feet only, but his hands and his head should be washed. Jesus replies that to wash the feet is enough, and he whose feet are washed is clean every whit.

Then follows another manifest interpolation. As Jesus must have washed the feet of Judas also, and subsequent events show that Judas was not clean, the evangelist is confronted by a difficulty—either Jesus did not know that Judas was to betray him (which would show that his knowledge of what was in man was limited, and therefore he was no prophet—see the account of the Pharisee and the woman who was a sinner) or Jesus made a false statement about Judas, or else his washing of the feet of Judas was ineffectual to make him clean any whit. So in verses 10 and 11 come the statement (plainly falsified by what goes before it) that Jesus said "and ye are clean, *but not all*," and the evangelist adds, "For he knew who should betray him; therefore said he, Ye are not all clean."

But why not all? Had the washing been ineffectual in Judas's case? If so, why? After this painful makeshift, the story goes on with the natural statement that after Jesus had washed the feet of his disciples, and taken his garments and sat down again, he begun to tell them why he had done this.

He had done it as an example to them, an example in humility. He was their Master and Lord, yet he had washed their feet. As he had done to them, let them do to each other.

After that comes two verses in the spirit of the previous ones. The evangelist thinks he has to make it intelligible why Judas is there, and why Jesus behaves to the guilty disciple as to the righteous disciples. So Jesus is made to quote Scripture to show that he had to do this. And then he is made to say that he tells them this before the time of his betrayal comes so that they may believe that he is the Christ foretold.

But why? They knew already.

All this again is extremely feeble in thought, and totally unlike Jesus. The same idea goes through the following verses of *John* XIII, from 21 to 30. These verses contain a story which it is hard to believe to be historical, inasmuch as it is impossible of occurrence.

Jesus goes back to the betrayal. He is troubled in spirit and says, "Verily, verily, I say unto you, that one of you shall betray me."

Why should Jesus say this? I see no purpose to be served by it. He is not shaming the betrayer out of his betrayal, for he knows that his betrayal by one of his own (one who "eateth bread" with him) is the preordained plan—foretold by the prophets, according to *John*. The disciples looked at each other, doubting of whom he spoke. And then Peter beckoned to one of the disciples whom Jesus loved (as if he did not love all of them, or all of them in an equal degree) and told him (as in a whisper) to ask Jesus of which of them he was speaking.

This, the disciple indicated did, saying, "Lord, who is it?" Whereupon Jesus (presumably also in a whisper, for the company was very small and everything would otherwise be heard), answered, "He it is, to whom I shall give a sop, when I have dipped it."

Although it says, at the beginning of the report, that the supper was ended, it is not ended, inasmuch as Jesus dips (in the patriarchal manner) in the common dish, and takes a portion of food out and gives it to Judas Iscariot.

This, of itself, is not important. What is important is that the disciple to whom Jesus had revealed the identity of the traitor was, from that moment, perfectly aware that Judas was to betray his master. It is also reasonable to think that he passed this knowledge on to Peter, who had first asked the question.

Then come two startling statements. One, that after Judas had taken the sop *Satan entered into him*. This *appears* to say the impossible thing, that the act of Jesus in giving the sop had been the cause of, or the signal for, the downfall of Judas, the reason of an occasion for Satan to take possession of him, thus making Jesus in some sort responsible at once for his own betrayal and for the damnation of the soul of Judas.

When the earliest of the notable critics of Christianity, Celsus, in the midst of many brutal criticisms, urged this objection, he was not wholly without justification, not seeing (what we now see plainly) that Jesus had been made responsible for words and acts which were utterly impossible to him.

After this statement (that Satan entered into Judas on his taking the sop from Jesus) it is reported that Jesus said to Judas, "That thou doest, do quickly," whereupon Judas immediately rose from the table and went out into the night.

Then follows the other startling statement, namely that "no

man at the table knew for what intent" Jesus spoke to Judas as he did, some thinking that, as Judas "had the bag" (that is to say was the treasurer of the little company, a fact we have never, I think, heard of before, except from the same disciple, on the occasion of the supper when the woman anointed Jesus's feet with ointment), Jesus had merely meant to say that he was to bring the things that were needed for the feast (still to come), or perhaps that he was instructing Judas to lose no time in giving something to the poor.

But here is the outstanding difficulty that one disciple at least, and two probably, knew from Jesus's own mouth that Judas was to betray him, that his end was very near. Therefore, there could be no possible excuse for two of the disciples not understanding that when Judas went out he went out to do the evil work which Jesus knew he would do, and that what Jesus had said plainly meant, "As you have to do this evil thing, do it quickly."

No shuffling can enable rational persons to escape from this conclusion, and inasmuch as it carries with it the fact that two disciples *knew* that Jesus was to be betrayed, and that Judas was to betray him, it leaves it as a mystery why the remaining disciples did not raise a hand or stir a foot to restrain Judas. In short, I find it an inconceivably foolish story, bearing clear marks of a much later origin than the event recorded. It is the fiction of many years later, when the Judas myth had only one form in the mind of the early Christians—that by the preknowledge of Jesus alone Judas betrayed him.

Nowhere else is there any indication that any of the other disciples even suspected Judas, except in the account of the anointing of Jesus by Mary of Bethany, where John's Gospel sends out of the blue (no hint of the like having gone before) that Judas was a thief, who had the bag, and had been known before (*there is no other rational inference*) to steal from the contents of it, for how else did John know that Judas was a thief?

What, then, am I compelled to conclude? Only one thing that I can see—that by far the larger part of *John* XIII is unhistorical; that it was created out of oral tradition, many years after the death of Jesus; that it is confused and contradictory at nearly every point; and that it gives a totally false and dishonouring picture of Jesus in his relation to Judas, who becomes almost his victim at one moment.

Observe, further, that the alleged explanation of Jesus's words to Judas (that he may have told him to go out to buy things for the feast) disposes of the idea that this supper was the Passover Feast at all, but an ordinary meal which took place *before* the Passover Feast, or at least that part which concerns the festival supper.

Whether the supper, in *John,* is or is not intended by the evangelist to be the feast of the paschal lamb is by no means certain. On the whole, I am compelled to think that John meant no such thing. There is no breaking of bread, giving thanks, and so on, no command to the disciples to do this in remembrance of him. Indeed, the later part of John's narrative (that which concerns the trial and crucifixion of Jesus) leaves a very clear impression that it cannot have been so intended, and that, according to *John,* the Passover Feast was to be eaten by the Jews *on the evening of the day on which Jesus died and was buried.* Also, that the first day of the Feast of Unleavened Bread and the Sabbath Day were the same day.

But nevertheless, the account in *John* from verse 31 of Chapter XIII onwards to the end of Chapter XIV, "Arise let us go hence," and perhaps even to the end of Chapter XVII, where (with the beginning of Chapter XVIII) we look on to the incidents in the garden of Gethsemane, may not have been written by John.

However this may be, it is certain that there is nothing in any of the Gospels of greater value than these passages in *John,* from Chapter XIII, 31 to the end of Chapter XVII, which are of the very essence of Christianity, whether they contain the authentic words of Jesus or not.

Whether they were all spoken by Jesus, or whether they were in great part a reconstruction by a later writer (whether John, the son of Zebedee, or another) they assuredly contain some of the sweetest and most unquestionable expressions of the Christ spirit, and it is difficult to think of Christianity without them.

What are they?

Jesus begins by saying (as if in reference to the going out of Judas on the errand of betrayal) that now is he glorified and God is glorified in him. Then he speaks of his forthcoming end, saying,

Little children, yet a little while I am with you. Ye shall seek me, and as I said unto the Jews [Why should he, a Jew, speaking to Jews, call their fellow-countrymen "the Jews," as one would speak of foreigners?] Whither I go, ye cannot come; so now I say to you. A new commandment I give unto you, That ye love one another; as I have loved you, that ye also love one another. By this shall all men know that ye are my disciples, if ye have love one to another.

Here is the authentic voice of Jesus. It is impossible to doubt. But, O God, what a commentary on the history of the Church through all the ages since!

Then follows a doubtful passage. Peter asks, "Lord, whither goest thou?" and Jesus answers "whither I go, thou canst not follow me now; but thou shalt follow me afterwards." Peter asks why he cannot follow him now, and says that he will lay down his life for his sake. Jesus replies, "Wilt thou lay down thy life for my sake? Verily, verily, I say unto thee, the cock shall not crow, till thou hast denied me thrice."

It is night and very late, and this merely means that in the short time before cock-crow Peter will be so far from laying down his life for his Master that he will have three times denied all connexion with him.

Now we return to undoubted history.

Then Jesus comforts his disciples in their sorrow at being about to lose him. Let not their hearts be troubled. As they believe in God they are to believe also in him. In his Father's house there are many mansions. He is going away to prepare a place for them, so that where he is they may be also. Whither he goes they know, and the way they know.

Hearing this, Thomas, one of the disciples, protests that they do not know where he is going, therefore how can they know the way?

To this Jesus answers, "I am the way, the truth, and the life; no man cometh unto the Father, but by me." Then he reproves them. "If ye had known me, ye should have known my Father also."

Philip, another disciple, says, "Lord, show us the Father, and it sufficeth us." Jesus says, "Have I been so long time with you, and yet hast thou not known me, Philip? He that hath seen me hath seen the Father. . . . I am in the Father, and the Father is in me."

After that he comforts them again, telling them that whatever they ask in his name he will do it. When he is gone he will pray to the Father, and he will give them another comforter who will abide with them for ever. And then he himself will return to them. He will not leave them comfortless. Yet a little while and the world will see him no more, but they will see him, and because he lives they shall live also.

Another disciple is puzzled by this, and asks how it is to be that Jesus will manifest himself to the disciples and not to the world.

Jesus answers that to those who love him and keep his words he will appear, and make his abode with them. But to those who do not love him, will not keep his sayings and obey his commandments, he will not manifest himself.

Is this a light cast forward on the stories of the Resurrection, and if so, is it historical, or the interpolation of a later age? There was long the constant objection of sceptical critics that nobody saw Jesus after his Resurrection, except his own people. He did not show himself to his enemies, although to do so would have been to shame them for ever, and perhaps to prevent the repetition of their persecutions.

Then comes a very difficult passage.

These things have I spoken unto you, being yet present with you. But the Comforter, which is the Holy Ghost, whom the Father will send in my name, he shall teach you all things, and bring all things to your remembrance, whatsoever I have said unto you.

I confess I see a later speaker here. Why should Jesus declare that it would be necessary that another should come in his name to teach them since *he* had been teaching? Had not his teaching been clear enough? And why should it be necessary that another should bring to their remembrance what he had said to them? Had not he so plainly spoken that they could never forget what he said?

I strongly suspect that this is an apology, made long after the death of Jesus, for putting words into his mouth of which his recorded sayings (made soon after his death) contain no account.

But now, again, comes the authentic voice of Jesus, Jesus alone:

Peace I leave with you; my peace I give unto you; not as the world giveth, give I unto you. Let not your heart be troubled, neither let it be afraid. Ye have heard how I said unto you, I go away, and come again unto you. If ye loved me, you would rejoice, because I said, I go unto the Father, for my Father is greater than I. . . . Hereafter I will not talk much with you, for the prince of this world cometh and hath nothing in me. But that the world may know that I love the Father; and as the Father gave me commandment, even so do I. Arise, let us go hence.

Incidentally, these words, "Arise, let us go hence," seem to me to show that Jesus and the disciples were not *sitting* at a table, but *reclining* about one.

Here is the clear, authentic voice of Jesus at last—no voice but the voice of Jesus. I think this is the end of the talk with his disciples after the supper.

But what about *John,* Chapters XV, XVI and XVII? First, let us see what they contain.

The supplementary chapters, as I read them, begin by Jesus saying he is the true vine and his Father is the husbandman. Every branch in him that does not bear fruit God takes away, and every branch that does bear fruit God purges that it may bring forth more fruit.

Observe that here Jesus makes no claim to be the equal of God, or part of God. He is merely one of the vines in God's vineyard.

Continuing, Jesus says that they (his disciples presumably) are his branches. As he is the vine they are the branches. And as a branch cannot bear fruit of itself, they cannot bear fruit except they abide in him. Without him they can do nothing. If they do not abide in him, they are as the branch which is cast forth and is burnt in the fire.

I confess this does not impress me deeply. I have no feeling yet that it is Jesus who is speaking. But then comes a surer note. "This is my commandment, that ye love one another, as I have loved you."

It is only open to the objection that Jesus said this in the same words only a few moments before (*John* XIII, 34). Would he repeat them so soon after? I think not. I feel that these last words belong to a later occasion.

But then comes a passage which is entirely new and very beautiful: "Greater love hath no man than this, that a man lay down his life for his friends."

This sounds like the authentic voice of Jesus. The objection to it is that it breaks suddenly into the idea of redemption—that the death which Jesus is about to die is a death of sacrifice and redemption, and nothing has yet been said on that subject in the farewell discourse in the Gospel of John.

The succeeding verses have for me no mark of the mind of Jesus. They are an explanation of the use of the word "friends." His friends for whom he is about to lay down his life are these who do whatever he commands them. They are not his servants, but his friends. In this explanatory passage the sacrificial death of Jesus descends to a lower level. He is not dying for a sinful world, but for his followers, his disciples. But then comes a new thought.

> If the world hate you, ye know that it hated me before it hated you. If ye were of the world, the world would love his own; but because ye are not of the world, but I have chosen you out of the world, therefore the world hateth you. Remember the word that I said unto you, The servant is not greater than his lord. If they have persecuted me, they will also persecute you; if they have kept my saying, they will keep yours also. But all these things will they do unto you for my name's sake, because they know not Him that sent me. If I had not come and spoken unto them, they had not had sin; but now they have no cloak for their sin. He that hateth me hateth my Father also. If I had not done among them the works which none other man did, they had not had sin; but now have they both seen and hated both me and my Father. But this cometh to pass, that the word might be fulfilled that is written in their law, They hated me without a cause.

Is there any good reason why I should not say that there is not in the Gospels a passage more utterly unlike Jesus? It suggests the work of two hands, both writing long after the death of Jesus, and with a space of time between them. Think of the scene in which they claim to be spoken. It is the night before the morning of the arrest, trial, condemnation and death of Jesus. The verse speaks of the world hating the disciples, but we know nothing of the world doing so down to that time. The Gospels contain no mention of the persecution of the disciples of Jesus until after they have taken up his work, and this was not until after the day of Pentecost.

Verse 20 differs from verse 19 in foretelling persecution for the disciples, and it is probably the work of the second writer. The succeeding verses, down to verse 25, read like the writing of one who has witnessed the persecution of the early Church and is seeking to reconcile the early Christians to their sufferings by telling them, through the mouth of Jesus, that he also had suffered, that they must suffer, and that their suffering was the proof of their fidelity and love to him and to God, and the persecutions of their enemies in the world was the proof that they hated God.

Verses 26 and 27 are imperfect versions of what Jesus had said only a little while before; the important phrases are the same. These later verses differ only in being less beautiful.

My conclusion, after careful reading of Chapter XV of *John*, is that it is not historic; that it was written (probably by two hands) long after the death of Jesus; but that it contains some passages which seem to be authentic memories of words actually spoken by him. Some of these are in the Synoptic Gospels.

Chapter XVI of *John* bears still more markedly the appearance of later origin. It begins (verse 2) with a form of prophecy. "They" (the enemies of the disciples) will put them out of the synagogues, and even kill them, and in killing them will think that they are doing God's service. They will do this because they have never known God, and never known him—Jesus.

Jesus says he has told them this that when the time comes they may remember that he told them. A poor reason. "But now I go my way to Him that sent me; and none of you asketh me, Whither goest thou?"

Is it humanly possible that Jesus can have said this? *It is not true,* therefore he did not say it. In Chapter XIII, 36, during the same evening, while Jesus and his disciples were reclining at the same table, Peter said to Jesus, "Whither goest thou?"

Is it possible that the writer of Chapter XVI did not write Chapter XIII, and that he did not even know of it?

Then Jesus (in verse 7) is made to return to the Comforter, saying,

> It is expedient for you that I go away; for if I go not away, the Comforter will not come unto you; but if I depart, I will send him unto you.

It should be observed that this is the fourth time in the address after the supper in which Jesus has spoken of the Comforter, and it is by far the least satisfactory.

What is the Comforter to do, according to this last reference? He is to reprove the world of sin, because they had not believed in him, but *that* Jesus himself had already done; of righteousness (or is it unrighteousness?) "because I go to the Father and ye see me no more" (observe this in relation to the Resurrection); and of judgment, "because the prince of the world is judged."

Jesus is then made to say a feeble thing—that he has yet many things to say to his disciples but they cannot bear them now. But when the Spirit of truth is come he will guide them into all truth; for he shall not speak of himself, but whatsoever he shall hear, that shall he speak, and he will show them things that are still to come. The Spirit of truth will glorify Jesus, "for he shall receive of mine, and shall show it unto you. All things that the Father hath are mine; therefore said I, that he shall take of mine, and shall show it unto you." The whole passage seems to me inexpressibly feeble in thought, and confused in expression. I can offer only a vague conjecture as to its meaning, which seems to be this: that the Comforter, who is not one with God or with Jesus, but a being who receives the messages of God, will come to the world after Jesus has left it, not to speak of himself, but to glorify Jesus, to tell the disciples of Jesus what he has not told them, and to foretell their future.

Then comes a further repetition. In verse 16 of Chapter XVI, Jesus says, "A little while, and ye shall *not* see me; and again, a little while, and ye *shall* see me, because I go to the Father."

Observe that in verse 10 he has said that the Comforter will reprove the world of righteousness, because "I go to the Father, *and ye see me no more.*" And next, that in verses 18 and 19 of Chapter XIV Jesus has said, "I will not leave you comfortless; I will come to you. Yet a little while, and the world seeth me no more; but ye see me; because I live, ye shall live also."

In this previous passage Jesus had said nothing about the little while in which they *shall not* see him, and he offers the difficult explanation that this is because he goes to the Father.

No wonder the disciples asked Jesus what he meant by it. His answer is given in a passage of great beauty, which has the authentic ring of the words of Jesus, but it is no answer, at least no direct answer, to the question.

> Verily, verily, I say unto you, That ye shall weep and lament, but the world shall rejoice, and ye shall be sorrowful, but your sorrow shall be turned into joy. A woman when she is in travail hath sorrow, because her hour is come; but as soon as she is delivered of the child, she remembereth no more the anguish, for joy that a man is born into the world. And ye now therefore have sorrow; but I will see you again, and your heart shall rejoice, and your joy no man taketh from you.

Commentators take the passage to mean that the disciples of Jesus will weep and lament when his death comes, and their enemies of the world will rejoice. But they will be like a woman in labour before the birth of her child, who, as soon as she is delivered of her child, is full of joy—he will come back from death and then their hearts will rejoice with a joy that can never be taken away from them.

This may be the right explanation, but it does not plainly say that he will rise from the dead, although it may be said to indicate that a little while after he disappears from their sight he will reappear, and then their sorrow at his death will be turned into overwhelming joy.

But, if this is the meaning, it is clear that it does not penetrate the minds of his disciples, although a little later, in quite another connexion, they are made to say, "Now are we sure that thou knowest all things, and needest not that any man should ask thee. By this we believe that thou camest forth from God."

To this Jesus makes the moving answer, "Do ye *now* believe?" But did they? Clearly, they did not.

After that he makes another prediction:

> Behold, the hour cometh, yea, is now come, that ye shall be scattered, every man to his own, and shall leave me alone; and yet I am not alone, because the Father is with me. These things I have spoken unto you, that in me ye might have peace. In this world ye shall have tribulation; but be of good cheer; I have overcome the world.

Chapter XVI, if historical, is either a prophecy of the Resurrection or of the second Advent. If it is a prophecy of the Resurrection, it is not understood by the disciples to be so, and their behaviour at the time of the death of Jesus will presently show that they did not so understand it.

Nor am I at all sure that they understood it to be a prophecy of the second Advent, for with this clear prediction firmly rooted in their minds—that Jesus would come again and all their sorrow concerning his death and the breakdown of that Messianic hope would then be wiped out—they could not have behaved as they *all* did after his Crucifixion—running away, hiding from the Jews.

The most natural explanation of Chapter XVI is that it is not a prophecy of the Resurrection, but the essay of a writer coming later than the Resurrection (or the belief in the Resurrection) and recording what had actually happened, namely, that at the death of Jesus the disciples were plunged in despair, but that as soon as the belief that Jesus had risen from the dead took possession of them they were like a woman who (after the pains of labour) had been delivered of her child, full of unquenchable joy.

It is very difficult to come to a conclusion on this point. Assuredly, Chapter XVI of *John,* if historical, is of the highest value.

Chapter XVII of *John* is a prayer by Jesus, with which, apparently, the supper gathering came to an end. It opens on a note of exaltation. The hour has come in which God is about to glorify His son, that His son may glorify God.

> As thou hast given him power over all flesh, that he should give eternal life to as many as Thou hast given him. And this is life eternal, that they might know Thee, the only true God, and Jesus Christ, whom thou hast sent.

Observe that for the first time (I think) Jesus speaks of himself here as "Jesus Christ." Observe, also, that for the first time in these after-supper speeches in the Gospels reference is made to the reason for the death of Jesus—*that he should give eternal life to as many as God gives him.* Further, observe, that the grounds for eternal life are belief, belief in God as the only true God and belief in Jesus Christ. Nothing about atonement for sin, about the sacrifice of Christ for the redemption of the world. The great theory of atonement made to God by Jesus in his death for the sins of the world is not so much as hinted at here in the definition of eternal life.

Then comes a statement of the theory that lies at the root of the fourth Gospel:

> And now, O Father, glorify Thou me with Thine own Self, with the glory which I had with Thee before the world was.

Verses 6–10 are the words of one who is less than the Father, and has carried out the Father's commands. Verse 11 strikes a new note. Not only does it cause Jesus to say that he is one with the Father, but he is made to say that he is "no more in the world." This (notwithstanding the phrase "I come to thee") suggests that it is spoken from Jesus in Heaven to his Father in Heaven, praying for the care of His children who are still on earth.

Almost the whole of the remainder of the prayer, down to the end of the chapter and the close of the supper scene, leaves on my mind the same impression.

The prayer is not the prayer of Jesus on the night of the Last

Supper, but long afterwards—after his followers on earth have suffered prison and martyrdom for his sake, and he prays for their protection, that they should be kept from evil, that they may hold fast to their faith, in spite of all suffering and all temptation, and that they should, in the end, be brought to where he is, and see and perhaps share the glory God has given him, and the love with which He has loved him from before the foundation of the world.

It is a great outpouring of prayer for his children in the world who have suffered greatly for his name's sake, that they may share his glory and God's love at last.

It is a great prayer, but I find it impossible to think of it as historical—as a prayer spoken on the Passover night of A.D. 30.

In order to believe that it was then spoken, it would be necessary that Jesus had already risen above the limitations of time, and projected himself a generation farther into the future—after the death of Stephen, Paul and James, after the scourging of his disciples, the destruction of Rome and the tortures under Nero of the Christians, who had taken the precious name of Jesus and died for it.

A more simple and natural explanation is that this great prayer, too, was the work of a later writer—not earlier than the end of the first century.

Did this writer write from memory of the actual words spoken by Jesus some forty years before? Or did he express the spirit of Jesus as he understood it, in this prayer, and put it into the mouth of Jesus? And, in doing so, did he transform a report into a prophecy, making it seem as if Jesus had prophesied all this which he (the actual writer) had lived through and (in part) had seen?

If the latter, is he to be regarded as a kind of forger? Or, if he has preserved the spirit of Jesus, is he not justified by his aim?

Or if Jesus did indeed foresee all that was to befall his disciples, by projecting himself into the future (thirty-five to sixty years at least), and told them what he saw before them, did he make them understand? Or if they did not understand, then (on that night of the Last Supper) did they come to understand after they realized (or believed they realized) that he had risen from the dead (becoming thereby "the first-fruits of them that slept," the Messiah, the Christ, the Son of God) and so attain the heroic power to go through suffering, martyrdom and death, knowing it had been foretold to them by the Christ, who had also foretold their great and eternal reward—that they would share his glory in the world to which he had gone?

Or is it sufficient, and more natural, to think that all the contents of these three chapters of *John,* being written after prison, martyrdom and death, when the hearts of the disciples were sinking under the hatred of the world, were intended to comfort them as the things that must be, that Jesus had foretold, though the record of his foretelling had until then been lost?

I find it hard to say. The one thing I greatly miss in these last addresses (in the four Gospels) of Jesus to his disciples is the *redemption,* the atonement, the nearing and intuition of death. I do not feel that it comes out strongly here—not nearly as strongly on the verge of his death as when his death was still far-off, as at Cæsarea Philippi.

Having gone carefully through the trial before Pilate I am now fully convinced that the writer of the Gospel of John did not intend to say that the Last Supper was eaten on the first evening of Passover.

Quite the contrary. He opens the account of it, speaking of a time "before" the Passover. He describes an ordinary meal. He does not give the slightest suggestion that the meal has any relation whatever to the festival of the liberation of the Jews from their Egyptian bondage which the Passover was, in the eyes of the Jews, intended to celebrate.

It is (taken in relation to the subsequent incidents, Gethsemane, the arrest, the trial, condemnation and death) plainly intended to take place on the Thursday evening. The arrest and other events are as plainly intended to take place on the Friday. The Passover was to be eaten by the Jews on the evening of the Friday, after the death and burial of Jesus. The day following (from Friday evening to Saturday morning) is plainly intended to be the day both of the Feast of Unleavened Bread and the Sabbath (for the Sabbath that year was "a high day").

Such is my reading. To substantiate it I should have to know whether the subsequent events *could* have taken place on the night of Thursday and the morning of Friday. Could Jesus and his disciples get out of the city at night on Thursday, or were the gates closed at sunset? Is it necessary (according to John's account) to think that the ordinary meal (described by John as a *supper*) could have taken place *before* the gates of the city were closed for the night?

That the arrest, trial, and so on *could* take place on the day before the Sabbath and Passover is natural enough. Moreover, that they *should* do so is in keeping with the desire of the Jews to get rid of Jesus before the crowds became excited by the feast, with its reminder of the coming of the Messiah.

That the supper in *John* is intended to be an ordinary meal, at which Jesus says farewell to his disciples, is shown by the absence in this Gospel of the breaking of bread. There is a definite foundation for the Eucharist in *John* VI, 48, 50: "I am the bread of life . . . which cometh down from Heaven, that a man may eat thereof and not die."

How, then, do we explain this difference between the Synoptic Gospels and John? That the Synoptics were written in that earlier period after the death of Jesus, when the Jewish-Christians were seeing Jesus in the Jewish prophecies, and interpreting the teaching of the Jewish rites. And that *John* was written later, when the Gentile-Christians, never too favourable to the Jews, wished to separate Christianity from Judaism. So the writer of *John,* probably a Greek, knew nothing of the Passover or the Last Supper. To him it was an ordinary meal to be repeated in remembrance of the Master after he was gone. In this sense, even the apostles had so regarded it at first. Their meeting for the breaking of bread took place on the first day of the week, and we do not see that any sanctity attached to it.

A little later, even by the Jews, it was turned into a Passover, with Christ as the lamb slain. Still later, by the Gentiles, it was turned back into the meal of remembrance.

V. After the Last Supper

In passing from the place of the Last Supper, Jesus would go through the city; the streets would be deserted, the people being indoors. He might hear voices through the open windows.

He might catch the last joyous part of the Passover service:

Chad Gadya! Chad Gadya! One only kid of the goat. And a cat came and devoured the kid which my father bought for two zuzim. *Chad Gadya! Chad Gadya!* And a dog came and bit the cat which had devoured the kid which my father bought for two zuzim. *Chad Gadya!*

What did the commentators say was the meaning of this jingle? The passing of the ancient empires—*Egypt, Assyria, Persia, Greece, Rome!* The procession of the ages, the passing of the ancient empires, the ultimate triumph of the people of God, when the Messiah came.

It is a great background to that passing to Gethsemane. Jesus and his followers behind him.

Perhaps a certain note of rejoicing, even of merriment, laughter mingling with the chorus, coming out to them as they pass the last house before they go through the gate into the silent country, and on to the Mount of Olives.

CHAPTER XXVIII

Gethsemane

I. *According to Matthew*

IT WAS CUSTOMARY to open the gates of the Temple at midnight on the Passover Festival night, to admit the people. The feast had to conclude before midnight, and it closed in a spirit of joy. The populace tramped to the Temple, and the streets, previously deserted, would be densely thronged when Jesus and his disciples passed through the city towards Gethsemane. Judas Iscariot and the soldiers would probably leave the vicinity of the Temple, with some of the rabble, shortly after midnight. When Jesus was taken back to the Temple—the high priest's house—it would probably be two in the morning.

He left the city at his leisure; on the road he allowed the disciples, now reduced to eleven, to see something of the weight of sorrow that oppressed him. There are five verses in *Matthew* (XXVI), which may reasonably be understood to pertain to what was said on the way out to the Mount of Olives and the garden of Gethsemane.

In verse 31 Jesus tells the disciples that they shall all be offended because of him that night, because it is written, "I will smite the shepherd, and the sheep of the flock shall be scattered abroad."

This obviously means that the disciples will take offence at Jesus because they will have to suffer by reason of him, and the form of the suffering will be that they will have to fly. But the next verse says that after he is risen again he will go before them into Galilee.

This verse has no obvious relation to what goes before, or what comes after it. Therefore, it is a manifest and rather impudent interpolation put into this place by an appallingly bad editor. Verse 33 takes up the theme of verse 31. Peter says that though all men should be offended because of Jesus yet he will not be offended.

To this protestation of loyalty Jesus replies that that very night before the cock crows, Peter shall deny him thrice.

The Jews had some fixed hours which they denominated the "cock-crows"; but the plain sense of the reply of Jesus to Peter is that before the dawn his fidelity would fail him and he would deny his Master. To the answer of Jesus, Peter replies that though he might have to die with Jesus yet would he never deny him. And all the other disciples say the same.

According to Matthew's Gospel, Judas was still with Jesus, inasmuch as the whole of the twelve sat down with him at supper, and it is nowhere said that Judas had left him. But we have already seen that he "rose from the table and went out into the night."

Then they came to a place called Gethsemane. Nothing is said in *Matthew* about the position of this place beyond the statement, that it was on the Mount of Olives. But the garden of Gethsemane is clearly indicated in the other Gospels. It was obviously beyond the Kidron brook and on the side of the Mount of Olives, being apparently near the foot of it.

When they had reached a secluded place where they were not likely to be disturbed, Jesus said to his disciples, "Sit ye here, while I go and pray yonder." And taking with him Peter and the two sons of Zebedee, "he began to be sorrowful and very heavy." He said to the three, "My soul is exceedingly sorrowful, even unto death; tarry ye here, and watch with me."

Then Jesus went a little farther, and fell on his face and prayed.

Clearly, he knew his death was near—the death he had spoken of last when the woman poured ointment on his head at Bethany —"she did it for my burial." Yet why this exceeding sorrow? Had his courage failed him as he came in sight of death? At Cæsarea Philippi, and all the way from there up to Jerusalem, and in Jerusalem and unto now, he had regarded his death as the crown of his life. Why should he now be exceedingly sorrowful? Countless followers of Jesus in the succeeding ages have gone to their death with something like joy—the triumphant sense of a victory about to be achieved in his name. Why should the heart of Jesus fail him? Was there any special cause? Had he to suffer a death no other had yet known—no other was ever to know? Or was his sorrow in any way associated with the thought of Judas? Had it added to the bitterness of death that one of his own family, whom he trusted and perhaps loved, was to betray him? Had

Judas deserted them at the very gate of Gethsemane? Had this been to Jesus the first positive knowledge of which one of his disciples was to be the traitor?

This is not a plausible explanation, for, according to Matthew's account, Jesus had already known at the Last Supper which of his disciples was to betray him, and had distinctly pointed to him in the presence of his fellow-disciples by answering the question, "Master, is it I?" with the words, "Thou hast said."

Or is the sorrow of Jesus the ordinary human pain of the man at the near approach of death and (in a worldly sense) of shame? Are we to conclude that the story of the victory he was about to achieve by redeeming mankind had not conquered this ordinary human feeling?

I am conscious that the emotion of Jesus in Gethsemane is very imperfectly explained by the Gospel of Matthew. I fail to understand it there. To me it is utterly and most painfully inadequate.

Jesus goes a little farther than the place at which he leaves Peter, James and John, and then falls on his face and prays. His prayer is, "O my Father, if it be possible, let this cup pass from me; nevertheless, not as I will, but as thou wilt."

Again, a painful sense of unexplained emotion. First, was the reference to the cup perhaps a reminiscence of the cup at the Last Supper (verse 27), when he took the cup and gave thanks? Next, is it conceivable that after Jesus had said, when giving the cup, that it was his "blood of the new testament, which is shed for many for the remission of sins," he actually lost heart and would have escaped from the penalty of shedding his blood for the remission of the sins of many, if he could have done so with the will of God? It is utterly incomprehensible.

After this prayer he returned to the three disciples, Peter, John and James, and found them asleep. What, in the meantime, had happened? Had Jesus seen the soldiers of the Temple coming? From the traditional site of Gethsemane, he might easily have seen any group of men who came round the hill on the western side of Kidron. It would be moonlight at that time of the month—about April 14. Besides, the coming party were carrying torches and lanterns.

The three had no apprehension of the near approach of his arrest, and of danger to themselves, such as they afterwards realized (when the time came), and had fallen asleep.

It was natural that they should sleep. They had passed through a day (and particularly a night) of great physical and emotional exhaustion. Two of them (Peter and John) had, according to *Luke,* been the disciples who had been sent to prepare the Passover supper, probably a hard day's work. And both they and James and the other disciples had gone through the deeply depressing supper itself, which (contrary to the ordinary Jewish Passover supper) had not been a joyous and triumphant festival, ending on a note of rapture, but (according to *Matthew*) a very sad meal, concerned with thoughts of betrayal, of treachery within themselves, and death.

It was, therefore, natural that they should sleep, and there is nothing to wonder at in this, unless Jesus, when he said, "Tarry ye here, and watch with me," told them plainly that he was to be arrested that night, and there.

I see no explanation of the warning of Jesus, but that he did tell them this, and that during the supper he forewarned them that his arrest was near.

How had he come by this knowledge? By divine inspiration? If so, why did he pray that the cup might pass from him, if God willed it, for, in that case, he must have known that God did not so will it? Or had he, as is more reasonable to think, been told by one of his secret followers among the priests (we know he had such) or within the Sanhedrin itself (we know that Joseph of Arimathæa and Nicodemus belonged to it) that he was to be betrayed that night, and that Judas was to betray him?

Jesus reproached his three disciples with the words, "What, could ye not watch with me one hour? Watch and pray, that ye enter not into temptation; the spirit indeed is willing, but the flesh is weak."

And this means that, according to Jesus, Peter, John and James did not really know of the coming danger, and that, not knowing it, they would fall into the temptation of running away from it when it fell upon them unawares. But what he says about the spirit being willing, but the flesh being weak seems to apply not more to the protestations of loyalty at all costs which they had just before made to Jesus, than to Jesus himself and the pledge he had made to God—to die for the remission of the sins of many. It is a painful, inadequate passage.

Jesus went away from the disciples, and prayed a second time, saying, "O my Father, if this cup may not pass away from me, except I drink it, Thy will be done." This is essentially the same prayer. There is no new thought whatever.

After this, Jesus returned a second time to where he had left the three disciples, and again he found them sleeping, for, says the evangelist, "their eyes were heavy."

Without reproaching them again, however tenderly, Jesus went away once more, and prayed a third time, saying the same words.

It is not irrelevant to ask who reported these prayers of Jesus, spoken while the three disciples nearest to him were asleep. Not Jesus himself, surely. What was in the mind of the evangelist when he wrote this down? That God revealed to him these words of Jesus when he was alone, and that he (Matthew) wrote them down under divine inspiration? I see no escape from the latter conclusion.

It is not by any means the only occasion on which the evangelists leave this as the only possible inference—that inasmuch as what they are writing could have come from no source except God (Jesus himself being, in most cases, out of consideration), He revealed to them the words which they recorded.

This is, as far as I can see, the chief argument in favour of the inspiration of the Scriptures—that the *writers themselves believed that God spoke through them*. But does it follow that God did speak through them? I fear not. God cannot be made responsible for stories of one utterance, or of one incident, which conflict with and eliminate all other such stories.

After this third prayer Jesus comes again to the three disciples and says to them:

> Sleep on now, and take your rest; behold, the hour is at hand, and the Son of Man is betrayed into the hands of sinners. Rise, let us be going; behold, he is at hand that doth betray me.

Here is a most painfully unintelligible passage. First, it is clear that before returning to his disciples the third time Jesus had seen or otherwise become aware that his arrest was to take place immediately. He had, apparently, seen his enemies approaching. Yet, although he had first asked his disciples to watch with him and had reproached them for not doing so, having fallen asleep, he now (when the moment of danger has come) tells them to sleep on and take their rest. More unaccountably, he tells them in the next breath to rise, that they might be going—not, surely, to escape, for that would be contrary to all his intentions, but, perhaps, to go and meet the multitude. I find the passage so unintelligible and self-contradictory as to be almost meaningless.

In short, with all reverence, I find the entire story of Gethsemane, as told in *Matthew,* to be utterly unworthy, lowering to Jesus in every respect, as showing him shrinking from the great fate which he had foreseen and had fearlessly come to Jerusalem to meet.

While Jesus was thus speaking to his disciples, "Judas, one of the twelve, came, and with him a great multitude with swords and staves, from the chief priests and elders of the people."

Judas had told them that as a sign to enable them to arrest Jesus, and not another, he would kiss Jesus.

"Whomsoever I shall kiss, that same is he; hold him fast," Judas had said. This is an incident difficult to believe, not merely because it is devilish, but because it is unnecessary. Every soldier of the Temple would know Jesus. No officer of the Temple would require to have identified the one man who had apparently figured in and about the Temple during the foregoing days more than any other.

So Judas stepped up to Jesus and said, "Hail, Master!" and kissed him.

Whereupon Jesus said, "Friend, wherefore art thou come?"

And then the persons with Judas laid hands on Jesus, and took him.

Then follows an incident of some consequence. Nothing has hitherto been said in *Matthew* about the disciples carrying swords. That comes in another Gospel (*Luke* XXII, 35–38) in an incident which comes between the Last Supper and the going out to the Mount of Olives. But here it is said in *Matthew* that at the moment of the arrest of Jesus one of his followers drew a sword and struck a servant of the high priest's, smiting off his ear. And that Jesus reproved his follower, saying, "Put up again thy sword in his place, for all they that take the sword shall perish with the sword. Thinkest thou that I cannot now pray to my Father, and He shall presently give me more than twelve legions of angels?"

The reproof, notwithstanding its note of exaggeration, sounds historical—sounds like the voice of Jesus. But it appears to show that the disciples had indeed feared arrest, and taken measures to protect themselves. It is scarcely conceivable that they had thought one sword, or two, or a sword for each, would enable them to withstand the Temple guard. What sort of force did they think would be sent to make the arrest? And, after all Jesus had said at the Supper, and long before it, had they been so far from a comprehension of his teaching as to think that he was to be saved by the use of the sword—apparently one sword? Is there any value to the incident, except such value as lies in the words of the reply of Jesus, that if temporal power had been required he could at any moment have obtained it by asking God to send him the spiritual strength of twelve legions of angels!

But the whole incident (especially as it is enlarged in later Gospels) has no appearance of being historical. It bears, for me, the unmistakable mark of a later hand than that of the original writer.

After the interpolation, as I think it, of the incident of the cutting off of the ear of the high priest's servant (XXVI, 51–54), the direct story goes on. Jesus turns to the multitude and says, "Are ye come out as against a thief with swords and staves for to take me? I sat (observe the word *sat*) daily with you teaching in the Temple, and ye laid no hold on me. . . . Then all the disciples forsook him and fled."

Such is the story of Gethsemane according to *Matthew,* a disturbing and often distressing and belittling story.

II. *According to Mark*

The general lines of the story, as told in *Mark,* are the same as in *Matthew.* The points are not of great consequence. The Agony of Jesus in the garden goes the length, in *Mark,* of his asking that he should be relieved of it. "And he said, Abba, Father, all things are possible unto Thee. *Take away this cup from me;* nevertheless, not what I will, but what Thou wilt."

Jesus does not reprove the follower who cut off the ear of the servant of the high priest.

After it is reported that they all (meaning the disciples) forsook Jesus and fled, it is said that there followed him a certain young man, who that night had a linen cloth cast about his naked body; and that the young men (apparently of the high priest's party) laid hold of him, but he escaped from them by leaving the linen cloth in their hands and flying away naked.

Who this young man was we do not know. Obviously, he was not one of the twelve. That he was in the garden at night (a *cold* night, as we are led to understand a verse or two later, when we are told that in the apartment of the servants in the palace of the high priest there was a fire), that he was clad in a linen cloth only, and that he left this in the hands of the people who tried to arrest him and fled away naked, almost suggests imbecility. We never, to my knowledge, hear of this young man again. Why he takes any place in the narrative of *Mark* it is not easy to understand. We lose all track of him, and there is no inkling of his part in the story of Jesus.

What I have said of the story of Gethsemane in *Matthew* seems to apply equally to the story in *Mark*. It is equally lowering to Jesus, and, in most respects, equally baffling.

III. *According to Luke*

The story of Gethsemane in *Luke* begins with the incidents of the swords. Before they leave the house in which they have eaten the Last Supper, Jesus says to his disciples (after telling Peter that he will deny him thrice before cock-crow that day), "When I sent you without purse and scrip, and shoes, lacked ye any thing?" The disciples answer, "Nothing." "But now," says Jesus, "he that hath a purse, let him take it, and likewise his scrip; and he that hath no sword, let him sell his garment, and buy one. For I say unto you, that this that is written must yet be accomplished in me, And he was reckoned among the transgressors; for the things concerning me have an end." And the disciples answer, "Lord, behold, here are two swords." Jesus replies, "It is enough."

In my judgment there is not in any of the Gospels a more palpable interpolation than this. The prediction is quoted in *Mark* (XV, 28), but in another connexion, where, after it is recorded that Jesus was crucified between two thieves, it is said, "And the scripture was fulfilled, which saith, And he was numbered with the transgressors."

Here in *Mark* the Scripture (wheresoever it comes from) has a natural explanation. But in *Luke* (XXII, 37) it has no apparent application whatever.

What meaning has it? Is it to be assumed that Jesus, presuming the attempt to arrest him that night, wishes to arm his disciples to withstand arrest? If so, what becomes of all the prediction of death, and the *will* to death, which goes before the demand for swords?

Is it conceivable that Jesus thought two swords "enough" to withstand the Temple guard who would be sent out (or brought out) by his betrayer? If so, how foolish it would make Jesus.

Is it conceivable that he meant that two swords would be sufficient to make a protest? But why a protest with swords, since his own word would be a hundredfold more effectual—if any effect were necessary?

And, finally, is it conceivable that after preaching the gospel of non-resistance Jesus should, the moment he himself was in danger, act on the principle of resistance, and involve his disciples in the consequences of it?

I cannot conceive of anything more palpably untrue to the character of Jesus, of the aim of Jesus and the mission of his life. And the sequel of this incident reduces it to something little short of folly.

That this incident is an interpolation is further shown by the fact that the warning to Peter—still more the last words to the disciples, as a whole, and here I think Luke's original story of the Last Supper ended (XXII, 30)—lacks a direct note.

"And he came out, and went, as he was wont, to the Mount of Olives; and his disciples also followed him" (XXII, 39).

Still no mention of Judas, who, according to all the Synoptic Gospels, must have been still with him.

On reaching the place (not mentioned by name, in *Luke*) he said to his disciples, "Pray that ye enter not into temptation."

The rest of the story of what happened in Gethsemane is so nearly like the story in *Matthew* and *Mark* as to suggest that it was taken from the same source, and perhaps borrowed from *Mark*. The only differences are:

(1) That in the midst of his Agony, there appeared an angel unto him from Heaven, strengthening him. The strengthening, however, does not appear to have been of much avail, for we are next told, that, being in an agony, his sweat was, as it were, great drops of blood falling down to the ground. This does not seem to have been intended by the evangelist to be accepted literally—

that Jesus sweated blood—yet some medical authorities have said that under conditions of extreme nervous agony the body of man does actually sweat blood.

(2) That Luke does not tell of *three,* but only of one return to the three disciples.

(3) The followers of Jesus are made to say, after the multitude have arrived to arrest Jesus, "Lord, shall we smite with the sword?"

This is a foolish thing to ask in view of the presence of the captains of the Temple with their swords and staves. And without waiting for the reply of Jesus, one of his followers smites with his sword and cuts off the right ear of the servant of the high priest.

On this Jesus says, "Suffer ye thus far." And then he touches the ear and heals the man.

It is difficult to think of any such miracle being worked with so little effect. In all other instances of miracles great effects are said to have been made on the onlookers. Here there seems to be no effect whatever. Nobody seems to have been impressed with the thought that the man whom they were arresting must have divine power, since he restores to its place the ear that has been cut off. Nobody refuses to arrest him after seeing the exercise of his divine power.

My conclusion is that in *Luke,* as in *Mark,* the story is an interpolation. It is an enlarged, a more unactual version of *Mark's* story, put in by a later writer.

By why was it interpolated? My inference is that it was interpolated much later than the original writing to justify the early Christians who wished to have the authority of Jesus for having an individual purse (while there is no reference elsewhere during the ministry of Jesus, and darkest disapproval of it among converts after the death of Jesus), and also the authority of Jesus to use the sword in self-defence, contrary to the spirit of the teaching of Jesus.

IV. *According to John*

The story of Gethsemane, according to *John,* is brief. It omits the Agony. In this it is immeasurably more true to the spirit of Jesus. He has determined to die. He is convinced that for him to die is the only way to redeem the world. It is a part of the scheme of God for the salvation of mankind. Then why the prayer to God? Why the failing heart? Why the reproaches to the disciples? None of this appears, or could appear, in John. It is contrary to John's conception of Jesus. In this Jesus loses something of his humanity, but his divinity gains greatly.

John also tells us how Jesus reached Gethsemane, if the place to him *was* Gethsemane. After he had said (*John* XIV, 31), "Arise, let us go hence," he went forth with his disciples over the brook Kidron, where was a garden. He had oft-times resorted to this garden with his disciples.

Judas knew the place. And, after leaving the scene of the Last Supper, and going to the Temple, and receiving a band of men and officers, he led them with chief priests and Pharisees, carrying lanterns and torches and weapons, to where he knew Jesus would be.

Jesus, knowing all things that should come upon him, went forth to meet the crowd—Judas standing among them, perhaps leading them—and said to them,

"Whom seek ye?"

They answered, "Jesus of Nazareth."

Jesus said, "I am he." When they heard this fearless admission, they fell back. The evangelist says, they fell to the ground, as if overpowered by the courage and majesty of the man they came out to arrest—who offered no kind of resistance, but fearlessly offered himself, delivered himself up. Apparently, they were speechless, and Jesus asked them again, "Whom seek ye?"

They answered as before, "Jesus of Nazareth." Jesus then said, "I have told you that I am he. If therefore ye seek me, let these go their way."

Clearly, he feared that his disciples might be taken with him as his accomplices. Or else he feared that all of them might be taken so as to prevent the possibility of their taking the wrong one.

All this is on the highest plane of tragedy and nobility. Every melodramatic and incomprehensible incident, all confusion of motive is gone. Jesus is carrying out the plan for which he came up to Jerusalem—to die. No kiss by Judas, no answering reproach however tender—"Friend."

Then comes the incident of the sword. It is attributed to Peter. Peter is said to draw a sword and to smite off the ear of the high priest's servant. The Gospel, for no particular reason, gives the name of the servant of the high priest. The name is Malchus. It is never heard of again. This revelation of the name of the servant is assumed to be proof that the writer of *John* was an eye-witness. It would be as reasonable to say that the writer of the apocryphal Gospel, which gives the names of the two thieves who were crucified side by side with Jesus, was an eye-witness. The name, Malchus, means nothing and proves nothing, and is quite useless.

The reproof of Jesus to Peter is most assuredly true to the spirit of Jesus, "The cup which my Father hath given me, shall I not drink it?"

This is the end of the story in *John,* except that the band and the captains and officers of the Jews take Jesus and bind him and lead him away.

V. *Conclusions*

If the incident concerning the sword is historical, it is only so as John tells it. As told by Mark it is scarcely believable. As told by Luke utterly unbelievable. Critics have said that the captains and soldiers who arrested Jesus were Roman. There is nothing to justify this. It is ridiculously incredible. To think that the Roman authorities would help the Jewish authorities to arrest a prisoner who was first of all to be accused of offences against the Jewish religious law is foolish. To say that after arresting him they should proceed, not to the Roman courts of the procurator, but to the Jewish palace of the high priest is to descend to the ridiculous.

That the Jewish authorities did sometimes, by false representations, enlist the help of the Roman authorities to arrest Jewish offenders, is shown by the arrest and trial of Paul by the captain of the castle in Jerusalem, who sends him to Festus, the procurator at Cæsarea. But that the Roman procurator clearly saw that he had no right to try Paul is shown by the letter of Festus to King Agrippa, who says that the Jews who had called for Paul's trial had deceived him, for he had found him innocent of any charge for which he could try him. (See *Acts* XXV, 18, 19.)

Therefore, it is clear that Jesus was arrested solely and only by the guards of the Temple, who were accompanied by all the hangers-on and riff-raff of whom there would be large numbers about the Temple that night, *if* it was the night of the Passover Feast.

As to the incident of the sword, it is at least conceivable that the impetuous Peter, who had valiantly protested against the idea that Jesus should suffer death at the hands of the Jews, and may have been indignant at the idea of the betrayal, may have armed himself (on leaving the place of the supper) and struck a blow with his sword at the servant of the high priest, who may have been officiously forward in laying hold of Jesus. But I confess to grave doubts of the whole incident from beginning to end, and in any form whatsoever.

In such a crowd where would Peter have been after such an offence? Not where we shall presently find him—in the palace of the high priest.

CHAPTER XXIX

The Trial

I. The Inquiry Before Annas

JESUS HIMSELF offered no physical resistance when the soldiers from the Temple came to arrest him in the garden of Gethsemane. All his disciples forsook him and fled. Two followed afar off. These were John and Peter. They got admission to the house of the high priest where Jesus was to be tried. Legally, there could be, and was, only one high priest—Caiaphas; but actually at that time there were two, Annas having the power that lay behind the high priest.

The narratives in the Gospels, although substantially the same, differ from each other in many important particulars concerning what followed upon the arrest.

How many trials and inquiries did Jesus go through? *Matthew* and *Mark* indicate two only. *Luke* indicates three. *John* indicates four, and possibly an inquiry besides.

It is probable, as John's Gospel says, that they took Jesus first to the house of Annas, which was on the Mount of Olives in close proximity to the garden of Gethsemane. In *John,* alone, it is recorded that after Jesus's arrest his first appearance was before Annas.

Annas had been high priest for several years. He was succeeded in the high priesthood by Joseph Caiaphas, who remained high priest for many years. Joseph Caiaphas is said by John to have been the son-in-law of Annas.

Josephus, who gives a full account of Annas, and says that five of his sons were high priests after him, and who mentions Joseph Caiaphas repeatedly, does not say that Caiaphas was the son-in-law of Annas. Therefore, the fact is doubtful. On the other hand, I think it highly probable that the man who was powerful enough with the Roman procurators (who appointed the high priests) to secure the succession of five sons might have done the same by a son-in-law. The matter is quite important; it concerns Jesus one way or the other.

The Gospels repeatedly speak of both Annas and Caiaphas as high priests, conveying the idea that there could have been two high priests at the same time. Critics have made much of this, saying that it was a slip, an error. It was not, except in the strictest sense. Josephus shows, by many references, that on the lips of the people of Jerusalem there were often many high priests at the same time; that the past high priests continued to be called high priests for as long as they lived after they had been deposed. Once a high priest, always a high priest, in name, at least. Naturally, the powers of the ruling high priest could only be exercised by the actual high priest of the time.

What was the position of Annas, after he had given place to Joseph Caiaphas?

Clearly, from many references, both in the Bible and in Josephus, it was one of great influence. He might be said to be the high-priest maker. He was a go-between of the ruling high priest and the procurator.

Further, he may have had an official position. There were two courts of the Jews, a lower and a higher one. The lower council (or lower Sanhedrin) was apparently a kind of court of first entrance. It passed the accused on to the higher and grand court of the Sanhedrin on good cause being shown. I think it in the highest degree probable that Annas was president of this lower court in the time of Caiaphas. This would make it imperative that a prisoner should first be accused before him. This has been the custom of the law in nearly all countries and all ages. It was so in Jerusalem.

In the time of Christ, the power of the president of the lower court must have been great. It would be at his instance that an arrest would be made (as to-day in our own legal procedure), not at that of the high priest, or high-court judge.

Another point. The high priest could not summon a court of the Sanhedrin without the consent of his Roman superior, who appointed him—the procurator. Proof of this important fact can be found in Josephus in the account of the proceedings which followed the illegal trial and execution of James, the brother of Jesus, by the son of Annas of the same name, who was threatened by the Roman procurator of his time, Albinius, with dismissal from his high-priesthood, for having summoned a Sanhedrin without his consent and illegally executed James.

All this (never, as far as I know, mentioned before) is of the utmost consequence in determining the proceedings which led up to the execution of Jesus.

Another point. It has repeatedly been said by critics, who regard as unhistorical the appearance of Jesus before Annas, that Caiaphas must have been the authority under which the arrest was made. Nothing of the kind. Jesus would be arrested under the authority of the president of the lower court, who, having satisfied himself that there was a case to go before the higher court, would find a true bill and send him to the president of the higher court.

Further, it follows that this has a bearing on the conduct of Judas. It would not be to Caiaphas and the Temple that Judas would go when he decided to betray Jesus. It would be to Annas. And it was easy for him to go to Annas, and difficult for him to go to Caiaphas. The high priest lived in the Temple, and the Temple was surrounded by officials. It would have required almost impossible cunning in Judas to reach Caiaphas without the fact becoming known to multitudes of Temple officials and vast numbers of other persons. It was not known even to the disciples that he had ever done so. I conclude that Judas never went to the Temple until the last hour before the arrest in Gethsemane, or, more probably, that he never went near the Temple at all.

What did he do? He went to Annas. Where? Here comes a flood of light on the betrayal.

Annas had a house, says Josephus, near the eastern gate of the Temple, on the Mount of Olives. Tradition has it that he had a sort of farm there for the breeding and sale of the birds and beasts sold for sacrifice at the altar. It was convenient, and (for the use of the Jews who came from distant countries) almost inevitable that such a place there should be, within easy reach of the Temple, and particularly of that court of the strangers in which the trading and money-changing were done.

This house of Annas's *outside* the eastern wall of Jerusalem must have been near the garden, whether the garden was Gethsemane or a place nearer the summit of the mount. It would also be near Bethpage, where (as tradition has it) Joseph of Arimathæa had a country seat or a farm.

Thus we have three important places (important to the history of Jesus) in close proximity, within a radius of about half a mile—Annas's house, Gethsemane and the seat of Joseph of Arimathæa.

Look at the story of the betrayal from the beginning and things now seem clear. After the supper at Bethany, Judas, according to the Gospels (all except *Luke*) took his first step. He had been rebuked and was a little estranged because of it. Also, he was, as I think, increasingly fearful for his own safety, and perhaps for the safety of his Master. At the supper at Bethany others were present besides the disciples. If the disaffection of Judas betrayed itself in his face, that fact would be observed. Is it not possible that some of the hostile Jews observed it, spoke to him, read his fears, interpreted his disaffection, and communicated it to Annas? And is it not simple to see that through that easy channel came Judas's first bargaining with the Jewish rulers? To go into Jerusalem and to the Temple was almost impossible to him. To go to Annas's house from Bethany was the easiest thing possible.

Thus, I conclude that Annas was the means whereby Judas's betrayal of Jesus was brought about. He was also the official (if he was president of the lower court) through whom *alone* it could be brought about.

Now, come to the night of the Last Supper. Whether Judas left the supper-chamber where John makes him leave it, or at the gate of the garden, as the critics think more probable, he would go (beyond doubt) to the house of Annas near by. This would be after midnight. He could do it so easily, without the slightest danger of being observed.

Annas would do the rest. Having prepared Caiaphas (by telling him of his commerce with one of Jesus's disaffected followers) for the arrest of Jesus, he would send down to the Temple for the Temple guard—not to the Castle of Antonia for the Roman cohort, which would be unnecessary foolishness—and with an hour or two the captains, the Pharisees, the elders and multitudes of the people who had come out after their festival feast and entered into the courts of the Temple for their joyful gatherings, when, after midnight, the gates of the Temple were reopened (they were always closed at sunset)—within an hour or two (say at 2 A.M.) the crowd, led by Judas, would arrive at the garden.

What then?

After the arrest, where would it be natural that the prisoner should *first* be taken? To the Temple, to the court-room of the Sanhedrin, or even to the palace of the high priest? By no means. The natural thing would be to take him to Annas, the president of the lower court, who had ordered the arrest.

Would they take him to Annas's house? I think certainly. The lower court probably (almost certainly) had a court-hall in the Temple, or near it. But it was not necessary to an eastern ruler that he must try a case in the regular court-house. He could try a case anywhere; in his own house, in anybody else's house, in the high road if need be—wherever he happened to be. We see this in the history of Herod Philip, who carried his judgment-seat about with him when he went on his journeys through his dominions, and held his court wherever and whenever the need arose. This practice descended in some countries down to the lifetime of persons still living or only lately dead. I could, myself, cite a case of a court being called and held in a public highway. There would, therefore, be nothing irregular in the holding of an inquiry first in the house of Annas. Convenience would suggest it, and necessity would require it.

So much by way of disposing of the great outcry of the wise critics against the account as given by John.

The description is undoubtedly a confused one. The story is imperfectly told. It is bemuddled by two verses in particular, which lead to uncertainty as to whether what is being described is taking place in the house of Annas or in the palace of Caiaphas.

The first of these is verse 13 of Chapter XVIII: "And led him away to Annas first; for he was father-in-law to Caiaphas, which was the high priest that same year."

Putting aside the fuss that has been caused by the words "high priest that same year" (which serves the critics to show that John did not know that the high-priesthood was not an annual appointment, and that Caiaphas had then been high priest for several years), we can see no reason for the second clause of the verse, unless it is intended to mean that they had led Jesus to Annas first *because* he was the father-in-law of Caiaphas—which seems to be nonsense, the relationship providing in itself no apparent justification for taking Jesus to the wrong place, if it was the wrong place.

The second of the two difficult verses is 24, which runs, "Now Annas had sent him bound unto Caiaphas the high priest." This seems to suggest that all that goes before is the record of what took place at the house of Caiaphas—an inference which is strengthened by the fact that otherwise not one word is said about what took place at the house of the high priest, and not a syllable of justification is given for the next step taken, namely that of Caiaphas sending Jesus to the judgment-hall of the Roman procurator.

But most critics, however hostile to John, conclude that what is reported from verses 13 to 27 is intended to be the record of what happened at the house of Annas—unless they except the denial of Peter, which they assign to the palace of Caiaphas. In this I think they are wrong, notwithstanding that all the three earlier Gospels (who record nothing of the appearance of Jesus at the house of Annas) place the denial of Peter in the palace of Caiaphas.

What, then, took place at the appearance before Annas as reported by John? Exactly and precisely what might have been expected to take place at a court of first instance.

Annas tried to find grounds for sending Jesus on a specific charge of blasphemy to the court of Sanhedrin, which alone had the right (his lower court certainly had not) to try a case of blasphemy and (in olden days) to inflict the punishment of blasphemy—death.

It is almost certain that this inquiry would be held in the common language of the people—Aramaic. Annas questions Jesus as to his disciples and his doctrine. Jesus answers:

> I spake openly to the world; I even taught in the synagogue and in the Temple, whither the Jews always resort; and in secret [mark this] I have said nothing. Why askest thou me? Ask them which heard me, what I have said unto them; behold, they know what I said.

This was good law, and a perfectly proper answer. Annas, as a judge, had no right to make a case out of the prisoner's own words. But Annas was not acting as a judge, and he was not holding a court. He was acting as an *agent provocateur,* and was trying to extort evidence from the prisoner himself to be used against him when he came to trial before the Sanhedrin.

He failed to do so. Jesus answered him as he deserved to be answered, "If you want to know what I said, don't ask me; ask the people who heard me."

It was a smashing retort to which there was no legal answer. And so one of the officers who had brought Jesus to Annas, feeling the crushing power of it, struck Jesus with his hand, saying, "Answerest thou the high priest so?"

To this Jesus replied, "If I have spoken evil, bear witness of the evil; but if well, why smitest thou me?"

It is another smashing answer. The blackguard could not possibly make a reply. Jesus had a right to hear the witness against him; his inquisitor had no right to try to make him a witness against himself. He had also a right to say this, to a high priest above all others, because *he* ought to know, and having said it no officer had a right to smite him.

We do not gather that Annas, who made no reply, reproved his officer for doing a brutal and illegal thing. We only see that, having utterly failed to secure any evidence whatever that justified him in sending Jesus to the court of the high priest (his investigation having, in fact, ended in nothing, in utter failure), he nevertheless sent him to Caiaphas.

It was inevitable that he should do so. That was of the essence of the plan. Critics who refuse to believe in the authenticity of the inquiry before Annas say that the answer Jesus made to Annas is a repetition of what he said at the moment of his arrest in Gethsemane.

This is not so. The words are in part the same, but the significance is entirely different. In Gethsemane he says (*Matthew* XXVI, 55) that he preached daily in the Temple, and they might have arrested him then and did not.

In the house of Annas (*John* XVIII, 20) Jesus says he has spoken openly in the Temple, and if the high priest wishes to know what he has said of his doctrine and disciples, he has only to ask the Jews who heard him.

A totally different thing.

II. *Peter's Denial*

And, now, here comes the incident of the denial by Peter. In all the other Gospels it takes place in the palace of Caiaphas in the Temple. But see how much more naturally it takes place, where John appears to place it, in the house of Annas.

John does not say that upon the arrest of Jesus in the Garden the disciples ran away. Neither does Luke say so. Only Matthew and Mark say so, and they say it in the same words ("they all forsook him and fled"), which shows that one copied from the other and, therefore, there is one witness only for the flight of the disciples against two which know nothing of their flight.

Nevertheless, in the light of the subsequent events (that the disciples were not present at the Cross, unless John was present, that they were not present at the so-called trial, unless Peter was present, and that they were within closed and locked doors for fear of the Jews after the Resurrection) I conclude that they *did* fly away and that Jesus was left alone.

What happened to ten of them that night we do not know. Whether they got back into the city is not said. The gates of the city were opened on the Passover night, and it is reasonable to think that in the crush and excitement of the crowded streets after the festival, and perhaps (a striking thought) in the midst of the excitement occasioned by the bringing in of the prophet of Galilee as a prisoner, they *did* get into Jerusalem and find shelter together in the room where we find them sixty hours later.

But there is one exception—Peter. Luke says that Peter followed Jesus afar off to the palace of the high priest. And John says the same. To which house did Peter follow his Master? I think to the house of Annas. That house was near to the garden. I see Peter flying off; then stopping in the darkness; repenting of his cowardice and returning at the tail of the crowd that were taking his Master away—with another disciple, who gets in, leaving Peter outside.

He arrives at the gate of Annas's house. What kind of house would it be? Would it be a semi-Roman house such as Josephus (and Keim) describes, connected with the Temple and built by Herod the Great? I believe not. The few indications in the Gospel story (in all the Gospels) show, I think, that it was an oriental house, a purely Jewish house. That means that it would be a house with an inner court, or patio, open to the sky, with rooms around it, opening off it, and with the doors often open.

The story of how Peter got into the house of the high priest, as told in the Gospels, is as follows:

In *Matthew* we read (XXVI, 58) that Peter "went in, and sat with the servants, to see the end." Later (69) when the high priest had pronounced Jesus guilty of death, we read that Peter "sat without in the palace," and that a damsel came unto him, saying, "Thou also wast with Jesus of Galilee."

Peter denied this, saying, "I know not what thou sayest."

Peter then went out into the porch where another maid saw him, and said, "This fellow was also with Jesus of Nazareth." Again Peter denied, saying, "I do not know the man."

After a while, others that stand by say to Peter, "Surely thou also art one of them [one of the Galileans] for thy speech bewrayeth thee." Then Peter begins to curse and swear, saying, "I know not the man." And immediately the cock crows, and Peter remembers that Jesus had said to him, "Before the cock crow thou shalt deny me thrice." And Peter goes out and weeps bitterly.

This story obviously requires that the two domestic servants should have gone to Gethsemane with the multitude who arrested Jesus and seen Peter there. If they were maids of the palace of Caiaphas in the Temple, the distance would be considerable. It is possible, but scarcely probable.

The story in *Mark* is the same as in *Matthew,* except that Peter is described as "sitting beneath the palace," a point that indicates a city house.

The story in *Luke* is that Peter sat by a fire in the hall, and that one of the maids looked after him, saying, "This man was also with him." And after Peter had made a similar denial to two men, the cock crew and "the Lord turned and looked upon Peter," and then Peter remembered the word of the Lord, and went out and wept bitterly.

Obviously, this story by Luke excludes that of Mark so far as it concerns Peter sitting "beneath the palace," unless we are to understand that the inquiry was held beneath the palace (an improbable thing), otherwise Jesus could not have "looked" upon Peter.

The story in *John* is that Peter stood at the door of the high priest's house until another disciple "who was known to the high priest" came out to him, spoke to the woman (mark, a woman doorkeeper) who kept it, and brought Peter in. There would hardly be a woman doorkeeper in the palace at the Temple. Obviously, they entered into a courtyard, or patio, for the people stood about a "fire of coals," for it was cold, "and they warmed themselves, and Peter stood with them."

What follows in *John* is the same, except that Peter's remembrance of what his Master had said, and his remorse, are not recorded.

Now from these stories I conclude:

1. That the house was an oriental house with a patio, and that it was therefore not in Jerusalem, but on the Mount of Olives.

2. That the fact of a woman porter suggests a country house, not the palace of Caiaphas or the Temple.

3. That the fire and the mention of the cold night suggest that Peter stood in the open air in the patio of a house on the mount, not in the underground chamber of a semi-Roman Herodian palace in the Temple.

4. That the incident of Jesus looking at Peter would be possible and natural if the house were an oriental house on the Mount of Olives, but quite impossible if Peter were in the basement of the palace of Caiaphas in Jerusalem.

Of the incident itself it is not necessary to say much. The prediction of Jesus that Peter would deny him was only meant to say that before the dawn of the next day he would do so. But cockcrow to the Jews had reference to specific hours, and the first of these was as early as midnight. Again, remember it was full moon that night (14th Nisan) and that cocks often crow in the moonlight, mistaking the light for dawn. But to attempt to put an exact literal form to the story would be futile. Jesus merely intended to reprove Peter's over-confidence.

Had he any prophetic knowledge of what was to take place with Peter? Did he foresee this exact scene? I think it is folly to consider this necessary. I also think the story of Peter's denial gathered these barnacles as it passed through the sea of time.

The only value of it to me is that it contributes to the atmosphere that makes me fairly sure that the first inquiry into the alleged offence of Jesus was made, as John says, in the house of Annas; that the house of Annas was outside the eastern gate of the city and near to Gethsemane; and that the proceedings were such as John describes—utterly ineffectual to the end they were expected to serve, and a complete failure.

But this only makes the next step—the inquiry before Caiaphas —the more illegal and iniquitous.

III. *Josephus, Keim and the Author's Notes*

Keim is quite sure that Jesus was led to the house of Caiaphas. According to Josephus, Annas was the son of Seth, and was made high priest by Cyrenius in A.D. 7. Annas was deposed by Gratus in the autumn of A.D. 14. He was followed in the high-priesthood by five of his sons—by Eleazar about A.D. 16, by Jonathan and Theophilus about A.D. 36 or 37; by Matthias about A.D. 42 or 43 and by Annas the younger about A.D. 63. Between Eleazar, as high priest, and Jonathan, there came Joseph Caiaphas, who is said (in the Gospel of John, but not by Josephus) to have been a son-in-law of Annas.

Caiaphas became high priest about A.D. 15 and had (according to Keim's reckoning) been eighteen years high priest at the time of the trial of Jesus.

Keim does not think that Annas was the first judicial examiner of Jesus, for he says, "This report of John's has been frequently regarded, even by critics, though without justification, not only as an unhistorical, but also as a factually true correction of the earlier Gospels." And he continues, "If Caiaphas was the actual, officiating and ruling high priest; if he was, on account of eighteen years dreaded administration, in the highest degree powerful, it was he, not his aged father-in-law (who had long since retired from office), who had the prerogative of hearing the report of the arrest and of first examining the prisoner."

This, in my judgment, is short-sighted nonsense. Where and when does a high court judge perform the duty of ordering the arrest and preside at the first examination of a prisoner? Thus Keim and many other critics are very contemptuous of John's report that Jesus first appeared before Annas. On the other hand Ewald, in his History of Israel, thinks it improbable that Jesus was taken directly to the chief high priest. Some critics regard Annas as the dominating power in the high-priesthood and Caiaphas as a mere lay-figure. But this defence of John's account is quite unnecessary. John is recounting a natural occurrence.

Keim thinks there can be no doubt whatever that the actual high priest, and not another, was the president of the judicial tribunal. It is quite unnecessary to doubt this. It is only necessary to doubt if in Jerusalem, or anywhere else, the higher judicial tribunal would be the first to examine any prisoner. I say it would most certainly *not* be the first. "Annas," says Keim, "did not pass sentence." Of course he did not. He merely sent Jesus on to Caiaphas, which he had no right to do on the evidence given, there being nothing to make a case for the higher court. It was done solely because Annas was determined to secure a conviction.

It will presently be seen that, contrary to nearly all criticism, Caiaphas did not pass sentence upon Jesus either. Jesus, in fact, was never tried by the Sanhedrin, or, if tried, was never condemned by it.

IV. *"That Other Disciple"*

According to *John* (XVIII, 15) Peter was taken into the house of the high priest by another disciple who had acquaintance with the high priest. Who was that other disciple? Our only information about this person comes from John. What does John say? He says that

> Simon Peter followed Jesus and so did another disciple: that disciple was known unto the high priest, and went in with Jesus into the palace of the high priest. But Peter stood at the door without. Then went out that other disciple, which was known unto the high priest and spake unto her that kept the door, and brought in Peter.

From the fact that the other disciple followed with Peter it might at first sight be concluded that he was one of the remaining ten (Judas being, of course, excluded). But examination shows this to be impossible.

Critics have said that it was the evangelist John himself. It is not John's habit to refer to himself by name, but it is in the last degree improbable that John, the son of Zebedee, the fisherman of Galilee, would be "known unto the high priest." Again, the denial of Peter has its origin in fear of being identified as a follower of Jesus and therefore an accessory to his offence, whatever it might prove to be. But John was equally an accessory, and in just the same degree, and yet he has not only no cause for fear, but he exercises the powers of a person favoured by the high priest. Again, the answer to Peter's protest—that he is a Galilean, for his speech betrays him—would as certainly apply to John, the fisherman of Galilee.

Finally, the maids of Annas's house, who recognized Peter as a man they had seen with Jesus in the garden (they might easily have been there, since the garden was only a short distance from their home, and the lanterns and torches of the crowd coming from Jerusalem might naturally draw them), might as naturally recognize John, except only that, according to the fourth Gospel, Peter had made himself conspicuous by using the sword.

So I rule out John as the other disciple.

Other critics suggest Mark as at once the young man who ran away naked and who later followed Jesus into the high priest's house and afterwards brought in Peter. This is too absurdly impossible to require answering.

Again, other critics suggest Matthew, as one who, in his former capacity as tax-gatherer, might have become known to the old high priest. But if known at all to Annas, Matthew (Levi) would be unfavourably known to a Jewish high priest, as one of the Jews who consented to do the most degrading work of their Roman masters, that of the publican who, in gathering tribute, was (as a Jew) expected to pry into the most intimate facts of his fellow-Jews' incomes.

So all the immediate disciples of Jesus are excluded. Who remains? One or other of the secret disciples of Jesus. He had many such. Two were very powerful—Nicodemus and Joseph of Arimathæa.

Remember that Joseph of Arimathæa was at hand—that he was probably a near neighbour and friend of Annas; that he was not yet known to be a disciple of Jesus. Here we have the leading facts necessary to the identification of the other disciple. I can have no doubt that this person was Joseph of Arimathæa, who took Peter into the house, or patio, of the high priest.

But that fact is not of itself important. What is important is that he was probably the reporter of what took place in Annas's house. Peter is the only other source of our knowledge, Jesus himself being, for obvious reasons, excluded; and Peter was clearly too much occupied with the protection of his own liberty to know exactly what occurred between his Master and the high priest.

A certain light on the "other disciple" is cast by the Gospel of John in the account of the Resurrection. After Mary Magdalene returned to the sepulchre and found it empty, she ran and told Peter and "that other disciple" whom Jesus loved. Incidentally, she and her companion are said in *Mark* (XVI, 8) not to have told any man, "for they were afraid."

But if it was John, the disciple, who knew the high priest and had this influence with him, why did he do nothing for his Master? He did not say a word at the trial either before Annas or Caiaphas. We never hear of anything he did, except appear at the foot of the Cross with the mother of Jesus.

There is, further, the suggestion of some critics that Lazarus, of all people, was the other disciple who, being known to the high priest, took Peter into the high priest's house. Hardly anything could be less probable. Clearly, the high priests had thought the story of Lazarus being raised from the dead an imposture.

They were angry that by this alleged imposture people were being led to believe in Jesus. Therefore, when Jesus disappeared (to Ephraim) they "consulted that they might put Lazarus also to death." Was it likely that this person (who, in their view, had lent himself to an imposture, with the obvious intention of forwarding Jesus's Messianic plans) would be in such favour with Annas that he would be allowed to be present at his house during the examination of Jesus?

Incidentally, the fact that they consulted to put Lazarus to death shows that they did not believe he had ever been dead. Otherwise, they would have reflected that the miracle-worker who could raise him from the dead once could do it again (after *they* had put him to death), and then they would be for ever confounded.

V. The Inquiry Before Caiaphas: According to Matthew

It is almost certain that the inquiry before Caiaphas would also be held in the common language of the people—Aramaic. Greek was understood by the Jews, but not generally spoken. Even Josephus says of himself that though he understands the elements of the Greek language he has so long been accustomed to speak the tongue of the Jews that he cannot pronounce Greek with sufficient accuracy.

In the following summary I omit the incident of the denial by Peter, because I assign it to the incident of the inquiry before Annas.

And they that had laid hold on Jesus led him away to Caiaphas, the high priest, where the scribes and the elders were assembled. [XXVI, 57]

It was then not later than 2 A.M. on the morning of Nisan 15th. How had it come to pass that at that hour the scribes and the elders were assembled at Caiaphas's house? It is possible that a number of them may have taken part with him in the Passover Feast.

It is possible that Judas, coming from the Last Supper of Jesus (which must have ended before midnight, and Judas left it some time before it ended, according to *John's* report), arrived at the palace of Caiaphas before the high priest's friends departed, and that he (Caiaphas) kept them there in the expectation that Jesus would shortly be arrested and brought to him, and desiring that Jesus should be disposed of before the city was stirring in the morning, so as to avoid any possible attempt at rescue on the part of the followers of Jesus among the people.

Further, it is possible (alternatively) that immediately on the departure of the Temple guard, with Judas, for the arrest of Jesus, Caiaphas sent round the city to summon as many of the scribes and elders as were within call for the purpose (and reason) I have given.

But what is not possible is that in this time he could have summoned the whole council of the Sanhedrin, many of whom would live at a distance.

Or, assuming that all, being devout Jews, were present in the Holy City at that time of the Passover, it is still improbable that within two hours or even three, the high priest could have gathered together the seventy members of the Sanhedrin or even as many as were necessary for a quorum.

But even assuming that all this was possible, it was obviously not possible for Caiaphas to fulfil all the traditions of the Jewish law in relation to the summons of the Sanhedrin.

On the other hand, we have two cases of the illegal summoning of the Sanhedrin in *Acts*—in the cases of Stephen and Paul—and this may give credence to the idea that Caiaphas (resenting, as all high priests must have done, the control of a Roman soldier over a Jewish court) did actually call a Sanhedrin. But if he did call a Sanhedrin it was illegally called, and therefore its proceedings must have been illegal.

My belief is that Caiaphas did not then, or at any later time, call a Sanhedrin to deal with the case of Jesus of Nazareth. Therefore, I conclude that the proceedings before Caiaphas were not a trial, but merely an inquiry—a kind of third degree investigation—intended to lead to a regular trial if necessary, but to dispose of Jesus irregularly if that seemed necessary to the safety and supremacy of the Jewish religious rule.

Now the chief priests, and elders, and all the council, sought false witness against Jesus, to put him to death; but found none; yea, though many false witnesses came, yet found they none.

Observe here that nobody makes mention of the fact that Jesus made a Messianic (kingly) entrance into Jerusalem, *riding on an ass.*

The Jews knew better than to mention a fact which the high priests would know told *against* their accusation. The riding on an ass was of itself proof that Jesus made no pretensions to kingship.

> At last came two false witnesses, and said, This fellow said, I am able to destroy the Temple of God, and to build it in three days.

To speak against the Temple was of itself a form of blasphemy (see Stephen's trial, *Acts* VI, 13. "This man ceaseth not to speak blasphemous words against this holy place, and the law." The council is then in the Temple. The accusers of Stephen go on to declare that they have heard Stephen say that this Jesus of Nazareth shall destroy this place).

> And the high priest arose and said unto him, Answereth thou nothing? What is it which these witness against thee? But Jesus held his peace.

Here is the most manifest travesty of a trial. Witnesses are brought at that early hour of morning, say 3 o'clock. Had a kind of whip been sent out through the city to fetch from their beds the persons who had (possibly) before played spy upon Jesus, and brought to the Temple authorities their stories of what he said, either publicly to the people, when he addressed them in the courts of the Temple, or privately to his disciples, when they pointed out to him the stones of the Temple, and he told them that before long every stone would be thrown down? ("There shall not be left here one stone upon another, that shall not be thrown down"—*Matthew* XXIV, 2.)

The foregoing reflects upon the other passage in which Jesus speaks of rebuilding the Temple in three days.

Obviously, the evidence was confused and conflicting. It is argued that this fact is evidence that the high priest had not made a deliberate preparation of a case against Jesus, or he would have seen to it that the evidence agreed. But here is clear proof that Caiaphas did not attempt to try Jesus in any legal sense. He did not ask if there were witnesses in defence. The Jewish law required that witnesses for the defence should be called if none approved of themselves. Caiaphas did not ask for any. He did not adjourn the inquiry to enable witnesses for the defence to be found, as Jewish law required he should do if he were presiding over the Sanhedrin.

The only witness for the defence was the prisoner himself. Caiaphas questioned Jesus only. This was not the act of a judge, but of an inquisitor. Caiaphas was not trying Jesus. He knew he was not trying Jesus. He was only seeking to obtain such admission from Jesus as would enable him to try him, and presumably condemn him to death.

> And the high priest answered him and said unto him [Jesus] I adjure thee, by the living God, that thou tell us whether thou be the Christ, the Son of God.

This seems to me impossible language from a Jewish high priest, who could not believe that God had any Son, or that the Galilean could be the Christ, not having been born under the only condition which, according to Scripture (as Caiaphas knew it), must apply to Christ. But Caiaphas might have said the same thing substantially in other words, as "I adjure thee by the living God, that thou tell us whether thou hast said thou art the Christ, the Son of God."

This is a natural form of speech for such a man as Caiaphas at such a time. But it would not come "out of the blue." Something must have suggested and, in a sense, provoked it. Some of the unreported witnesses must have said that Jesus had claimed to be the Christ, the Son of God.

> Jesus saith unto him, Thou hast said: Nevertheless I say unto you, Hereafter shall ye see the Son of Man sitting on the right hand of power, and coming in the clouds of Heaven.

The first clause of Jesus's reply can only be taken as an affirmative answer to the high priest's question. The second half of it is irrelevant, except as far as it claims for Jesus the fulfilment of the prophecy of Daniel. But why *Nevertheless?* I see no logical meaning in the link between the two clauses. Not in spite of the fact that Jesus was the Son of God, but *because* he was so, they would see him sitting on the right hand of power, and coming in the clouds of Heaven.

My conclusion is that Jesus's reply was limited to the first clause, and that the second clause was added by the evangelist or by some later writer. The first clause was sufficient. It was of the essence of what Caiaphas wanted Jesus to say. He would not have been greatly concerned if Jesus had said he was the Messiah, the servant of God. Many, many had said so already, and many more were to say so in the years to come. But that Jesus should say he was the Son of God was the unpardonable offence in the eyes of the Jewish high priest. The law of Moses asserted that God was one, that there was no other God, therefore that God could have no Son.

For Jesus to say (which, in effect, he did) that he was the Son of God was blasphemy. It was, according to Jewish law, blasphemy which must be punished by death. From the moment Jesus said this there could be only one end—Jesus must be put to death.

> Then the high priest rent his clothes, saying, He hath spoken blasphemy; what further need have we for witnesses? Behold, now ye have heard his blasphemy. What think ye?

And to this the scribes and elders and chief priests, and "all the council" answered "He is guilty of death."

This is not a condemnation to death, but according to Jewish law. It is merely what the words say, it is a declaration that Jesus is guilty of that crime which is punishable by death.

VI. According to Mark

> And they led Jesus away to the high priest, and with him were assembled all the chief priests and the elders and the scribes. [XIV, 53]

The proceedings reported by Mark are the same as those reported by Matthew, neither more nor less nor different.

When the witnesses break down, because they do not agree, the high priest stands up in their midst and asks Jesus why he does not answer that which is witnessed against him (which is nothing, because it is conflicting), and when Jesus makes no reply the high priest says,

> Art thou the Christ, the Son of the Blessed? And Jesus said, I am; and ye shall see the Son of Man sitting on the right hand of power, and coming in the clouds of Heaven.

Then the high priest asks, "What need we any further witnesses? Ye have heard the blasphemy; What think ye?" And the evangelist adds, "And they all condemned him to be guilty of death."

It is the same story, and the employment of the words "condemned him" and so on, does not make any difference in the natural interpretation of the words—Jesus is not condemned to death by a court of trial, but by a court of inquiry. Observe that the words "they *all* condemned him" conflict with *Luke* (XXII, 50, 51) that Joseph of Arimathæa was a councillor and that he had *not* consented to the deed of the council.

VII.   *According to Luke*

Then took they him, and led him, and brought him into the high priest's house. [XXII, 54]

Luke seems to indicate that, for some time after being brought to the hall of the high priest's house, Jesus was in the hands of the high priest's servants, who maltreated him barbarously. Luke also seems to say that the incident of the denial by Peter also took place during this evil time when the servants were maltreating Jesus.

The scene occurred in the hall of the high priest's house, and apparently the only persons present, besides Peter and the high priest's servants, were the Temple guard, who had arrested Jesus in the garden, "the place," as Luke calls it.

Then, "as soon as it was day," the elders of the people and the chief priests and the scribes came together, and led Jesus from the hall into the council-chamber. In the council-chamber their investigation took place. It is the first inquiry (not the second meeting of the council), and it is even less a trial in *Luke* than in *Matthew* and *Mark.*

There is no report of any witness, although at the end a reference to the futility of further witnesses is mentioned. Jesus is asked if he is the Christ, and he answers, "If I tell you, ye will not believe. And if I also ask you, ye will not answer me, nor let me go."

Apparently, he means by the last clause, "If I ask you why you have brought me here, you will not answer me." But here, again, as in *Matthew* and *Mark,* he quotes the prophecy which says, "Hereafter shall the Son of Man sit on the right hand of the power of God."

Whereupon the chief priests say, "Art thou then the Son of God?" And Jesus answers, "Ye say that I am."

Understanding this to be an admission (which it is, although not so obvious an admission as in *Matthew,* nor so direct an answer as in *Mark*) the chief priests (not specifically Caiaphas) say,

"What need we any further witness? For we ourselves heard of his own mouth."

Obviously, this admission of Jesus that he was the Son of God was understood by the high priest to be equivalent to saying that he *was God*. It was a distinct claim, not merely to divinity, but to *Godhead*. The conclusion does not differ from that in *Matthew* and *Mark*. Jesus had committed blasphemy, but there is no talk of condemnation. Jesus is not, in *Luke*, condemned to death in the palace of Caiaphas.

VIII. *According to John*

If the proceedings reported in verses 19–23 of Chapter XVIII take place in the house of Annas, nothing is reported in *John* of the proceedings in the palace of Caiaphas.

IX. *Conclusions*

My conclusions are that Jesus was never brought to trial by the Jews, and therefore never condemned to death by the Jews, although the chief priests, scribes, elders, and others said he was "guilty of death."

I do not think that the Sanhedrin was summoned, or that it sat, but it is obvious that during the night, or (according to *Luke*) early in the morning, a number of the members of the council of the Sanhedrin (some of the Gospels say *all*) sat with Caiaphas to examine witnesses against Jesus (none in defence of him) and hear his answer.

I think their object was purely to make an investigation, an inquiry to extort (if possible) a confession from Jesus. And he did make a definite declaration—that he was the Son of God. This was blasphemy and deserving of death. The Jewish religious classes must see that he be put to death. The law of Moses required that he should be stoned to death. What were they to do?

It is significant how limited, according to the Gospel narrators, was the range of the evidence against Jesus.

1. He was not charged with Sabbath-breaking.

2. He was not charged with working miracles by collusion with Satan.

3. He was not charged with violating the custom of the Jewish fathers about the washing of hands before eating.

4. He was not charged with claiming the right to forgive sins.

5. He was not charged with condoning adultery, as in the case of the woman taken in adultery.

6. He was not charged with consorting with publicans, sinners and Gentiles, as in the case of the Canaanite woman near Tyre.

All these offences against Jewish law he had been guilty of, according to the Pharisees; but nothing apparently was said about them.

He was, indeed, charged with speaking contemptuously, or worse, of the Temple, and that was an offence punishable by Jewish law.

The one aim of the so-called judges was to obtain evidence that he had said he was the Son of God. They got him to say so, and that was enough. It was everything. There could be only one end— Jesus must die. How was he to be brought to his death?

CHAPTER XXX

The Trial (Continued)

I. The Morning Meeting of the Sanhedrin

ACCORDING TO *Matthew,* "When the morning was come, all the chief priests and elders of the people took counsel against Jesus to put him to death" (XXVII, 1).

Apparently, this means that they sat in council to consider what steps should now be taken to bring to his death the man who had said that he was the Son of God. No report of the proceedings is given by John; if the council was held in secret, no report could be given except by a member of the council. If any secret disciple was present at the council, he gave no report to the writer of the first Gospel or to his predecessor, the writer of the document on which he based his memoirs. We know what the result of the deliberations were only by what was done next. Jesus was bound and led to the judgment hall of Pontius Pilate, the procurator (governor).

According to *Mark,* the same occurred. "And straightway in the morning the chief priests held a consultation with the elders and scribes and the whole council, and bound Jesus and carried him away and delivered him to Pilate" (XV, 1).

The words "the whole council" are understood to mean the whole Sanhedrin. Nothing is reported of the proceedings. Only the result is recorded.

Luke records nothing about a private meeting of the council to consider what is to be done with Jesus after he has said (thus they understood him) that he was the Son of God. The inquiry itself took place in the morning, and at the close of the report of it we are told that "the whole multitude of them arose, and led him unto Pilate." Their chief priests, priests, elders and people took Jesus immediately to the Roman procurator.

As in *Luke,* nothing is reported in *John* of any private council to consider what was to be done with Jesus. He was immediately led off to the judgment hall of Pilate.

Notwithstanding that neither *Luke* nor *John* speaks of any private meeting of the so-called council after the inquiry, I take the view that such a meeting was (as *Matthew* and *Mark* say) held.

It was probably equivalent to the private meeting of the council held later to inquire into the case of Peter and his fellow-apostles (*Acts* V, 27–40), when Gamaliel asked that the apostles should be "put forth a little space," while he gave his fellow councillors his opinion of what should be done with them.

The necessity for such a private council was very urgent in the case of Jesus. The inquiry had led to no practical results. As the investigation before Annas had been fruitless, so the inquiry before Caiaphas had left the council powerless. They had convinced themselves, on the declaration of Jesus himself, that he was guilty of an offence against the Mosaic law which called for his death. But they had no power to inflict death. What were they now to do? It was a difficult question.

The difficulty was enhanced by the differences in religious belief which prevailed among themselves. Who and what were the members of the council? They were Sadducees, Pharisees, the scribes of both Sadducees and Pharisees, the elders of the people.

These differences had given the inquiry its character. Thus, the Pharisees believed in the resurrection of the dead; in angels and devils; in the coming of a Messiah and of a kingdom of Heaven; they were strict observers of the ritual of the law of Moses—the keeping of the Sabbath, the washing of hands before eating, and so on.

Jesus had been guilty of offences against the Mosaic ritual as they understood it. But there had been no attempt to charge him with these at the council, or even to ask for evidence in respect of them. In any event, such offences would not have brought the results they desired—the death of Jesus.

The Sadducees did not believe in the resurrection of the dead, in angels and devils, or in a Messiah and the coming of a kingdom of Heaven.

Therefore it had been of small consequence to them whether Jesus was, or was not, guilty of offences against this aspect of Mosaic law. They believed in God and His ordinances; in the Temple as His sacred abode; in the law of Moses.

That Jesus had violated their faith in the unity of God by claiming to be His Son, to share His divinity, to perform His miracles by virtue of that divinity, to be the king of the Jews, being the Son of God, the Christ, the Messiah—all this was of the first consequence to the Sadducees.

If they had been the highest type of their sect they could not have tolerated such a man. They must have put him to death. The law of Moses required that they should stone to death such a pretender.

But they were not the highest type of Sadducee, and they had lower interests also to serve. They were the ruling classes among the Jews at this time. They held, in long succession, the high priesthood.

This position should have been succeeded to only by hereditary descent from Aaron. But that succession had long ago been broken. They now held their position by the will of their Roman masters. The mouthpiece of their Roman masters was the procurator. The procurator of the moment was Pontius Pilate, whose hostility to the Jewish people they too well knew.

What then? They saw that as Jesus claimed to be the Son of God, his followers claimed that he was the rightful king of the Jews. A long tradition attached to the idea that a king of the Jews would arise; from where they did not know, except that he was to belong to the family of David, and that (perhaps) he was to be born in Bethlehem; that he was to work miracles such as no man had ever worked before, raising the dead being one of them, and that he was to take possession of the throne of David by the supernatural help of flights of angels descending from the clouds of Heaven.

Pretenders to this name, this power, and so on, had arisen before and had been put down—often with much shedding of blood, and much upheaval of the Jewish condition.

One such case had been that of Judas of Galilee, nearly twenty years earlier. It had curtailed the power of the Jewish hierarchy. It had led to deep humiliations, such as placing the vestments of the high priests under lock and key by the Roman procurator, so that no religious festival could possibly be held without his consent.

It had led to the withdrawal from them of the power over life and death, so that the punishment of death could not be inflicted by the Jewish rulers, but only by the Roman rulers.

It had, almost certainly, led to the necessity of obtaining the consent of the Roman procurator before a Sanhedrin (the highest Jewish court) could be summoned.

All this was galling to the Jews as a whole, but especially galling to the ruling classes among the Jews—the Sadducees.

And what was the position now? A Galilean peasant said he was the Son of God, the Christ, the Messiah, therefore the king of the Jews. A vast multitude of the people believed him. When he had entered Jerusalem a few days before they had hailed him as the king of the Jews. They were looking for the realization of their dream—partly a political dream, partly a religious one.

The Pharisees had heard of this Galilean before, and had frequently tried in vain to compass his downfall, both for his offences against the Mosaic customs and for the violent insults he had heaped upon themselves. If the Sadducees had heard of him, they had paid little attention until a few days before his entrance into the Holy City. Then a rumour had reached them that within two miles of the Holy City, in the village of Bethany by the Mount of Olives, he had raised from the dead a man who had been four days in his grave.

It was the eve of Passover, when hundreds of thousands, perhaps millions, of Jews (from all parts of Palestine, and from all the countries round about in which the Jews were dispersed) were flocking into Jerusalem to celebrate the greatest event in Jewish history—the liberation from the bondage of Egypt. They were greatly excited by the Passover. It revived and raised to the highest pitch their Messianic dreams—of a deliverer who would come in the name of the Lord, drive out their cruel taskmaster, who had taken possession of their country, restore the throne of Israel, and establish the promised kingdom of God.

And now here was a man who said he was that king of the Jews, and had apparently so proved it by miracles, as to do what no man had ever done before—raise the dead.

When they heard and thought of all this they had asked themselves what would happen. Being men of the world, they had no illusions. They did not, for one moment, believe in the Messiah, the worker of miracles. They did not believe he had raised a man from the dead, or done any of the wonderful works ascribed to him. They did not believe in the coming of any Christ. They did not believe in any Son of God. But if a vast multitude of the Jews did believe, and if they followed after him, the only consequence would be an attempt to transform their dream into a reality. It would be a vain and fruitless attempt, but what would be the end of it?

The end would be that the Roman army, then in Jerusalem to keep the peace at this season of fanatical excitement, acting under the orders of their tyrannical, relentless and bloodthirsty procurator, who had already twice or thrice within a few years shed Jewish blood like water—that the Roman soldiery would put down the insurrection with a strong hand.

But the procurator would not stop there. He would report the whole seditious proceeding (which to him would have only a political aspect, the expulsion of the Romans from Palestine) to his master, the Roman emperor. And what would the Roman emperor do? He would take the nation entirely away from the Jewish people, and put his procurator in the position of absolute ruler, thus wiping out even the measure of self-government which his predecessor (the emperor Augustus) had left to them after the suppression of the last great fanatical insurrection—that of Judas the Galilean.

And then? The ruling classes among the Jews—the Sadducees —would lose their places.

The Romans would not be any longer content with the right to nominate the high priest (who was essentially the Jewish prime minister); he would wipe the Jewish high priest and prime minister out of existence, destroy every religious right now possessed by the Jews, suppress the Jewish faith, and establish the religion of Rome —paganism with all its barbarities and superstitions.

All this the high priest, Caiaphas, had seen as a possibility, before Jesus of Nazareth had come into Jerusalem, and to prevent him from coming he had, apparently, set a price on his head.

If he had held his hand it had been from fear of his own people, who were running after the Galilean, and might rise against their rulers—in their gross ignorance and superstition.

But at length the time had come when this man had fallen into their hands. It was the night before the real beginning of the festival. Their rival sect, the Pharisees (nearly always opposed to them), had, in this instance, made common cause with them, and so it had come to pass that, by unanimous consent (or almost unanimous consent), they had concluded that the prophet of Galilee, who was so great a danger to the Jewish nation, the Jewish faith, and especially to the Jewish rulers, should be put out of the way.

But still remained this difficulty. Only the Roman procurator could order the man's death. If they of themselves killed him (claiming the authority of their own religious law) the procurator would soon lay them by the heels. Pilate would do to Caiaphas what he did to Annas, a generation later, when Annas, without his authority, executed James, the brother of Jesus.

No, Pilate must put Jesus to death. But how were they to lead him to do so? It was idle to go to him with the evidence which had satisfied themselves. It was useless to say to him, "This man claims to be the Son of God." "What God? Your God? I know nothing of your God. And what is it to me that, according to your Jewish religion, your God can have no Son? The religion I know recognizes that a God may have a Son."

Thus they (the Jewish rulers) saw that they had to strike a new line of attack. They were to charge Jesus not with blasphemy, but with sedition—sedition against the ruling power, the Roman power.

It is true that they (the Jewish rulers) had no love of the Roman power, and no desire to maintain it, except so far as, in the case of the Sadducees, it maintained their own supremacy; but it was now necessary to *appear* to stand up for it, to be anxious for its maintenance.

This thought led them back quickly, led Caiaphas, in particular, back to what he had said while Jesus was at Bethany. Only they had to give it a new colouring. They were to present themselves before Pilate as persons who desired to suppress the insurrection which was threatened by the presence in Jerusalem of a man who said he was the king of the Jews, the descendant of David, and who had behind him an immense multitude of ignorant people who believed him, and would act on his word.

Against all this there may have been a certain dissent. If Joseph of Arimathæa and Nicodemus (secret followers of Jesus) were present at the early morning council in the palace of Caiaphas, after the inquiry, they may have urged the objections which Gamaliel afterwards urged in the case of Peter and the apostles,

Take heed to yourselves, what ye intend to do . . . Refrain from these men, and let them alone, for if this counsel or this work be of men, it will come to nought. But if it be of God, ye cannot overthrow it; lest haply ye be found even to fight against God.

But if such objections were heard (we read that Joseph of Arimathæa, an honourable councillor, had not consented to the general decision) they were overborne by the council as a whole.

The decision was taken to deliver Jesus to the Roman power, to lead him to the Roman procurator, not to wait to be the victims of the possible insurrection (with the necessity of being on their defence against the possible charge of Pilate that they had helped the insurrection, or, if not helped, they had not resisted it, not throttled it in time), but to be themselves the first movers on the side of the Roman power, even if they had thereby to oppose what the Jewish people might believe to be the ancient Jewish hope—the Messianic hope.

It was a base intrigue, but not an unnatural one. And, apart from the selfish desire of the Sadducees to protect their own sect, class and power, there was a certain reasonableness and inevitableness in it. Caiaphas saw plainly that there was no room in Jerusalem for both Jesus of Nazareth and Joseph Caiaphas. One or other must fall. Naturally, he concluded that it was Jesus who must fall. It is unnecessary to think that this was an insincere as well as selfish decision. Caiaphas and Annas believed they had to protect the Temple and all it stood for.

They had to protect the nation and preserve whatever power remained to it. This man from Galilee, with his enormous popular following, was threatening all that. He must die. There was no other way.

Thus the decision was arrived at in that private sitting of the chief priests, scribes, elders, and others, after the public inquiry. For once, all the Jewish rulers were united. Even the Pharisees were united to the Sadducees. Thus it was that their old enemy, who had confounded them in the eyes of the people, who had exposed their gross ignorance of the spirit of the law in their respect for the letter of it, who had degraded them and denounced their insincerities and hypocrisies—thus it was that he was to be brought low. However, in analysing the reasons which led to the decision arrived at during the morning sitting of the Sanhedrin, it is not possible to forget the effect of the recent insurrection by Barabbas, or of Caiaphas's reported declaration that it was better that one man should die than that the whole nation perish. It is impossible to take a just view of the situation down to this moment (the summoning of the Sanhedrin for its formal morning sitting) without being just to the Jewish rulers. To be just to the high priests it is necessary to see what was the offence to which Jesus was believed to have confessed.

He had declared in plain words that he was the Son of God. This, according to Jewish religious law, was blasphemy. What was blasphemy by Jewish law? It was an attempt to draw the people away from the worship of the Lord their God.

How terrible was this offence in earlier ages may be seen in *Deuteronomy* XIII, where it is explained that no man shall walk after that prophet or dreamer of dreams who leads the people away from the worship of God as the law proclaims it. The prophet or dreamer who does this shall be put to death. If it be a man's brother or his son or his daughter or his wife or his friend who is as dear to him as his own soul, yet if he attempts to turn you away from God, as God has revealed himself to you through Moses from the Mount of Sinai, you shall not only not listen to him, or conceal him or shield him, but you shall openly condemn him, witness against him and bring him to his death.

He shall be stoned, and while he is being stoned your eye shall not pity him and neither shall you spare him. You shall be the first to put him to death. By your hand shall he first fall, and then by the hands of the people, because he has sought to turn you away from the God who brought you out of the land of Egypt, from the house of bondage.

The scene of the stoning shall be terrible. He (the guilty man) shall kneel, and you shall put your hand on his head in the presence of the people; then you shall take off your garments and cast the first stone at him, and then—the whole, infuriated multitude are let loose upon him.

Such was the death of which Jesus was "worthy," according to the judges who had sat over him in the night. But although it was so commanded in their law, they were powerless to carry it out. Their Roman masters forbade it. What, then, were they to do? This man, Jesus, *must* die. But how? By what means could it be brought about?

This was the question before the Sanhedrin in the morning. That, and that only, was why they were met. Not for a formal, full-dress trial and condemnation.

II. *The Smiting Scene*

Meantime, while the chief priests had been holding counsel together, a shocking scene had been enacted in the rooms beneath their council chamber. At the close of the public inquiry Jesus had been committed to the care of the Temple guard, and the servants of the high priest. What had they done with him? This is the story according to *Matthew* XXVI, 67:

> Then did they spit in his face, and buffeted him; and others smote him with the palms of their hands, saying, Prophesy unto us, thou Christ, Who is he that smote thee?

As these words stand in *Matthew,* it appears as if the chief priests had done these outrages. But is it conceivable that this can have been intended by the evangelist? It seems at first sight to be too great a slander on the Jewish priesthood to believe it. And one of the other evangelists (Luke) liberates them from the charge of such barbarity.

But why trouble to defend these precious judges from participation in the actual smiting? Did not Annas allow his servant (without remonstrance) an hour before to smite Jesus with the palm of his hand? And, later, did not the blackguardly son of Annas *order* his servant to smite Paul in the mouth? Why trouble to defend these barbarisms?

According to *Mark* (XIV, 65), after the last words of the high priest and the words "And they all condemned him to be guilty of death"—

> And some began to spit on him, and to cover his face and to buffet him, and to say unto him "Prophesy"; and the servants did strike him with the palms of their hands.

This would go farther than *Matthew* in incriminating the chief priests in these barbarities by the mention of the servants who struck him, but for the obvious inference that the servants are perhaps mentioned only to distinguish them from the guards.

Luke gives this barbaric scene before the inquiry, not after it, as in *Matthew* and *Mark*—in the night (XXII, 63):

> And the men that held Jesus mocked him, and smote him. And when they had blindfolded him, they struck him on the face, and asked him, saying, "Prophesy, who is it that smote thee?" And many other things blasphemously spake they against him.

John does not give this barbaric scene, either before or after the inquiry in the palace of Caiaphas; but during the trial before Pilate he gives (as will be seen later) a scene of yet greater barbarity.

It is all shocking. Matthew and Mark do certainly leave the impression that the judges took part in the outrage. Mark attempts to modify its horror by saying that the servants did the striking. The difference is not much. Luke, a cultivated Greek, appears to have been unable to believe that the scene, as reported to him (there are no eye-witnesses indicated by him except the hostile Jews), was enacted by responsible judges, rulers of the Jews, and others; educated and presumably enlightened men; and, therefore, he places the whole of the wretched scene before the beginning of the inquiry and indicates that it took place in the *hall* of the high priest's house. That this hall was not the council chamber in which the examination took place is clearly indicated in *Luke* (XXII, 66), when he says that "as soon as it was day the elders of the people and the chief priests and the scribes came together, and led him into their council." Was this council (chamber) in the same house in the upper part of the town, as some think—as the traditional site now shows? I think not.

Nothing could be clearer than that Luke believed the scandalous scene was enacted in the hall during the dark hours of waiting for the judges or examiners by the Temple guard which had arrested Jesus in the garden.

III.   Jesus and Caiaphas

What Caiaphas had heard about Jesus we partly know. He may have heard lies from the Pharisees who had visited Jesus in Galilee, and gone back with bitter hearts, having had their vaunted knowledge openly exposed. "Let them go," said Jesus, when the disciples told him he had offended the Pharisees. They had gone, probably telling themselves that their time to square accounts with him would come when he (Jesus) came to Jerusalem, which they could not doubt he would.

But Caiaphas, the high priest, would probably know little about Jesus until he was on the point of entering Jerusalem.

Jesus, on the other hand, would know all about Caiaphas—how for eighteen years that "serpent" and "oppressor" had held his usurped place as high priest by playing the part of time-server and lickspittle to the Roman procurators. Jesus would know his man to the soles of his feet. His bearing towards his questions would be partly coloured by that knowledge.

IV. The Witnesses

Observe that the evidence recorded (the speech of Jesus regarding the pulling down of the Temple and its rebuilding) is such as would appeal to the presiding judge (Caiaphas, the Sadducee) as a grievous offence.

Observe that this evidence is actually truthful as regards the words, although false as to their significance. And yet observe that all the witnesses are described by the evangelists (Matthew and Mark) as false witnesses.

Again observe that no other evidence is recorded; that nothing is said about breaking the Sabbath, and so on.

But observe that the final question of the high priest which obtains the declaration of Jesus, which is alleged to be blasphemy, seems to suggest that some of the witnesses must have said that Jesus claimed to be the Christ, the Son of God.

Once more observe that none of the disciples or the followers of Christ offers evidence in his defence.

None of them appears to be present—unless Peter was present. According to *Mark,* Peter, although in the house, was not in the court-room, but in the room beneath the palace. In any case, Peter not only shrank from giving evidence, but denied his Master, or had already at the house of Annas denied him. If he had gone off weeping, he had not returned. None of the disciples had followed Jesus to the house of the high priest except Peter (who did less than nothing for him), unless it was John.

If John was the "other disciple" he did not say one word for his Master either before Annas or before Caiaphas.

In like manner none of the other companions of Jesus followed him, or attempted to defend him. Lazarus, who had been raised from the dead by him, did not care to establish that fact. Bartimæus, who had been cured of his blindness a few days before at Bethany, did not present himself. Mary of Bethany, who had washed the feet of Jesus with her tears and wiped them with the hair of her head, did not come. The sinners, the publicans, the paralysed, the lepers, the possessed of devils were all absent from this inquiry. (Only in the apocryphal gospel of *Nicodemus* does this vast army of the people he had healed come to bear testimony on his behalf.) Why? Is it to be understood that the doors of the palace of Caiaphas were locked against anybody who had a word to say for Jesus? If so, this was no trial in accordance with Jewish law, but only in open defiance of Jewish law.

Was it because the whole dastardly transaction was taking place in the middle of the night, when few could know and none would believe it possible that the life of the prophet of Nazareth was at stake?

If so, the examination was in open defiance of Jewish law. And if the Sadducees were, as is said, strict observers of the letter of the judicial law, it is only possible to infer one of two things: (1) that the high priest and the elders were deliberately carrying on an illegal trial, or (2) that they never for a moment pretended to themselves that they were conducting a public trial.

I am compelled to come to the latter conclusion.

Keim, (speaking of the second sitting of the council in the morning, the sitting of the whole Sanhedrin) urges as a reason for it that the high priest was anxious to obey the letter of the law, which required that sentence should not be pronounced on a prisoner found guilty of the capital crime on the same day as his condemnation.

But this is palpable foolishness. If, as he says, the "trial" before Caiaphas began at 3 A.M. and the final meeting of the whole Sanhedrin was held at 6 A.M. it was the same day on which Jesus was found guilty of death and sentenced to death. In any case, there is the fact, which Keim forgets, that the Jewish day counted from evening to evening. So even if Caiaphas thought he was carrying out the law, actually he was violating it.

No, I am satisfied that there was no Jewish trial—that Jesus was not tried at all by the Jews. The trial before Pilate will prove this in the fact that Pilate, at one moment, tells the accusers to take Jesus and try him themselves. Why did he say this? Because he knew that Jesus had not yet been tried by the Jewish court authorized to deal with cases of life or death.

How should he know that? Because if the Jewish rulers had held a Sanhedrin to try a man for his life they must have come to him for permission to do so, and they had not. All they had done was to send a man with an accusation that Jesus was breeding sedition by claiming to be (contrary to Roman law) the king of the Jews.

Incidentally, it is obvious that it was of the essence of Roman government that the procurator should possess the power of deciding whether a Sanhedrin should or should not be held. It was within the power of the Roman authority alone to say whether one of their subjects should be condemned to death.

The Jewish authorities had not asked for the right to hold a Sanhedrin for the trial of Jesus on the capital charge; therefore Jesus could not be tried on the counts on which the Jews sent Jesus to him, Pilate.

Once more, in the conduct of the council at their morning sitting, I recognize the unseen hand, compelling the Jewish rulers to carry out the preconceived plan, or, to put it better, leaving them free to do so or not, but knowing in advance what course they would take.

After the declaration of Jesus in reply to Caiaphas, the smaller tribunal which had examined him could have cast Jesus out of the synagogue or banished him—done the worst they had the power to do. But no, they were determined to do what they had not the power to do—to put Jesus to death. It was possible to do this only by calling in the Roman procurator—by using the hand of the enemy of the Jewish nation. To "save" the Jewish nation they had to use the Roman nation to destroy one of their own people who was obnoxious to them because he had committed blasphemy against God—against the Jewish religious law.

So the unseen hand seemed to force them to send Jesus to Pilate.

V.   The Night Sitting

In the palace of Caiaphas, Jesus was evidently led into the inner chamber of the house. Luke says he was taken from the hall (where he had been tortured) into the council—meaning, without doubt, the council chamber. Keim thinks the house was approached by a quadrangle, enclosed by the wing of the house, and that in this quadrangle the guards had lighted a fire. I have already disposed of this by showing that this was the form of Annas's house, and that it was there that the fire was lighted, and the denial of Peter took place.

Luke times the trial at the break of day, Matthew and Mark in the night. A morning trial would have many things in its favour—the legal practice, as well as the impossibility of calling judges and witnesses in an hour.

This is explained by the argument that the Jewish rulers had been (for days probably) preparing with Judas for Jesus's arrest, and that the judges *might* have been eating the Passover at the high priest's house.

"On the other hand," urges Keim, "the nocturnal examination of Matthew and Mark is genuinely Sadducean. All the details fit together—hot haste of the decision, swift collection and eclectic composition of the tribunal, adroit questioning, hastily determined harshness of the sentence."

But there was no sentence. Luke gives none, and Matthew and Mark only cause the examiners to say that Jesus is guilty of death —a phrase bearing a different significance.

One commentator says that a night sitting in the mere house of the high priest was held to be illegal. But there was no attempt at giving legality to the proceedings. It was not a trial, and Pilate (as we shall presently see) knew there had been no trial. Keim says the examination before Caiaphas left nothing for the morning Sanhedrin to discuss—only a hurried ratification of the conclusion arrived at.

Of course, it is hereby maintained that the nocturnal examination was by no means a mere preliminary inquiry, as has recently been so often asserted, but, as the sources themselves give it, a formal and definite judgment.

Keim argues that it was quite possible to bring the judges together in the middle of the night by sending out bailiffs from house to house as soon as the high priest got word from Judas about the place where and the time when Jesus could be arrested.

This sounds to me like unimaginative nonsense. A third of the Sanhedrin, twenty-three judges, would be sufficient to give validity to the decisions of the court. This was the minimum number for a Sanhedrin. The Gospels speak of a council. Is it the same thing?

"According to the Gospels, it may have been about 3 A.M.," says Keim. The Gospels say nothing about the hour. They only say that at the end of the examination the cock crows! *Luke* says it was as "soon as it was day." *John* "it was early."

Who reported the proceedings? If Peter was not present, if John was also not there, inasmuch as he gives no account of the proceedings in the palace of Caiaphas, who was the source of the evangelist's knowledge? Keim hints at Joseph of Arimathæa or Nicodemus. I think it a reasonable surmise. But it has to be remembered that the Gospels were written long after this event, and some of the soldiers, some of the Jews, even some of the priests, may have become converts in the morning, and *then* given the evangelists their recollections of what took place.

VI. The Scene of the Inquiry

Keim says:

The transaction [the examination before Caiaphas] was not wanting in that degree of propriety and legality which was preserved in the reign of terror of the later zealots. The Sadducean leaders were masters of form as well as of law-abiding legality. As in the ordinary sittings in the Temple, which were imitated as closely as possible, the judges would sit in a semicircle upon cushions or carpets with legs crossed. The high priest sat in the middle and the most influential and the wisest of the councillors at his side. [Annas, perhaps] The accused stood before the high priest, and was at first guarded against ill-treatment. To the right and left of the crescent were the two clerks of acquittal and condemnation. There were also the servants of the court—with swords and thongs, to guard the prisoner, to call in the witnesses, and ultimately to execute the sentence.

With regard to the witnesses Keim says, "the Mosaic law of the examination was rigorously employed."

No such thing. The Mosaic law, according to the Talmud, was that where the words of witnesses agree their testimony was firm. But, according to the evangelists, the words of the witnesses did not agree, and yet their words were held firm. There is the fact, however, that the evangelists were followers of Jesus.

Keim has a lot of palpable nonsense about the judges hastening from evidence to evidence, and refusing to be satisfied by any, and therefore not being disposed to lie. If this was so, the evangelists most unjustly suppressed the fact to their injury. But obviously they did no such thing. They gave every indication of a frivolous inquiry with an end in view, and the desire to arrive at a predetermined conclusion.

We see no accuser. The high priest makes himself the accuser.

All this is in complete defiance of Jewish law, as it is of the law of all modern civilized countries. No counsel for the defence was given to Jesus. He was vouchsafed no opportunity of calling counter-witnesses. The Jewish practice of beginning by raising the points in favour of the prisoner was not followed.

Of course, Judas was not called. Keim says this was from "a sense of propriety." What nonsense! No sense of propriety influenced Caiaphas for a moment. It was a part of the bargain with Judas not to call him. Besides, the Jews knew enough of the power of mind of Jesus to be afraid that if they put Judas to witness against his Master, Jesus would expose him in thirty seconds. Had he not done so with both Pharisees and Sadducees within the past few days?

Keim finds it a proof of the absence of conspiracy that the witnesses contradicted each other—there had not been time to coach them into harmony. These conflicting witnesses had not even been instructed of the penalties of perjury. As if they were in any danger!

The Jewish rule was that witnesses should be examined in the order of their age, beginning with the oldest. Then there was the Jewish practice of testing and cautioning witnesses. Not a sign of it. But it may have occurred. Keim says it is a Jewish fable that it was necessary to call witnesses by a herald for forty days in the case of a capital charge. This, in the eyes of Jewish critics, is proof that there was nothing to say for Jesus, since not a witness for the defence appeared.

All this is foolishness. Not a witness dared appear, as he believed, without risking his liberty, perhaps his life.

According to the Jewish fable, the verdict was by no means precipitated. Evidence of the innocence of Jesus was sought for, but in vain. Keim says "the judicial murder could not more eloquently be endorsed than by this apology."

VII. The Evidence Against Jesus

There is very little evidence reported. Matthew states that the chief priests and elders say that "though many false witnesses came, yet found they none"—until there came "two false witnesses" who agreed that Jesus had said he would destroy the Temple. But evidence was certainly adduced. What was it? We can quite reasonably judge of this from the previous accounts of the ministry.

First we have to bear in mind the undeniable fact that the so-called court consisted of two strongly opposed sects. Each of these would have its witnesses. These witnesses would see the offences of Jesus from the point of their own sect. Thus the Pharisees would see Jesus's offence in Sabbath-breaking; in neglecting the custom of washing before meals, in the alleged commerce of Jesus with evil spirits, as shown by his power of casting out devils (in the name and by the power of Satan); in consorting with persons of low and bad character, of association with publicans (the extortionate servants of the Romans) who, as in the case of Zacchæus of Jericho, had robbed people by making false accusations against them, probably in the Roman courts, of eating and drinking with such persons, of having women of notoriously evil life always about him; of excusing and defending them against the just charges of those who stood by the Mosaic law, as in the case of the woman taken in adultery.

Then, on the other hand, the Sadducees would see Jesus's offence in his pretensions to what they thought impossible miraculous power. Not believing in the resurrection of the dead, they might adduce the rumour of the raising of Lazarus at Bethany as a case of deliberate imposture to serve a manifest political purpose. This "fellow" wanted to enter Jerusalem in the character of the Messiah who, when he came, was to do works such as no other man had ever done. So, by collusion with Lazarus and his family, this manifest trick was concocted. The Sadducees had never doubted that it was a trick. If they had doubted, they would not have dared to arrest and kill a man who had raised another man from the dead, and to kill, also, the man who had been raised from the dead. To attempt such a thing would be palpable folly. It would be fighting against God. It would also be exposing themselves to inevitable contempt on the part of the people.

So the evidence of the Sadducees would almost certainly be to expose this folly concerning Lazarus.

Then there would be the explanation of Jesus's flight to Ephraim and his return to Bethany on the eve of the Passover, from the Sadducean point of view—Jesus had wanted sufficient time to elapse for the miraculous story to take hold of the ignorant and superstitious minds of those who had come up for the Passover, inflamed by the fanatical passion which that festival inspired.

Next, the Sadducean evidence would almost certainly relate to the Messianic entrance into Jerusalem. To this they would give a political (not a religious) colour. The Sadducees were by no means strong on the Messiah. They distrusted the Messianic movement. They were afraid that the Messianic hope would work mischief to the nation. They were quite sure it would destroy their own sect. It was founded on a theory which they rejected—the theory of the Resurrection. Therefore, they fastened on the political character of Jesus's entrance into Jerusalem—this peasant pretender who could not overthrow the Roman power, but could bring out the Roman soldiers, and lead to limitless bloodshed.

Then the Sadducean evidence would turn to the offence of Jesus in speaking contemptuously of the Temple, the sacred symbol of God's authority, the place of the Holy of Holies, the very seat of authority, and the home of God on earth.

Such would, I think, be the subjects of the evidence brought against Jesus in the inquiry before Caiaphas in the night. But it would not only be difficult for the witnesses to agree about any of these offences, it would be nearly impossible for the court to take a unanimous view of their gravity. What the Pharisees thought of great consequence the Sadducees thought of little consequence.

On the question of immortality (of life from the dead, therefore of the raising of Lazarus) there might easily be a difference of opinion. On the question of the Messianic entry into Jerusalem there might be a difference of opinion. On the cleansing of the Temple there might possibly be a violent opposition of opinion. Therefore, the witnesses were not the only ones who found it difficult to agree—the so-called judges found it difficult.

So the inquiry may have lasted long. If it began at 3 A.M. it may have gone on until 5 A.M.

But at last there came an issue on which both sects were competent to agree. Probably some of the witnesses attested that certain of the disciples had declared (in spite of Jesus's repeated warnings to them that on that subject they should say nothing) that Jesus said, and they believed, that he was the Christ, the Son of God.

That question united Pharisees and Sadducees.

The high priest put the question to Jesus. He admitted that he was the Son of God. And in answer to the first shout of derision from the judges and their minions he threw David and the prophet Daniel into their midst like a thunderbolt, and told them that they should yet have proof of this by seeing the Son of Man (himself) coming in power from the clouds of Heaven.

After that there was nothing to do but to bring Jesus to his death.

Derision gave way to wild anger. The high priest rose and rent his clothes—a custom not peculiar to high priests, for Paul and Barnabas did the same (*Acts* XIV, 14) when at Lystra the people took them for gods—"the gods are come down to us in the likeness of men"; they ran in among them and cried, "We also are men . . ."

At the examination before Caiaphas, Jesus was charged with seducing the people by false teaching. So far as we know he was asked no questions before Caiaphas about any false political teaching. He was not even asked why he permitted himself on his entry into Jerusalem to be hailed as the king of the Jews. Or by what authority he turned the money-changers out of the Temple. If these semi-political, semi-religious questions were put to Jesus we hear nothing about it at the examination before Caiaphas.

We do not (to our astonishment) hear anything about it in the trial before Pilate, as we shall see later.

The reason for the former omission (the cries at the entry into Jerusalem) was, perhaps, because the Sadducees were not by any means sure of the Messiah; and it was a Sadducean high priest who was presiding, therefore, he could have had no desire to raise an issue that might possibly lead to differences with the Pharisees by his side.

And the evidence of questions about the cleansing of the Temple may have been similarly inspired by a desire on the part of the Pharisees to avoid an issue that might expose the corruption of the Sadducean high priests—Annas, perhaps, in particular.

The two parties of rascals had to watch each other as well as Jesus. They knew what Jesus could do if he tried. He had divided them before.

Sayings of Jesus at Jerusalem were finally adduced. There was no denying them. The words of the witnesses were literally true. The spirit of them was entirely gone.

That other questions besides those about the Temple were raised is almost certain, but on these the witnesses disagreed and contradicted each other. Clearly, the examiners could not accept them. But the witnesses about the Temple did agree, and the high priest fastened on to that evidence.

"I testify that this man said he could destroy the Temple of God and build it again in three days."

"And I testify that I also heard him say so."

Something like this must have occurred.

Then some reference to his entry, to his reply to the Pharisees about the "very stones crying out," may have followed. There must have been something said to suggest the high priest's own question, for the question must have been repugnant to him. Only under provocation would he even talk about the "Son of God," not believing in any such being, revolting against the idea of any such thing. Jesus was silent. When Jesus was challenged to say if he had any answer to the one question on which the witnesses agreed, to the one word of testimony against him which would stand, he made no reply.

Why did he not reply?

Because the testimony itself in that case was true, though the literal meaning attached to his words was false. And perhaps the spiritual meaning he (Jesus) would have given to his words would have seemed to his examiner to be a still deadlier condemnation of him.

Strauss says Jesus did not answer because he did not recognize the tribunal. Renan says because he saw that his examiners were only seeking pretexts. De Witte says Jesus was silent in contempt.

Keim asks if the high priest was not driven, by Jesus's silence, to put the final question. Also, Keim says that when Caiaphas, "the serpent of the house of Annas" put his last question, Jesus was compelled to answer it. Why? Because, although provedly silent before the torturing witnesses, he was sensitively candid when put upon his honour, and could live and die enthusiastically conscious and jealous of the great idea of his life. Therefore, when Caiaphas said, according to *Matthew,* "I adjure thee by the living God, that thou tell us whether thou be the Christ, the Son of God," or, according to *Luke,* "Art thou the Christ?", Jesus was bound to reply.

Keim uses Luke's question first, and Matthew's question last, making two parts of one interrogation. This is interesting and reasonable.

Then why did Jesus, silent in the face of other questions, speak now? Keim's answer is as follows:

> In the face of such an appeal to the Holy God made by the mouth of the high priest of God, whom men were bound to obey as God, Jesus could no longer be silent, though to speak would be to run the risk of signing his own death-warrant.

But where does Keim get this? Where does Jesus say he so regards the high priest Caiaphas? Nowhere at all. What reason is there for thinking his obedience was due to this man as to God? Nowhere at all. First, Jesus knew that in the strict sense of the Mosaic law Caiaphas was not the high priest at all. He was merely the servant of the Roman procurator imposed upon the Jewish people in the position of the high priest. More, and higher, Jesus believed that he stood closer to God than all or any high priest that had ever lived. But not from any duty of obedience to this miserable "serpent of the house of Annas" did Jesus speak.

Why then? My answer is clear. The time had come for him to drop the veil with which he had covered himself since the Messianic proclamation at the source of the Jordan—to say, "Thou hast said it."

But Jesus says more. He quotes from *Daniel* and from the *Psalms,* saying, "Nevertheless I say unto you, hereafter you shall see the Son of Man sitting on the right hand of the power of God, and coming in the clouds of Heaven."

"Nevertheless, I say unto you." Why this? Why does he say more than "Yes"? What added value do the words from *Daniel* and the *Psalms* give his answer? Why "nevertheless"?

Keim says that they had for him laughter, or that Jesus, in the helplessness of his forlorn position, as a poor prisoner without a supporter to stand by him, had expected a burst of derision at his simple though sublime reply, and therefore added the authority of Scripture and prophecy.

Keim also thinks that the words of *Daniel* and the *Psalms* carried the pretensions of the man of Galilee to the highest point of monstrosity in the mind of Caiaphas. He might not believe in the prophecy—or attach importance to it—but that this man before him should dare to quote these well-known words of the Jewish prophet as applying to himself was an outrage so frightful that he could not control himself in the presence of it.

Therefore, his passion burst forth, and, leaping to his feet in anger and scorn, he rent his priestly linen clothes, bared his breast and cried to his fellow-examiners, "He hath spoken blasphemy; what further need have we of witnesses? Behold, now ye have heard his blasphemy. What think ye?"

And his fellow-examiners answered, "He is guilty of death," for, according to ancient law, blasphemy to the extent of making paltry man equal to God was punishable by death.

Keim says that Caiaphas, in full conviction, now called for a vote. There is not a particle of justification for the statement. There is not a word about a vote, either then or at any time.

Light says that the collection of votes (in writing) was dispensed with in the time of Jesus, and even the declaration "Guilty" was dispensed with. Abraham Geiger says Jesus was justly condemned. Grätz says Jesus was at least the victim of a misunderstanding. Goethe's famous distich justifies the cross of the fanatic. Renan, from the standpoint of orthodox Judaism, thinks there was nothing to be said. From a higher point, there may have been much to say.

On the Jewish side it is said the verdict on Jesus was a most moderate one—one almost unfavourable to his own people. Jewish critics in all ages have complained of the violation of all legal forms in the story in the Gospels. Christians say, "Private murder by the foes of Jesus."

Was Jesus condemned? I think he was not. In none of the Gospels is it even vaguely suggested that Jesus was properly condemned and sentenced, as:

Jesus of Nazareth, for the sin of blasphemy you are condemned by the court and sentenced to the penalty of death.

There was nothing like that.

For this aggressive confession Jesus, like other though lesser heroes of the truth, was condemned, in good faith, by the men of the old school. They had instituted a tentative trial with bad means, but on the ground of his own voluntary confession, (was it voluntary if they had torn it out of him by putting him on his oath before God?) they closed the trial with sincere conviction. And if one pities them for their indefinite perception of the things which take place between Heaven and earth, yet it must not be overlooked that the new truth had only struck them in fragments—

in this person of the poor prisoner who had boasted of his rights and privileges and even of the "throne of God," and called the prophets to witness to them, over the heads of the paltry little witnesses who were all the high priest had been able to bring to his condemnation—David and Daniel against these nameless little Jews who had perhaps played the part of eavesdroppers for the pay of the priests!

VIII. The Mishandling of Jesus

"The passionate mood excited by the closing appeal," says Keim, "and the sentence of condemnation against Jesus [it was not a *legal* condemnation, and not a sentence] put an end to the dignity of the assembly, and lawlessness and mishandling of Jesus commenced."

It was the rule to mourn and fast on the day of a capital verdict, but we do not hear that these men mourned or fasted.

Honourable Sanhedrists, and particularly the outwardly courteous but inwardly brutal Sadducees, did not control the impulses of their Oriental blood. Did they not think they had the authority of Moses, himself, for what they did? Had not *Deuteronomy* (XVIII, 22) told them that, when a prophet spoke presumptuously, they were not to be afraid of him? So they fell upon Jesus in their anger and abhorrence, spat in his face and buffeted him and smote him on the mouth.

I am afraid there is no escape (*Luke* notwithstanding) from the conclusion that what *Matthew* and *Mark* imply is that Jesus's examiners themselves (including, perhaps, the high priest himself) committed these atrocities. The evangelists may be wrong, but looked at from the Jewish point of view it is not unnatural. No more monstrous thing had ever been said than what the prisoner had said—that he was the Son of God, and that it was the psalmist and the prophet who had spoken what he had repeated. Observe, that the maltreatment is purely Jewish in the sense that it has reference only to the outrage which Jesus (by his declaration before Caiaphas) had committed against the sacred law of the Jews. The ruffians blindfold him and strike him, and then call upon him to prophesy who had struck him. The maltreatment in the palace of Caiaphas was purely in derision of Jesus's claims to be the Christ, the Son of God. They had a religious, not a political significance. They were meant to say, "If you are the Son of God and therefore know everything, tell us this paltry thing with your eyes bandaged—who strikes you?"

Later, when Jesus is similarly tortured in the house of Pilate, we shall see that the derisive maltreatment is directed to the quite different political end of showing his helplessness and folly as a king. They crown him and put the sceptre of kingship in his hand, and bow to him, and so on.

All this establishes for me the authenticity of both narrators of the maltreatment. Each of its own kind. It shows the complete difference, too, between the examination before Caiaphas and the trial before Pilate.

Attempts have been made to show that the story of the maltreatment had been suggested to the evangelists by passages in the Old Testament.

Most of these passages contain such trivial virtual resemblance to the Gospels as to be not worth looking up—*Isaiah* I, 6, I *Kings* XXII, 24.

They show the futility of feeble and unimaginative minds. The blindfolding in *Luke* and *Mark* is, for example, referring back to the incorrect conception of *Isaiah* LIII, 5.

It is all very poor stuff.

IX. *The Morning Sitting*

To refer once again to the morning sitting of the Sanhedrin, Keim, in common with nearly all modern critics, occupies himself with an endeavour to prove (1) that this was an actual and regular sitting of the whole Sanhedrin; (2) that it was not held in the palace of Caiaphas, but in the regular chamber allotted to the full council, and, therefore, that Jesus had to be taken to it—perhaps through the streets of Jerusalem; (3) that it was intended to fill up with legitimate legal exactness what was lacking in the night sitting of the Sanhedrin, at which he was "condemned" by a morning sitting which would be more exactly in accordance with Jewish law.

I think all this is totally wrong. I agree that the sitting in the morning was probably one of the whole Sanhedrin (or of as many as it was possible to gather together at the early hour of 6 A.M.); but I see no reason, except in one line in *Luke* (XXII, 66, "and led him into their council"), and that line refers to the first sitting, not the second, to say that the council chamber was not in the house, or attached to the house, of Caiaphas; and, finally, I see no reason whatever for thinking that the morning meeting of the whole Sanhedrin was intended to confirm or ratify the discussion of the night sitting of the partial Sanhedrin.

My reasons are:

(1) That we do not hear authoritatively that Jesus was present at the morning Sanhedrin, and without his presence no final sitting for purposes of trial or sentence could be anything but a foolish farce; we do not hear of any witnesses being present; or (if witnesses were unnecessary after Jesus's confession, as the high priests would think it) any pleading of guilty, or anything equivalent to guilty, on the part of the prisoner on whom (according to the critics) it was the object of the morning Sanhedrin to pass sentence.

(2) If the morning sitting of the council had been that of a Sanhedrin to try and sentence a man on a capital charge, the high priest must have had permission from the procurator to hold it, and we know of no such permission being asked for or given. For holding such a Sanhedrin without his permission Herod the Great executed a Sanhedrist, and for doing the same later, at the death of James, the brother of Jesus, the younger Annas was censured.

Caiaphas may have resented the power of the procurator, Pilate, and regarded him as a usurper of power over the sacred courts of the Jewish faith; but he knew his man too well deliberately to ignore his clear rights (without which his position as procurator would have been a foolish farce) and then deliberately to go to him, or send to him, to say he had done so. No, Caiaphas did no such foolish thing as to send Jesus to Pilate as one who had been condemned to death by a Sanhedrin about which (as is clearly evident by later events) Pilate knew nothing.

If, then, the morning council was not a legal Sanhedrin, what was it, for what was it called and what did it do? All this seems to me perfectly clear. It was, I think, admittedly a gathering of the members of the Sanhedrin. There would be the high priests Caiaphas and Annas; scribes of both the Sadducean and Pharisaic sects, elders (signifying lay officials and dignitaries), and, in general, laymen who occupied personal social positions.

The council thus constituted would consist of the two chief religious parties—Sadducees and Pharisees. At that time the parties were almost equally divided in numbers (as far as we can see), but the Sadducees had the great advantage of being in office.

The high priest, Caiaphas, would naturally preside, and the next place in distinction, that of vice-president, would be occupied by the ex-high priest, Annas.

What was this Sanhedrin? It is not altogther certain that it was a formally recognized judicial power. There is the fact that from the time of Herod the Great to A.D. 66–68, the Jewish historian, Josephus, had little or nothing to say about it.

What we hear of it (from Josephus) in Herod's time is a significant story. It is that down to Herod the Great's time this assembly of the seventy or seventy-one had been all-powerful in Palestine. It could even call the king to account. It had called Herod himself (although he had nominated the high priest) to its tribunal to answer to a charge which might have led to his condemnation to death. Being aware of this power of the Sanhedrin, Herod obeyed the call, but took a large body of soldiers with him. The high priest was appalled. One old Sanhedrist protested. This was a thing they had never seen before—that one who was summoned by the highest court of the Jews (king or no king) should come with an army to defend him, with his hair oiled and combed, like a conqueror, not like a prisoner with dishevelled hair, ready to take his judges' lives if they gave their verdict against him. The end of that transaction was that Herod *did* in fact take the lives of some of the Sanhedrists, and that thenceforward no meeting of the Sanhedrists could be called without the consent of the ruling secular power.

That had been the position throughout Herod the Great's life and that of his son, Archelaus. And when the Romans came, they had clearly exercised the same right of controlling the meetings of the Sanhedrin in all serious cases—particularly in cases of life and death. It was natural that they should do so. If the Roman authority had not the last word on life and death their power was a farce.

Such, then, was the position of the Sanhedrin on that morning of the 15th Nisan when it met to "take counsel against Jesus to put him to death" (*Matthew* XXVII, 1).

Now come to the position of the reorganized Jewish authority.

It could exist—but only by permission. It could act—but only in a limited way. Think what gall and wormwood this would be to the Jews. Their Sanhedrin had, since the exile, held limitless power. And now it could not execute a miserable highway robber, without going to the Roman procurator, and saying, "By your leave."

But, however they may have smarted under their humiliations, the Sanhedrin that assembled on the morning of the 15th Nisan was in no mood to defy the Roman procurator, Pilate. First, because their president, Caiaphas, a cunning person, had owed his appointment to one of Pilate's predecessors, and could be deposed by Pilate himself. Next, because he had held his high priesthood a great many years (perhaps longer than any other high priest) by his skill at time-serving, at keeping a sort of peace between his own people, the Jews, and their masters, the Romans.

The Pharisees might not be so anxious to play the double part, but Caiaphas, and with him, Annas, would most surely wish to give no more offence to Pilate than was necessary.

So there they were.

Keim says that this assembly of the seventy was presumed to have met at the call of the high priest in the official judgment hall in the Beth-Din, and no longer in the house of Caiaphas. But there is nothing to show that the judgment hall was not connected with the house of Caiaphas, nothing whatever in the Gospels, or in Josephus, to show that they were separate buildings. The localities cannot at this day be with certainty defined. According to the Talmudists, the original meeting-place of the Sanhedrin was in the inner court in immediate propinquity to God, to the Temple and the Altar. On Sabbath days and festivals, however, the sessions were transferred to the Beth Midrash, the temple synagogue, between the outer courts and the court of the women.

My inference is that both the house of the high priest and the meeting-place of the Sanhedrin were in the spaces of the outer court of the Temple. So if Jesus was taken from the house of Caiaphas on the morning of the meeting of the Sanhedrin he was probably never taken into the open air, but passed from chamber to chamber.

The brevity of the reports in the Gospels leaves the inference (1) that nobody was there who could or would report the proceedings; (2) that Jesus was not present, nor any of the witnesses.

Keim thinks the high priest would simply report to the full

assembly the confession of Jesus at the night "local," to ask the final question, "Guilty or not guilty?" and the business of the president of the Sanhedrin would be to pass the formal sentence of death (after a vote had been taken, either in writing or orally). After that there would be nothing to do but to send Jesus to Pilate and say in effect, "We, the Sanhedrin, have found this man guilty of an offence requiring his death, and all that remains to you to do is to execute him."

My own view of the proceedings at the morning meeting of the Sanhedrin I have given in a former note. Briefly, it was to find a plausible way of so presenting Jesus to Pilate that he (Pilate) would be compelled to put him to death.

Never were men in a more grotesquely tragic position.

Rarely or never can they have had such a piece of work to do. Ordinarily, their business was to protect their fellow-countrymen from the Roman authority. It seems almost certain that they had had this to do quite recently in the case of Barabbas, whose life they were so eager to claim at the Passover. The Roman power arrested a Jew, and all the judicial power of the Jews was called to wrest him, if possible, from the hands of the Romans.

But, behold, here they were about to reverse all that. They, the Jewish authority, were going to present a Jew to the Roman power and call on it to execute him.

It might, in a rare event, do that where a Jew was an outrageous enemy of his own people. But it was very difficult to prove that Jesus was an enemy of his own people. Clearly, his own people did not think so. The Jewish rulers knew that so well that they were afraid the people might defend and rescue him and snatch him out of their hands.

Nevertheless, the Galilean must die. He had been guilty of blasphemy—the most terrible crime in the Jewish code of laws. It was not possible that he could live and the law of Moses live also. Incidentally, it was not possible that Jesus of Nazareth could live and the Sanhedrin (which always killed the prophets) could live. Also that Caiaphas, in particular, could live as high priest exercising the authority with the people that was proper to a high priest, and at the same time Jesus of Nazareth.

But there was no legal way of putting an end to Jesus except that of persuading Pilate to put an end to him. How were they to do that? I think this was the whole business of the morning meeting of the Sanhedrin—not the ratification of the night proceedings at all.

It was a shockingly ironical task. They, the Jewish powers, who resented the presence of the Roman powers; looked upon them as usurpers; would have turned them out of the country if they had had the power; who had twice before complained to the emperor at Rome about the bloodthirsty cruelties of this particular procurator, and the perpetual extortions and tyrannies of his servants; they were to go to Pilate, with Jesus of Nazareth, and say:

> Here is a Galilean who actually says he is the king of the Jews, and has been, by this claim, sowing dissension all the way down from Galilee and, until yesterday, in Jerusalem itself. We send him to you to put him to death because we think he, unlike ourselves, is a traitor to Cæsar. We want no Jewish king. We want nobody to rule over us but Cæsar. Therefore, having examined this man, and received his open and free and audacious confession that he does indeed claim to be the king of the Jews, and that in due time we shall all see him come in power to take possession of his kingdom, we hereby send him to you and call upon you to crucify him.

What would Pilate say? Would he, like Festus, a generation later, see through all this imposture, and say, this charge by the Jews merely comes from "their own superstitions," and has really no sincerity in its assumed anxiety for the stability of the Roman rule in Palestine?

I am compelled to conclude that there would be sensible and acute minded among the seventy who would see this as a possibility. But I am also compelled to conclude that in the excitement of the hour, in the imminent danger, which Caiaphas and Annas would urge, of the people taking the side of Jesus if they allowed the day to dawn fully before they disposed of him, or getting him at least into Roman hands, the level-headed and righteous men, with few or no exceptions (Joseph of Arimathæa and Nicodemus would count for little among so many, even if they were present and courageous enough to speak, which is doubtful), would yield to the general will and let Caiaphas have his way. As for the Pharisees, they would hail the welcome coalition of the Sadducees as the promptest way of getting rid of the adversary who, both in Galilee and Jerusalem, had denounced and shamed them.

So the "judicial" murder was committed—not by a vote or sentence, but probably by a written charge sent by the high priest in his character as president of the people's Sanhedrin, addressed to Pontius Pilate.

I think the seventy would conclude that Pilate would be only too eager to bring by the heels a man who was carrying off the allegiance of perhaps hundreds of thousands of the Jews now assembled in Jerusalem for the dangerously inflaming feast of the Passover.

So they sent Jesus bound to the judgment hall of Pilate.

I think the Temple guard would take him, and that the chief priests and elders would accompany him, carrying the charge of the Sanhedrin in the handwriting of the high priest. I do not think either of the high priests went to Pilate's judgment hall with Jesus. They might easily think it did not accord with the personal dignity of the high priest (president of the Sanhedrin, whose powers of life and death the Romans had usurped) to go and stand before Pilate. I feel quite sure they did not go.

On the other hand, I do not exclude the possibility that Caiaphas and Annas were present at Pilate's court. We know that the younger Annas was present at the court of Pilate's successor at Cæsarea to try Paul.

Close observation of the Gospel narratives shows that when Caiaphas is mentioned he is carefully called the "high priest." So with Annas. But the hierarchy which appear before Pilate are called "chief priests," and, as far as I can judge, this is intended to indicate a difference.

I think this meeting of the Sanhedrin occurred about six o'clock in the morning. And that about (or before) seven in the morning, while the greater part of the inhabitants of Jerusalem, and certainly the strangers from Galilee and the Jews from distant countries, who had kept their feast until midnight, and after that had wandered about the streets and the courts of the Temple until, perhaps, two in the morning, *were still asleep in bed.*

Once more, in my reading of the business of the morning meeting of the Sanhedrin, I see the working of the unseen hand. These seventy men, and particularly the two men who presided over them, were in the grip of an *unseen power which compelled them to do what they did.* They hated to do it, but there was no other way. They had to put themselves into the hands of their enemies in order to protect themselves from their own.

And now, what was Pontius Pilate to do?

CHAPTER XXXI

Before Pilate

I. The Language of the Trial

IN WHAT LANGUAGE the trial before Pontius Pilate was held we are not told. But it is fairly certain it would be *Greek,* the common language of the Mediterranean coast. We know that Greek was the language spoken by the Romans in Jerusalem in the time of Paul, for in *Acts* (XXI, 37), Paul asks the captain of the castle (who was obviously a Jew made a Roman), if he may speak to him, and the captain asks, "Canst thou speak Greek?" But if the trial before Pilate was held in Greek, did Jesus understand it? I think certainly. We hear nothing of an interpreter when Jesus answers Pilate. Pilate would certainly not know Aramaic or Hebrew. But Josephus shows that the Jews all knew some Greek, through trading with Greeks and Romans who did not speak Hebrew or Aramaic.

II. According to Matthew

When they had bound Jesus on the morning after the inquiry in the palace of Caiaphas they "led him away and delivered him to Pontius Pilate the governor. . . . And Jesus stood before the governor" (XXVII, 2, 11).

This, of itself, is a sufficient answer to the statement of critics that Jesus was arrested by some of the Roman cohort from the tower of Antonia. He was led away and *delivered* to Pontius Pilate. If the soldiers of Pilate already held him under arrest they would not deliver him. He was led.

There is no indication here of where Jesus was delivered to Pilate—whether inside the judgment hall or outside.

. . . and the governor asked him, saying, Art thou the king of the Jews?

Where did this idea come from? There is no hint of it in the inquiry before Caiaphas, except so far as that the Christ who was to come was, according to the prophets, to be the king of the Jews. But Pilate would know nothing of the Jewish prophets. Whence, then, had come this idea that Jesus might be the king of the Jews? Had it been a part of a written charge drawn up by the morning Sanhedrin? Or had there been preceding evidence before Pilate saying that the offence with which Jesus was charged was that he was a pretender to the throne of Palestine?

It was according to Roman law to make a prisoner a witness against himself. A sentence was rarely pronounced until the accused had convicted himself or confessed. We see this in the letter of Pliny the Younger to his emperor about the Christians. We see it also in Tacitus again and again. If the prisoner did not confess, he was usually put to torture. That an instructed race could have thought torture a way to the truth is bewildering. It must, in the majority of cases, have been the way to a lie. But it was necessary, because the Roman law could not kill unless the accused admitted its right to do so.

So Pilate questioned Jesus. "Art thou the king of the Jews?"

Jesus answered Pilate's questions quite clearly enough, "Thou sayest," or "Thou sayest so." This could only be taken as an affirmative reply.

"And when he was accused of the chief priests and elders, he answered nothing."

We do not hear what the accusations were. Naturally, they would be such as agreed with the Sadducean case against Jesus. It was clearly of no use to advance the accusations of the Pharisees—the breaking of the Sabbath; the non-washing of hands; the expelling of demons by the power of Satan; the general disregard and even violation of the Jewish fathers; the insults hurled at the Pharisees. What would Pilate care about all this? He would smile at it as part of the "superstition," with which, later, Festus told Agrippa that as a Roman he could have nothing to do.

In like manner the Sadducees would make before Pilate no accusation of blasphemy. It would not shock Pilate that Jesus should say he was the Son of God. He (as a pagan) was familiar with the idea that an ordinary, or extraordinary, man should be said to be the son of a god. Many of his own people had been said to be the sons of gods. Julius Cæsar was said to be the son of a god. Augustus was called the "divine." It was certainly not a thing for which to put a man to death that he said he was of divine origin, or that his followers said so of him. The Jewish rulers must have known this perfectly. That they *did* know it is shown by their behaviour at the very first clash they had with Pilate, when he tried to bring the Roman standards (with the image of Tiberius as a divinity on them) into Jerusalem and perhaps into the Temple.

So the Jewish rulers, in accusing Jesus before Pilate, would give the religious crimes of Jesus (which had been sufficient to damn him at their Jewish inquiry) a political colouring, in order to make them equally damning in a Roman court. Therefore, the accusation would be that Jesus had called himself a king—the king of the Jews. This was true in a sense in which the chief priests were presenting it to the mind of Pilate. They would speak of his kingly entry into Jerusalem. Pilate would laugh at that. The idea of a Galilean peasant riding on an ass, with a crowd of unarmed peasants about shouting hosannas, and calling him a king, and that by this force he was in any way dangerous to the Roman power, the rule of the emperor, as represented by him, as he had come into Jerusalem just before from Cæsarea with armed men in chariots or on horseback—all this would be manifest foolishness to Pilate.

The Jewish rulers must have had something else in their minds. What was it? Then the accusers would go on to talk of the air of sovereignty which Jesus had given himself in cleansing the Temple. Once more, the picture of the Galilean prophet with a whip sweeping the cheating money-changers out of the Temple would make Pilate smile. That this was a pretender to the throne of Cæsar in Palestine was too childish. But its very childishness would betray the motive of the accusers. It was envy. This man had got the hearts of the people. All their little world was running after him.

Again they would accuse him of his offence against the Temple, the natural home of the sovereignty of the king of the Jews. But what did Pilate care for their Temple? He had outraged it once, and tried to outrage it more than once. It was, for him, the central seat of their Jewish superstitions, where they kept their God seated, imprisoned.

Finally, they accused Jesus before Pilate of the one offence which counted with him—that of forbidding the Jews to pay tribute to Cæsar. Had he done this? He questioned Jesus. "Then said

Pilate unto him, Hearest thou not how many things they witness against thee?"

Jesus answered never a word. The governor marvelled.

Nothing is said of what was going on in the mind of Pilate. We can only judge of this by his next action. He prepared to release Jesus. Here is a difficulty. Jesus was not strictly, down to this moment, a prisoner at all. He had not been tried. He had not been condemned. Certainly he had not been tried and condemned by the Roman court. He had only been presented by the Jewish authorities on the capital charge. Yet Pilate talked of "releasing" him.

He had a right by custom to release a prisoner (tried and condemned and under sentence to the Roman authority) at the time of the Passover. This was a concession to Jewish feeling—to set free a prisoner of their own selection at the feast that celebrated their national liberty. When this custom originated is not known with certainty, but it is clear that it existed before the time of Pilate.

It chanced that at that moment the Roman prisons contained a prisoner named Barabbas. We know nothing about him from Matthew, except that he was a notable person. The previous winter had been a hard one for the people of Jerusalem. Very heavy taxation had been laid upon them by Pilate. There were revolts. One of these revolts was led by a man named Barabbas. In the fighting he killed a Roman sentry. For this he was arrested and condemned to death. He was a Jew. The Romans held him, and it would appear probable that he had to die at that Passover, there being many reasons for thinking that the Romans liked to select the Jewish feast days as the days for the execution of Jewish prisoners guilty of offences against Roman law.

So Pilate, having come to the conclusion that the Jews had delivered Jesus to him out of envy, and being perhaps frightened by an appeal his wife had made to him on Jesus's behalf, had taken a favourable view of Jesus. This notwithstanding that he had admitted that he was the king of the Jews. Perhaps convinced by the unreported evidence against him, to which Jesus made no reply, that the sense in which he claimed to be the king of the Jews was not in the least a political one, and therefore did not concern Rome, Pilate exercised his right of pardoning a prisoner in favour of the so-called prisoner, Jesus. He said to the accusers of Jesus, "Whom will ye that I release unto you? Barabbas, or Jesus which is called Christ?"

The chief priests and elders persuaded the multitude that they should ask for Barabbas, and destroy Jesus. And when Pilate repeated his question, "Whether of the twain will ye that I release unto you?" They answered, as before, "Barabbas."

Then Pilate said, "What shall I do then with Jesus which is called Christ?" and they replied, "Let him be crucified."

Observe here that, in playing upon the name Christ (a name probably quite unknown to him until then), Pilate had begun to realize the origin of the motive which had led the Jewish high priests to send Jesus to him—this man was claiming a place and an authority far higher than theirs, he was claiming to be the religious king of the Jews. But this circumstance, down to the present point, appears only to have amused Pilate.

"What evil hath he done?" he questioned. But they cried out the more, "Let him be crucified."

If anything happened immediately after that (as seems certain), Matthew does not record it. The next thing we see is Pilate in a much more serious mood.

When Pilate saw that he could prevail nothing, but that rather a tumult was made, he took water, and washed his hands before the multitude, saying, I am innocent of the blood of this just person [a letter from his wife, sending him a message while he sat on the judgment seat, had called Jesus "this just man"] ; see ye to it.

Then answered all the people and said, "His blood be on us, and on our children."

"His blood be upon us" (See *Acts* V, 28). The apostles who had been warned by the high priests (Annas and Caiaphas are named in *Acts* IV, 6) not to preach Jesus, are now addressed as followers by the high priests. "Behold ye have filled Jerusalem with your doctrine, and intend to bring this man's blood upon us."

I think this passage tends to prove the authenticity of the cry of the Jews in answer to Pilate. And then Pilate scourges Jesus, and delivers him to be crucified.

Such is the story, according to *Matthew,* of the "trial" of Jesus before the Roman procurator, Pontius Pilate. It is not a trial, but a grotesque farce. Nothing more obviously incomplete as a report, or more utterly contemptible as a trial, is it easy to conceive. Here is the representative of the Roman empire, sent there by his emperor to maintain public security, of which the chief part is security of life, and to dispense justice according to Roman (not Jewish) law. The religious court of the people he governs send him a prisoner, charged with treason to the Roman emperor, with being a pretender to the throne of Palestine, which, by right of conquest, belongs to Rome.

This governor asks the prisoner if he is the king of the Jews, and the prisoner admits it. But the governor, on examining the evidence of the accusers, sees that the sense in which the prisoner claims to be king is not political, but religious, and therefore does not concern his court at all. Being, therefore, satisfied that the prisoner is innocent of the charge of treason against the Roman emperor, that he has been sent to him by his fellow-Jews because they wish to get rid of one of whose claims they are envious and afraid, he wishes to pardon and release him according to a custom which enables him to do so at that moment, with the consent of the Jewish people.

But the rulers of the Jewish people persuade the multitude to cry out for another prisoner, and when the governor asks what he is to do with the man they have brought before him they cry, "Let him be crucified."

"But what evil has he done?" asks the governor, and the only answer he gets is the same insistent cry, "Let him be crucified."

What then? The Roman sees that he cannot prevail upon the accusers to let the innocent man be released; also he sees that if he releases him against the envy and bad passions of the prisoner's accusers, there will be a tumult, so he says in effect, "Very well, let him be crucified, only do not blame me for the death of this 'innocent person.' The responsibility must be yours."

On this the accusers are so sure that the death of the prisoner is right in the sight of God that they say, in effect, "If he is not put to death justly, let his blood be on our heads and on the heads of our children."

Hereupon, the Roman governor, sent to Palestine to preserve public security and to maintain justice, scourges Jesus and delivers him to be crucified, having first, without doubt, pronounced from his judgment seat the sentence of death on the man he has declared to be innocent.

The whole story, as it stands in *Matthew,* is so appalling as to be unbelievable. We must know more of the inner facts before we can accept such a travesty of Roman justice as historical. Pilate was plainly an unjust judge. Everybody must have known he was an unjust judge.

Incidentally, it is objected that the washing of hands before pronouncing a sentence for which a judge would not stand morally responsible was a Jewish custom, and that therefore a Roman judge would not employ it. The answer is that, having used his words in vain, Pilate adopted the outward sign which he knew would be best understood by the Jewish people.

Incidentally, also, it would appear probable from Pilate's mention of Barabbas that this man was to be executed that same day, and that he was released at the cost of Jesus being sent to the Cross.

The mention in *Matthew* (XXVII, 19) of Pilate's judgment seat (Pilate sitting here when his wife sends her message pleading for Jesus) seems to show that the proceedings either took place indoors, or, if out of doors, in an open courtyard on the raised platform of which there was a seat for the judge.

III. *According to Mark*

Mark, like Matthew, leaves it uncertain whether Jesus was tried indoors or out of doors. Mark, like Matthew, makes Pilate begin by asking Jesus if he is the king of the Jews, and by Jesus replying, "Thou sayest it." Mark follows the same line as Matthew, without any material change. He tells us about Barabbas, that he "lay bound with them that had made insurrection with him, who had committed murder in the insurrection," thus showing that Barabbas had committed serious overt acts of sedition, whereas Jesus had committed no overt act whatever, unless the cleansing of the Temple could be considered so. Yet the Jews called for Barabbas in preference to Jesus, and Pilate released him instead of Jesus.

There is nothing to say about the trial as reported in *Mark* that has not been said about the trial as reported in *Matthew*—that it is a travesty of Roman justice, and that Pilate is manifestly an unjust judge, a judge who executed a man whom he *knew* to be innocent.

IV. According to Luke

"And the whole multitude of them arose, and led him unto Pilate" (XIII, 1).

In eastern manner, they seem to have been sitting during the inquiry before Caiaphas. Only Jesus, the prisoner, and his guards, would stand. The judges, so-called, would, of course, be seated.

Once more, nothing is said about the place at which they presented Jesus to Pilate, whether indoors or out of doors.

> And they began to accuse him, saying, We found this fellow perverting the nation, and forbidding to give tribute to Cæsar, saying that he himself is Christ a king.

Here, for the first time, is an intelligible beginning to the trial before Pilate, making plain the origin of Pilate's first question addressed to Jesus.

"And Pilate asked him, saying, Art thou the king of the Jews? Jesus answered, Thou sayest it."

Then Pilate is reported to have said to the chief priests and to the people, "I find no fault in this man."

Why? If Jesus admitted that he was the king of the Jews, and if to claim that rank was to be a pretender to the power and rank claimed by the Roman emperor, and enjoyed by him, why did Pilate say he found no fault in him? On the face of it, Jesus must have been, in the eyes of the Jews, a traitor to the ruling power. But the next verse shows that something more must have been said than is reported.

> And they were the more fierce, saying, He stirreth up the people, teaching through all Jewry, beginning from Galilee to this place.

Obviously, the Jews had forced the note of Jesus's treason to the Roman power, his claim to sovereignty, his forbidding people to pay tribute to Cæsar.

> And as soon as he knew that he [Jesus] belonged to Herod's jurisdiction, he sent him to Herod, who himself also was at Jerusalem at that time.

What had been the accusations, according to *Luke*, made against Jesus, by the Jewish chief priests? We hear of one only—that he perverted the people and forbade them to give tribute to Cæsar.

The reason Jesus is said to have given was that he was the king of the Jews, being the Christ.

Whether this charge was driven home (as probably in Caiaphas's palace) by accounts of how Jesus had given himself the airs of a king, by entering Jerusalem with a large crowd who were saluting him as the son of David, by lashing the traders out of the Temple, and by talking about destroying the Temple that had been built by Herod the Great, and rebuilding it himself, we do not know.

All we know is that Pilate, having heard the accusation of the chief priests and the admission of Jesus that he was the king of the Jews, said he found no fault in him.

It is impossible not to conclude that Pilate realized from the form of the accusation and from the witnesses (if there were any—Luke does not speak of any, but only of general clamorous denunciations as from a crowd) that Jesus was not really a political pretender to the sovereignty of Palestine, but only a religious dreamer, who was accused of claiming to fulfil in his own person certain Jewish prophecies of 500 or more years ago, which said that a deliverer of the Jewish people, a Christ, would come, and that this Christ would be the king of the Jews.

Thus Pilate must have seen through the transparent artifices whereby the Jews had turned an offence committed by Jesus against their Jewish religious law, and an attack being made by him on Jewish religious authority, as represented by his present accusers, the chief priests, into an offence against the emperor of Rome. Seeing this, Pilate quite clearly said, "Of the offence with which you charge this man he is innocent as far as *I* am concerned."

On hearing this ruling (which they might have foreseen if they had been clear-sighted men, or men not blinded by passion or terror) the chief priests went on to emphasize the offence of Jesus in creating disorder. In making this claim, in teaching that he was the Christ, the king of the Jews, he had been stirring up the people throughout Jewry, and, lately, all the way down from Galilee to Jerusalem.

Here Pilate saw at once a difficulty and a way of escape from it. If it were true that this man was stirring up the people, it might be that he would give trouble. He might be thinking of nothing but a religious kingship, but who could be sure that they, the people, might not think of a political kingship?

Pilate saw this; but could he banish the man for that? It would be dangerous to do so. These Jews were not his friends. They had reported against him twice to the Roman emperor. He had been told to deal more tenderly with the people he was sent to govern. If the word went to Rome that he paid no heed to rebellious teaching, and it resulted in an insurrection, it would be difficult for him to explain that it was harmless and rather fantastic and certainly superstitious teaching in itself, and that it would have been unjust to execute a man for the misconception of his teaching by the ignorant masses.

What might be the result if he did not execute the man? Another sharp rebuke from his emperor. What would be the result if he did execute the man? A still sharper rebuke from Rome on the report of any sane Jew who was clear-sighted enough to see that he had killed a man who had committed no overt act of rebellion, who showed no sign of committing such an act—merely to satisfy the desires of a gang of envious priests who found that their world was deserting them and following a rival?

Such was Pilate's predicament when he heard that Jesus had been committing the offences with which he was being charged not only there, in Judæa, in Jerusalem, but in Galilee.

He seems to have said, "Galilee? Why do you say he began in Galilee?"

The answer must have been, "Because he is a Galilean, and came up here from Galilee."

Here, then, for a moment, seemed a way of escape for Pilate. If this man was a Galilean, why should not he be sent back to Galilee? That was outside his jurisdiction as Roman procurator. It was in the jurisdiction of another governor appointed by Rome—Herod Antipas, the tetrarch. Why should not he send this man to Herod? There seemed excellent reasons why he should do so. First, it would enable him (Pilate) to escape from his own difficulty with the Jews in Jerusalem. Next, it would give him a good excuse to Rome if an overt act of insurrection were ever committed by this man or his followers in future. Next, it would remove him from the possible danger of intruding upon the rights of Herod Antipas over his subjects, an offence he had lately committed, about which Herod Antipas had complained to Rome, and for which the emperor had reprimanded him.

Then he seems to have remembered that it was the custom of

Herod Antipas to come to Jerusalem for the feast of the Jewish Passover. This was the time of the Jewish Passover. Herod Antipas was in Jerusalem now. He would send this man to his rightful judge, the governor whose subject he was in the name of Rome. He would send him to Herod, and so get rid of him and the difficulties of his own position.

So Pilate adjourned his court and sent Jesus over the way to Herod Antipas.

What did he expect Herod to do? He could not have expected him to try the man in Jerusalem and on finding him guilty (of treason to the Roman emperor, in claiming to be the king of the Jews) execute him in Jerusalem.

That Pilate could never have dreamt of. He would have been the first to prevent any such thing. It would mean a sure offence on his part. He was there to govern Judæa, and to allow another governor to take life on his territory must have been unthinkable.

What, then, if this incident is historical, did Pilate expect to be the result of his sending Jesus to Herod? The only reasonable answer is that he would expect him to ask for power of extradition, to take this Galilean, this sower of sedition against their common master, Tiberius, back to Galilee, to be tried there, and, if found guilty, executed there.

The whole of this incident of Herod Antipas has been pronounced unhistorical by many critics on various grounds: (1) that it appears in Luke's Gospel only; (2) that it is a palpable effort on the part of the early Christians, who struggled to cast all the blame of the death of Jesus on the Jews and to exculpate or excuse Pilate, to implicate *all* the Jewish authorities in the guilt of Jesus's death; (3) that it was a preposterous thought that Herod could try and punish even his own subjects on another ruler's territory; (4) that the proceedings at Herod's palace are out of harmony with the earlier accounts of his attitude towards Jesus.

But I have, in the foregoing, indicated my reasons for thinking that Pilate would naturally make this attempt to escape from his own difficulties.

Now let us see what Herod did.

And when Herod saw Jesus, he was exceeding glad; for he was desirous to see him of a long season, because he had heard many things of him; and he hoped to have seen some miracle done by him. [XXIII, 8]

As this indicates a light and rather amused attitude towards Jesus, it is thought to be out of harmony with the earlier account of Herod's attitude towards Jesus, where it is described as being one of terror of Jesus as a worker of miracles, based on the belief that Jesus was none other than John the Baptist raised from the dead.

But that is a misconception of the earlier passages. In *Luke* (IX, 7–9 and XIII, 31, 32) we have the record of two previous occasions on which Herod Antipas was concerned about Jesus. In the first of these it is said that Herod the tetrarch was perplexed by what he heard of Jesus, and concluded that he must be John (whom he had beheaded) risen from the dead. His reason for this was that Jesus was healing and working marvellous miracles. Therefore (according to *Luke*) Herod desired to see Jesus. But if Herod gave the miracles of Jesus as his reason for thinking he was John risen from the dead, he was obviously lying, for John had worked no miracles, and therefore he could have no fear of Jesus, as the risen John, based on the miracles.

Herod's desire to see Jesus had probably nothing to do with the miracles, and nothing to do with any idea that Jesus was John risen from the dead. It was more probable because Jesus had denounced divorce, and therefore condemned Herod's marriage with Herodias, that Herod desired to see him, and to do with him as he had done with John.

The second of the moments at which Herod is reported to interest himself in Jesus is when Jesus is on his way to Jerusalem from Cæsarea Philippi, and passing through Samaria he is warned, by certain of the Pharisees, to leave Herod's territory, otherwise Herod (who is obviously looking for him) will kill him.

It follows then that, when Pilate sends Jesus to Herod, the pleasure of the latter at seeing Jesus is in strict keeping with the spirit of the previous occasions on which he had desired to see him and had failed.

Herod was just as eager as ever to see an end put to this prophet of Galilee, more powerful than John the Baptist, and more to be feared by reason of his enormous following in Galilee.

But he saw at a glance through Pilate's purpose. It was to get *him* to dispose of this dangerous person, whom the people regarded as a prophet and would probably rise up to defend. More, he saw that the danger to himself in Galilee, if he were to take Jesus back there, try, condemn and execute him, would be immeasurably more certain and assuredly more swift than any danger that could fall upon Pilate from Rome.

Herod knew (what. Pilate did not know) the full meaning of this alleged claim of Jesus to be the king of the Jews. He was half Jew himself, and a Jewish ruler, therefore he understood the meaning and the power of the Messianic hope. The only interest he had ever had in the miracles of Jesus of Nazareth was that they had inspired this Messianic hope in Galilee.

In his own territory there were vastly more people than there could be in Judæa, who believed that Jesus of Nazareth was the Christ, therefore the king of the Jews.

Therefore, for him (Herod) to claim this prisoner as his subject, whom he had a right to try and punish, would be to encounter the fanatical opposition of his own subjects, who regarded Jesus as a prophet, the greatest of the prophets.

Should he, therefore, fall into Pilate's trap, of taking Jesus back to Galilee? By no means. He had got into too much trouble already, by killing John the Baptist, to court a greater disaster— the possible rebellion of all the people.

What, then, did Herod do?

He questioned Jesus in many words. It is not difficult to imagine what manner of words they were. They probably related to his miracles, to his entrance into Jerusalem and to his claim to be the son of David. But what his questions were matters little. Jesus answered nothing. Why should he?

The scene of these two face to face is dramatic enough. The incestuous adulterer, who had broken every law of Moses, and Jesus. His silent contempt must have irritated Herod.

Meantime, the chief priests and elders who had followed Jesus to Herod's house stood and vehemently accused Jesus. And to them also Jesus made no answer. What did Herod decide to do? To send the prisoner back to Pilate with a message implying his unwillingness to take out of Pilate's hands a prisoner whose offence had so obviously been committed in Pilate's territory, whose arrest had been made there, and who had there come under the condemnation of the Jewish Sanhedrin.

As for Jesus's claims to be the king of the Jews, Herod affected to regard this with derision. This mock king! This mountebank! This Nazarene journeyman who claimed to be the son of David, foretold by the prophets! How ridiculous!

There was only one way to deal with such a pretender—to crown him with ridicule.

Herod did so. His "men of war" mocked Jesus, arrayed him in a gorgeous robe (no doubt a kingly robe) and sent him back to Pilate—no doubt with a courteous message of thanks. Herod had been long aggrieved by Pilate's conduct. This sending of Jesus to him had been a flattering overture of friendship. Herod received it as such and returned the compliment.

"And the same day Pilate and Herod were made friends together; for before they were at enmity between themselves."

Thus I find the incident of the appearance of Jesus before Herod a natural one. It rings true to the situation, and to what we know of the character of both men.

Incidentally, I find it reasonable to think that Herod Antipas saw that Pilate would be compelled, by the pressure of the Jewish rulers, to condemn and execute Jesus, and felt that this would be a good end to the career of one whose future activities in Galilee might be very disagreeable to himself.

The fact is obvious that Herod saw through the scheme of Pilate, and that while not openly resenting it he told himself that he was not going to be caught in that trap. If Pilate was in danger from the ruling classes in Jerusalem, he (Herod) was in still greater danger from the people in Galilee, who might tear him limb from limb if he again attempted to destroy a prophet of God.

While it is true, as some critics say, that it was not Herod's intent to *save* Jesus, it was very strongly to his interest to save himself, and have nothing to do with the death of Jesus, although he wished him dead.

Jesus was brought back to Pilate. Pilate's scheme for liberating himself from responsibility for the fate of Jesus had failed. But his strength had been increased by this refusal of Herod to take Jesus. So he resumed the hearing of the case. He called back the chief priests and the rulers of the people, brought back the prisoner, and said,

Ye have brought this man unto me, as one that perverteth the people, and, behold, I, having examined him before you, have found no fault in this man touching those things whereof ye accuse him.

That is to say, "I do not find this fellow has perverted the nation, and forbidden to give tribute to Cæsar or pretended to be a king in the sense of a worldly king and rival of Cæsar."

No, nor yet Herod: for I sent you to him, and, lo, nothing worthy of death is done unto him.

In brief, Herod has not condemned him, though he may have said he was a troublesome agitator, disturbing the people. "I will, therefore, chastise him and release him."

Here is an almost unbelievable thing. The Roman law recognized the right of torture, and if Pilate had still any lingering idea that Jesus was a political pretender aiming at securing the throne of Palestine and thus casting out Cæsar, a thing he regarded with derision as a ridiculous impossibility, it is conceivable that he might have ordered Jesus to be scourged, in order to extort a confession which would justify punishment. But no such thing. He was only going to scourge him as a preliminary to releasing him.

Why scourge him if he found no fault in him? Why not rather scourge his false accusers? Does Pilate think, and did Herod say, that although Jesus had never set up as king of the Jews he had disturbed the people and therefore ought to be scourged and sent away with a warning not to disturb the peace of the country again? This monstrous conduct would be quite in the spirit of the time and country. It was done not long afterwards to Peter and then to Paul. But the injustice and barbarity of it is none the less appalling.

Pilate's proposal to dispose of the case of Jesus in this way was rejected by the Jews. They called (as in *Matthew* and *Mark*) for the release of Barabbas, "who, for a certain sedition made in the city, and for murder, was cast into prison."

Pilate, willing to release Jesus, makes another appeal to the Jews, but they cry out, "Crucify him! Crucify him!"

Pilate asks, for the third time, "Why, what evil hath he done? I have found no cause of death in him, and I will therefore chastise him, and let him go."

But the Jews are insistent, with loud voices, requiring that Jesus might be crucified. And the voices of the people and the chief priests prevailed. So "Pilate gave sentence that it should be as they required." He released to the Jews the man who for sedition and murder had been cast into prison, and he delivered Jesus to their will.

Such is Luke's account of the trial of Jesus before Pilate. Another appalling story. Not a word to account for Pilate's motive in condemning to death a man whom he knew and declared to be innocent of the crime with which he was charged. One outrage after another against the first principles of Roman law.

We have still to look for Pilate's motive for his outrageous conduct. Here he behaves like a coward and a fool, and an utterly unjust judge.

V. *According to John*

Then led they Jesus from Caiaphas unto the hall of judgment; and it was early; and they themselves went not into the judgment hall, lest they should be defiled; but that they might eat the passover. [XVIII, 28]

Observe from the first John's clear design (in the face of the earlier Gospels, which it is impossible he should not have known, which he did know because he quoted from them in various passages) of saying the trial was not on the morning after the eating of the Passover, but on the morning of the day on which the Passover was to be eaten after sunset. Observe, next, that this choice of time will presently involve John in various difficulties, among them being that of conducting a trial according to procedure which is next to impossible to believe any Roman governor would, for one moment, tolerate; (1) that, contrary to the strict requirements of Roman law, he should never bring the accusers and accused face to face; (2) that he should himself make a constant, humiliating and quite ridiculous perambulation to and fro between the so-called prisoner indoors, and his accusers out of doors.

"Pilate then went out unto them"—somebody apparently having gone into the judgment hall where, possibly, Pilate was already sitting on the bench, presented the prisoner, and told him the Jews would not come in lest it make them unclean for their own festival if they should enter a Gentile house on that day of preparation for their own holy day.

It is hard to believe that a Roman procurator (especially one who, like Pilate, was on bad terms with the Jews, and plainly held them and their religion in contempt) would humble himself in this way. What he would more probably do would be to tell them to leave their prisoner and come another day. Or, if they urged necessity (the necessity of safety for him, Pilate, and for Cæsar) and the possible danger of an uprising of the people if the matter were not dealt with at once, Pilate would more probably send for his man and tell the Jews to go about their business, and come back when they could do so without dishonouring the procurator by making him a kind of peripatetic messenger between their prisoner and themselves. In short, it is nearly impossible to believe that Pilate, leaving Jesus inside the judgment hall, would come out to the Jews in the open space in front of it. That he did so is a foolish story, probably invented by the writer to escape from his difficulty of placing the trial on the day before the Passover.

"Pilate then went out unto them and said, What accusation bring ye against this man?" So he had not received a written accusation from the morning Sanhedrin.

"They answered and said unto him, If he were not a malefactor, we would not have delivered him up unto thee."

Anything more impudent than this it is difficult to conceive. It implies, also, an utterly false idea of the position of the procurator in relation to the Sanhedrin. It seems to say, "It should be sufficient to you that our sacred court have found him to be a malefactor worthy of death, and all that remains to you is to put him to death. The Jews knew better than that. They knew that the power over life and death which the Roman authority reserved to itself would have been a silly farce if the procurator had been required to ratify the condemnation of the Jewish court without inquiry of his own. The Roman law required to be satisfied that death was deserved. Therefore the procurator would (must) hold a court, confront the accused and his accusers, hear the evidence, question the prisoner, and form his own judgment and pass sentence or acquit on his own responsibility.

"Then said Pilate unto them, Take ye him, and judge him according to your law." The Jews answered, "It is not lawful for us to put any man to death."

Observe here two things, (1) that Pilate did not know or believe that Jesus had been tried by the Jews at all down to that moment, and (2) that if he did know that their Sanhedrin had tried him, or made an inquiry into his offence, he regarded its decision with contempt. In short, Pilate did not recognize any proceedings against Jesus previous to his own. Also that he did not wish to have anything to do with Jesus's case, suspecting from the first that it was some sort of squabble between the Jewish rulers and one of their own people.

Having received this reply from the Jews, and realizing that it was a case of the capital crime, Pilate, according to this astonishing story of John, entered into the judgment hall again and called Jesus, and said, "Art thou the king of the Jews?"

Obviously, John has omitted something. There is nothing reported by him which could have suggested this question. In saying they had no power to put a man to death, the Jews must have said that Jesus deserved death as a pretender to the kingdom of the Jews. Pilate must have thought it astounding that the Jews themselves presented a criminal for capital punishment for questioning the right of the emperor to rule over them, and of one of their own race (this man or any other) to oust him and take his place.

"Jesus answered him, Sayest thou this thing of thyself, or did others tell it thee of me?"

Jesus saw that Pilate could not have conceived such an idea for himself. It must have been put into his mind. And Pilate also clearly saw that only a Jew, not a Roman, could have conceived such an idea.

"Pilate answered, Am I a Jew? Thine own nation and the chief priests have delivered thee unto me. What has thou done?"

This is perfectly in order thus far, according to Roman law, except that the question ought to have been asked in open court, in the presence of the accusers.

"Jesus answered, My kingdom is not of this world; if my kingdom were of this world, then would my servants fight, that I should not be delivered to the Jews."

This is a perfectly natural answer. It says, "It is true I claim to be a king, but not a temporal king, not a king with an earthly kingdom. My kingdom is a kingdom of another world, an unseen world, a spiritual world. I am a spiritual king. If I had been a king of this world my servants would have fought for me, and I should never have been taken by the Jews."

This is a perfectly straight answer, and Pilate fully understands it. "Art thou a king, then?" he asks.

"And Jesus answers, Thou sayest that I am a king. [Meaning Pilate says rightly that Jesus is a king.] To this end was I born, and for this cause came I into the world, that I should bear witness unto the truth."

Pilate understands that also, but his Greek culture (such as it is) leaps to his mind at that moment, and he asks, "What is the truth?" Meaning by that "Who shall say what is the truth? Is there any such thing as the truth?"

Down to this moment Pilate has behaved well, except that he has not insisted on all this dialogue with Jesus taking place in open court. He is, however, fully satisfied that Jesus is no pretender to the throne of Judæa. He is no enemy of Cæsar's. He is a religious fanatic, who believes that in some other world than this (Pilate has heard of that other world) he, the accused, will be a king of the Jewish people.

Pilate went out again to the Jews, and said unto them, "I find in him no fault at all," meaning "I do not find this man a malefactor; he is not leading any political revolt against the Roman power, and that is all I have to think about—all I am here to prevent."

Then he remembers that there is a Jewish custom (when and by whom started is uncertain, but probably by Herod the Great) that at the time of the Passover, the time of rejoicing for the recovery of the liberty of the Jews from the slavery of their Egyptian taskmasters, a Jewish prisoner should be released to the Jewish people.

This meant that the Jews should nominate some Jew lying in prison (probably for some political offence against the Roman authority), and ask that he should be set at liberty at this time of Jewish rejoicing, and that the Roman procurator should give them the man they asked for.

Remembering this custom, Pilate suggested that he should release Jesus, calling him (out of his perfect knowledge of the motives which had caused the Jews to charge Jesus) "the king of the Jews."

Observe that John also sees nothing wrong in this situation. He does not see that, according to Pilate's view, Jesus has not yet been tried by the Jewish courts, and therefore cannot have been condemned, and that he has certainly not yet been condemned by Pilate's own court.

"Then cried they again, saying, Not this man, but Barabbas." And to point the irony of the situation the evangelist says, "Now Barabbas was a robber."

Now here comes an incredible incident. Pilate, who has heard what the Jews have had to say about Jesus, and has told them that they ought to try him according to their own law, who has examined Jesus and come to the conclusion that he is innocent of the accusation made against him of claiming to be the king of the Jews, and has said that he "finds no fault in him at all"—this Roman governor now takes Jesus and scourges him.

If Pilate had had any uncertainty about Jesus's testimony—if he had really suspected him of withholding some incriminating fact about his pretensions as a political king—he would have been perfectly justified, by the usages of the Roman courts, in putting him to torture, to extract a fuller confession. This was constantly done at that time in the courts in Rome. It was done later by Nero with the Christians, when he wished to find scapegoats for the destruction of Rome by fire. It was even done by Pliny the Younger when he had to deal with Christians on their trial. But Pilate had no intention of putting Jesus to torture for such purposes. He was simply giving way to a passion for brutality, possibly in order to pacify the Jews and to allay their lust for blood, and so help him at least to save Jesus's life.

What follows is a shocking outrage on the Roman name, a hideous stain on Roman justice. And the high reputation of the Roman soldier for mercy to his adversary goes down to the very dregs with it.

> And the soldiers [obviously Pilate's soldiers] plaited a crown of thorns and put it on his head, and they put on him a purple robe [the colour of royalty] ; and said, Hail, king of the Jews ! And they smote him with their hands.

Of all this horrible maltreatment, Pilate, a knight of Rome, procurator of the Roman empire, was fully conscious, and if he did not assist at it, he authorized it.

> Pilate therefore went forth again, and said unto them [the assembled Jews outside], Behold, I bring him forth to you, that ye may know that I find no fault in him.
> Then came Jesus forth, wearing the crown of thorns and the purple robe ; and Pilate said unto them, Behold the man !

It is not easy to follow the process of thought in the mind of Pilate during this scene. What does he think he is doing? In common phrase, what is he after? If he wished to pacify the Jews, to allay their thirst for blood, he (being a man who did not mind eating his own words that the man was innocent) might have scourged Jesus; but why insult the Jews and laugh at them by dressing the prisoner up in mock regal robes, with a crown made of thorns, and then bring him out and say in effect, "Behold the man! What am I to do with him?" It was the act of a brute, but also of a fool. If he wished the Jews to let him escape from the iniquity of sending an innocent man to death he was behaving in the way most likely to defeat his purpose. Naturally, the Jews raged at the sight of this mockery of a king, and cried out, "Crucify him! Crucify him!"

Then the fool in Pilate went one step farther. "Take ye him, and crucify him," he said, "for I find no fault in him."

Pilate knew perfectly that if the Jews had taken him at his word he would have been the first to lay them by the heels. The Jews could not crucify any man. If they had been able to do so, Pilate might as well have gone home for all the use he was to his imperial master. The Jews knew this and they answered, "We have a law, and by our law he ought to die, because he made himself the Son of God."

Observe here that the Jews overstepped themselves. They were forgetting the political offence of Jesus, and letting out the secret of his religious offence. But the effect was great on Pilate, nevertheless.

Pilate was indeed familiar with the idea of a human being having been understood to be (or claiming to be) the Son of God. That was not a crime by Roman law. What was a crime (or worse) was scourging a Son of God, holding him up to common derision. Pilate found himself afraid. Was this man whom he had scourged and mocked a Son of God?

He "went again into the judgment hall," evidently taking Jesus back with him, and says to Jesus, "Whence art thou?"

Jesus gives him no answer. Pilate is amazed. "Why don't you speak to me?" he says. "Don't you know that I have power to crucify you, and power to release you?"

Jesus answers, "Thou couldest have no power at all against me, except it were given thee from above."

Observe here the operation of the belief (more strongly expressed than ever before and at a more threatening moment) which Jesus has held ever since the scenes at the source of the Jordan, that everything that is happening to him, everything that will happen, is under the will of the unseen powers. Jesus tells Pilate that what he is doing, and all he can do, is according to the will of God.

Incidentally, this is all he says to Pilate at this moment, and it must have been later that uninstructed and unimaginative minds added to his simple and sublime words the paltry and illogical words that follow, out of sequence and without any intelligible idea: "therefore he that delivered me unto thee hath the greater sin."

If, as is assumed, the "he" referred to is Caiaphas there is no logical reason for the statement. Caiaphas, equally with Pilate, must have been powerless to do anything to Jesus except it were given to him from above.

Next, observe that the thought of higher powers controlling his actions made a sensible impression on his conduct, as the idea that he had been dealing with a "Son of God" had done before. Jesus had merely carried on the same spiritual idea, and it had fallen on Pilate as another blow.

"And from thenceforth [after Jesus had, in fact, threatened Pilate with higher powers than his own] Pilate sought to release him."

What he did is not reported in *John*. The natural inference is that he attempted to explain to the Jews the sense in which Jesus claimed to be the king of the Jews—a spiritual sense, not a political sense. But the Jews knew all he could say on that subject—and more. They knew that if they once admitted that Jesus held a spiritual kingship there was an end to their old doctrine of the unity of God. They saw that it carried with it the theory of the Son of God, which was blasphemy to the Jewish faith. It was (from their point) of no use to try to explain this to Pilate. He simply would not understand a word of it. He had been brought up in a faith which saw no harm, but only good, in the idea of a plurality of Gods—of God the Father and God the Son, or what amounted to much the same thing in his view.

So the Jews did the only things such men would do. They drove home the political charge against Jesus, telling Pilate again that this "fellow" was claiming to supplant Cæsar as the sovereign of Palestine. Therefore if he (Pilate) did not put this man down he was no friend of Cæsar's.

"Whosoever maketh himself a king speaketh against Cæsar."

Here entered the dilemma already dealt with in the notes on the story as revealed in the earlier Gospels. Pilate remembered his difficulties, his frequent reproofs from Tiberius, and reflected on the danger of his downfall if another such report—a more serious one, that he had tacitly encouraged sedition—were made. Pilate saw himself as a martyr—for what? To save this obscure Galilean peasant, who had set himself up as a prophet and gathered a multitude of more or less ignorant followers. Why should he? Justice? Did it call on him to run the risk of lifelong dishonour for the sake of this obscurity?

Under the fire of this temptation, Pilate, being a coward, fell. He hated these Jews, who for envy, as he thought (not seeing the force of their temptation, which was at least as great as his), were forcing his hand, compelling him to kill an innocent man.

He ordered Jesus to be brought out, sat down on his judgment seat in the place called the Pavement (clearly a place in the open air), and said, bitterly, "Behold your king!"

The blistering irony of this (as he thought) was too much for the Jews, and they cried, "Away with him! Crucify him!"

Pilate's irony cut deeper. "Shall I crucify your king?" he asked. And the chief priests answered, "We have no king but Cæsar."

Was there ever such a situation? Was Pilate duped by it? Not for one moment. He knew the chief priests cared nothing for Cæsar, and would have eagerly overthrown him if they could—but not this way, not at the hands of a man who would claim to do so by divine right as God.

Incidentally, it was similar to the later case of Joan of Arc, only worse, since Joan only claimed to be the servant of God, not the daughter of God.

Pilate saw one way of escape. He took it.

"Then delivered he him therefore unto them to be crucified. And they took Jesus, and led him away."

Such is the appalling story of the trial of Jesus, according to John. It is a breathless and thrilling story, but an utterly shocking one, in its lying (in effect), its deception, its concealment of real motives, its cowardice on the part of Pilate. The ultimate effect of it is that Pilate was an unjust judge, as in the earlier Gospel stories, condemning to death an innocent man, knowing him to be innocent of the crimes with which he was charged.

The tremendous power of the story comes, in my judgment,

from the sense of all the parties to it acting (being compelled to act) under the will of higher powers. No Greek tragedy carries this sense so far, so unrelentingly.

First, Jesus is acting under the higher power which has, in his view, willed that he should die, and therefore he is silent when he might easily defend himself; he allows palpable lies to be told about him which he might easily disprove; permits statements of fact to be urged against him which he might easily explain. He, unlike Pilate, later, makes no effort to silence his adversaries. He lets them have their will.

When he speaks at the inquiry at the Sanhedrin (the night sitting) it is only that he shall not run away from the claim he has made to his disciples. When he speaks before Pilate, it is only to clear away the mud and scum of the worldly idea which the chief priests (perfectly well knowing what they were doing) had plastered on to his claim to a kingdom.

Next, the Jewish rulers are acting under the influence of higher powers in destroying the man who was cutting at the root of their faith in denying its cardinal doctrine—the divinity of God. They could not have done otherwise than destroy such a man. In a sense, Jesus was justly sent to his death by them. But such was the entanglement of their political position that they could only send him to his just death (according to Jewish law) by a criminal concealment of their real motive, by a criminal reversal of their real grounds of objection to him, and by deliberate lying about their desire (for such it amounts to) to maintain the Roman power in Palestine—a thing their people were hungering and thirsting to destroy.

Finally, and perhaps above all, Pilate was acting under the higher powers, in condemning an innocent man (knowing him to be innocent) in order to save himself.

Thus the whole drama is a drama of a controlling influence of higher powers. This, for me, is a convincing proof of the authenticity of the substantial and essential part of the whole story—that Jesus was betrayed into the hands of the Jewish rulers by one of his own followers; that the Jewish rulers were compelled by their religious law to conclude that he was worthy of death; that they were forced by their political position as a subject race to hand him over to the Roman power for execution, and finally that the representative of the Roman power was compelled, by the peril of his own personal position, to send him to his death.

It is pertinent to ask, "Who reported this trial of Jesus by Pilate?" Obviously, not any of Jesus's disciples. They were all (Peter included) in hiding for fear of the Jews—thinking they might suffer as the accomplices of their Master.

It may have been Joseph of Arimathæa, or perhaps Nicodemus, who communicated the story of it to the disciples when (perhaps years after the event) they began to write. But more probably it was one, or many of the Jews or Romans, who, being present at the trial, became Christians afterwards.

Was the procedure as John described it? I think most assuredly it was not. It violates every known principle of Roman law. The first principle was that a prisoner and his accusers should stand face to face. If we did not know this (as we so well do) from Roman history, we should learn it from the Scriptures themselves.

In *Acts* (XXV, 16) we read that Festus, addressing himself to Agrippa, says:

> It is not the manner of the Romans to deliver any man to die, before that he which is accused have the accusers face to face, and have licence to answer for himself concerning the crime laid against him. Therefore, when they [the Jewish accusers of Paul] were come hither, without any delay on the morrow I sat on the judgment-seat, and commanded the man to be brought forth.

If we are to accept the story of John's Gospel, the Roman procedure adopted by Festus was deliberately violated by his predecessor Pilate. It is not believable. Neither is it for a moment conceivable that there was anything in the facts of the forthcoming festival which required a change in procedure.

The trial of Jesus before Pilate, according to *John,* is a farce, a very meaningless farce. It is no trial at all. Jesus is only brought out to his accusers for two short moments. The first of these is the moment (out of utter contempt of the Jews, as I think, not out of sympathy and compassion and a desire to conciliate his enemies, as other critics say—as if any sane man actuated by such emotions, would bring out Jesus crowned with thorns and in the mock disguise of a king) when Pilate says, "Behold the Man!" and the other is the moment when Jesus (not having heard, except at second hand from Pilate, one word of the accusations made against him) is brought out to be declared guilty of sedition and sentenced to death, as, it may be, in words like these:

> I find thee, Jesus of Nazareth, guilty of treason against the emperor Tiberius Cæsar, of having claimed to be the king of the Jews, and of stirring up the country to resist Cæsar's power, and to drive his soldiers out of the country, and I sentence thee to be crucified on the Cross, until you are dead.

All this (or whatever took place which resembled it) is in utter violation of the first principles of Roman justice.

I cannot believe it. But I think I see how the evangelist John came to give this grotesque picture of the procedure in a Roman court of law. Having convinced himself from the outset that Jesus did not eat the Jewish Passover, and that his last supper with his disciples was an ordinary meal which had no relation to the Passover, and was not burdened by its significance in any way whatever, John became entangled (or thought he did) in the difficulty of keeping the accusing Jews outside the house of Pilate while he had to present Jesus before the judgment-seat, which he thought was within.

I do not think it was within. There are various facts in Roman history which show that it was sometimes (perhaps generally) out of doors.

In conclusion, I find it impossible to believe in the going and coming of Pilate between Jesus and the priests. I think that he sat in his usual place on the judgment-seat outside his palace, that Jesus stood before him, and that his accusers were face to face with him from first to last; that nothing occurred between them in private (a ridiculous supposition, in my view); and that the only break was when (according to *Luke*) Jesus was sent to Herod Antipas.

VI. *Peter's Reference to Pilate*

There is a reference by Peter (after the death of Jesus) to the part played by Pilate (*Acts* III, 13). After Peter and John, going into the Temple by the gate Beautiful, heal a lame man, they are surrounded by people who are amazed at the miracle, and to them Peter speaks. He accuses them of having delivered up Jesus, "and denied him in the presence of Pilate, when he was determined to let him go."

Thus Peter exonerates Pilate of the death of Jesus, and casts the chief blame on the people. If Peter made this partial statement, he knew the facts (as recorded in the Gospels) imperfectly. The event was soon after the death of Jesus, and it may very well be that the full facts had not yet become known to Peter.

Certainly we see, not here only but in many places, that the apostles in the early days held Pilate in a certain esteem as one who would have saved Jesus if he could have done so.

We shall see later that in after years Christians took this view very strongly. One section of the Church canonized Pilate's wife, who had sent a message to Pilate while he was on the judgment-seat warning him against doing any harm to that "just man" Jesus.

Stephen, in like manner (somewhat later), cast the responsibility of the death of Jesus on the Jews, and said nothing about the guilt of the Roman governor.

> Which of the prophets have not your fathers persecuted? And they have slain them which showed before of the coming of the Just One; of whom ye have been now the betrayers and murderers. [*Acts* VII, 52]

This is the attitude of the Early Christians always. The Jews are responsible, not the Roman authority. It is true, nevertheless, that Peter on the Day of Pentecost (*Acts* II, 23) recognizes that Jesus has been "delivered" up to his destroyers "by the determinate counsel and foreknowledge of God," yet he says that they (the Jews) by "wicked hands have crucified and slain."

CHAPTER XXXII

The Crown of Thorns

I. The Time of the Trial

HISTORIANS SAY that it was usual for the Roman procurator to begin his sittings very early in the morning, even at sunrise, which at the time of the trial before Pilate would be about 6 A.M. Incidentally, it is said in *John's* Gospel to be the sixth hour of the preparation of the Passover. The sixth hour would be noon. But according to *Mark* (XV, 25) Jesus had by that time been three hours crucified, having been put on the Cross at the third hour, 9 A.M.

It is pointed out by Keim that the governor's house in which the trial before Pilate was held was not where legend has placed it, on the north side of the Temple near the fortress of Antonia, but in the upper city on the south-west of the Temple hall. If so, Jesus would have to pass through many of the streets of Jerusalem. Why did not the multitude of his followers see him? Why had not the disciples, if they had already returned to the city, conveyed the news of his arrest to the multitudes who had thronged the Temple every morning to hear him? If, as the Synoptics say, it was the morning of the first day of the unleavened bread, it would be a holiday, and most of the people would be still in bed after the feast and merrymaking of the night before. But if, as John indicates, it was the day before the first day of unleavened bread the streets of the city would be full at 7 A.M.

II. At Pilate's House

Tradition shows the ancient house of Pilate on the north-west of the old Temple site. Later, such a house became a barrack. But it often happened that the Roman governors inhabited the splendid edifices of the local kings in all the countries that Rome conquered. It was so at Cæsarea (as we see in *Acts*), and it is more than probable that it was so in Jerusalem.

912

As late as the beginning of the Jewish war, and therefore a generation earlier than the trial of Jesus before Pilate, the palace of Herod the Great was well preserved by the Romans, and Josephus says its magnificence was indescribable and incomparable. He refers to several palaces built by Herod the Great. In one place he says, "Herod built himself a palace in the upper city, raising the rooms to a very great height and adorning them with the most costly furniture of gold, and marble seats, and beds; and these were so large that they could contain very many companies of men. These apartments were also of distinct magnitudes, and had particular names given to them, for one apartment was called Cæsar's, another Agrippa's."

Probably this was the palace inhabited by Pilate, to which Jesus was taken. Robinson, in his *Biblical Researches,* states how he looked for this palace near the western tower. Others think it stood by the eastern tower. Its position is still uncertain. Josephus refers to the long stretch of the palace, and its parks southward from the three towers. Here are sufficiently contradictory statements. A modern writer does not hesitate to give a detailed description of the palace to which Jesus was taken. Keim says:

It was situated on the north-west side of the upper city, contiguous to the first city wall, but with three white towers. It was at once a tyrant's stronghold and a family pleasure-house. A wall of thirty cubits in height surrounded it, crowned with towers at regular intervals. It was capable of accommodating a small army. It had a magnificent prospect over Jerusalem and had two colossal marble wings, far surpassing even the splendour of the Temple.

Among its magnificent chambers was a great dining-room for men, furnished with one hundred tables and couches, and therefore capable of accommodating three hundred diners, three to each table. The floors were covered with the rarest stones, the ceilings were of gigantic beams, gorgeously decorated. Outside there were great colonnades. Beyond these were magnificent parks with broad walks, deep canals and cisterns for water. A proud residence for a Roman knight (for such Pilate was), yet inhabited only for a few days every year—particularly at Easter with its dreaded insurrections of the Jewish people longing for freedom—which had to be held in check.

"The rulers of the Gentiles lord it over them, those that wear soft raiment are in king's palaces." Thus had Jesus formerly given expression to the repugnance of Galilean simplicity to emperors and temporal dominion; and now he, himself, fettered, passed through the gates of a king's palace.

Did the palace contain a judgment-seat inside or outside the walls? Probably outside. Roman justice required that trials should be public and open to all.

What was Pilate's mood? Keim thinks it might easily be favourable to Jesus from the first. He had no reason to love the Jewish nation. On the contrary, he had some excuse for hating them. They had twice, at least, complained of him to his master, and once he had been sharply reprimanded. Therefore, the haughty and perhaps brutal Roman might be more sympathetically disposed towards the accused than towards his accusers. But there was a limit to his sympathy, his fear. He had good reason to expect that if he made a false step the Jewish multitudes might complain of him again, and that might be the end of his rule in Judæa.

It was in this spirit that he behaved during his trial of Jesus. Yet we are left with the impression that even Pilate would have spared Jesus if the clamour of the Jews had not been so strong, and if the fruits of his long misrule had not been so bitter for him.

The proceedings before Pilate took place in all probability in the open air and in front of the palace. The Romans favoured publicity in trials. The procurator Florus, in A.D. 66, caused his seat of judgment to be set up here before the palace of Herod, in which he resided, and caused the high priests and the notables of Jerusalem to stand around his seat. It was while sitting so, according to Josephus, that he caused Bernice, the Jewish queen, to come barefoot before him as a suppliant.

So it was that Jesus came. The earlier Gospels suggest that the proceedings take place partly here and partly within the palace— Jesus being within. The place of the sentence is, according to tradition, Gabbatha, a Hebrew word meaning "a hump"—a raised place between the palace and the high outer walls. Thus, on the quadrangular and crescent-shaped wooden or stone tribunal, which was erected upon an elevated spot and commanded the court, Pilate sat upon his official seat, to pronounce sentence at least. The earlier part of the proceedings between Pilate and the accusers of Jesus might take place on the Pavement, the top landing of the steps leading up to the palace.

Keim sees the scene as follows:

> Beside Pilate would be the counsel, or assessors, of the court, friends, Roman citizens. The steps leading up would be occupied by

the Sanhedrists who had come to deliver up their prisoner. There was sitting room on the tribunal for the accusers and the accused—when they were Romans. But for the subjects of Judæa this honour did not apply. Jesus in particular was required to stand.

III.   At the Palace of Caiaphas

The maltreatment of Jesus at the house of Pilate is a totally different incident, with a totally different meaning, from the maltreatment at the house of Annas and the palace of Caiaphas.

According to *Matthew* (XXVI, 67, 68), after the high priest had rent his clothes and his fellow councillors had said that Jesus was guilty of death

> Then did they spit in his face, and buffeted him; and others smote him with the palms of their hands, saying, Prophesy unto us, thou Christ, who is he that smote thee?

It seems clear that the people who spat in Jesus's face were the councillors who had said he was guilty of death. Whether it was they, also, who smote him with the palms of their hands, and called upon him to say who had smitten him, is not so clear, because it might be assumed that Jesus knew the Sanhedrists and would have no difficulty in saying who had smitten him unless he were blindfolded, or the ruffians struck him from behind.

Mark's account of the maltreatment (XIV, 65) is the same as in *Matthew,* except that Mark says they covered his face before they smote him and called on him to prophesy.

According to *Luke* (XXII, 63), after Peter had gone out weeping bitterly we read:

> And the men that held Jesus mocked him, and smote him. And when they had blindfolded him, they struck him on the face, and asked him, saying, Prophesy who is it that smote thee? And many other things blasphemously spake they against him.

This was before Jesus had appeared before Caiaphas.

According to *John* (XVIII, 21, 22), in the house of Annas an officer of the high priest struck Jesus because he had told the high priest to ask the Jews what doctrine he had taught in the Temple. In the middle of the trial before Pilate, the procurator orders Jesus to be scourged.

Some unspeakable critics say this was an act of deep and sensitive humanity on Pilate's part. Humanity? To scourge Jesus, to let his soldiers put a crown of thorns on him, to call him, in manifest mockery, the king of the Jews, and to smite him with their hands; and then for the benevolent and sensitive judge to bring him forth in his ridiculous garb, and say to the crowds of Jews, "Behold the man!"

IV.   The Scene of the Mocking

There are three different stories in the Gospels of the scene of the mocking of Jesus. In order to see which is the true one it is necessary to examine them carefully and in detail.

The story according to *Mark* is, probably, the earliest of the three.

After Pilate had yielded to the demand of the Jews that Jesus should be crucified, and when he had scourged him until the blood came, he delivered him to the soldiers, naturally and obviously the Roman soldiers, who led him away into the hall called Prætorium, and they called together the whole band of soldiers.

There they clothed him with purple, plaited a crown of thorns and put it about his head, and saluted him, "Hail, King of the Jews!" They smote him on the head with a reed, and spat upon him, and bowing their knees to him they pretended to worship him.

And when they had mocked him, they took off the purple cloak from him, and put his own clothes on him, and led him out to crucify him.

The story according to *Matthew* was, probably, the second to be written.

After Pilate realized that his efforts to save Jesus from death did not prevail, but rather tended towards the making of a tumult, and after he had washed his hands in public as a sign of his innocence of the blood of an innocent person, and he had delivered Jesus to be crucified (in other words, had condemned him to death), and after he had scourged him, the soldiers of the governor (Roman soldiers) took Jesus into the common hall and gathered the whole band of the soldiers, and they stripped Jesus and put on him a scarlet robe, plaited a crown of thorns and put it on his head, put a reed in his right hand, and bowed the knee before him and mocked him, saying, "Hail, King of the Jews!"

They spat upon him, took the reed out of his hand and smote him on the head, and after they had mocked him, they took the robe off him, put his own raiment on him, and led him away to be crucified.

This account seems to me to be not only revolting but senseless and intolerable. Why should the Roman soldiers do this? Had they any grievance against Jesus? None whatever. Did they believe that Jesus was guilty of the crime charged against him by the Jews? It is highly improbable that they believed it. Their master, Pilate, did not believe. They had seen him wash his hands of the guilt of his death, and they had heard him again and again, and down to the last moment, declare Jesus to be innocent and a just person.

Did they think they would please Pilate by this scene of revolting brutality to one whom he had pronounced innocent? It is impossible to believe it.

Did they suppose they were showing honour to Cæsar, their emperor, by dressing up a pretender and impostor in mock robes of royalty? Cæsar would hear nothing about it.

Were they merely enjoying a wild debauch of cruelty in their common hall among themselves? It is almost too silly a thing to think about. Were they not Roman legionaries, or, failing that, Roman auxiliaries, and did they not pride themselves on the dignity of their conduct in war and peace? They had always done so. And although examples of barbarous conduct on the part of Roman soldiers are to be found in history, such another example of needless barbarity to a helpless man (whom their governor did not believe to be guilty, and whom he had been compelled to condemn to death out of sheer fear of Jewish representations to Rome on what he knew would be a hypocritical and lying accusation) is not to be found in Roman history.

There is not a vestige of motive to account for the Roman soldiery behaving with this barbarity to Jesus. On the contrary, there would have been a motive for their revenging themselves on the Jewish authorities by any means that lay within their power.

Finally, if the disgusting scene took place in the common guard room of the Roman soldiers, who was there to report it? The legionaries were hardly likely to do so.

The story according to *John* is in some measure more believable. After Pilate had convinced himself that Jesus had committed no political crime, and had told the Jews that he (as the Roman governor) could find no fault in him, and after Pilate had failed to get Jesus released as the prisoner whom he was by custom required to release at the Passover, at the choice of the Jews, Pilate scourged Jesus, which he had no right to do, before condemning him to death by crucifixion, and then his soldiers plaited a crown of thorns, and put it on the head of Jesus, piercing his temples as their rough hands crushed it down, and then in ribald mockery they flung over his shoulders a soldier's cloak of the imperial colour, and said, in sham homage as they bent the knee before him, "Hail, King of the Jews," and smote him with their hands.

Then Pilate came out to the Jews again, taking Jesus with him, in his mock crown and mock robe of royalty, and presenting him to the Jews he said, "Behold the man!"

There were no cheers, nor wishes that his life might be prolonged. Upon seeing Jesus, thus clad and stricken and bleeding, the chief priests and the officials cried out, "Crucify him, crucify him!"

Pilate answered, "Take him and crucify him yourselves; I find no fault in him."

The Jews replied, "By our law he ought to die, because he has made himself the Son of God."

Pilate became afraid at hearing that, and taking Jesus back into his judgment hall he said, "Whence art thou?" but Jesus did not reply.

Pilate asked Jesus why he did not answer. Did he not know that he (Pilate) had the power to crucify or to release him. Jesus told him he had no power whatever except what was given to him by God.

Pilate's fears took another form then, and he tried to obtain the release of Jesus. But then the Jews cried out, "If you let this man go you are no friend or servant of Cæsar. Whosoever makes himself a king speaks against Cæsar."

Pilate was utterly beaten. He brought Jesus out again and taking his place on the judgment-seat he said to the Jews, "Behold, your King!"

"Away with him, away with him, crucify him!" cried the Jews.

The pagan Pilate, with scarcely veiled contempt for the barbarian rabble before him then asked, "Shall I crucify your king?"

"We have no king but Cæsar," answered the Jews.

Then Pilate delivered Jesus to be crucified, and they led him away.

The motive of the mocking scene is clear in *John*. The story by John shows that if Jesus was dressed up and mocked by the Roman soldiers, it was by the direct order of Pilate, in order that he might show his contempt of the Jews by presenting Jesus to them in the character of a king.

The development of motive in Pilate is as follows:

1. He does not believe that Jesus has made a political claim to kingship, and thinks he sees that the chief priests have made the charge against Jesus out of envy of his influence with the people.

2. He tries to get him released by persuading the Jews to accept him as the prisoner whom the Roman governor by custom releases at the time of Passover.

3. When the Jews refuse the release of Jesus and demand the release of a common robber, Pilate's anger and contempt suggest to him a form of derision.

4. He causes Jesus to be first scourged as a common disturber of the peace, and then dressed up as a mock king, with a purple robe of royalty on his back, a crown of thorns on his head.

5. In this guise he brings him out to the Jews and says in derision, "Behold your King!"

It is a brutal and almost intolerable thing for a Roman governor to do to an innocent man, not yet tried and not condemned; but Pilate has his object.

The Jews know, as Pilate knows, that the only sense in which Jesus claims to be a king is a spiritual sense; but what of that? Rome will find that difficult to understand. And, furthermore, although this man may have no political aims, no desire to be a temporal king, yet his ignorant followers may understand that he has such ambitions, and may try to make him a temporal king.

The perils are twofold: (1) the peril to Rome of the multitude breaking into open insurrection; (2) the peril to Pilate himself from the representations which the Jewish authorities may make to Rome.

6. Therefore, in sheer fear, Pilate condemns Jesus to death, although he believes him to be innocent.

7. But his contempt and hatred of the Jews has now reached its height, and in sending Jesus to crucifixion he writes, or causes to be written, in Hebrew, Greek and Latin, the accusation on which he has condemned him, and orders that it shall be nailed on the Cross:

JESUS OF NAZARETH
THE KING OF THE JEWS

8. The Jews are furious at this derision, and say to Pilate: "Write not, the king of the Jews, but that he said, I am the King of the Jews."

To this Pilate answers, in his anger and contempt, "What I have written I have written."

Pilate's last words are easily understood. They are his justification to Rome. "This man was the king of the Jews, according to the mass of the people. As the king of the Jews I condemned him to death." The Jews have threatened to appeal against Pilate to Rome. Pilate puts himself right before Rome by hitting back at the Jews. It is *he* who has condemned their king, not *they* who have compelled him to kill a man called Jesus of Nazareth.

9. Thus Pilate turns the tables on the men who have forced his hand; he shuts their mouths on that subject for ever; and puts a black mark against them in the eyes of Rome.

10. In his next report to Rome Pilate would say, "There have been further tumultuous political scenes in Jerusalem, and I have had to put to death a man named Jesus of Nazareth who was called 'the king of the Jews.'"

The inferiority of this story is that a Roman governor treats an uncondemned man as if he had been found guilty, in order to show his contempt of the Jews, his enemies.

The story, according to *Luke,* is as follows. After Herod had questioned Jesus and received no answer, and after the chief priests and scribes had vehemently accused Jesus, Herod, with his men of war, set him at naught and mocked him, and arrayed him in a *gorgeous* (some of the Latin versions render this word *white*) robe and sent him again to Pilate.

Here the motive is clear. Herod was the son of the last of the kings of the Jews. He had hoped to be king of the Jews himself. By his father's first will it was intended that he should be king of the Jews. When his father's final will made him king only of

Galilee and his brother Archelaus king of Judæa, Herod went to Rome to appeal against his brother's claim. The result was that Herod became merely the tetrarch of Galilee, but he never ceased to covet the kingship of Galilee. He was finally deposed (a few years later) in an attempt to prevail upon the emperor to make him king. He had lived an evil life and was unpopular with his people.

One of his people, the prophet John the Baptist, had denounced him as a breaker of the law of Moses, and therefore one who ought to cease to be a ruler and to be excommunicated, perhaps stoned to death. He had killed John, and this had caused him to be hated by his subjects. This man, Jesus of Nazareth, was another and more dangerous prophet. He had preached a doctrine which made him (Herod) not only a breaker of the law of Moses, but an outlaw from all the children of God. He had called him "that fox."

Herod's father (Herod the Great) had, according to tradition been so far from welcoming the coming of the Messiah that he had destroyed the young male children of Bethlehem in the hope of destroying him with them. To say that Herod Antipas would adopt any attitude except one of hostility to a supposed Messiah is to talk nonsense. He had long wanted to get this Jesus of Nazareth into his power. When Pilate did him the courtesy of sending Jesus to him he was glad. His day had come. But, unless he was a fool, he knew he had no jurisdiction over his own subject in Jerusalem for an offence committed in Judæa.

He saw through Pilate's motive in sending Jesus to him. He was not to be caught in the trap of repeating (even if he had the power, which he had not) in the case of Jesus the stupid mistake he had made in the case of John the Baptist.

But there was no reason why he should not express himself through the person of the pretender, by making him a subject of sport and derision. So, before sending him back to Pilate with a polite message, he caused his soldiers to dress Jesus up as a mock king and so *sent him back,* as if saying, "This is what I think of the king of the Jews! An actor! A mountebank! A charlatan!"

Are we to assume that the mocking by the Roman soldiers was rehearsed by the Jewish soldiers of Herod in advance?

V. Conclusions

I reject the story in *Matthew* and *Mark*. I think the truth lies in a combination of the stories in *Luke* and *John*. I think it was according to the character of the envious reprobate that Herod was to think of deriding Jesus and the claims he made and the claims made for him by dressing him up as a king and sending him back in that guise to Pilate. Then when Pilate received him back from Herod he took Jesus again to the Jews in his courtyard and said, "Behold your king!" I think he was prompted to do this by the motives indicated in my summary of the story according to *John*. I think the rest of the story is as recorded in *John*.

I consider it not improbable, indeed highly probable, that Jesus went to the Cross in the clothes in which Herod clothed him, and that the garment for which the Roman soldiers cast lots was not his own toil-stained garment, in which he had travelled from Cæsarea Philippi and slept in, on the Mount of Olives, but the "gorgeous garment" which Herod had thrown over his head in derision of his claims as king. That Herod intended the gorgeous garment as a mark of honour is preposterous.

Looking over these accounts of the maltreatment of Jesus after his arrest, I see one outstanding and significant difference between his maltreatment in the house of the high priest and in the houses of the temporal rulers, Pilate and Herod Antipas.

In the house of the high priest the maltreatment and mockery is directed solely against Jesus's claim to be the Messiah, the Christ, the Son of God. Hence the blindfolding, the calling upon him to prophesy, meaning that if he were a god he would know things without seeing them.

On the other hand, the maltreatment and mockery in the houses of Pilate and Herod is all directed to hold up to derision Jesus's supposed claim to be a temporal king. Hence, the crown of thorns, the purple robe, the bowing before him in obedience, the "worshipping" him, the salutation of "Hail, king of the Jews!" The attitude to him is totally different. In the one place he is a sham prophet. In the other places he is a sham king.

This corresponds perfectly to the charge or accusation, and is to me one more convincing proof of the authenticity of the story of Jesus's arrest, trial and condemnation. If the story had been a legend, a myth, somebody would have slipped and tripped up on this secondary point.

Nobody does in the Gospels. The only slipping up is found in the apocryphal Gospels written centuries later by ignorant people who did not understand, and particularly in the Acts of Pilate, written probably in the first century, the writer being a palpably ignorant person, giving a false account from the first line to the last, except so far as he borrows from and caricatures the Gospels.

In considering the maltreatment of Jesus we have to remember that he was fettered. He was first bound in Gethsemane. Still bound in the house of Annas. Still bound when sent from the house of Caiaphas to Pilate. Then he was probably liberated from his fetters while under trial before Pilate. Probably bound afresh to be sent to Herod, and liberated again on being returned to Pilate.

Obviously, Jesus was not bound while being maltreated by the Roman soldiers, for they put a reed in his hand. But almost certainly he was bound afresh when sent to his Crucifixion.

Probably it was because he was fettered on going to Calvary that another was made to carry his Cross. There is no apparent justification for the legend, perpetuated by Christian art, that Jesus carried his Cross at first and then broke down from exhaustion.

Taken altogether, the arrest, trial and condemnation of Jesus makes one of the basest stories of heartless selfishness in human history. One looks in vain for one unselfish impulse.

Some of the scenes accessory to the trial, such as the incidents of Judas and Peter, are shocking. The act of betrayal by Judas is to a certain degree mitigated by his repentance, his suffering and his death by his own hand. The act of denial by Peter is mitigated by his remorse, and by the fact that the world could have known nothing about his offence if he himself had not revealed it— put himself in the stocks. But there are moments when I hardly know which seems to me the worst act.

The conduct of the other disciples is cowardly and contemptible, only to be excused on the ground of their gross ignorance. They never for one moment understood Jesus while he was alive. The women who followed Jesus alone showed loyalty, love and courage, down to the last moment. It was a woman who stood by his grave.

But the great fact, transcending all other facts in the history of this great crime, is that while the Jews, the Roman governor and the disciples behaved throughout with gross selfishness, Jesus was behaving with an unselfishness such as the world had never witnessed.

He was going to his death as he believed, and repeatedly declared, to redeem the world. When, by a word, he could have saved himself, he did not say it. He stood silent against the basest and falsest charges.

Why? Because he believed that God had appointed that he should die for the world which in its blindness was killing him.

It is difficult to say which of the two leading parties to the wrongful condemnation of Jesus is the more culpable—the Jews, who made what they *knew* to be a false accusation against Jesus (they had tested his loyalty and found it right), or Pilate, who sent to death a guiltless man. The one party was getting out of the way a man who was likely by his influence to destroy their power. The other was merely saving himself from danger at the hands of his Roman masters, from the lying reports which he thought the Jews would not hesitate to make against him—that he had refused to put to death a man who was plotting against the rule of the Roman emperor.

In short, I see no escape from the conclusion that, judged from the point of law, the trial of Jesus was an almost farcical outrage on justice (both in its hurried and irregular procedure and in the verdict), an outrage on common morality and an irremovable blot on the priests of the old Judaism.

I see nothing to justify it. The Jewish priests were indeed fighting for their existence, but they had no right to exist. The Roman governor was indeed fighting for his governorship. But the Jewish priests and the Roman governor behaved in the full result like criminals. They killed an innocent man, *knowing him to be innocent*.

The chief priests handed Jesus over to the Roman court, altering the charge, so that the offence was not blasphemy against God, but treason against Cæsar. Therefore the condemnation and crucifixion of Jesus can only be accounted for on the ground that the chief priests did not believe that Jesus was the Son of God.

Did Jesus believe he was the Son of God—not merely the Messiah, the messenger or servant of God? I think he most certainly did. If he had not done so he might have escaped from death at the hands of Pilate by calling witnesses to prove that he had been a perfectly loyal subject of Cæsar, paying his tribute, and so on. But he knew that he was the Son of God, and therefore the king of the Jews, as of all men, and that if his teaching prevailed it *must* destroy Cæsar and all such rulers, as well as the Temple with its priests.

Did the disciples believe Jesus was the Son of God? Obviously, not during his lifetime. They thought he was the Christ, the messenger and servant of God, and they believed he would do as the prophets said the Messiah would do—establish a king of Heaven by re-establishing the throne of David.

But after his death and resurrection the disciples did indeed believe that Jesus was more than the Messiah—the Christ was more than the Messiah; he was the Son of God; he had ransomed man from sin by his death and made his atonement with God.

I cannot account for the subsequent lives of the disciples—for the sufferings which they cheerfully bore, for the martyrdom they went through and gloried in—except on the ground that they believed Jesus to be the Son of God.

In the fourth Gospel that belief goes to the utmost length. John believes that Jesus had been with God from before the beginning of the world; that he existed before Abraham. That Jesus did not attach importance to the fact (if such it was) that he was by blood lineally descended from David is shown by the passage in *Matthew* (XXII, 44) in which Jesus quotes David as saying, as about the Christ, "Lord, sit thou on my right hand till I make thine enemies thy footstool." David called Christ the Lord. How then could the Christ be David's son?

I think Jesus attached a much higher meaning to the name Christ than belonged to the name Messiah.

VI.   The Attitude of Jesus Towards His Trial

If the Jews had not actually believed that the claim of Jesus to be the Christ-King, the Son of God, was an imposture, they would not have dared to ask Pilate to crucify him—it would have been fighting against God.

And if Jesus, on his part, had not as firmly believed that he was the Christ-King, the Son of God, he could not possibly have stood silent when he was charged with offences which he could easily have disproved.

It was because Jesus actually believed himself to be the Christ-King, the Son of God, and that he was to die at the instigation of his people and at the hands of the Romans, that he stood practically silent at his trial, and allowed himself to be condemned to death.

At the same time it was because the disciples, notwithstanding their repeated assurances of loyalty to death, had either never truly believed that Jesus was the Christ-King, or because their belief had suffered a paralysing shock when he was arrested, and had been killed by his condemnation and by his Crucifixion as a common malefactor, that they fled away from his side in his last hours.

It is not possible, therefore, to account for the Crucifixion on any other ground *than that Jesus believed he was the Son of God.*

In like manner it is impossible to account for the fact that the chief priests called on the Roman procurator to crucify Jesus except on the ground that he claimed to be the Son of God, and that the chief priests thought he was not and that to say he was the Son of God was blasphemy, for which the law of Moses required that a man should die.

All this does not exclude the personal desire of the priests to get rid of a troublesome person who would destroy their class, but it rises above it, and puts the chief priests on a higher level.

Nowhere in the story of Jesus is the unseen power presiding over and predetermining his destiny seen to be operating more clearly and powerfully than in the course of the trial before Pilate.

The efforts made by the Jewish authorities to bring him to his death, the helplessness of the Roman governor to resist these efforts to destroy a man who, though guilty of blasphemy according to Jewish religious law, was innocent of sedition and treason according to Roman civil law—all this, with the lying, concealment and duplicity attending it, and all leading up in the end to the condemnation of Jesus, is a picture of human helplessness in the hands of higher powers, such as does not exist anywhere else in history or yet in imaginative art, such as the Greek drama.

It is overwhelming in the impression it makes of inevitableness. We feel that nothing can resist it. A mighty higher power is rushing events on and on to the end it finally reaches. Jesus had to die this death. It *MUST* have been.

CHAPTER XXXIII

The Way of the Cross

I. *The Attitude of Pontius Pilate*

THE POSITION IS that Jesus has been condemned to death by the Roman governor for beginning a seditious insurrection. It has not gone far; it has not reached any overt act of rebellion. But one man, Jesus, has claimed the sovereignty of Palestine and its inhabitants. Jesus has said he is the king of the Jews. In saying so he has in effect denied the sovereign rights of the Roman emperor. Jesus and Cæsar cannot exist together. A great multitude of the Jews are accepting Jesus in the character of the king of the Jews.

Therefore, the only course open to the representative of the Roman emperor is to put an end to Jesus—to get him out of the way. The Roman way of putting an end to a traitor is to treat him as the Roman law treats brigands, burglars and thieves generally—to crucify him, the form of punishment which is the lowest, the cruelest and the most contemptuous.

It is true that, although the Roman governor has condemned Jesus to death as a traitor to Rome, he does not believe that Jesus has been guilty of any treason to Rome. On the contrary, he believes he is innocent of any kind of treason. He sees that he is claiming only a kind of spiritual kingship. To Pilate this spiritual kingship is a kind of harmless folly. A man might properly be whipped for it, because it is disturbing the minds of foolish people —the rabble—and might possibly lead to trouble of some sort. But that is all.

Pilate would have much preferred not to punish Jesus of Nazareth with death, since he had done nothing to deserve death. But he has yielded to the importunate demands of the Jews that Jesus should be crucified, because he thinks that they will otherwise make complaint against him to Rome. He has had bitter experience of their complaints on two former occasions when he

927

was in the wrong. And now that he is in the right he is far from sure that he will not suffer, be reproved, perhaps removed, perhaps banished, seeing that the Jews have such a plausible case— a man contesting the rights of the Roman emperor to rule as king over the Jews.

Pilate has seen through the artifice of the Jews. They have been merely using him (and the power of Rome) to do what they cannot legally do for themselves—put to death a man who has offended against Jewish law. If they had been able to stone Jesus, they would have stoned him without more ado. He had been guilty of blasphemy in saying he was the Son of God, and that was an outrage which their laws punished in old days with death. But since they were now under the Roman occupation, and had no power over life and death, they must wait for their Roman masters to execute Jesus. Happily, the offence against Jewish law could be made to look like an offence against Roman law. This was a fundamental offence. The offence of Jesus against Jewish law was a religious offence. But translated into the terms of Roman law it was a political offence. So Rome must do what they (the Jews) could not do—it must put Jesus of Nazareth to death.

Pilate saw all this, and was angry that by a kind of blackmailing he was to be compelled to do what he did not want to do—put a man to death for an offence against the Roman occupation who was really innocent of any such offence. If Pilate had been a braver or better man he would have said, "Do your worst against me. Report me to Rome if you like. Say that in releasing this man I am not a friend of Cæsar's, whose servant I am expected to be. Rome may possibly listen to you. I may perhaps find it difficult to make Rome understand that you are using it as a means to your own ends—a means to carry out your ridiculous religious laws which Rome would naturally condemn and despise. Rome may decide against me, and remove me and even banish me. But no matter! I know I have no right to put this man to death; and come what may to myself *I will not do it.*"

But Pilate was not the man to take this course. He was a coward and a bully, and therefore he submitted to the threats of the Jews. But he despised the Jews, and made no disguise to them of his contempt.

Such is the point reached when Pilate gives Jesus up to be crucified.

Pilate had called as witnesses only the priests and the rulers of the people. He had not called the common people. Nor did the common people come to him. Nor did Nicodemus and Joseph of Arimathæa among the rulers raise their voices when Pilate was waiting and watching for an excuse to save a man whom he knew to be guiltless. All this occurred between the evening of Thursday and the morning of Friday.

Thus the class that brought about the condemnation of Jesus was that of his lifelong enemies the Pharisees, the elders, the rulers, the rich men and the chief priests, whom he had denounced as hypocrites, as whited sepulchres, as grinders of the faces of the poor, to whom he had denied the kingdom of Heaven that was to come, on whom he had prophesied all woes, hunger, wailing, outer darkness, and damnation.

To bring about the betrayal of Jesus this class had resorted to a base trick, and to effect his condemnation they had lied foully, consciously and openly, and played, in relation to the Roman powers, the part of hypocrites, professing a zeal for Cæsar which they did not feel.

Jesus, on his part, had allowed himself to be the victim of falsehood. He could have explained what he meant by calling himself the Son of God, but he did not. He could have denied that he had forbidden people to pay tribute to Cæsar, but he did not. He could have shown that he had set up no claims to be the king of the Jews, but he did not. He was not allowing himself to be condemned in error. He was in truth the Son of God, and the king of the Jews, and Cæsar had no right to men's tributes, but why should he attempt to explain? Besides, had he not come to die? And was it not part of his gospel that man should not resist evil? He could bear it, for God was with him.

II. The Disciples After the Condemnation

When it became known among the followers of Jesus that he had been condemned to death, the consternation would be great. The poor whom he had taught, the sinners whom he had forgiven, the sick whom he had healed, the blind to whom he had given sight, all the rags and tatters of the Jews and Gentiles would gather in the streets of Jerusalem—the streets in which he had done no violence, in which he had put forth his hand so often to heal, to comfort and to bless. They would gather, too, about the house of the two women at Bethany.

Perhaps the disciples, as the men most in danger, had hidden themselves. Perhaps the mother of Jesus, hearing of his sentence, had conquered all other feelings in her motherly love, and, separating herself at all costs of anger from her kinsfolk, had hastened from Nazareth to Bethany. She may have remembered certain visions she had while bearing Jesus, and recalled her sense of God's purposes with him. Jesus had recalled them all, though not as she had then expected. She saw things plainly now, and remembered the song of her heart "My soul doth magnify the Lord. . . . He hath put down the mighty from their seats, and exalted them of low degree. He hath filled the hungry with good things, and the rich he hath sent empty away." That had been the gospel of Jesus. The song of her heart while Jesus was yet within her womb had been the keynote of all the doings of his life. Now Mary realized all.

The two Marys would be closely drawn together at this time of trouble. They would follow Jesus from the house of Pilate to that of Herod, and from Herod's house, clad in his mock regal robes, back to Pilate's. They would see him mocked and smitten and blindfolded. They would understand why he submitted. But among the multitude of the followers of Jesus there would be the beginning of the misgivings that Jesus foresaw. Some had hitherto been in awe of his supernatural powers. Why could he not now save himself? The faith of these waxed cold.

But the faith of others waxed more hot. Jesus would yet assert his power. He would never die on the Cross. Let the priests and the Pharisees go on. They could not kill him. He would take himself out of their hands at the last moment. He would even descend from the Cross before their eyes. He could not die. Had he not said that the kingdom of Heaven was near? Had he not said that he was himself to rule in that Kingdom? How then could he die?

But these were only a few. The great body saw nothing but disaster. Jesus had fallen, and the gospel of the Kingdom had gone. The Kingdom had been a dream. Things were not to be reversed; the poor were not to inherit the earth; the rich were not to be cast down; the sinners were not to be received back by their Father in Heaven. All that had been a vain vision. Jesus was to die.

Then another group of believers, forgetting the Kingdom, giving no thought to the prophet, remembered only the man. Him they mourned as a companion lost, a tender friend, and a powerful ally. No respecter of persons, no truckler to the great, he was fierce before the strong, gentle only to the poor and the weak and the downtrodden and heavy-laden. The sweetest, meekest, strongest, bravest soul in all the world of God. This company was mainly a company of women; and they were bewailing and lamenting him. Chief among these was the woman who ministered to him—Mary Magdalene—and with her, perhaps, the other Mary, his mother. To these Jesus turned and said:

> Daughters of Jerusalem, weep not for me; but weep for yourselves, and for your children. For, behold, the days are coming in the which they shall say, Blessed are the barren, and the wombs that never bare, and the paps which never gave suck. Then shall they begin to say to the mountains, Fall on us; and to the hills, Cover us.

The women must have understood him.

Perhaps the company of women and the poor that followed him were those only that mourned the man. Afar off, following slowly, waiting and watching for the deliverance of Jesus from the hands of his enemies, were those who had known his healing power—the blind who had been in darkness, and could see their healer going up to Calvary with the Cross behind him. These were looking for fire from Heaven to destroy the soldiers and the priests and the Pharisees, and to set the Master free.

Yet farther back may have been the disciples, in terror lest they should share the fate of Jesus. And perhaps alone, not near to these but afar off, hiding himself, trying to see unseen, in terror, half in hope—Judas, waiting and watching. Who shall say he was not there?

The way of the Cross from the hall of judgment to Calvary would not be the narrow and twisting Via Dolorosa, but along a broad military road that ran to the Damascus Gate. But this is by no means certain. For some fifteen centuries the Church of the Sepulchre has been accepted as the true site of the Crucifixion. Of course, the Romans might have crucified Jesus within the walls of Jerusalem; but Pilate was not likely so far to outrage Jewish susceptibilities. John says the place was "nigh unto the city." It is named by three of the evangelists by the Hebrew word Golgotha. Luke says Calvary, and gives no interpretation, and they all define it as meaning "the place of a skull."

III. Crucifixion

Crucifixion was a purely Roman form of punishment. It was unknown in Mosaic law, wherein the punishment of death was by stoning. Why, then, did Jesus so frequently speak of the Cross? It is the badge of suffering, also of death. It is frequently in his mind. When his end seems near, he appears to hint at death by crucifixion—*"when I am lifted up."* What does all this mean? Did he expect to die by crucifixion? If so, he expected to die at the hands of the Romans. Perhaps Jews frequently died by crucifixion at the hands of the Romans. When they threatened the public peace, or claimed to dispute the sovereignty of Rome, they were, no doubt, crucified.

But Jesus had made no attempt to disturb the powers of Rome. If he claimed to be the king of the Jews there is no sign that he ever dreamt of driving the Romans out of Palestine. Why, then, his frequent references to the Cross and Crucifixion?

There are frequent references to the Cross in the words of Jesus to his disciples (see *Matthew* X, 38). Those who shall be saved must take up their cross and follow him.

All these references lead to the suspicion that after the death of Jesus, and in memory of the death he died, the writers of the Gospels put words and phrases into his mouth which were not likely to have been spoken by him. Jesus can have had no thought that he was to die on the Cross—that he was to carry the Cross— to take it up and carry it. All this looks like an afterthought. Did he, by divine foreknowledge, know that he was to die the death of the Cross? Then why his cry from the Cross, "Why hast thou forsaken me?"

Crucifixion was thought by the Romans to be a shameful death. Therefore, they doomed slaves to crucifixion. They frightened robbers, thieves and rebels with crucifixion. Cicero speaks of it as a most cruel and disgraceful death, painful, lingering and ignominious. Origen and other early Fathers say that crucified persons often lived two days on the Cross. The piercing of the hands and feet caused intense suffering. The sufferer screamed. The wounds throbbed, burned and bled. The strain on the body led to strain on the heart. It often happened that after a few hours the heart was ruptured. There was great thirst. Sheer humanity led the onlookers to offer an opiate or a sop of narcotic drink to deaden and stupefy. The executioner generally allowed this to be done.

The cross, itself, was not so high as is generally supposed. Sometimes there was a projecting bar which served for a seat or support for the body, and there was occasionally a rest for the feet. Sometimes, instead of being nailed, the feet were bound with cords.

On arriving at the place of crucifixion the victim was stripped of his clothes, and after receiving a cup of wine, sometimes medicated to stupefy against pain, he was nailed to the cross. Sometimes this was done while the cross was lying on the ground, and then the cross was raised and dropped into a hole that had been dug for it. In some cases the cross was raised first, and then the victim was hoisted up to it and nailed. This would give most trouble to the executioners and most agony to the condemned.

Always there was a transverse piece near the top of the upright beam, for the outstretched arms. On the piece of the upright beam above the transverse piece the head rested, and then to this, too, it was usual to fix a superscription giving his name and stating the offence for which he was being crucified.

The superscription on the Cross at Calvary is supposed to have been derision of the Jews on the part of Pilate. Nothing of the kind. It was Pilate's self-defence. Having been forced by the Jews to execute an innocent man (one whom he believed to be innocent of the charge made against him), Pilate determined to protect himself from his masters the Romans, as well as from any double-dealing on the part of the Jews, by making a public statement of the crime for which he had condemned Jesus. Jesus was the king of the Jews. He had condemned him for that treason against Tiberius. If in the future any trouble arose, if his conduct was called in question, he would turn to the witness of his public superscription—*the King of the Jews*.

Thus the tragic revenge of Pilate on the Jews for the pressure they had brought to bear on him. They had threatened him. He had had to yield. But he would protect himself by charging the Jewish people. This man Jesus was their king. He (Pilate) had had to put him down in defence of his master, the emperor. They (the Jews) could not open their lips without disclosing their double-dealing. They had forced him, but now he had them in his hands—the King of the Jews! So Pilate thought to protect himself in the eyes of Tiberius with this expression of the Jews. A bitter revenge! A deserved one!

In my view this interpretation of the superscription on the Cross raises the incident to great heights of sinister tragedy.

Crucifixion was a lingering punishment and a painful one, since the wounds in the hands and feet did not lacerate any large vessel. Death came by the slow process of nervous strain and exhaustion, added in some cases to thirst and hunger. As mentioned before, Origen and other early Fathers said that crucified persons often lived two days on the cross. Under the Diocletian persecution a man and his wife who suffered in the year 286 are said to have hung nine days and nights. In the same year, twin brothers of an illustrious Roman family were, it is said, bound to two pillars, with their feet nailed, and remained so for a day and a night, and then were stabbed with lances. There are many stories of crucified persons being stabbed on the cross to hasten death. On the other hand, it was one of the terrors of the cross, held out to criminals, that their bodies would be left in suspense until the ravens picked their bones clean. To be denied sepulchre was an added terror.

The remarks attributed to Pilate about the sudden death of Jesus show that death on the cross was generally slow. The answer given to him by the Roman soldiers leaves no doubt that Jesus was actually dead, unless we are to assume that they had their own reasons (such as bribery) for saying he was dead when he was not. The exclamation of the Roman centurion, "Truly this man was the Son of God," is interpreted by believers as proof that Jesus had power to lay down his life and to take it again, being in their view proved by the words spoken immediately before, "Into Thy hands I commend my spirit."

Against this is the story of Matthew, which appears to show that not the words of Jesus, but the natural phenomena of the quaking of the earth, the rending of rocks, and the graves opening, and the dead rising, caused the centurion to say, "Truly this was the Son of God"—meaning that nature had undergone convulsions at his death. It was a widespread belief among pagan nations that both at the birth and death of divine persons nature showed commotion. In *Mark* it is merely the fact that Jesus cried in a loud voice *after* he had previously said, "My God, my God, why hast thou forsaken me?" that caused the centurion to say, "Truly this man was the Son of God."

A very illogical conclusion on the centurion's part from such facts.

In *Luke* the words of the centurion followed most nearly after the words of Jesus, and have most appropriateness. Jesus was submitting to the will of God, and commending his spirit to God, therefore the centurion said, "Certainly this was a righteous man," a very different and much more natural exclamation. Tertullion says, "He spontaneously dismissed his spirit with a word." The early Fathers fastened on to the words of Jesus as proof that the centurion regarded the death of Jesus as miraculous. It sounds like nonsense. Lightfoot defends the statement that Jesus died voluntarily by his words in *John* X, 17, 18: "I lay down my life, that I may take it again. No man taketh it from me, but I lay it down of myself. I have power to lay it down, and I have power to take it again." But these words of Jesus were fully explained by the fact that he deliberately went up to Jerusalem—they had no reference to the immediate incident of his death.

The loud voice with which Jesus cried from the Cross after all his sufferings in Gethsemane and at his trial is advanced as further proof that he was still a strong man when he died, and therefore he died of his own free will. Such writers will not allow themselves to recognize the fact that on his human side Jesus was nothing more than a man. They say he deliberately dismissed his soul when his work was finished. The apostles, Stephen and Peter, had no such illusions. They said plainly that Jesus had been murdered by crucifixion.

That Jesus died as a man is abundantly shown by all the four narratives. He was not a physical weakling, as some of the early monks would have us infer. He had been a strong man, undergoing fatigue from long journeys, and prolonged periods of fasting and privation. When he died it was from complete exhaustion, accelerated perhaps by some physical accident due to exhaustion. He died from agony of mind; from agony of body; resulting probably in a sudden rupture of the heart. The heart was the organ chiefly attacked by the incidents of the last weeks of the life of Jesus.

This is an explanation in complete harmony with all we know of the sufferings of mankind in general from prolonged and acute heart strain, when all the passions are brought into play.

The contrast between the loveliness of the Judæan springtime and the agony-broken figure on the Cross torn by the apparatus of crucifixion was terrible to a degree which the people of these later centuries do not clearly realize. Many of them see in thought the horrors of earthquake and darkness that accompanied and followed the Crucifixion, and all the terrors of the rent rocks and the upheaval of all nature; but very few, and especially few among modern women, ever visualize what Jesus himself looked like in these supreme and awful hours. When they see him in imagination upon the Cross, they see him clean, well toileted, attractive in appearance, and full of dignity, as when he had prepared himself for the last night's supper. Why do they never see him as he actually was, with his hair wet and sticky with sweat and blood, and his face scarred with blows and smeared with the foulness of the streets—which had been flung at him—and with the spittle of the Roman soldiers, and his body contorted and piteous, as well as horrible to see, with his agonies and his wounds and the marks of his scourgings? Is their faith not strong enough to bear the contemplation of him in the grim light of Truth?

Jesus suffered all the excruciating agonies of crucifixion and his sufferings were not mitigated by his divinity. He actually died on the Cross. To deny that he died in the human sense is to deny everything that is fundamental to Christianity. No man can be a Christian who denies it.

Let us now review the four stories of the four evangelists in relation to the Crucifixion.

IV. According to Matthew

It was now (although *Matthew* does not mention it) a little before nine o'clock in the morning, so swiftly had the trial and condemnation of Jesus taken place. It was the month of April, and at that hour in Jerusalem the sun would be up, and the city would be stirring. A crowd would certainly gather. The soldiers set out with their prisoner, and "led him away to crucify him."

Two other prisoners, common thieves, were to be crucified the same morning, but whether they went to the place of execution at the same time as Jesus, Matthew does not say. Probably they did. The place of execution was called Golgotha (meaning the place of a skull). Clearly, this was not in Jerusalem itself, but in some natural formation of earth and rock outside the city. It was not far from the city. A natural opening in the hilly land beyond, making, as seen from the gates of the city, the shape of a skull. Such was Golgotha.

The victim had by Roman usage to carry his own cross. It was beneath the dignity of a Roman soldier to carry it.

Clearly (though again, Matthew does not say) the torture to which Jesus had been subjected during the night at the hands of the brutal soldiers had so weakened him that he could not carry his Cross. It is not unreasonable to believe the tradition which speaks of the spurring of him on when his strength failed him under the burden, and that he fell. One can believe that the Roman soldiers had small patience with the delay. This job must be got over. Perhaps they had been told to get it over, lest the rabble who only a few days ago had come down the hill with Jesus, shouting "Hosanna," might make an effort to rescue him.

Accident helped them. They came upon a man of Cyrene, named Simon, and they compelled him to carry the Cross, while Jesus, almost certainly fettered, walked in front of him. It was a common practice of the Roman soldiery (a kind of unwritten right) to compel any passer-by to carry burdens for them.

On reaching Golgotha the Roman soldiers crucified Jesus. Matthew does not give any account of the Crucifixion itself. We know from secular history (Josephus) what kind of execution it was.

The two thieves were crucified at the same time, one on the right hand and the other on the left.

When the act of crucifixion was finished, and while Jesus hung on his Cross, the soldiers began to divide his clothes among themselves. This was according to custom. We are told that the clothes of a crucified prisoner were the perquisite of his executioners. According to *Matthew* the soldiers cast lots over the garments. It is a frightful picture—the Saviour on the Cross above, and below his executioners on the ground casting dice as to who should have his clothes!

It was also usual to fix on the head of the cross a paper stating the name of the condemned, and his crime. On the paper set over the head of the Cross of Jesus was written:

THIS IS JESUS THE KING OF THE JEWS

Obviously, this superscription was the work of Pilate, a last derisive stab at the Jews who had forced his hand.

Golgotha was not far from a high road. Those that passed by, coming into Jerusalem, and going out of it, looked up at Jesus and reviled him, wagging their heads and saying, "Thou that destroyest the temple and buildest it in three days, save thyself. If thou be the Son of God, come down from the Cross."

Matthew, anywhere, does not report Jesus as saying that he would destroy the Temple and rebuild it in three days, but other evangelists do.

The chief priests also are at the Cross, and they mock Jesus, saying among themselves, probably so that he can hear, "He saved others; himself he cannot save. If he be the King of Israel, let him now come down from the Cross, and we will believe him. He trusted in God; let Him deliver him now, if He will have him; for he said I am the Son of God."

The chief priests are now more sure than ever that the pretensions made by Jesus (that he was the Christ) are fully disproved by his helplessness. He had no power in himself, or he would now exercise it for himself. And God does nothing for him—therefore God is disowning him. The thieves also who were crucified with him, cast his former pretensions and his present helplessness in his teeth. It is not said in *Matthew* that one of the thieves became penitent.

This reviling scene goes on, according to *Matthew,* from nine o'clock in the morning until twelve o'clock noon. Then the sun of the Palestinian morning disappears, and darkness gathers. The darkness is "over all the land," and it lasts for three hours, until three o'clock in the afternoon. It is an earthquake: "the earth did quake and the rocks rent."

About three in the afternoon Jesus cried with a loud voice, "Eli, Eli, lama sabachthani" (*"My God, my God, why hast thou forsaken me?"*). Until now he had thought he could drink the cup God had given him to drink, he could meet the whole agony of the death God had intended him to die. But his strength of soul, as well as body, was failing him. Perhaps he was asking himself, "Why? What is the good? Will any such good come of all this as I have believed and foreseen? Is it for this that I have given up so much? So many of the joys of life? Has it all come to—this?"

It is even possible that the Devil, who had tempted him before, returned to tempt him again at this last extremity of his strength, and whispered, "You see what it has all come to—this? If you had only listened to me, I could have given you everything. Above all, happiness and power."

His soul was sinking.

Then it appears that in a moment of recovered spiritual strength he became conscious of all this. He had expected God's strength to be with him to the very last, to support him to the end, no matter what he had to go through. Was God forsaking him at the moment when he needed Him most? He was.

"My God, my God, why hast thou forsaken me?"

The great human cry—the cry of the man. The great divine cry —the cry of an awaking God.

If any of the Palestinian Jews heard the cry of Jesus they must have understood it. We are not told that they did hear it. But the Roman soldiers hear it. They do not understand Aramaic, but they have heard about Elias. During the past few days especially, the name has been on every Jewish tongue. Elias is the Jewish prophet who did not die, but was taken up to Heaven in the body, and will (according to the Jews) come again to re-establish the Jewish nation and create the kingdom of God which they believe will be the end of the world. So the Roman soldiers (clearly the foreigners who do not understand the cry of Jesus) say, "This man calleth for Elias."

One of the Roman soldiers understands that Jesus is in great agony. He runs, takes a sponge, fills it with vinegar, attaches it to a reed (a long stick), and holds it up to Jesus that he may drink.

But his fellow-soldiers say, "Let be, let us see whether Elias will come to save him."

Then Jesus cried with a loud voice and died.

It is probable that he died literally of a broken heart, due to the prolonged strain of body and spirit.

Apparently, Jesus died at three o'clock in the afternoon of the day before the Sabbath of the Passover. It was dark—there was an earthquake. Matthew reports that during this earthquake and perhaps at the time of the death of Jesus, the veil of the Temple was rent in twain, from the top to the bottom. (This was the veil that hid the part assigned to the people from the Holy of Holies into which the priests alone entered.) The earth quaked and the rocks were rent.

It is three o'clock, the ninth hour; Jesus died in the dark.

The disciples of Jesus were not there. They were still hiding from the Jews of the Temple, fearing they might share the same fate as Jesus. Not one came near Jesus at that last moment. But some women were braver. They were Galilean women. They had ministered to him of their substance. They had followed him from Galilee to Jerusalem. One of them was Mary Magdalene, "out of whom he had cast seven devils." Another was Mary the mother of James and Joses. Another was the mother of John and James, the sons of Zebedee.

These women were looking on from "afar off." They saw Jesus die, if not too far away. It was three o'clock in the afternoon. The darkness (of the earthquake) continued until that hour.

Jesus died in the dark.

V. *According to Mark*

The story of the Crucifixion as told in *Mark* does not differ in any important particulars from the story as told in *Matthew*. So closely are they related that they suggest that one was copied from the other, the greater part of the words being the same, and the order of incidents being identical.

Certain differences there are, and these may have been due either (1) to the later copy (whichever it may have been) being made from memory (in that case a very retentive memory), or (2) that the second reporter had, from more exact knowledge, deliberately altered the earlier versions.

The following are the chief similarities and disparities:

After Pilate had scourged Jesus, his soldiers led him away into the hall, called Prætorium. The revolting scene of the mocking of the royalty of Jesus is the same.

Simon the Cyrenian is said to be "coming out of the country." He is also described as the father of Alexander and Rufus. Simon may have been coming, on the morning of the day before the Passover, to Jerusalem from some place in which he lived, or worked, to keep the feast. His sons Alexander and Rufus became Christians.

The drink which the Roman soldiers offer Jesus is described by Mark as wine mingled with myrrh, not (as in *Matthew*) vinegar mingled with gall. Probably much the same thing.

The reason of the soldiers casting lots for the garments of Jesus is more clearly explained by Mark (although obvious enough in *Matthew*) that each man might know what he should take.

The superscription over the Cross was merely:

THE KING OF THE JEWS

Scripture is quoted as being fulfilled in the fact that Jesus was crucified between two thieves ("And he was numbered with the transgressors"). Absurd and trivial.

The story in *Mark* does not say anything about an earthquake, the rocks being rent, the graves being opened.

The third woman afar off (unnamed in *Matthew*) is called Salome in *Mark*. Salome was the name of the mother of James and John.

VI. *According to Luke*

It will be observed that the story of the Crucifixion in *Luke* also has its points of difference.

Jesus walked to Calvary ahead of Simon, who was carrying the Cross. There followed Jesus a great company of people (and of women) who bewailed and lamented him. Jesus turned to the women and said, "Daughters of Jerusalem, weep not for me. . . ." The place of execution was called Calvary. When they crucified him, with the malefactors, one on the right hand and one on the left, Jesus prayed for his executioners, and perhaps for the Jewish enemies, saying, "Father, forgive them; for they know not what they do." And they parted his raiment and cast lots.

And the rulers also derided him, saying, "He saved others; let him save himself, if he be Christ, the chosen of God."

Thus, the scoundrels of Jews returned to their original ground of grievance against Jesus (that of blasphemy against God, not treason against Cæsar) when they had at last effected his condemnation and nailed him to the Cross.

The soldiers joined with the people who stood by in mocking him, and offering him vinegar. Luke, being an Alexandrian, probably did not know that a kind of vinegar was the usual drink of the Roman soldier, a sort of sour wine.

Luke records that the superscription over the Cross was written in Greek, Latin and Hebrew, and that it said:

THIS IS THE KING OF THE JEWS

One of the malefactors railed at Jesus, saying, "If thou be Christ, save thyself and us." The other malefactor rebuked the first, saying, "Dost not thou fear God, seeing thou art in the same condemnation? And we indeed justly; for we receive the due reward of our deeds, but this man hath done nothing amiss."

Then, as if converted to belief in Jesus, he said, "Lord, remember me when thou comest into thy kingdom," and Jesus answered, "To-day shalt thou be with me in Paradise." Was this promise fulfilled?

It was not, if we are to believe the later story told in *John* (XX, 17) that Jesus forbade Mary Magdalene to touch him, *because* he had not yet ascended to his Father—in other words, he had not yet entered Paradise. Where had he been? In hell, as the Church said?

In the story as in *John* (eight days after his Resurrection) he had still not ascended, and yet he told Thomas to put his hands in his wounds. One is tempted to ask, Where does the story of the penitent thief come from? Who reported the incident? The Roman soldiers? The Jews? Mary the mother? John? How did the thief know anything about the innocence of Jesus? It reads like fiction, bad fiction.

It was then three in the afternoon. The same darkness and rending of the veil of the Temple, but nothing about an earthquake or about the graves opening and the dead arising.

Jesus cried with a loud voice, "Father, into thy hands I commend my spirit." And having said this he died. No failure of his soul as in *Matthew* and *Mark*.

As in *Matthew* and *Mark,* Jesus died at the ninth hour—three in the afternoon. The darkness was still over the earth. It lasted until the ninth hour. As in *Matthew* and *Mark.* Jesus died in the dark.

I think it fair to assume with Luke that Jesus went to his Crucifixion in the "gorgeous robe" which had been thrown over his head in derision by Herod Antipas, and that this garment (not the toil-stained garment in which he had travelled from Cæsarea Philippi to Jerusalem, and in which he had slept on the Mount of Olives) was the garment for which the soldiers cast lots. "And they parted his raiment, and cast lots" (*Luke* XXIII, 34).

VII. *According to John*

In the Gospel of John we are told that Jesus bears his Cross. There is no mention of Simon as carrying the Cross. The place of Crucifixion was "nigh to the city." John says it was Pilate who wrote the title above the Cross. It was in Hebrew, Greek and Latin, and it ran:

JESUS OF NAZARETH
THE KING OF THE JEWS

The chief priests of the Jews said to Pilate, "Write not, the king of the Jews, but that he said, I am king of the Jews." Pilate answered, "What I have written, I have written."

The soldiers, in dividing the garments of Jesus, cast lots for his coat, because it was "without seam, woven from the top throughout." This again was "that the Scripture might be fulfilled, which saith, They parted my raiment among them, and for my vesture they did cast lots."

John alone makes reference to the presence of Mary the mother of Jesus at Calvary:

"Now there stood by the Cross of Jesus his mother, and his mother's sister, Mary the wife of Cleophas, and Mary Magdalene." Jesus, seeing his mother, and the disciple whom he loved, said to his mother, "Woman, behold thy son!" Then he said to the disciple, "Behold thy mother!" And from that hour that disciple took her into his own home.

There are obvious difficulties here. How did the mother of Jesus come to be at the foot of the Cross? We do not hear in any of the Synoptics that she was one of the three who came up with him from Galilee. The last time we heard of her she was coming with his brethren to restrain him and carry him away, thinking he was beside himself.

Among the brethren was Joses, who afterwards became the first bishop of the Christian Church at Jerusalem. In *Acts* the mother of Jesus and the brethren are with the disciples within forty days after the Crucifixion. Why should Jesus have given Mary into the care of John? We have no reason to believe that John (if he was the son of Zebedee) had a home of his own. We have reason for thinking he was a very young man. And how did John come to be by the Cross? The other disciples had fled away, and were in hiding for fear of the Jews. John must have fled also. It is not to be believed that he was the disciple who took Peter into the high priest's house at the trial of Jesus.

Jesus, knowing all things were now accomplished, said, "I thirst." He then said, "It is finished," bowed his head and died.

VIII. Conclusions

There are no *essential* differences between the stories of the Crucifixion as told in the four Gospels; but there are many minor differences.

The two first, *Matthew* and *Mark,* are practically identical, and are either copied from each other, or from a common source. *Luke* owes something either to *Mark* or *Matthew* or the common source, but adds something of his own. Luke's story is the least suggestive of the supernatural, being the story of the death and burial of an innocent man, who was good to the end and who touched the spectators with a sense of great pity.

John's story is an entirely independent one, being deficient in some important points of the other stories, having various additions (particularly of the presence of the mother of Jesus at the Cross) and frequent references to prophecy. It is not so human as the other narratives. The human story is in *Matthew* and *Mark.* It makes no preparation for the Resurrection.

I think the stories in the four Gospels are on the whole, historically harmonious.

We are told in *Matthew* (XXVII) that as the fateful procession came out from the hall of judgment they found a man of Cyrene, Simon by name; him they compelled to bear the Cross. It was usual to make the condemned carry his cross. The reason why Simon was called upon to carry it is not to be found in *Matthew, Mark* or *Luke.* In *John,* as we have seen, Jesus did carry his Cross. But the other Synoptics speak of Simon. Why did Simon carry the Cross?

My conclusion is that Jesus was in fetters. This would be for the same reason that he was fettered in Gethsemane on the way to Annas, and again on the way from Annas to Caiaphas and again from Caiaphas to Pilate, because the authorities, knowing "the world was running after him" were even yet afraid that an attempt might be made by the people to rescue him. There were "multitudes" in Pilate's court. It would now be between 8 and 9 o'clock in the morning. Jerusalem would by this time be fully active. Even the Roman soldiers, of whom there might be many, could not run any risks in the narrow streets of the city if a disturbance arose. Therefore, Jesus was again fettered. He would be fettered hand and foot.

Consequently he would be unable to carry so cumbrous a burden. It was considered utterly beneath the dignity of a Roman soldier to carry the Cross, and they compelled the first Jew they met on coming out of the soldier's quarters. This Jew was named Simon.

It is a pitiful thought that the precautions against an uprising of the people for the rescue of Jesus proved to be quite needless. Not a soul among his immediate adherents appeared. The disciples, even those who had made the loudest protestations of going to death with him, were not in sight. The people Jesus had cured did not come. Blind Bartimæus, Lazarus, the mighty army of them— many of whom might be expected to come up to the Passover, or to follow him up after they had been healed—none was there. Only perhaps a seething mob of his enemies, crying, "Away with him! Crucify him!" And all this only a few days after the entry into Jerusalem, with the branches and cloaks and the cries of "Ho-sanna." What a picture!

"And when they were come unto a place called Golgotha . . ." There is no indication of where this place was. But it must have been outside the city walls. This was necessary. An execution within the city would have been a violation of Jewish custom, which even Pilate would not attempt. It must have been the usual place of execution. We are not told that it was the place outside the walls that was nearest to the palace of Pilate, otherwise it would have been on the south-western side of Jerusalem. There is nothing in *Matthew* to say where Golgotha was.

"They gave him vinegar to drink mingled with gall; and when he had tasted thereof, he would not drink."

Crucifixion was a horrible, fearful punishment, and therefore humanity suggested a stupefying drink to deaden the sense of pain. Jesus refused this drink. He intended to suffer to the utmost.

The Roman soldiers conducted the Crucifixion, and then parted his garments, having stripped him for crucifixion. The clothes of a condemned prisoner are understood to have been a perquisite of the executioners. Observe here that nothing is said about dividing Jesus's money. Clearly, he had no money. When Jesus died he had not a penny in his pocket, or we should have heard of it. Never is there a suggestion from his bitterest enemies that he made money by his mission.

"And sitting down they watched him there." A terrible scene. The man on the Cross. The soldiers sitting in front of him.

"And set up over his head his accusation written, This is Jesus the king of the Jews."

"Then the soldiers, when they had crucified Jesus, took his garments, and made four parts, to every soldier a part."

Does this mean that there were only four Roman soldiers at the Crucifixion? It is incredible. With the great company of the people who sympathized with Jesus it is unbelievable that Pilate would trust his captive and two malefactors to four soldiers. There were more, probably a large body of soldiers, but only four executioners—four were enough to crucify—the rest would keep the crowd away, and in order.

"And also his coat, now the coat was without seam; woven from the top throughout."

Was this garment the gift of one of the Galilean women who ministered to him? It is most unlikely. Apparently the soldiers thought it valuable, and it is therefore probable that it was the mock regal robe in which he had appeared in the Prætorium.

They said "Let us not rend it, but cast lots for it, whose it shall be, that the Scripture might be fulfilled, which saith, they parted my raiment among them, and for my vesture they did cast lots."

This passage comes from *Psalms* XXII, 18: "They part my garments among them, and cast lots upon my vesture." Once more David is lamenting to God about his own forlorn condition. He is not prophesying the fate of a future Messiah.

The adaptation of this passage of Scripture to the incident of the soldiers casting lots for the coat of Jesus casts grave suspicion on its authenticity. It suggests that the casting of lots is the afterthought of the apostles, who, after the death of Jesus, were scouring the Scriptures for every passage that could possibly seem to apply to his life.

Apart from this the incident makes a thrilling scene—the dying man on the Cross, the four Roman executioners, having stripped him to crucify him, casting lots for his garments. It is a fearful picture.

Now comes a startling episode.

Now there stood by the Cross of Jesus, his mother, and his mother's sister, Mary the wife of Cleophas, and Mary Magdalene. When Jesus therefore saw his mother, and the disciple standing by, whom he loved [I dislike this recurring phrase intensely; he loved all of them, but this one, John, presumes to say that the Master loved him especially; perhaps John was the youngest, and almost a boy, and hence he may have had more tenderness of manner shown to him], he saith unto his mother, Woman, behold thy son! Then saith he to the disciple, Behold thy mother. And from that hour that disciple took her unto his own home.

Had the mother of Jesus been one of the company of women who had come down with him from Galilee? If so, we never hear of it. Only twice before have we heard of the mother of Jesus during the ministry of Jesus—at the wedding in Cana; and when she thought he was beside himself and she came with his brothers to take him away.

It would be natural that she should come up for the Passover, with others of the household in Nazareth, her husband, Joseph, presumably being dead, and hearing of the arrest and condemnation of her son, she might quite naturally, have been brought by John. Equally naturally the Roman authorities might have permitted the mother of the crucified to approach the foot of the Cross, and allow his disciple to accompany her.

The words of Jesus are, however, difficult. He is committing his mother to the care of one of his disciples, the youngest of them, perhaps. It has been said that, leaving her himself, he wished to provide for her protection. But he had left her from the day he departed from Nazareth (if that was still the family home) to begin his ministry. And then what need had she of the protection of John, if she had other sons? If it is said (as it has been) that she had probably estranged them (being themselves estranged from Jesus, not believing in him), the answer is that forty-eight hours later they were (according to *John*) to be found sitting with her among the disciples. And then, is it likely that John had any home of his own at that time? Or must we conclude that he took the mother of Jesus to Zebedee's house? Is there anything in John's subsequent history (outside the irresponsible foolishness of apocryphal Gospels) to encourage the idea that Mary the mother was ever afterwards with him?

And then is it not recorded that one of the brothers of Jesus became the head of the Church at Jerusalem, and remained so until about A.D. 66 or 68? If Mary the mother died, as tradition says, about A.D. 56, is it at all probable that she did not die at the home of her son James, the bishop of Jerusalem?

But what is the value of the incident? It does not account for any special knowledge by John of the early life of Jesus, for John says nothing about his birth, infancy, and early life. We have to go to *Matthew* and to *Luke* for these—both remote sources.

"After this, Jesus knowing that all things were now accomplished, that the Scriptures might be fulfilled, said, 'I thirst.'"

There was a vessel of vinegar (the common drink of Roman soldiers) standing there. One of them gave a drink to Jesus on a sponge. After receiving it, he said, "It is finished," and died.

All this suggests that Jesus was living long enough to see all the Scriptures fulfilled that had reference to him, and having seen all fulfilled he said, "It is finished," and died.

It is difficult to accept such a story, except as the opinion of the evangelist. The words may have had a far higher significance— that he had finished the work that God had given him to do.

It was the preparation day—Friday, at three o'clock. The Sabbath was near, and this Sabbath was also to be the Passover—the first day of unleavened bread. The Jews held it against their custom that an executed man should be hanging on the cross during the Sabbath—so they asked Pilate (probably sending to him for that purpose) to allow the legs of the three men to be broken, so as to hasten death, that their bodies might be taken down and buried. Pilate appears to have consented to this, and the soldiers broke the legs of the two malefactors, but coming to Jesus, and finding that he was already dead, they did not break his legs. One of the soldiers, however, pierced his side with a spear, and the evangelist reports that "forthwith came there out blood and water."

As if foreseeing that this would be disbelieved, the evangelist makes a special point of saying that he saw it, and that the record he makes of it is true. Further, he says it that you (his readers) may believe. Also, he says that the incident is the fulfilment of two passages of Scripture, one of which says that "a bone of him shall not be broken," and the other that "They shall look on him whom they pierced."

It is very obvious that the place of Crucifixion was near a highway along which people passed. The chief priests, scribes and elders had followed from Pilate's palace to see the execution carried out. It is significant that, once outside the house of the Roman governor, the feature of a political offence on the part of Jesus was dropped, and the Jewish authorities reverted to the grounds of offence they had at the inquiry before the Sanhedrin—the offence of Jesus's claim to be the Son of God, no longer of his claim to be a rival to Cæsar.

IX. *The Two Thieves*

"The thieves, also, which were crucified with him, cast the same in his teeth" (*Matthew* XXVII, 44)—that if he were the Son of God, let God deliver him.

It is possible, but intensely inhuman. Nevertheless, it is conceivable that in their agony the two thieves may have uttered this utterly illogical taunt. It is useless to point out how illogical or how barbaric.

In *Mark* it is mentioned that two thieves were crucified with him, one on the right hand and the other on his left. And it is also said that "they that were crucified with him reviled him."

In *Luke* it is said that "there were also two other malefactors, led with him to be put to death," and that they were crucified one on the right hand and the other on the left.

But here comes this additional incident:

> And one of the malefactors which were hanged railed on him, saying, If thou be Christ, save thyself and us. But the other answering rebuked him, saying, Dost thou not fear God, seeing thou art in the same condemnation? And we indeed justly; for we receive the due reward of our deeds; but this man hath done nothing amiss. And he said unto Jesus, Lord, remember me when thou comest into thy Kingdom. And Jesus said unto him, Verily I say unto thee, To-day shalt thou be with me in Paradise.

In *John* it is said that two others were crucified with him, on either side one and Jesus in the midst. But nothing further is said about them. Thus, all four Gospels say that two thieves were crucified with Jesus, one on each side of him. But two say they reviled him. One says nothing about what they did. And Luke alone says that one reviled him and the other reproved the reviler, and begged Jesus to remember him when he came into his Kingdom. Apparently the malefactor knew the mission of Jesus. He understood by it that Jesus was going to a heavenly Kingdom. He did not share the opinion of the disciples (now in hiding) that it was an earthly kingdom which Jesus was about to set up. Surely this passage was written at the end of the first century (not earlier), when the hope of the coming of an earthly kingdom was dying out or dead!

"And Jesus said unto him, Verily I say unto thee, To-day shalt thou be with me in Paradise."

But if by Paradise Jesus is understood to have meant Heaven, in the presence of God (not in the intermediate place the Jews believed in, where the souls of men waited for the Judgment, while their bodies lay in the grave), it was a promise not fulfilled, for, as we shall see presently, at dawn on the first day of the week (about forty hours later) he told Mary Magdalene he had not yet ascended to his Father, he had not yet reached Heaven. The apocryphal Gospel of the second century (the Gospel of Nicodemus) tries to explain this by bringing both Jesus and the malefactor into Hades, immediately after their death on earth.

Luke's is a doubtful story. There is nothing to account for the conversion of the thief. It presupposes that he believed in Jesus before he was himself arrested, tried and condemned to death.

It is not indicated, in *Matthew*, at what hour Jesus was put on the Cross, but it is said that from the sixth hour (that is 12 noon) there came darkness over the land, and that it lasted until the ninth hour (3 P.M.).

And about the ninth hour (3 P.M.) Jesus cried with a loud voice, "Eli, Eli, lama sabachthani"; that is to say, "My God, my God, why hast thou forsaken me?" The cry is in the Aramaic language, the native language of Palestine, the language commonly spoken in Jerusalem as well as in Galilee. Jesus's mother-tongue. The words themselves are a quotation from the Scriptures (*Psalms* XXII, 1). The lamentation of David about himself.

Was it consistent with the character of Jesus that he should so cry out? Why did he think God had forsaken him? Were his physical sufferings so much greater than he had expected? Many men have died painfully. Was he suffering the pain of the punishment of all the sinful world? Or was he suffering from the sense of his abandonment by his disciples? It was enough, but had he not foreseen it?

"Some of them that stood there, when they heard that, said, This man calleth for Elias."

The "some of them" must have been persons who did not know the Aramaic language. Therefore they cannot have been Jews—

born Jews. They may have been Jewish-Greeks. Or more probably they may have been the Roman soldiers. But if the latter, what suggested to them that Jesus (in the word Eli) was calling for Elias? The Romans would know nothing of the Jewish prophets. Even if they had heard (as they might) that Elias was one of the chief of the Jewish prophets, they would not be likely to know the intricate fact that Elijah was, according to Jewish prophecy, to appear at the same time as the Jewish Messiah, whom Jesus, according to his accusers, was claiming to be.

"And straightway one of them [again them] ran, and took a sponge, and filled it with vinegar, and put it on a reed and gave it him to drink."

A preparation of vinegar was a customary drink of Roman soldiers, therefore our first thought is that the man who gave it to Jesus (out of reach on the Cross, and therefore only to be handed up on a sponge at the end of a reed) gave it out of an impulse of compassion for the sufferer, whose agonies had forced a loud cry from him.

"The rest said, 'Let be, let us see whether Elias will come to save him.'"

This shifts the incident from the Romans, back to the Jews. The Romans would have no idea of a dead (or translated) prophet coming back from the spirit world to succour the dying Messiah. But the Jews might think of that as a possible thought of Jesus.

"Jesus, when he had cried again with a loud voice, yielded up the ghost."

Thus far, the story in *Matthew,* making allowance for slight difficulties, is plain, simple and direct. What follows is full of very serious difficulties.

> And behold, the veil of the Temple was rent in twain from the top to the bottom; and the earth did quake, and the rocks rent; and the graves were opened; and many bodies of the saints which slept arose, and came out of the graves, *after his Resurrection,* and went into the holy city, and appeared unto many.

Observe that this convulsion of nature plays no further part in the story of Jesus than to affect the mind of the Roman centurion. The incident of the saints waking, but not coming out of their tombs until after the Resurrection of Jesus, does not correspond with Jewish belief. It is a ridiculous picture—the saints alive in their tombs and waiting some thirty-six hours before coming out. It requires another theory of the place of the dead.

> Now when the centurion, and they that were with him, watching Jesus, saw the earthquake, and those things that were done, they feared greatly, saying, Truly this was the Son of God.

There does not seem to me a line or phrase in this that can possibly have belonged to the story as originally written by the author, Matthew. It is all saturated in legend and myth. The rending of the veil of the Temple, if it happened, could not have been known until later, and is in itself only possible as a supernatural incident, and only valuable as being intended to convey a symbolical meaning. The earthquake and the opening of the graves and the arising of the saints who had slept are incidents which (having produced no subsequent events) are beyond belief; the anticipated assertion that *after the Resurrection* (no mention of the Resurrection having been made before) the dead saints went into Jerusalem and were seen there by many is a transparent afterthought, partly intended to meet the difficulty that it was believed by St. Paul and others that Jesus was the "first fruits of them that slept"; and, finally, the words attributed to the Roman centurion after he had marvelled at the things which had occurred in the hour of Jesus's death—"Truly this was the Son of God"—are a manifest attempt to put into the mouth of a pagan a conclusion which was utterly impossible to him unless (and until) he became a convert to Christianity.

In my opinion the whole passage from Chapter XXVII, 51–54 betrays unmistakably in substance, in thought and in style, the mark of a much later writer. It is an interpolation which is, I think, in every way damaging to the historic value of the story of the Crucifixion.

> And many women were there beholding afar off, which followed Jesus from Galilee ministering unto him; among which was Mary Magdalene and Mary the mother of James and Joses, and the mother of Zebedee's children.

I find it profoundly moving that only the women of Jesus's company came into the zone of danger; not one of the disciples came. It cannot be said that they did not know that their Master was being led to his Crucifixion. The women knew; therefore they

would know. It cannot be said that perhaps they had not yet got
back to Jerusalem, for thirty hours later we find them there. Only
the women came, and of these those who had loved much.

"And there followed him a great company of people, and of
women, which also bewailed and lamented him."

Who were these people, a great company? I am satisfied that
they were not the avowed followers of Jesus; that they most certainly were not his disciples. I think they were the ordinary inhabitants of Jerusalem and the people who had come from distant
places to keep the Passover, perhaps many Galileans among them.

I think they lamented the fate that had befallen him; but the
second clause of the verse pertains only to the women. Once more
we have the pathetic fact that the women alone had the courage to
show sympathy.

> But Jesus turning unto them [the women] said, Daughters of
> Jerusalem weep not for me, but weep for yourselves, and for your
> children. For behold, the days are coming, in the which they [the
> children] shall say, Blessed are the barren, and the wombs that never
> bare, and the paps which never gave suck. Then shall they begin to
> say to the mountains, Fall on us, and to the hills, Cover us. For if
> they [the rulers of the Romans and Jews this time] do these things
> in a green tree, what shall be done in the dry? [*Luke* XXIII, 28–
> 31]

What are we to understand by this moving passage? Clearly
that Jesus foresees the downfall of the existing order. It needed
no divine insight to do so, only a clear brain. Such a condition as
the one of which he was himself the victim, in which, by the corruption of the Jewish religious classes, their subjection to the
Romans, and the Roman usurpation of power in Palestine, could
not last. It must all end in complete disaster. The Jewish people
would suffer. They would be dispersed. The children of the women
who were weeping for him would weep for themselves. Daughters
of Jerusalem, weep for yourselves, and for your children. I cannot doubt that this passage is historic. It has the authentic voice
of Jesus. It was spoken probably in a pause in the slow progress
of that fateful procession from the city to the rising ground of
Calvary.

When Jesus is crucified he cries, "Father, forgive them, for they
know not what they do." This, too, is in the true spirit of Jesus.

Throughout the Gospel stories of the Crucifixion we see the

purely human side of Jesus. His love of man. His self-sacrifice. This is the end of it—the great spirit ending in ignominy and shame. The great pathetic human story. His own people destroying him. The heartrending pathos of it. So the world has dealt with all the great prophets. It has stoned them all. This is how they end.

Then the scheme of God is clearly apparent. God had sent His prophets. The world had not listened. It had gone on its evil way. At last He sent His Son. A part of Himself. To call the world of men back to Him by speaking through him. Now the world had slain His Son. Man killed his God.

But the end is not yet. As from the tombs of the prophets the Spirit of God had spoken to the world of men, so out of the tomb of the Son of God the salvation of man was yet to come. God would not suffer His Holy One to see corruption.

The great sun that will rise above the tomb!

Those who read the Gospels carefully must see that during the six hours Jesus was on the Cross his sufferings, which could hardly fail of being great, never clouded his mighty mind or disturbed his divine soul—until the end. The few words he spoke from the Cross show that the pains of his body did not compel him, for so much as an instant, to think only of his own condition.

"My God, my God, why hast thou forsaken me?"

At the very close of the sixth hour he uttered a piercing cry and died.

I conclude that, worn out by long strain and suffering, which never conquered his unconquerable will, a swift and sudden access of physical pain killed him in great agony—may be that he died of an instantaneous rupture of a vessel of the heart. I feel sure that his death was terribly painful.

CHAPTER XXXIV

The Three Days

I. *At the Foot of the Cross*

THE PEOPLE GATHERED round the Cross. Mary Magdalene at the foot of it, weeping; Mary the mother, beside her; some other women, and a few men and some children who loved Jesus. But the wailing of these was unheard in the derision and merriment of those who rejoiced to see Jesus die. The priests and elders and Pharisees and rulers of the people and rich men generally wagged their heads at him. He could save others, why could he not save himself? Let him come down from the Cross if he could! Look now and see what his miracles had been worth! They had been all a sham, and imposture! This man had no powers from God. If he had been the Christ, the chosen of God, now God must save him. God did not. God was letting him die. He was no Son of God. He was a son of Beelzebub.

And the soldiers had mocked him also, while they divided his clothes among them and cast lots for them. One of the two robbers also mocked at him and said, "If thou be the Christ, save thyself and us." But the other reproved his fellow, saying that they were punished justly, but "this man hath done nothing amiss." And then, turning to Jesus, he said, "Lord, remember me when thou comest into thy Kingdom." And Jesus said, "To-day thou shalt be with me in Paradise." Did this come to pass?

It was the hour of the last temptation of Jesus. If he could conquer the devil this time every tittle of the law would be fulfilled. He had seen himself insulted and derided, spat upon and smitten in the face, clad in mock robes of a king and crowned with a mock crown of thorns. This was the death he had come to, and he could bear it, for God was with him. Through the lips of the priests and Pharisees he heard the Devil tempt him to forget God or curse Him. He must have heard the Devil whisper, "God has been with you in many miracles. God has let you cleanse the leper, and give sight to the blind, and bring back the dead to life. But God who has given you power to do so much for others does nothing for yourself." He must have shut his ears to this, for the angel of God strengthened him, and God was with him.

He saw the soldiers mock at him, the passers-by make sport of him. And the Devil must have whispered, "Is it for men like these that you are here on the Cross instead of walking the world like other men?" But he prayed, "Father forgive them, for they know not what they do."

From the Cross he must have seen afar off the company of those who waited and watched for the manifestation of his power, and for the fire from Heaven that was to consume his enemies. He must have known that these would go away humbled and crushed, for they must see him die and then their faith would wax cold. And the Devil must have whispered, "Have you been so long with these people and still they do not know you?" And that must have gone to his heart.

He must have seen his disciples still farther off, looking on in fear and trembling, thinking first of themselves and of the safety of their own lives. And the Devil must have whispered again, "See, did you not say that the spirit was willing but the flesh was weak? Did you not tell them to pray lest they fell into temptation? Where are their brave vaunts now? Look, are these the chosen ones to be baptized with your baptism?" And his heart must have sunk.

Perhaps he saw Judas Iscariot far off, hiding in the clefts of the rock, peering out with eyes of shame. And the Devil must have whispered, "Thus is your gospel dishonoured in the eyes of men by treason from within. Your gospel was to conquer human passions, but in him has human passion conquered your gospel? Look, he has preferred before you that poor harlot at your feet." And his heart must have sunk lower still.

Finally, at the foot of the Cross he must have seen many poor women, and two above all. One was his mother, and the world had separated her from him until now when he was to go from the world. The other was the woman who had been a sinner, Mary Magdalene, who had followed him and ministered to him; who had washed his feet with her tears and wiped them with the hair of her head; whose tears had brought tears to his own eyes; whose sorrows had been sorrows to him; who had seen his reproach, his shame in the eyes of the world, and who had clung to him to the last.

And the Devil must have whispered, "Look at her. She is there. You put aside that human love for the sake of your gospel. Your gospel was for the poor. Where are the poor now? Where are those whom you healed? Where are the blind to whom you gave sight? Where is Lazarus to whom you gave back life? They are all gone. What is the end of it all? Yonder crowd on the hillside is going off. They see that God is not to snatch you out of the hands of your enemies. You are dying. And only that woman is there— that harlot—only she, and such as she. And this is the end!"

And then Jesus cried with a loud voice, saying, "My God, my God, why hast thou forsaken me?"

But the angel came and strengthened him, for the angel must have whispered, "Look up, be strong, only hold out a little longer, only resist the Devil now, and all will be well. He is coming to you when you are weakest, he is preying on your human infirmities. But why throw away the labour of a life with one cry of submission now? That life has been well spent. You have kept the laws of God. You have shown that man may keep them. You have justified the ways of God with men. Only finish it now, and as long as man lives men will bless you, and speak of this hour, and picture it, and see you dying a conqueror. Other servants of God the world has slain. Now the world slays God's beloved Son. But your death will call men to repentance. It will ransom all who believe in you. Sinners will fall before your Cross, the poor will kneel there. You will be their King, their Comforter. None other name will they know under Heaven. This is to be your empire for ever and ever."

And then Jesus answered, "Father, into thy hands I commend my spirit."

It was only the sixth hour, but the darkness of night fell over the land. Three dark hours passed, and then feeling death upon him, Jesus cried with a loud voice, a voice of triumph, "It is finished"; and so died, a man only in flesh, a god in the spirit.

The Roman soldiers saw him die, and the centurion said, "Truly this man was the Son of God."

II. Mary the Mother of Jesus

If Mary the mother of Jesus was (as *John* alone says) at the foot of the Cross, her presence there may be accounted for by inference as follows:

She had lived with the carpenter's family during the earlier part of the ministry of Jesus. When Jesus left Nazareth and set out on his homeless wanderings, I think his mother remained with her kinsfolk and perhaps sided with them against Jesus. It is reasonable to assume that she did so reluctantly and with pain. I think when she went with "the brethren" of Jesus to take charge of him, thinking he was beside himself she did so with deep motherly solicitude for his welfare. I do not at all think she was one of the Galilean women who followed him to Jerusalem when he came up on his last journey. If she had been, it is impossible that we should have heard so frequently of other women, and so rarely of the one woman above all others who might have been with him.

It is shuffling to say that the presence of the mother of Jesus by his side must be taken for granted. The mother of Jesus not only may have come up to the Passover at the same time that Jesus came up to his death, but it is almost certain that she had done so. She came to the Holy City every year with her husband. And if Joseph was now dead, as seems more than probable, it is fairly certain that she would come up with the sons, particularly with James, who was perhaps a strict Pharisee, totally out of sympathy with Jesus.

The arrest of Jesus, and the report which would inevitably reach her in Jerusalem of his trial and sufferings, his condemnation and Crucifixion, would wring and agonize her motherly heart. She would then hasten in love and fear to his feet, and the most ruthless of Roman soldiers, and the hardest of Jewish high priests, would not forbid her approach. I find it difficult to believe that John (the son of Zebedee) could have been at the foot of the Cross. He was a person suspected of complicity in the blasphemies alleged against Jesus, and he must have been hiding in the company of Peter. A little later we are told that they were together on the Sunday morning, when they ran in company to the tomb. But if John was at the Cross it could only have been as the helper of the suffering mother of Jesus, who, it must be remembered, was old for that period and country, probably about fifty.

In coming to Jesus in his hour of need at the call of motherhood, Mary may have had to break with her people. This may have been either known to Jesus or divined by him. And seeing John and his mother standing together, John, a young and almost certainly unmarried man, devoted to him, and beloved by him, this fact may have prompted Jesus to the desire that his mother might be cared for by John, now that she was heartbroken and desolate. This is the only human interpretation of the words he addressed to his mother, "Woman, behold thy son," and to the disciple, "Behold thy mother!"

If, after the Resurrection, as Paul seems to say, Jesus appeared to James (and that James his brother, not either of the other two Jameses), the situation becomes one of intense poignancy of emotion, charged with a profound and almost tragically human appeal. But we have no record of that appearance, nothing but the mention of it.

What, then, about Mary in relation to James, now converted to the faith? Why did she not return to James, her son? Was it out of regard for the inner-consciousness of Jesus as to her position, or was it partly because James may have been married and had a wife, while John, so far as we know, remained unmarried to the end? John tells us that "from that hour that disciple took Mary into his own home." But during the days following the Ascension Mary the mother of Jesus, with his brethren, was (according to *Acts* I, 14) with his other disciples in the upper room, where they abode, probably abiding with them there, for John is said to be living there. From this we derive three inferences:

1. That if John had a home at that time he remained in Jerusalem.

2. That both Mary the mother of Jesus and the other brethren were with him there.

3. That the appearance of Jesus to James must have taken place within the period which elapsed between the Crucifixion and Pentecost.

Later, John the Evangelist was alone, an exile to the Isle of Patmos. He was then a very old man.

James, the brother of Jesus, had long before been murdered, and Mary (probably thirty years older than John) was almost certainly long dead.

Where or when she died we do not know. Tradition says it was at Ephesus when she was about fifty-seven years of age. If so, and if John the Evangelist was John the Ephesus, the story in the Gospel of John that Mary the mother of Jesus was at the Cross is supported (1) by known facts (2) by the reference in *Luke* to her presence in Jerusalem with the apostles in the time between the death of Jesus and his Ascension. But we do not hear of her at the burial of Jesus, and there is no mention of her at the moment of his first appearances after the Resurrection. He does not (according to the Gospels, *Acts* or St. Paul) appear to his mother after he has risen from the dead. That is serious. Our human side is hurt by this omission on the part of Jesus to comfort the one tender heart that would be most wounded by his death, and would have most joy in the certainty of his survival.

There is, however, the argument that by his death on the Cross, his hour having come and passed, he ceased to be human, and that at the Resurrection he had returned to his divinity, no longer man but God. All this strikes me as being of first-class importance.

III. Prophetic References

It is usually assumed that the act of breaking the bones of the two thieves on the cross on either side of Jesus was merely intended to hasten death, in order that the crucified ones might not remain on the cross on the Sabbath Day of the Jews. It was presumably the fact that Jesus was found to be already dead, requiring no such treatment, which prompted one of the Roman soldiers to pierce his side with a spear, thus, in effect, fulfilling the prophecy that no bone of him should be broken.

The prophecy "a bone of him shall not be broken" is quoted from *Exodus* (XII, 46), where it refers to the flesh eaten at the Passover. Again *Numbers* (IX, 12) once more referring to the feast, obviously the Passover, on the fourteenth day of the second month : "They shall leave none of it unto the morning, nor break any bone of it ; according to all the ordinances of the Passover they shall keep it."

The giving of the gall is supposed, in like manner, to fulfil the prophecy of the *Psalm* (LXIX, 21) : "They gave me also gall for my meat, and in my thirst they gave me vinegar to drink." But the psalm cannot, as a whole, be thought to come from the mouth of Jesus. Then why pick out one passage, detach it from the rest, and say *this* foretold Jesus, when the other passages clearly do not?

This is one of the infirmities of the prophetic references so frequent throughout the New Testament. One or two lines, sometimes one phrase, applies and is detached from its sequence ; all the rest is foreign to the event understood to be foretold. Vinegar was the ordinary soldiers' drink. A sour wine. The Roman soldier gave it to Jesus to quench his thirst. It did so. It was an act of mercy. But the soldier makes excuse for it—to keep Jesus alive in order to see whether Elias will come to save him.

The execution of Jesus was a murder, but it was a legalized murder. Everything was apparently in order. He died the death of the lowest criminal. He died the cruelest of deaths. Yet it was inevitable. It had to be. Not because the prophets had foretold this end, but because the future could not be what it has been if the death had not been so.

If this had been the absolute end of the life history of Jesus, what would have been the result? If there had been no further incident of any kind to come, where would Jesus be to-day in the eye of the world and the experience of the human soul? Would he be where Thaddæus is and Judas the Galilean—revolutionaries who had rebelled against corruptions in the Jewish religion?

IV. The Burial of Jesus

It was still but two or three hours later than 3 P.M. on that spring day when a rich man of Arimathæa, named Joseph, appeared on the scene of the Crucifixion. He was secretly a disciple of Jesus, and he went boldly up to Pilate and begged for the body of Jesus, that he might bury it in a new grave of his own. With Joseph came Nicodemus (the one who had come to Jesus by night) bringing a hundred-weight of a mixture of myrrh and aloes. The hundred-weight is significant, as also is the fact that Mary Magdalene and the other Mary were present, and saw Jesus buried in this vast quantity of spices for the burial. This incident conflicts with the reference made by Jesus himself, at the supper at Bethany, to the ointment which Mary is using as by anticipation of his burial. It is true that Jesus, except by divine intuition, could not have foreseen the act either of Nicodemus or of the two Marys.

The reference to Joseph as a rich man has suggested that he gave money to Pilate for permission to give the body of Jesus human burial. Later it is suggested that one of Pilate's successors hoped that even Paul (who had nothing but what he worked for) would bribe him, or get some rich friend like Joseph to do so. But bad as Pilate's record in other respects is, veniality of this kind is nowhere charged against him. He merely gave permission to a Jew who happened to be rich, and therefore influential, to take the body of the dead "king of the Jews" after he had done with it, and do what he pleased with it. The matter was one of indifference to Pilate then.

Joseph of Arimathæa is described as "an honourable councillor," obviously meaning a member of the Sanhedrin, held in high esteem. He is said to have gone in *boldly* to Pilate to crave the body of Jesus. It wanted some courage to do so. If he was a member of the council he had not protested. Was he absent? Was he also absent from the trial by Pilate? He came to ask for the body. It would, to Pilate, imply sympathy, a certain high respect for the dead prophet. It would sound in Pilate's ear like an accusation against an unjust verdict. He wished to give honourable burial to a dead criminal.

Pilate said nothing that is recorded about this. But he expressed surprise that Jesus was dead so soon. He asked the centurion (who had said "Truly this man was the Son of God"), and the centurion having assured him that Jesus was actually dead, Pilate gave Joseph the right to take down Jesus's body.

And when Joseph, with the help of Nicodemus, had taken the body down from the Cross, "he wrapped it in a clean linen cloth, and laid it in his own new tomb, which he had hewn out of the rock; and he rolled a great stone to the door of the sepulchre." This last fact is significant since it implies that the sepulchre was thereby made secure.

We do not always realize how very brief was the interval of time which elapsed between the Last Supper and the final episode of the burial of Jesus. But according to the Gospel calculations the arrest in the garden of Gethsemane, the series of trials, the Crucifixion, and the burial, all took place within so short a period as seventeen hours. Thus the picture at the close of the Crucifixion is of Jesus being hurried, almost hustled, into his grave, so that he might be buried before sunset on the evening of the Sabbath and of Passover.

It is further important to observe what space of time was covered between the burial of Jesus and his Resurrection. The interval is commonly believed to have extended to three full days. "On the third day he rose from the dead." But the first of the three days was almost at its close before the descent from the Cross. Jesus was buried at 5 P.M. on Friday. He lay in the tomb one hour before 6 P.M. which began the second day. He lay all the twenty-four hours of the second day, Sabbath, until 6 P. M. Then from that hour on Saturday (Sabbath), the end of the second day, until, say, 6 A.M. on Sunday. Thus:

1st day — 1 hour

2nd day — 24 hours

3rd day — 12 hours

Jesus was therefore about thirty-seven hours in the tomb, not three days.

V. After the Crucifixion: According to Mark

Joseph of Arimathæa is described by Mark as "an honourable councillor, which also waited for the kingdom of God." This suggests that Joseph was a member of the Sanhedrin. He is said to go to Pilate on the evening of the Crucifixion, "because it was the preparation, that is, the day before the Sabbath." Pilate, marvelling that Jesus was already dead, called for the centurion to say if this were so. Being satisfied, he gave the body of Jesus to Joseph.

Mark is in agreement with Matthew in giving only two names of the followers of Jesus as being present at his burial—Mary Magdalene and Mary the mother of Joses. They "beheld where he was laid."

Mark's story is simpler than Matthew's. It is realistic in nearly all its details.

VI. According to Matthew

After the death of Jesus, or at the moment of his death,

the veil of the Temple was rent in twain, from the top to the bottom; and the earth did quake, and the rocks rent; and the graves were opened; and many bodies of the saints which slept arose, and came out of the graves after his Resurrection, and went into the holy city, and appeared unto many.

Here is a very different story. That many dead bodies of the saints arose is a fact of which there is no mention elsewhere. Is it possible that if it had occurred the Jewish enemies of Jesus dared have gone one step farther against his followers? Such a miracle would have closed their mouths for ever. And what about the special importance of the Resurrection of Jesus if many arose from the dead? A legend—a very foolish legend—stuck in later.

Then the Roman centurion and the soldiers who were watching Jesus on the Cross, were terrified what they saw, the earthquake, the darkness, and so on, and associating the physical manifestation with the Crucifixion of one who had claimed divine origin, they said, "Truly this was the Son of God."

The obvious meaning of this is that the earthquake, occurring while Jesus was dying on the Cross, and reaching its crisis at the moment of his death, played upon their fear, and they told themselves that after all it must be true—a greater than Elias had come; God Himself had fallen on the earth in all His power, and told the children of men that what they have done is a crime.

God was speaking.

The disciples of Jesus were not near to Jesus at his death, according to *Matthew*. The impulse which had caused them to fly from him at the moment of his arrest in Gethsemane was still keeping them away. They were afraid that they might suffer the same fate as Jesus. They would be accused of being his accomplices and accessories in his claim to be the king of the Jews, attempting to re-establish the throne of David.

The charge which the maid in the high priest's palace made against Peter was that she wished to fasten this measure of guilt upon him. And Peter's denial of Jesus meant that he wished to escape from the danger of being arrested as an accomplice of Jesus in his seditious attack on the Roman powers. The disciples had not even yet got any farther than this. They still believed that Jesus had come to Jerusalem to establish his Kingdom—the Kingdom of the Christ which had been foretold. He had not established it. On the contrary, he had been arrested, condemned and crucified for attempting to establish it. Therefore their faith was shaken. They had believed he was the Christ. But could he be the Christ? The Christ was to conquer the powers of the world, establish the kingdom of God.

All this had fallen to a welter of wreck and ruin.

In the evening of that day, apparently some time before six o'clock, for that is when the Jewish Sabbath began, a rich man named Joseph of Arimathæa (a town not far from Jerusalem), a disciple of Jesus's, went to the Roman governor and begged for the body of Jesus that he might bury it. Pilate commanded his soldiers to give the body to Joseph of Arimathæa.

Joseph took the body down from the Cross (or it was taken

down by the Roman soldiers, we are not told which), wrapped it in a clean linen cloth, and buried it in a new tomb, which had been hewn in the rock, and rolled a great stone to the door of the sepulchre, and then departed.

Such sepulchres were not uncommon outside the walls of Jerusalem. They were generally hewn out of the rock of the side of a hill, not underground, and the door was therefore an upright one, like the door to a house, and the stone was usually a flat stone, running in a groove in front of the opening of the tomb.

The darkness is said to have lasted until three o'clock; we are not told whether the light came thereafter, and whether at six o'clock (the beginning of the Sabbath) it was clear. It may have been still cloudy or dim, or the air may have been full of the dust of the earthquake. Jesus was buried in a hurry, to get the burial over before the beginning of the Sabbath. Jesus died in the dark. It may be that he was buried in the dark.

According to *Matthew,* the only followers of Jesus, apart from Joseph, who saw where he was buried were Mary Magdalene and the other Mary (the mother of James and Joses). Others may have been there, but we do not hear of them. Perhaps the chief priests heard of this burial of Jesus by Joseph of Arimathæa, and it gave them cause for a certain anxiety.

The next day, that followed the day of the preparation, the chief priests and Pharisees came together unto Pilate, saying, Sir, we remember that that deceiver said, while he was yet alive, After three days I will rise again. Command, therefore, that the sepulchre be made sure until the third day, lest his disciples come by night and steal him away, and say unto the people, He is risen from the dead.

If this occurred, the last error would be worse than the first. The people who had believed that Jesus was the Son of God would then be sure of it from the facts, without any precedent in the history of the world, that he had risen from the dead.

Did the chief priests believe that Jesus would rise from the dead? Not for a moment. They were Sadducees chiefly and did not believe in resurrection at all. But they knew that the common people did believe in the Resurrection, and that they had heard that Jesus had said he would rise in three days. His disciples would try to justify his prophecy by removing his body. Therefore, they made this application to Pilate.

Pilate may have seen the danger of insurrection in this. The people would assuredly go mad with wrath against a government which had executed a god. The consequences would be shocking. He, too, might say the body had been stolen by the disciples, but the people would not believe him and there would be bloodshed. On the other hand Pilate may have been as contemptuous of the fear of the Jews as he had been of the previous charge. He may not have recognized the danger that any foolish people would believe that any man could rise from the dead. Therefore, he would not make himself ridiculous by putting his own soldiers to watch the grave of the dead man for three days. But, with the same contempt for the Jews, he said, "Ye have a watch; go your way, make it as sure as ye can." As it might be, "I don't say I credit this absurd story, but to make sure that there is nothing in it, or that the followers of this dead man make no capital out of it, go and watch over the grave for yourselves."

So the chief priests, who had soldiers of their own connected with the Temple and the Jewish courts (the same that had arrested Jesus in Gethsemane), sent them to the sepulchre, and they made it sure, *sealing the stone* rolled against the door by Joseph, and setting a watch outside the tomb.

Thus ends Matthew's story of the death and burial of Jesus. Now comes the first step towards the story of the Resurrection.

It is, on the whole, a natural and vivid picture. Omitting the occurrence of the earthquake, there is nothing in it that seems outside human experience.

VII. *According to Luke*

The centurion said, "Certainly this was a righteous man"— nothing about the Son of God, or any suggestion of the supernatural protest against the crucifixion of Jesus.

The prayer of Jesus that God would forgive his enemies and his promise of Paradise to the penitent thief are enough to account for the centurion's words, "Certainly, this was a righteous man." Thus the centurion, though not converted to the belief that Jesus was the Son of God, as in the earlier Gospels, is sympathetic to Jesus, and feels that he may have been unjustly put to death. It is not the manifestations of nature which in *Luke* make him say so, but the divine spirit of the dying man, who forgives the dying malefactor, does not revile his executioners, but merely commends his soul to God.

And all the people that came together to that sight, beholding the things which were done, smote their breasts, and returned.

This moving passage shows that there was a great company of helpless people from Jerusalem who thought Jesus had been unjustly dealt with, and were deeply touched by his sufferings. The sense of the pity of the public at the death of a good man, one who had probably not deserved his death. The death scene in *Luke* does not give any suggestion of the death of a god.

Arimathæa is said to be a "city of the Jews"; another indication that the writer of *Luke* was neither himself a Jew nor was he writing for Jews.

Joseph is described as a councillor who had not consented to the counsel and deed of his fellow councillors. He was clearly one of those who were afraid of being turned out of the synagogue. He is also said to have "himself waited for the kingdom of God." Here is a right understanding of the coming of the Kingdom as taught by Jesus. The malefactor had the conception that grew out of it many years later.

Joseph is said by Luke to have taken the body of Jesus from the Cross. Again the women who came up with Jesus from Galilee are alone mentioned as being present at his burial and seeing how and where the body was laid. This somewhat conflicts with the idea coming later in *John*, that the tomb was in *immediate* proximity to the place of Crucifixion—they "followed after." There is nothing said about Nicodemus or about the hundred-weight of spices, also coming later in *John*. The women returned (to Jerusalem, no doubt) and prepared spices and ointments, and rested the Sabbath Day.

VIII. *According to John*

It was the Day of the Preparation. Therefore the Jews who did not wish the body of Jesus to remain on the Cross on the Sabbath Day (which this time was a high day, Passover) besought Pilate that the legs of the three men might be broken, that they might die quicker, and their bodies be taken away.

Apparently, Pilate consented, for the soldiers broke the legs of the two thieves, but when they came to Jesus, and saw that he was already dead, they did not break his legs. But, apparently to make sure, one of the Roman soldiers pierced his side, whereupon there came forth blood and water.

This was thought to be a miracle, and John makes special affirmation of its truthfulness, referring to Scripture again. This was done that the Scriptures might be fulfilled which said, "A bone of him shall not be broken." And again, "They shall look on him whom they pierced."

There is nothing in *John* about Pilate's surprise on hearing that Jesus is dead.

Joseph of Arimathæa goes *secretly* to Pilate "for fear of the Jews," asking for the body of Jesus. Nicodemus also comes and brings a mixture of myrrh and aloes (about a hundred pound weight). They wind the body in linen clothes with the spices, "as the manner of the Jews is to bury." Obviously John's Gospel was not written for the reading of Jews.

There would be nothing of the nature of a coffin. The body would be laid in a cradle-like bed (or trough) cut out of the floor of the rock tomb. There was a garden near the place of the Crucifixion, and in the garden a new tomb in which never man had yet lain. The garden was a garden of tombs—a cemetery. It was near to Calvary; in the same cutting out of the rock, or near it. There they laid Jesus, because it was nearing the Sabbath. "For the sepulchre was nigh at hand." The inference is that Jesus was buried very hurriedly before six o'clock on the day of Preparation before the Sabbath. Jesus was hurried into the earth. Nothing is said in *John* about the women from Galilee being present at the burial.

Observe that from the moment of the burial of Jesus nothing more is heard of Joseph of Arimathæa. He is not heard of again in the Gospels. He does not appear at the time of the Resurrection. He is not mentioned in the Acts of the Apostles, or in the Epistles, except in certain of the apocryphal Gospels (chiefly written from the second to the fourth centuries). He never appears again.*

IX. *The Three Days*

On that night of the 14th Nisan the disciples must have lost their last hope. If they fled from their Master in Gethsemane after

---

*There is a tradition that Joseph of Arimathæa being sent to Britain by the apostle St. Philip, about the year 63, settled with his brother disciples at Glastonbury.

he had said, in effect, that he did not intend to call down legions of angels to help him to withstand his enemies, and thereby redeem Israel, as they had, down to that moment, believed he would do, what now was their condition?

Their Master was dead and buried. Their Messiah, their Christ, had by his death (and particularly by the way of his death, as a cursed one on the tree) falsified every Messianic hope. He had not been the Messiah. He had been one of the false Messiahs. At the best he had been a teacher who had deceived himself, and led them to deceive themselves. He was utterly crushed. Death had put an end to their expectations. They had spent their time following him in vain. As soon as might be they must return to their old way of life. They must go back to Galilee and take up afresh the broken threads of their lives. After dreaming dreams and seeing visions of themselves sitting on thrones to judge the children of Israel in that new Kingdom which the prophets had foretold, and which Jesus had (consciously or unconsciously) led them, or permitted them, to cherish, they were to go back to their homes, humble and ashamed.

But not yet. For fear of the Jews, who might still arrest them and punish them as accomplices of their dead Master, they must keep themselves in hiding yet awhile. They must sit behind closed doors. They must wait.

I see all this selfish feeling mingled with love for their Master. They weep for him. Perhaps they reproach themselves for making no effort to help and save him, for wishing to share his fate, going to prison with him, dying with him, as they had protested they would—Peter, Thomas. I see the women returning from Golgotha, until the evening of the day, and the beginning of the Sabbath; I see them preparing the spices and ointments with which they intend to anoint his body. Then the beginning of the Sabbath, which (according to the fourth Gospel) is also the feast day.

The disciples sit within doors. They hear the people in the neighbouring houses, saying and singing the passover service until the impressive moment when the door is thrown open to allow Elijah to enter. At that moment, Jesus, the Messiah, is in his grave outside the walls of the city.

At a later hour they hear the people trooping joyously through the streets to the Temple, which will be thrown open at night.

It was on that same night that Judas destroyed himself. He had seen Jesus die. From afar, alone, he may have witnessed all—the blows, the spear-thrust, perhaps had heard the laughter and caught the words of derision. He may have seen Mary at the foot of the Cross, heard her weeping, looked upon her agony. When the darkness fell, and others fled in dismay, he may have crept nearer, for he could do so unobserved, fearing nothing, for what had *he* to fear? He may have listened from behind the Cross, and heard the last cry.

When the body had been taken down, it may have been his first impulse to run and help. Then he may have drawn back, partly from fear of the living face of Mary, partly from dread of the dead face of Jesus. He may have stood afar and watched them as they buried Jesus, and he, too, may have seen where the Master was laid. Mary and Judas alone of all that had followed Jesus, of all he had healed and loved—the woman who was a sinner, the man who had betrayed him—may have been there when they laid him in the tomb.

Then Judas may have crept away, shrinking from every face. He had sinned against the Holy Ghost. There was no hope for him in life, no mercy in death. He would destroy himself.

Jesus was now at God's right hand. Was he witnessing against him? He had betrayed Jesus to his death, but Jesus alone knew why he had done so. Jesus might pity him and forgive him. If only he could go to God's throne and fall at the feet of Jesus, and cry to him to forgive him, and ask God to forgive him too! Judas fled into the potter's field that the priests and elders bought with the thirty pieces of silver he had cast back to them, and there he hanged himself.

The following day, Saturday, the Sabbath, was spent by the followers of Jesus in deepest gloom. Those who mourned the man were in tears, and those who had believed that the prophet could not die were in despair. From the one class Jesus, the comforter of the poor and heavy-laden, was taken away. They would never hear his voice again, and never again look upon his strong and tender face. There would be no one now to say, "Come unto me all ye that labour," no one to take the side of the poor, no one to defend the sinner, no one to defy the arrogance of the rich. The poor and meek who had heard him gladly would hear him no more. To those who had trusted in the prophet there was an awful void. The Kingdom would not come. All had been a vain illusion. Jesus was dead, and lost for ever.

In this mood they gathered together in secret, in dark places of the city, coming and going by stealth, talking in whispers, not daring to walk the streets in the light lest some one of the Pharisees, ceasing his prayer at the corner, cry out, "This one is also a Galilean."

To all of them in that hour the religion of Jesus was dead. The men of Galilee must go back to Galilee; the ways of the world must begin again where they had been broken off when the man of Nazareth arose with his glad tidings three years ago. They are done. Their last hope is gone. Yet over them hovers the wings of an almighty event. They are unconscious of it. It is the last thing that can come to their minds.

But there was one to whom Jesus, though dead, still lived. That was Mary Magdalene. For her he could not die. Nay, he had but now begun to live in her heart. Mary had followed Jesus in the devotion of a disciple. He had been her saviour, her protector, her saint. She had lain at his feet. She had felt towards him as Simon felt when he said, "Depart from me, O Lord, for I am a sinful man." She had followed him with the devotion of a dog. To her he had been the worker of miracles, the raiser of Lazarus, the rebuker of the Pharisees, the compassionate Master.

All this had lasted three years. But the very death that had rebuked the high faith of the one class, and depressed the heart of the other, had lifted up the heart of Mary, and helped it to know itself. Jesus, the raiser of the dead, was dead himself. Like any other man he had suffered and given up the ghost. Like any other man he had been smitten and spat upon and derided. Like any other poor human malefactor, powerless to help himself, he had submitted to it all. On the Cross he had cried out under suffering as any other man might cry out. And like any other man his body had been embalmed and laid to rest in a tomb. But all this only brought him the closer to Mary. It made him a man to her.

But Jesus was dead. She could never see him again. The stone was rolled against the door of his tomb. He was gone from her for ever. All that she could do was what other women did. She could pay him funeral honours.

So on Sunday morning very early she went off hurriedly to the grave. On the way there she must have been telling herself of another such journey near to that place, perhaps upon that spot. It was when her brother Lazarus lay four days dead, and Jesus came and called for her, and she went out to meet him, and wept at sight of him, with a fresh access of grief, and Jesus wept with her. Together they had walked this path until they had come to the door of the tomb. Jesus had ordered that the stone should be removed, and when that had been done, she had seen into the dark cavern of the grave. Then he had cried, "Lazarus, come forth!" And her brother had come out at his word.

Thinking thus, she came upon the place of the tomb of Jesus, and there she found the stone rolled away and the grave open! At first she thought of one thing only. The body of Jesus had been stolen from the tomb of Joseph. The Pharisees had done this evil thing that they might carry their enmity even beyond life, and heap contempt upon the corpse of their enemy. What had they done with the body? Into what dishonoured grave had they cast it, what river, what ditch? She began to weep.

Suddenly she was conscious of the presence of someone near her. She thought it was the gardener of that garden of graves, and, without turning her head, cried while tears blinded her eyes, "Sir, if thou have borne him hence, tell me where thou hast laid him, and I will take him away." Then she heard a familiar voice ring in her ears and echo in her heart. It spoke her own name, "Mary!" She looked. It was Jesus. Then he, like Lazarus, had risen! Ah, what had he said again and again, that after three days he must rise again! He *was* risen! Again she did what she had done before: she flung herself at his feet, and would have washed them with her tears.

He motioned her not to touch him; he looked at her with a great tenderness, and then he faded from her sight for ever. But she rose with a new joy. He was risen! Jesus was not dead! He lived! He had appeared to her! To her first of all women, to her first of all mankind!

CHAPTER XXXV

The Resurrection

I. *According to the Four Gospels*

NOW COMES THE MOMENT of greatest exaltation. Here, one would expect the evangelists would rise to the highest pitch of emotion, the greatest intensity.

The story is about to be told of how Jesus did that which no man had ever done before—rise from the dead. The circumstances of his rising, the events attending it, the appearances he makes to his followers, perhaps to his enemies who have put him to death, confounding them (it may be) by sight of their utter impotence to destroy the Son of God—this is what they have now to describe in their narrative of the scenes of the Resurrection.

Yet how do they describe it? Is there any good reason why I should not say—what I deeply and most painfully feel—that they describe it in a series of passages so remote from reality, so crude, so contradictory, so confused, so pitifully puerile that it is difficult or impossible to accept the story as it has come down to us?

After the vivid reality of the story of the arrest, trial and Crucifixion, these stories of the Resurrection leave the impression of feeble make-believe. Hardly a passage of any of them does not challenge question. They do not seem to be the work of any of the pens which produced the earlier parts of the four Gospels. It is difficult to determine which of the Gospels has the most satisfactory account of the Resurrection. None of them, taken separately, commands belief. Taken together they almost demand disbelief. It is not merely (hardly at all) that they describe incidents which are outside human experience, but that they describe things which do not agree with themselves. And then the pitiful feebleness of the narrations as mere narratives! They bring back to memory the apocryphal Gospels of the second and succeeding centuries, being just as jumbled, inconsequent and inconclusive.

Can it be possible that the Resurrection formed a part of the original story of Jesus? We *know* that a belief in the Resurrection of Jesus came early, very early, as early as the Day of Pentecost following the Passover, during which Jesus died. But these accounts given in the Gospels are not any part of the story told by Peter and Stephen. It is not until much later (as late as Paul after his second coming to Jerusalem) that we catch any echo of these stories. Did they come into existence in the meantime? And how did they come into existence? Were they invented (consciously or unconsciously) to meet criticism, to account for what the Jewish world found a stumbling-block and the Greek world foolishness? Is their self-contradiction to be accounted for by the possibility that they came into being at various periods during the first seventy or more years after the death of Christ? Do they reflect the progress of Christianity during that period, and indicate the objections it had to meet, and the means it adopted to overcome them?

It is a grave question. Let us see, if we can, what the original germ was, out of which grew the belief that Jesus rose from the dead—whether in a purely spiritual or a corporeal body.

Remember, Jesus had never during life really said that he would rise from the dead. The passages in which he is made to speak of rising on the third day are palpably unhistorical. Assuredly, they made (as we shall now see most vividly) no impression whatever on the minds of his disciples. As seen in the text they are all, without exception, palpable interpolations. In like manner, and as a consequence, Jesus never said *why* he should rise from the dead on the third day. He never said what he would do after he had risen from the dead on the third day. He never said how long he should remain on the earth after he had risen from the dead on the third day. He never spoke of ascending to Heaven after this period of renewed life. The only possible reference to anything akin to this is in the passage in *John* XVI, 16, "A little while, and ye shall not see me; and again, a little while, and ye shall see me, because I go to the Father."

II. *According to Matthew*

"Now the next day, that followed the day of the preparation [this would be the Sabbath] the chief priests and Pharisees came together unto Pilate [on the Sabbath they came to Pilate, and contrary to Jewish law, and the Pharisees did it, not merely the Sadducean chief priests] saying, Sir, we remember that that deceiver said, while he was yet alive, After three days I will rise again" (XXVII, 62).

When had Jesus said this (if he ever said it at all) except to his disciples, and then only under a pledge of secrecy, such as "he straitly charged them and commanded them to tell no man that thing"? In any case he speaks to his disciples and to them only, never to the people generally. Unless we are to assume that the disciples broke his command to keep silent this thing (and all it stood for, that he was the Christ) it was false that the chief priests could know that Jesus had said he would rise after three days, and false that they should say they remembered that he had said so.

Command therefore that the sepulchre be made sure until the third day, lest his disciples come by night, and steal him away, and say to the people, He is risen from the dead, so the last error shall be worse than the first.

But what had Pilate to do with the sepulchre? It belonged to Joseph of Arimathæa. And what had Pilate to do with the body of Jesus any longer? He had given it to Joseph. And why should the chief priests go to Pilate to ask him to protect the grave, since they had a guard of their own, and to protect the graves of the Jewish dead from molestation was very specially the duty of the Jewish authorities? It is all so unnatural and so unnecessary.

Pilate said unto them, Ye have a watch; go your way, make it as sure as ye can.

This was ordinary common sense. Pilate was not in any case going to set the Roman soldiers to work to prevent a hypothetical possibility—the opening of a grave and the stealing of a body. Why should he? Besides, he had nothing to fear for himself any longer. Even if the disciples did steal the body of the man whom he had tried for treason, and then gave it out that he had risen from the dead, having said he would rise in three days, the Roman emperor would not listen to such an idle tale, the Roman religion having no place for the idea of a man rising from his grave.

So Pilate would see no danger to himself in this except in the esteem of the followers of Jesus himself, and what would that matter to him? Besides, that the story is incredible is apparent in the fact that it asks Pilate to enter into consideration of the *reli-*

gious issues concerned in Jesus's case. He knew nothing of such religious issues at the trial, while Jesus was alive. That these issues are now forced upon him in the story after Jesus is dead shows that it is a fabrication of Christian-Jewish minds, to whom the religious alone is present.

"So they went, and made the sepulchre sure, sealing the stone, and setting a watch." And it is remarkable that the chief priests and elders do all this on the Jewish Sabbath which forbids work of any kind. Surely this is obviously intended to be an answer to critics who said, long after the event, that the body was stolen by the disciples of Jesus!

The remainder of the story of the watch is yet more incredible. This is on the Sabbath. The watch are at the sepulchre on Saturday and on Sunday morning. And between these times there is a great earthquake; an angel of the Lord descends from Heaven, and rolls back the stone from the door and sits on it.

Observe the comparison of natural with supernatural powers to account for the rolling away of the stone—the earthquake and the angel. "His [the angel's] countenance was like lightning, and his raiment white as snow; and for fear of him the keepers [the watch] did shake, and became as dead men."

How long the keepers remained so is not reported, but we are told that in the morning the watch came into the city and told the chief priests what had happened, whereupon the chief priests consulted the elders and took counsel with them, and finally gave "large money" to the soldiers, telling them to say that Jesus's disciples had come by night and stolen him away while they slept.

> And if this [the fact that the body of Jesus has been stolen] comes to the governor's ears [Pilate's] we will persuade him, and secure you.

So the men take the money and do as they are told, and that is the explanation of the Resurrection of Jesus which is reported down to the day when that part of the Gospel is written.

This section of the story is feeble in the last degree. The soldiers saw the angel; they tell the chief priests they saw the angel, but that supernatural manifestation makes no impression on either, so the priests fabricate the story (and the soldiers took money for telling the lie) that although set to watch they fell asleep, and that while they were asleep (and therefore could know nothing of what was happening) the disciples of Jesus came and stole his body.

Further, that if the story of the stealing of Jesus's body comes to the ears of Pilate the chief priests will persuade him of the truth of this story and so protect them, Pilate having nothing to do with the matter and being naturally quite unconcerned about it.

It is all very lame and feeble. It was obviously designed to meet the criticism raised by the Jewish enemies of Christianity—that even if the grave in which Joseph of Arimathæa had laid him was empty (as perhaps it was) the disappearance of the body could be accounted for in the way described. There is, however, one thing this idle story of the watch does. It shows that the fact that the grave was empty was known to the Jews, and that they devised this story of the stealing to account for it, and (in answer) the Christians devised the further story of the watch to answer the story of the stealing.

But while presenting this Jewish explanation of the Resurrection of Jesus, and giving his own version of its base origin, the writer of the last chapter of *Matthew,* offers the Christian story of the Resurrection, which is as follows: Just before dawn on Sunday morning, Mary Magdalene and the other Mary (that is Mary the mother of James and Joses) came to see the sepulchre, and found the stone rolled away from the door, and the angel sitting on it. To allay the fear of the women the angel said,

> Fear not ye, for I know that ye seek Jesus, which was crucified. He is not here; for he is risen, as he said. Come, see the place where the Lord lay. And go quickly, and tell his disciples that he is risen from the dead; and, behold, he goeth before you into Galilee; there shall ye see him; lo, I have told you.

The women then leave the sepulchre in fear and great joy and run back to take word to the disciples.

On the way, they meet Jesus who salutes them, saying, "All hail!" Whereupon they kneel to him, hold him by the feet and worship him. "Then said Jesus unto them, Be not afraid; go tell my brethren that they go into Galilee, and there shall they see me."

It is impossible not to shrink from comment on this most feeble and meaningless repetitive story. We are not told that the women did as they were bidden. Later, as we shall see, we are told that they did, and that they did not.

The story in *Matthew* next reports that the eleven disciples then went into Galilee into a mountain where Jesus had appointed them. But we have no record in any of the Gospels of Jesus appointing to meet his disciples in Galilee, or any mention of a mountain. In another account, as we shall see, he meets them on the seashore.

"And when they saw him, they worshipped him, but some doubted." The meaning of this last clause is difficult to determine. It may mean that some did not see him, or did not believe that he was risen from the dead.

> And Jesus came and spake unto them, saying, All power is given unto me in Heaven and in earth. Go ye therefore, and teach all nations, baptizing them in the name of the Father, and of the Son, and of the Holy Ghost. . . .

The first clause is a reproduction of words Jesus is reported to have spoken during life; the second clause is (as far as I know) the first statement of the Trinity made in the Gospels.

> . . . Teaching them to observe all things whatsoever I have commanded you; and, lo, I am with you alway, even unto the end of the world. Amen.

The final passage is a very feeble close to the great story of the life of Jesus. It is difficult to think that the writer believed any of the great things which lie at the foundation of Christianity: (1) the divinity of Jesus; (2) his redemption of the world by the sacrifice of himself for its sin. It is a tame statement of the work of an ordinary human being that his teaching and commandments should be observed. All the greatness of the Christ-story has evaporated in this utterly feeble account of the Resurrection as recorded in *Matthew*. My conclusion would be that the author of the book of *Matthew* did not write one word of this closing chapter (XXVIII). It has the mark of the far feebler hands of the writers of the apocryphal Gospels of the second century.

Finally, what end is served by this Resurrection as it is told by *Matthew?* None whatever. Jesus says and does nothing in his resurrected existence that he had not done during his natural life. *If* he had told his disciples to meet him in Galilee he only repeats himself. It is true that he announces the power that has been given him, and proclaims the Trinity, but both passages are, in the highest degree, impossible. In short no purpose whatever has been served by this version of the Resurrection.

III. According to Mark

And when the Sabbath was past, Mary Magdalene, and Mary the mother of James, and Salome, had bought sweet spices, that they might come and anoint him. And very early in the morning the first day of the week, they came unto the sepulchre at the rising of the sun.

According to Jewish reckoning the Sabbath was over at 6 P.M. of the night before. This is Sunday morning at sunrise (6 A.M.). Critics say this is the first statement of the beginning of the Christian division of time. But if so, it is only so in the mind of the writer of the Gospel of Mark. We have no evidence that the Christian-Jews counted time in this way until long afterwards, the reference in *Acts* XX, 7, notwithstanding. It was strictly the beginning of the first day of the week, the hours between 6 P.M. Saturday and 6 A.M. Sunday being the Watches of the Night.

The statement referring to the anointing conflicts with the statement in *Matthew* that they saw Jesus buried, and with the statement in *John* that Nicodemus had wrapped the enormous quantity of a hundred-weight of myrrh and aloes in the linen in which Jesus was buried. Either they were not there at the burial, or they did not know that the body had already been protected by such preservatives. The use of preservatives against the decay of the body of the dead was a custom of the Jews (see *John* XIX, 40). They tried to preserve the body from "seeing corruption," while the soul was, according to the belief of the Pharisees, waiting in Hades for the final resurrection. Incidentally, this incident shows that the women had been brought up as Pharisees. If they had been Sadducees they would have believed that the body perished, and that there was an end after death of both body and soul.

On the way to the tomb they were asking each other whom they should get to roll away the stone, for it was very great. But when they got there they found that the stone had already been rolled away and that the tomb was open. The women obviously knew nothing about an earthquake or, if they did, they did not think of it as an explanation of the rolling away of the stone. It is said, however, that they entered into the open tomb, and saw a young man sitting on the right side, clothed in a long white garment. They were affrighted; but he said to them:

> Be not affrighted; ye seek Jesus of Nazareth, which was crucified; he is risen; he is not here; behold the place where they laid him. But go your way, tell his disciples and Peter . . .

Why the disciples *and* Peter? Does not this suggest that the passage was written after Peter had become a claimant to the headship of the Church? If so, it must have been written after the death of James, the first Bishop of Jerusalem, and after Peter went to Rome—say A.D. 68—thirty odd years after the events now being recorded.

> . . . that he goeth before you into Galilee; there shall ye see him, as he said unto you.

Why this? Does it need this tremendous incident of the Resurrection of Jesus to repeat the old message, if it was ever spoken by Jesus during his life, as the words of the angel say it was?

> And they went out quickly, and fled from the sepulchre; for they trembled and were amazed; neither said they anything to any man; for they were afraid.

Here we find astonishing facts. The women are so terrified that they fly. The idea that Jesus should rise from the dead had never occurred to them. The fact of their bringing spices to preserve his body shows that they thought his body was for ever dead. If Jesus had said to his disciples that he would rise on the third day, the disciples never communicated this to them, although the chief priests (in *Matthew*) claim to remember that he said so.

Then observe that they say nothing to any man about the empty tomb, and that they do not deliver to the disciples and Peter the message about Galilee which the angel gave them. It is said that they were afraid. But are they afraid of their own senses? Did they doubt if they had really seen and heard? Did it occur to them that it had all been a vision? Observe that all this is contradicted by stories in later Gospels. Here is the end of the first of the two stories in *Mark*. What does it amount to? Nothing, but that three devoted women, going to the tomb of Jesus about 6 o'clock on Sunday morning, found the tomb open, the body gone, and saw an angel who told them to go back and tell the disciples that Jesus had risen and would meet them (as he said) in Galilee.

Clearly, the second story in *Mark* is a fragment of which the opening appears to be lost. It begins by saying that when Jesus had risen, early on the first day of the week (Sunday), he appeared first to Mary Magdalene, alone (out of whom, it is said, Jesus had cast seven devils). What he said to her or she to him, or what passed between them is not recorded. Nor is it said where he appeared to her.

Next, it is said (contrary to the first story in *Mark*) that she went and told them that had been with him, as they mourned and wept. This clearly refers to the disciples and followers, and pictures them within the closed doors of their lodging in Jerusalem, where they were concealing themselves from the Jews, as recorded in *John*.

The disciples and followers of Jesus when they heard from Mary that Jesus was alive, and that she had seen him, would not believe her. In *Matthew* she (with the other women) saw Jesus when she was returning from the tomb to Jerusalem. Then *Mark* says Jesus appeared to two of the disciples themselves, or more probably his followers, as they walked into the country, and that these two returned and told the rest of the disciples and followers, and that the disciples and followers of Jesus did not believe them either.

> After that he appeared in another form, unto two of them, as they walked and went into the country. [Clearly, the missing part of the story must have said something about the form in which Jesus appeared to Mary Magdalene.] Afterward he appeared unto the eleven [Judas being gone] as they sat at meat, and upbraided them with their unbelief and hardness of heart, because they believed not them which had seen him after he had risen.

I confess this seems to me very inadequate. If he had upbraided them with forgetting that he had told them he would rise again on the third day there would have been some reason in his upbraiding. But short of this, what possible ground for upbraiding was there in the difficulty they found in believing that a dead man would rise from the grave and live again, before the Last Day on which alone such manifestations of divine power were promised?

Again, there is a break in the narrative, and then Jesus delivers certain messages. He tells his disciples to go into all the world and preach the Gospel to every creature. He has said this, in substance, during his lifetime.

> He that believeth and is baptized shall be saved; but he that believeth not shall be damned.

This, too, he may be understood to have said; but by no means so crudely, almost brutally.

Then he tells the disciples what signs there shall be that people believe:

> In my name shall they cast out devils; they shall speak with new tongues; they shall take up serpents; and if they drink any deadly thing, it shall not hurt them; they shall lay hands on the sick, and they shall recover.

In short, the sign that they believe in him and will be saved is that they shall perform the lesser of the miracles which he himself performed. The greater of the miracles performed by Jesus during his lifetime they are not promised the power to perform, but they are promised the power of speaking with tongues (presumably in languages they have not learned).

And that is all. Nothing about the great purpose of his life—to call the world back from its sins, to redeem the world, to make atonement to God for the sins of man, to call on sinful man to accept Jesus as his intermediary with God, by whose sacrifice in death he was to be saved. Not a word of all this great story!

> So then, after the Lord had spoken unto them, he was received up into Heaven, and sat on the right hand of God.

This is no realistic statement. The disciples could not see him take his place by the right hand of God. The statement is not an historical statement in any sense whatever.

> And they [the disciples] went forth, and preached everywhere, the Lord working with them, and confirming the word with signs following. Amen.

This last verse suggests to me a much greater hand, finding the *Mark* narrative pitifully insufficient, and trying to cover the great mission of the disciples in a few general words. If such they are, they would be added much later.

With all reverence I say that a feebler account of a great event it is not possible for any intelligence to conceive. It is confused. It is repetitive. It is a jumble of things written elsewhere. It is a commonplace story as of a commonplace event occurring to a commonplace person. Some of its passages, read literally, are down to the bottom level of stupidity. It is necessary to remember that none of the best manuscripts contains this feeble alternative story.

What, then, is the value of the supplementary Resurrection statement as narrated by Mark? Nothing whatever. If Jesus rose from the dead, and said and did not more than this, his Resurrection was unnecessary. The greatest event in human history was valueless. Jesus in life was a great being. In his Resurrection he was a little being.

Observe that down to this moment Jesus in the Resurrection has said nothing that corresponds to the value of what he said during his life. He is not actually the same man. His characteristics are smaller and even meaner. His language lacks all its former distinction. His ideas lack all their former elevation. He resembles the spirits which speak through media in modern séances. He has lost nearly every quality of distinction, or even ordinary ability, which he showed in life. He is scarcely recognizable in anything he does or says. The great adventure of death and the hereafter which he has passed through has taught him nothing. At least he says nothing about it. We hunger and thirst to know what is to us unknown, and he has nothing to tell us. All he does is to say over again, in a much fuller way, what he has previously said in life. He talks about one life only, nothing about the great life he has entered upon.

And just as we are so frequently compelled to feel that the spirit has taken the colour of the medium through whom he speaks, having his limitations of thought and speech, so here we are compelled to feel that the reporters of the Resurrection have imposed upon Jesus their own minds and characteristics, their own passions (sometimes very little ones), their own limitations of knowledge, their own small aspirations.

Not a glimpse have we yet got of the Jesus of the Last Supper or of Gethsemane after he has passed through death. Not a suggestion of the Jesus of the great sacrifice for the sins of the world, or the Redemption. Not even a hint of the Being who has done what no human creature has ever done before, broken the power of death and come back to life.

Down to this point the Resurrection stories in the Gospels seem to excuse, if not to justify, the scorching words addressed to the Christians by Celsus, a pagan sceptic of the second century: "You utter fables and you do not even possess the art of making them seem likely. . . . You have altered three, four times and oftener the texts of your own Gospels in order to deny objections made to you."

IV. According to Luke

Remember, in approaching Luke's account of the Resurrection, what he claims for himself at sitting down to write—that he has taken it in hand to set down these things which are most surely believed among the Christians, as they were declared unto them from the beginning by those who had been eye-witnesses and ministers (preachers) of the word (the gospel of Jesus).

This, then, is Luke's story, so derived.

On the first day of the week, very early in the morning, the women of Galilee (Mary Magdalene and Joanna and Mary the mother of James, and other women), who had seen where Joseph of Arimathæa had buried Jesus, came to the sepulchre, with the spices and ointments which they had prepared the night before, for the anointing of his body. They found the stone rolled away from the sepulchre, and, entering into it, they did not find the body of the Lord Jesus.

As they stood perplexed, they became aware that two men (two angels, not one, as in the earlier Gospels) were standing by in shining garments. The women were afraid, and "bowed down their faces to the earth," whereupon the two men (angels) said,

> Why seek ye the living among the dead? He is not here, but is risen; remember how he spake unto you when he was yet in Galilee, saying, The Son of Man must be delivered into the hands of sinful men, and be crucified, and the third day rise again.

It was then the third day truly, but only in a strained sense. If Jesus was buried at, say, one hour before sunset on Friday, and this was 6 A.M. on Sunday morning, he had been one full day and one hour of the preceding day and about twelve hours of a third day in the grave—thus about thirty-seven hours altogether.

The women remembered his words. But nowhere that I can recall are we told in the Gospels that he ever said these words to the women, or to anybody except his twelve disciples, and to them only (or generally) under a pledge of secrecy, that they are to say nothing about this until he is risen.

The women return to Jerusalem from the sepulchre and tell all these things to the eleven disciples and all the rest of Jesus's followers.

Observe that *Mark* (XVI, 8) has said they were too afraid to tell. The disciples and followers of Jesus do not believe the words of the women, thinking them idle tales. But nevertheless Luke tells us that Peter "ran unto the sepulchre," and looking down he saw the linen clothes in which Jesus had been buried, and then he returned, "wondering in himself at that which was come to pass."

Observe that the story of the women and the words they repeated from the two angels had wakened no recollections in Peter. Apparently he remembered nothing that Jesus had said about rising from the dead on the third day. The tomb was empty; the body of Jesus was gone; nothing else seems to have occupied the mind of Peter. What had become of the body of Jesus?

As for the stories of the women about the angels they had made no impression on Peter, so far as we can see. They were hysterical visions, such as devotional women have. That was all, down to that moment.

Then comes an incident of great importance. Two of the disciples (or more probably one disciple and one other follower of Jesus), Simon the Canaanite and Cleopas, went out that same day (Sunday) to a village called Emmaus, which was about seven miles outside Jerusalem, a place difficult of access even yet, except on horseback or on foot. And, as they walked together talking of the things that had happened, Jesus himself drew near to them and walked beside them. They did not recognize him. We are told that this was because their "eyes were holden," not that his appearance had been changed during the period in the grave, but that they were supernaturally made blind to his identity with the Master they had lived with so long.

Jesus spoke to them, asking what was the subject of their conversation, which made them so sad as they walked and talked. Then one of the two, Cleopas, said, "Art thou only a stranger in Jerusalem, and hast not known the things which are come to pass there in these days?"

This is significant as showing that, in their view at least, only a passer-by, a stranger, could fail to know of the Crucifixion of

Jesus. Clearly, they thought it was a matter of immense and universal interest, not an insignificant event, as certain critics have said. And there were perhaps millions of persons in Jerusalem then.

"What things?" asked Jesus—not at all a sincere question. And the men said, "Concerning Jesus of Nazareth, which was a prophet mighty in deed and word before God and all the people."

Mark this, Jesus was still "a prophet mighty in deed and word" to his disciples, *nothing more*. He had died as the Christ, but that fact had not even yet become known to them. Had they, down to that hour, *ever* known it? Although Peter and the others had said—as far back as the days at the source of the Jordan, at Cæsarea Philippi, and after the Transfiguration—that Jesus was the Christ, the Son of God (*if* they had then said it), it had been nothing more than lip-service. They can never really have believed it. If they had really believed that their Master was the Son of God could they have fled away from him, in Gethsemane; could they have hidden away from the Jews during his trial and his Crucifixion, or must they have stood by his side in the same confidence that God would stand by His own?

I am compelled to believe, from a review of all the facts, that the disciples down to this moment did not really believe that Jesus was divine, that he was the Christ. He was to be a prophet, as other men had been prophets and had been put to death by the rulers of the Jews.

"And how the chief priests and our rulers delivered him to be condemned to death, and have crucified him." This, according to Jewish belief, they could never have done if he had been the true Christ.

Then comes significant words. "But we trusted that it had been he which should have redeemed Israel . . ."

This was the hope with which they had followed Jesus up to Jerusalem. It was only when he disappointed this hope by allowing himself to be arrested, and saying he would not call down the angels of Heaven to defend him, that they had fled away and left him. Observe, also, that the idea of the Messiah was not, in their minds, synonymous with the Son of God. He was the servant of God. They hoped Jesus was that servant, and that he would redeem Israel. They did not think he was the Son of God, a part of God, *that idea had never yet entered into their minds.*

Then comes a difficult line: "And beside all this, to-day is the third day since these things were done."

What do they mean? Have their words any meaning? Is it merely the mention of the lapse of time or are they thinking of the women's report of what the angel had said about the third day?

Yea, and certain women also of our company made us astonished, which were early at the sepulchre; and when they found not his body, they came, saying, that they had also seen a vision of angels, which said that he was alive. And certain of them which were with us [Peter and others] went to the sepulchre, and found it even so as the women had said [merely that the tomb was empty] but him they saw not.

Now comes the great moment of the story. It is the first real indication we get in the Gospels of the true meaning of the Resurrection.

Jesus, still unknown to his two followers, says (*Luke* XXIV, 25):

O fools, and slow of heart to believe all that the prophets have spoken; ought not Christ to have suffered these things, and to enter into his glory? And beginning at Moses and all the prophets, he expounded unto them in all the Scriptures the things concerning himself.

They were now near to the village of Emmaus, and Jesus made as though he would go farther. But the two men constrained him to stay the night with them, saying it was towards evening and the day was far spent.

Jesus went in to tarry with them. It may have been the house of Simon the Canaanite, for the Canaanites were scattered over all the provinces of Palestine. It is not likely to have been an inn, because the road to Emmaus can hardly have been a highway to anywhere.

Jesus ate with the two men. It is significant that he assumed the position of host, breaking the bread and blessing it and giving it to the others.

As he did this, their eyes were opened and they knew him.

Why then? Had his way of breaking bread recalled the Last Supper? If so, it could have recalled it to the disciple only, the twelve only being present at it. Or had they recognized the usual way in which Jesus had presided over the meals of his fellowship?

It was Jesus. This, according to Luke's account, was the first time any of the followers of Jesus had seen him. In the morning of that day Mary Magdalene had found the tomb of Jesus open and empty, and she had been told by two angels that he had risen from the dead. And Peter had found the tomb empty. But this was the first time, according to *Luke,* when anybody had seen the risen Jesus. And it was now evening of the first day of the week—Sunday.

Apparently, as soon as the two men had realized that it was Jesus, he vanished out of their sight.

They had seen him. They knew for themselves the astounding fact that he had risen from the dead. Their Jewish belief in what happened to the dead must have been shaken to its foundations. Their theory of death and the grave and the intermediate state of rest for the souls awaiting the judgment (where, according to their old belief, the prophets of old, as far back as Moses, lived and waited), must have collapsed within them.

Jesus lived. He was not merely a prophet mighty in deed and word. He was the Son of God—the one of whom they had just been hearing—the one foretold in the Scriptures, although they had never thought of it until now.

The two men looked at each other and said, "Did not our heart burn within us, while he talked with us by the way, and while he opened to us the Scriptures?"

They were understanding both Jesus and the Scriptures for the first time.

So, within the same hour, in their feverish excitement, as men to whom a new revelation had come, hitherto undreamt of, they returned to Jerusalem, and found the eleven disciples and the followers of Jesus who were with them, and said, "The Lord is risen indeed [what the angels told the women is indeed true] and hath appeared to Simon."

Why Simon only? Why not Cleopas also?

While they were telling the company what had happened to them at Emmaus, and on the way to it, and how they had recognized Jesus in the act of breaking of bread, suddenly Jesus himself appeared to them. He stood in the midst of them and said, "Peace be unto you."

Here we have clearly the visitation of Jesus recorded in the earlier Gospel (*Mark* XVI, 14) in the doubtful story which does not appear in the best manuscripts. But what he says in *Luke* is quite different from what he says in *Mark*. In *Mark* he upbraided them for not taking the word of those who had seen him, after he had risen, and then told them to go into all the world, and promised them exemption from dangers and miraculous powers over evil.

In *Luke* there is nothing of this. First, we read that the assembled company is terrified, thinking they are looking upon a spirit. Next, Jesus allays their terror by assuring them he is no spirit, and telling them to satisfy themselves that he is a living man of flesh and bones, by handling him (particularly by showing them his hands and feet where the wounds, or the marks of the wounds, of his Crucifixion are still to be seen). Next, by asking for food, and eating before them a piece of broiled fish and of a honeycomb. Finally, he reverts to what he had said to the two on the way to Emmaus, reminding them that these were the words which he had spoken to them while he was with them in life—that all things that were written of him (in Moses and in the prophets) had to be fulfilled—"thus it behoved Christ to suffer, and to rise from the dead the third day, and that repentance and remission of sins should be preached in his name among all nations, beginning at Jerusalem."

Here, then, is the meaning of the Resurrection—that Jesus rose from the dead to break down for us the old Jewish idea, and to prove that he was not only a prophet mighty in deed and word, not only the Christ, in the old sense of a messenger and servant of God, but the divine Son of God; for had it not been foretold in the Scriptures from Moses and the prophets downwards that the true Christ would die and rise again, and had he not died and risen again? "And ye are witnesses of these things." That is to say that, having appeared to them, they could henceforward testify to all the nations ("beginning at Jerusalem" may or may not have been an interpolation) that they had seen him after he had risen.

In this narrative of Luke I see two stories, probably written at widely separated times. The first was the story of the appeal of Jesus to the Scriptures as proof of his divinity as the Christ, in the sense of the Son of God. I think this story probably became current in the early days after the Crucifixion, and that it became the essence of the teaching of the apostles.

The second story was that of Jesus's corporeality in his Resurrection, and I think this was conceived long afterwards. Some of the Jews had long believed in a spiritual resurrection to come at the time of the coming of the Messiah, at the time of the Judgment. And it may be (it seems certain) that after Pentecost critics of the preaching of the apostles told them that their vision of Jesus had been only a ghost, a phantom of their deluded imaginations, never seen by anybody outside their own interested circle of believers, that he was not a reality, a being that ate and drank and walked the world, but a spirit that entered rooms whereof the door was locked, appearing and vanishing contrary to all experience of possibility.

To meet this criticism the disciples appear to have conceived (sincerely believing, perhaps, that they remembered the fact) that on the first occasion of appearing to them Jesus had replied to this suspicion in their own minds and had banished it by telling them to handle him, to look at the marks of the wounds of his Cross, and finally by asking for food (as if hungry) and eating it before their eyes.

But then arises another thought. If, as Jesus is made to say, he had told his disciples while he was with them in life that "all things must be fulfilled which were written," why was it necessary that he should rise from the grave in order to tell them the same thing again?

Was it that his first saying had made no impression upon them, that they had never really grasped the idea that he was more than a prophet; that he was the Son of God, and that by his death he was to bring remission of sins and the atonement of man with God; and, therefore, it was necessary that he should rise from the dead, and by so breaking all the laws of nature, and so disturbing all the theories whereby the Jewish religion had hitherto lived, he might prove, and they might witness to all the world, that he was the Son of God?

Here, again, arise questions. Did Jesus actually say all these things during his lifetime? Did he say that Moses and all the prophets foretold him? Or was this put into the text of the Gospels long afterwards (or conceived of after his death) in order to justify the preaching of the apostles?

Luke's account of the only appearance Jesus makes to his followers (apart from the appearance to the two on the way to Emmaus) closes by a warning Jesus gives them that they are not to leave Jerusalem until they are endued with power from on high.

Observe that this conflicts with the message of the angel to the women in *Matthew* (XXVIII, 7) and of Jesus to the women on their way back from the tomb to Jerusalem, that they are to go back to Galilee and there they will see him. But then Mary Magdalene and the women of Galilee do not, in *Luke,* see their risen Lord at all.

Then comes Luke's story of the Ascension, dealt with in a later section.

V. *According to John*

As in the three previous Gospels, Mary Magdalene comes to the sepulchre first. In *John* she is alone, as she is in the second story in *Mark.*

This fact, that the story that Jesus has risen from the dead begins with a devoted woman, is highly significant. It would be folly to put it aside or not to give due weight to it.

There is an obvious break between the first and second verses of Chapter XX. Something has been omitted. Clearly, it has said that the tomb was open and that she found it empty, the body of Jesus gone. She runs to Peter and to John (the "other disciple whom Jesus loved") and said, "They have taken away the Lord out of the sepulchre, and we know not where they have laid him."

Peter and John then run to the sepulchre to see for themselves. John (the younger man) reaches it first, outrunning Peter.

He finds the sepulchre open, and stooping down and looking into it, but not "going in," he sees the linen clothes in which Jesus had been buried. Then comes Peter, and he goes into the sepulchre, and sees, not only the linen clothes but also the napkin that had been wrapped about the head. Then John enters the sepulchre and sees this also and believes. What does he believe? That the body is gone? Nothing else is indicated.

"For as yet they knew not the Scripture, that he must rise again from the dead." Often as Jesus is reported to have told them, they did not know it. Did he ever tell them? Or, if he told them, is it not certain from this that they never understood him?

Then the two disciples went away to their own home. This must mean to their lodgings in Jerusalem (not in Galilee) where we shall presently find them.

While the two men are at the sepulchre, or after they have gone, Mary Magdalene returns to it. She is weeping. And as she weeps she stoops down and looks into the sepulchre. There she sees two angels in white, sitting one at the head and the other at the feet of where the body of Jesus had lain. Remember, that according to earlier Gospels she had seen where he was buried.

The angels spoke to her. "Woman, why weepest thou?" She answered, "Because they have taken away my Lord, and I know not where they have laid him." To this, no reply by the angels is recorded. But it is reported that when she had said this she turned back and saw Jesus standing near, but did not know it was Jesus.

Had his appearance changed? Or were Mary's eyes also "holden" as the eyes of the two men on the way to Emmaus had been? Jesus then said to her, "Woman, why weepest thou?"

The same question as that of the angel.

"Whom seekest thou?"

A rather disingenuous question, almost suggesting a made-up story. He must have known quite well whom she was seeking.

Mary, supposing him to be the gardener, said, "Sir, if thou hast borne him hence, tell me where thou hast laid him, and I will take him away."

It is difficult to know what idea is in Mary's mind. Does she look at him and think he looks as the gardener might look? Incidentally, none of the Gospel stories gives any thought to the obvious matter-of-fact question of what garments Jesus wore after his Resurrection, his own having gone with the Roman soldiers, and the linen of the grave-clothes still remaining in the tomb. And if the gardener, why should she think he had taken the body out of the sepulchre, which belonged to Joseph of Arimathæa, assuming that he had any right to remove it, or that, out of hostility to the dead, he had done this act of sacrilege to gratify his own feeling? And if he had removed and laid it elsewhere (one of the apocryphal stories says he threw it in a stream or ditch), what reason had she to think he would tell her how it had disappeared, and, finally, how did she think she was to carry it away?

But from this childish simplicity we come back in the next verse to what seems to be the authentic history. Jesus says to her, "Mary!"

"She turned herself [this suggests that she had not turned to the gardener and therefore had not seen him, but only felt the presence of somebody behind her] and saith unto him. . . . Master!"

The next verse indicates a natural gesture of the woman (she is evidently kneeling at the moment) to embrace the feet of Jesus, whereupon he says,

Touch me not; for I am not yet ascended to my Father . . .

This conflicts with the promise to the thief on the Cross, "To-day shalt thou be with me in Paradise," unless we are to understand that Jesus had in the meantime been in that intermediate place of many states and conditions, and that Paradise was one of them—a blessed one—otherwise the promise to the thief has no grace of forgiveness and blessing in it.

. . . but go to my brethren and say unto them, I ascend unto my Father, and your Father; and to my God, and your God.

This scene is in its essence very beautiful. Mary Magdalene goes to the disciples and tells them she has seen the Lord, and what he has said to her.

And in the evening of the same day (Sunday) when the disciples are assembled in their own room, with the doors shut for fear of the Jews, Jesus comes and stands in their midst and says, "Peace be unto you!"

Here is clearly the same scene, at the same time, as in *Luke* (XXIV, 36) and in *Mark* (XVI, 14), but the essential part of what occurs is different.

First, Jesus convinces the disciples of his corporeality by showing them his hands and his side (his feet, also, in *Luke*), the marks of the wounds he received on the Cross and therefore of his identity. The disciples are glad, and Jesus says, "As my Father hath sent me, even so send I you." And when he had said this, he breathed on them, and said unto them, "Receive ye the Holy Ghost."

Observe that, according to *John,* Jesus confers the Holy Ghost on his disciples on the Sunday of his Resurrection, whereas at the same interview, as it is reported in *Luke,* he tells them to tarry in Jerusalem until it is conferred upon them, and that this (as we shall see later) is what, according to *Acts,* occurred.

Further, Jesus confers powers upon his disciples of remitting or retaining sins.

One incident occurs here, which has the appearance of having been added after the first writing, and with a manifest purpose. At this appearance of Jesus to his disciples one of them is absent—Thomas.

When, later, the disciples told him they had seen the Lord, he doubted so vehemently as to say that he would not believe that Jesus had risen unless and until he could see in the hands of Jesus the print of the nails of the Cross, and thrust his hand into his side, and feel the place of the wound made by the spear.

After eight days this satisfaction is granted to him. Jesus appears to his disciples again in the same place, under the same conditions, salutes them as before with the words, "Peace be unto you!"

And then he calls on Thomas to touch his hands and thrust his finger into his side and thereby to believe. After Thomas has done so, he cries, "My Lord and my God!"

Whereupon Jesus says, "Thomas, because thou hast seen me, thou hast believed; blessed are they that have not seen, and yet have believed."

In no other incident of the Resurrection stories is there clearer evidence of an effort to meet the criticism of a later age. The time had come when people in Palestine, or more probably in distant countries, who had not seen Jesus either during his lifetime or after his Resurrection, were saying to the apostles, "You tell us he appeared to you; you may believe on the strength of what you saw, what you were eye-witnesses of; but what reason have we to believe?"

This story of the appearance to Thomas, therefore, was conceived to show that to believe because one has seen is blessed, but far more blessed is it to believe when one has *not* seen.

> And many other signs truly did Jesus in the presence of his disciples, which are not written in this book.

Why were they not written, when every word and fact would have been evidence of gold?

But now come to the heart and essence of the whole story, and the reason of the Resurrection of Jesus.

> But these are written, that ye might believe that Jesus is the Christ, the Son of God; and that believing ye might have life through his name.

This is plainly the end of John's Gospel as it was originally written.

So the heart and soul of the Resurrection is the sheer fact that Jesus, unlike all other men who had ever lived since the beginning of the world, had died and been buried, and had then risen from the dead and was there appearing to his people.

This makes short shrift of the miracle of the raising of Lazarus, but there is no resisting it. Jesus died and rose again. By that great fact it was to be known and for ever believed that Jesus was more than man—that he was the Son of God.

But that is not all. Being the Son of God he had come to the world for a specific work. During his lifetime he had told what that work was—to redeem the world from the burden of its sin before God, to make atonement unto God.

Why is this not said here of all places? Why have we to wait until fifty days later (until Pentecost) to hear this from the lips of Peter? Why have we to wait until Paul, years later, explains the great mystery?

CHAPTER XXXVI

The Resurrection (Continued)

1. Did Jesus Foretell His Resurrection?

NEW TESTAMENT writers assert that the Resurrection of Jesus was a fulfilment of prophecy. St. Paul writes that Jesus has been raised on the third day according to the Scriptures. But where do the Scriptures, that is the books of the Old Testament, say that the Messiah is to be *raised on the third day?* We are told that as Jonah was three days and three nights in the belly of the whale, so shall the son of man be three days and three nights in the heart of the earth (*Matthew* XII, 39, 40). The answer to this is that Matthew's story is not in accordance with the facts. Jesus was about thirty-seven hours in the grave.

There is the passage in *Hosea* (VI, 2) which seems to mark the period of the Resurrection of Jesus after his death: "After two days he will revive us: in the third day he will raise us up, and we shall live in his sight." But nowhere is this adduced in the New Testament or yet in the apostolic fathers as prophetic of Christ's Resurrection.

The first Isaiah (writing in seventh century B.C.) says (XXVI, 19) :

> The dead men shall live, together with my dead body shall they arise. Awake and sing, ye that dwell in dust; for thy dew is as the dew of herbs, and the earth shall cast out the dead.

Thus the belief in individual resurrection dates back to the earlier Isaiah who wrote before the Assyrian invasion.

It is significant that in his great final speeches Jesus says much about his Second Coming, but nothing (that I can see or remember) about his Resurrection from the dead. My impression is that the passages which speak of his approaching death bear in all cases the stamp of truth, but that the salient clause about rising again on the third day never seems to be necessary to what he is saying, or to produce any sensible effect on his disciples.

996

The disciples understand him perfectly when he says he must die at the hands of his enemies, and sometimes they resist it violently, saying it shall not come to pass; and sometimes they indicate their Jewish belief that the Messiah does not die, and therefore he (being the Christ) should not die, too. But there is, as far as I can remember, no indication that the disciples pay any serious attention to the statement that he is to rise again on the third day. The Jews knew nothing about such rising from the dead. Their only thought about resurrection was that it was to be at the last day, in the hour of judgment, when the Messiah should appear in the clouds and all his people should go up to meet him (as Paul says) in the air.

I cannot think that the idea of a third day Resurrection from the grave ever entered into the consciousness of any of the disciples. If it had done so it is inconceivable that they should have run away from Jesus in Gethsemane, or hidden themselves during his trial and execution and after it. If they knew he was absolutely and undeniably the Lord, they would have had no fear for him or for themselves.

But when Mary Magdalene came to them on the morning of the first day of the week with the story that Jesus had risen from the dead, and she had spoken with him, everything was changed. In the fact (as they believed it to be) that Jesus had risen, a new idea came to them. Is it possible then it was in this way (and this alone) that the idea of the Resurrection began? What followed is not too difficult to account for. What did Jesus mean by the Resurrection on the third day? What lay behind the idea that having died for the redemption of man, and been buried, he should rise on the third day? Why the third day, and not the second or the same day? Was it to be a corporeal rising or a rising of a spiritualized body? In the Epistle of Ignatius an utterance is attributed to Jesus which is not to be found in any of the Gospels: "Take, handle me, and see that I am not a bodiless demon."

Clearly, the demons whom Jesus cast out were understood to be bodiless. They were spirits—evil spirits.

The Gospels and *Acts* say he remained on earth as an ordinary human body, exactly (down to the wounds made at the Crucifixion) as he had been put into the tomb, for thirty days, moving about Palestine, from Jerusalem to Galilee, and being seen by various disciples (all of them in the end, his brother James, and finally five hundred). Why was this? What was Jesus doing during those thirty days which he had not done in his ordinary existence before his death? Is it to be said that the fact that he was a resuscitated body, that he was a man who had been dead and was now alive again, was to work so strongly on his disciples and followers as to compel belief or strengthen the belief that failed them when death befell him? If so, why could not the resuscitated body of Lazarus produce the same results? What was the scheme of salvation involved in these thirty days' existence and wandering in Palestine before his ascension to Heaven?

Jesus had said on the Cross that he would be that day in Paradise. He was not, for on the first day of the week he told Mary Magdalene that he had not yet ascended to his Father. The Church teaches that during the days between his death and his Resurrection he descended into hell. But he never said in life (so far as I can remember) that he had any intention of doing so. What, then, does the Resurrection and the Ascension *do?*

Is it possible that both Resurrection and Ascension are the afterthoughts of the disciples, and that Jesus had no part in creating them? Is it possible that all the references to the third day on which he would rise again were the creation of the time that came *after* the first day of the week? Is it possible that Jesus conceived of two great things only, (1) that he should die as a sacrifice for sinful men; (2) that in God's time he should return from Heaven to establish the kingdom of Heaven on earth?

Is it certain that the insertion of the many conflicting and perplexing stories of his Resurrection on the third day and his Ascension on the thirtieth was the product of the time, following his death, when the apostles were hard put to it to account for the death of him whom they believed to be the Son of God?

All this requires careful thought, and most exact reading. If it proves to be a reasonable way of looking at the latter events it may, or may not, strip Christianity of one of its most powerful appeals. Would it disturb the belief of St. Paul, by disturbing the grounds of his conversion? I think not. Would it disturb Pentecost? I am not sure.

I see the spiritual conviction taking hold of the disciples that Jesus is not dead, but lives; and that in due course (they thought within their own time) he would come again, and do all that the Messiah was foretold by the prophets to do—to establish the kingdom of God on earth. Of one thing I feel sure—that such a reading (if it is a possible one) would put Jesus abreast of the belief of our own time. Our later age would not have to part with any of the cardinal doctrines of the Christian faith (Incarnation, Atonement, and so on); but only the material things of which it has no experience and cannot believe.

This is grounded on the idea that the Scriptures (the Gospels and the Epistles of Paul and Peter) present a theory of the character and mission of Jesus which was created by the people of that time to meet the spiritual needs of that time. And that, in many ages since, this portrait of Jesus has undergone changes necessary to bring it into harmony with the changing times. Finally, that it is now necessary to make a picture of Jesus that will be agreeable to the spirit of the modern world.

This can best be done by getting down to the naked reality of the historical Jesus, and, in doing so, stripping away all that has been added to the historical Jesus by the necessities of the earlier ages.

On looking (rather hastily) through the Gospels for references by Jesus himself to his Resurrection, I am startled to find how few they are, and how unconvincing.

I find the following: *Matthew* XVI, 21; XVII, 9, 23; XX, 19. *Mark* IX, 9; IX, 31. *Luke* IX, 22; XVIII, 33. *John* XVI, 16. (Observe that in the great passage in *John* [XII, 23–36] in which Jesus foretells his death, he says nothing about rising from the dead.)

Many of these are duplicates, and probably would be reduced by much more than half on careful analysis. In several cases they consist of the words "and on the third day he will rise again from the dead." The reference in *John* is the passage in which Jesus said, "and again, a little while, and ye shall see me."

And then there is the story of the watch put upon the tomb lest the body should be stolen, to carry on the picture that he had risen because he had said he would rise. Besides there are certain short verses saying he will go before them into Galilee, presumably after his Resurrection.

On examining these passages I see:

1. That in none of the cases except one does the phrase about rising again on the third day bear any clear relation to what goes before or comes after it.

2. That in no case except one does the promise of the Resurrection make any apparent impression on the minds of his disciples. In one case they are reported to ask each other what this rising from the dead can mean, showing that the idea that Jesus would rise out of the grave after his burial never really penetrated their consciousness while he was alive.

3. That the context in nearly every case shows that the disciples were only concerned about the thought that Jesus should die; that they resented this thought, partly out of their love for him, and partly because it was opposed to all their Jewish conceptions of what should befall the Christ. But the idea that, though he was to die, he was to return to them within three days, and be the same to them as he then was—of this assuredly there is no indication in anything they say or do either at the moment or later, down to the first day of the week.

On the first day of the week they were *all* so completely ignorant that Jesus was to rise from the grave on the third day that some of the women went to the tomb to embalm (in a primitive way) his dead body (to put preservative spices about it), and when the general body of them was told by one of the women that he had risen from the dead they thought she was beside herself.

After this time, and his appearance among them in a room whereof the doors were closed, after a second such appearance, and after various appearances to other persons in other places (including five hundred in Galilee), they did indeed remember that he had foretold his Resurrection from the dead.

But had he?

Which are we to believe—that he did indeed foretell his Resurrection on the third day and that his disciples did not understand what he was talking about, and forgot all about it until it actually came to pass; or that he did not foretell it, and that after he had actually risen, or after the disciples believed he had risen, after he had already appeared to them, they honestly made themselves believe that he had foretold that at just the time it did occur he would rise out of the grave?

I confess (with some reluctance) that the latter explanation is the one which commends itself to my intelligence; in view of the clear fact that, although Jesus is reported to have said plainly that he would rise from the dead on the third day, nobody seems to have believed for a moment that he would rise or had risen or could rise.

Keim says:

> His last words triumphed over death and the grave and his fall. It is true he never said nor knew anything about a rising again of his weary body.

But this brings us to a very serious question. Did Jesus actually rise from the dead in the sense indicated in the Gospels?

The stories of the Resurrection in *Acts* and in *Galatians* are in the last degree conflicting. If I had to harmonize them, as a condition of my belief, I should have to throw the whole thing up. No two stories bear out each other. In every case each story eliminates all others. In one point only do they agree—that Jesus actually appeared to his followers after his death and burial. They do not give any clear idea of *why* he appeared to them. He does not say anything after his Resurrection which compares for so much as a moment with the great things he said immediately before his death. In sober truth the Jesus of the Resurrection is an uninspired and rather commonplace being, often saying very poor, feeble and apparently valueless things. He has lost all the greatness he had in his last speech in the Temple, his last speech on the Mount of Olives, at his trial before the high priests and before Pilate, and again as a dying man on the Cross.

It is a startling fact, not to be denied by any one with imagination and power of thought, that in his days on earth after his Resurrection all the virtue has gone out of him. He talks as the spirits are said to talk to the spiritualists, saying very worthless things, out of harmony with their minds as we knew them in life, and often out of harmony with their character.

What, then, is my conclusion from all this? With great reluctance it is:

1. That Jesus did not foretell his Resurrection, and that the lines here and there which are appended to his foretelling of his death were added after his death by the writers of the Gospels— or to the oral stories which were the foundations of the Gospels —not deliberately, not out of deliberate intention of putting statements into his mouth which he did not speak; but in a kind of honest self-deception, as "This thing happened, therefore he must

have said it would happen, although it had passed out of our recollection until it took place."

2. That the story of the watch that was put upon the grave and of the subsequent base happenings (the bribing of the Jewish soldiers to say that the disciples had stolen away the body while they were asleep) is manifestly and almost impudently unhistorical.

3. That Jesus did not rise from the dead in the sense described in certain of the Gospel stories—as a human body in every way the same as the body which about thirty-seven hours before had been put into the grave, with the wounds of the Cross (apparently healed) upon it, and with the same human appetite of hunger, a claim which is belied by the other conditions of the resurrected body, such as that it can pass through closed doors.

I know these are bold conclusions, and that they threaten to cut at the root of Christianity, as it is now understood.

That the disciples did honestly and firmly believe in the Resurrection it is impossible to doubt. It was this which brought back their faith in the Messiah, the Christ, when his death on the Cross had most surely killed it, and nothing remained to them after his death but love for the man. It was this that made them shake off their fear, and come out of hiding and face death at the hands of the Jewish and Roman authorities on the day of Pentecost, nay, almost court death, that they might share the fate of their Master and his glory. It was this absolute faith in the Resurrection of Jesus which converted Paul, and thereby carried Christianity into the Gentile world—made it a world religion.

To disturb the belief in the Resurrection of Jesus is therefore a terribly serious thing.

My answer to all this is that while I deny the bodily Resurrection of Jesus (or rather see nothing in the Gospels that justifies my belief in it as an historical occurrence) I do not deny that Jesus appeared to the disciples after his death, and thereby revived their fallen faith.

This does not require that I should accept any of the Resurrection stories as they have come down to us. In my judgment there is not one of them that has not been coloured by the necessities of the time in which they were narrated. Those necessities do not apply to our time, and therefore we are not required to accept the colouring.

That Jesus, after his death, conveyed to the consciousness of his followers the firmest and most confident belief that notwithstanding his death he still lived, and that all he had foretold about his second coming would come to pass in God's own time—this is the measure of my belief in the Resurrection of Jesus. But I think it is the essence of it. It is all that St. Paul had to assure him that Jesus still lived. If it was sufficient for Paul it is sufficient for me. I do not need the material proofs of Thomas. It is because the Church has put itself in the position of Thomas, and demanded the same physical proofs of the Resurrection as he demanded, that the Resurrection story has presented difficulties—is still presenting difficulties.

To reconsider and restate it (in the spirit of St. Paul) is the first necessity of the Christianity of our own age.

The foregoing suggests the obvious thought that there may be a way of stripping away from the traditional portrait of Jesus and the reports of his words and his mission the accretions of all the ages since his death. These accretions were made in the effort to accommodate him to the spiritual minds of the various ages, and to answer the criticism of the sceptics and to make converts for Christianity. For instance, the first effort of the disciples must have been to make converts of their fellow Jews, and this suggested the study of the Scriptures, so as to prove that he was the Messiah who had been foretold. Next, the effort would be to meet the desires and difficulties of the Greek converts, and this may have suggested the earlier supernatural stories (as of his Virgin Birth). And so on and on, at every stage of his life, and through all the years down to the making of the canon at last. Thus every age made the Jesus it wanted.

Is it not reasonable to think that in order to make a portrait of Jesus such as the twentieth century wants, we should not add anything but should strip away all the accretions of the earlier centuries, the Middle Ages, and even the apostolic times and get back, if possible, to the naked historical Jesus?

II. *The Gospels' Account*

Objections to the story of the Resurrection may reasonably come from the facts (1) that it is claimed that his actual body, with its marks of his sufferings on the Cross, with the appetite for food, and so on, had risen; (2) that it was seen by a great number of persons both in Jerusalem, other parts of Judæa and in Galilee, for forty days or more; and that Jesus walked to and fro in Jerusalem in the midst of his "furious enemies," though he was neither taken nor seen by them.

We may well decide in favour of the account of the Resurrection that is most simple and free from perplexing difficulties. Take, for example, the appearance to the women on the way back from the grave to Jerusalem. This account is vitiated by the mention of the guard whom they see hurrying back to their masters with the story of what happened during the night. That the story of the guard is an impossible combination of Jewish and Christian legend I am firmly convinced.

The evangelical writers only agree as to a few of the appearances of Jesus after his Resurrection. Their accounts of the localities of his appearances exclude each other in many cases. Clearly, either no one of the evangelists knew what had been said by the other, or (more probably) the later writers interpolated new and conflicting stories at various periods according to the needs of their time, their own place and the condition of the Christian community in which they lived. This liberates the original writers from responsibility for a great deal of contradiction and confusion.

III. The Corinthians Account

Outside the accounts in the Gospels are the accounts in *Corinthians*. St. Paul's Epistle to the Corinthians was written probably about the year A.D. 59 therefore a little less than thirty years after the Resurrection. It requires us to believe, which may very well be true, that many members (the greater part of the five hundred) of the primitive Church were then still living, and that among them were several of the apostles, and perhaps several other eye-witnesses.

Paul (I *Corinthians* XV, 4–8) says:

And that he was buried, and that he rose again the third day according to the Scriptures . . .

[To what Scriptures does Paul refer? Does he mean the Old Testament Scriptures? If so, where is it said that the Messiah was to rise again on the third day after burial? If he refers to the

Gospels as Scriptures, then we are compelled to believe that some of the Gospels, in some form (perhaps an early form) existed before A.D. 59, the date at which, in *Corinthians,* Paul is writing.]

. . . And that he was seen of Cephas, then of the twelve [actually there were only eleven at that time, the twelfth to take the place of Judas not being chosen until afterwards, more than forty days later, when the lot fell upon Matthias]. . . . After that, he was seen of James; then of all the apostles. And last of all he was seen of me also, as of one born out of due time.

Thus, the whole of this passage (I *Corinthians* XV, 4–8) suggests that the "Scriptures" referred to by Paul are the Gospels, which existed before the time when he wrote his letter to the Corinthians about thirty years after the Resurrection.

All this is extremely important as showing that Gospels were in existence much earlier than is now commonly supposed. Some of these Gospels may be the earlier versions of *Matthew, Mark, Luke* and *John.* Or they may be Gospels which are entirely lost. Where, for example (a very important point), have we now any Gospel account of how Jesus appeared to Cephas, or to his brother James? This last appearance must have been of immense significance. It may account for James's conversion to belief in Jesus, which the Gospels, as they have come down to us, do not attempt to explain.

Some great event seems to be here faintly indicated by St. Paul —Jesus convincing his unbelieving and even unsympathetic brother that he was the Christ.

IV. *The Appearance to St. Paul*

When Paul places the earlier appearances of Jesus in the same class with the appearance to himself, we are compelled to conclude that they were of the same kind. Of what kind was the appearance of Jesus to Paul, according to his own account? It is impossible to regard it as an external, objective, physical appearance. Paul does not see, still less does he touch Jesus; he does not, like Thomas, put his hand in the wounds. He is struck blind and has no evidence of the presence of Jesus, except a *voice.* But that is enough for him. It is proof to Paul that Jesus has risen from the dead and that he lives. He believes Jesus is the first and only one that has so risen from the dead and lived. Jesus is the "first fruits of them that slept." Hence Paul is convinced.

He has heard nothing about Lazarus. It is more than a mere mood of mind in Paul, as it was more than a mood of mind in Stephen. Paul actually heard, though the people with him did not hear Jesus. Stephen actually saw, though the people stoning him did not see Jesus.

It was a distinct external appearance, although limited to the person who was to become conscious of it. The ears of others were deaf to it, the eyes of others were blind to it.

V.   St. Paul's Story of the Resurrection

For I delivered unto you first of all that which I also received, how that Christ died for our sins according to the Scriptures; and that he was buried, and that he rose again the third day according to the Scriptures; and that he was seen of Cephas, then of the twelve. After that, he was seen of above five hundred brethren at once; of whom the greater part remain unto this present, but some are fallen asleep. After that, he was seen of James; then of all the apostles. And last of all he was seen of me also, as of one born out of due time. [I *Corinthians* XV, 3–8]

This story of the Resurrection by Paul differs materially from any of the stories in the Gospels. No longer is it Mary Magdalene to whom Jesus first appeared, but apparently he appeared first to Cephas. No longer does he appear to the eleven disciples (Judas being gone), but to the twelve (which seems to include Judas, and wipe out the story of the betrayal). Of the appearance to the five hundred at once nothing is said in the Gospels, which do, however, as we shall presently see, tell of his appearance to Simon on the shores of the Lake of Galilee. And finally, he appears to James, clearly the brother of Jesus, who afterwards became the head of the Church, but whom we last saw in hostility to Jesus and almost deriding him. What would we give for the story of his appearance to James! With this reference only it fades out of history.

St. Paul's doctrine of the reason of the Resurrection is given in I *Corinthians* (XV, 12–26). The substance of it is that they are wrong who, in Paul's time (as is clearly evident and a most important fact), were still saying there was no resurrection (Paul clearly knew nothing of Lazarus) from the dead for man in general, although Jesus may have risen. If there were no resurrection from the dead, then Christ had not risen. And if Christ did not rise from the dead then the whole fabric of the faith in Christ collapses. Then their preaching is vain. They are false witnesses. If God did not raise up Christ, then the dead do not rise. And if the dead do not rise then Christ is not risen. And if Christ is not raised their faith is vain, and they are still in their sins—the sins inherited from Adam. And all that died in the doctrine of Christ have perished. If they merely have hope in Christ in this life—if he is merely a great teacher of righteousness—then they are of all men the most miserable.

But *because* Jesus rose from the dead they are saved. By man came death into the world, and by man came the Resurrection of the dead. All men died in Adam, and in Christ they all become alive. And now Christ is with God, but he is coming in the end, and then he will reign, until he has put all the enemies of God under his feet. And then Christ himself will be subject to God, and God will be all in all.

Such is Paul's explanation of the Resurrection. But nothing of all this great message is given in the feeble, confused and confusing stories in the Gospels.

VI. An Incident in John

St. John's Gospel has one further incident. It is in a chapter obviously added long after the original writing, and intended to serve an obvious purpose. In the last chapter in *John* (XXI) we are told that Jesus showed himself again to the disciples at the sea of Tiberias. His disciples are there, having forgotten the injunction of Jesus to remain in Jerusalem until the Holy Spirit descends on them. They have given up all thought of carrying on the mission of Jesus, and have gone back to their old vocation as fishermen. They have broken up and only seven are there, and one of then (Nathanael of Cana in Galilee) is, so far as we know, not a former disciple.

Peter says, feebly enough, "I go a-fishing," the others say, "We also go with you." They go out on the lake and fish all night but catch nothing. In the morning, when they are returning Jesus is standing on the shore. They do not know him. Their eyes again are "holden." Jesus says, "Children, have ye any meat?" and they answer, "No." He calls to them to cast their net on the right side of the ship. They do so and were unable to draw it for the multitude of fishes. Then the "disciple whom Jesus loved" (John, the assumed writer) says to Peter, "It is the Lord."

When Peter hears this he puts on his fisherman's coat (apparently the weather is hot, for it is the end of April or beginning of May and he has been naked) and gets into the sea, as if to walk ashore in his eagerness. The other disciples get into a smaller boat, and drag their net behind them. When they are all ashore they see that there is a fire there with fish cooking and bread. Jesus tells them to bring some of the fish they have just caught. Peter drags the net to land. It contains 153 fishes, and yet the net is not broken. At that great moment they have counted the fish.

Then Jesus says, "Come and dine." None of the disciples dared ask him "Who art thou?" because, says the writer, they knew. Jesus takes the bread and gives it to them and he gives the fish also.

When they have dined Jesus says to Peter, "Simon, son of Jonas, lovest thou me more than these?"

To this amazing question Peter replies, "Yea, Lord, thou knowest that I love thee." And Jesus answers, "Feed my lambs." Again a second time Jesus asks the same question and gets the same reply, whereupon he says, "Feed my sheep." A third time he asks the same question, and Peter, being grieved at being three times asked, makes the same answer, whereupon Jesus says once more, "Feed my sheep."

After that Jesus is said to describe (for no reason that is apparent) the death of martyrdom by which Peter will die, and then he says, "Follow me." Peter follows him a few paces and then, turning about, sees the disciple whom Jesus loved coming behind him, whereupon he says, "Lord, and what shall this man do?" Apparently he means, "Shall this man also die of martyrdom?" Jesus answers, "If I will that he tarry till I come, what is that to thee? Follow thou me."

Then the writer interposes to correct an error which had spread abroad among "the brethren" (clearly the language of a much later time) by saying that Jesus did not say that John should not die; but only that if he willed that he should remain alive until Jesus came again, what was it to Peter?

The writer closes by saying that the disciple in question (the disciple whom Jesus loved) is he who has written the Gospel of John, and "we [the brethren in general] know that his testimony is true."

Finally, there is a verse which, in its utter ineptitude, reads like something out of the feeblest of the apocryphal Gospels of the second century.

> And there are also many other things which Jesus did, the which, if they should be written every one, I [some unknown writer] suppose that even the world itself could not contain the books that should be written.

Is there any good reason why I should not say, what I strongly feel, that this last chapter of the Gospel of John is an outrage on the memory of Jesus?

Why was it written and when? We can only offer a suggestion based on what we know of the history and dissensions of the early Church. Several things are clear.

1. That the whole scene is untrue if the other Gospel stories are true.

2. It is an attempt (the only one, as far as I can see, except the reference to Jesus appearing to certain of his followers in a mountain) to carry out the prediction of the angels at the sepulchre, and of Jesus when met by the Galilean women on their way back from the sepulchre to Jerusalem, that after his Resurrection he would rejoin his disciples (for no apparent reason) in Galilee.

3. The early Church in Jerusalem was clearly presided over by James, the natural brother of Jesus, and to whom both Paul and Peter at an earlier time had had to present themselves and account for their ministry.

4. James was stoned to death about A.D. 56 and after that the presidency of the Church became a matter of dispute between the two larger groups into which it had become, in some degree, divided, the group of Peter and the group of Paul.

5. I conclude that this story was originated, either then or later, by a partisan of the group of Peter, and the object was to put into the mouth of Jesus another phrase that could be interpreted as an emphatic selection of Peter as the head of the Church. He loved Jesus more than the others. He was to die as Jesus himself died!

One further point comes out parenthetically. Verse 23 shows the current idea which existed a generation after the death of Jesus concerning what was to befall the *living* followers of Jesus. At his coming they were not to die. Those who were still alive at the time of his coming would live for ever.

Verse 24 suggests that this chapter was written after the Gospel of John had got into circulation. It is commonly believed that *John* was first circulated about A.D. 90. Therefore, this chapter was probably interpolated between that time and the time of the death of John in (about) A.D. 92.

It is significant that according to *Acts* (I, 6) the disciples had not abandoned their original hope of the restoration of the kingdom of Israel, even after Jesus rose from the grave (or at his last appearances among them), just before his Ascension. They asked of him, saying, "Lord, wilt thou *at this time* restore the kingdom of Israel?" And Jesus reproves them by saying that which he had said during his lifetime, that it is not for them to know when the kingdom of God will come. This is highly significant.

VII. Comparing the Gospel Stories

Here is a table of the events concerning the Resurrection as narrated in the four Gospels.

1. He appears to Mary Magdalene and the other Mary (*Matthew* XXVIII, 9).
2. He appears to Mary Magdalene alone (*Mark* XVI, 9).
3. Peter runs to the grave (*Luke* XXIV, 12).
4. Peter and John run to the grave (*John* XX, 4).
5. Peter looks in the grave (*Luke* XXIV, 12).
6. John looks in the grave (*John* XX, 5).
7. Peter sees the clothes lying alone (*Luke* XXIV, 12).
8. Peter sees the clothes, and the napkin not lying with the clothes (*John* XX, 6, 7).
9. Peter goes home (*Luke* XXIV, 12).
10. Peter and John go home again (*John* XX, 10).

My conclusion is that most of these incidents, instead of strengthening each other, eliminate and destroy each other. What locality did Jesus indicate for his appearance after his Resurrection?

1. "But after I am risen again, I will go before you into Galilee" (*Matthew* XXVI, 32). Look at the text, and one sees that these words have no relation to what goes before and comes after them. Jesus has been saying that his disciples (they have left the scene of the Last Supper, sung a hymn and gone on to the Mount of Olives) will be *offended* because of him that night, and that it will be with him as it is written in the prophets that when the

shepherd is smitten the sheep of the flock will be scattered abroad. In plainer words he is saying, "I am about to be taken prisoner, and you will run away and leave me to save yourselves."

This is what goes before the passage about Galilee. What follows has no reference to Galilee, but it has a very immediate and distinct reference to what Jesus has said about the shepherd being smitten and the sheep being scattered.

"No," says Peter, "though all men shall be *offended* because of thee, yet will *I* never be offended." Then Jesus tells him that before the cock crows he will deny him thrice.

Was there ever a more obvious interpolation than verse 32, about going before the disciples into Galilee? It is a very clumsy and stupid interpolation by a totally illiterate editor.

2. "But go your way, tell his disciples and Peter that he goeth before you into Galilee; there shall ye see him, as he said unto you" (*Mark* XVI, 7). This would have no value apart from the passage in *Matthew*. As the passage in *Matthew* is, in my view, a manifest interpolation, this is also valueless.

It is also entirely destroyed by the second version of Jesus's appearance after the Resurrection in the same chapter in *Mark,* where it is shown that after he had appeared first to Mary Magdalene he appeared (1) to the two disciples walking in the country, (2) to eleven of the disciples as they sat at meat, and nothing is said there either about the disciples going to Galilee (as in the earlier version they were told to do) or about Jesus going to meet them there, as he is said to have told them he would.

3. "Then said Jesus unto them [the women he met when they were on their way back to Jerusalem] be not afraid; go tell my brethren that they go into Galilee, and there shall they see me" (*Matthew* XXVIII, 10).

The eleven disciples go into Galilee and see him on a mountain, where Jesus had appointed to meet them. We know nothing of such an appointment, and it conflicts with the other records of his appearance in Galilee on the shore.

4. A full account of how Jesus showed himself to his disciples at the Sea of Tiberias (*John* XXI).

It is a shocking story, as showing:

1. That the disciples had so far forgotten their ordination as apostles of Jesus as to return to the occupation, as fishermen, from which, at the beginning, he had called them.

2. That if this is to be explained and excused on the ground that they had obeyed his order to go out to Galilee, they were so destitute of every thought of him that they did not know him when they saw him; that not until he had helped them to catch fish did one of them (John) say, "It is the Lord"; that when they came ashore they dared not ask him who he was ("knowing that it was the Lord," a preposterous and impossible junction of ideas and motives); that Jesus did nothing by this appearance except glorify Peter, put him in a position of superiority to his fellow-disciples, predict the method of his (Peter's) death, and finally indicate (indirectly and not very clearly) that John should not die until he (Jesus) came again. "Tarry till I come."

It is a wholly futile story. John knows nothing of any direction of Jesus to the disciples to go into Galilee, and he makes Jesus show himself to his disciples on the day of his Resurrection in (apparently) Jerusalem, and again eight days later in Jerusalem. But his concluding chapter gives the foregoing account of the appearance of Jesus on the shores of the Lake Tiberias. A more palpable addition to the first story by John there could scarcely be. The chapter immediately preceding the last in *John* is the obvious close of John's Gospel.

And many other signs truly did Jesus in the presence of his disciples, which are not written in this book. But these are written that ye might believe that Jesus is the Christ, the Son of God; and that believing ye might have life through his name.

After this comes the feeble, ineffectual story of the appearance at Galilee.

In *Luke* there is no record of an appearance in Galilee, and Jesus never says he will meet his disciples in Galilee. Moreover, Jesus is made to say to his disciples in Jerusalem, "Tarry ye in the city of Jerusalem, until ye be endued with power from on high."

In *Acts* (I, 4) there is a more definite injunction that the disciples should not depart from Jerusalem "but wait for the promise of the Father, which, saith he, ye have heard of me." Thus Jesus commanded the disciples to remain in Jerusalem until Pentecost. If it is true that on the day of his Resurrection Jesus appeared to his disciples and commanded them not to leave Jerusalem until Pentecost (which is what it came to), then it is not true that he commanded them within the same period to go into Galilee that he might appear to them there.

The commentators, who can harmonize any contradiction to their own satisfaction, pretend to believe (a) that Jesus merely meant, Do not change your abode from Jerusalem, but feel at liberty to take walks as far as Galilee; (b) that Jerusalem, in the mouth of Jesus, meant the whole of Palestine, and that he was only telling his disciples not to set out on their evangelical missions until after Pentecost. It is difficult to see how persons of common honesty, not to say common sense, can so shuffle with plain facts. A witness in a court of law who attempted to shuffle so with plain facts would be told to stand down instantly as a person whose testimony was much worse than worthless.

Other commentators again attempt to show that the visit to Galilee was after Pentecost, but this requires us to accept the further and yet greater absurdity that Peter after his speech on the Day of Pentecost returned to his former occupation, as if nothing had happened and no great life-task lay before him as is witnessed by his commonplace words, "I go a-fishing."

It is all very foolish. And the inspiring motive of this interpolation of the incident of Galilee is clear. In the early days of the Church there was strife for authority between the leaders in Jerusalem, and to establish the unquestionable supremacy of Peter all this conflicting, ineffectual and dishonouring story was interpolated.

The first news that the grave of Jesus was open and the body gone came to the disciples by the mouths of the women.

What women? Was it by the mouth of Mary Magdalene alone? John gives Mary Magdalene alone. Why did they go to the grave? Not certainly out of any expectation of the Resurrection. Did they go to embalm the body? If so, had they not seen what Nicodemus had already done? Did they know that a stone had been rolled before the grave? Apparently they did, for they asked themselves who was to roll it back for them, recognizing their weakness as women.

At what time did they go? All agree that it was on the Sunday. At what hour? One says it was "as it began to dawn" (*Matthew*). Another that it was "at the rising of the sun" (*Mark*). *John* says it "was yet dark." "Very early in the morning" (*Luke*). The differences are totally immaterial.

The divergencies as to the rolling away of the stone do not amount to a great deal, although they are sufficient to make the story doubtful. It is impossible to say of any of the miracles, "This is what happened, not that."

Now come to the burial and Resurrection of Jesus.

In John's Gospel Joseph of Arimathæa and Nicodemus bring a mixture of myrrh and aloes (about a hundred-pound weight, an enormous quantity) and wind it in the linen clothes with the spices "as the manner of the Jews is to bury." Nothing is said about anybody else being present at the burial.

On the first day of the week, Mary Magdalene comes to the grave, while it is yet dark, and sees that the stone of the sepulchre has been "taken away." Nothing is said about why she comes, or whether she brings spices or whether others are with her.

In *Luke,* it is Joseph of Arimathæa who is mentioned as having taken down the body, wrapped it in linen and buried it. That he did this alone is improbable; but nobody else is mentioned—Nicodemus is not mentioned—and it is not said that Joseph laid preservatives in the linen.

But in *Luke* it is said that the women who had come up with Jesus from Galilee saw where and how Jesus was buried.

Strauss mentions that it would then (April 14) be *full moon.* An important point. Does this justify our conceiving a mental picture of Jesus resting in the tomb, on the night after the Crucifixion, under the white light of the Syrian moon? The scene would be quiet then (the watch not being there then in any case, for the chief priests did not ask for the watch until the Sabbath morning). All the tumult was over, the disciples were in hiding. Even the Galilean women were at home, preparing their spices.

On the first day of the week, very early in the morning, the Galilean women came back "Bringing the spices which they had prepared, and certain other things with them." They found the stone rolled away from the sepulchre. The stone was not laid on the tomb. It was rolled across the mouth of it. The women entered in and did not find the body of the Lord Jesus. Then they saw two men in shining garments who (as the women bowed down their faces to the earth) said to them, "Why seek ye the living among the dead?" It is all very impressive.

The men said, "He is not here, but is risen. Remember how he spake unto you *when he was yet in Galilee,* saying the Son of Man must be delivered into the hands of sinful men, and be crucified, and the third day rise again." The women then remembered and returned to the eleven. The disciples thought their words idle tales and believed them not.

Now as to *Mark*. Joseph of Arimathæa buried the body of Jesus in fine linen, and rolled a stone before the door of the sepulchre. Nothing is said about Joseph or anybody else bringing preservatives in the linen. Mary Magdalene and Mary the mother of Joses beheld where Jesus was laid.

Then when the Sabbath was passed (it was passed at sunset on Saturday) Mary Magdalene and Mary the mother of James (is this the same Mary as the mother of Joses?) bring sweet spices, and come to the tomb of Jesus to anoint the body. It is very early in the morning (so clearly not the Saturday evening, but the Sunday morning) and "the rising of the sun."

As they approached the tomb they asked themselves who was to *roll* away the stone from the door of the sepulchre, "for it was very great." But they found that it was already rolled away. They *entered in* and saw a young *man* (only one young man in *Mark*, not two as in *Luke*), and he told them Jesus of Nazareth was risen, and they were to go and tell his disciples that he was going before them into Galilee, and there they should see him as he said they would.

Thereupon the women went quickly away, but said nothing to anybody because they were afraid.

Here the first version of the Resurrection in *Mark* stops abruptly, and it is generally understood that the end of it has been lost. But there is a totally different version subjoined, which is most certainly not a continuation of the first version.

In this second version Jesus appeared first to Mary Magdalene. It *may* be said that this second version began later than the early hours of Sunday morning. She told the disciples while they were mourning and weeping. The disciples would not believe her.

Then Jesus appeared to two of his disciples as they walked in the country. These two told the "residue" (vile phrase suggesting a later writer). The "residue" did not believe either.

Afterwards (*when* is not said) he appeared to the eleven as they sat at meat, and upbraided them for not believing those who had seen him after he had risen. Then he told them to go into all the world and preach the gospel to every creature. And he that believed should be saved, and he that did not believe should be damned.

A pretty lot these eleven were to go into all the world on such an errand. They had not believed themselves until they had actually seen him.

The conclusion of Mark's second version is feeble in the last degree. Most certainly I should say it was by another and much inferior writer.

Finally, as to *Matthew*.

Joseph of Arimathæa wrapped the body of Jesus in a linen cloth, and buried it in a new tomb. Nothing is said about preservatives. He *rolled* the great stone to the door of the sepulchre.

The next day (the Sabbath day, clearly) the chief priests and Pharisees go to Pilate to ask him to command a watch. All this is dealt with later, for it very clearly is a story of very much later date. The only important point is that it is said that the guard "sealed the stone" (XXVII, 66).

Then "as it began to dawn" on the Sunday, Mary Magdalene and the other Mary came to the sepulchre. Nothing is said in *Matthew* about their having seen the burial of Jesus, or why they came to the grave. Nothing about spices.

There had been an earthquake, the evangelist says. An angel of the Lord had descended and *rolled* back the stone from the door and *sat on it* (a difficult thing to understand). The keepers were terrified, and became as dead men.

And now here are the clearest possible indications of a later interpolation—the whole story of the watch being interpolated. For verse 4 of Chapter XXVIII, is a distinct break in the narrative, which clearly runs on from "his raiment was white as snow" to "and the angel answered and said unto the women . . ."

The message of the angel is the same as in the other Gospels. The women run off quickly to take word to the disciples. On the way Jesus meets them and salutes them. They kneel and hold him by the feet. He bids them tell his brethren that they should go into Galilee and there they should see him.

Then come five verses of the fabricated story of the watch.

Then the chosen disciples go into Galilee, and in a mountain there Jesus appears to them. Some of them worship him; some doubt him. He speaks to them and tells them to go and teach all nations, baptizing them in the name of the Father, and of the Son, and of the Holy Ghost.

My inference would be that the whole of the conclusion of *Matthew's* story is of later date. At all events it is feeble and unconvincing.

The reference to baptism is not in keeping with the earlier

instructions of Jesus, as when he sends out the twelve and afterwards the seventy. Jesus did not attach great importance to baptism.

He did not talk of the Trinity.

VIII. The Appearance at Galilee

The appearance of Jesus to the disciples on the shores of the Lake of Galilee (*John* XXI, 11, 12) bears to my view no suggestion of reality at any point whatever.

1. It is prepared from a series of statements put into the mouth of Jesus, and into the mouth of the angel at the tomb, which are the most palpable and even impudent interpolations. No child in the study of story could fail to see that they have in every case been put in by an utterly clumsy and incompetent hand; that the verse before links on to the verse after; and that the reference to Galilee is a foreign thing that breaks the trend of the story, and has nothing to do with the thing being said.

2. It is belied by the fact that the disciples do not, and probably dare not, leave Jerusalem during the period between the Crucifixion and the Day of Pentecost.

3. It makes the disciples pitiful ingrates and fools in forsaking their Master and the mission he has committed to them, and in going back to their former occupations as men who were trying to wipe out of mind a period of painful disillusionment.

The answer that they were merely waiting for the appearance he had foretold, when he should appear to them in Galilee, has no authority in the only record of the event (*John* XXI), and is merely an excuse to account for their stupidity and pusillanimity (*if* they returned to Galilee).

4. It requires that we believe that the disciples did not know Jesus on seeing him standing on the shore, and that this is meaningless, unless it is to be assumed that after his Resurrection he adopted a different personality, an argument belied by the incident of his first appearance to the disciples in the upper room, where the disciples recognized him instantly, but supported by his first appearance to Mary Magdalene at the tomb, when she mistakes him in the half-dark for the gardener, and also by the incident of the two disciples on the road to Emmaus, who do not recognize him until they see him in the act of breaking bread.

5. It requires us to believe that in the early morning while the disciples were fishing in vain on the lake, Jesus was lighting a fire of coals on the shore, with fish and bread laid thereon.

6. It is foolish and childish in saying that after the disciples had come ashore, and Jesus had asked them to "Come and dine," none of them dare ask him, "Who art thou?" because they knew he was the Lord.

7. The story of the appearance on the shore at Galilee merely stops and does not end. We do not know what happened at the end of it, what became of Jesus or what the disciples did.

Did he disappear as a spectre, leaving the disciples on the shore? What, then, became of him? What became of them? At what period did they return to Jerusalem?

All we have is a very feeble, and probably quite untrustworthy, assertion that John the Galilean was the disciple whom Jesus loved, that it was he who testified of the things written in the Gospel which now bears his name.

It is a lamentable, childish, and dishonouring story, utterly value-less as proof of the Resurrection and serving no purpose except that of further emphasizing the leadership of Peter in the Church of the future.

CHAPTER XXXVII

After the Resurrection

I. The Five Hundred Witnesses

IT IS SAID by St. Paul that Jesus was seen of 500 persons in Galilee.

Where did Paul learn this? When? Was it from Peter during the few days he spent with him in Jerusalem after his (Paul's) three years in exile in Arabia? But Peter never refers to the multitude of witnesses. Mark's Gospel (assumed to be written by Peter's inspiration) does not mention the 500, unless it is in that concluding chapter which is supposed to be lost. *Luke* does not mention the 500 witnesses. On the contrary, both *Mark* and *Luke,* as they have come down to us, complete the story of the Resurrection to the exclusion of the incidents of the 500 witnesses.

Then, think of the incident of the 500 witnesses in its inevitable effect on the time. Five hundred persons prepared to say that "I have seen in the flesh one who was supposed to be put to death," must have made some impression. It is incredible that such a fact would have been hidden. It would become known. And being known (even as a report) to the high priests, what would they have done? They would most certainly have taken measures to silence a report so damning to themselves. That they had led to the crucifixion of a god! That the man Jesus of Nazareth had actually been what he claimed to be! That he had committed no blasphemy!

If the high priests had taken that view, they must have hidden their heads. But they did no such thing.

The next time we hear of them they are denouncing the people who have the audacity to say that Jesus rose from the dead. Or suppose they had heard the story and had not believed it, what would they have done? They would have hailed the repeaters of the story before the Sanhedrin and punished them.

They did not—until much later when "filled with indignation they laid hands on the apostles" (see *Acts* V, 17, 18).

Or, again, suppose that Pontius Pilate had heard that people (as many as 500 of them) were going about saying that they had seen, talked and eaten with the man whom he had ordered to be crucified —what would he have done?

He would have remembered that Joseph of Arimathæa had asked permission to bury Jesus, and he would have sent for Joseph and said, "Did not you tell me that you wished to bury that man? *Did* you bury him? What happened then?"

And would not Pilate have sent for his centurion and said, "When I asked you if the man had been any while dead, did you not tell me that it was so? What about this report by 500 that he is alive and walking about? Was he not dead? Had he only fainted? Was he resuscitated? If so, by whom? By Joseph of Arimathæa? Then both you and Joseph must account to me for what you have done."

Of if Pilate had been glad of an excuse to ignore and forget the whole miserable matter, would not the Jews, who had set on the tomb a watch which had failed, because (by their own invented account) the disciples of Jesus had come by night and stolen the body away while they slept, have called on Pilate to re-arrest Jesus as one who had not died at all, and therefore had never suffered the penalty of his condemnation, but had, by trickery, escaped it, and was now walking in Galilee free?

The whole story of the 500 witnesses is incredible. That a little group of disciples should, in their secret room behind closed doors, tell each other that he who had been put to death had risen again, and that forty days later, in the religious ecstasy of Pentecost, they should talk openly of his Resurrection *and say he was now ascended into Heaven,* and that both the high priests and Pilate should have turned a deaf ear to all this, thinking it the foolish talk of over-excited fanatics—all this is credible.

But that 500 persons should be walking about Galilee telling a plain circumstantial story that they had seen and spoken to a man who had been dead and buried, and that nobody took special notice of this—all this is unbelievable.

Furthermore, and as a final point, with such a cloud of testimony, what further witness to the truth of the claims of Jesus could the world want? Why should there have been any doubt? Why did not the gospel of Jesus take complete possession of the whole Galilean world—instantly?

But instead of doing so the faith in Jesus as a risen Saviour had to fight its way through persecution, prison, courts, and so on.

Is the Resurrection, therefore, a myth? By no means. It requires to be stripped of the unnecessary, the unbelievable. It is the difficulty that besets the faith of all great beings (and Jesus above all) that his followers always try to prove too much. In trying to prove too much they destroy belief instead of increasing it.

The Resurrection of the Spirit of Jesus is clearly established. It is established on simple testimony which we cannot doubt.

All this effort to establish by numbers of witnesses, by the testimony of his wounds, his ability to eat and drink, as a man, and then ascend to Heaven with all his organs, as a man—all this hurts, detracts, destroys.

II.   Dr. Headlam's Arguments

Dr. Headlam (bishop of Gloucester) states as his opinion that "It is impossible to harmonize the accounts given in the four Gospels *because they are incomplete and to some extent inaccurate."* But this is feeble.

It is impossible to harmonize them because they are contradictory in statements of fact, and because one includes scenes which others render impossible. Yet Dr. Headlam believes that "there is still poor evidence for the Resurrection of Jesus having been physical in the sense that (in whatever respects his new body may have been different from his old body) it involved, at any rate, the disappearance of the old body from the tomb."

Not necessarily. In one account we have only Mary Magdalene's evidence that the tomb was empty, and in two accounts that the empty tomb was that of Jesus. But in all the Gospels the risen body was so far the old body that it bore the scars of the Cross, and in at least two of the accounts it ate and drank, and thus possessed the ordinary cravings and organs of digestion as the old body. Nothing, therefore, could be essentially different in the new body from the old one, if the narratives in the Gospels are to be taken as they stand. There is the plain fact that Jesus, according to one account, ascended to Heaven with an undigested meal in his body.

No, the stories of the Resurrection in the Gospels have to be read in the light of the time in which they were written, and probably rewritten again and yet again, to meet the objections of a people (in many countries) who, though familiar with the idea of life in a hereafter, were totally unprepared for belief in a resurrection from the dead—the miracles of Jesus notwithstanding.

There are three facts to go upon: (1) the fundamental belief in the Resurrection in the primitive community; (2) the fact of the empty tomb of which he (Headlam) will not at all allow that St. Paul's account shows that he had no knowledge; (3) a considerable number of narratives bearing witness to the fact that the disciples had seen the risen Lord. Something happened which entirely changed the character and attitude of the disciples.

The last clause is undoubtedly true. It is the fundamental truth. While Jesus was alive the disciples heard him say again and again (according to the Gospels) that after three days he would rise again; but there is not a word to show that they grasped his meaning. If they had done so their conduct on his arrest, during his trial, after his condemnation and during his Crucifixion, and for some time later must have been entirely different. Without being fools they could not have run away from one who was so far omnipotent that he was shortly to conquer death. They could not have been afraid of what the Jews would do to them, as accomplices in the alleged blasphemy of Jesus, if they had absolutely believed that it was not blasphemy.

It was only after the conviction forced itself upon them (whether from report from Mary Magdalene or by the witness of their own eyes) that Jesus had actually conquered death and risen from the dead, and was so far the same in body that he could ask them to touch him, that he could speak to them, that he could eat and drink with them, it was only *then* that they were confident that their Master was what they had called him—the Son of God, the Christ.

But does all this establish the conflicting accounts of the Resurrection? Does it require that he should be seen again and again by the same disciples under different conditions, while adding nothing whatever to the original story that is of the essence of it? Does it justify the appearance on the shores of Galilee, which is full of improbability and has no apparent motive but that of putting special authority into the power of Peter? Does the story of the Resurrection get any additional authority from the evidence of Paul (much later) that Jesus was seen by 500 pairs of eyes?

Does it require the ineffectual story of his appearance to the two disciples walking to Emmaus?

Does it need the story of the second visit to the room of the disciples in order that Thomas may put his hands into the wounds of Jesus and be reproved?

Are the evidences of the Resurrection the stronger for these stories, so obviously the product of a later date, so clearly afterthoughts, so manifestly meant to meet the objections of an age that had never before heard of a body rising out of the grave after death, and walking about and eating and drinking as before in life?

Is it not enough to accept the Resurrection on the grounds on which St. Paul accepted it on the road to Damascus, without seeing any body, any face, only hearing a voice from Heaven, which announced to him that Jesus of Nazareth still lived?

Is it, too, not enough to account for the something that had happened "entirely to change the character and attitude of the disciples," that three days after the Crucifixion, death and burial of Jesus they had come to believe, whether merely by the report of Mary Magdalene (which at first they disbelieved), or by that, plus their own actual sight of him in the room with them, appearing suddenly among them, when the doors were locked, speaking to them, assuring them, charging them, and then going off as suddenly as he came?

This belief never changed. The disciples never wavered in it. When the high priests challenged it and would have punished them for it (inasmuch as it charged them with the worst error of crucifying a god), and did actually stone Stephen for it, the disciples went on saying it, and saying what was implied by it, namely that the man who had conquered death was divine, was Christ, was God, and they went to their deaths for saying it, not only in their own country but also in Rome.

Surely *this* is the real evidence of the Resurrection, and it is nine parts more spiritual evidence of a spiritual Resurrection, of which, down to that moment, the world knew nothing.

My own view is that all this hunger after physical proof of the Resurrection is injuring the belief in it, that all these shifting and shuffling supplementary stories in the Gospels (put in, as I believe, long after the original Gospels were written) have acted as agents towards the rejection of belief in the Resurrection.

Whatever the value of the material and physical proofs of the Resurrection of the body of Jesus exactly as it was put into the tomb by Joseph of Arimathæa, I think they have been of less than no value in the centuries since.

The believer in Jesus does not need the evidence of the wounds, of the broiled fish, and the other material and not very noble and certainly very perplexing proofs.

The Resurrection of Jesus is sufficient for the believer on the grounds on which St. Paul received it. He needs no other evidence.

III. What Jesus Foretold

According to the Gospels, Jesus predicted his Resurrection just as clearly as he predicted his death. As often as he said that he was to die, and indicated clearly that he was to be crucified, he added that on the third day he would rise again from the dead.

Now here is something which no clearness and depth of human intellect could have enabled himself to foresee. How did he come by that knowledge—that after his death he should arise again? If he meant that his physical body which had gone through death, and could in ordinary course begin corruption, should rise up, as if from sleep, and walk the world again, as if no such thing as death had ever occurred to it, then he could only have known this by divine teaching, by direct revelation from powers higher than human powers—in a word by God. Or if not by God then he knew he *must himself have been God*.

But here arises an important question. What did Jesus actually mean by rising again? And by rising again on the third day?

Did he mean that his cause, his mission, after coming to sudden death in his own person, would rise again in a very short time to renewed life? Is this the only meaning which the disciples attached to his prediction? If they had understood his words literally, that on the third day he was actually to rise out of the grave, could they have behaved as they are reported to have behaved? If Mary went alone to the grave in the early dawn on Sunday morning, did she go expecting the fulfilment of his prophecy that he would rise again?

When she had ocular proof that his body was not there would she have lamented and asked the man whom she mistook for the gardener if he had taken the body of her Lord away? Or if she went to the grave with the other Mary, were they not so far (so utterly far) from expecting that Jesus would have risen from the dead that they took spices to embalm his body against too rapid corruption? And could the disciples have been astonished when Mary returned to them and told her story? Would they have regarded as an idle tale the literal fulfilment of what Jesus had repeatedly told them would actually take place? Would the disciples have returned to Galilee, and resumed their former occupation as fishermen, if they had really understood that within three days after his death their Master would rise from the grave to another and much greater life? Surely, one thing is beyond question—that the disciples never really grasped the idea which Jesus intended them to understand, that on the third day after his death he would literally and physically rise from the grave.

What did they understand by his words? Or did he ever speak these words at all? And were the words "on the third day I will rise again from the dead" put into his mouth after the event had, in the belief of the apostles, actually taken place? Further, did Jesus use the words in the figurative sense that his mission would not die, but rise out of his tomb to a new and greater life? It is impossible to accept this. More than once the words are used with such literalness, and in such close proximity to words that could not possibly be understood except in a literal sense (reference to his Crucifixion, being "lifted up"), that it is wholly and utterly impossible to think that in a single sentence he would pass from literal speech to metaphysical speech.

IV. The Vital Problem

I am compelled to conclude that Jesus did positively say that on the third day he would actually rise from the dead. But how did he come by this idea, this strange thought, without parallel in the world before him?

No man, unless Lazarus, had ever before died, been buried, and then, after an interval, short or long, risen out of the tomb, and lived again on the earth. It is a startling, incomprehensible thought. Did it come from God? Was it a divine revelation to him? Did he know it, as he is said to have known all things, because he *was* God? Was he thinking of the prophecy of David—that God's Holy One could not be left to corruption? "For thou wilt not leave my soul in hell; neither wilt thou suffer thine Holy One to see corruption" (*Psalms* XVI, 10). Was his belief in his Resurrection built on his confidence in prophecy, his certainty of what that prophecy told of him?

Is his reference to Jonah having been three days in the belly of the whale as a type of the three days which he is to be in the bowels of the earth to be taken as the expression of his foreknowledge of the period of time in which he would be in the grave and the time of his burial?

Is his reply to his disciples about the Temple, that if they destroy it in three other days he will raise it up afresh, also to be understood, as the evangelist says, to refer to his foreknowledge that the temple of his body would in three days be raised from destruction to new life?

Though Jesus did not indeed speak of his future Resurrection, it was none the less foreknown to him. How was it foreknown? In a supernatural manner, by means of the prophetic spirit, the higher principle that dwelt with him, by means (in short) of his divine nature? Or did he know it in a natural manner by means of his human reason? If by the former, there is nothing more to say. But if by the latter, what operation of his human reason can possibly have told Jesus that after being actually dead and buried he should come to life again and rise out of the grave?

Here is the vital problem.

Thrice at least in the Gospels Jesus is made to establish his belief in his Resurrection on the third day on prophecy. First, in the reference to Jonah. Second, in the reply about Herod in which he said:

> Go ye, and tell that fox, Behold, I cast out devils, and I do cures to-day and to-morrow, and the third day I shall be perfected.

This is not a definite and literal statement about the time of his Resurrection. As a definite statement it proved to be untrue. As a figurative statement it might bear no reference to the Resurrection.

Third, when going up to Jerusalem for the last time from the neighbourhood of Jericho, and he says to the twelve:

> Behold, we go up to Jerusalem, and all things that are written by the prophets concerning the Son of Man shall be accomplished. For he shall be delivered unto the Gentiles, and shall be mocked, and

spitefully entreated, and spitted on. And they shall scourge him, and put him to death; and the third day he shall rise again.

It is here said that the disciples understood none of these things. All this occurred *before* his Resurrection. *After* his Resurrection (as when he talks with the disciples on their way to Emmaus) he reproaches them with not knowing that what had happened *must* come to pass:

> O fools, and slow of heart to believe all that the prophets have spoken. Ought not Christ to have suffered these things, and to enter into his glory? And beginning at Moses and all the prophets, he expounded unto them in all the Scriptures the things concerning himself.

But here comes the difficulty, *that nowhere is any single passage given* as having been interpreted by Jesus as referring to his Resurrection. The whole burden of the conversation with the disciples is about the marvel of the Resurrection, which the disciples find it hard to believe, notwithstanding the testimony of the women who had seen the vision of the angels "which said that he was alive"; and yet Jesus is not represented as quoting one word of Old Testament prophecy in justification of his statement that his Resurrection was prophesied. Nor can we ourselves find anything in the prophecies of the Old Testament which would justify us in saying the Resurrection of Jesus was foreknown. The Jonah passage has no obvious reference to the Resurrection, it is merely made to typify it.

Is the Resurrection to be conceived as a miracle? Was it within the divine power of Jesus to foresee that miracle? Why did he not speak so plainly about his Resurrection as to prevent the possibility of any misunderstanding on the part of his disciples, or any such ridiculous and cowardly behaviour as they were obviously guilty of after his death?

Are the references to prophecy in the New Testament to be understood as we understand the illusions of one who has looked at the sun and cannot see anything that meets his gaze. Were they so blinded by their enthusiasm for the new Messiah that they saw him in every page of the Old Testament? This is Strauss's view. I see no way of refuting it.

V. My Own Conclusion

My conclusion, after long and serious thought, is that Jesus did not tell his disciples that after three days he would rise from the dead, meaning by that as a physical being, such as he had been in life. Or that if he *did,* his disciples did not so understand him—that he was to die, to be laid in the grave, that he was to remain there three days, and was then to rise afresh to human life.

If Jesus told his disciples that he was to rise in three days, and if they did not understand him (or understand him in the way in which he should have been understood), he was at fault, because if he knew all things, and if no man needed to tell him anything, he must have known that they did not understand him. If he knew that they did not understand him, he had no ground for reproaching them (after the Resurrection) as he does in the second Resurrection story in *Mark* (XVI, 14) in which he is said to have "upbraided them with their unbelief and hardness of heart, because they believed not them which had seen him after he was risen." *They,* in the case of this story, were Mary Magdalene and the two disciples walking into the country only, for when they told the "residue" that they had seen him the "residue" did not believe them.

If Jesus told his disciples that he was to rise again in three days, and if they understood him to speak literally, not figuratively (as of some spiritual rising of his faith, his mission), their conduct from the moment of his arrest, and particularly after his trial and Crucifixion, is beyond all possibility of human belief. They had been told that their Master was to do what never man had done, he was to conquer death; they had told him that they believed he was the Christ who was to bring in the kingdom of Heaven, and he had acquiesced in that name; and yet they ran away, hid away, fled from the police of the Temple who had arrested him, in obvious fear of being themselves arrested as his accomplices, and remained hidden.

Such conduct in men who knew what they must have known, if Jesus had actually told them that he was to rise again from the grave in three days, passes all limit of belief. It was the act of fools and cowards. In a word it is utterly unbelievable on any basis of sanity on the part of the disciples.

Assuming that they had really grasped the idea that their Master was to conquer death, and therefore turn to naught all the machinations of his enemies, what would have been their natural course of conduct? Surely they would have stood by him, they would have been with him at the inquiry of the chief priests; they would have witnessed for him in the trial before Pilate; they would have risked any peril to themselves, because they would have known that within three days the acts of the enemies of Jesus would be confounded, and the Christ, risen and glorified by the triumph over death, would straightway establish the kingdom of God.

They acted entirely differently. One of them, Judas, was so ignorant of, or so indifferent to, the idea of the Resurrection which was to come to pass in three days that he betrayed his Master when he must have known that within three days his Master would have it within his power to punish him. Another was so ignorant of the idea of the Resurrection that he denied that he had ever known his Master; the other ten hid themselves behind closed doors during his trial, during his Crucifixion (leaving a few of the women to look on at it from afar off), and all the following day—Saturday.

In short, the attitude of the disciples seems to have been as follows:

1. At Cæsarea Philippi, and at various times afterwards, they were told that he was to suffer many things and be killed, and after three days he was to rise again.

2. They rebelled against the idea of his suffering and being killed, and they were rebuked for their rebellion. But they did not then, or at any time, say anything about the forthcoming Resurrection, suggest that they had ever heard of it, or, having heard of it, had understood what it meant.

3. Again, as they approached Judæa on their way up to Jerusalem, they are told what things are to happen to them—that in Jerusalem Jesus is to be delivered to the high priests, and they shall condemn him to death and deliver him to the Gentiles, and mock him and scourge him, and spit upon him, and kill him, and the third day he shall rise again. But again they gave no hint that they had any conception of the Resurrection. They set themselves to a foolish rivalry about the places they were to occupy when his time of glory came.

4. On the journey up to Jerusalem they were repeatedly told the same story; but the only thing that seems to have fully entered into

their consciousness was that they were going up to the triumph of Jesus—that the kingdom of God would immediately appear.

5. That they entered Jerusalem with their Master in this confident expectation, and that their hosannas to the son of David, and those of the crowd, were meant to express their confident hope that the new era was on the point of beginning.

6. That little by little, during the few remaining days of the life of Jesus in Jerusalem, he set himself to make them realize that his glory was to come through suffering and death, and that slowly they did realize this—that he was surrounded by dangers, that he was being betrayed into the hands of the authorities by one of themselves. I think this prompted them to talk foolishly about buying swords to protect him, and perhaps led one of them (Peter) to buckle one foolish sword about his waist.

I think this sense of impending danger was strong upon them during the Last Supper, that it oppressed their hearts as they sang the hymn, and then walked with him through the dark city to the garden of Gethsemane; and was weighing them down when he told them that his soul was exceedingly sorrowful unto death.

7. I think that at that time they felt that his arrest was certain; but they did not know when it would take place, or what he would do. When it did actually take place the last of their hopes of the establishment of the Kingdom fell to wreck, and they fled away to save themselves.

8. In their hiding they were probably ashamed of their cowardice, but saw no merit in exposing themselves to danger. Jesus had failed them. Or (without reproaching him) their faith in him had failed. They had made a mistake. He was arrested, condemned, crucified, buried. As soon as it was safe they would steal away from Jerusalem, return to their own country, Galilee, and resume their former occupations.

9. Then Mary Magdalene at the early dawn of Sunday morning (the first hour at which she could go without breaking the Sabbath, on the Holy Day of Passover) went to the place of the burial of Jesus, not to take spices for the preservation of his body, but to pay the devotion of her love by kneeling before the tomb in which his body lay.

And now, what about Jesus himself? Did he know that he was to rise from the grave on the third day? If so, did he know by divine inspiration? By his own divine knowledge, knowing all things? By prophecy? Or by any natural means or process of reason?

It is impossible to say he did not know without denying his divinity. If he knew by virtue of his divinity there was no need to know by prophecy. It was impossible that he could know by natural means, by unaided process of reason; for nothing of the kind had ever occurred before, and there was nothing but divine intuition to say that such a thing could or would ever occur. But is it to be believed that he told his disciples that he was to rise again on the third day by virtue of what the Scriptures had foretold of him?

There is no indication, as far as I can see, that during his lifetime he ever claimed prophetic authority for the prediction that he was to rise again on the third day.

It is only *after* the Resurrection that either he or anybody else claims prophetic authority for the Scripture, for the fact which now has taken place. In conversation with the two disciples on the country road to Emmaus he is said to reproach them with their surprise that his Resurrection should have taken place on the ground that it had been foretold in the Scriptures. But there is not one word of Scripture quoted to justify this reproach. And I do not know of any word of Scripture in which it is said that Jesus is to rise again on the third day. The only references to the third day in the Old Testament Scriptures bear no reasonable relation to the Resurrection of Jesus. It is useless to contend with the people who think they do.

Again, after he has risen (see *Luke* XXIV, 40, 44–46) Jesus having shown them the marks in his hands and feet, told his disciples that he had said to them while he was living with them "that all things must be fulfilled, which were written in the law of Moses, and in the prophets, and in the psalms, concerning me. . . . Thus it is written, and thus it behoved Christ to suffer, and to *rise from the dead the third day,* and that repentance and remission of sins should be preached in his name among all nations, beginning at Jerusalem."

But the difficulty is that we have no record that the Scriptures ever said that he was to rise from the dead on the third day.

In short, my conclusion is: (1) that Jesus never in his natural life told his disciples that on the third day he would rise again from the dead; (2) alternatively, that if he did tell them so, they did not understand him, and that there is no evidence whatever that during his lifetime they had any conception whatever of the Resurrection; (3) that Jesus could not have reproached or upbraided his disciples for not believing the evidence of those who had seen him after his Resurrection, inasmuch as they had no other conceivable ground for believing the incredible thing than their word, which might be an "idle tale," a dream due to hallucination.

But does it follow from all this that Jesus did not rise from the dead? And that he did not rise after (or within) three days? By no means.

I believe in the Resurrection of Jesus. I believe he rose from the dead after (or within) three days. But I do not find it necessary to believe any of the physical stories that surround the story of the Resurrection. I do not believe in the story of the Jewish watch. I do not believe in the stories of Peter and John and their run to the grave. I do not believe in the appearance of Jesus to Mary Magdalene and the other Mary on their way back to Jerusalem. I do not believe in the story of the angel who sat on the stone; of the two angels who sat within the tomb; of the reminder of the promise of Jesus to meet them in Galilee. I do not believe that he met the disciples on the shore in Galilee, or on the mountains in Galilee. I do not believe the story of Thomas and the sign of the wounds in the hands and side; the eating of broiled fish, either in Jerusalem or in Galilee (on the shore).

I believe Jesus rose in the sense indicated by St. Paul in I *Corinthians* XV. *He died a temporal body. He rose a spiritual body.* He appeared to Mary Magdalene. He appeared to his disciples when they were together within closed doors. Perhaps he ascended to Heaven from the Mount of Olives from the midst of his disciples, who then returned to their homes in Jerusalem.

I think all the rest of the Resurrection story was imported into it long after the event—to answer sceptical objections; to buttress up the belief of Jewish converts from Scriptures; to meet the objections of the Gnostics who had begun to doubt the corporeality of Jesus, his actuality. To meet, too, the objections of those who were saying that the Resurrection was only a vision, a dream, a hallucination.

But I believe the Resurrection (in Paul's sense) was an absolute reality, that it does not need to be buttressed up by passages from prophecy of doubtful relevance, or manifestly of no relevance at all.

I believe the whole Christian faith rests on the foundation that Jesus of Nazareth, having alone, of all human beings, conquered death, risen again and appeared among men, was the Son of God.

My belief in the Resurrection of Jesus does not require all the materialistic evidence (often very poor and unconvincing) which seems to have been necessary to most of the Jews and Gentiles of nearly two thousand years ago. It is not necessary to me.

The belief of St. Paul did not require it.

What was the quality and nature of the body of Jesus after the Resurrection? Was it a physical or a spiritual body of Jesus which appeared to the disciples?

According to *Matthew,* when the women were hastening back from the grave to Jerusalem they met Jesus, and they fell down and embraced his feet in veneration. It was therefore a real physical body.

Luke and *Mark* tell the story of the appearance of Jesus to the two disciples on their walk into the country. In *Mark* all this narrative is in few words. In *Luke* we are told that Jesus goes with the two disciples and breaks bread with them. It must have been a real body which broke real bread. But the next moment Jesus mysteriously disappears from the sight of the disciples. So the real body becomes a spiritual one.

Was it the sight of the wounds in his hands or the breaking bread that caused the disciples to recognize him?

In the assembling of the disciples in Jerusalem when Jesus suddenly appeared in their midst, they at first thought he was a ghost. But to dispel this idea he shows his hands and feet to them, and makes them touch him, and then calls for food and eats some broiled fish. Therefore it was not a real physical body which entered the locked room by supernatural means, but it *was* a real body which ate, and could be touched and handled.

Mark and *Luke* add, as the close of the earthly life of the risen Jesus, that he was taken away before the eyes of the disciples. This indicates the disappearance of a supernatural body. The disappearance is described in *Acts* (I, 9) as occurring in a cloud. Once more a supernatural body. In *John* Jesus stands behind Mary Magdalene as she is turning away from the grave and calls her by name. His voice is real. But *voice* is constantly used in the Scriptures by invisible spirits.

Jesus forbids Mary Magdalene to touch him. This may be said to indicate a spiritual body. The reason he gives does not tally with the fact in the other Gospels, that he incites the disciples to do what he has forbidden Mary to do—touch him. Therefore, nothing can be made of the incident. But when Thomas sees the risen Jesus he does actually touch the place of his wounds, and this proof of the physical reality of Jesus is what makes Thomas cry, "My Lord and my God."

When Jesus appears to his disciples in Galilee on the mountain we know nothing of his body. But when he appears on the shore of Tiberias his body is real, for he dines with the disciples, obviously taking the food even as they did.

Later, when Jesus appears to Paul, his body is not present. Only his voice is heard. What happened at his appearance to James (presumably his brother) we do not know. What happened at the appearance to the 500 we do not know, except that he spoke and may therefore have been a voice only. Whether he ate and drank, and was touched by them, we do not hear.

Either the body of Jesus after his Resurrection was a natural body, subject to the laws of a human body, or it was a supernatural body, not subject to these laws—the physical and organic laws of real life, such as digestion, the inability to pass through a solid substance like a wall or a door, to rise in the air, to vanish from human sight.

Many passages in the Gospels speak of a perfectly natural and human life on the part of Jesus after the Resurrection. Had he a physical and earthly corporeality, or was it a heavenly corporeality? If he consumed earthly food his corporeality was obviously of the earth. If he walked with two men on the earth his body was of the earth. On the other hand if he merely appeared and disappeared, as to Mary Magdalene at the grave, to the disciples in the closed room in Jerusalem, his corporeality may have been heavenly.

The explanation that he disappeared and reappeared in a natural manner, merely evading observation, will not bear consideration. Either he was a real person, or he was a spiritual being, subject to none of the laws of a physical body.

The efforts of the Rationalists to account for the events of the life of Jesus after his Resurrection by banishing the miraculous breaks down instantly. It is either one or the other. We must either acknowledge the physical evidences (eating, drinking, walking, and so on), and thereby accept the idea of a real physical body, or reject this, and thereby accept the idea of a spiritual manifestation. The idea that a body which consists of solid matter can pass without hindrance through other solid matter outrages common knowledge.

Attempts to explain the appearance of Jesus in the closed room by saying that somebody opened the door to him is to reduce the whole story to absurdity. The door was shut and remained so, and yet Jesus appeared in the room—that is the plain sense of the narrative, and all the rest is nonsense. The supernatural will not admit of being removed or explained away without the whole narrative being destroyed, together with its sense and significance.

That Mary Magdalene took Jesus to be the gardener because he had borrowed the gardener's clothes is just one of countless examples of the absurdities to which the totally unimaginative Rationalists descend when they try to account for facts contrary to the laws of nature by materialistic explanations.

Did Jesus, after his Resurrection, return to a purely natural existence, such as he had had before his Crucifixion? It is ridiculous to think so. It makes his death and burial a purposeless farce, a thing that might as easily have been avoided. Why did he die? Why was he buried? What is all the fuss about, if the death of Jesus was not real, was not irrevocable, was not a final thing?

Does this forbid the belief in the Resurrection? By no means. It only makes impossible the idea of the Resurrection of the natural body that was laid in the grave. There was no going back on the fact that the life of Jesus as a natural man *ended* on the Cross. On the Cross Jesus actually died. There he died for the first and last time. And when he lived again it was not as a man merely (if at all), but as a God, no longer subject to the laws of pain and death, no longer eating and drinking earthly food, but above all this, having no need of all this.

How, then, do I account for all the narratives in the Gospels which give these stories of physical reality? By the unbelief of the disciples of Jesus, who had not witnessed his spiritual appearances and could not conceive of them; who, like Thomas, could not believe until seeing. Also, I account for this by the effort of the early Christians to convince the unbelieving Jews.

Just as they had to resort to such stories (not necessarily deliberate fabrications, but the insensate growth of legends as they passed from mouth to mouth) to account for the fact that Jesus had risen from the grave at all, so they had to resort to such stories to convince the unbelieving world that they were not merely dreaming, that they were not mere visionaries, intoxicated (however innocently) by their faith. They must lay hold of something real. So they laid hold of the fact of the wounds in the hands and feet of Jesus, that Thomas had thrust his hand into the side of Jesus, that Jesus had actually overcome their fear that he was only a phantom who had taken possession of their sight, by calling for food, so that they might see him eat.

It was no more than the struggle of poor, unenlightened, unimaginative human nature in simple men and women to convince others that what they had seen was real; and, above all, to go on *believing this themselves*. A very important point.

That they did believe in the actual reality of the risen Lord cannot be doubted by anyone who considers what they did to prove their belief. They died for it—hundreds, thousands. They lived for it, not one year, but ten, twenty, thirty years and more through endless and most cruel persecution, when they might have escaped all their sufferings by a word, by saying, "I thought so, but I deceived myself, I must have done so; I really saw a phantom, but it was the spirit, and not the body of Jesus."

There are other minor difficulties. For example, the stone was rolled away from the tomb. Why? To allow the risen body to come forth. But the same body, the same night, entered into the upper room when the doors were closed. Therefore, the rolling away of the stone was not necessary to the risen Christ.

Then one must ask, What clothes did Jesus wear during the forty days he was on the earth after the Resurrection? He had been naked on the Cross. His own clothes had been taken away from him by the Roman soldiers. The linen in which Joseph of Arimathæa had wrapped his body was lying in the empty tomb. The napkin which the Jews wrapped about the head of the dead was there. What had become of the hundredweight of preservatives which Nicodemus had buried with Jesus we do not hear. Nothing is said about it, whether it was there or had gone. In what clothes had he gone out? If his were a corporeal body he must have been clothed. He was not recognized at first by many of those to whom he appeared; was it because he wore other dress?

I dismiss all such considerations by saying that the body which rose from the tomb was the spiritualized body described by St. Paul. The body which, according to Paul, we must all have at the universal Resurrection. Therefore, the clothes disappear in this consideration. The clothes Jesus wore in life he would seem to his disciples to be wearing still.

The women who came with Jesus from Galilee beheld the sepulchre, and how the body of Jesus was laid. They were apparently the only persons who saw Jesus buried. Early on the Sunday morning they brought spices, intending to put them with the body. But they found the stone (of which there is no previous mention in *Luke*) rolled away from the sepulchre. Later, they returned to the eleven, and at first were not believed. Then (*Luke* XXIV, 12) "Peter ran to the sepulchre [no mention of anybody else with him] and stooping down, he beheld the linen clothes laid by themselves."

Peter did not take the linen clothes away with him. A sensible man, not too excited, would have done so, in order to say to Joseph of Arimathæa, "Are these the linen clothes in which you buried him? If so, where is the body? What has happened? Is it true, as he said, that he has risen from the dead?"

In *John* the linen clothes and the napkin that had been about the head of Jesus are made yet more of.

Yet it does not occur to either Peter or John to take the linen clothes as evidence that Jesus had gone. Peter, in John's Gospel, goes into the sepulchre, and sees the linen clothes and napkin. John had arrived first, but he had only stooped down and looked in. Peter had arrived second, and he went in. Then John went in also, and "he saw and believed." Believed what? That the body of Jesus had gone? John's Gospel clearly means more. "For as yet they knew not the Scripture, that he must rise again from the dead."

"Then the disciples went away again unto their own home."

Nevertheless, the same day (XX, 19), after Mary Magdalene had told the disciples that she had seen the Lord, being within doors (which were shut for fear of the Jews) Jesus appeared to them. Were the disciples in Jerusalem or on their way back to their own homes in Galilee? Were Peter and John not there, within closed doors when Jesus appeared? It is one of two things, both stories (eliminating each other) cannot be true.

Or is it conceivable that Peter and John were both in that upper room and received that ordination from Jesus, and yet went back to their own homes and occupations in Galilee, as if it all had been a foolish dream?

I find the story utterly shocking in its stupid self-contradiction.

Jesus breathes on his disciples, confers on them the Holy Ghost, gives them power to remit sins (XX, 22), and yet in the next chapter the disciples are back in Galilee, having returned to their occupation as fishermen (Peter said "I go a-fishing"), and therefore utterly disregarding the instructions of Jesus. And he appeared to them on the seashore, dined with them, and talked to Peter.

It is all unutterably confusing, stupid and even childish.

VI.　Concerning the Holy Ghost

When was the Holy Ghost bestowed upon the disciples?

In *John* (XX, 22) we read that Jesus, appearing among his disciples in the upper room when the door was closed, breathed on them and said, "Receive ye the Holy Ghost."

But, according to Luke's last chapter, Jesus appeared to his disciples after his Resurrection, told them that they were to tarry in Jerusalem until they were endued with power from above. And that they received this power from above on the Day of Pentecost, seven weeks after the first day of the week on which, according to *John,* he had breathed upon them, and said, "Receive ye the Holy Ghost."

Naturally, the harmonizers have been at work on this conflict of evidence and concluded that the text in *John* should be not "receive ye," but "ye shall receive." Equally naturally, the harmonizers in getting out of the lesser difficulty played with the bigger one, for they make the symbolic action which is the act of granting the Holy Spirit unnecessary, and therefore ridiculous.

By his breathing on them he *conferred.* By their being breathed upon they *received.* If not, the whole passage is foolishness.

VII.　Before the Ascension

"Without the Resurrection," says Tieftrunk, "the history of Jesus would terminate in a revolting catastrophe; the eye would turn away with melancholy and dissatisfaction from an event in

which the pattern of humanity fell a victim to imperious rage, and
in which the scene closed with a death as unmerited as sorrowful. . . . The history of Jesus requires to be crowned with the
expectation towards which the moral contemplations of every one
are irresistibly drawn."

Klausner's view of the Resurrection is that the story is not a
deception, but that the Galilean disciples, and afterwards Paul,
saw their Lord and Messiah *in a vision*. In short, the Resurrection
is *spiritual,* not *material.*

VIII. *Jesus and Baptism*

During his ministry, Jesus has said little about baptism. It has
not figured prominently in his teaching. He himself has not
baptized. The references to baptism by his disciples are not
uniform, and therefore not satisfying. But in the accounts of
what he says after he has risen, great prominence is given to
baptism.

In *Matthew* (XXVII, 19), he says, "Go ye therefore, and teach
all nations, baptizing them in the name of the Father, and of the
Son, and of the Holy Ghost." This is, perhaps, the earliest statement of the Trinity. In *Mark* (XVI, 16)—the second version of
the Resurrection—are the words: "He that believeth and is baptized shall be saved; but he that believeth not shall be damned,"
language totally out of harmony with the spirit of Jesus while he
lived. It is followed (verse 18) by other words that are probably
not by Jesus—all the foolishness about immunity after drinking
any deadly thing.

In *Luke* Jesus makes no mention of baptism. In *John* he gives
no command about baptism. But in *Acts* very much is made of
baptism. Peter, on the Day of Pentecost, cries:

Repent, and be baptized every one of you in the name of Jesus
Christ for the remission of sins, and ye shall receive the gift of the
Holy Ghost. [II, 38]
Then they that gladly received his word were baptized, and the
same day there were added unto them about three thousand souls.
[II, 41]

Here comes the important consideration. Where were these
3,000 baptized? If the scene of their baptism was Jerusalem, where
was the water for the immersion of 3,000? There were only two

known pools of water in or near Jerusalem—the pool of Siloam and, after the coming of Pontius Pilate, Solomon's pool. But these were both wanted for drinking purposes.

There is, however, the fact that the impotent man was helped into the pool of Siloam when the water was troubled. This must be allowed for. Jordan was fully twenty-two miles from Jerusalem by road. A journey of forty-four miles for the baptism! It is incredible. How could the apostles baptize so many in one day? If all twelve baptized it would give 250 to each. Once more incredible.

There is the possibility of sprinkling instead of immersion. But that immersion was the rule of John the Baptist is clearly shown by his searching for a part of Jordan where there was much water. Then sprinkling instead of immersion was not practised by the Church until the third century apparently.

The conclusion is either that the first chapters of *Acts* were not written until long after the Crucifixion and the events they record, or that they were written by somebody who did not know Jerusalem or even Judæa.

My inference would be that the prominence given to baptism in the Resurrection stories is one more proof that they are of later date, some of them at least, and that, in particular, the words put into the mouth of Jesus are in great part the invention of writers coming long after his death.

By that time (whatever the date, probably the second century) the need of a sign of allegiance to the Christian community became a necessity. Hence the revival of John's baptism, and the attaching of it to Jesus. The words are Peter's, not Jesus's. "Repent and be baptized . . . for the remission of sins."

Finally, this contributes to my conclusion that some of the Resurrection stories are to be read as the product of far later times than the general body of the stories of the death and burial.

IX. *Evidence of the Gospels*

Nothing is more obvious, and few circumstances are more difficult and painful, to one who wishes to accept the Gospel stories as nearly as possible in the form in which they come down to us, than the fact that all the critics seem to make a special point of spiritualizing away the humanity of Jesus during his lifetime; so far as to make him supernaturally born, fast for long periods, be carried through the air by Satan, disappear in crowds, walk on the sea, and then of *materializing* him after his death and Resurrection, so far as to make him exhibit the wounds of the Cross, apparently healed although only some thirty-six hours have passed since they were inflicted upon him, call for bread to appease apparent hunger, eat solid food, light fires and begin to cook a meal.

This contradiction is intelligible to me only in the light of the criticism of Christianity which went on after the death of Jesus, and the repeated efforts being made by the early Christians to meet the criticism:

1. To prove that he was a being superior to all other men.

2. To disprove the statement that he was a phantom, or an idea, and had never had any real existence.

X.   *General Conclusions*

If we put aside the thought of the physical resurrection of Jesus, and conceive of the resurrection of a spiritualized body, the burial of a temporal body and the rising of a spiritual body, the burial of a corrupt body and the rising of an incorruptible body, the more serious difficulties of the Resurrection disappear.

Jesus appears to Mary, and calls her (as she believes) by her name, bidding her to go to the brethren his disciples and tell them that he has risen, as he had promised, that he still lives, and that he is not dead, and therefore all he has foretold about himself has come to pass.

Mary Magdalene goes to the disciples in their hiding-place and tells them this story, and at first they cannot believe her. But on the evening of the same day, while they are gathered together, talking of what has befallen them, and particularly of Mary's story of how that morning she saw Jesus and spoke to him, and then recalling one by one the words he had spoken to them when they did not understand him, about dying and rising again, suddenly Jesus appears to them in their midst and tells them to carry on his work, and that as many as receive his gospel and believe in him as the Son of God shall have everlasting life.

But one difficulty still remains. If the actual physical body of Jesus which had been nailed to the Cross, and was afterwards buried by Joseph of Arimathæa, was not raised, what became of it?

To this I have no answer. I refuse to believe that that tortured body, with all the marks of its suffering upon it, was the one that rose from the dead. But I cannot say whether it went through a form of spiritualization, making the corruptible incorruptible. Apparently, this was Paul's belief—that the body buried in the earth died away, but from it came a heavenly body, a spiritual body, an incorruptible body.

If this heavenly body was the body that rose from the tomb in Joseph's garden, we must set down as myth the stories about the wounds in the hands and side, as well as the two stories (in the Synoptics and in *John*) of Jesus eating food with his disciples.

It should not be forgotten that among the legends of the Resurrection there is that which says that Joseph of Arimathæa, who had buried Jesus in the garden because the time before the Passover Day was short, and because the sepulchre was close to the place of Crucifixion, never intended it to be a permanent burial; and that fearing that some indignity would be shown to the body of Jesus by the lower class of the Jews, who, thinking he was the Messiah about to set up a temporal kingdom, had followed Jesus in the past and were now mad, in their disillusionment as they believed, in finding that he was only a man like other men, subject to the common lot of humanity, death (whereas the Messiah was never to die)—that Joseph, fearing this, went early in the morning of the first day, rolled the stone away from the sepulchre, took the body out and buried it again in another place, unknown to anybody except, perhaps, Nicodemus.

In favour of this story there is another legend, that the body of Jesus was actually taken from the river or ditch into which the gardener threw it and dragged through the streets of Jerusalem.

Against it is the fact that the burial clothes of Jesus are said to have been left in the sepulchre, and that both Peter and John saw them there, whereas the dead body (wherever it was intended to rebury it) would still, presumably, want grave clothes.

Again, there is the legend that, suspecting Jesus was not dead, Joseph opened the grave in the night of the burial, that Jesus was stripped of his grave clothes in order that, as a sick man, he could be carried without suspicion through the streets, but actually died soon after from the sufferings he had passed through, and was then buried by Joseph and Nicodemus in some unknown place.

Finally, there is the legend that Jesus never really died, and that, knowing this, Joseph went to the tomb and resuscitated him, and he went away from Judæa and lived for many years longer, probably among the Essenes.

But, of course, all this presupposes concealment amounting to fraud upon the part of Joseph, and criminal concealment on the part of Jesus, as well as frank admission that he came to realize that his ministry from first to last had been a failure, and his pretensions imposture.

Also, that Jesus should remain all his subsequent life in ignorance of the fact that thousands of his disciples were dying for their faith in him.

Of course, all these legends are too preposterous for further words. Nothing remains but that Jesus died and was buried, and that first through the medium of one devoted woman, and finally through the conviction of ten of the disciples, who were convinced that he appeared to them, he rose from the dead, and that he still lived, and that they were so certain of this that thousands of them suffered prison and persecution and death for it, and that five years (perhaps) later an enemy of Jesus became the chief of his apostles by reason of his firm conviction that Jesus had risen from the dead and had spoken to him from the clouds.

Of one thing I feel very sure—that the foundation of Christianity lies in the belief in the Resurrection of Christ; that without this there may be a Christian morality, but there can be no Christian religion. The Resurrection of Christ from the dead was to Paul the very essence of his faith. I see no faith without it. But what was it that rose—a physical body, or a spiritual body? I say a spiritualized body. And it does not matter to me what became of his physical body that hung on the Cross, whether it was spirited away, and its dust still lies in some unknown Syrian grave, or whether it was the seed out of which the incorruptible body sprang. I prefer to believe the latter.

CHAPTER XXXVIII

After the Resurrection (Continued)

I. *The New Idea of the Messiah*

DURING THE PERIOD of his life with his disciples, Jesus had constantly impressed them more and more with the belief that he was the Messiah. It is impossible to get away from this. But his death was a shock to this belief, for, to the Jewish mind, the Messiah was not to die. The earlier Jewish idea was that the Messiah should have eternal life. In the first shock of this fact their belief in Jesus as the Messiah was annihilated. But their affection for the man remained.

At what period did the new idea come to them that the Messiah was to die and to rise again from the dead? Was it when Mary Magdalene brought them word that the grave was empty and she had seen and spoken to the risen Jesus? Or was it when the two disciples going into the country were spoken to by Jesus, who showed them that the Scripture (as well as Jesus himself) had always said that these things should be?

What *was* the new idea, and where in the Old Testament was it found? It was that the Messiah was to suffer and die. In the Emmaus story we are told that Jesus, beginning at Moses, and all the prophets, expounded unto them in all the Scriptures the things concerning himself—namely that Christ ought to have suffered such things, and to enter into his glory (*Luke* XXIV, 26).

Where did Jesus find them? In *Psalms* (XVI, 10) "Thou wilt not leave my soul in hell, neither wilt thou suffer thine Holy One to see corruption." This was understood to explain the Resurrection, that it must take place. The passage in *Isaiah* (LIII, 7), "He is brought as a lamb to the slaughter, and as a sheep . . ." was understood to explain his death.

Whether they had any relation to Jesus, whether they were prophecies of Jesus, is another matter. That the disciples believed they were prophecies is certain. This impression deepened and strengthened, became deepest in the women.

Then there was the fact that the grave in which Jesus was buried was empty. That the disciples believed it to be empty is apparently certain. How much evidence they had that it was empty we are not sure. Mary Magdalene said so. The other Mary may have said so. We do not know definitely of anybody else.

What had become of the body? An angel in one Gospel, two angels in another, told the women that Jesus had risen, as he had promised.

What did the disciples do? Did they *immediately* proclaim the fact to all the world, and in the face of their enemies, that the crucified Jesus had risen? Apparently, they did not. They spoke about it among themselves. But unless we can accept the story about the Jewish guard (a very difficult thing to do) they said nothing about it before their enemies until the Day of Pentecost. That was forty days after.

But even then it would have been possible for the chief priests to refute them by ocular demonstration at the grave. They could have reopened the grave and disclosed the decaying body of Jesus. They did not do so. And yet the disciples went on saying, "He is not there. He has risen from the dead."

The one unanswerable reply of the chief priests, if the grave had not been empty, would have been to say, "He is not risen from the dead. He is here, what is left of him, going to corruption." They did not do this. The obvious reason is that they could not. They knew the grave was empty. So they said to the disciples: "Yes, we admit that his body is gone. You stole it out of the grave." And to this the disciples made answer with the story about the Jewish guard.

In the Gospels, the disciples were convinced on the second morning after the death of Jesus that he had risen. Weiss regards the death of Jesus as real, and the narratives of the grave being found empty as later fabrications, and the appearance of the risen Jesus as merely objective, magical facts—psychological visions.

II. My Own Story of the Resurrection

My own conclusion is that Jesus did actually die; that he was buried; that during the Saturday or early Sunday morning an earthquake (such as apparently took place during the Crucifixion) did actually take place; that during this earthquake the stone in front of the tomb was actually rolled away (it almost certainly ran in a groove).

What happened to the body of Jesus which had hung on the Cross I do not know; one of the Jewish traditions was that the keeper of the garden dragged it out of the tomb at night and flung it into a ditch, or shallow and muddy river that ran near. This may have been suggested by Mary Magdalene's words: "Sir, if thou have borne him hence, tell me where thou hast laid him, and I will take him away."

It may have undergone some spiritualizing change such as Paul describes in I *Corinthians* XV. If so, it bore no longer the marks of his sufferings on the Cross. It was no longer a physical body. It was a spiritual body.

I think Mary came in the very early hours of Sunday morning with no other thought than that of adding the spices to the body of her Lord—a reverential love token—if she should get anybody to roll away the stone for her. She had not come the day after the Crucifixion because it was the Sabbath. But she came in the earliest dawn—before the rising of the sun—at the first moment at which she could find her way back to the place in which she had seen him, whom she loved, committed to the grave. I think she found the stone rolled away by the earthquake and that her first thought was that his body had been stolen. She began to weep. Then she saw two angels, one at the head and the other at the feet of where the body of Jesus had lain. I think this was the vision of an excited woman.

They said to her, "Woman, why weepest thou?" And she answered, "Because they have taken away my Lord, and I know not where they have laid him." "Sir, if thou have borne him hence, tell me where thou hast laid him, and I will take him away." Clearly, she was thinking that following on the dishonour shown to Jesus by his Crucifixion had been the dishonour of his body, which might have been thrown out of the new grave into a ditch— as an ancient tradition says it was.

Then she hears her name, "Mary!" She looks up and sees it is Jesus, and exclaims, "Master!" as she throws herself on to her knees and tries to embrace his feet.

"Touch me not," he says, "for I am not yet ascended to my Father. But go to my brethren and say unto them, I ascend unto my Father and unto your Father; and to my God and your God."

All this is very touching. And once it is granted that the dead survive, and make themselves manifest to the living, it becomes a very simple and real story. It requires us to believe that the spirit of Jesus did actually appear to the eyes of this most loving of his followers, or that she firmly believed that it did.

What happens then? Mary hastens back to Jerusalem. She finds the disciples where she had left them, in hiding from the Jews. She tells them that she has seen Jesus, and what message he has sent them.

All this from *John;* and it is reasonable to take a passage here from *Luke* (XXIV, 11). Her words seem to the disciples like idle tales. They are still under the shock of their disillusionment about Jesus as the Messiah, who had falsified their hopes. They have not yet come to the idea that the Messiah must (according to the Scriptures) suffer and die and rise again, because God cannot suffer His Holy One to see corruption. So they do not believe Mary Magdalene.

What happens next may be as Luke says (John records two visits of Mary Magdalene, one before she takes the news to Peter and John, and one afterwards), that Peter and John go off to the tomb and find it empty, as Mary Magdalene had said. They find the linen clothes lying there, and the napkin that had been about the head of Jesus, lying apart, and they believed. What did they believe? Only that the grave was empty, that the body of Jesus was gone. They had not yet come to the belief that he had risen from the dead; that the Scriptures said he must rise.

And then?

The same day, at evening, being Sunday evening, when the doors were shut where the disciples were assembled for fear of the Jews, Jesus came and stood in the midst, and said, "Peace be unto you."

Was this merely a vision on the part of the disciples?

Merely a subjective impression, due to the exalted moods of their minds arising out of their knowledge of the empty grave, out of their gathering recollection of what Jesus had so often said to them while he was alive, that on the third day he would rise again? Were they snatching back from memory some new meaning for his familiar words which, during his life with them, they had not understood? Did it happen that in the exaltation of their minds, all the air of the room tingling with excitement, somebody, more susceptible to such visions than the others, suddenly cried, "Look, he is here," and then *all* saw him?

Or was it actually true that Jesus did appear to them in his spiritual body, as he had appeared to Mary by the side of the empty tomb?

With all sincerity I believe this; that he did actually appear to them—that this was his Resurrection. I cannot believe that for thirty years thereafter the disciples could have gone through the pains of persecution and death for any less certainty. They believed that Jesus had appeared to them and spoken to them after he had been dead and buried. They were ready to be scourged for that belief, to go to their deaths for it, to be burnt at the stake for it.

Not for one moment will I believe the appearance of Jesus was a mere form of optical delusion, a result of spiritual intoxication. I believe it was a reality—Jesus had risen. He did appear.

But here I stop. I do not find it necessary to follow John (or whosoever wrote into his Gospel) with verse 20 about his hands and his side. I skip that verse, and go on to verses 21 and 22. That ends this section of the story for me.

Of the stories of the Resurrection told in the four Gospels it is impossible for me to say that I find any of them entirely convincing. After the firm reality of the story of the trial, death and burial they leave the impression that one is carried into the world of legend, contradictory and confusing legend. They do not seem to me, in any case, to agree either with themselves or with each other.

Luke says Jesus ascended on the first day of the week (probably in the dark). Therefore, he was only one day on the earth after his Resurrection. *John* speaks of him as appearing a second time to his disciples on the ninth day after his Resurrection. *Acts* says he was forty days on the earth after his Resurrection. *Matthew* causes Jesus on the first day of the week to bid Mary Magdalene to tell his disciples to go into Galilee and there they shall see him. Also, the angels in *Matthew* tell Mary the same about Galilee.

Luke causes Jesus on the first day of the week to tell his disciples to tarry in the city of Jerusalem until they have been "endued with power from on high," obviously meaning that they should wait there for the Pentecost.

Matthew causes the disciples to go into Galilee before they have been "endued with power from on high." *Matthew* says the disciples saw Jesus in Galilee on a mountain as he had appointed them. *John* says Jesus saw his disciples in Galilee on the seashore.

The contention of theologians (beginning with Clement of Alexandria) who say that the injunction in *John* about tarrying in Jerusalem is to be read as referring to the whole of Palestine, and therefore including Galilee, is unworthy, almost degrading. Jesus never elsewhere speaks of Galilee as Jerusalem, very much the contrary.

The first story of the Resurrection in *Mark* (XVI, 1–8) conflicts at the outset with the second story (XVI, 9–20).

St. Paul, preaching in Antioch, and telling the story of the death, burial and Resurrection of Jesus, says:

> And when they [the Jews] had fulfilled all that was written of him, they took him down from the tree, and laid him in a sepulchre. But God raised him from the dead. And he was seen many days of them which came up with him from Galilee to Jerusalem, who are his witnesses unto the people.

Observe Paul says he was seen in Jerusalem after his Resurrection. Paul does not say Jesus was seen in Galilee.

The story in *Mark* that the disciples in Jerusalem did not believe the story of the disciples who had seen and spoken with Jesus in the city does not agree with the story of the same incident in *Luke,* where nothing is said of the disciples not believing them. This is a secondary point. The story in *Luke* that the women who had followed Jesus from Galilee brought spices on the first day of the week (obviously with the intention of anointing the body of Jesus) shows that they did not know (what is recorded in *Matthew*) that the tomb had been sealed by the Jewish watch. This again is secondary.

The stories of Jesus eating broiled fish with the disciples (*Luke*), and of his eating with the two disciples at Emmaus (also *Luke*), and of his eating with the disciples on the shore of Galilee (*John*) shows that his body had all the needs and organic functions of a human body. Yet his ascent into Heaven from Bethany (*Luke*), immediately after eating, shows that his body was not subject to the ordinary laws of natural bodies. With its material functions (proper to life on the earth) unfulfilled, it rose through the air into the heavens.

The story of the Resurrection has one anticipatory phrase in *Matthew* (XXVII, 51), where it is said that during the Crucifixion

> the veil of the Temple was rent in twain, from the top to the bottom; and the earth did quake, and the rocks rent, and the graves were opened; and many bodies of the saints which slept arose, and came out of the graves *after his Resurrection,* and went into the holy city, and appeared unto many.

Nothing further is ever said about this incident. I think it is legendary. If the "saints" mentioned were old Jewish prophets, surely the Talmud would tell us something concerning so great an event. If "saints" mean the Christian dead, surely the Gospels or *Acts* or the apostles (Paul and Peter) would have some notion of such a tremendous incident.

It is never mentioned again. It is a manifest legend, an interpolation of a much later period. The period is probably not earlier than the beginning of the second century, when the persecuted Christians were for the first time being called saints, and Jerusalem was being called the Holy City.

The three verses (*Matthew* XXVII, 51–53) are manifest interpolations of the story of the death of Jesus, which goes directly from verse 50 to 54.

III. Conclusions

My own conclusions are a general view of all the evidence. I believe:

1. That the disciples had not understood Jesus when he told them he was to rise on the third day.

2. That they were all in hiding during the three days following the Crucifixion, fearing to be arrested by the Jews (or Romans) as accomplices in the crime of Jesus in his treason against Cæsar.

3. That Mary Magdalene (probably the woman who was a sinner in *Luke*) in her great love of Jesus went on the Sunday morning with spices to anoint his body.

4. That she found the stone rolled away from the door to the tomb. That this was probably due to the earthquake.

5. That the body of Jesus was gone and that, not knowing what had become of it, she suddenly remembered that he had said he would rise again on the third day. That the scene of "Mary,"

"Rabboni" took place, or Mary believed it took place. That she did not touch him. That when he disappeared she returned to the disciples to tell them the Lord's word had been fulfilled—he had risen.

6. That the disciples were sitting together in their hiding-place, weeping for the loss of their Master and the downfall of their hopes.

7. That the disciples were at first unwilling to believe her, thinking her love had led her to imagine the story.

8. That while they were disputing together and belief in Mary's story was getting hold of them, Jesus suddenly appeared in their midst (the doors being closed against surprise from the Jews). That this was his spirit.

9. That he spoke to them, saying what is said in *Luke* (XXIV, 44–49). And, again, much of what he is said to say in *Acts* (I, 4–8).

10. That he then disappeared, or, as they believed, he led them back through Jerusalem to the Mount of Olives, and from there (near Bethany) his spirit ascended into Heaven, and a cloud received him out of their sight. It was night.

11. That they returned to Jerusalem in a condition of great emotional excitement. Everything was changed for them. They understood what had hitherto been dark. Jesus had risen. He would restore the Kingdom to Israel. They had to wait.

Summing up, my views are as follows:

I do not believe in the bodily Resurrection.

I do not believe that Jesus showed his wounded hands and side.

I do not believe that the disciples failed to know him.

I do not believe he ate broiled fish in Jerusalem, or in the house at Emmaus, or on the shore of Galilee. It requires belief in a material body raised from the dead.

I do not believe in his appearance to the two disciples on the road to Emmaus, or that he ate with them, and that they only recognized him in the breaking of bread—presumably as at the Last Supper; one of them, Cleopas, had not been present at the Last Supper, which was confined to the twelve.

I think this scene was written after it became necessary to obtain the authority of Jesus for finding that the Scriptures had witnessed to him from the beginning. This must have been very early after the Crucifixion.

I think this scene was devised to give the authority of Jesus to the idea that all Scriptures foretold him.

I do not believe in the scene in Galilee; or in the authenticity of the verse in which Jesus says they were to meet him in Galilee. I think this scene was devised at the time when it became necessary to obtain the authority of Jesus for the position of Peter as the central power in the Church.

I do not believe in the story of the Jewish watch. There is no possible reporter for it, unless we assume a converted member of the watch.

I think it is a Christian legend to gain anti-Christian evidence of the empty tomb.

I do not believe the story of the saints rising from their tombs, broken open by the Resurrection. It takes the importance out of the Resurrection of Jesus, and has not a particle of historical probability. It is of no spiritual value to the story of Jesus.

In short, I believe in the spiritual Resurrection of Jesus. Not that the apostles thought he spoke to them; but that he did actually speak to them. That nobody who had died had ever spoken to the living before; and by this they knew he was the Christ.

If I am asked do I believe in the empty tomb, I answer:

1. That there is no evidence that the empty tomb was that of Jesus except the evidence of Mary Magdalene, who saw him buried in what may have been half darkness.

The evidence of Peter and John is valueless; they did not see him buried.

The evidence of the Jewish watch is valueless; the story is a myth.

Only one other witness could be called—Joseph of Arimathæa. If he had said "the empty tomb in which I laid Jesus," or if Nicodemus had said so, the fact would have been established. But we never hear anything more, I think, about either Joseph or Nicodemus.

2. Alternatively, if I believe it was the tomb of Jesus, and it was empty, I may also believe that (a) the earthquake opened it, as it is said to have opened the other tombs; (b) that Joseph took the body away and buried it elsewhere to escape the dishonour which might have been shown to it. We hear nothing more of Joseph until legend brings him to Glastonbury with the Holy Grail and the staff which he thrusts into the earth.

I believe in the Resurrection of the Soul of Jesus. He survived and appeared to his disciples. I am not concerned about what happened to his body. But if his body rose, I think it was a spiritualized and incomplete body. I think this was the theory of St. Paul, who did not require proof of the physical Resurrection of Jesus for his own conversion. He heard a voice from Heaven. That was enough for him.

Even after Jesus has appeared to his disciples they do not fully understand him. They ask him whether he could now restore again the kingdom of Israel.

He answers that that is in God's hands. He alone can determine that. Meantime, the Holy Spirit will come to them shortly, and they are to go out to the uttermost parts of the earth, preaching his message in his name, and as many as believe it will be saved from the penalty of their sins.

As he ascends to Heaven, and they look after him in amazement, angels tell them that he will come again—appearing in the clouds.

With this hope they return to Jerusalem with great joy. Their eyes, which have been closed, are now open. They understand at last. Their Master is not dead. He has only left them for a little while. In a little while they will see him again.

He will come in the clouds, and then the great Kingdom will be re-established.

It will be as they had always expected; only more gloriously, more magnificently, more divinely. The Christ is alive, and will live for ever. The hopes they had cherished, and had for three black days thought crushed, will be fulfilled. The heavenly Kingdom they had foreseen will be established on the earth, presided over by their Master, and lasting beyond the end of time and perhaps for eternity.

CHAPTER XXXIX

The Ascension

I. The Forty Days

THAT Jesus should have been forty days wandering about Palestine after the Resurrection before he ascends to Heaven presents a picture (as recorded in the Gospels, in *Corinthians,* and in *Acts*) irreconcilable with itself, and utterly humiliating, futile and almost degrading.

During this period he is described as going about in his body as he lived during what we call his lifetime, bearing marks of the wounds he received on the Cross (in his side and hands if not in his feet), eating and drinking, giving proof that he is not a ghost but a real physical being, appearing in rooms through closed doors, disappearing no one knows how, sitting at meat with two disciples, then suddenly vanishing from their sight, exercising a power of dematerializing and again materializing himself.

What work during this period does he do?

Beyond offering proof that he has actually fulfilled his prophecy while he lived, that he would rise from the dead, he does nothing that he has not done already during life. And what he is reported to have said after his Resurrection is immeasurably lower as teaching, poorer as morality, than what he said while he was in his first life.

Compare such great passages (spoken during his earthly life) as "O Jerusalem, Jerusalem, which killest the prophets, and stonest them that are sent unto thee; how often would I have gathered thy children together, as a hen doth gather her brood under her wings, and ye would not" (words which one cannot better by reason of the emotion with which they are charged) with the unspeakable aridity, barrenness, want of emotion and even of power of expression (a transcendant quality always in the *real* Jesus) of such words and promises as the following, supposed to be spoken by Jesus after his Resurrection: "And these signs shall follow them that believe; in my name shall they cast out devils; they shall speak with new tongues; they shall take up serpents; and if they drink any deadly thing, it shall not hurt them . . ."

To say that these poor, sterile words are the words of Jesus, after he had passed through death, after he had risen from the grave, and immediately before ascending to the Father, is to say an unbelievable thing.

How are we to account for the decline in Jesus after his Resurrection? His greatness has gone. He has nothing to say after coming from the grave, which he has not said during life ten thousand times better. What he says after the Resurrection is utterly unworthy of the great and lofty spirit who spoke at the Last Supper and in Gethsemane. The charges he gives his apostles after he rises from the dead are poor and mean and paltry, compared with the charges he gave them during his lifetime.

All the grandeur of soul has gone. He is nothing but a poor little leader of a group of evangelists.

Further, after his Resurrection, he has attached to himself a number of dogmas and ceremonials, of which he either knew nothing, or to which he attached little importance, during life.

During life he paid little regard to baptism. He never himself performed baptism. He did not cause his disciples to be baptized when he called them, or when he sent them out to preach. Now, after the Resurrection, he tells them that baptism is essential to salvation. "He that believeth and is baptized shall be saved; but he that believeth not shall be damned" (*Mark* XVI, 16).

This is not Jesus speaking. It is some poor churchman coming later, probably much later.

The scene of Jesus appearing to the two disciples on the way to Emmaus is by far the most significant of the appearances after the first appearance to Mary Magdalene, and the appearance to the disciples in the closed room.

It is intended to (or serves to) open the eyes of the disciples to the fact that what he had predicted during life has actually come to pass, and that it had been foretold in the Scriptures.

I think this incident is of later origin, but it serves a useful purpose.

But of what use is the appearance of Jesus on the mountain in Galilee? We know nothing of what he said there. He added nothing that the disciples did not already know in Jerusalem.

Again, of what use is the appearance on the shore of the Lake of Galilee? He says nothing that he had not said before and better during his lifetime. Even the superiority he gave to Peter is better expressed in the scene (perhaps partly apocryphal) at Cæsarea Philippi: "On this rock I will build my Church."

Even the prediction (apparently) that the beloved disciple should not die until Jesus came again is better made (with less prevarication) in what he said during life.

Again, what of the appearance to James? If, as seems probable, it was his brother James, was any account of what passed between them ever written? Did Paul know what he said? If it was important (as it must have been, in the circumstances of the former relation of Jesus to his brother, and the brother's subsequent relation to the early Christian Church), how does it come to pass that Paul says nothing about it?

Finally, what about the appearance of Jesus to the more than 500 brethren at once, "of whom the greater part remain unto this present, but some are fallen asleep?" Did he say nothing to them that made it necessary that he should appear to them after death?

What supplementary message did he bring from the grave?

If it is argued that, by appearing to something like 500 persons during the seven weeks of his wandering over Palestine after his Resurrection, he was establishing beyond all possibility of doubt the fact that he had actually risen, how does it come to pass that, having been seen by so many, there could ever afterwards be so much as one single moment's doubt about the fact of his Resurrection? How could the Jews doubt the word of so many? How could the chief priests go on to their persecutions and the stoning (utterly illegal apparently) of Stephen, if 500 separate persons of their own race were ready to declare that they had seen him, that many of them had spoken, eaten and drunk with him?

If once the conviction forced itself upon the chief priests that Jesus may actually have risen from the dead, how could they continue denouncing the people who said he had risen, without the paralysing fear that they were (as Gamaliel said) fighting against God?

It is all utterly incredible.

But against this vain and rather degrading story, that Jesus wandered about in his real-life body for seven weeks after his Resurrection, I place the fact that during that time he said nothing and did nothing that was in the smallest way worthy of the great being who, during the same period of about seven weeks from leaving Cæsarea Philippi to his death on the Cross, had said the greatest words man had ever uttered, performed the greatest miracles man had ever performed, and died the greatest death.

In short, my conclusion is that the seven weeks story is a puerile fiction, imposed upon the Gospels and perhaps upon Paul, long after the writing of the Gospels, and perhaps after the writing of Paul's Epistle to the Corinthians.

On the other hand it is possible to pass from the puerilities of the stories in the Gospels to the account of the life of Jesus on earth after his Resurrection which appears in the first chapter in *Acts*.

What does this say?

It says that

> he showed himself alive after his passion by many infallible proofs, being seen of them [his apostles] forty days, and speaking of the things pertaining to the kingdom of God. And being assembled together with them, commanded them that they should not depart from Jerusalem, but wait for the promise of the Father, which, saith he, ye have heard of me.
>
> For John truly baptized with water; but ye shall be baptized with the Holy Ghost not many days hence.
>
> When they therefore were come together, they asked him, saying, Lord, wilt thou at this time restore again the kingdom to Israel?

Clearly they had not even yet cleansed themselves of the muddy imperfection of their worldly hopes of a worldly kingdom. The Messianic hope with them was still Jewish.

To their question Jesus replies (1) that it is not for them to know the times or the seasons which the Father hath put in his own power; (2) but that they [the disciples] shall receive power, after the Holy Ghost is come upon them, and they shall be witnesses to him both in Jerusalem and in all Judæa and in Samaria, and unto the uttermost parts of the earth.

And after saying this (and no more that is recorded) he is taken up in a cloud and out of their sight.

This occurs on the Mount of Olives, and while they look towards Heaven as he goes up, two men in white apparel stand beside them and say:

> Ye men of Galilee, why stand ye gazing up into Heaven? This same Jesus, which is taken up from you into Heaven, shall so come in like manner as ye have seen him go into Heaven.

After that the disciples return from the Mount of Olives to Jerusalem. And there they abide together in an upper room, waiting for the coming of the Holy Ghost.

This account in *Acts* is certainly less purely imaginary than some of the accounts in the Gospels of the appearances of the risen Jesus, but it does not amount to a great deal.

Still the risen Jesus who has passed through the great adventure of death has nothing to say that he did not say in his human life, except that they are not to leave Jerusalem until the Holy Ghost descends upon them.

According to the Gospels they *do* leave Jerusalem, and go into Galilee. And some of the harmonizers pretend to account for this by saying that Jerusalem meant Judæa, and Judæa meant Galilee, and Samaria. It did nothing of the kind, anywhere or at any time.

II. Stories of the Ascension

Neither the Gospels nor the apostles in their epistles give any great prominence to the circumstances of the Ascension. There is no really clear and distinct account of the Ascension. Even the apocryphal writings say little about it. Only one of them, the Epistle of the Apostles, has an abridged version of the story in the Gospels. It speaks of thunder and lightning and an earthquake, and of a bright cloud which bore Jesus up into the sky; of the voices of many angels rejoicing and singing praises. When Jesus drew nigh to the firmament his apostles are said to have heard the voice of Jesus saying, "Depart hence in peace."

The apostles believed that their Master had not only risen from the dead, but had ascended, in his natural body (immediately after eating a meal) to the supernatural world. They thought Heaven was a place in the sky; and that he took his place there by God's right hand. Therefore, Jesus, in his human body, is in a distinct place as in his human body, in the plenitude of his humanity actually sitting on a throne in the sky. And in this character, and from that place, he looks down on the world, the universe, and in due time he will descend to the world to judge the living and the dead.

All this is so archaic as to be almost past belief of the early Christians. As a record of an actual happening it is of no use to the modern mind. It has to be understood as a poetical figure or it is worthless to Christianity. It belittles Christianity. It materializes Jesus not only in this world, but in Heaven. It also materializes God.

The report of the Ascension comes to us in three different narratives.

Mark says merely (in his second and more doubtful version of the Resurrection) that having spoken to his disciples, telling them what to do, and what their protection should be (that they should take up serpents, drink deadly things and not be hurt), Jesus "was received up into Heaven, and sat on the right hand of God."

This is the baldest of the three Ascension stories.

In *Matthew* there is no account of the Ascension of Jesus to Heaven. Apparently, Matthew knows nothing about it. And if he had Mark's Gospel at hand (as clearly he had) when he wrote his own Gospel, Mark's Gospel either cannot have contained that second account of the Resurrection which is added to the first, or if it did contain it, which is improbable, Matthew rejected it.

Luke's account of the Ascension is that after telling his disciples to tarry in Jerusalem, until they should be endued with power from on high, Jesus led them out as far as to Bethany, and having there lifted up his hands and blessed them, he was parted from them, and carried up into Heaven, whereupon the disciples worshipped him and then returned to Jerusalem with great joy.

In John's Gospel, also, there is no account of the Ascension.

Neither following the account of his second appearance to the disciples for the purpose of convincing Thomas (an account which closes with a benediction that is apparently intended to be the end of the Gospel) nor yet in the subsequent chapter about the meeting of Jesus and his disciples on the shore of the Sea of Tiberias, when they eat there with him, and Jesus indicates to Peter by a negative phrase the time of his Second Advent (within the period of the lifetime of John)—in neither of these accounts in *John* is there any reference to the Ascension of Jesus into Heaven.

But in *Acts*, Luke (if he is the writer of the whole, or of the opening chapter, which I see reason to doubt, inasmuch as the opening chapters of *Acts* conflict at various points with the Gospel of Luke) gives a full and detailed account of the Ascension, which agrees scholastically with the Gospel of Luke, and supplements it.

In *Acts* we read (1) that after Jesus had, through the Holy Ghost, given commandment to the apostles whom he had chosen,

> . . . to whom also he showed himself alive after his passion by many infallible proofs, being seen of them forty days, and speaking of the things pertaining to the kingdom of God; [none of this is told us in the Gospels; we have to look elsewhere for it] and, being assembled together with them, commanded them that they should not depart from Jerusalem, but wait for the promise of the Father . . . while they beheld, he was taken up, and a cloud received him out of their sight.

Now this meeting of Jesus with his disciples for the last time, according to the ordinary course of the narrative, would appear to have taken place on the Mount of Olives (Luke's Gospel says at Bethany).

And while the disciples (when, or at what time of day or night we are not told) looked steadfastly towards Heaven as Jesus went up, two men in white apparel stood by them, and addressing them as men of Galilee, asked them why they stood gazing into Heaven:

> This same Jesus, which is taken up from you into Heaven, shall so come in like manner as ye have seen him go into Heaven.

After that they return from the Mount of Olives to Jerusalem, and there they abide together in an upper room—Peter, James, John, Andrew, Philip, Thomas, Bartholomew, Matthew, James, the son of Alphæus, Simon Zelotes and Judas the brother of James.

Here are eleven of them living together in the upper room in Jerusalem, waiting for the time when (according to Jesus) the promise of the Father would be conferred upon them.

And there they continued with one accord in prayer and supplication with the women who had come up with them from Galilee. Also, with Mary the mother of Jesus, and with his brethren.

This carries one step further the reference in *John* to Mary at the Cross. The brothers of Jesus, hitherto hostile, were now, after his Ascension on his side, and waiting with the others for the pouring out of the Holy Ghost. But here is a great chronological difficulty. This period of waiting is clearly described as following after the Ascension from the Mount of Olives, and yet in verse 3 of the same chapter of *Acts,* we read that Jesus showed himself alive and was seen by his apostles forty days.

The Feast of Pentecost came seven weeks (say forty-nine days) after the Passover, or fifty days after the Crucifixion, by which we are to understand, (1) that for forty days Jesus appeared to his disciples after his Resurrection; (2) that at the end of the forty days he ascended from the Mount of Olives; (3) that for ten days more his apostles, lived and assembled for prayer in the upper room in Jerusalem; (4) that at the end of the nine days came the Feast of Pentecost, at which the Holy Ghost descended upon the apostles and disciples (they are said to have numbered altogether about 120); (5) that in the meantime the apostles had appointed Matthias to take the place of Judas; and (6) that on the Day of Pentecost, when they were all together with one accord in one place, there suddenly came upon them a sound from Heaven as of a rushing mighty wind.

III. Summary of the Foregoing

Thus the three Ascension stories in *Mark* and *Luke* and *Acts* conflict as to the time when they occur. In the Gospels of Mark and Luke the Ascension takes place on the same day as the Resurrection. In *Acts* it occurs forty days after the Resurrection. Did Luke, after writing his Gospel, find out that he had made a mistake, and did he correct it in *Acts?*

If the Ascension of Jesus took place after his Resurrection in the presence of his eleven disciples, and in the ways described in two of the Gospels and in *Acts,* there is the astonishing fact that Matthew and John must both have been present at it, and yet they say nothing about it. The Ascension is only reported by Mark in his Gospel and by Luke in his Gospel, and by Luke (apparently) in *Acts,* and yet neither Mark nor Luke could have been an eye-witness of the event.

If Mark is to be considered the mouthpiece of Peter, the answer is that he only records the Ascension in his second version of the Resurrection, and with none of the incidents given by Luke, and no reference to the Mount of Olives as the scene of the Ascension, but clear indication of a totally different place—the room in which the apostles dwelt in Jerusalem. If again, Luke is to be understood as having given an account inspired by Paul, there is the fact that Paul himself was not an eye-witness of the Ascension, and that there is no authority except Luke himself for the story of the Ascension from the Mount of Olives.

The effect of the two Gospels which do not mention the Ascension, *Matthew* and *John,* is that the story of the life of Jesus on earth tails off to a vague and ineffectual obscurity. It closes rather than ends.

Commentators try to explain the silence of Matthew and John about the Ascension, which they must have witnessed if it had occurred, by stating that they thought it unnecessary to tell afresh a story which had already been told. But the story had never been told harmoniously. It had been told in two narratives which contradicted each other in essential particulars. If, therefore, Matthew and John had witnessed the Ascension (whether from the room in Jerusalem or from the Mount of Olives) they *must* have wound up their own stories by showing which version of the Ascension was the true one.

That they did not do this convinces me (1) that they had not witnessed the Ascension; (2) that they had not read either Mark's story or Luke's, or yet the story in *Acts.* In short, my conclusion is that the Ascension of Jesus was not witnessed by the disciples; but that they all believed that it took place is abundantly clear from references throughout the New Testament to the present position of Christ in Heaven, at the right hand of the Father.

It is also beyond question that they regarded the place of Heaven as somewhere in the sky—the firmament to which Elijah had to rise in order to reach Heaven. The conversion of Paul shows that he too thought that the heavens in the sky were the seat of God, and therefore from there Jesus must descend accompanied by angels when he came to establish his Kingdom.

Evidently the apostles were not troubled by physical difficulties, such as the laws of gravitation, or by the fact that a human body which had exercised the functions of digestion was passing from the sphere (the earth) in which they were natural to a sphere which (so far as we know) can have no use for them. Or, if the apostles and disciples thought of these difficulties, they frankly regarded the Ascension as a miracle—some of them as a miracle which in ordinary course must occur to the risen body of Jesus; others (apparently) as a miracle which had actually taken place before the eyes of the first of the disciples.

I think the story of the Ascension is of much later date than the rest of the story of the life of Jesus, and was probably designed to meet the objections of the sceptics of the end of the first century, who were saying that Jesus had never died at all, but had been taken down from the Cross while still alive, resuscitated and then carried off to some secret place, perhaps to some Essene monastery.

To confute this it became necessary to say (1) that Jesus had actually died; (2) that he had actually risen again as a natural man, and been seen of several hundreds; (3) that he had actually eaten and drunk and passed from Judæa to Galilee (eager as the high priests would have been to recapture him on the first whisper that he had escaped death, or to run away in terror at the idea that God had snatched him out of the hands of death), and, finally, that he had actually ascended into Heaven before the eyes of his disciples, and that angels had appeared to them and said in effect, "Be comforted, as ye have seen him rise into Heaven, so you will see him some day come down from Heaven."

IV. My Final Conclusion

My first conclusion is that nine-tenths of the difficulties presented by the stories of the Resurrection and Ascension come of the fact that we read (and in the Gospels are encouraged to read) of the risen and ascending body as if it were the actual body that died and suffered on the Cross.

This of itself is from first to last beset with difficulties.

1. The difficulty of the promise of Jesus to the penitent thief that this day he would be with him in Paradise, followed by his forbidding Mary Magdalene after the Resurrection to touch him, because he had not yet ascended to his Father—whatever that injunction may mean.

2. The difficulty of his appearance to the disciples in the upper room where the doors were closed (coming through the door or walls as if the materials of door and walls were no obstacles) and immediately afterwards calling upon the disciples to look at his hands and side, and to see him eat food as proof that he was not a spirit, but a man like themselves. And again his sudden parting from them as he had appeared to them.

3. The difficulty of his appearance to the disciples on the road to Emmaus, his sitting at meat with them, and then his sudden disappearance.

4. The difficulty of his convincing Thomas of his physical

reality, as the human being who hung on the Cross and was wounded in hands and feet and side, and immediately afterwards passing away from the disciples as only a disembodied spirit can be thought capable of doing.

5. The difficulty of his leaving behind him the linen in which his naked body had been wrapped by Joseph of Arimathæa, and going about Palestine and appearing to more than 500 persons in garments about which we hear nothing—how obtained or what they were.

Further, his eating fish, and thus accepting the conditions of a human body, with its laws of appetite and digestion, and then, immediately afterwards, leading his disciples up to the Mount of Olives and there defying the laws of gravitation, and the laws of human life, by rising into the air and disappearing in a cloud to a sphere in which a physical body, which walked the earth and required food to sustain itself, would, so far as we know, not be required.

But put aside this theory, with all its bewildering and belittling difficulties of a clash with natural laws, of a physical body such as lived on the earth, precisely the same body, with the wounds of the Cross still fresh (although in thirty-six hours apparently healed, so that the wounded side no longer bled, and the hands through which the nails had been driven no longer suffered and the feet that had been nailed did not make it hard to walk) ; put aside all this inconsequent and totally unexplainable theory, and conceive the Resurrection in the spirit of St. Paul (I *Corinthians* XV), not as the rising of the same natural body which had hung on the Cross and been wrapped by Joseph of Arimathæa in white linen and laid in the tomb, but of a spiritual body that had undergone the change which, according to Paul, all the bodies of men must undergo before the final Resurrection of the last day; a change that will come about in the twinkling of an eye at the last trump, causing the dead which have been buried in corruption to rise incorruptible, the mortal to put on immortality—conceive of this, and think that (still according to Paul's interpretation) Jesus, the body of Jesus, was the first to go through this change, and nine-tenths of the difficulties of the fact of Christ's Resurrection and Ascension disappear.

1. It gets rid of the difficulty of the promise (if ever made) to the penitent thief, since the moment Jesus died on the Cross his

soul may have been in Paradise with God, and the soul of the thief with him.

2. It gets rid of the difficulty of his appearances to Mary and his injunction to her not to touch him, though the reason for this injunction would have to be ignored.

3. It gets rid of the difficulty of his appearance to the two disciples on their way to Emmaus, although it requires that the eating would probably have to be abandoned.

4. It gets rid of the difficulty of his appearance to the disciples when they are gathered together in the upper room with the closed doors, when he appears to them and then disappears from them.

5. It appears to offer a possible explanation of the scene on the shores of the Sea of Tiberias, although that incident is obviously in conflict with the injunction Jesus gives to his disciples to remain in Jerusalem until the Spirit descends on them.

6. It even makes intelligible the scene of the Ascension from the Mount of Olives, where the disciples (waiting in expectation of the coming of the Holy Spirit) may very well have had the habit of going up to that spot (sacred to the memory of some of the greatest manifestations of their Master's power, the deepest hours of his affectionate relation with them), going up there after nightfall, in the starlight or moonlight seeing him ascend and become hidden by a cloud. And then being addressed (or believing themselves to be addressed) by somebody who reminded them of the prophecy of Daniel, that as they had seen Jesus rise, so according to the last of the prophets he was to descend when he came in his glory, surrounded by angels, to establish the kingdom of God and to judge all the earth.

Thus the spiritual body (according to Paul's theory) accounts for nearly, if not quite, everything.

And if the early disciples abandoned this theory (which may well have been their first belief), it was almost certainly only under the pressure of scepticism without, which told them they were merely fanatical dreamers and that there was no tangible reality about either the story of the Resurrection or of the Ascension. So they made all the secondary incidents of the story to prove that the Jesus who rose from the grave was not a ghost, but a flesh and blood man, the same man in every respect that had hung on the Cross.

I find this satisfying both to my mind and to my soul. The other theory, of a natural body, I find very painful and almost revolting. Carried to its utmost length, it requires us to believe that the Jesus who rose into Heaven, and sat on the right hand of God, was still the man of tortured, wounded and disfigured body, who had been scourged and mocked and smitten and spat upon, and finally nailed on to a tree, and then hustled into a new grave.

The idea of the firmament as the scene of Heaven gives me no trouble. I find it in nearly all Hebrew literature as far back as the idea of a belief in the Resurrection goes. First, I find it in all Hebrew literature as the scene of the seat of God.

It is not distinctly said where Enoch goes with God; only that he walked with God, and that God took him. But chariots and horses transport Elijah to the skies. Moses, at the close of the last of the books attributed to him, is said to have gone up, at the command of God, to the top of Pisgah, the mountain that is over against Jericho (the city of palms) on the eastern side of the Jordan, and there, within sight of the land which God had promised to Abraham, Isaac and Jacob, as far as to the utmost sea (which we now call the Mediterranean), to have died. And God is said to have buried him in some unknown place, and "no man knoweth the place of his burial to this day."

According to Josephus, the end of Moses was different. He did not die. He was in a certain valley with Joshua and Eleazar, and was about to embrace them when, on a sudden, a cloud came over him and he disappeared. Although he wrote in the Holy Books that he died (this implies that he wrote the end of the last of his books after his disappearance), this was out of fear, lest it should be said that because of his extraordinary virtue he went to God.

Philo, the great Jewish writer of the time of Christ, makes only the soul of Moses ascend to Heaven.

The scene of the death of Moses, according to the Scriptures, is one of utter splendour, grandeur and dignity. The great prophet, who has spent his life bringing his people out of captivity in Egypt to lead them into the land which God had promised to their fathers, not being permitted to enter it himself, but being taken up to the top of the highest mountain to look at it, and then dying and being buried by God.

The Ascension of Jesus of Nazareth as told by Luke has points of resemblance to this. Christ is taken up in a cloud. His deserted people see him ascend. He is lost to their sight on his way to God, by Whose right hand he will sit in Heaven.

The hope that he will come again as he has gone up—only supported by legions of angels, to establish the kingdom of God on earth, to judge all mankind, to separate the good from the evil.

Were the disciples thinking of this scene of the death of Moses when they saw Jesus ascending from the Mount of Olives? But then the greater events—the second coming of Jesus. The greater than Moses, the Son of God, to come in His glory.

He was to come soon. Had it not (as they believed) been promised them that he would come within the lifetime of certain of themselves—that one of them at least (John) should not taste of death until all this came to pass?

Meantime—what?

They were to go into all the world and call on all men to repent, to believe, so that they might be numbered among the redeemed when the Redeemer came again.

A great scene.

V. The Four Gospels and Acts

The accounts of the Ascension of Jesus in the Gospels are few, meagre and very perplexing.

Matthew records nothing about the Ascension. He leaves Jesus on earth after the Resurrection (in a corporeal body), but does not say how long he remains on earth or what becomes of him.

Mark has a short passage which is in no sense realistic. It occurs at the end of his second, and doubtful, account of the Resurrection. After Jesus has appeared to his disciples on Sunday night, in Jerusalem, and told them they shall be exempt from prison and shall heal the sick:

> So then, after the Lord had spoken unto them, he was received up into Heaven, and sat on the right hand of God.

Here, the only inference to be drawn is that, just as he had appeared to them as a spirit, so he disappeared as a spirit. How the disciples knew that he was received up into Heaven and sat on the right hand of God, the evangelist does not attempt to say.

Luke has a somewhat more circumstantial story. On the night of the day of the Resurrection, after Jesus had been with his two followers at Emmaus, and they had hurried back to the eleven disciples in Jerusalem, Jesus appeared in their midst, a corporeal being, and he ate before them, and spoke to them. Then, without any apparent lapse of time (the same night it would seem)

. . . he led them out as far as to Bethany, and he lifted up his hands, and blessed them. And it came to pass, while he blessed them, he was parted from them, and carried up into Heaven.

John has no account of the Ascension, and neither after the account of Jesus's appearance to the disciples (in a corporeal body) on the Sunday night, in their own room in Jerusalem, when the door was shut for fear of the Jews, nor after his second appearance in the same place, when he convinced and reproved Thomas, and finally breathed the Holy Spirit upon the disciples, nor yet on the shore of Galilee, when he spoke to Peter and about John, are we told what became of him, how long he remained alive in Palestine, where he went, or when he ascended into Heaven.

But *Acts* describes a realistic scene.

In Chapter I (3, 4, 9,) we read that Jesus remained forty days on the earth after his Resurrection, that he showed himself alive by many infallible proofs; that he spoke of the kingdom of God; that he told his disciples not to depart from Jerusalem, but to wait for the promise of the Father as he had given it them during his lifetime; and he was "taken up [into Heaven] and a cloud received him out of their sight."

This scene occurred, as we are afterwards told, on the Mount of Olives (the mount called Olivet); and that while the disciples looked steadfastly towards Heaven, as he went up, two men stood by them in white apparel and said:

Ye men of Galilee, why stand ye gazing up into Heaven? This same Jesus, which is taken up from you into Heaven, shall so come in like manner as ye have seen him go into Heaven.

That is the whole story of the Ascension as it is described to us in the New Testament.

We know no more about it. It is a strange story in some of its details. After eating, and being in a corporeal body, Jesus ascends into Heaven, in opposition to all we know of the law of nature, and carrying into another sphere a body proper to our sphere, but not, so far as we know, possible to any other.

VI. *What Jesus Said after His Resurrection*

Returning from the Mount of Olives to Jerusalem, after the Ascension, the disciples (the remaining eleven) lived together in an upper room. There they continued with one account, in prayer and supplication, with the women who came up with them from Galilee, and with Mary the mother of Jesus, and with his brethren.

This is the second mention of Mary the mother of Jesus, as joined with his disciples, the first being in John's Gospel, where she appears at the foot of the Cross.

This time the mention is apparently by Luke, for the first verse of the chapter (I) in which Mary the mother of Jesus and his brethren are mentioned as belonging to his followers speaks of "the former treatise, O Theophilus," pointing clearly to the Gospel of Luke.

They are waiting in Jerusalem for the fulfilment of "the promise of the Father," for the baptism of the Holy Ghost, the power which they shall receive when the Holy Ghost is conferred upon them.

There were then of apostles and disciples together about 120. Peter stands up in their midst and speaks of Judas. He says that David spoke concerning Judas, who had been the guide to them that arrested Jesus.

He is obviously referring to *Psalms* (XLI, 9) : "Yea, mine own familiar friend, in whom I trusted, which did eat of my bread, hath lifted up his heel against me."

Having referred to this prophecy, he narrates the story of Judas's death, and (apparently) follows it up with two verses which must have been written long afterwards, that the field which Judas bought for himself was known to all dwellers in Jerusalem, inasmuch as that field is called in their proper tongue, Aceldama, that is to say the "field of blood"—the field in which the soil contains a quality which makes dead bodies decay in it. "For it is written in the book of *Psalms,* Let his habitation be desolate, and let no man dwell therein; and his bishopric let another take."

Obviously, verse 19 must have been written long after the event, not merely some forty odd days after. Verse 20 may have been spoken by Peter.

Then he goes on to say that of the men who have companied

with them all the time that the Lord Jesus went in and out among them, beginning from the baptism of John, must be ordained one to take the place of Judas, and be a witness with them to his Resurrection.

This gives a certain support to the theory that others besides the apostles saw the risen Christ.

So they appoint two, and then pray to the Lord, who knows the hearts of all men, to show them which of the two shall be chosen to take part in the ministry and apostleship from which Judas by transgression fell, "that he might go to his own place." They then cast lots, and the lot falls upon Matthias, and he is numbered with the eleven.

VII. Pentecost

Then comes the story of the Day of Pentecost. The disciples have either not gone to Galilee, and resumed their former occupations as fishermen, or they have returned to Jerusalem within the forty days in which Jesus is wandering through the land, for at the end of that time they are all with one accord in one place (obviously in Jerusalem), when suddenly there comes from Heaven a rushing mighty wind, and there appear to them cloven tongues as of fire and they sit upon each of them, and they all begin to speak with other tongues than their own. And then Peter, standing up with the eleven, speaks to the multitude of Jews of all nations which have gathered for the festival of Pentecost, telling them that what they are witnessing is what was foretold by the prophet Joel, saying that God had said that in the last days he would pour out his Spirit upon all flesh. "And it shall come to pass that whosoever shall call on the name of the Lord shall be saved."

Then Peter proceeds to apply all this to Jesus of Nazareth, describing him as

. . . a man approved of God among you by miracles and wonders and signs, which God did by him in the midst of you, as ye yourselves also know; him, being delivered by the determinate counsel and foreknowledge of God, ye have taken, and by wicked hands have crucified and slain. Whom God hath raised up, having loosed the pains of death, because it was not possible that he should be holden of it. [David, speaking concerning him, had foreseen that God would not leave his soul in hell, nor suffer His Holy One to see corruption.]

Therefore, says Peter:

Men and brethren, let me freely speak unto you of the patriarch David, that he is both dead and buried. . . . Therefore being a prophet, and knowing that God had sworn with an oath to him, that of the fruit of his loins, according to the flesh, he would raise up Christ to sit on his throne. He seeing this before spake of the Resurrection of Christ, that his soul was not left in hell, neither his flesh did see corruption.

This Jesus hath God raised up, whereof we all are witnesses. Therefore being by the right hand of God exalted, and having received of the Father the promise of the Holy Ghost, he hath shed forth this, which ye now see and hear. Therefore let all the house of Israel know assuredly, that God hath made that same Jesus, whom ye have crucified, both Lord and Christ.

After this outburst of metaphysical reasoning to account for the Resurrection of Jesus as a divine and foreseen event, as a thing foretold by David as promised to himself, but (David being dead and buried) carried into effect in the person of his son, according to the flesh, the people listening (the Jews from all countries who have come up for the festival, as well as the Jews of Jerusalem), are pricked in their hearts, and say to Peter and the rest of the apostles, "Men and brethren, what shall we do?"

Whereupon Peter says:

Repent, and be baptized every one of you in the name of Jesus Christ for the remission of sins, and ye shall receive the gift of the Holy Ghost.

Further, Peter tells them, as John the Baptist had done, to save themselves from "this untoward generation," and they gladly receive his word, and are baptized, 3,000 on the same day.

It is a most astonishing story. It does not sound like reality. When was it written? Did the events actually occur within seven weeks of the Crucifixion? Or does the internal evidence show that the story was written long after the events recorded, when the Church found the need of proving the Resurrection by prophecy, when it was struggling to make Christians of the Jews who believed prophecy and still looked for the Messiah, when some symbol was necessary to mark and cut off the believer, and baptism (of which Jesus most assuredly had not made much) seemed necessary.

The lesser difficulties of the story are great enough. Three thousand baptized in Jerusalem in one day. It seems to have been physically impossible. Twelve apostles could not have baptized so many.

It all reads like a story written long afterwards by somebody who did not know Palestine, and did not know *all* the Gospels, and did not know Peter.

What is Peter's argument on the day of Pentecost? This:

1. Jesus of Nazareth was a man approved by God, as was seen by the miracles and signs and wonders which God did by him. ·

2. He was, by God's foreknowledge and counsel, taken by the Jews, who by their wicked hands crucified him.

3. But he rose from the dead because death could not hold him. David, when speaking concerning him, had predicted his Resurrection when he said that God would not leave his soul in hell, or suffer His Holy One to see corruption.

Observe that David is here speaking, not of his successor according to the flesh, but of himself.

4. But that inasmuch as David had actually seen corruption, and is both dead and buried, the only possible interpretation is that he was speaking as a prophet, and, as such, was remembering that God had sworn an oath to him that of the fruit of His loins He would raise up another to sit upon His throne.

Here David, *Psalms* (CXXXII, 11), is making God speak: "Of the fruit of thy body will I set upon thy throne."

5. *Therefore,* David through God was speaking of the Resurrection of Christ, that his soul should not be left in hell, neither should his flesh see corruption.

6. *Therefore* this Jesus hath God raised up. The proof that he is raised up is that he is the son of David, therefore he is the Christ.

7. Therefore, let all the house of Israel know assuredly that God hath made that same Jesus, whom we have crucified, both Lord and Christ.

More briefly, because Jesus of Nazareth has risen from the dead he was the son of David and the Messiah.

Now this was a speech made to the Jews and for the Jews. The Jews were waiting for the Messiah. The Messiah must fulfil the conditions of prophecy. Jesus alone of all men had fulfilled these conditions in the one fact that his body had not seen corruption, and that his soul was not left in hell. Consequently, the Jews must know assuredly that Jesus was both Lord and Christ.

It is an argument totally unlike anything recorded as having come from Peter during the lifetime of Jesus. Never once, when his Master lived, does he (as far as I can remember) seek to convince himself that Jesus is the Christ by any reference to prophecy, or yet to the relation according to the flesh to David. It is all a metaphysical argument which must have come to Peter after he had become convinced that Jesus had risen from the dead.

Although Jesus had told him and his fellow-disciples that after three days he would rise again, it had never once occurred to him to connect this with David. In order to connect it with David he has to persuade himself that, because the prophecy had not applied to David himself, therefore it must have been meant to apply to one of his descendants. And the only one it could apply to was the man Jesus, who had actually risen, who had not seen corruption.

The argument has a suggestion of casuistry quite foreign to anything we have previously been prepared to find in the mind of the fisherman of Galilee. It is utterly untrue to the type of his mind, and can only be explained by assuming that the Holy Ghost on the day of Pentecost made of Peter a different man, with different knowledge, different ways of thought.

I confess I do not like it. It leaves on me the impression of the writing of a totally different person, trying to convert the Jews by reference to prophecy, found necessary to their conversion.

Such is the last chapter in the life of Jesus and the first in the history of his Church.

VIII. After Pentecost

The disciples' former fear fell away from them. They hid themselves no longer in an upper room, but went up together to the Temple, performed miracles in the name of Christ, and preached in his name, openly braving the persecution of the Jewish authorities, and charging them with putting to death the Son of God, calling him also the Holy One and the Just and the Prince of Life, saying that God had raised him from the dead, and that they were the witnesses of it. Above all, showing that all that happened to Jesus at the hands of his enemies, the Jewish authorities, had been foretold by God through the mouths of His prophets.

And, finally, calling upon men to repent and be converted, that their sins might be blotted out, "when the times of refreshing" should come from the presence of the Lord, and He should send Jesus Christ, whom the heavens must receive, until the time of restitution of all things; which God had spoken by the mouth of all His holy prophets since the world began.

Thus they claimed that from the beginning God through His prophets had foretold Jesus. Moses had truly said to their fathers:

A prophet shall the Lord your God raise up unto you of your brethren, like unto me; him shall ye hear in all things whatsoever he shall say unto you. And it shall come to pass, that every soul, which will not hear that prophet, shall be destroyed from among the people. . . . Ye are the children of the prophets, and of the covenant which God made with our fathers, saying unto Abraham, And in thy seed shall all the kindreds of the earth be blessed.

Unto you first, God, having raised up His Son Jesus, sent him to bless you, in turning away every one of you from his iniquities.

Later, in the very presence of the rulers, elders and scribes, of Annas, the high priest, and Caiaphas, gathered together at Jerusalem (the very men who had led to the Crucifixion of Jesus), Peter, "filled with the Holy Ghost," proclaimed:

Jesus Christ of Nazareth, whom ye crucified, whom God raised from the dead . . . This is the stone which was set at nought of you builders, which is become the head of the corner. Neither is there salvation in any other; for there is none other name under Heaven given among men, whereby we must be saved.

Such is the great transformation which takes place in the disciples during the first seven weeks which follow the Crucifixion.

The weak, timid men, who had run away and hidden themselves, come boldly out, being convinced of the Resurrection of their Master, and proclaim him as the Messiah, the son of David and the Son of God who had been foretold by the prophets.

The words Jesus had spoken to them during his lifetime come back to them now with a new meaning.

They have no longer any fear. They serve the supreme power. Nothing can touch them. They face Annas and Caiaphas and the elders with a new courage. They defy them.

They are willing to bear persecution, no matter in what form— scourging, imprisonment, death. They are so far from shrinking from this that they count themselves honoured to suffer in *his* name. They court martyrdom, for the glory of sharing in his sufferings. The more they suffer for him the more their glory.

The behaviour of the chief priests in the face of this—it was almost paralysing. It is a bold challenge, a defiant charge. *You* who crucified him are the accursed of God. That is the spirit of their charge.

They gather a great following. Thousands come to them. Their fearlessness cannot be gainsaid.

What the Roman authorities do we cannot gather from the narrative. The greater force of the attack of the disciples is clearly against the Jewish rulers. On them they lay the burden of the death of Jesus. Although his death was preordained, yet their wickeness was none the less, for they brought it to pass. They *forced* the hand of the Romans. When Pilate would have saved the life of Jesus, they compelled him to crucify him, preferring the commonest thief and murderer to the Lord of all.

The story of those first years of the little Christian Church would be a thrilling story if only we had the material to fill it up.

END OF BOOK II.

BOOK III

After Christ

CHAPTER I

The Second Advent

I. The Disciples after the Ascension

THE STORY of what followed the death, Resurrection and Ascension of Jesus is told by Luke and in the Acts of the Apostles. The question to be considered is, What was the gospel as seen in the words and acts of the first apostles of Jesus immediately after he left them? What did they understand him to be? What was he in the world for? What was Christianity to the first Christians?

On returning to Jerusalem from the Mount of the Ascension the disciples are changed men. All their fear of the chief priests and others has gone. They see without difficulty now. Whereas, hitherto (between the Crucifixion and the day of the Resurrection—the three days), they thought they had deceived themselves, or perhaps misunderstood Jesus, they now realize that they had been right. He was indeed the Christ. They remembered what he said to them about rising on the third day, and he had risen. They remembered what he had said about returning to God, and he had returned to God.

They remembered what he had said about coming again in the clouds of Heaven to re-establish the kingdom of Heaven on earth, and he would come again. They remembered that he had told them his return would be soon, that some of their little company should not die before they had seen him coming back, with the power of God's angels behind him, and he would come soon, before all of them died, and then they would share his glory. They remembered that he had said they would sit with him on twelve thrones to judge the twelve tribes, and all this would come to pass.

He had told them to wait in patience until the coming again of their Lord, for only God could will when that should be, and they would wait.

They remembered that he had told them that before the coming of the great day there would be wars in the world, earthquakes, the rising and falling of nations, and that all this should be the sign to them that the day was near.

They remembered that he had told them that at the Judgment all mankind would be saved if it believed on him, that God had sent him, and that his word was God's word to man. They remembered that he had told them they were to go on while he was away, preaching the gospel he had brought to the world, and that in his name they were to work miracles.

They knew that he had told them that the world to which they were to dedicate their lives would persecute and kill them, as it *had* persecuted and killed him; but that this was to be their glory, not their shame, the sign of their victory, not of their defeat.

Such was the change that had taken place in the apostles. And what had brought it to pass?

The Resurrection of Jesus from the dead.

No man had ever risen before. He alone had conquered death. Only God could conquer death.

But the evidence of his Resurrection was not alone their strength. They saw now, as never before, all that the Scriptures foretold of Jesus from the beginning. Everything they had witnessed had been prophesied, from Moses downward.

We see the apostles back in Jerusalem. They are concealing themselves from the chief priests no longer. They may be seized, tried, condemned to death, executed. But that did not matter. It was what had happened to their Master, and they would glory in the suffering they shared with him. They were to remain in Jerusalem—not fly away—until the Spirit of God came to them to strengthen and inspire them.

So during these forty days they had never been in Galilee at all. Some of the commentators try to avoid this difficulty by saying that "Jerusalem" covered "Galilee." It never did so in the mouth of Jesus.

In the opening of *Acts* we see them waiting for this great moment. They are all there, except the apostle who has fallen from them, living together in an upper room, continuing in prayer and supplication. With them are the faithful women who had followed Jesus from Galilee to Jerusalem. With them, also, according to *Acts,* is Mary the mother of Jesus, and the brothers of Jesus.

How these came, by what impulse (having been hostile to Jesus when we heard of them last), we are not told.

II. *The Day of Pentecost*

At length the great day comes.

It is the day of the Jewish Feast of Pentecost, the beginning of the harvest. It is fifty days after the Passover—the time of the death of Jesus. The apostles, the women and the followers—all Jews—are gathered together in one place. It is nine o'clock in the morning.

The disciples are suddenly conscious of great happenings. There comes a sound from Heaven as of a rushing of a mighty wind. Great tongues of fire seem to come and sit on each of them.

It is no illusion; they are convinced of its reality. They find themselves suddenly endowed with a new spirit—possessed of powers they have never had before. They begin to speak with tongues hitherto unknown to them. It is the coming of the Holy Ghost, which the master had foretold.

The extraordinary facts became known in Jerusalem.

There are, at this time, in the city, great numbers of foreign Jews who have come up for the feast as well as others—Parthians, Medes, Elamites, dwellers in Mesopotamia, in Cappadocia, in Pontus and Asia, Phrygia, Pamphylia, Egypt, Libya, Cyrene, strangers from Rome, Cretes, Arabians. There are Jews and proselytes. They are all amazed. They hear the apostles speaking in their own language. What does it mean? Some onlookers think the men must be demented.

Peter stands up and speaks.

"Ye men of Judæa, and all ye that dwell at Jerusalem . . ." he begins, "hearken to my words."

Jesus of Nazareth, who had lived among them, and whom they had taken and by wicked hands crucified, had been raised up by God.

The prophet David had spoken of him. Knowing that God had sworn an oath to him that of the fruit of His loins, according to the flesh, He would raise up the Christ to sit on His throne, this Jesus had God raised up.

Of the Resurrection of Jesus they were all witnesses. This was no illusion. They had not been dreaming dreams. They had not been seeing visions. Not to everybody, but to his own people, Jesus had appeared. He had appeared in the flesh. They had been sure of his bodily presence. He had eaten and drunk with them. And then he had risen into Heaven. And now he was sitting on God's right hand in Heaven.

Therefore let all the house of Israel know assuredly, that God hath made that same Jesus, whom ye have crucified, both Lord and Christ.

In these words, Peter, having overcome all his former fear of the priests, throws in their faces their crime.

The result is that some of the Jews are pricked in their hearts and ask what they should do.

"Repent, and be baptized every one of you in the name of Jesus Christ for the remission of sins." Thus Peter testified and exhorted, saying, "Save yourselves from this untoward generation."

It is the message of John the Baptist over again.

Many receive the word and are baptized. It is said 3,000 that same day. "Fear came upon every soul; and many wonders and signs were done by the disciples."

Such is the story of the coming of the Holy Ghost on the day of Pentecost.

It sounds like the illusion of men intoxicated by a great new impulse. It is to be noted that, as often as men are converted and baptized (the same in Paul's case as in Peter's), the Holy Ghost is said to come on them and they speak with tongues and prophecy (see *Acts* XIX, 6).

Some of it sounds like physical impossibility, such as the baptizing of 3,000 in one day in Jerusalem by twelve apostles (Judas's place being filled) at that time of the year, when water is scarce in Jerusalem, and the nearest river, the Jordan, is twenty-two miles away, and the pools of Solomon and Siloam contain barely enough drinking water for the people of the crowded city.

Apparently, no notice is taken of all this by the priestly classes who, fifty days before, caused Jesus to be put to death. Neither is any notice of it taken by the Roman governor, who crucified Jesus for saying no more about himself than his followers are now saying about him.

The great multitude of converts are said to continue steadfastly in the apostles' doctrines and fellowship, and in the breaking of bread and in prayer.

In the first period of peace for the infant Church an attempt is made to live according to the teaching of Jesus. Their way of believing in Jesus is that of putting his teaching into actual operation. Therefore, to avoid the greed he condemned, the inequalities of rich and poor which he denounced, they establish a commune.

They have all things in common, selling their possessions and parting with them to all men, as every man had need. Nobody lacked; poverty disappeared among the followers of Jesus. Other efforts they make to carry into life the teaching of Jesus. It impresses the people.

How long this condition lasts we are not told, and have only secular history to help us to an opinion.

The disciples and their followers frequent the Temple. They pass freely from house to house, praising God and having favour with all the people. Their number increases to 5,000.

Meantime, the two leading disciples, Peter and John, begin to work miracles, such as Jesus had worked before them. They declare to the unbelieving Jews that they do this not by their own power of holiness, but by that of Jesus, whom they (the Jews) had killed.

It was true that both they and their priestly rulers had done this through ignorance, but being shown by the word of the prophets that the man they had crucified had been the Christ, whom God had sent to bless them, they turn away from their iniquities.

After a time (how long we are not told) the priests, the captain of the Temple and the Sadducees begin to realize that the teaching of the disciples is a bitter reproach.

One day Annas, the "high priest" (Luke perpetuates his technical error and thus indicates the identity of the writer of *Acts* with the writer of the Gospel of Luke), and Caiaphas, and many of the kindred of the high priests called for the disciples and said, "By what power and by what name have ye done this?"—performed miracles. Then Peter, "filled with the Holy Ghost," without fear, repeats what he has said before.

The miracles they perform are in the name of Jesus Christ of Nazareth, "whom ye crucified," and whom God raised from the dead. There is no other name under Heaven than that of Jesus whereby men might be saved.

The priests perceive that Peter and John are unlearned and

ignorant men, and marvel at the authority with which they speak. They hear that Peter and John had been with Jesus.

The priests in council consider together what they should do, and decide that they must threaten the apostles that they must no more speak or teach in the name of Jesus.

This was a natural decision. If it had been blasphemy in Jesus to say he was the Son of God it was no less blasphemy in the apostles to say he had been the Son of God. Therefore the offence of the apostles was not only as great as that of Jesus but greater.

They added the further charge against the priestly class of having killed the Son of God, and supported the charge by saying that the divinity of Jesus had been proved by his Resurrection, and by the word of the prophets, whose Scripture his life had fulfilled.

More than that, the preaching of the apostles (Peter, in particular) was bitterer to the priestly class than any bitter thing Jesus had said of them, in so far as it propounded the doctrine that they (the priests) had by God's foreknowledge been the instruments of this iniquity.

At length (at what period is still uncertain), after the new community had still further increased, and Peter in particular was performing miracles even in Solomon's porch in the Temple, "the high priest rose up, and all they that were with him (which is the sect of the Sadducees), and were filled with indignation, and laid their hands on the apostles, and put them in the common prison."

III. Gamaliel

By what miraculous means the apostles were liberated from prison *Acts* tells at length.

They were brought again before the priests, who said, "Did we not command you that you should not preach in this name? Yet you have filled Jerusalem with your doctrine. You are trying to bring this man's blood upon us."

To this, Peter replies that they have to obey God, not man; that the God of their fathers had raised up Jesus, whom they (the priests) had slain; that God had exalted Jesus to be a prince and a saviour to give repentance to Israel and forgiveness of sins.

When the priests hear this again they are cut to the heart, and take counsel to slay the disciples.

Apparently, a council of the Sanhedrin is called. At this council a Pharisee, named Gamaliel, a descendant of the great Jewish Rabbi, Hillel, counsels prudence. "Take heed what you do to these men," he says. He quotes history—Theudas, Judas of Galilee—to show that to kill the men would be unwise. The burden of his advice is, "Leave these men alone. If their message be of men it will come to naught. If it be of God you cannot overthrow it, and to resist it will be to fight against God."

At that sitting the Sanhedrin agree with Gamaliel. And, as a result, they do to the apostles what Pilate wished to do to Jesus— they beat them and let them go, commanding them again not to speak in the name of Jesus.

This produces no effect on the disciples. They have no fear. They only rejoice that they are counted worthy to suffer shame for the name of Jesus. It is what he had told them would happen —they would be scourged in the synagogues. So, without ceasing, in the Temple and in every house, they go on to teach and preach Jesus Christ.

Time passes (again *Acts* does not tell us how long), the number of the disciples is multiplied.

> And the word of God increased: and the number of the disciples multiplied in Jerusalem greatly; and a great company of the priests were obedient to the faith.

Why not? Peter and his fellow-apostles were still Jews. They still taught in the synagogues. They were saying nothing yet that a Jew might not believe: (1) that Jesus was by his Resurrection proved to be the Christ whom Scripture had foretold; (2) that to believe God had sent him, and that they were to accept his word as God's word, was the way of salvation; (3) that he had died on the Cross that everyone who believed in him might be saved from the penalty of his sin; (4) therefore Jesus had died for men, by which they must be the children of the promise—of Abraham.

IV. *What Jesus Said: According to Matthew*

It is important to know what Jesus himself said concerning his second coming.

After his denunciation of the scribes and Pharisees (*Matthew* XXIII) for shutting up the kingdom of Heaven against men and for devouring widows' houses, he continues with the following flaming passages:

Woe unto you, scribes and Pharisees, hypocrites; For ye compass sea and land to make one proselyte, and when he is made, ye make him twofold more the child of hell than yourselves.

Woe unto you, ye blind guides, which say, Whosoever shall swear by the Temple, it is nothing; but whosoever shall swear by the gold of the Temple, he is a debtor.

Ye fools and blind, for whether is greater, the gold, or the Temple that sanctifieth the gold?

And whosoever shall swear by the altar, it is nothing; but whosoever sweareth by the gift that is upon it, he is guilty.

Ye fools and blind; for whether is greater, the gift, or the altar that sanctifieth the gift?

Whoso therefore shall swear by the altar, sweareth by it, and by all things thereon.

And whoso shall swear by the Temple, sweareth by it, and by Him that dwelleth therein.

And he that shall swear by Heaven, sweareth by the throne of God, and by Him that sitteth thereon.

Woe unto you, scribes and Pharisees, hypocrites! for ye pay tithe of mint and anise and cummin, and have omitted the weightier matters of the law, judgment, mercy, and faith; these ought ye to have done, and not to leave the other undone.

Ye blind guides, which strain at a gnat, and swallow a camel.

Woe unto you, scribes and Pharisees, hypocrites! for ye make clean the outside of the cup and of the platter, but within they are full of extortion and excess.

Thou blind Pharisee, cleanse first that which is within the cup and platter, that the outside of them may be clean also.

Woe unto you, scribes and Pharisees, hypocrites! for ye are like unto whited sepulchres, which indeed appear beautiful outward, but are within full of dead men's bones, and of all uncleanness.

Even so ye also outwardly appear righteous unto men, but within ye are full of hypocrisy and iniquity.

Woe unto you, scribes and Pharisees, hypocrites! because ye build the tombs of the prophets, and garnish the sepulchres of the righteous.

And say, If we had been in the days of our fathers, we would not have been partakers with them in the blood of the prophets.

Wherefore ye be witnesses unto yourselves, that ye are the children of them which killed the prophets.

Fill ye up then the measure of your fathers.

Ye serpents, ye generation of vipers, how can ye escape the damnation of hell?

Wherefore, behold, I send unto you prophets, and wise men, and scribes; and some of them ye shall kill and crucify; and some of them shall ye scourge in your synagogues, and persecute them from city to city;

That upon you may come all the righteous blood shed upon the earth, from the blood of righteous Abel unto the blood of Zacharias son of Barachias, whom ye slew between the temple and the altar.

Verily I say unto you, All these things shall come upon this generation.

O Jerusalem, Jerusalem, thou that killest the prophets, and stonest them which are sent unto thee, how often would I have gathered thy children together, even as a hen gathereth her chickens under her wings, and ye would not!

Behold, your house is left unto you desolate.

For I say unto you, Ye shall not see me henceforth, till ye shall say, Blessed is he that cometh in the name of the Lord.

After the entrance into Jerusalem, Jesus went out of the Temple (*Matthew* XXIV) and his disciples came with him to show him the buildings of the Temple. An unnecessary thing. These unlettered Galilean fishermen showing the buildings of the Temple to Jesus.

And Jesus tells them that at some time, not indicated, there will not be one stone left upon another of these stones of the Temple.

They then go up into the Mount of Olives and the disciples come to him privately and ask when shall this thing happen? And assuming it to mean the end of the world they ask what shall be the sign of the coming of the end of the world.

Jesus thereupon answers:

(1) that they are to take care that no men deceive them, for many impostors will arise, saying, "I am Christ";

(2) they will hear of war and rumours of wars, but they are not to be troubled, for the end will not be yet;

(3) nation shall rise against nation, and kingdom against kingdom, and there will be famines and pestilences and earthquakes in many places, and all these will be the beginning of sorrows;

(4) they shall be persecuted and killed, and hated of all nations for his sake; many shall betray one another and hate one another; many false prophets shall arise, and because iniquity shall abound (apparently within the Church itself) the love of many shall wax cold;

(5) but he that shall endure to the end (that is whose faith does not fail) shall be saved;

(6) his gospel of the Kingdom shall be preached in all the world as a witness to all nations and—then shall the end come.

(7) When they shall see the abomination of desolation spoken of by Daniel, the prophet (*Daniel* IX, 25–27) : "Know therefore and understand, that from the going forth of the commandment to restore and to build Jerusalem unto the Messiah the prince shall be seven weeks, and threescore and two weeks; the street shall be built again, and the wall, even in troublous times. And after threescore and two weeks shall Messiah be cut off, but not for himself; and the people of the prince that shall come shall destroy the city and the sanctuary; and the end thereof shall be with a flood, and unto the end of the war desolations are determined. And he shall confirm the covenant with many for one week; and in the midst of the week he shall cause the sacrifice and the oblation to cease, and for the overspreading of abominations he shall make it desolate, even until the consummation, and that determined shall be poured upon the desolate"—when they shall see this, they are to stand in the holy place.

Then let the people who are in Judæa fly to the mountains. They are not to wait, to return home to save anything. Woe unto the women who are with child in those days, and woe unto those that are suckling children. They are to pray that the flight they have to make will not be in winter or on the Sabbath Day . . . (when they would be forbidden by the law of Moses to fly).

There shall be great tribulation, such as there has not been since the beginning of the world until that time, or ever shall be. Unless those days of tribulation be shortened, nobody alive shall be saved. *Yet for the elect's sake they shall be shortened* (apparently an interpolation).

(8) Again a repetition about the false Christs and false prophets who in those days will show signs and wonders that will almost deceive the very elect. (This—XXIV, 23, and the next verse—reads like commonplace interpolation, and not in the least like Christ speaking.)

"Behold, I have told you before."

Where? Except in this chapter? Or does this mean "I have prophesied?"

As the lightning cometh out of the east, and shineth even unto the west, so shall also the coming of the Son of Man be. For wheresoever the carcase is, there will the eagles be gathered together. [XXIV, 27–28]

What does this mean in this connexion?

Immediately after the tribulation of those days shall the sun be darkened, and the moon shall not give her light, and the stars shall fall from Heaven, and the power of the heavens shall be shaken. And then shall appear the Son of Man in Heaven; and then shall all the tribes of the earth mourn, and they shall see the Son of Man coming in the clouds of Heaven with power and great glory. And he shall send his angels with a great sound of a trumpet, and they shall gather together his elect from the four winds, from one end of Heaven to the other. [*Matthew* XXIV, 29–31]

He expects his elect to be all over the earth by the time of the end, and they shall be in Heaven also from one end to the other; in other words, a vast number will have died and passed into Heaven.

Then after a very feeble use of the similitude of the fig-tree, which tells us it is summer by putting forth its leaves, Jesus goes on to say when this time of his coming will be. It will be within the period of the generation then living. This generation shall not pass until all these things shall be fulfilled. But of that day and of the hour no man knows anything, even the angels know nothing. Only God knows.

As it was in the days before the Flood, when men ate and drank and married and knew nothing about the impending Flood until it came upon them, so it will be with the coming of the Son of Man.

So sudden shall it be that two shall be working in the field and one shall be taken and the other left. Two women shall be grinding at the mill, and one shall be taken and the other left. "Watch therefore; for ye know not what hour your Lord doth come."

Be ready, for in the hour when you think not the Son of Man will come.

Another parable (the parable of the ten virgins) to show the necessity of being ready (*Matthew* XXV, 1–12). The moral is, "Watch therefore, for ye know neither the day nor the hour wherein the Son of Man cometh."

Another parable (the parable of the talents) to show the necessity of making ready for the coming.

Then comes the Great Vision of the Judgment:

When the Son of Man shall come in his glory, and all the holy angels with him, then shall he sit upon the throne of his glory. And before him shall be gathered all nations; and he shall separate them one from another, as a shepherd divideth his sheep from the goats. And he shall set the sheep on his right hand, but the goats on the left. Then shall the King [Is this the first claim of the Messiah to be King?] say unto them on his right hand, Come, ye blessed of my Father [the King is not the Father], inherit the Kingdom prepared for you from the foundation of the world. [XXV, 31–34]

Then follows what is perhaps the most beautiful passage put into the mouth of Christ. Critics have doubted if Christ ever spoke it. But if not Christ, who ever spoke anything so deeply moving, so profound, yet so simple and searching?

Why are those on the King's right hand to inherit the Kingdom prepared for them from the beginning of the world?

For I was an hungred, and ye gave me meat; I was thirsty, and ye gave me drink; I was a stranger, and ye took me in;

Naked, and ye clothed me. I was sick, and ye visited me; I was in prison and ye came unto me.

Then shall the righteous answer him, saying, Lord, when saw we thee an hungred, and fed thee? or thirsty, and gave thee drink?

When saw we thee a stranger, and took thee in? or naked, and clothed thee?

Or when saw we thee sick, or in prison, and came unto thee?

And the King shall answer and say unto them, Verily I say unto you, Inasmuch as ye have done it unto one of the least of these my brethren, ye have done it unto me.

Then shall he say also unto them on the left hand, Depart from me, ye cursed, into everlasting fire, prepared for the devil and his angels:

For I was an hungred, and ye gave me no meat; I was thirsty, and ye gave me no drink:

I was a stranger, and ye took me not in: naked, and ye clothed me not: sick, and in prison, and ye visited me not.

Then shall they also answer him, saying, Lord, when saw we thee an hungred, or athirst, or a stranger, or naked, or sick, or in prison, and did not minister unto thee?

Then shall he answer them, saying, Verily I say unto you, Inasmuch as ye did it not to one of the least of these, ye did it not to me.

And these shall go away into everlasting punishment: but the righteous into life eternal.

This is, perhaps, the sublimest picture in the Scriptures, the picture and prophecy of the Kingdom. It tells of the coming of the end of the world, and the establishment of a new order.

Why is the world to come to an end? Because of the hypocrisy and wickedness of the ruling classes, and the sufferings they are inflicting on the weak and poor.

When is it to come to an end? Clearly, the answer to the direct question of the disciples points to a period similar to, if not identical with, that of the destruction of Jerusalem. The sign of the end is what is described—wars, famines, pestilences, earthquakes in many places, the persecution of the followers of Jesus, the defection of many, the rise of many false Christs, and so on.

Nevertheless, the gospel of Jesus will be preached over all the world before the end comes.

This may have to be understood in the spirit of the age, all the world meaning the same as its equivalent in the Temptation.

If, therefore, the period of the destruction of Jerusalem is clearly indicated by Jesus, his prophecy (if such it was) has proved to be false. That period is nineteen hundred years behind us, and yet the events predicted by Jesus as certain to come immediately after it have not even yet taken place.

Out of this arise many considerations.

(1) Did Jesus actually speak the words here put into his mouth? If so, he was prophesying, and that part of his prophecy was true which concerned the destruction of the Temple and the downfall of Jerusalem, which took place forty years later, namely A.D. 70. But that part of his prophecy which says that this generation shall not pass away until the Son of Man is seen coming in the clouds of Heaven has not proved to be true. And this deals a serious blow to the claim of Christianity.

(2) Were these words put into the mouth of Jesus after the event, that is to say after the destruction of Jerusalem in A.D. 70? If so, they are an imposture, for they claim to be actually spoken about A.D. 30, whereas they could then not actually have been written until forty years afterwards.

(3) The theory of many critics that they were not spoken by Jesus in A.D. 30 but written by his followers after A.D. 70, and were therefore not prophecy but mere reporting, reduces one of the strongest claims of Christianity (that Jesus knew everything before it took place and no man had need to tell him anything) to the level of rank falsehood.

(4) It is mainly on this supposition, that these chapters (*Matthew* XXIII, XXIV and XXV), so far as they concern historical events, are reports, not prophecy, that critics doubt if the wonderful passages contained in them were Christ's.

(5) My answer to this is, (a) if the historical part is mere reporting, and therefore substantially true (including the destruction of the Temple and the downfall of Jerusalem), what are we to say of that part of the reporting which has not yet proved true —namely the account of the coming of Christ in the clouds and the Judgment? In short, if these chapters were not spoken in A.D. 30, but written in A.D. 70, why should they have included an account of the supernatural events (the second coming and the Judgment) which the reporter must have known had not taken place and of which there was not then the remotest probability that they would take place in the near future? (b) if these wonderful passages were not spoken by Jesus, by whom could they have been written? What record have we of any other human creature who spoke or wrote like that?

The passages, as a picture of the crash and downfall of the old world, as a vision of the judgment of that world, and as a prediction of the new world to be set up in its place, are, in my opinion, superior to anything at all like them in any literature the world knows, or, so far as we are aware, has ever known. Such nobility of conception, such majesty of phrase, such imagination, such humanity are not to be found in Dante or in Milton, or yet in Isaiah. If not Jesus, who? There is no answer.

If Jesus did not conceive the picture of the Judgment, and speak the words beginning, "When the Son of Man shall come in his glory, and all his holy angels with him . . ." and ending with "but the righteous into life eternal," who did? To this there is no answer. And the only real ground on which it can be said that Jesus did not speak them is that they contain too detached and exact a report of what took place forty years after his death. (c) My conclusion is that these great chapters are by Jesus, that they resemble his ways of thought, his methods of expression, his closeness to humanity, and those of nobody else whatever.

But the more certain we are that this account of the destruction of the old world, the creation of the new, and the second coming of Christ has the authority of Christ, the more perplexed we are by the fact that the most material part (that which concerns the Judgment and the Second Coming) has not taken place, although it was, apparently, expected to take place within the lifetime of the generation living when Jesus spoke.

Was Jesus wrong? Did his prophecy break down? Is it still unfulfilled? If so, does not Christianity therein suffer a grievous blow? Is it possible any longer to think of Jesus as a prophet who knew everything? Is it possible to think of him as the Son of God? Or are we to take refuge in some other explanation of what he said about the present generation not passing away until all these things he has foretold have been fulfilled?

Are we to shelter ourselves in Peter's explanation that our way of counting a thousand years in God's reckoning is the same as a day to us?

It is impossible, without juggling, to take refuge in this makeshift. We cannot take one half of a passage literally and the remaining half figuratively. Either Jesus thought his second coming was to take place during the lifetime of some of his disciples or he did not.

If he *did* think so he was clearly wrong. Jesus has not come to earth a second time. The scenes he describes, the Judgment, have not taken place.

If he did not think so, what *did* he think?

In this great vision of the destruction of the world, the Judgment of mankind, the separating of those who are worthy to inherit the Kingdom which has been prepared for the righteous from the foundation of the world from those who are not worthy, nothing that I can see is said about the atoning power of Christ's sacrifice of himself, of his redemption of man from the punishment of sin, from the atonement with God which is wrought by Christ for all who believe—who accept him.

The Judgment is based on ordinary terms of justice—those who have loved righteousness go into life eternal, while those who have lived unrighteously go into eternal damnation. As far as I can see, there is no intervention of a Redeemer, no indication of a Saviour, a God-man (such as *Hebrews* expounds) who steps in and saves man from the just penalty of his sin.

So far *Matthew* on the Second Coming.

V. According to Mark

Again, as in *Matthew*, Jesus speaks after the entry into Jerusalem.

There is no essential difference between Matthew's account and Mark's of the signs that are to go before the beginning of sorrows. Jesus foretells more precisely what persecutions are to be suffered by his disciples; how they are to be delivered up to the councils, *beaten* in the synagogues, brought before the *rulers and kings* for his sake, *for a testimony against them.*

> And the Gospel must first be published among all nations. . . . Now the brother shall betray the brother to death, and the father the son; and children shall rise up against their parents, and shall cause them to be put to death. And ye shall be hated of all men for my name's sake; but he that shall endure unto the end, the same shall be saved.

Then the reference to the abomination of desolation spoken of by Daniel. Then the false Christs.

> But take ye heed; behold, I have foretold you all things.

Here is a distinct affirmation that Jesus was prophesying, not merely reporting after the event. If this is not true, then the later writers (after A.D. 70) were making Jesus a liar.

Thus, Mark's account of what Jesus said about his Second Coming is the same as in *Matthew,* with the difference that it is not so full, so splendid, so human, and that it does not give an account of the Last Judgment. But it does give a briefer picture of the falling of the stars of Heaven, and the coming of the Son of Man in the clouds with great power and glory, and his sending his angels to gather together his elect from the four winds, from the uttermost parts of the earth to the uttermost parts of Heaven.

This clearly indicates a much greater lapse of time than forty years or the time of the "present generation." His gospel is to be preached over all the world, his elect are to be in the uttermost parts of the earth and the uttermost parts of Heaven.

All this points to a more simple explanation—that Jesus foretold the destruction of the Temple and the downfall of Jerusalem as coming within the time of the present generation, but that before the Second Coming of Christ a far greater interval should occur, and that when the Son of Man should come in the clouds of Heaven his followers would be so many and so widespread that they would have to be called, not from the boundaries of Palestine, but from the uttermost parts of the earth and Heaven.

So much for what Jesus says of his Second Coming in *Mark*.

VI. *According to Luke*

Jesus was on his way from Galilee to Jerusalem. He passed through the midst of Samaria and Galilee (XVII, 11). The Pharisees demanded of him to say when the kingdom of God (which he was always preaching) should come.

He answered that the kingdom of God came not by observation. They could not say, "It will be here," or "It will be there," *because the kingdom of God was within them.* The days would come when they would desire to see one of the days of the Son of Man, and they should not see it. People would say, "See here" or "See there." But Jesus tells his disciples not to go after such people. As the lightning that lighteneth out of one part under Heaven, shineth unto the other part under Heaven, so shall also the Son of Man be in his day.

In other words, the Son of Man would come everywhere at the same time. But before he came he must suffer many things and be rejected of this generation.

As it was in the days of Noah so it will be in the days of the Son of Man. People ate and drank in Noah's day, married wives, and were given in marriage, until Noah entered the Ark and the flood came and destroyed them all. (Jesus believed the Noah story of the flood.)

In the same way, in the days of Lot, people ate and drank and bought and sold and planted and builded, but the same day that Lot went out of Sodom it rained fire and brimstone from Heaven and destroyed them all.

It would be so in the day when the Son of Man would be revealed. His coming would be sudden and unexpected. Let him that is on the housetops not come down for anything he has in the house. And let him that is in the field not return home to recover what he has there. If any man wished to save his life he must lose it. Whosoever shall lose his life shall preserve it.

So sudden shall be the day of the Son of Man (the sign of the end of the world) that two men shall be in one bed, and one shall be taken and the other left; two women shall be grinding corn together, and one shall be taken and the other left. Two men shall be in the field, and one shall be taken and the other left.

Then his disciples asked, "Where, Lord?" And Jesus answered, "Wheresoever the body is, thither will the eagles be gathered together."

I confess I do not clearly understand. The "body" is the dead carcass; the eagles are the birds of prey which live on the dead carcasses. What is the parallel? And, indeed, what is the meaning of the passage?

Then follow two parables (XVIII). The first (the parable of the judge and the importunate widow) I find difficult to apply to the foregoing discourse on the Second Coming of the Son of Man.

The second parable (that of the Pharisee and the publican going up to the Temple to pray) I also find difficult to associate with the discourse upon the Second Advent.

Then comes the incident of the little children who are brought to Jesus after his disciples had rebuked the people who brought them. Again I find it difficult to find any connexion between this incident and the discourse on the Second Coming.

Next, there is the incident of the ruler who said, "Good Master, what shall I do to inherit eternal life?" and is told at length to sell all, distribute to the poor and follow Jesus.

All are very beautiful, but are separate incidents, or parables, which stand each on its own. Hence, I think the first verse of Chapter XVIII is without any proper meaning, so far as concerns the italicised words *to this end*. If this means (either in the view of the original writer or of subsequent editors) that the contents of Chapter XVIII are intended to illustrate the discourse in Chapter XVII, I think it is utterly wrong.

After this comes the passing through Jericho and the entry into Jerusalem.

The next direct reference to the end of the world comes in verses 41–44, Chapter XIX, while Jesus is entering Jerusalem.

When he came near to the city and beheld it, he wept over it, saying:

If thou hadst known, even thou, at least in this thy day, the things which belong unto thy peace! but now they are hid from thine eyes. For the days shall come upon thee, that thine enemies shall cast a trench about thee, and compass thee round, and keep thee in on every side, and shall lay thee even with the ground, and thy children within thee; and they shall not leave in thee one stone upon another; because thou knewest not the time of thy visitation.

Then he goes into the Temple and casts out them that buy and sell there.

Here is a prophecy of the destruction of Jerusalem which, although almost identical in spirit, is fuller than that in *Matthew* (XXIV).

In *Luke,* however, the prophecy is spoken while Jesus is approaching Jerusalem, and before he has entered it. In *Matthew* it is spoken after he has entered Jerusalem, after he has cast out of the Temple those that bought and sold there, after he has spoken in the Temple, after he has denounced the Pharisees, after he has lamented over Jerusalem ("O Jerusalem, Jerusalem, thou that killest the prophets . . . Behold, your house is left unto you desolate").

After this (*Luke* XX) comes, what I think, the crowning parable of Jesus—the parable of the vineyard let out to husbandmen.

I take this to be an illustration of God's treatment of His chosen people. God gives them the world to live in. He sends His prophets to guide them. The husbandmen kill the prophets, one by one. At length God sends His beloved Son, thinking the husbandmen will reverence him. They kill God's beloved Son also.

Then God comes and utterly destroys the husbandmen, and gives the vineyard to others.

The Jews who are listening to this parable (the chief priests and scribes) say "God forbid!"

Jesus understands them, and answers:

What is this then that is written, The stone which the builders rejected the same is become the head of the corner? Whosoever shall fall upon that stone shall be broken; but on whomsoever it shall fall, it will grind him to powder.

The chief priests and scribes see that the parable is spoken against them. They perfectly understand Jesus to mean that, if they reject him, the promise given to Abraham will be transferred to the Gentiles. Therefore, they seek to lay hands on him, and are only restrained by fear of the people.

So they watch him, and set spies to work to feign sympathy with his doctrine, so they may betray him into saying something that will enable them to deliver him into the power and authority of the governor.

This means, obviously, the Roman governor. The idea of getting the Roman power to dispose of Jesus as a traitor to Cæsar has already come to them.

Then came the question about paying tribute to Cæsar. But these last passages do not immediately concern the Second Coming and what Jesus says about it.

Again, after the entry into Jerusalem.

Some spoke of the Temple and how it was adorned with goodly stones and gifts. Jesus said, "As for these things which ye behold, the days will come, in the which there shall not be left one stone upon another."

The disciples ask him when these things shall be, and what the sign will be that they are coming to pass.

He answers them as in *Matthew* and in *Mark* ("delivering you up to the synagogues . . ." from which it is clear that the synagogue had power to punish).

There are passages added and passages taken away, and some special and direct references to Jerusalem, as:

And when ye shall see Jerusalem compassed with armies, then know that the desolation thereof is nigh. [XXI, 20]

Then after the "woe unto them that are with child . . ."

And they shall fall by the edge of the sword, and shall be led away captive into all nations, and Jerusalem shall be trodden down of the Gentiles, until the times of the Gentiles be fulfilled.

Then the distress of nations, the sea and waves roaring . . . :

And then shall they see the Son of Man coming in a cloud with power and great glory. And when these things begin to come to pass, then look up, and lift up your heads, for your redemption draweth nigh. . . . So likewise ye, when ye see these things come to pass, know ye that the kingdom of God is nigh at hand.

Then the time is decided.

Verily I say unto you, This generation shall not pass away, till all be fulfilled.

Except that it does not picture the last Judgment with the division of the good from the evil, what Jesus says of his Second

Coming is practically the same in *Luke* as in *Matthew* and *Mark*. In *Matthew* and *Mark* he says it all after his entrance into Jerusalem and when sitting with his disciples on the Mount of Olives. In *Luke* he says some of it in answer to the Pharisees on his way from Galilee to Jerusalem, and some of it (concerning the destruction of Jerusalem) immediately before entering the city.

In *Luke's* record, as in *Matthew's* and *Mark's,* Jesus gives a detailed account of what is recorded by Josephus as having happened forty years later at the fall of Jerusalem.

Are we to believe that he foresaw all this? Or that somebody, writing after A.D. 70, merely reported it and put his report into the mouth of Jesus, making him say, "I have told you beforehand."

If the latter is true, that the passages are merely reports, then the first three Gospels are in this most important particular (of Christ's prediction of the fall of Jerusalem) sheer fiction.

If the former is true (that Jesus was prophesying, that he really foresaw the fall of Jerusalem and the destruction of the Temple forty years before these events took place) we are in a still more difficult position. We are compelled to say that inasmuch as Jesus also most clearly predicted that his Second Coming would follow immediately on the events foretold (the fall of Jerusalem and destruction of the Temple, the persecution of his people—all which did actually happen, including the martyrdom of Stephen, of his own brother James, of Peter, of Paul), and before the present generation should pass away, his foreknowledge failed him about the most important of all—the beginning of the new dispensation, the establishment of the kingdom of God, the Second Coming of the King, the Christ, the Messiah, the Son of Man in the clouds in power and glory, the redemption of God's people, the gathering of mankind from the uttermost parts of the earth and Heaven and (as in *Matthew*) the Last Judgment.

It is true that in *Luke* this picture of the Last Judgment does not appear, but all else has its parallel.

Here, then, we are confronted by the same tremendous difficulty.

If Jesus predicted that within the lifetime of persons living in his time (in A.D. 30) all this should come to pass, and if it has not come to pass, if indeed nearly 2,000 years have gone by and it has not come to pass—how then are we to accept him as one who knew everything, as a prophet taught of God, as the Son of God, as the Christ?

Has Christianity failed in this first test of its truth? Did it indicate a false sign of the end of the world? Were the words of Jesus about his Second Coming rendered untrustworthy by the fact that the greatest word of all (the fall of Jerusalem might have been foreseen in a material way by any man of clear vision forty years before it came to pass) broke down, proved false?

What is the answer to this most terrible charge?

VII.   *According to John*

In John's Gospel there is no such distinct statement of the signs and wonders which are to precede the end of the world as there are in the Synoptic Gospels. But there are incidental references in the same spirit, though I doubt if they can be said to convey the idea of the Second Coming, or the realization of the prophecy of Daniel of Christ coming in the clouds attended by angels. Nor do I at present see any such definite reference to the destruction of the Temple and the fall of Jerusalem as in the Synoptics. Indeed, these may be said to have no place in *John*.

After Jesus has cast the dealers out of the Temple he is asked by the Jews what sign he can show of his authority to do these things, and he answers, "Destroy this Temple, and in three days I will raise it up" (*John* II, 19).

The Jews answer that the Temple was forty-six years a-building, and could he rear it up in three days?

The evangelist says he was speaking of the temple of his body, and that after he was raised from the dead they remembered that he had said this to them. He also says they believed the Scriptures. But where do the Scriptures say that Jesus is to be raised from the dead after three days?

The Temple was Herod the Great's Temple. It was begun about 25 B.C. Therefore, in A.D. 29 it had been about eight years finished.

Then in *John* (V, 24) Jesus says the hour is coming when the dead shall hear the voice of the Son of God and they that hear shall live. . . . Again, that God had given him authority to execute judgment, because he is the Son of Man. Again, that the hour is coming in which all that are in the graves shall hear his voice, and shall come forth, they that have done good to the Resurrection of life, and they that have done evil to the Resurrection of damnation.

Later (*John* VII, 33) "Yet a little while am I with you, and then I go unto Him that sent me."

Still later (*John* VIII, 21) "I go my way, and ye shall seek me, and shall die in your sins; whither I go, ye cannot come."

Again (*John* VIII, 51) "If a man keep my saying, he shall never see death."

Constantly, in John's Gospel, Jesus refers to his being "lifted up." He will draw all men to him when he is lifted up, and so on.

The people answer him:

> We have heard out of the law that Christ abideth for ever; and how sayest thou The Son of Man must be lifted up? Who is this Son of Man?

Jesus evades the question.

Clearly, the Jewish Christ was to live for ever. The law said so. But Jesus said he was to die—by the act of death he was to draw all men to him. What did he mean?

Chapter XIV of *John* gives, perhaps, the clearest statement in the fourth Gospel of what Jesus thought of the future.

They were not to let their hearts be troubled. In his Father's house were many mansions. He was going to prepare a place for them. If he went away he would come again and receive them to himself, that where he was there they might be also. He would pray the Father that He would give them another Comforter, that he might be with them for ever.

> Yet a little while, and the world seeth me no more; but ye see me; because I live, ye shall live also. [XIV, 19] . . . . Peace I leave with you, my peace I give unto you; not as the world giveth, give I unto you. Let not your heart be troubled, neither let it be afraid.

They had heard him say:

> I go away, and come again unto you. If ye loved me, ye would rejoice, because I said, I go unto the Father, for my Father is greater than I. And now I have told you before it come to pass, that, when it is come to pass, ye might believe.

For the farewell admonition of Jesus at the Last Supper nothing is more beautiful than passages in *John* (XV, 12–27, XVI inclusive):

> This is my commandment, That ye love one another, as I have loved you.

Greater love hath no man than this, that a man lay down his life for his friends.

Ye are my friends, if ye do whatsoever I command you.

Henceforth I call you not servants; for the servant knoweth not what his lord doeth: but I have called you friends; for all things that I have heard of my Father I have made known unto you.

Ye have not chosen me, but I have chosen you, and ordained you, that ye should go and bring forth fruit, and that your fruit should remain: that whatsoever ye shall ask of the Father in my name, he may give it you.

These things I command you, that ye love one another.

If the world hate you, ye know that it hated me before it hated you.

If ye were of the world, the world would love his own: but because ye are not of the world, but I have chosen you out of the world, therefore the world hateth you.

Remember the word that I said unto you The servant is not greater than his lord. If they have persecuted me, they will also persecute you; if they have kept my saying, they will keep yours also.

But all these things will they do unto you for my name's sake, because they know not him that sent me.

If I had not come and spoken unto them, they had not had sin: but now they have no cloke for their sin.

He that hateth me hateth my Father also.

If I had not done among them the works which none other man did, they had not had sin: but now have they both seen and hated both me and my Father.

But this cometh to pass, that the word might be fulfilled that is written in their law, They hated me without a cause.

But when the Comforter is come, whom I will send unto you from the Father, even the Spirit of truth, which proceedeth from the Father, he shall testify of me:

And ye also shall bear witness, because ye have been with me from the beginning.

These things have I spoken unto you, that ye should not be offended.

They shall put you out of the synagogues: yea, the time cometh, that whosoever killeth you will think that he doeth God service.

And these things will they do unto you, because they have not known the Father, nor me.

But these things have I told you, that when the time shall come, ye may remember that I told you of them. And these things I said not unto you at the beginning, because I was with you.

But now I go my way to him that sent me; and none of you asketh me, Whither goest thou?

But because I have said these things unto you, sorrow hath filled your heart.

Nevertheless I tell you the truth; It is expedient for you that I go away: for if I go not away, the Comforter will not come unto you; but if I depart, I will send him unto you.

And when he is come, he will reprove the world of sin, and of righteousness, and of judgment:

Of sin, because they believe not on me;

Of righteousness, because I go to my Father, and ye see me no more;

Of judgment, because the prince of this world is judged.

I have yet many things to say unto you, but ye cannot bear them now.

Howbeit when he, the Spirit of truth, is come, he will guide you into all truth: for he shall not speak of himself; but whatsoever he shall hear, that shall he speak; and he will shew you things to come.

He shall glorify me: for he shall receive of mine, and shall shew it unto you.

All things that the Father hath are mine: therefore said I, that he shall take of mine, and shall shew it unto you.

A little while, and ye shall not see me: and again, a little while, and ye shall see me, because I go to the Father.

Verily, verily, I say unto you, That ye shall weep and lament, but the world shall rejoice: and ye shall be sorrowful, but your sorrow shall be turned into joy.

A woman when she is in travail hath sorrow, because her hour is come: but as soon as she is delivered of the child, she remembereth no more the anguish, for joy that a man is born into the world.

And ye now therefore have sorrow: but I will see you again, and your heart shall rejoice, and your joy no man taketh from you.

And in that day ye shall ask me nothing. Verily, verily, I say unto you, Whatsoever ye shall ask the Father in my name, he will give it you.

Hitherto have ye asked nothing in my name: ask, and ye shall receive, that your joy may be full.

These things have I spoken unto you in proverbs: but the time cometh, when I shall no more speak unto you in proverbs, but I shall shew you plainly of the Father.

At that day ye shall ask in my name: and I say not unto you, that I will pray the Father for you:

For the Father himself loveth you, because ye have loved me, and have believed that I came out from God.

I came forth from the Father, and am come into the world: again, I leave the world, and go to the Father.

His disciples said unto him, Lo, now speakest thou plainly, and speakest no proverb.

Now are we sure that thou knowest all things, and needest not that any man should ask thee: by this we believe that thou camest forth from God.

Jesus answered then, Do ye now believe?

Behold, the hour cometh, yea, is now come, that ye shall be scattered, every man to his own, and shall leave me alone: and yet I am not alone, because the Father is with me.

These things I have spoken unto you, that in me ye might have peace. In the world ye shall have tribulation: but be of good cheer; I have overcome the world.

Finally, Jesus's deeply moving prayer for his disciples:

That they all may be one; as thou, Father, art in me, and I in thee, that they also may be one in us: that the world may believe that thou hast sent me.

And the glory which thou gavest me I have given them; that they may be one, even as we are one:

I in them, and thou in me, that they may be made perfect in one; and that the world may know that thou hast sent me, and hast loved them, as thou hast loved me.

Father, I will that they also, whom thou hast given me, be with me where I am; that they may behold my glory, which thou hast given me: for thou lovedst me before the foundation of the world.

O righteous Father, the world hath not known thee: but I have known thee, and these have known that thou hast sent me.

And I have declared unto them thy name, and will declare it: that the love wherewith thou hast loved me may be in them, and I in them.

CHAPTER II

The Second Advent (Continued)

I. A General Summary

I DO NOT SEE that in *John,* as in the Synoptic Gospels, Jesus prophesies the destruction of the Temple or the fall of Jerusalem, or the end of the world, or the coming of Christ in the clouds of Heaven, as described by Daniel, or the Last Judgment.

He does indeed speak constantly of going away, and sometimes of coming back. He is going back to the Father to prepare a place for his people; he will leave behind him a Comforter; then he will return to take his people back to the Father.

He does not say that God will give him authority to judge mankind, and to give the resurrection of life everlasting to the good and the resurrection of damnation to the wicked.

But there is no indication of a millennium. Of any kingdom of God to be established on earth. No indication of the time at which he is to come back. Nothing about these things coming to pass within the lifetime of the present generation.

In short, I do not see that there is in John's Gospel any clear indication of a Second Advent on earth at all.

In the Synoptic Gospels, on the other hand, although they differ at many points, the theory as it comes from the mouth of Jesus is, I think, as follows:

1. That he must die.

2. That he will rise again.

3. That he will ascend into Heaven (though this is not very clear as a prophecy, or yet as a report of what took place).

4. That within the present generation (the Temple having been destroyed in the meantime, Jerusalem having fallen, many wars, famines, pestilences, and earthquakes having occurred in many parts of the world; the gospel having been preached to all nations; the disciples having suffered shocking persecution, scourgings, tortures, death and so on) he would come again.

5. That he would come in the clouds, as Daniel had foretold, surrounded by a mighty host of angels. That his disciples would then sit with him in judgment upon mankind. That he gave to the good resurrection, to the bad extermination.

Now if this was all put into his mouth by persons writing after the event of the fall of Jerusalem, that is to say forty years after his death, Jesus, as he is presented in the Synoptic Gospels, is made an impostor.

If, on the other hand, it was all spoken by Jesus in A.D. 30, although a great deal of what he predicted did indeed actually take place, yet the fact that the fundamental event (the Second Coming of Christ) did not take place, has not yet taken place, this deals such a blow to the claims of the founder of Christianity to be the Christ, the Son of God, that it is difficult to see how Christianity can survive it.

II.　After Reading Strauss

Strauss says:

> Immediately after the time of tribulation, the darkening of the sun and moon, and the falling of the skies and the shaking of all the powers of Heaven would usher in the appearance of the Messiah, who, to the dismay of the dwellers on earth, would come with great glory in the clouds of Heaven, and immediately send forth his angels to gather together his elect from all the corners of the earth. . . . All this, as it came to pass, would be as plainly discernible as the approach of summer by the budding of the fig-tree, but only God would know exactly when it would come to pass. Mankind, after their usual manner (as in the time of Noah and Lot), would let all this overtake them in thoughtless security, until the very presence of the Messiah compelled them to see it. . . . Hence, watchfulness was necessary—illustrated by the parables of the master of the house and the thief, and the wise and foolish virgins. Finally, there would come a solemn judgment which the Messiah would hold over all the nations, in which he would award blessedness and misery.

Now, as it will be seen, eighteen centuries since the destruction of Jerusalem, and an equally long period since the generation contemporary with Jesus (which was not to pass away until all these things were to be fulfilled) the events predicted (the *greatest* of them) have not taken place, and the advent of the Christ seems as far off as ever.

Was the prediction of Jesus erroneous?

Already in the first age of Christianity, when the return of Jesus Christ was delayed longer than had been expected, scoffers asked: Where is the promise of his coming? for since the fathers fell asleep, all things continue as they were from the beginning of the creation (2 *Peter* III, 4).

To this taunt of the scoffers Peter is reported in his Epistle to make the quibbling and foolish answer that "one day is with the Lord as a thousand years, and a thousand years as one day."

Peter's next answer is that the Messiah does not come within the time of his promise because (as he himself foresaw to be possible) when he came he might find no faith in the world. Therefore, not wishing that any should perish, but that all should come to repentance.

Therefore, says Peter (and he calls Paul as witness with him), beware lest ye also fall away from steadfastness.

All this is very like wriggling. Jesus made a definite prediction that the end of the dispensation in which he lived should come within the present generation. It did not come within that time. What are we to say? That his prophecy was erroneous? Or that he never made the prophecy? It is one of two things apparently.

Critics of what is called the Fragmentalist School say that no promise throughout the Scriptures is more definitely expressed, or has turned out more frequently false, than this, which yet forms one of the main pillars of Christianity.

Was it an error on the part of the disciples?

Strauss says:

Paul in the second epistle to the Thessalonians (as well as Peter in his second epistle), resorts to the absurd expedient of appealing to the divine mode of reckoning time. The prediction (if made) cannot be evaded. If made, and not fulfilled, it inflicts a fatal wound on Christianity.

Did Jesus really intend to place the two series of events (the fall of Jerusalem and the end of the world) in immediately chronological succession?

There are reasons to think he did not. That it was only the power that was to come within the present generation. The end of the world was to come only after the gospel had been preached to all the nations, which could not possibly be within forty years after the Christian Church had become so widespread that the elect had to be called from the uttermost parts of the earth, and their dead from the uttermost parts of Heaven.

I see no solution but this, and if it breaks down at any point, from the fact that the verse about the present generation not passing away applies sometimes to one series of events and sometimes to both, it is because the disciples were not clear about either, and mixed them up.

Some of the fathers of the Church (Irenæus and Hilary) lived in the primitive expectation of the return of Christ, and referred the entire prediction from its commencement in *Matthew* XXIV to its end in *Matthew* XXV to the still future return of Christ to judgment.

This interpretation nullifies itself, apparently by admitting that Jesus really began by talking about the destruction and making that the basis of his predictions.

To modern rationalism this Second Advent of Christ is in every form annihilated. Christ of the Second Advent is as much a lost cause to such so-called Christians as the coming of the Messiah is to so many so-called Jews.

It is abundantly clear that there are two distinct epochs referred to in Christ's prediction, for the period of the destruction of the Temple does not suit the later period of the destruction of the world.

Quite erroneously, appeal is made, in support of the merely figurative meaning of the prediction, to the prophetic pictures of the divine day of Judgment—*Isaiah* XIII, 9, XXIV, 18; *Jeremiah* IV, 23; *Ezekiel* XXXII, 7; *Joel* III, 3; *Acts* II, XVII.

In these prophetic passages eclipses of the sun and moon, earthquakes and the like are described as prodigies which will accompany the predicted catastrophe.

Finally, Peter expects that the outpouring of the spirit will be succeeded by the appearances in the heavens which will be signs of the *Great Day of the Lord.*

Obviously, all this transparent nonsense was deeply imbedded in the minds of the people of the time of Jesus. *These were to be the signs.*

It is objected that an enormous interval of time is supposed to elapse between the two parts of the prophecy, that which refers to the fall of the Temple, and that which refers to the end of the world. But lapses of time are constantly indicated in the text of the Gospels, sometimes long intervals, sometimes short, often of many months.

Further, remember that in the one case Jesus is made clearly to indicate the time within which the destruction of the Temple and the fall of Jerusalem were to take place (within the lifetime of the then present generation); in the other case he is made to say that the time is indefinite, and is only known by God—it is impossible to determine it.

The evangelist has joined together, not in the best order, distinct declarations of Jesus.

That Jesus did not deliver his predictions without intermission (as in *Matthew*) is shown by the fact that Luke gives them in two places, under different conditions, and with an interval of time between.

Then arises the question (on which the chronology of the Gospels also depends), did the primitive Church really expect the Second Advent of Jesus within the generation in which it lived?

The affirmative answer is thought to be given in various passages of the New Testament, that the primitive Church did expect the speedy return of Christ, and the end of the present period of the world.

"And they are written for our admonition, *upon whom the ends of the world are come*" (I *Corinthians* X, 11).

"We shall not all sleep, but we shall all be changed" (I *Corinthians* XV, 51).

"The Lord is at hand" (*Philippians* IV, 5).

"That we which are alive and remain unto the coming of the Lord" (I *Thessalonians* IV, 15).

"For the coming of the Lord draweth nigh" (*James* V, 8).

"For the end of all things is at hand" (I *Peter* IV, 7).

"Even now are there many anti-christs, whereby we know that it is the last time" (I *John* II, 18).

"Which must shortly come to pass" (*Revelations* I, 1).

"If therefore thou shalt not watch, I will come on thee as a thief, and thou shalt not know at what hour I will come upon thee." "Behold, I come quickly" (*Revelations* III, 3, 11).

"Behold, I come quickly." "For the time is at hand." "Behold, I come quickly." "Surely I come quickly" (*Revelations* XXII, 7, 10, 12, 20).

From the foregoing it becomes apparent that down to the date of the writing of the last word in the New Testament, whatever it may be, the belief in the near coming of the Christ was strong and was taken in the primitive Church.

And that when scoffers held it up to derision as time went on, and Christ did not come, Peter and Paul resorted to the expedient of counting time by the heavenly reckoning—a thousand years as one day.

Strauss thinks it is impossible not to see that Jesus places the two events (the destruction of Jerusalem and the end of the world) in immediate connexion, and he decides that the attempt to discover an immense interval between the destruction of Jerusalem and the end of all things has failed.

III.   What Did Actually Happen?

What did actually happen of that which Jesus foretold—if he foretold it?

It is difficult to be a Christian and to reconcile oneself to the thought that Jesus made a prediction which time has proved to be false, namely, that the end of the world and the Last Judgment should follow immediately after the destruction of the Temple and the fall of Jerusalem. Nearly 1900 years have passed since the destruction and fall, and the end of the world seems as far off as ever.

It is no less difficult for the non-Christian to believe that in the same discourse a mind so logical as that of Jesus could have made two statements which were utterly irreconcilable—that these things (meaning all that is predicted in the discourse) will occur within the present generation (that in which he was himself then living, say thirty to forty years), and that no man knew when it should occur, and only God knew.

Further, it is difficult to believe that the entire fulfilment of the prophecy of the end of the world, the Second Coming of Christ and the Last Judgment can have been expected by Jesus to come shortly, since it specifically required that things should first be done on earth which must obviously occupy a very long time, many ages, and which have clearly not taken place even yet, namely that before the end came the gospel must be preached to all nations, and that when the Christ came the second time, he would call his elect from the uttermost parts of the earth and the uttermost parts of Heaven. This means that many ages must have passed, that the followers of Christ must have extended to every part of the earth, that many of them must have died and gone to Heaven, and that only then Christ would come in his glory to call together the family of men and sit in his final judgment.

Matthew united nearly all the sermons of Jesus in one sermon—the Sermon on the Mount—contenting himself thereafter in general by saying "he preached" and so on, without recording what he said; so Matthew brought the whole prophecy of Jesus concerning the events that were to follow his death and precede his Second Coming into one prophecy, whereas Luke divides the prophecies of Jesus at least into two, spoken at different times and in different places.

In the case of the prophecy which concerns the destruction of the Temple and the fall of Jerusalem, it is important to observe that, looking back in history, nearly all that Jesus predicted came to pass. The story, as told by Josephus, is often strikingly like the prediction of Jesus. Wars, pestilence, earthquakes and famines did actually befall Palestine. The Temple *was* destroyed, and not one stone was left above another. Jerusalem was encompassed by the armies of Titus; a trench *was* actually dug about it, even after Titus had pronounced such a trench impossible of construction, owing to the attacks of the inhabitants of the city from the walls. People did attempt to fly away, and some perished in their flight and some got safely away.

And, after all this had occurred, and the Jewish people (according to their old manner) began to attribute the misfortunes which had been permitted by God to fall upon them, to their sins, and God's punishment of their sins, false Christs did arise and carry the people away with them into the deserts. Josephus himself, as governor of Galilee, had to deal with at least one such impostor and deceiver. Such men persuaded the people to follow them into the wilderness, promising signs and wonders which would be performed by the providence of God. And we read that in one case Felix brought them back and punished them.

All this, then, was fulfilled to the letter. Indeed, so completely did the historical facts correspond with the word of Jesus that critics have asked if it was not possible that the words were not his at all, but those of a reporter who was writing after the event the things which he had actually witnessed.

I do not take this view. I think Jesus, seeing deeper than other men, saw these things as events that must inevitably come to pass, having regard to the relation in which the Jewish people stood to their Roman masters, the corruption of the Jewish rulers and the aims of the Roman authority. The details of the sure downfall of the Temple, the central seat of Jewish hostility to Roman domination, and the fall of the Jewish Jerusalem, without which the total subjugation of Palestine could not be brought to pass, were such as would flash upon almost any imaginative mind.

Therefore, I do not see that the prophecy of the fall of Jerusalem need have come to Jesus by any but natural means, except so far as it was by the exercise of what we might call a supernatural intelligence.

The second part of the prophecy which concerns the end of the world stands on a totally different footing. It is possible that in predicting the final catastrophe Jesus was influenced by the prophecy of *Daniel* (IX, 27). It is true there is a belief that the passages in *Daniel* which refer to the desecration of the Temple concern Antiochus Epiphanes, and thus concern events long past, not events to come, and therefore that the interpretation put upon them by Jesus was a mistaken one.

The second half of the prophecy, too, which also (apparently, like the first half) affirmed famines, wars, pestilence, earthquakes, the falling of stars and general commotion of the heavens to be the harbingers of the coming of the Messianic kingdom, was familiar to prophecy, not in *Daniel* alone.

The day of the coming of Jehovah, after great tribulation, had been described in *Isaiah* XIII, 9; *Joel* I, 15; *Zephaniah* I, 14; *Haggai* II, 6; *Zechariah* XIV, 1; *Malachi* III, 1.

The idea, therefore, of such tribulations as Jesus described, preceding the Messianic kingdom of the saints (*Daniel* VII–XII), also found expression in later Jewish writings.

This has led many writers to think that Jesus drew his material for the signs of the end of the world from a circle of ideas which had long been current among the Jews. In Jewish writings we find the idea that the birth of the Messiah would coincide with the destruction of the sanctuary, but Strauss thinks the idea came later than A.D. 70 in Jewish writings, and was intended to console the dispersed Jews at the lowest depths of their misery.

It may be that Jesus attributed the prophecies of Daniel to refer to events still to happen. Inasmuch as the prophecy of the coming of the Christ in the clouds had *not* followed the defeat of Antiochus, he and his people may have concluded that it referred to an event still to come.

There is the important fact that the disciples understood the two parts of the prophecy to be one—that after the death they did actually expect that he would return shortly. The epistles contain repeated reference to his coming—his coming soon, to his coming by night, to their belief that they were living in the last days, that Jesus who had died in humiliation was shortly to return in glory. And as time passed, and one by one their own company grew smaller by death, and they found themselves with few remaining of those who had stood with him when Jesus prophesied, and as they were confronted by the scoffers, who told them in effect that their prophet had prophesied falsely, and that he was therefore an impostor, they had to satisfy their faith in him by talking about the heavenly reckoning of a thousand years as one day.

Then there is the further important fact that while the three first Gospels say much of the Second Advent, John's Gospel says little. It is true that the idea of the Second Coming of Christ can be adduced from *John;* but it takes no such distinct and definite place in the fourth Gospel as in the Synoptics. And yet, according to *Mark* (XIII, 3), John was present when Jesus made his prophecy. He, alone, of all the evangelists, was present. But he says nothing of that startling scene in which Jesus foretold the end of the world, the awakening of the dead, the appearance in the clouds, and the Last Judgment!

How are we to account for his silence? Is it (as I think) the fact that the writer of the fourth Gospel was certainly not the evangelist, not the Son of Zebedee, the Galilean fisherman, who was present, but somebody else, who was certainly not present when the prediction was made?

But how did it come to pass that knowing, as he must have done, that Matthew, Mark and Luke had told this story he ignored it? Was it that he did not believe it? Was it that he was writing at a much later period than the writers of the three earlier Gospels, and was under the influence of the Gnostics, who had arisen in the interval, and whose view of the description given in the prophecy about the end of the world would not have admitted of a literal interpretation? Did the writer of John's Gospel so far share the

Gnostic view that he tried to "resolve the external and the future into the internal and present."

On the other hand, it is clear that the author of the fourth Gospel admits that Jesus was to come into the world to judge, but it is difficult to think this referred to his first presence in the world.

"It is also true," says Strauss, "that a certain interpretation of the Jesus of John's Gospel supposes him to intimate that his return was not far distant."

IV. Conclusions

My own conclusions briefly are:

1. That Jesus foresaw the destruction of the Temple and the downfall of Jerusalem by the natural operation of his clear intellect.

2. That he believed and said it would come soon—within the present generation. That what he said was afterwards fulfilled to the letter.

3. That by supernatural insight he foresaw the end of the world. That this was to come after his gospel had been preached all over the world, and the whole of mankind had warning.

4. That he accepted the predictions of the prophets that the end of the world and the coming of the Messiah would take place after that physical upheaval, that deep moral degradation.

5. That he used the language of Daniel to describe what would follow—the Second Coming of the Christ in glory to judge the righteous and the evil.

6. That he would be the Christ who would preside over the great assize.

7. That the time of it may be any time, but the conditions described by Jesus do not even yet exist.

8. Therefore, Jesus cannot be charged with being a false prophet because the end of the world has not yet come.

CHAPTER III

The Legend of Jesus

I. The Task of the Apostles

THE BELIEF in the supernatural birth of Jesus by the conception of the Holy Ghost and the medium of a virgin (apparently forced upon the early Christians, after the tour of the apostles, by the objections of their critics) led to stories of supernatural powers displayed by him in his childhood and boyhood.

Again, the apostles, when they went out to convert the world, had to meet the difficulty of proving the divinity of Jesus by his mighty works. The pagan world expected "works" of their divinities. Even the Jewish world (scattered abroad as well as remaining at home) had to be convinced that Jesus (assuming that they accepted the story of the eye-witnesses, out of belief in their truthfulness, that he rose from the dead) had performed the works that were foretold of the Messiah. It was speedily found that it was not enough to show that he had healed the sick of countless diseases, that he was such a physician of the body as the world had never before seen.

It was not even enough to prove to the pagan world that he had cast devils out of the people who were supposed to be "possessed" of them. They had their sorcerers who claimed and were believed to do that. And the Jews were convinced that by the power of the chief of devils, Beelzebub, other devils could be cast out. It was necessary to go further for Jesus. So, one by one, not necessarily by any conscious intention to deceive, but by the pressure of necessity and the mysterious power of the human mind for self-deception, it came to pass that the miracles of Jesus began to transcend all human law whatever, to defy it and set it at naught.

Thus he was reported, for no good purpose that the modern mind can recognize, to change water into wine, to feed 5,000 persons with a few loaves and fishes, and to walk by night on the sea.

Further, it was not enough that he should do what Elijah had done, call back to life the newly dead whose spirits, by long tradition, still floated about them after the powers of life were gone. He must be able to raise from the dead one who had been four days dead, whose body had gone to corruption, and whose soul (according to ancient Jewish belief) had descended to that hell, or Hades, where all souls waited, from Adam downwards, for the day of judgment.

It was not at first observed that this made foolishness of the very foundation of their faith, that Jesus was the Messiah foretold by the prophets *because* he was the first who had triumphed over death in the Resurrection.

The apostles plainly knew nothing of this claim. The raising of Lazarus was unknown to them in the circumstantial form in which it has come down to us. They could not have believed the story of what happened in Bethany, according to the Gospel of John, or they could never have said what they did say about the Resurrection of Jesus. The one thing eliminates the other. If they knew anything of the raising of Lazarus it must have been another story, different in essential particulars.

Examined closely, all these accretions to the miracles of Jesus betray their later origin by careful examination of the facts. Thus, the miracle of the feeding of the five thousand breaks down by close observation of its own evidence as to time and place. The same applies to the miracle of the walking on the sea, the turning of water into wine, and the destruction of the Gadarene swine. Nobody who knows the country in which these miracles are said to have taken place can fail to see that they never occurred, could never have occurred, in the way described. They carry their condemnation within themselves, and are therefore totally unlike the authentic miracles of Jesus which, far more marvellous, are also far more believable.

Most of these stories are dead and gone with the futile apocryphal writings which contained them. Of such stories are those of the sermons he preached while in his cradle—of the clay birds to which he gave life while at play with his playmates; of the curses that fell upon children who struck him; of the supernatural power he had of helping his father at his work as a carpenter.

But one at least found its way into the Gospels—the story of how at twelve years of age he disputed with the doctors in the

Temple. This story is equally dishonouring to Jesus, as a son who had forgotten the natural anxiety of his parents, and to the parents, who had been neglectful of the child who was to be "set for the fall and rising again of many in Israel." But its origin and intention are obvious—to answer the objections of those scoffers who were asking how it had come to pass that for thirty years of his life Jesus had been apparently unaware that he was the Messiah.

Equally, the objection of sceptics, like Celsus, that, if Mary the mother of Jesus had been told by the Angel Gabriel that she would conceive a child who should be called the son of the Highest, and that the Lord God would give him the name of his father, David, and that of his Kingdom there should be no end, it was surprising that she never afterwards gave a hint of any knowledge of his great power and destiny, but, on the contrary, behaved throughout life as if she had never heard anything of the kind, and, on one occasion, as if she thought he was beside himself—this objection had to be answered by some exhibition of such knowledge on her part.

In this respect also the apocryphal writings are full of idle stories, but one story has been introduced into the Gospels—the story of the marriage feast in Cana of Galilee—which was obviously intended to show her foreknowledge of her son's miraculous powers.

Examination of this story, also, whether in the light of the topography of the country, the particulars of time given in the Gospels, or of the great juncture in the life of Jesus at which this incident is said to have occurred, also shows plainly that it was no part of the original narrative, or that the story of the miracle was written long after the death of the three or four disciples who could have been eye-witnesses of the not very uplifting event.

It is not only an impossible story as to time and place; it is, like each of the other apocryphal miracles that have found their way into the Gospels, *useless for the purpose it was intended to serve,* and generally dishonouring to Jesus.

Thus we see how the legend of Jesus grew, both during the lifetime of the apostles and, more particularly, after their death.

Other additions to the legend came later, when the Church of Jesus began to establish itself, and when to do so it had to make its terms, both with Judaism, in its birthplace (Palestine) and with paganism abroad.

II. The Miracles

I am thoroughly convinced that the so-called miracles referred to in this section were the invention of a later age than that of the apostles, and came into being in other countries than Palestine. Of these events the original eye-witnesses of the life of Jesus on earth can have known nothing. They were nearly all Galileans, and therefore, it is impossible that they could have made the multitude of mistakes which appear in the records of these events. They bear, in all cases, the mark of the foreign hand. Palestinians could not have written these parts of the Gospels. The outside writers (Greeks probably), or the owners of the original Gospels who interpolated these events, had probably no thought of falsifying them. But no one who looks closely into the Master's mysteries, and knows the ground on which they are said to have occurred, can doubt that the authors had no compunction about making these changes and additions. They believed they were doing God's service in silencing objectors like Celsus and his predecessors.

The test to which I would bring every miracle of Jesus would be, To what end was it permitted? If the end seems to be fruitless or inadequate or injurious, I reject it, but not until I find that on grounds of physical as well as spiritual law it is impossible of acceptance.

It is then a part of the legend of Jesus.

Immediately after the disciples became convinced (as they did most positively) that their Master had risen from the dead, legends began to gather about him.

It is quite unnecessary to say that any of them, least of all those who had lived with him, consciously invented anything. They were comforted with one great fact—that he who was dead was alive again, and, as they believed, had ascended into Heaven.

This was a fact so absolutely contrary to all human experience that they were compelled to account for it. They accounted for it by an appeal to the Scriptures. In the Scriptures they believed they found the great fact foretold. The Messiah was to break the power of death, to rise from the grave and ascend into Heaven. Jesus, their Master, had done that, therefore he was the Christ.

III.   Recording the Life of Jesus

Such was the foundation of their faith. Then they set themselves to reconcile it with their recollection of what he had said and done in life. In doing so, they were absolutely sincere and honest. They had not the smallest desire to deceive themselves or others. But they were subject to precisely the same laws as those which have always operated on the human soul at times of great emotion.

One man remembered something, or believed he remembered it, communicated his recollection to others, and instantly they all remembered. This is the everlasting fact of human experience. And when the time came to write down what they remembered of the life and sayings of Jesus while he was with them on earth, they wrote these recollections. They had no compunction in doing so. It was according to the literary morality of their age to put words into the mouth of a dead man which perhaps he had not exactly spoken, and to make him do what he had not exactly done, if only they were "according" to his spirit, his character and the undoubted facts of his life.

It was not a characteristic of the Jewish mind only to find this a proper and even estimable thing to do. The best Roman mind did the same thing at the same time, and for long years afterwards. Thus, while Josephus, at the end of the first century, again and again put words into the mouths of historical Jewish characters for which he had no possible historical authority, Tacitus again and again put long speeches into the mouths of men (long dead) of which he could not have had the smallest report. They were true to the spirit of the dead person, and that was enough. To the literary morality of those ages all over the world this was quite justifiable.

In the case of the Gospels, their authors (as a learned divine says) felt no compunction in correcting or enlarging them so as to support their own theories or to reply to their critics. Towards the end of the second century St. Dionysius, the bishop of Corinth, complained that his letters had been altered, and that people did not hesitate to falsify the "words of the Lord." Celsus, the pagan writer of the second century, taunts the Christians with altering the texts of their Gospels, two, three and four times, to meet the objections made against them. In this light we must look upon the growth of the legend of Jesus.

IV. Accounting for the Resurrection

During the lifetime of the apostles, the legend went on by slow degrees. After they were dead it increased by leaps and bounds. In going out to preach, the apostles had, from the very first day, the Day of Pentecost, to stand up against one great difficulty. They had to account for the Resurrection of Jesus, which was the foundation of their faith in the eyes of the multitudes (outside their own numbers), who had had no experience of it, for Jesus had not appeared after his Resurrection to any except his friends. He had risen on the third day, and they had to account to the outside world (as well as to themselves) for that first fact.

They did so by remembering, what they frankly admit they had totally forgotten, that he had told them over and over again that he would do so. Therefore, without a thought of self-deception, they tacked on to their obviously authentic recollection of his prediction that he would be put to death the statement that he would rise from the dead on the third day.

Seven times they made him say so, and when we look at the passages (as they were written down afterwards) we see that six times they have no possible relation to what goes before or comes after them, and that on the seventh occasion the words are mentioned only to be immediately dismissed from further consideration.

The next difficulty of the apostles was to meet the objection of the critics of their faith in the Resurrection, who mocked as the people of Athens mocked St. Paul when he asked them to believe in a faith which required them, as its first condition, to believe in something they had never seen and was utterly outside human experience.

Therefore, somebody remembered that Jesus himself had said that, while it was good to believe what one had seen, it was blessed to believe what one had not seen, and took by faith.

In this way, most obviously, comes the story of the second appearance of Jesus to the disciples to convince Thomas, who at first could not believe because his physical senses were not satisfied.

The reality of the Resurrection of Jesus, on which the apostles had, down to the Day of Pentecost, built their faith, suddenly encountered severe objections among many.

It was realized that while the evidence of the prophets was convincing that a Messiah was to come, and that he was to suffer such and such things, it was difficult to convince people who had not seen unless they gave overwhelming proof that the whole story was not a delusion, a dream, a thing born of the excited imagination of its first authors.

To the disciples it was at first sufficient that Mary Magdalene said that on the site of the sepulchre Jesus had appeared to her, and spoken to her; that to two of the apostles, walking out into the country, with minds oppressed by the terrible things that had happened, breaking down all the hopes they had so long cherished and for which they had left all to follow the beloved Master, the Master himself had appeared, and spoken to them; that the same night, when the disciples were gathered together within closed doors in their hiding-place in Jerusalem, in sorrow and tears for their beloved Master who was lost to them, suddenly he had appeared to them and comforted them, saying, "Peace be with you"; and finally, that when about forty days later they had gone up, perhaps at night, to the top of the Mount of Olives, the place most intimately associated with him by their dearest memories, to pray and sing, out of sight and hearing of their enemies, suddenly, in their ecstasy and their faith that they were to rejoin him in the hereafter, they saw him in their midst, and he ascended to Heaven before their eyes, and they told each other that as they had seen him go up they would see him return to establish a greater kingdom than they had dreamt of during his life, the kingdom of God, itself.

But they soon realized that while all this was convincing enough for themselves, they could only impress the fact upon those who were willing to accept their word that they had actually seen and heard and experienced all this. For those who would not take their word, they had nothing to offer that commanded belief. That the dead should rise was beyond their power of belief. That Jesus of Nazareth, whom they had seen walking the streets of Jerusalem, had broken the everlasting law, and overcome the common lot of humanity—death—was not to be accepted on the mere word of this group of uninstructed fishermen out of Galilee.

Even later, when a man of learning, St. Paul, said the same

thing, they could not believe it on his word only, so that he said, when he came to trial before the Jewish king, Agrippa, "Why should it be thought a thing incredible with you, that God should raise the dead?" And then he was compelled to drive home the seemingly incredible story by telling an almost equally incredible story from his own life, which drew from Agrippa the remark, "Almost thou persuadest me to be a Christian."

Thus it came to pass that, having nothing to offer except the evidence of their own senses that Jesus was risen and therefore was the Christ, they had to meet the objection that the being who had appeared to them in their time of sorrow and great excitement had only been a phantom, a ghost, a thing born of their own imagination, by giving a tangible and corporeal reality to the body of the risen Christ.

Out of this hard necessity came the other stories of the Resurrection and the additions to the first story, namely, that when Jesus appeared to Mary he had spoken to her, and she had been at the point of touching his feet; that when he appeared to the disciples going into the country, they had prevailed upon him to eat with them, and they had recognized him by his way of breaking bread, and that when, perhaps two hours later, he had appeared to them all in the room, he had asked them if they had anything to give him to eat, and he had eaten before their eyes, and finally that he said he was not a ghost, and in proof of it had asked them to touch the wounds in his hands and side which he had received on the Cross.

Later, this materializing of the risen Jesus went further, as when it became necessary (probably long afterwards and for other reasons) to establish the direct headship of Peter they remembered that Jesus had always said (what they had neither understood when he uttered the words nor acted upon them immediately after his death) that he would meet them in Galilee, and that he prepared a meal for them on the shore of the lake and (apparently) ate with them. And, finally, he again defied all the laws of ordinary human existence by eating immediately he ascended into Heaven.

Thus, the apostles, in the early years, met the objections of unbelievers by making the risen Christ a being who ate and drank and was in all respects the same after his Resurrection as he had been before his death.

Again, as the apostles went out into the world to carry the gospel, according to his command, they had to meet criticisms of another kind. In the Gentile world, in particular, they had to meet the difficulties of his human origin. Pagan faiths had never taken their religion from mere human beings. In Persia, Mithras, whose cult was then in the ascendant, was a semi-supernatural being, born out of a rock and apparently fully grown. The deities of Greece and Rome (at that time) came by a kind of cross between human mothers and divine fathers. In this way only could humanity accept the idea of a Saviour who was to redeem the world.

So, at what period we do not exactly know, the divinity of Jesus and his sinlessness (a necessary condition of his claim to be the Messiah, according to the latest prophecies) were established by the story of a supernatural birth.

When the two nativity stories in *Matthew* and *Luke* were first conceived we do not know. We do not even know when they were written down. It is abundantly clear that they came much later than the Gospels in which they appear, and that they were interpolated into them. They form no essential part of them. They can be removed, and nothing that remains wants explanation. Being interpolated, a great deal needs explanation. They give no light to what follows them. They are out of harmony with nearly everything that comes afterwards. They have no relation to the Epistles which the apostles wrote to the Churches they established abroad.

Except for occasional and very difficult passages, they do not appear to have been at any time within the first generation a part of the rock on which the apostles built their Church.

They do not agree with each other except in two isolated facts— the fact that Jesus was supernaturally conceived of a virgin mother, and that he was born in the city of David. In essentials they totally eliminate each other. They transform the Founder of the Faith from Jesus of Nazareth to one who (in the case of Matthew's story at least) could only be properly and legally described as Jesus of Bethlehem, a Judæan, not a Galilean.

They connect him (one of them by necessary conditions, the other by a mere phrase) with the time of Herod the Great, in which, according to Luke's chronology, he cannot possibly have been born.

Above all, they are manifestly useless for any purposes of the life and mission of Jesus while he lived, or at the dark hour of his death. They did not contribute in the very least to his life's work as the Messiah.

Nevertheless, they were apparently necessary to meet the enormous difficulties of the disciples (not certainly the first apostles, who seem never to have known anything about them) of making converts among pagan peoples. And they have contributed since in holding the faith of pious people.

V. The Apostles in Jerusalem

After the Ascension the disciples, still living in their room in Jerusalem, come out of their hiding without fear, the place where they assemble being filled with a sound from Heaven as of a mighty rushing wind. A great new wave of courage comes over them. They resolve to go out fearlessly and confront the rulers who had crucified Jesus with the statement that he had been the Messiah foretold in the Scriptures—the Christ who was to redeem Israel from the bondage of her tyrannical masters, and re-establish the throne of David—a Messiah who was to redeem them from the bondage of sin and make them at one with God through His Son, Jesus Christ.

They go boldly into the Temple, and preach their new gospel. Multitudes of Jews from foreign countries come to see and hear them. Many of the astonished listeners are pricked to their hearts, and say, "Men and brethren, what shall we do?" And Peter answers, "Repent, and be baptized every one of you in the name of Jesus Christ for the remission of sins, and ye shall receive the gift of the Holy Ghost."

Then happens the miracle performed by Peter on the lame man, lying at the gate of the Temple.

"Silver and gold have I none," says Peter, "but such as I have give I thee. In the name of Jesus Christ of Nazareth rise up and walk."

The astonishment of the people—wonder and amazement, mingled with fear of the consequences.

Then the priests and the captain of the Temple, coming upon the scene, arrest Peter and John, and bring them next day before Annas and Caiaphas and two others, John and Alexander, new names among those of the ruling authorities.

The authorities ask by what name and power they are doing

these things, meaning by implication, "Are you doing miracles such as this by the power of the Devil?"—the old Jewish belief.

Peter replies that they were doing them by the name of Jesus of Nazareth, whom they (the Jews) had crucified, but whom God had raised from the dead.

The priests take alarm from the fact that such teaching will have the effect of bringing the blood of Jesus upon them in the eyes of the people. The priests first threaten the apostles, and then let them go, finding no means of punishing them.

The apostles go, but, "filled with the Holy Ghost," they continue to preach their gospel with boldness. They then set up a society founded on the common possession of all things. Probably this was the system under which they had lived in community with Jesus during his life on earth. The converts sell their lands and other possessions, and lay the money at the apostles' feet. But this system, which had been workable in the little company of Jesus and his twelve disciples (poor men all of them), became difficult when it was applied to society in general—a large body of converts, some poor, some rich.

Apparently, in a little while the system suffers a check from the strain put by it on human impulses. There are certain tragic happenings—a man and his wife falling dead on being convicted of being false to their pledge.

Out of this and similar happenings come other incidents. The high priests rise up against them again. The captain of the Temple arrests the apostles and brings them before the Sanhedrin. They are tried for sowing sedition against the rule of the authorities. A member of the Sanhedrin (never heard of before), Gamaliel, a doctor of the law, counsels toleration. He regards the Christians as a company of fanatics whom it is best and wisest to leave alone. His advice prevails; the apostles are scourged and sent away with the command that they shall not again speak in the name of Jesus.

But they continue on their way, glorying in their stripes, rejoicing that God had "counted them worthy to suffer shame" for the sake of their Master.

Still they taught in the Temple, and in private houses, the gospel of Jesus—that he was the Christ, and that he had died for the remission of men's sins.

Not yet were the apostles forbidden the Temple, and clearly they were free of the synagogues.

VI. The Stoning of Stephen

Then, very early, a new figure arose among the apostles—Stephen, "full of faith and power," who did great wonders and miracles. A certain jealousy of him led to his betrayal by fellow Jews of the synagogue. He was condemned to the elders, the scribes and the council as a man who had been heard to speak blasphemous words against Moses and against God, the law and the Temple, saying among other things that this Jesus of Nazareth would destroy the Temple and change the customs of Moses.

On this charge (hardly different from that which was brought against Jesus himself) Stephen was brought before the council on his trial. We do not know that permission to hold a Sanhedrin was asked of the Roman procurator, although the accusation was again such as, according to Jewish law, was worthy of death.

Stephen made a great defence, recounting the history of his people from the time of Abraham's coming from Mesopotamia to live in Charran down to the time of Moses, who had said that the Lord would raise up a prophet like unto him, and so on, to the time of David and Solomon and the prophets who had pointed to the coming of the Just One (Jesus) of whom they (the judges before him) had been the betrayers and murderers.

On this the council appears to have outraged the Jewish law in Stephen's case even more violently than in the case of Jesus, and to have ignored the Roman prerogative over the death penalty. They cried out on Stephen and ran upon him, cast him out of the city and stoned him to death.

Stephen was firm to the last. While his judges were gnashing their teeth on him, he looked up steadfastly to Heaven and "saw Jesus standing on the right hand of God." As he was being stoned he cried, "Lord Jesus, receive my spirit." And as he knelt down, he cried, "Lord, lay not this sin to their charge," and so died.

The exact date of this incident is unknown. We do not hear that the Sanhedrin were called to account for their outrage on Roman law. But the high priest, Caiaphas, is never again mentioned in *Acts*. Here he drops out of Bible history, and what becomes of him is only known from outside sources. Josephus says little about him. But it is certain that he ceased to be high priest in A.D. 36 which was probably the year of Stephen's death. Pilate, himself, was recalled to Rome in A.D. 36, and arrived in A.D. 37, immediately after the death of Tiberius.

But that a great crisis in the life of the Christian Church at Jerusalem came immediately after the death of Stephen is fully established.

In *Acts* VIII, 1, we read that "at that time there was a great persecution against the Church which was at Jerusalem; and they were all scattered abroad throughout the regions of Judæa and Samaria." It is, however, significant that *Acts* adds, "except the apostles."

CHAPTER IV

St. Paul and St. Peter

I. Saul of Tarsus

OUT OF THE PERSECUTION of the disciples arises a new and great figure. A young man is described as standing by while Stephen is being stoned.

. . . the witnesses laid down their clothes at a young man's feet, whose name was Saul.

Whether this means that the "witnesses" were the men who stoned Stephen to death, and that they had thrown off their clothes to stone him, is to me not altogether certain. That is its obvious meaning, although by some ceremonial there may have had to be legal witnesses to the stoning, and these took off their outer clothes and the high priest rent his garments.

Stoning was the punishment according to *Leviticus* (XXIV, 16) for any man who blasphemed the name of the Lord. This was Stephen's offence according to the Sanhedrin.

In *Deuteronomy* (XIII) the following injunction is given. It says, in effect: "The man who attempts to turn you away from the Lord your God, although he be your brother or your son or your daughter or your wife you shall stone him, and not look upon him with the eye of pity. Your hand shall be the first to put him to death; then the hand of the people."

The function of the witnesses is indicated in *Deuteronomy* XVII, 6, 7. By two witnesses shall a man be found worthy of death. . . . These two witnesses shall be the first to stone the man. Afterwards, the people shall stone him.

So it is clear that the witnesses who laid their clothes at the feet of Saul were the two (or more) suborned witnesses who had sworn falsely that they had heard Stephen say that "this Jesus of Nazareth should destroy the Temple and change the customs of Moses."

Down to this moment what do we see?

1. That the apostles derived their belief in the divinity of Jesus from the Scriptures, wherein, they believed, his death and Resurrection had been foretold.

2. That Jesus, the Son of God, had given his life for the remission of man's sins.

3. That only by accepting his name could men avail themselves of that salvation.

4. That this salvation by Jesus was first of all for the children of Abraham—for the Jews.

They preached this doctrine openly in the Temple, in the synagogue; were imprisoned and perished for doing so, but rejoiced in their sufferings, because they were for Christ.

That finally one of their number, Stephen, was stoned to death, in defiance of Roman law, by order of the Jewish council.

That there then came a dispersion of the early Church, and that many fled from Jerusalem into other parts of Judæa (assuming these two were legally distinct) and into Samaria.

Nothing yet about the doctrines of the faith which concerned the sacrament of the Lord's Supper. The sacrament of baptism is "for the remission of sins," but whether as a witness or as a purifying ordinance is not quite certain.

Nothing yet about the Holy Ghost as a third party in the Godhead.

The utmost that can be properly read into the story of the early days after the death of Jesus is that Jesus was the Son of God, and therefore the Godhead if it yet consisted of two persons, consisted of two persons only.

Saul's appearance in the early incidents is only faintly indicated in *Acts*. Clearly he took a large part before the martyrdom of Stephen.

Who was Saul? After his conversion we know him better by the name of Paul.

He was a Jew born in Tarsus, a city of Syria. He was a Pharisee, and had been brought up in the strictest sect of the Pharisees. He was also a Roman citizen by birth—he was "free born." This means that his father had been a Roman citizen before him.

There were at least two ways in which a Jew might become a Roman citizen. One was by purchase, apparently at a very high price.

It is clear that this could not have been the way in which Saul's father became a Roman citizen. At least, we have no reason to think Saul had inherited wealth. All through his life as an apostle he worked with his hands for his living. Towards the end he lived on the alms of his converts.

The other way by which a Jew could become a Roman citizen was by distinct and conspicuous services to the Roman empire. This is probably what Saul's father had done in Cilicia before Saul was born.

But the family of Saul must have remained Jewish by faith. It was not the way of Rome to interfere with the religion of the people whose countries they conquered, who could believe what they liked, as long as their religion did not trespass upon the rights of the state. The Jews never entirely grasped this fact. They associated government with God. Hence they continually asked Rome to punish the offenders against their religion, and Roman rulers always refused to do so.

Saul, in his early youth or manhood, left Tarsus for Jerusalem. This was in order to join the rabbinical school of Gamaliel.

Gamaliel was a grandson of the great rabbi Hillel, and like him, although a Pharisee, a Jewish liberal in theology. But his liberalism went no farther than a free interpretation of the customs of the Jewish fathers—the right observance of the Sabbath, the keeping of feasts and the washing of hands. Beyond this, Gamaliel (like his grandfather) was a rigid Jew, who would be outraged by any failure of faith in fundamentals.

It is not certain that Saul was in Jerusalem during the trial and death of Jesus. It is fairly sure that he never saw Jesus in the flesh. It is improbable that his master, Gamaliel, was a member of the Sanhedrin when it met to consider what should be done about this Galilean who claimed to be the Son of God, and therefore was worthy of death, though they could not inflict it. If he had been a member he would probably have counselled the same toleration as he did when Peter and the apostles were brought before the council. If so, we should probably have heard it. His counsel might have prevailed. On the other hand, he might have been borne down by the majority, and especially by the high priests who were Sadducees, and thought their positions, as heads of the Jewish people, were in peril.

But if Saul saw nothing of Jesus himself he must have begun to deal with the apostles not long after Jesus's death.

The story of the arrest, trial and death of Stephen shows that Saul was already at work in an effort to stamp out the new religion.

There is no reason to think he was less than sincere. In later life he was always tolerant to the Jews who were persecuting and imprisoning him, as he had persecuted and imprisoned earlier Christians. He granted them full credit for being sincere and zealous for the purity of their faith. He was a great Jew at this time.

Saul's position in those days of his youth is quite clear. He sincerely thought that these men, the Christians (as they were afterwards called), were destroying the purity of the Jewish religion. They were preaching a new God—a God of two members. This was to him as great an outrage on Jewish belief as if they had preached pure paganism. And it was more dangerous, because it claimed to be founded on the Jewish Scriptures, and to have its foundations in Hebrew prophecy. Therefore, it was blasphemy to the religion that had been brought down from Sinai by Moses.

And what had Moses ordered should be done to the dreamers of dreams who tried to draw people off from the worship of God? They were to be condemned by the highest religious tribunal and then stoned to death.

The procedure was very severe and very solemn, if also very brutal. It is described in the foregoing pages.

But somebody had to set all this procedure in motion. Saul, the young man of the school of Gamaliel, undertook this task. He went out against Peter and his converts to exterminate them. Clearly, he acted the part of informer. He went from house to house in Jerusalem, rounding up the people who were preaching this gospel—that a man named Jesus, who had been justly put to death for claiming to be the Son of God, had risen from the dead, and therefore was greater than David and Moses and Abraham whose bodies were still lying where they were buried, and whose souls were still resting and waiting in Hades for the final Judgment Day.

I see Saul as the informer upon Stephen, who (like Peter and the rest) was making no secret of his belief that Jesus had risen from the dead and was now at God's right hand in Heaven. To Saul this was heresy worthy of death. He was quite sure of the actual facts about Jesus. It might be true (probably was) that the tomb in which Jesus had been buried by one of his own (secret) followers had been found open and empty, and the body gone on the third morning after its burial, but this was merely because his disciples had come in the night and stolen it away, and then given out their lying story.

It seems very probable that Saul was the informer in the case of Stephen, and that it was he who secured the lying witnesses who brought about his condemnation. It does not follow that Saul knew this to be lying. It is probable that he was the means of paying them, but again it does not follow that he knew he was paying to swear Stephen's life away.

When the execution came he took the part of the informer formally to look on, and at his feet the witnesses laid down their clothes when they were about to cast the first stones at the prisoner.

When, exactly, this happened, we do not know. It was probably not a great while after the Crucifixion—probably in A.D. 36. It was an outrage on Roman law. The Jewish council had taken the law into their own hands, and put Stephen to death against the strict law of their Roman governors. They do not seem to have been called to account for it. There is no certainty that they were punished. Caiaphas remained for a time high priest. What had happened? We do not know for certain. Did the whole thing occur in the absence of Pontius Pilate? Was it after Pilate's own recall, and before another procurator had taken his place? We shall see later, by a comparison of dates.

II.   The Conversion of Saul

After the death of Stephen, Saul renewed his activities. We read (*Acts* VIII, 3) that he made havoc of the Church, entering into every house, and haling men and women, committed them to prison.

As a consequence, the Christians of Jerusalem fled from the city, and took refuge in other parts of Judæa and in Samaria—all except the apostles, who apparently did not fly away.

In doing this, Saul was entirely sincere. According to his light he was doing God's service. It was exactly what Jesus had foreseen would happen. Saul was a true Jew, honestly believing that he was acting rightly.

Then came a crisis in Saul's career. Breathing out threatenings and slaughter against the disciples of the dead prophet Jesus, the dreamer of dreams, he asked the high priest to give him letters, empowering him to go up to Damascus (to which some of the Christians had escaped) to arrest the heretics he found there and bring them bound to Jerusalem.

On the way to Damascus a great thing happened to him, perhaps the second greatest event in Christian history. Luke tells the story in *Acts,* and afterwards Saul himself tells it at least twice. There are minor differences in their stories, but substantially they are the same.

Saul was on his way, his soul burning, as he believed, with zeal to destroy the enemies of the faith, and just as he had come near to Damascus, perhaps while he was thinking deeply of the almost supernatural confidence of the Christians in their faith, and of the cheerfulness with which they went to their deaths for it at his hands, smiling as Stephen had smiled, a great light suddenly shone upon him at midday, which blinded him temporarily, and a voice came from Heaven, saying, "Saul, Saul, why persecutest thou me?"

"Who art thou, Lord?" asked Saul.

And the voice from Heaven answered, *"I am Jesus, whom thou persecutest."*

Was it a reality? Was it an illusion?

Saul was convinced. This was the voice of Jesus of Nazareth who had died and been buried, yet was alive. No other man who had died and been buried was alive. Abraham, Isaac, Jacob, Moses himself, David, they were in their tombs. But this Jesus lived. Only a voice from the sky, but Saul required no other evidence. He did not, like Thomas, need to put his hands into the wounds of the Cross. He did not, like the five hundred odd other disciples, want the tangible evidence of one who ate and drank and walked with them for forty days.

Jesus had, in some sort, appeared to him also, and he was satisfied.

It was no dream to him, no vision. He at least thirty years after it, repeated it again and again, and never had one moment's doubt of it. He died for his faith in it.

Saul ceased to be a persecutor of the Christians, and became himself a Christian. Saul became Paul.

His religion was at first very simple. It was solely and fully founded on his belief in the Resurrection of Jesus of Nazareth. Later, it appears to have become enlarged by intercourse with the apostles, especially Peter, and above all by his conversions among the Gentiles.

In his blindness he was led into Damascus by his travelling companions, who did or did not see the light and did or did not hear the voice—the evidence is conflicting. Three days after he recovered his sight and began to preach Christ in Damascus.

The Jews, at first astonished, became watchful, and tried to kill Paul. He escaped from Damascus and went up to Jerusalem to see the apostles.

There, too, his conversion was at first suspected, but, giving proof of his sincerity, he was accepted, and began on his great career as an apostle of Jesus, born out of his time.

From that time forward the chronology of his life becomes difficult.

III. St. Paul's Early Travels

Paul himself says (*Galatians* I, 17; II, 1), contrary to *Acts,* that he did not go up to Jerusalem, but into Arabia, returning again to Damascus, staying three years, then going up to Jerusalem (where he saw James, the brother of Jesus); then he went to Syria and his own country, Cilicia, and after fourteen years went again to Jerusalem. Whether this means fourteen years in all or seventeen years is not quite clear.

After that Paul travelled far and wide; established societies in many countries; returned once more to Jerusalem; was finally arrested; claimed the rights of a Roman citizen to be tried only by Cæsar, and was sent to Rome. This seems to have been about A.D. 60.

Incidentally, many things happened that are of high moment. He resisted and overcame the theory of the Church at Jerusalem that salvation was only for the Jews. He became the apostle of the Gentiles. He refused to recognize circumcision as the necessity of discipleship. He had been baptized himself and he baptized, but he does not seem to have observed any other sacrament. When he claimed his rights as a Roman citizen he was turning down the right not only of Annas, as high priest, to try him; he was also turning down the right of the Roman procurator to try him, or even the Jewish king, Agrippa II, to try him. Only the Roman emperor could try him. He appealed to Cæsar (incidentally called Augustus, who was long dead) and to Cæsar he was sent. The Cæsar at that time was Nero.

Arriving in Rome, he did not find many Christians, although they had been there for ten years, arriving probably about A.D. 50. Perhaps it was a small group, holding their meetings in secret and afraid to make themselves known.

He was first met by a company of "brethren" at the "Three Taverns" on the Appian Way, and afterwards put into a house of his own, with a Roman soldier to guard him, while he waited the convenience of the emperor to try him. He remained two years there.

He had a right to receive visitors in his lodging, and the chief of the Jews came to see him. They told him they had received no letter about him from Jerusalem, whether for good or bad. They had heard of the new sect of the Christians, and everywhere it was spoken against. Evidently, no real Christian propaganda had begun in Rome.

He preached his gospel to these Jews, both out of the law of Moses and out of the prophets, and some of the Roman Jews believed and some did not. Certainly, Peter did not come to him, and when his time of necessity came the brethren do not appear to have helped him.

Ultimately (apparently, about two years after his arrival in Rome) Paul was tried by Nero and acquitted. This would be about A.D. 62. As far as we know, he then went down the northern shores of the Mediterranean, possibly as far as Spain.

Then came the destruction of Rome by fire in A.D. 62, and Nero, who was himself suspected, found a scapegoat in the Christians. Many were burnt and some crucified.

Paul either came back to Rome or was brought back. He was tried a second time by Nero, and, as we shall see later, condemned to death.

Paul's activities as an apostle had taken him to many cities, chiefly Gentile cities, pagan cities. There he had to preach a gospel which could be understood by Gentiles. This he did in Athens with only small effect, but elsewhere (as in Corinth and Antioch) with great effect.

He preached in synagogues in Jerusalem; he was for a time

permitted to preach in the Temple in Jerusalem. Therefore, his gospel could not have been considered entirely hostile to the Jewish faith. His constant claim was that it was founded on the law and the prophets. Nevertheless, sooner or later, the Jews threw him off, and he was scourged and imprisoned, and had to make various flights to save his life.

His doctrine, although apparently difficult, is not complicated. His faith is first of all based, as I have shown, on his confident belief that Jesus of Nazareth had risen from the dead, and the proof of it to him was that he had heard his voice from the sky, also, that great numbers of others had actually seen him in the flesh walking on the earth after his death and burial.

The fact was of paramount importance to Paul, no other man whatever (he knew nothing, apparently, about Lazarus) having risen from the dead before. In the Resurrection of Jesus, Paul found his reason for believing that Jesus was the Christ.

Jesus was by the flesh descended from David (Paul knew nothing about the supernatural birth of Jesus), but he was the chosen son of God. It was a divine Christ who would establish a kingdom of God. He thought that Kingdom would come before long. Meantime, he thought his duty was to do what John the Baptist had done, but with greater knowledge than John had possessed—to call people to repentance, and so escape the punishment which Christ would have to impose at his coming (in the Judgment) upon those who lived and died in sin, and to have part in the redemption which Christ had won by his death for those who accepted it—who believed in him and wished to make their peace with God, to become one with God.

Thus Paul preached the redemption of the world from its sins by the death of Jesus. This was, by God's will, the way atonement was to be made.

As to the end of things, Paul believed that all men would die as Jesus had died, and all believers would be raised from the dead as Jesus had been raised. The way of the Resurrection was not the old Pharisaic idea, yet it was essentially similar.

The body which was laid in the grave would undergo a spiritualizing change, such as the seed which is sown in the soil undergoes in growing up for the harvest. This would occur at the coming of the Christ. He would come in the clouds, and those who were in their graves would rise in their spiritualized bodies, and those who were still alive at Christ's coming would be changed in an instant, in the twinkling of an eye, and together they would ascend and meet Christ in the sky as he came again to establish the kingdom of God. That Kingdom would be established on earth. Paul never committed himself to any prediction of *when* it would be established.

His letters to his converts were of great value. Not all that are attributed to him are clearly by him. Some (such as *Hebrews*) bear unmistakable marks of another hand—Apollos, a powerful rhetorician, perhaps—not being in Paul's style at any moment.

Finally, Paul believed that the gospel of Christ was for all the children of men—not for the children of Abraham only.

IV. St. Peter

The life and work of Peter, after Christ, are simpler. The man who had at Cæsarea Philippi declared that Jesus was the Christ, the Son of God, and had afterwards behaved as if he had never really understood what he had said, who had fled from Jesus, denied him, hidden from the Jews for fear of sharing the fate of his Master, became a transformed being the moment he was convinced that Jesus had risen from the dead.

From that moment Jesus was indeed the Christ to him, the redeemer of the world, not merely the son of David, destined to restore the throne of David, but the Son of God, destined to establish on earth the kingdom of God. His faith in Jesus was also based on what he believed the prophets to have said of him. He believed Jesus was preordained to be the Christ from the foundation of the world and made manifest in his time. And the duty of his disciples (of himself above all others) was to call men to repentance for their sins, so that they might share in the redemption which Christ had won (as if from God) by his death.

Therefore, he preached Christ crucified, and desired nothing more than to share in the fate of his Master.

I do not think Peter was at any time the head of the Church at Jerusalem. That position was held by James, the brother of Jesus, who joined the Church at some moment unknown, after Jesus had appeared to him in his Resurrection. Whether James (who had not been an apostle, but had been almost hostile to Jesus) was appointed to his bishopric by reason of special gifts, or because of his relationship to Jesus we do not know. But we see that for many years (down to his martyrdom) both Peter and Paul deferred to him, reported to him and submitted to him.

Peter seems to have remained a Pharisee to the end. He believed that after his death Jesus descended into hell and preached to the saints. This seems to have been Hades, where Abraham, Moses and David were waiting for the Judgment. What possible use the preaching of Jesus in hell can have been I do not see. And I do not see any other meaning of Peter's statement.

Peter at first shared the idea that the gospel of Jesus was only for the Jews. He was apparently still of this opinion when he wrote his first Epistle to certain of the Churches established abroad. But he was converted from this partly by a vision at Jaffa (in the house of Simon the tanner) and partly by a controversy with Paul.

I cannot see that he ever looked upon the Holy Ghost as a part of the Godhead. I think this doctrine of three persons in one God did not exist until the fourth century, although the Church in a somewhat earlier period had prepared for it. Peter and Paul knew nothing about it. I do not find it in the Apostles' Creed.

Peter practised baptism (not, I think as a regenerating rite), but I see no reason to think he attached any spiritual significance to the bread and wine (and other food, apparently) taken in the meals eaten in remembrance of the Last Supper.

I do not see that he knew anything about the supernatural birth of Jesus, or made any authentic reference to the incidents of the nativity told in *Matthew* and *Luke*.

He believed Jesus to be descended from David. He interpreted the most detailed passages of the prophets as references to Jesus. He often seems to me to reason backwards, as one who says, "Because Jesus rose from the dead after three days his body never saw corruption, therefore he was foretold in the *Psalms,* and the "holy one" spoken of in the *Psalms* was Jesus, so Jesus was the Christ.

I think Peter believed that Christ would come again within the lifetime of some of his disciples, and that he was often troubled as time passed and he did not come. Nevertheless, I do not at all believe that he wrote the second Epistle that bears his name, or that he made shift to silence the "scoffers" by talking about a thousand years as one day. I think this second Epistle is a forgery written in the second century, because it speaks of Peter's death as still to come.

It is certain that Peter went to Rome, but not until after Paul's first trial and after Paul had left Rome, perhaps even after Paul's death.

I think he probably arrived in Rome shortly before or shortly after the fire in A.D. 64, and was made the first bishop of Rome. I see no historical reason for thinking he was there in A.D. 42 as Catholics believe.

Peter was crucified in Rome. But I do not think the postscript to *John* (XXI) was written until long after the event, when it was thought necessary to establish the supremacy of the bishop of Rome over all other bishoprics. This was probably about A.D. 757 when Stephen III was the bishop in Rome, and tried to establish his succession from Peter, and Peter's ordination direct from Jesus.

I have examined the Catholic claim for Peter as the founder of the Church in Rome, and its bishop from about A.D. 41 or 42, and that he remained Bishop until his martyrdom in A.D. 67, as it is stated in Canon Barnes's book, "St. Peter in Rome." I find it characteristic.

He begins by saying (what is generally stated by the early fathers) that Peter did not leave Jerusalem until twelve years after the Crucifixion. If so, it is clear that Peter was not the head of the Church in Jerusalem during this time. James was the head. He says James was probably martyred in A.D. 42 or 43, which does not appear to agree with Josephus, unless it means James, the son of Zebedee, not the brother of Jesus.

He says that when Paul arrived in Rome he found Christians there and apparently an organized Church, which may have had its origin in St. Peter's labours. Nothing of the kind can be found in history.

If so, it is astonishing that, as Peter must have been in Rome during the whole period of Paul's residence there *Acts* says nothing about him. It is equally strange that Peter did not help Paul in his poverty in Rome, which is described in the last chapter of *Philippians,* written from Rome to acknowledge the alms sent to him by the Philippians.

In short, I see nothing in *Acts* to justify the statement of the Catholic Church that Peter was in Rome while Paul was there, but much to discredit it.

Barnes quotes Jerome's statement that "Simon Peter . . . in praise of the apostles, after an episcopate at the Church of Antioch . . . came to Rome in the second year of Claudius." The second year of Claudius was A.D. 42.

Barnes quotes the postscript of John about the conversation of Jesus with Peter concerning the manner of his death, as proof that Jesus foretold Peter's death by crucifixion. This requires us to believe the postscript was written before A.D. 67, while John's Gospel is attached to A.D. 90. If it was written at (or more probably long after) A.D. 90 it was a report, not a prophecy, unless it is believed that Christ's prophecy was made immediately after his Resurrection and not written down until long years afterwards.

The statement that the passage about Peter stretching forth his hands and another girding him is a description of crucifixion is almost childish in its literary inefficiency. If it is a description of crucifixion it is a very bad one.

The statement that Peter did not leave Jerusalem until twelve years after the Crucifixion and yet arrived in Rome in A.D. 42 requires that the Crucifixion took place in A.D. 30, which it did not, unless the facts of John's Gospel are false in their chronology, for some of the events recorded in *John* as having occurred during the lifetime of Jesus did not take place until three to four years after A.D. 30, and John's Gospel itself requires nearly three years for the ministry.

Barnes quotes various archæological statements to prove that Peter was in Rome as bishop for many years. They belong to a much later period, and have no real value. The portraits of Peter and Paul which are said to be reproductions from contemporary originals are impossible from nearly every point of view.

To think that portraits of two obscure men (as they must have been) put to death because they were leaders of what was believed in the time of Nero (and long afterwards) to be a shameless and even disgraceful sect should have been made by Jewish converts (who were forbidden by their former Jewish religion to make portraits of anybody) is childish. Moreover, the reproductions of the portraits do not justify the belief that they represent such men as we know Peter and Paul to have been. They are false to the characters of both as we know them.

Taken altogether, I share the opinion that Peter did really visit Rome, but not until after Paul's first trial, or possibly after his death, say, A.D. 62, or about the time of the burning of Rome (64); that he wrote his first Epistle from Rome, and that he was crucified in Rome (probably about A.D. 67); but that Peter did not establish the Christian Church in Rome, and neither did Paul. I think the Roman Church was probably founded about A.D. 50 by Christianized Jews from Antioch or Palestine, and that Renan's account of the foundation of the Roman Church by Peter and Paul is an invention which was intended to prove the apostolic origin of the episcopate.

I think the postscript to *John,* about Jesus's appearance on the seashore, was written not long before this, in order to put into the mouth of Jesus authority for the statement that through Peter came the apostolic succession of the Roman episcopate.

Of James the Gospels and *Acts* tell us little. The Gospels do not mention him by name. They refer to him generally with his other brothers as brethren of Jesus.

For purposes of dogma, the early Church afterwards made James and his brethren the half-brothers of Jesus, or sometimes his cousins. There is not a particle of evidence for this either in the Gospels, in *Acts* or in the Epistles. It is solely and only intended to establish the belief that Mary had no children before Jesus and none after him, and that, having given supernatural birth to Jesus, she lived and died a virgin.

V. James

Whatever the relation of James and the other brethren to Jesus, it is clear that they did not believe in him at the beginning. It is probable that, during his ministry, they were hostile to him. At one moment they thought he was beside himself. At the only other moment at which they take any active part in his life they seem to be taunting him. Jesus showed them no favour. If it is true that on the Cross he committed his mother to the care of John, the apostle, he ignored them.

Only in a line in *John* are we told that James (presumably) appeared with their Master among the disciples after Jesus's death. Yet Paul tells us that Jesus appeared to James after his Resurrection.

This, in the absence of all other information, must be assumed to be to James (what a like occurrence was to Paul) the moment of James's conversion.

After that we learn that, at some period undetermined, James became the head of the Church at Jerusalem.

Why he was chosen for this high place over the head of Peter does not appear. Clearly, the story told in the last chapter of *John* of Jesus's distinct ordination of Peter, as head of his Church, as well as the passage in which Jesus, at Cæsarea Philippi, says that on Peter he builds his Church, was not then written or the facts were not common knowledge to the early Christians.

I think James became the head of the Church at Jerusalem solely because of his close relationship with Jesus. We know of nothing else that gives him any title to the superiority.

His headship is unquestionable in *Acts*. Not Paul only, but Peter reports to him their doings and experiences outside Jerusalem.

VI. Mary the Mother of Jesus

We hear little about Mary the mother of Jesus, either in the Gospels or in *Acts*.

Only on three occasions does she appear in the active life of Jesus, apart from the Nativity stories and the last story of John's Gospel, at the Cross and in the room in Jerusalem where Jesus appears after the Resurrection.

The first is where she comes to the Temple to find Jesus when he is a boy of twelve.

The second is where she comes to Jesus at the wedding feast at Cana.

The third is where she comes with her other sons to see Jesus (in Galilee), thinking he is beside himself.

In *John* she is at the foot of the Cross and afterwards in the room with the disciples after the Resurrection.

Thereafter she disappears out of the history of the Gospels and *Acts*.

In *Matthew* and *Luke* she appears in relation to the Nativity. Nowhere else in the New Testament are these incidents of the Nativity referred to.

She appears in various apocryphal Gospels, at the trial of Jesus and on the way to the Cross and elsewhere. Her death is also recorded in the apocryphal writings, and her burial.

When, in the fourth century, the rule of faith of the Church was summed up in the Apostles' Creed, she was described as the

Virgin Mary. This idea of her virginity, down to the birth of Jesus, had been recognized earlier, but apparently not during the lifetime of the apostles.

In the nineteenth century A.D. her own immaculate conception was made a dogma of the Catholic Church.

At the beginning of the twentieth century some of the religious orders asked for the dogma of the Assumption—that the body of Mary was transported into Heaven immediately after his death. This may yet be granted, and then the mother of Jesus will share with Jesus himself the dogma which covers the Resurrection and Ascension.

Although the Nativity stories may be of later origin and therefore not historical, they may be based on historical knowledge of her general character. These represent the mother of Jesus as very young at his birth, very fair and gentle.

Where she died and when is not recorded in Scripture, and the apocryphal writings give conflicting accounts.

This is nearly all we know (on the authority of Scripture) of what happened after his death to the chief persons in the earthly life of Jesus.

CHAPTER V

The Enemies of Jesus

I. *Pontius Pilate*

WHAT WE KNOW of Pilate after the death of Jesus comes chiefly from Josephus. He tells us that a "Jew," who had been driven from his own country by an accusation laid against him of transgressing the Jewish laws, found his way first to Rome, and professed to instruct men in the wisdom of the law of Moses. For an act of sheer robbery committed upon Fulvia, a "woman of quick dignity," he, with four partners in his crime and the Jews in general, was banished from Rome by the emperor Tiberius. He made his way back to Samaria, and was there the author of a tumult which led to Pilate's downfall. He took a vast multitude of the Samaritans to Mount Gerizim, which they looked upon as the most holy of mountains, promising them that he would show them there the sacred vessels which Moses had laid in that place.

The people to the number of 4,000 followed him, armed, for some reason, and were preparing to go up the mountain in a great multitude when Pilate, hearing of what was going on, and concluding that the real object was a political sedition of another pretended prophet, probably claiming to be, like Jesus of Nazareth, a Messiah, and aiming at the overthrow of the Roman occupation of the country, took possession of the roads with a large band of horsemen and footmen, fell upon the Samaritans, slew a great many, put others to flight and took a great many alive. The leader escaped; but Pilate ordered that on being captured he should be slain.

It was probably a blunder on Pilate's part. The false Messiah may have been a man of base character, as his career in Rome indicates, but the Samaritans did not take that view. As soon as the tumult was appeased they appealed, over the head of Pilate, to the governor of Syria, Vitellius, the superior of the procurator of Judæa, accusing Pilate of the murder of those who had been killed in what they declared to be a harmless and holy religious quest. So Vitellius sent a friend of his, Marcellus, to take control in Judæa, and ordered Pilate to go to Rome to answer before the emperor to the accusation of the Samaritans.

Pilate had no choice but to go, but before he reached Rome, the emperor, Tiberius, was dead (he died in A.D. 37), and his successor, Caligula, ordered him to be deprived of his office as procurator and banished. Here Pilate passes out of authentic history, but tradition says that he was never allowed to go out of Rome; that the vengeance of the Samaritans (or perhaps of the Jews of Judæa, whom he had so often offended) overtook him, and he was thrown into the Tiber. Later tradition has a story of how his body found its last home in the Lake of Lucerne, where, under the shadow of the mountain called Pilatus, it rises once a year at Easter and is seen to wash its hands.

It is thought by some writers that the "Jew" of Josephus (who escaped) was the "Egyptian" spoken of by the captain of the castle who rescued Paul in Jerusalem from the Jews, and said, "Art not thou that Egyptian, which before these days madest an uproar, and leddest out into the wilderness four thousand men that were murderers?" This is possible, but by no means sure. The incident in Samaria occurred about A.D. 37; the attack upon Paul was in Jerusalem about A.D. 52. Other false prophets may have arisen in the fifteen years between, but there is enough resemblance to make the guess reasonable.

It is also possible that the illegal stoning of Stephen took place in the period after Pilate's departure, and before the appointment of his successor, Marcellus. It took about a month to reach Rome from Jerusalem.

This was about A.D. 37 (Keim says before Easter A.D. 36), ten years after Pilate's first coming as procurator into Judæa.

So that three years after the Crucifixion the Roman governor who ordered the death of Jesus of Nazareth came to an ignominious end.

The two events are perhaps not wholly independent of each other, since the charge under which Jesus died may have led to the suspicion in Pilate's mind which provoked his attack upon the Samaritan prophet and the slaughter of his followers.

II. Joseph Caiaphas

The downfall of Caiaphas, the High Priest, who was perhaps the chief agent in the condemnation of Jesus of Nazareth, came about two years later—A.D. 39.

The case of Caiaphas's deposition is not clear. His high-priesthood began in A.D. 18 and lasted until A.D. 36. Keim says that he, like Pilate, was deposed by Vitellius, the governor of Syria, in A.D. 36. Pilate, says Keim, had been deposed by him before Easter A.D. 36, and Caiaphas at the close of the Passover A.D. 36. Thus Caiaphas continued in his office only about two months after Pilate ceased to be procurator.

Had both events any relation to the massacre in Samaria? It is by no means improbable. That Pilate's was the direct signal to it is sure. Is it not possible that Caiaphas, who about two years before had caused Pilate to kill Jesus on the ground of his assumed political pretentions, caused him, in like manner, to follow up and destroy the followers of the later pretender in Samaria? That the deposition of Caiaphas and the recall of Pilate occurred within a month, perhaps, of each other, suggests this explanation. That the ends of Pilate and Caiaphas were both brought about by Vitellius adds to the probability of the same cause.

If so, it is not straining probabilities too much to say that the downfall of Caiaphas was also related to the Crucifixion of Jesus of Nazareth.

The junction of these events is partly indicated by Josephus, who narrates the coming of Vitellius into Jerusalem at the time of the Passover immediately after telling of the recall of Pilate. He says Pilate tarried in Judæa ten years. This could not be exactly right if Pilate first came as procurator in A.D. 27. But good authorities say he came in A.D. 26, which would make his stay in Judæa ten years in A.D. 36. Josephus says Vitellius came to Jerusalem at the time of the Passover. This was the Passover of A.D. 36.

Vitellius came to Jerusalem to protect the Samaritans against the arrogance of Pilate. At the Easter of A.D. 36 or (it may be) 37, he appointed Jonathan as high priest in succession to Caiaphas, and seven weeks afterwards deposed him and appointed his brother, Theophilus. One writer, Hitzig, explains Jonathan's dismissal by saying that he (in the absence of a procurator) carried out the execution of Stephen, and that he was, on that account, like the younger Annas at a later date (A.D. 63) speedily deposed.

Against this is the fact that Josephus makes the presence of a procurator (Marcellus) unquestionable, and it is difficult to explain the gift of the high-priesthood to the brother of a deposed priest who had been guilty of a flagrant breach of the law.

But in reply to this it may very well have occurred that the new procurator, Marcellus, may not yet have known his power over the Sanhedrin, and in any case may have had no desire to repeat the error of his predecessor, Pilate, by interfering in the just death of a sedition-monger, as he would consider Stephen to be.

On the whole, it seems reasonable to conclude that the same cause which brought about the downfall of Pilate brought about the downfall of Caiaphas; that both these events came along after the Crucifixion of Jesus and were both related to it by being provoked by the mood of mind which the death of Jesus had created in the procurator and high priest alike.

Thus, then, fell the second of the enemies of Jesus—swiftly, after his Crucifixion.

It should be observed that some writers say that the same Christian hand which interpolated into Josephus the passage about Jesus made chronological changes to separate Jesus from the seditious Samaritan.

III. Herod Antipas

The downfall of Herod Antipas came about two, or at most, three years after that of Pilate and Caiaphas.

That Herod Antipas was from first to last an enemy of Jesus cannot be questioned by any close student of the facts. Jesus, himself, had no illusions on that subject. He called him a fox, got out of his way, and finally refused to plead in the presence of the incestuous adulterer, the murderer of John the Baptist.

Many writers place the death of John the Baptist by order of Herod Antipas between Pentecost and Tabernacles A.D. 35. Keim places it one year earlier. I see reasons for placing it two years earlier—A.D. 33.

Josephus's account of the end of Antipas separates his downfall entirely from Jesus. He says that after Caius (Caligula) became emperor in succession to Tiberius (A.D. 37) he appointed Agrippa to be king (not procurator) of Judæa.

Agrippa I died in A.D. 44 leaving a very young son (about seventeen) to succeed him. Agrippa was the brother of Herodias, the wife of Antipas. He had been a friend of Caius in his tumultuous youth, and after being sent out of Rome by Tiberius he had been compelled to throw himself on the charity of Antipas (his sister's husband) in Galilee.

Antipas, for his wife's sake, had given Agrippa, who was a spendthrift and deeply in debt, a menial office (as inspector of the Galilean markets) ; later they quarrelled and parted.

Then Tiberius being dead, and Agrippa's friend, Caius, being emperor, Herodias saw her scapegrace brother assuming royal rank in Judæa, while her husband (who had been his benefactor, and was the son of Herod the Great) remained merely procurator.

It is said that Herodias saw her brother in Rome in his kingly splendour in the spring of A.D. 37, most probably at the Feast of Tabernacles, passing through the crowds to display his vanity with all an upstart's ostentation of royal splendour, wearing the diadem and gold chain the new emperor had given him, and accompanied by guards he had brought from Alexandria.

This had excited all the womanly jealousy and envy of Herodias, who, wishing for her husband an equal rank and for herself general dignity, incited her husband to sail to Rome to ask the emperor to make him, also, king.

Antipas was unwilling to do this, knowing that, Tiberius (his former friend) being dead, he had no great reason to expect favours from Caius. But Herodias persisted in her importunities, with the result that in A.D. 39 Antipas, much against his will, journeyed to Rome on this errand, and Herodias went with him, carrying costly presents to the new Cæsar.

But as soon as Agrippa heard that Antipas and his sister Herodias had set off for Rome, he followed them, and arrived soon after them. And while Antipas was with the emperor at his palace in a little city of the Campania outside Rome, pleading to be made king, Agrippa arrived and made grave charges against him (Antipas), accusing him of conspiracy with Sejanus (the favourite of Tiberius) in opposition to the succession of Caius, and particularly of having made an armoury sufficient for 70,000 men to oppose him. The emperor demanded to know from Antipas if it was true that he had accumulated such an army, and Antipas, being unable to deny it, the emperor thought this a sufficient proof of Antipas's intention to revolt, and so he not only refused to make Antipas king, but took his tetrarchy away and banished him perpetually.

As for Herodias, knowing she was the sister of Agrippa, he told her he would not banish her, and out of regard to her brother he would make her a present of her own money, which otherwise would have been confiscated. But Herodias refused both mercies, redeeming her past iniquities in some degree by saying, "As I have been a partner with my husband in his prosperity, so will I be a partner with him in his misfortunes."

Thereupon, the emperor, in great anger, sent her into banishment with Antipas, and gave her estate to her brother, Agrippa.

Thus two other enemies of Jesus passed out of the page of history. This was in A.D. 39.

Herod Antipas was for forty-three years (from Augustus to crazy Caligula) tetrarch of Galilee. When he married the daughter of Aretas, the Arabian king, I do not know. He built the city of Tiberias about A.D. 22 (near the hot springs of Emmaus) and called it after the emperor Tiberius.

In A.D. 33 his brother, Philip, died, and (probably in the same year) he went to Rome to beg Tiberius to add his brother's territory to his own. Tiberius did not do so. On that visit (probably) he met Herodias, who was the wife of another brother, living in private life in Rome.

Before he brought Herodias to Tiberias, his Arabian wife fled back to her father, Aretas, who made war on Antipas to revenge his daughter.

I think the murder of John the Baptist took place late in A.D. 33 when Antipas went out to meet Aretas, who was coming down from his own capital, Petra, to invade Antipas's territory, Peræa.

The war between Aretas and Antipas lasted until A.D. 36, and ended in a serious reverse for Antipas.

It was in the spring of A.D. 37 (Tiberius having died in March) that Caius was made Emperor Caligula.

It was probably in A.D. 38 that Herodias saw her brother Agrippa in his royal splendour in Rome.

It was in A.D. 39 that both Antipas and Herodias were banished.

Such was the end of the only temporal ruler under whom Jesus lived.

IV. Annas

Only Annas remains to be accounted for. He had been high priest before Caiaphas, and after his own deposition had retained influence enough with the people to make it worth while for the Roman procurators to take council with him when, one by one, they appointed his successors. Thus, as seems clear, he secured the nomination of six members of his own family. Joseph Caiaphas is said (not altogether reliably) to have been his son-in-law. It is certain that five of his sons were high priests in succession. The last to hold this position was his namesake, Annas, the younger, who fell by the procurator for an illegal act in summoning a Sanhedrin without his consent, and executing James, the brother of Jesus.

It might well be thought that with the downfall of the last of his family the power of Annas, the elder, would cease. But it is too much to believe that he lived to see this downfall. And when or how he died we do not know with certainty. Renan says (on what authority, except that of the apocryphal writings, I do not know) that Annas, who was "above all things guilty of the death of Jesus," continued to wage an implacable war against the disciples and family of Jesus, and brought to death its first martyr, remained to the end "the happiest man of his age," and ended his life overwhelmed with honours and consideration, without ever doubting for an instant that he had rendered great service to his religion and his nation.

The source of this account is never quite unimpeachable, and it is rendered a little difficult in this instance by the fact that the sons of Annas were constantly in difficulties with the Roman procurators, having often dispensed with the consent of the latter to gratify their vanity and violent instincts, and were frequently dismissed at short notice and after exercising their office only a very short time. But the story of Annas's end seems reasonable and may very well be true. I see him dying in his bed at his seat near to his farm on the Mount of Olives, in the continued enjoyment of the wealth he had long earned by selling doves and fowls for the sacrifices at the altar (if sacrifices continued), and the perquisites of the tables of the money-changers whom Jesus had cast out of the Temple.

Such, then, was the last of the men who had been the chief actors in the drama which brought Jesus to his death.

It is impossible to say that they fell either as the direct or indirect cause of their crime against Jesus, although two of them (Pilate and Caiaphas) may be said to have fallen as the result of the condition of mind within themselves and in the general Jewish populace which the Crucifixion of Jesus brought to pass.

One thing is sure. They all came to an end well within six years (perhaps four or five) after the Crucifixion of Jesus. Thus a swift Nemesis overtook them. The little country in which they had strutted through their little day knew no more about them. They left nothing behind them to perpetuate their memory except the fact of the part they played in Jesus's death. But for this they would have sunk into obscurity.

Excepting for the two little stories about the bringing of the Roman standards into Jerusalem, and the robbery of the treasury of the Temple to pay for the supply of more water, Pilate appears in Jewish history solely as the Judge who condemned Jesus to death. He never appears in Roman history except as the governor under whom Jesus suffered. Joseph Caiaphas never appears anywhere in authentic history in any other connexion, and Annas, for all his influence while he lived, is lost in the pages of history but for the part he played in bringing Jesus to the Cross.

Let us say he died in his comfortable bed in his house on the Mount of Olives. It is the last place of nearly all such men—who are all things to all men. While he had found the Roman procurators useful to him, the Roman procurators had found him useful to them. It had been good to have such a go-between where governors were so completely out of touch with the people they had to govern, in race and in faith. Neither could understand the other, but a man like Annas could understand both. So let us say he died at a great age, covered with honours.

So ends the first generation of the enemies of Jesus. Another generation of the enemies of Jesus's followers were coming on, and what they did, and what came of it, will presently appear.

CHAPTER VI

The Church of Christ

I. Jerusalem the Home

WHETHER Jesus ever meant to establish a Church is to me more than doubtful. The few (very few) passages in which he speaks of his Church bear marks of being by later writers than the writers of the Gospels. As Dionysius says, they were written (in the second century) by people who did not hesitate to falsify the "words of the Lord."

Their object in doing so was worthy, but it was often unwise and led to mischief.

Of the history of the early Church the chief authority is the Acts of the Apostles, helped out in important particulars by the letters of Paul and by the other apostles and evangelists.

The Book of *Acts* is chronologically very confused and confusing. Dates, as we know them from history, are tossed about to our frequent bewilderment. This is due, no doubt, to the fact that it had many writers—that owners of copies had no compunction in putting in and taking out passages, and sometimes altering the order. Generally we find the following details:

After the death of Jesus his disciples continued to make Jerusalem their central home. They had certain conflicts with the Jewish authorities, who thought that by their preaching they were trying to make them responsible for the death of Jesus, to bring his blood upon them; but on the whole they were left comparatively free to propound their new doctrine openly. They were not forbidden to worship and to teach in the synagogue, and even in the Temple. They constantly did so, speaking openly of Jesus as risen from the dead, and therefore the Christ.

The Jews, who disbelieved this, appear to have had only one answer—that he did not rise from the dead, and that the explanation of the fact that on the third day his tomb was empty was that during the night his disciples had stolen his body in order to give colour to their declaration that he had risen.

1152

Altogether, according to early writers, the early Church lived in Jerusalem for at least twelve years after the Crucifixion.

There was one notable break. At the time of the stoning of Stephen the Christians were driven from Jerusalem into other parts of Palestine—Samaria, in particular, not, as we might have expected, particularly into Galilee. It is surprising how little we hear of Galilee in the story of the early Church, as told in *Acts*.

But there is one stranger fact. We are told (*Acts* VIII, 1) that after the persecution of the Church of Jerusalem by Saul of Tarsus, following the stoning of Stephen, they of the Church were scattered abroad throughout the regions of Judæa and Samaria, *except the apostles*. This was apparently about two years after the Crucifixion. Why the apostles, of all persons, should have been permitted to remain in the central home of Jerusalem, while Saul was making havoc of the Church by entering into private houses and haling obscure men and women and committing them to prison, passes understanding.

There was no need to search for the apostles. They were preaching openly the Gospel that the man, Jesus, had been killed by the influence of the leaders of the Jews with Pilate, the procurator, and that he was the Christ—therefore, that the Jews had killed the Christ.

But, according to *Acts*, it is clear that Peter remained in Jerusalem and came and went freely between Jerusalem and other parts of Judæa. Later, we are told (*Acts* IX, 31), after the conversion of Saul and his return to Jerusalem, that "then had the Churches rest throughout all Judæa and Galilee and Samaria." Apparently, this means that the Church's great enemy, Saul of Tarsus, having been converted to the side of the apostles, they were left in peace. It was only partly true, as *Acts* afterwards shows.

During this time of rest, what was the Gospel the apostles were preaching?

It was the Gospel of the salvation of the world from sin by the death of Jesus, the Christ. They said Jesus was the promised and expected Messiah, the Son of God, that the proof of this was that he had risen from the dead, as the prophets had said the Messiah would rise; that he would come again to the world and establish a kingdom of God into which his followers would be admitted and from which the wicked would be excluded.

They were, for a long time, permitted to preach this Gospel in the Temple and in the synagogue of the Jews. It is difficult to see any difference between it and the claim which Jesus made for himself on his appearance before Caiaphas, and for which, through various machinations, he died. It was the same Gospel for which Stephen died. And yet the apostles were permitted to preach it.

Why was this? My conclusion is that the Jews did not at that time understand the early Church to mean that Jesus was God. He might be divine, as the angels were, and a greater than any of the angels. He might have existed from the beginning of things by the side of God, and God might have chosen him to be the Redeemer of the world from the penalty of its sins. But he was not distinctly a part of the Godhead.

This was, I fully believe, what the Jews in general understood the early Church of Jesus to be teaching. It is inconceivable that they could have allowed the apostles to teach in the Temple if they had believed them to be teaching that Jesus was God. I confidently feel that the apostles had not yet come to the point at which (later) they believed Jesus to be God. He was Christ and the Redeemer, and divine, but they were still Jews, and they did not believe that God had any partner. To be His Son (even in the particular sense in which they applied the word to Jesus) did not mean that Jesus was one with God.

Later, as we shall see, their successors went farther, and did not hesitate to uphold their views (as Dionysius says) by putting words to support their opinion into the mouth of Jesus himself in the Gospels.

The Gospel preached by the early Church did not affirm the Holy Ghost to be part of the Godhead. The apostles thought of it as a divine spirit sent by Jesus in Heaven to inspire and comfort them during their sojourn on earth. They thought the Holy Ghost was the special gift of Jesus, and that it came to them at the moment of their baptism in his name. It did not come to the people who were baptized in the name of John. It gave them the power of tongues; it gave ignorant and illiterate men the power of speaking in languages they had never learned. One of the objects of this was that they could thereafter go out into the world and preach the Gospel to people of foreign nations in the language of those nations. Beyond this, and the ever-sustaining power of faith which it gave them, the Holy Ghost had no function in the early Church. Nobody ever spoke of the Holy Ghost as a part of the Godhead. In two or three passages in the Gospels and *Acts* and the letters of the apostles it is so described, but these are clearly contrary to the spirit of the books as a whole, and may very naturally have been added (they are sometimes superscriptions) by the owners of the manuscripts in a later age.

The apostles certainly remained in and about Jerusalem for a long time after the Crucifixion. Either they had not heard Jesus say that they were to go out into all the world and preach the Gospel to every sinner, or they had not understood his command. It was not until the Jews who did not believe made their residence difficult, and the apostles had differences among themselves, that they went out into the world.

One reason for this was that the majority of the early Church had a narrow view of the mission and salvation of Jesus. They thought it was for the Jews only. The stock of Abraham was the only one to whom he was sent. For them only was his salvation. They alone were to be redeemed by the sacrifice of his blood.

To defend this they called Jesus himself to witness. They put into his mouth, without the smallest intention of falsification, words which he could not possibly have spoken without being untrue to the whole burden of his teaching almost from first to last.

For instance, they made him speak to the Canaanite woman outside Tyre as if her sick daughter was no more than a dog. "It is not meet to take the children's bread, and to cast it to dogs" (*Matthew* XV, 26).

This outrage on the spirit of Jesus was committed without thought of evil. But it was none the less shocking. If it had been allowed to stand as the word of Jesus it would have meant that the millions of Christians now living would be as dogs in the eyes of the Founder of our faith.

Sooner or later the belief of the early Church was bound to break down. It broke down within itself. The apostles came to believe that the Gospel was *first* to the Jews and *afterwards* to the Gentiles. But the moment they began to preach to the Gentiles they found another difficulty—on the Gentile side. The story of the early Jewish Christians was that if the Gentiles were to share in the salvation of Christ they must become Jews. This required that they should observe the customs of the Jews—above all, the Mosaic custom of circumcision. That was a grievous stumbling-block. Many of the

Gentiles would not submit to an ordeal which revolted them. Some of the apostles were on their side.

The members of the Church who were scattered far and wide after the death of Stephen preached the Gospel only to the Jews. But men of more liberal views, from Cyprus and Cyrene, arose and preached the Gospels to the Grecians in Antioch. This scandalized Jerusalem, and the Church there sent one of themselves, Barnabas, to Antioch to show them the error of their ways. But Barnabas, who was a good man, was himself persuaded, and he went to seek Paul, who was in his country, Tarsus. Paul came to Antioch and took the side of the liberals.

The result was much disputing in the early Church. The dispute was carried up to Jerusalem. The Pharisees, who had become Christians, were naturally rigid for the observance of the law of Moses regarding circumcision. Peter took a less definite view. The fact that Gentiles received the Holy Ghost in baptism was proof enough for him that God had given them the right to belong to His people. That was all that really mattered. Paul was passionate in his protest against circumcision as an essential condition of the membership of Gentiles in the Church, holding that circumcision availed nothing, nor non-circumcision, but only faith which worked love.

James, the head of the Church in Jerusalem, a man of balanced and temperate mind, pronounced judgment. He said that God had clearly chosen to take the Gentiles into the fold of His chosen people, therefore his sentence was that they should not trouble them to observe the strict rule of the Jews, but only require them to abstain from pollutions of idols, from fornication, and from things strangled, and from blood. This satisfied the early Church, and the long and bitter struggle came to an end.

It had been a long warfare, and the story of it occupies much space in *Acts*. But it was very important to the future of the Church. Without it, and the result of it, Christianity would have remained no more than a sect of Judaism.

But the decision of the early Church of Jesus to accept the Gentiles on their own terms contributed to separate them from the unbelieving Jews. These Jews would not have the uncircumsized Gentiles in their synagogues and in their Temple.

That was the beginning of the final separation of the Jews from the early Christian Church. Hitherto, the followers of Jesus had been only another kind of Jews. Now they were their open enemies.

The Jews denounced the apostles, and Paul took up the challenge. It had been necessary, he said (so far he was a Jew and remained so to the end), that the word of God should first be spoken to the Jews, but, seeing they put it from them *and judged themselves unworthy of everlasting life,* he would turn to the Gentiles.

Paul's biting tongue had made the breach unbridgeable.

The great preachers of the early Church went out into the world. It is worthy of note here that the date of Paul's first visit to Antioch is by inference given as A.D. 64. For this is the accepted date at which Christians are mentioned in history. But this is impossible. This is the date of the burning of Rome. But *Acts* (XI, 26) says, immediately after reporting the coming of Paul to Antioch, his residence of a year there, and the success of his preaching, that the disciples were first called Christians in Antioch. This must be an anticipatory statement, but in verses 27 and 28 we are confronted by another statement which appears to show that the writer is thinking, not of A.D. 64 but of A.D. 44. He says that prophets came from Jerusalem and prophesied that a great dearth would come throughout the world in the days of Claudius Cæsar. Now Claudius was made emperor in A.D. 41 and the dearth came four years earlier, in A.D. 37.

Perhaps this is only a part of the chronological confusion of *Acts.* I think the date of Paul's first coming to Antioch was somewhere between the two dates A.D. 41 and A.D. 64, nearer the former than the latter. We shall see later that he was in Cæsarea (Samaria) about A.D. 52.

While the great preachers of the early Church were in distant parts of Palestine and in foreign countries, the Church in Jerusalem continued under the headship of James, the brother of Jesus.

From time to time the preachers came back to report to James the results of their work. Clearly, therefore, Peter was not the head of the Church in those days. If Jesus had made him the rock on which he built his Church, his word of authority had not yet been recognized. Whither Peter went during many succeeding years it is difficult to determine. The Catholic Church says he went (about A.D. 41) to Rome; that he established the Church there, became its bishop and remained so until A.D. 67, when he was put to death by crucifixion. The Book of *Acts* gives no hint of this. Peter drops out of its direct story, but it is clear from the closing chapters that its writer (almost certainly Luke) did not know anything about Peter being in Rome when Paul arrived there; or during the two years in which he lived in his own house there, chained to a Roman soldier; or when he was tried and acquitted by Nero, and again tried and condemned and executed.

II. Paul's Travels

Of Paul's doings *Acts* gives a much fuller and clearer story. Paul travelled far and established societies in many places—Antioch, Corinth, Galatia, Ephesus, Thessalonia, Athens and elsewhere.

He was obviously a poor man, and he always insisted on living by his own labour (he was a tentmaker, a common occupation in those days, when caravan journeys necessitated the constant use of tents in desert places).

He kept in constant touch with his converts, sending them letters of encouragement, expostulation, counsel, and so on.

The earliest of these letters (the first Epistle to the Thessalonians) appears to have been written about A.D. 48, a date which makes havoc of his own statement that he spent seventeen (or it may possibly have been fourteen) years in his own country and in Arabia, for he wrote that epistle, it is said in the superscription, in Athens, which must have been after he had spent a year in Antioch and some time in Jerusalem.

Sometime before the beginning of the reign of the Jewish king Agrippa II, son and successor of Agrippa the Great, Paul returned to Palestine through Tyre, with the intention of going up to Jerusalem. He was warned not to go, but he persisted in doing so. When the day came for his departure from Tyre, the Christians there, with their wives and children, followed him out of the city and set him on the way, and together they kneeled down on the shore and prayed.

A day or two later he reached Cæsarea, in Samaria, and there he was besought not to go up to Jerusalem lest he, like his Master before him, should be delivered into the hands of the Romans. But he was determined to go.

He said:

> What mean ye to weep and to break mine heart? For I am ready not to be bound only, but also to die at Jerusalem for the name of the Lord Jesus. [*Acts* XXI, 13]

So he went up and called to see James and the elders, and told them of the work he had done in foreign and pagan lands. And James and the Church rejoiced; but the unbelieving Jews cried out against Paul that he had brought uncircumcized Greeks into the Temple, and the crowds threw him out of the sacred building.

There was an uproar; the Roman chief captain received Paul and bound him, intending to scourge him, but, after Paul had told him he was both a Jew and a Roman, he spirited him away to the Roman procurator at Cæsarea to save him from Annas the younger (son of the Annas of Christ's time) and a group of confessed assassins.

The procurator, Felix, was a base type of man, but he saw that Paul had committed no offence against Roman law, and would have liberated him if he (Paul) or any of his friends had bribed him. To please the Jews, however, he left Paul in prison in the castle formerly belonging to Herod the Great.

There he lay imprisoned for two years, and then another procurator, Festus (A.D. 60–64), followed Felix (A.D. 52–60), and he brought Paul to trial before the Jewish king, Agrippa. This must have been the second Agrippa, who reigned from about A.D. 44 (unless there was regency for four years, making it A.D. 48) to 100, his reign having begun on the death of his father, when he was seventeen years of age.

King Agrippa II would have liberated Paul if Paul had not claimed to be judged by Cæsar, for which reason Agrippa sent him to Rome. This must have been somewhere about A.D. 52 to 60, nearer the former date than the latter.

III.   The Doctrines of Paul

Paul arrived in Rome midway between those two dates. Here he waited two years before being tried by Nero. During that time he wrote many of the letters to his converts which are preserved in the New Testament, but several of the letters were written earlier.

Paul taught in his epistles that Jesus was the Christ. He based this belief on the fact of his Resurrection. He knew that Jesus had risen from the dead, because Jesus had spoken to him from the sky when he was on his way to Damascus.

He found in the prophets the prophecies of which this primary fact was the fulfilment. In becoming a Christian, Paul never ceased, according to his own view, to be a Jew. He certainly claimed to believe in Jesus *because* he believed in Moses and the prophets. In speaking to the Jewish king, Agrippa, he appealed to Agrippa's belief in the law and the prophets as the reason *why* he should believe in Jesus and his Resurrection from the dead.

The prophets had said that Christ would rise from the dead, that God would not permit his soul to remain in hell or his body to see corruption.

The soul of Jesus had not remained in hell, and his body had not remained in the grave. To no other man ever born in the world (from Adam downwards) had this occurred. Jesus was the first who had risen from the dead, the first who, before the great day of judgment, had ascended to Heaven. Therefore, Jesus was the Christ.

This was the foundation of Paul's teaching in his letters to the societies he founded.

Then came his teaching on the mission of Jesus, the meaning of Christ coming to the world. It was to redeem mankind from sin. God had willed it that by the sacrifice of the blood of Jesus the sins of men might be wiped out. The condition of that salvation was the acceptance of it.

Next came the teaching of Paul on his own mission and that of his fellow apostles.

It was to tell the world that soon, perhaps very soon, the end of the world would come, and then all mankind would be judged, both living and dead. God had appointed a day on which He had ordained, whereof He had given assurance by raising him from the dead. Christ would come again to judge mankind. Those who accepted the salvation of Christ would become members of a Kingdom of Heaven which Christ would establish on earth. Those who rejected it would be cast out. Therefore, it would be their mission to cry out to the world, "Make haste! Flee from the wrath to come, and win for yourselves eternal redemption."

What was Paul's belief concerning Jesus and the Holy Ghost?

I do not think Paul believed that Jesus was God. To be the Christ was to be God's divine son, but not necessarily a part of the Godhead. Only through Christ could man be reconciled to God, but even that did not mean that Christ was God.

Nor do I think he believed that the Holy Ghost was a part of the Godhead. It was the Spirit of God shed upon His anointed—His saved children. It was shed only upon those who came to God through Christ.

When, on one occasion, Paul asked certain of the supposed converts in Ephesus whether they had received the Holy Ghost, they answered that they did not even know whether there was any Holy Ghost. Then he asked in whose name they had been baptized, and they answered John the Baptist's.

Upon this he told them that they must be baptized in the name of Jesus. They were so baptized, and immediately the Holy Ghost descended upon them. To Paul, the Holy Ghost was the Spirit of God given to men through the medium of Christ. It was not otherwise a part of the Godhead.

In what light did Paul regard baptism?

I think Paul regarded baptism solely as a sign, a badge which the believer wore to show that he had accepted the belief in Jesus as the Christ, and his redemption by Christ's sacrifice of himself for his sins by dying for them on the Cross. I think he believed baptism to be the rite whereby the Christ signified admission into the company of the followers of Christ.

I do not at all think he intended to teach that baptism was in itself a redeeming rite. Paul performed baptism himself, and called for baptism, much more than Jesus ever had done; but I am by no means sure that he considered it necessary to salvation, any more than he thought circumcision necessary, or that he believed the man who died unbaptized would necessarily fall into the number of the unredeemed when the day came which God had appointed to judge the world by that man whom he had ordained.

What did Paul teach about the sacrament of the Lord's Supper?

I do not think it is true that he adapted the love-feasts of the early Christians, who were accustomed to meet on the first day of the week for brotherly meals in remembrance of Christ, to the pagan cults in which the god was eaten.

I do not think that his teaching (I *Corinthians* XI, 20–29) justifies the general inference that Paul prepared the way for the Catholic mass, which requires belief in the presence of the body and blood of Christ in the food partaken of at the Lord's Supper.

What did Paul teach about the second coming of Christ?

I do not think he thought of it as coming to pass within the lifetime of the existing generation. I do not, at this moment, see any indication that Paul thought it would come to pass before the last of the disciples died.

· He believed it was near, and that it would happen suddenly, when nobody was expecting it, and he argued, therefore, that everybody must be prepared.

What did Paul teach about the kingdom of Heaven?

I think he expected it would come on earth; that Christ would appear in the clouds; that the dead who had died in time (in faith in him) would rise out of their graves to meet him in the sky; that the living also would meet him, and that all this would come to pass by an instantaneous transformation of the physical body of man into a spiritual body.

I am persuaded that he saw a spiritual kingdom of Heaven established, but whether on the physical earth or in the heavens I do not know.

Did Paul believe in personal immortality?

I assume that he believed in personal immortality, and that this was to be a necessity of his belief in a personal God and a personal Christ.

If he was influenced, as he appears to have been, by Greek thought, he was not so far influenced as to believe in an eternity of an impersonal spirit to which all good souls would belong as an indivisible part.

IV. The Doctrines of Peter and the Author of Hebrews

Peter, in his epistles, taught substantially the same as Paul. But Peter remained to the end more of a Jew than Paul in his belief in the Jewish rites and customs. Peter believed more firmly than Paul that the second coming of Christ was to be not only soon, but within the lifetime of some of the disciples who had lived with him.

Even if, as seems certain, the second Epistle of Peter is a forgery of the second century (and in that case a very shameless forgery), I think he suffered almost as much as the later writer did from the taunts of the unbelievers, who, seeing the disciples of Jesus dying off one after the other, while still Christ did not come, "scoffed" at them as followers of one who had been a false prophet.

I take it that the author of *Hebrews,* whether Paul or Apollos or another, thought essentially the same thing as Paul—almost more powerfully than Paul, and yet without his flashes of inspiration.

All the leading men among the early Christians appear to have held substantially the same doctrine. They also encountered the same difficulties. But they were more serious in Paul's case than in the case of the others.

The weakness of Paul's case when he preached from Mars Hill, at Athens, was that, after he had propounded his great argument that God was a spirit, the Lord of Heaven and Earth, who did not dwell in temples made with hands, and was not to be worshipped through things of silver and stone made by hands; that He had made of one blood all nations of men, and that (as the great poets had said) in Him all men lived and moved and had their being; he had to ask the Greeks to accept his personal word for it that a man named Jesus had lived and died and been buried, and had then risen from the dead and was again alive.

This the Greeks, with a few exceptions, could not believe, and so they mocked Paul, and he shook the dust of Athens off his feet and went to Corinth, and so forward on his long wanderings.

One thing was necessary to Paul and his fellow apostles—they must mightily convince people by the Scriptures and by personal testimony that Jesus was Christ.

V.   The Epistles

The epistles were written from various places, Paul's chiefly from Rome during the two periods of his imprisonment. One of the last, probably the second Epistle to Timothy (Timothy was then, or later, ordained the first bishop of the Ephesians) was written, it is believed, in Rome when Paul was either awaiting his second trial before Nero, or had already been tried and condemned and was awaiting his execution.

They were intended to be read aloud in the various Churches which Paul had established, and each letter was passed from Church to Church.

One marvellous thing about them is that they have been preserved. Another, that they have suffered so little at the hands of their owners. Perhaps it was hard to insert interpolations in the writings of Paul; they were so closely knit, and, as the writer of the second Epistle of Peter says, "hard to be understood."

They were intensely realistic and contained much beside doctrine, which we still have to consider in a later section.

Thus did the early apostles found the Church of Christ. It is clear that it was the aim of the apostles to establish Churches throughout the world. They thought this form of organization was the best way in which to circulate the Gospel.

But whether Jesus himself (in spite of occasional passages in the Gospels) ever thought of founding a Church I am very far from sure. I incline to the opinion that he never did; that he thought faith an individual thing which concerned the soul of the believer, and was not to be bound by doctrines of laws or customs or rites. Man, I think, stood alone to him, before God.

If he were living now I believe he would say that every man must be his own high priest, his own pope.

VI. Passages from Paul's Epistles

In his epistles Paul only occasionally quotes Jesus, one instance being the following:

> For this cause shall a man leave his father and mother, and shall be joined unto his wife, and they two shall be one flesh.

Other notable passages are:

> Put on the whole armour of God.
> I, therefore, the prisoner of the Lord.
> Let not the sun go down on your wrath.
> Ye are sealed unto the day of redemption.
> Faint not at my tribulations for you, which is your glory.

And the memorable passage referring to the glorious doctrine of the Resurrection:

> So when this corruptible shall have put on incorruption, and this mortal shall have put on immortality, then shall be brought to pass the saying that is written, Death is swallowed up in victory. O Death, where is thy sting? O grave, where is thy victory? The sting of death is sin, and the strength of sin is the law. But thanks be to God, which giveth us the victory through our Lord Jesus Christ.

VII. The Gospel Preached by the Early Christians

The Gospel preached by the early Christians (the apostles, who are eye-witnesses, by Paul, by Apollos, and others) is clearly enough indicated in the epistles of the Revelation.

Paul based his belief in Jesus as the Christ on the fact (1) that he had risen from the dead, and appeared to him by hearing and to others by sight; (2) that the prophets had foretold the Christ as one who would rise from the dead, and whose body would never see corruption; and (3) that no other than Jesus had ever risen from the dead and not seen corruption (*Acts* XXVI, 22, 23).

He expounds this Gospel from his appearance before King Agrippa at Cæsarea (probably *about* A.D. 58) : "King Agrippa, believest thou the prophets?" (*Acts* XVI, 27). Constantly he claimed to prove by the Scriptures that Jesus was the Christ.

The obvious defect in Paul's reasoning was that he had to ask his hearers, as in Athens, to take his unsupported word for it that Jesus had risen from the dead. This was the disadvantage under which all the apostles laboured. If they made converts they made them by establishing faith in *themselves* and their testimony on that point.

Paul's foundations of scripture, as stated in *Acts* XIII, 16, 23, 29 and XVII, 31, are in *Psalms* II and XVI :

Thou art my Son; this day have I begotten thee.
Neither wilt thou suffer thine Holy One to see corruption.

The promised one would not die. Jesus did not die (absolutely), therefore Jesus was the promised one.

Of this man's [David's] seed hath God, according to his promise, raised unto Israel a Saviour, Jesus.

David died and saw corruption, but he whom God raised up of the seed of David did not see corruption. Christ must needs have suffered and risen again from the dead, and their Christ was Jesus.

God appoints a day in which He will judge the world by that man whom He hath ordained. He has given assurance of him by raising him from the dead (*Acts* XVII, 31). Paul says he believes all that is written in the law and the prophets; *therefore*, he believes Jesus is the Christ. He thinks that God made all nations of one blood (*Acts* XVII, 26). Jesus was the Son of God, "made of the seed of David according to the flesh." He was the Son of God according to the spirit of holiness by the Resurrection from the dead.

VIII. Paul's Scheme of Redemption

Paul's scheme of redemption is fully stated in *Romans* III, 24, 25; V, 9–11, 14; and in VI, 9, 10, in which he says:

Knowing that Christ being raised from the dead dieth no more; death hath no more dominion over him. For in that he died, he died unto sin once: but in that he liveth, he liveth unto God.

Thus Paul's Christianity rests on the Resurrection. He asks us to believe his word that Jesus rose from the dead, and then proceeds to show by the Scriptures that the Christ had so to rise.

For the fullest statement of Paul's belief about the Resurrection see I *Corinthians* XV.

Here we see that Paul founds redemption entirely on Christ's Resurrection. Christ died for our sins according to the law. And he was buried and rose from the dead. If there be no Resurrection from the dead then is Christ not risen. And if Christ is not risen then is our preaching vain and our faith is vain. If the dead rise not then is not Christ raised; and if Christ is not raised we are still in our sins. If we have hope in Christ only in this life then we are of all men most miserable—that is to say Christ as a teacher of morality is not a Saviour.

It is by no means certain that *Hebrews* (although ascribed to Paul in the New Testament and said to have been written from Italy by the hand of Timothy, Paul's companion) was written by Paul. It bears in its more rhetorical style marks of another hand— a very powerful hand. The writer may have been Apollos, a Jew born at Alexandria, described as an eloquent man and mighty in the Scriptures (*Acts* XVIII, 24). He had been baptized by John. But two friends and housemates of Paul, Aquila and Priscilla, made him a believer in Jesus as the Christ.

The writer gives what is, on the whole, the fullest and best account of the scheme of the Redemption, and the meaning of Christ's sacrifice as taught by the apostles in the generation after his death. The essence of their teaching and the soul of Christianity as they understood it is found in *Hebrews* II, 9; VII, 14–16; IX, 10–28; X.

The writer of *Hebrews* is very explicit on the Redemption.

Jesus, by the grace of God, tasted death for every man (*Hebrews* II, 9). He is the captain of our salvation through his sufferings.

He was made even like other men that he might make reconciliation for the sins of the people. As he suffered and was tempted he is able to succour those that are tempted. In Jesus we have not a high priest who cannot be touched with the feeling of our infirmities, "but was in all points tempted like as we are, yet without sin."

In the days of his flesh (while he lived) he

offered up prayers and supplications, with strong crying and tears unto Him that was able to save Him from death. . . . Though he was a Son, yet learned he obedience by the things which he suffered. And being made perfect, he became the author of eternal salvation unto all them that obey him.

This (*Hebrews* V, 7–9) obviously refers to the cries and prayers of Jesus on the Cross.

IX. *The Priesthood of Christ*

Jesus was made priest "not after the law of a carnal commandment, but after the power of an endless life" (*Hebrews* VII, 16).

"This man [Jesus], because he continues ever, hath an unchangeable priesthood. Wherefore, he is able also to save them to the uttermost that come unto God by him, seeing he ever liveth to make intercession for them." He is a high priest, "holy, harmless, undefiled, separate from sinners, and made higher than the heavens" (*Hebrews* VII, 24–26).

He does not need, like earthly high priests, to offer up sacrifices daily, first for his own sins and then for those of the people; for this he did once when he offered up himself.

The author of *Hebrews* on the theory of sacrifice:

Once every year into the second tabernacle went the high priest alone, not without blood, which he offered for himself and for the errors of the people.

But Christ being come a high priest, by a greater and more perfect tabernacle, not made with hands, neither by the blood of goats and calves, but by his own blood he entered into the holy place, having obtained eternal redemption for us.

If the blood of bulls and goats testified to the purifying of the flesh, how much more shall the blood of Christ, who, through the eternal Spirit, offered himself without spot to God!

For this cause he is the mediator of the new testament, that by means of death, for the redemption of the Transgressions that are under the first testament, we who are called might receive the promise of eternal inheritance.

Christ is not entered into a holy place made with hands, but into Heaven, and is now appearing in the presence of God for us. He must often have suffered since the foundation of the world, but now once in the end of the world hath he appeared to put away sin by the sacrifice of himself.

As it is appointed to men once to die, but after that the Judgment, so Christ was once offered to bear the sins of many, and unto them that look for him shall he appear the second time without sin unto salvation.

It is not possible that the blood of bulls and of goats should take away sin (*Hebrews* X, 4).

In burnt offerings and sacrifices for sin thou hast had no pleasure. . . . I [Jesus] come to do Thy will, O God.

By this we are sanctified through the offering of the body of Jesus Christ once for all.

The offerings of the priests can never take away sins. But this man Jesus, after he had offered one sacrifice for sins for ever, sat down on the right hand of God.

And the Lord says, "And their sins and iniquities will I *remember no more.*"

The writer of *Hebrews* sees the day of God approaching:

For yet a little while and he that shall come will come, and will not tarry.

Meantime, the disciples are to assemble together, exhort each other. He foresees a fearful judgment which will devour the unrighteous. It is a fearful thing to fall into the hands of the living God.

He paints a terrible picture (*Hebrews* XI, 35–40) of the sufferings of the children of God in the past, describing how, from the time of their bondage in Egypt, they were mocked and scourged and suffered bonds and imprisonment, were stoned and sawn asunder, were tempted and slain with the sword; how they wandered about in sheepskins and goatskins, being destitute, afflicted, tormented, in deserts and in mountains and in dens and caves of the earth—yet, he says, all these having received a good report by faith *received not the promise.*

But God has provided better things for us. Seeing we also are compassed about by a great cloud of witnesses, let us lay aside the sin which doth so easily beset us, looking to Jesus, the author and finisher of our faith, who for the joy that was set before him endured the Cross, despising the shame of it, and is now set down at the right hand of the throne of God.

Jesus is the mediator of the new covenant. And if they escaped not who refused him when he spoke to them on earth, how little likely we are to escape if we turn away when he speaks from Heaven!

God is a consuming fire.

Jesus sanctified the people through his blood.

This is the essence of the teaching of the apostles during the generation after the Crucifixion. There can be no mistaking it. We must take it or leave it. To deny it is to turn our backs on the foundations of Christianity. If it is wrong, then Christianity is wrong. But surely this is the doctrine which, right or wrong, has conquered the world!

CHAPTER VII

The Twelve Years Rest

I. The Early Church

IT IS IMPOSSIBLE not to believe that the early Christians found joy in the downfall of the enemies of the Master—so quickly one after another. Within four or five years after the Crucifixion the three principal enemies had disappeared—Caiaphas, Pilate, Herod Antipas. Only one leading figure remained, and his time would come soon.

Now the Church settled itself down as an organized unit in Jerusalem. After the death of Stephen, many of the Christians were scattered abroad throughout the regions of Judæa and Samaria, except the apostles.

It is difficult to understand why the apostles, of all others, should have been permitted to remain; that while private converts were hunted out as a result of a secret inquisition from house to house, apostles like Peter, who openly declared their faith in the public places (including the Temple and synagogues), should have been allowed to live in Jerusalem.

They were not afraid. They would have gloried in persecution, making no terms with their persecutors, casting their accusations in their teeth, charging them with killing their Messiah, foretold by the prophets, thinking martyrdom a way of showing the fate of their Lord and joining him the more quickly in his heavenly glory—why should the apostles, in the fierce explosions of the illuminism, have been spared?

It is difficult to find an explanation. But it may be that the toleration of certain of the leaders of the early Church was due to the coming of a tactful, temperate and wise man, who became the head of it.

This man appears to have been James, the brother of Jesus. When he joined the early Church we do not know. How he came to join it we are not definitely told, although Paul indicates it.

1170

That the brothers of Jesus had been against him is clearly enough stated in the Gospels. James must surely have been one of the brothers whose unbelief in Jesus is recorded. At one moment he had thought Jesus beside himself and had gone with his mother and brothers to take him away, thereby (apparently) to protect him against himself. At another moment he had taunted Jesus with remaining so long in Galilee instead of going up to Jerusalem, where his teaching, his claims and his miracles might be put to the test of the best judges.

But after that we have three significant references. The first is to the presence of the brothers of Jesus with their mother in the upper room in Jerusalem where, after the Ascension from the Mount of Olives, the apostles are in prayer and supplication. The second (*Galatians* I, 19) is where Paul says that on going up to Jerusalem for the first time, three years after his conversion, to see Peter, he saw also James, the Lord's brother, and none other. The third is where Paul, in numbering the evidences of Jesus's Resurrection, says that Jesus appeared to James also—obviously Jesus's brother—not James the son of Zebedee, who would be present when he appeared to all the remaining eleven disciples (Thomas excepted) on the night of the day of his Resurrection.

Of this great scene of Jesus's appearance to his unbelieving brother we have no other record—what the world would give to have the record of that great moment!

But it is probable that after James, like Paul (perhaps by a similar revelation), became convinced that Jesus had risen from the dead, he joined himself to the apostles.

It is clear that he became the head of the early Church in Jerusalem—and it is probable that he was so when Paul went up to see Peter and saw James also, and no other.

At what time it came to pass that James acquired this headship of the Church we are not told. It was probably after the execution of Stephen, when the apostles and converts were dispersed. How it came to pass we do not hear. Was it because of the absence of Peter? Was it because of James's near relationship to Jesus?

Probably the latter. But it is clear that in the early Church in Jerusalem he stood above Peter and all the apostles, although not himself a disciple from the first, but a late-comer like Paul.

Obviously, the incident of Jesus having chosen Peter to be the rock on which he built his Church was, down to that time (perhaps five years after his Crucifixion), unknown or disregarded.

Peter was obviously a wandering evangelist for some time after the death of Stephen. Paul, by his own account, was in Arabia. As often as they returned to Jerusalem during many years thereafter they reported to James.

The body of converts over whom James presided in Jerusalem probably continued to live in community. Apparently they continued, both then and for a long time afterwards, to frequent the Temple and the synagogues, but they held prayer-meetings in their own homes, and elected elders of their own. The members earned their own living and there was no paid priesthood.

They may have continued to keep the Jewish Sabbath, for were they not all Jews down to this time? But they also kept Sunday, the day of the Resurrection. On the evening of this day (the first day of the week) they met for their meal in remembrance of their Master. We do not yet hear of any mystical significance attaching to this meal.

It is probable that at these private gatherings they read aloud the records of the sayings of Jesus that were beginning to be written by those of the disciples who had heard them. It is almost certain that the writer of these sayings was Matthew, perhaps the only one of the company who had the pen of a ready writer.

It is not hard to believe that over these records there were frequent disputations. Some would recall other words, and these would have to be added. Some might recall different words, and they would have to be discussed. Perhaps an agreement as to what Jesus had said was not always arrived at, and hence some of the differences in the various reports of his words as they have come down to us.

James would have no easy task to maintain harmony among his zealous company. What we read of him in *Acts* shows that he was a wise and temperate adjudicator. His "sentences" on points of difference between the disciples are usually moderate, rarely or never extreme or fanatical.

His office would consist largely in keeping peace among the brethren, in settling such quarrels as might arise among them, in managing the common purse, in granting relief to the poor, and in directing the evangelical activities of the Church.

Intensified by their expectation of the approaching end of the world, and the coming of the kingdom of Heaven, they would fall into excesses. Apparently, they did not encourage marriage. Why marry and bring into the world children who would be exposed to the wrath that was so soon to come? They practised extreme asceticism; not only in food and clothing, but also in the control of their natural passions and appetites.

> There are some eunuchs, which were so born from their mother's wombs; and there are some eunuchs, which were made eunuchs of men; and there be eunuchs, which have made themselves eunuchs for the kingdom of Heaven's sake. He that is able to receive it, let him receive it.

Some carried these principles to the excess of mutilating themselves in obedience to what they believed to be the divine command.

> Wherefore if thy hand or thy foot offend thee, cut them off, and cast them from thee; it is better for thee to enter into life halt and maimed, rather than having two hands or two feet to be cast into everlasting fire. And if thine eye offend thee, pluck it out, and cast it from thee; it is better for thee to enter into life with one eye, rather than having two eyes to be cast into hell fire.

They had no compunction in putting these words into the mouth of the Master, fully persuading themselves that he had spoken them, or that they were the essence of his teaching, although they are, as we see them now, both in the letter and the spirit, untrue to his character.

In their devotion to the Master they went the length of denouncing affection for their own kindred.

> If any man come to me, and hate not his father, and mother, and wife, and children, and brethren, and sister, yea, and his own life also, he cannot be my disciple.

Rarely in the history of the world can asceticism have taken a more formidable shape. Later, it was to bring them terrible tragedies.

But let us not too hastily conclude that these passages were not spoken by Jesus, more or less in the form given to them. They were according to his fiery and imaginative way of illustrating spiritual truths by phrases drawn from actual life. They can never have been intended to be taken literally. As literal teaching they are impossible, just as Christ's teaching about eternal punishment is impossible. Hell, as Jesus describes it, would be an unthinkable absurdity if his words were subjected to literal interpretation. There could be no such physical hell. It is not possible. Later, as we shall see, a literal interpretation was fastened on his words by others to serve their own often unworthy purposes.

On one important subject there was long and serious discussion in the early Church. This was the difficult subject of whom the kingdom of Heaven was intended for. Being Jews, they believed it was for the Jews only. They quoted the authority of Jesus himself for saying so.

When they recalled the incident of the curing of the daughter of the Canaanite woman who came out to him from the coasts of Tyre and Sidon (*Matthew* XV, 28 and *Mark* VII, 25), they did not hesitate to put words into his mouth in defence of their belief (that his mission was only to the Jews) that were little short of brutal. The woman had cried, "Have mercy on me, O Lord, thou son of David"; he had answered (first to his disciples) "I am not sent but unto the lost sheep of the house of Israel," and afterwards, to the woman herself begging him to have mercy on her sick daughter, "It is not meet to take the children's bread and to cast it to the dogs."

There are some 650 millions of Christians in the world now, nearly all Gentiles (few of them being of Jewish blood), and if these sayings of Jesus were historical the Founder of our Faith called us dogs.

There is not an enlightened Jew in the world to-day who will believe that their great brother from the Galilean hills ever said anything so brutal. He never could have said it. It was contrary to his spirit and the meaning of his mission. But the early Christians believed this was his doctrine, and the first serious quarrel in the early Church of Jerusalem arose out of that blunder.

The quarrel was brought to a head by an incident that happened to Peter.

In Cæsarea (Samaria) there was a Roman centurion of the Italian band. His name was Cornelius. He was a devout man who prayed to God always, gave much alms, and had a good reputation among the Jews.

Clearly, he had heard the preaching of the dispersed apostles and evangelists and wished to become a Christian. But there was the impediment that he was not a Jew, and he was troubled to know what he could do. He dreamt that an angel appeared to him and told him to send to Joppa (Jaffa) for one Simon Peter, who was then lodging with one Simon the tanner. The centurion sent two of his servants and a soldier.

When these men were approaching Joppa, Peter, being hungry and having to wait while his food was made ready, went up on to the housetop to pray. It was midday, when the sun would be hot, and he fell asleep and dreamt. He thought he saw descending from Heaven a vessel containing all manner of beasts forbidden as food by the law of the Jews, yet a voice told him to rise, kill and eat. He answered that he had never eaten anything that was common or unclean. To this the voice replied, "What God hath cleansed, that call not thou common."

At that moment the servants from the centurion arrived and delivered their message, asking Peter to come to him. Peter went, and on entering the house of the Roman centurion at Cæsarea he said, "You know that it is an unlawful thing for a Jew to keep company with one of another nation, but God has told me to come, and I am here. Why have you sent for me?"

The centurion told him, and Peter said, "Of a truth I perceive that God is no respecter of persons, but in every nation he that feareth him, and worketh righteousness, is accepted by Him."

Then Peter preached his gospel according to Jesus to the centurion, and his people believed and were baptized, and Peter lodged with them several days.

But rumours of these happenings at Cæsarea reached Jerusalem, and Peter was called back to the Mother Church to account for his conduct in preaching the Gospels to, baptizing, and living and eating with them.

Peter thereupon told what had happened from first to last, and when the elders heard it they were satisfied and said, "Then hath God also to the Gentiles granted repentance unto life."

This was the great event. It was the first step towards making the Church of Jesus a world Church—Christianity a world religion.

And the credit of that great first step is to Peter.

II.   The Story of Agrippa

Agrippa visited Rome about the year A.D. 39, and he returned to the territory assigned to him after the fall of Antipas—Galilee and Peræa, as well as the territory north of them which had previously been Philip's. He lived first in Tiberias, the city that had been built by his predecessor. He was a good Jew, and began immediately to show favour to the Jewish people.

There had been a house tax and he removed it. Other good things he did for his Jewish subjects, and the greatest of them was done shortly after he became king of Galilee.

The occasion of it was as follows:

While Agrippa was good to the Jews, Caius, his friend, patron and benefactor, became increasingly hostile. Caius had conceived the idea that the Jews, not only in Palestine but throughout his empire, were his enemies.

There arose a tumult in Alexandria between the Jews and the Greeks, the Greeks charging the Jews with neglecting the honours that belonged to Cæsar. While all other subjects of the Roman empire built altars and temples to Caius, and received him as they received gods, the Jews alone refused to do so. The result was a riot in which indignities were shown to the Jews, such as that Jewish women were compelled to eat pork.

Against this treatment the Jews sent an embassy to Rome to claim the same right to live according to their religious law as they had enjoyed under Tiberius and Augustus. Caius received this embassy badly. The head of the embassy was an Alexandrian Jew of world-wide eminence, named Philo, not altogether an orthodox Jew, but a great philosopher of liberal religious principles, whom modern writers have not too wisely called "the spiritual brother of Jesus."

According to Philo's account there were two embassies—three Jews and five Greeks, and they came to Rome that the emperor might judge between them. Caius's mind was soon made up, for was not one side standing for him and the other for a God he did not know anything about.

Hardly had Philo begun to present the case for the Jews when Caius behaved like a madman, working himself into a towering rage and flinging Philo out of his palace.

The result was that Jews throughout the world hated Caius, particularly the Jews of Judæa. To punish this spirit of antagonism, Caius gave orders to the governor of Syria to make an invasion into Judæa, and if the Jews there would not admit of his statue being erected in the Temple at Jerusalem, and worshipped as that of a god, to conquer the city and province by war, and then to do it. The governor set about obeying his emperor's orders, but the Jews answered, "If you are entirely resolved to set up the statue in our Temple you must first kill us, for we cannot permit such things to be done as are contrary to the laws of our forefathers."

Seeing this stubborn resistance, and that he could not carry out Caius's will without a great deal of bloodshed, the Syrian governor wrote a letter to Caius with the object of dissuading him from his mad design.

Now Agrippa, who continued to be the close friend of Caius, chanced to be in Rome at the time that the governor's letter arrived, and he asked the emperor to a feast of great magnificence. Not to be outdone by the hospitality of his subjects, King Caius returned this compliment by asking Agrippa to a feast of his own of still greater splendour.

At this feast Caius drank freely, and being more merry than usual, he made in the presence of his notables a speech in Agrippa's honour, which concluded with the assurance that everything he had was at Agrippa's service, and he had only to ask anything and it should be granted him.

It was at first the scene over again of Antipas and Salome on the eve of the execution of John the Baptist, but the end was different. Agrippa replied with grace, tact and unselfishness, fully knowing how dangerous a thing he was going to say.

"Since thou, O my Lord," he said, "think I am worthy of thy gifts, I will ask nothing relating to my own felicity, but I desire something that will make thee glorious for piety, and may be an honour to me among those who inquire about it—I will ask that thou wilt no longer think of the dedication of that statue of thine which thou hast ordered the governor of Syria to set up in the Jewish Temple in Jerusalem."

It was the last petition Caius had expected, but the scene was once more the same as that in Herod Antipas's fortress above the Dead Sea. In the presence of his guests he dared not dishonour his promise, so he said he admired Agrippa's virtue and would do what he requested.

So he wrote to the governor of Syria, telling him that if he had not already erected the statue he was not to trouble any further about it.

The story of how Agrippa had saved the Temple from desecration was not long in reaching Jerusalem, and it added greatly to his popularity among his own people, who had been saved from the madness of Caius, who had wanted to compel them to transgress the religious worship of their country and call him a god.

Caius died a miserable death by murder, being left outstretched on the ground, naked, or with no such covering as became the dead, and with his wife lying over him with streaming hair and face wet with his blood.

Agrippa supported her cause for a time and then went over to the new emperor.

Claudius Cæsar made Agrippa king of Judæa and Samaria, so that when he returned to Palestine he was sovereign of the whole of the kingdoms over which his grandfather, Herod the Great, had reigned.

A Roman procurator was still retained by Rome (as during his grandfather's time), but Agrippa pleased his people greatly by setting up his home in Jerusalem, almost certainly in his grandfather's palace, the house in which Pilate had lived and Jesus had been condemned to be crucified.

He also delighted the Jews by hanging up within the Temple, over the treasury into which Jesus saw the widow drop her mite, the golden chain which Caius had given him, as a demonstration of how the greatest dignity and importance may have a fall and how God sometimes raises up His servants from the lowest misfortunes.

Having been very poor, he was now rich, with an income derived largely from taxes, equal to about £400,000 of British money.

He was very liberal in his gifts to the Jews, though some of them (such as that of strengthening the walls of their city) excited the suspicion of his emperor; and others seem to have been out of keeping with the spirit of his people—such as the gift of a theatre where 700 prisoners condemned to death fought 700 others until all were killed.

We have no right to say that any of this vast number of condemned men in so small a country as Palestine at this same time were Christians, though they may have been, for the land was still, as during the time of Jesus, overrun by brigands.

Agrippa observed all the Jewish feasts, but if he was a good Jew he cannot by any stretch of language be said to have been a good friend to the Christians.

Notwithstanding various proclamations by Claudius calling upon his subject-kings, governors and procurators to let the subjects of the Roman empire in foreign countries live in religious matters according to their own laws and conscience, Agrippa lost no time in laying his hand on the little Church in Jerusalem.

We read in *Acts* that about this time (A.D. 42) Herod (Agrippa) the king stretched forth his hand to vex certain of the Church; that for some cause, not given but easily guessed at, he killed by the sword James the brother of John (the two sons of Zebedee, the old fisherman of Galilee) ; and that when he saw that this pleased the Jews he arrested Peter also and locked him up in prison, intending to try him after Easter, for it was then the eve of the Passover.

While Peter was waiting for his trial the little group of his brethren continued to pray for him, and on the night before the day appointed by Agrippa for Peter to be brought before him, he (although sleeping between two soldiers and bound by two chains) was liberated from prison by what he believed to be supernatural agency.

Coming to himself in the streets outside the prison, Peter was sure that an angel from Heaven had delivered him from the hand of the king and from the expectation of the Jews, which could only be that he, like James (Zebedee), would be put to death.

He found his way through the night to the home of one of his Jerusalem converts, Mary the mother of a young man called John Mark, supposed to be the disciple who had been known to the high priest, and gained admission to his palace for Peter, when Jesus was about to be tried.

Many of the brethren were gathered in Mary's house for prayer, perhaps for Peter, that God might carry him through his ordeal in the morning.

Peter knocked at the door, and a young woman, named Rhoda, came to open it. Before she had done so she heard Peter's voice without, for in eastern manner he was calling the customary salutation of a visitor before entering a house—"God be with you, and all that are here."

In gladness, and perhaps in fear, she ran back and told the brethren that Peter stood before the gate. They answered her that she was mad; but she constantly affirmed that it was so, and then they said, "It is his angel."

Meantime, Peter continued to knock, and when at length they opened the door and saw him they were astonished.

Peter beckoned with his hand to them to hold their peace; told them how the Lord had brought him out of prison; instructed them to tell all to James, the head of the Church, and then went away "into another place."

As soon as it was day the soldiers of the prison were in dismay at the escape of their prisoner. They were unable to account for it; but Agrippa had no difficulty in doing so, and having examined the jailers, he condemned them to death, and then, leaving Jerusalem, went down to Cæsarea, the capital of Judæa, where the Roman procurator still kept his army of occupation and the king had one of the houses and judgment-seats of his grandfather.

That was the last of Agrippa's journeys. In spite of his tumultuous popularity, he had enemies even among his own people, though as long as he had life and health he had his own ways of dealing with them. One of these was a man named Simon, who, being learned in the law, called an assembly at Jerusalem during Agrippa's absence in Cæsarea to shew that he was not living holily, that he was not really a Jew, and that he ought to be excluded from the Temple. Agrippa sent for the man, invited him to his box in the theatre, where they were seen together by the people, asked him in a low and gentle voice what he had done contrary to the law, made him a present, and sent him back conquered, convinced and content.

The Acts of the Apostles mentions in passing another of Agrippa's reconciliations with his enemies. Agrippa had been highly displeased with the people of Tyre and Sidon for reasons whereof history gives a meagre account. It seems probable that, among other offences, he suspected them of harbouring some of his enemies, even such of them as were threatening his life. Agrippa was a ruler of resource, and he soon made the people of Tyre and Sidon realize that the trade of their country was at his mercy, for could he not stop the passing of the caravans from their ports not only into Palestine but also into Mesopotamia and Egypt?

So they came to him in a spirit of humility, made his chamberlain, Blastus, their friend and intermediary, and so secured reconciliation.

It was the last of Agrippa's triumphs. In honour of it, apparently, the people of Cæsarea made a festival to celebrate vows for his safety. A great multitude of the notables and populace of the city and provinces came to it, and about noon, when the sun was at its height, Agrippa arrived, clad in a wonderful garment made wholly of silver. As he entered his box, and took his seat on his throne, his garment was illuminated by the reflection of the sun's rays upon it, and he looked so resplendent that the people were at first speechless and spellbound, and then they burst out in loud and frantic cries, "It is not a man. It is a god. Have mercy upon us!"

Agrippa did not rebuke them, or reject their impious flattery, and the gladiatorial games went on, perhaps such as those at which men condemned to death destroyed each other.

But presently, looking up, he saw an owl sitting on a rope over his head, and taking this for an evil omen he became suddenly depressed. Almost immediately afterwards (according to the Jewish historian Eusebius) "a pain came in his belly" and presently became violent. The royal flatterers carried him out of the theatre, and, as he was going, he turned on them and said, "You lied to me, saying I was immortal, and now I am being hurried home to die."

He lived five days longer, rolling in agony on the ground and weeping, and then he died, worn out by his sufferings.

And then came the climax of his fate. As long as he was alive the women and children of Cæsarea sat in the streets in sackcloth, offering prayers for his recovery. But the moment he was known to be dead, the men, including some of the king's own soldiers, who had called him a god five days before, shouted and sang and drank themselves drunk with joy in the public places.

Nor did they stop at insulting the dead king himself. Agrippa had left four children behind him, a son, seventeen years of age, who was then at school in Rome; a daughter named Berenice, who was married and gone, and two other daughters of six and ten years of age, Mariamne and Drusilla, who had lived at home with him, and the inhabitants of Cæsarea, having broken into the king's house and carried off the statues of his two daughters, exposed them to unspeakable indignities, and finally put them on the tops of the public brothels.

So died the last of the Herods who count for anything in history. They had undoubtedly done some good, but also much harm. With few exceptions they were an evil family, cunning, sensual, adulterous, incestuous, dogmatic, degenerate, having many wives but few children, often none at all. Within a hundred years they had almost all been wiped out.

Nevertheless, Agrippa was a great king and a great Jew. The Christians of his time, who saw the hand of God in everything, said the angel of the Lord smote him, and he was eaten of worms, because "he gave not God the glory."

This, according to the reckoning of Josephus, was in A.D. 44.

III.　The First Quarrel among the Christians

To the people of that age these tumultuous events must have seemed to be of immense importance, for reports of them reached Rome and set the empire itself in motion, with its procurators, and governors and kings. But in the long course of the centuries they have proved to be only a passing show compared with something of far more moment to the world that had been going on about the same time in a back street, perhaps, in Jerusalem.

Where Peter went to after he fled for his life from Agrippa, leaving by night the house of Mary, the mother of Mark, for "another place," we do not know.

The narrative in *Acts* follows mainly the story of Paul.

We are told that, hearing of the success of the disciples who had been scattered abroad after the stoning of Stephen, the little Church at Jerusalem sent Barnabas, a new-comer and a good man, probably a brother of Mary of Jerusalem, and uncle of John Mark, his sister's son, full of faith, as far as Antioch, to strengthen the converts there. With his help many other converts were made, and he found it necessary to call for assistance. He remembered Paul, whom he had known at Damascus. Paul was then at Tarsus, and Barnabas went up for him and brought him to Antioch. Paul remained at Antioch for a year, and the Church increased greatly under his ministrations.

Down to this time the converts of Paul had apparently been all Jews.

It has been frequently said by rationalist critics that the disciples were first called Christians in A.D. 64 in Rome, when the city was burning, and that the name was given to them in derision by their enemies.

This will not do. If the New Testament is to be believed the disciples were first called Christians in Antioch about A.D. 44, by themselves, and as a badge of glory. We shall presently see they were also called Christians in Canaan long before the fire in Rome.

A widespread famine came during the reign of Claudius (secular history fixes the date of it as several years earlier), and Paul and Barnabas went up from Antioch with relief from the Church there (every man having given according to his ability) to the brethren at Jerusalem, who were still living the communal life according to the strict precepts of Jesus, which had required that they should take no thought for the morrow—"give us *this* day our daily bread."

Then Paul and Barnabas, taking John Mark with them, returned to Antioch and continued their ministrations. But they lived in the belief that they must obey the direction of the Spirit within them, and finally the Spirit told them that they must go further. So, after fasting and prayer, the Christians of Antioch laid their hands on the heads of Paul and Barnabas and sent them away.

They sailed to Cyprus, and went on through various places to another Antioch (in Pisidia), and there Paul preached with great power but not with complete acceptance. His gospel was grounded on the law and the prophets, and therefore he preached in the synagogues. But now he thought that by the death of Jesus of Nazareth the law of Moses had not only been justified and completed but superseded.

This did not please the Jews, and there was much division. But it pleased the Gentiles, and at a gathering to which the whole city came he preached his doctrine again.

Against this the Jews rebelled, and Paul and Barnabas told them (not without irony) that it had been necessary that the word of God should be spoken first to them, but seeing they put it away from them, and judged themselves unworthy of everlasting life, they would henceforward go to the Gentiles.

This was the beginning of a great movement.

Expelled by the Jews from their coasts, the apostles went to Iconium, preaching to both Jews and Gentiles, and from there to the pagan cities of Lycaonia and there they had, at first, a great if embarrassing success. Partly as a result of a cure they had performed on a cripple, the people thought gods had come to them in the likeness of men, and it was as much as the apostles could do to prevent the people from offering sacrifices to them.

But Jews came from Antioch and Iconium and so turned the tide against the apostles, that they were stoned in the streets, and in one place Paul was dragged out of the city and left for dead. He recovered, went on to other cities, and finally sailed back to Antioch, to give an account to those who had sent them out of the work they had fulfilled, which included establishing Churches among the Gentiles and ordaining elders from among the Gentiles themselves.

Then came a check in their activities. Certain unauthorized Jews from Judæa came to Antioch and told the Gentile converts that unless they were circumcised after the manner of Moses they could not belong to the Church of Christ.

This led to further divisions, and to settle once for all the question of the validity of the conversion of the Gentiles, Paul and Barnabas and others went up to Jerusalem.

The apostles and elders of the Mother Church of Jerusalem came together to consider the matter. Peter, who, from the "other place," had returned to Jerusalem, was present also at the conference, and James, the brother of Jesus, as head of the Church, presided.

The report of the proceedings in *Acts* is meagre, and it has to be read partly in the light of certain passages in Paul's Epistles.

The sect of the Pharisees were rigid in their demand that the Gentile converts should be commanded to observe the law of Moses, which required that they should be circumcised. This meant that before they could be recognized as members of the Church of Jesus they should become Jews.

Paul, who was a man of vision, saw that this would be a stumbling-block to the Gentiles, who would resent circumcision, thinking it a degrading rite when executed after infancy. Besides, according to Paul's views, circumcision was not only unnecessary, but wrong, the law of circumcision established by Moses having been superseded by the coming of Christ.

Apparently, Peter spoke first. He reminded the brethren that a good while ago through his work at Cæsarea God, who knows all hearts, had brought it about that the gospel had been preached to the Gentiles, putting no difference between them and the Jews, therefore, why tempt God by putting a yoke upon the neck of the disciples which neither their fathers nor they could bear.

More than this, however, Peter must have said, although it is not reported in *Acts,* and we have to look elsewhere for the sequel.

It is clear that while Peter held that the Gentiles should be accepted into the Church they should conform to the rites and the laws of Moses—not in baptism only, but also in circumcision.

To this Paul replied warmly, saying that through him, too, and his companion Barnabas, God had wrought miracles and wonders among the Gentiles.

More than this he must have said, although we have to look for it later on in one of his letters. The covenant that was made to Abraham and fulfilled in Christ was not annulled by the law that came through Moses 430 years after. The law had only been their schoolmaster to bring them to Christ, and now that Christ had come there was no longer any need of a schoolmaster. They were all children of God, and the seed of Abraham by faith in Jesus, and therefore there was neither Jew nor Greek among them, neither bond nor free, for they were all one in Christ.

This was startling doctrine. It seemed to them to tear to shreds the pride of the Jews that they were a peculiar people, a chosen generation, a holy nation, a royal priesthood, and therefore that the kingdom of Heaven foretold by Jesus was to them alone.

Clearly, there were hot words between Peter and Paul, some of them personal. Apparently Paul thought Peter was, as we now say, sitting on the fence. "I withstood him to the face, because he was to be blamed," said Paul afterwards, speaking of the encounter as having occurred earlier at Antioch, but Paul's chronology is not always reliable, and it is in every way more probable that it occurred here.

Knowing that at Antioch Peter had first eaten with the Gentiles, and then, when James visited them, had separated himself from them, out of fear of the head of the Church, and that others, including Barnabas, had dissembled with him, he said to Peter, "If thou, being a Jew, livest after the manner of the Gentiles, and not as do the Jews, why compellest thou the Gentiles to live as do the Jews?"

It was a deadly thrust, and it cut deeply. The company was sharply divided, Barnabas being alienated from Paul and the young John Mark siding with his uncle, Barnabas, and with Peter, his mother's friend and his own.

At length, silence being restored, James, as head of the Church, gave judgment. It was a marvel of wisdom. Going back to the greatest of the prophets, he showed that God, who knew everything from the beginning of the world, had first visited the Gentiles, to take out of them a people to his name, and then said he would return to rebuild the tabernacle of David after it had fallen down, and accept all the Gentiles who helped to do this.

Therefore, his judgment was that they should not trouble the brethren of the Gentiles who had turned to God, but write to them at Antioch and elsewhere, telling them that the apostles and elders and the whole Church there assembled, having heard that certain persons had been subverting their souls by saying, "Ye must be circumcised and keep the law," denied that they had given any such commandment, and now they laid no greater burden upon their Gentile brethren than that they should abstain from meats offered to idols, and from blood, and from things strangled and from fornication, showing that they had no longer any part or lot with the pagans, and if they did that they did all that was necessary, and so "Fare ye well."

To this the assembly agreed, and two of the chief men of the company, Barnabas and Silas, who had hazarded their lives for their faith in Jesus, were chosen to go back to Antioch with Paul and Barnabas and carry the decree.

Thus ended the first of the disputes of the early Church.

Henceforward the Gentiles, without becoming Jews, were to be free of the Christian Church. The gospel of Jesus, his redemption and his Kingdom, were no longer to be the sole inheritance of the Jews only, but to belong to all nations.

It was a great and fateful decision; perhaps the greatest and most fateful in the history of humanity.

The tragic fate of Agrippa at Cæsarea, with its noisy and shameful consequences and even tumult made in Rome, with the discharging of centurions and the marching of armies, sinks into insignificance when compared with the long sequence of mighty events in the future history of the world which were to come of this dispute among a handful of unknown men in a back street in Jerusalem.

Paul is usually thought to be the author of the decision without which the Christian Church, as such, might possibly have become no more than a Jewish sect and died out in fifty years, and was indeed the spirit behind it. But the real author of it was James the brother of Jesus. Foster father of Christianity! He found Christianity in the ghetto and opened the gates of the world to it.

IV. The Parting of the Apostles

The Church of Jerusalem submitted to the decree of their leader, but it is not certain that they all agreed. The dispute had awakened personal feelings, which were in some cases too strong for further companionship.

A few days after the four ministers had returned to Antioch and delivered their letter to the Gentile converts amid rejoicings, Paul asked Barnabas to go back with him to every city in which they had established assemblies, that they might see how they fared. But Barnabas would only go with Paul if his nephew John Mark went with them also. Paul would not have John, so Barnabas and John went one way while Paul and Silas went another.

What became of Peter we do not know with certainty. The traditions of the Roman Church, apocryphal writings, occasional references in the early fathers, certain inscriptions in and about Rome, together with the opening verse of the first Epistle of Peter (the second Epistle being a manifest forgery of a later century) seem to indicate the scenes of his life. But the Scriptures say nothing of that.

After the assembly in the house of James in Jerusalem, Paul and Peter, so far as we know from the Scriptures, parted company.

The two great apostles of Christianity never met again.

CHAPTER VIII

The Missionary Work of St. Paul

I. His Ministry among the Gentiles

FOR THE NEXT twelve or fourteen years the history of Christianity (as far as we know it from the Bible, supported by the authentic records of secular history) is the story of St. Paul—his wanderings, his work, his struggles, his sufferings, his successes, his failures.

What a task was before him! He was going out to convert the Gentiles. They were not barbarians, but often, in their own ways, enlightened people, living sometimes in great cities, sometimes in seats of learning, in one case in the central heart of the culture of the world—the birthplace of the Greek philosophers, the great thinkers, the great poets of the world.

And what was the message he was taking with him?

First, that a certain book of the Jews called the Law and the Prophets (which most of them might never have heard about) had foretold from far back the coming of one who would save mankind from its hard taskmasters, and above all from the everlasting penalty of its own sin and wickedness; that this Saviour had come in these latter days, and that the proof of his being the Promised One, the Messiah, the Christ, the Saviour of mankind, was that being dead he was still alive; that he had risen from the dead, which no other man from the beginning of the world had ever yet done, and was now sitting on the right hand of God; that he would come again, soon, very soon, none could say how soon, to judge the world, to separate the righteous from the unrighteous, to set up a kingdom of Heaven on earth, and that to share his salvation and fly from the wrath of God, from eternal damnation, it was necessary to believe in him, to accept him, and be baptized in his name.

And who was this Christ? Only a Jewish journeyman of a little city in the Galilean hills called Nazareth, which most of them had never heard of before, but nevertheless he was the Son of God

1188

and had been with God from before the beginning of the world; he had fulfilled in his life all the conditions of the prophets made in the Jewish book of the Law and of the Prophets; he had been rejected by the rulers of his own people; he had died at their insti- gation by Crucifixion, but that this had been his glory, not his shame, for he had thereby taken the curse that would otherwise have fallen on man; and his death had been his sacrifice for man's sin, the means whereby he had purchased man's everlasting redemption from punishment and his reconciliation with God.

And what proof had he to give them that this Jesus of Nazareth, whose name they had never heard before, had risen from the dead? The word of many witnesses (whom he had left behind him in Palestine) who had seen him face to face after he had been three days in the grave; and, if they doubted that, his *own word,* the evi- dence of his own senses, for after his death and burial this Jesus had appeared to him in a shining light on his way to Damascus, and had spoken to him from the sky, telling him to go out into the world and take the message of his Resurrection to all men, for redemption was not for the Jews only, but for all mankind, since God had made of one blood all nations of men that dwell on the face of the earth.

Could they doubt him? Did they think him a blind fanatic? Had he not in times past been the deadliest of the enemies of Jesus, per- secuting those who believed in him, as blasphemers against God, hunting them from house to house, from city to city, entering into the Jewish synagogues and delivering them up to judgment and death?

Such was the message Paul carried out to the Gentiles. It takes one's breath away to think that Paul expected them to accept it, on his own word mainly, and the evidence of documents they did not recognize.

What happened to him?

For the history of his pilgrimages we have one authority and perhaps one only—that of the Acts of the Apostles, believed to be written by Luke, but clearly only partly written by him. In his second Epistle to the Corinthians (XI, 24–33) Paul himself gives a long summary of journeyings, adventures, persecutions, priva- tions and other sufferings, which are not alluded to by Luke, and one of the early fathers (Clement of Rome) speaks of five imprisonments. But *Acts* contains the only fairly consecutive story, and we are compelled to follow that, verifying it and illustrating it by the known facts of history.

With his companion, Silas, at first, and afterwards (as time went on) with others who became his converts and followers, Paul passed over many hundreds of miles of the Mediterranean coasts, going to and fro, backwards and forwards; he had no programme, no mapped-out tour. He believed he was guided and directed from day to day by the Holy Spirit. When at the beginning of his ministry, in a vision of the night, he thought a man appeared to him, saying, "Come over into Macedonia and help us," to the chief city of Macedonia he went.

He was poor, and like all the primitive clergy of the Church, unsalaried, always earning his own living by working with his hands, just as did the rest of the early Christian community. His trade was that of a tent-maker, a calling greatly in demand in those days when much of the travelling on land was by caravan over long stretches of uninhabited deserts. In one place he came upon a man and his wife of the same craft, Aquila and Priscilla, who had come from Rome where the emperor Claudius had lately expelled the Jews, and they worked and lodged together for a year and a half. He did the like everywhere, keeping himself by his own labour and being "at charges" to nobody.

As his means allowed, and the necessities of his mission required, and, above all, as he believed the Holy Spirit moved him, he passed from place to place, from country to country, sailing in trading ships on the sea, and generally walking afoot across the land. In the criss-crossing of place-names in *Acts* it is not always easy to follow the chronology of Paul's movements, but it is certain that he visited (sometimes more than once) Philippi, other cities in Macedonia, Thessalonica, Galatia, Athens, other cities in Greece, Corinth and Ephesus.

In some of these places he stayed years, in others months, in others weeks, in others days.

He found Jews nearly everywhere, and always visited them first, never allowing that he had ceased to be a Jew in becoming a Christian. Where there were synagogues, he did not hesitate to enter them and teach in them, for he would not admit for a moment that the gospel he preached was not in accordance with the law and the prophets. Where there were no synagogues, or where he was expelled from them, he preached in the streets and the marketplaces, on the seashores, or by the river-sides outside the cities.

He had both good fortune and bad. From the Jews in general he had almost constant opposition. They took the view that had been taken by the ruling religious classes in Jerusalem in the last days of Jesus, that the new gospel was blasphemous, because it claimed for Jesus of Nazareth that he was the Son of God. Therefore, they did to Paul what their fellow-Jews had done to his Master—condemned him to the Roman authorities as a sower of sedition, who was turning the world upside down, and doing things contrary to the decrees of Cæsar by saying there was another king, one Jesus.

Some of them followed him from city to city with this denunciation, thereby creating uproar among the citizens and compelling the Roman rulers to send Paul and his companions away as troublers of the peace.

Sometimes the Roman rulers withstood the misrepresentations and drove the Jews from the judgment-seat to which they had dragged the apostles, telling them that if Paul were guilty of wrong or wickedness they would listen to them, but if they had nothing to complain of but questions of words and names and matters of their own law, they would be no judges between them.

But even in cities that were mainly or entirely pagan, Paul had his difficulties.

In Philippi, a young woman who was thought to be possessed of a spirit of divination, and was in fact a fortune-teller, followed Paul and his companion about for some days with disturbing cries; but afterwards, she was converted, and then her masters, seeing their hope of gain was gone, laid hold of the apostles and dragged them to the magistrates, saying they were Jews who were teaching customs which were not lawful for them to receive, being Romans.

The magistrates, without examination, ordered Paul and Silas to be beaten until they bled, and then cast them into prison, where the jailer put them into an inner dungeon, and fastened their feet in the stocks.

But the apostles took their shame as glory, for their Master's sake, and at midnight the other prisoners heard them praying and singing praises to God.

Later, there was an earthquake, and we are told that the foundations of the prison were shaken, its doors were thrown open, and everyone's bands were loosed.

Seeing this, and thinking that his prisoners must surely have escaped, the jailer, on awaking from sleep, drew his sword and would have killed himself, but Paul cried, "Do thyself no harm, for we are all here."

On that the jailer came trembling to Paul and his companion, as to holy men, threw himself at their feet, washed their sores, and asked what he should do to be saved.

Next day the magistrates sent sergeants to say, "Let those men go." But Paul, who was proud of his Roman citizenship, said, "No; they have beaten us uncondemned, being Romans, and cast us into prison, and now they wish to thrust us out privily. Let them come themselves and fetch us out."

The magistrates came in humble mood, brought them out and begged them to leave the city.

Again, at Ephesus, Paul had the vested interests of the pagans up against him. It was the central city of the goddess Diana, and a silversmith named Demetrius, who lived by making silver shrines to her, seeing his craft in danger from the religion of Christ, which in those days did not call for crucifixes, stirred up his fellow-craftsmen against the preachers who were telling the people that the gods made by hands were no gods, and to worship them was superstition.

The result was that the whole city was thrown into confusion, and two of Paul's companions in travel were dragged into the theatre to account for their conduct.

But when one of the two attempted to make his defence he was shouted down by the crowd, some crying one thing, some another, some hardly knowing why they cried, except that they saw the temple of Diana insulted and the glory of their city threatened.

Paul, who had the heart of a lion, tried to follow his comrades into the theatre, but was restrained by his friends and thus saved from death by the fanaticism of the pagans.

For two hours the tumult continued, the people crying, "Great is Diana of the Ephesians," and then the town-clerk (a Roman official) commanding silence, said, "You have brought here these men who are neither robbers of churches nor blasphemers of your goddess. If Demetrius and the craftsmen have anything against them the law is open, but let the matter be determined by a lawful assembly. Meantime, do nothing rashly, be quiet, lest you be called to answer for this uproar."

It was the voice of Gamaliel over again, and it prevailed, so Paul and his companions escaped in safety.

But when the apostles were free from physical perils they had other difficulties in the promulgation of their faith which were perhaps more serious.

Twice, at least, Paul visited Greece, and once he went up to Athens. He spoke Greek, for that was the common language of the Mediterranean coast. Also, he knew something of the Greek poets, as we see by a paraphrase he made from one of them, not long dead. Waiting at Athens for two of his companions to join him, he looked round and saw that the city was given over to idolatry. So he began to dispute both with the Jews in the synagogue and with the Greeks in the market-place.

Certain Epicurean and Stoic philosophers overheard him, and asking each other, "What does this babbler say?" they invited him to tell them what his new doctrine meant.

From Mars Hill, the open air forum, he made a speech which shows at once the strength and the weakness of the first appeal of Christianity.

"Men of Athens," he said, "I perceive that in all things ye are too superstitious. As I passed by and beheld your devotions, I found an altar with this inscription, 'To the Unknown God.' Whom therefore ye ignorantly worship, I come to declare to you."

Then he attacked their idolatry. God had made the world and everything in it; He was Lord of Heaven and earth; He did not dwell in temples made with hands—why, then, should they think that the Godhead was like gold or silver or stone, graven by art and man's device, and believe that God was to be worshipped in the works of men, seeing that He had made man Himself, that as certain of their poets had said, Man was His offspring, and in Him they lived and moved and had their being? Time had been when God tolerated this ignorance, but now He commanded all men everywhere to repent of their sins, and had appointed a day when He would come to judge the world in righteousness and had ordained a man to sit in judgment.

Who was this man? Jesus of Nazareth. Only a Jewish journeyman, yet the Son of God from before the beginning of the world. And what was the proof of his ordination? That he had died and that God had raised him from the dead.

When the schoolmen of Athens heard of the resurrection from

the dead, and found themselves called upon to accept a new religion, a new statement of man's place in God's scheme of the universe, on the strength of Paul's personal word that Jesus of Nazareth had risen from the grave, they mocked and left him.

Paul, himself, was undismayed. His faith in the prophets of his own people, and his unbroken belief in the Voice that had spoken to him from the sky on his way to Damascus, carried him through mockery as well as persecution. It also carried multitudes along with him.

There is no greater error than to suppose that Christianity appealed at first only to the ignorant and uninstructed. Some of Paul's converts everywhere were among the most enlightened and learned—in Athens Dionysius, the Areopagite, a scholar who in later times was to be the victim of a series of flagrant forgeries; in Ephesus an Alexandrine Jew, named Apollos, hitherto a disciple of John the Baptist, an eloquent man, mighty in the Scriptures, believed by many to be the author of the Epistle to the Hebrews, perhaps the clearest of all expositions of Christianity, and a piece of rhetoric that need not fear comparison with the noblest passages in Cicero and Demosthenes; and above all Luke "the beloved physician," who wrote, from the accounts of listeners and eye-witnesses, some of the most beautiful parables in the Gospels, which is to say certain of the most perfect pieces of literature in the world.

But it was among the simple rather than the wise, the children in heart and brain to whom Jesus had liked best to speak, that Paul found his largest following. They brought back to their sick the handkerchiefs and aprons with which they had touched Paul's body, and the diseases were said to depart from the afflicted and the evil spirits to go out of them. Wizardry and the black arts generally were a common source of profit in the countries Paul was travelling through, but people who practised curious arts brought their books together and burnt them, although they had cost much, and the earnings they had made had gone with them. It was believed that he worked miracles, and when the young man fell out of the window of a room on the third story in which the apostle was preaching, and Paul went down and embraced him and said, "Trouble not yourselves, for his life is in him" no one doubted that he had raised the young man from the dead.

Paul minced no words with his Gentile converts, sometimes

calling their pagan habits by hard names, but nevertheless they loved him. Tradition says he was rather an ugly little man, yet women were devoted to him. He liked to have "honourable" women about him, and, according to certain of the apocryphal writings, scandal did not spare him in respect of one of them.

But the faith of the simple had a deeper source still. They took Paul's word for it that the man called Jesus had risen from the dead, and believed that he would have died rather than deceive them. Above all, they heard in Paul's preaching another voice than his, the voice from within, the universal voice, speaking of sin which must be atoned for if they were to escape from everlasting punishment and make their peace with God. The laws of Moses could not do that for them, nor devotion to Diana, nor vague supplications to an unknown Deity, nor any sacrifices of bullocks and rams, but only the blood of the Son of God Himself.

If this was fanaticism it was the most formidable wave of it that had swept through the souls of men since the scenes in the hills and valleys of Galilee.

Everywhere and in spite of every kind of persecution Churches were established in the faith and increased in numbers daily. They consisted of Jews as well as Greeks, and both paid a bitter price for following him. Shut out from the synagogues and the temples, they were compelled to meet in their own houses, Jews and Gentiles together, secretly and generally at night. When Paul had to go forward on his pilgrimage he laid hands on some, and appointed them to be elders to protect the flock from the wolves that would fall on them when the shepherd was gone.

He wrote to them constantly. His letters must have been many, although only fourteen have come down to us, and not all of these are authentic.

That any remain seems little short of miraculous unless we assume that, believed to be sacred, they were preserved as the words of God. We have the first Epistle to the Thessalonians. This is the earliest piece of Christian literature known to the world, and it was written, as far as we can judge, about A.D. 48. It gives a marvellous picture in short space of the man writing, the people being written to, the age they lived in, and the faith they held in common. The superscription alone tells everything:

Paul, and Silvanus, and Timotheus, unto the Church of the Thessalonians, which is in God, the Father and in the Lord Jesus

Christ; Grace be unto you, and peace, from God our Father, and the Lord Jesus Christ.

It has been well said that if this alone had fallen into the hands of one of the Roman philosophers of the time it must have left him speechless. "God I have heard of," he would have thought, "but who is this Lord Jesus Christ? And who are these Jews who call themselves by Roman names?"

But, unknown to Rome, the tide of the new faith was rising. Before the end of Paul's mission, there were, probably, thousands of Christians on the Mediterranean coast. Nothing daunted the little Jew who believed he was especially ordained of God to call in the Gentiles. It was almost as if he thought he had to wipe out from the record in the Book of Life the scores, perhaps hundreds, of martyrdoms he had inflicted on the saints in Jerusalem in the days when he hounded them out of the synagogues, and compelled them to curse Christ or go to their deaths like Stephen.

Thus fourteen years passed, and then Paul's strength began to fail him. He could hardly have been much more than fifty years of age, yet he called himself "old Paul," and no wonder. Scourged, beaten in the public streets, thrown into dungeons uncondemned, stoned and cast out of the cities for dead, or escaping from his enemies in the night, according to his own account, three times flogged, twice shipwrecked, a night and a day in the sea, in peril of robbers, of the heathen, of his own countrymen, of his open enemies, of false brethren, in hunger, in thirst, in cold and nakedness, and perhaps beset through it all by a chronic disease—he saw his pilgrimage coming to an end. Yet the Spirit that was always speaking to him in his weariness and painfulness told him he must return to Jerusalem for the last time and then see Rome.

How often he had broken his missionary journeying by visits to Palestine we do not know with certainty, but this time, on his way back, he passed through Macedonia and Achaia, and there he gathered up contributions from his Gentile converts towards the support of the little parent Church in Jerusalem, which was probably still living in community and consequently poor. It had ministered to them in spiritual things, he said; therefore it was their duty to minister to it in carnal things.

When his time came to turn his face homewards, he sent for the elders at Ephesus to meet him at Miletus.

He told them he was bound in the Spirit to go up to Jerusalem, although he did not know what might befall him there. But neither bonds nor afflictions moved him, and he did not count his life dear, if only he could finish with joy the ministry he had received from God. He had nothing to regret. He had kept the faith. He had preached the kingdom of Heaven, and therefore he was pure from the blood of all men. He had coveted no man's silver or gold or apparel. His own hands had ministered to his necessities, and he had laboured to support the weak, remembering the words of Jesus that it was more blessed to give than to receive. And now he had to say farewell to them, for they would see his face no more.

The elders wept and kissed him, sorrowing most because he had said they should see his face no more, and then accompanied him to the trading ship that was to take him home.

He landed at Tyre, for it was there the ship had to unlade her cargo.

Tyre was a notoriously wicked city, an island port, inhabited chiefly by sailors from all parts of the world. We do not know that any of the evangelists had visited it. Even Jesus himself seems to have stopped on its borders. But Paul found disciples there, and perhaps it is permitted to us to think they may have been the friends and descendants of the Canaanite woman who, praying for mercy for her afflicted daughter (if the story is authentic), said the Christ-like words: "Truth, Lord, yet the dogs eat of the crumbs which fall from their master's table."

Paul stayed some days with the disciples at Tyre, and when he spoke of going up to Jerusalem they begged of him not to, but seeing he was determined to go they brought him on his way as far as the shore outside the city, and there they knelt and prayed.

Only those who know the place can feel to the full the emotion of that moment. On the desolate shore south of the Sodomite city, with the blue waves breaking white over the reefs in front, the apostle, old before his time, surrounded by the men and their wives and children on their knees, singing, with only the sea to hear them, the psalm of their father David:

> The Lord is my shepherd, I shall not want. . . . Yea, though I walk through the valley of the shadow of death, I will fear no evil, for thou art with me; thy rod and thy staff they comfort me.

Two days later Paul reached Cæsarea. James, the evangelist, who had fled from Jerusalem during the persecutions by Paul which followed the stoning of Stephen, was now living there, with four daughters believed to have the power of prophecy. News of Paul's arrival soon reached Jerusalem, and another prophet came down to Cæsarea. He took Paul's girdle and binding his own hands and feet with it, perhaps to make the similitude of a prisoner in the stocks, said, "So shall the Jews at Jerusalem bind the man that owneth this girdle, and shall deliver him into the hands of the Gentiles."

Seeing this, Paul's companions besought him not to go up to Jerusalem. Paul was moved, but immovable.

"What mean ye to weep and to break mine heart?" he said, "for I am ready not to be bound only, but also to die at Jerusalem for the name of the Lord Jesus."

"The will of the Lord be done," they answered, and taking up their carriages (their travelling baggage) they went up with him afoot to Jerusalem, probably setting out on their long day's journey at dawn in the morning.

II. The Temper of Jerusalem

There had been serious happenings to the Church in Jerusalem since that meeting in the house of James, the brother of Jesus, and though there are illuminating references in *Acts* we have to go to sources outside for a full account of them.

The son of Agrippa, seventeen years of age at the death of his father, had been thought to be too young to govern his father's kingdom, so Agrippa's brother, Herod, the king of Chalcis, was given authority over the Temple and its treasury and the choice of the high priests, while Cuspius Fadus was made procurator of Judæa.

Fadus had proved to be a relentless enemy of the Jews and Herod of the Christians. Together, for eight years, they had kept Palestine in perpetual tumult and turmoil. Clearly, there had been a great deal of religious activity, although the Jewish historian calls it by another name. Men whom the Jews thought divinely inspired had been continually appearing. One such was Theudas (not to be confounded with the person of the same name mentioned by Gamaliel at the trial of Stephen), who persuaded a great part of the people to take their effects and follow him to Jordan, promising to divide the river, as Moses had divided the Red Sea on the flight of the Israelites from Egypt. Apparently, this was intended to lead the Jews out of the land in which they were crushed by their Roman taskmasters, but Fadus sent a troop of horsemen after them, fell upon them unawares, slew many of them, captured their leader, cut off his head and carried it back to Jerusalem.

Fadus was recalled and another procurator (first Alexander and then Ventidius Cumanus) took his place, but he was no more merciful than his predecessor, and two sons of Judas the Galilean, trying to follow in the footsteps of their father, were crucified.

Meantime, Herod of Chalcis appointed to the high priesthood Ananias (not to be confounded with the high priest by courtesy who had conspired against Jesus), and together with Fadus's successor he contributed (not without cause) to a tumult in Jerusalem at the time of the Passover, which resulted in the destruction of 20,000 Jews, who were crushed to death in the narrow streets about the Temple while flying from the Roman soldiers.

Then Herod died, and the procurator and high priest quarrelled over certain tragic consequences of the custom of the Galileans to come to their festivals in Jerusalem through Samaria (as mentioned in *Luke*), whereupon both the high priest and the procurator were sent by the governor of Syria to Rome where the emperor Claudius sided with the high priest and banished the procurator, appointing Felix in his place. This was in A.D. 52.

Felix was no better than the man he had succeeded. We are told in *Acts* that he had a Jewish wife, named Drusilla. This was the youngest daughter of Agrippa, one of the two daughters whom as children the people of Cæsarea had insulted after the death of their father. When Felix, who, according to the Roman historian Tacitus, had many wives, first met Drusilla she was the wife of a pagan prince and a woman of great beauty. Felix, falling in love with her, did what Antipas had done before him—persuaded the lady to forsake her husband and marry him, promising to make her a happy woman.

Meantime, Agrippa, the younger, a young reprobate with devil's dues in him, had been made king of his father's dominions in A.D. 48, and he continued Ananias in his high priesthood. Claudius Cæsar was now dead, and Nero, at seventeen years of age, had become emperor (A.D. 54), and he in like manner continued Felix in his office.

Better matched than before, the procurator and the high priest

LIFE OF CHRIST

now showed no mercy to the enemies of either church or state. Some of these, claiming, like John the Baptist, to be divinely inspired, led the people into the wilderness, where they performed, or were said to perform, wonders and signs by the providence of God. One such person was an Egyptian, whom the Jews took to be a prophet, although the historian calls him a robber. Gathering 4,000 Jews, he led them up to the Mount of Olives, saying that from hence, at his command, the walls of Jerusalem would fall down, and then they would enter and possess the city. Felix followed them up with horsemen and footmen, killed 400 and took 200 alive, the Egyptian escaping and being heard of no more except in the Bible story.

Without even reading between the lines of the Jewish historian it is not difficult to say what these insurrections were—outbursts of futile and pitiful nationalism on the part of the poorer and more pious Jews against the extortions, the fleecing and the tyranny of the Roman procurator, helped out by the interested acquiescence of the high priests, bad men both.

Meantime, in the midst of these eruptions of tyranny and fanaticism, the little Church at Jerusalem had had to walk warily. The one thing it had had to avoid was open rupture with the Temple. Under the temperate guidance of James it had hitherto done so. Clearly, it had not taken sides with any of the rebels against the Roman authority or the Jewish hierarchy. As a result it had greatly increased in numbers, many Jews having joined it under the impression that Christianity was only another and more inspiring form of Judaism. It cannot too often be said that the early Church in Jerusalem had never, for one moment, thought that in becoming Christians they had ceased to be Jews, and turned their back on the law of Moses and the rites and customs of the religion of their forefathers.

But now in these latter years, apparently between A.D. 54 and A.D. 58, a great danger threatened it.

It had come from Paul. Rumour had reached Jerusalem of what Paul had been doing in distant countries. The unbelieving Jews scattered abroad in Corinth, Thessalonica, Ephesus and elsewhere, who had tried to punish Paul for blasphemy, and had had him snatched out of their hands by the Roman deputies and governors, had been writing to their fellow-Jews and to the high priests at Jerusalem denouncing him as a heretic.

His heresy had been twofold, first in preaching to the Gentiles and receiving them into the company of Jews without circumcision, and, next, in discouraging the people of his own race from circumcising their children and thus teaching them to forsake Moses. This was a crime punishable only with death. The man who was guilty of it was not fit to live. Such was the temper of Jerusalem when Paul set out for home, and such were the facts known to his friends at Cæsarea when they tried to restrain him from returning to Jerusalem.

III. Paul in Jerusalem

Paul had desired to reach Jerusalem by the Day of Pentecost (the feast equivalent to the modern harvest thanksgiving), and apparently he did so. The city was then full of foreign Jews, many of them from Asia, and other countries in which he had travelled.

Probably he arrived at night, after his long journey over the rough road from Cæsarea. Next day he went to see James, and found all the elders of the Church with him.

The brethren received him gladly, and after he had delivered to them the contributions sent by the converts in Macedonia and Achaia, he told them the story of what great things God had wrought by his ministry among the Gentiles, saying nothing that we know of about the price he had paid for them.

When they heard it they rejoiced, and then they, on their part, told Paul of the multitudes that had been added during his absence to the Church at Jerusalem.

After that, there was more to say, and it was not easy to say it.

> Thou seest, brother [it was clearly the voice of James], how many thousands of Jews there are in Jerusalem that believe; yet they are all zealous of the law. But they have been informed of thee that thou teachest the Jews among the Gentiles to forsake Moses, not to circumcise their children or to walk after the customs.

It was right that he should have taught the Gentiles that they need lay no burden of Jewish rites and customs upon themselves, for had they not written two letters to them to say so? But with the Jews the case was different. The Jews must keep the law and so must their teacher.

The matter was urgent. The multitude of Jews who had joined

the Church would hear of Paul's arrival and would come together to see him. What should he do?

This is what they thought he should do.

They had four men in Jerusalem at the moment who had a vow on them. Let Paul take these four men and purify himself with them, so that all might know that the stories they had heard of his apostacy were nothing, that he walked orderly and kept the law.

Paul obeyed the command of the head and elders of his Church, took the four men, and next day entered the Temple with them.

But before the seven days of purification were ended, a number of the Jews from Asia, who had seen Paul in the meantime walking in the city with a pagan convert from Ephesus, and had supposed that this was one of the four men whom he had brought into the Temple, stirred up the Jews of Jerusalem against him, crying, "Men of Israel, help! This is the man who teaches all men everywhere against the law, and now he has brought Greeks into this holy place and polluted it."

At this the Jews laid hold of Paul, flung him out of the Temple and shut the doors on him.

The Temple courts and corridors, usually full of people during the Feast of Pentecost, as well as the narrow streets about them, in which 20,000 persons had, not long before, been crushed to death, were soon in a state of tumult. The people were buffeting and beating Paul as if trying to kill him. Word reached the Roman captain of the guard that Jerusalem was in an uproar, and he ran down with soldiers, rescued Paul from the crowd, commanded that he should be bound with two chains, equivalent to handcuffs and anklets, and demanded to be told who he was and what he had done.

In the general clamour some said one thing and some another, and when the captain could learn nothing with certainty he ordered that Paul should be carried to the castle.

The crowd followed through the streets of Jerusalem, crying, "Away with him," and the violence of the people became so threatening that the soldiers had to lift their prisoner up the steps on to the bridge that led to the castle gate.

As Paul was being hurried into the castle, he asked the captain if he might speak to him.

"Canst thou speak Greek?" asked the captain. And then, having concluded that Paul was a criminal, who had probably attempted to rob the Temple, he said:

"Art thou not that Egyptian who before this day made an uproar and led 4,000 murderers into the wilderness?"

"I am a Jew of Tarsus, a citizen of no mean city," said Paul, "and I beseech thee to suffer me to speak to the people."

From the steps of the castle Paul was permitted to do so. He spoke in Hebrew, and when the people heard the sacred language of the synagogue, they were silent and listened.

He told them who and what he was—a Jew like themselves, brought up in their own city, at the school of Gamaliel, being taught according to the strictest manner of the law of their fathers, and as zealous towards God as they all were that day.

More than that, in his youth he had done what they were now doing; persecuted to the death those whom he had believed to be enemies of the law, both men and women.

But after that the Lord had spoken to him. On his way to Damascus, with authority from the high priests of the time to bring the brethren who had fled to that place back to Jerusalem to be punished, a blinding light had shone upon him, and a voice from Heaven had cried, in the Hebrew tongue: "Saul, Saul, why persecutest thou me?"

It had been the voice of Jesus of Nazareth, risen from the dead, and he had answered, "What shall I do, Lord?" And then, and again later, he had been told what he was to do. He was to be baptized to wash away his sins, and then he was to go far hence to the Gentiles all over the world, to open their eyes, and turn their darkness into light, that they, too, might receive forgiveness of sins, and share in the inheritance of those who were sanctified by faith.

At that last word the silence of the audience was broken. The Jews were enraged. The information they had received from foreign countries was true. The man had admitted everything. He had been corrupting the chosen people. So they lifted up their voices and cried:

"Away with such a fellow from the earth. He is not fit to live."

The chief captain commanded that Paul should be brought into the castle. But he was not satisfied with Paul's explanation, and thinking he had been keeping something back, he did what his emperor in Rome was at that time doing constantly—ordered that his prisoner should be examined by scourging, so that he might reveal the true reason why the Jews were crying out so frantically against him.

While Paul was being bound, with the examining officers standing by, he did what his Master, who was only a Jew, could not do when, thirteen years earlier, on the same spot, or near it, he was scourged by Roman soldiers at the command of Pilate—turned to the centurion who was to carry out his ordeal and asked, "Is it lawful for you to scourge a man that is a Roman, and uncondemned?"

The centurion took that paralysing word to the chief captain, who came back to Paul and said, "Tell me, art thou a Roman?"

Paul answered, "Yea."

The chief captain, in spite of his Roman name, Claudius Lysias, was probably a Greek, who had purchased his Roman citizenship in order to become an officer in the Roman army. He said, "With a great sum obtained I this freedom."

"But I," said Paul, perhaps with a lift of the head, "was free born."

The examining officers were dismissed, Paul was sent to his cell, and the chief captain returned to his own apartments.

But still the chief captain, being a pagan, was perplexed, and on the morrow, that he might know with certainty wherefore Paul was accused by the Jews, he called the chief priests and their council to the castle and set his prisoner before them.

It was a kind of informal inquiry, rather than a Sanhedrin, probably held in the open air, in front of the castle, the high priest sitting in the middle of a half-circle, and the prisoner in front of him, with an officer of the Temple on either side.

When Paul was called upon to speak, he said, "Men and brethren, I have lived in all good conscience before God until this day."

This was said to prove his sincerity as a Jew, but to the high priest, Ananias, it was a blasphemous falsehood, and he called upon the officers of the Temple who stood by Paul to smite him on the mouth.

That was too much for the fiery little Jew, who, lacking his Master's sublime self-control in a similar circumstance, but using some of his language, cried, "God smite thee, thou whited wall;

for seekest thou to judge me after the law, and commandest me to be smitten contrary to the law?"

The rest of the proceedings were disorderly. Perceiving that, while his chief judge was a Sadducee, some of his council belonged to the opposing sect, Paul cried out that he was a Pharisee, the son of a Pharisee, and the only ground of his offence was that he had been preaching the doctrine of the resurrection from the dead—the Resurrection of Jesus of Nazareth, who had appeared to him on his way to Damascus.

This divided the council. The scribes and the Pharisees said they found no fault in the man; and if a spirit or an angel had spoken to him from the sky let them not fight against God.

It was the voice of Gamaliel again, but this time it provoked violent dissension, and the chief captain, fearing lest Paul should be pulled in pieces between the contending parties, ordered his soldiers to take him from them by force, and bring him into the castle.

The chief captain saw now that Paul was no murderer like the Egyptian or pretender Theudas, but, if he had to keep the peace, what was he to do with the man? The Jews themselves found his own answer.

Next day forty of the Jews bound themselves together under a curse, saying they would neither eat nor drink till they had killed Paul. They had a plan for doing so, and according to the Christian historian they took it to the chief priests and elders.

It was this: that the council should ask the chief captain to send Paul down to their own chamber, in order that they might inquire more carefully into his case, and that on his way between the castle and the Temple (about a quarter of a mile) they should fall on him and kill him.

It seems almost incredible that the most fanatical high priest should have been so foolhardy as to participate in such a perilous conspiracy, but there is reason to believe that he did.

There was a nephew of Paul, the son of his sister, living in Jerusalem at that time, and, hearing of the conspiracy, he obtained entrance to the castle and revealed it to his uncle, whereupon Paul, calling one of the centurions, asked him to take the young man to the chief captain, for he had something to tell him.

The chief captain must have received the request of the high priest by this time, for he acted like one who had no doubt of the young man's story. He ordered that soldiers should make ready to go to Cæsarea immediately, and then wrote a letter to Felix, the procurator, telling what had happened and saying he was sending the prisoner and commanding his accusers to follow him.

In the middle of that night Paul, riding a beast and accompanied by seventy horsemen, left Jerusalem for Cæsarea. He never returned to Jerusalem.

This must have been in the summer of A.D. 58.

IV. Felix and Festus

Antonius Felix behaved according to his kind. He had good reason not to offend the high priest if he could avoid doing so, therefore he committed Paul to Herod the Great's judgment-hall (his prison) to await the arrival of Ananias and the elders.

They were in no hurry to come, but after five days they arrived, bringing with them a public orator, or advocate, named Tertullus.

This man, a Jew and a lawyer, was just as incapable as the priestly classes of realizing that the Roman empire had firmly and highly resolved to have nothing to do with questions of religious law and custom among their subject peoples. He began the trial of Paul with the customary flattering of the Roman judge, saying that the Jewish people were thankful for the great quietness they had enjoyed under the rule of the most noble Felix.

It was false. Felix had then been six years procurator of Judæa, and nearly every day in his calendar had been stained with its trail of blood. He then proceeded to denounce the prisoner.

Paul was a pestilent fellow, a mover of sedition among all Jews throughout the world, and a ringleader among the sect of the Nazarenes. Lately he had profaned the Temple, and when they took him and would have judged him according to their law, the chief captain Lysias had taken him with great violence out of their hands and commanded them to accuse him before the governor.

If Felix had been as eager to serve the cause of Roman justice as he was anxious to please the high priest and his council, the trial must have come to an end the moment Tertullus sat down. But he beckoned to Paul to reply, and the old man did so in a brief and biting speech.

He said it was only twelve days since he returned to Jerusalem, and during that time nobody had seen him raising up the people either in the Temple or the city or the synagogues. If Jews from Asia had anything to say to the contrary, why had they not come to say it there?

But to one thing he freely confessed—that after the way the high priest and his elders called heresy, he worshipped the God of his fathers and believed everything that was written in the law and the prophets.

That was his real offence in the eyes of his accusers—not merely that he had gathered into the family of the Jews the Gentiles who might refuse their governance, but that he had believed that there should be a resurrection from the dead, which they did not believe, being Sadducees.

Felix had now no excuse for not seeing that the accusation against Paul was a matter outside his jurisdiction. But as the prosecution had charged the Roman chief captain with obstructing the Jewish authorities in the exercise of their own law, he adjourned the inquiry until Lysias could come down from Jerusalem.

Lysias never came down. To keep peace with the high priest Felix knew better than to call him. So Paul remained at Cæsarea two years on parole to a centurion.

Meantime Felix, who, according to the Roman historian, had broken nearly every law of his country, with his Jewish wife Drusilla, who had outraged the law of Moses in leaving her husband and living in adultery with a pagan, sent for Paul on certain days and heard him on his faith in Christ.

It was the scene over again of Herod Antipas and Herodias calling for John the Baptist during his imprisonment in the grim old fortress by the Dead Sea. Paul did not spare the guilty pair. He spoke not only of righteousness and temperance, but of judgment to come, for he believed in hell as well as Heaven. Felix trembled. "Go thy way for this time," he said. "When I have a more convenient season I will call for thee."

The more convenient season never came. After two years, Felix was removed from his procuratorship of Judæa and Samaria and finally accused at Rome, and thinking "to show the Jews a pleasure" he left Paul bound.

His successor, Porcius Festus, who came early in A.D. 60 was a better man altogether, with a high sense of Roman justice. Three days after his arrival at his headquarters in Cæsarea, he went up to Jerusalem, and there the high priest and the notables approached him about Paul. The apostle was muzzled and chained, but as long as the old dog lived there was no knowing where he would break out next, so they wanted him dead and done with.

Following some further parleying with the priests, Paul was asked by Festus if he would go up to Jerusalem to be judged by him, after he had met his accusers face to face—a binding condition of Roman law, although Pilate, fourteen years before, according to the writer of the fourth Gospel, had forgotten it.

Paul refused. "I have done no wrong to the Jews," he said, "therefore no man may deliver me unto them. I appeal to Cæsar."

He was within his rights. It says something for Roman justice that the humblest citizen of the Roman empire, in the smallest of its dependencies, being accused of a crime punishable with death, could appeal over the heads of the judges of his own people, his own king and even the Roman governor, to the emperor himself.

Some days later King Agrippa the younger came to Cæsarea to pay his respects to Festus. He was thirty-one years of age, and not much of a Jew, although Josephus praises him. In his graceless youth in Rome he had been openly charged with criminal conversation with his sister Berenice. And now with his wife, another Berenice, he was returning to the place in which his father had met his miserable end.

Festus told Agrippa about the man whom Felix had left behind, and how the high priest and the elders desired to have judgment against him. But their accusations seemed to concern questions of their own superstitions only, and of one Jesus, whom the Jews said was dead but Paul affirmed was alive. He had wished to take the man up to Jerusalem to be tried by him, in the presence of the high priest and his people, but being a Roman, he had demanded to be heard by Cæsar. Yet how was he to send a prisoner to his lord the emperor without signifying the crimes that were laid against him?

"I will hear the man myself," said Agrippa.

On the morrow, Agrippa came to the place of hearing, in great pomp with his queen, and Paul was summoned.

Paul's defence was both moving and subtle. Stretching forth his hand, after the manner of the Romans, thus conciliating Festus, he conciliated the king also, who was only half a Jew, by saying he was happy to answer for himself before one who was expert in all the laws and customs of the Jews. He was a Jew of Jews; and because he lived in hope of the promise God had made to their fathers, he stood accused before his king that day.

After that he told once more his great story of the Voice that spoke to him from the sky on his way to Damascus, and what it had told him to do. How could he be disobedient to that heavenly vision? He could not. Therefore, he had gone out to the Gentiles, saying nothing except those things which Moses and the prophets had said would come—that Christ should suffer, that he should be the first that should rise from the dead, that he should call all men to repentance and show light both to the Jews and Gentiles, having made of one blood all nations of men that dwell on the face of the earth; and that this Christ was Jesus of Nazareth, who had been put to death and buried, but was alive again.

Festus was as much bewildered by all this as the Epicureans and Stoics on Mars Hill had been, and cried, "Paul, thou art beside thyself. Much learning doth make thee mad."

"I am not mad, most noble Festus," said Paul. "The king knows these things, for they were not done in a corner. King Agrippa, believest thou the prophets? I know thou believest."

Agrippa was afraid to deny the prophets, although he had broken their precepts. "Almost thou persuadest me to be a Christian," he said.

And Paul replied, "I would to God, that not only thou, but also all that hear me this day, were both almost, and altogether such as I am, except these bonds."

The king rose, and speaking to the queen and the governor apart, he said, "This man might have been set at liberty if he had not appealed unto Cæsar."

But Paul had appealed to Cæsar, and to Cæsar he must go. A little later, in the charge of a centurion, he set sail for Rome.

This must have been in the autumn of A.D. 60.

V. Towards Rome

Why Paul refused to be tried by the high priest and his council is clear. Although they could not stone him to death while Festus was in Judæa, they could cast him out of the synagogues and cut him off from his people, both at home and abroad. And why he appealed to Cæsar is no less certain. It was not to save his life, for

Festus could have done that, but, by escaping from the condemnation of the Sanhedrin, to keep his inheritance as a Jew, on which above all else, except his apostleship, he prided himself.

But perhaps he had another reason. Not on the road to Damascus only, but everywhere and always he believed voices from Heaven were speaking to him. One of these voices had told him, in certain of his darkest hours, to be of good cheer, for after he had been to Jerusalem he would go to Rome. And now that he was going, though he was going as a prisoner, his heart was light.

With his centurion as guard, a number of other prisoners and their guards, and his "beloved physician" Luke as companion, he sailed northward, past Tyre, the infamous island seaport with its thicket of ships' masts in the rocky harbour, like a forest of pine trees in winter, and its tall houses standing up against the sky like turrets. They are all down now, and twice a day the sea is awash over them. On the hills behind Tyre were the cedars of Lebanon, the glistening sources of the Jordan and the snowy heights of Hermon.

Next day they put in at Sidon, where Paul was permitted to say farewell to his friends, and then stood out for the coasts of Asia, sailing over the Sea of Cilicia, with his native place Tarsus, "no mean city," ten miles inland, a gray speck to the north on the rolling uplands. Paul was seeing it all for the last time.

Owing to contrary winds they passed under Cyprus, and then drove across to Myra, a city in Lycia. There the centurion found a ship from Alexandria laden with wheat and bound for Italy, and Paul and his fellow-prisoners were re-embarked in her. They were now 276 souls in all, including the soldiers and the crew.

With a strong south wind blowing, sailing was slow and dangerous and they took shelter in the "Fair Havens," in Crete, but on leaving these they were caught in a cyclone, and being in danger from the storm they cast out the ship's tackling, and afterwards the wheat of her cargo.

For many days and nights they saw neither sun nor stars, and the shipmaster and his crew lost all hope of saving their ship or their lives. But Paul's confidence never failed him. In this hour of greatest peril his Voice spoke to him again telling him to have no fear, for he must reach Rome, and be brought before Cæsar, therefore neither he nor his shipmates would come to harm.

"Be of good cheer, sirs," he said, "for I believe God will do even as He told me, and not a hair shall fall from the heads of any of you."

At this they all took heart, and ate, having fasted before, and at length, seeing land, they hoisted their mainsail and made for it. But falling into a place where two seas met, their ship ran aground, and stuck fast, and the vessel was broken to pieces by the violence of the waves.

Then the soldiers were for killing the prisoners lest they should swim ashore and escape, but for Paul's sake his centurion dissuaded them from this, and on planks and boards every soul came safe to land.

They were then on the island of Melita, and it was winter, but after staying three months there they found another ship from Alexandria, the *Castor and Pollux* bound for Puteoli, the modern Pozzuoli, on the Bay of Naples. And with a fair wind following, they sailed north under the fiery hills of Italy on their last stretch to Rome.

VI. St. Paul in Rome

It is clear that more material things than his heavenly voices were calling Paul to Rome. There was a church there, and he wished to visit it. He must have known as early as A.D. 49 that the Jews had been expelled from Rome, for it was then that he met Aquila and Priscilla at Corinth "lately come from Italy," having been banished by the emperor's edict. Yet six or seven years later he wrote from the same city to the Romans, saying that their faith was "spoken of throughout the world."

Some happenings of importance to the Church in Rome must have taken place in the meantime. What they were and what their experiences had been, we may partly see later, when we come to consider the public life of another apostle of Christianity.

In his letter to the Romans, Paul mentions a number of names which we have never heard before. Obviously, some of them were his own people who had gone to Rome before him. Others may have been, like Aquila and Priscilla, Roman Christians whom he had met during the years of their exile. To all he sends affectionate salutations.

"I have been much hindered in coming to you," he says; but whensoever after his next visit to Jerusalem he makes a journey into Spain, he will come to them.

He landed from his ship with his centurion and his companion Luke, at Puteoli, and found some of the Christians of that place were waiting for him. A few days later he went afoot to Rome. It would be spring, and the flowers of Italy's sunny land would be blooming by the wayside. At the "Three Taverns" about twenty miles outside Rome, the brethren of the Roman Church met him, and when he saw them he thanked God and took fresh courage.

At the gates of the city the brethren appear to have left him, for we never hear of any of them again. His centurion delivered him to the captain of the guard, who may have been an officer of the royal regiment, but more probably was a policeman from the prefecture.

The emperor, as we shall see, was too much occupied at that time with more amusing activities to hear Paul's case immediately, so the Roman-Jew who had appealed to Cæsar over the heads of his own rulers had to wait for his leisure.

He waited two years for it, living in the meantime in his own hired house, at his own expense, with a soldier to guard him night and day.

Strangely enough, no trace of the locality of this house remains in Roman traditions. Perhaps it was in proximity to the royal palace, for Paul was in frequent contact with servants of the royal household, and some of them became his friends and converts. Perhaps it was in the neighbourhood of the barracks of the soldiers, to meet their convenience in changing guard. But more probably it was in some mean quarter of the Trastavere, under the shadow of the Janiculum, with the turbulent waters of the Tiber in front and a clear view to the left of the paved way to the circus on the hill of the Vatican, to which Cæsar drove in his chariot to take his pleasure in gladiatorial shows.

For six years Paul's voices had called him to Rome. He had come to it in chains.

CHAPTER IX

The Missionary Work of St. Paul
(Continued)

I. St. Paul in Rome

THERE MAY HAVE BEEN no Christians living within the walls of Rome at the time of Paul's arrival, but there were many Jews, and three days later Paul sent for the chief of them.

He told them that although he had nothing of which to accuse his nation he had been compelled to appeal to Cæsar, and he had called them together that they might know that for nothing worse than his faithfulness to the hope of Israel he had been bound with the chains in which they saw him.

What more he said then we can only surmise from the answer they made him—that they had received no letters about him from Judæa, and as for the sect called the Nazarenes they desired to be told what he thought about them, since everywhere in Rome they were hearing them condemned.

A day was appointed for this purpose, and the chief of the Jews came again to Paul's lodgings and there, from morning to evening, he showed them out of the law of Moses and out of the prophets that Christ was foretold, and that he had come in the person of Jesus of Nazareth.

Some of them believed, but the majority did not believe, for it is clear that Paul drove them out of doors, with biting words from *Isaiah,* saying their ears were dull of hearing and their eyes were closed, and the salvation of God was henceforth to the Gentiles.

Paul then set himself to the only task remaining to a prisoner— the writing of further letters to the Churches he had founded among the Gentiles.

Six of these letters have come down to us, stamped with his name as having been written in Rome, and though it is possible that he wrote many more during the two years of his imprisonment, it is not certain that all we have are authentic.

1213

Apparently, they were dictated to disciples he made in Rome, for the Roman authorities left him at liberty to receive all that came to him, and (his material disability apart) it was not easy for him to use his own hand, which was chained day and night to a soldier.

The letters were usually sent by hand to their destinations, with instructions that each of them was to be read aloud to the Church to which it was addressed, and then passed on to the other Churches.

Men of learning in all ages have disputed about their dates, their authenticity and their teaching, and century after century their judgments on these points have changed, and they are still changing. On one thing only have they agreed—that the letters of the prisoner from his obscure lodging in Rome have shaken the world to its foundations.

Searching in thought, majestic in phrases, charged with nearly every emotion that moves the human heart, they have so woven themselves into the language of man that passages from them have become a part of the common speech of all peoples. In this respect there is nothing to compare with them except the words that were spoken among the hills of Galilee.

For centuries after they were written they influenced profoundly the greatest of minds. One of these said of one of Paul's letters, "It is my wife; I have betrothed myself to it." Others questioned and condemned them on historic, chronological, psychological and even doctrinal grounds, and still others pronounced certain of them to be spurious. Some of these differences came out of the thunders of sectarian quarrels, and some of the smoke that issued from "the narrow apertures of single texts."

It is not the duty of the historian to discuss the teaching of Paul's letters, except so far as it casts a light on the history of Christianity. But in discharging this task (having no dogmas to attack or defend) he sees how far Paul was, in his letters written in Rome, from the Christianity which was soon to follow him.

The flash and play of Paul's brilliant pen, in which two voices often seem to be speaking at once, may have confused learned men, in all ages, but the steady gaze of the independent mind has no difficulty in seeing what he intended to say for himself.

First, that Jesus of Nazareth was the greatest being that ever lived on the earth—that he was the Christ; that the Christ was greater than the rabbis or even the prophets had said; that he had been with God from before the beginning of the world and would be with Him until after the end of it; that through him and by him God had given redemption and salvation to all His sinful children, and that at his name every knee should bow.

So high did St. Paul place Jesus above all other men, so completely within the realm of the divine, that sometimes as we read his letters we are startled by the thought that he is writing about one who, little more than twenty-five years before, was walking in the streets of Jerusalem with persons who were still alive and had eaten and drunk with him.

Yet Paul does not intend to speak (and never, except in one questionable passage, does speak) of Jesus as a part of the Godhead. On the contrary, he says more than once that God is one, and there is no other God than one.

Next, Paul in his letters intends to speak of the Holy Ghost as the divine spirit which Christ sent to his brethren on earth, after he had left them and ascended into Heaven, to comfort them, to strengthen them, to guide them and to inspire them, but never does he say that the Holy Ghost is a part of the divinity.

Next, Paul in his letters does not say anything about the mystery of the Holy Trinity, three persons in one God, for if he had done that he would never have stood up in the synagogue, and all his life he had been doing so.

Again, Paul in his letters does not speak about the "hypostatic union," which was later to be known as the mystery of the Incarnation. He believed with the prophets that Christ, and therefore Jesus, was the son of David according to the flesh, but he never says that at his birth Jesus was not subject to the common rule. He speaks constantly of "Our Lord," but never of "Our Lady."

He refers to the mothers and even to grandmothers of certain of his converts, but he never mentions the mother of Jesus. He speaks little of the facts of Jesus's life on earth, apart from the supreme ones of his death and Resurrection. He has never heard the report of the raising of Lazarus or, if he has, he has refused to believe it, since it would have destroyed his great proof that Jesus was the Christ, and that this was proved by the fact that he was the first to rise from the dead.

He quotes frequently Moses and Elijah and Isaiah, but rarely Jesus. Most of the great sayings in Galilee, the wonderful parables about the kingdom of Heaven and the sublime utterances on the

Mount of Olives must have been unknown to him, or they would have burst again into flame on his fiery lips.

He believed in baptism, although, like his Master, he rarely practised it, and then not always by immersion (for sometimes that was impossible); but this was his only sacrament, and he thought it an outward sign of an inward repentance, and he would have shown as short shrift to the Gentile Christians who rejected the unbaptized as he did to the Christianized Jews who refused the uncircumcised.

He continued the brotherly meals which the early apostles ate on the first day of the week in remembrance of the Resurrection, but (notwithstanding certain difficult words in one of his letters) he thought the body and blood of Jesus was in the souls of believers, not in the bread and wine consumed by them.

He believed that Christ would come again, but he knew nothing of the time of his coming, that it would be within the lifetime of the first disciples, and therefore he did not watch their mortality as if expecting to see Christ's Second Advent before the last of them had fallen asleep.

He believed in the resurrection of all just men, just as he believed in the Resurrection of Christ, but it would be a spiritual resurrection, not of the natural body, which had been laid in the grave and gone to corruption, but of a celestial body that had none of the wounds and inferiorities of life on it, as Christ's body had had none of the scars of the Cross.

He believed in hell, but it was the hell of the lost soul, which, like the soul of the rich man while Lazarus was in Abraham's bosom, would see the Heaven of love and purity and forgiveness for ever out of its reach, not the physical hell of everlasting fire which would consume without consuming—an unthinkable thing which his instructed mind could not conceive of for a moment.

Above all, though his words were sometimes "difficult," Paul sent out his gospel in no uncertain form, and it was also very human and very clear. It was founded solely on faith, and grounded on three supreme propositions; First, that deep in the heart of man, great and small, rich and poor, wise and simple, there was the consciousness of sin; that however he might shuffle off the burden of his transgressions against his fellow-men in this world by bearing their worldly penalties, or against himself by forgetting them in the pleasures and temptations of this life, an eternity was before him, in which his naked soul would stand face to face with his Master, and then his sins would be sins against God.

Next, that man was helpless to save himself from everlasting consequences of eternal justice; and last, that his heavenly Father had ordained that Jesus, His beloved Son, His Christ, had so loved him that he had died to wipe out his sin, and make his peace with God.

Such, speaking broadly, was the gospel which Paul sent out to his Churches among the Gentiles. In this, to the greatest of the early Christians, stood all Christianity.

But through the splendid web of his sublimest thoughts runs the homely woof of his personal affections. He remembers his converts in far-off countries, and writes to them as a father might write to his children.

Sometimes he chides and rebukes them, checking their vainglory and denouncing their vices, commanding them to compose their quarrels like brothers, and not to let the sun go down on their wrath. But usually he cheers them with praise, telling them to be of good comfort, to stand fast in the faith, to quit themselves like men, to be strong, to put on the whole armour of God, knowing that a crown of victory and joy is coming to them.

He mentions a great number of them by name, lest any should think they are forgotten. One of them is his "son," begotten to him during his imprisonment; another is his "true yoke-fellow." He never forgets the women. Some are born to honour and some to dishonour; but it is the duty of man to be tender to all of them.

"I intreat thee," he says, ". . . help those women which laboured with me in the gospel . . . Whose names are in the Book of Life."

They are in his book also. Nearly half the names in his letters are the names of women. "Salute your mother and mine," he writes, and sometimes it is "my sister and thine." The old man must have been absolutely irresistible.

His own spirit is half way home, but he does not forget the things of earth. He makes frequent mention of the duty of love between wife and husband. Like his Master, he disapproves of divorce, but he does not forbid it, for he says that if a woman's husband is dead, or has put her away, she will be doing no wrong if she marries again. He thinks it is good to be married, but since the day of Christ may be near, and their thoughts should be centred on that, it is better not to be married, as he is not.

As for the affairs of this world it is not worth their while to be entangled in them, inasmuch as they are heirs to the unsearchable riches of the world that is to come.

But in spite of his constant thought of his children, the old father is lonely. Sitting in his chains in his lodgings in Rome he has few visitors. He has some that are Roman citizens and have become converts, and among them members of the household of Cæsar himself. And then there is Luke, the beloved physician, who is frequently with him, and above all, Timothy, who has given proof of himself as a son. But of the Christianized Jews of Rome, to whom he wrote from Corinth that their faith was being spoken of throughout the whole world, we hear nothing. None of the thirty he mentioned before appeared again, even as the writers of his letters. Perhaps they were forbidden to come to him, and that is part of the mystery which shrouds the cradle of Christianity— the almost impenetrable darkness which it is the business of the historian to pierce.

He was not only lonely, he was poor. Cut off by his imprisonment from his trade as a tent-maker he had to depend on his Churches to minister to his necessities. Some of them to whose spiritual needs he had contributed forgot his bodily ones. But one (his beloved Church at Philippi) remembered them more than once, and his letter of thanks for the last of their gifts is among the most moving things in literature.

"I rejoiced in the Lord greatly," he says, "that now at the last your care of me hath flourished again."

Not that he desired a gift, and not that he would speak of want, for he had learned in whatever state he was to be content. He knew both how to be full and to be hungry, to abound and to suffer need.

"Notwithstanding ye have done well, that ye did communicate with my affliction—and so, God bless you!"

Simple, manly, sensitive, proud! Only the common phrase expresses it. Paul was a great gentleman.

Thus the two years passed in which the apostle was in prison in his own hired house in Rome. And now, after the clattering of horses' hoofs, the roll of chariot-wheels, and the flourish of trumpets across the Tiber, as week by week the emperor went up to his pleasures at the circus, the time had come when Cæsar could snatch an hour to hear the Roman-Jew from Palestine, who had appealed to him over the heads of his high priests and kings.

II. The Emperor Nero

Who and what was the emperor for whom Paul was waiting?

Nero Claudius Cæsar Drusus Germanicus, whose proper name was Lucius Domitius Ahenobarbus, had been born in Antium in A.D. 37, the year of Stephen's martyrdom in Jerusalem.

When he was two years of age his mother Agrippina had been banished for treasonable conspiracy by her brother the emperor Caius. When he was three, his father had died. He was then sheltered by an aunt, who handed him over to the care of two slaves, a barber and a dancer. After Caius's death, Claudius, his successor, recalled Agrippina, and she rewarded him for his mercy by spending ten years in getting his wife disgraced and destroyed. Then Claudius had married her, and her next step had been to get the emperor to adopt her son, over the head of his own, as his successor, naming him Nero.

When he was fifteen, Nero had been married to the emperor's daughter, and when he was seventeen his mother, in fear lest Claudius's son should be taken back into the favour of his father, and recover his rightful inheritance, had caused her husband to be poisoned and her own son to be proclaimed sovereign by the Prætorian guards.

Such had been the first act in the life drama of one of the most infamous of men. The second was with the equally infamous woman, who had made her son emperor not for his sake, but to gratify her love of power. He was a youth of savage temper and ungovernable selfishness, and she had pandered to the vehemence of his sensual passions so as to leave him no time or inclination for public affairs, and herself in a position to control them. The lengths to which she had carried her son to degradation would be scarcely believable if it were not vouched for by the greatest of Roman historians.

But he had often bettered her bad instructions. Not satisfied with the women of his court, he had been known to disguise himself in the clothes of a civilian and go out at night to amuse himself with the wives of the citizens and even the women of the streets, and it is said that on one such adventure the sovereign was soundly trounced by an indignant lover or husband.

He was a creature of childish vanity. At fourteen he had been admitted to the priestly college, but now he fancied himself as a philosopher, a poet, an orator, a musician, a soldier, a charioteer, above all an actor. His senators were shocked that their emperor should lower the imperial dignity by playing the buffoon upon the stage, but the populace were delighted, and he was cheered in the streets and the theatre.

This went on until A.D. 55 or 56. That was about the date of Paul's Epistle to the Romans, in which he tells them that their faith was being spoken of throughout the world. What had happened in Rome to bring them such celebrity is one of the lost chapters in the early history of Christianity, and where nothing is known with certainty it seems pardonable to put together facts which appear to penetrate the otherwise impenetrable darkness.

When Nero had reached eleven years of age his mother had prevailed upon Claudius to recall from unmerited banishment the younger Seneca, a statesman and philosopher, that he might become tutor to her son. In that capacity his influence for a few years had been as good as the character of his pupil permitted; and when he saw that Nero's mother, in her lust of power, was degrading him as an emperor, he resisted her and so made her his enemy.

We know Seneca now as a writer of effeminate prose and ranting verses, and perhaps as the author of Nero's speeches; but apparently he had another claim to consideration. Three and a half centuries later some of the doctors of the Latin Church reckoned him among the Christians, and a correspondence between Seneca and Paul was known to Jerome and Augustus. It was a forgery, but it appears to pierce the darkness.

The Roman histories say that there were 20,000 to 30,000 Jews in Rome about this time, but they were certainly not all Christians. The Christians were few, but perhaps they were troublesome, for they were making no disguise of their opinion of what was going on in Rome. As we shall see later, they were chiefly Christianized Jews, and, with memories of the captivity, they were calling Rome the modern Babylon, "the great whore, the mother of harlots and abominations."

Apparently, they were openly rebuking Nero's debauchery and extravagance. But worse than that, they were probably taking no part in the civic life of the city of their adoption, finding it impossible to reconcile their civil duties with the claims of their religion. Being men of peace, they were almost certainly resisting conscription. Believing the end of the world was near, they were not marrying and producing children, to become citizens of Rome and soldiers of the emperor. This gave them the appearance of being ridiculous visionaries promulgating a pernicious superstition. Tacitus speaks of them later as enemies of mankind. It is a charge that is frequently preferred against the Christians of the following century.

For such passive anarchists and revolutionaries the mother of Nero could have no place in Rome, and if Seneca sided with them; that was one more reason why they should be compelled to leave it.

If the Christians were expelled from Rome at this time (A.D. 55) their going would make no small stir. They might not be many in numbers, but they were not unimportant. Such of them as came from Jerusalem would be poor, for long ago they had sold up their possessions and put the proceeds into the common purse. But such as had returned from Antioch, Corinth and Ephesus may have been rich. There would be the confiscation of businesses, forcible eviction, pillage and perhaps martyrdom. No wonder the noise of it had been heard throughout the world.

But if the Christians had been driven out of Rome between A.D. 54 and the time of Paul's letter, they had not gone far. Probably, they had settled in the little villages of the Campagna. This may have been the reason why they had met Paul as far out as the "Three Taverns," but had not seen him, as far as we know, to his lodgings inside the walls, or visited him during the two years following.

During this time the wheels of life had been moving fast with Nero, Seneca's influence had waned, and the emperor had taken a mistress, Poppæa Sabina—no "religious woman," as the generally-accurate Josephus calls her, having got her out of date and place. From that hour onward the struggle for Nero's evil heart had been no longer between a man and a woman, but between two women, equally avid of power—the mother and the mistress.

The mistress had won. But the mother had made an appalling

fight for the influence over the emperor which had been slipping away from her. We shiver at the record of some of the temptations she had employed to oust her rival. She was still a beautiful woman, hardly more than forty years of age, and it is said that one night she dressed herself up in her most gorgeous clothes and jewels, and thinking Nero's satiated appetite would welcome a new sensation, she went into his room to tempt her own son to seduce her.

She had failed, and paid the price of her importunity. Nero had first put his mother into "honourable confinement." Then he had caused a shipmaster to take her out to sea on a pleasure excursion, to upset the ship and to drown her. The night had been bright with stars and the sea unruffled. Agrippina had been reclining on a couch, talking cheerfully, with two of her friends, when at a given signal, a canopy, loaded with lead, had fallen on them. One of the three had been killed outright, but the mother of the emperor had escaped without serious injury. Seeing this the sailors had tried to turn the ship over, but they had failed to act together, and the result had been that Agrippina had dropped gently into the water. She had swum ashore, and although she had been only too sure of her son's share in the plot to destroy her, she had despatched a man friend to inform him that by the mercy of the gods and her own happy star, she had escaped from a serious accident.

Nero had offered her no sympathy, and she had been half dead with terror, not knowing what her ultimate fate was to be, when a company of guards had broken into her villa, and found their way to her bedroom. There the miserable mother had been lying in a dim light with a single female attendant. The emperor's assassins had struck her on the head with a bludgeon and the centurion in charge of the murder had drawn his sword for the death-stroke, when Agrippina, exposing the womb that had borne her son, cried, "Strike me here," and so perished under a volley of blows.

Such had been the barbaric end of the most infamous woman that had ever stained the sacred name of mother. This had been in A.D. 59. A prolonged carnival had been held in Rome that year in honour of the matricide.

Next year Nero divorced his wife, the daughter of Claudius, and married his mistress. Poppæa profited by Agrippina's error and encouraged Nero to become emperor for himself. For the first time he began to occupy himself with affairs of state, sitting as judge in the courts and making speeches in the Senate.

His judgments were said by his flatterers to show the wisdom of Solomon and his orations the eloquence of Cicero.

This went on down to the traditional date of Paul's trial, A.D. 62. There can be little doubt that Nero himself heard Paul's appeal, there being no other reason why the apostle should have waited so long for his trial. Somebody must have told Cæsar at last that an old Roman-Jew from Palestine had appealed to him against his own people and he snatched an hour to hear him.

There is no historical record of the event, but we have little need to imagine anything, for is it not all written out by anticipation in the New Testament?

The scene must have been arresting. First, the young redheaded emperor, twenty-five years of age, with diamonds and pearls on his bare arms and neck, coming hurriedly on to the judgment seat, followed by his guards and chamberlains; and then the old man in the dock, in his woollen habit and girdle, but calm and unafraid, for he had had two years in which to compose his soul.

In all history there is no more striking illustration of the irony of human life than the scene of Paul at the bar of Nero. Paul, who had denied himself everything. Nero, who had denied himself nothing. On the judgment seat the man in the imperial purple, stained by every crime—his mother's murder, his wife's, his dearest friend's—steeped in innumerable vices of body and soul. On the other hand, the white-haired prisoner, "the best man in the world."

Clearly, the high priests and elders were not there, to appear against Paul, and the proceedings were to consist of the letter of the procurator in Judæa and (after the manner of Roman procedure) the cross-examination of the accused.

"Come, let us have done quickly. What is the charge against this person?"

What the charge was we can scarcely say. It must have seemed as unreasonable to Festus after the examination before King Agrippa as before it—to send a prisoner to his lord in Rome without signifying the crimes laid against himself. But though Paul had committed no offence against the Roman authority, the high priests and elders of Jerusalem were threatening, and Festus had to do his best with his bad material.

"To the most mighty, venerable, most divine and most terrible, the august Cæsar, Porcius Festus, governor of the East, sends greetings. This man, Paul, O most mighty, is a Jew of Cilicia, of the city of Tarsus, but a free man born. He was left to me by Felix, and on my going up to Jerusalem the chief priests and elders of the Jews demanded judgment against him, saying he ought not to live any longer, being a pestilent fellow, a mover of sedition among the Jews throughout the world, and a profaner of their Temple.

"But when I brought him face to face with his accusers according to our manner as Romans, I found nothing in him deserving of death, but only certain questions of the Jewish superstition and of one Jesus, whom the Jews said was dead but Paul affirmed was alive.

"Therefore both I and my friend, the excellent King Agrippa, would have set him at liberty, but the chief priests objected, and Paul himself appealed to Cæsar's judgment seat. Therefore, that peace may be preserved in this province, I have made bold to send him to you."

If the trial went on a moment longer after this, and Paul was called upon for his defence, he must have stretched forth his hand and repeated what he had said at Cæsarea.

"I have done none of the things, O Cæsar, whereof my people accuse me. Nor did they find me profaning the Temple or raising the people either in the synagogues or the city. I stand here to be judged, O Cæsar, because I have been faithful to the hope and promise of my fathers, that the Christ should come, and that the proof that he had come already was that in Jesus of Nazareth he had been raised from the dead."

If after that Paul was permitted to continue he must have told once more his great story of what befell him on his way to Damascus.

"At midday, O Cæsar, I saw a great light from Heaven, above the brightness of the sun, shining round about me, and heard a voice saying from the sky . . . So I could not be indifferent to the heavenly vision, O Cæsar. . . ."

If Paul got that far he would get no farther. The divinity on the judgment seat would be at the end of his patience.

"Gods, what is this? Are the Jews quarrelling again? And who is this Jesus, who is alive and dead at the same time like the cats in the cat pit? Why am I bothered with such foolery? Send the man away at once. Send him away."

And then the pearls and the diamonds would go glittering out of the judgment hall, followed by the grinning guards and chamberlains.

Paul had waited two years for the hearing of his appeal to Cæsar. It was probably disposed of within five minutes.

III. The Neronian Persecution

Whither Paul went after he was acquitted by Cæsar we do not know. When we hear of him next he is in Macedonia. But it seems certain that he must have gone first to the brethren outside the walls. Seven years before he had written:

"I beseech you that you strive with me in your prayers that I may come to you."

But if he came to them at length, it seems certain that he did not stay with them long. The events of the next years show that they had increased greatly in numbers. Probably some great new leader had arrived whose fiery zeal was making many converts among the Romans of the Campagna, and Paul was not the man to build on another's man's foundations. Therefore, it is reasonable to conclude that he quickly carried out his intention of visiting Spain, to which his heavenly voices had so often told him he must go after he had been to Rome.

Paul probably sailed from Ostia. There were trading ships from there to the various seaports of the Mediterranean. By one of these he may have travelled in company with Luke, his friend and physician. Along that southern coast, now occupied with such different activities, to where the western extremity of Europe is washed by the Atlantic, he must have taken his gospel to the Gentiles.

It was the same old gospel, but touched, as we plainly see, by the new fire of his wrath at what he had heard while he lay in his chains in Rome. None was righteous, no, not one. Yet God in His love of man had sent His beloved Son to die that their sins might be forgiven them. There was salvation for sinners who accepted his sacrifice, and the mercy of God was the same to all men that dwelt on the earth.

But the day of Christ was coming, when he would judge the world and separate the righteous from the unrighteous. What then would be the pride of the flesh compared with the glory of the Spirit, which was all in all? Wealth was a flower that faded, and the pomp of this world would be as dust and ashes in the presence of the imperishable riches of Christ. Better weep by the waters of Babylon than laugh in the carnivals of Rome.

Paul's success on the southern coast must have been great. We have it on the authority of a writer who came not much later that there were 60,000 Christians in the towns and villages of the Mediterranean.

If Paul went to the West he must have returned to the East. We hear of him at Miletus and finally at Troas. How long he was away on his journey, whether two years or three, or longer, we do not know.

Meantime, the wheels of life had been going fast for Nero. Two years of egregious mismanagement of imperial affairs had been interspersed with appalling pleasures. He could not keep himself from crime either in his business as an emperor or his amusements as a man. That he might gain credit with the citizens, against the hostility of the Senate, who were impatient of his excesses, he made feasts in the public thoroughfares. But the most profligate of his entertainments were either held by him in his own house or given in his honour in the houses of his friends.

The Roman historian tells of one such entertainment in a garden in the neighbourhood of the Pantheon. The garden contained a basin, or pool, and a banquet was set out on a barge built for the purpose, and rode by youths who were chosen according to their age and proficiency in libidinous practises. On the banks of the pool were brothels, occupied by ladies of rank, who joined with public prostitutes, stark naked, in every kind of indecent gesture and language. The emperor himself took part in this orgy and went through a mock marriage, taking the part of a bride in a bridal veil, and going through a mimicry of everything that night conceals as between husband and wife.

But fast as the wheels of life were going for Nero, the wheels of his fate were overtaking him. News reached Rome of disasters in Britain. The "barbarians," whom it had taken a hundred years to conquer, had broken into rebellion. Out of Colchester, which had a Roman colony since A.D. 50, the legionaries had been driven by the Britons with terrible slaughter and the imperial forces had barely preserved London.

In the following year came news of a disaster at home. An earthquake had led to the partial destruction of Pompeii. And then, in July, A.D. 64, a calamitous fire broke out in Rome itself. It began in that lower part of the city which adjoined the emperor's circus, among wooden shops full of inflammable merchandise. The destroying flames swept up to the heights of the Palatine and the cliffs of the Esquiline with a rapidity which outstripped all efforts to cope with them. The fire burned for six days in the south and then broke out afresh in the northern region of the Lata. Before it could be quenched more than half of Rome had been destroyed.

The inhabitants of the city were panic-stricken. The shrieks of women, the weakness of the aged and the helplessness of the young created scenes of unparalleled horror.

The Romans had told themselves, through many proud generations, that when Rome fell the world would fall. They had to find a scapegoat and they found it in Nero. The disaster was held to be a manifestation of the gods against the emperor.

Colour was given to this belief by the fact that Nero had been out of Rome at Antium when the fire began, and that he remained away for some days afterwards. It was said that on the hot July nights he went on to the roof of his villa on the Campagna to watch the burning of the city as a gorgeous spectacle, and that while looking at the fury of the flames and listening to their roar he recited, in a frenzy of delight, some verses of his own describing the destruction of Troy.

The legend grew. At length it was rumoured in Rome that the emperor himself had been the cause of the fire, having in his vanity conceived the idea of destroying the city in order to rebuild it under his own name—Neronia.

It was the last thing such a man could have dreamt of doing. Rome was the city of the world, the history of the empire in stone. Nero was then only twenty-seven years of age, but if he had lived to be a hundred he could never have rebuilt it. And meantime he would have been an emperor sitting in the ashes of a capital in ruins.

Hearing the rumours, Nero was like a man waking from a delirious sleep. He hurried back from the country and fought hard to put out the fire. It was too late. Suspicion born of fury is harder to kill than to create. The populace hooted him in the streets and the senators denounced him, calling him to his face by every name of contempt from a mountebank to a monkey.

He, too, had to find a scapegoat, and he found it in the Christians. It was they who had set fire to the city, as their revenge for being expelled from it.

Nothing could have been more fabulous or foolish. The most elementary knowledge of the Christians and their faith would have shown any instructed Roman that to set fire to Rome would have been an act of incredible folly.

Most of them were Christianized Jews, waiting day by day for the end of the world, when Christ, according to the last of their prophets, and the supposed prediction of their Master, would come in the clouds surrounded by legions of angels, to sweep away the modern Babylon of Rome, with its idolatrous temples and to re-establish the throne of David in Jerusalem.

But to some extent the Christians had laid themselves open to suspicion. It was known that out on the Campagna (perhaps already in the catacombs) they had been wont to meet together on the first day of the week, before it was light, to sing a hymn to Christ as to a God, and to eat a meal together in memory of his Resurrection. The Romans had heard that these meals were not always innocent ones—that they were scenes not only of drunkenness and gluttony but of indescribable abominations.

It was not entirely untrue. Paul, himself, in writing to the Romans, eight years earlier, had found it necessary to denounce the vices which the Gentile Christians in the Roman Church had brought out of paganism into Christianity; and not many years later the Lord's Supper was forbidden in Rome by imperial edict.

But at this moment of delirium after the fire the accusation against the Christians went further. Writing about thirty years later the Roman historian says that at the time of the fire the Christians were so detested for their abominations that they were thought worthy of the direst punishment, whether they were guilty of the fire or not.

Clearly, the abominations meant were not merely gluttony or drunkenness, or yet incest, for these were notoriously the view of their emperor and nobles at home and their subject kings throughout the empire. It was cannibalism. This seems to show either that an early version of the Gospels was already known and misunderstood in Rome, or that by some malevolent reports of their enemies the Christians were believed to practise at their love-feasts the rite of eating and drinking the body and blood of a substitute for their God.

Fastening on this, in his simulated rage, Nero showed no mercy. The pretence of procedure he adopted to carry out his will was the extremity of legalized crime. The prefect of Rome at that time was one Flavius Sabina. He is described by contemporary historians as a "man of gentle nature, abhorring bloodshed." His gentle nature did not deter him from dragging the Christians out of the Campagna and compelling them to confess under torture that in the darkness of night they had stolen into Rome and thrown lighted torches into open windows.

On such evidence Nero proceeded to deal with them. It was almost as if he said, "You made this fire and now you shall perish in it." The death of the Christians he turned into a diversion. Some of them he nailed to crosses, some he covered with the skins of wild beasts and then threw them to the dogs, some he flamed to death for the purpose of lamps in the streets when daylight failed, and a great number he tied to stakes in his garden and burnt alive, while he raced round them in a chariot and his bad women and worse men looked on and laughed.

But terrible as the story is, it has its aspect of glory. We know from a Roman writer, who came not many years later, that from this, as from all such tortures or persecutions, the Christians might have escaped if they had been willing to curse Christ and worship the image of Cæsar. Some of them may have done so, but clearly the greater part refused life at such a price. "While the world standeth," they said, "we stand by Christ." We can see what occurred. While the flames burnt, and the smoke choked them, such of them as were Christianized Jews sang the psalms of their fathers.

> I will lift up mine eyes unto the hills, from whence cometh my help. My help cometh from the Lord, which made Heaven and earth.

In the light of such scenes how little and mean look the great writers of the past who tell us that if not for arson, then for their hatred of mankind, "the people called Christians by the vulgar" deserved neither mercy nor pity!

IV. How St. Paul Met His Death

News of the fire, and what followed it, passed rapidly over the Roman empire. Paul must have received it. Tradition says he was then at Ephesus, and was sent back to Rome. It is more probable that he was at Troas, and returned of his own free will. It was according to the character of the man who had gone back to Lystra, after he had been stoned in it and then cast out as dead, to go back to Rome, that he might stand by such of his brethren as survived, when their backs were, as we say, against the wall.

In what way he protested against the monstrous tyranny of Nero we do not know, but we know what price he paid for it. He was cast into prison again, not a hired house this time, but apparently a dungeon. Of his life there we have a full and moving autobiography. It is written out at length in his three last letters, sometimes called his pastoral epistles.

He was lonelier than ever now—the great man is always lonely. He had made more converts than he could keep. Those of Nero's household, perhaps naturally, he never saw again. At his preliminary examination before the magistrates his followers had forsaken him, loving this present world. His friends were far away in Asia, having turned away from him, being ashamed of his chains.

"I pray God it may not be laid to their charge," he says.

Only Luke is left.

Yet Paul's strong soul does not fail him. He has always known that in these last days perilous times would come. In the midst of a crooked and perverse nation, he is prepared for whatever God may send him. Death itself has no more dominion over them that die in Christ.

We can only judge of the length of Paul's second imprisonment by the approximate date of his letters. Apparently it was a long one. As time passed before he was brought to his final trial, he seems to have encouraged a certain hope. He writes to Timothy, son of a Jewish woman and of a Greek, and now the head of the church at Ephesus, begging him to "do his diligence" to come to him. There are several homely and human touches. Clearly, it had been summer when he flew from Troas in hot haste to plead for his friends in Rome, and now that the winter is coming, he asks

Timothy to bring a cloak that he had left behind him. As soon as he sees how it is to be with him he will write to him again.

"Prepare me a lodging also, for I trust that through your prayers I shall be given unto you."

Later, he loses hope of life and prepares for the end. He is "Paul the aged," and he is ready to enter into his rest. He says, "We bring nothing into this world, and it is certain we can carry nothing out of it." He would like to see Mark, as if wishing to be reconciled to him. He commends to Timothy's care Onesimus, the son he had "begotten in his bonds."

Perhaps this boy had been a servant, perhaps a slave, of Philemon's, and having robbed him and run away, had come under the influence of Paul and been converted. And now Paul pleads for him to his injured master.

"Receive him as a brother," he says, "and if he hath wronged thee or oweth thee ought, put that to my account."

He is ready to depart and be with Christ, for that is far better. He has nothing to regret. "I have fought a good fight," he says; "I have finished my course; I have kept the faith."

Some men's sins go before them; some follow after. Nero's did both. A pestilence due to overcrowding followed the fire in Rome, and to meet the needs of homeless people Nero made apparently praiseworthy efforts to rebuild a portion of the city. But while the spectre of Death was striding through the land, he also built himself another palace, with shady woods and artificial lakes, and called it his Golden House. He also erected near by a colossal statue to himself as god of the sun. They are all down now, and the owls hoot by night in the ruins of the Colosseum which was shortly afterwards erected on their site.

In the year after the fire he killed his wife Poppæa in a fit of savage rage by kicking her on the abdomen when she was pregnant. His temper had become ungovernable, and during the next two years he murdered Seneca, his former tutor, and many others who were distinguished for integrity and virtue.

Perhaps this was the time of the second trial of Paul, therefore its result was a foregone conclusion. We would give much for an authentic record of the scene, but even conjecture cannot go far astray. It would be the same as before and yet tragically different. The miserable creature on the judgment seat, loud-voiced and boisterous, but nervous and irritable and in daily and hourly terror of assassination. And then the old man in the place of the prisoner, calm and unafraid, not putting his life at a pin's fee.

There can be little doubt of what the charge against Paul was this time—that of denouncing the persecutions of the Christians and of inciting the people against the edicts of the emperor. The trial would be over in a few minutes. The pestilent fellow who had dared to be a mover of sedition against Cæsar would be found guilty, and being a Roman, sentenced to death, not by crucifixion but by the sword.

They show you the traditional place of execution a few miles outside Rome. It is a peaceful spot now. Behind a line of tall eucalyptus trees, in the church of a Trappist monastery, you see the white marble column to which Paul is said to have been bound; and the three marble basins which are believed to be wells that sprang up where his head fell and bounded.

But as you look at all this, the white column, the wells and the church fade away and you are carried back nearly 2,000 years, and are in the yard of a barrack on the Roman campagna. There, in your mind's eye, you see it all as it must have been.

It is an early morning in winter, and the air is keen and frosty on the Roman marshes. The sun is rising over the farthest slopes of the Alban Hills, and Rome, with its many temples to its many gods, lies half-hidden under the morning mist. Perhaps a few trembling women, as on a former and still greater occasion, are looking on from a distance.

In the middle of the barrack yard there is a stout wooden stake, like a ship's mast cut in half and standing upright.

A line of soldiers come from their sleeping-huts and range themselves in front of the stake. Then the old prisoner walks out with the headsman beside him. His hair is like the snow of winter on his bare head, but his step is firm. Death has no dominion over him, and he is not afraid. He is ready to die and be with Christ, for that is far better.

When he stands by the stake his eyes are to the sunrise. He looks up at it and his scarred old face breaks into the smile of young Stephen—perhaps at sight of the same vision. He is hearing his voices for the last time.

Not a word is spoken. Two of the soldiers step up, strap him to the stake (after the Roman method of execution by beheading), and then fall back. His lips move for a moment.

"I have fought a good fight; I have finished my course; I have kept the faith."

The soldiers stand at the salute, every right arm stretched out from the shoulder. After all they are Romans. Friend or foe, there is no honour too high for the man who meets death with a brave front.

So passed the greatest of the Christians. Dauntless soldier of the Cross, you taught us how to die.

V. The End of Nero

In the year of Paul's death, Nero, who professed to be a worshipper of Greek art, visited the cities of Greece, and in Athens the "god of the sun" had a reception that was different from that of Paul. But on coming home he found black looks awaiting him. He had plundered all Italy to pay for his extravagance, and the spectres of poverty and death were stalking through the land.

The thunders of Heaven were now rolling about him. After a while his Prætorian guards, who had proclaimed him sovereign, rose against him with the object of making another man emperor, and the Senate declared him to be an enemy of his country.

Seeing this was the beginning of the end, he shut himself in his palace. Through the gilded chambers of his Golden House, now as empty as a mausoleum, he wandered, like a lost soul, alone. The report came that soldiers were on their way to arrest him, and he found that his sentinels had deserted their posts.

He knew this was the beginning of the end. In some pitiful disguise, he stole out of Rome in the night and took refuge in the villa of a freed-man four miles away. The soldiers tracked and followed him, and as they were hammering at the door to burst it open, the "god of the sun," to save himself from arrest and the certainty of being carried through the streets as a prisoner, committed suicide. His vanity remained with him to the end and ran into his death rattle. His last words are said to have been:

"What an artist is lost in me!"

Thus died in his thirty-first year the foulest thing that ever dragged through the dung of the beast the noble name of man.

CHAPTER X

St. Peter's Last Years

I. *Peter's Missionary Wanderings*

MEANTIME a great figure in Christian history must have been moving unseen behind the black cloud of these terrible events. And it is necessary to go back. . . .

Of Peter we have heard nothing in Scripture since he parted from the apostles in the house of James in Jerusalem, except in a passing reference, which is clearly uncanonical, in one of the letters of Paul, and in two letters supposed to be his own.

Of the second of these two letters it is difficult to speak with patience. It was not admitted into the canon of the New Testament until the fourth century, and ought never to have been admitted at all, being plainly and palpably a forgery, written at least 100 years after Peter's death, and describing a condition of Christianity which existed then but could not possibly have existed earlier.

But the first letter is, in substance if not in words, as plainly genuine, and we shall have to consider it later in dealing with the time in which it was produced.

Apart from these two documents we have nothing in the Bible to say where Peter was, or what he was doing, during the twenty-two years which passed between his departure from Jerusalem and the year in which he is usually believed to have died.

There are men to whom important things are always happening, and Peter was one of them. Everything we read of him in the Gospels and in the first chapters of *Acts* shows clearly that he could not have lived a year, a month, or even a week, without vivid experiences. When we part from him in Jerusalem he is at the climax of his zeal and the height of his impetuous and masterful spirit. Therefore, it is not unreasonable to assume that his next succeeding years must have been crowded with incidents of the greatest importance in the history of Christianity. Yet the Bible is silent about all of them.

It is an incalculable and everlasting loss, perhaps the greatest loss in Christian history. If there had been anybody by Peter's side during those twenty-two years to do for him what Luke did for Paul, we should, perhaps, have had such a record of struggles and sufferings, of triumphant successes, and no less triumphant failures, as would have matched Paul's in its vigour and intensity.

But there have been historians in all ages unwilling to believe that the Bible is to be accepted as the only authority in Christian history. The doctors and fathers of the Latin Church have, from the first, taken up this position, and so far as it concerns Peter the Catholic Church may be said to be founded upon it.

The lost story of the last years of Peter's life as told by the Catholic historians begins as far back as the death of Christ. This occurred according to their chronology, not later than A.D. 29 or the Easter of A.D. 30. During the twelve years following the Crucifixion none of the apostles left Jerusalem, although all the Church is said to have been scattered abroad after the martyrdom of Stephen. It was in A.D. 41, according to the Catholic historians, that Peter, flying for his life from the tyranny of the elder Agrippa, left the house of Mary of Jerusalem by night and "departed and went into another place."

Taking her son Mark with him, he went first to Antioch and then to Pontus, Galatia, Cappadocia and Asia. At Pontus he made two notable converts, Aquila, the tent-maker, afterwards spoken of by Paul, and Priscilla, his wife, who belonged to a superior class. The proof of this is that there is a Church at Pontus still, named after the family of Priscilla and believed to have been founded by Peter.

Prompted by Priscilla, who had friends in the capital of the empire, Peter then went on to Rome. With his three companions, Priscilla, Aquila and Mark, he sailed for Italy from some port in Asia Minor and landed at Naples, where he established a Church and consecrated a bishop, now called St. Aspreno, but otherwise unknown to history.

From Naples he made his way past Capua, along the Appian Way, and entered Rome at the Porta Capena, now known as the Gate of San Sebastiano. This must have been in A.D. 42, because

Jerome, a father of the Church, writing in the fifth century, and repeating the record of another father, Eusebius, writing in the third century, says that Peter came to Rome in the second year of Claudius, who was made emperor in A.D. 41.

On arriving in Rome, Peter, according to the Catholic historians, first made his home in a house taken by Aquila and Priscilla on the hill called the Aventine. The proof of this is that there is still an inscription of the twelfth century, recording the event, in the crypt of a modern church which stands on the site of the dwelling.

The Aventine was occupied until lately by monasteries and vineyards, but as an Israelite cemetery at the time of Peter's arrival, it was a kind of uncivilized ghetto, densely populated by the poorer Jews. In the home of Aquila and Priscilla, Peter set up an altar for the celebration of the holy mysteries, making many converts from among the noble classes, and the evidence is first that Paul, writing many years later, speaks of a Church in the house of Aquila and Priscilla in Rome, and next, that a plank from the altar is still in the Church of St. John Lateran.

But Peter's stay on the Aventine was short, because the rulers of the Jews in Jerusalem sent picked men to sow dissension among his converts, and therefore he removed to a more distant part of Rome. This was the district called Nomentana, a few miles outside the walls, beyond the gate of Porta Pia.

There, on the fringe of the Campagna, Peter set up his episcopal chair. The proof of this is, first, that as early as the sixth and seventh centuries pilgrims came to Nomentana from all parts of the world to venerate the "chair in which St. Peter sat"; next, that the chair itself is now in the Cathedral of the Vatican; and finally, that it has two iron rings on either side of it, such as are still used for the poles employed in carrying the Sovereign Pontiff shoulder high on his *sella gestatoria,* when he blesses his people in the Vatican Cathedral. This is believed to show that Peter had the rank of a bishop and was the first bishop of Rome.

For several years hereafter Peter remained at Nomentana with his minister Mark, who employed himself (with Peter's knowledge, but without his co-operation) in writing an account of what the apostle was telling the people of the sayings and doings of Jesus in Galilee and at Jerusalem. The proof of this is that one of the eldest fathers of the Church, named Papias, who wrote about

A.D. 115, and was a hearer of the apostle John, had put it on record that such was the origin of the Gospel of Mark.

Peter made many converts at Nomentana, chiefly among the Jews of the Campagna, creating a great communion, and becoming the bishop of Rome there, and this is the fact to which Paul refers when he says, in his letter to the Romans, written from Corinth several years later, that much as he wishes to preach the gospel among them he is not the man to "build on another man's foundations."

But then came the expulsion of all Jews from Rome, by the emperor Claudius, in A.D. 49, and Peter had to go with the rest of the Jewish people. But though the edict of expulsion was rescinded by Claudius's successor in A.D. 56, Peter did not return to Rome until A.D. 62, and that accounts for the fact that Paul, in writing to the Romans about A.D. 56, and saluting the members of the Church that had gathered there again, mentions many names but omits Peter's.

On leaving Rome, Peter left a Gentile assistant in charge of his bishopric, sent Aquila and Priscilla to Corinth, and Mark, with his manuscript gospel, to Alexandria, and then to Antioch; and it was there and then that Paul "withstood him to the face."

But remaining in Antioch only long enough to organize a Church there, Peter went on to Jerusalem in A.D. 50 to preside over the first council of the Church, which was to decide upon the admission of the Gentiles. After that he went back to Antioch, established an episcopate there, stayed six or seven years, and then, the ban on the Jews being removed, returned to Rome, by slow stages, arriving for the second time in A.D. 62, resuming his bishopric at Nomentana and remaining head of the Roman Church until his death.

Such is the story of the last years of Peter's life with which the Catholic historians fill the silence of the Bible. The most devout of them will hardly deny that it is founded chiefly on legend and tradition. But the historians of the Protestant communion go much farther. They say it conflicts not only with the chronology of the Bible, but with the known facts of history. Jesus of Nazareth did not die as early as A.D. 29–30, or the account in the Gospels of the marriage of Antipas and Herodias and the beheading of John the Baptist must be deliberate fiction, because these events did not occur until three years later. Peter did not fly to Rome from the tyranny of Herod Agrippa in A.D. 41 because the Jewish king did not come to Jerusalem until Easter of that year, or execute James, the apostle, until the year following, or imprison Peter until a few months before his own death in the first months of A.D. 44.

Peter did not preside over the council of the Church in Jerusalem in A.D. 50, because it took place at least five years earlier, since Paul, who was present, made various long journeys before he met Aquila and Priscilla in Corinth, when they had "lately come from Italy" after the expulsion of the Jews from Rome. And, finally, there is no evidence whatever that Peter was ever in Rome at all, except that an old man of the middle of the second century said that when he was a boy he heard another old man of the end of the first century say that when he was a child he saw Peter in Italy and heard him preach there.

But the historian who belongs neither to the Catholic nor the Protestant communion finds little occasion for contention. Admitting the clash of chronology, he sees no reason to deny that Peter was in Rome. If he was not there, it is impossible to account for the silence of Scripture except on the assumption that he was dead. And the fact that while the Churches at Jerusalem, Antioch, Alexandria and Constantinople have disappeared the Church of Rome has held the position of the Mother-Church of Christendom is proof enough that, almost from the first, it has been believed to have been founded by one who held the apostolic succession.

Yet, granting the general truth of the Catholic tradition, the detached historian finds the apostle enshrouded by it in such a cloud of magnifying and glorifying legend as obscures and falsifies both him and the early history of Christianity.

What, then, must be the story of the last years in the life of Peter, if we carry it on from what we know of the man himself in the Gospels?

II.   Peter in Naples

The first thing to remember is that Peter was a Galilean fisherman. Almost certainly his father, Jonas, was a fisherman before him. He was born in the Galilean Bethsaida, which stood on the western side of the lake, between Capernaum and Magdala. Those of us who know the spot (now a narrow cove covered with rank grass among a wilderness of stones) can easily see what Peter's birthplace must have been—a fishing village with its naked back to the broad camel road which came down from Syria and went on to Egypt, and with its feet in the inland sea.

Being so small it might have many prayer-houses, but no synagogue and no resident rabbi, and consequently no schoolmaster. Therefore, it is not unlikely that Peter was entirely untaught and could neither read nor write. He would nevertheless know the prophets and the *Psalms,* for he would hear them on the Sabbath in the prayer-houses. He would also know, as well as his mother-tongue, a sort of Galilean Greek, for that would be necessary to him from his earliest boyhood, when he sold his father's fish to the people of the caravans who came down through Galilee from Tyre.

When he became a man he would join his father in the boat, and the sudden storms of the Lake of Galilee would make him a sailor as well as a fisherman. He would spend most of his nights on the water, and some part of his days on the shore, mending his nets and tackle.

Such would be Peter, when with Andrew, his brother, he was casting their net into the sea at the moment his Master called him and they left all and followed him. We do not know what his age was then, but he was probably of something like the same age as Jesus himself, and the oldest of the disciples. Neither do we know what he was like to look upon, but he was almost certainly such a man as his birth and upbringing had made him—a rugged sailor-man, with big limbs, hard hands, and a lusty voice, impulsive and masterful, but with a tender vein, too, cheery and generally happy, not easily depressed, and afraid of nothing and nobody.

Apparently he was a widower, for though we read of a visit which Peter paid to his mother-in-law at Capernaum, we hear nothing of his wife, either then or at any time. To dispute with the people who see a reference to Peter's wife in the closing passage of his first Epistle would be to waste words. In nothing was the Jewish rule of life more strict in those days than that men should minister to the necessities of their women if they had to go away from them. We may be fairly sure that Peter had no children.

On the death of his Master no one would be more sure that it was their first duty to gather his people together, and then go out into the world to carry his gospel to the dispersed among the Gentiles. After the meeting in the house of James in Jerusalem, when

Mark went away with Barnabas and Silas with Paul, it is more than likely that Peter would go off alone.

He would probably sail from Cæsarea in one of the trading ships from Italy which lay out in the open roadstead while goods for the Roman army of occupation were put ashore in boats, and then go on to one of the ports of Asia Minor. He was poor, perhaps without a penny, and the sailor-man would almost certainly work his passage.

Where he landed we do not know, but we see that he must have made his way overland through Cappadocia to Pontus, which was near the eastern end of the Black Sea, and then westward by short stages, through Galatia to Bithynia. These were Roman colonies at that time, chiefly inhabited by pagans, but with a considerable Jewish population.

Wherever possible Peter would work at his trade as a fisherman, he would be as little likely as Paul to allow himself to be a burden to others. That would be a wild coast to fish on, but even the wind called Euroclydon, which afterwards frightened Paul's shipmates, would have few terrors for the sailor who had fished the Lake of Galilee.

His courage would make him friends, and his friendships would make him converts. He might not be able to read or write, but we know he could speak with a heart of fire and a tongue of flame. His mission would be chiefly to his own people, and when the great urge came to him to go farther with his message, he would lay his hands on his best and wisest and so make them elders of the little flock he was leaving behind, just as the wandering rabbis in the synagogues at home used to make their ministers.

It was probably from some unknown port in Asia Minor that Peter sailed for Italy, in another trading ship, but under the same conditions. He would land wherever his ship had to unload her cargo, perhaps at Ostia or Brindisi, but more probably at Naples. That would be as early as the end of A.D. 45. Peter was, as far as we know with certainty, the first Christian to set foot in Europe.

Naples was no inconsiderable town even then, and it had thousands of Jews among its inhabitants, for Judaism was a recognized religion among the Romans. So we see the rugged sailor-man going up to the synagogue on his first Sabbath morning, for Peter, like Paul, never ceased to be a Jew.

It would be seen that he was a stranger, and it would be

rumoured that he was lately come from Jerusalem, therefore, the minister, according to custom, would ask him if he had any word for the congregation.

We know what Peter's word would be—the same in substance as on the Day of Pentecost.

"Ye men of Israel, the God of Abraham and Isaac and Jacob, the God of our fathers hath sent me with glad tidings."

What had they been saying in their service? "I believe with perfect faith in the coming of the Messiah, and though he tarry I will wait patiently for his coming."

The Messiah had come! He was Jesus of Nazareth, and though the rulers of the Jews had in ignorance crucified and slain him, God had raised him from the dead, for he was the Son of God, and there was no other name known among men, whereby they could be saved.

It was then hardly more than ten years since the tragic happenings in Jerusalem, and it is not unlikely that nobody in Naples had ever heard of Jesus before. The rabbi would interrupt, and leading Jews, learned in the law, would protest.

Yes, but what else had they said in their service? "I believe with perfect faith that God is one and that He alone is God." Therefore, the man who said that any other man was God was a blasphemous heretic, and by the law of Moses he ought to be stoned.

There would be commotion; dissension, perhaps indignant cries, and as likely as not Peter would be cast out of the synagogue. No matter! Had not the same thing happened before—in Nazareth?

Peter would still be poor. We see him lodging in the huddled-up tenements that faced the old brown fortress of Procida which stood even then on its egg-shaped island by the edge of the sea. And because he would be no more willing there than elsewhere to be a burden to others, we see him fishing by night in the bay, under the shadow of Vesuvius and in the ever clear waters about Capri, and coming down from his room next day, after his rest, to talk to the Jewish women who sat on the pavement in the Italian sunshine, with their children on their knees.

It would be the same story over again, but touched with a tenderer message. Did they believe in the holy prophets, as their mothers had done before them? Then they must believe in Jesus of Nazareth, a man approved by God, by miracles and wonders and signs whereof he himself was a witness. He was standing by

God's right hand in Heaven now, but he would come again soon, very soon, they would see him coming in the clouds, and all his holy angels with him, and then their sons would be no more slaves to pagan kings or servants to hard taskmasters, but as many of them as accepted his sacrifice would be saved from their sins because he had purchased them with his blood.

One by one and day by day the women would bring down their husbands to hear the sailor-man's marvellous story, until the pavement would be too full, and then they would gather in an upper room for prayer and praise and the breaking of bread, for "the innocent meal," in joyful remembrance of the Resurrection.

Thus the dark days would pass, and with the turn of the year the great urge would come again to Peter—to carry his Master's message to the uttermost parts of the earth. So the men of Naples, with their wives and children, would take him on his way, until they were out of the city, and then on the road to the north they would kneel down and pray, and part from him with tears.

III. *Peter in Rome*

It would be spring in that lovely land. The roses would be in bloom by the wayside and the vines in blossom in the vineyards. As Peter strode along with a high step and with his "carriage" (his knapsack) on his back, he would sing, in his lusty voice, the songs of his fathers.

> The Lord is my shepherd, I shall not want. He maketh me to lie down in green pastures; he leadeth me beside the still waters. He restoreth my soul.

As often as he passed through towns and villages he would deliver his messages. His receptions would be various. Sometimes he would be welcomed with joy, and there would be a bed for him such as the Shunammite woman made for Elisha. But sometimes he would be beaten in the streets and scourged in the marketplace, or cast into prison or stoned and then dragged outside the city walls and left for dead.

Peter's head would be "bloody but unbowed." Had he not been told in advance that all this would happen? And was it not his glory and his crown to suffer shame in the name of his Master?

Weakened, faint, hungry perhaps, with his handkerchief bound about his forehead, what wonder if, as he strode along, he saw visions and dreamed dreams? As Paul was always hearing voices, so Peter was always seeing visions, and he saw them now as never before.

He was going to Rome. He had heard of it all his life. "Strangers from Rome," had been with them at Pentecost. There were tens of thousands of the children of Abraham there, and he was taking the word to them that would save them from their sins, for was he not the apostle to the Jews?

There were hundreds of thousands of pagans there, too, and he would show them the folly of their superstitions, that the Godhead was not like things of gold and silver and stone fashioned by man's hand, but a Spirit made manifest to man in His holy Son Jesus, who had died to redeem them.

And then Cæsar lived there also. That had been a name of terror to him ever since he was a boy. His image was on every coin for which he had sold his father's fish on the caravan road through Galilee. He had sent Pilate the procurator, who had crucified Jesus of Nazareth, saying he had called himself the king of the Jews.

He would see Cæsar. Yes, he would confront him face to face, as the prophets of old had confronted the kings of Israel. He would tell him that Jesus had not meant what Pilate had supposed, and the high priests of his own people had pretended, but something quite different. And then Cæsar would tremble before him as Saul had trembled before Samuel. Or if he refused to listen and to lift his hand from God's chosen people, he would warn him of the blood and fire and vapour of smoke that would come with the terrible day of the Lord.

O come, let us exult before the Lord, for the Lord is a great God, and a King above all gods.

But as the days passed, each longer than the day before it, a change would come over Peter. Unconsciously, the rugged man, ignorant and untaught, would begin to feel the power and mystery of the Roman empire—that mighty, relentless, pitiless monster which marched over all the nations of the earth and subdued them to its will.

We see him passing Capua under the Alban mountains. We see him on the last day but one of his journey. He is on the Appian

Way, some miles beyond the "Three Taverns," lying down to sleep under the shelter of the tombs in the heaviness of the evening. When he raises his head in the morning another vision rises before him. It is a great white city, larger and more magnificent by far than Jerusalem, the city of Solomon, which he had always believed to be the oldest and greatest in the world. Marble palaces and temples, rotundas and amphitheatres, with their arches and colonnades, standing on its seven hills, and shining under the blue sky in the early morning.

The Romans at that time were building a vast barracks a few miles outside the walls for their ever-increasing army. Peter must have passed it in approaching Rome, and perhaps, as he did so, the Prætorian guard came out on their high-stepping horses, going to the imperial palace on the Palatine, aglitter in their accoutrements and swearing at the rugged man on the road with the blood-stained bandage about his head, and whipping him out of their way.

No matter! God was greater than Cæsar. He had taken a shepherd out of the sheepcote and made him a King above all Kings, and of his seed, according to the flesh, had come One who was the Saviour of the world. So, with a lift of the head, the rugged man, footsore and wayworn, but full of the fire of the Holy Ghost, went on to the great pagan city to conquer it for Christ.

Perhaps it is all a dream. But in the silence of Scripture and the confusion of the fathers, who will say that it was not in this way that Christianity came to Rome, rather than with the pomp of apostolic processions, and with the dignity of episcopal chairs which no human creature ever heard of until 221 years later? For it was in that year when Paul of Samosata was severely censured at a council of the Christians in Antioch for seating himself on a high throne—an act considered unseemly in a disciple of Jesus Christ.

After that the events of Peter's life shorn of their episcopal grandeur, would probably be much as the Catholic historians say. It would be in the fifth year of Claudius (not the second, which is impossible) that Peter came to Rome. He would enter it at the Porta Capena, now San Sebastiano. At the gate, he would ask the guards the way to the Jewish quarter, and be directed to the Aventine.

Arriving there he would be quickly surrounded by a close crowd of Roman Jews, curious to know where he came from, and trying hard to understand his Galilean Greek when he inquired for a lodging. He would be taken to the house of two good souls who feared God and sometimes received poor strangers. These would be Aquila and Priscilla, and they would become Peter's first converts. After a few days other Jews would join them, and then there would be gatherings in Aquila's house on the first day of the week for prayers and praise and the breaking of bread, and that would be the beginning of the Church of Rome.

In a little while Peter would preach in the streets and perhaps baptize in the river in the isle of Ospadata, where the turbulent old Tiber runs slow.

By this time the rabbis would be asking questions about the new sect which the Galilean fisherman had brought from Jerusalem. Before long there would be no small discussion and disputation at the meetings on the Aventine, and the police would be looking on with suspicion.

Fearing trouble with the prefecture, Aquila would advise Peter to remove to Nomentana, a marshy district outside the walls, also inhabited by Jews, as (according to Juvenal) were many other districts around Rome. They were the poorest and meanest of their race, "the ragpickers and mendicants," of the Roman historians, "the people born to slavery," according to Cicero, the human scavengers of the city only to be seen when they shuffled through the streets in the muffled night or in the echoing morning.

Here, and among these outcasts of civilization, Peter would set up his Church. It is not improbable that down to the last days of his life this was his home, and that he never reached the hill of the Vatican until the fateful day that was to witness the end of it.

There is a river which runs under the road of Nomentana still, and it would probably be in that, or in the pools with which the marshes abounded, that Peter baptized his converts. Apparently he made many of them, or the history of the next years must have been different. And it would be as true of the gospel there, as it had been in Palestine, that the common people heard it gladly.

Two years seem to have passed in comparative peace, then came the first of the Roman persecutions. The hostile Jews of the Aventine, hearing that the fisherman from Galilee was gathering multitudes of the ragpickers and mendicants of Nomentana with his blasphemous new sect, must have come out to destroy it. We know that there were serious disturbances, and that the soldiers from the neighbouring barracks were sent to suppress them.

News of what was happening so near to the city seems to have come into Rome, but with little comprehension of the cause of the trouble. A heathen writer, Suetonius, who appears to have believed that Jesus of Nazareth was still alive and living on the edge of the Roman campagna, tells us that there were continual riots among the Jews there, in which one Christus (Christos) was the ringleader.

At length the news reached the emperor Claudius. He knew as little as his learned men of the meaning of what was happening at Nomentana, and being unable to distinguish between the people who cursed the name of their Christos and the people who worshipped it, and seeing they both were of the same race, and believing them to be enemies of Roman civilization, he expelled all Jews from Rome and the country round about it.

This was in A.D. 49, and Peter must have fled from Rome with the rest of his countrymen. There can be little doubt that he went to Antioch, which was the capital of Syria. The ancient city on the banks of the Orontes, now called Antakia, must have seemed to him only second to Rome as a scene for Christian evangelization. It had been Greek down to sixty-four years before Christ, when it had passed with Syria to the Roman republic. In the time of Peter it was the seat of the Roman governor of Syria, and of the army of the empire in the East. It was from there that the soldiers had come to Palestine at the call of the procurators, to suppress Judas the Galilean, the Jew of Samaria, the Egyptian of Jerusalem and the Arabian king, Aretas.

It was called "Antioch the Golden," which was probably a tribute to its magnificence. The writers of antiquity speak of it with equal enthusiasm and scorn. It was proud of its reputation for letters and the arts. The Romans held it in contempt, but their emperors, for reasons of their own, had always cultivated its favour, and not only Tiberius, Caius and Claudius, but also Herod the Great, had contributed to its grandeur.

It was almost entirely pagan. Its divinities were Daphne and Apollo, the gods of beauty and licentiousness. It was subject to earthquakes, and its inhabitants (as frequently happens in places liable to convulsions of nature) were turbulent and dissolute. In Peter's time its population was probably about 100,000, chiefly

Greek (although speaking Peter's mother tongue, Aramaic), but with no inconsiderable proportion of Jews.

Such was the city to which Peter made his way in A.D. 49, when the Jews were expelled from Rome. He cannot be said to have founded the Church in Antioch, for Paul and Barnabas had spent a year there, six years before this, but undoubtedly he raised its structure.

That would be no light task to such a man as Peter, the rugged sailor, "ignorant and untaught." In that demoralized community, he would be subjected to every kind of derision, indignity and persecution—beatings from his fellow-Jews, scourgings from the Romans, arrests, threats and imprisonments. That the story of all this is lost to us in probably due to the disability that he could not write, and had nobody of his own fellowship to write for him. But that his fiery soul triumphed in the end seems to be proved by the fact that to this day the Antiochean patriarchite claims Peter for its author.

Peter's task in Antioch must have been not only a hard but a long one. Chrysostom, who was born there, says that Peter remained six or seven years in Antioch. We can well believe it. Having regard to the spirit of the man, we can only wonder that he ever left it.

While in Antioch Peter must have heard that Claudius was dead; that another emperor was reigning in his place; that his edict expelling the Jews from Rome was annulled, and that Aquila and Priscilla and perhaps many of their well-to-do fellow-exiles of the Jewish faith were returning to their homes. This must have been in A.D. 59, but it was probably not until A.D. 62, as some of the other fathers say, that Peter went back to Rome, taking Mark, perhaps, with him.

He cannot have found things as he expected. Owing to events already recorded, the Jews alone would be living within the city, while the Christians would be outside the walls.

We know, with as much certainty as we know anything, that on his second arrival in Rome Peter returned to his former home at Nomentana. What he did there during the two years following still lies under the cloud that shrouds the cradle of Christianity. Paul was in prison in Rome at that time, but we do not hear that the apostles ever met. The account given by Irenæus (writing in the second century) of how, on Paul's liberation after the first trial, they preached together and founded the Church of Rome is a predominant but impossible fiction. Equally unreliable is the legend attached to the little modern church outside the Porta Pia, in an apocryphal letter of Dionysius the Areopagite whom Paul converted at Athens, giving the words they exchanged when they passed each other on the road, each going to his martyrdom. Nothing is more clear than that from the day they parted in Jerusalem the apostle of the circumcision and the apostle of uncircumcision each went his own way.

Two years after his return Peter must have witnessed the burning of Rome. What efforts he made during that terrible time to protect his helpless people, when they were being dragged by the police of the prefecture from the marshes of Nomentana to a mock trial and then to the gardens of the emperor, we do not know. Against the enormities of legalized crime that were then committed, his bravest efforts would be of little avail. The only wonder is that he himself escaped them. Writers of authority believe that he died in the Neronian atrocities. The opinion is plausible but not conclusive. That Peter did not perish in the fire of Rome, but lived to be the victim of a later persecution seems to be established by facts of great importance.

IV.   Peter's Teaching

That Jesus, between his death and Resurrection, was in hell was first indicated by Peter in his sermon on the Day of Pentecost (*Acts* II, 25–27). It is based on *Psalms* XVI, 9–11, and reads in Peter:

> For David speaketh concerning him, I foresaw the Lord . . . Therefore did my heart rejoice, and my tongue was glad; moreover also my flesh shall rest in hope; because thou wilt not leave my soul in hell, neither wilt thou suffer thine Holy One to see corruption.

The passage has no apparent reference to the Christ. It is with all that goes before and comes after plainly intended to refer to the Psalmist.

Peter's application of the Psalm to Jesus is based on the argument that David himself is dead and buried and is not ascended into the heavens, but Jesus is. Clearly Peter reasoned backwards. Because Jesus had risen from the grave and his body had not seen corruption, he was the Christ.

Hence, what should the people do?

They should repent and be baptized in the name of Jesus Christ, for the remission of sins.

To whom was this gospel, according to Peter, to be preached?

"To the Jews first, and afterwards to as many as the Lord our God shall call."

This priority of the Jews was also founded by Peter on the *Psalms* 132, 11. "The Lord hath sworn in truth unto David . . . Of the fruit of thy body will I set upon Thy throne."

The first effect was that the followers parted their possessions. They had things in common. "And sold their possessions and goods and parted them to all men, as every man hath need."

How long this order of life in community lasted we do not know, but we know it had certain tragic happenings.

Meantime, they returned to the Temple, and "broke bread" from house to house, apparently on Sundays.

Peter's gospel again:

Repent ye therefore, and be converted, that your sins may be blotted out, when the times of refreshing shall come from the presence of the Lord; and He shall send Jesus Christ, which before was preached unto you; whom the Heaven must receive until the times of restitution of all things, which God hath spoken by the mouth of all His holy prophets since the world began. For Moses truly said unto the fathers, A prophet shall the Lord your God raise up unto you of your brethren, like unto me; him shall ye hear in all things, whatsoever he shall say unto you. And it shall come to pass, that every soul, which will not hear that prophet, shall be destroyed from among the people.

Is this an interpolation? It reads like it, being a break in the flow of the sentences.

Yea, and all the prophets from Samuel and those that follow after, as many as have spoken, have likewise foretold of these days. Ye are the children of the prophets, and of the covenant which God made with our fathers, saying unto Abraham, And in thy seed shall all the kindreds of the earth be blessed. Unto you first God, having raised up His Son Jesus, sent him to bless you, in turning away every one of you from his iniquities.

All this is clear enough. It shows that Peter and the apostles did not say that Jesus had said of himself that he was the Christ, but that the prophets from the beginning had foretold Jesus as the Christ; that through Jesus the people of God were to be saved; that this salvation was to the children of Abraham first and afterwards to as many as the Lord might call.

Clearly, this preaching had a great appeal for the Jews. It made it easy for them to become converts. We are told (*Acts* IV, 4) that many of them that heard the word in those early days believed, and that the number was about 5,000. And that these were baptized in one day, an impossible thing in Jerusalem, if the baptism was by immersion.

Peter and the apostles preached the Resurrection of Jesus from the dead. This angered the priests, the captain of the Temple and the Sadducees (observe that the Pharisees are not mentioned in this connexion), and therefore they took Peter and put him under constraint overnight.

Next day the rulers and elders and scribes, including Annas, the high priest, Caiaphas, and John and Alexander (not heard of before) and many of the kindred of the high priest, gathered in council, called the apostles and asked them, "By what power, or by what name, have ye done this?"

Their question was in reference to a miracle they had performed on a lame man.

Peter replied that they had performed the miracle in the name of Jesus of Nazareth, whom God had raised from the dead. Of Jesus, he also said that there was no other name under Heaven given among men whereby men could be saved.

Thus, Peter preached the redemption of the world from its sins by the death and Resurrection of Jesus.

Observe that the high priests do not at this time (or ever) dispute the statement that Jesus had risen from the dead. But they forbid Peter and John to teach in the name of Jesus, and then (finding no means of punishing them, because of the people— the same old fear) send them away.

The apostles continued to preach this gospel and worked further miracles in the name of Jesus. At this, the high priest arrested them and put them in the common prison.

An angel set them free in the night and next morning they were back in the Temple, preaching. The captain of the Temple brought them (with some danger to himself, lest he should be stoned by the people, who were with the apostles) before the council.

Clearly, the first days after Pentecost brought a strong popular wave in favour of the apostles, and therefore of Jesus. A great body of the people were now convinced that he was the Son of God, foretold by the prophets, and as a consequence they were hostile to their religious rulers who had crucified him.

Again, Peter is called upon by the high priest to say why he has filled Jerusalem with his story about Jesus, with the result that he is bringing "this man's blood upon us." This obviously means that the acceptance of the preaching of Peter had reflected upon the high priest and the council for the condemnation and Crucifixion of Jesus.

Peter's answer is that God had raised up Jesus and they (the rulers) had hanged him on a tree; but Jesus was now exalted to God's right hand to be a prince and a Saviour, for the repentance of Israel and the forgiveness of sins. Therefore, they must obey God in declaring this gospel, not their rulers in keeping silence about it.

Hearing this, the rulers were cut to the heart and took counsel to slay them. But a Pharisee of the council, Gamaliel, held in high esteem as a doctor of the law, counselled toleration.

He said that in earlier days men of the same kind as the apostles had risen and fallen, although they had for a time obtained followers. One such was Theudas [who arose about A.D. 7], who had boasted himself to be somebody and had gathered 400, but they had been scattered and his movement had come to naught. Another had been Judas of Galilee [we know of him] who drew away many people, but he, too, had perished, and his followers had been dispersed. So let these men [the followers of the dead man Jesus] alone. If their work was of man it would come to naught. But if it were of God they [the council] could not restrain it, and to attempt to do so would be to fight against God.

It is difficult to believe that the first Epistle of St. Peter, any more than the second Epistle, was either written or dictated by the apostle. In none of the arts is the vehicle of expression more sensitive to the life, the upbringing and the surroundings of the artist than the art of the writer. Peter was a sailor, yet never for a moment in this Epistle, as always in his sayings and sermons reported in the Gospels and in *Acts,* do we hear the voice of the sea and feel the breath of the ocean. The writer of the first Epistle of Peter was almost certainly a landsman, familiar, like Jesus of Nazareth, whose words he echoes, with the grass and the flowers of the field.

But the measured rhetoric of the letter, with its laboured linking together of clause with clause, is not more unlike the forthright speech of Peter than its spirit is foreign to his character. Nothing is more clear than that Peter was a stalwart soul who knew no humility due to inferiority of class, and had never hesitated to denounce the iniquities of people in high places. Yet in this letter we see him telling such of his followers as are servants to submit to their masters "with all fear"—he who had been afraid of no man. To honour the king—that king being Nero! Almost he claims divine origin for the king's kingship—he who must have heard that Nero's mother had poisoned her husband to make him emperor! He says that the king's governors have been sent for the punishment of evildoers and the praise of them that do well, and therefore they must obey them, for "so is the will of God"—he who must have known that the king himself had sent one of them to murder his mother for the sake of his mistress!

As we read the rather turgid expression of all this servility we ask ourselves, "Can this be Peter, the fearless fisherman of Galilee, the impetuous and masterful man who, according to the Gospels, struck off the ear of the servant of the high priest to protect his Master, who, after the Resurrection, charged the Jews in the Temple with crucifying Christ when Pilate would have let him go, who answered Annas and Caiaphas when they commanded him to speak or teach no longer in the name of Jesus; 'Whether it be right in the sight of God to hearken unto you more than unto God, judge ye'?"

"This is not Peter," we say; "it is false to the spirit of the man as we knew him in the Gospels."

A learned German writer of our own time tries to escape from the clash of characteristics by saying that the body of the letter was probably anonymous, while the beginning and end of it were added a hundred years later. But escape is impossible. The first Epistle of Peter was authorized by the apostle, whoever held the pen for him. To read it aright, we must read it not in the light of its theology, but in the light of its history, the light of the time and place in which it was written. The place was Rome, and the time was shortly after the fire, for to no other time or place does the essential part of it apply.

The persecutions of the Christians was nothing more than a passing event to Nero, an excuse, a demonstration.

After it was over, and he had made some frantic efforts to house his homeless people, he went on as before, abating in no degree his normal life of pleasure. But the shame of it remained with the Romans, particularly with the Senate, and they did their best to hide from the rest of the world the enormities which had been committed in obedience to the barbaric humour of one man. Apparently, they imposed a rigid censorship on letters leaving Rome, and this accounts, in some measure, for what troubles us in Peter's Epistles.

But the fact that scenes which would have disgraced the records of a savage chieftain had occurred in the head-centre of Roman culture was becoming known, and could not be denied. Hence the Roman rulers had to devise some show of self-defence, and we know that they did so. While condemning the inhuman persecution of the Christians, and even admitting that they might not have been guilty of arson, they denied that the punishment had been inflicted upon entirely innocent persons. And to save the face of Rome before the world, they sent out an edict to all parts of the empire, requiring that the Christians should be watched, as a pernicious sect who were suspected of practising (apparently at their "innocent meal") the most atrocious abominations, including gluttony, drunkenness, incest and cannibalism.

Clearly, this was the occasion of Peter's letter. He foresaw the possibility of Roman governors in distant colonies doing what the emperor had done, and therefore he tried to pre-warn them of the kind of persecution that might fall on them.

His letter was not written, as might have been expected, to the Church at Antioch, whose position must have been most perilous, for that would have awakened the suspicion of the Roman police, if by any misadventure the bearer of it, Silvanus, had fallen into their hands. It was written to "the strangers scattered throughout Pontus, Cappadocia, and Bithynia," Roman colonies far away, and it was dated from Babylon, a cipher name which would have no such meaning for the Romans as for the Christians—chiefly Jewish Christians, to whom it was addressed.

With the horrors he had lately witnessed in Rome still present to his sight, Peter was writing as one who felt a heavy responsibility for the bodies as well as the souls of his converts. Calling himself an elder, and writing to the elders of the Churches in Asia Minor, hardly knowing how much they knew, he offers, under cover of a pastoral letter, his counsel in advance of the trials they will have to undergo. He tells them they are to spend their time of sojourning in fear; but they are to humble themselves before the mighty hand of God, that He may exalt them in due time, after they have suffered awhile. He says all flesh is as grass, and all the glory of man as the flower of the field; the grass withers and the flower thereof falls away, but the word of the Lord endures for ever. He reminds them of their great inheritance. They are a chosen generation, a royal priesthood, a holy nation, a peculiar people, and as strangers and pilgrims in the country in which they live, they are to have an honest conversation among the Gentiles, although they speak of them as evil-doers, that they may glorify God in the day of visitation.

Finally, and above all, he speaks at first by metaphor, and then plainly of the "fiery ordeal" which is to try them.

"Beloved," he says, "consider it not strange concerning the fiery ordeal which is to try you."

Can anything be clearer? Peter is telling his converts in distant places, as plainly as he dare speak, the strange and unbelievable thing that they may have to be burnt alive. He is also telling them that if that fate befalls them they are to rejoice, inasmuch as they will be partakers of Christ's sufferings.

Surely this, not its doctrinal teaching, is the essence and intention of Peter's letter. If so, the letter is proof enough of the fact that he lived through the first Roman persecution. That he died in a second persecution is indicated by facts which seem no less clear.

The first Epistle of Peter must have been written in A.D. 65, if it was written, or authorized, by Peter at all. During that year and the two years following, the whole of the known world seems to have been full of trouble. Fearful convulsions of nature were falling upon it everywhere. There had been an earthquake in Antioch in the reign of Caius; another in the reign of Claudius; and now a third in the reign of Nero. There were wars, too, with terrible slaughter, in Armenia, in Gaul, in Britain, and revolts in Palestine and other countries.

Above all, there was a mad riot of debauchery at home. Nero's jerry-built Golden House, which he had thrown up in a year or two, was a scene of such wickedness as no human creature had ever witnessed before. Its gardens had become an open brothel with "the god of the sun" as brothel-keeper. It was almost as if Satan had taken possession of the world, and was using man for his own destruction.

The Roman historian tells us that the gods themselves seemed to mark out these crimson-stained years by storms and pestilence. The Campagna was devastated by a hurricane which overthrew houses, woods and crops, and whose fury reached almost to the city. In Rome itself, persons of every grade were carried off by a plague, though the eye could discover no sign of distemper in the air. The houses were filled with dead bodies and the streets with funerals. No sex, no age escaped the scourge. Slaves and freeborn alike perished amid the lamentations of wives and children, who were themselves in many cases burnt on the same pyre beside which they wept and watched.

To Peter all this would be as the sign of God's wrath upon His children. More, it would be the sign of the fulfilment of the time foretold by Christ when he would come again to judge the world and to establish the kingdom of Heaven on earth.

We have no reason to think that Peter, any more than Paul, knew anything of the saying attributed to Jesus, that certain of his disciples should not taste of death until they had seen the coming of his Kingdom. But nothing is more sure than that the first generation of Christians had a profound belief that the end of the world was near.

"The time is at hand" was their constant watchword.

When questioned about the time of his second coming the Master had generally refused to commit himself to any definite reply. He had said that God alone knew when it should be, and he himself did not know the day or the hour. But he had also said that the time of the end would come as a surprise such as had fallen on the world in the days of Noah and Lot, when the waters had suddenly submerged the land and when fires of brimstone had, without warning, consumed the cities of the plain.

Had he not said that when his disciples saw distress upon the earth, with the sea and the waves roaring, with signs in the sun and the moon and the stars, with men falling by the edge of the sword, with the nations giving way to gluttony and drunkenness, they would know that the day of visitation was at hand? But had he not also said that when they saw these things they were to lift up their heads, for their redemption was near and they would see the Son of Man coming in a cloud with power and great glory?

What wonder if, to such a man as Peter was, the terrible, glorious, triumphant foretold time was here—it was now. It would be a call to him from Heaven to make his last and greatest effort.

He was an old man now, sixty-six at least, perhaps, bruised and broken by twenty years of persecution, but his great soul would be aflame. With the strength of his faith he would leave his home at Nomentana and go through the towns and villages around Rome, calling the people to repentance.

"Repent, for the kingdom of Heaven is at hand." It would be the old message, but with a new force behind it.

The effect would be great and instantaneous. The pagan population of the Campagna who had turned a deaf ear to his religion of the Jewish prophets, his gospel of the Resurrection, would listen to him when he foretold the near ending of the world.

We see what would happen. The prayer-meetings in the streets, the camp-meetings in the fields, the weeping and wailing, the cries of supplication, the shouts of thanksgiving, the pouring out which Peter would believe to be the Holy Ghost.

If this was another such explosion of fanaticism as occurred in Jerusalem on the Day of Pentecost, it was a far more formidable one.

If there were 5,000 converts then, there would be 50,000 now. The paroxysm of terror among the population of the Campagna would surround the city as with a ring of fire.

The Roman rulers could not long be indifferent to the movement that was going forward outside the walls. Perhaps they tried to think of it as the temporary insanity of an ignorant rabble, whose expectation of the approaching end of the world made them the laughing-stock of serious thinkers. More probably they looked upon the people engaged in it as the civilized nations now look upon anarchists and communists—not, indeed, as serious dangers to the state, but as disturbers of peace and security of society.

Of the religious significance of the movement they would not have the faintest comprehension. It is among the amazing facts of history that not until twenty-five years later did the wisest of the Romans come to know anything about Christianity or to learn the first facts about its founder. Meantime, stripping the movement entirely of the supernatural, they would give it the most matter-of-fact explanation. The miserable peasantry on the marshes, reduced to starvation by the national calamities, and still more by the extortionate taxation imposed upon them to pay for Nero's extravagance, were making tumultuous protest. In this they were assisted, perhaps inspired, by a Jewish pretender, sometimes called Christos, sometimes Jesus of Nazareth, who made ridiculous claims to world dominion, and said he was sent by God to establish a kingdom of Heaven on earth, in which the poor would become rich and the rich would become poor, and the world would be turned upside down. This person was probably living (did not his followers always say he was alive?) somewhere among the Alban Hills, waiting for the moment when his ringleaders had excited the disaffected people to such a pitch of frenzy that they thought they could pour into the city and take possession of it.

The chief of those ringleaders was an old Jew, named Simon, sometimes called Peter, utterly ignorant and untaught, but with such a power of working on the emotions of the mobs by the speeches he made to them in his Galilean Greek or broken Latin that there was no saying what might not happen. Therefore the first thing to do was to lay that old Jew by the heels; so a company of the guards, fully armed, would be sent out to take him, guided, perhaps, by a spy from the prefecture.

V. "Quo Vadis?"

Tradition tells us that Peter was not easily arrested. The mysterious power that seems to protect the man with a mission until his destiny is fulfilled, appears to have protected Peter; when he was expected to be here he was there, and when there here. And then who will say that the sympathy of the soldiers themselves did not sometimes help him, unknown to himself, to evade capture? The fire that had blazed in Jerusalem would not fail him in Rome. "Never spake man like this man"—it would be the story of the officers in Judæa over again.

There is a tradition of that time which is so natural, so beautiful and so moving that we feel almost compelled to believe it to be true. It is associated with the little oratory on the Appian Way called Quo Vadis. When Peter's arrest seemed certain, a company of his followers came to him and said that though they knew he despised his life in the service of his Master, yet they begged him to bear its burden a little longer for their sake by flying from Rome until his danger was over.

Reluctantly, Peter consented and set out on his journey. But before he had gone far on the road he had another of his visions. He thought he met Jesus coming towards him as if going into Rome.

"Whither goest thou, Lord?" said Peter.

"To my Crucifixion," said the Vision.

"Wilt thou be crucified again, Lord?" said Peter.

"Yea, again," said the Vision, and then it disappeared.

Peter stood perplexed for a moment, pondering on the meaning of the vision, and then seeing that it meant that by God's will his Lord was to be crucified a second time in his own person, he turned about, ashamed at the weakness that had tempted him to escape, and returned to Rome and—death.

This would be early in A.D. 67, if Jerome is right in stating that Peter died two years after Seneca, for Tacitus says Seneca died in A.D. 65.

It is altogether unlikely that Peter like Paul was tried by the emperor. If, on entering Rome twenty-two years before, with a blood-stained bandage about his head, he had any dream of confronting Cæsar face to face, it was not to come true. The fathers tell us that Nero was then on his visit to the cities of Greece, and that Peter was tried by his rulers.

They would make short work of him. The charge would be political—that of inciting the riff-raff of the Campagna against the throne and person of the emperor. There would be no lack of witnesses, and the sentence would be the only possible one, for he was a Jew.

"Crucify him! Crucify him!" It would be the old cry over again.

Opinion has long been divided about the place at which Peter suffered death. The antiquaries of Rome are now satisfied that it was on the southern side of the Vatican hill, where Nero's circus stood before the fire, near to the point at which the chariots turned in the gladiatorial shows, and not far from the site of the palace now occupied by the Pope.

Origen, an Alexandrian priest, who had lived in Cæsarea and must have been familiar with Jewish traditions, was the first to say that Peter was crucified head downwards, by his own request, thinking himself unworthy to die in the way of his Master. It is not impossible. That method of crucifixion was common in the East, and Seneca says it was not unknown in Rome. But it is more probable that Peter, in his humility, made the request that he should suffer this further degradation rather than that the Roman guards should put themselves to the trouble of reversing the cross to meet the whim of a common criminal who had been a ringleader in an insurrection among ragpickers and mendicants.

It is said that a road ran past the place of Peter's crucifixion. If so, it is not improbable that the passers-by, as formerly at Jerusalem, wagged their heads at the dying man, and that among them (pitiful witnesses to human infirmity!) would be some of his hysterical converts of the Campagna, who, finding that his predictions about the end of the world had not been fulfilled, were there to taunt and insult him. His friends from Palestine must have deserted him. It would be two years since Silvanus went to Asia Minor, and we have no reason to think that even Mark remained. Peter would be utterly alone.

The district in which the cross was raised still keeps, by a corruption, the name of Montoria, and it is perhaps an error of identification that from the fourteenth century down to our own day the place of Peter's crucifixion has been believed to be the summit of the Janiculum, and within the church of S. Pietro in Montoria.

If imagination could have its way, it is there we should still place the scene of Peter's crucifixion. It is a wonderful spot. No one even now can look on it at first without emotion—the many-domed city below, encircled by the arms of the Alban Hills, and with its face scored deep with the tragedy and tears of twenty-five centuries. But to Peter, in that hour of equal victory and defeat, it must have been far more moving—the white marble temples of Mars, of Saturn, of Juno, of Jupiter, of Marcellus—the pride and glory of the pagan capital of the world!

If it is permitted to the dying to look into the future, is it forbidden to us to believe that Peter, on his cross, broken and bleeding, and more than half naked, saw all this pomp and magnificence pass away in a few years—dropping down to where it still lies in the dust and ashes of the old Rome—and a new city rising out of the ruins to be the capital of Christendom?

Rugged old exile and saint, when your eyes closed in death on that scene of so much sin and suffering, did they open at home on a sweeter and purer one—the springs of Jordan, with the tall cedars of Lebanon on your left and on your right the heights of Hermon, whose snow-capped crown is the first to catch, over the mists of morning, the light of the rising sun? And did you hear again the beloved voice which, through all the years of your cruel persecution, had whispered in your ear—"Thou art Peter: on this rock I build my Church!"

CHAPTER XI

The Four Gospels

I. The Mother Church

WHEN WE ASK OURSELVES what was happening to the Church at Jerusalem during the long period of the suffering and death of Peter and Paul in Rome, we plunge again into the cloud of darkness about the cradle of Christianity which Voltaire declares to be impenetrable.

We have seen the Mother Church returning to Jerusalem a short while after the dispersion which followed the death of Stephen. They have found the possessions which they had pooled at the time of their foundation confiscated. They have been undismayed by their poverty, feeling it to be a condition more proper to followers of Jesus, who had himself been poor, and had told them to take no thought for the morrow, what they should eat or what they should put on, but to trust to the Heavenly Father to feed them as He feeds the birds of the air and to clothe them as He clothes the flowers of the field.

We have seen, too, how this trust in God had to meet the hard facts of nature. A prophet had foretold a great dearth throughout the world, and it had come in the early years of the reign of Claudius Cæsar. Then Paul and Barnabas had gone out to the Churches they had established abroad on an expedition of relief for them.

They had gone out again on a similar errand a few years later. And then Paul had brought alms to them from the Churches in Macedonia when he came up to Jerusalem for the last time.

After that we have heard nothing about them. Whether they stood by Paul at the time of his arrest in Jerusalem and his imprisonment at Cæsarea we are not told. Whether they ever visited him during the two years of his imprisonment under Felix, or sent Luke unto him to Rome, we do not know. Whether he wrote from there to the Church at Jerusalem, as he wrote to other Churches, and whether they heard of his first trial and acquittal, and his second trial and death, we never hear.

Still more strange is the silence about the Mother Church during the ministry of Peter. If he communicated with them, or they with him, after he sailed to Asia Minor, or at any time during the tumultuous days down to his martyrdom, we hear nothing about it.

A black darkness in Scripture fell upon not fewer than ten years in the life of the Church at Jerusalem. Have they been exterminated, or at least banished, from Palestine since Paul's departure?

Almost the only answer we get is from tradition and outside history. From these we learn that the Mother Church was still alive and still at Jerusalem, until a few years before the death of the apostles. Apparently it lived about twenty-five years altogether, some of them peaceful years, and some very tragic. There is just light enough to pierce the darkness of their history.

The Church at Jerusalem was never really a Church in the modern sense of the word. Like all the other Christian Churches of the first generation it was merely an assembly. Our vision is so dazzled by the grandeur that has surrounded it in the course of the centuries that we find it hard to realize how humble were its beginnings.

No other religion that has ever made any progress in the world began so humbly. Christianity was born among the hills and valleys of Galilee, and brought up in the streets of Jerusalem. Its founder, in the eyes of the majority of his fellow-countrymen, was merely a common criminal who had come to a degrading death at the hands of the Romans for making ridiculous pretensions, and causing a number of country people to believe on him. He created no religious organization, and neither did his immediate followers.

The little Church at Jerusalem had no tabernacle, no rites, no ceremonies, no sacrament except baptism, and no salaried clergy. A priest of the third century put it on record that James, the brother of Jesus, was the first bishop of Jerusalem, and that James's episcopal chair was to be seen there down to his own day. Nothing in the world could be less probable. The Mother Church of Christendom was almost certainly a little band of lay brothers, living in community, with James as their elder or head, and perhaps (who can say anything to the contrary?) Mary, the mother of Jesus, as the only woman in the household. The men were probably all unmarried; and as many as could do so worked at their trades, like other men of the same class in Jerusalem. They were Jews, and they frequented the Temple, observing the custom of their fathers. They kept the Jewish Sabbath, and they also kept the early hours of Sunday, when they gathered before dawn in the common room of their private house to break bread in remembrance of the Resurrection of their Master. To this weekly gathering they welcomed all their little fellowship, who would come, in the darkness of Sunday morning, with lamps in their hands, in their slippered feet over the white stones of the narrow streets.

Their house would be a simple dwelling like that of Mary of Jerusalem, with a courtyard behind a high wall with a gate or door in it, such as Peter knocked at on the night he escaped from prison, when Rhoda answered him. The stormy period of their first persecution being over, they would live for several years at peace with their Jewish fellow-citizens, particularly James, who was called the Just, because of his reputation for righteousness. It is even said that sometimes the scribes and Pharisees would come to consult with him on questions of doctrine.

The central brotherhood of the Church of Jerusalem would all be disciples of Jesus, the remnant of the twelve whom we never hear about after his Crucifixion. They were not evangelists like Peter and John and others, who with Paul and Barnabas were founding Churches in pagan countries. But nevertheless they were the recognized elders and fellows of the Church everywhere, and their apparent office was to compose the differences which arose among the other Churches, to baptize converts, to attend on the sick and to minister to the dying. Silver and gold they had none, but such as they had they gave to all who asked of them.

Such was the little Church of Jerusalem during its first years, as we see it in tradition, and in secular history. And now we ask ourselves whether, during the period in which Scripture says nothing about it, and perhaps from the beginning, its members had not dedicated their lives to some great silent task. And if so, what was it?

For an answer to that question we have to go back to Scripture, and when we find it there the scales seem to fall from our eyes, and a great light to penetrate the darkness. In his letter to the Romans Paul says, when he has asked alms of the converts in Macedonia and Achaia for the "poor saints in Jerusalem," "For if the Gentiles have been made partakers of their spiritual things, their duty is also to minister unto them in carnal things."

Is it improbable that not being evangelists, the brotherhood of the Church at Jerusalem are ministering to the foreign Churches in the only way possible to them—that of compiling the first rough draft of the first three Gospels?

II. The Scriptures

The literature in many languages which deals with the authorship and chronology of the books of the New Testament is a long study. It is doubtful if anybody could master a tenth of it if he lived as long as Methuselah. Nor does it concern the historian, except so far as it affects the movement of events. But because it does this in some degree it is necessary to make a rapid review of it.

During the first three or four centuries of the Christian era learned men, chiefly priests, were throwing grappling-hooks into the uncharted sea of legend and tradition, to find out who had been the writers of certain Christian documents which had come down to them; when they were written and where. They had no idea of any sanctity attaching to the documents. One of them in the fourth century made a rough and ready paraphrase of them, and another, in copying them, omitted passages which he did not like, and even added others.

During the next fourteen centuries this attitude was altered. A certain number of the documents, sorted out from many others, were embodied in a canon of the Church, and thereby became sacred. They were then believed to be the inspired and revealed word of God, spoken through men who were only the passive instruments of the Divine Spirit. This belief became obligatory upon any child of the Church, and for a Christian to question any line or word of Scripture was to expose himself to swift excommunication. The fourteen centuries offered no apologies and no explanations. It was a spiritual sphinx, silent and inexorable.

During the past two centuries the pendulum has swung to the opposite extreme. The books of the New Testament have been examined, like all other books, by their own internal evidences only. Tests of philosophy, psychology, and, as far as possible, of history, have been brought to bear upon them. The result has been that their divine origin has, in general, been denied; that they have been declared to be very human books; man-made and man-disfigured, the writings of many authors, writing in many ages; often confused, sometimes contradictory, partly legendary and even mythical, although in substance truly historical.

Naturally, the four Gospels, as containing the four biographies of the Founder of Christianity and of the fullest account of his teaching, have been the most hotly contested, and the first three of them, taking all the ages through, have been the most searchingly examined.

Thus the Gospel of St. Matthew, according to the early fathers, was undoubtedly written by the apostle of that name, who was formerly a tax-gatherer in the service of Herod Antipas, and was sitting in the custom-house at Capernaum when Jesus called him. He put together and wrote "a collection of the sayings and discourses of Jesus in the Hebrew language, and each man interpreted them as he was able." In this form they were used by the two or three generations following the apostolic age. But St. Matthew also wrote his Gospel in Greek, and as late as the Reformation the Greek version was accepted as the work of the Galilean taxgatherer. His Gospel was probably put into circulation not long after the Crucifixion; it is the only one of the first three Gospels that bears the name of an apostle, and therefore it has the higher authority.

According to the modern theologians much of this is false and even foolish. There is no certainty that the tax-gatherer was the writer of the Gospel that bears the name of Matthew. It is certainly the work of a Jew, and is addressed to the Jewish people, but only to the Jews of the Dispersion; and that did not occur until something like fifty years after the Crucifixion. It contains passages which must have been copied from other Gospels that had been circulated earlier. The signs of dogmatic reflection contained in it show clearly that it was composed late in the first century, and therefore it is impossible to assign it to any earlier period than A.D. 80 to 100.

The Gospel of St. Mark according to the fathers, was written by John Mark, the son of Mary of Jerusalem. Mark became a convert of Peter in the troubled days when the first of the apostles frequently sought refuge from the persecutions of the first Agrippa in the house of the good women to whom he went by night at the moment of his greatest peril. When Peter set out for Rome, Mark, who was then young, but had had a certain scnooling, went with the illiterate fisherman as his dragoman or interpreter. He wrote his Gospel while in Rome; getting his information about Jesus from Peter, who speaks of him as "Mark, my son." When the Jews were expelled from Rome by Claudius in A.D. 49, Mark sailed to Egypt, and when he arrived at Alexandria he was carrying his lately-composed manuscript in his hand. His Gospel was in Greek, and it was intended for the Gentiles. It contains a number of unimportant details which clearly show that it was written either by an eye-witness or by one who had been instructed by an eye-witness, and therefore it is to be accepted as essentially the Gospel of St. Peter.

Modern historians say that it is one of the best attested facts of Gospel history that all this was so. They quote as their earliest authority one John, a priest of the first century, who wrote in a book which is lost that he had heard John the apostle say that Mark was the follower and interpreter of Peter. Also, they quote a priest of the second century, named Papias, who said in a tract which is also lost that he had received this information from one who had frequently heard it repeated by an elder of the first generation.

But the modern theologians say that much of this must also be untrue; that Mark was not in Rome in A.D. 49, because he was then travelling elsewhere with his uncle Barnabas; that another priest, Irenæus, of the third century, says that Mark wrote his Gospel after Peter's death in A.D. 67; that there are many internal proofs that this must have been so; that while the Gospel of Mark may be accepted as the first of the three Gospels it cannot be placed earlier than A.D. 68; that, while it is vivid and direct in narrative, it is not to be regarded as the work of an eye-witness, or yet of the interpreter of an eye-witness, since Mark as a writer is too fond of making scenes, of showing off before his Gentile readers his knowledge of his native tongue, when passages in the original language are quite unnecessary, and by displaying his familiarity with trivial details of Christ's life, which nobody could possibly have remembered after so long an interval.

The Gospel of St. Luke, according to the fathers, was written by an outsider, and is therefore the more valuable as a witness. Luke was the son of a Greek physician, belonging to southern Italy. His father settled in Rome, where Julius Cæsar had conferred the rights of Roman citizenship on all Roman physicians; therefore Luke, like Paul, as the son of his father, was a Roman citizen. He was born about A.D. 30, and consequently had never known Christ. But in early life he had become an adherent of the synagogue, perhaps a proselyte of the gate (a kind of half-Jew, who accepted the Jewish God but rejected circumcision), and travelling in Macedonia he had met Paul and become a Christian.

In A.D. 58 Luke, according to the fathers, heard that Paul was imprisoned at Cæsarea, and he went there to visit him. He enjoyed the liberty of Felix to visit Paul and to minister to him. While doing so he conceived the idea of writing a full, ordered and connected history of all the known facts in the life of Jesus. In this task Paul could give him little help, not having known Jesus in the flesh; so Luke spent some part of the two years of Paul's imprisonment in going about Galilee, gathering up stories from eye-witnesses and investigating events. In doing so he not rarely lost his way, as Luther says (and as such of us as know the country can see), and sometimes misunderstood the Aramaic which was the common language of the Galileans. But he brought back a body of very moving memoirs, chiefly in the form of parables about the kingdom of Heaven, which he had taken down from the lips of the people and turned into his beautiful Greek. Thus, according to the fathers, the Gospel of Luke was written before A.D. 60, when Luke sailed from Cæsarea with Paul for Rome.

The modern theologians say that much of this, also, is obviously incorrect. Luke's Gospel could not have been written between A.D. 58 and 60, because it contains quotations from the *Antiquities* of Josephus which were not published until A.D. 92. Also, because it causes Jesus to describe the fall of Jerusalem, although that event did not take place until A.D. 70. Therefore the earliest date which can be assigned to the composition of the Gospel of Luke is A.D. 80 to A.D. 92.

On the shifting sands of all this legend and tradition, calculation and conjecture, the historian finds it difficult to walk with safety. There is no finality, no certainty. The names and dates of yesterday are not those of to-day, and those of to-day are not likely to be those of tomorrow. Above all, there is no human history, and the real-life persons of the Gospel story (including the Founder of Christianity himself) are no more than ghosts that are seen flitting over a balcony by the light from a curtained window.

The historian in quest of the human story finds himself not rarely siding with the early fathers and against the modern theologians, who have scarred the Gospels through and through for him with human difficulties. There is, for instance, the case of the passage in *Luke* which is supposed to describe the fall of Jerusalem. Clearly, it is one of two things—either a prediction or a report. If it is a prediction of the fall of Jerusalem, Jesus is a prophet. If it is a report written after the event, and put into the mouth of Jesus before the event, Luke is a forger and Jesus is a false prophet. More than that, inasmuch as the passage says that the time of the events described will be the time of the Second Coming of Christ, it follows that if Luke wrote his report after the fall of Jerusalem, knowing that the Second Coming of Christ had not taken place, Luke is not only a forger but a fool, and Jesus is not only a false prophet but a phantom, who has no right to a place in history.

It is impossible not to respect, and in some cases to reverence, the sincerity, the scholarship and the lifelong devotion to a great task with which learned men in many countries have devoted their lives to the study of the authorship and chronology of the Gospels. But it is equally impossible for the historian not to think that the learned men may have taken the wrong road to their destination, and that a quicker and surer way to a right understanding of how and when and by whom the Gospels were first written would be to look at the simple human necessities which called them into being. What were these? Where did they arise? What was their sequence according to the laws of the human heart?

That takes us back with tired footsteps, but with the torch of St. Paul's inspiring text in our hands, to the little house of the Mother Church in Jerusalem.

III. *The Spiritual Flame*

That little house in Jerusalem contained a group of simple men, most of them from Galilee, and probably quite unlettered. They had been held together from the first by one great devotion—love for their Master. For this, they had given up everything—the joys of home and wife and children. Nothing is more sure about Jesus of Nazareth than that he inspired the deepest love among those who came nearest to him. Sometimes it seems as if he asked nothing of his disciples but that they should love him. They loved him at the most tragic moments of their lives with a tenderness which we can scarcely think about without tears.

One proof of this stands out above all other proofs. On the third night after his death and burial, when they thought he had failed them, disappointed all their hopes of him, perhaps deceived them or been himself deceived, wasted their lives, exposed them to the pity of their friends and the derision of their enemies, and perhaps to the danger of punishment from the Roman rulers, as being his accomplices in the cause for which he had been condemned, they gathered together in an upper room, in the company of his mother and brothers—for what? To revile his memory? No, but out of their undying love of the man, to weep for the loss of him.

As time went on the love of their Master was not the only thing which held them together. He was not really dead; he was alive, and they lived daily and hourly in the hope of his return. He would come again soon, very soon, and meantime it was for them to watch and wait and to keep his lamp alight and trimmed, as for a wedding procession, which might come unawares.

This great expectation ringed their little house round as with a spiritual flame through which the things of the world could not come. It was nothing to them that procurators and high priests came and went, and that emperors rose and fell. The one thing that mattered was that their Master was not dead and in his grave, as the world supposed, but standing at the right hand of God, and that he was coming again to establish the kingdom of Heaven on earth. They were the only remaining eye-witnesses of his earthly pilgrimage, the only ones (except their brother apostles, who were in foreign countries preaching the glad tidings and founding Churches) who had lived with him and eaten and drunk with him, and seen and heard all he said and did. Round about them in distant places were the multitudes of their fellow-men who had accepted the words of eternal life—Jew and Gentile, bond and free, but all children of their Heavenly Father now, by the grace of the Lord Jesus Christ. And not having the gift of tongues, but being full of the Holy Ghost, it was for them to find spiritual food for all who needed it. That was the office to which they had dedicated their lives, and it would not be long before they were called upon to exercise it.

If human nature was the same then as it is now, the foreign Churches would soon find that after the apostles had been with them, and then passed on to other cities, the torment of emotion excited by their preaching had been followed by a wave of depression and doubt. This would fix itself first on the central doctrine of their new faith—the doctrine of the Resurrection.

One of the foreign Churches, in Ephesus perhaps, would write to the Mother Church at Jerusalem to say that it had been easy enough to believe the doctrine of the Resurrection while Paul, with his flaming sincerity, had been among them—that though Abraham and Moses and David were in their graves, and their tombs were still with them, the tomb of Jesus of Nazareth was empty, because he was risen from the dead, being the only man since the beginning of the world who had so risen, and therefore he was the Christ. But now that they were left to themselves, a creeping sense of doubt was coming over them. Could it be true, this amazing story, so contrary to all human experience? Or had it been due to the ecstasy, the spiritual exaltation, even intoxication, of one man? Were there any other witnesses?

The little Church at Jerusalem would leap at that call for spiritual help. They would remember those fifty days between the Crucifixion and Pentecost, when doubts had assailed the hearts of some of themselves, after the Magdalene had come from Calvary with the story, which they could not at first believe, that her Lord had appeared to her, and then recall the cloud of witnesses on the road to Emmaus from Galilee and elsewhere which had swept away all their misgivings.

We can see what they would do. They would write it all down on parchments, attach the sheets to wooden rods (just as they had seen the scribes do with chapters of the Torah intended for the use of the little synagogues in remote places in the country), and then send them out to Ephesus, with the Church's request that, after they had been read aloud to the brethren there, they should be passed on to the other Churches and finally returned to them.

Such would be the first call to the Church at Jerusalem for spiritual things, and the next would come quickly after it. Another of the foreign Churches, in Pontus perhaps, would write to say that while Peter was with them he had repeated some of the words which Jesus himself had spoken. They were so wise, so searching, so beautiful, so comforting to the hearts of the poor who were compelled to live under the heel of hard task-masters. No man had ever spoken like that man, for he had the words of eternal life. And now they wished to have a record of them, if possible, that they might read them on Sunday mornings at the breaking of bread, and so hear the voice of the Master again.

We can see what the little brotherhood would do in answer to that call also. They would appoint one of their number to write out the sayings and discourses of Jesus. It might very well be Matthew, the tax-gatherer, for he would have a ready pen and perhaps a retentive memory. He would write on his parchments as much as he could remember of the eight discourses which we now call the Sermon on the Mount, attach them to their wooden rods and then send them out, with the same request as before.

Later, another of the foreign Churches would write to Jerusalem to say that the apostles had told them of the mighty works which the Master had done while he went about doing good. They were so marvellous in their power, their mercy and their tenderness. They could never hear enough of them. They knew that prophets worked miracles, but such of them as were Jews also knew that when Christ came he would work such miracles as the world had never before witnessed. Could they have a full account of the miracles of Jesus?

Once more, we see what the little brotherhood would do. And if this was in A.D. 49, when Mark arrived in Alexandria, he would come up to Jerusalem (for there would be nothing else, as far as we can see, that he could or would do) with his lately-composed Gospel in his hands. It would be received with joy, and, if it were said to have been written under Peter's eyes, with delight. So it would be copied out on other sheets of parchment, and sent round to the foreign Churches with the same request.

Still later, the foreign Churches would write to say that the time had come when they, who were chiefly strangers so far away, wished to look upon the Lord as he lived, as he had been seen by those who had been eye-witnesses from the beginning, and were now ministers of his word. Could they not have an account of his life among them?

This would come to the little brotherhood in Jerusalem, like the cry from their inmost heart. It would carry them back to their early days at home, when they were called by a voice they could not resist from their boats in Galilee; when they had to keep back the crowds in Capernaum which thronged about their Master and worshipped him; when they had him to themselves, on the banks of the Jordan, and he spoke to them, first of all people in the world, the parables of the kingdom of Heaven which were more beautiful than the flowers in the grass beside him and sweeter than the river at his feet.

And if this was in A.D. 60 when Paul was being sent to Rome, and if Luke, before going with him, sent up from Cæsarea the Gospel he had written during the two years of the apostle's imprisonment, and if it reached the Church at Jerusalem with the inspiration of Paul himself (why should it not, since Paul afterwards called it "our Gospel"?), it would be received with rapture.

What matters about its errors in geography, if the spirit was here and it showed a perfect understanding of all things from the very beginning that were most surely believed among them? So this, too, would be copied out on its sheets of parchment, attached to its wooden rod and sent out to the foreign Churches.

One by one the parchments would come back to Jerusalem but not as they had left it. They would be scored all over with other writings. Thousands would have read them while they were away; and among the number would be many Christians who had been scattered abroad after the death of Stephen. Some of these had seen Jesus in the flesh, and perhaps not a few believed they knew better than the apostles what he had said and done, at moments when he spoke to them alone, no one else being near enough to hear him—the blind man whom he led out of Capernaum, the woman at the well in Samaria, the poor sinner in the house of the Pharisee who had washed his feet with her tears and dried them with the hair of her head.

So the parchments would be revised, collated, gathered together under the names of their principal authors, copied afresh and sent out again—not the writing of three men now, or yet thirty, but perhaps three hundred.

Would this be the way the first three Gospels came into being, at the urgent call of the hungry hearts of the early foreign converts? Or would it be at the casual will of writers who, according to learned commentators, wrote long after the events they recorded —Mark, twenty years after the death of Peter, and Luke as long after the death of Paul?

Was this what the Mother Church was doing during those years in which Paul was asking alms of the foreign Churches for the "poor saints" in Jerusalem, on the ground that they were ministering to them in "spiritual things"?

And if the spiritual things were not these first versions of the first three Gospels, what other things could they be?

They are lost to us now in the native tongue of the people in which the greater part of them must have been composed. Or we see them only in the Gospels as they have come down to us, after feeling their way through many versions in another language, and after the changes of text and story which the prophets and doctors of the Latin Church a hundred years later thought necessary, while fighting for their faith against the more highly trained intellects of the pagan philosophers, who accused them of making fables and not possessing the art of making them seem likely.

"Some of you," said Celsus, in the second century, "like men who, when drunk, hurt their own selves, have altered four times and oftener, the texts of your Gospels, in order to deny objections made to you."

Of one thing we may be sure, that crude, inconsequent, repetitive, out of order, as these early documents may have been, they were the pure doctrine, the true story, and the pure tradition of Christ and the Christian religion.

And then the Gospels, which modern theologians are constantly looking for. Are they what we call the Nazarene and Ebonite fragments? What we would give to recover them!

IV. The Assumption

In the ninth chapter of *Acts* we are told, a little out of chronology, that "the Churches had rest through Judæa, Samaria and Galilee." This peace, as we now know, began at the death of the elder King Agrippa, a few days before Easter A.D. 44, and continued until shortly after the death of Festus, the procurator, in A.D. 64. Not long before the latter date, the first shadow of the cloud that was coming fell on the Church at Jerusalem.

Mary the mother of Jesus died.

Of Mary we know little from Scripture. We do not hear who she was, who her parents were, where she was born, or to what condition of life she belonged. Apart from the two stories of the Nativity, there are only four incidents in the Gospels in which she appears, and two of them are plainly apocryphal. To anybody who knows Palestine, and has entered into the heart of Jesus, the incident of the marriage feast at Cana of Galilee, in whatever light regarded, is both physically and spiritually impossible and painful. To anybody who remembers the history of John's wandering life, or thinks of Mary's after the time of the Crucifixion, the incident at the Cross in the fourth Gospel in which Jesus commits his mother to the care of the apostle, and he takes her to his home, is incredible from the point of his possibilities and unnatural from hers.

The Scriptures tell us as nearly as possible nothing about Mary. The apostles never speak of her. St. Peter says nothing about her, and St. Paul, who is constantly referring to women in his letters, and sending his salutations to them, the mothers and sisters of his converts, never mentions the mother of Jesus. She says little for herself, either. If all the words she is reported to have spoken, apart from the hymn in *Luke,* were put together, they would scarcely be sufficient to make the shortest paragraph.

We do not hear where she died or when, or anything about her burial. A cloud covers her which it seems impossible to pierce. And yet she lives so vividly in Christianity that to remove her name would be like taking the heart out of it. For a vast multitude of Christians, through many centuries, she has been adored and worshipped with a devotion only second to that given to her Son.

Somehow, we scarcely know how, the world has created for itself a beautiful picture of her. She is a pure, sweet woman, full of mercy and tenderness. Fresh from the study of the women of the pagan world, with their gross carnality, their lust of power, their ruthless atrocities committed to control the destinies of men, Mary seems to us the last and the most beloved of the sisterhood of beautiful women of the Bible, who were faithful wives and tender mothers. But that does not explain the mystery of the ages. Why has Mary laid her hand so lastingly on Time that we cannot think of the history of the world without her? Is there something in the heart of man to which, in spite of her silence, she has spoken?

Outside the Bible a vast apocryphal literature has gathered about her. Some of the more enlightened of the early fathers know very little about it, and the few that do know appear to discountenance it. Some of it may have been of early origin, but apparently the greater body of it came into existence in the third century and was created by monks and friars. According to them her father was Joachim of the tribe of Judah. He was a shepherd and lived in Jerusalem, although, as far as we can see, there was not a clear acre of pasturage within a radius of miles around that stony place at that time. Her mother was Anna, and she was long childless, like so many women of the Bible who were afterwards to give birth to remarkable children.

Mary was sinless. She had not sinned when Adam sinned. The time had not come when anybody would dare to say, "I am the Adam of my own soul." To these old monks in their cells, obsessed by thoughts of sex, the mark of original sin in a woman was that she should be the mother of a child according to natural order. For this reason, therefore, among other reasons, Mary was born supernaturally.

From her third to her twelfth year she was brought up in the Temple, being fed by angels in the form of doves. Then she was given in marriage to an old man named Joseph, on condition that he took a vow of lifelong celibacy. After the birth of Jesus, Mary had no more children. The brothers and sisters referred to in the Gospels were the sons and daughters of another Mary, the daughter of Joseph by an earlier marriage and the wife of Cleopas; therefore, they were the cousins of Jesus.

Mary was in Jerusalem, keeping the Passover, at the time of the Crucifixion, and John the apostle called her to the Cross. On the way she uttered many woeful cries, and continued to cry when she got there. After Jesus had committed her to the care of the apostle she lived in his house, but she also travelled with him into distant countries.

When she died is not certain. Some say in A.D. 56; some in A.D 64. But she is buried in Jerusalem. Her tomb may be seen there to this day. It is in an underground Russian church at the foot of the Mount of Olives, and hard by the traditional garden of Gethsemane. As you go down the broad steps to it, the Russian monks show you, by the light of their candles, two other tombs on either side—one of them being the tomb of Joseph and the other of Joachim and Anna. At the bottom is the tomb of Mary, but her body does not rest in it, and, except for a moment, has never done so. After the apostles had closed the tomb in burying her, suddenly a dazzling and miraculous blaze of light burst out of it and rose to the sky, and by this they knew that the body of Mary, just as she had died, had ascended into Heaven. This is now called the Assumption, and although it is not yet a dogma of the Church, the successors of the monks of the third and fourth centuries hope it will soon become so.

At the close of the third century, at Alexandria, Mary was first called the Mother of God. In the fifth century at Ephesus she was first called the Holy Virgin and Mother of God. From that time forward she was believed to be the only bridge between man and the Almighty, and was used for purpose of prayer and intercession. It was said that Jesus had revealed it to her in a vision that if she asked for anything in his name God would grant it. One of the popes prayed to her to ask for the protection of his armies in battle. So the mother of the Prince of Peace became the goddess of war!

No right-hearted man could wish to speak without respect of a belief which has commanded the homage of millions of his fellow-creatures, and still moves their hearts to its deepest devotion. But is it not in this rhodomontade of bad romance that we find the key to the mystery of the ages—that Mary is the most beloved of all the daughters of women? The mother of mothers, the saint of every Saturday through sixteen centuries.

Let us get back to the simple humanities of the little house in Jerusalem.

Perhaps Mary went from the Cross back to the house of John in Galilee, and then followed him on his long and perilous missionary journeys in Asia Minor. More probably, in the larger designs of Providence, she remained in Jerusalem. If she was there at the time of the Crucifixion she was almost certainly there in A.D. 44, in the house of James, a righteous man, and the head of the Mother Church which was then at peace after the death of the elder Agrippa.

When we say we know nothing about Mary, we are wrong. We know one fact which seems to be above and beyond all other facts whatever—she was the mother of her Son. Knowing this, we seem to know everything. What he did she did, and in due time we see her becoming the mother of Jerusalem.

She is growing old now and she has seen a great sorrow, for a sword has indeed pierced through her soul also. Everybody in the city knows it, and there is not a head, from that of the humblest citizen to that of the proudest Pharisee, that does not bow to her as she passes through the streets. As surely as the needle goes to the magnet, sorrow goes to sorrow, and the women of Jerusalem whose sons have fallen by the cruelty of hard task-masters, the tyranny of Roman rulers, or yet by their own waywardness, find their way to the house of the little brotherhood. She receives all who come to her, whether Christian or Jew. So silent is she that down to the last some of them cannot remember that they have ever heard the sound of her voice, but they have felt her soft hand on their wet cheek and gone away comforted.

She receives the women who are sinners, also the outcasts who, according to the stern rule of their fathers, should not cross the threshold of a good woman's house; and though she has scarcely spoken to them, they feel as if they have heard her say, "Her sins, which are many, are forgiven, for she loved much."

She is the pulse of the house of the little group of apostles, busy day by day with their long task of providing spiritual food for the foreign Churches. When she enters the room in which they sit together at their work it is the same as if a lamp has come into the gathering gloom, and every strained face softens to a smile. They are her sons, and she is the mother of all of them.

So the years pass, in the peace of the Churches, until A.D. 62. The apostles are by this time growing old also. James will not be less than sixty, and the others are not much younger. But she is by much the oldest of all, and the time comes when she has to share the common lot of humanity.

She is so patient in her pain that they can never be quite sure or know when she is suffering. For some months, perhaps, they live between the dark confines of hope and fear. But the black camel comes at last that kneels at the gate of all.

We can see it as if we were there. Perhaps it is, as the monks say, a bright day in summer. In her upper chamber she is in bed, which is a pile of thick cushions on the carpet. Around her the old brothers are kneeling with clasped hands, James at the head, and nearest to the pale face on the pillow. The women of Jerusalem are in a close throng on the stairs and in the courtyard. The windows are open and the sounds of the city are heard from without; the water-carrier, bent almost double under his goat's skin, clattering his can as he goes by; the camel grunting on his way up the cobbled streets with her double panier of dates from Jericho. From farther off comes the trumpet of the Roman soldiers who are changing guard in the cloisters, and the horn of the minister in the priest's court in the Temple.

The sweet old eyes open with a smile. Nothing is there for grief, nothing for tears. Death has no terror for her and the grave no victory. She is parting from her children, but only for a while, and in the sure hope of the Resurrection.

When the end comes and the old men rise to their feet, it seems as if the sun, which had been shining a moment ago, has gone out and the chamber has suddenly become dark. On the stairs and in the courtyard the women are weeping.

Perhaps the brothers think of burying her in Jerusalem. More probably they decide to carry her back to Galilee that she may rest with her husband and her parents, and perhaps some of her children, in the obscurity from which they have never emerged.

Early next day, while the breeze of morning in that silent land is passing through the air, like an angel's whisper, the old brothers are carrying their burden through the narrow silent streets, followed by a long train of the women of Jerusalem. Outside the northern gate they set it down for some moments and the women go by it and touch it, one by one, as if asking for the saint's last benediction. Then they take it up again, and the women, with their hands to their mouths, stand there to watch them, as they pass away, the little group of six or seven elderly men, becoming smaller and smaller as they go over the bare forehead of Scapius, towards the sandy roads of Samaria and the deep plain that reaches to the foot of the hills of Galilee, and so on to the nameless grave in Nazareth on which the Syrian stars look down.

But she was not dead. She can never die. Through all the centuries since her silent presence has been with every old mother who has lost a son and with every young one who has borne a child.

Mater Dolorosa—Mother of Sorrows? Yes, but the mother of her Son as well. And that is the key to the mystery of the ages.

V. *The Martyrdom of James*

After the traditional date of the death of Mary, the mother of Jesus, the shadows closed rapidly on the little Church of Jerusalem. Two events of consequence occurred within the next few days—

the martyrdom of James and the dispersion of the brotherhood. Scripture is silent about both, and though outside history gives us a circumstantial story of what was done, it provides no explanation of the reasons for it. What new clash with the Jews or break with the Romans caused the prolonged peace of the Church to be broken so suddenly by incidents of almost barbaric violence? We are left to come to our own conclusions. And it is not difficult to do so.

At the beginning of A.D. 60 the Church at Jerusalem must have been occupied for nearly twenty years in sending out spiritual food to the foreign Churches. Their primitive Gospels had been the records of what they had themselves seen and heard of the life of their Master during his pilgrimage among them. Their writers would be eye-witnesses, or the spoken word of eye-witnesses. Their writings would begin with the beginning of the ministry of Jesus and end with his death and Resurrection. They would contain nothing about the years of which the writers themselves knew nothing.

But that would not be enough for the foreign converts. They would wish to learn something of the early life of their beloved Master, of his birth, his childhood, his mother's home, as well as to look with their own eyes on the places in which he had done his mighty works, from which he had sent out the glad tidings that had given them a new hope in life and death.

It would be a natural impulse. What happens now would happen then. In the course of years, hundreds, perhaps thousands of younger pilgrims would visit Palestine. It would be easy to do so. Trading ships were sailing constantly in those days from the ports of Cyprus, Asia Minor and Macedonia to Tyre and Cæsarea.

Like the pilgrims of later ages, the early pilgrims to the country of Jesus would probably see less than they had expected, and hear little more than they had heard already. It is hardly likely that their chief objective would be Jerusalem, for that had been the scene of his sufferings and it would still be the seat of his enemies. In Galilee they would probably find that Luke had been before them, and gathered up all there was to know. Unless some of the brothers and sisters of Jesus were still alive they would find few remaining eye-witnesses. If it was enough for them to look on the Lake of Galilee and to trace the footsteps of their Lord they would perhaps go back satisfied; but there would be little else to satisfy them. It would all be so long ago. We are told that the Churches in Galilee had greatly multiplied during the years of peace, but their members would, for the most part, belong to a second generation. The sick and blind and lame who had crowded about the miracle-worker in the streets of Capernaum would be gone, and the miracles themselves not remembered.

Nazareth itself would perhaps have forgotten that it had rejected him, and if it had any recollection of him at all, it would probably be of the shame he had brought upon it at his death, when its name was written, possibly in derision, over the head of his Cross. If the pilgrims asked for the place in which Jesus was born there would be nobody to say where it was or had been. It would be sixty-four years since then, and only old people of eighty could be expected to remember that when they were young an obscure Galilean girl had married an obscure Judæan man and given birth to a son.

But if the converts from foreign countries took little away with them they must have left much behind. It is not more pitifully true that a prophet is not without honour save in his own country than that a prophet has honour at home as soon as it is seen that he has honour abroad. The repeated visits of pilgrims from distant places would open the eyes of the people of Galilee to the fact that one of the gods of the earth had lived among them. They would then remember the home of Mary, the workshop of Joseph, the well at which the mother of Jesus had drawn water, the miracles which the miracle-worker had performed in his cradle, in his childhood, and in his boyhood. A vast body of legend would spring up about Jesus, the germs of the fabulous stories which, two or three centuries later, were written out in the foolish and sometimes mischievous books we call the apocryphal Gospels.

Perhaps these legendary stories would be no more than the satisfaction of a desire on the part of Christians and Jews to fill up the gap of the earlier years in the life of Jesus of which the apostles at Jerusalem knew nothing. But this would be a mood of mind in the Church in Galilee which the pagan religions would run out to meet. There was no part of Palestine at that time more closely in touch with paganism than Galilee. From north, south, east and west the pagans were continually passing through it. There was a caravan route from the extreme west of Asia Minor by which the merchants of Greece came with their merchandise through Cilicia and Syria to the little towns of Galilee on their way back to Egypt. The Greek merchants would bring their religions with them, and one of the most widespread bore a strange kinship to Christianity. This was the mystery religion called the Mother and Youth.

Under a supreme deity, the mother was the earth-god, whose duty it was to preside over agriculture, and to rejoice and weep with her children. Associated with her was a youth, generally her son, but supernaturally born, for in the purer forms of the religion the mother was a virgin. He was the king of his people and a god-man, and he stood midway between the supreme deity and mankind, being both human and divine, subject to the sufferings of humanity but free from the sin which man had contracted in a premundane period, when he was spirit, without body.

When the crops failed from long droughts, or there were earthquakes, eruptions and wars it was a sign of the wrath of the supreme god. Then the king had to die to appease the deity and so save the world from destruction. The festival of the saviour was a day of mourning, for it was the day of his death, but it was followed by a day of rejoicing, which was the day of his resurrection. After that, all would be well with the people, because the "faithful son" had by the sacrifice of his life won their salvation.

The struggle between the divine and the human elements in the god-man and his mother were often deeply moving. Sometimes the human element would for a while overcome the spiritual. As the day of sacrifice approached, the mother would carry her son away on lonely wanderings into the mountains or desert places to escape from the doom of death which was the penalty of man's sin. She was like the mother of sorrows and he was like the man of Gethsemane. "O, my Father, if this cup may not pass from me except I drink it, Thy will be done."

VI. *Mithras and Mithraism*

Another mystery religion passed through Galilee in the early days of Christianity. It came from the East by way of Arabia and Damascus. This was the religion of Mithras, a Persian god, who was also born supernaturally, but out of a rock, for the human woman had no place of honour in the eastern mystery religions. Mithras was the god of light, which fructified the earth and was the first cause of life. He, too, was a king, and both human and divine, standing midway between the supreme god and mankind, and therefore free from sin. He was also a dying god, and the saviour of the people from the wrath of the supreme deity. Associated with him was a divine bull which was slaughtered when the deity was wrathful with man for his sins, and then the god-man was bathed in the redeeming blood. This purification through sacrifice brought redemption to the sin-laden people, and an ultimate immortality, in which man was for ever regenerate.

Mithraism was like the religion of the Christians not only in its share of salvation, but also in its rites and ceremonies. The Mithraic worshippers practised baptism with sacred water. They had also a eucharist, in which bread and wine were mingled in a cup, over which their priest pronounced sacred words.

If all this bears a startling resemblance to Christianity, the Christians of the modern world need not be dismayed. Neither need they follow the early fathers (Justin Martyr, A.D. 150, and Tertullian, A.D. 200) in calling Mithraism "a diabolical attempt to emulate the mysteries of the divine sacraments." Most certainly it was not that.

It was a stage in the divine movement of the ages in which the soul of man was struggling to pierce the darkness which divided him from the mysterious Author of all.

Learned men have traced the mystery religion of the Mother and Youth as far back as the grey antiquity of 1500 B.C. The cult of Mithras was born in Persia, in 60 B.C., and flourished in Cilicia in the time of St. Paul. The former was strong in Greece, Asia Minor and Syria in the days when Christianity was born in Palestine. The latter contested the supremacy of Christianity during the first four centuries of the Christian era.

It was carried by the Roman soldiers along the Danube and the Rhine to Cologne, and up the Thames to London, where the remains of its monuments are to be seen to this day. When it fell before Christianity it left its mark upon its conqueror. Nobody then knew, as nobody now knows, when Jesus of Nazareth was born. Some of the early fathers said it was on March 20th; others on April 20th; still others on January 6th. December 25th was the birthday of Mithras. It became the birthday of Jesus also.

But what chiefly concerns us now is that the two pagan religions of Mithraism and the Mother and Youth were vivid and vigorous in the early days of the Church, when the Greek and Persian merchants were passing in their caravans through Galilee. What effect did they have on early Christianity? Were they the first authors of what we call the legendary Jesus? And were they the indirect cause of the calamities which fell upon the Church between A.D. 64 and 68?

VII. Recapitulation

It is impossible to regard the birth-stories in the Gospels as the records of actual happenings. They are obviously conceived in the spirit of legend and written in the language of myth. Never for a moment have they any reality. They were certainly not composed in collusion. In every incident, except one, they contradict and clash with each other.

In the story in *Luke* the original home of the parents of Jesus is in Nazareth. In the story in *Matthew* it is already in Bethlehem. In *Luke* the visit of the angel who foretells the forthcoming birth of the Messiah is to Mary, in Galilee. In *Matthew* it is to Joseph in Judæa. To attempt to harmonize these inconsistencies by saying that in the time between the two angelic visitations Joseph and Mary had removed from Galilee to Judæa is to destroy the sequence of events. In *Luke* a decree of Augustus is the reason for the removal of Joseph and Mary from Nazareth to Bethlehem. In *Matthew* they are already in Bethlehem, and there is no mention of the decree of Augustus. In *Luke* the announcement of the birth of Jesus is by means of a visit of angels to shepherds in Bethlehem and a revelation of the Holy Ghost to an old man and an old woman in the Temple. In *Matthew* it is by means of a star which appears to astrologers in the East. In *Luke* the parents of Jesus return to Nazareth forty days after his birth. In *Matthew* they make a long journey into Egypt before coming to Nazareth.

The incident in *Luke* of the taxing or enrolment has no foundation in history. To establish its authenticity it is necessary to show that the taxing or enrolment took place during the lifetime both of Herod the Great and of Jesus of Nazareth. No taxing or enrolment took place in the lifetime of Herod the Great that was within the lifetime of Jesus, if we are to accept the statement in the body of Luke's Gospel that Jesus was beginning to be thirty years of age in the fifteenth year of Tiberius.

A census was made in Herod the Great's time by Augustus in 8 B.C. which would make Jesus about 38 years of age (not 30 as Luke says) in the fifteenth year of Tiberius.

The massacre of the children of Bethlehem recorded in *Matthew* is not mentioned in *Luke,* and it is not supported by history. There were three contemporary (or almost contemporary) historians, and one of them appears to account for the doings of nearly every day in the last years of Herod, but he says nothing about that atrocity. Power of life and death was not possessed by Herod the Great (though he may have arrogated it in his anger), for while he was on his death bed he had to send swift messengers to Rome to obtain permission from the emperor to execute two of his sons who were conspiring to poison him.

The birth stories in *Matthew* and *Luke* must have been unknown to the persons chiefly concerned in them. If Mary circumcised her child, she must have thought of him as an ordinary son of Abraham, who could only thus enter into the everlasting covenant of God and not be cut off from his people, but if he was supernaturally born he was a being apart and not of the seed of Abraham at all. If she went through a period of purification she must have thought of herself as an ordinary Jewish woman, but if she had conceived supernaturally she had never been impure and was still a virgin.

The birth stories have nothing to do with the historical Jesus. Apparently, he never thought of Bethlehem as his birthplace or as the birthplace of Joseph. Certainly he never spoke of it, and although he was frequently within an hour's walk of it, he seems never to have entered Bethlehem. He never called himself the son of David or permitted others so to call him. The idea in the minds of the people that he was in actual fact descended by flesh and blood from David, the king of Israel, must have mitigated the indignities and brutalities to which he was subjected during his life. The idea that he had been supernaturally born and was therefore a god-man must have terrified his Jewish enemies as much as the idea that he was the Son of God alarmed Pilate for a moment at his trial. But no such idea ever, as far as we know, entered into anybody's mind, or yet into his own, from his cradle to his grave.

The birth stories must have been unknown to the first generation of the Christians. They are not mentioned in any other part of the Gospels. The punitive Hebrew Gospels, sometimes called the Nazarene and Elamite fragments, are said, by writers who read them, to have begun with the ministry of Jesus, and contained nothing about his earlier life. The preaching of St. Peter and St. Paul made much of the supernatural Resurrection of Jesus, as proof that he was the Christ, but it made no claim for his divinity on the ground of his supernatural birth.

It is impossible to say when the birth stories were written. To say that the first of them was written by Luke is to assume that an instructed chronicler would say vaguely in his first two chapters that Jesus was born in some indefinite period during the reign of Herod the Great, and then to say presently in his third chapter that Jesus was born many years later, in the first year of what we now call the Christian era. To say that the second of the birth stories was written by St. Matthew is to assume that an intelligent writer would say, at the beginning of his Gospel, that Jesus was by birth and parentage a Judæan, only properly to be called Jesus of Bethlehem, and then, in the body of his Gospel, that he was a Galilean and to call him Jesus of Nazareth.

When tradition attempts to harmonize these manifest contradictions it makes confusion worse confounded. It says that the supernatural birth of Jesus was a secret known only to Mary and Joseph. But to account for the fact that if they had carried their secret to their graves it would have been useless to themselves and to mankind, tradition says that Joseph revealed it to Peter, and Peter to Matthew, forgetting that, according to another tradition, Joseph was dead before Peter was called. Tradition also says that Mary revealed the secret to Luke, forgetting that she can never have seen Luke, except once, while she withheld it from John, whose mother she had become by command of Jesus.

But above all other proofs that the incidents of the birth stories have no foundation in reality there is the fact that from beginning to end they serve no purpose of God or man. If we are to think, as we must, that God's intention in all these supernatural manifestations—the angelic visitations to Mary and Joseph, the star in the East, the many dreams and visions, the appearance of the angels to the shepherds at Bethlehem, and the revelations of the Spirit to Simon and Anna—was to announce to the world the advent of the Great Being who was to save it from its sins, we are compelled to conclude that God's intention failed.

Against this shocking insult to the Deity the spirit of the believer revolts. It cries out for another explanation of the birth stories, and happily the explanation is not far off. There is always something more true than the material part of the truth, and that is the soul of it. The incidents of the birth stories were no more a record of actual happenings than were the incidents in the apocalyptic writings which were then being revived in Palestine, and were even, as we shall see presently, to have a large and perhaps fatal development in the Book of Revelation. They were allegories, true in essence, but not true (perhaps not intended to be true) to facts. To trace the origin of the birth stories to their source, to show why they came into existence, and when and at what call of the soul of man, we must go far back.

VIII.   The Israelite Religion

Two facts in the history of religion seem, as far as human knowledge goes, to be beyond question—first, that there has never been a time when man did not believe in the existence of a supreme God, who ruled and created all things, and next, that there has never been a time when man has not been conscious of sin. In the earliest forms of what we call pagan faith this original sin began, as we have seen, in some prematerial existence when man was all spirit, without body.

On being cast out into the body and becoming man, the spirit brought the burden of its sin with it. But God was a merciful God, and on receiving a great sacrifice He permitted the sinful spirit to throw off its sin and return to Him. That sacrifice, in pagan religions, had to be made by a being who was half divine and half human, to stand as a mediator between God and man. He took the body and form of a man, but was born in another sort of nature, as in the case of Mithras, or by the union of a minor god or goddess, as in the case of the Mother and Youth. His sacrifice was that of his life. Only by blood could man's soul be saved.

Such perhaps was the earliest form of pagan religion, but it speedily degenerated. The man-god fell in love with the daughters of men and thereby created a great many other god-men, and thus the original idea of a mediator between God and man became a gross and impure superstition.

Then came the Israelite religion, which proclaimed the great truth that God was one, that there were no other gods, that He was the Creator and Ruler, the sole Deity in all the world, and that He had no semi-gods and no partners. This, at one stroke, wiped out the sensuality which had grown up in the heart of paganism.

The God of Israel was a great, mighty, and awful God, and man, His creature, had sinned against Him. Man's sin had not begun in a prenatural existence, but in this world. At the beginning of the world, immediately after its creation, God had placed the first man and woman, Adam and Eve, in a garden, and given them His command. They had disobeyed His command, and that was the origin of sin. For this offence of the first man and woman, God had not only cast the two sinners out of the garden, but had ordered that all their offspring, through all generations, should bear the burden of their sin and suffer its punishment.

Nevertheless, the God of Israel was also a merciful God, and the Father of His people. He did not desire the death of His children, but that they should repent and live. To enable them to repent He gave them a mediator. This mediator was not a semi-god. He was not a being half human and half divine, as in the pagan religions. He was God's own Spirit written out in a Book.

That Book was the Torah, a sacred writing, dictated by God Himself to certain of His saints, and containing His commandments. As men lived by these commandments they entered into the kingdom of God, and for them the kingdom of God would be within them. When all men lived by God's Torah there would come a blessed condition. A Messiah, pure and good and holy, who was waiting in Heaven until all men obeyed God's commandments, would be born, and he would establish the kingdom of God on the earth, and it would last for ever.

This Messiah was not to be a man-god. He was to be a son of man. He was to be the son of a very human man, who had sinned deeply and suffered much, but was nevertheless a man after God's own heart. The Messiah was to be the son of David, the greatest of the kings of Israel, and when he came he was to be born in Bethlehem.

Such was the Israelite religion in early days, and though it underwent many modifications during the ages, and its people passed through many tribulations, it remained essentially the same down to the beginning of the first century of our own era. God was one. There were no other gods. He was the God of the Jews. The promise given to David was to the Jews only. The kingdom of God was for the Jews alone. The nations and races outside could only be admitted to the promise of the Kingdom by becoming Jews. If any Jew rejected the Torah or failed to observe its commandments, he was to be cast out.

Then came Christianity.

CHAPTER XII

The Four Gospels (Continued)

I. Their History

HAVING READ the four Gospels very carefully, not less than one hundred times, and having copied them out with my own hand at least four or five times, and having read many scores of commentaries upon them by writers in many countries and in many ages, my considered opinion about them, roughly stated and without entering into detailed criticisms, is as follows:

1. They were not, as they have come down to us, written under the inspiration of God.

2. At every point, on nearly every page, they betray the hand of man, very fallible man, liable to errors and making very palpable mistakes as to time, geography, customs, motive and prophecy.

3. Never in the world of letters have there been books which could be more properly described as man-made books.

4. The four Gospels are most surely not the work (as they have come down to us) of the apostles whose names they bear.

5. It is probable that when written they were never intended to bear that character.

6. Just as Tacitus repeatedly put into the mouths of historical characters of an era far earlier than his own words of which it was impossible that he could have had any report, so the writers of the Gospels often put into the mouth of Jesus words which it was impossible for them to say he had spoken.

7. It was the accepted literary morality of the first and second centuries of the Christian era that this could quite properly be done, and that nothing more was intended than to convey the impression to the reader that what he was reading was the writer's version of what the person speaking would and perhaps must have said in general, not in particular. In short, that it was, according to the belief of the writers, true to the spirit of the man, his known character and opinions.

8. Hence it came to pass that the Gospels are said to be "according" to this, that or the other apostle, meaning that it was according to his spirit, and perhaps his meaning, not necessarily and always according to his *word*.

9. In this way, the four Gospels came into being, and thus they may have passed under many hands before they reached the form in which we have them.

10. I think the four Gospels are not the work of four men but of many men, writing at different periods, changing and copying according to their own views of what was said and what had happened, and influenced by the ever-altering demands of their time.

11. Thus, following the method of commentators early and late, I find that each of the Gospels had many authors and many forms.

12. Of these authors and forms I give the following as my rough statement:

(a) I think that the view long held that there was no writing about Jesus for many years after his death, for the reason that the disciples expected that he would come again very soon, and therefore to make any sort of historical record for future ages would be unnecessary (inasmuch as there would be no future ages to need them), is a mistake.

(b) It is reasonable to assume, and almost certain, that immediately, or as soon as they were at ease from persecution, after the death of Jesus his disciples began to set down in writing all they could remember of his sayings, his sermons and his parables. That if this had not been so we should not have possessed the large body of his utterances contained in the Gospels, and they would not, *on the whole,* have borne so strangely their harmony of character as the words of the same speaker. Or (as seems probable) they were written in collaboration and probably in the same house. Or at least the first three Gospels were—in whole or in part.

(c) I think that when the little group of disciples first came to the making of these reports of the words to which they had listened, and of which they wished to preserve the memory, they found that there was only one among them who possessed the pen of the ready writer, all the others being illiterate men, fishermen generally, who probably could neither read nor write.

(d) The apostle who held the pen for these first records of the sayings of Jesus was undoubtedly St. Matthew. I think Matthew wrote in his native tongue, Aramaic—the language in which Jesus usually spoke. I think the reports he made were probably read aloud in the synagogues and elsewhere at their meeting-places, and that they were added to and corrected from the recollections of the other disciples—not the twelve merely.

(e) Therefore the first book of the sayings of Jesus (mentioned by Papias) was probably the joint work of all the disciples in Jerusalem during the early days of the Church.

(f) I think these sayings of Jesus satisfied the early Christians who lived in Palestine and were Jews, but that when Peter and Paul went out on their missionary errand the converts they made among the Gentiles, and among the Jews dispersed among the Gentiles, called not only for the sayings of Jesus, but for some account of his life, and particularly, at the beginning, for some account of his miracles, for it was upon his power to work miracles that much of their faith in him as the Messiah had to rest. It was just as if they said, "You tell us Jesus of Nazareth was the Messiah and the Son of God. Well, prove it to us by showing us that he did the marvellous works which the Scriptures prophesied the Messiah when he came would do."

(g) I think this was the call that led to the writing of the first of the Gospels. I think the first of the Gospels was almost certainly the Gospel according to Mark. I mean the first complete Gospel, after the fragments had been gathered together. My reason for thinking so is that it is the shortest, the plainest, the most direct; and it is impossible to believe that any longer Gospel would be made into a shorter one at a time when there was so great a cry for all that was known, while it is entirely reasonable to think that a longer Gospel, with fuller information, would be written after a shorter one, to supplement it from other sources.

(h) I think, therefore, the first story of the life and ministry of Jesus was that of St. Mark. It may have been written by Mark, perhaps in Greek, probably in Aramaic, perhaps in Rome and apparently for non-Jews. But as Mark was almost certainly a very young man, and did not himself remember the events he had to record, I think it reasonable to conclude that he was inspired by the recollection of an older apostle who had known Jesus at least from the time of the beginning of his ministry—that is to say from his first appearance in Capernaum.

(i) Therefore, I think Mark wrote from the recollections of Peter, and, apart from other reasons for fixing the date of the first Gospel, it was probably written during one of the periods of Peter's imprisonment, when, cut off from the active work of preaching, he occupied his time in dictating to Mark, or in talking to him of the facts in the life of Jesus which Mark was about to record—either in Cæsarea or (more probably) in Rome, before the expulsion of the Jews (and therefore the Christians, who were then chiefly Jews) from Rome.

(j) I think this early *Mark* is almost certainly not the Gospel as it has come down to us. Our *Mark* contains evidences that the writer of the Greek version was not a Jew, whereas Mark was a Jew, born probably in Jerusalem. I think Mark's original Gospel was probably written in his own and Peter's native tongue, Aramaic. Our *Mark* is probably not the original *Mark*.

(k) I think that after this first biography of Jesus there were various others, and that the rapid growth of the Church, under the missionary labours of St. Paul particularly, led to a great hunger for Gospels.

(l) At what period St. Luke's Gospel came is uncertain, but I think it reasonable to conclude that many Gospels of doubtful authenticity had been written before it, but that Matthew's Gospel (as distinguished from the "sayings") was not yet written and that *Mark* was the only accredited Gospel when Luke wrote. I think it probable that Luke wrote in Cæsarea about A.D. 58–60, while Paul was in prison there under Felix.

(m) I think Luke wrote with Matthew's "sayings of Jesus" (not with his Gospel) before him, and with the original *Mark* before him. Luke also had access to certain reports of the parables of Jesus which Matthew had not included in his "sayings"; but by whom these parables were written I do not know—nor does anybody. I think it possible that the actual words of the parables in *Luke* may have been Luke's own, for he was clearly an accomplished writer if (as it is natural to think) the exordium of his Gospel is his, and if it remains to this day as he wrote it.

I do not think it necessary to conclude that even Luke's Gospel, as originally written, is the *Luke* we possess. But of the four Gospels I incline to think our *Luke* is the nearest to the original

Luke. Luke was not a Jew, and his Gospel shows it. He was a Roman citizen, and probably wrote in Greek. He was not writing for Jews, and his Gospel shows that also. He had a very imperfect knowledge of the geography of Palestine, and his Gospel shows that as well. He was not very well informed on Jewish history and religion, and his Gospel gives painful proof of it. His Gospel shows that passages are missing from it.

But he was a friend of Paul, and what Paul could tell him he used. What Paul knew of the life of Jesus was clearly not a great deal. Paul was probably not yet in Jerusalem (or yet Palestine) at the death of Jesus. He was almost certainly not at Jesus's trial and Crucifixion. What he knew of Jesus must have been gained (1) from the enemies of Jesus during the period in which he was persecuting the Christians, and (2) from Peter and the Christians in Jerusalem during the few days (very few) in which he visited them after his conversion, and again after his retirement into Arabia and his escape from Damascus, and before the beginning of his mission. I think *Luke* was first written in Greek. Luke was a Gentile from, perhaps, Alexandria, but coming from Rome, and earlier still from his father's house in the south of Italy. His father was a doctor who had, perhaps, been made a Roman citizen by settling in Rome where (by an edict of Julius Cæsar) all doctors became Roman citizens—the title becoming hereditary—disease (malaria) being rife in the Campagna and all doctors very welcome.

(n) I think probably the Gospel of Matthew (the finished, revised and, completed or *altered* Gospel) followed the Gospel of Luke (for Luke, who quotes from *Mark* does not copy from *Matthew,* and clearly does not know *Matthew*). I think the Gospel of Matthew was probably written first in Aramaic. Certainly the fragments on which it was based were written in Aramaic.

I think the Acts of the Apostles was then written partly by Luke—also in Greek. Partly by others. The beginning and the end were almost certainly by Luke.

(o) This is, roughly and briefly, my view of the first writing of the first three Gospels. I think the original versions of all three, and of the Acts of the Apostles also, were made between A.D. 64 and 68, the date of the death of Peter and perhaps of Paul.

(p) What further versions were afterwards made I do not know, and apparently nobody can ever know. Clearly, the nativity stories were not in the earliest versions of *Matthew* and *Luke*. I think that after the fall of Jerusalem and the dispersion of the Jews (A.D. 70), down to the return of John from Patmos about twenty years later, there was a great deal of literary activity among the Christians. I think this activity was chiefly among the Greek and Roman adherents to Christianity, and that the new versions of the Gospels, "according" to this or that disciple, were sensibly coloured by the needs of the Church at the periods at which they were made—the necessity of meeting and combating criticism. Many passages were interpolated; many miracles were added, many parables were superimposed, and many facts of the life of Jesus were changed to give authority to the constantly changing views about his character and mission.

(q) Thus I think the nativity stories in *Matthew* and *Luke* were inserted long after the original Gospels were written. My reason for this is (1) that they are not in any way borne out by any other parts of the Gospels in which they appear; (2) that they do not agree with each other in any single particular except that of the supernatural conception, and the fact of the birth at Bethlehem; (3) that the facts recorded contradict, supersede, exclude and eliminate each other even as to date (the dates of *Luke* being impossible to *Matthew*), and no honest mind has ever yet succeeded in harmonizing them or, I think, ever will; (4) that they are manifestly the product of a different type of mind with a different kind of imagination, Matthew's story being essentially oriental and probably coming from the Far East, and having its origin in the legendary land from which other stories of supernatural birth came—such as the story of the birth of Mithras, whose cult lived at the same time as the early Christian Church, contested its success and for a short period appeared to surpass it in its appeal.

(r) In like manner I think a good deal of material that is damaging to our view of the teaching of Jesus was introduced into the new versions of the Gospels as they were made during these thirty years and many later years, such as the pernicious teaching of the parable of the unjust steward, which Christian apologists for centuries have tried, with most pitiful and almost abject results, to harmonize with the character and teaching of Jesus. Above all, as to the divinity of Jesus and what he himself said on that subject.

So much for the probable history of the first three Gospels. And now we may consider the fourth Gospel.

The Gospel according to St. John was for a long period thought to belong to the second century. Some commentators placed it late in the second century. More recently its date of origin has come gradually closer to the Crucifixion. It is now generally believed to have been written between A.D. 90 and the end of the first century. This view is partly based on the effort to establish its authorship, to prove that it was from the pen of the apostle John, who at that period had lately returned from his exile in Patmos, and seems to have died about A.D. 92.

I have carefully considered it for a long period in the hope of finding traces of the apostle of Galilee. I find no trace of him anywhere. Or, if at all, only in little touches of what we may call "local colour," and they are of little or no value.

The little touches of reality in the narrative which I formerly thought indicated that the writer was an eye-witness of the events recorded no longer seem necessarily to attach themselves to John the Apostle, but to have descended from him.

They might very well have been derived from him either at the period of the production of the book or earlier. They might have been interpolated by the writer at John's suggestion if the book were read over to him before it was put into circulation. But none of them requires belief that John the Apostle wrote the Gospel. Much the contrary.

Against the contention that John wrote the Gospel is the fact that although a native of Capernaum and present with Jesus during the comparatively long period of the short ministry in which Jesus made his home there, the witness of his miracles in and about Capernaum, and a hearer of his sermons on the plain of Gennesaret, he says nearly nothing about them that had not been said about thirty years before by the writers of the Synoptic Gospels. Assuming (which we reasonably may) that John was the youngest of the twelve, and that he was probably not more than twenty at the time of the death of Jesus, we have to account to ourselves for the fact that the memories of early manhood, of first association with Jesus, of the tremendous incidents of the early discipleship (all calculated according to the laws of memory to leave the deepest and most vivid impression upon his mind) left little or no impression on him whatever.

If it is said that John did not report the doings of these early Galilean years because they had already been reported in the earlier Gospels, the answer is the same as to all the wilderness of similar objections in relation to the omissions in the Synoptic Gospels, namely, that while silent about facts which would, in obedience to natural law, be most vivid in John's memory, he repeats incidents which *are* in the earlier Gospels, and indeed almost reproduces literally the reports of them.

On the other hand, while the Gospel of John proves that the writer did not know the Galilean ministry, or, knowing it, did not attach sufficient importance to it, he did know very intimately the ministry in Judæa and particularly in Jerusalem. Everything that happened in and about Jerusalem he knows well. He knows Jerusalem better than he knows Galilee. He attributes to the ministry in Jerusalem and Judæa incidents which the earlier Gospels more reasonably attach to Galilee and Peræa. The giving of sight to the man born blind is an obvious case of this kind. At the period at which, according to *John,* Jesus performs this miracle in Jerusalem, he is, according to the Synoptics, performing a similar miracle on the banks of the Jordan. The balance of probability in this case is strongly with the Synoptics.

But there is the further and more serious argument against the contention that John the Apostle was the writer of the Gospel bearing his name, that the spirit and theory of the book are utterly unlike those of the disciples as we see them in the Synoptic Gospels. The spirit of the fourth Gospel is obviously and strongly marked by the Greek spirit which came into Christianity after the fall of Jerusalem and the dispersion of the Jewish-Christians among the Gentiles.

Jesus is no longer merely the Messiah in any of the accepted senses. He is the absolute Son of God. He is God. He was with and of God from the beginning. He will be with God to the end. There was no spiritual development in Jesus during his life on earth as a man. He knew all from the first. Nothing was hidden from him. It needed not that anybody should tell him anything. Everything was foreordained. Nothing happened that had not been foreseen and expected by him.

All this is totally unlike the Jesus of the Synoptic Gospels, where Jesus attains to this stage only at the end. In the Gospels of the Synoptics Jesus could not have been charged with blasphemy (according to the Jewish theory of blasphemy) down to the moment of his own evidence at the inquiry before the high priests, except in relation to what he said about the Temple. In John's Gospel he was guilty of blasphemy (according to Jewish standards) in the beginning and all through his ministry. There is not a moment in which (according to John's narrative) he did not blaspheme in the Jewish sense. His disciples were also guilty of blasphemy in relation to him. In particular, John the Baptist was guilty of blasphemy in relation to Jesus. His first words about Jesus are, from the Jewish point of view, blasphemous. There was no period of the ministry at which Jesus might not have been arrested and tried on a charge of blasphemy according to old Jewish law, and condemned to death. He blasphemed to the woman of Samaria—a woman of the lowest type of life. He called himself the Son of God nearly all through his public life.

Is this in any degree like the thought of John the Apostle? Think of what he was—an untaught fisherman of Capernaum. It is *possible* that at the beginning of his discipleship he could neither read nor write. We hear very little of what he says or does during the lifetime of Jesus. He hardly ever speaks, and when he does it is usually rather selfishly and foolishly; and he is sometimes sharply reproved—as when he asks Jesus to call down fire from Heaven to destroy the Samaritan village that has refused to receive Jesus; as when, with his brother James, he asks Jesus to give him a higher place than that of his fellow-disciples in the Kingdom which they expected to be established soon. He is frequently described as the disciple whom Jesus loved, and as lying in the bosom of Jesus. We see no reason for this preference (if such it is) except that he was probably much younger than the other disciples, and was therefore treated by Jesus as an affectionate boy.

It is assumed by some careless commentators that he is the disciple who, being known to the high priest, was permitted to be present at the inquiry before the council; but this is a manifest error on which it is unnecessary to waste further words. It is said (by John alone) that he was at the foot of the Cross with the Virgin Mother. This is in the highest degree improbable, inasmuch as he had fled away from Jesus at the arrest in Gethsemane, and, like the rest, must have been in hiding from the Jews, lest they should be arrested as the accomplices of the pretender to the kingship of the Jews. It is said (also in *John* alone) that to him Jesus committed the care of his mother, and he took her to his house. Once again, this is highly improbable, because he was almost certainly a very young man at that time, possibly not more than twenty, unmarried and without a home (remember that his mother was travelling with Jesus and his disciples), while Mary the mother could as easily have been. entrusted to the care of James who could not have been much younger than Jesus himself, probably thirty-two years, and who became the head of the Church at Jerusalem within a few years of the death of Jesus.

There is nothing known to me that justifies the belief that this simple and not very conspicuous disciple, indeed rather featureless and indifferent person, formerly a fisherman of Capernaum, was the writer of a Gospel, which was based on a theory of Christ's divinity from the beginning that came into being many years after the Crucifixion, and was cultivated and perhaps brought into being by the cultured classes. Only once during the life of Jesus does any of the disciples make a clear pronouncement of Jesus's character as the Son of God—Peter at Cæsarea Philippi.

Taking a general view, I am of opinion that the fourth Gospel was written by a Jewish-Christian living in Jerusalem, probably a rabbi. I think this person was perhaps John the Presbyter, perhaps John of Ephesus. Also, I think he knew John the Apostle, and that when he wrote his Gospel he gave it out in the apostle's name, because John was the apostle and had had direct and close personal relations with Jesus, and therefore his name carried authority. Alternatively, I think the writer was a Gentile living in Alexandria.

I think John the Apostle, the fisherman of Capernaum, may have given John the Presbyter or John of Ephesus some touches of reality—very few, for very few touches of reality are to be found in the fourth Gospel, which is almost as idealistic as *Revelation,* and probably came from the same pen, except that portion of *Revelation* which rather obviously comes from a far earlier eastern and purely legendary source.

If we were compelled to believe that John, the son of Zebedee, the fisherman of Capernaum, wrote the fourth Gospel, we should have to account for the fact that when ninety years of age, or perhaps more, he remembered incidents of the greatest importance which accounted more for the Crucifixion of Jesus than any of the other incidents recorded in the earlier Gospels. And that he waited about fifty-five years after the death of Jesus to record these important incidents.

One such incident is the miracle of the raising of Lazarus. Nobody can read the first three Gospels carefully without seeing that there is no sufficient reason shown why Jesus should have been arrested and tried and condemned and crucified just *when* these events happened. Why the haste? Why not before or later? Why at all until there was some real danger to the Jewish power or the Roman power? No such danger is indicated in the first three Gospels. But the danger is made clear in the fourth Gospel.

The fourth Gospel explains all this. It may be that during the thirty years between the circulation of the Synoptic Gospels and the writing of the fourth Gospel questions like these were being asked by the educated Gentile-Christians in Alexandria and elsewhere. *Why was Jesus arrested just then?* The fourth Gospel supplies the answer. It is to be found in the miracle of the raising of Lazarus, the effect it produced and was likely to produce, especially at that moment of the Passover, when Jerusalem contained vast multitudes of Jews who looked forward to a Messiah who would do just such things—raise men from the dead.

If this miracle had been known to the Synoptic writers it is difficult to believe that they could have kept it back for thirty years at least. Yet Matthew and Peter, as well as John, were at Bethany on the day when Lazarus was raised from the dead—if that is the right way to describe what happened—and Matthew and Mark say nothing about the tremendous event. Remember, also, that Paul can have known nothing about it, for his chief claim for Jesus's divinity is that he was the first fruits of them that slept—the first to rise from the dead—but while all the prophets, including David, had seen corruption, Jesus had not done so, and this was God's sign to the world that Jesus was the Christ—His proof.

II. The Canon

The foregoing represents my general view of how the four Gospels came into existence. But it does not show what they were at the beginning or how they became what they are now.

There is no manuscript to show what any of them were in their first forms. Only references by writers such as Papias indicate what the early Christian writings may have been.

We gather what they were rather by the silence of the earliest writings about incidents of great importance than by what is said. Thus we hear nothing from the earliest writers of the story of the Nativity, and from this we are reasonably justified in thinking that the stories of the Virgin Birth in *Matthew* and *Luke* were put into the Gospels after the period at which the Gospels were first written. It is incredible that so great a claim to divine origin should not be mentioned either in the rest of the Gospels themselves or in any of the earliest Christian writers. It is doubtful if anything is said about the Virgin Birth until at least thirty years after the Crucifixion.

What we see, in tracing the history of early Christian literature, is that in every generation new Gospels were being written, also new versions of the early Gospels. There was an immense hunger for knowledge of Jesus, his life, his acts, his words, and this produced an immense literary activity which lasted until the end of the second century. A vast number of apocryphal Gospels were written. Some of them are worse than valueless, being repellent. Others are merely childish and trivial, and appear to come out of the very babyhood of human intelligence. They borrow from the early Gospels and make them look foolish. The conscience of the Church cast off a great many of these forgeries after short life. Others lived on and did harm, making much conflict of opinion.

In the course of time the Gospels survived which appealed most strongly to the Christian heart. These were the four which have come down to us. But they did not come down unscathed by legend, myth and other forms of falsification. As the copies of the four Gospels passed from Church to Church they underwent many changes. Apparently, many passages were interpolated. Some sayings, some parables, some miracles were added, generally for easily recognized reasons. Into the copies of the four Gospels scribes inserted what they thought best in certain of the apocryphal Gospels. These changes would naturally reappear in the next and next copies, until it would be difficult to distinguish between the new and the old, the authentic and the apocryphal. Many of these false passages seem to remain to this day.

The apostolic fathers were well aware of all this, and hence they adopted no reverential attitude towards the manuscripts. Origen certainly does not believe in the literal word of God. He adopts a free attitude of tone towards the Gospels as he does to the Old Testament. Justin Martyr is so little minded to worship the letter of the Gospels that he makes a free rendering of them for himself. It was not until much later that they came to be regarded as the Word of God.

But towards the third century all this begins to present difficulties to the Church, which wants some standard, some fixed version, that it can accept and teach from.

Out of this need came the congress in the fourth century which examined all the Christian writings purporting to come from the earliest days, and finally selected the four Gospels.

By what means did it select the four Gospels? First, no doubt, by honestly and industriously investigating the authenticity of all the Christian writings down to that period. Which were oldest? Which most supported by the testimony of the early Christian fathers? But the great test of all would be this: Which of the Gospels appeals most to the human spirit? Which brings most comfort, gives most joy? Thus the needs of the human spirit was the ultimate test.

Having chosen these four Gospels, and cast out the others, the Church thereby created a canon. Naturally from that time onwards the canon became infallible. It became necessarily and automatically the inspired Word of God. It was no longer to be doubted. Much in the four Gospels which had been questioned a little before by the most enlightened of the apostolic fathers could be questioned no longer. Thus, the canon was made. It has ever since been the sure word of God. The Roman Church has never doubted it.

It does not doubt it now. It never can doubt it without overthrowing the decision of the congress of the fourth century. And that can never happen.

A large part of Christendom has continued this faith in the Gospels as the inspired word of God. It is all true to vast numbers of persons belonging to all the Churches, or none of it is true. They say you cannot pick and choose from it. You must take it all or leave it altogether. Such was the attitude of the Churches down to recent days. It is still so in some sections of the Churches.

But all the time the four Gospels have contained matter which did not exist in them at the beginning, matter which was perhaps accidentally copied into them by scribes (without authority) from apocryphal Gospels, from hearsay, from legend, matter which was deliberately (not necessarily dishonestly) put in without authority.

The task of biblical criticism during the past hundred years has been to work back on the Gospels in order to find their original form. This has been a task of immense difficulty. It can only be carried on by students who know the history of the Gospels, how they came into existence, and what varying conditions of belief they have passed through; what languages they have been translated into from the original language, and what changes of meaning have come through translation.

Above all, the task of working back on the Gospels to find what they were at the beginning and what conclusions we must draw from their manifestly irreconcilable differences, can only be attempted by students who are prepared to face the possibility (1) that they are most clearly not the directly inspired Word of God, but the work of very fallible men, of many men, writing in different ages and under the influence of different phases of the Christian faith; and (2) that therefore the Gospels must be judged of exactly as we judge of many other books, must be tried by and stand or fall by their own internal evidences, as well as by external historical evidences.

III. Their Literary Qualities

Nothing is more common in commentators than unmixed adulation of the Gospels as literary products. Even the writers who are most sceptical of the teaching of the Gospels are among the most enthusiastic about their literary form. This enthusiasm disturbed and perplexed me for a long time. Reading the Gospels in dry light I could see little to justify their vast reputation as great works of literature. I distrusted my judgment and tried again and again (perhaps through a hundred readings of the Gospels) to see their great literary qualities. I did not see them. On the contrary I was constantly being disturbed by their crudity, by their inconsequence, by their want of form, by their poverty of construction, by their needless repetition, by their baldness of style, by their limited vocabulary, but, above all, by their utterly bad story-telling, not in one instance only (as in the case of the story of

John the Baptist which is told shockingly badly in all the Gospels, although least badly in *Luke*), but in many other instances.

When a master of style such as Renan says, *"Luke* is the most beautiful book in the world," it is impossible not to listen. I thought over this judgment until I saw that *Luke* was an extraordinary mixture of the very good (from the literary point) and the very bad. The very bad is the narrative part, which is confusion confounded. The very good are the reports of the sayings of Jesus, the sermons and, above all, the parables. The parables as given in *Luke* are beyond doubt the most beautiful series of literary products in the whole range of literature. Some of the speeches of Jesus as given in *Luke* are unquestionably the most beautiful utterances of which literature contains record.

Where did Luke, who (if he wrote the whole of his Gospel, which I seriously doubt) could not tell a connected story in order, get these wonderful reports? Did he write the parables himself from oral tradition of their substance? Had he any original documents? If the latter, how did it come to pass that the beautiful documents escaped Matthew?

But then comes, for me, a larger question. There were manifest contradictions in the character of Jesus as presented by the Gospels. How are these to be accounted for?

Jesus was said to have foretold the fall of Jerusalem. Did he foretell it? Or were the passages put into his mouth written thirty-five years after his death, and were they, therefore, reports, not prophecies?

If so, the Gospels were not only not the inspired word of God, they were in some passages deliberate imposture. They claimed that Jesus said in A.D. 35 (or earlier) what Luke or somebody else wrote after A.D. 70.

This troubled me extremely, and I had the impulse more than once to throw the Gospels up altogether, not only as man-made books, but books that had been very shamefully and dishonestly man-made—making Jesus a creature of fiction, of myth, and leaving his historians in the position of forgers.

IV. Composite Productions

But after a time I saw more clearly that they were composite productions, that many hands had been at work in the writing of them, at many periods, that the intention had not been to deceive, but inasmuch as there was no clearly recognizable and consistent picture of Jesus to be made by accepting all of them, by combining them, it was necessary to deal with them as a judge would deal with the evidences of the various witnesses in a court of law, weighing each man's evidence against itself and each witness's evidence against the evidence of the other witnesses, accepting whatever is in harmony with the manifest character of Jesus, and rejecting what is palpably false to that character.

This made it easier to look for the historical Jesus in the Gospels. But it began by requiring that I should abandon once for all the idea that the Gospels were the work of many men; that they had been written into again and again as they passed in manuscript from congregation to congregation and encountered the difficulties of faith which arose from age to age—difficulties from which the early Christians thought they had to be protected by authority.

What, then, had I to do? I had to read and interpret the four Gospels actually as I should read and interpret any other books. To form the clearest possible general impression of the character and mission of Jesus, and to bring everything in the Gospels to that test—*which is the test of the human spirit*. Is this like Jesus? Is it possible to Jesus? If not, out it must go.

V. *Inspiration*

The belief in the Gospels as the inspired word of God is based on the same grounds as the belief in the Old Testament as the inspired word of God.

The foundation of it is the idea that man is God's highest creation, and that for his welfare God has spoken to him through certain of the highest types of man, his prophets and seers, to instruct him, to guide him and forewarn him.

Thus (according to that theory) he inspired the words believed to be written by Moses in what are called the Books of Moses, beginning with the story of the creation of the world and the birth of man, and going on, by the pens of other writers and prophets, through the history of one section of his people down to the days almost immediately preceding the birth of Jesus of Nazareth.

In like manner, it is believed that God inspired the apostles of

Jesus and his other disciples and followers of the first century after his death to write the story of his life and his miracles and the reports of his sermons, sayings and parables, with all that therein related to his mission on earth.

Such is the faith at the root of the belief in the Scriptures (including the Gospels) as writings directly inspired by God. Man held the pen, but God dictated what they wrote. They could not help writing what God dictated. Their own will did not operate in any way.

If such a belief can be maintained, it is impossible to do otherwise than to accept the whole of the Scriptures and the whole of the Gospels without question, and to subject them to no further criticism than is necessary, to ascertain if any changes have been made in their passage through the ages, and from language to language and from race to race.

No fundamental statement of fact or faith can for so much as a moment be questioned, and the work of the student of the Scriptures is solely and only to make apparently conflicting passages agree with each other, to harmonize apparently inharmonious stories and statements of belief.

Such is the basis of belief in the Scriptures as the inspired word of God, and it is open to obvious and grave objections. It requires us to believe:

1. That God spoke, during various periods of the world's history down to the century after the death of Jesus (but has never spoken since), to a small company of men, putting it into their minds to write, and telling them exactly what to write.

2. That what God is believed to have told these men to write does not always agree one account with another, and does not agree with what we know from other sources about the matters with which they deal.

3. That on the contrary much of what God is believed to have inspired men to write, although so circumstantially related, can only be accepted as poetry that makes no claim to reality; that much of it is self-contradictory, and much of it is in violent opposition to what our heart and conscience tells us are the works and attributes of God.

4. That these contradictions in the written word of the Scriptures, these limitations of knowledge, are natural and easy of explanation if the Scriptures are read as the work of men who

may have been inspired by God to write, but were left by Him free to write as they thought best.

5. That this conflict within the Scriptures very properly leads us to ask if man has been right or even reasonable in assuming that God, wishing to speak to man, to instruct, guide and forewarn him, can ever have used the pen of man for that purpose, and thereby exposed His inspired words to the thousand dangers of change and misinterpretation, and even of the imposture and fraud of the interpolator who for his profit or for the maintenance of his Church, or for the prosperity of his state, has inserted teaching of his own invention into the divine record.

6. That in the larger issue it leads us to ask ourselves if God, who had His vast universe, with all its wondrous phenomena, its laws, which make life what it is—if God who regulates the movements of the earth and the stars, determines the order of summer and winter, makes the wind to blow and the rain to fall, if God, who had all this vast and mighty medium through which to speak to man, to teach him, to guide him and to warn him, can ever have thought of speaking to man, solely or mainly through a book—a frail, perishable thing, written on paper or parchment, produced in one period of the life of man on this planet, and liable to be lost or changed or destroyed, or to be changed and superannuated by the altering necessities of man's life.

7. That in the light of these thoughts, is it not presumptuous and foolish of humanity to think that the Bible, whether the Old Testament with its prophets, or the New Testament, with its Gospels, is God's word to man—His inspired Word?

8. That a Book so soiled by ignoble uses, as the Bible has been, so open to question as the Gospels are, on nearly every page, so full of records which are impossible of reconcilation by minds that are both honest and free, should continue to be regarded as the literal Word of God, His only message to man, His law, is not a help to belief, but a grave hindrance, not a means of accepting Jesus, but an impediment to his acceptance.

9. That we have no way to a right understanding of the Gospels except that of reading them in exactly the same spirit and with the same mind as we read other books; we have no way of proving them except on their own evidence; no way of seeing what kind of being Jesus of Nazareth was except that of searching the history of the Gospels to find out, as far as now remains possible,

who wrote them and when they were written, what they were at the beginning, and how and for what reason they were altered during succeeding ages.

In order to accomplish this the first thing we have to do is to put aside the idea that they are the inspired Word of God unless and until, and wheresoever their internal evidences give proof of it.

10. In conclusion, my own view is that a reasonable distinction may be made between Inspiration and Revelation. That the Gospels were revealed by God to man I do not believe. That some of their teaching was inspired by God I find no difficulty in believing. God has inspired all great writers to write, but He has not revealed to them what they should write.

VI. Conclusion

Thus, by the end of the first century or perhaps the beginning of the second century, the Christian community in various places, chiefly in Jerusalem, Alexandria and perhaps Rome, had created (or revealed, whichever it may be), in Jesus of Nazareth, a being such as had never before existed on the earth as a man.

1. He was born in the days of Herod the Great, and events of grave public importance attended his birth and early childhood of which there is no record in external history, or in the Gospels themselves outside two chapters.

2. He was not born in the ordinary course of nature, of a human father and human mother, but of a human mother only, by the intervention of the Divine Spirit, and this immaculate conception was understood to free him from the taint of sin.

3. Throughout life he was a sinless being.

4. He possessed powers which entirely transcended those of the material man. He heard voices from the sky, which no other man heard. He saw sights in the heavens which no other man saw. He was carried by a supernatural being from place to place, apparently through the air. He was visited on the mountain by persons who were long dead and had long disappeared from the earth. He walked on the tumultuous sea, and rebuked the storm. He fed thousands of persons by multiplying a few loaves and fishes. He gave sight to persons who had been born blind. He cured the deafness of persons born deaf. He gave the power of speech to persons born dumb.

In a moment he made a man who had been born deaf and dumb to hear and speak—thus instantaneously conferring upon him not only the gift of hearing and speaking but also the full knowledge of a language which he had never heard. He made blind men describe the things they had never seen. He raised from the dead a man who had been four days in the grave, and after corruption had set in. Finally, he died himself and after three days he rose from the dead, and appeared to some five hundred and fifty persons at various times, living seven weeks on the earth and moving from place to place, sometimes like a dematerialized spirit, sometimes exercising the ordinary functions of a human being, eating and drinking as a man.

At last he ascended into the sky from the summit of a mount near Jerusalem in the presence of many witnesses.

5. In all this he was believed to be fulfilling the prophecies which had been made with respect to him from the beginning of the world, and these prophecies were quoted as witnesses to his life's story. Nearly every act of his life had been foretold by the prophets. He did nothing that had not been preordained. He suffered nothing that had not been a part of God's plan, with respect to him, foretold by him, by God's spokesmen throughout the ages. The most trivial as well as the most important events of his life had been foreseen and recorded in advance.

6. The object of this life of Jesus of Nazareth on earth had been to redeem humanity from sin, to make atonement for Man to God, to reconcile him to his Maker. He was the Christ, the Messiah, the messenger of God, a part of God, the Son of God, who had existed with God from the beginning and would be with God to the end.

7. This scheme of God with respect to him was that at some time after his Ascension, some time known to God only, it might be early or late, this divine Being would reappear on the earth coming in the clouds of Heaven (as he had ascended in the clouds), establishing in the world a kingdom of God, such as existed in Heaven, ruling over it as its king, judging humanity, separating the evil from the good, consigning the former to everlasting destruction (perhaps to everlasting torture), and giving the latter a condition of everlasting blessedness.

How much of this existed during the lifetime of Jesus of Nazareth? How much of it was believed by his parents, his disciples, his apostles, by those who were with him constantly and were the eye-witnesses of his life and death? By what stages did this picture of Jesus of Nazareth come to be made?

What necessities called for it, perhaps little by little? What were the conditions of the early Church which brought it into existence?

What did persecution do to create this picture?

What did the natural doubts of persons within the early Church do to make this picture?

Is it possible, by any process of elimination, by any effort to bring passages of the Gospels into relation to the known history of the early Christian Church, to account for what is confused and contradictory in the story presented in the four Gospels?

The effect of the spiritualizing efforts of the primitive Church after the Resurrection was to spiritualize Jesus. They spiritualized his birth by the immaculate conception. They spiritualized his descent, which was made to be from David. They spiritualized his mother, his father. In the end they were found to have spiritualized Jesus out of all human existence.

Then the enemy, both within the Christian camp and outside of it, came along and declared that he never had any human existence; he was a phantom; an idea; he stood for ideals.

Or he was a spirit moving through the world, working miracles, raising people from the dead, rising from the dead himself, ascending through the air to Heaven.

At this the early Christians took alarm. If Jesus had never been a man he did not fulfil the mission marked out for him. So they set to work to prove that he had been a real man, who ate and drank, both while in life and after the Resurrection. This was the only way to prove the reality of his work; of his miracles, of his actual death on the Cross and of his actual Resurrection from the dead.

Unless these were proved, nothing was proved. Christianity was nothing but a dream. Man could not suffer persecution and die for a dream. It could only do this for a reality.

Then came the passages of Scripture which emphasized this reality. Coming on the top of the passages which emphasized his spirituality, they sometimes made an apparent, if not a real, contradiction. The result was a portrait which the world could not recognize either as real or unreal, as human or divine.

What, then, have we now to do if we would get back to the historical Jesus?

We have to strip away the layers of supernaturalism and anti-supernaturalism and try to see what lies beneath—what the solid foundation of facts was on which this composite picture was painted.

Shall we thereby get back to a hard, matter-of-fact unspiritual personality—at best a teacher of morals?

I think not. I am sure not. We shall get back to the true spiritual Being—the Son of God.

END OF BOOK III